FROMMER'S

COMPREHENSIVE TRAVEL GUIDE

CANADA '94-'95

by Alice Garrard,
John Godwin, and
Marilyn Wood

PRENTICE HALL TRAVEL

NEW YORK • LONDON • TORONTO • SYDNEY • TOKYO • SINGAPORE

Authors

Alice Garrard: Nova Scotia, New Brunswick, Prince Edward Island, Newfoundland &
   Labrador, Montréal, The Laurentians & the Estrie Region, Québec City & the Gaspé
   Peninsula

John Godwin: Getting to Know Canada, Planning a Trip to Canada, Alberta, British Columbia,
   The Northwest Territories, The Yukon

Marilyn Wood: Ottawa, Toronto, The Golden Horseshoe & East Along the St. Lawrence,
   Southern & Midwestern Ontario, North to the Lakelands, Winnipeg, Saskatchewan

FROMMER BOOKS

Published by Prentice Hall General Reference
15 Columbus Circle
New York, NY 10023

Copyright © 1980, 1982, 1984, 1986, 1988, 1990, 1992, 1994 by Simon & Schuster, Inc.

Excerpts from "The Spell of the Yukon" by Robert W. Service from *The Collected Poems
   of Robert Service* reprinted by permission of McGraw-Hill Ryerson Limited, Canada;
   Dodd, Mead & Company, U.S.A.; and Ernest Benn Limited, England.

ISBN 0-671-86793-8
ISSN 1044-2251

Design by Robert Bull Design
Maps by Ortelius Design and Geografix Inc.

Frommer's Editorial Staff

Editorial Director: Marilyn Wood
Editorial Manager/Senior Editor: Alice Fellows
Senior Editors: Lisa Renaud, Sara Hinsey Raveret
Editors: Charlotte Allstrom, Thomas F. Hirsch, Peter Katucki, Theodore Stavrou
Assistant Editors: Margaret Bowen, Christopher Hollander, Alice Thompson, Ian Wilker
Editorial Assistants: Gretchen Henderson, Douglas Stallings
Managing Editor: Leanne Coupe

Special Sales

Bulk purchases (10+ copies) of Frommer's Travel Guides are available to corporations at special
discounts. The Special Sales Department can produce custom editions to be used as premiums
and/or for sales promotion to suit individual needs. Existing editions can be produced with
custom cover imprints, such as a corporate logo. For more information write to: Special Sales,
Prentice Hall Travel, 15 Columbus Circle, New York, NY 10023.

Manufactured in the United States of America

CONTENTS

LIST OF MAPS

INVITATION TO THE READERS

In researching this book, we have come across many fine establishments, the best of which we have included here. We are sure that many of you will also come across appealing hotels, inns, restaurants, guest houses, shops, and attractions. Please don't keep them to yourself. Share your experiences, especially if you want to comment on places that have been included in this edition that have changed for the worse. You can address your letters to:

Author (see copyright page)
Frommer's Canada '94–'95
Prentice Hall Travel
15 Columbus Circle
New York, NY 10023

A DISCLAIMER

Readers are advised that prices fluctuate in the course of time and travel information changes under the impact of the varied and volatile factors that affect the travel industry. Neither the authors nor the publisher can be held responsible for the experiences of readers while traveling. Readers are invited to write to the publisher with ideas, comments, and suggestions for future editions.

SAFETY ADVISORY

Whenever you're traveling in an unfamiliar city or country, stay alert. Be aware of your immediate surroundings. Wear a moneybelt and keep a close eye on your possessions. Be particularly careful with cameras, purses, and wallets, all favorite targets of thieves and pickpockets.

AN IMPORTANT NOTE ON PRICES

Unless stated otherwise, **the prices cited in this guide are given in Canadian dollars,** which is good news for American readers because the Canadian dollar is worth 25% less than the American dollar, but buys nearly as much. As we go to press, $1 Canadian is worth 75¢ U.S., which means that your $100-a-night hotel room will cost only U.S. $75, and your $6 breakfast costs only U.S. $4.50.

CHAPTER 1

GETTING TO KNOW CANADA

For an American, a trip to Canada is like going abroad and staying home at the same time. Therein lies the peculiar charm of the U.S.'s big, amiable neighbor to the north.

The surface features of the country evoke instant familiarity. Its currency and traffic regulations, slang terms and fashion styles, supermarkets, fast-food chains, and TV commercials, plus a thousand other home touches, can give you the impression that you've strayed into a vast elongation of your own backyard. Yet Canada is also unique, and exploring those differences will be the most fascinating aspect of your trip.

For a start, the sheer amount of elbow space makes you dizzy. Measuring 3.8 million square miles (200,000 more than the United States), Canada ranks second in size after Russia. This colossal expanse, however, contains only 25½ million people—barely three million more than California. What's more, the overwhelming majority of them cluster in a relatively narrow southern belt that boasts all the nation's large cities and nearly all its industries. As you head north, the landscape becomes emptier and emptier, until you reach an endless majestic wilderness almost devoid of human habitation.

The big metropolitan centers of the south—chic Montréal, dynamic Toronto, panoramic Vancouver—resemble somewhat better scrubbed and considerably safer counterparts of major U.S. cities. The silent north of the Yukon and Northwest Territories—where 51,000 people dot 1½ million square miles—remains a pioneer frontier, a mysterious vastness stretching to the Arctic shores, embracing thousands of lakes no one has ever charted, counted, or named.

Officially, Canada is a member of the British Commonwealth of Nations, but its ties with the Old Country are sentimental and historical rather than political. Britain's Queen Elizabeth II is also queen of Canada, which makes the country—theoretically—a monarchy. In practice, executive power rests with the prime minister and Parliament. Canada today is as independent as any member of the United Nations.

Yet the bonds of tradition remain: some quaint, some beautiful, some very useful indeed. They become visible in towns like Victoria, as regally English as Big Ben, in the scarlet coats and bearskins of the soldiers "trooping the colour" at Government House in Ottawa, in the profusion of British merchandise in the stores and Olde English shingles and inn signs all over the country. Less visible but most pervasive is law enforcement, which keeps Canada's streets safe and its ratio of criminality minuscule by U.S. standards.

Canada's traditional hospitality, however—which can be overwhelming—has nothing to do with any particular ethnic background. It is the essence of a pioneering people not yet far removed from an age when hospitality could mean the difference between death and survival. The stranger you fed and sheltered today might do the same for you tomorrow. It's an almost legendary characteristic of Newfoundland, Canada's youngest province. There, a quest for directions often leads to an invitation to a meal of the local specialty, salt beef and bannock. Or more likely, an offer of a noggin of "screech," an absolutely fiendish high-proof rum guaranteed to straighten curly hair and keep drowning sailors afloat in a North Atlantic gale.

1. A CAPSULE HISTORY

DATELINE

- **1608** Samuel de Champlain founds the settlement of Kebec — today's Québec City.
- **1642** French colony of Ville-Marie established, later renamed Montréal.
- **1720** Fort Toronto built as a French trading post.
- **1759** British defeat French at the Plains of Abraham. Fall of Québec City.
- **1763** All of "New France" (Canada) ceded to the British.
- **1775** American Revolutionary forces capture Montréal, but are repulsed at Québec City.
- **1813** Americans blow up Fort York (Toronto) in the War of 1812.
- **1841** Act of Union creates the United Provinces of Canada.
- **1855** By royal decree the lumber village of Ottawa becomes Canada's capital.
- **1869** The Hudson's Bay

(continues)

The Vikings landed in Canada over 1,000 years ago, but it was the French who got the first toehold in the country. In 1608 Samuel de Champlain established a settlement on the cliffs overlooking the St. Lawrence River—today's Québec City. This was exactly a year after the Virginia Company founded Jamestown. Hundreds of miles of unexplored wilderness lay between the embryo colonies, but they were inexorably set on a collision course.

The early stages of the struggle for the new continent were explorations, and there the French outdid the English. Their *coureurs de bois*—adventurous fur traders—their navigators, soldiers, and missionaries opened up not only Canada but most of the U.S. At least 35 of the 50 United States were either discovered, mapped, or settled by the French, who left behind some 4,000 place names to prove it, among them Detroit, St. Louis, New Orleans, Duluth, and Des Moines.

Gradually they staked out an immense colonial empire that, in patches and minus recognized borders, stretched from Hudson Bay in the Arctic to the Gulf of Mexico. Christened New France, it was run on an ancient seignorial system, whereby settlers were granted land by the Crown in return for military service.

The military obligation was essential, for the colony knew hardly a moment of peace during its existence. New France blocked the path of western expansion by England's seaboard colonies with a string of forts that lined the Ohio-Mississippi Valley. The Anglo-Americans were determined to break through, and so the frontier clashes crackled and flared, with the native tribes participating ferociously. These miniature wars were nightmares of savagery, waged with knives and tomahawks as much as with muskets and cannon, characterized by raids and counterraids, burning villages, and massacred women and children. According to some historians, the English introduced scalping to America by offering a cash bounty for each French scalp the native braves brought in!

The French retaliated in kind. They converted the Abenaki tribe to Christianity and encouraged them to raid deep into New England territory where, in 1704, they totally destroyed the town of Deerfield, Massachusetts. The Americans answered with a punitive blitz expedition by the famous green-clad Roger's Rangers, who wiped out the main Abenaki village and slaughtered half its population. By far the most dreaded of the tribes was the Iroquois,

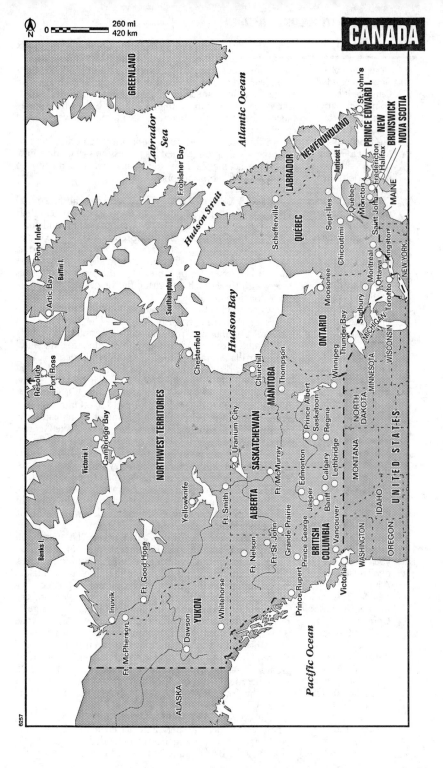

CANADA

0 260 mi
420 km

DATELINE

Company sells Rupert's Land to Canada. It becomes the Province of Alberta.

1873 Creation of the Northwest Mounted Police — the Mounties — now called Royal Canadian Mounted Police (RCMP) and rarely mounted.

1875 West Coast community of Gastown incorporated as the city of Vancouver. The Northwest Mounted Police builds the log fort that developed into the city of Calgary.

1885 Rebellion of the Métis under Louis Riel in western Saskatchewan.

1887 The Transcontinental Railroad reaches Vancouver, connecting Canada from ocean to ocean.

1896 The Klondike goldrush brings 100,000 people swarming into the Yukon.

1905 The former trading post of Edmonton, barely a year old as a city, declared capital of Alberta.

1906 The Toronto Cycle and Motor Company builds the first Canadian automobile.

1914 Canada enters World War I alongside Britain. Some 60,000 Canadians died in combat.

1920 The Northwest Territories
(continues)

who played the same role in the Canadian east as the Sioux (another French label) played in the American west. Unspeakably cruel, the Iroquois were also astute politicians who learned to play the English against the French and vice versa, lending their scalping knives now to one side, then to the other. It took more than a century before they finally succumbed to the whites' smallpox, firewater, and gunpowder—in that order.

In this border warfare a young Virginian officer named George Washington learned his profession—including how to take a licking. In 1754 the French defeated his unit in Ohio and took him prisoner.

THE FALL OF QUEBEC There were only about 65,000 French settlers in the colony, but they more than held their own against the million Anglo-Americans, first and foremost because they were natural forest fighters—one Canadian trapper could stalemate six redcoats in the woods. Mainly, however, it was because they made friends with the local tribes whenever possible. Thus the majority of tribes sided with the French and made the English pay a terrible price for their blindness.

When the final round began in 1754, it opened with a series of shattering English debacles. The French had a brilliant commander, the marquis de Montcalm, exactly the kind of unorthodox tactician needed for the fluid semiguerrilla warfare of the American wilderness.

Britain's proud General Braddock rode into a French-Indian ambush that killed him and scattered his army. Montcalm led an expedition against Fort Oswego that wiped out the stronghold and turned Lake Ontario into a French waterway. The following summer he repeated the feat with Fort William Henry, at the head of Lake George, which fell amid ghastly scenes of massacre, later immortalized by James Fenimore Cooper in *The Last of the Mohicans*. Middle New York now lay wide open to raids, and England's hold on America seemed to be slipping.

Then, like a cornered boxer bouncing from the ropes, the British came back with a devastating right-left-right that not only saved their colonies but also won them the entire continent.

The first punches were against Fort Duquesne, in Pennsylvania, and against the Fortress of Louisbourg, on Cape Breton, both of which they took after bloody sieges. Then, where least expected, came the ultimate haymaker, aimed straight at the enemy's solar plexus—Québec.

In June 1759 a British fleet nosed its way from the Atlantic Ocean down the St. Lawrence River. In charge of the troops on board was the youngest general in the army, 32-year-old James Wolfe, whose military record was remarkable and whose behavior was so eccentric that he had the reputation of being "mad as a march hare." When King George II—who, whatever his other failings, did not lack wit—heard the rumors, he snorted: "Mad, is he, what? Then, by Jove, I wish he would bite some of my sane generals!"

The struggle for Québec dragged on until September, when Wolfe, near desperation, played his final card. He couldn't storm those gallantly defended fortress walls, although the British guns had shelled the town to rubble.

Wolfe therefore loaded 5,000 men into boats and rowed upriver to a cove behind the city. Then they silently climbed the towering cliff face in the darkness, and when morning came Wolfe had his army squarely astride Montcalm's supply lines. Now the French had to come out of their stronghold and give battle in the open.

The British formed their famous "thin red line" across the bush-studded Plains of Abraham, just west of the city. Montcalm advanced upon them with five regiments, all in step, and in the next quarter of an hour the fate of Canada was decided. The redcoats stood like statues as the French drew closer—100 yards, 60 yards, 40 yards. . . . Then a command rang out, and—in such perfect unison that it sounded like a single thunderclap—the English muskets crashed. The redcoats advanced four measured paces, halted, fired, advanced another four paces with robot precision—halted, fired again. Then it was all over.

The plain was covered with the fallen French. Montcalm lay mortally wounded, and the rest of his troops were fleeing helter-skelter. Among the British casualties was Wolfe himself. With two bullets through his body, he lived just long enough to hear that he had won. Montcalm died a few hours after him.

Today, overlooking the boardwalk of Québec, you'll find a unique memorial to both these outstanding men—a statue commemorating both victor and vanquished of the same battle!

THE U.S. INVASION The capture of Québec determined the war and left Britain ruler of all North America down to the Mexican border. Yet, oddly enough, it was this victory that generated Britain's worst defeat. For if the French had held Canada, the British government would certainly have been more careful in its treatment of the American colonists.

As it was, the British felt cocksure and decided to make the colonists themselves pay for the outrageous costs of the French and Indian Wars. Hence the taxes slapped on all imports—especially tea—that infuriated the colonists to the point of open rebellion against the Crown.

But if the British misjudged the temper of the colonists, the Americans were equally wrong about the mood of the Canadians. Washington felt sure that the French in the north would join the American Revolution, or at least not resist an invasion of American soldiers. He was terribly mistaken on both counts.

The French had little love for either of the English-speaking antagonists. But they were staunch Royalists and devout Catholics, with no sympathy for the "godless" republicans from the south. Only a handful changed sides, and most French Canadians fought grimly shoulder to shoulder with their erstwhile enemies.

So Washington's three most aggressive generals came to grief over French resistance. The daredevil Vermonter Ethan Allen and his Green Mountain Boys were taken prisoner at Montréal. Montgomery fell before Québec, while the ambitious Benedict Arnold was driven back with defeat on his record and the first seeds of treason ripening in his heart.

Thirty-eight years later, in the War of 1812, another U.S.

army marched up the banks of the Richelieu River where it flows from Lake Champlain to the St. Lawrence. And once again the French Canadians stuck by the British and flung back the invaders. The war ended in a draw, but with surprisingly happy results. Britain and the young United States agreed to demilitarize the Great Lakes and to extend their mutual border along the 49th parallel to the Rockies.

LOYALISTS & IMMIGRANTS   One of the side effects of the American Revolution was an influx of English-speaking newcomers for Canada. About 50,000 Americans who had remained faithful to King George, the United Empire Loyalists, migrated to Canada because they were given rough treatment in the U.S. They settled mostly in Nova Scotia and began to populate the almost empty shores of what is now New Brunswick.

After the Napoleonic Wars, a regular tide of immigrants came from England, which was going through the early and cruelest stages of the Industrial Revolution. They were fleeing from the new and hideously bleak factory towns, from workhouses, starvation wages, and impoverished Scottish farms. Even the unknown perils of the New World seemed preferable to these blessings of the Dickens era.

By 1850 more than half a million immigrants had arrived, pushing Canada's population above two million. And now the population centers began to shift westward, away from the old seaboard colonies in the east, opening up the territories eventually called Ontario, Manitoba, and Saskatchewan.

With increased population came the demand for confederation, largely because the various colony borders hampered trade. Britain complied rather promptly. In 1867 the British Parliament passed an act creating a federal union out of the colonies of Upper and Lower Canada, Nova Scotia, and New Brunswick. British Columbia hesitated over whether to remain separate, join the United States, or merge with Canada, but finally voted itself in. Remote Newfoundland hesitated longest of all. It remained a distinct colony until 1949, when it became Canada's 10th province.

THE REBELLION OF THE METIS   Geographically, Canada stretched from the Atlantic to the Pacific Ocean, but in reality most of the immense region in between lay beyond the rule of Ottawa, the nation's capital. The endless prairies and forest lands of the west and northwest were inhabited by about 40,000 people, over half of them nomadic tribes. They lived by hunting, fishing, and trapping, depending largely on buffalo for food, clothing, and shelter. As the once-enormous herds began to dwindle, life grew increasingly hard for the nomads. Adding to their troubles were whisky traders peddling poisonous rotgut for furs, and packs of outlaws who took what they wanted at gunpoint.

Ordinary law officers were nearly useless in this environment. In 1873 the federal government therefore created a quite extraordinary force: the Northwest Mounted Police, now called the Royal Canadian Mounted Police (and now rarely mounted). The scarlet-coated Mounties earned a legendary reputation for toughness, fairness, and the ability to hunt down wrongdoers. And unlike their American counterparts, they usually brought in prisoners alive.

The Mounties proceeded to tame the west, and did so with astonishingly small numbers. One trooper alone would clean up a settlement, throw out the liquor traders, and clap the armed thugs in irons. When Chief Sitting Bull's tribe of Sioux drifted into Canada after the battle of the Little Big Horn, the government sent five Mounties to force them to a reservation. Custer had tried it with 400 U.S. Cavalry and died in the attempt. The Mounties accomplished the feat without ever drawing their guns, evoking Sitting Bull's comment: "Now I know why the queen needs so few men to uphold her peace."

But even the Mounties couldn't handle the desperate uprising that shook western Saskatchewan in 1885. As the railroad relentlessly pushed across the prairies and the buffalo vanished, the people known as Métis felt they had to fight for their existence. The Métis, offspring of French trappers and native women, were superb hunters and trackers. The westward expansion had driven them from Manitoba to the banks of the

DID YOU KNOW . . . ?

- Canada is the habitat of the largest as well as the smallest land mammal in North America—the wood buffalo and the pigmy shrew, respectively.
- Canada is 200,000 square miles bigger than the United States, but has only three million more people than California.
- The first-ever singing commercial was aired by a religious radio station in Toronto in 1926.
- The name "Canada" is derived from the Huron term *kanata,* meaning settlement.
- Canadian militia—not British troops—torched the Washington White House during the War of 1812. They did it to retaliate for the Americans' burning of Parliament House in what was then York—today's Toronto.
- Québec City is the only walled town on the American continent.
- Frederick Law Olmsted, the man who designed New York's Central Park, also designed Mount Royal Park in Montréal.
- The Klondike goldfields in the Yukon were the richest gold deposits ever found on earth.
- In Cambridge Bay, Northwest Territories, the sun shines 24 hours round the clock during summer months.
- The Battle on the Plains of Abraham, Québec City, fought in 1759, was the only combat in history in which *both* opposing commanders were killed.
- There are more Native Canadians (Indians) living today than existed at the arrival of the white man.
- Montréal has the only existing museum devoted to humor.
- During World War II, with Britain threatened by invasion, the entire gold reserve of the Bank of England was shipped to Canada.

Saskatchewan River, where some 6,000 of them now made their last stand against iron rails and wooden farmhouses. They had a charismatic leader in Louis Riel, a man educated enough to teach school and mad enough to think that God wanted him to found a new religion.

With Riel's rebels rose their natural allies, the Plains tribes, under chiefs Poundmaker and Big Bear. Together they were a formidable force. The Métis attacked the Mounted Police at Duck Lake, cut the telegraph wires, and proclaimed an independent republic. Their allies stormed the town of Battleford, then captured and burned Fort Pitt.

The alarmed administration in Ottawa sent an army marching westward under General Middleton, equipped with artillery and Gatling machine guns. The Métis checked them briefly at Fish Creek, but had to fall back on their main village of Batoche. There the last battle of the west took place—long lines of redcoats charging with fixed bayonets, the Métis fighting from house to house, from rifle pits and crude trenches, so short of ammunition that they had to shoot lead buttons instead of bullets.

Batoche fell (you can still see the bullet marks on the houses there) and the rebellion was completely crushed shortly afterward. Louis Riel was tried for treason and murder. Although any court today probably would have found him insane, the Canadian authorities hanged him.

RAILROADS, WHEAT & WAR The reason that the army was able to crush Riel's rebellion so quickly was also the reason for its outbreak: the Canadian Pacific Railway. The railroad was more than a marvel of engineering—it formed a steel band holding the country together, enabling Canada to live up to its motto, *A Mari Usque ad Mare*— "From Sea to Sea."

Although the free-roaming prairie people hated the iron horse, railroads were vital to Canada's survival as a nation. They had to be pushed through, against all opposition, if the isolated provinces were not to drift into the orbit of the United States and the Dominion cease to exist. As one journalist of the time put it: "The whistle of a locomotive is the true cradle song and anthem of our country."

If Canada had adopted a national color, it probably would have been yellow—for wheat. As the country's transportation system developed, the central provinces emerged as one of the world's biggest breadbaskets. In one decade wheat production zoomed from 56 million bushels to over 200 million, which put Canada on a par with the U.S. and Russia as a granary.

And despite the bitterness engendered by the execution of Riel, in the following year Canada elected its first prime minister of French heritage. Sir Wilfrid Laurier had one foot in each ethnic camp and he proved to be a superlative leader—according to some, the best his country ever produced. His term of office, from 1896 to 1911, was a period in which Canada flexed its muscles like a young giant and looked forward to unlimited growth and a century of peaceful prosperity—just like an equally optimistic American neighbor to the south.

With the onset of World War I, the Dominion went to war allied with Britain and likewise tried to fight it on a volunteer basis. It didn't work. The tall, healthy Canadians, together with the Australians, formed the shock troops of the British Empire and earned that honor with torrents of blood. The entire Western Front in France was littered with Canadian bones. The flow of volunteers became a trickle, and in 1917 the Dominion was forced to introduce conscription. The measure ran into violent opposition from the French-speaking minority, who saw conscription as a device to thin out their numbers.

The draft law went through, but it strained the nation's unity almost to the breaking point. The results were ghastly. More than 60,000 Canadians fell in battle, a terrible bloodletting for a country of 7¼ million inhabitants. (In World War II, by contrast, Canada lost 40,000 from a population of 11½ million.)

The one benefit Canada reaped from the slaughter was an acceleration of industrial development and an enormous boost to mining activity. In the postwar years Canada emerged not merely as an agricultural exporter, but as a budding power in the mineral and manufacturing fields.

TOWARD WORLD POWER   Between the wars the fortunes of Canada more or less reflected those of the United States, except that Canada was never foolish enough to join the "noble experiment" of Prohibition. Some of its citizens, in fact, waxed rich on the lucrative bootlegging trade across the border.

But the depression, coupled with disastrous droughts in the western provinces, hit all the harder in Canada. There was no equivalent of Roosevelt's New Deal in the Dominion. The country staggered along from one financial crisis to the next until the outbreak of World War II totally transformed the situation. The war provided the boost Canada needed to join the ranks of the major industrial nations. And the surge of postwar immigration provided the numbers required to work the newly developed industries. From 1941 to 1974 Canada doubled in population and increased its gross national product (GNP) nearly tenfold.

With the discovery of huge uranium deposits in Ontario and Saskatchewan, Canada was in the position to add nuclear energy to its power resources. And the opening of the St. Lawrence Seaway turned Toronto—which lies more than 1,000 miles from the nearest ocean—into a major seaport. The project, incidentally, did the same for Chicago, Buffalo, and Detroit on the U.S. side. When Queen Elizabeth and President Eisenhower jointly opened the colossal seaway in 1959, it represented the biggest technical undertaking ever completed by two countries working in partnership.

All these achievements propelled Canada into its present position: the sixth-ranking manufacturing and trading nation on the globe, with a standard of living higher than that of the United States. But, simultaneously, old and never-banished ghosts were raising their heads again.

TROUBLE IN QUEBEC   As an ethnic enclave the French Canadians had won their battle for survival with flying colors. From their original 65,000 settlers they had grown to over six million, and had done so without receiving reinforcements from overseas.

The French Canadians had preserved and increased their presence by means of large families, rigid cultural cohesion, and the unifying influence of their Catholic faith. But they had fallen far behind the English-speaking majority economically and politically. Few of them held top positions in industry or finance, and they enjoyed relatively little say in national matters.

What rankled most with them was that Canada never recognized French as a second national language. In other words, the French were expected to be bilingual if they wanted good careers, but the English-speakers got along nicely with just their own tongue. On a general cultural basis, too, the country overwhelmingly reflected Anglo-Saxon attitudes rather than an Anglo-French mixture.

By the early 1960s this discontent led to a dramatic radicalization of québecois politics. A new separatist movement arose that regarded Québec not as simply one of ten provinces but as l'état du Québec, a distinct state and people that might—if it chose—break away from the country. The most extreme faction of the movement, the Front de Libération du Québec (FLQ), was frankly revolutionary and terrorist. It backed its demands with bombs, arson, and murder, culminating in the kidnap-killing of Cabinet Minister Pierre Laporte in October 1970.

The Ottawa government, under Prime Minister Pierre Trudeau, imposed the War Measures Act and moved 10,000 troops into the province. The police used their exceptional powers under the act to break up civil disorders, arrested hundreds of suspects, and caught the murderers of Laporte. And in the provincial elections of 1973, the separatists were badly defeated, winning only six seats from a total of 110.

The crisis calmed down. In some ways its effects were beneficial. The federal government redoubled its efforts to remove the worst grievances of the French Canadians. Federal funds flowed to French schools outside Québec (nearly half the schoolchildren of New Brunswick, for example, are French-speaking). French Canadians were appointed to senior positions. Most important, all provinces were asked to make French an official language, which entailed making signs, government forms, transportation schedules, and other printed matter bilingual. Civil servants had to bone up on French to pass their examinations and the business world began to stipulate bilingualism for men and women aiming at executive positions. All these measures, it should be noted, were already afoot before the turmoil began, but there is no doubt that bloodshed helped to accelerate them.

UNION OR SEPARATION? Ever since this violent crisis, Canadian politicians of all hues have been trying to patch up some sort of compromise that would enable their country to remain united. They appeared close to success when they formulated the so-called Meech Lake accord in the 1980s—only to see it destroyed by a whole series of opposition moves stemming not only from French Canadians but also from Native Canadian groups. The separatist Parti Québécois rallied its forces and staged a political comeback. The rift between Québec's French and English speakers is today wider than ever.

Québec's premier set up a commission to study ways to change the province's constitutional relationship with the federal government in Ottawa. This, in turn, aroused the ire of other provinces, who failed to see why Québec should be granted a "special"—meaning privileged—position within Canada. So the proposals, memorandums, and referendums go on and on; each one vetoed by the other camp and none coming closer to a solution.

By now most Canadians are heartily tired of the debate, though nobody seems to have a clear idea how to end it. Some say that secession is the only way out; others favor the Swiss formula of biculturalism and bilingualism. For Québec the breakaway advocated by francophone hotheads could spell economic disaster. Most of Canada's industrial and financial power is located in the English-speaking provinces. An independent Québec would be a poor country. But all of Canada would be poorer by losing the special flavor and rich cultural heritage imparted by the presence of "La Belle Province."

2. THE PEOPLE

Canada's people are even more diverse than its scenery. In the eastern province of Québec live six million French Canadians, whose motto *Je me souviens*—"I remember"—has kept them "more French than France" through two centuries of Anglo domination. They have transformed Canada into a bilingual country where everything official—including parking tickets and airline passes—comes in two tongues.

The English-speaking majority of the populace is a mosaic rather than a block. Two massive waves of immigration—one before 1914, the other between 1945 and 1972—poured 6.5 million assorted Europeans and Americans into the country, providing muscles and skills as well as a kaleidoscope of cultures. Thus Nova Scotia is as Scottish as haggis and kilts, Vancouver has a Germanic core alongside a Chinatown, the plains of Manitoba are sprinkled with the onion-shaped domes of Ukrainian churches, and Ontario offers Italian street markets and a Shakespeare festival at—yes, Stratford, Ontario.

You can attend a Native Canadian tribal assembly, a Chinese New Year dragon parade, an Inuit spring celebration, a German *Bierfest,* a Highland gathering, or a Slavic folk dance. There are group settlements on the prairies where the working parlance is Danish or Czech or Hungarian, and entire villages that speak Icelandic. For Canada has not been a "melting pot" in the American sense, but rather has sought "unity through diversity" as a national ideal.

INDIANS There are actually more Native Canadians living in Canada today than existed at the time of the first white settlements. Anthropologists have estimated that the original population was about 200,000. The native population began to decline with the arrival of the Europeans. By the early 20th century it was down to almost half, and common belief labeled the native peoples a dying race. At the last census, however, the total number had reached 282,000.

Ethnically Canada's native peoples are the same as some tribes in the U.S. Some tribes, such as the Cree, Sioux, and Blackfoot, are found on both sides of the border. In Canada they belong to 10 distinct linguistic groups, subdivided into widely differing local dialects. Their customs, religion, and methods of hunting and warfare were very similar to those of tribes near the border in the United States. The treatment they received, however, was rather different.

In the 1870s—before most white settlers reached the west—the Canadian government began to negotiate a series of treaties with the prairie tribes. By the end of the decade most of the western tribes had agreed to treaties in which they surrendered their lands in return for guaranteed reservations, small cash payments for each individual member, supplies of seeds and tools, and assistance in changing over to farming for a livelihood. By and large, with a few inglorious exceptions, those treaties were kept.

The Canadian government wielded much greater control over the white settlers than its counterpart in Washington. It was thus able to prevent the continual incursions by gold prospectors, buffalo hunters, railroad companies, and squatters that sparked most of the Indian wars south of the border. The Mounties, as distinct from the U.S. Cavalry, actually protected native tribes. As the Blackfoot chief Crowfoot said: "The police have shielded us from bad men as the feathers of birds protect them from the winter frosts. If the police had not come, very few of us would have been left today."

The decline of the native population was due mainly to sickness brought in by the whites. In addition, tens of thousands of erstwhile nomadic hunters simply couldn't bear a life tied to one patch of soil; they died from sheer discouragement, unwilling to continue an existence that appeared joyless and stale.

IMPRESSIONS

You won't find any Canadians in the North, only mad dogs and Scotsmen.
—WELSH SCIENTIST, REMARK QUOTED BY ALISTAIR HORNE,
CANADA AND THE CANADIANS, 1961

A Canadian is someone who knows how to make love in a canoe.
—PIERRE BERTON, 1973

Today the country has 574 separate Native Canadian communities, known as "bands." A few—a very few—of them still roam the northern regions. The others share 2,110 reserves, although less than two-thirds actually live on reservations. Today they are successful farmers, nurses, builders, secretaries, doctors, teachers, clergy, salespeople, and industrial workers, both on and off the reserves. In 1973 the government accepted a proposal by the National Indian Brotherhood by which increasing numbers of bands now manage their own schools. Instead of trying to erase their past, the new school curricula include history and native-language courses for children who have almost forgotten their native tongues.

This is only fair, since the very name "Canada" derives from the Huron word for settlement, kanata.

INUIT "Inuit" means "people," and that is what the Canadian Eskimos call themselves. So remote was their native habitat, so completely isolated from the rest of the world, that they were unaware that any people except themselves existed.

The Eskimos are a unique people, the Canadian branch even more so than the others. There are only around 80,000 Eskimos in the entire world, forming part of four nations: Russia, the United States, Canada, and Denmark (in Greenland, which is a Danish possession). This makes the Eskimos the only natives of the same ethnic group to live in both Asia and America.

Some 22,000 Inuit live in Canada today, and we have no idea how many there might have been originally. They inhabited the far north, the very last portion of the country to be explored, much later than the other Arctic lands of the globe. While their cousins elsewhere were trading with the white settlers, the Inuit initially had limited contact with Europeans.

The Inuit were traditionally coastal people who lived by fishing and by hunting seals, whales, and polar bears. These animals supplied their food, clothing, light, and heat (in the form of blubber-fueled lamps and stoves), and were utilized to their last shred of skin. The Inuit's earliest contact, therefore, was with whalers, frequently with tragic results. The Inuit were gentle people, intensely hospitable and so averse to violence that their language had no term for war.

When the first British and American whaling ships touched Baffin Bay in the 1820s, they found that the Inuit had no conception of private property, of food and clothing that was not shared with whoever needed it. The Inuit marveled at the white sailors' wooden whaleboats, firearms, iron tools, and glass bottles—none of which they had ever seen. They had no idea of the dangers associated with these wonders.

Murder and rape were the least of them. Liquor was far more destructive, but worst of all were the diseases the whalers introduced. For all its harshness, the Arctic was a healthy region, free of bacteria. The Inuit might starve and freeze to death, but they rarely succumbed to illness. As a result their bodies had no resistance to the measles, smallpox, and tuberculosis that the whites brought in along with their rum and gadgetry.

The Inuit—particularly their children—died like flies. The only doctors available to them were a handful of missionaries, usually with very limited medical supplies. Today's Inuit, therefore, are a race of survivors, the strain that somehow battled through a century that killed uncounted numbers of their kind.

It was not until the 1950s that the Canadian government took serious steps to assure the Inuit their rightful place in their Arctic homeland. As air transportation and radio communications broke down the isolation of the far north, the government introduced improved educational, health, and welfare services. The Inuit are now full citizens in every respect—not in name only—electing members of the Territorial Council of the Northwest Territories and running their own communities.

They have ceased to be nomads and have moved into permanent settlements. But

---

IMPRESSIONS

Such a land is good for an energetic man. It is also not so bad for the loafer.
—RUDYARD KIPLING, *LETTERS TO THE FAMILY*, 1908

unlike the prairie tribes, the Inuit are still basically hunters, although nowadays they use rifles instead of the traditional harpoons. But don't compare their hunting with weekend activity. The Inuit hunt in order to eat, and no one is more ecologically conscious than they are. Everything in their prey is used—a walrus represents a miniature supermarket to an Inuk—and they kill nothing for pleasure and not one animal more than is absolutely necessary.

The Inuit Tapirisat (Inuit Brotherhood) is their nonpolitical organization dedicated to preserving the Inuktetut language and culture and to helping them achieve full participation in Canada's society. This would include legal rights to some of the enormous lands the Inuit once roamed and utilized, but without establishing fixed borders for their domain. Some of these areas have been found to contain valuable deposits of oil, natural gas, and minerals, which makes the question of ownership more than merely academic.

If you want a glimpse of the Inuit soul, look at their art, which you'll find in stores all over Canada. Their artistry shouldn't surprise you: The Inuit are perhaps the greatest needle (fishbone) experts in the world, and their completely waterproof sealskin kayak canoe is possibly the best-designed vehicle in marine history.

But Inuit carvings of people and animals have a quality all their own. They are imbued with a sense of movement, a feeling for anatomy, almost a smell. Their expressions are so hauntingly lifelike, yet so curiously abstract, that they give you an eerie notion of having seen them before in some strange dream.

3. WILDLIFE

Canada has many of the same animals as the northern United States, but in larger quantities and spread over wider areas. You still come across brown bears and grizzlies in British Columbia and the Laurentians of Québec; buffalo in Alberta; elk and moose in Saskatchewan; and deer, skunks, raccoons, and beavers in most of the provinces.

The fewer the people, the richer the animal life, which is why the Northwest Territories, the Yukon, and the northernmost regions of Québec boast the most numerous fauna—huge white polar bears lumbering over ice floes; musk-oxen and caribou grazing on the tundras; seals and walruses waddling along the shorelines; and occasional packs of wolves prowling the forests.

Most of these animals are now protected (although in the case of seals and polar bears, not enough). But Canada is an absolute paradise for sportfishing: Some call it the greatest fishing hole in the world. Hundreds of thousands of lakes, rivers, and streams teem with all the major freshwater species, while the Atlantic and Pacific coasts are home to striped bass, bluefin tuna, sharks, and the entire gamut of deep-sea fish.

Each region has one or several favorite species: rainbow trout (called Kamloops trout) in British Columbia, Atlantic salmon in Labrador, bluefin tuna in Prince Edward Island, brook trout in Nova Scotia, northern pike and walleye (pickerel) in Québec, smallmouth bass in Manitoba, and arctic grayling and char in the Yukon and Northwest Territories.

As a general rule, the farther north you go, the more fabulous the fishing—and the shorter the season for it. In the Yukon and Northwest Territories, open-water fishing extends from June to late September and is at its best just after the ice is gone from streams and lakes—the latter half of June through the first half of July. The water in these Arctic regions is very cold and game fish fight harder than they do in the south, an added attraction for some.

Some of the finest fishing in Canada is a fly-in proposition: The fishing camps and lodges can be reached only by aircraft. We'll describe some of the package plans available when we deal with the provinces concerned. A week-long fishing excursion—including flights, meals, and guides—varies as much as from $400 to $850 per person, according to the time of year and the location of the camps.

IMPRESSIONS

I saw a great and wonderful country; a land containing in its soil everything that a man desires; a proper land, for proper men to live in and to prosper exceedingly.
—FIELD-MARSHAL LORD MONTGOMERY, 1946

I don't even know what street Canada is on.
—AL CAPONE, 1931 REMARK QUOTED IN ROY GREENWAY, *THE NEWS GAME*, 1966

Each province and territory has its own licensing regulations, simple in some parts of the country, more complicated in others. Fishing permits are readily available, but if you go for Atlantic salmon in New Brunswick, for instance, the rule is that nonresident anglers must hire guides in required numbers: one guide per angler in a boat, but only one guide per three wading anglers. Don't ask us why.

The cost of fishing licenses varies also. The tourist information offices in each province will give you booklets listing all the red tape wrapped around the rods in their particular realm.

4. RECOMMENDED BOOKS & FILMS

BOOKS

GENERAL Two of Canada's outstanding and internationally popular writers in different fields are Farley Mowat and Pierre Berton. The former deals mainly with wildlife, the latter with historical themes; both are immensely enjoyable to read. Their works would fill several shelves, but their best-known books are probably Mowat's *Never Cry Wolf* and Berton's *My Country*.

For other aspects Canadian, try:

Oh Canada! Oh Québec!, Mordecai Richler (Penguin Books, 1992)
Klondike, Pierre Berton (M & S, 1972)
Riel to Reform, George Melnyk (Fifth House, 1992)
Canadian Anecdotes, Douglas Fetherling (Broadview Press, 1988)
Towards a Just Society, Thomas Axworthy & Pierre Trudeau (Viking, 1990)
My Father's Son, Farley Mowat (Key Porter Books, 1992)
The Patriot Game, Peter Brimelow (Key Porter Books, 1986)
Stolen Continent, Ronald Wright (Viking, 1992)
Canada Firsts, Ralph Nader (M & S, 1991)
In the Eye of the Eagle, Jean-Francois Lisée (HarperCollins, 1990)

FICTION Margaret Atwood and Mordecai Richler are among the best-known contemporary Canadian novelists. Most of Ms. Atwood's books are set in Toronto, including her famous *Life Before Man.* Richler's most celebrated work, *The Apprenticeship of Duddy Kravitz,* deals with lower-class Jewish life in Montréal and was made into a hit movie. The equally famous poet-balladeer Leonard Cohen is difficult to define and best heard on one of his records, such as *Songs of Love and Hate* and *Death of a Ladies Man.*

For an eclectic sampling of contemporary Canadian fiction, try:

The Cat's Eye, The Handmaid's Tale, and *The Robber Bride,* Margaret Atwood
Beautiful Losers, Leonard Cohen (Viking, 1966)
The Americans Are Coming (humor), Herb Curtis
The Tin Flute, Gabrielle Roy (translated from the French; McClelland and Steward, 1980)
White Desert, Jean Ethier-Blais (translated from the French; Véhicule Press, 1991)

The Meeting Point, Austin Clarke (1967)
The Progress of Love, Alice Munro
The Suicide Murders (detective mystery), Howard Engel (1988)

FILMS

Canadians have earned more acclaim for their animated shorts and documentaries than for full-length features. The reason for this is that the shorts are uniquely Canadian—Anglo or Franco—and bear the unmistakable stamp of their origin. Full-length films, on the other hand, tend to be coproductions with American and British companies and a mix of directors and actors that makes it difficult to sort out the actual Canadian element. Even such a quintessentially Canadian theme as *The Apprenticeship of Duddy Kravitz* (1974), starred American Richard Dreyfuss in the lead. And the enthralling historical drama *The Black Robe* (1991) was directed by Australian Bruce Beresford.

The titles below, while Canadian in setting, mostly represent the same kind of mixture.

I Confess (1953), directed by Alfred Hitchcock
The Dog Who Stopped the War (1984)
The Care Bears Movie (1985), starring Mickey Rooney
The Decline of the American Empire (1986)
Jesus of Montréal (1989), directed by Denys Arcand
Agnes of God (1986), with Anne Bancroft and Jane Fonda
If Looks Could Kill (1991), with Linda Hunt
Dead Ringers (1988), starring Jeremy Irons

PLANNING A TRIP TO CANADA

I strongly recommend that you read this chapter before you set out on your trip. It could save you money, luggage space, time, and possibly aggravation. It contains capsuled tourist know-how: when to come, what to bring, the documentation you'll need, and where to make inquiries.

It's all very basic stuff, but you'd be surprised how a little foreknowledge can make the difference between a smooth and a bumpy excursion. The purpose of this chapter is to package the information you need so you can concentrate solely on the business of enjoying yourself. And we can't think of a worthier cause.

1. INFORMATION, ENTRY REQUIREMENTS & MONEY

SOURCES OF INFORMATION Canadian consulates do *not* dispense tourist information. All such information is handled by the various provincial offices.

• Alberta Economic Development and Tourism, City Centre, 10155 102 St., Edmonton, AB, T5J 4L6 (tel. toll free 800/661-8888).
• Discover British Columbia, Parliament Building, Victoria, BC, V8V 1X4 (tel. toll free 800/663-6000).
• Travel Manitoba, 155 Carlton St., Winnipeg, MB, RC3 3H8 (tel. toll free 800/665-0040).
• Tourism New Brunswick, P.O. Box 12345, Fredericton, NB, E3B 53C (tel. toll free 800/561-0123).
• Newfoundland and Labrador, Dept. of Development, P.O. Box 8700, St. John's, NF, A1B 4J6 (tel. toll free 800/563-6353).
• Nova Scotia Dept. of Tourism, P.O. Box 456, Halifax, NS, B3J 2R5 (tel. toll free 800/341-6096).
• Northwest Territories Economic Development and Tourism, P.O. Box 1320, Yellowknife, NWT, X1A 2L9 (tel. toll free 800/661-0788).
• Ontario Travel, Queen's Park, Toronto, ON, M7A 2E5 (tel. toll free 800/668-2746).

- Prince Edward Island, Dept. of Tourism and Parks, P.O. Box 940, Charlottetown, PEI, C1A 7M5 (tel. toll free 800/565-0267).
- Tourisme Québec, C.P. 20,000, Québec City, PQ, G1K 7X2 (tel. toll free 800/363-7777).
- Tourism Saskatchewan, 1919 Saskatchewan Dr., Regina, SK, S4P 3V7 (tel. toll free 800/667-7191).
- Tourism Yukon, P.O. Box 2703, Whitehorse, YK, Y1A 2C6 (tel. 403/667-5340).

For general information about Canada's national parks, contact **Environment Canada,** Inquiry Center, Ottawa, ON, K1A 0H3 (tel. 819/997-2800).

ENTRY REQUIREMENTS U.S. citizens or permanent residents of the United States, or British, Australian, New Zealand, or Irish nationals, require neither passports nor visas. You should, however, carry some identifying papers such as a passport or birth, baptismal, or voter's certificate to show your citizenship. Permanent U.S. residents who are not U.S. citizens must have their Alien Registration Cards.

Customs regulations are very generous in most respects, but get pretty complicated when it comes to firearms, plants, meats, and pet animals. Fishing tackle poses no problems, but the bearer must possess a nonresident license for the province or territory where he or she plans to use it. You can bring in free of duty up to 50 cigars, 200 cigarettes, and two pounds of tobacco, providing you're over 16 years of age. You are also allowed 40 ounces of liquor or wine.

One important point for teen travelers: Any person under 19 years of age requires a letter from a parent or guardian granting him or her permission to travel to Canada. The letter must state the traveler's name and duration of the trip. It is therefore essential that teenagers carry proof of identity; otherwise their letter is useless at the border.

For more detailed information concerning Customs regulations, write to: Customs and Excise, Connaught Building, Sussex Drive, Ottawa, ON, K1A 0L5.

MONEY Canada figures in dollars and cents, but with a very pleasing balance: The Canadian dollar is worth around 75¢ in U.S. money, give or take a couple of points' daily variation. So your American traveler's checks get you 25% or 26% more the moment you exchange them for local currency. That makes a difference in your budget. And since the price of many goods is roughly on a par with the U.S., the difference is real, not imaginary. You can bring in or take out any amount of money, but if you are importing or exporting sums of $5,000 or more, you must file a report of the transaction with U.S. Customs. Most tourist establishments in Canada will take U.S. cash, but for your own advantage you should change your funds into Canadian currency.

If you do spend American money at Canadian establishments, you should understand how the conversion is done. Often there will be a sign by the cash register that reads "U.S. Currency 20%." This 20% is the "premium," and it means that for every U.S. greenback you hand over, the cashier will see it as $1.20 in Canadian dollars. Thus, for a $8 tab, you need pay only $6.40 in U.S. bills. Great, isn't it? Well, yes and no.

When you cash U.S. traveler's checks at a bank, most banks will charge you a $2 fee per transaction (not per check). Hotels, restaurants, and shops don't charge fees as a rule, but their exchange rate may be somewhat lower than the current figure. The best advice I can give you is always to ask first.

The worst place to cash your checks is at airports, which always offer the lowest exchange rates of all. The tops (providing you have Amex traveler's checks) are American Express offices, which charge no fees and give peak exchange rates. It's a wise precaution to bring in sufficient Canadian cash to pay for an initial cab or bus and a meal.

A final word: Canada has no $1 bills. The lowest paper denomination is $2. Single bucks come in brass coins bearing the picture of a loon—hence their nickname, "loonies."

AN IMPORTANT NOTE ON PRICES

Unless stated otherwise, **the prices cited in this guide are given in Canadian dollars,** which is good news for U.S. travelers because the Canadian dollar is worth 25% less than the American dollar, but buys nearly as much. As we go to press, $1 Canadian is worth 75¢ U.S., which means that your $100-a-night hotel room will cost only U.S. $75, and your $6 breakfast costs only U.S. $4.50.

Here's a quick table of equivalents:

Canadian $	U.S. $
$ 1	$ 0.75
5	3.75
10	7.50
20	15.00
50	37.50
80	60.00
100	75.00
200	150.00

2. WHEN TO GO

CLIMATE Canada has a more uniform climate than the U.S., since it contains neither tropical nor desert regions. In the southern and central portions the weather is the same as in the northern United States. As you head north the climate becomes arctic, meaning long and extremely cold winters, brief and surprisingly warm summers (with lots of flies), and absolutely magical springs.

As a general rule, you can say that spring runs from mid-March to mid-May, summer from mid-May to mid-September, fall from mid-September to mid-November, and winter from mid-November to mid-March. Pick the season best suited to your tastes and temperament, and remember that your car should be winterized through March and that snow sometimes falls as late as April. September and October are best, in fact fantastic, for color photography.

Evenings tend to be cool everywhere, particularly on or near water. In late spring and early summer you'll definitely need a supply of insect repellent if you're planning bush travel.

To give you an idea of temperature variations, here is a list of some of the summer and winter extremes in various spots:

Location	Summer	Winter
Québec	77°	5°
Nova Scotia	74°	21°
Ontario	81°	−2°
Manitoba	80°	−12°
Alberta	76°	1°
British Columbia	74°	31°
Yukon	67°	−4°
Northwest Territories	69°	−26°

With the huge size of some provinces and territories, you naturally get considerable climate variations inside their borders. Québec, for instance, sprawls all the way from the temperate south to the Arctic, and the weather varies accordingly. British Columbia shows the slightest changes: It rarely goes above the 70s in summer or drops below the 30s in winter.

HOLIDAYS National holidays are celebrated throughout the country; meaning that all government facilities close down, as well as banks, but some department stores and a scattering of smaller shops stay open. If the holiday falls on a weekend the next Monday is observed.

New Year's Day, January 1	Labor Day, September 6
Good Friday, April 9	Thanksgiving, October 11
Easter Monday, April 12	Remembrance Day, November 11
Victoria Day, May 24	Christmas Day, December 25
Canada Day, July 1	Boxing Day, December 26

The following are the major provincial holidays, observed only locally:

Heritage Day, August 2, Alberta
British Columbia Day, August 2, British Columbia
Civic Holiday, August 2, Manitoba, Ontario, Nova Scotia, Saskatchewan
New Brunswick Day, August 2, New Brunswick
Discovery Day, June 21; Memorial Day, July 1; Orangeman's Day, July 12; St. George's Day, April 26; St. Patrick's Day, March 15; Newfoundland and Labrador
St. Jean Baptiste Day, June 24, Québec

3. HEALTH & INSURANCE

You don't need any special shots or vaccinations to get into Canada, and the local medical facilities are as good as—sometimes better than—those in the U.S. However, if you use any kind of regular medication it's a good idea to bring a prescription from your doctor giving the *generic* term for your medicine, since a particular brand name may not be available.

The kind of health and accident insurance you may need for your trip depends entirely on the insurance you already have. Check your policy and find out if it covers you in a foreign country. If not, several companies exist that specialize in supplementary insurance, including **Travel Guard International,** 1145 Clark St., Stevens Point, WI 54481 (tel. toll free 800/821-2828); and **International SOS Assistance,** Box 11568, Philadelphia, PA 19116 (tel. toll free 800/523-8930).

4. WHAT TO PACK

The wearables in your luggage naturally depend on the time of year you come and whether you're out to ski or to swim. But there are a few items we recommend taking along in all of our travel books—the result of wisdom acquired in many years of solid globe-trotting:

(1) A travel alarm clock, which renders you independent of hotel wake-up calls. (2) A washcloth in a plastic bag—although nearly all Canadian hotels supply them for their guests, a few do not. (3) A small flashlight, particularly if you're driving. (4) A very small screwdriver. (5) A magnifying glass to read the tiny print on maps. (6) And if you intend to go to Québec, an English-French dictionary.

As far as clothing is concerned, include at least one warm sweater, a warm coat, and a light overcoat, even in summer as Canada is prone to cold snaps. Although Canadians tend to be fairly casual in their apparel, it's wise for men to bring along a jacket and tie in case you run into one of the few restaurants that still refuse to serve you without them. And, vitally important, everyone should pack at least one pair of sturdy, no-nonsense walking shoes. A lot of holidays have been ruined because every pair packed either hurt or fell to pieces.

Since Canada hums on the same current and uses the same plugs as the U.S., you can take any electrical gadget you wish. But do yourself a favor and don't take too many. They weigh too much and take up more luggage space than their use justifies. Do, however, pack one of those small travel umbrellas—Canada gets plenty of rain, even in summer.

A final note on packing in general—travel light. Never bring more luggage than you yourself can carry without assistance. Porters aren't always available at air terminals and rail stations, and those handy luggage carts have a habit of vanishing just when you need one. The ideal tourist kit consists of one suitcase and a shoulder bag.

5. TIPS FOR THE DISABLED, SENIORS, SINGLES, FAMILIES & STUDENTS

FOR THE DISABLED Canadian city pavements are sloped for wheelchair travel, and the larger hotels and airports have washrooms designed for the disabled. A great many restaurants and tourist attractions feature wheelchair accessibility. There are several books that deal specifically with travel for the handicapped, including *Travel for the Disabled,* by Helen Hacker ($19.95); and *Wheelchair Vagabond,* by John G. Nelson ($14.95). The latter is a guide to RV or automobile travel.

These titles, and others, are available from the **Disability Bookshop,** P.O. Box 129, Vancouver, WA 98666-0129 (tel. toll free 800/637-2256).

FOR SENIORS Few countries in the world are as attentive to the needs of senior citizens as Canada. People over 60 receive discounts on tickets and fees for almost everything from public transport to movie and museum admissions, as well as excursions, sightseeing tours, and even some hotels, restaurants, car rentals, and entertainment places. Price reductions for seniors range from 7% to 15%, sometimes depending on the day of the week or the season. These discounts are usually well displayed, but in the case of tours, hotels, and restaurants inquire about them *first,* not when you're paying the bill.

There is a large and growing number of American organizations that arrange travel programs for seniors. The biggest group is the **American Association of Retired Persons (AARP),** 1909 K St. NW, Washington, DC 20049 (tel. 202/662-4850).

The **National Council of Senior Citizens,** 1331 F St. NW, Washington DC 20004 (tel. 202/347-8800), publishes a monthly newspaper for its members, containing the very latest travel information of interest to seniors.

Both these organizations issue ID cards for members, showing their seniority.

FOR SINGLE TRAVELERS Solo touring in Canada entails no special risks, but—as everywhere—has financial drawbacks. Hotel rooms are invariably cheaper (per person) for duos than for singles. The same applies to car rentals. Youth hostels display notices with offers to share car or camping costs, but you'd better take a careful look at whoever is doing the offering. Newspapers in the larger cities announce parties and excursions for singles, which are strictly potluck—they range from delightful to dismal. The best of this breed are the special-interest functions—for hikers, stamp collectors, folk dancers, ecologists, etc.—since they start off bringing together travelers with at least one interest in common.

FOR FAMILIES Robert Benchley once said that there are two ways to travel: first class and with kids. This is slightly less true today than it used to be. International airlines go out of their way to provide facilities for children: free Baby Travel Bags for infants, or games, toys, crayons, and coloring books for the older set. "Mini meals" for children are also available, but you have to order them when you make your reservation. Strollers can be taken only as far as the aircraft door; they're stored in the hold during flight. Therefore a "papoose"-type baby carrier comes in handy at transit stops.

Rates for juveniles in Canadian hotels vary considerably. They range from heavy discounts to no charge at all for children sharing a room with their parents. The same goes for cots and rollaway beds, which may come gratis or at nominal fees. (See the following chapters for listings of individual hotels.) Very few hotels, however, provide play areas or special entertainments for children.

All public transport offers discount fares for kids, and most tourist attractions, museums, theaters, exhibitions, and tours let them in at half price. A number of restaurants serve children's meals, which sometimes consist of reduced adult portions, more often of such standard juvenile favorites as hamburgers, spaghetti, or pancakes. Please note that these meals are often time-bound—i.e., not available after 8pm.

FOR STUDENTS   The handiest document a traveling student can carry is the International Student Identity Card. This is issued only to full-time students (of any nationality) and entitles the bearer to an array of discounts on rail, bus and ferry services, theaters, festivals, museums, exhibitions, lectures, and most sightseeing tours. You can get the card at the **Council on International Educational Exchange,** 205 E. 42 St., New York, NY 10017 (tel. 212/661-1414).

Council Travel is a branch of the above outfit and located at the same address. The Council arranges charter tours for students and has a list of special bargain trips available. Apply for the Council catalog on student travel.

6. ALTERNATIVE/ADVENTURE TRAVEL

Canada offers countless opportunities for outdoor adventures, from skiing to dogsledding to canoeing. Many of the companies that offer organized trips and many of the best spots for such activities are described in detail in the chapters that follow. So turn to the chapter on the destination that interests you for ideas on what's available.

NATIVE CANADIAN CAMPS   This is no doubt the most excitingly different type of accommodation in our listings, but not everybody's holiday brew. These facilities are offered by Canada's native peoples, and they range from family recreation areas to remote fishing and hunting lodges. The more remote, the more fascinating—but also the more expensive. Those lying in the real wilderness can be reached only by charter aircraft. And in order to enjoy the unexcelled hunting and fishing they offer, you need local guides, considerable equipment, and a certain amount of physical stamina.

The samples below will give you an idea of the variety of camps available. But they can't convey the sheer fascination of hitting the trail with a native companion, someone linked to the country by bonds of blood and heritage and willing to impart some native lore to you:

Burnt Church Reserve: This is the fishing reserve of the Burnt Church people in northern New Brunswick. It has campgrounds, trailer parks, and motel facilities, and fishing from lobster boats. Write to: Chief Frank Paul, Burnt Church Indian Reserve, Burnt Church, NB, E2A 3Z2.

Big Trout Lake Indian Reserve: Here's a log cabin and an adjacent cookhouse in Ontario, with fishing for lake trout and northern pike and hunting for moose, bear, grouse, and woodland caribou. Access is by aircraft. Write to: Mr. Aglias Chapman, Big Trout Lake, ON, P0C 1G0, via Central Patricia.

Silvester Jack: This is a big-game hunting camp in the Yukon Territory, with black bear, grizzly, moose, caribou, and superb fishing for trout and grayling. Hunters reach the base camp by boat; dogs are used for packing out to spike camps. Write to: Mr. Silvester Jack, Atlin, BC, V1J 4J3.

Pointe-Bleue Reserve: This tourist camp with gas station and stores is in central Québec, with hunting for moose and grouse, and fishing for lake trout, Atlantic salmon, and whitefish. It features tribal dances, canoe races, and sports competitions. Rail and bus transportation are from Québec City. Write to: Chief Harry Kurtness, Pointe-Bleue, PQ, G5M 1E8.

BICYCLING ADVENTURES Air Canada and Rocky Mountain Cycle Tours offer a combination package for pedal pushers that also leaves time for optional hiking, horseback riding, or river rafting. Titled "Kananaskis Country Explorer," this takes you over uncrowded mountain roads in the Rockies between Calgary and Banff and includes a barbecue cookout and lodgings in cozy backcountry inns. The cost is U.S. $510 for three days and two nights. Contact **Rocky Mountains Cycle Tours,** 537 4th St., Box 1978, Canmore, AB, T0L 0M0 (tel. 403/678-6770).

CANADIAN RIVER EXPEDITIONS This company was founded in 1972 as Canada's first river-rafting outfitter. It offers a variety of rafting adventures that take you through some of the most majestic and unspoilt landscapes on the continent and introduce you to the wildlife found in British Columbia and the Yukon Territory. The various expeditions are designed for different tastes and degrees of adventurousness — some shooting rapids, others consisting mainly of gentle floating. All of them have expert guides and supply everything needed for the trip, including camping gear.

For further details and bookings contact: John Mikes, Jr., **Canadian River Expeditions,** 3524 W. 16th Ave., Vancouver, BC, Canada V6R 3C1 (tel. 604/738-4449). Some of their offerings include:

- a six-day rafting and hiking journey through the Yukon Kluane National Park. This trip emphasizes natural history and visits the watershed of the Alsek River. Starts from Whitehorse. The cost is U.S. $1,420.
- an 11-day Chilcotin-Fraser expedition, looping by yacht, seaplane, raft, and train through British Columbia's coastal, forest, and mountain regions. Starts at Seattle or Vancouver. Cost is U.S. $2,325.
- a 12-day Tatshehenshini-Alsek journey, from the Yukon's Kluane National Park through the most remote region of British Columbia into Alaska's Glacier Bay National Park. Goes through untouched wilderness territory populated by grizzlies, mountain goats, and eagles. Starts at Whitehorse. Cost is U.S. $2,295.

ADVENTURES FOR WOMEN OVER 30 Founded more than a dozen years ago, **Rainbow Adventures** offers programs for women, whether they're in their 30s or their 70s, to experience new cultures, to get in touch with nature and the outdoors, and to enjoy an active vacation. Their offerings span the globe, but there are usually programs featuring travel to Canada — in the summer of 1994, for example, Rainbow Adventures offers a week-long horsepacking trip through the Canadian Rockies and Banff National Park for $1,295, and a week-long helicopter hiking trip in British Columbia for $1,995.

For details and an up-to-date list of their programs, contact Rainbow Adventures, Inc., 1308 Sherman Ave., Evanston, IL 60201 (tel. 708/864-4570).

7. GETTING THERE

BY PLANE

Canada is served by almost all the international air carriers. The major international airports in the east are Halifax, Toronto, and Montréal; in the west they're Winnipeg, Edmonton, Calgary, and Vancouver.

FROM THE U.S. Direct flights to Canada leave from the following major U.S. cities:

Boston, Chicago, Cleveland, Dallas, Honolulu, Houston, Los Angeles, Miami, New York, and San Francisco. You can realize substantial savings on fares by purchasing one of the many special excursion fares available. Many of these special excursion fares (which usually feature minimum-maximum stays and advance-purchase requirements) offer a 50% discount (or more) on regular economy fares. So be sure to check with the airlines and try to take advantage of these opportunities.

All major U.S. carriers fly to Canada, but **Air Canada** has more flights to more Canadian cities from the U.S. than any other airline. There are seven flights daily from New York to Montréal and Toronto; four flights daily (weekdays) from Newark to Toronto as well as direct service to Calgary, Vancouver, and Halifax during the summer; four flights daily from Boston as well as service to Halifax and Saint John, N.B.; two flights daily from Miami to Toronto and one to Montréal; daily flights to Toronto and Montréal from Tampa; daily flights from Chicago to Toronto, Montréal, Calgary, and Vancouver; daily flights from Los Angeles to Calgary, Edmonton, Winnipeg, Toronto, and Montréal; daily flights from San Francisco to Calgary, Edmonton, Toronto, and Montréal; and two daily flights from Houston to Toronto.

Below are some samples of roundtrip airfares to Canada, given in U.S. dollars:

New York–Montréal:	coach $324, business class $356, first class $534
Chicago-Calgary:	coach $660, business class $836, first class $1,254
Los Angeles–Toronto:	coach $780, business class $1,140, first class $1,700
Boston-Halifax:	coach $382, business class $484
Houston-Toronto:	coach $578, business class $910, first class $1,332
Miami-Montréal:	coach $624, business class $754, first class $1,134

Air Canada offers discounted fares with certain ticketing and reservation restrictions (see below). It also offers a year-round "Freedom Flyer" program especially tailored for senior citizens. On this program travelers 60 years and over get a 10% discount on *all* the airline's fares, including the lowest bargain fares, to destinations in North America as well as Britain and the Caribbean. A companion of any age can fly with the senior at the same fare, providing both travel together. For flexibility the "Freedom Flyer" program also offers discount rates to multiple destinations in Canada with the "Multi-Stop" plan—on flights originating in the U.S. that can include four to eight different stopovers. Tickets for all these discount trips must be booked 14 days in advance.

For further information call Air Canada toll free at 800/776-3000.

FARES FROM OUTSIDE THE U.S. Currently your cheapest direct-flight options fall into three categories, the first of which is the APEX fare (Advance Purchase Excursion), or Super APEX fare, which is usually valid from seven to 60 days and must be purchased at least 21 days in advance. These requirements do vary (minimally, though), not only from airline to airline but also from one part of the world to the other. The second category is the GIT fare (Group Inclusive Tour), which requires a minimum of five people traveling together on a complete air-and-land itinerary. Tours using these fares must include your hotel and sightseeing and may be purchased from your travel agent or airline. You must stay abroad a minimum of seven and a maximum of 21 days. Tickets must be issued and land arrangements paid for more than seven days before departure. Again, the rules vary somewhat depending on the airline and the geographic area. The third option, the Excursion fare, usually requires a minimum stay of seven days and a maximum of 60. The ticket usually allows a limited number of stopovers at a surcharge generally ranging from $25 to $50 each. There are no advance-purchase requirements on this one. These, then, are your least expensive options.

Canadian Airlines International, the result of a merger of four major carriers, provides great scope for getting into Canada from the far points of the globe as well as for coast-to-coast travel within the country. It operates twice-weekly flights from Sydney, Australia, and Auckland, New Zealand; 10 times weekly from Tokyo; five times weekly from Hong Kong; twice weekly from Bangkok; and weekly from the Peoples' Republic of China to Vancouver and Toronto. From South America there's twice-weekly service from Rio de Janeiro and São Paulo to Toronto, with connections across Canada. From London (Gatwick) and Manchester, respectively, there's one flight a day to Toronto.

GOOD-VALUE CHOICES   Charter Flights   A charter flight is an economical option for a onetime transit to a fixed destination. It can prove a real bargain if you're willing to book months ahead, pay in advance, and don't change your mind about going. There are usually severe penalties if you cancel. Charter flights may also be canceled if the tickets don't sell out. *Always* check the restrictions on your charter contract before paying. One of the major charter flight organizers is the Council on International Educational Exchange (Council Charters), 205 E. 42nd St., New York, NY 10017 (tel. toll free 800/223-7402).

Bucket Shops   Officially called "consolidators", these outfits buy block tickets from airlines and sell them at heavily discounted prices—sometimes 35% to 40% below regular fares. Bucket shops advertise in the travel sections of newspapers and frequently the same companies arrange charter flights as well. Terms of payment vary, but since their supply of tickets varies also you have to be flexible in your travel dates to take advantage of them. One of the largest consolidators is **Access International,** 101 W. 31st St., Suite 1104, New York, NY 10001 (tel. toll free 800/825-3633).

Standbys   The simplest and least reliable method to cut traveling costs. You turn up at the airport and hope that a seat is available at the low standby rate. Only good if your schedule is in no way time-bound. Not advisable during holidays or any other peak period.

Courier Travel   Air couriers are employed by companies that fly important documents or equipment around the world and want someone to accompany the goods. It is a popular fallacy to assume that couriers travel free. They don't, but only pay a fraction of the regular fare. The usual rate is 50% less, but it can go as low as 20%, depending on the cargo, the destination, and the urgency of the flight. The courier has to make do with a cabin bag—he or she gets no luggage space. Otherwise the rules are casual. You should be reasonably neatly dressed, hold a valid passport, and should not drink liquor during the flight. It's a great plus if you're familiar with the airports you're flying from and to. Above all, you should be prepared to fly at a moment's notice; though in most cases you get several days' warning.

There are several air-courier firms you can join, as well as the **International Association of Air Travel Couriers,** 8 S. "J" St., P.O. Box 1349, Lake Worth, FL 33460 (tel. 407/582-8320). For a $35 annual fee the company will send you regular newsletters and bulletins informing you about available courier jobs.

Ⓕ FROMMER'S SMART TRAVELER: AIRFARES

1. Shop around all airlines flying to Canada.
2. Watch out for new routes starting up—they usually have introductory promotional prices.
3. Keep calling airlines until the last possible moment—additional low-fare tickets often become available as the departure date nears.
4. Fly on a weekday. Weekend prices are frequently higher.
5. Try to travel during the traditional slow periods: after Thanksgiving and before Christmas, during March and April, in late May or early June.
6. Ask about frequent-flyer programs that will give you bonus points.
7. Find out about fly-drive package deals. They won't save you airfare but may sharply reduce car-rental rates.
8. Inquire about ground transportation before you arrive. Airport shuttle buses charge only a fraction of cab fares.
9. Bucket shops frequently have last-minute fares even lower than the slashed prices they advertise.

BY TRAIN

Amtrak serves the East Coast with four main routes into Canada. The *Adirondack*, which starts at Penn Station, New York, is a day train that travels daily via Albany and upstate New York to Montréal. The *Montrealer* travels nightly from New York's Pennsylvania Station through Vermont to Montréal. The *Maple Leaf* links New York City and Toronto via Albany, Buffalo, and Niagara Falls, departing daily from Penn Station. From Chicago, the *International* carries passengers to Toronto via Port Huron, Michigan.

From Buffalo's Exchange Street Station you can make the trip to Toronto on the Toronto/Hamilton/Buffalo Railway (THB), which is a two-car Budd train. In Toronto you can make connections to Montréal, Ottawa, and so on.

Connecting services are available from other major cities along the border in addition to these direct routes. Call Amtrak (tel. toll free 800/USA-RAIL, or 800/872-7245) for further information, and to check the fares given below, which are, of course, subject to change.

SAMPLE RAIL FARES

	Coach Fare One-Way	Round-trip Excursion
New York–Montréal	$69	$90–$101
New York–Toronto	$101	$121–$161
Chicago–Toronto	$95	$105–$133

Remember that meals are not included in these prices; you must pay for meals on the train when you receive them, or carry your own food.

BY BUS

Greyhound is the only bus company that crosses the border into Canada from the U.S. Its routes are so extensive that you should be able to travel from almost anywhere in the U.S. to any destination in Canada, perhaps making a few changes along the way. In many cases the bus can be faster than the train, a little cheaper, and routes are flexible if you want to stop off on the way. On the other hand they are more cramped, meals are at rest stops, and you may find yourself stopping at 20 or more cities on transcontinental routes. All fares beyond a certain distance from your point of departure revert back to the top Greyhound rate. All rates are subject to change, so check with your local Greyhound office. You should also look into discount fares and their special unlimited-travel passes. Rates vary from season to season, but sometimes the discounts are incredible. More information and rates will be yours by calling Greyhound at 212/971-6363 for the East Coast routes or 213/620-1200 for West Coast service.

BY CAR

Hopping across the border by car is no problem as the U.S. highway system leads directly into Canada at 13 points. Once across the border you can link up with the Trans Canada Highway which runs from St. John's, Newfoundland, to Victoria, British Columbia—a total distance of 5,000 miles.

BY FERRY

Ocean ferries operate between Maine and Nova Scotia and between Seattle and Victoria, British Columbia. For details, see the relevant chapters.

PACKAGE TOURS

There are so many different types of package tours going to Canada that it would take an entire chapter to describe just the major ones. You get fly-drive, fly-coach, fly-rail, and fly-bike packages; some tailored for city sightseeing, others for hitting the hiking trails, some with an accent on history, some on sports, and one even for theater fans.

Some entail stays in luxury hotels, others in country inns, still others in bed-and-breakfast establishments. Most of them operate in conjunction with airlines, but don't necessarily include your airfare in the package price quoted. The samples below will merely give you an inkling of your choices.

Air Canada has a "Go As You Please Self-Drive" package to Newfoundland in combination with Brian Moore International Tours. This includes round-trip airfare to St. John's from a dozen U.S. departure cities, use of a rental car for three days, plus accommodation vouchers for three nights in either hotels or inns. Prices vary according to the accommodation you choose, starting at U.S. $753 per person. Contact **Brian Moore International Tours,** 116 Main St., Medway, MA 02053 (tel. 508/533-4426).

Canadian Airlines International operates an array of package tours in conjunction with the Canadian Holidays Company. One of their best bargains is a two-night jaunt to Toronto, starting in Florida, for a total price of U.S. $294. This includes round-trip airfare from Orlando, plus two nights of hotel accommodation based on double occupancy. This trip must be paid in full 60 days before departure.

Another venture by the same team are the Fly/Rail packages, offering a range of scenic rail trips after your flying start. The airfare from the U.S. is not included, and the discounted train fare depends how far and in what degree of comfort you wish to roll, giving you maximum flexibility. For example it's U.S. $298 from Montréal to Edmonton in coach class.

For these and half a dozen other packages contact **Canadian Holidays,** 3507 Frontage Rd., Suite 220, Tampa, FL 33607 (tel. toll free 800/237-0190).

8. GETTING AROUND

As I've stated several times before, and will undoubtedly mention again, Canada is a land of immense distances. Which means that transportation from point A to point B forms a prime item in your travel budget as well as your timetable. To give you some idea of the mileage you're dealing with, here are some sample distances (in miles) between major cities, as the crow flies or the jet jets: Montréal to Vancouver, 3,041; Vancouver to Halifax, 3,897; Toronto to Victoria, 2,911; Winnipeg to St. John's, 3,159; Calgary to Montréal, 2,299; St. John's to Vancouver, 4,723; Ottawa to Victoria, 2,979.

BY PLANE Canada has two major transcontinental airlines, **Air Canada** and **Canadian Airlines International.** Both fly overseas routes as well, and together with their regional partner companies, handle most of the country's air transportation. There are also numerous small local outfits, but these will concern us only when we get into their particular territories.

Within Canada, Air Canada operates daily service between 18 major cities, and their schedules dovetail with a string of allied connector carriers such as Air B.C., Air Ontario, Northwest Territorial Airways, etc., to serve scores of smaller Canadian towns.

Here are a few sample fares to give you an idea of the cost of air travel in Canada. All prices quoted are economy class: Montréal to Toronto, $213; Toronto to Winnipeg, $457; Ottawa to Toronto, $176; Vancouver to Calgary, $252; Edmonton to St. John's, $954.

But Air Canada also offers an array of package deals specially tailored to trim the costs of your vacation jaunts. Collectively these packages come under the title "Air Canada's Canada." This term covers a whole series of travel bargains that range from city packages to fly-drive tours, escorted tours, motorhome travel, ski holidays, and Arctic adventures.

I don't have the space to give you more than an inkling of the tour possibilities involved. For detailed information get the brochure from an Air Canada office, or have it sent to you by calling toll free 800/776-3000.

BY TRAIN Most of Canada's passenger railroad traffic (Canadians say railway) is carried by the government-owned **VIA Rail.** This nationwide network suffered a near-lethal budget trimming campaign in January 1990, which cut passenger service by more than 50%. Since then, however, VIA Rail has staged a remarkable comeback—by public demand—and today you can traverse the continent very comfortably in sleeping cars, parlor coaches, bedrooms, and roomettes. Virtually all of Canada's major cities are connected by rail, though service is less frequent than it used to be. Some luxury trains, like *The Canadian,* boast dome cars with panoramic picture windows, hot showers, and elegant dining cars.

The one-way sample fares quoted below will give you an idea of train-travel prices: Montréal-Edmonton, $361; Ottawa-Montréal, $32; Toronto-Ottawa, $69; Vancouver-Winnipeg, $281.

You can also purchase a Canrailpass that gives you 12 days of unlimited travel throughout the VIA national network, providing you do this within 30 days. A Canrailpass costs $489 in high season, $329 in low season.

Seniors aged 60 and over and students receive a 10% discount on all fares. Fares for children up to 11 are half the applicable adult rate.

For information about services, times, and fares call VIA Rail toll free at 800/561-3949.

The Rocky Mountaineer   Billed as "The Most Spectacular Train Trip in the World," it may very well be that. Operated by the privately owned Great Canadian Railtour Company, this sleek blue-and-white train winds past foaming waterfalls, ancient glaciers, towering snowcapped peaks, and roaring mountain streams. *The Rocky Mountaineer* gives you the option of either traveling east from Vancouver, west from Jasper or Calgary, or taking a round-trip. The journey entails two days on the train, one night in a hotel, and lets you see the Rocky Mountains as you never would behind the wheel of a car.

The train operates from late May into October, entirely in daylight hours. In peak season, June 5 to September 22, the fare is $499 per person, based on double occupancy. This includes meals and your hotel room on the stretch from Vancouver to Banff or Jasper. If you want to go on to Calgary it's another $49.

For information and bookings contact the **Great Canadian Railtour Company,** Suite 104, 340 Brooksbank Ave., North Vancouver, BC, V7J 2C1 (tel. toll free 800/665-7245).

BY BUS   There are seven main bus lines operating in Canada, including the familiar Greyhound. Bus travel is the cheapest form of transportation available (if you exclude your thumb), and the coaches have the same degree of comfort you'll find in the U.S. The bus stations, incidentally, are almost equally as drab, except that they're somewhat better swept and considerably safer. Again, a few sample fares: Vancouver-Banff, $92.50; Winnipeg-Halifax, $237.55; Vancouver-Toronto, $271.75.

We'll deal with the sightseeing and excursion tours offered by various bus lines in the appropriate chapters.

The companies that run interprovincial services are **Greyhound** (tel. 403/260-0877), and **Voyageur** (tel. 613/238-5900). In the summer of 1993, Voyageur offered a TourPass that included 14 days of unlimited travel throughout Ontario and Québec for $159. Ask if they have any similar good-value passes available during your trip.

BY CAR   Rentals   Canada has scores of rental-car companies, including the ubiquitous **Hertz, Avis,** and **Budget.** Nevertheless, rental vehicles tend to get very tight during the tourist season, from around mid-May through the summer months. Your wisest step would be to reserve a car as soon as you decide on your vacation.

The biggest and most thoroughly Canadian car-rental outfit is **Tilden Interrent,** a third-generation family enterprise that began in 1924 with three cars in a rented garage in Montréal. Today Tilden Interrent has a fleet of 19,000 vehicles in 400 locations coast to coast, plus affiliates in the U.S., Latin America, Europe, the Middle East, the Pacific area, and Africa.

While rates are in a constant state of flux, to put it mildly, the Tilden prices, which are highly competitive, will give you an idea of the costs involved at the time of writing—there is no guarantee that prices will be the same a few months from now. Tilden Interrent cars come in different classifications, including four-passenger economy vehicles, mid-size, full size (five passengers), sporty, premium, six-passenger luxury, seven-passenger vans, and 15-passenger minibuses. The company offers a special Vacation Plan that is tailor-made for motoring visitors. The plan is good for a seven-day week (which you can start on any day of the week) and covers three vehicle categories: E car (economy), M car (mid-size), F (full size), or a five- to seven-passenger minivan. No-smoking vehicles are available in all categories. You pay $234 per week for an E car, $261 per week for a mid-size, $285 per week for an F, and $371 per week for a minivan. Each rate includes 1,400 free kilometers (853 miles); above that you pay 15¢ per kilometer (about 25¢ per mile). In all except economy models, air conditioning is included.

You have to reserve at least one day prior to arrival and your car must be returned to the original rental station.

Tilden rentals offer what I believe is an "industry first" in the form of a Roadside Assistance Program. This means that in case of an accident, breakdown, dead battery, flat tire, dry gas tank, getting stuck, or locking yourself out of your car you can call a 24-hour number and get an immediate response for roadside help anywhere in Canada. The toll-free number is 800/268-9711.

To book a car or get additional information while in the U.S., contact **National Car Rental** (tel. toll free 800/CAR-RENT). In Canada contact the local stations listed in this book or Tilden Interrent headquarters at 250 Bloor St. East, Suite 1300, Toronto, ON, M4W 1E6 (tel. toll free 800/387-4747).

The rates include standard liability protection, but not personal accident insurance, and the collision damage waiver that eliminates your deductible payment in case of an accident.

Gasoline   As in the United States, the trend in Canada is toward self-service gas stations. In some areas, in fact, you may have difficulty finding the other kind. And although Canada—specifically Alberta—is a major oil producer, gasoline is not particularly cheap. Gas sells by the liter, and pumps at around 55¢ to 60¢ per liter ($2.20 to $2.40 per gallon); prices vary slightly from region to region. Filling the tank of a medium-sized car will cost you roughly $19.

Driving Rules   Wearing seat belts is compulsory (and enforced) in all provinces, and Canada's highway system is excellent until you reach the far north, where gravel roads take over. But driving conditions differ sharply within the various cities. This is due partly to urban renewal, partly to the temperament of the locals. Calgary, for instance, has a complex pattern of one-way streets, the intersections festooned with so many signs that it can take several minutes to read them. To make up for this, it has the politest and most patient motorists in the entire country. In Montréal, on the other hand, they drive with maniacal Gallic panache (read "very badly") and you'd better use whatever you know of defensive motoring, because the others sure don't.

 CANADA

Business Hours   Banks are open Monday to Thursday from 10am to 3pm, and Friday until 6pm. Stores are generally open from 9:30am to 6pm on weekdays, with extended hours on Friday; on Saturday and Sunday, they're likely to be open from 10am to 5pm.

Climate   See "When to Go," earlier in this chapter.

Currency   See "Information, Entry Requirements, and Money," earlier in this chapter.

Customs   See "Information, Entry Requirements, and Money," earlier in this chapter.

Documents Required   See "Information, Entry Requirements, and Money," earlier in this chapter.

Drug Laws   Drug laws are similar to those in the United States, but they're more strictly enforced.

Electricity   Canada uses the same electrical current as does the U.S., 110–115 volts, 60 cycles.

Embassies and Consulates   All embassies are in Ottawa, the national capital; the U.S. embassy is at 100 Wellington St., Ottawa (tel. 613/238-4470).

You'll find U.S. consulates in the following locations: Nova Scotia—Cogswell Tower, Suite 910, Scotia Square, Halifax, NS, B3J 3K1 (tel. 902/429-2480); Québec—2 place Terrasse-Dufferin (P.O. Box 939), Québec City, PQ, G1R 4T9 (tel. 418/692-2095), and Complexe Desjardins, South Tower, Ground Floor, Montréal, PQ (tel. 514/398-9695); Ontario—360 University Ave., Toronto, ON, M5G 1S4 (tel. 416/595-1700); Alberta—Room 1050, 615 Macleod Trail SE, Calgary, AB, T2G 4T8 (tel. 403/266-8962); British Columbia—1095 W. Pender St., Vancouver, BC, V6E 2Y4 (tel. 604/685-4311).

There's also a British consulate general at 777 Bay St., Toronto (tel. 416/593-1267), and an Australian consulate general at 175 Bloor St. East, Toronto (tel. 416/323-1155).

Emergencies   In life-threatening situations, call 911.

Gasoline   See "Getting Around," earlier in this chapter.

Holidays   See "When to Go," earlier in this chapter.

Liquor Laws   Beer and wine are sold in supermarkets and most grocery stores; spirits are sold only in government liquor stores. The minimum drinking age is 19.

Mail   Canadian postal rates are different from those in the U.S., and all mail posted in Canada must have Canadian postage. Canadian postal codes, which are absolutely essential for delivery, are a sequence of numbers and letters.

Maps   Maps are easily obtained at information offices, at the offices of the Canadian Automobile Association, and at special map stores.

Newspapers and Magazines   The only national daily is the Toronto-based *Globe and Mail.* Cities have their own local newspapers, and the *New York Times* is sold at most large newsstands. So are *Time* and *Newsweek.* Larger cities produce the monthly *Where,* available free in many hotels and specifically aimed at visitors.

Radio and TV   By far the best and most informative programs are produced by the government-owned Canadian Broadcasting Corporation (CBC) for both television and radio.

Safety   With the exception of a few small urban patches, Canada is a considerably safer country than the U.S. Nonetheless, whenever you're traveling in an unfamiliar city or country, stay alert. Be aware of your immediate surroundings. Wear a moneybelt and keep a close eye on your possessions. Be particularly careful with cameras, purses, and wallets, all favorite targets of thieves and pickpockets. It's your responsibility to be aware and alert in even the most heavily touristed areas.

Taxes   In January 1991 the Canadian government imposed a new 7% federal tax, the GST, on virtually all goods and services. Some hotels and shops include the GST in their prices, others add it on separately. When included, the tax accounts for the odd hotel rates, such as $66.04 a day, that you might find on your final bill: The GST is also the reason you pay 50¢ for a newspaper at a vending machine, but 54¢ over a shop counter: The machines haven't been geared for the new price.

Thanks to a government provision designed to encourage tourism, you can reclaim the GST portion of your hotel bills and the price of goods you've purchased in Canada—in due course. The minimum GST rebate is $7 (the tax on $100) and the claim must be filed within a year of purchase. You must submit all your original receipts (which will be returned) together with an application form. Receipts from several trips within the same year may be submitted together. Claims of less than $500 can be made at certain designated Duty Free shops at international airports and border crossings. Or you can mail the forms to Revenue Canada, Customs and Excise, Visitors' Rebate Program, Ottawa, ON, K1A 1J5. You can get the forms in some of the larger hotels, in some duty-free shops, or by phoning 613/991-3346 outside Canada, or toll free 800/66-VISIT in Canada.

The rebate does not apply to car rentals or restaurant meals. And the GST is not levied on airline tickets to Canada purchased in the United States.

Time   There are six times zones observed in Canada. In the winter, when it's 7:30 Newfoundland standard time, it's 6 Atlantic standard time (in Labrador, Prince Edward Island, New Brunswick, and Nova Scotia); 5 eastern standard time (in Québec and most of Ontario); 4 central standard time (in western Ontario, Manitoba, and most of Saskatchewan); 3 mountain standard time (in northwestern Saskatchewan, Alberta, eastern British Columbia, and the Northwest Territories); and 2 Pacific standard time (in the Yukon and most of British Columbia). Each year, on the first Sunday in April, daylight saving time comes into effect in most of Canada and clocks are advanced by one hour. On the last Sunday in October, Canada reverts to standard time. During these summer months, all of Saskatchewan observes the same time zone as Alberta.

Tipping Very few Canadian hotels or restaurants add service charges to their bills. The usual tip for hotel maids is $1 to $2 per day, for porters 50¢ to $1 for bags carried. Waiters, cab drivers, hairdressers get around 15% of the total bill.

Youth Hostels The Canadian Hostelling Association has changed its title to Hostelling International–Canada. The National Office is at 1600 James Naismith Dr., Suite 608, Gloucester, ON, K1B 5N4 (tel. 613/748-5638). The name change is a sensible move since these hostels have long catered to patrons of all age groups. You can get a membership card of the International Youth Hostel Federation through American Youth Hostels, Box 37613, Washington, DC 20013 (tel. 202/783-6161).

NOVA SCOTIA

Nova Scotia wears its Scottish allegiance as proudly as any Highlander wears a kilt. From town names like Inverness, Iona, and New Glasgow, to the musical dialect of the province's old-timers, Scottish culture and traditions are remembered and revered.

But Nova Scotia is not completely Scottish in tradition. The Micmac were here long before the first European settlers came—and the first European settlers were French. A Scottish colony, established a few years after Samuel de Champlain's first settlement (1605), did not survive. The French one did, and soon its colonists filled the valley of the Annapolis Basin. And Halifax, named for a Yorkshire town, has more of London about it than it has of Edinburgh.

Toasting the queen in Halifax, watching the Highland Games in Antigonish, visiting the Acadian memorials at Grand Pré, learning of Micmac history and lore—all these take second place to the beauty of the land itself. The rugged coastlines scooped with rows of small coves, the dramatic mountain scenery of Cape Breton's highlands, and the lush, fertile fields lining the Fundy shores are the real Nova Scotia, beautiful and hospitable to all who come here.

Assuming that most visitors coming by land will cross from New Brunswick on the Trans Canada Highway, this chapter is arranged to start at Amherst, coming south to Halifax, and then touring the peninsula on the motor routes mapped out by the provincial tourist authorities. Then it's off to Cape Breton Island, Nova Scotia's most exciting tourist destination.

SEEING NOVA SCOTIA

INFORMATION For information about Nova Scotia, call these toll-free numbers: in Canada, 800/565-0000; in the United States, 800/341-6096. In Halifax or Dartmouth, call 902/425-5781.

For printed information before you go, write to **Nova Scotia Tourism,** P.O. Box 130, Halifax, NS, B3J 2M7 (tel. toll free 800/341-6096 in the U.S., or 800/565-0000 in Canada). Request the free, 300-page *Nova Scotia—The Doers and Dreamers Complete Guide,* so useful for its driving information; accommodations and campgrounds listings; and descriptions of the province's many scenic trails, parks, historic sites, festivals, and museums.

When you get to Nova Scotia, any travel bureau or information center operated by the provincial authorities will help you find a room through the Check In system. While a good number of Nova Scotia hostelries participate in the system, not all do; often the ones that don't are the less expensive ones. But it's good to know that assistance is available.

A NOTE ON TAXES Almost all goods and services in Nova Scotia are subject to a

WHAT'S SPECIAL ABOUT NOVA SCOTIA

Scenic Drives
☐ The time-honored and road-tested Cabot Trail.
☐ The picturesque Lighthouse Route into Nova Scotia's seafaring past.

Cape Breton Island
☐ The fabled Nova Scotia highlands.
☐ An astounding national park.
☐ The embodiment of Nova Scotia's French heritage.
☐ Memorable resorts, bed-and-breakfasts, and out-of-the-way places.

Historic Sites
☐ The Citadel in Halifax.
☐ The Fortress of Louisbourg.
☐ Grand Pré, near Wolfville.
☐ Port Royal Habitation, near Annapolis Royal.

☐ Alexander Graham Bell National Historic Site in Baddeck.

Industry Museums
☐ The Miners' Museum in Glace Bay.
☐ The Fisheries Museum of the Atlantic in Lunenburg.

Music
☐ Singers like Anne Murray, Rita McNeil, and the Rankin Family.
☐ Ceilidhs (kay-lees), old-fashioned gatherings with friends and a fiddle.

Summer Festivals
☐ The Nova Scotia Tattoo in Halifax, July 1–7.
☐ The Antigonish Highland Games in mid-July.

11% provincial tax (which applies to your accommodations, too—even in B&Bs) and a 7% national government tax (GST). Nonresidents are eligible for a tax rebate on goods purchased but not used in the province; they are also eligible for a rebate (GST only) on accommodations, except for camping fees.

GETTING THERE   By Plane   Halifax is the air hub of the Atlantic Provinces. Air Nova, the commuter partner of Air Canada, provides direct service between New York (Newark Airport) and Halifax, twice a day in summer, otherwise one flight a day Sunday through Friday. The airline also serves Sydney and Yarmouth in Nova Scotia, as well as 13 other destinations in Atlantic Canada (tel. toll free 800/776-3000 in the U.S., 800/565-3940 in Maritime Canada). Halifax, Sydney, and Yarmouth are also served by Air Atlantic, the commuter partner of Canadian Airlines International (tel. 902/427-5500, or toll free 800/426-7000 in the U.S., 800/665-1177 in Maritime Canada, and 709/576-0274 in Newfoundland). KLM's charter airline, Martinair, flies into Halifax three times a week from Amsterdam (tel. toll free 800/777-5553 in the U.S.).

By Rail   Halifax has limited rail service, with one train arriving from Montréal via Sherbrooke, Québec, and Saint John, and Moncton, New Brunswick, on Tuesday, Friday, and Sunday, and from Montréal via Campbellton, New Brunswick, and Mont Joli (Gaspé), Québec, on Monday, Thursday, and Saturday. For specific schedule and fare information, call VIA Rail (tel. toll free 800/561-3949 in the U.S.). For information on getting to Montréal from the U.S., call Amtrak (tel. toll free 800/USA-RAIL).

By Bus   Acadian Lines, 6040 Almon St. (tel. 902/454-8279 Monday to Friday from 9am to 5pm, 902/454-9321 other hours), has routes connecting Halifax with Amherst (and buses from New Brunswick), Sydney, and Yarmouth, as well as Bangor, Maine (check with Greyhound). The Halifax-Yarmouth buses connect with the ferries to Bar Harbor and Portland, Maine. Acadian also has daily service between Halifax and Charlottetown, P.E.I., via the Caribou–Wood Islands ferryboat. On Cape Breton Island, Acadian will take you to points from which you can connect with other

AN IMPORTANT NOTE ON PRICES

Unless stated otherwise, **the prices cited in this guide are given in Canadian dollars,** which is good news for U.S. travelers because the Canadian dollar is worth 25% less than the American dollar, but buys nearly as much. As we go to press, $1 Canadian is worth 75¢ U.S., which means that your $100-a-night hotel room will cost only U.S. $75, and your $6 breakfast costs only U.S. $4.50.

Here's a quick table of equivalents:

Canadian $	U.S. $
$ 1	$ 0.75
5	3.75
10	7.50
20	15.00
50	37.50
80	60.00
100	75.00
200	150.00

lines to Inverness, Baddeck, and Newfoundland. In Halifax, McKenzie Bus Lines has daily departures for Yarmouth and the South Shore (tel. 902/454-9321).

By Car and Ferry Coming overland by car, one enters Nova Scotia from New Brunswick, probably along the Trans Canada Highway, entering at Amherst. Then there are the ferry connections: from Prince Edward Island (Wood Islands) to Caribou, N.S.; from Newfoundland (Port aux Basques) to North Sydney, N.S.; from New Brunswick (Saint John) to Digby, N.S.; and from Maine (Bar Harbor and Portland), to Yarmouth, N.S. At this writing, there is serious talk of inaugurating ferry service between Boston and Halifax. Ferries to other Atlantic provinces are covered in the chapters dealing with the provinces they serve. The ones from Maine are popular, convenient, and fun.

Portland/Yarmouth: From Portland, Maine, one service connects with Yarmouth, at the southwestern tip of Nova Scotia, saving 858 miles of driving: Prince of Fundy Cruises operates the MS *Scotia Prince* on daily voyages during the busy summer months. The ship departs Portland at 9pm almost every day in season, arriving in Yarmouth at breakfast time after an 11-hour cruise. Departure from Yarmouth is at 10am, arriving in Portland around 8pm. One-way fares are $75 in season ($55 off-season) for adults, half price for children ages 5 to 14 accompanied by an adult. Vehicle fares depend on the season: The charge in high summer is $98 one way per car, $80 in the "shoulder" seasons of mid-May to late June and early September to late October. Cabins on the night trip from Portland cost anywhere from $32 to $95, and suites are $165, or $20 to $60 and $165, respectively, off-season. (Note that all these prices are in U.S. dollars, and credit cards are accepted for fares.) Prince of Fundy Cruises sponsors money-saving package deals including round-trip specials; "mini-cruises" that give you bargain-priced round-trip tickets, cabin, and meals (but no car passage); and tours that include ferry passage for car and passengers, and then rooms in hotels and motels on a predetermined route. A travel agent can fill you in on details, or contact Prince of Fundy Cruises, International Terminal, Portland, ME 04101 (tel. 207/775-5616, 902/742-6460 in Yarmouth, or toll free 800/341-7540, 800/482-0955 in Maine; call collect from elsewhere in Maritime Canada). Needless to say, reservations are a must during the busy summer months.

Bar Harbor/Yarmouth: Between Bar Harbor, Maine, and Yarmouth, N.S., sailings are aboard the Marine Atlantic's MV *Bluenose,* which operates year-round on the six-hour run. In high season, late June to mid-September, departures are daily, from Bar Harbor in the morning, from Yarmouth in the late afternoon. Fares are $41.50 per adult, $51 per car, and $22.10 per child 5 to 12; off-season, there are only a few departures in either direction each week, and fares drop to $28 per adult, $47 per

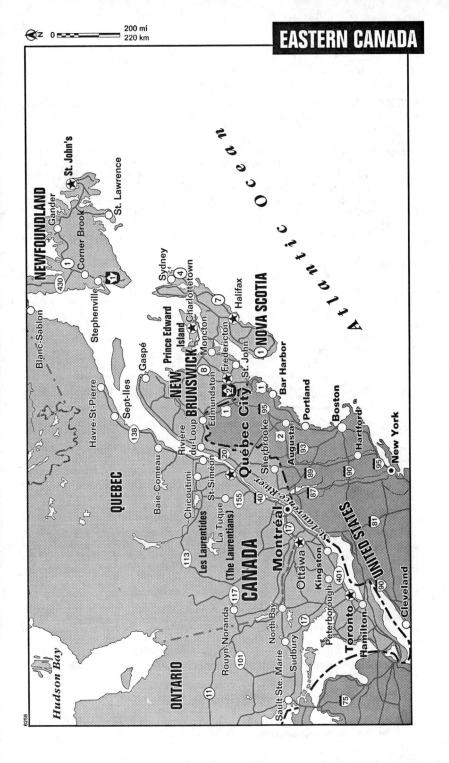

EASTERN CANADA

N

0 200 mi
   220 km

NEWFOUNDLAND

St. John's
Gander
Corner Brook
St. Lawrence
430
1
Stephenville

Blanc-Sablon

Havre-St-Pierre
St-Pierre
Sept-Iles
138

QUEBEC

Baie-Comeau
Chicoutimi
St-Siméon
Rivière-
du-Loup

Gaspé
Sydney
4
Charlottetown
Prince Edward
Island
Moncton
7
Halifax
NOVA SCOTIA
1
NEW
BRUNSWICK
8
Fredericton
St. John
Edmundston

Québec City
1
12
20
Sherbrooke
2
95
Augusta
93
89
87
90
95
Portland
Boston
Bar Harbor
Hartford
New York
81
Atlantic Ocean

La Tuque
La Tuque (The Laurentians)
155
40
St. Lawrence River
Les Laurentides
113
117
Montréal
17
Ottawa
Kingston
401
90
Cleveland

Rouyn-Noranda
101
North Bay
Sudbury
17
Peterborough
Toronto
Hamilton
75

CANADA
UNITED STATES

ONTARIO
Sault Ste. Marie
11

Hudson Bay

6258

car, and $11.05 for children. Day cabins are available. Fares are payable in U.S. dollars in Bar Harbor, in Canadian dollars in Yarmouth. For reservations, call toll free 800/341-7981 in the U.S., or call Bar Harbor at 207/288-3395. You can also write: Marine Atlantic Reservations Bureau, P.O. Box 250, North Sydney, NS, B2A 3M3.

GETTING AROUND Once you arrive in Nova Scotia, you can get around fairly well by local buses. But Nova Scotia is truly road-trip lovers' paradise, so try to bring your own wheels, or rent some. You'll find no better driving anywhere.

Car-rental agencies based in Halifax include Budget, 1588 Hollis St. and at the airport (tel. 902/454-8501, or toll free 800/268-8900); a local company called Byways, 2156 Barrington St. (tel. 902/429-0092, or toll free 800/668-4233); Avis, on the corner of Sackville and South Park and at the airport (tel. 902/873-3523); Dollar, 1498 Lower Water St. and at the airport (tel. 902/453-5400, or toll free 800/800-4000); Thrifty, 6390 Lady Hammond Rd. and at the airport (tel. 902/422-4455, or toll free 800/367-2277); and Tilden, 1130 Hollis St. (tel. 902/422-4439, or toll free 800/387-4747). You should reserve your rental car in advance during the busy summer months, particularly if you plan to arrive in Yarmouth by ferry and then rent a car to continue your travels.

FISHING If you plan on angling for Atlantic salmon, speckled trout, or any other fish, write for the brochure *Nova Scotia Travel Guide*, put out by the Department of Tourism and Culture, P.O. Box 456, Halifax, NS, B3J 2R5. It gives specific river recommendations and regulations, as well as the best periods for catching whatever fish you wish. For up-to-date license and regulation information, write to the Department of Natural Resources, Extension Services-Support, P.O. Box 68, Truro, NS, B2N 5B8. For Atlantic salmon, contact the Department of Fisheries and Oceans, P.O. Box 550, Halifax, NS, B3J 2S6 (tel. 902/426-3928).

1. FROM AMHERST TO HALIFAX

AMHERST

Coming from New Brunswick, the first town you reach across the Nova Scotia border is Amherst (pop. 9,700), right at the edge of the Tantramar marshes. Those who stop at the well-stocked Provincial Tourist Office just off the Trans Canada Highway will be welcomed to the province with true Nova Scotian hospitality.

If need be, staying the night in or near Amherst is no problem. Just after passing the Tourist Office, look for the LaPlanche Street exit, the one to take for Amherst's basic roadside motels. Ask for brochures at the Tourist Office.

Amherst was home to four of the 25 fathers of Canadian Confederation—an impressive contribution to national history—and the **Four Fathers Festival** is held here for 10 days in September. An annual **Blueberry Harvest Festival** is held here the first week of August, celebrating Nova Scotia's ranking as the world's top exporter of the delicious fruit.

The "Sunrise Trail," outlined by Nova Scotia's Department of Tourism, starts in Amherst and stretches along the province's northern coast all the way to the Canso Causeway, entrance to fabled Cape Breton Island. To follow it, take Highway 6 to the coast and proceed east, passing inlets, beaches, and villages along the way (see Section 6 in this chapter).

Many travelers opt instead to head southeast from Amherst along Highway 104 toward Truro and Halifax, stopping en route to pay homage to a world-famous singer, who happens to be a native Nova Scotian.

SPRINGHILL

Take Exit 4 off Highway 104 onto Route 2 to enter Springhill, 19 miles (30km) from Amherst. The former mining community, with fewer than 5,000 people, is home to

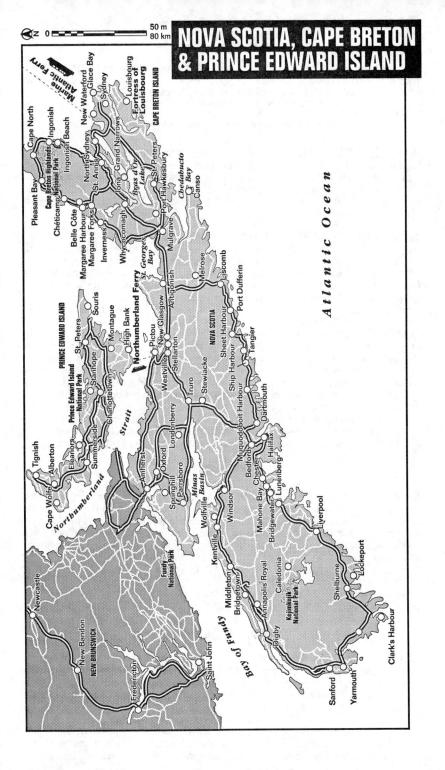

NOVA SCOTIA, CAPE BRETON & PRINCE EDWARD ISLAND

Atlantic Ocean

CAPE BRETON ISLAND

Glace Bay
Louisbourg
New Waterford
Sydney
Fortress of Louisbourg
North Sydney
Ingonish
Ingonish Beach
Cape North
St. Ann's
Grand Narrows
Iona
Bras d'Or Lake
St. Peters
Cape Breton Highlands
Cape Breton Highlands National Park
Pleasant Bay
Chéticamp
Belle Côte
Margaree Harbour
Margaree Forks
Inverness
Whycocomagh
Port Hawkesbury
Mulgrave
St. George's Bay
Chedabucto Bay
Canso

Marine Atlantic Ferry

Melrose
Liscomb
Port Dufferin

PRINCE EDWARD ISLAND

Souris
Montague
St. Peters
Northumberland Ferry
High Bank
Pictou
New Glasgow
Antigonish
Stellarton
Westville
NOVA SCOTIA
Sheet Harbour
Tangier
Prince Edward Island National Park
Stanhope
Charlottetown
Summerside
Eleanors
Truro
Stewiacke
Ship Harbour
Muquodoboit Harbour
Dartmouth
Strait
Tignish
Alberton
Cape Wolfe
Northumberland
Amherst
Oxford
Springhill
Londonderry
Parrsboro
Minas Basin
Windsor
Bedford
Chester
Halifax
Mahone Bay
Lunenburg
Bridgewater
Wolfville
Kentville
Liverpool
Lockeport

NEW BRUNSWICK
Newcastle
New Bandon
Fundy National Park
Middleton
Bridgetown
Annapolis Royal
Caledonia
Kejimkujik National Park
Shelburne
Bay of Fundy
Fredericton
Saint John
Digby
Sanford
Yarmouth
Clark's Harbour

N
0
50 m
80 km

IMPRESSIONS

There is no mistaking the spirit of sane and realised nationality, which fills the land from end to end precisely as the joyous hum of a big dynamo well settled to its load makes a background to all the other shop noises.
—RUDYARD KIPLING, *LETTERS TO THE FAMILY*, 1907

the Springhill Miners' Museum, which has underground tours and exhibits, and is a pilgrimage site for countless Anne Murray fans.

From Springhill, you can link up with the Sunrise Highway to go to the seaside town of Pictou and on to Cape Breton Island (see Section 6 of this chapter). Or you can head to Halifax, Nova Scotia's historic capital city, 124 miles (200km) away via Truro.

ANNE MURRAY CENTRE, 36 Main St. Tel. 902/597-8614.

The country and pop singer was born and grew up in Springhill, and in this museum, the community pays a touching tribute to one of its own and takes visitors down a musical memory lane. You'll hear Murray's most famous songs, for sure, but you'll also see a lock of baby hair (1945), a catcher's mitt, a pink prom dress, a school blazer, glowing report cards, an early guitar, a college degree in physical education (1966), and a wedding certificate (1975). Fame came in 1969, with the recording of "Snowbird," followed by the Grammy award–winning "Love Song" in 1974, "You Needed Me" in 1978, "Just Fall in Love Again" in 1979, and many other chart-topping songs and albums. The silver, gold, and platinum records are displayed here, along with glitzy gowns, magazine covers, and photos with John Lennon, Bernadette Peters, Dionne Warwick, and others. Videos portray Anne Murray welcoming visitors to the museum, performing in concerts and television specials, and as a young woman sitting around a table with her parents and brothers. Today she lives in Toronto and continues to enrich the world with her music, which is sold in the museum shop. Allow at least an hour for a visit.

Admission: $5 adults, $4 seniors, $3.50 children 7–14, $2 children 3–6.
Open: Mid-May to mid-Oct daily 9am–5pm; otherwise, by appointment.

TRURO

Equidistant from Springhill and Halifax (100km, or 62 miles, from either), Truro was first home to Native Canadians, who called it Cobequid, and then to Acadians and to Loyalists. The first Bible Society in North America was founded here in 1810, and the first oatmeal was manufactured in 1820. The town also claims Canada's first condensed milk factory, the first railway workers union, the first school of agriculture in Atlantic Canada, and the first long-distance telephone service and incandescent lighting in the province. In the late 19th century, Truro was known as the "Hub of Nova Scotia" because railways linking the province converged here. Today its population numbers 13,000, and it is a center for transportation (road, not rail), manufacturing, and agriculture.

WHAT TO SEE & DO

Each August the Nova Scotia Provincial Exhibition, an agricultural and amusement fair, is held here, at 1,000-acre **Victoria Park,** one of the most dramatically beautiful city parks anywhere. A deep gorge cuts through the park, filled by a clear stream that cascades from level to level among the rocks. It's only a 700-foot stroll to Howe Falls from the parking area.

Truro is also known for the tidal bore that rushes up the Salmon River from the Bay of Fundy via Cobequid Bay. The bore is a rushing current that can develop into a wall of water several feet high. Usually, the days of the full moon in August or later in autumn bring the bore in like a torrent. To witness this phenomenon, consult the current tide table or call Dial-a-Tide (tel. 902/426-5494), and plan to be at **Tidal Bore Park** at least 10 minutes prior to high tide. This twice-daily event can be viewed at night courtesy of powerful floodlights. The park is located at the riverbank on the grounds of the Palliser Restaurant (see below).

WHERE TO STAY & DINE

BEST WESTERN GLENGARRY, 150 Willow St., Truro NS, B2N 4Z6. Tel. 902/893-4311, or toll free 800/528-1234. Fax 902/893-1759. 90 rms. TEL TV **Directions:** Take Exit 13 off Highway 102.
$ Rates: Motel, $64–$68 single; $68–$72 double; hotel, $80–$85 single, $85–$95 double. Extra person $10. Children 18 and under stay free in parents' room. Discount for seniors. AE, CB, DC, ER, MC, V.
Part of the Truro Trade and Convention Centre, the Best Western has both motel and hotel units, as well as a licensed dining room, lounge and piano bar with entertainment nightly. Most rooms are air-conditioned; some have minibars. Added pluses include an indoor and outdoor pool, Jacuzzi, and sauna. Day rates are available.

PALLISER, Tidal Bore Rd. (P.O. Box 821), Truro, NS, B2N 5G6. Tel. 902/893-8951. 40 rms. TV
$ Rates (including hot and cold buffet breakfast): $39 single; $41 double. Extra person $4. AE, DC, ER, MC, V.
Most of Truro's recommendable hostelries are out of town by the highway, overlooking the tidal bore, and with any luck, you won't even have to move from the comfort of your room to see this phenomenon. At the Palliser Resort, for instance, the marshy estuary of the Salmon River is all around you. The Palliser and its companion motel are at the end of Tidal Bore Road near Exit 14 from Highway 102. Most of the motel's units have baths and showers, others have showers only; all have cable color TV.
The Palliser Restaurant is well known among the locals for its pine-paneled dining room, decorated with colorful plates high along the walls and a large coat-of-arms. Windows look onto the Salmon River, just in case the tide rises during your mealtime (it's lit at night). Food at the Palliser, served between 7:30am and 8:30pm, is solid and tasty rather than exotic, and a full dinner will run you about $20. Wine, beer, and drinks are served.

Bed-and-Breakfast

JOHNSON'S EAGLE ROOST, 1702 Salmon River Rd., Truro, NS, B2N 5N2. Tel. 902/895-4797. 3 rms (with 2 shared baths). **Directions:** Three miles (5km) east of town via Queen Street.
$ Rates (including full breakfast and evening snack): $35 single; $45 double or triple. **Closed:** Oct 2–May 30.
I heard about this place from someone in Halifax who spent her honeymoon here and recommended it highly. Three comfortable rooms share two full baths, a TV/VCR lounge, games room, sun deck, and veranda overlooking the Salmon River. Owners Jim and Juanita Johnson provide a friendly welcome, not to mention a big breakfast and an evening snack. School-age children are welcome.

SHUBENACADIE PROVINCIAL WILDLIFE PARK

At the town of Shubenacadie, follow signs for Route 2 north to the park, which is 24 miles (38km) south of Truro and 40 miles (65km) north of Halifax. Set in natural woodland, the park gives visitors a close look at the animals and birds that inhabit this province, along with a few imported species. Shubenacadie is truly a park, too—it's not a zoo. Animals are kept in large enclosures rather than in cages, and most of the birds aren't restrained at all. Ducks, swans, reindeer, moose, and cougar are only some of the species you'll see. The Creighton Environment Centre is at the park entrance, and a 35-acre picnic area is adjacent to the wildlife display area. There's also a children's playground, gift shop, and canteen. Park hours are 9am to 7pm daily mid-May to mid-October, and admission is free (donations welcome). To get here, take Exit 10 off Highway 102.

---

2. HALIFAX

299 miles (481km) NE of Yarmouth; 99 miles (159km) SW of Truro

GETTING THERE   See "Seeing Nova Scotia," earlier in this chapter. Useful transportation numbers include: Acadian Lines, for bus information (tel. 902/454-9321); Air Canada (tel. 902/429-7111); Canadian Airlines International (tel. 902/427-5500); and VIA Rail (tel. 902/429-8421).

Halifax is the British heart of Atlantic Canada. Maritime metropolis, capital of Nova Scotia, airline hub, and home to five universities, it feels the pulse of eastern Canadian life. And yet in the depths of its romantic soul, Halifax dreams of England and of things English.

A quick look at history explains why Halifax is unabashedly Anglophile. Nova Scotia was explored by the English, but settled by the French, Irish, and Scots—all except for Halifax, which was founded under the benevolent and watchful eye of George Montague Dunk, earl of Halifax. The earl was president of England's Board of Trade and Plantations in 1749, when the town was founded under the auspices of that board. Halifax was fortunate in many things, but above all in that it could derive its name from the earl's bailiwick—the Yorkshire city of Halifax—rather than from the earl's family name. (Imagine if the city had been named "Dunk"!) Founded by this English body, Halifax was to be Britain's commercial center and naval stronghold in the New World, two duties that Halifax performs to this day. For this purpose, the board recruited settlers from England rather than from other British lands.

The location picked for the city was superb, on a hilly peninsula surrounded by one of the world's great natural harbors (not to mention it's the second largest—after Sydney, Australia). Fortresses crowned the hills in early times, and pastures surrounded them. A few of the grand fortresses survive, and the pastures have been turned into parks: Halifax is one of the greenest cities you'll visit. But location, green space, and water views don't account totally for its charm. Although this city shoulders the responsibilities of a regional as well as a provincial capital, of a major port, of a business and communications center, it's not gigantic. With a population of more than 114,000, Halifax has all the vibrant activity and cultural opportunities of a much larger city, but none of the crowding and sprawl found in more populated urban areas.

Keep in mind, then, that when you get to Halifax you'll be walking up and down its hillside a lot, and that the sun will play hide-and-seek with the fog. And don't be surprised to see a color photograph of Her Majesty Queen Elizabeth II gracing a wall in every shop and office. And also, as in London, remember that pedestrians have the right-of-way and crosswalks are sacrosanct—in Halifax, as elsewhere in Canada, stop your car whenever you approach a crosswalk if a pedestrian has stepped off the curb to cross. Otherwise you'll set yourself up for a scolding (or a citation) from a police officer in a very Canadian way—firm but polite.

THE BIG BANG   The major piece of information to know about this city is that everything in Halifax was affected, in one manner or another, by the Great Halifax Explosion of December 6, 1917, the world's most powerful human-made explosion until the bombing of Hiroshima. A munitions ship, the *Mont Blanc,* was laden with eight million pounds of TNT when it collided with another ship, the *Imo.* Two thousand Haligonians were killed outright or later died of their wounds, and about 9,000 others survived with injuries. Half the city was flattened by the blast, or by the fires that broke out immediately afterward. Damage was in the tens of millions of

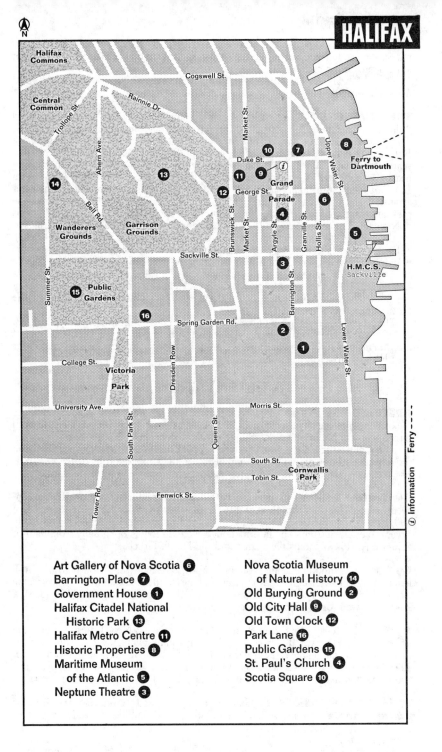

HALIFAX

Halifax Commons
Central Common
Cogswell St.
Rainnie Dr.
Trollope St.
Ahern Ave.
Bell Rd.
Market St.
Duke St.
George St.
Grand Parade
Upper Water St.
Ferry to Dartmouth
Wanderers Grounds
Garrison Grounds
Sackville St.
Brunswick St.
Market St.
Argyle St.
Barrington St.
Granville St.
Hollis St.
H.M.C.S. Sackville
Summer St.
Public Gardens
Spring Garden Rd.
College St.
Victoria Park
University Ave.
Dresden Row
Morris St.
Lower Water St.
South Park St.
Queen St.
Tower Rd.
Fenwick St.
South St.
Tobin St.
Cornwallis Park

(i) Information   Ferry - - - -

Art Gallery of Nova Scotia **6**
Barrington Place **7**
Government House **1**
Halifax Citadel National
  Historic Park **13**
Halifax Metro Centre **11**
Historic Properties **8**
Maritime Museum
  of the Atlantic **5**
Neptune Theatre **3**

Nova Scotia Museum
  of Natural History **14**
Old Burying Ground **2**
Old City Hall **9**
Old Town Clock **12**
Park Lane **16**
Public Gardens **15**
St. Paul's Church **4**
Scotia Square **10**

dollars, even at 1917 prices. The blast was so strong it shattered windows in Truro, 60 miles away, and rattled dishes in Cape Breton and Prince Edward Island. For a look at a memento of the catastrophe, examine the sculpture in front of the Halifax North Memorial Library at 2285 Gottingen: It's made partially with metal from the ill-fated *Mont Blanc.*

THE *BLUENOSE* You won't have been in Halifax long before you hear the word "Bluenose" mentioned. These days, the reference may be about the *Bluenose II,* which sails in Halifax harbor. But the legend has to do with its predecessor, the *Bluenose,* a majestic ship that once was the pride of the Atlantic fishing fleet. Two years after that ill-fated explosion detailed above, the *Bluenose* was launched in nearby Lunenburg, 70 miles from Halifax. The ship—161 feet (49m) long with a 125-foot-high (38m) mainmast and 10,000-square-foot sail—won numerous races against eager challengers, notably those from New England, and garnered the prestigious International Fishing Vessel Trophy in 1921, 1922, 1931, and 1938; it was only defeated once, in 1930. In 1933 the *Bluenose* represented Canada in the Chicago World's Fair. Over the years, it had only one captain, Angus Walters (1881–1968), although different crews were aboard for racing and for fishing. In 1939, when its working days were over, Captain Walters purchased his beloved ship to prevent its sale at auction, but three years later, it was sold to the West Indies Trading Company as a freighter. In 1942, the *Bluenose* struck a reef on Haiti and sank. Some say the image of the graceful schooner, imprinted on the Canadian dime, is more recognizable than the Nova Scotia flag.

The *Bluenose II,* a replica of the legendary ship, was built in Lunenburg in 1963, and Captain Angus sailed on its maiden voyage to Bermuda. If you catch a glimpse of the *Bluenose II* in Halifax harbor, its giant sail billowing against the sky, catch your breath and journey back in time, if only for a moment.

ORIENTATION

ARRIVING By Plane Halifax International Airport is approximately 25 miles (40km) north of the city on Highway 102. A "share a cab" (the taxi has a fare in both directions) will be around $18, while a regular cab is about $32 plus tip.

The **Aerocoach City Shuttle** (tel. 902/468-1258) provides transport between the airport and downtown hotels, making more than a dozen trips daily; the fare is $11 one-way, $18 round-trip (children under 10 accompanied by an adult ride free).

By Train Trains arrive in Halifax from Montréal at 3:20pm daily except Wednesday. The train station is at 1161 Hollis St. (tel. 902/429-8421, or toll free 800/872-7245 in the U.S.). The train to Montréal and points west leaves Halifax daily except Tuesday at 2pm. The information/ticket window is open daily from 9am to 5:30pm. A walkway joins the station and the Hilton Hotel.

By Bus Greyhound bus line from New York, Voyageur from Montréal, and SMT from New Brunswick connect with Acadian Lines for destinations in Nova Scotia; the Acadian Lines bus station in Halifax is at 6040 Almon St. (tel. 902/454-9321), a 20-minute walk or short cab ride to the downtown hotels.

By Car Highway traffic funnels into Nova Scotia via New Brunswick and the Trans Canada Highway. Drivers going through Maine may choose to shorten their driving time by taking the ferry at Bar Harbor or Portland to Yarmouth, Nova Scotia. There is also car-ferry service from Saint John, New Brunswick, to Digby, Nova Scotia, and from Wood Islands, Prince Edward Island, to Caribou, Nova Scotia.

TOURIST INFORMATION There is a well-stocked **Nova Scotia Tourist Information Centre** (tel. 902/424-4247) in the Red Building, Historic Properties, open daily from 8:30am to 7pm June to mid-September, to 4:30pm weekdays the remainder of the year.

The province also maintains information offices at the Halifax International

Airport (tel. 902/873-1223) for arriving passengers and along Route 102 at the airport interchange (tel. 902/873-3608).

Tourism Halifax, in the Old City Hall (P.O. 1749) on Duke Street at Barrington (tel. 902/421-8736; fax 902/421-6448), is open daily in summer, usually from 8:30am to 6pm (to 8pm on Thursday and Friday), from 9am to 4:30pm weekdays only during the remainder of the year. Check the bulletin board for current goings-on about town.

CITY LAYOUT   Halifax occupies a peninsula. The heart of the old town was between Bedford Row, on the water, and the Citadel, a star-shaped fortress occupying the hilltop behind the town. Today this same area is the heart of downtown Halifax.

The downtown area is laid out on a grid, so it's easy to get around, and most likely any place you're looking for is within five or 10 blocks. If you're unsure, call and ask for directions.

Halifax is a compact city and visitors will basically be in the downtown area, where the hotels, restaurants, attractions, and nightspots are concentrated. Most are clustered around the waterfront and the Grand Parade. Slightly farther away are the restaurants and shops along Spring Garden Road, and the Public Gardens, though you can certainly walk there. Directly across the harbor from Halifax, Dartmouth, with a population of 67,000, is so close it can almost be counted as a neighborhood. If you enter Halifax via the MacDonald Bridge, you'll drive through Dartmouth.

GETTING AROUND

BY PUBLIC TRANSPORTATION   Local buses cost $1.15 per trip for adults, 65¢ for seniors or children 5 to 12; if you need a transfer, ask for it when you board. For routes and timetables, call 902/421-6600.

BY CAR   All the major car-rental agencies are here, including Avis (tel. 902/873-3523), Budget (tel. 902/454-8501), Hertz (tel. 902/873-3700), National/Tilden (tel. 902/873-3505), and Thrifty (tel. 902/422-4455). The 873 exchange indicates Halifax airport locations.

Metered parking is 25¢ for 15 minutes, and can be purchased for up to one or two hours, but free before 8am and after 6pm weekdays, as well as all day Saturday, Sunday, and holidays. If you're fined, a parking ticket will run you $7.50. Oversize vehicles may be parked in the lots along Lower Water Street across from the Brewery. Parking in the open lot at Purdy's Wharf, on the waterfront, next to the Sheraton Hotel, costs $4.50 a day.

BY TAXI   There are over 800 licensed taxi operators in Halifax. Nearly the entire alphabet is represented, from Aero Cab (tel. 902/445-3333) to Casino (tel. 902/429-6666) to Yellow Cab (tel. 902/422-1551).

ON FOOT   This is the best way to see Halifax, which is infinitely walkable. Tourism Halifax also provides a self-guided tour in its *Visitor Guide,* and organized walking tours are available. In inclement weather, take advantage of the pedways linking many of the downtown stores, hotels, and office buildings (the *Visitor Guide* has a map of them); you can work your way indoors all the way from the Sheraton to Citadel Hill.

FAST FACTS

American Express   The American Express office is located at 5523 Spring Garden Rd. in the City Centre Atlantic (tel. 902/423-3900).

Babysitting   Ask at your hotel, or contact Mothercare Sitter Service (tel. 423-3833).

Bookstores   A Pair of Trindles Bookshop (tel. 902/423-7528), in the Old Red Store in Historic Properties, deals exclusively in books by Canadian authors, both nonfiction and fiction. Good generic bookstores include The Book Room, 1664 Granville St. (tel. 902/423-8271), or Entitlement The Book Company, 5675 Spring Garden Rd. (tel. 902/420-0565).

If you're looking for international magazines and newspapers, you'll find everything including the *New York Times* and *USA Today* at Blowers Paper Chase, 5228 Blowers St. (tel. 902/423-0750). It also sells a large assortment of notecards and is open conveniently late, until 10pm Sunday through Thursday, until 11pm Friday and Saturday.

Business Hours   Banking hours are Monday through Wednesday from 10am to 4pm, on Thursday and Friday to 5pm. Stores are open Monday, Tuesday, Wednesday, and Saturday from 9:30am to 5:30pm, and Thursday and Friday from 9:30am to 9:30pm. Some shops downtown open on Sunday, from noon to 5pm.

Drugstores   The Shoppers Drug Mart, 5514 Spring Garden Rd. (tel. 902/429-2400), is large and open 24 hours a day.

Emergencies   Call the Halifax police (tel. 4105, no prefix; 421-6840, nonemergency); Poison Control Centre (tel. 902/428-8161); fire (4103, no prefix); Halifax Infirmary, 1335 Queen St. (tel. 902/496-2781); or the 24-hour Help Line, for an emotional crisis (902/421-1188).

Laundry and Dry Cleaners   Clarks Cleaners, in the Scotia Square Upper Mall (tel. 902/423-3456), provides same-day dry cleaning Monday through Saturday, but get it in by 9am to get it back by 5pm.

Library   The Halifax City Regional Library is at 5381 Spring Garden Rd. (tel. 902/421-6983). Look for the towering statue of Sir Winston Churchill, by Oscar Nemon, in front.

Liquor Laws   Liquor sales in Nova Scotia (including wine and beer) are restricted to government stores. Most liquor stores in Halifax are open Monday through Saturday from 10am to 6pm. The Scotia Square store has a good selection.

Post Office   The Halifax Central Post Office, 1680 Bedford Row, is open Monday through Friday from 7:30am to 5:15pm (tel. 902/426-2293).

Religious Services   Services in St. Paul's Anglican Church, between Barrington and Argyle Streets at the Grand Parade, are on Sunday at 8:30 and 10:30am, and 11am on Wednesday. For other times call Halifax Tour Information (tel. 902/429-2240). Established in 1750, St. Paul's, was the first Protestant church in Canada.

Taxes   Most items are subject to an 11% provincial sales tax in Nova Scotia, plus a 7% federal goods and services tax (GST).

Weather   For a weather report, call 902/426-9090.

WHAT TO SEE & DO

Strictly speaking, the Nova Scotia Museum is spread throughout Nova Scotia in 25 different locations. Historically significant houses, farms, and old industrial sites have all been incorporated into this grand museum plan, which includes two museums in Halifax. Pick up a copy of the descriptive booklet about the museum network, *Discover Nova Scotia's Heritage,* from the tourist office.

GUIDED TOURS   Take a Double Decker Tour. The bright red bus departs several times a day from Historic Properties and the Sheraton Hotel for a two-hour city tour, which costs $13 for adults, $11 for seniors 65 and older, and $6.50 for children 5 and older. Tours are offered from mid-June to mid-October (tel. 902/420-1155).

Or hop aboard a Gray Line tour, operated through the **Acadian Lines** bus company (tel. 902/454-9321); you can combine a regular city tour ($15) with a harbor tour ($25 for the two), or visit Peggy's Cove ($22), which is described at the end of this section. The company picks up passengers at the major downtown hotels.

Some tours go even farther afield: Besides offering 2½ to 3 hour tours of Halifax and Dartmouth for $15, Cabana Tours, 3227 Kempt Rd. (tel. 902/455-8111), goes to Peggy's Cove ($12) and the Annapolis Valley ($47), and it offers a three-day package to Cape Breton Island starting at $465. It offers a four-hour tour of Halifax and Peggy's Cove year-round for $30.

Get a different view of Halifax and an exhilarating feeling on a harbor cruise. Choicest of these is a trip aboard the majestic, 18-person-crew ✪ *Bluenose II,* a replica of Canada's trophy-winning two-masted schooner, which has the largest sail in the world (12,500 square feet, 2,500 square feet more than the original). A 161-foot-long (49m) boat with a 125-foot (38m) mainmast, it's moored at Privateers'

Wharf, and while it does hoist sail and leave Halifax a few times in summer, most Tuesdays through Sundays it is available for harbor tours. Half the space on the three daily sailings may be reserved in advance; the remainder is first-come, first-served, and it gets snapped up quickly. Pick up tickets at Privateers' Wharf. The cost for the two-hour cruise is $14 for adults, $7 for seniors and children 12 and under (tel. 902/422-2678 in July and August, 902/424-5000 year-round).

Several other harbor tours and fishing trips, depart regularly from Cable Wharf, within walking distance of Privateers' Wharf. For information about them, contact **Murphy's on the Water** at Cable Wharf (tel. 902/420-1015).

The cheapest water tour of all costs only 85¢ one way (50¢ for kids 5 to 12), and begins at the foot of George Street, off Water Street, in Historic Properties. It's the Halifax-Dartmouth ferry, which has been plying the waters of the harbor since 1752 in one form or another. Boats powered by horses turning a windlass on deck have been replaced by many-horsepowered engines, but the "mini-cruise" is as enjoyable as ever—especially for the price. The compact blue-and-white boats operate from about 6:30am to 11:30pm Monday through Saturday, and from the first weekend in June to the last weekend in September on Sunday from noon to 5:30pm.

Prefer to walk? Tourism Halifax has come up with a **⑨ self-guided walking tour and map,** included as part of the *Greater Halifax Visitor Guide.* If you want a knowledgeable companion to walk with you, contact DTours (tel. 902/429-6415), which offers 90-minute strolls for about $3 per person, from June to October; other months by appointment.

THE TOP ATTRACTIONS

ART GALLERY OF NOVA SCOTIA, 1741 Hollis, at Cheapside. Tel. 902/424-7542.

As much folk museum as art gallery, the Art Gallery of Nova Scotia is housed in a heritage property, the stately Dominion Building (1868), a former Customs house, post office, bank administrative building, and courthouse. The four levels of gallery space inside are modern, primarily displaying the works of Maritime artists, among them Maud Lewis (1903–70), known as the mother of Nova Scotian folk art (the province's Grandma Moses). The well-known folk art gallery is on the mezzanine level. Other exhibits feature Canadian, European, and British paintings, and Inuit art. The outstanding shop on the ground floor sells jewelry, pottery, conversation-piece clothing, and folk art. Look in the Art Sale and Rental shop on the opposite side of the entry from the museum shop; it actually rents out paintings to museum members for about $16 a month, with an option to buy.

Admission: $2.50 adults, $1.25 seniors and students, $5.50 family; children under 12 free. Free to all on Tues.

Open: June–Aug Tues–Wed and Fri–Sat 10am–5:30pm, Thurs 10am–9pm, Sun noon–5:30pm; Sept–May Tues–Fri 10am–5pm, Sat–Sun noon–5pm.

THE CITADEL, Citadel Hill. Tel. 902/426-5080.

When Cornwallis and his band of settlers founded Halifax in 1749, they knew the town was to be a military and naval defense point as well as a commercial center. One of the first projects they undertook was to build a crude fortress atop the hill behind the docks, and then to link it to other forts in a line of defense. In 1825, a long-lasting masonry Citadel, the one you'll visit today, was built. Begun at an estimated cost of £116,000, the Citadel was not completed until 1856, at a cost of more than twice that. By 1870, it became obsolete—artillery had become powerful enough to damage its three- to six-foot-thick walls. But prior to that, enemy commanders must have thought twice about attacking such a formidable fortress.

The Citadel has been a National Historic Park since 1956, and is Canada's most visited historic site. Peer down into the wells, one of which could hold almost 19,000 gallons of water. Marvel at the seemingly impregnable powder magazines. Take in the panoramic views of the city and its harbor. A guide will take you around for free if you inquire at the information center, on the left as you enter. Slightly before noon is a good time to visit, when soldiers in period uniforms prepare for the firing of the noonday cannon, a blast that has been an everyday occurrence here since the mid-19th century.

Admission: Mid-June to Labor Day $2 adults, $1 children 5–16, $5 family; free for seniors and children; free the rest of the year.
Open: Mid-June to Labor Day daily 9am–6pm; the rest of the year daily 10am–5pm.

HISTORIC PROPERTIES, Halifax waterfront.

A group of restored 19th-century buildings at the Halifax waterfront is a wonderful place to begin exploring the city. The buildings house the tourist office, along with many shops, restaurants, and casual eateries. The *Bluenose II* is moored here, at Privateers' Wharf. You can easily walk from here along the waterfront, past the Dartmouth ferry dock and Cable Wharf, to the Maritime Museum of the Atlantic, or do it the other way around.

MARITIME MUSEUM OF THE ATLANTIC, 1675 Lower Water St. Tel. 902/424-7490.

Right on the waterfront, this impressive museum is a combination of a modern new building and an old historic one, the William Robertson & Son building. Outside the entrance to the museum, note the plaque to native son Samuel Cunard (1787–1865), who founded Cunard Steam-Ship Company. (His first ship, the *Britannia,* began service July 4, 1840, between Liverpool and Halifax; in the early days, it carried a few cows on board so that its well-heeled passengers could have fresh milk during the 14-day crossing.) Inside the museum, visit Robertson's store (to the left of the entrance), which for more than a century sold marine hardware, from fishhooks to harpoons to canvas for making sails; on the level above it, an exhibition called "The Age of Sail" incorporates a deckhouse from a coastal schooner in a moving way. To the right of the entrance, in the new wing, you'll discover artifacts from the *Titanic,* including a deck chair, and Queen Victoria's barge, donated by Queen Elizabeth in 1959. In the upper level of the new wing, in an exhibit called "The Age of Steam," more homage is paid to Samuel Cunard, and numerous objects from the permanent collection are displayed informally in "visible storage." An observation deck overlooks the harbor. Behind the museum, and part of it, the CSS *Acadia* is moored. Built in 1913 in England, the ship always worked in Canadian waters, charting the coasts of Nova Scotia, Newfoundland, and Labrador until it retired in 1969. Go aboard to admire the cabins of Honduras mahogany and English oak and to see how the officers and crew lived. Allow a couple of hours to tour the entire museum.

Admission: June to mid-Oct $2.25 adults, 50¢ children 5–16, $5.50 family; free Tues 5:30–8pm. Mid-Oct to May free every day.
Open: June to mid-Oct Mon and Wed–Sat 9:30am–5:30pm, Tues 9:30am–8pm, Sun 1–5:30pm; mid-Oct to May Tues 9:30am–8pm, Wed–Sat 9:30am–5pm, Sun 1–5pm.

OLD BURYING GROUND, at Barrington St. and Spring Garden Rd.

If you love to roam through the tombstones of old cemeteries, don't miss this large, impressive one. The final resting place for Halifax's first citizens, it was opened in 1749, when the city was founded, and was in use until 1844. More than 12,000 people were buried here, though only 10% of the graves are marked, many of the stones from the 1700s. The Welsford Parker Monument at the entrance honors two Haligonians who died in the Crimean War. It was erected here in 1860, before Canadian Confederation, and restored in 1989. No rubbings are allowed in the cemetery.
Admission: Free.
Open: Daily 9:30am–5:30pm.

ST. PAUL'S CHURCH, on the Grand Parade between Barrington and Argyle Sts. Tel. 902/429-2240.

At one end of the Grand Parade stands the first Anglican cathedral established outside of England and Canada's oldest Protestant place of worship. Part of the building, which dates from 1750, was fabricated in New England—in fact, the original timbers were cut in Boston, then a British colony—and it was erected in Halifax with the help of a royal endowment from King George II. St. Paul's has fine

stained-glass windows, and dozens of little memorial plaques put up in honor of past parishioners. It also has an interesting and mysterious attraction: In the Halifax explosion of 1917, the third window on the Argyle Street side smashed and looks distinctly like the silhouette of a man. Some claimed it had an uncanny resemblance to the first assistant curate, Jean Baptiste Moreau, who served at St. Paul's. A piece of flying debris from that same explosion is lodged in the wall over the doors to the nave.
    Admission: Free.
    Open: Daily 9am–4:30pm; Sun services 8:30 and 10:30am.

MORE ATTRACTIONS

DALHOUSIE ART GALLERY, 6101 University Ave. Tel. 902/494-2403.
    On the university campus, this gallery offers changing exhibits of historical and contemporary art, often with a regional theme.
    Admission: Free.
    Open: July–Aug Tues–Sun 1–5pm; the rest of the year Tues 11am–5pm and 7–10pm, Wed–Fri 11am–5pm, Sat–Sun 1–5pm.

GRAND PARADE, at George and Argyle Sts.
    Once the drilling ground for Halifax's militia, the Grand Parade is now a central square in the city, a magnet for city workers who want to eat lunch outside and get a little sun in summer, or simply be part of the downtown scene. Free concerts, from blues to brass, are given here in summer from noon to 1pm, usually on Wednesday, Thursday, and Friday. Performances associated with local festivals, notably the International Tattoo on July 1–7 and the Buskerfest in August, also take place here. The streets surrounding the Grand Parade are lined with popular restaurants, and historic St. Paul's Church stands at the Prince Street end of it.

GOVERNMENT HOUSE, 1451 Barrington St.
    Before Government House, the official residence of the province's lieutenant-governor, the provincial governor and his wife lived in a wooden house on this same site, which, according to Lady Frances Wentworth, wife of then-governor Sir John Wentworth, was about to collapse into its own cellar by the year 1805. The provincial assembly voted to build a nice stone mansion for the couple and in 1897 the Wentworths moved in—as have every lieutenant-governor and family since then. Although Government House is not open to visitors, you can pass the imposing original entrance on Hollis Street near the corner of Bishop; then go around to the other side, on Barrington Street, and compare the more modest entrance used today.

HMCS *SACKVILLE,* behind the Maritime Museum of the Atlantic. Tel. 902/429-5600.
    The HMCS *Sackville,* named after the town of Sackville, New Brunswick, is the only remaining Canadian World War II corvette out of 111 such convoy escorts built in Canada for the Royal Canadian Navy (11 more were built for the U.S. Navy). Built in 1941, it has been restored to its wartime configuration, to serve as a memorial to the 110,000 men and women of Canada who served in the navy during World War II, all volunteers. A 15-minute audiovisual presentation, *Battle of the Atlantic,* is shown on the hour and the half hour. The statue beside the boat is *The Wave* (no, it's not a whale), by Nova Scotia artist Donna Hiebert Davison.
    Admission: Free.
    Open: Mon–Sat 10am–5pm, Sun noon–5pm. **Closed:** Oct–May.

NOVA SCOTIA MUSEUM OF NATURAL HISTORY, 1747 Summer St., near Bell Rd. Tel. 902/424-6671.
    Located west of the Citadel, and part of the Nova Scotia Museum system, it houses exhibits on Nova Scotia's natural history, wildlife and peoples, industries, marine life, and famous individuals in modern galleries. There are temporary shows, as well.
    Admission: $2.25 adults, 50¢ children 5–16, $5.50 family; free Wed 5:30–8pm.
    Open: Mid-May to mid-Oct Mon–Tues and Thurs–Sat 9:30am–5:30pm, Wed 9:30am–8pm, Sun 1–5:30pm; the rest of the year, 9am–5pm (to 8pm Wed).

OLD CITY HALL, 1841 Argyle St. Tel. 902/421-6448.

Built in 1890, it is graced with the largest wooden flagpole made of one piece of timber in the world. The mayor of Halifax holds an informal afternoon tea here on weekdays in July and August. Visitors are welcome to come, meet the mayor, sip tea, and tour the building. Use the Grand Parade rather than the Argyle Street entrance.

Admission: Free.

Open: Teatime, July–Aug Mon–Fri 3:30–4:30pm.

OLD TOWN CLOCK, Citadel Hill.

When you pass along Brunswick Street, you get a glimpse of the distinctive Old Town Clock, designed by the duke of Kent, Queen Victoria's father, while he was commander of the Citadel (1794–1800). It was built in London, and erected here in 1803. The duke valued punctuality in his soldiers and in the townsfolk, and he liked tinkering with things mechanical. Designing the clock made him happy on both counts.

PROVINCE HOUSE, Hollis St., near Prince St. Tel. 902/424-8967.

The seat of the Nova Scotia Legislative Assembly, this handsome Georgian mansion of weathered stone was finished in 1819, and the assembly has occupied it ever since. You can tour Province House with a guide for free. You'll visit the chamber of the Legislative Assembly, as well as the Red Chamber, a sumptuous room with fine oil paintings, the seat of Nova Scotia's Legislative Council until it was disbanded.

Admission: Free.

Open: Mid-June to mid-Sept Mon–Fri 9am–6pm, Sat–Sun 9am–5pm; other months Mon–Fri 8:30am–4:30pm, except holidays.

PARKS

In the beautiful ✪ **Public Gardens,** ducks and swans cruise across the glassy surfaces of ponds, fountains play in the breeze, and the sweet fragrance of flowers greets you as soon as you enter. The 18-acre formal English gardens have been soothing the souls of Haligonians since Queen Victoria's reign. The main gates were shipped from Scotland in 1890. Watch for a summer schedule of free band concerts, performed in the red-topped gazebo. The gardens, bounded by Sackville Street, South Park, Spring Garden Road, and Summer Street, are open daily from 8am to sunset.

Point Pleasant Park, at the southern tip of Halifax peninsula, is a marvelous 186-acre forest laced with 10 miles of walking trails and dotted with picnic spots and views. Park your car in the lot near the end of Young Avenue, the southern extension of South Park Street. No cars are allowed past here, so you must proceed on foot. Established in 1866, Point Pleasant Park has an old martello tower, one of the cylindrical defense towers erected throughout the British Isles and eastern Canada in the 19th century.

A 20-minute boat ride from Cable Wharf, **McNab's Island** provides 1,200 acres of land to enjoy—beaches, walking trails, and the remains of military fortifications to explore. Murphy's on the Water (tel. 902/420-1015) and East Coast Charters (tel. 902/422-3608) provide transportation. A trip here makes a fine afternoon outing, and boats make the trip several times daily from Cable Wharf in July and August and on weekends in June and September.

SHOPPING

Historic Properties, on the waterfront, is filled with little shops selling everything from T-shirts and tapes to household items to books about Nova Scotia, and it's fun to wander from one to the next. One, the Harbour Swan, is a pleasant, all-purpose gift shop with something for everyone. Nearby, in the Sheraton Hotel, the Houston North Gallery, 1919 Upper Water St., specializes in and sells Inuit art and Nova Scotia folk art; its main gallery is in the town of Lunenburg. Local folk art is also sold in the shop of the Art Gallery of Nova Scotia, downtown at 1741 Hollis St.

Scotia Square, a tremendous development bounded by Barrington, Duke, Market, and Cogswell Streets, has more than 100 shops and services on two levels—clothing and shoe stores, gift shops, airline outlets, a tailor, florist, copy shop—in short, a Halifax in microcosm.

Right across the street is **Barrington Place,** at 1903 Barrington St., with a number of fashionable boutiques, notably Lady Jane's, on the second level, which sells stylish costume jewelry, and the Micmac Heritage Gallery, on the ground (Granville) level, selling quality native crafts.

The smaller (and less confusing) **Maritime Centre**, at 1505 Barrington at the corner of Spring Garden Road, has two levels of shops and a food court frequented by the many office workers who inhabit this building and the surrounding ones.

At 5657 Spring Garden Rd. and Dresden Row, half a block from the Public Gardens, the upscale **Park Lane** has three stylish floors filled with fashionable shops, an eight-screen cinema, and a food court. The tree-filled atrium lobby adds an inviting touch.

The blocks along Spring Garden Road between Queen Street and Park Street provide a pleasant stretch for shopping and strolling. There's even a designer sock shop, at no. 5495.

WHERE TO STAY

The "very expensive" designation is for double-occupancy rooms from $135 to $175; "expensive," from $100 to $130; "moderate," from $65 to $95; and "inexpensive," from $40 to $60.

VERY EXPENSIVE

HALIFAX HILTON, 1181 Hollis St. (corner of Terminal Rd.), Halifax, NS, B3H 2P6. Tel. 902/423-7231, or toll free 800/HILTONS in the U.S., 800/268-9275 in Canada. Fax 902/422-9465. 291 rms, 16 suites. MINIBAR TV TEL

$ Rates: $115–$145 single; $135–$165 double; from $145 suite. Extra person $20. Children of any age stay free in parents' room. Weekend rates and packages available. AE, CB, DC, DISC, ER, MC, V. **Parking:** Outdoor, free.

⭐ The Halifax Hilton represents an appealing combination of old and new. Built in 1929, it has the special character of a fine old hotel, but with its $18 million facelift in 1990, it's also quite gorgeous, with rooms furnished in sand and blush colors, prints on the walls, and one queen or two three-quarter beds. The harbor-view rooms are tops, and you can gaze down at the cruise ships that dock behind the hotel. Rooms in the older section have ceiling fans, while those in the newer section are air-conditioned. The alcove suites, with balconies, are lovely. The wide hallways lack the institutional look of so many newer hotels. The hotel accepts pets. Right next to Halifax's VIA Rail terminal, and six blocks from the center of town, it provides a complimentary shuttle bus to the downtown area.

Dining/Entertainment: There's the Chart Room, for breakfast and lunch buffets and dinner, and the nautically themed Pier 21 lounge.

Services: Same-day dry cleaning and laundry, shop, hair salon, bathrobe on request, in-house movies, babysitting.

Facilities: Concierge, executive floor with lounge, small indoor pool (open 6am to 11pm) and fitness room, sauna, Jacuzzi, tennis court, no-smoking floors.

PRINCE GEORGE HOTEL, 1725 Market St., Halifax, NS, B3J 3N9. Tel. 902/425-1986, or toll free 800/565-1567 in Canada. Fax 902/423-6048. 196 rms, 9 suites. A/C MINIBAR TV TEL

$ Rates: $150–$160 single; $160–$170 double; from $190 suite. Extra person $15. Children under $18 free with parents. Weekend rates and honeymoon packages available. AE, CB, DC, DISC, ER, MC, V. **Parking:** Underground, $6 a day.

This is the city's most centrally located hotel, perfect for those who prefer to walk everywhere. The Prince George has comfortable, tastefully decorated rooms with either a king or two double beds, hairdryer, toiletries, coffee and tea maker, and windows that open. Add to that a commendable staff. It is connected by an underground passage to the Metro Centre and World Trade Centre.

Dining/Entertainment: The Terrace Room serves breakfast only, and there's also a quick, inexpensive breakfast wagon in the lobby. Bistro-style Georgio's restaurant and bar serves food from 11am to 11pm (drinks until 2am). Guppy's Bar, with an entrance on Grafton Street, features dancing to fifties, sixties, and seventies music, and karaoke on Tuesday night.

Services: Automated message service, complimentary newspaper Monday to Friday, in-room movies, same-day valet, shoeshine, babysitting service.

Facilities: No-smoking floors, an indoor pool, two outdoor terraces, concierge floor, meeting rooms, shop.

SHERATON HALIFAX, 1919 Upper Water St., Halifax, NS, B3J 3J5. Tel. 902/421-1700, or toll free 800/325-3535. Fax 902/422-5805. 332 rms, 21 suites. A/C TV TEL

$ Rates: $99–$175 single or double, depending on numerous factors; from $200 suite. Extra person $20. Children under 18 stay free with parents. Packages and weekend rates available. AE, CB, DC, ER, MC, V. **Parking:** $6 a day.

  The impressive Sheraton Halifax has been ingeniously nestled into the city's most historic area, its design blending harmoniously with the waterfront and the handsome old buildings of Historic Properties. The rooms, which were newly refurbished in 1993, have color schemes that feature greens and coral, are spacious, and have either one king or two double beds. The baths have hairdryers, makeup mirrors, and clotheslines, and when you look in the closet you'll find that rarity of rarities—removable hangers. The rooms overlook either the water, Historic Properties, the city, or the pool—all pleasant views. The pretty indoor pool is under a skylight.

Dining/Entertainment: Harborfront restaurant, which serves lunch and dinner, becomes a bar with dance floor after 9pm; the Grand Banker restaurant serves three meals a day; and the Edible Express is a take-out deli. In the lobby there's a lavish buffet spread for Sunday brunch, 11am to 2pm; and on nice days lunch is served outside on the Boardwalk Grill.

Services: Concierge, same-day dry cleaning and laundry, in-room movies, complimentary coffee-making equipment, room service (6am to midnight).

Facilities: Two no-smoking floors, indoor pool, extensive fitness center (6:30am to 10pm), saunas, Jacuzzi.

EXPENSIVE

CAMBRIDGE SUITES, 1583 Brunswick St., Halifax, NS, B3J 3P5. Tel. 902/420-0555, or toll free 800/565-1263. Fax 902/420-9379. 200 rms. A/C MINIBAR TV TEL

$ Rates: $92–$110 single; $102–$120 double. Children under 18 stay free with parents. AE, DC, ER, MC, V. **Parking:** Indoors, $4 per day.

Across the street from the Citadel, Cambridge Suites provides a comfortable home away from home for vacationing families and business travelers. Each unit comes with queen-size beds, two telephones, a remote-control TV with in-room movies, a hairdryer, and a dining/living area, as well as a microwave, refrigerator, dishes, and cutlery. There are no-smoking rooms and laundry facilities. And the bathroom mirrors are heated so they remain steam-free. Particularly outstanding is the rooftop fitness center (open 6am to 10pm), which overlooks the city and has a whirlpool, sauna, free weights, and exercise bikes. There's also a sun deck and terrace barbecue. On Wednesday nights, the hotel manager hosts a barbecue for guests (it costs $9 for steak or chicken and fixings, with a free cocktail and hors d'oeuvres; children get free burgers and hot dogs).

DELTA BARRINGTON, 1875 Barrington St. (corner of Duke), Halifax, NS, B3J 3L6. Tel. 902/429-7410, or toll free 800/268-1133. Fax 902/420-6524. 201 rms, 1 suite. MINIBAR TV TEL

$ Rates: $104–$120 single or double, $170 suite. Extra person $15. Weekend rates packages available. Children 18 and under stay free in parents' room and eat for half price; those 6 and under eat for free. AE, DC, ER, MC, V. **Parking:** $7 (no in/out privileges); $11 valet, at Scotia Square, across the street.

The Delta Barrington has a refreshingly casual ambience. Its country-style but modern accommodations are enveloped in a century-old building that is part of Historic Properties. The guest rooms feature pine furniture, painted chests, lots of hunter green touches, and a painted trimming around the ceiling. They have two three-quarter beds, coffee makers, large baths, and—shades of the good old days—windows you can open. Signature rooms are much larger and have a queen- or king-size bed, and massage shower heads and oversize towels in the bath. The courtyard rooms are particularly quiet. The hotel is surrounded by inviting little shops and cafés and is only half a block from the Halifax tourist office.

Dining/Entertainment: McNab's country-style restaurant, serving three meals a day, including soup, salads, a lobster dinner, and, in summer, a buffet breakfast; for imbibers, there's the Trader's Lounge.

Services: In-room movies.

Facilities: Fitness room, Jacuzzi, indoor pool with a glass partition that opens onto a sun deck; meeting rooms.

Bed-and-Breakfast

HALLIBURTON HOUSE INN, 5184 Morris St., Halifax, NS, B3J 1B3. Tel. 902/420-0658. Fax 902/423-2324. 30 rms (all with bath or shower), 3 suites. TV TEL

$ Rates (including continental breakfast): $90 single; $100 double; from $120 suite. Extra person $15. Children under 18 stay free in parents' room. Discount for AAA members and seniors. AE, DC, ER, MC, V. **Parking:** Limited, but free.

Halliburton House is actually three adjacent buildings. The office, restaurant, and library are in the former home of the longest-serving Supreme Court justice of Nova Scotia, which was built in 1809. All the rooms are different: Some are particularly large, others have balconies or high ceilings, some have minibars, all have either a fan or an air conditioner. Two of the suites have working fireplaces, and the two-level family-loft suite has a full kitchen. The restaurant has a reputation for good, sometimes exotic food (seafood and beef dishes interspersed with pheasant, alligator, buffalo, and wild Arctic musk-ox); it's open daily for breakfast, lunch, and dinner, for guests and others; prices are inexpensive at lunch, expensive at dinner. In warm weather, you can dine in the pleasant tree- and flower-filled garden. Halliburton House has been operated as an inn since 1987; smoking is still accepted here.

MODERATE

Bed-and-Breakfast

STERNS MANSION, 17 Tulip St., Dartmouth, NS, B3A 2S5. Tel. 902/ 465-7414. Fax 902/466-8832. 5 rms (all with bath). TV

$ Rates (including breakfast): $55–$65 single; $65–$75 double; rooms with Jacuzzi $90 single, $100 double. Honeymoon and golf packages available. MC, V.

In a quiet, residential area of Dartmouth, Sterns Mansion is as romantic a place as you're likely to lay your head. The rooms have been thoughtfully filled with Victorian antiques and eclectic collectibles; candles, dimmer switches, and fun toiletries add to the mood. Two rooms feature swimming pool–size Jacuzzis. Guests may enjoy musical instruments, games, books, and a VCR in the living room, as well as a back patio and barbecue. The four-course breakfast starts off with a wake-up beverage served in your room. In the evening tea and cakes are served downstairs. The honeymoon packages are tempting to anyone (not just honeymooners) in need of spoiling. If you're a golf fan, be sure to ask about the Nova Scotia golf-tour packages. The B&B, which permits neither smoking nor pets, is a short walk from the ferry to Halifax or a quick drive away, and just 20 minutes from the airport.

THE WAVERLEY INN, 1266 Barrington St. (between Morris and South Sts.), Halifax, NS, B3J 1Y5. Tel. 902/423-9346, or toll free 800/565-9346 in the Maritimes. Fax 902/425-0167. 32 rms (all with bath). A/C TEL TV

$ Rates (including continental breakfast and snacks): $55–$85 single or double. Extra person $10. MC, V. **Parking:** Free, behind the house; entrance to lot on Morris Street.

 I first learned of this inn through a Frommer traveler, who was thrilled to discover it. Indeed, it is a find, starting with the location (six blocks from the center of Halifax), and followed by the reasonable rates, the make-yourself-at-home touches like a 24-hour pot of coffee and free snacks from 6am to midnight, the antique furnishings, and the warm host, A. J. Leventhal, who claims running an inn is better than golf any day. The parlor boasts a high ceiling and stained-glass window. The rooms are filled with oak and mahogany furniture; each has a ceiling fan, and an air conditioner in the window. Baths have either a tub or shower. No. 110 is an old-fashioned room on the ground floor with two double beds with high headboards; no. 124 is the house's most elegant room, with mahogany vanity, chest, and beds. The smaller rooms on the third floor are less expensive. Guests may sit out on the second-floor deck, and swim at the YWCA across the street. The house was built in 1866 and became an inn 10 years later—welcoming such notables as Oscar Wilde (who stayed in pretty room no. 124), P. T. Barnum, and Anna Leonowens, the tutor and nanny of the children of the king of Siam and better known simply as Anna in *The King and I*. To his credit, Mr. Leventhal, who'll greet you like a long-lost relative, is working hard to restore the Waverley Inn to its former grandeur.

NEAR THE AIRPORT

THE INN ON THE LAKE, P.O. Box 29, Waverley, NS, B0N 2S0. Tel. 902/861-3480. Fax 902/861-4883. 37 rms, 4 suites. A/C TV TEL
$ Rates: $75–$85 single; $85–$95 double; from $175 suite. Extra person $15. Children under 12 stay free. AE, ER, MC, V. **Parking:** Free.

Only 10 miles from the airport, the Inn on the Lake aptly calls itself a "small country club hotel." Innkeepers Sue Bartlett and Ron Nelson gave up big-city life to carve out this serene niche for themselves and others. Set on five acres of park alongside Lake Thomas, it features comfortable rooms, many of them lavishly renovated; suites, some with two levels, have kitchens, fireplaces, and Jacuzzis. There's an outstanding dining room that prepares fresh seafood in innovative ways, a bar, tennis courts, shuffleboard, volleyball, and water sports. Guests can swim in the pool or the lake. If you don't want to deal with a rental car, they provide an airport shuttle for free.

BUDGET

HERITAGE HOUSE HOSTEL, 1253 Barrington St., Halifax, NS, B3J 1Y2. Tel. and fax 902/422-3863. 14 rms (6 with bath).
$ Rates: $12.75 Canadian AYH members, $15.75 Canadian nonmembers, $16.75 nonmembers of other nationalities. $25 room with private bath. V.

Next to Halifax's YWCA in the historic Joseph Seeton House (1864) and opposite the Waverley Inn, Halifax's downtown hostel opened in 1992 and the interior still reflects how run-down the once-beautiful house had become. Still, it represents an economical respite for those who pass its way. Most accommodations are in dorms with four to eight beds in them, and there are two shared baths. Three family rooms accommodate up to four people. Doors to the rooms are painted lavender, also the color of the carpet. There's a common room with books and magazines, a laundry, a modest kitchen, a dining room, lockers, a pay phone, and a bulletin board. The building, which is smoke-free, is 1½ blocks from the railway station.

YMCA, 1565 S. Park St. (P.O. Box 3024), Halifax, NS, B3J 3H1. Tel. 902/423-9622. Fax 902/425-0155. 53 rms.
$ Rates: $31 single; $42.50 double. Weekly and monthly rates available. MC, V. **Parking:** Street only.

For those on a budget, especially individuals, another good choice for accommodations is the YMCA, which is well located across from the pretty public garden. It houses both men and women (over 18), in single rooms with one twin bed per room; there's a shared bath for men, another for women. Guests may use the pool, gym, racquetball court, and weight room at no extra cost, and they pay only a small fee (about $5) to use the health club on the premises.

YWCA, 1239 Barrington St., Halifax, NS, B3J 1Y3. Tel. 902/423-6162. Fax 902/423-7761. 27 rms.
$ Rates: $31 single; $47 double. Weekly and monthly rates available. V. **Parking:** Free.

The women's counterpart to the YMCA is the YWCA, also in a good location, somewhat closer to downtown than the YMCA. The YWCA, 1½ blocks from the train station, houses women only and offers guests free access to its kitchen, large pool, weight room, and TV lounge. There are a couple of double rooms, though most are singles. The bath is shared.

WHERE TO DINE

Note the restaurant hours: This city stays up and eats fairly late into the night.

Keep an eye peeled for "Taste of Nova Scotia" signs in restaurant windows; they're your best bet for a memorable meal in Halifax or elsewhere in the province. Members of this prestigious group are known for quality food that emphasizes Nova Scotia's produce and recipes, good service, and pleasant atmosphere. You can get a guidebook listing the member restaurants at most visitor information centers.

The restaurants recommended below have been categorized according to the price of the majority of their dinner main courses. "Very expensive" is more than $20; "expensive," $15 to $20; "moderate," $10 to $15; and "inexpensive," less than $10.

VERY EXPENSIVE

FIVE FISHERMEN, upstairs at 1740 Argyle St., at the corner of George St. Tel. 902/422-4421.
   Cuisine: SEAFOOD. **Reservations:** Recommended.
$ **Prices:** Appetizers $4.50–$8; main courses $17–$30; specials $17. AE, DC, ER, MC, V.
   Open: Dinner Mon–Sat 5–11pm, Sun 5–10pm.
Halifax is known for its seafood, and a great deal of it is served up in style at the Five Fishermen. Complimentary plates of mussels, as well as a salad bar, start things off. Main courses run the underwater gamut, but some, such as Digby scallop fettuccine and lobster thermidor, have a special appeal. You can also choose "hot rocks"—slabs of granite on which you sizzle your seafood at your table. The homemade desserts include apple pie, truffle cake, cheesecake, ice cream, and sherbets.

The Five Fishermen is a pretty but casual place, in the second-oldest building in Halifax, an old schoolhouse that's been redone with handsome etched-glass doors, authentic Tiffany lamps, antique coatracks, and exposed stonework. It's in the same complex, and under the same ownership, as the more inexpensive eateries Atrium/My Apartment and Lawrence of Oregano, and the jazz and blues club Cheers.

EXPENSIVE

LA MAISON GALLANT, 1541 Birmingham St., off Spring Garden Rd. Tel. 902/492-4339.
   Cuisine: FRENCH. **Reservations:** Recommended.
$ **Prices:** Lunch items $8–$10; dinner appetizers $5–$11, main courses $13–$17. AE, CB, DC, MC, V.
   Open: Mon–Sat 11:30am–5pm; dinner daily 5–11pm.
⭐ Owner and attentive host Jerry Gallant has created a quiet, pretty setting where you can sit out in the patio on summer evenings or in intimate dining areas anytime. The focus here is on French cuisine in all its incarnations—from France, Québec, the Caribbean, and Louisiana. At dinner, start with an appetizer of jumbo shrimp with garlic and olive oil, escargots, squid, or any of the pâtés, followed by broiled halibut filet with Cajun spices, poached salmon with béarnaise sauce, or stuffed chicken breast with a fresh-herb sauce. Lunch runs the gamut from sandwiches to seafood, with several pâtés to tempt you.

RYAN DUFFY'S, 5640 Spring Garden Rd. Tel. 902/421-1116.
   Cuisine: STEAK/SEAFOOD. **Reservations:** Recommended.
$ **Prices:** Main courses $13–$23. AE, MC, V.
   Open: Lunch Mon–Sat 11:30am–3pm; dinner Mon–Wed 5–11pm, Thurs–Sat 5pm–midnight, Sun 5–10pm.
This steak and seafood house is known primarily for its steaks, cooked over wood charcoal with a blend of spices. Steak prices—from tenderloin filet to New York

strip—are determined by the ounce and are displayed on a chalkboard at the front desk. Lunch is served in casual Duffy's Bar and Grill, and you can get light fare, including soups, salads, nachos, pasta, and pizza, as well as heartier selections. The bar stays open until 2am nightly except Sunday, when its hours are 5 to 11pm.

UPPER DECK RESTAURANT, on the third floor of the Privateer's Warehouse, Historic Properties. Tel. 902/422-1289.

Cuisine: SEAFOOD. **Reservations:** Recommended.
$ Prices: Appetizers $5–$9; main courses $11–$23. AE, DC, ER, MC, V.
Open: Dinner Mon–Sat 5:30–11pm, Sun 5:30–10pm.

Privateer's Warehouse features three eateries stacked one on top of the other, and this one, on the top floor, is definitely tops for dining. The Upper Deck features unabashed nautical decor and even a crow's-nest balcony. Fine dining and excellent service have made the establishment a favorite of Haligonians and visitors for years. You might choose their Waterfront Grill (salmon steak, scallops, and shrimp), Cajun or pan-fried halibut or haddock, lobster thermidor, or bouillabaisse. From the grill, consider chicken, Cajun style or in phyllo pastry and served with a lemon peppercorn sauce; juicy six- or eight-ounce steaks; lamb with a garlic and feta stuffing; or peppered pork loin with a spicy raspberry sauce. The desserts are equally tempting, and the wine list is substantial. Down one level, at the Middle Deck restaurant, the emphasis is on pasta and the prices are lower (tel. 902/425-1500); after dinner, the Lower Deck, on the ground level, can supply some lively Maritime music (tel. 902/422-1289).

MODERATE

McKELVIE'S, 1680 Lower Water St. Tel. 902/421-6161.

Cuisine: SEAFOOD. **Reservations:** Recommended at dinner.
$ Prices: Appetizers $4–$7; lunch main courses $6–$9, dinner main courses $9–$20; three-course dinner $20. CB, DC, ER, MC, V.
Open: Mon–Sat 11:30am–10pm, Sun 4:30–10pm.

In a former firehouse dating from 1903, McKelvie's is so seafood-oriented that a boat is part of its decor. This is a pretty place, with latticework, exposed bricks, and a relaxed atmosphere. The menu features appetizers such as the Solomon Grundy (marinated herring with a creamy mustard and dill sauce), as well as excellent soda bread and bannock. At lunch, you can get omelets, chowder and a sandwich, pasta, or a grilled chicken or fish sandwich. At dinner, consider the likes of calamari, Digby scallops, bouillabaisse, lobster, haddock, halibut, and swordfish. Prices drop by more than half at lunchtime, and from 4:30 to 6pm, "early bird specials" are featured. There's also a children's menu.

SALTY'S, upstairs at Privateers' Wharf. Tel. 902/423-6818.

Cuisine: SEAFOOD. **Reservations:** Recommended for upstairs dining room.
$ Prices: Lunch items $3–$14; dinner appetizers $5–$9, main courses $9–$20. AE, DC, ER, MC, V.
Open: Lunch Mon–Fri 11:30am–2:30pm; dinner daily 5–10pm; bar daily 11:30am–1am.

If you're out for dinner in Historic Properties, look for Salty's, overlooking the harbor. The view of the boats and sea gulls drifting by is as good as can be. The menu features pastas and fresh Atlantic seafood such as scallops, salmon, halibut, shark, and swordfish; if you've a penchant for steak, it's available, too. Lunch, served in the restaurant and in the pub on the main floor, leans heavily toward short orders, from buffalo wings to fish-and-chips to pizza. Salty's pub, popular for its view, outdoor patio, and weekend entertainment (8pm to midnight Friday and Saturday), essentially serves the lunch menu all day, until 10pm.

SILVER SPOON CAFE AND RESTAURANT, 1813 Granville St. Tel. 902/422-1519.

Cuisine: INTERNATIONAL. **Reservations:** Recommended at dinner.
$ Prices: Lunch appetizers $4–$7, main courses $5–$9; dinner appetizers $4–$9, main courses $10–$19; three-course jazz brunch $10; three-course fixed-price dinner from $19. AE, DC, ER, MC, V.

Open: Lunch Mon–Sat 11:30am–2:30pm; brunch Sun 11:30–3pm; dinner Mon–Sat 5:30–10pm.

 In a renovated historic building, this is one of the city's most pleasant restaurants for dining, ambience, and service; the downstairs café and pretty upstairs dining room both serve lunch and dinner, the dining room menu is more extensive, and the seafood dishes are particularly popular. All the breads, pastas, and desserts are made from scratch right here. For lunch the menu touts green salad with warm Brie and fresh-fruit chili salsa, smoked chicken fajitas, quiche, and salmon cakes. At dinner, numerous pastas may be ordered as appetizers or main dishes, or you might start with mussels or Thai spring rolls, followed by cashew chicken or roulade of sole. The house salad is a mini-vegetable garden. Save room or come back for one of their 12 desserts, including a particularly gooey one called "Sweet Mouthful." They can accommodate special diets.

There is also a Silver Spoon Café at 5657 Spring Garden Rd. in the Park Lane shopping complex (tel. 902/422-1616). It serves the same diverse menu, and is open for lunch and dinner Monday through Saturday. It's also licensed.

INEXPENSIVE

Market, Grafton, and Argyle Streets between George and Blowers Streets are lined with trendy cafés, lounges, and restaurants. Most run daily lunch specials announced on convenient outside bulletin boards. Typical of them is the **Lawrence of Oregano Beverage Room,** across from Parade Square, at 1727 Argyle (tel. 902/422-6907), which claims to construct the best sandwiches in town.

PEDDLER'S PUB, Granville St., Barrington Place. Tel. 902/423-5033.
   Cuisine: LIGHT FARE. **Reservations:** Not needed.
$ Prices: Menu items $1–$5. MC, V.
   Open: Mon–Sat 11am–midnight, Sun noon–10pm.
This casual establishment on the Barrington Place pedestrian mall ranks high on the list of local favorites for a glass of beer, pub food, and a chat. Two of the most popular menu items are the chicken wings and the steak special, both under $4. On a warm, sunny day, grab a table outside. The Peddler's Pub is two blocks from Historic Properties. A local group called Ken & Alex & the Swell Guys has been performing here on Saturdays from 3 to 6pm since 1980.

SATISFACTION FEAST, 1581 Grafton St., between Sackville and Blowers. Tel. 902/422-3540.
   Cuisine: VEGETARIAN. **Reservations:** Not needed.
$ Prices: Menu items $1–$10; specials $5–$10. AE, MC, V.
   Open: Breakfast Mon–Sat 7–11am; brunch Sun 10:30am–2:30pm; lunch Mon–Sat 11:30am–4pm; dinner daily 4–10pm (to 9pm Mon–Thurs in winter).

Bright, airy, simple, and appealing, Halifax's vegetarian restaurant, in a simple wood-frame house, has a reassuring name: Satisfaction Feast. Owner Sarita Earp provides a peaceful atmosphere, where the smell of fresh-baked bread issues from the kitchen. Breakfast is a casual, self-serve affair. Other times, you can order, among other possibilities, a savory soyburger, a stuffed pita, a hefty salad, a pasta or stir-fry meal, pirogies in garlic/cheese sauce with Caesar salad, the curry of the day, and side orders of tofu, steamed veggies, and brown rice. At lunch you can have soup and a sandwich or salad for $5; three-course dinner specials are $10. Do save room for dessert: peanut butter balls, fruit crisps, cheesecake, assorted pies and cakes, and blueberry grunt, a Nova Scotia favorite. All items are available for take-out; fresh bread, muffins, and cookies are on sale beside the cashier.

SPECIALTY DINING
Breakfast

TRIDENT BOOKSELLERS & CAFE, 1570 Argyle St. Tel. 902/423-7100.
   Cuisine: LIGHT FARE. **Reservations:** Not needed.
$ Prices: Most items $1–$3. MC, V.
   Open: Sun 10am–6pm, Mon 8:30am–6pm, Tues–Sat 8:30am–10pm.

For those who like to sip coffee and read at the same time, this is the perfect spot to do it—a combination bookstore selling secondhand books and remainders, and an adjoining café. The menu is short and to the point: muffins, pastries, and a wide choice of hot and iced teas and coffees, including cappuccino, café mocha, espresso, and café au lait by the bowlfuls. The decor and ambience are restful: brick walls, mahogany paneling, fresh flowers on the tables, the work of local artists on the walls, soft classical music playing in the background, and copies of the daily paper, the *New Yorker, Harper's,* and *The Economist* for folks to peruse.

Picnic Fare

You can supply yourself with beans, vitamins, nutritious bread, organic produce, and any of hundreds of herbs (for cooking or curing) at **Supernatural Foods,** 1505 Barrington St. (tel. 902/423-8630), in the Maritime Mall. They have the best selection of herbs I've ever seen.

You can also buy groceries at the **Deli Food Market,** on the lower level of Scotia Square; at **Sobey's,** 1120 Queen St.; and at the **Spring Garden Grocery,** 5640 Spring Garden Rd.

EVENING ENTERTAINMENT

THE PERFORMING ARTS

CONCERTS   Halifax's outspokenly modern **Metro Centre,** downtown at 5284 Duke St., draws crowds for sports events and concerts alike. Entertainers here have included such stars as Paul Simon, Rod Stewart, and Céline Dion. The center is currently the home of the Halifax Windjammers basketball team, and there is a small, free Sports Hall of Fame opposite the box office. Tickets for concerts cost $20 to $30; for basketball games, $5 to $15. The box office is open Monday to Friday from 11am to 5pm (tel. 902/451-1221 to place orders, 902/451-1202 for recorded event information).

THEATER   The **Neptune Theatre,** 5216 Sackville St., at Argyle (tel. 902/429-7070), is small and unprepossessing, but has offered some of the city's liveliest drama and comedy since 1980. The season runs from October to May, with no productions mounted in summer. The 1993–94 season included *Dancing at Lughnasa, All Fall Down,* and *Les Misérables.* Tickets are $17 to $26, with a discount for students and senior citizens Sunday through Thursday. The box office is open Monday to Saturday from 10am to 6pm, later on performance days.

Productions are also staged at the **Rebecca Cohn Auditorium** in the Dalhousie University Arts Centre, University Avenue and Seymour Street. Watch for newspaper listings of current events.

DINNER THEATER   The **Grafton St. Dinner Theatre,** 1741 Grafton St. (tel. 902/425-1961), offers two musical comedies and shades of sockhops, swingtime, and speakeasies. Recent productions have included *Class of '61* and *Heaven Can Wait.* The dinner choices are prime rib, poached salmon, or chicken Kiev.

For a step further back in time—into the 1840s—try the dinner (a seafood medley), music, and theater experience offered by the **Historic Feast Co.** (tel. 902/420-1840) at Historic Properties. Shows change from season to season, but rest assured, a lively cast of characters is always on hand—and good fun's a-brewing.

Both companies have nightly performances and charge about $30 per person.

THE CLUB & MUSIC SCENE

CABARET   The **Misty Moon Cabaret,** at 1595 Barrington St. (tel. 902/423-8223), and the **Palace Cabaret,** 1721 Brunswick St. (tel. 902/429-5959), throb with the beat of live band music nightly. The action doesn't heat up until after 10pm, but continues until 3:30am. The cover charge varies with the popularity of the groups but is usually from $2 to $12 at the Misty Moon and from $3 to $5 at the Palace. The Palace is open nightly, the Misty Moon Wednesday to Sunday.

LIVE MUSIC   A lot of local and national talent flows through Halifax's clubs and lounges. Newspaper listings and free entertainment sheets can keep you up-to-date on who's playing where.

In Historic Properties, the ✪ **Lower Deck Pub,** in Privateers' Warehouse at street level (tel. 902/425-1501), is the best place to hear rousing folk songs from the Maritime coasts, led by a songster and roared by several hundred happy listeners. Local bands play Monday through Saturday, and the music starts at 9:30pm. Expect to pay $2 to $3 admission Wednesday through Saturday. Only beer and wine are sold.

For live jazz, head for the **Birmingham Grill,** 5657 Spring Garden Rd. (tel. 902/420-9622), any night of the week. The balcony overlooking the street is popular in summer.

DANCING The **Harbourfront Bar,** at the Sheraton, 1919 Upper Water St. (tel. 902/421-1700), is actually a restaurant that converts to a bar with a popular dance floor nightly at 9pm. The location, overlooking the water, is part of the appeal; there's a deck and live local entertainment in summer.

Guppy's, in the Prince George Hotel, on the corner of Grafton and George Streets (tel. 902/425-1986), spins discs from the fifties to the nineties and appeals to all ages. The staff even gets into the act here, performing their own dance number around midnight.

Most of the bars in Halifax have small dance floors, and you're welcome to kick up your heels on them.

THE BAR SCENE

Generally called lounges or beverage rooms, bars abound in Halifax and they're all busy weeknights, but packed on Thursday, Friday, and Saturday evenings.

Tops with locals and visitors alike, the ✪ **Granite Brewery,** 1222 Barrington St. (tel. 902/423-5660), is eastern Canada's first and only "brew pub." Their brews are produced and sold exclusively on the premises. Both are top-fermented, unpasteurized, and unfiltered. Stop by for a 12- or 18-ounce glass, or try their "Best Bitter" beer, made with an 80-year-old strain of English yeast, or the "Peculiar" beer, an old-style dark English ale with a sweeter taste. No hard liquor is served, only beer and wine. Pub atmosphere thrives here, especially upstairs, where food is served.

CINEMAS

The megatheater (eight-screen) **Famous Players Park Lane Cinemas,** in the Park Lane Mall, 5657 Spring Garden Rd. (tel. 902/423-5866), shows first-run general-audience movies. At the opposite end of the spectrum is **Wormwood's Dog and Monkey Cinema,** at 2015 Gottingen St. (tel. 902/423-3433), offering intellectual, foreign, and Canadian films.

AN EXCURSION TO PEGGY'S COVE

Peggy's Cove (pop. 90) is a small fishing village on Highway 333 due west of Halifax, 27 miles (43km) away. Don't be put off by the telephone lines. The scenery gets prettier as the road gets curvier. Figure on driving no more than 42 to 48 m.p.h. (70 to 80kmph) on a good stretch.

The picturesque village sits in the midst of a spare, boulder-strewn landscape, with old clapboard houses, fishnets drying, lobster traps crowding the wharves, and a winking lighthouse atop the smooth, sea-washed coastal rocks. The village is like many another Nova Scotia fishing village, only more perfectly picturesque, and very close to Halifax. For these reasons it has acquired a reputation almost like that of the Cabot Trail or the Annapolis Valley; guidebooks and tourist bureau personnel steer armies of visitors toward the one narrow dead-end street in the village, and the result is that what most tourists see in Peggy's Cove is other tourists.

Should you bother to go? Yes, under certain conditions. First, don't go on a foggy day. The village would be picturesque in the fog if one were alone there, but you won't be. Second, go off-season if you can, in early June or mid-September, and get there as early in the morning as possible. Park in the public lot at the entrance to the village—it's well marked by signs—and don't take your car down the narrow street to tangle with the tour buses. Remember, there's nothing wrong with the village itself. It's beautiful, and it is now protected from commercial development by the government of Nova Scotia. There's nothing wrong with the tourist traffic either, except when too many people come at the same time. While you're in the village, you can have a meal at its only restaurant, the efficiently run **Sou'Wester** (you can grab a bite at the counter if tour groups fill the tables), or post a letter or card from the tiny post office located in the lighthouse.

3. THE LIGHTHOUSE ROUTE TO YARMOUTH

Nova Scotia's Lighthouse Route follows the southwestern coast along Highway 103 from Halifax to Yarmouth, passing through or near dozens of quaint coastal villages and several interesting small cities.

You can stop at Peggy's Cove on your way from Halifax (see "An Excursion to Peggy's Cove," above). If you've already paid a visit to this picturesque hamlet, leave Halifax by Highway 103 heading west and south. Your first stop will be the charming town of Chester. If you're pressed for time, you can follow the Lighthouse Route only as far as Lunenberg, only 70 miles from Halifax and a wonderful drive in itself.

CHESTER

You must leave Highway 103 and take Highway 3 to reach Chester (pop. 1,120), a pretty little New England–style village by the sea, 42 miles (70km) southwest of Halifax. Chester was in fact settled in 1759 by people from New England and England, who called the place Shoreham. A hundred years later, it had become a summer vacation retreat, with fine homes and four hotels.

Pirates used to rove this coast, but now all you'll see are pleasure yachts, particularly in mid-August for **Chester Race Week,** the largest sailing regatta in Atlantic Canada.

If you drive into town and follow King Street to the shore, then turn right on South Street, you'll come to a pretty gazebo, the Chester Yacht Club, a monument of a soldier in kilts to commemorate the town's World War I heroes, and some beautiful views.

The **Chester Tourist Booth,** on Highway 3, is open from 9am until 6pm daily, June through September (tel. 902/275-4616). The knowledgeable staff will provide a map of Chester complete with a suggested walking tour. This is also the best source of current information about Big Tancook Island.

In the center of town there is a large pharmacy called Pharmasave where you can stock up on essential travel items like vitamins, sunglasses, toothbrush, magazines, newspapers, film, batteries, and snacks. It's open Monday to Saturday from 8:30am to 9pm, Sunday from noon to 5pm (tel. 902/275-3518).

WHAT TO SEE & DO

Besides a walk around this pretty town and a look in its several art galleries and craft shops, consider taking a ferry ride out to Big Tancook Island in Mahone Bay. The ferry, for passengers only (no cars), makes four round-trips Monday through Thursday, more on weekends and holidays. There is a small charge for the 4.8-mile (8km) trip. The excursion, including a browse through the town of Tancook, will take most of a day.

If you're in town in the evening in July or August, you might take in a play or musical event at the air-conditioned **Chester Playhouse,** 22 Pleasant St. (tel. 902/275-3933, or toll free 800/363-7529 in Nova Scotia and Prince Edward Island); tickets cost about $15, less for students and seniors.

ROSS FARM MUSEUM, Hwy. 12. Tel. 902/689-2210.
Another short excursion from Chester takes you about 20 miles (32km) north

along Highway 12 to the Ross Farm Museum. The farm, a "living museum," is part of the Nova Scotia Museum, and on your visit you'll be transported right back to a working farm in 19th-century Nova Scotia. Children particularly love to see the farm animals and ride in a horse-drawn wagon or sleigh. Originally settled by William Ross almost two centuries ago, the farm was home to five generations of Rosses before becoming a museum.

Admission: $2 adults, 50¢ children 5–16, $5 families.

Open: June to mid-Oct daily 9:30am–5:30pm (otherwise, call for limited schedule).

WHERE TO STAY

CAPTAIN'S HOUSE INN, 129 Central St. (P.O. Box 538), Chester, NS, BOJ 1J0. Tel. 902/275-3501. Fax 902/272-3502. 9 rms (all with bath).
$ Rates (including continental breakfast): $65 single; $75 double. Extra person $10. AE, DC, ER, MC, V. **Parking:** Free.

Near the Chester Yacht Club, the Captain's House inn is a marvelous old mansion dating from 1822, set among trees and lawns overlooking the water. It's a memorable choice for dining in Chester, with its formal service and gourmet seafood. Start with the house pâté or mussels and proceed to the salmon, halibut filet, or stuffed chicken. Lunch is served daily from noon to 3pm, including Sunday buffet brunch; dinner is from 5:30 to 10pm daily. Lunch will run $10 to $15, brunch $23, and dinner $30 to $35. The inn has nine rooms, each with a private full bath; you can request a television or telephone in the room.

MECKLINBURGH INN, 78 Queen St. (P.O. Box 350), Chester, NS, BOJ 1J0. Tel. 902/275-4638. 4 rms (none with bath).
$ Rates (including full breakfast): $50 single; $59 double; $79 triple. V. **Closed:** Late Oct–May.

Consider this little inn—with wood floors, pine furnishings, and an apple garden and a 40-foot well in back—your own secret hideaway. The rooms are named after islands in Mahone Bay: Gooseberry and Mrs. Finney's Hat, for instance. Three of them have a double bed and sofa bed; one has two twins; and they all share two big full baths. Bottles of Perrier, Hershey's Kisses, and tartan robes are placed in the rooms for guests' enjoyment. There is also a living room with TV and VCR, and a balcony where guests may lounge in a red Adirondack chair and listen to the sounds of evening. The inn was built in 1890 and to a great extent was always operated as a rooming house and inn; in 1990, it was renovated by the present owner and innkeeper, Suzan Frazer, a native of Chester and an accomplished cook, a sailor, and a world traveler. Suzi feeds her visitors around a big dining room table (originally a cutting table in a milliner's shop). She'll even pack them a picnic lunch on request. The inn is a block or so from the Chester Theater, and a few blocks from the Tancock Island ferry dock. The name Mecklinburgh was the first name of the body of water now known as Mahone Bay.

WHERE TO DINE

FOC'SLE, 42 Queen St., at Pleasant St. Tel. 902/275-3912.
Cuisine: LIGHT FARE. **Reservations:** Not needed.
$ Prices: Most items $3–$7. No credit cards.
Open: Mon–Sat 11am–2am, Sun noon–8pm.

Wet your whistle at Foc'sle, a congenial local watering hole with everything from draft beer to the hard stuff, along with inexpensive pub food. The second-oldest tavern in Nova Scotia, it opened in 1949. There's a pool table for any takers.

MAHONE BAY

Entering from the east on Highway 3, the first thing to strike you after the scenic beauty of the town of Mahone Bay (pop. 1,230) is that the Mahonians must be religious folk: five steeples rise above the town, three of them reflected in the waters of the bay. For the record, they're St. James Anglican, the United Baptist, St. John's Lutheran, the Calvary Temple, and the United Church. A sign at the entrance to the town says "Mahone Bay, 1754. We love the beauty around us and welcome you to share it."

The **Settlers Museum,** on Main Street near the center of town, houses period antiques and an outstanding collection of ceramics. Mahone Bay has craft shops, galleries, and boutiques waiting to be explored. Out of the town's wooden boat–building heritage has sprung Atlantic Canada's only **Wooden Boat Festival,** held annually the last week in July.

The helpful **Tourist Bureau** will be on your right as you come into town. It's open from May through October from 10am to 5pm (from 9am to 7:30pm in midsummer). Mahone Bay is located 62 miles (100km) from Halifax, and 15 miles (24km) southwest of Chester.

WHERE TO STAY

SOU'WESTER INN, 788 Main St. (P.O. Box 146), Mahone Bay, NS, B0J 2E0. Tel. 902/624-9296. 4 rms (all with bath). TEL

$ Rates (including full breakfast and evening tea): $55 single; $65 double. Extra person $15. MC, V.

For lodging in Mahone Bay, a sure bet is the tidy Sou'Wester Inn, formerly the home of a local shipbuilder, where your hosts, Ron and Mabel Redden, are anxious to make your stay an enjoyable one. Over complimentary full breakfast and evening tea, or a leisurely chat on the veranda, they'll help you plan scenic drives or shore hikes, or share their piano, books, and parlor games with you. All rooms have private bath with shower or tub. No smoking or small children, please.

WHERE TO DINE

ZWICKER'S INN, 662 Main St. Tel. 902/624-8045.
   Cuisine: INTERNATIONAL. **Reservations:** Recommended.
$ Prices: Lunch items $3.50–$9 ($21 for lobster in season); dinner appetizers $4–$8, main courses $9.50–$19. AE, DC, ER, MC, V.
   Open: Daily 11:30am–9:30pm. **Closed:** Dec 24–26.

⭐ Near the Sou'Wester Inn, Zwicker's is a good place for lunch or dinner (so much so a reader recently wrote to say so), and it's fully licensed. Lunch features homemade soups, sandwiches, an omelet, and fish and meat selections, while the dinner menu is more extensive, with homemade pasta, rabbit in white wine sauce, chicken breast in lemon cream sauce, roast duck with black currants, prawns provençale, and much more. Besides good food, the pretty restaurant has lace curtains at the windows, five eating nooks, no-smoking areas, and roses on the tables.

LUNENBURG

Continuing along Highway 3, a few minutes' drive will bring you into Lunenburg (pop. 3,015), a charming seaside town with exceptional houses. Lunenburg, 69 miles (111km) from Halifax, is the fishing center of Nova Scotia's fishing industry; the champion racing schooner *Bluenose* was built here in 1921, as was a replica of it, in 1963.

The town was settled in 1753, and many of its first inhabitants were Germans; in fact, German was heard in the streets of Lunenburg well into the 1800s.

You'll no doubt notice the large red-roofed building with a spire and black trim at the western end of Lawrence Street. It looks like a resort but is actually the former **Lunenberg Academy** (1895), now a National Heritage Site. Today the building houses an elementary school, so give up any notion of checking in.

Lunenburg has been associated with locally produced pudding and sausage. Lunenburg pudding is a meat dish, and possibly a German settler's idea of pâté. Lunenburg sausage is served hot and may be spicy. Nova Scotians stock up when they visit here.

The **Lunenburg Tourist Bureau** (tel. 902/634-8100), in a lighthouse at the top of Blockhouse Hill Road, books rooms, answers questions, and supplies a map of the town and a walking tour brochure that showcases its splendid architecture. It also sells illustrated Heritage Society books on the houses of Lunenburg. The bureau is open from 9am to 9pm daily in high summer; there's a lookout deck in the top of the lighthouse. To get there, follow Lincoln Street up the hill.

WHAT TO SEE & DO

A major event is the **Crafts Festival** in mid-July. During this weekend over 25,000 visitors descend on the little town. The goods for sale are of excellent quality and artistry, and the prices are quite reasonable. It's followed in August by the **Lunenburg Folk Harbour Festival,** with an emphasis on Maritime music, and the **Nova Scotia Fisheries Exhibition and Fishermen's Reunion,** where traditional skills like scallop shucking and fish filleting are put to the test.

A fine place to see folk and Inuit art is the **Houston North Gallery,** at 110 Montague St. (tel. 902/634-8869).

East of the Fisheries Museum of the Atlantic, along the waterfront, scallop draggers tie up and unload. Farther east, at the end of Montague Street, are the Scotia Trawler Shipyards, where fishing vessels are winched into dry dock for hull maintenance. The original *Bluenose* and *Bluenose II* were built here, as was the *Bounty* for the movie *Mutiny on the Bounty.*

Before leaving Lunenburg, take a walk or a drive through the older part of town, up on the hill. Right by the Town Hall at Duke and Cumberland Streets is the second-oldest church in Canada after St. Paul's in Halifax: **St. John's Anglican Church,** a lovely old clapboard building painted white with dramatic black trim; its oak frame was brought here from Boston. **St. Andrew's Presbyterian Church,** a block away at King and Townsend, has a 5.5-foot copper codfish weathervane atop its spire, doubly symbolic.

All the grand old houses of the town just beg to be noticed.

FISHERIES MUSEUM OF THE ATLANTIC, on the waterfront. Tel. 902/ 634-4794.

Stay to the right when you drive into town and you'll find your way almost immediately to the town's major attraction. The Fisheries Museum encompasses large red wharfside buildings that used to be a fish-processing plant, the wharf itself, and the two vessels tied up at the wharf that you can tour: the salt-bank schooner *Theresa E. Connor* and the trawler *Cape Sable.* Inside the buildings you'll explore three floors of exhibits, including an enlightening one on the legendary *Bluenose* and its equally famous captain, Angus Walters (both were featured on a stamp in 1988), a 20-tank aquarium (don't miss the heavyweight lobster), a theater, a demonstration room where you'll see how to clean and filet fish, and a working dory shop. A gift shop, a fast-food area, an outstanding restaurant (see "Where to Dine," below), and ample free parking are available. When you enter the museum, ask when the next film screening will take place and then time your visit to the ships and the indoor exhibits with that in mind.

Admission: $2.25 adults, 50¢ children over 5, $5.50 family ticket.
Open: Daily 9:30am–5:30pm. **Closed:** Oct 16–May.

WHERE TO STAY

BLUENOSE LODGE, 10 Falkland St. (P.O. Box 399), Lunenburg, NS, B0J 2C0. Tel. 902/634-8851, or toll free 800/565-8851. 9 rms (all with bath).
$ Rates (including full buffet breakfast): $60–$65 single; $65–$70 double. Extra person $15. Packages available. Nov–Mar, by reservation. MC, V. **Parking:** Beside the house and on the street.

This old Lunenburg mansion, set in a big yard surrounded by trees, has an inviting tiled entry and country decor. The rooms are pretty, and vary in size and decor; all come with bath (shower, no tub). No smoking is allowed in the bedrooms, only in the sitting area on each floor. The inn's dining room, Solomon Grundy's, is open for breakfast from 8 to 9:30am, and for dinner from 5:30 to 9pm. Seafood is the strong item on the dinner menu, and you can also order Lunenburg pudding, a traditional pâté of pork and spices served with rhubarb relish, or the three-course daily special. Look for the towering celery-colored Victorian house with blue-gray trim. Innkeepers Ron and Grace Swan provide a warm welcome.

COMPASS ROSE INN, 15 King St. (P.O. Box 1267), Lunenburg, NS, B0J 2C0. Tel. 902/634-8509, or toll free 800/565-8509. 4 rms (all with bath). **$ Rates** (including breakfast): $55–$65 single or double. Packages available. AE, ER, MC, V.

The Compass Rose Inn is a lovely restored 1825 Georgian home with wonderful ambience, decor, cuisine, and location, right downtown, only one block above the harbor. The interior of the house reflects the period, with comfortable antiques and rooms with iron beds covered with quilts. The licensed dining room, open to the public, always draws a crowd for its local and house specialties and reasonable prices. Lunch is served daily from 11:30am to 2:30pm; dinner from 5 to 9pm. The Compass Rose Inn also has a guest lounge, an outdoor garden patio, and a gift shop. The owners, Suzanne and Rodger Pike, operate another bed-and-breakfast, the Lion Inn (ca. 1835), a few blocks away.

KAULBACH HOUSE HISTORICAL INN, 75 Pelham St. (P.O. Box 1348), Lunenburg, NS, B0J 2C0. Tel. 902/634-8818. 8 rms (6 with bath). TV **$ Rates** (including full breakfast): $50–$75 single; $50–$80 double. Packages available. AE, MC, V. **Open:** May–Oct; Nov–Apr, by reservation only. **Parking:** Behind the house or on the street. **Closed:** Two weeks at Christmas.

This striking house (ca. 1880) with mansard roof and dormer and bay windows, has been lovingly restored by its young, enthusiastic owners, Karen and Enzo Padovanio, who have painted it the color of pink champagne. Six of the rooms have private bath with a shower (no tub); two others, which have single beds, share a bath with a clawfoot tub. Room no. 1, on the ground floor, is particularly pretty; room no. 6, the Tower Room, has a queen-size bed with two sitting areas overlooking the harbor. There are two seatings for the three-course breakfast, at 8 and 9:15am; it's served family style. It's fully licensed, so guests can sip sherry in the Victorian parlor. Drinks and meals are for guests only; they get room service, too. No small children or pets, please.

LUNENBERG INN, 26 Dufferin St. (P.O. Box 1407), Lunenberg, NS, B0J 2C0. Tel. 902/634-3963, or toll free 800/565-3963. 6 rms (all with bath), 1 suite. **$ Rates** (including full breakfast): $60–$80 single; $65–$85 double. Packages available. MC, V. **Parking:** In front of the house; limited.

This richly appointed inn (1893), beside the old railroad station, is a neighbor to the Bluenose Lodge. Its pretty living room has a fireplace and ceiling fan and is filled with games, magazines, and videos for guests' enjoyment. All rooms have a private bath, and the suite fills the entire third floor and has a Jacuzzi. There is no smoking except in the sitting rooms, or on the front porch or upstairs balcony. The inn has a liquor license, but hosts Faith and John Piccolo serve only their guests. Faith also runs the deli-café in town, La Bodega, where you can eat in or take out bagels, croissants, or fresh baguettes. The Lunenburg Inn is lovely, but is on a triangular lot quite close to the road. You can walk to town from here.

TOPMAST MOTEL, 76 Masons Beach Rd. (P.O. Box 958), Lunenburg, NS, B0J 2C0. Tel. 902/634-4661. Fax 902/634-8660. 16 rms (all with bath). TV TEL **$ Rates:** $50–$60 single or double; $65–$70 housekeeping unit. Extra person $5. Children under 5 stay free. AE, MC, V.

For motel-lovers, Lunenburg has an excellent one, located next to the golf course high above town. All the units at the Topmast Motel have balconies; all but one overlook the harbor, and a few are no-smoking rooms or housekeeping units. The view from here is simply spectacular. The hospitable and personable owners, Agnes and Don Wilson, encourage their guests to use the barbecue and picnic tables, and will provide a VCR if they want to rent videos. Small pets are accepted. The motel is within walking distance of a tennis court and the golf course.

WHERE TO DINE

Even if you're not a guest at the Bluenose Lodge or the Compass Rose Inn, you can still have a meal there (see above).

CAPT'N ANGUS SEAFOOD RESTAURANT, 2nd floor, Fisheries Museum of the Atlantic. Tel. 902/634-3030.
Cuisine: SEAFOOD. **Reservations:** Recommended if you want a table by the window.
$ Prices: Lunch and dinner appetizers $3.50–$6; lunch main courses $5–$14; dinner main courses $8–$20; daily specials $9–$15. The federal, but not the provincial, tax is included. AE, DC, ER, MC, V.
Open: Lunch daily 11:30am–4pm, dinner daily 4–9pm. **Closed:** Oct–May.

A reader tipped me off to this place, on the second floor of the Fisheries Museum but open longer hours. Its multipaned windows overlook the water and, beyond it, the Bluenose Golf Course, and the decor is jaunty, with nautical flags, painted buoys looking a lot like folk art, and old photos. The lunch and dinner menus are similar, though the latter offers more appetizer and beef selections, and you can expect fish chowder, fish-and-chips (a house specialty), fisherman's platter, angels on horseback (scallops wrapped in bacon), garlic shrimp scampi, Solomon Grundy (marinated herring and onion with sour cream), and "hot rocks"—scallops, shrimp, sirloin, or chicken sizzling on a hot slab of Nova Scotia granite. I opted for a delicious dinner special of fishcakes with cucumber-and-onion salad, fluffy soda biscuits, *real* iced tea, and a megapiece of gingerbread with whipped cream—all for $13. The service is enthusiastic here, and it's fully licensed.

EN ROUTE TO SHELBURNE

Bridgewater (pop. 7,000) is aptly named, as you'll discover if you pass through the town instead of bypassing it on Highway 103. The bridge over the LaHave (rhymes with "gave") River gives you a view of the railroad sidings that in past years brought Bridgewater its prosperity. You may also take the ferry from LaHave to Bridgewater and save 45 minutes of driving. Today a tire-manufacturing plant is the main commercial concern.

For a cultural stop in Bridgewater, try the **DesBrisay Museum,** on Jubilee Road, which houses the collections of Judge Mather Byles DesBrisay, who died in 1900. The objects here are from Lunenburg County's heritage: from the natural environment to the works of local artists and manufacturers. Besides the permanent collection, the DesBrisay has modern galleries for major traveling exhibits. Hours are 9am to 5pm Monday through Saturday and 1 to 5pm Sunday from mid-May through September; October to mid-May it is open Tuesday through Sunday from 1 to 5pm. Admission is free, and parking and picnic facilities are available (tel. 902/543-4033).

The DesBrisay Museum also operates the Wile Carding Mill, a five-minute drive across town. Built in 1860, the water-powered mill once carded the wool brought here by farmers from the region. During sheepshearing season in May, it operated 24 hours a day, six days a week. The mill is open from June to September, Monday to Saturday from 9:30am to 5:30pm and Sunday from 1 to 5:30pm.

The next large town along the Lighthouse Route is Liverpool, near which there's a turnoff for **Kejimkujik National Park,** known simply as "Keji" to Nova Scotians (tel. 902/682-2772). Kejimkujik is filled with glacial lakes and streams, stands of pine and hemlock, and bogs. The park lures outdoor enthusiasts with a large backcountry area for hiking, canoeing, and wilderness camping. Kejimkujik has a visitor reception center, nature interpretation program, supervised beach, and canoe and bicycle rental service. The principal campground is at Jeremy's Bay, just off Highway 8, with 329 semiserviced sites at $10.50 per night.

SHELBURNE

"A Loyalist Town," like many others along the South Shore, Shelburne was settled by families loyal to the Crown who opposed the American Revolution. Some 3,000 immigrants arrived in Shelburne in the 1780s, increasing its population to 10,000 people, so that the tiny village, then called Port Roseway, was nearly unrecognizable.

By the early 1800s, it had become the third-largest town in North America. It still has the third-largest natural harbor in the world.

Many old Loyalist houses still stand in the town, now home to only 2,245 people. The **tourist bureau** at the foot of King Street, beside the water (tel. 902/875-4547), open from 9am to 9pm mid-May to mid-October, will provide you with a walking-tour guide for the town as well as information on day tours around the county.

WHAT TO SEE & DO

With your walking-tour map from the tourist bureau, track down the **Ross-Thomson House** on Charlotte Lane, a thriving store during the boomtime of Shelburne at the end of the 1700s. Part of the Shelburne Historic Complex (along with the Shelburne County Museum, the Dory Shop, and Tottie's Crafts, all on or just off Dock Street), it is open daily June to mid-October from 9:30am to 5:30pm for free, courtesy of the Nova Scotia Museum and the Shelburne Historical Society. The house has been restored to its condition of the 1780s, and fitted out as a store of the time would have been. Visit the front store, with its long counter, stacks of hides, and barrels of provisions; the clerk's room; the sitting room; two bedrooms upstairs; and the kitchen in the basement (enter from the back of the house).

Nearby on the shore is a working cooperage firm, across the road from the Cooper's Inn. It is still making barrels the old-fashioned way, carving the staves from blocks of wood. Stacks of staves set out to dry fill a field across the road from the coopers' workshop.

The **Shelburne County Museum** is housed in the historic building at the corner of Dock Street and Maiden Lane (tel. 902/875-3219). Besides temporary exhibits, the museum has permanent collections concentrating on Loyalist history, and the shipbuilding activities so prevalent in Shelburne County a century ago. The museum is open mid-May through mid-October from 9:30am to 5:30pm every day; in winter, hours are 9:30am to noon and 2 to 5pm Monday through Saturday.

WHERE TO STAY & DINE

Bed-and-Breakfast

COOPER'S INN, 36 Dock St., at Mason St. (P.O. Box 959), Shelburne, NS, B0T 1W0. Tel. 902/875-4656. 5 rms (all with bath).
$ Rates (including full breakfast): $55–$75 single or double. AE, MC, V. **Closed:** Mid-Oct to end of Mar.

Cooper's Inn is a fine choice for a historic bed-and-breakfast. The recently renovated 1785 house was built for the local cooper, but today has jazz or classical music wafting throughout the living and dining rooms. A breakfast of fruit and homemade breads and muffins is included in the room price. Children are welcome; the owners, Cynthia and Gary Hynes, have a youngster of their own.

Dinner, served nightly from 5:30 to 8:30pm, is beautifully prepared with fresh ingredients and light sauces and presented by Gary Hynes and served by candlelight. A typical meal might include a warm salad of chanterelles and snow peas, followed by rack of lamb or tuna "filet mignon," garnished with several fresh vegetables, and for dessert, homemade ice cream or plum tart. Expect the bill, including tax and tip, to run $50 for two.

A Motel

CAPE COD COLONY MOTEL, Water St. (Hwy. 3; P.O. Box 34), Shelburne, NS, B0T 1W0. Tel. 902/875-3411. Fax 902/875-1159. 23 rms. A/C TV TEL
$ Rates: $40 single; $45 double. Extra person $5. Children under 10 free. AE, DC, DISC, ER, MC, V.

Shelburne's motels are west of the center of town on Highway 3, and of them, the Cape Cod Colony Motel is one of the handsomest. It has fully equipped rooms and well-tended grounds with tables, umbrellas, and a swing. Guests are provided with complimentary coffee. The dining room is open from 7am to 10pm daily.

WHERE TO DINE

CLAUDIA'S DINER, 149 Water St. Tel. 902/875-3110.
   Cuisine: LIGHT FARE. **Reservations:** Not needed.
$ **Prices:** Most items $2–$11; dinners $8–$15. V.
   Open: May–Sept Mon–Wed and Fri 7am–9pm, Thurs 7am–7pm, Sat 9am–2pm, Sun noon–9pm. Oct–Apr Mon–Fri 9am–9pm, Sat 9am–2pm, Sun noon–7pm.
For down-home cooking, early risers and others may want to head for Claudia's Diner. Here you'll find all your favorite—and some typically Nova Scotian—breakfast, lunch, and dinner short orders: grilled cheese sandwiches, hamburgers with the works, chicken fingers, fish chowder, lobster sandwiches, all manner of seafood and fries, pork chops, and liver and onions. All the dinners come with juice or soup, a freshly baked roll, potatoes (your choice), coleslaw, and tea or coffee. Homemade desserts run the gamut from doughnuts and cinnamon rolls to pies. Yes, there is a Claudia.

HEADING WEST EN ROUTE TO YARMOUTH

If you're still deep into the 1700s as you leave Shelburne, continue your historic explorations at Barrington (pop. 355), west of Shelburne on Highway 103, at the Barrington River. The **Barrington Woolen Mill** began operation in 1884, industrializing an activity that had been carried on in private homes since pioneer days: the manufacture of yarn, cloth, and blankets from locally grown raw wool. The mill was initially powered by water, and later by steam; its production narrowed to yarn in the 20th century and ceased altogether in 1962. Part of the Nova Scotia Museum, it displays much of its original machinery, and the staff demonstrates spinning. Touring the mill is to discover how cloth was made in the 19th century. Managed by the Cape Sable Historical Society, it is open mid-June to the end of September Monday to Saturday from 9:30am to 5:30pm, Sunday 1 to 5:30pm. Admission is free. A picnic area is beside the river.

WHERE TO DINE

OLD SCHOOL HOUSE RESTAURANT, Barrington Passage. Tel. 902/637-3770.
   Cuisine: LIGHT FARE. **Reservations:** Accepted but not usually needed.
$ **Prices:** Most items $1–$17. AE, MC, V.
   Open: Mon–Sat 11am–8pm, Sun noon–8pm.
In Barrington Passage, a 20-minute drive from Shelburne, there's a marvelous place to stop for a meal. As the name hints, the renovated building was a former schoolhouse, but once you step inside you'll barely be able to visualize desks, chairs, and chalkboards. The meals are well priced, wholesome, and filling: lobster or chicken-breast dinners, a New York–style Reuben or corned beef sandwich with Swiss cheese, sauerkraut, and mustard on rye bread; charbroiled fish-and-chips; fruit salad; and much more. Complement it with a bottomless cup of coffee.

YARMOUTH

"The Gateway to Nova Scotia," Yarmouth (pop. 7,620) is the terminus for ferryboats from Bar Harbor and Portland, Maine. Yarmouth has a number of hotels, inns, and motels to accommodate visitors, but they book up early, so reservations, are important, particularly in summer. If you can't get a reservation, consider staying in Digby or Shelburne.
   For tourist information, drop by the huge, modern **provincial visitors' center,** at 342 Main St., perched above the ferry docks—you can't miss it as you come off the boat. An observation deck on top provides a partially obstructed view. For more detailed local information, check with the **Yarmouth County Tourist Association,** P.O. Box 477, Yarmouth, NS, B5A 1G2 (tel. 902/742-5355; fax 902/742-6644).

WHAT TO SEE & DO

YARMOUTH COUNTY MUSEUM, 22 Collins St. Tel. 902/742-5539.
Wander up Collins Street, off Main Street between the ferry terminal and Frost Park, to the Yarmouth County Museum. Exhibits are nautical as well as general, with ship models and paintings, rooms decorated authentically to date from various periods in Yarmouth's history, and artifacts illuminating the way Yarmouthians have earned their livings in times past. The museum won the Canadian Parks Service Heritage Award in 1989.
  Admission: $1 adults, 50¢ students, 25¢ for children; family maximum $2.50.
  Open: June to mid-Oct Mon–Sat 9am–5pm, Sun 1–5pm. Mid-Oct to May Tues–Sat 10am–noon and 2–5pm.

FIREFIGHTERS MUSEUM OF NOVA SCOTIA, 451 Main St. Tel. 902/ 742-5525.
Yarmouth also is home to the Firefighters Museum of Nova Scotia, right in the downtown shopping district. The rich collection of equipment shows how firefighters have battled blazes from 1819 to the present. From early horse-drawn apparatus and an 1880 Silsby Steamer, through a 1926 American LaFrance hand-drawn pumper and a 1931 Model A ladder truck, to a 1933 Chevrolet Pumper, the place is heaven for anyone who has ever loved the big red machines. The gift shop sells postcards and souvenirs of interest to firefighters and those who admire them.
  Admission: $1 adults, $2 families.
  Open: July–Aug Mon–Sat 9am–9pm, Sun 10am–5pm. June and Sept Mon–Sat 9am–5pm. Oct–May Mon–Fri 10am–noon and 2–4pm.

WHERE TO STAY

A few Yarmouth hostelries are within a block of the ferry docks; others, within a mile or so—walking distance if your bags are light. Still others are on the outskirts of town, and for these last ones you'll need a car or a cab.

Bed-and-Breakfasts

MURRAY MANOR GUEST HOUSE, 225 Main St., Yarmouth, NS, B5A 1C6. Tel. 902/742-9625. 3 rms (none with bath).
$ Rates (including full breakfast): $45 single; $55 double. V.
Murray Manor, which has been described as a Gothic-style English cottage, has a great location: a block from the ferry terminal (at the top of the hill), right at the edge of a lovely residential neighborhood, and only a few steps from the downtown shopping area. Innkeepers Joan and George Semple offer only three rooms (one with a four-poster queen-size bed, one with a double bed, one with four-poster twin beds), so reserve ahead. The rooms share 1½ baths. Guests may read or watch videos in the library. The Semples will pick you up, if you arrive without transportation.

VICTORIAN VOGUE BED AND BREAKFAST, 109 Brunswick St., Yarmouth, NS, B5A 2H2. Tel. 902/742-6398. 6 rms (1 with sink and toilet).
Directions: Turn left on Main Street after leaving the ferry terminal, then right on Parade Street, and left on Brunswick. It's at the corner of Huntington Street.
$ Rates (including breakfast): $30–$60 single; $45–$60 double. Extra person $10. MC, V.
A mile or so from the ferry, you'll find the charming Victorian Vogue Bed and Breakfast. An 1872 Queen Anne Revival, the house features five fireplaces, a three-story turret, stained-glass windows, and an abundance of oak and birch throughout. The rooms share two baths, though one room has its own sink and toilet. Congenial owner-innkeeper Dawn-Marie Skjelmose invites you to "linger in the past." Her breakfast menu includes oat cakes, muffins, brown bread, maple-apple upside-down pancake, and orange rings.

A Motel

BEST WESTERN MERMAID MOTEL, 545 Main St., Yarmouth, NS, B5A 1S6. Tel. 902/742-7821, or toll free 800/528-1234. Fax 902/742-2966. 45 rms. A/C TV TEL

$ Rates: $89–$96 single, double, or triple. AE, ER, MC, V.

A bit farther out of town along Main Street, which becomes the road to Digby, the Best Western has its own heated swimming pool, laundry facilities, gift shop, and rooms on two floors; five rooms have kitchenettes. A licensed restaurant, Captain Kelley's (see below), is five doors away. The motel is only three minutes from the ferry and shopping; the same management operates the less-expensive Capri Motel nearby (tel. 902/742-7168; fax 902/742-2966). Well-behaved pets are accepted at both places.

WHERE TO DINE

CAPTAIN KELLEY'S RESTAURANT, 577 Main St. Tel. 902/742-9191.
   Cuisine: SEAFOOD. **Reservations:** Recommended.
   $ Prices: Appetizers $1–$5; main courses $5–$14. AE, ER, MC, V.
   Open: Dinner daily 4–8pm.

Captain Kelley's Restaurant is located in a sea captain's big, white house, a 20-minute walk from the ferry docks. One of the most popular dining places in Yarmouth, it has both downstairs and upstairs dining, with some old pieces and antique-style touches that result in a half-modern, half-old-time decor. Prices are moderate, and popular menu items include Nova Scotia lobster, prepared most anyway you like it, casseroles, hot sandwiches, and clam, scallop, or haddock dinners. The wine list is short and good, but can get expensive. Captain Kelley's Sports Pub, in the same house, is open from 11am to 1am daily.

4. THE EVANGELINE TRAIL & ANNAPOLIS VALLEY

In 1605 Samuel de Champlain founded the first European settlement in Canada, other than the short-lived camps of the Vikings. Champlain's foothold was near Annapolis Royal, on Nova Scotia's Annapolis River near a fine natural harbor. In the century to come, Champlain's career would see him become governor of Canada and lieutenant-general of New France, and French fortunes throughout the lush farmlands and forests of Nova Scotia would thrive. The land not yet called "Nova Scotia" would be dotted with French settlements.

Although these early settlers of Acadia (or Acadie, the French name for Nova Scotia) came from the same homeland as those who settled in what is now Québec, their history was to take a very different course. Before French and English interests in the New World came to the point of armed struggle in the Seven Years' War (1756–63), the British had largely taken control of Acadia. They knew there would be war, and they believed that Acadia's French-speaking inhabitants would secretly struggle for French victory. The British governors decided on a bold and ruthless plan: All Acadians who would not openly pledge allegiance to the British sovereign must be deported from the land. The deportation order came in 1755, and French-speaking families throughout the province were forcibly moved from their homes, many resettling in the French territory of Louisiana where their "Cajun" (Acadian) language and culture are still alive today.

To replace the Acadians, shiploads of Scottish and Irish settlers arrived from the British Isles, and the province soon acquired the name Nova Scotia, the New Scotland.

But the Acadian people, a hardy lot before and after the expulsion, began to return to the land their ancestors had first settled after the hostilities ended. Canada was firmly under British rule, and Acadian farmers were no longer seen to be a "fifth column." Many French-speaking people journeyed back to the rich Annapolis Valley, to cultivate farms and fishing grounds in peace, on good terms with their British and Micmac neighbors, just as they had been before the deportation. They remain here to this day.

The Evangeline Trail, named for the heroine of Longfellow's romantic poem, will lead you through the original land of the Acadians. Tidy towns and villages, each with its church of wood or stone, its shops filled with traditional crafts and farm products, along with brilliant bursts of wild flowers, line Highway 1, alternating with stately towns built in British colonial style.

EN ROUTE TO DIGBY

Along the Evangeline Trail between Church Point and Digby you'll pass a couple of churches of note; they are often open, but if not, check at the rectory next door and ask if you can take a look. Striking **St. Mary's Church,** on a hill (to your left) in Church Point, is the largest and tallest wooden church in North America. The contractor could neither read nor write, and all the labor was voluntary. The spire extends 185 feet (56.3m) and has ballast (40 tons' worth) in the base to steady it from the buffeting of the winds that blow in off St. Mary's Bay. A bilingual guide is on hand to give tours of the church from June to mid-October, and there is a religious museum on the premises.

The granite **St. Bernard Church,** in the village of the same name on Highway 1, is an example of the unity and self-sacrifice of the Acadian people who built it, one course of stone blocks per year from 1910 to 1942. The stone was hauled from the railroad siding by ox team, then cut and dressed with hand tools. The church is open every day for visitors.

WHERE TO STAY

BAYSHORE BED & BREAKFAST, Hwy. 1 (P.O. Box 176), Saulnierville, NS, B0W 2Z0. Tel. 902/769-3671. 3 rms (1 with bath).
$ Rates (including full breakfast): $30 single; $35–$40 double; $50 family room. No credit cards.
If you're smitten with the area, check into the Bayshore Bed & Breakfast. The best part of this circa-1830 Cape Cod–style cottage overlooking St. Mary's Bay is the owner, Ted Murphy, whose great-grandma hailed from here (her photo's on the wall). He spent his summers here as a child and will enthusiastically answer any questions you have about the area and suggest activities for you. He and his wife, Connie, originally hail from Massachusetts. They rent out a small family room (consisting of two rooms and a private bath with a shower) that is quiet and overlooks the water, as well as one room with a double bed and another with a twin bed that share a bath with shower. Guests can use the TV room and VCR (Ted, a former actor, is partial to Bette Davis videos). Rooms come with "a full breakfast—your call." An 18-hole golf course is a mile away, and a lake for swimming is a 10-minute drive away.

WHERE TO DINE

LA RAPURE ACADIENNE, Hwy. 1, Church Point. Tel. 902/769-2172.
Cuisine: ACADIAN.
$ Prices: Most items $3–$6. No credit cards.
Open: Daily 8am–5:30pm.
Pâté à la râpure ("rappie pie" in English), an Acadian specialty that appeared soon after 1755, transforms cooked grated potatoes and meat, fowl, or shellfish into what looks like a four-pound potpie (the crusty brown shell is potato). Sample this fare at La Râpure Acadienne (don't blink or you'll miss it as you pass through Church Point). With only one table inside and two picnic tables outside, plan on take-out. Beef or chicken pâté à la râpure costs $5; you pay 75¢ more for clams; ask for a copy of the recipe.

DIGBY

Leaving Yarmouth on Highway 1, the first town of size along the Evangeline Trail is Digby (pop. 2,560), famous for its scallops gathered from the Bay of Fundy and for "Digby chicken" (locally cured smoked herring).

The town takes its name from Robert Digby, a British admiral who commanded the HMS *Atlanta,* which brought 1,500 Loyalists here from New England in 1783. One of them was John Edison of Newark, New Jersey, the great-grandfather of the inventor Thomas Alva Edison, the "father of electricity" (who was born in Ohio in 1847).

Digby is the southern terminus of Marine Atlantic's MV *Princess of Acadia,* a car-ferryboat connecting the town with Saint John, New Brunswick. (For details on ferry crossings, see the section on Saint John in Chapter 4.)

Digby also has a Laundromat on First Street (near St. Mary's Street), which you may well need by now, and there are plenty of motels and bed-and-breakfasts if you decide to stay the night.

The **Evangeline Trail Visitor Information office,** in town by the water, is open daily from 9am to 5pm in early June, from 9am to 8:30pm daily for the summer (tel. 902/245-5714). It can supply you with information about the entire province. The **Nova Scotia Information Centre** is on the shore road to the ferry, opposite the Annapolis Basin and just before the Pines Resort Hotel. It's open daily from mid-May to mid-October.

WHERE TO STAY

Digby itself has several motels and restaurants, but many others are scattered in the outskirts, especially in the resort hamlet of Smith's Cove, a few miles east along Highway 1.

ADMIRAL DIGBY INN, Shore Rd. (P.O. Box 608), Digby, NS, B0V 1A0. Tel. 902/245-2531. 46 rms. TV TEL

$ Rates: $54–$62 single or double. Extra person $6. Children under 12 stay free. Senior citizen discount. AE, DC, DISC, ER, MC, V. **Parking:** Free. **Closed:** Nov–Apr.

Three miles from Digby and only half a mile from the Marine Atlantic ferry dock, the Admiral Digby is the closest hostelry to the boats—and therefore full-up most of the time, so reserve well in advance. The large, clean motel-style rooms fill two floors, have cable color TV, private bath, and radio, and offer fine views of the water. The indoor, heated swimming pool is handy on days when the sun can't cut through the fog, and the licensed dining room provides sustenance, and a memorable view, from 5 to 9pm. There's a Laundromat for guests' use, and the easygoing innkeeper, Doug French (a country music fan from way back), will check you in, answer your questions, and sell you snacks and aspirin as needed. Reserve two or three weeks ahead July through September.

PINES RESORT HOTEL, Shore Rd. (P.O. Box 70), Digby, NS, B0V 1A0. Tel. 902/245-2511, or toll free 800/667-4637. Fax 902/245-6133. 143 rms, 32 cottages. TV TEL

$ Rates: $108 single; $122 double, from $180 suite, from $244 cottage. Extra person $20. Children 17 and under stay free with parents. Golf and other packages available; meal plan optional. AE, CB, DC, DISC, ER, MC, V. **Parking:** Free. **Closed:** Mid-Oct to mid-May.

One of Nova Scotia's three resort hotels operated by the provincial government is in Digby, right on the road to the ferry dock. The Pines Resort Hotel, which has welcomed wayfarers since 1929, is a mammoth 143-bedroom mansion in French-Norman style, surrounded by 32 one-, two- and three-bedroom cottages, and set on a 300-acre tract of forests and lawns, with spectacular views of the Annapolis Basin. To make the Pines a complete summer resort, there is an 18-hole (par 71) golf course, tennis courts, shuffleboard, croquet, a huge outdoor glass-enclosed heated swimming pool, and a fitness center with exercise equipment, sauna, and Jacuzzi. A playground will delight children, and will also keep them conveniently occupied most of the day. Whale-watching, deep-sea fishing, a theme park, and historical attractions are nearby. Cottages come with living room and fireplace, veranda, and bedrooms to accommodate one to eight people; the price of the cottage depends on how many people occupy it. Some of the cottages have minibars. The Pines' pretty dining room is open to the public for lunch and dinner.

WHERE TO DINE

RED RAVEN PUB, 100 Water St. Tel. 902/245-5533.

   Cuisine: LIGHT FARE. **Reservations:** Not needed.
$ **Prices:** Appetizers $2–$8; main courses $6–$10. V.
   Open: Sun–Mon 11am–9pm, Tues–Sat 11am–2am; Sat–Sun brunch 10am–
   2pm.
This laid-back local place serves filling, no-frills food and has a children's menu.
Among the menu items, you'll find seafood chowder, hot chicken and zucchini fingers,
poutine with cheese and gravy, scallops, clams, steak, burgers, and hot turkey.
Upstairs there's a lounge with a great view, a bar well stocked with Keith's pale ale and
Labatt Blue, a pool table, and video games. The pub is well situated overlooking the
water and has a deck.

EN ROUTE TO ANNAPOLIS ROYAL

Nova Scotia's theme/amusement park, **Upper Clements Park** (tel. 902/532-7557,
or toll free 800/565-PARK in Atlantic Canada) is located in Clementsport, only 4
miles (6km) from Annapolis Royal. The attraction features rides (paddleboats, bumper
cars, and Atlantic Canada's only wooden roller coaster); entertainment featuring
Nova Scotia music and street performers; crafts exhibits and demonstrations; a
children's petting farm; a dozen shops selling local crafts and souvenirs; a variety of
restaurants; and theme weekends such as "Down on the Farm" and "Acadian
Weekend." Open daily from 10am to 7pm in July and August, and on weekends only
in late May, June, and September. Admission is free (though that may change in 1994),
and so is parking.
   From Upper Clements Park, a tunnel leads to a provincial wildlife park, where you
might spot moose, Sable Island ponies, and bald eagle. And, as incongruous as it may
sound, a Chinese theme park re-creating the past 600 years of Chinese history and
culture may open nearby in 1994.
   Theme parks aside, the Annapolis Valley is verdant with farms and forests. From
the road you'll have sweeping vistas across the Annapolis Basin and River. As the
highway turns corners, small villages, each with a neat little church, come into view.
   At Cornwallis, the highway goes through a huge Canadian Forces base before
heading on again toward the "capital" of the region and the birthplace of Canada,
Annapolis Royal.

ANNAPOLIS ROYAL

Samuel de Champlain built his original *habitation* at a place not far from the modern
town of Annapolis Royal (pop. 740). The fortified enclosure put up by these earliest of
French settlers had long since passed into ruin by the time a modern reconstruction
effort was begun. The replica is now Port Royal National Historic Site.
   The town changed locations in the area over the years as the French and English
battled for control of the narrow mouth of the Annapolis River, where it empties into
the Annapolis Basin. In 1710 the English won decisively, setting up a garrison at the
French town of Port Royal and changing its name (to honor Queen Anne) to
Annapolis Royal. Until the deportation of the Acadians, Annapolis Royal was an
English enclave in a region of French-speaking people.
   The **Annapolis Royal District Tourist Bureau,** in the old Railway Station at
the end of Victoria Street (tel. 902/532-5769), is open daily from mid-May to
mid-October from 9am to 7pm; request their brochure with a walking tour and scenic
drives. The **Nova Scotia Visitor Information Centre** is in the Annapolis Tidal
Power Project on Route 1 (tel. 902/532-5454).

WHAT TO SEE & DO

The **O'Dell Inn Museum** (ca. 1869), a Victorian stagecoach inn on Lower St.
George Street, has been fully restored, with downstairs rooms filled with Victoriana
depicting aspects of life a century ago: a wedding room complete with bride; a
mourning room with coffin plaques, memorial pictures, and wreaths of hair from the
dear departed. A dollhouse adds a lighter note. The museum, along with the
Robertson-McNamara House (ca. 1784), on the same street, is open and free to
the public in summer only, daily from 9:30am to 5:30pm.

Other historic buildings include the **Adams-Ritchie House,** which is still standing (it now houses Leo's café and restaurant), and the **Farmers Hotel** (ca. 1710). Besides seeking out these places, you'll want to spend some time wandering up and down Annapolis Royal's residential streets, which are lined with stunning Victorian houses, and enjoying the tranquillity of its historic gardens.

ANNAPOLIS ROYAL HISTORIC GARDENS, 441 St. George St. Tel. 902/532-7018.

On a 10-acre tract in the middle of town, you have the pleasurable opportunity of understanding the botanical history of the Annapolis region. There's an Acadian Garden, just like those tilled by the first settlers; a Governor's Garden, in the colonial style of the 1740s; a Victorian garden; a rose garden complete with a maze made up of 2,000 bushes; and an Innovative Garden, which demonstrates trends in gardening techniques. There's also a lookout over a 50-acre marsh and wildlife sanctuary for waterfowl-watchers.

Admission: $3.50 adults, $3 children and seniors, $9.75 families.
Open: May–Oct daily 9am–dusk. **Closed:** Nov–Apr.

ANNAPOLIS TIDAL POWER PROJECT, 236 Prince Albert Rd. Tel. 902/532-5454.

By now you've heard about the Bay of Fundy tides, "highest in the world." Well, several years ago they were put to work generating electricity. You'll pass the turbine station of the Annapolis Tidal Power Project as you cross the causeway to Granville Ferry or Habitation. Stop and have a look in the Interpretive Centre, which tells you all about harnessing the tides for useful work.

Admission: Free.
Open: Mid-May to mid-June daily 9am–5:30pm; mid-June to Aug daily 9am–8pm; Sept to mid-Oct daily 9am–5:30pm. **Closed:** Late Oct–early May.

FORT ANNE NATIONAL HISTORIC SITE, entrance on St. George St. Tel. 902/532-2397.

In the center of Annapolis Royal, this fort was built, though never actually completed, by the French at the beginning of the 1700s. It still saw a lot of action in the fierce sieges and battles that raged around here. Today the powder magazines and the largely rebuilt officers' quarters buildings are still standing, and artifacts discovered on the site have been arranged to outline the turbulent history of the town and the fort. Take a stroll through the adjacent cemetery, too, for a look at the ancient headstones.

Admission: Free.
Open: Mid-May to mid-Oct daily 9am–5pm; the rest of the year Mon–Fri 9am–6pm. **Closed:** Holidays.

NORTH HILLS MUSEUM, Granville Ferry. Tel. 902/532-2168.

Part of the Nova Scotia Museum Complex, the North Hills Museum, a mile from Annapolis Royal, in Granville Ferry, is the repository of the Robert P. Patterson Collection of Georgian furniture, ceramics, glass, silver, and paintings. Mr. Patterson (1908–74) was a Toronto banker-turned-collector and antique-shop owner, who in 1964 purchased the 18th-century Amberman house in Granville Ferry to house the collection (and himself), and renamed it North Hills after North Mountain, which rises behind it. In 1974, he bequeathed the house and its contents to the Nova Scotia Museum.

Admission: Free, but donations appreciated.
Open: Mon–Sat 9:30am–5:30pm, Sun 1–5:30pm. **Closed:** Late Oct–May.

PORT ROYAL HABITATION NATIONAL HISTORIC SITE, four miles past Granville Ferry. Tel. 902/532-2898.

The Port Royal Habitation, a fur-trading post established by Sieur de Omns and designed by Champlain, was the first permanent settlement (1605) by Europeans north of St. Augustine, Florida. It was burned by a British raiding party in 1613, and several hundred years later archeological digs unearthed some of the foundations. In 1938–39, it was reconstructed by the Canadian government. What you'll see when you visit is rustic and simple—looking much like an escapee from another century in the midst of more modern dwellings built much later—but it also is thrilling. As you walk through the bunkrooms, chapel, kitchens, storerooms, and the governor's lodgings, costumed interpreters will help you better understand what it must have been like to be here in the early 17th century, thousands of sea miles from France, with unknown people and perils around them. It's no wonder the "Habitants" founded the "Order of Good Cheer," the fraternal body dedicated to making each evening's meal a happy and memorable banquet, and to dispelling gloomy thoughts of fear and loneliness. They survived, as did Canada, which in a real sense began right here. To visit the Habitation, cross the Annapolis River, drive through Granville Ferry, and continue another four miles. The view from here is dramatic.

Admission: Free.

Open: Daily 9am–6pm. **Closed:** Late Oct–early May.

WHERE TO STAY

At least half a dozen elegant Victorian houses have been converted to receive guests in this historic and exceptionally pretty town. One, the Garrison House Inn, also has a fine dining room. You'll spot several inns along St. George Street, also known as Highway 8, the road into town from Digby.

BREAD AND ROSES COUNTRY INN, 82 Victoria St. (P.O. Box 177), Annapolis Royal, NS, B0S 1A0. Tel. 902/532-5727. 9 rms (all with bath).

$ Rates (including breakfast): $55 single; $70–$80 double. Extra person $10. MC, V.

This red-brick Victorian mansion with a circular driveway and vine-covered porch, off St. George Street, is topped by a slate roof and filled with fine woodwork, tile fireplaces, and Inuit and folk art. The rooms are furnished with thoughtfulness and affection by owners Richard and Monica Cobb, and with many period pieces from the 1880s, when the house was built. Two of the rooms have queen-size beds. Breakfasts are big and plentiful, and the Cobbs serve complimentary tea and cakes in the parlor in the evening. Monica is a fine artist who works in stained glass, and you'll see some of her creations in the house (including lovely Room 1). Old photographs of the Cobbs' ancestors add to the ambience of the house, one of only a few brick houses in Nova Scotia. The Cobbs request no smoking, pets, or children under 12, although their own small pooch is on the premises.

GARRISON HOUSE INN, 350 St. George St. (P.O. Box 108), Annapolis Royal, NS, B0S 1A0. Tel. 902/532-5750. Fax 902/532-5501. 5 rms, 1 suite (all with bath).

$ Rates: $48–$65 single; $53–$68 double. Extra person $10. Honeymoon package available. AE, MC, V. **Parking:** On the street; across the street from the inn is best. **Open:** June–Oct; possibly weekends the rest of the year.

Surrounded by a white picket fence, the Garrison House Inn is directly across from Fort Anne in the center of town. With this location, it's not surprising that it actually was built as an inn in 1854. It still serves meals to travelers and townsfolk alike, and offers lodging in five rooms and one two-room family suite. The public rooms are filled with bouquets of lupine, peonies, and Johnny-jump-ups. The country-style bedrooms have comfortable beds and good lighting, and they are quiet. Room 7, the "crow's nest," at the back of the house, is the perfect place to get away from the world. Children are welcome.

Even if you don't stay here, come for a meal in the inn's pretty dining room ($5 to $10 for lunch, $20 to $25 for dinner) or afternoon tea (only $4). Lunch is served from noon to 2:30pm, tea from 2:30 to 4:30pm, and dinner from 5:30 to 9pm. Choose from 10 main dishes, prepared with your health in mind; among them, pork tenderloin with citrus-ginger chutney, fresh pasta with Thai chicken, and Acadian jambalaya. I enjoyed fresh haddock with herbs, served on a bed of beet leaves, with vegetables (brussels sprouts, cauliflower, snow peas, and carrots) steamed to perfection, followed by heavenly strawberry-rhubarb pie. Breakfast is available but is not included in the room rate. There is a private bar just for guests. Innkeeper/chef/sommelier Patrick Redgrave does a superb job, and Angela, who has worked here since 1983, is the waitress by whom all others should be judged.

QUEEN ANNE INN, 494 Upper St. George St. (P.O. Box 218), Annapolis Royal, NS, B0S 1A0. Tel. 902/532-7850. 10 rms (all with bath).
$ Rates (including full breakfast): $44–$70 single; $50–$80 double. MC, V.

Of the many extravagances of Victorian architecture, this 22-room house, built in 1865 in the Second Empire style, has to be among the most delightful. And it's as incredible on the inside as it is on the outside. Three parlors with sky-high ceilings are filled with antiques. Most of the rooms are large, with full bath; some have only a shower, such as romantic Room 4. Fresh flowers often greet you when you enter the room. It's hard to imagine now, but a large stuffed moose used to stand in the entrance hall. The congenial innkeeper, Mr. Leslie Langille, who helps his guests plan their activities and gives them tea and cookies every evening, has recently renovated and reopened the Hillsdale Inn (1849), across the street. You can easily walk to the center of town from the Queen Anne Inn, which is a no-smoking property.

Places to Stay in Nearby Granville Ferry

Just to the north, less than a mile away across the Annapolis River, lies the village of Granville Ferry (pop. 535). It's what you see when you gaze across the river. You pass through here on the way to visit the Port Royal National Historic Site, four miles away, and you might prefer making it your headquarters.

THE MOORINGS, P.O. Box 118, Granville Ferry, NS, B0S 1K0. Tel. 902/532-2146. 3 rms (none with bath).
$ Rates (including full breakfast): $38 single; $42 double. Extra person $10. V. **Parking:** Across the road. **Closed:** Nov–Apr, except by reservation.

The Moorings, formerly a sea captain's home, is a guesthouse with three bedrooms with bay windows overlooking the Annapolis Basin and its 25-foot tides. The restored late-19th-century house has all the grace and beauty the times could give a home, while the owners' fine collection of contemporary paintings and photographs provide a modern complement. There are two large sitting rooms, one with a fireplace, library, and TV. Two of the handsomely decorated bedrooms have a private sink and toilet; the three rooms share two baths, one with an enormous old-fashioned tub. "We bought the house because the tub fit me," says lanky innkeeper Nathaniel Tileston, who is a transplanted American. He and his wife, Susan, are both artists, and their creative touch shows up everywhere. The Moorings, probably this area's first bed-and-breakfast, has welcomed guests since 1972.

NIGHTINGALE'S LANDING, Granville Ferry, NS, B0S 1K0. Tel. 902/532-7156. 2 rms (none with bath), 1 suite.
$ Rates (including full breakfast): $35 single; $40–$50 double; $55 suite. Extra person $10. V. **Parking:** In back of the house. **Closed:** Late Oct–early May, except by reservation.

Staying here is like overnighting in Auntie Mame's house, filled with deliciously exotic furnishings, reflecting all the places in the world effervescent owner Sandra Nightingale has lived. There's a Chinese screen made from a lemon tree, an English sideboard, an entire room devoted to Germany. There are even some furnishings from New England. The two bedrooms are filled with whatnots and share a large bath, while the suite has its own bath (shower only). The ambience here is informal, and tea is served in the afternoon or evening. Enter through the front, not the side, door. No smoking or pets, please.

WHERE TO DINE

Besides the Garrison House Inn (see above), there are a couple of other fine choices for dining in Annapolis Royal. You should stay at least two days in the area and sample all three.

LEO'S, 222 St. George St. Tel. 902/532-7424.
Cuisine: LIGHT FARE.
$ Prices: Breakfast items $1–$3; lunch items $3–$6; dinner appetizers $3–$4, main courses $7–$10. MC, V.
Open: Summer breakfast daily 9–11am, lunch daily 11:30am–3pm, dinner daily 5:30–9pm; the rest of the year daily 9am–5pm.

Ⓢ For a quick bite at breakfast or lunch, or a more leisurely dinner, head for Leo's, in the oldest building (1712) in English Canada. The coffee's good here any time of day, and the tea list runs the gamut from Love Potion no. 9 to Bengal spice. At lunchtime, you can't beat the hefty sandwiches, with a multitude of ingredients (only veggies, if you choose) bookended with slabs of 12-grain bread; two hearty soups are prepared daily. The dinner menu changes often, but features pasta and fish dishes. A long-standing favorite is Leo's Famous Linguine, tossed with scallops, tomatoes, and green onions in a saffron cream sauce. Desserts include cakes, pies, and cheesecake. Special diets and children's tastes can be accommodated. The country café is downstairs; the dining room and a deck, upstairs. Hats off to the 24-year-old owner and chef, Paula Buston.

NEWMAN'S, 218 St. George St. Tel. 902/532-5502.
   Cuisine: SEAFOOD. **Reservations:** Recommended.
$ **Prices:** Lunch soups $4, main courses $7.50–$14.50; dinner appetizers $5–$9, main courses $12–$25; daily specials $16–$22. V.
   Open: July–Aug lunch daily 11:30am–5pm; dinner daily 5–9pm. June and Sept lunch Tues–Sun 11:30am–5pm; dinner Tues–Sun 5–9pm. May and Oct lunch Tues–Fri 11:30am–2:30pm; dinner Tues–Fri 5:30–8:30pm; Sat lunch 11:30am–5pm, dinner 5–8:30pm; Sun noon–8:30pm. **Closed:** Nov–Apr.
Newman's promises outstanding food in pleasant surroundings at moderate prices, and the menu changes daily to assure the freshest products. Consider homemade baguettes and pâté, vichyssoise, Greek salad, homemade lamb sausage with pine nuts, charcoal-broiled gravlax, curried pork with mango chutney, Nova Scotia mutton chops, local black bear braised in red wine, cornmeal johnnycakes, and a serving of tiramisu or strawberry, blueberry, or peach shortcake big enough to feed a family of four. They serve select wines, but the house wines are quite drinkable and laudably inexpensive.

EN ROUTE TO WOLFVILLE & GRAND PRE

Bridgetown (pop. 1,050) and Lawrencetown (pop. 550), on Highway 1, are fine old towns with lots of graceful Victorian houses and lofty shade trees. If you pass through Lawrencetown in mid-August, plan to spend a few hours touring the region's largest agricultural fair, the **Annapolis County Exhibition.** The highway passes the exhibition grounds.

   Past Kingston (pop. 1,590) you have a choice of roads: Old Highway 1 continues on its meandering course through the countryside, while the newer, faster Highway 101 will speed you toward Grand Pré and Halifax.

   Just before Grand Pré, you'll pass Kentville and Wolfville, which have good inns and restaurants. Named after the duke of Kent in 1826, Kentville (pop. 4,980) has become the largest community in the Annapolis Valley. The **Apple Blossom Festival** is held annually during the last week of May.

WOLFVILLE

When the Acadian settlers were driven from their homes in 1755, British settlers rushed to move in. Wolfville (pop. 3,235) was founded by British colonial farmers from Connecticut, also known as the New England Planters, who established a settlement and named it Upper Horton. Later called Mud Creek, it took its final, more dignified moniker from Judge Elisha DeWolfe, one of the town's Connecticut founders.

   Wolfville flourished from agriculture and shipping, and in 1838 Acadia University (Canada's ninth oldest) was founded here. Today it has 3,800 students and a 250-acre campus.

   The **tourist office,** set in Willow Park fronted by a fountain (you'll spot it easily as you drive along elm-lined Main Street), is open from 9am to 7pm daily from late June to Labor Day; otherwise, 9am to 5pm daily. Come here to find out where and when to see the world-famous tidal bore, pick up brochures, and get information about the town or the entire region. Be sure to ask for the "Self-Guided Walking Tour."

WHAT TO SEE & DO

One of the first Georgian houses built in Wolfville, the **Randall House** (1808), 171 Main St. (tel. 902/542-9775), is furnished primarily with the late-19th- and early-20th-century belongings of the descendants of New Englanders who settled this district from 1760 to 1770. A private home until 1949, it is now open to the public from mid-June to mid-September, Monday to Saturday from 10am to 5pm, and Sunday 2 to 5pm. Admission is free.

The **Acadia University Art Gallery,** in the Beveridge Arts Centre, at the corner of Main Street and Highland Avenue, showcases contemporary local, national, and international art in a variety of media year-round. Summer hours are daily noon to 5pm (tel. 902/542-2201, ext. 373).

Favorite pastimes of local folks in Wolfville include the simple pleasures of watching the tides and the birds. To see the tides right in town, pick up the walking trail across the road from the Blomidon Inn and follow it to the water's edge (the highest tides are in the Minas Basin, however, and the best place to see the tidal bore is along the Meander River near Windsor).

For some unique birdwatching, make your way downtown just before dusk to the old chimney beside the liquor store on Front Street, which attracts a swarm of chimney swifts (and a flock of human onlookers). The chimney was once part of an old milk factory, and when the town realized the birds' fondness for it, it built a small nature center around it rather than tear it down. The tourist office can provide more information.

IN NEARBY STARR'S POINT   About four miles from Wolfville, in tiny Starr's Point (pop. 96), stands the **Prescott House Museum,** part of the Nova Scotia Museum Complex. The Georgian-style house was built around 1814 and is furnished with period antiques. Its original owner, Charles Ramage Prescott, was a merchant and horticulturist who introduced several varieties of apples to Nova Scotia and helped found the Fruit Growers' Association here. The house and grounds are open to the public June to mid-October, Monday to Saturday from 9:30am to 5:30pm, and Sunday from 1 to 5:30pm. Admission is free (tel. 902/542-3984). To get there, take Route 358 to Port William and turn left.

WHERE TO STAY & DINE

BLOMIDON INN, 127 Main St. (P.O. Box 839), Wolfville, NS, B0P 1X0. Tel. 902/542-2291. Fax 902/542-7461. 22 rms, 4 suites (all with bath). TEL
$ Rates (including continental breakfast and afternoon tea): May–Oct $59–$94 single; $69–$104 double; $109 single suite, $119 double suite. Extra person $12. Nov–Apr rates drop 30%–40%. Packages with dinner available. AE, ER, MC, V.

The Blomidon Inn was built in 1877 by Capt. Rufus Burgess, a shipping magnate whose ships often returned laden with ballast of exotic woods from the tropics, used lavishly in the construction of his house. In fact, the opulence of this towering red house filled with working fireplaces and antiques could be intimidating but for the warmth of the staff. Ten of the genteel rooms and suites are in the original house; two rooms have fireplaces; one room and one suite have Jacuzzis. Those in the annex are similar in decor but have plush carpeting instead of wood floors, and air conditioning (versus large ceiling fans in the older rooms), and old-fashioned wooden toilet seats. The Blomidon also has two beautiful parlors; a pub serving light fare that's open Thursday and Friday nights, with jazz occasionally on Friday nights; a large deck out back; a tennis court (ask for balls and rackets at the front desk); shuffleboard; games; and grounds filled with trees, including a spectacular chestnut in front of the house.

Even if you don't stay here, consider lunch (daily 11am to 2pm) or dinner (daily 5 to 9:30pm) in the outstanding dining room. Three-course table d'hôte dinners cost $18 or $25; an à la carte dinner will run $30 to $35 and includes a complimentary sorbet, such as lemon sherbet with amaretto, served before the main course. Choices include poached salmon, sirloin steak, vegetarian crêpes, or the Blomidon's own Chicken Elizabeth, boneless breast of chicken with crabmeat, spinach, and Swiss cheese in a puff pastry with hollandaise sauce. Top it off with raspberry syllabub, gingerbread with lemon sauce, Dutch apple tart, or English walnut and coffee torte. Tea, which is included in the room rate, is served daily from 3 to 5pm. Dinner reservations are recommended.

TATTINGSTONE INN, 434 Main St. (P.O. Box 98), Wolfville, NS, B0P 1X0. Tel. 902/542-7696. Fax 902/542-4427. 10 rms, 1 cottage (all with bath). A/C TEL
$ Rates: $78–$108 single or double; $138 cottage. AE, ER, MC, V.
For those who want hotellike amenities, such as a telephone in the room, a tennis court, an outdoor heated swimming pool, and a steamroom, search no farther than the Tattingstone Inn, decorated like an English country house. In the main house are five rooms, with tall four-poster queen-size beds, comfortable upholstered chairs, a writing table, and marble fireplace (no. 2 is a particularly pretty room, and no. 3 is a popular choice of honeymooners). In the Carriage House, there are four rooms, also with four-poster beds but simpler decor. The more rustic Toad Hall is a private cottage with a queen-size bed in the sleeping loft, a fireplace, and a sofa bed. Guests may relax in the music room and the library. For an additional $5, you may have breakfast in the sunny breakfast room. The gourmet dining room is open daily from 5:30 to 9:30pm. No smoking, please. Betsey Harwood is the innkeeper.

VICTORIA'S HISTORIC INN, 416 Main St. (P.O. Box 308), Wolfville, NS, B0P 1X0. Tel. 902/542-5744. 10 rms (all with bath), 1 suite, 4 motel units. TV TEL
$ Rates: $49–$108 single or double; $118 suite. Extra person $10. Full breakfast $3.75. Packages available. DISC, MC, V.
Victoria's, a white gingerbread house with wicker chairs on the porch, is a grand home built for a prosperous apple merchant in 1893. The rooms are pretty, each one distinctive and decorated with country furnishings. All have wingback chairs and cable TV with remote control; some have air conditioning. VCRs are available for use in the rooms, the most elegant of which are on the second floor. Rates depend on the size of the room and whether or not the bath has a Jacuzzi. Breakfast is not included in the cost of the rooms, but you can order a full breakfast for $3.75. Dinner is available in the licensed dining room, but make a reservation as soon as possible. The cuisine is French, prepared by a chef from Québec, and the dining room is open May to October, Tuesday through Sunday, from 5:30 to 8:30pm (daily during summer months). Smoking is not allowed in the bedrooms or dining room but is permitted in the parlor. Reserve early in summer. Carol and Urbain Cryan are the cordial hosts.

In Nearby Port Williams

PLANTERS' [BARRACKS] COUNTRY INN, 1468 Starr's Point Rd. (R.R. 1), Port Williams, NS, B0P 1T0. Tel. 902/542-7879. Fax 902/542-4442. 9 rms (all with bath). **Directions:** Pick up Route 358 (to Port Williams) west of Wolfville and watch for signs for the inn; turn right onto Starr's Point Road at the flashing light and drive another two miles.
$ Rates (including full country breakfast): $49–$79 single; $69–$109 double. AE, MC, V. **Closed:** Mid-Dec to mid-Jan.
On a country road about four miles (6km) from Wolfville, the historic Planters' (Barracks) Country Inn sits on five acres of land in one of the oldest buildings in Kings County. The early-Georgian-style building (1778) started out as Fort Hughes, constructed here by the British to oversee the resettlement by some 8,000 New England Planters of the farmland evacuated (under duress) by the Acadians in 1755. It was later used as a customs house for the Port of Cornwallis. Of the nine guest rooms, six are in the main house, and three in the Customs House, which also houses the Acacia Croft Tearoom, open daily from noon to 5pm from mid-March to mid-December for lunch or afternoon tea with clotted cream and strawberry jam. The bedrooms, large and decorated in Victorian style, come with robes, hairdryers, old-fashioned tubs, and way-back issues of the *Saturday Evening Post;* an added treat, they have at least three shuttered windows. The rooms are carpeted to cut down

on noise, but the wide-board floors have been left in the public areas. In the main house, there is a large kitchen with a walk-in fireplace and a downstairs lounge, where guests may watch television or play Othello or Scruples. A tidal river and old graveyard are behind the house. Guests enjoy tennis courts, complimentary mountain bikes, and a backyard barbecue set in a lovely garden. The inn is licensed for guests, and dinner can be arranged with 24 hours' notice. Planters is the type of place you'll want to savor, so allow time to enjoy it, not just sleep in it. Grace and Ted Fraser are the accommodating innkeepers, and special acknowledgment goes to Jennie Speito, the owner and head gardener, for the authenticity of this historic restoration.

WHERE TO DINE

CHEZ LA VIGNE, 17 Front St. Tel. 902/542-5077.
Cuisine: FRENCH. **Reservations:** Recommended.
$ Prices: Lunch appetizers $4–$8, main courses $7–$17; dinner appetizers $6–$9, main courses $15–$20. MC, V.
Open: Daily 11am–10:30pm.

Among the better-known restaurants in Wolfville, Chez La Vigne is owned and operated by talented Swiss chef Alex Clavel, who opened it in 1982. The atmosphere here is quietly French, the music and lighting soft, the food delicious. The lunch menu, which includes salads, grilled chicken breast, smoked turkey, pasta dishes, omelets, and vegetarian crêpes, is served all day long, for those who prefer a lighter meal. Among the dinner appetizers are mussels, escargots, and seafood antipasto, while main courses include rack of lamb, filet mignon, Digby scallops, and Nova Scotia salmon. The restaurant is downtown, at the corner of Front and Central Streets, off Main Street. There is outdoor seating.

THE COFFEE MERCHANT, 334 Main St. Tel. 902/542-4315.
Cuisine: LIGHT FARE.
$ Prices: Most items $1–$6. MC, V.
Open: Mon–Fri 7am–11pm, Sat–Sun 8am–11pm.

If you're looking for a place for breakfast, if you need to take a break from touring, or if you need a coffee break, go no further than the Coffee Merchant. You'll find five types of coffees to choose from: regular, medium, strong, decaf, and the special of the day. They also sell iced coffee or tea, muffins, killer cheesecake, ice cream, sandwiches, and bagels, along with packaged coffees and teas and related paraphernalia. There's more seating here than first meets the eye: at tables on the sidewalk, inside, in the back, and in the back courtyard. This is a great place to meet the locals. At happy hour, from 5 to 7pm, all the coffee is 65¢.

GRAND PRE NATIONAL HISTORIC SITE

Acadian history's saddest times began at Grand Pré (pronounced like "pray"), which was the center of Acadian settlement in the early 1700s. The fierce French-British struggles for the rich lands of Nova Scotia caught these early French-speaking settlers right in the middle. Unwilling to give up their cultural connections with France, unable to bring themselves to be British, they were deported swiftly and in great numbers. The deportations began in 1755, urged on by British governors and generals whose forces were locked in a life-and-death struggle with the French. The prize was Nova Scotia. Some 14,000 Acadians were ejected from their homes by 2,000 Loyalist troops, families were inadvertently sundered, and many were to die searching for new lands that would accept them.

They boarded ships only with what they could carry, and their homes and belongings were burned to discourage their return. They attempted to settle along the Atlantic seaboard, as far south as Georgia, but because they were French-speaking and Catholic, they were doubly ostracized. Only in Maryland were they accepted. In Virginia, a boat carrying 1,150 Acadians was refused entry and sent to England, where its passengers were put in prison and later repatriated to France. By the early

19th century, the Acadians had ventured as far as the Falkland Islands, the West Indies, and Europe; four million live in Louisiana today.

To get to Grand Pré National Historic Site, take Exit 10 off Highway 101. If you're driving from Wolfville, it's easy to miss the turnoff—turn at the sign for Evangeline Beach and if you see a sign for Windsor, you've gone too far. (Parking for the site is to your right just after the railroad tracks.)

Grand Pré National Historic Park is a memorial garden dedicated to the Acadians who suffered through the deportation, to those who returned, and also to those who have always lived in the province—and still do today. The memorial stone church, built in 1922 in typical French style (a typical Acadian church would have been wooden) on the site of the original church where the deportation order was read, has never been consecrated as a house of worship. Rather, it has always been a memorial, and inside it holds not pews, but exhibits detailing the history of the Acadian people (start with those to your right).

You'll read sad letters of petition written to Massachusetts officials by impoverished Acadians asking for assistance. The stained-glass window over the door of the church is by Acadian Terry Smith-Lamother, a Baton Rouge–born, longtime resident of Halifax; the red lines represent separation; the orange arc, the artist's hope that the Acadian culture will survive. A small park and gardens surround the church, and in front of it is a statue of Longfellow's tragic heroine, Evangeline. Follow the path to the garden and the old blacksmith's shop with its huge bellows. From here, gaze out at the surrounding farmland reclaimed from the marsh in the 18th century. An air of emptiness and sadness pervades Grand Pré, a fitting place to ponder the irrevocable machinations of history.

This historic site is open from mid-May to mid-October from 9am to 6pm daily. Admission is free.

WINDSOR

Farther along the Evangeline Trail, and only 12 miles (20km) from Grand Pré and 43 miles (70km) from Halifax, lies Windsor, best known as the birthplace of Judge Thomas Chandler Haliburton (1796–1865), fondly remembered as the humorist who created the character Sam Slick, a Yankee clock peddler from Slickville, Connecticut. In Slick's voice, Haliburton penned such enduring slogans as "raining cats and dogs," "going to the dogs," "barking up the wrong tree," "quick as a wink," and "facts are stranger than fiction." (The young Mark Twain was an avid reader of Haliburton.)

Haliburton House (1836), his home and 25-acre estate, is now open to the public, though it is much altered since the days when he lived in it. The author moved to Middlesex, England, after the death of his first wife, and he is buried there. Period Victorian furnishings fill the house, though most are not original to it; there are also illustrations from the Sam Slick books and information about Haliburton (tel. 902/798-2915).

Windsor is also home to the Queen Anne–style **Shand House** (1891), a striking presence with a tall square tower atop Ferry Hill. The house can best be described as elegant on the outside and functional on the inside. Only four people ever lived in it: Clifford and Henrie Shand and their two children, Gwendolyn and Errol. Upon the death of Gwendolyn Shand in 1982, it became a branch of the Nova Scotia Museum Complex. At her request, the interior has not been restored. Many of the furnishings were made locally (tel. 902/798-8213).

You'll see signs directing you to both the Shand and the Haliburton House when you arrive in Windsor. Both are part of the Nova Scotia Museum Complex and are open from June to mid-October, Monday to Saturday from 9:30am to 5:30pm, and Sunday from 1 to 5:30pm (tel. 902/798-2915). Admission to both is free.

The **blockhouse** at Fort Edward National Historic Site is the only such structure still standing in Nova Scotia. Built in 1759, it is the oldest one in Canada. The blockhouse was a major assembly point for Acadians during their expulsion from the area in 1755. There is an interpretive display here. It's open daily from mid-June to Labor Day, from 10am to 6pm; admission is free.

Windsor, it should be noted, grows some of the world's largest pumpkins, and if you pass through on Canadian Thanksgiving Day, in October, you'll get to see some of them at the **World Pumpkin Festival.** The Hants County Agricultural Exhibition, the oldest agricultural fair in North America, is held here annually in September.

5. MARINE DRIVE

East of Halifax, the jagged southeastern coast of Nova Scotia stretches as far as Cape Canso. Rivers and streams descend from the hills to enter the sea—the highway seems to cross a river every few miles. This region is more sparsely settled than the southwest coast or the Annapolis Valley, and the driving along Marine Drive, alias Highway 7 (reached from Halifax via faster Highway 107), is slow and circuitous. For that reason, I recommend skipping the first and last parts of the drive. Instead, follow Highway 102 out of Halifax as if heading to the airport, connect with Highway 212, and then Highway 224, which will deposit you on the coast (and Marine Drive) at Port Dufferin. From here you can explore nearby Liscomb Mills and Sherbrooke, and easily link up with Pictou, Antigonish, Cape Breton Island, and the fabled Cabot Trail.

PORT DUFFERIN

Port Dufferin, a two-hour drive from Halifax, is small to the point of being minuscule, which is precisely its appeal. One comes here to relax, to gaze out to sea, or to go to sea for an afternoon—and to eat well, of course.

WHERE TO STAY & DINE

MARQUIS OF DUFFERIN SEASIDE INN, R.R. 1, Port Dufferin, NS, B0J 2R0. Tel. 902/654-2696. 8 rms. TV

$ Rates (including continental breakfast): $65 single; $75 double. Extra person $10. Children under 2 free. Packages available. MC, V. **Closed:** Mid-Oct to mid-May.

In Port Dufferin (pop. 160), the road winds around Beaver Harbour and past the delightful Marquis of Dufferin Seaside Inn, a small eight-room motel in which the recently upgraded rooms have TVs, but all have such a splendid view of the harbor, with patio doors opening onto private balconies, that those TVs are hardly ever turned on. Besides, there is a 22-foot sailboat to charter, as well as rowboats, canoes, bikes, and maps for hiking. Congenial hosts Eve and Mike Concannon arrived in Port Dufferin from England in a roundabout way, after 20-odd years in Philadelphia. Their award-winning (no-smoking) dining room features fresh seafood and local products, with meat selections, as well; it serves dinner only, nightly from 6 to 8pm.

LISCOMB MILLS

Liscomb Mills, 105 miles (170km) from Halifax, is home to the most rustic of the three resorts operated by the Nova Scotia government, Liscombe Lodge. You might choose to base yourself here and as an excursion, follow Highway 7 northeast along the St. Mary's River 16 miles (25km) to Sherbrooke Village, the biggest attraction along Marine Drive (see below).

WHERE TO STAY & DINE

LISCOMBE LODGE, Liscomb Mills, NS, B0J 2A0. Tel. 902/779-2307, or toll free 800/341-6096 in the U.S., 800/565-0000 in Canada. Fax 902/779-2700. 30 rms, 15 chalets, 5 cottages (including 5 suites). TV TEL

$ Rates: $83–$90 single; $95–$103 double; $230 suite. Extra person $10. Children 17 and under stay free in parents' room. Packages and optional meal plan, with breakfast and dinner, available. AE, DC, ER, MC, V.

Liscombe Lodge is a complex of 15 small chalets, five deluxe four-bedroom cottages, and a guest lodge clustered around a central lodge surrounded by trees and fronting on the seashore. Rooms rates are similar for the lodge, cottages, and chalets, although two bedrooms in a cottage, with the exclusive use of the living room, may be rented as a private suite. The chalets have fireplaces and little porches for sitting; cottages are more elaborate, with four bedrooms each, plus a common living room with a fireplace, and verandas. The guest lodge contains superior rooms, each with a balcony overlooking the marina. In 1993, the lodge added an enclosed swimming pool and fitness center. Nature trails, tennis, biking, boating, and fishing, including deep-sea charters, also fill one's days at Liscombe Lodge, and the days pass all too quickly. The main lodge's dining room is open to guests and passersby alike from noon to 2:30pm for lunch, and 5:30 to 9pm for dinner. The smoked fish is prepared in the resort's own smokehouse, and the salmon is cooked in an outdoor pit, an old Micmac method. Guests are served breakfast from 7 to 9:30am, and sandwiches and beverages are available throughout the day.

SHERBROOKE

Sherbrooke is a small community, home only to 400 people, but also to the major attraction along Marine Drive, Sherbrooke Village. Once you've explored it, you may be in the mood for a rural drive. If so, continue along Marine Drive (Highway 7), following the St. Mary's River through lush farmland, where herds of dairy cattle graze slowly in rich pastures, and now and then you'll see a sign inviting you to pick your own strawberries at a farm by the road. Take them up on the offer: Fresh Nova Scotia strawberries are a taste sensation.

WHAT TO SEE & DO

SHERBROOKE VILLAGE, Sherbrooke. Tel. 902/522-2400.
   Sherbrooke Village is less than a mile off Highway 7, and signs clearly point the way. Unlike other "living museums" you may have visited, it is not an old town or colony assembled from various buildings brought to the site or reconstructed. Rather, it is a small town that changed very little between its gold-rush days (yes, there was a gold rush here) in the 1860s and the middle of the present century. Restoration work consisted of putting the town in order and opening it to the public. You'll visit two churches (one still in use), craft workshops, the schoolhouse, pharmacy, print shop, blacksmith shop, tailor's shop, jail, temperance hall, working post office, and a hotel that operated from the 1860s to 1918 and now serves meals and take-out drinks and ice cream. The townspeople, dressed in costumes from the 19th century, keep to the schedule tolled by the town bell. Even if you arrive after closing time, you may still drive through Sherbrooke Village (and into another era). The entry is left open because a few local families actually still live here.
   Admission: $2 adults, 50¢ children under 16.
   Open: Daily 9:30am–5:30pm. **Closed:** Oct 16–May 14.

WHERE TO DINE

BRIGHT HOUSE, Main St. Tel. 902/522-2691.
   Cuisine: LIGHT FARE. **Reservations:** Recommended.
$ Prices: Lunch items $6–$8; dinner appetizers $2–$6.50, main courses $12.50–$15.50. MC, V.
   Open: June and Sept–Oct daily noon–8pm; July–Aug daily 11:30am–9pm.
   Closed: Nov–May.
Everything about Bright House is appealing, from the wood floors and hanging plants to the hooked rugs and the friendly service. The fine old house (1850) has been restored in the spirit of Sherbrooke Village, and it opened as a restaurant in 1975. The couple who own the house, Wynneth and Gordon Turnbull, do the cooking and serving, so the food and service have an exceptionally personal touch. The lunch menu is small, featuring a lobster salad plate, minced beef pie, chicken potpie, home-baked beans, English cold plate, quiche of the day, and cheese melt. At dinner, you might start with seafood chowder or the house pâté with herb bread, and follow it with fresh halibut, haddock, or sole, roast beef, or steak-and-kidney pie. The prices are eminently reasonable, and alcohol is served. Bright House sits right at the corner in Sherbrooke where the side road goes off to Sherbrooke Village. It can get busy on Saturday and Sunday evenings.

6. THE SUNRISE TRAIL: PICTOU-ANTIGONISH SEGMENT

Nova Scotia's Northumberland shore is sprinkled with farms, fisheries, some industry, and several warm-water beaches. Why beaches this far north? The waters of the Northumberland Strait, between Nova Scotia and Prince Edward Island, are sheltered from ocean currents, and said to be the warmest in all of Canada, New England, or even the Mid-Atlantic states.

Following this coastline, the Sunrise Trail stretches east from Amherst (see Section 1 of this chapter) to the Canso Causeway (see Section 7), the entry point to Cape Breton Island. Highlights for many travelers on the Sunrise Trail include admiring (or taking) a sleek, white Prince Edward Island ferry to or from Caribou (it's not a Nova Scotia town, just a ferry landing) and visiting nearby Pictou, the historic point of entry for Scottish settlers in "New Scotland," and Antigonish, site of the province's annual Highland Games. In this region, the skirl of bagpipes is never far away.

For ferry information, call 902/566-3838. To travel from Amherst to Pictou (or Caribou), follow Highway 6, which is part of the Sunrise Trail.

PICTOU

Once a Micmac town, Pictou (that's *Pick*-toe; pop. 4,415) was chosen as home by a band of settlers from Philadelphia in 1767. They were joined in 1773 by the first shipload of immigrants to arrive from the Scottish Highlands aboard the *Hector,* many more of whom were to arrive in succeeding years.

Most visitors never see Pictou, as they rocket by on Highway 106 to or from the Prince Edward Island ferry at Caribou. Little do they know they're missing the chance to visit not just a pretty Nova Scotia town, which it certainly is, but also the historic "birthplace of New Scotland."

The **Nova Scotia Tourist Office,** just to your left as you come off the rotary into Pictou, is open daily from 8am to 8pm. If you are traveling on I-104, you'll pass a tourist information cabin about 18.5 miles (30km) south of town. The cabin is blue, so it's easy to spot, and it's next door to a small market (handy if you need to stock up on supplies). It's open 8am to 8pm daily in summer.

To travel from Pictou to Antigonish, you may continue along the coast-hugging Sunrise Trail (Route 245 to Route 337), or take the faster, more direct Highway 104.

WHAT TO SEE & DO

Follow the signs for Braeside, and you'll soon come upon the **Northumberland Fisheries Museum,** in the gabled former Canadian National Railway station (1904). An original fisherman's bunkhouse is authentically furnished, and there are many old items related to the fishing industry, including a "spar and boom" used in a lobster boat in the late 1800s. Take a look at the *Silver Bullet,* a locally built boat three times victorious in Pictou's Lobster Carnival races, which have been held in early July since 1934. A visit here is free, though donations are appreciated; it's open in summer only, from 9:30am to 5:30pm Monday through Saturday, and from 1:30 to 5:30pm on Sunday.

Free tours of the **Grohmann Knives factory,** at 116 Water St. (tel. 902/485-6775), are given weekdays at 9 and 11am and at 1pm June through September. The company was founded by a Czech, Rudolph Grohmann, in 1957 and is still family-owned and -operated. The factory outlet store, at the same address, sells kitchen knives, chef's sets, two- or three-piece gift sets, pocketknives, belt knives, outdoor knives, scissors, and manicure sets. Hours are 9am to 5pm Monday through Saturday.

The nine-hole **Pictou Golf and Country Club** (tel. 902/485-4435), just outside of town on Beeches Road, is set picturesquely on the water and is open to the public. Club rental is $6 with a $15 deposit; the greens fee is $13 weekdays, $15 weekends and holidays.

The **Hector Festival,** held for five days in mid-August, pays tribute to the area's Scottish heritage.

HECTOR HERITAGE QUAY, 29–33 Caladh Ave., Pictou waterfront. Tel. 902/485-8028.

The centerpiece of the Hector Heritage Quay is a full-size replica of the *Hector,* now under meticulous reconstruction. The original ship brought the first Scots to Nova Scotia in the 18th century, starting a major migration. The story of their voyage (which took almost two grueling months) and their early life is told in the interpretive center, in a large post-and-beam building put together with wooden pegs instead of nails. In one exhibit, you'd swear you were on the boat with them. Explanatory texts are enlivened with quotes. A carpentry shop and blacksmith shop are also on the premises.

Admission: $3.50 adults, $3 seniors and children 12–16 per person; children under 12 free; $9 families.

Open: June to mid-Oct daily 10am–8pm; mid-Oct to May Mon–Fri 9am–5pm.

MCCULLOCH HOUSE, off Hwy. 106, in Pictou. Tel. 902/485-4563.

Thomas McCulloch, a Presbyterian minister, educator, and naturalist, had this house built in 1806 with bricks and stones supposedly brought over from Scotland as ballast in ships. Little changed since that time, it's not grand, as McCulloch was not a rich man or Pictou a wealthy place. Rather, it's a monument to the early "civilizers," people who came to the wild backwoods of Canada and brought with them a feeling for the finer side of life. The McCulloch House, with its original furniture and artifacts from the town's early history, is Pictou's installation of the Nova Scotia Museum Complex. Reverend McCulloch's ornithology collection, some of which is on display, was proclaimed one of the finest of its kind in North America by the naturalist J. J. Audubon, who visited him here.

Admission: Free; donations appreciated.

Open: Mid-May to mid-Oct Mon–Sat 9:30am–5:30pm, Sun 1–5:30pm. **Closed:** Late Oct–early May.

WHERE TO STAY & DINE

CONSULATE INN, 115 Water St., Pictou, NS, B0K 1H0. Tel. 902/485-4554. 3 rms (all with bath). TV

$ Rates (including continental breakfast): $45–$70 single or double, depending on the room. Extra person $10. Not suitable for small children. AE, MC, V.

The Consulate Inn, with its welcoming red awning, is aptly named: Housed in a stately stone building that was a U.S. consulate back in 1865, it has three large rooms, each with full private bath, and a pretty living room upstairs. Guests also enjoy the back patio and lawn. The owners, Claudette and Floyd Brine, lived in Bermuda for 25 years before coming back to Pictou. The inn has a popular dining room serving dinner nightly from 5 to 9pm (lunch is available for groups only); the fixed-price meal is $18 to $20, and à la carte choices are available.

PICTOU LODGE RESORT, P.O. Box 1539, Pictou, NS, B0K 1H0. Tel. 902/485-4322. Fax 902/485-4945. 45 rms and suites (all with bath). TV TEL

$ Rates: $89 single; $99 double; from $89 suite. DISC, MC, V. **Closed:** Mid-Oct to early May.

Imagine a retreat by the sea, deluxe log cabins and a lodge in a secluded, serene spot. You have it in Pictou Lodge, with 29 well-constructed units, divided into one- and two-bedroom suites and three-bedroom log cottages, many with stone-hearth fireplaces, fully equipped kitchenettes, living rooms, and wonderful screened-in porches overlooking the ocean or lake. The main lodge, a log showpiece, houses the dining room, where lunch and dinner are served daily. A complete seafood or steak dinner, including tax and tip (but not wine), will cost $30 to $40. Pedal and rowboats are available for guests. Pictou Lodge, ably run by owners Carol Ann and Peter Van Westen, is on Brae Shore Road, equidistant from Pictou and the P.E.I. ferry, three miles (five kilometers) in either direction.

WALKER INN, 34 Coleraine St. (P.O. Box 629), Pictou, NS, B0K 1H0.
   Tel. 902/485-1433. 10 rms (all with bath). TV
   $ Rates (including continental buffet breakfast): $55–$60 single; $63–$75 double. Extra person $10. AE, MC, V.
Run by a young, enthusiastic Swiss couple, Theresa and Felix Walker, this inn features pretty rooms in a carefully renovated house dating from 1865. Each of the rooms has its own particular charm, but all come with cable TVs, baths with showers, and good lighting (a real plus in my book). There is a library for guests' use and meetings. A three-course dinner is available by reservation. There's a parking lot one block away, as well as on-street parking right out front. Pictou's main street, Water Street, dead-ends into Coleraine. The inn is a minute's walk from the Hector Heritage Quay.

WHERE TO DINE

FOUGERE'S, Ferry Rd. Tel. 902/485-6984.
   Cuisine: SEAFOOD. **Reservations:** Recommended.
   $ Prices: Appetizers $4–$8; main courses $13–$22. MC, V.
   Open: Dinner Mon–Sat 5–10pm, Sun 4–9pm.
Just out of town is a treat of a place tucked off Shore Road, off to your left just before the turnoff for the Caribou ferry—Fougère's, which takes its names from the jovial owner and chef, Ben Fougère. Ben attributes his long-standing success to the fact that "we specialize in good food." The restaurant is known for its seafood, not to mention "the best French onion soup this side of Montréal," but the menu also features roast beef, leg of lamb, pork chops, and a roast turkey dinner. Ben cuts his own beef and is proud of his kitchen, inviting anyone who's interested to tour it. The wine list, supervised by Bernice Fougère, who also acts as hostess, includes French labels.

STONE HOUSE CAFE & PIZZERIA, 12 Water St. Tel. 902/485-6885.
   Cuisine: LIGHT FARE. **Reservations:** Not needed.
   $ Prices: Most items $3–$12. MC, V.
   Open: July–Aug Sun 9am–midnight, Mon–Thurs 8am–midnight, Fri–Sat 8am–2am; the rest of the year, Sun noon–midnight, Mon–Thurs 11am–midnight, Fri–Sat 11am–2am.
For a bite to eat, stop in at the Stone House Café & Pizzeria. Start with the seafood chowder (chock-full of lobster!), and then venture on to a salmon steak, served with vegetables and potato. The menu is full of snack choices, including pizza, if you're only moderately hungry. A bottomless cup of coffee is 80¢, so guzzle away. There is additional seating in back and on the patio overlooking the harbor. Fully licensed.

ANTIGONISH

Halfway between Halifax and Sydney, Antigonish (pronounced Anti-ga-*nish;* pop. 5,205) has become a way station on the drive to Cape Breton Island for Nova Scotians and visitors alike. But other things draw people to this pretty town situated at the junction of several major roads. Prime among them are the annual Highland Games, held early to mid-July and attended by devotees of Scottish sports, pipe bands, and dances (see "What to See and Do," below).

   The campus of St. Francis Xavier University (affectionately referred to as "St. F. X." by students and locals) has been a beautiful and significant part of the Antigonish town scene since the university's founding in 1855. Today its students number more than 2,300, and its distinctive senior ring with the large X is said to be one of the most easily recognizable rings in the world.

   St. Ninian's Cathedral (built 1867) is the seat of the Roman Catholic bishop of Antigonish.

   The friendly and helpful **Nova Scotia Tourist Office,** well signposted and easy to spot when you come into town (take Exit 32, off Highway 104), is at 56 West St. (tel. 902/863-4921, or toll free 800/565-0000). It's open July and August from 8am to 8pm in summer, and 8am to 5pm in June and September.

WHAT TO SEE & DO

Antigonish's lavish display of Highland lore, art, strength, and skill—the **Highland Games**—has been held annually since 1861, usually Friday through Sunday in mid-July. For the price of admission (about $7), you may enter and leave the grounds as often as you please throughout the day; they ink-stamp your hand. To get there, proceed down Main Street to Columbus Field, by Right's River.

At one end of the field are the Highland dancers, at the other brawny athletes are throwing the hammer, broad-jumping, and "tossing the caber," while pipe bands march and skirl in between. Highlights of the day are the dance finals, the massed pipe bands—hundreds of bagpipers marching and playing together—and the caber toss. The latter event is a marvel. The caber, a log peeled of its bark, about 26 feet long and six inches in diameter, is lifted and tossed end-over-end by any of the thick-muscled athletes who can handle it. It takes immense strength and skill to get the mammoth tree trunk into the air, then straight up like a flagpole as it goes over, and few can do it.

But not even the caber toss can compete with the massed pipe bands for sheer emotional thrill. After competing all day for points in playing, marching, uniforms, and bearing, the bands come together in an unforgettable display of Scottish color, glitter, and ceremony. The bands alone are worth taking the trouble to schedule your Nova Scotia visit so as to catch the Highland Games at Antigonish. For more information, tickets, or entry forms, contact the secretary at **Antigonish Highland Society,** 274 Main St., Antigonish, NS, B2G 2C4 (tel. 902/863-4275). The office is located in Room 206 of the Town Hall building.

Festival Antigonish, a summer-long extravaganza of theater, including dramas, musicals, and revues, is held at the Bauer Theatre on the university campus in July and August.

WHERE TO STAY

Should you be coming for the Highland Games, or during graduation week in mid-May, make your reservations well in advance. The town's inns and motels fill up quickly. If they're full-up, get a reservation on the far side of Antigonish (in whichever direction you're headed) and plan to visit the city for the day or half a day.

OLD MANSE INN, 5 Tigo Park, Antigonish, NS, B2G 1M7. Tel. 902/863-5696 or 902/863-5259 off-season. 5 rms (3 with bath), 1 apt. **Directions:** Take Exit 32 from Highway 104, come into town; when you see the William Alexander Henry Building (Government of Canada) on your right, turn left—you'll end up on Hawthorne Street; take the second left, onto Tigo Park, and another immediate left, into the driveway of the Old Manse.

$ Rates (including full breakfast): $30 single; $36–$50 double; $80 two-bedroom suite. Extra person $10, child $8. Weekly rates available. No credit cards. **Closed:** Labor Day–June.

A renovated 1874 Victorian house with a lot of character, the Old Manse Inn sits up on a hill just a five-minute walk from the downtown district. Besides being one of the town's more interesting places to stay, it's also among the least expensive. Three downstairs bedrooms have private bath, while the two bedrooms upstairs share a large full bath. Room 4 (adjacent to the shared bath) is pretty, with tall windows and an interesting angle to the ceiling. Room 3, with two twin beds, is large and light. The two-story apartment, great for families, has a private entrance, two upstairs bedrooms, a full bath downstairs, a large kitchen, and a comfy TV room. Prices for all accommodations, including the apartment, include a full breakfast with fresh farm eggs, bacon, homemade jam and muffins, cereal, and tea or coffee made with spring water. Guests enjoy lounging in the chairs on the porch, at the picnic table, and in the well-tended yard. Barbara and Leonard Pluta, originally from Poland, and their staff provide a warm welcome. He teaches at the university.

WANDLYN INN, 158 Main St., Antigonish, NS, B2G 2B7. Tel. 902/863-4001, or toll free 800/561-0006 in the U.S., 800/561-0000 in Canada. Fax 902/863-2672. 34 rms. A/C TV TEL

$ Rates: $58–$74 single; $60–$80 double. Ask about senior discounts and special rates. AE, DC, ER, MC, V.

The Wandlyn Inn is a friendly, modern place in the Scottish tradition. Each of the nicely appointed rooms has either two double beds or one double bed plus a sofa bed, along with a cable TV. Guests may also enjoy the Elmwood Café and the quiet Library Lounge (it lives up to its name) on premises, and free use of the university's health facilities, including a pool and weight room. The inn is right downtown.

WHERE TO DINE

SUNSHINE CAFE AND TEA ROOM, 194 Main St. Tel. 902/863-1194.

Cuisine: VEGETARIAN. **Reservations:** Not needed.

$ Prices: Sandwiches and salads $4.75–$5.25; daily specials $6.75. MC, V.

Open: Summer Mon–Fri 8am–8pm, Sat 8am–5pm; the rest of the year Mon–Sat 8am–5pm.

Fresh vegetables, grains, nuts, fruits, and cheeses are the main ingredients at the Sunshine Café and Tea Room, a vegetarian restaurant and store. Wholesome sandwiches and salads are offered, as are daily specials, posted on a board on the sidewalk. This is a great place to stock up on healthy snacks for the Cabot Trail drive or to get sandwiches to go if you're in a hurry. There's free parking in the lot behind the café and metered parking on the street. Eat inside at small tables or, on pleasant days, out on the front porch.

7. CAPE BRETON ISLAND

Cape Breton Island, the wild and beautiful eastern end of Nova Scotia, is actually several islands surrounding the many-armed, 450-square-mile Bras d'Or Lake (pronounced Brah-*door*), the largest saltwater lake in the world and home to the largest population of bald eagles in North America. The mountainous country of Cape Breton kept it from being heavily settled, although it was just this remoteness that appealed to hardy Scots settlers who founded small towns back in the mountains. They named the towns for familiar places in Scotland, with the occasional Micmac name left in place.

Cape Breton is still very much a land of rugged highlands, dramatic mountains and valleys, rocky coasts, tranquil lakes, and "large days" (that's island talk for the unforgettable kind). Except for Sydney and Glace Bay, twin industrial centers in the northeastern reaches of the island, Cape Breton towns are small, often with no more than a dozen houses, a general store, and a post office.

North Sydney, a suburb of Nova Scotia's second-largest city, is the departure point for ferries to Newfoundland. The Fortress of Louisbourg, south of Sydney, is undoubtedly Cape Breton's most impressive and exciting historical site.

Driving your own car is the best way to see Cape Breton, and the time-honored drive—in fact, one of the world's great drives—is along the Cabot Trail through the northern tip of the island in Cape Breton Highlands National Park.

The exploration of Cape Breton mapped out here starts at Canso Causeway, the only road to Cape Breton from the mainland, and heads north to the national park. From the park, roads take you south to North Sydney and Louisbourg, and then west to the shores of Bras d'Or (it means "Golden Arm") before returning to Canso Causeway.

Before setting out, you should know about Cape Breton's unique bed-and-breakfast program. Motels and inns are sprinkled along Cape Breton's roads, but they fill quickly in summer. To encourage tourism at modest prices, local authorities have organized lists of Cape Breton residents with spare rooms to rent. You'll see the distinctive "Cape Breton Bed & Breakfast" signs frequently along the road. A house may have only one, or several, rooms for rent, but the cost will always be about $35 for one, $40 for two sharing a bed, breakfast included. The tourist bureau can provide you with a leaflet listing the participants in the program.

AN IMPORTANT NOTE ON PRICES

Unless stated otherwise, **the prices cited in this guide are given in Canadian dollars,** which is good news for U.S. travelers because the Canadian dollar is worth 25% less than the American dollar, but buys nearly as much. As we go to press, $1 Canadian is worth 75¢ U.S., which means that your $100-a-night hotel room will cost only U.S. $75, and your $6 breakfast costs only U.S. $4.50.

Here's a quick table of equivalents:

Canadian $	U.S. $
$ 1	$ 0.75
5	3.75
10	7.50
20	15.00
50	37.50
80	60.00
100	75.00
200	150.00

OVER THE CANSO CAUSEWAY

The Canso Causeway, connecting Cape Breton with the mainland, opened in 1955. At 217 feet deep, it is the deepest causeway in the world. The bridge across it deposits you in the town of Port Hastings (pop. 495), where the busy tourist bureau (tel. 902/625-9991), is open daily from 9am to 7pm (to 9pm in July and August). Port Hastings and nearby Port Hawkesbury have a cluster of motels and restaurants to serve those who cross at nightfall.

CHOOSING A ROUTE   Once over the Canso Causeway, you must decide how to tour Cape Breton. First to Louisbourg, then Bras d'Or Lake, and finally around the Cabot Trail? Or first to the Cabot Trail? And which way around the Cabot Trail—clockwise or counterclockwise? Visitors debate the pros and cons of each direction, but it really doesn't matter which way you choose. The roads are excellent and safe and the scenery is gorgeous, whichever way you go. The information center at the Chéticamp gateway is much larger than the one at Ingonish, however, and it provides a much more extensive orientation to the park.

If you have only a few days to explore the whole of Cape Breton Island, head straight for the Cabot Trail. I suggest taking the western, or clockwise, route. The entry into the park is dramatic here, and the information center exceptionally helpful.

You may be tempted to follow the coast via the **Ceilidh Trail** (pronounced *Kay*-lee) along Route 19 to link up with the Cabot Trail, but it's more time-consuming than picturesque until you reach Mabou. Instead, take Route 105 to Whycocomagh, then head west 18 miles (29km) on Route 252 to Mabou and pick up the Ceilidh Trail there. A "ceilidh," by the way, is an old Scottish tradition, alive and well on Cape Breton Island, that is basically an impromptu kitchen party; all you need is some tea, a fiddle, and some friends.

From Mabou, follow the Ceilidh Trail north to Margaree Harbour to link up with the Cabot Trail. Follow it to Chéticamp and Cape Breton Highlands National Park, then loop around to Ingonish and Baddeck.

If you have a couple of days to explore the park, consider staying in centrally located Dingwall (Chéticamp, Pleasant Bay, and Ingonish are other alternatives) and use it as your base of operations for daily excursions. Trying to go back and forth from Mabou, Margaree, or Baddeck in one day can be taxing (though doable if necessary), and it leaves no time to explore the highlands in a leisurely way.

From Baddeck, there are several possibilities: Head east to explore the unforgettable Fortress of Louisbourg or the Miners' Museum at Glace Bay; to Sydney Mines, to stay in an excellent bed-and-breakfast; to North Sydney to take the ferry to Newfoundland; or if time is tight, scoot back to Whycocomagh and the Canso Causeway to return to the mainland.

Be forewarned that local drivers don't always use turn signals, so keep an eye out for them. Such is island life.

WHERE TO STAY & DINE NEAR PORT HASTINGS

MACPUFFIN MOTEL, Rte. 4 (P.O. Box 558), Port Hawkesbury, NS, B0E 2V0. Tel. 902/625-0621. Fax 902/625-1525. 32 rms and suites. A/C TV TEL
$ Rates: $59 single; $67 double; $99 suite. Extra person $8. Discounts available in May–June and Oct. AE, ER, MC, V.

About half a mile (1km) past the Canso Causeway (it'll be on your left) stands the MacPuffin Motel, a tidy two-story wooden building with brick-and-green trim and flower boxes and hanging baskets galore. It has clean, modern rooms with cable TV, in-room movies, handmade puffin quilts on the beds, and full baths. Breakfasts and dinners are served in the motel's licensed dining room. For guests' enjoyment, there is a heated indoor swimming pool, exercise room, games room, gift shop, laundry, and a swing set for the kids. The same management owns the MacPuffin Inn, which is closer to the causeway, but I prefer the motel. Ask for a room in back to eliminate any noise from the highway.

WANDLYN INN, Reeves St. (Box 759), Port Hawkesbury, NS, B0E 2V0. Tel. 902/625-0320, or toll free 800/561-0000. Fax 902/625-3876. 74 rms.
$ Rates: $58–$73 single; $67–$95 double. Extra person $8. Children under 18 free with parents. AE, ER, MC, V.

Only 3 miles (5km) from the Canso Causeway, the Wandlyn Inn is the area's most modern hostelry. Besides comfortable rooms, guests will find a large outdoor pool, a small indoor pool, a kids' pool, a Jacuzzi, a fitness center, Sampler's Café, and a helpful staff. Willy's Lounge has occasional entertainment. Room service is available.

WHERE TO DINE IN PORT HASTINGS

HASTINGS HOUSE RESTAURANT, at the rotary, just past the causeway. Tel. 902/625-3346.
Cuisine: HOME COOKING. **Reservations:** Not needed.
$ Prices: Most items $2–$13. MC, V.
Open: May to mid-Oct daily 6:30am–11pm; mid-Oct to May daily 11am–9pm (sometimes closed off-season).

If you're hungry, swing by Hastings House, a licensed restaurant known for its hefty portions and conveniently long hours. You'll spot it to your left, on the hill overlooking the rotary and causeway. The burgers are a mere $2; hearty lunch specials, about $6; and dinner specials, served after 4pm, not much more. Main courses include rib steak, pork chops, and roast turkey, all served with potatoes, vegetables, coleslaw, rolls, and coffee. It's a casual place that's popular with families. Joan and Martin Chisholm are the owners and the cooks, too. They also sell cassettes of local musicians (buy the "Sounds of Nova Scotia," Volume 2, if it's available) and baked goods to go.

WHYCOCOMAGH

A tiny village of 410 souls, Whycocomagh (pronounced Why-*cog*-ah-mah) is near a Micmac reservation and a provincial park, and is right on the northwestern bay of Bras d'Or Lake. Here you'll find (should you need them) a bank (on Main Street), post office, gas station, and, on the main road, the wonderful **Farmer's Daughter Country Market,** open April through September from 9am to 9pm, and selling fruit, vegetables, and baked goods, including yummy ginger cookies.

From here the road to Mabou is lined with "marshmallow fields." You'll find them in Prince Edward Island, too. Don't tell the kids, but the humongous "marshmallows" are really bales of hay placed in big, white plastic bags to keep them dry. (My grandfather, a Georgia farmer, would have been amused by the sight of them.)

MABOU

The peaceful village of Mabou (pronounced *Mah*-boo) is home to 595 people, among them the locally famous Rankin family singers. You'll see their cassettes in many souvenir shops and gift stores on the island. There's a lot to do in this area, and Mabou makes a wonderful base for explorations or just soaking up the natural beauty and harmony here. And don't be surprised if you find yourself at your first ceilidh or kicking up your heels at a local square dance.

WHAT TO SEE & DO

In the summer, visit the **Mabou Village Gallery,** where the work of local artist Suzanne MacDonald is exhibited and sold; the oils and limited serigraphs are particularly good (tel. 902/945-2060).

Square dances are held less than a mile out of town, in west Mabou, nightly in summer and every Saturday night the rest of the year. A local fiddler plays, and people of all ages are welcome, at this nonalcoholic event.

For a pretty drive, go out Mabou Harbour Road to Mabou Coal Mines Road and follow it about 3.7 miles (6km) to the wharf. You can also ride out to the lighthouse at Mabou Harbour (watch for bald eagles). There's a hiking trail here as well.

GLENORA DISTILLERY, Rte. 19. Tel. 902/258-2662.

On 200 acres, 5.6 miles (9km) north of Mabou stands the only single-malt whisky distillery in North America, a black-and-white complex with a distinctive cupola and a seven-foot holding tank in front. On the tour of the Glenora Distillery, you start at the Mash House, where the sugar is extracted from the barley (which is imported from Rotterdam) and proceed to the Still House, where the distillation process takes place. The water that is used comes from McClellan's Brook, out front, chosen for its mineral content, purity, and good taste. You'll even get to sample "Cape Breton Silver," which has been likened to Irish "patuchka." One visitor called it "the best damned moonshine I ever had." The aging process takes five years. Glenora's first batch of single-malt whisky (10,000 bottles) will be ready in 1996 and will be sold worldwide (they're already taking orders). It also blends and bottles white and dark rum.

Admission: $2 adults, children free.

Open: Daily 11am–4pm.

MOTHER OF SORROWS PIONEER CHAPEL AND SHRINE, Rte. 19. No phone.

This small chapel honors the area's pioneer settlers and is surprisingly touching. Flip the switch to your right at the entry to hear recorded a capella chants.

Admission: Free; donations accepted.

Open: July–Aug daily 10am–4pm.

WHERE TO STAY IN MABOU

CLAYTON FARM B&B, Rte. 19 (P.O. Box 33), Mabou, NS B0E 1X0. Tel. 902/945-2719. 3 rms (none with bath). Directions: About half a mile (1km) south of town on Route 19; look for the sign and the big red barn.

$ Rates (including full breakfast): $35 single; $45 double. Extra person $10. No credit cards.

This 195-acre working farm has been in Isaac Smith's family since 1835, and he and his wife, Bernadette, love to share it with visitors. ("I get up in the morning and wonder who's traveling towards here today," Bernadette told me.) The upstairs guest rooms are large, with wrought-iron beds and a fan; they share a cheery bath big enough to have chairs and a chest in it. There is also a wonderful sitting nook upstairs. For breakfast, expect oatcakes and jam, Acadian pancakes with maple syrup, local sausage, and endless coffee and conversation. Other typical activities at Clayton Farm include sitting on the porch, walking down the lane behind the house, and swinging under the canopy of linden trees beside the house. The farm is dramatically situated, surrounded by water on three sides, and the views are stunning. If you like red Aberdeen Angus cattle, Isaac will be happy to show you his. Bernadette is a musician with a particular interest in Celtic music, and ceilidhs are common occurrences in her kitchen. There's a nightly square dance just down the road in summer.

DUNCREIGAN INN, Rte. 19 (P.O. Box 59), Mabou, NS, B0E 1X0. Tel. 902/945-2207. 3 rms (all with bath), 1 suite. TV
$ Rates: $55–$65 single or double; $80 suite. Extra adult $10, extra child $5. MC, V.

Trimmed with blue bonnets, columbine, lupine, irises, peonies, and lady's mantel, the Duncreigan Inn is perfectly situated, overlooking the harbor and the white spire of St. Mary's Church. It is also elegant, quiet, architecturally appealing, and beautifully decorated with antiques. Ingenious European-style windows tilt into the rooms to provide a pleasant breeze. Room 2 is large and lovely, with a view that is beautiful by day and dramatic by night. The inn, which is owned and run by Eleanor and Charles Mullendore, is open year-round and has a gift shop that sells paintings and Inuit carvings. They can supply guests with a telephone or VCR or rent them a canoe and two mountain bikes; Eleanor is happy to help plan local activities.

The licensed dining room, open Tuesday through Sunday from 5:30 to 8:30pm, features main dishes that include homemade yeast rolls and pasta, salmon, lobster-stuffed chicken breast, and charbroiled tenderloin steak. The three-course dinner is $24; the four-course dinner, $27.50. Or you may order à la carte; some folks come by just for their antipasto plate, soup, and dessert. Reserve a table beside the bow window.

WHERE TO DINE IN MABOU

MULL CAFE, Rte. 19. Tel. 902/945-2244.
  Cuisine: LIGHT FARE/DELI FOOD.
$ Prices: Lunch items $2–$10; dinner items $9–$15. MC, V.
  Open: Daily 11am–9pm (dinner served from 5pm).
If you're blitzing through here on your way to the Cabot Trail, you can get take-out at this popular local café. The deli sells a variety of meats and cheeses, soft drinks, and bottled water. Lunch items include soups, salads, fish, pasta, veggie fritters, nachos, deli sandwiches, grilled chicken, burgers, and a daily stir-fry. Dinners—grilled or charbroiled halibut, scallops, lemon chicken, or steak with vegetables and rice or potato—are filling, and the desserts, such as brownie pudding pie and strawberry daiquiri cream puffs, are tempting. It's licensed.

WHERE TO STAY & DINE NEAR MABOU

GLENORA INN & DISTILLERY, Rte. 19 (P.O. Box 181), Mabou, NS, B0E 1X0. Tel. 902/258-2662, or toll free 800/341-6096 in the U.S. (800/492-0643 in Maine only), 800/565-0000 in Canada. Fax 902/258-3133. 6 rms (all with bath), 3 suites. TV
$ Rates: $68–$78 single; $78–$88 double; $108 suite. AE, MC, V. **Closed:** Nov–Apr, except by arrangement.
In a tranquil setting alongside McClellan's Brook, 5.6 miles (9km) north of Mabou, the region's only distillery is also an inn, providing lodging and meals. It is perhaps best known for its outstanding dining room, open for three meals a day. At dinner, start with seafood chowder, salad, or mussels, then order chicken, Atlantic salmon, New York strip, or steak-and-kidney pie, then cap the evening with cranachan, a Scottish dessert of cream and fresh fruit flavored with Smugglers Cove rum, or a brownie doused with Bailey's Irish Cream, or Smugglers Cove rum cake, or a nonalcoholic cheesecake. Appetizers run about $5, main courses $13 to $17 ($6 to $8 at lunch). The dining room and adjoining pub, both fully licensed, are sometimes the stage for local step-dancers, fiddlers, and Gaelic singers. There is a small gift shop.

HAUS TREUBURG GUEST HOUSE, Hwy. 19 (P.O. Box 92), Port Hood, NS, B03 2W0. Tel. 902/787-2116. Fax 902/787-3216. 4 rms (2 with bath),

3 cottages. **Directions:** From Mabou, take the second exit for Port Hood and follow Main Road.

$ Rates (including full breakfast): $45–$55 single; $50–$70 double. Extra person $5. Cottages $85 daily, $425 weekly. MC, V. **Closed:** Mid-Oct to mid-May.

 Elvira and Georg Kargoll transplanted themselves from Germany and established this charming inn in Port Hood, 9 miles (15km) south of Mabou, in 1986. The four rooms are comfortable, with good reading lighting; the two that have a private bath also have a telephone and television; the other two rooms share a large, full bath (of these, no. 4 is particularly nice). The three popular cottages overlook the ocean and come with a large sitting room, a kitchen, a separate bedroom, a large, full bath, and a deck with barbecue.

The Kargolls serve a wonderful full German breakfast with homemade bread and much more, and in the evening their highly praised dining room, which opened in 1989 with Georg as chef, offers a five-course fixed-price dinner, by reservation only, for $29 (inn guests may eat à la carte). The cuisine is a mix of Italian and French, and the menu changes daily. You might find homemade French baguettes, gravlax, cream of tomato soup, Greek salad, salmon or halibut steak with potatoes Romanov or green noodles, followed by apple strudel or cognac sorbet. Dinner is served daily from 7 to 10pm. Lighter fare, along with cappuccino and espresso, is served in the cozy bar/lounge.

Port Hood has sandy beaches and some of the warmest waters in eastern Canada. Look for the white shingled house with brown trim set back from the road, on the left after the Co-op food store.

THE MARGAREE VALLEY

The Margaree Valley is so pretty and peaceful that you may choose to linger here. It's an area perfect for hiking, canoeing, sandy beaches, golf, and salmon and trout fishing. Once a world-class salmon-fishing river, the Margaree River is now experiencing a comeback. Eight "Margarees" are clustered in the Margaree Valley: Upper Margaree, Southwest Margaree, Margaree Forks, Margaree Center, Northeast Margaree, the Margaree Valley, East Margaree, and Margaree Harbour.

WHERE TO STAY & DINE

DUCK COVE INN, Margaree Harbour, NS, B0E 2B0. Tel. 902/235-2658.
Fax 902/235-2592. 24 rms (all with bath). TV
$ Rates: $50–$60 single; $60–$75 double. Children under 12 free. Special rates available for seniors. AE, MC, V. **Closed:** Nov–May.
The Duck Cove Inn overlooks the mouth of the Margaree River from its perch on the hillside above the Cabot Trail, just outside the village of Margaree Harbour. The motel-style rooms have two double beds and a full bath; six of them have balconies. I prefer the larger units in the uphill block; they lack balconies but still have the river view. The inn's licensed dining room is open nightly from 5:30 to 8pm. There's a laundry for guests, and management can arrange canoe and bicycle rentals, and whale-watching and fishing trips. Golf and saltwater beaches are nearby. The Duck Cove Inn has been around since 1934; its current owner, Gordon Lawrence, who is also a teacher, since the early 1980s.

NORMAWAY INN, Egypt Rd. (Box 121), Margaree Valley, NS, B0E 2C0.
Tel. 902/248-2987, or toll free 800/565-9463. Fax 902/248-2600. 9 rms (all with bath), 19 cabins. **Directions:** Two miles (3.5km) down Egypt Road; follow the signs.
$ Rates: Rooms or cabins, $75 single ($110 with breakfast and dinner); $75–$114 double ($150–$190 with breakfast and dinner); with Jacuzzi $15 extra. Extra person $10 ($40 with breakfast and dinner). Discounted room rates after 4pm, day of check-in, on availability. Special packages available. MC, V. **Closed:** Mid-Oct to mid-June, except by special reservation.

 At the end of a pine-lined lane on a country road in the Margaree Valley, the Normaway Inn sits in a world of its own, on 250 private acres. Practically surrounded by hills, the wood-shingled inn with green trim, designed by an architect from Yonkers, New York, and built in 1928, has long had a reputation for outstanding hospitality and food. Since 1944, it has been owned and run by the MacDonald family, and lively, engaging David MacDonald is the current innkeeper. Besides nine inn-style rooms, many with original furnishings, the main lodge has a cozy living room with a fieldstone fireplace, filled with books, games, and comfy couches. A folksinger and guitar player perform here almost every evening in summer, and there are nightly movies, Wednesday-night barn dances, and plenty of reading nooks. Scattered among the trees near the tennis court are 19 one- and two-bedroom cabins, all with lively red decor, radio/cassette players, and full bath. Some have wood-stove fireplaces, Jacuzzis, and screened-in porches with swings. The inn rents mountain bikes and can arrange salmon-fishing expeditions with guides.

In the Normaway's renowned dining room, bright and cheery decor and hardwood floors complement tasty fare. Dinner runs about $30, and the homemade desserts are terrific. Reserve your table in advance.

A Nearby Place to Dine in Belle Côte

Just past Belle Côte, be prepared to be stopped in your tracks by the convention of scarecrows outside Ethel's Take-Out, a good place for cold drinks and short orders.

CROSSROADS RESTAURANT, Belle Côte. Tel. 902/235-2888.
   Cuisine: HOME COOKING. **Reservations:** Not needed.
$ Prices: Most items $2–$12. MC, V.
   Open: Daily 7am–11pm.
Across the bridge from Margaree Harbour, up the hill, and to your left stands the Crossroads Restaurant, a popular local place open long hours all year. You can get a variety of food here, including burgers, hot and cold sandwiches, soups, salads, milk shakes, and dinners (from 11am) served with fries and veggies. Licensed, with take-out available, it's in the hamlet of Belle Côte (pop. 230).

CHÉTICAMP

The "Hooked-Rug Capital of the World," the gateway to Cape Breton Highlands National Park, and the center of Acadian life on the island's north shore, Chéticamp (pop. 3,000) is a pleasant French-speaking fishing town famous for its folk art and handcrafts shops. At first the prices of the hooked rugs and smaller hooked items seem high, but not so when you consider that one 12-inch square with no design takes eight hours to complete.

The folk art here is wonderful, and Cape Breton Highlands National Park is only three miles away.

WHAT TO SEE & DO

There are numerous craft stores in Chéticamp, most notably **Flora's,** just south of town, which has a mind-boggling amount of merchandise (not inexpensive) and an adjacent ice-cream parlor.

Whale-watching excursions leave from the dock in the center of town.

BILL ROACH FOLK ART/SUNSET ART GALLERY, Rte. 19. Tel. 902/224-2119.
   If you only have time to stop at one place in Chéticamp, make it the Sunset Art Gallery, about a mile north of town, on a bend in the road, to your right. The gallery displays the work of local Acadian artist Bill Roach, whose carvings are whimsical, winsome, and wonderful. Like other folk artists, Bill is self-taught; he began whittling before he went to school, and his three sons are following in his footsteps. He works mostly in pine and cedar and follows the natural shape of the wood to create fish, birds, roosters, cats, mice, sea gulls, and even six-foot giraffes. Bill and his wife, Linda, who runs the gallery, are on hand to talk with visitors. Prices range from $50 to $3,000, and they'll mail the work home to you if you decide to buy, though there's absolutely no pressure to do so. The most popular item is a colorful crowing cock. The studio also sells the work of a few other local artists, as well as handmade quilts at good prices.
   Admission: Free.
   Open: Summer daily 9am–6pm; otherwise, by appointment.

MUSEE ACADIEN AND CRAFT CO-OP ARTISANALE, 774 Main St. Tel. 902/224-2170.

Upstairs, in the Handcrafts Cooperative, hooked rugs and other craft items are on sale, as well as local music, including the "Sounds of Nova Scotia," volumes I and II, and recordings of the Rankin Family. Downstairs, the two-room Acadian Museum houses a small collection of artifacts from Acadian traditional life; there's often a guide on the premises, eager to show you around. A small café in the same complex serves lunch and dinner (see Restaurant Acadien in "Where to Dine," below).

Admission: Free.

Open: Mid-May to mid-Oct daily 7am–9pm. **Closed:** Late Oct–early May.

LES TROIS PIGNONS, Rte. 19. Tel. 902/224-2642.

Just north of town, to the right, is the colorful (red, white, and blue) Les Trois Pignons, a combination information center, gallery, and museum. The museum houses the eclectic collection—furniture, dolls, bottles, and tools from Canada, the United States, and Europe—of Marguerite Gallant, a local woman who worked in the States for 25 years as a caregiver in private homes. Also on display, and of particular note, are 20 historical tapestries by local artist Elizabeth LeFort, whose work has hung in the White House, Buckingham Palace, and the Vatican. Dr. LeFort dyed her own wools, and some of her creations have more than 500 colors in them. Les Trois Pignons (the name means the "Three Gables") can supply information about the region, and it sells books on the area.

Admission: $2.50 per person; children under 12 free.

Open: Summer daily 9am–6pm; the rest of the year Mon–Fri 8:30am–4:30pm.

WHERE TO STAY

LAURIE'S MOTEL AND DINING ROOM, Rte. 19 (P.O. Box 1), Chéticamp, NS, B0E 1H0. Tel. 902/224-2400. Fax 902/224-2069. 48 rms, 7 suites. TV TEL

$ Rates: July–Sept $55–$75 single; $65–$87 double; from $100 suite. Off-season $50–$65 single or double. Extra person $7. Children under 12 free. MC, V.

Laurie's Motel and Dining Room, an old Chéticamp standby and one of the largest motels in the region, was established by Mr. Laurie Chiasson in 1938. In the Highlander section, the downstairs rooms are large, with two double beds, a sitting area, and an enormous bath; upstairs rooms are smaller but they have a balcony overlooking the Highlands. Suites and connecting units are also available; the honeymoon suite has a king-size bed, Jacuzzi for two, private patio, and complimentary roses and champagne for $125. The motel, which is carpeted throughout, features a welcoming lobby, a lounge with occasional Acadian entertainment free for guests only, Laundromat, VCR and bicycle rentals, in-room movies, and a courteous, bilingual staff. The on-premises restaurant is licensed, specializes in seafood, and is open for breakfast (7 to 11am) and dinner (5 to 9pm) in July and August, with more restricted hours the rest of the year.

WHERE TO DINE

LE CHALOUPE, Whale-Watching Tour Wharf, Main St. Tel. 902/224-3710.

Cuisine: HOME COOKING. **Reservations:** Not needed.

$ Prices: Appetizers $2–$5; lunch main courses $3.50–$11, dinner main courses $8–$13. AE, MC, V.

Open: Daily 11:30am–9pm.

In the center of town, this is a pleasant spot simply to sit, sip something, and look out over the water. If you're hungry, they've got sandwiches, mussels, good spicy chili, as well as ham, fish, and chicken dinners with mashed potatoes or fries, vegetables, coleslaw, and bread. It's a light, airy, and clean place, with seating on the deck, inside, and upstairs.

RESTAURANT ACADIEN, 774 Main St. Tel. 902/224-3207.

Cuisine: ACADIAN/HOME COOKING. **Reservations:** Not needed.

$ Prices: Lunch items $2–$9; dinner items $6–$12. AE, MC, V.
   Open: Mid-May to mid-Oct lunch daily 11am–4pm, dinner daily 4–9pm; mid-Oct
   to mid-May daily 9am–7pm.
In this small café, Acadian women dish up light lunches, suppers, and snacks. The
menu is fairly extensive. For instance at lunchtime, choose from meat pies, a variety of
sandwiches, hamburgers, fish chowder, or salad. The dinner menu features cod
fishcakes, fresh breaded scallops, lobster or crab salad plate, or a codfish, smelt,
turkey, or pork chop dinner. All the dinners come with vegetables, potatoes served a
variety of ways, homemade roll, and coffee or tea. If you've room for dessert, mull
over the possibilities: berry pies, lemon or butterscotch meringue pie, strawberry
shortcake, blueberry or raisin pudding with hot syrup, or gingerbread with hot syrup.
It's real home cooking, heavy on sugar, though. The café is licensed to serve beer and
wine.

CAPE BRETON HIGHLANDS NATIONAL PARK

It's one of Canada's most spectacular parks—and that's saying a lot, as so many are so
exceptionally beautiful. The Cabot Trail begins at Baddeck, heads to Chéticamp, and
then in a few miles enters the national park to wind up into the dramatic scenery of
the mountains. Camping areas, picnic sites, and scenic lookouts are spaced at good
intervals along the trail. The famous drive, which measures almost 70 miles (113km)
from Chéticamp to Ingonish (a town on the eastern shore with many tourist services),
was created along with the park, in 1936. En route, in the Grand Anse Valley, you'll
pass one of the largest and oldest uncut stands of hardwood timber in the Atlantic
Provinces. The drive can easily be done in a day, or even half a day, but take a picnic
and enjoy a leisurely pace.
   During your drive, plan to stop at several of the well-marked lookout points. You'll
also see many hiking trails; a booklet describing all the trails, giving lengths and hiking
times, is available at park offices. Ask for it, and any other information, at the modern
Information Centre at the gateway to the park. There's an outstanding bookstore on
the premises, along with exhibits and a play area for kids. In summer it's open from
8am to 8pm daily. Several hiking trails begin from here, and there's also a picnic area
and a children's playground.
   If you plan to make any stops in the park (as opposed to driving straight through),
you'll have to pay a user's fee of $5 a day, or $10 for four days, per car.
   The highway wanders outside the boundaries of the national park at several points,
including Pleasant Bay, Cape North, and South Harbour. At these points you can buy
gasoline and food, or even find lodging for the night.

EN ROUTE TO DINGWALL

The first "inhabited area" in the Highlands you'll happen upon is the small
community of Pleasant Bay (pop. 295), nestled between MacKenzie Mountain and
North Mountain. You can take a 2½-hour whale- and seabird-watching tour with
Pleasant Bay Boat Tours (tel. 902/224-2547). If you're ready for a break from
driving, or if nightfall is about to overtake you, Pleasant Bay offers the **Mountain
View Motel** (tel. 902/224-3100) and the **Black Whale** seafood restaurant, a rustic
place that does little to disturb the forest scenery. Both are open from June to
mid-October.
   From here, the Cabot Trail climbs North Mountain, 1,460 feet high (445m). Even
if you're not a hiker, take time to stop at the **Lone Sheiling** (watch for the sign). This
replica of a Scottish sheep crofter's thatched hut is set amid 300-year-old maple trees
just off the highway. The half-mile trail to the hut is easy and pleasant. You can walk
there and back in 10 minutes. The hut, by the way, was built to provide a visual,
cultural "link" between life in the Scottish Highlands and that in the Cape Breton
Highlands of "New Scotland."
   Continuing along the Cabot Trail, before the turnoff to Beulach Ban Falls, just
when you think you've seen about as many lupines as a person can see, you'll come
upon an entire mountainside of purple ones, in bloom early in the summer. This

stunning sight makes the drive worthwhile even if the lovely Aspy River Valley is shrouded in fog.

DINGWALL

Dingwall is ideally located for those who plan to take two or three (or more) days to explore and enjoy Cape Breton Highlands National Park. You can stay in either a rural bed-and-breakfast or a remote and romantic coastal resort with one of the finest dining rooms in Nova Scotia. Both are conveniently located just a few kilometers off the Cabot Trail.

Above all else, this is a place to enjoy nature. Walk along the sandy beaches of Aspy Bay, or in the old gypsum quarry, with its interesting rock formations and pools.

Go birdwatching. This area full of bald eagles, merlin falcons, great blue herons, seabirds, and swallows.

Take a three-hour whale-watching and seabird tour with **Aspy Bay Tours** in Dingwall (tel. 902/383-2847), or a 2½-hour tour with **Capt. Dennis Cox** in nearby Bay St. Lawrence (tel. 902/383-2981).

For an indoor activity, visit the **North Highlands Community Museum** to learn about the history of the area, and see relics from the *Auguste* shipwreck. The museum, in a log cabin, is free, and open daily 11am to 6pm June to mid-October.

You can fill your car up with gas at the station across the street from the museum.

Where to Stay and Dine

THE MARKLAND, Dingwall, NS, B0C 1G0. Tel. 902/383-2246, or toll free 800/565-0000. 12 rms (all with bath), 8 cabins. TV TEL

$ Rates (including buffet breakfast): $60–$80 single, $80–$110 double, depending on season; $115–$135 cabins. Extra person $12. Children under 12 stay free with parents (meals not included). Packages available. AE, MC, V.

Stillness pervades the Markland resort, except perhaps for the sound of waves. The accommodations are simple and understated. The rooms, in four buildings with three units each, each have tongue-and-groove paneled walls (including the bathroom), high ceilings with a fan, a sitting area with queen-size sofa bed, a queen-size bed so comfortable it deserves special mention, soft bedcovers and towels, a picture window overlooking the water, and, incongruously, a television (reception is blessedly poor). The one- and two-bedroom cabins are similarly furnished, but with cathedral ceilings and a full kitchen with a microwave and stove (guests can also order pizza from nearby Northern Lights Pizzaria; call 902/383-2171). The two-bedroom cabins have double instead of queen-size beds. All the cabins come with complimentary cassette players, so you can create your own mood. Cabin no. 8 sits in the woods overlooking the ocean, and cabin no. 1 is tucked off by itself in the woods—both very romantic. In the public sitting room, a puzzle lies half-finished on a table, people chat or read (books on the area are for sale), and though the Markland is not known as a family resort, children do come here, and often sit quietly transfixed by a video while their parents dine leisurely nearby. Ann MacLean, the gracious manager, has compiled a list of 50 things to do at the Markland, starting appropriately with "relax and do nothing at all." You may also vegetate in the lawn chairs or gazebo (or watch the glorious sunrise from here), use the barbecue, take a dip in the outdoor pool, play lawn games, enjoy a complimentary canoe or bicycle, gaze at the stars (there are no other lights to interfere), and much more. The Markland, about an hour from Chéticamp and the entrance to the park, is a perfect spot from which to explore the park. It is a perfect spot, period.

One of the best meals I had in Atlantic Canada was at the Markland, late on a particularly busy night when the chef had run out of almost everything! At dinner, appetizers run $5 to $7, main dishes, $17 to $19. Expect to feast on homemade breads, fresh-from-the market salad, steamed mussels, lamb médaillons, chicken breast with cheese and crab stuffing, and blackened shark with lemon butter sauce. (Lunch items cost a reasonable $5 to $8.) The wonderful breakfast buffet is served from 7:30 to 11am; lunch, from 11:30am to 3:30pm; and dinner, from 6 to 9:30pm.

OAKWOOD MANOR, P.O. Box 19, Dingwall, NS, B0C 1G0. Tel. 902/383-2317. 4 rms (none with bath). **Directions:** Turn off the Cabot Trail and take the road toward Bay St. Lawrence—*not* the road to Dingwall; drive 2.8 miles (1.7km) and look for the sign directing you to turn left to Oakwood Manor.

$ **Rates:** $32 single; $40 double. Extra person $8. No credit cards. **Closed:** Mid-Nov to Apr.

Oakwood Manor is on a winding country road less than two miles off the Cabot Trail. Each of the four guest rooms has a sink in the room; they share two full baths. It's located down a short country road that opens onto picture-perfect acreage and a series of weathered barns.

EN ROUTE TO THE INGONISHES

Stop by pretty **Neil's Harbour,** reminiscent of Peggy's Cove, near Halifax, though not quite as picturesque. The fishing village has a distinctive Newfoundland flavor and heritage, with houses built close to the water.

South of Neil's Harbour, **Lakie's Head lookout,** in the park, is a particularly scenic spot, with a natural play of rocks, sea, wind-sculpted trees, and wildflowers.

If you have at least half an hour for a side trip, turn off the Cabot Trail to **Mary Ann Falls** and drive four miles (6.5km) along a dirt road to this pretty, moderately sized waterfall that spills into a secluded swimming hole. This drive takes about 12 minutes, and you might even spot a red fox (as I did) running along the road. There's also a pleasant picnic area here.

A popular hike in this part of the park is along the trail to the top of **Broad Cove Mountain.** On Tuesdays in summer, the Broad Cove campground is the site of interpretive evenings and Scottish concerts.

THE INGONISHES

At the southeastern entrance to Cape Breton Highlands National Park, strung along eight miles (13km) of the Cabot Trail, are the villages of Ingonish, Ingonish Centre, and Ingonish Beach (pop. 570)—otherwise known as the Ingonishes. Most of the national park recreational facilities—golf, tennis, hiking trails, boating, and sailing, and the fine sandy beaches in both Ingonish and Ingonish Beach—are in this area, as are the park's administrative headquarters.

There is a small information center for the park, at its entrance, in Ingonish. Maps are available.

WHERE TO STAY & DINE

KELTIC LODGE, Middle Head Peninsula, Ingonish Beach, NS, B0C 1L0. Tel. 902/285-2880, or toll free 800/565-0444. Fax 902/285-2859. 72 rms, 26 cottages. TV TEL

$ **Rates** (including breakfast and dinner): $169–$184 single; $233–$248 double. Extra person $74. Children 4–17 half price on room and meals. Packages available. AE, DISC, ER, MC, V. **Closed:** Mid-Oct to Dec, Apr–May.

If your budget will allow it, the only place to stay in this area is at the breathtaking Keltic Lodge, at the end of a birch-lined drive on a vast estate. You'll be greeted by colorful lawn chairs and views that go on forever. Rooms are rented in the baronial Main Lodge, the modern White Birch Inn, and in two- and four-bedroom cottages; rates vary with accommodations. For outdoor enthusiasts, the lodge offers a large pool, a freshwater lake, a mile-long beach, three tennis courts, and a seven-mile-long, 18-hole golf course with resident moose and deer. (You have to walk the course; carts aren't allowed because it's part of the national park.)

Even if you can't stay at this fabulous place, drive up for a peek at it—and perhaps stay for a meal in the Purple Thistle dining room. The table d'hôte breakfast costs $11, lunch $18, and dinner $36. There's a dress code for dinner. There is the more casual Atlantic Restaurant, as well as Corson Lounge. The Keltic Lodge is one of three resorts run by the Nova Scotia government.

SOUTH TO BADDECK

The Cabot Trail heads southwest from the Ingonishes to rejoin the Trans Canada Highway at South Gut St. Ann's. Along the way, you'll pass Wreck Cove (pop. 38) and the **Wreck Cove General Store** (tel. 902/929-2929). This is a good rest spot where you can buy cooked lobster, sandwiches, and camping and other supplies, fill up the gas tank, or simply get a cheap cup of coffee for 25¢. A covered picnic area with a barbecue pit is available from 7am to 9pm daily, June through September, or take yourself and your snack south to the pretty **Plaster Picnic Park** down the road about 8 miles (12.5km); it's on the left. Wreck Cove is about an hour and 10 minutes from Baddeck.

Before meeting the highway, the Cabot Trail passes by the tiny hamlet of St. Ann's (marked as Goose Cove on some maps) where you'll see the **Gaelic College of Celtic Folk Arts,** founded in 1938 (tel. 902/295-3411). Set on a 350-acre campus, it offers summer courses in the Gaelic language and music, playing the bagpipe and drum, Scottish country dancing, Cape Breton step dancing, and kilt making and weaving. At the end of the summer session there's a festival called the Gaelic Mod, with dance competitions and lots of merriment. If you pass by the first Thursday through Sunday in August, you'll catch it.

The college has an excellent craft shop, selling kilts, quilts, Nova Scotia songbooks, and much more. In the same building there is a small museum with exhibits on Scottish clans, life, dress, and music, as well as a statue of the "Cape Breton Giant," Angus MacAskell, who was seven feet, nine inches tall and weighed 425 pounds. The larger-than-life MacAskell was born in Scotland in 1825 and died in St. Ann's in 1863. Admission is $2 (children under 12 free), and hours are 8:30am to 5pm daily July and August, and Monday to Friday only from mid-May to June and September to mid-October (closed the rest of the year).

When you reach the Trans Canada Highway (Highway 105), you can go left (east) to Bras d'Or Lake, North Sydney, and Louisbourg, or right (west) to Baddeck and back to the Canso Causeway via Whycocomagh. Both routes are outlined below, beginning with Baddeck.

WHERE TO DINE

LOBSTER GALLEY, South Gut St. Ann's, at the intersection of the Trans Canada Hwy. 105 and the Cabot Trail (Exit 11). Tel. 902/295-3100.
  Cuisine: SEAFOOD. **Reservations:** Not needed.
  $ Prices: Appetizers $2–$7; main courses $7–$23; daily fish special $16. AE, MC, V.
  Open: May–June and Sept–Oct daily 11am–9pm; July–Aug daily 10am–10pm.
  Closed: Nov–Apr.
In South Gut St. Ann's, near the Gaelic College, the Lobster Galley is a good place for lunch or dinner. The Lobster Galley's forte is fresh lobster from its own pound and a wonderful view. The lobster special starts at $17 for a near one-pounder, and the price goes up with the size of the lobster. The concise menu also features toasted garlic cheese bread, seafood chowder, lobster bisque, St. Ann's Bay mussels, deep-fried bay scallops, pasta primavera, sole stuffed with scallops and crabmeat, poached or grilled Atlantic salmon, chicken and vegetable stir-fry, and vegetarian lentil casserole. And save room for the popular German apple cake or bumbleberry tart with English cream.

BADDECK

Baddeck (pronounced Bah-*deck*) is one of Cape Breton's most delightful old resort towns, famed for its tranquil beauty and fine views of St. Patrick's Channel, part of Bras d'Or Lake. Surprisingly, this small town (pop. 965) also has a place in aviation history, being the spot where one J. A. D. McCurdy made the first heavier-than-air flight in the British Empire, on February 23, 1909.

But Baddeck has an even greater claim to fame: Inventor Alexander Graham Bell came to spend his summers here, and Baddeck is now the proud site of the Alexander Graham Bell National Historic Site, with exhibits devoted to Bell's life and work.

Bell was a Scot, born in the old country in 1847, later moving to Canada and then to the U.S., but Baddeck was his choice of locations for a summer estate, called "Beinn Bhreagh" (Gaelic for "Beautiful Mountain") and still in the Bell family.

The inventor of the telephone was not a single-track genius by any means. Bell put his lively intelligence to work in the solution of medical and surgical problems, and to probe the mysteries of flight, besides his widely known experiments with electricity and speech devices.

WHAT TO SEE & DO

ALEXANDER GRAHAM BELL NATIONAL HISTORIC SITE, Chebucto St. (Rte. 205). Tel. 902/295-2069).

Although you can't visit "Beinn Bhreagh," the Alexander Bell estate, you can visit this great, modern museum, filled with exhibits detailing his life and work, particularly his experiments with the *Silver Dart,* an early airplane, and the HD-4, an early type of hydrofoil boat, the original hull of which is displayed. This is one of the most engaging museums I've ever visited. Through the use of photographs, childhood anecdotes, compelling exhibits, and an excellent film, it not only presents Bell's accomplishments but reveals his love for this part of the world and for his family, and paints a touching portrait of his long marriage to Mabel Hubbard. Both are buried at Beinn Bhreagh. Once you've seen the exhibits, go up to the museum's roof for the fine view of Baddeck Bay and Bras d'Or Lake.

Admission: Free.

Open: July–Sept daily 9am–9pm; the rest of the year daily 9am–5pm.

WHERE TO STAY

AUBERGE GISELE, 387 Shore Rd. (P.O. Box 132), Baddeck, NS, B0E 1B0. Tel. 902/295-2849. Fax 902/295-2033. 60 rms, 3 suites (all with bath), 3 housekeeping units. TV TEL

$ Rates: $50–$75 single; $55–$85 double; $95 housekeeping unit for two to four people; from $125 suite. Extra person $8. Children under 10 free. Honeymoon packages available. AE, ER, MC, V. **Closed:** Nov–Apr.

The Auberge Gisele is on the hillside along Shore Road. Forty-six of its rooms, including the three suites, are air-conditioned and in a striking new complex, a short stroll from the parking area. You can drive right to the door of the units in the older, equally comfortable but less modern complex. All rooms have hairdryers, and overlook the inn grounds or Bras d'Or Lake. The suites have kitchenettes and fireplaces. Cordial owner/manager Helen Sievers speaks English, French, and Ukrainian; her mother-in-law, Gisele, opened this place in the 1950s as a tourist lodge. Today's more elegant incarnation features a whirlpool, sauna, solarium, and the only licensed lounge in Baddeck, with a fireplace and dance floor. A conference room and coin-operated laundry are on the premises.

If you're just dropping in to dine, hours are 7:30 to 9:30am and 5:30 to 10pm. At dinner you may be surprised by some of the original and intriguing dishes served by the German chef; pasta, meat dishes, and fresh seafood served with garden vegetables range in price from $14 to $22. The dining room has a smoking and a no-smoking section (the former affords a view of the well-tended grounds; the latter is more intimate), and there's an inviting patio for dining al fresco.

DUFFUS HOUSE, 2878 Water St. (Box 427), Baddeck, NS, B0E 1B0. Tel. 902/295-2172. Fax 902/752-7737. 9 rms (3 with bath), 1 suite.

$ Rates (including breakfast): $50 single; $55–$70 double; $90 suite. Extra person $10. Children 6 and older are welcome. V. **Closed:** Mid-Oct to May.

Duffus House, right down at the water's edge with a private dock, is actually two houses, side by side. Between them, they offer nine guest rooms, three with private bath (the other six sharing three baths), and one suite with a private sitting room that opens onto a patio. Most rooms have sinks. Rates include a home-baked breakfast in a country kitchen. Both houses date from the mid-19th century and are filled with wood, forest colors, and rustic charm. Guests enjoy four sittings rooms, a library, and a garden and large pond out back. Duffus House, built around 1850 and lovingly run by Judy and John Langley, is on Water Street, one block off the main street. You can park on the street in front of the brown-shingled house or behind the white house that's beside it. The Baddeck boardwalk and the center of town are within walking distance.

INVERARY INN RESORT, Shore Rd. (P.O. Box 190), Baddeck, NS, B0E
1B0. Tel. 902/295-3500, or toll free 800/565-5660. Fax 902/295-3527. 137 rms, 3 efficiency apts. TV TEL

$ Rates: Mid-June to mid-Oct $81–$120 single; $89–$120 double. Extra person $8. Lower off-season rates available. AE, MC, V.

The Inverary Inn, a collection of tidy chocolate-brown buildings with white trim, has that lazy summer resort feel to it, with a squadron of red rockers on the porch and piles of magazines and paperbacks in the comfy living room. Set back from the road deep within its spacious grounds and flowering gardens are a private beach, pool, and children's playground, and there are complimentary boat cruises and bicycles, canoes, paddleboats, tennis courts, a hot tub, sauna, and indoor pool. Winter activities include cross-country skiing, snowshoeing, and tobogganing. Fishing trips, tours, and sleigh rides can be arranged. The Inverary's rooms are spread out: in the main lodge, in 10 cottages, including three efficiency apartments, and in a motel-type building. Family rooms are available. Some of the rooms have fireplaces; in some, the decor is country style, and in others it's modern.

The air-conditioned dining room is open to the public as well as inn guests for breakfast (7 to 10am) and dinner (5 to 10pm). At dinnertime feast on the seafood chowder, poached halibut and salmon with hollandaise sauce, dessert, and coffee, and expect a bill, with tax and tip, of about $35. The Fish House, also on the premises, offers lunch and dinner in a less formal atmosphere and specializes in . . . you guessed it.

TELEGRAPH HOUSE, Chebucto St. (P.O. Box 8), Baddeck, NS, B0E
1B0. Tel. 902/295-9988. 16 inn rms (12 with bath), 13 motel units, 5 cabins, 5 cottages. TV

$ Rates: $52–$75 single, $52–$85 double, depending on type of accommodation. Extra person $8. Rates drop Dec–May. AE, MC, V.

Telegraph House is best described as a country house, even though it's in the center of town. The big gray house with white shutters and an inviting front porch has been in the same family for four generations and, under the energetic supervision of Mary Dunlop, offers its guests "open fireplace" hospitality. Alexander Graham Bell stayed in Room 1 in the late 1880s (photographs of him hang there). A sweet twin room with a separate entrance is off the porch, but you have to climb two flights of stairs to get to the other rooms. Or you can stay out back in the higher-priced motel annex, in one of the pretty rooms with wood-beam ceilings, or in one of the cabins or cottages, one of which has a kitchenette. On all but the warmest days a fire crackles in the inn's living room fireplace.

The dining room specializes in country cooking, with lots of fresh seafood and "time-tested" desserts, including oatcakes made from a century-old recipe. On the menu you'll find fishcakes, barley-based chicken soup, shepherd's pie, chicken or seafood casserole, and (at dinner) baked Canada ham, roast turkey or chicken, meat loaf, and half a dozen fish and seafood dishes. Breakfast costs $3 to $6; lunch, $5 to $11; dinner main courses, $10 to $17. Breakfast is served from 7 to 11:30am, lunch from 11am to 2:30pm, and dinner from 5 to 8:30pm.

WHERE TO DINE

BELL BUOY, Chebucto St. Tel. 902/295-2581.
Cuisine: SEAFOOD. **Reservations:** Not needed.

$ Prices: Lunch items $5–$12; dinner appetizers $3–$7, main courses $9–$20; three-course dinner $28. AE, DC, DISC, ER, MC, V.

Open: Lunch daily 11am–5pm; dinner daily 5pm–10pm. **Closed:** Nov–May.

There are several eateries in the center of Baddeck and this is one of the most pleasant. At lunch, choose from sandwiches (clubs to seafood melts), a vegetable basket, stuffed filet of sole, Caesar salad, a cold lobster plate, burgers, or eggs Benedict. At dinner, go light with the Bluenose chowder and a lobster sandwich, or pull out all the stops with steamed mussels or marinated herring for starters, followed by a bountiful fish or seafood dinner, and a dessert like Grandma used to make. There's a menu for "little buoys and gulls." Service is courteous and quick. The Bell Buoy is licensed and open conveniently late.

HERRING CHOKER DELI, Hwy. 105. Tel. 902/295-2275.
Cuisine: DELI. **Reservations:** Not needed.
$ Prices: Most items $3–$7. No credit cards.
Open: Lunch daily.

If you're headed back to Whycocomagh and the Canso Causeway, the Herring Choker Deli, only six miles west of Baddeck, before the turnoff for the Cabot Trail, is an unexpected find. The deli and its companion bakery join forces to serve sandwiches on freshly baked bread, fresh-roast coffee, and such deli fare as smoked fish and meat, and Canadian cheeses. Soup and a sandwich eaten inside, on the deck, or take-away, runs about $5; so does lox and cream cheese on a bagel with tomato and onion. A "herring choker" is a fisherman.

THE SYDNEY AREA

The only city on Cape Breton Island, Sydney is Nova Scotia's third-largest metropolis (pop. 29,450) and one of Canada's steel manufacturing cities. It was founded by British and Loyalist settlers in 1785 and over the years has attracted a rich variety of immigrants, including Irish, Scottish, French, Spanish, Portuguese, Ukrainian, Lebanese, Polish, and others—an ethnic mix that is reflected in its cuisine and cultural activities. St. Philip's, in Sydney, is the only African orthodox church in Canada.

In the 20th century, Sydney figured prominently in a couple of historic events: From here in early March 1909, Adm. Robert Peary departed on his successful expedition to the North Pole, and it was to Sydney that he returned. And in May 1915, the survivors of the torpedoed *Lusitania* landed in Sydney.

In the seaport town of North Sydney (pop. 7,820), 15 miles from Sydney, Newfoundland-bound ferries depart for Port aux Basques and Argentia. And 17 miles from Sydney, in Sydney Mines (pop. 8500), you'll find one of the finest bed-and-breakfasts and dining rooms in Nova Scotia, the Gowrie House, a convenient base for day trips to the Fortress of Louisbourg and the Miners' Museum in Glace Bay.

WHAT TO SEE & DO

Check to see if the Rankin Family or other well-known Nova Scotia singers or fiddlers are performing at the **Savoy,** the 1928 Victorian-style theater on Lower Union Street in Glace Bay, and take in a show (tel. 902/849-1999).

FORTRESS OF LOUISBOURG NATIONAL HISTORIC SITE, Hwy. 22, Louisbourg. Tel. 902/733-2280.

The great Fortress of Louisbourg is a historical curiosity. Construction began shortly after the Treaty of Utrecht (1713) took away the French bases in Newfoundland, and Cape Breton, another French possession, became the country's major base for cod fishing in the Grand Banks. A prosperous commercial town grew up within the massive fortified enclosure, and while the fortifications looked impregnable and daunting to the untrained eye, bad positioning of the fort virtually predestined it to be captured. When the English laid siege to the place in 1745, the design flaws were immediately apparent and the fortress fell in less than two months. The peace treaty handed the defeated stronghold right back to its French defenders, but by 1758 Louisbourg was under siege by the English once again and this time was lost for good.

Proven to be of limited usefulness, the great fortifications were blown up and the French town abandoned, but when Cape Breton's coal mines were shut down in the 1960s, a large and hearty force of workers was free to begin resurrecting the fort and town as they had been two centuries before, to create the Canadian government's largest historical reconstruction project. Today visitors to the Fortress of Louisbourg National Historic Site can easily picture themselves in the prosperous French base. In summer, its streets, houses, kitchen gardens, workshops, and storerooms are filled with more than 100 people in period dress and their accoutrements from long ago. Bread is baked daily in the old ovens, chickens and geese waddle here and there, and the inns and taverns serve meals and refreshments of the kind popular when Louisbourg flourished. This is Canada's best time machine.

If it's a clear day as you zoom down Highway 22 approaching the park, take a short detour to view the fortress from across the harbor at Lighthouse Point; the road will be to the left before you reach the center of the modern town of Louisbourg. This spot is one of the best places to photograph the fortress and grasp its grand dimensions. When you arrive at the fortress, park at the Visitor's Centre, buy your tickets, and take the time to view the exhibit on the ramp to the lower level. Then board the free bus, which will take you the mile or two to the site. Maps, booklets, and the people of Louisbourg themselves will fill you in on everything, from the colony's history to the crafts they are pursuing. You can easily spend three or four hours opening doors and exploring buildings and buttonholing guards in the "Bastion du Roi" (the central part of the fortress) with questions about where the soldiers slept, what they ate, why they couldn't marry, and what they had to do to be tossed in the guardhouse.

To get the most out of your visit, you have to plan ahead: Come early in the day; wear shoes that will be comfortable on rough, cobbled streets; and without fail, bring a sweater or windbreaker and preferably some waterproof garment, since fog and drizzle can sweep in unexpectedly.

Admission: $6.50 adults, $3.50 children over 5, $16 family pass covering two adults and their children.

Open: June daily 9:30am–5pm; July–Aug daily 9am–6pm; after Sept 1, hours revert to those of June (limited access during off-season). A sign on Highway 22 well north of Louisbourg warns you of current closing times, but the best way to avoid disappointment is to come in the morning, or at least right after lunch.

MINERS' MUSEUM, Glace Bay, 22 miles (35km) from Louisbourg. Tel. 902/849-4522.

For an inside look at the industry that shaped industrial Cape Breton, take a 20-minute guided tour of the coal mine at the modern Miners' Museum in Glace Bay (pop. 20,000). The tours are conducted by retired miners, many of whom have spent most of their lives working in the mines. It's damp and cool down below, and the subterranean tour is not for those with bad backs (expect low ceilings); but those who take it will be rewarded with thorough explanations of the coal-mining process and the fascinating tales of the experienced guide. Protective clothing is provided, but you should wear sturdy, comfortable shoes and bring a sweater (it's 50°F underground). In the Miner's Village, you'll find reconstructed miners' homes from 1850 and 1900, a small company store, and a restaurant serving home-cooked meals at reasonable prices. It's open from 9am to 10pm, mid-June through September only. Inquire about concerts by the excellent mining chorus, The Men of the Deeps. When you get to Glace Bay, just follow the many signs a mile to the museum; they're plentiful.

Admission (including the film, which you should see before the tour): $2.75 adults, $1.75 children. Extra charge for mine tour $2.25 adults, $1.25 children.

Open: Early June–early Sept daily 10am–6pm (to 7pm Tues); the rest of the year Mon–Fri 9am–4pm.

WHERE TO STAY & DINE

GOWRIE HOUSE BED & BREAKFAST, 139 Shore Rd., Sydney Mines, NS, B1V 1A6. Tel. 902/544-1050. 10 rms (4 with bath).

$ Rates (including full breakfast): $51–$68 single; $58–$75 double; from $110 suite. Extra person $12. MC, V. **Closed:** Nov–Mar.

⭐ Frommer's has received many letters of praise about the Gowrie House, so it comes with multiple recommendations. The house, built between 1820 and 1830, remained in the same family until 1975, when the current owners bought it. There are four guest rooms in the gray-shingled main house, set in five acres of exquisite grounds with towering trees. They are decorated with an impressive mix of antiques and other collectibles, and share two full baths. The four suites, in the garden house behind the main house, have rich wall coverings, queen-size beds, working fireplaces, television, and private bath; one is decorated solely with pre-1870 Cape Breton furniture. The inn's dining room serves a four-course dinner with a meat or fish main course nightly, June through September. The price is $32, and there is only one seating at 7:30pm, so reservations are a must. The amiable innkeepers, Clifford Matthews (also the chef) and Ken Tutty, inspire interaction among the guests. Gowrie

House, which is no-smoking, is five minutes away from the Newfoundland ferries, and 45 minutes from the Miner's Museum and Fortress of Louisbourg.

HEADING BACK TO THE MAINLAND

From the eastern reaches of Cape Breton, including Sydney Mines, North Sydney, and Louisbourg, two routes lead back to the Canso Causeway and the mainland.

VIA IONA

Highway 223 follows the shore of St. Andrew's Channel to Grand Narrows, where there's a bridge across the Barra Strait to the village of Iona (pop. 120) (before autumn 1993, a small ferryboat got people across). Iona is home to the 43-acre, open-air **Nova Scotia Highland Village Museum,** 10 historic buildings on a hillside overlooking the Barra Strait that depict the life of the early Scottish settlers in the region (tel. 902/725-2272). **Highland Village Day** is celebrated here the first Saturday in August.

Where to Stay and Dine

HIGHLAND HEIGHTS INN, Rte. 223 (P.O. Box 19), Iona, NS, B0A 1L0. Tel. 902/725-2360. Fax 902/725-2800. 26 rms (all with bath). **Directions:** At the Barra Strait, take a short ride over the bridge (or on the Little Narrows ferry, if it's running), then turn right.

$ Rates: $62 single; $68 double. Extra person $8. Packages available. MC, V. **Closed:** Late Oct–May.

Adjacent to the Nova Scotia Highland Village Museum and along the Bras d'Or scenic drive, the Highland Heights Inn can provide lodging, meals (including a picnic lunch), bicycles, a walking map, a great view, and the Cape Breton hospitality of hosts Sheila and Bruce MacNeil and their staff. Each motel-style room has two double beds and a full bath. The licensed dining room, open from 7am to 9pm, features country cooking, seafood specialties, and homemade breads and pastries. The Canso Causeway is 50 minutes away.

VIA ST. PETERS

The other route west from North Sydney is Highway 4 south and west to St. Peters (pop. 670), a historic town on St. Peters Bay. The beauty of the little town is best appreciated from across the bay at Battery Park. As you drive into St. Peters, take the road to the left immediately before the canal, which was dug in 1854. Along with a great view you'll find picnic tables and a few signposts describing the history of the town. Staying the night is no problem (see below).

From St. Peters, Highway 4 goes east to Port Hawkesbury and Port Hastings, where it joins the Trans Canada (Highway 105) to cross the Canso Causeway back to the mainland. The Nova Scotia mainland is filled with great beauty, but everyone leaving Cape Breton Island feels a pang when it comes time to say good-bye.

Where to Stay and Dine

INN ON THE CANAL, P.O. Box 9, St. Peters, NS, B0E 3B0. Tel. 902/535-2200. Fax 902/535-2784. 20 rms (all with bath), 1 cabin. TV TEL

$ Rates: Room or cabin $60 for one to four people. AE, MC, V.

This big log lodge, beside the bridge, only ⅓ mile (.5km) east of town, opened in 1989, and has been busy ever since. The rooms are comfortable, with soft colors, two double beds, and a full bath; the 14 upstairs rooms have cedar paneling. The cabin in back is perfectly perched above Bras d'Or Lake; it has tongue-and-groove paneling, a carpeted sitting area, a smallish bedroom with three-quarter bed, and a full bath (no kitchen). About this place, one person wrote in the guest book: "It's as good as home." The pretty, licensed dining room does pride itself on home-cooked meals and friendly service. It's open from 7am to 9pm in summer, until 7pm the rest of the year. Occasionally the inn hosts country bands or a square dance. The inn is only half an hour from the Canso Causeway. It books up early, so call ahead.

NEW BRUNSWICK

Just between us, vacationers who blast through New Brunswick in their rush to reach other Maritime Provinces are missing out: This province is rich in heritage inns that rival any in Canada for accommodation and cuisine. It's rich in savings (just cross the border from Maine and compare), and in travel destinations, including some of the oldest cities and towns in Canada, founded by Loyalist (and British) refugees from the American Revolution.

Consider the lovely old summer resort town of St. Andrews (the Cape Cod of Canada), the genteel reaches of FDR's beloved Campobello Island, and the city of Saint John, home of the Fundy tides, highest in the world. Inland, there are the delights of the tiny artists' hideaway, Gagetown, and the province's small, pretty capital, Fredericton, on the bank of the Saint John River.

The beaches along the shores of the Northumberland Strait beckon wayfarers with "some of the warmest waters north of Florida." All told, New Brunswick has 1,400 miles of coastline.

Small French towns and villages dot New Brunswick's northern shores, which are peopled by the descendants of those Acadians who were once driven from their traditional homes. You may be surprised to learn that French-speakers make up almost 38% of New Brunswick's population, and the province is officially bilingual.

SEEING NEW BRUNSWICK

INFORMATION For tourist information, from anywhere in Canada or the continental U.S., dial toll free 800/561-0123 to get the New Brunswick tourist authorities. In addition, it's good to know that provincial tourist bureaus located at major entry points will assist you in finding accommodations during the summer through their "Dial-a-Night" hotel reservations service, available free at any bureau. For printed information, contact Tourism New Brunswick, P.O. Box 12345, Fredericton, NB, E3B 5C3.

Whether you enter New Brunswick from the state of Maine or from Québec, remember that this province and all the other Atlantic Provinces except Newfoundland and Labrador operate on Atlantic time, which is one hour ahead of Eastern time. Set your watch ahead one hour as you cross the border, summer or winter.

A NOTE ON TAXES One costly detail is the 11% sales tax added to all restaurant and hotel prices, plus an additional 7% goods and services tax. The rates quoted in the New Brunswick chapter of this book do not include tax unless specifically stated. Very few items are exempt, and posted prices never include the sales tax. Avoid being unpleasantly surprised by figuring an additional 18% into the stated price. Exceptions include some articles of clothing, footwear, bed-and-breakfasts with three or fewer beds, camping fees, and, of all things, take-out food orders.

GETTING THERE New Brunswick, the "gateway to Atlantic Canada," is the crossroads linking the rest of Canada to Prince Edward Island, Nova Scotia, Newfoundland, and Labrador.

WHAT'S SPECIAL ABOUT NEW BRUNSWICK

Bilingual Culture
- ☐ Officially a bilingual province, New Brunswick is 38% French-speaking (97% on the Acadian Peninsula).
- ☐ The French-language Université de Moncton.
- ☐ Living history in re-created villages—British and French.

Natural Phenomena
- ☐ Reversing Falls in Saint John.
- ☐ The Fundy tides at Fundy National Park.
- ☐ Magnetic Hill in Moncton.
- ☐ The tidal bore on the Petitcodiac River in Moncton.

World-Class Attractions
- ☐ Roosevelt Campobello International Park, incorporating the beloved summer home of FDR.
- ☐ King's Landing Historical Settlement, on the St. John River near Fredericton.

Heritage Inns
- ☐ Some of Canada's best.
- ☐ Historic houses.
- ☐ Gastronomic feasts.

Beach Towns
- ☐ St. Andrews by the Sea, the Cape Cod of Canada.
- ☐ Shediac, home of the Lobster Festival in July.

Fun Ferry Links
- ☐ Letete to Deer Island to Campobello Island.
- ☐ Blacks Harbour to Grand Manan.
- ☐ Free provincial ferries between Saint John and Gagetown.
- ☐ Saint John to Digby, Nova Scotia.
- ☐ Cape Tormentine to Borden, P.E.I.

By Plane   Within New Brunswick and the other Atlantic Provinces, the local carriers are **Air Nova,** the commuter partner of Air Canada (tel. toll free 800/776-3000 in the U.S., 800/565-3940 in Maritime Canada, 800/563-5151 in Newfoundland), with destinations in Fredericton, Saint John, Moncton, Bathurst, and St. Leonard; and **Air Atlantic,** the commuter partner of Canadian Airlines International (tel. toll free 800/426-7000 in the U.S., 800/665-1177 in Canada), with destinations in Fredericton, Saint John, Moncton, Charlo, and Chatham.

By Rail   VIA Rail Canada will carry you by rail between Rivière-du-Loup, Québec, via Matapédia, Campbellton, Bathurst, Newcastle, Moncton, and Sackville to Amherst, N.S. The train is the *Ocean,* which departs daily on its run from Montréal. There are sleeping cars as the trip from Rivière-du-Loup to Moncton takes about 10½ hours.

Within New Brunswick, railcars make the 87-mile (141km) trip between Moncton and Saint John three times a week (Monday, Thursday, and Saturday) in less than two hours. For more specific information, call VIA Rail (tel. toll free 800/561-3949 in the U.S., 800/561-3952 in the Maritime Provinces, 800/361-5390 in Québec) between 6am and midnight.

By Bus   New Brunswick's provincewide bus network is served by the **SMT** company, with headquarters in Saint John (tel. 506/458-3500). SMT buses connect with the daily Greyhound coaches that come direct from Washington via New York, Boston, and Portland. From St. Stephen, you can catch a bus to Moncton, or Amherst, N.S., or any point along that route, including St. Andrews, St. George, Blacks Harbour (for Grand Manan Island), or Saint John. Change buses in Saint John for points farther along: Moncton, Fredericton, or destinations in Nova Scotia or Québec.

By Car   From Maine, the best way to come to New Brunswick (in this writer's opinion) is via U.S. 1 to Me. 189 to Lubec. Cross from Lubec to Campobello Island;

AN IMPORTANT NOTE ON PRICES

Unless stated otherwise, **the prices cited in this guide are given in Canadian dollars,** which is good news for U.S. travelers because the Canadian dollar is worth 25% less than the American dollar, but buys nearly as much. As we go to press, $1 Canadian is worth 75¢ U.S., which means that your $100-a-night hotel room will cost only U.S. $75, and your $6 breakfast costs only U.S. $4.50.

Here's a quick table of equivalents:

Canadian $	U.S. $
$ 1	$ 0.75
5	3.75
10	7.50
20	15.00
50	37.50
80	60.00
100	75.00
200	150.00

from here, take the ferry to Deer Island, and then the free government ferry from Deer Island to the mainland. It's scenic and historic—and a New Brunswick–style adventure (you'll happen upon other free ferries in your travels here). Full details appear a bit farther on in this section.

Entering via St. Stephen, take I-95 to Me. 9, to Calais, Maine, whence two bridges lead across the St. Croix River into St. Stephen, New Brunswick.

Those headed straight for New Brunswick's capital city of Fredericton may want to take I-95 to Me. 6 to Vanceboro—on the New Brunswick side it's St. Croix (and nearby McAdam). But think twice before passing up the delightful shores of the Bay of Fundy.

From Québec City and the south shore of the St. Lawrence, the Trans Canada Highway (Highway 105) crosses the wilds of Québec and northwestern New Brunswick to enter the St. John River Valley, and thence to Fredericton. If you've just come all the way around Québec's Gaspé Peninsula, cross via the bridge at Pointe-à-la-Croix to Campbellton, and head south on Highway 11.

Most visitors to New Brunswick arrive by car from Maine. If you're among them, note that the road leads directly to one of the province's loveliest destinations: Campobello Island. Not far away is the more remote island getaway, Grand Manan, and, on the mainland, the charming seaside town of St. Andrews.

GETTING AROUND You can rent a car at the airport in Saint John, Fredericton, or Moncton. For instance, contact **Tilden Car Rentals,** to name one company, in Saint John (tel. 506/696-3340), in Fredericton (tel. 506/446-4105), or in Moncton (tel. 506/382-6104). Call Tilden direct at these numbers or dial toll free 800/328-4567 to National Car Rental within the U.S. Other car rental companies, such as Avis, Budget, and Hertz are well represented in New Brunswick; call your local branch for the correct number.

1. CAMPOBELLO ISLAND & ST. STEPHEN

If you are driving into New Brunswick from Maine, as most people do, the two first points of entry you come to are Campobello Island, the summer home of Franklin and Eleanor Roosevelt, and St. Stephen, the birthplace of the chocolate bar.

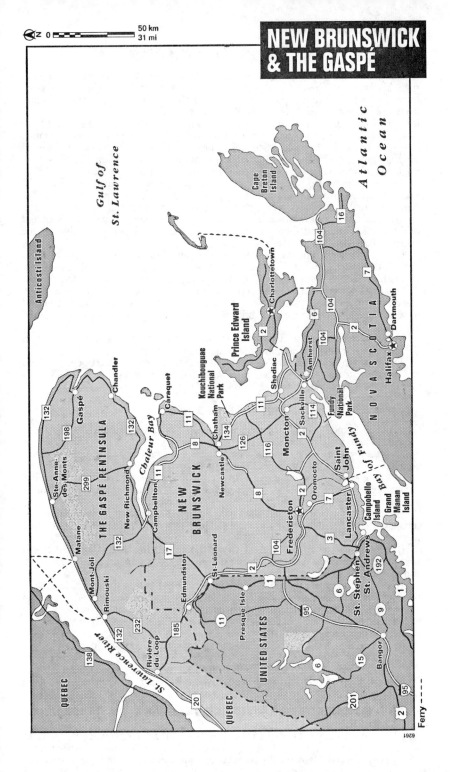

NEW BRUNSWICK & THE GASPÉ

50 km
31 mi

Ferry – – – –
6261

CAMPOBELLO ISLAND

A Canadian island with an Italian-sounding name on which an American president spent his summers: These little mysteries are not at all as difficult to believe as they first seem. Campobello is indeed part of Canada, even though the major access road comes from Lubec, Maine. And the "Italian" name is nothing more than the name of a former Nova Scotian governor—William Campbell—with two "o's" added for panache. When the island was granted to Capt. William Owen by Governor Campbell in 1767, it was still part of Nova Scotia. The province of New Brunswick was founded 17 years later, in 1784, when large numbers of United Empire Loyalists fled New England to live in King George III's still-loyal dominions to the north.

Franklin Delano Roosevelt's father, James, bought some land on the island in 1883, at a time when many important city people were building summer "cottages" at Bar Harbor, Passamaquoddy Bay, and other northern American coastal locations. Young Franklin—to solve that last mystery—came here long before he was president of the United States, and spent many a summer rowing, paddling, and sailing on the waters and hiking through the woods.

In 1920, FDR ran for the vice presidency—and lost. Taking on a banking job instead, he looked forward to a relaxing summer at Campobello in 1921. On August 10 of that year the first signs of sickness showed, and two weeks later the doctors diagnosed FDR's crippling disease as polio. When he left the island in September, he had no way of knowing that the few more times he would see the summer cottage and his Campobello friends would be brief weekend visits—as president of the United States.

In 1960, the movie *Sunrise at Campobello,* starring Greer Garson and Ralph Bellamy as Eleanor and Franklin Roosevelt, was filmed here.

The tourist information center, just over the bridge to your right, is open from 9am to 7pm, May to mid-October (tel. *506/752-2997*). Campobello Island is 243 miles (392km) from Portland, Maine.

WHAT TO SEE & DO

Campobello Island is only three miles wide and 10 miles long, and it's a pleasure to drive it, bike it, walk it, and swim off it.

At **Herring Cove Provincial Park,** there is a camping area, a nine-hole golf course, and a mile-long sandy beach with unsupervised swimming.

At **Friar's Head,** park and walk up the hill to the observation deck, which has interesting descriptions of what you're gazing out at, including "the Bay of Fundy, known for its bad temper and bountiful seafood harvest."

Walk out to the bog, which is filled with bird song and low-growing vegetation—sphagnum moss, cloudberries, and shrubs. There's an observation deck overlooking the bog and rocky coastline.

Drive all the way to the end of the island to admire **East Quoddy Head Lighthouse,** the most photographed lighthouse in eastern Canada; as an added treat, you might sight some sea life, too.

You're sure to notice the graceful fishing weirs used to trap schools of herring in these waters. The weirs, circles of long poles stuck into the seabed and projecting above the waterline, form frames for the netting that encloses the circle. Once in the weir's net circle, few fish find their way out before the fishing boats come and lift the nets, catching tons at a time.

Be prepared to battle blackflies and mosquitoes if you come in June.

For some indoor activity, look in pretty **St. Anne's Anglican Church,** in Welshpool, where the Roosevelt family worshiped when they stayed here. Also in Welshpool, shop at **Island What-Nots,** where local arts and crafts are sold on consignment.

ROOSEVELT CAMPOBELLO INTERNATIONAL PARK, Rte. 774. Tel. 506/752-2922.

The day-to-day lives of the great and powerful are fascinating to explore in detail, and a visit to the Roosevelt house on Campobello gives one a peek at the early years of this incredibly courageous man who went on to become governor of New York and president of the United States after having been crippled by polio. It is no less intriguing to see how a well-to-do family spent its summers at the turn of the century, with long and leisurely days filled by sports, games, and family fun. Servants saw to the chores, and even they must have enjoyed getting away from the city to such a beautiful spot. The Roosevelt Cottage is now part of a vast 2,800-acre nature preserve administered jointly by Canadian and American parks services. Guides at the reception center will point out the path to the 34-room Roosevelt Cottage, purchased for Eleanor and Franklin by his mother in 1909, but be sure to see the 15-minute film, *Beloved Island*, with an introduction by FDR, Jr., before you go. They can also map out various walks (8½ miles' worth) in the park. Also don't miss the oval picture window in the nearby Kuhn Cottage, also in the park and open to the public. Prior to your visit, you may want to write for information to Roosevelt Campobello International Park, P.O. 97, Lubec, ME 04652; or P.O. Box 9, Welshpool, NB, E03 3H0.

Admission: Free to the park and the Roosevelt cottage.

Open: Sat prior to U.S. Memorial Day (the Sat after Canadian Victoria Day) through U.S. Columbus Day (Canadian Thanksgiving), daily 10am–6pm Atlantic (Campobello) time (9am–5pm Eastern time); last cottage tour 4:45pm. **Closed:** Mid-Oct to late May.

WHERE TO STAY

There are half a dozen places to stay on Campobello Island, and the tourist information center has information on and directions to them all.

LUPIN LODGE, Rte. 774 (P.O. Box 16), Welshpool, NB, E0G 3H0. Tel. 506/752-2487. 10 rms (all with bath).

$ Rates: $62–$72 single with bath; $72–$125 double with bath. Extra person $20. AE, MC, V. **Closed:** Late Oct–May.

Located on a hill between the park and Welshpool, the Lupin Lodge offers the "poshest" accommodations on Campobello, with rooms that combine log construction with tongue-and-groove interiors. The restaurant is open from noon to 9pm.

OWEN HOUSE, Rte. 774, Welshpool, Campobello, NB, E0G 3H0. Tel. 506/752-2977. 8 rms (4 with bath), 1 suite. **Directions:** Drive to Welshpool and turn left after St. Anne's Church; take an immediate right and you'll be in the driveway.

$ Rates (including full breakfast): $50 single without bath, $55 single with bath; $55 double without bath, $65 double with bath. Extra person $15. V. **Closed:** Late Oct–May.

Owen House (ca. 1835), a retreat on a point of land overlooking the bay, is popular with artists, photographers, and bicyclists. (Greer Garson stayed here during the filming of *Sunrise at Campobello*.) The owner, Joyce Morrell, is a painter whose still lifes and local scenes are filled with vibrant colors. The house provides inviting nooks for guests, including a glassed-in porch accented with models of sailing ships and driftwood, a sitting room made cozy with a nightly fire in the hearth, and a beautifully set dining room where a breakfast of limitless pancakes, sausage, juice, and coffee is served family-style at 8:30am. The old-fashioned bedrooms have wallpaper, white curtains at the windows, single or double beds, and board floors. The four bedrooms on the second floor all have private baths (Room 1 overlooks the water; Room 4, in back, has a bay window), and the smaller four on the third floor share a bath with a shower. The two-room suite is ideal for families. Reserve early.

WHERE TO DINE

FRIAR'S BAY RESTAURANT, Welshpool. Tel. 506/752-2056.
Cuisine: HOME COOKING. **Reservations:** Not needed.
$ Prices: Appetizers $1–$3; main courses $6–$18. V.
Open: Daily 8am–8pm, often later in July–Aug. **Closed:** Late Oct–May.
Friar's Bay Restaurant sits on the beach side of the road, not far from the international

park. Made of rough wood boards inside and out to preserve Campobello's woodsy feeling, it has modern bay windows so you can take in the marvelous sea view. Gull-topped posts and fishing weirs appear and disappear in the morning mist as you start the day with a filling country breakfast for about $5. At lunch or dinnertime, equally economical and filling repasts are served up, and can be accompanied by beer, wine, or a cocktail. The Canadian baked ham is excellent, and you can also get chicken, lobster, smoked mackerel, pollock, or haddock, all served with a yeast roll, potato, and vegetables. The waitress is likely to call you "dear," no matter what your age is. The same folks run the motel across the road.

AN EXCURSION TO DEER ISLAND

As long as the weather's not too stormy, a ferry operates between Campobello and Deer Island, a small fishing community with some houses, one road, and a little café. Signs direct motorists to the ferry docks, where the boat leaves about every 1½ hours—seven trips a day in each direction, lasting about 45 minutes. The ferry, actually a steel barge pushed by a determined tug, has the capacity to carry 15 full-size cars, even motorcoaches, casually attached to the side. Fees to or from Campobello are $11 per car and driver, and $2 for each additional passenger up to a maximum charge of $16 per car.

When you get to the ferry dock (whether on Campobello or Deer Island), don't be surprised if you're all alone. That's a good sign: You'll be first in line. If the ferry's not running that day, a posted sign will tell you so. Ferries normally operate from 9:15am (first trip from Deer Island) and 10am (first trip from Campobello) to 6:15pm and 7pm (last trips, respectively); the ferry runs only from the last weekend in June until mid-September. Nonscheduled trips can be arranged for several vehicles, although you'll have to dicker over the fare. By the way, those lining up at Deer Island dock for the ferry to Campobello should make sure they're in the proper waiting lane. The ferry to Eastport, Maine, departs this dock as well. If the Campobello ferry isn't working for some reason, you can take the ferry to Eastport (20 minutes), founded in 1780 and one of the finest deep-water ports on the East Coast, and drive another 45 minutes to Campobello from there. For more information, contact **East Coast Ferries** (tel. 506/747-2159).

Between Deer Island and Letete, New Brunswick (on the mainland), there's a free-of-charge ferry service run by the government, in operation continuously from 7am to 10pm during July and August, to 9pm the rest of the year, weather permitting.

ST. STEPHEN

Residents of Maine and New Brunswick, while the best of friends, cling to memories of their ancestors' fervent support for, respectively, George Washington and George III. With the success of the American Revolution, United Empire Loyalists flocked across the frontier into Canada so as not to be disloyal to the monarch. "Loyalist" and "Revolutionary" towns preserve this good-natured rivalry.

But things are different in St. Stephen (pop. 5,100) and its neighbor, Calais, Maine (sounds a lot like "callous"). Folks in these two towns, cheek-by-jowl on the St. Croix River, make a point of telling visitors how they ignored the affinities of *both* sides during the War of 1812. St. Stephen even supplied powder-poor Calais with gunpowder for its Fourth of July celebrations! By the time the war came, families in the twin towns were so closely intermarried that no one wanted to take the time to sort out who should be loyal to whom.

A New Brunswick **information center** (tel. 506/466-7390) is handily located on King Street, half a mile from Customs. Besides the helpful staff and large selection of brochures, it has a money-exchange counter and a gift shop selling provincial arts and crafts. There's a picnic area outside. Hours are 8am to 9pm daily May through Labor Day and from 9am to 7pm daily after Labor Day to mid-October. St. Stephen is 232 miles (374km) from Portland, Maine.

WHAT TO SEE & DO

These days residents celebrate their unique "plague on both their houses" philosophy with an **International Festival** in the first week of August. The two bridges over the river between the two towns are thronged with merrymakers moving back and forth—through the watchful but benevolent eye of Customs, of course—and Canadian and American flags fly everywhere.

Loyalists of a different sort also flock to St. Stephen during the International Festival, these to attend the chocolate fantasy dinner, the "choctail" hour, or the great chocolate-chip-cookie-decorating affair, all part of the annual **Chocolate Fest.** This chocolate extravaganza is justifiable as St. Stephen is home to **Ganong Chocolatier,** which invented the chocolate bar in 1910—quite some claim to fame.

Founded in 1873 and Canada's oldest candy company, Ganong was Canada's first company to make lollipops, in 1895, and to sell heart-shape boxes of chocolates on Valentine's Day, in 1932. Factory tours are given only during Chocolate Fest, and only by advance reservation. The store, at 73 Milltown Rd., near the U.S. border, displays and sells more than 80 kinds of chocolates (try the "chicken bones," a favorite since 1885); it is open 9am to 8pm Monday through Friday, 9am to 5pm Saturday, and 11am to 5pm Sunday (tel. 506/465-5611).

WHERE TO STAY

BLAIR HOUSE, 38 Prince William St. (P.O. Box 112), St. Stephen, NB, E3L 2W9. Tel. 506/466-2233. Fax 506/466-5636. 3 rms (all with bath).
$ Rates (including full English breakfast): $35–$40 single; $40–$53 double. Extra person $10. MC, V.

The Blair House offers a relaxed, freewheeling ambience behind an elegant mid-19th-century facade. Each of the bedrooms has a full bath and ceiling fan; the two with a double bed are roomiest. The real draws here are hosts Betty and Bryan Whittingham, a warm, outgoing couple originally from England. Don't be surprised if they offer you kippers for breakfast. You can also look forward to tea and cookies on arrival, tea or coffee in your room in the morning, and an evening snack. Besides credit cards, the Whittinghams accept traveler's checks and U.S. dollars for payment. The house, which is set back from the street and has an English garden in front, is only 3½ blocks from the town's main street.

WHERE TO DINE

PIZZA DELIGHT, Milltown Blvd. Tel. 506/466-4147.
Cuisine: PIZZA. **Reservations:** Not needed.
$ Prices: Most items $3–$13. No credit cards.
Open: Sun–Thurs 11am–11pm, Fri–Sat 11am–1am.

If you've got kids in tow (and even if you don't), you may be happy to know there's a Pizza Delight in the heart of downtown. Its location right on the water is pleasant, and its hours are conveniently long. Besides pizza (prices start at less than $3), the menu also features pasta and sandwiches. There's outdoor seating.

---

2. ST. ANDREWS

19 miles (30km) SE of St. Stephen, 50 miles (80km) W of Saint John

GETTING THERE   Head east from St. Stephen on Highway 1, and turn south on Highway 127, to reach what may be the most delightful town in all New Brunswick.

ESSENTIALS   The St. Andrews Tourist Bureau is on Highway 1, on the outskirts of town (tel. 506/466-4858). You can stop here or drive into town and visit the St. Andrews Welcome Centre, 46 Reed Ave., at Harriet Street. It's open daily from 9am to 6pm in May and September, to 8pm in July and August (tel. 506/529-3000). The rest of the year, contact the Chamber of Commerce, in the same building (tel. 506/529-3555), or write the chamber, P.O. Box 89, St. Andrews, NB, G0Y 2X0.

The story of the founding of St. Andrews (pop. 1,800) is as romantic as the pretty town's seaside location. Loyalists in disagreement with the American Revolution moved north out of American towns to the safe harbor of British-controlled land at Fort George (later Castine, Maine). Now, Castine is a breathtakingly beautiful spot, and when these same Loyalists found that the new British-American boundary was to be the St. Croix River (at St. Stephen) and not the Penobscot (at Bucksport, Maine), they were at a loss. But they found a way. Pushing and shoving their newly built wood-frame houses onto ships, they *sailed* the entire town northward until they were again in British lands. The place they picked for their new—and final—settlement was at the tip of a peninsula in Passamaquoddy Bay: St. Andrews.

Luckily, the hardy and enterprising St. Andrians were not disturbed again, even during the War of 1812. The town had several blockhouses built for defense, but the war never reached Passamaquoddy. Prosperity came after the war with the shipbuilding trade, but as the century wore on and iron ships replaced wooden ones, St. Andrews felt the weight of stagnation. Just in time it found a new industry: tourism.

The great Canadian Pacific Railway Company owned the line that ran from Québec to the southern New Brunswick coast, and they put up a grand hotel in St. Andrews. Company directors and managers built sumptuous summer "cottages" in the vicinity, and today St. Andrews tells its history in its houses: Many of the 90 or so houses brought from Castine or erected about that time are still standing proudly, along with those raised by magnates in the 19th-century lumber and shipbuilding boom. These turn-of-the-century houses and the sumptuous, continually modernized Algonquin Hotel lend St. Andrews an air of gentility rare along the coast.

Today the town remains a summer visitors' haven, but it's beautiful in September and October, as well, and ever a wondrous place to admire the stars. Whenever you visit and however you choose to spend your time, you'll love it here.

WHAT TO SEE & DO

Take it easy. That's what a St. Andrews summer is all about. At your leisure, shop for crafts, dine, stroll, play golf, swim, or take boat tours or whale-watching or diving excursions in Passamaquoddy Bay.

Touring **Passamaquoddy Bay** is an adventure. Sandbars loll in the waters here and there, little evergreen-cloaked islets seem to float on the calm morning sea, and clouds of morning mist glide slowly along the shore. The frequent fogs bring a sense of mystery and romance, but they also bring a thrilling chill—sometimes just the thing to cool off a week of hot summer weather.

Like the Bay of Fundy, Passamaquoddy Bay is subject to the world's highest tides. The steepness of the shoreline, the narrowness, and the orientation of Fundy all contribute to the twice-daily rushing in and out of immense volumes of water.

If the weather's cool, **swimming** is available in the Algonquin's heated pool—at a small charge. If the weather's warm, though, indulge in a salty splash in the waters of **Katy's Cove.** While the cove, east of town, opens onto Passamaquoddy Bay, the small cove inlet keeps the cold tides from rushing in and chilling the water as one might expect.

Other good beaches—these open to the surf—are at the two provincial parks near St. Andrews. **Oak Bay Provincial Park** is on Highway 1 to the west, and **New River Beach** is to the east on the same road, past the town of St. George.

Hankering for a game of golf? The **Algonquin Golf Club's** nine- and 18-hole courses are open to the public, and you can rent clubs and carts (tel. 506/529-3062).

When you're strolling or driving around, be sure to see some of the old homes along Montague Street, and don't miss the **Greenock Presbyterian Church** (1824), at Montague and Edward Streets, a graceful and comely colonial structure with a unique steeple with a green oak emblazoned on it.

At the corner of King and Queen Streets, the **Sheriff Andrews House** (1820) is a restored home, now a museum, where student guides in period dress show you around for free. It's open from 9:30am to 4:30pm daily July through September (tel. 506/529-4470).

Cottage Craft Ltd., founded in 1915 and in the Ross family since 1945, represents 150 local knitters. The shop sells yarns, handwoven tweeds, handmade cardigans and pullovers, including the Fundy fisherman sweater and the traditional New Brunswick yoke sweater, wool jackets, short coats, stuffed animals made of wool and yarn, mittens, headbands, socks, and blankets. Sweaters for adults start at $115; for children, $55. It's open Monday through Saturday from 10am to 5pm (tel. 506/529-3190).

Blue Peter Books, 171 Water St. (tel. 506/529-4466), has a good selection of books on the Maritime Provinces, including some steeped in local color, like *Funny Fables of Fundy* and *The Miramichi Axe Murder.*

ATLANTIC SALMON CENTRE, on Chamcook Creek. Tel. 506/529-8889.
In a picturesque setting about five miles east of St. Andrews via Route 127, the Atlantic Salmon Centre gives visitors a close-up look at the "king of fish" in a natural spawning habitat. The modern interpretation center has exhibits on the Atlantic salmon, and a nature trail through the woods and along the creek.
Admission: $1.
Open: Spring and summer daily 10am–6pm; autumn Thurs–Mon 10am–5pm.
Closed: Winter.

HUNTSMAN AQUARIUM MUSEUM, Brandy Cove Rd. Tel. 506/529-4285.
Slightly northwest of town, this attraction takes you into the fascinating world of marine biological research as it's carried out here, in St. Andrews's largest industry after tourism. The "Please Touch" aquarium inhabited by starfish, sea cucumbers, lobsters, and the sea potato has become a family favorite. There is also an artistic seaweed exhibit and plenty of photographs. The seals are fed at 11am and 4pm.
Admission: $3.50 adults, $2.50 children, $3 seniors, $10 maximum family rate.
Open: May–June and Sept–Oct daily 10am–4:30pm; July–Aug daily 10am–6pm. **Closed:** Nov–Apr.

ROSS MEMORIAL MUSEUM, 188 Montague St., at King. Tel. 506/529-1824.
The Rev. Henry Phipps Ross and his wife, Sarah Juliette Ross, Quakers and American summer residents here, willed their 1824 neoclassic house and 87-acre estate to St. Andrews as a museum. The Rosses were collectors and world travelers (who died within eight days of each other in 1945), and the house is filled with antique furniture, carpets, paintings, and other decorative art objects. Juliette Ross was the daughter of the president of the Bradstreet firm that was to become Dun and Bradstreet. The house opened as a museum in 1980; from 1920 to 1934, it housed the Charlotte County Cottage Crafts, the dream child of Dr. Grace Helen Mowat.
Admission: Free.
Open: Late May–June and Sept to mid-Oct Tues–Sat 10am–4:30pm; July–Aug Tues–Sat 10am–4:30pm, Sun 1:30–4:30pm. **Closed:** Late Oct to mid-May.

ST. ANDREWS BLOCKHOUSE NATIONAL HISTORIC SITE, northwest end of Water St. No phone.
This is the sole surviving wood fortress of the 12 built along the coast of New Brunswick at the outbreak of the War of 1812. The original walls are 12 feet thick; the furnishings are reproductions. Centennial Park is across the street.
Admission: Free.
Open: June and the first couple of weeks in Sept daily 9am–5pm; July–Aug daily 9am–8pm.

WHERE TO STAY & DINE
HOTELS/INNS

ALGONQUIN HOTEL, 184 Adolphus St., St. Andrews by the Sea, St. Andrews, NB, E0G 2X0. Tel. 506/529-8823, or toll free 800/441-1414 in the U.S. Fax 506/529-4194. 250 rms and suites. MINIBAR TV TEL **Transportation:** Limousine transport from the Saint John airport, 70 miles (113km) away, by prior arrangement with the hotel, $29 per person one way.

$ Rates: $121–$166 single; $136–$181 double; from $235 suite for one to four people. Children 18 and under stay free in parents' room. Half board (breakfast and dinner) available for about $40 per person per day extra. Packages available. AE, CB, DC, DISC, ER, MC, V. **Closed:** Mid-Oct to mid-May.

⭐ The splendid Algonquin Hotel (1889) is an Elizabethan-inspired castle of white stucco, dark timbers, and a red-tile roof set in the midst of its own park and surrounded by myriad things to do. The rooms and suites, all different, are modern and comfortable, despite the hotel's age (105 and counting), and they all come with hairdryers. A new wing opened in 1993, with 45 pretty rooms and nine three-room suites; all have two queen-size beds, kitchenettes, and air conditioning. CP Hotels operates the Algonquin, as it has for the better part of the century, with top-flight food, service, and personal attention. The hotel may be out of your range, but do come by and see it, or browse the excellent gift shop.

Dining/Entertainment: Meals are served in the Passamaquoddy Veranda for lunch or dinner, or the adjoining glassed-in Van Horne Veranda, overlooking the front gardens; the lunch buffet is $12, Sunday brunch $18. There's also a pleasant, informal coffee shop, open 7am to 9pm daily. In the evening, wander down to the Dock Side Pub, where there's a band every night except Sunday, when it's closed. The Library Bar has piano music.

Services: Babysitting, room service, video rentals.

Facilities: 18-hole oceanside golf course, nine-hole woodland course, outdoor heated pool, tennis, biking, shuffleboard, aerobics classes, croquet on the lawn, rooftop garden; a health club with squash, racquetball, free weights, and a Jacuzzi; convention center.

BED-AND-BREAKFAST

PANSY PATCH, 59 Carleton St. (at Adolphus), St. Andrews, NB, E0G 2X0. Tel. 506/529-3834. Fax 506/529-4724. 2 rms (none with bath), 1 suite (with bath).

$ Rates (including full breakfast): $75 single or double; $150 suite. Extra person $15, child $10. MC, V. **Parking:** In the drive or on the street. **Closed:** Oct–May.

Located across the street from the Algonquin, the Pansy Patch looks like a miniature reflection of its neighbor, with its distinctive turret, white exterior, and green trim. The upstairs guest rooms are furnished with antiques and share a large bath. Breakfast is served in the glassed-in porch or on the back deck. A prix-fixe dinner is available for $30 with 24 hours' notice. On the premises, there is also a shop selling antiques and out-of-print and rare books. In fact, every item on the lower floor, including in the living room and dining room, is for sale! Call ahead to reserve a room, especially on weekends; they have a two-week cancellation policy. No smoking.

ROSSMOUNT INN, Rte. 127 (R.R. 2), St. Andrews, NB, E0G 2X0. Tel. 506/529-3351. Fax 506/529-1920. 17 rms (all with bath). **Directions:** Head a couple of miles from St. Andrews on Highway 127 headed north and east toward Bocabec.

$ Rates: $85 single; $95 double. Extra person $10. MC, V. **Closed:** Jan–May.

⭐ Perched on a hillside above the road, the three-story Rossmount Inn is set impressively on a wildflower-strewn lawn and furnished with period pieces and plush carpets. The front guest rooms are particularly popular, and no-smoking rooms are available. On the 87-acre estate, guests enjoy an outdoor swimming pool with licensed patio, nature trails, and fields of lupines. Children are welcome. Webber and Alice Burns are the cordial hosts.

The inn's acclaimed, pretty dining room is open to guests and the public. Meals are prepared with fresh, seasonal ingredients; expect to find pasta, Bay of Fundy scallops, grilled rosemary chicken, and catch of the day on the menu. Appetizers run $5 to $8.50, main courses $12 to $20. High tea is served daily from 3:30 to 5:30pm, and the bar is open from 2pm to 1am nightly.

SEA GARDEN, 469 Water St., St. Andrews, NB, E0G 2X0. Tel. 506/529-3225. 1 cottage.
$ Rates: $45 one person; $50 two people. No credit cards.

In a quiet, secluded spot at the far end of town, the Sea Garden could just as easily be called the Secret Garden. Owners Anne and John Mackeen rent out a single flower-trimmed, shingled cottage. The little hideaway, which looks beyond a picket fence to the bay and fishing weirs, has a bath with shower. Book early. Nonsmokers, please.

SEASIDE BEACH RESORT, 339 Water St. (P.O. Box 310), St. Andrews, NB, E0G 2X0. Tel. 506/529-3846. 24 rms.
$ Rates: $50–$65 single; $55–$75 double. Extra person $5. MC, V. **Closed:** Nov–Apr.

Here you're only four blocks from the heart of downtown St. Andrews, but it won't seem that way. The comfortable units, which include six two-bedroom apartments, all have kitchens and are spread over spacious, serene grounds overlooking St. Andrews Harbour. Everyone may use the barbecues, picnic tables, sun decks, and rowboats. Pets are welcome. There's parking in back and a supermarket a few blocks away. Gracious hosts Fran and Bob Campbell are part of the reason that families return here again and again.

SHIRETOWN INN, 218 Water St. (P.O. Box 145), St. Andrews, NB, E0G 2X0. Tel. 506/529-8877, or toll free 800/528-1234 in the U.S. Fax 506/529-3044. 36 rms. TV TEL
$ Rates: From $68 single; from $85 double. Extra person $8. Children under 12 free. AE, DC, ER, DISC, ER, MC, V.

The Shiretown Inn, now part of the Best Western chain, is Canada's oldest hotel, built in 1881, on the site of another hotel dating from the early 1800s. A bit worn but comfortable and welcoming, it is centrally located (you can walk everywhere from here) and old-fashioned in style. Ask for a front or even-numbered room; Room 202, facing the street and bay, is particularly nice. There's a downstairs sitting room, a reading room on each floor, and an oceanview lawn across the street, where the same management operates the Smuggler's Village Waterfront Suites, kitchenette-equipped units that sleep two to seven people and have a view of the water (rates start at $75 to $95); register at the Shiretown Inn. You can eat breakfast, lunch, and dinner on the Shiretown's dining room or front-porch terrace, and take in the passing parade of strollers and sightseers. The hotel is open year-round.

ST. ANDREWS MOTOR INN, 111 Water St. (P.O. Box 40), St. Andrews, NB, E0G 2X0. Tel. 506/529-4572. Fax 506/529-4493. 33 rms (all with bath). A/C TV TEL
$ Rates: June–Sept $90 single or double; off-season $80 single or double. Extra person $10. AAA and senior discounts available. AE, ER, MC, V.

Within walking distance of downtown, the St. Andrews Motor Inn has large rooms, each with remote-control TV, a full but small bath with a separate sink, and a balcony or patio. Most rooms have two queen-size beds, and seven come with a kitchen. There are also no-smoking rooms. Other pluses: the indoor heated pool overlooking the bay, and the complimentary coffee and doughnuts served in the morning. Pets are welcome. It's open year-round.

WHERE TO DINE

L'EUROPE, 48 King St. Tel. 506/529-3818.
Cuisine: INTERNATIONAL. **Reservations:** Recommended.
$ Prices: Appetizers $5–$14; main courses $15.50–$32. V.
Open: Dinner Tues–Sun 6pm–midnight. **Closed:** Oct–Apr.

For a dinner that is as memorable as it is filling, book a table at L'Europe. The restaurant looks like a Swiss chalet with myriad flags fluttering out front (Canadian and American among them); inside, three small dining areas are embellished with linen, candles, and flowers. All meals come with homemade pâté, Black Forest farmer bread, a salad plate, vegetables, and rice or potatoes. There are half a dozen soups, including Hungarian and French onion, and hot and cold appetizers such as escargots, cabbage rolls, and a herring plate. Main courses, among them whole trout fried in butter with almonds, Cornish hen, duck à l'orange, and jumbo shrimp, are all creations of talented owner/chef Anita Ludwig. The daily special is about $17, or you may make a meal of two appetizers. The wine list is a long one.

LIGHTHOUSE RESTAURANT, Water St. Tel. 506/529-3082.
  Cuisine: SEAFOOD. **Reservations:** Recommended.
  $ Prices: Lunch items $5–$9; dinner appetizers $4–$8, main courses $10–$21. MC, V.
  Open: Lunch daily 11:30am–2pm; dinner daily 5–9pm.
Lobster's the specialty—boiled while you wait and served with potato salad at lunch and a baked potato at dinner. You can also expect whatever's fresh off the boat to show up on the menu (and your plate). Start with steamed clams or lobster bisque, and if you eschew the lobster, consider the gourmet's delight, with scallops, jumbo shrimp, and filet of haddock. There are also sirloin, chicken, and haddock dinners, and a children's menu. The pretty dining room, with blue café-style curtains and tablecloths and artfully draped fishing nets, overlooks the bay and every table has a wonderful view of Navy Island, Deer Island, and the cottages of St. Andrews. Service is friendly. It's fully licensed.

MITCH'S/GABLES, 143 Water St. Tel. 506/529-3440.
  Cuisine: LIGHT FARE. **Reservations:** Not needed.
  $ Prices: Appetizers $4.50–$6.50; main courses $5–$18. MC, V.
  Open: Daily 11am–11pm.
Mitch's by day, Gables by night, this casual place, in an 1870's seaside shanty, serves generous portions of fresh food: nachos, lobster rolls, veggie burgers, steamers, soups, salads, and grilled cheese and lobster sandwiches. There's a children's menu, too. In summer, it's fun to sit out on the back deck—the only I've ever seen encircled by a picket fence and trees. Enter through the alleyway at lunchtime. It's so popular, you can expect slow service.

PASSAMAQUODDY FISH 'N' CHIPS, Town Wharf. No phone.
  Cuisine: SEAFOOD.
  $ Prices: Most items $2–$12. No credit cards.
  Open: Daily 11am–9pm. **Closed:** Late Oct–May.
Avoid the crowds and waits in local restaurants by heading out on the wharf, as so many locals do, for some fish-and-chips from the take-out window. This is no frills dining at its best. No seating, no restrooms. The fish-and-chips costs $4.25 or $6.15, and you can also get a lobster roll, a seafood platter, ice cream, milk shakes, soda, and juice.

EN ROUTE TO GRAND MANAN ISLAND

Traveling east from St. Andrews on Highway 1, the next place of note is St. George (pop. 1,200), a tiny town with a paper mill, the oldest Presbyterian church in Canada (1790), and the beautiful cascade of **Magaguadavic Falls,** which plummets 100 feet. Beyond it, turn off onto Highway 778 and then Highway 776 to go south to Blacks Harbour (pop. 1,400), the jumping-off point for a cruise to Passamaquoddy's island sanctuary for birds and humans, Grand Manan.

3. GRAND MANAN ISLAND

30 miles (48km) from St. Andrews

GETTING THERE By Ferry Ferries (two of them, the new and the old *Grand Manan*) from Blacks Harbour depart six times a day in each direction Monday through Friday June 30 to Labor Day (five times on Saturday and Sunday, and three times daily off-season), and in the busy summer months the line of cars waiting to board the ferry can be so long that some people don't make it on and will have to wait for the next sailing. Allow lots of time to get there and to return, and a good amount of time to stay. Put your car in the waiting line as soon as you arrive or—to avoid the disappointment of not making the boat—leave your car in Blacks Harbour and just sail over as a passenger.

You can go for the day, taking the first morning ferry and returning by the late-afternoon one, but this can be a lot of sailing (and waiting in line) for one day as the voyage takes 1½ hours one-way. Fares are $24 per car, $8 per adult, $4 per child 5 to 12, and $2.75 per bike, round-trip, paid on the return voyage. In other words, if you never come back, you never pay. For information, call Coastal Transport Ltd. on Grand Manan at 506/662-3724; in Saint John, call 506/636-3922 (their office is at 400 Main St.). Remember, no reservations are accepted—it's first-come, first-served.

ESSENTIALS   There is no official tourist information office on the island, but you may obtain information in St. Andrews or at Black's Harbour before you board the ferry. Or ask the helpful folks at the Compass Rose (see "Where to Stay and Dine," below).

SPECIAL EVENTS   If you're on Grand Manan during the first week in August, you'll catch the annual Rotary Festival. The week-long celebration starts with the Miss Grand Manan Pageant and culminates with a parade, barbecues, and fireworks display. The days between are filled with shows, sporting events, and suppers.

There is something special about islands that makes them the best choice for a relaxing vacation, and Grand Manan Island (pop. 690) in the Bay of Fundy is the perfect example. Anchored far out in Fundy's waters like a mammoth aircraft carrier, it is visited daily by almost 250 different kinds of feathered "aircraft," which find it the perfect spot to touch down. John James Audubon first discovered the exceptional variety of bird life on Grand Manan in 1831, and lesser but equally enthusiastic ornithologists have been coming here to peek at puffins, arctic terns, and the occasional bald eagle ever since.

Another draw for scientists is Grand Manan's geology, split between fantastically ancient six-billion-year-old formations and much, much younger volcanic deposits. But most people come just to relax, to take walks through the rocky countryside or along the rugged, cove-indented shores, to catnap in meadows of wildflowers, and to experience that island feeling of remoteness from the worries of the world.

As one visitor put it: "When we were there, time just stopped."

WHAT TO SEE & DO

Exploring is the thing to do—on foot or by bike, one you've brought with you or one you rent. Grand Manan is about 15 miles (24km) long by 5 miles (8km) wide, definitely a walker's paradise as far as size is concerned. The **Red Trail** to the **Hole-in-the-Wall** rock formation (30 minutes away) starts from the Marathon and takes you to **Whale Cove,** where novelist Willa Cather spent her summers. Another walk takes you to **Swallowtail Light,** a picturesque lighthouse of the sort that always appears in tourist brochures and seems unreal—until you see it towering above the rugged seashore, winking in the night.

Farther afield, **Dark Harbour** is the island's dulse-gathering and -drying center. This edible seaweed is packaged and sold in snack-size bags, and shops advertise that you can munch it "just like potato chips." It does make a good flavoring for soups, but first-time tasters might be well advised to approach it gingerly. Exotic, yes. For low-sodium diets, no.

Anywhere you see **fishing boats,** you can check out the possibilities of setting out in the morning with the herring fishing crews for their daily catch. When the boats return, you can follow the fish's progress from net to weir to smokehouse. Smoked mackerel, herring, and salmon are among the finest delicacies produced by this seafood-rich island. The various smokehouse operations start up in late July and continue into fall and winter.

Grand Manan has its own museum in Grand Harbour. The **Grand Manan Museum** has a collection of the many varieties of birds that visit the island, plus displays explaining the island's unique geology. Artifacts from the island's Loyalist past are here, too. From mid-June to mid-September you can visit between 10:30am and 4:30pm Monday through Saturday, and 2 to 5pm on Sunday (tel. 506/662-3524).

Whatever you do, don't leave Grand Manan without getting a glimpse of the playful **puffins,** the big-beaked birds, resembling toy-size penguins, that are the island's mascots. Puffins' fishing abilities are simply amazing, and in the clear Fundy waters they dip beneath the surface and swim swiftly like seals to catch their small prey. A puffin's wings, amazingly, are as effective deep in the water as they are high in the air. **Seawatch Tours** (tel. 506/662-8296) runs a charter-boat service from Seal Cove Wharf to Machias Seal Island, Monday to Saturday from June through August.

Ocean Search offers a full day at sea with a hot lunch and plenty of tea, coffee, and juice. A marine biologist is on board, and there's a film or slide show in the evening (tel. 506/662-8488).

WHERE TO STAY & DINE

COMPASS ROSE, North Head, Grand Manan, NB, E0G 2M0. Tel. 506/ 662-8570, or 506/446-5906 off-season. 9 rms (none with bath). **Directions:** When you leave the ferry, turn left onto the main road.
$ Rates (including breakfast): $45 single; $54 double. Extra person $6. V. **Closed:** Nov–Apr.

Fairly close to the wharf, the Compass Rose is actually two charming old houses with hardwood floors and bedrooms simply furnished with pine and looking out to sea. Guests get to know each other around Franklin stoves in sitting rooms. Cecilia Bowden is your host.

Early birds just off the first-run ferry can wake up with morning coffee and splendid muffins at the Compass Rose dining room for $1.75, served from 9 to 11am. The menu for the rest of the day is equally enjoyable: chowder, lobster stew, house pâté, lobster rolls, and seafood lasagne and prices range from $3 to $13, most $7 or $8. Lunch is served daily from noon to 2pm, afternoon tea from 3 to 4pm, and dinner Monday through Saturday from 6 to 8:30pm.

---

4. SAINT JOHN

60 miles (96km) from St. Andrews, 56 miles (90km) from Fredericton

GETTING THERE The ferry from Digby, N.S., deposits you right in Saint John. Someone is on board the ferry in summer to provide maps and brochures, so you should disembark knowing fairly well where you're going. From St. Andrews, follow Highway 127 to Highway 1 east and follow it to Saint John.

ESSENTIALS Saint John has four municipal tourist information centers: one is at Reversing Falls Bridge over the Saint John River on Highway 100 (tel. 506/658-2937); there is the Visitor and Convention Bureau, on the 11th floor at City Hall (P.O. Box 1971), Saint John, NB, E2L 4L1 (tel. 506/658-2990); located at Market Slip near Market Square Complex is the Little Red Schoolhouse (tel. 506/658-2855); and on Highway 1, on the west side of the city, is the fourth (tel. 506/658-2940). These places will be happy to supply you with city maps and tide tables so you won't miss the action at Reversing Falls Rapids. The office at Reversing Falls is open daily from 9am to 9pm. The other information centers are open daily from 9am to 8pm.

SPECIAL EVENTS Should you come to Saint John the third week of July, be sure to ask about the city's Loyalist Days celebration, when everybody dresses up in colonial costumes for a reenactment of the Loyalists' landing of 1784. Special programs and concerts, parades, and pageants fill the festival week.

During the Festival by the Sea, held annually for 10 days in mid-August since 1985, Saint John comes alive with Canadian culture, everything from Highland dancers from Nova Scotia to Ukrainian dancers from Manitoba; a different culture is highlighted each day.

People in Saint John (pop. 125,000) are justifiably proud of their city, New Brunswick's largest and one of Canada's most Irish. Nowhere, except in publications written by "foreigners," will you see "St. John" rather than "Saint John." As Pittsburgh and Edinburgh must have that final "h," Saint John must be spelled out. St. John's is the capital of Newfoundland—no relation, and more than one person I've heard of has gotten them confused when booking a flight.

Saint John is called "the Loyalist City" because it was incorporated by settlers from the revolutionary United States, but it was actually "founded" by Samuel de Champlain on St. John the Baptist's Day in 1604. It took a while after Champlain's visit for the French to set up a fort here for trade with the friendly natives and defense against the unfriendly English, and after that first fort was built (1631), it changed hands frequently.

The English were well established by 1783, when thousands of Loyalists flocked to the shelter of the British Crown in Canada. The Loyalist City is actually the oldest incorporated city in Canada, for these early settlers established their town on a legal basis way back in 1785.

The Loyalists who founded Saint John were hardworking and industrious types who soon turned their city into one of the world's greatest shipbuilding ports. When the wooden ship was replaced by the iron one, Saint John's builders followed suit, and the city has never lost its close connection with ships and the sea.

The city can get foggy, but local citizens don't seem to mind; in the back of their minds there may lurk the idea that fog, being very English, is in fact patriotic, and the best possible weather for the Loyalist City. Besides, when landlubbers in Fredericton and Moncton are sweltering in summer's sticky heat, in Saint John it's cool, even on sunny days.

In recent years, downtown Saint John has undergone a renaissance. The waterfront has been tidied up, and a modern convention center built with all the accoutrements: luxury hotels, shopping concourses, restaurant complexes, office towers. Though it may drizzle, conventioneers don't mind, as they can walk from the Hilton, which is right on the water, through the new series of buildings almost to King's Square without so much as getting their feet wet.

But unquestionably the biggest tourist draw to this ancient and honorable town is the bewildering phenomenon of the Saint John River's "Reversing Falls," a Fundy high-tide trick worth seeing (see "What to See and Do," below).

Famous native sons of Saint John include actors Donald Sutherland and Walter Pidgeon; Louis B. Mayer, founder of Metro-Goldwyn-Mayer and, in 1927, the Academy of Motion Picture Arts and Sciences; Nathan Cummings, founder of the National Tea Company (Consolidated Foods of Chicago); K. C. Irving, one of Canada's leading industrial magnates and reportedly one of the eight richest men in the world (it's his name you see on so many gas stations); and T. H. Estabrook, inventor of the tea bag.

The movie *Children of a Lesser God,* starring William Hurt and Marlee Matlin, was filmed in Saint John in 1985, and Matlin won an Oscar for best actress for her work.

WHAT TO SEE & DO

The city is awaiting the grand reopening of the **Imperial Theatre** (1913), as a center for performing arts. In its heyday, it hosted such luminaries as Ethel Barrymore, Harry Houdini, Edgar Bergen, and John Philip Sousa. In the 1930s and 1940s, the theater was mainly used to present "talkies." The intricate interior plasterwork from the old theater is being reproduced, and the original chandelier refurbished and rehung. All the seats offer an unobstructed view because the balcony is supported, not by columns, but a heavy steel truss.

To get to know the city, take a self-guided walking tour along Saint John's **Loyalist Trail,** filled with historical landmarks. The tourist information center (see above) can supply you with a map and brochure, or link you up with a free 90-minute walking tour at 10am or 2pm in July and August (it includes 15 minutes in the market). Highlights of the walk include the old County Courthouse, with its unsupported spiral staircase, an architectural marvel; Trinity Church, built in 1880 to replace an earlier church destroyed by Saint John's Great Fire of 1877 (the British royal arms over the west door is a replica of the coat-of-arms taken by Loyalist immigrants from the rebellious town of Boston); St. John's Stone Church, on Carleton Street at the end of Wellington Row, the city's oldest church building (1825), made completely from stone brought as ballast in ships from England, with a 12-story steeple crowned with a six-foot-long salmon done in gold leaf; the City Market (1876), where the art and craft of the city's wooden shipbuilding carpenters is immediately apparent; and the Loyalist Burial Ground, east of King's Square, with tombstones dating back to 1784.

The tourist office can supply maps and brochures for two other self-guided walking tours: The Victorian Stroll winds through the tree-lined, 19th-century residential streets of downtown Saint John, with an introduction to the architecture of the elegant old homes along the way. Prince William's Walk explores the merchant heritage of the city.

At the corner of Prince William and Princess Streets, you'll see the curious Chubb Building, on the northwest corner. It was erected in the latter part of the 19th century by one George Chubb, whom you'll see on the facade in the guise of a grinning gargoyle. Besides himself, Chubb had all his children and half the city's political leaders immortalized on the facade in little rosettes.

Farther along, at the southern end of Prince William Street at St. Patrick's Square, you'll see the city's distinctive Trinity Lamps, better known as the "Three Sisters." Visible from as far as five miles away, they once guided ships safely into the harbor.

To see some of the city's prettiest homes (some now posh apartments), wander around Queen Square and along Germain Street. The striking painted teak doors are part of the city's Irish tradition.

If you'd like to take home a souvenir of authentic New Brunswick fine arts or crafts, drop by a shop called **Handworks,** at 116 Prince William St. (tel. 506/652-9787), in the old City Hall. It's open year-round. You can buy local folk music at **My King of Music,** 57 Canterbury St. (tel. 506/652-3797)—or hear it live at **O'Leary's,** 46 Princess St. (tel. 506/634-7135), Thursday through Saturday. There's no cover; go early to get a seat.

Bands are on stage at the boardwalk, in front of Market Square, all summer long.

BARBOUR'S GENERAL STORE, King St. Tel. 506/658-2939.

Down the hill at the end of King Street, on Saint John Harbour, you'll be transported a century back in time to the kind of store our grandparents and great-grandparents thought of as modern and up-to-date. From the cracker barrel to the spice cupboard, from the salt cod to the spats, from whisky to molasses, everything is in its place. While you can't buy the ancient pharmaceuticals, you can get a free snack of dulse, New Brunswick's edible seaweed that for many is an acquired taste. The tourist information center is next door, in the Little Red Schoolhouse.

Admission: Free.

Open: Daily 9am–7pm. **Closed:** Late Oct–early May.

LOYALIST HOUSE, 120 Union St. Tel. 506/652-3590.

This is Saint John's oldest unchanged building, dating from 1817, and typical of the homes of United Empire Loyalists. A locally prominent, well-to-do Loyalist family (originally from New York), headed by David Daniel Merritt, had the house built in Georgian style and furnished with the elegant furniture of the time. It would be home to five generations of Merritts. Guides from the New Brunswick Historical Society are glad to point out the house's charming details.

Admission: $2 adults, 25¢ kids.

Open: July–Aug Mon–Sat 10am–5pm, Sun 1–5pm; Sept–June Mon–Fri 10am–5pm.

REVERSING FALLS, Hwy. 100, on the bridge over the Saint John River.

Many Saint John citizens are careful to boast of "Reversing Falls Rapids" rather than "Reversing Falls"—the difference in names is important. Don't expect to see a waterfall with tides leaping 100 feet up the rocks, a phenomenon that the name "Reversing Falls" might be expected to conjure up in the imagination. But what you'll see is equally amazing in natural terms, although not visually as spectacular.

At the bridge over the Saint John River on Highway 100 is a small building housing a tourist information center, a restaurant serving short orders of seafood, and a viewing point. A 20-minute film collapses the action-time of the tides and explains the amazing process whereby the Saint John River empties into the Bay of Fundy at low tide, rippling swiftly under the bridge as any good river should. But as the tide rises, a "slack" period is reached when no water moves and the river's surface is as still and calm as a millpond's. Then, slowly, the flow of water reverses, and soon a swift current is speeding under the bridge and up the Saint John River as the powerful Fundy tide rolls in. At high tide another slack time is reached, the water is calm again, but not for long. Soon the tide begins to recede, beginning the process all over again.

High tide comes twice a day (around 10am and 4pm, but check the exact times); tide tables are handed out everywhere. If the observation booth is too crowded, watch from the little grassy park nearby, or from Riverside Falls View Park, which is on the east side of the bridge, to the north, more or less behind the New Brunswick Museum.

Admission: Free; film $1.25.
Open: Daily 7:30am–10pm; film shown hourly 9am–8pm.

AIKEN BICENTENNIAL EXHIBITION CENTRE [ABEC], 20 Haven Ave. Tel. 506/633-4870.

Opposite the YM-YWCA, ABEC presents touring and local exhibitions of art, science, and technology in its five galleries. A room is devoted to hands-on exploration by children. Live performances are given here, as well. Call for an up-to-date schedule of events. The building dates from 1904 and was originally a public library financed by Andrew Carnegie. The entry has an enormous stained-glass skylight.

Admission: Free.
Open: Summer daily 10am–5pm; winter Tues–Sun 11:30am–4:30pm.

CANADA GAMES AQUATIC CENTRE, 50 Union St. Tel. 506/658-4715.

Rain or shine, kids and adults can relax downtown at Saint John's indoor playground. Built for the 1985 Canada Games, it's been going strong ever since. Lifeguards watch over the eight-lane Olympic-size pool, the leisure pools, and the tot pool. For added fun, there is a double-looping water slide, a Tarzan rope, whirlpools, saunas, and two weight and exercise rooms, as well as a sports medicine clinic (consultations only, and you need a referral from a medical doctor; call 506/658-1415 for more information).

Admission: General admission to swim or take an exercise class $4.25 adults 18 and older, $3.50 students 18 and older and children 13–17, $3.20 children 12 and younger. Family rate for four people $12.95. Use of fitness-center facilities $6.
Open: Daily 6:30am–8pm; public swims and fitness programs vary from day to day.

CARLETON MARTELLO TOWER, across from Reversing Falls.

If the fog's not so dense, cross the bridge over Reversing Falls and look for the sign that points the way to the left up the hill to Saint John's Carleton Martello Tower. The tower is open to visitors, with guides on hand. Martello towers, grand cylindrical stone defense fortifications like this one, were built throughout England and Ireland in the early years of the 19th century, and over a dozen were put up in North America as well.

Admission: Free.
Open: Daily 9am–5pm. **Closed:** Late Oct–early May.

CHERRY BROOK ZOO, Rockwood Park. Tel. 506/634-1440.

Another clear-day activity is a visit to the Cherry Brook Zoo, a 20-acre enclave in the northern section of Rockwood Park, which itself is a few miles north of the city. No doubt it would be strange to have one's first encounter with a gentle brown lemur, a golden lion tamarin, or a black wildebeest in Saint John, New Brunswick—but that's exactly what the zoo holds in store.

Admission: $3.25 adults, $2.25 seniors and students, $1.40 preschoolers; children 2 and younger free.
Open: Daily 10am–dusk.

JEWISH MUSEUM, 29 Wellington Row, at Union St. Tel. 506/633-1833.

The Jewish Museum chronicles the history and lifestyle of Saint John's Jewish community, which was founded in 1858 and numbered as many as 300 families from the 1920s to the 1960s. (It's smaller today.)

Admission: Free.

Open: May–June and Sept Mon–Fri 10am–4pm; July–Aug Sun 1–4pm. **Closed:** Oct–Apr.

MOOSEHEAD BREWERY, 89 Main St., West Saint John. Tel. 506/635-7000.

Another sightseeing possibility is a guided tour of the Moosehead Brewery, which bottles virtually every bottle of Moosehead beer sold in the world. Tours last about an hour; sign up for one at the Moosehead Country Store, 49 Main St., which also sells souvenir items with the Moosehead logo. On the tour, you will be conducted through the brewing and bottling process from start to finish. Moosehead takes great pride in its standing as Canada's oldest independent brewery, and you'll find your guide knowledgeable and enthusiastic. You will be, too, after sampling a bit of the product (on the house) at the end of the tour.

Tours: June 15–Aug Mon–Fri 9:30am and 2pm.

NEW BRUNSWICK MUSEUM, 277 Douglas Ave. Tel. 506/643-2349.

In the New Brunswick Museum, paintings and displays of sailing vessels outline Saint John's maritime past, while cases holding colonial uniforms and weapons, furniture, and other memorabilia from the New Brunswick of two centuries ago. Natural-science specimens are also on display. Founded in 1842, the museum claims the original copy of Clement Moore's beloved poem "'Twas the Night Before Christmas." It also has a Discovery Centre for children, an extensive library and archives, and a shop that sells gifts, books, and reproductions from the museum collections (also sold in the Gallery Gift Shop in the City Market). The museum is near Reversing Falls; to get there, coming from downtown, make a sharp right turn just before the Reversing Falls Bridge; the museum is a few blocks up on the left.

Admission: $2 adults, $1 students, children under 4 free, family pass $5.

Open: Museum daily 10am–5pm (Discovery Centre only is closed noon–1pm); library and archives daily 1–5pm or by appointment.

PARTRIDGE ISLAND, in Saint John Harbor. Tel. 506/635-0782.

Only half a mile offshore and open to the public since 1993, 24-acre Partridge Island was the first quarantine station in North America. From 1830 to 1938, 13 hospitals were built here, and diseased immigrants and sailors quarantined in them. Some 1,200 immigrants and some city residents are buried in the six graveyards on the island. Most of them were Irish immigrants, and a 20-foot-high Celtic cross has been erected in their memory. There is also a memorial to Jewish immigrants. From 1800 to 1945, the island was fortified to defend the port, as numerous concrete installations attest. Join one of the 2½-hour tours of the island. The island has twice been designated a National Historic Site. Tours leave from Market Slip, near Loyalist Plaza at the foot of King Street; however, they may be suspended for environmental studies. Call ahead.

Admission: $10 for the tour.

Open: May–Oct; no set daily schedule.

ROCKWOOD PARK, Mount Pleasant Ave. Tel. 506/658-2829.

Due north of downtown Saint John, Rockwood Park is a much loved and used 2,000 acres filled with the things that make human beings happy: lakes for swimming, boating (even bumper boats), fishing, and ice skating; an enclosed picnic area; hayrides in summer; a children's petting farm; a playground; miniature golf; and campgrounds for tents and trailers, with toilets and hot showers.

NEARBY ATTRACTIONS

IRVING NATURE PARK, off Sand Cove Rd. Tel. 506/634-7135.

★ A gift to the people of New Brunswick and visitors from the J. D. Irving Ltd. company, this 450-acre park seems eons removed from civilization, rather than only about two miles from downtown Saint John. A well-maintained mile-long one-way dirt road loops around it, hugging the shore and passing a number of covered picnic areas and parking spots. Pull into one if you want to walk to the water's edge, follow one of the four hiking trails (from .8 to 4 miles), or sit on a split-log bench and soak in the tranquillity. You're likely to see seabirds and migrating birds, seals, deer, and the occasional porcupine. Stop at the entrance and get a map and further information from the park rangers, and give yourself at least a half an hour to drive around this special spot along the Fundy coast. If you plan to hike, wear sturdy shoes. To get here from Saint John, take Highway 1 West to Exit 107A; go over the overpass, through the flashing yellow light to the top of the hill (when Bleury Street ends); turn right onto Sand Cove Road and drive 2 miles (3km). Impressively modern outhouses have been provided.

Admission: Free.

Open: Daily dawn–dusk; hikers year-round, vehicles June–Nov only.

BUS TOURS

For an overview of the sights, the bus tour, offered June to October by the **Saint John Transit Commission** (tel. 506/658-4700), might be just the ticket. Buses depart from Rockwood Park campground at 12:15pm, Barbour's General Store at 12:30pm and Reversing Falls at 1pm. Highlights of the three-hour guided tour are Market Square, Fort Howe, Reversing Falls, the martello tower, and King's Square. Adults pay $15 and children under 15 pay $5. Call ahead to confirm.

WHERE TO STAY

If you insist on blitzing through Saint John and only want basic accommodation for one night, head out to Monawagonish Road, where the motels are clustered. They tend to be old but are clean and economical.

HOTELS

DELTA BRUNSWICK, 39 King St., Saint John, NB, E2L 4W3. Tel. 506/648-1981, or toll free 800/877-1133 in the U.S., 800/268-1133 in Canada. Fax 506/658-0914. 243 rms, 12 suites. A/C MINIBAR TV TEL

$ Rates: Summer $75 single or double; rest of the year $115 single, $125 double. From $135 suite. Extra adult $15. Children 18 and under stay free in parents' room. Children 6 and under eat free. Ask about weekend "getaway" rates. AE, DC, DISC, ER, MC, V. **Parking:** Adjacent to hotel, valet $10, self-park $7.

Atop the bustling Brunswick Square shopping complex, this is downtown Saint John's largest hotel. Rooms are large, bright, and decorated with soft colors; you can open the windows, which isn't always the case in large hotels. Each room has a coffee machine, and in-room movies are available. The baths are stocked with big, fluffy towels. The third floor has been refurbished. Besides the hotel's own restaurants and lounges, there are lots more in the rest of the complex. It's on King Street, the main downtown thoroughfare, and is linked by covered skywalks to Market Square, Canada Games Aquatic Centre, and the Saint John Trade and Convention Center. Because the hotel is so large, request a room fairly near the elevator; otherwise, you could be in for a hike.

Dining/Entertainment: Shuckers seafood restaurant, open for three meals a day; Shuckers bar, with piano entertainment nightly; Delta Club business lounge, for light lunches and snacks, as well as afternoon tea that's open to the public.

Services: 24-hour room service, dry cleaning.

Facilities: Indoor swimming pool, whirlpool bath, saunas, exercise room, and a children's playroom; meeting rooms; business center; no-smoking rooms.

SAINT JOHN HILTON, One Market Square, Saint John, NB, E2L 4Z6. Tel. 506/693-8484, or toll free 800/445-8667 in the U.S., 800/268-9275 in Canada. Fax 506/657-6610. 167 rms, 30 suites. A/C MINIBAR TV TEL

$ Rates: Summer $89 single or double; rest of the year $110 single, $120 double.

From $150 suite. Extra person $12. Weekend rates and packages available. Children under 18 stay free in parents' room; children under 12 eat free. AE, DC, DISC, ER, MC, V. **Parking:** Underground, $8.25 a day.

 Perched right at the edge of the harbor and the city's only hotel on the water, the Hilton has the best location in town and an impressively friendly staff. You can see Reversing Falls from here ("Just get a harborview room") and walk to many attractions and restaurants. Rooms are large, with sand-and-seafoam green decor and furniture made from New Brunswick pine; most have two double beds (though five rooms are equipped with Murphy beds). Guests have use of a voice-mail system, and there are in-room movies available. Baths feature local marble and have hairdryers and lots of counter space. The hotel is connected to lively Market Square and to the Trade and Convention Centre, reachable by an enclosed walkway. When you enter the lobby, expect a warm welcome by Snookie the parrot.

Dining/Entertainment: The pretty Turn of the Tide restaurant serves three meals a day, including a breakfast and lunch buffet, Sunday brunch; the Brigantine Lounge overlooking the harbor, has a pool table, games area, big-screen TV, and piano music from 5 to 9pm Monday through Saturday.

Services: 24-hour room service, dry cleaning, babysitting, business support services.

Facilities: Small indoor swimming pool, Jacuzzi under a large skylight, saunas, exercise room, four no-smoking floors, meeting rooms.

INNS

DUFFERIN HALL, 357 Dufferin Row, Saint John, NB, E2M 2J7. Tel. 506/635-5968. Fax 506/674-2396. 6 rms (5 with bath).

$ Rates (including full breakfast): $40 single without bath, $45 single with bath; $50 double without bath, $55 double with bath. Extra person $10. Weekend packages available. Children younger than 10 free. MC, V.

If you've got an early ferry to Digby, or are arriving tired and in need of immediate pampering, consider overnighting only four blocks away from the ferry landing on a quiet, tree-lined street. The house, which once belonged to former premier and chief justice of New Brunswick, J. B. M. Baxter, has a leaded-glass front door, a lounge with a stained-glass window, and a paneled dining room, where a full breakfast is served every morning. New owners since 1993, Axel and Margret Begner, originally from Germany, have decorated the house splendidly, with European furnishings: china, silverware, candleholders, oak furniture (much of it made from one enormous tree—ask them the story), soft duvets on the beds, old-fashioned lights, and overstuffed chairs. The library/bar, with two stained-glass windows and floor-to-ceiling bookshelves, and Italian marble table and vase, is a showplace. The inn is no-smoking.

The dining room features seasonal menus with European-style cooking and fresh Canadian ingredients. Axel is a master cook and pastry chef (he makes his own pastas, pastries, and pâtés); Margret is a dietician. Expect such tempting dishes as potato-leek soup, escargot quiche, coconut chicken breast, a shrimp and scallop duet, veal steak Italian, and rack of lamb. Dinner appetizers run $5 to $10, main courses $15 to $27, or you can indulge in a four-course meal for $38.50. Lunch is served in summer only from 11:30am to 2:30pm Tuesday through Sunday, dinner year-round from 5 to 10pm, Tuesday through Sunday. It's licensed. Downtown Saint John is a five-minute drive away; the martello tower, a popular attraction, even closer.

PARKERHOUSE INN, 71 Sydney St., Saint John, NB, E2L 2L5. Tel. 506/652-5054. Fax 506/636-8076. 9 rms (all with bath). TV TEL

$ Rates (including breakfast): $65, $79, or $95, depending on room size. AE, MC, V. **Parking:** Free.

The Parkerhouse Inn, a stunning Victorian house (1891) that was once the scene of grand balls in Saint John, is adjacent to the renovated Imperial Theatre and a block from King's Square. Its bedrooms are decorated with period and country antiques, cloud-soft bedcovers, and plush linens, and they have large private baths with color-coordinated bathrobes. The inn also features a curved staircase, a wall displaying the owner's collection of beaded and chain-mesh purses, fireplaces, stained-glass windows, woodwork galore, smoking and no-smoking areas, a small gift shop, a licensed dining room serving breakfast and dinner (served 5 to 9:30pm) to guests and the public, and a solarium (now an intimate dining nook). Innkeeper Pam Vincent has gone out of her way to see that guests feel pampered; they even get a morning paper with breakfast. The inn is popular with honeymooners and business travelers alike.

BED-AND-BREAKFAST

CRANBERRY'S, 168 King St. East, Saint John, NB, E2L 1H1. Tel. 506/657-5173. 2 rms (none with bath), 1 suite (with bath).

$ Rates (including breakfast): $40 single; $45 double; $65 suite. No credit cards.

Cranberry's is an engaging house with an engaging host, Janice MacMillan, who has been everything from the house mother at a girls' school to the personnel manager of a large company and is now a human resources consultant and the warm welcomer of wayfarers. There are only two bedrooms at Cranberry's (so book early), and they share a large bath. One room has two twin beds; the other, actually a family suite, has a double bed and an adjoining child's room with bear trim around the ceiling. Janice has thoughtfully filled the bath with toiletries, including toothbrushes, shaving cream, and shampoo, and lots of magazines. There is also a suite with private bath, living room, and kitchen. For guests' enjoyment, the house also has a living room, dining room, back patio, and TV/reading room filled with more magazines and crayons for the kids. Janice insists that "nobody leaves without something for their pocket"; I got cranberry fudge. The location is central, a few blocks from King's Square and City Market, and near the Loyalist Burial Ground.

INNS NEAR SAINT JOHN

INN ON THE COVE, 1371 Sand Cove Rd. (Station B), Saint John, NB, E2M 4X7. Tel. 506/672-7799. Fax 506/635-5455. 3 rms (all with bath). **Directions:** From Saint John, take Route 1 West to Exit 107A; go over the overpass, through the flashing yellow light to the top of the hill (when Bleury Street ends); turn right onto Sand Cove Road and drive one mile (2km) to the inn (on your left). The Irving Nature Park is half a mile (1km) farther.

$ Rates (including full breakfast): $55–$90 single; $60–$95 double. Discounts for stays longer than one night; two-night Romance Package available. MC, V.

West of Saint John and an easy 10-minute drive away, the Inn on the Cove has a picture-perfect place on the water, with a picture window to go with it. Gaze out at Partridge Island, and seals, ducks, and Canada geese. The three-level house (you'll enter on the third level) was built in 1910 by Percy Manchester, Alexander Graham Bell's gardener in Baddeck. The three guest rooms are lovely; one has a working gas fireplace, wallpaper imported from England, and a picture window; another, a particularly large bath; another, its own Jacuzzi with a view of the bay (this one books up quickly). It would be hard to find hosts more welcoming than Ross and Willa Mavis. If you enjoy puns, get ready to match wits with Ross. He and Willa, both avid naturalists, share the cooking and create the atmosphere of relaxation and good cheer here. If you plan to have dinner at the inn, reserve a day in advance. A licensed, no-smoking inn, it's 10 minutes from Saint John.

SHADOW LAWN, 3180 Rothesay Rd. (P.O. Box 41), Rothesay, NB, E0G 2W0. Tel. 506/847-7539. Fax 506/849-9238. 8 rms, 2 suites (all with bath). TEL TV **Directions:** Take Route 1 East from Saint John to Exit 121; go down the hill to the end of Fox Farm Road; turn right onto Rothesay Road and continue 1.8 miles (3km); the inn will be on your right.

$ Rates: June 15–Oct 15 $69–$89 single or double, $125 suite; Oct 16–June 14 $58–$75 single or double, $89 suite (one-night deposit required in advance). Extra person $10. MC, V.

Only about eight miles northeast of Saint John, in the affluent town of Rothesay, the Shadow Lawn Inn (1871) takes its name from its tree-lined lawn out front. Amazingly, the towering house with a circular drive and pretty yard, was built as a summer home, in 1871. The guest rooms are all different, but they all have antique beds, high ceilings, hardwood floors, and private bathrooms. In no. 1, for instance, there is a couch in front of a fireplace; no. 4 is old-fashioned with a canopy bed and bath with a clawfoot tub. Two rooms are air-conditioned. One of the suites has a Jacuzzi, the other a kitchenette. Any meal in the well-reputed dining room is memorable; you might start with homemade rolls, proceed to a salad splashed with an excellent dressing, and move on to beef Wellington or poached Atlantic salmon embellished with cauliflower and snow peas, then a cheese course. End your meal triumphantly with baked Alaska and coffee or tea. The two front dining rooms are in the original house, the back one is in a 1993 addition. Reserve your table (6 to 8pm nightly except Sunday), and dress for dinner. The hosts are Pat and Marg Gallagher. The airport is 10 minutes away.

ST. MARTINS COUNTRY INN, Hwy. 11, St. Martins, NB, E0G 2Z0. Tel. 506/833-4534. Fax 506/833-4725. 10 rms, 3 suites (all with bath). TEL

$ Rates: $57 single or double; $65 and $80 suite. Extra person $10. Packages available. MC, V.

Due east of Saint John some 35 miles (60km), via Highway 111 past the Saint John airport, this restored Queen Anne mansion commands 100 acres of land overlooking the Bay of Fundy. The magnificent St. Martins Country Inn, in the fishing village of St. Martins, has eight working fireplaces, three dining rooms, two graceful drawing rooms, and romantic bedrooms, decorated with floral bedspreads, rugs, and wallpaper. (The Captain's Room, one of the suites, is more modern, with a brass bed and wall-to-wall carpeting.) The bridal suite has a four-poster bed, sitting room, and Jacuzzi; five of the rooms have fireplaces. Built in 1859, the inn, which is actually the twin to a villa on the French Riviera, is owned and beautifully run by Myrna and Albert LeClair. There's a small pond in front of the house and hiking trails behind it. Open year-round.

The inn's dining room serves three meals a day (breakfast is not included in the price of a room). Lunch is served daily from noon to 3:30pm (most items $5 to $9), dinner from 5:30 to 10pm (appetizers $5 to $10, main courses $15 to $27).

WHERE TO DINE

GRANNAN'S SEAFOOD RESTAURANT AND OYSTER BAR, City Market. Tel. 506/634-1555.

Cuisine: SEAFOOD. **Reservations:** Recommended in the evening.

$ Prices: Appetizers $3–$13; main courses $5–$30. AE, ER, MC, V.

Open: Mon–Sat 11:30am–midnight, Sun 11:30am–10pm; drinks nightly until 2am.

A favorite is Grannan's Seafood Restaurant and Oyster Bar, a relaxed and hearty place in the center of Market Square. You can expect big portions and moderate prices. Seafood, of course, is the main draw here—the Captain's Platter has been called the "Cadillac of all meals"—but you can also get good prime rib. At lunch there is light fare, including sandwiches and salads, and in summer, patio dining features barbecue. The desserts, like "Bananas Foster," flamed at your table, are reliably rich. Fifties-style Chevy's Bar, next door, is under the same ownership.

INCREDIBLE EDIBLES, 42 Princess St. Tel. 506/633-7554.

Cuisine: INTERNATIONAL. **Reservations:** Recommended.

$ Prices: Appetizers $3–$11; lunch main courses $7–$18; dinner main courses $9–$23. AE, DC, MC, V.

Open: Lunch Mon–Sat 11am–4pm; dinner Mon–Sat 4–10:30pm.

Incredible Edibles is best known for its scrumptious cheesecakes (from marble chocolate amaretto to French mint), but you can get less-calorie-filled fare, too. Along with the daily specials, including omelets, there are salads, pasta dishes, house pizza, and pita sandwiches filled with lobster or spicy stir-fry. Add to that hot-and-sour shrimp soup and seafood stew, and in the evening, grilled salmon, steak au poivre, and catch of the day. A meal should run you $7 to $12, depending on your appetite, and you can enjoy it in one of several dining areas, including an outdoor patio. It's licensed.

REGGIE'S RESTAURANT, 26 German St. Tel. 506/657-6270.

Cuisine: DELI/LIGHT FARE. **Reservations:** Not needed.

$ Prices: Most items $2–$7. MC, V.
Open: July–Oct daily 6am–9pm; Nov–June daily 6am–7pm Breakfast served until 11am.

Since 1969, Reggie's Restaurant has been serving eat-in or take-out homemade soups, chowders, smoked-meat sandwiches, and burgers to a loyal following. It's a great place for breakfast, especially for early risers, who might choose bagels, pancakes, or bacon and eggs, and much more. Lunch and dinner choices are equally numerous. It's licensed, and, yes, there is a "Reg."

SPECIALTY DINING

Head for **Market Square,** that modern complex right on the waterfront downtown. Within the complex, and spilling out onto the sidewalks and plazas nearby, are close to a dozen eateries of every conceivable type. That unique sculpture in front of the square, by the way, is an unusual clock tower with no hands or face. Rather, a serpent represents the world and four figures represent the passing of time, and they rotate every six hours. Made of Honduras mahogany, the Market Square Timepiece also incorporates benches to provide weary passersby with some time out. Created by John Hooper, from Hampton, New Brunswick, it was placed here in 1984. (Hooper also created the engaging sculpture *People Apart Moving Together* at the entrance to the Trade and Convention Centre; the artist is depicted in the center, with the beard.)

In the Food Hall at Market Square are various fast-food shops. You can pick up a pizza, or egg rolls and chow mein, or a burger, or fried chicken—the list goes on. The Food Hall has common tables where you can put away your purchases.

For a light lunch, snack, or picnic, you'll find everything you need in the **City Market,** off the northwest corner of King's Square, at 47 Charlotte St. A genuine historic site, and a stop on the Loyalist Trail (see "What to See and Do," above in this section), the City Market has been going strong since 1876. Check out Vern's Bakery for sweets, Lord's Lobster for fish and chowder, and Slocum & Ferris for sausages and dulse. At Jeremiah Hamilton, Esq., you can get cold cuts, cheese, vegetables, fruits, local honey, and ice cream—or have them make you a deli sandwich. The Whale of a Café has whale-size salads, and you pick the ingredients (ask for a half portion and tell them to go easy on the dressing). From a number of stalls, you can buy a bag of dulse (dried seaweed); you'll either like the taste or hate it, so ask for a sample first. There's a solarium with seating for lunchtime patrons. The City Market carpenters were shipbuilders. Can you tell? The market is open Monday through Thursday and Saturday from 8:30am to 5:30pm, to 9pm Friday.

THE FERRY TO DIGBY, N.S.

Marine Atlantic's MV *Princess of Acadia* plies the Bay of Fundy between Saint John, N.B., and Digby, N.S., year-round, making the crossing in approximately two hours and 45 minutes. In the peak summer period from mid-June through September, the ship carries its load of 159 cars and 650 passengers three times a day (two times on Sunday) in each direction. Crossings are less frequent the rest of the year. Summer fares for adults are $20 one-way; seniors, $15; and children 5 to 12, $10. Charge for a car is $45. You should have reservations: in Saint John, call 506/636-4048; in Digby, 902/245-2116; in the U.S., toll free 800/341-7981.

EN ROUTE TO FREDERICTON

Two roads lead from Saint John to Fredericton. Highway 7 is fast, but not memorable, while Highway 102 North follows the sinuous banks of the Saint John River north through a valley of patchwork fields, heavily laden apple trees, and hamlets where church suppers and quilting bees still take place.

If you are planning to visit Gagetown (and I heartily recommend it), consider a third alternative that provides a pure New Brunswick experience involving backroads and three short ferry crossings, all free:

Head out Route 1 east from Saint John to Rothesay (you'll already be there if you're staying at Shadow Lawn Inn). From Rothesay go to Gondola Point via Highway 100 west to Highway 119 and follow the signs. Take the ferry across Kennebecasis

Bay. Then drive along Route 845 east to Kingston, where you'll take Route 850 to get the second ferry, across Belleisle Bay. From here, take Route 124W to the third and final ferry, to Evandale and Route 102 north.

The ferries simply make the short trips back and forth all day long. The longest I ever waited for one was 10 minutes. This is a delightful way to travel, especially since so little is free anymore.

GAGETOWN

Time seems to have bypassed the village of Gagetown (pop. 620, and not to be confused with the Gagetown military base), nestled on the bank of Gagetown Creek, along Route 102. The creek feeds into the Saint John River, and Route 102 leads on to Fredericton, but you'll be tempted to linger here a while.

Gagetown is a village of artists and craftspeople. You can see their handiwork at the outstanding **Acacia Gallery of Canadian Art** (tel. 506/488-2591), on Front Street beside the Steamers Stop Inn, and at the **Loomscrofters** shop, housed in an old trading post (1761) beside the river and selling handwoven tartans and afghans made to order (tel. 506/488-2400).

The past is chronicled in the **Queen's County Tilley House Museum,** across from the Steamers Stop Inn, where a guide will show you around, explain how people lived in the early days of the town, and point out such treasures as the household gadget that coined the phrase "pop goes the weasel," a musket used in the American Revolution, an 18th-century ice-cream scoop, and a fine collection of arrowheads. In the former home (1786) of Sir Leonard Tilley, one of the fathers of the Canadian Confederation, the museum is open mid-June to mid-September from 10am to 5pm daily; from mid-September to Canadian Thanksgiving (U.S. Columbus Day), open weekend afternoons or by appointment. Admission is $1 for adults, 25¢ for students (tel. 506/488-2966).

Next door to the museum stands **St. John's Anglican Church** (1880). Loyalists and their slaves are buried in the cemetery.

Where to Stay and Dine

STEAMERS STOP INN, Front St. (P.O. Box 155), Gagetown, NB, E0G 1V0. Tel. 506/488-2903. Fax 506/488-2888. 7 rms (1 with bath).

$ Rates: $40 single; $45–$55 double without bath, $65 double with bath. Extra person $10. Packages available. MC, V. **Closed:** Weekdays in May and Sept; Oct–Apr.

⭐ This is the valley's most delightful small hotel. From the broad veranda facing Gagetown Creek, part of the Saint John River, to the cluster of five intimate dining rooms and the Victorian decor in the sitting room and bedrooms, the Steamers Stop Inn creates its own special ambience. The rooms have floral wallpaper, high-backed beds, and antique furnishings. There are horseshoes, canoes, kayaks, and a dock for guests' enjoyment.

The country cooking here is a treat. Come for lunch, served daily from noon to 4pm, or dinner, from 8 to 9pm. If you're in town for the all-you-can-eat Sunday brunch buffet, served from 11am to 3:30pm, more's the better. Lunch runs $4 to $10, and evening meals range in price from $13 to $23. The special is usually $15, and the great fiddlehead soup is $4.25. It's licensed. Vic and Pat Stewart are the welcoming hosts. Reserve your room a few days ahead.

5. FREDERICTON

35 miles (56km) N of Gagetown, 56 miles (90km) N of Saint John

GETTING THERE From Saint John, take fast Highway 7 north, or the more scenic Highway 102 north. From Gagetown, follow Highway 102 north.

ESSENTIALS The main source of maps and information in the city is right inside the door of the Victorian red-brick Fredericton City Hall, at 397 Queen St. (at York Street), by the river (tel. 506/452-9500). It can provide the excellent *Fredericton*

Visitor Guide, which has a good walking tour, as well as a free "Tourist Parking Pass," which allows out-of-province visitors to park free at meters and in town lots. You can always park free on Saturday and Sunday. It's open all week from 8am to 8pm mid-May through August, to 4:30pm in September, and Monday through Friday from 8am to 4:30pm the rest of the year. Or write ahead to the City Hall Visitors' Information Centre, 397 Queen St. (P.O. Box 130), Fredericton, NB, E3B 4Y7.

The City of Fredericton maintains another information center, on the Trans Canada Highway near the Hanwell Road exit, no. 289 (tel. 506/458-8331 or 506/458-8332), open every day during the summer tourist season from 9am to 5pm, 8am to 8pm in the peak travel season.

New Brunswick's capital city on the banks of the Saint John River is older than the province itself. Three hundred years ago the Saint John River, named Woolastook by the Micmac and Maliseet tribes, was a good place to fish, and settlements dotted its shores. By the end of the 1600s the French had built a fort here where the Saint John and Nashwaak rivers meet, and soon afterward a civilian settlement was established, and named for St. Anne.

When the British took control of French North America in the mid-1700s, they took over the site of St. Anne's, but it was really the influx of Loyalists fleeing the American Revolution who shaped the city—and the province. Some of the first Loyalists settlers didn't survive their first winter here, in 1783, dying from the cold and other hardships brought on by living in tents and log huts.

At first part of Nova Scotia, New Brunswick was declared a separate province in 1784 when the flood of Loyalists brought a population boom. The new province's first chief executive, Gov. Thomas Carleton, put his finger on the map at St. Anne's, marking it as the capital city and renaming it in honor of King George III's second son, Frederick, bishop of Osnabrück.

Today Fredericton (pop. 47,500) is a genteel, easygoing place with a village green and a river walk. It hardly seems a government town at all. The province's most famous native son, Lord Beaverbrook, had an enduring affection for the city, as evidenced by several generous gifts, including its fine arts gallery and playhouse.

Fredericton is home to two universities. One, the University of New Brunswick (1785), shares the honor of being the oldest public university in North America with the University of Georgia. It also once was home to the New Brunswick Baptist Seminary, the first college in Canada to admit men and women on equal footing and not to require religious tests. The city that was named for a bishop and royal scion is also, not so surprisingly, the seat of an Anglican bishopric.

WHAT TO SEE & DO

The starting point for any Fredericton tour should be **Officers' Square,** on Queen Street between Carleton and Regent, the site of free summer band concerts on Tuesday and Thursday evenings at 7:30pm. Pipe bands, marching and military bands from the city and the region, provide the music; you provide your own blanket, cushion, or chair. Lord Beaverbrook, New Brunswick's famous native son, is immortalized in a statue that stands in the square.

Actually a fine downtown park today, Officers' Square once was the city's military parade ground, and the quarters for officers of the British garrison, built between 1839 and 1851 and flanking the square's western side, now house the York-Sunbury Historical Society Museum.

From here, walk to old **City Hall** (1876), at Queen Street and Phoenix Square, and pay your respects to "Freddy the Nude Dude," who hangs out in the fountain (1885)

IMPRESSIONS

Fredericton is the unmarred and unscratched relic, the perfect museum piece, and with that final rarity in our time, a complete unconsciousness of itself, for it has never been discovered, extolled, or exploited by the traveller.
—BRUCE HUTCHINSON, *THE UNKNOWN DOMINION,* 1946

out front. Inside, in the Council Chamber, where the mayor and city councillors meet, hang 27 wool tapestries tracing the history of Fredericton, and someone is usually on hand to show them to you. The tapestries were created by two local artists, Gertrude Duffie and Dr. Ivan Crowell, in honor of the capital city's bicentennial in 1985.

Near City Hall, the **New Brunswick College of Craft and Design,** founded in 1950s and the only college-level school in Canada devoted to the development of craftspeople and designers, offers courses in pewter, pottery, and weaving. The work of some of its pewtersmiths is in the Smithsonian museums, but you can see it more immediately at **Aitkens Pewter,** 81 Regent St., founded in 1972 by Martin Aitken when he was only 17 years old (tel. 506/453-9474). Outstanding pottery, along with children's clothes and books, is sold at **Table for Two,** 349 King St. (tel. 506/455-1401).

Nearby, at 514 Queen St., is the small, free **New Brunswick Electricity Museum,** open September to June from 9am to 4:30pm Monday through Friday; in July and August, it's open daily, with longer hours (tel. 506/458-6805).

The favorite activity of many locals and visitors is strolling along the **River Walk,** which you can pick up anywhere downtown. It actually stretches about three miles, from the Sheraton hotel, along the bank of the Saint John River and the Green, past the Waterloo row houses (Fredericton's prettiest stretch of houses), to the remains of an old Loyalist cemetery, with a marker and a couple of tombstones dating from 1783 (it's just beyond Morell Park; follow the road beside the baseball field). I walked River Walk one way and took a cab back to my hotel (Student Taxi; tel. 506/459-8294); you might choose to walk only part way, but don't miss the row houses.

At the intersection of Brunswick and Church Streets, look at **Christ Church Cathedral,** built between 1845 and 1853 as the seat of Fredericton's Anglican bishop. From mid-June to Labor Day, free tours of the church are given daily: on weekdays between 9am and 8pm, on Saturday 10am to 5pm, and on Sunday after church, from 1 to 5pm (tel. 506/450-8500).

If you'd rather bike than walk, rent a bicycle from **Savage's,** 449 Queen St. (tel. 506/458-8985). Or if renting a canoe or kayak and exploring the Saint John River appeals to you, head for the **Aquatic Centre,** downtown on the river (walk to it or take the Victoria Health Centre driveway off Queen Street); they offer short courses in canoeing, kayaking, and rowing, as well as three-day river ecology tours for adults and families or teens (tel. 506/458-5513).

Don't leave town without at least a quick auto tour of the lovely hillside that cradles two universities: the **University of New Brunswick** (founded 1785) and **Saint Thomas University** (1910). The University of New Brunswick's Art Centre hosts summer exhibits in Memorial Hall on the UNB campus (Baily Drive), open Monday to Friday from 10am to 5pm, on Sunday from 2 to 4pm (tel. 506/453-4623).

On Wednesday from 4:30 to 9pm and Saturday from 6am to 1pm, the **Boyce Farmers' Market,** on George Street between Regent and St. John, is a delight to explore, with more than 100 stalls selling not only fresh fruits and vegetables, but all sorts of homemade edible goodies and craft items as well.

For evening entertainment fall, winter, and spring, attend a play at the **Playhouse,** Queen Street, a gift of Lord Beaverbrook to the city and the province, built in 1964. Call 506/458-8344 for the latest information on works staged by Theatre New Brunswick, the resident company. The season runs from September to mid-May.

Any season of the year, you can hear blues at **The Exchange,** above Trumpers café, at 366 Queen St. (tel. 506/459-2911).

OLD BURIAL GROUND, bounded by Brunswick, George, Regent, and Sunbury Sts.

The historical town plot, it was in use from 1787 to 1878 and is the resting place for the remains of Loyalists families and British settlers and soldiers, the province's first officials and clergy, and the founders of Fredericton. (There is also a small Loyalist cemetery near Morell Park, at the end of River Walk but only a couple of tombstones remain.)

Admission: Free.
Open: Daily 8am–9pm.

**YORK-SUNBURY HISTORICAL SOCIETY MUSEUM, west side of Offi-
cers' Sq. Tel. 506/455-6041.**

Housed in the old officers' quarters of the British regiments, the museum is filled
with exhibits depicting local military and civilian history from the native period to the
Loyalists to the pioneers to the recent past. On the third floor, be sure to see—are you
ready?—the taxidermically preserved 42-pound frog. Fredericton's legendary
Coleman frog was the pet of one Fred Coleman, a local innkeeper who adopted it as
a youngster and nurtured it to record-breaking size. The museum features seasonal exhibitions of a historic nature of contemporary New Brunswick fine arts and
crafts.

Admission: $1 adults, 50¢ seniors and students, children under 6 free, $2.50
family pass.

Open: May–June and early Sept Mon–Sat 10am–6pm; July–Aug Mon, Wed,
and Fri–Sat 10am–6pm, Tues and Thurs 10am–9pm, Sun noon–6pm; autumn
Mon–Fri 9am–5pm, Sat noon–4pm; winter Mon, Wed, and Fri 11am–3pm or by
appointment.

SOLDIERS' BARRACKS, Queen and Carleton Sts. Tel. 506/453-3747.

For a look at where the soldiers (not the officers) lived, check out the Soldiers'
Barracks (1827), completely restored a few years ago. (The entrance is off Carleton,
not on Queen.) A room has been set up as it would have been when 19 infantrymen
occupied it over 100 years ago. In the same compound stands the Guard House
(1828), the lockup where men who disobeyed orders or regulations were held. It's now
a museum of military memorabilia, and like the Soldiers' Barracks, is free.

Admission: Free.

Open: Daily 10am–6pm. **Closed:** Labor Day–May.

LEGISLATIVE ASSEMBLY BUILDING, Queen St. Tel. 506/453-2527.

The seat and symbol of democracy in New Brunswick since 1882, it was restored
in 1988. Guides are on hand to show you the architectural and decorative highlights in
the Assembly Chamber: Waterford crystal chandeliers, and two large portraits of King
George III and his consort, Queen Charlotte. (The province was named for the king's
ancestral family seat, Brunswick, in Germany.) In the front of the chamber is the
Speaker's Chair, which is just that when the Speaker of the House presides over a
session of the assembly. But when the queen's representative, New Brunswick's
lieutenant governor, attends a session of the assembly, the chair becomes the
"Throne," symbol of the monarch's reign. Be sure to see the handsome spiral
staircase at the end of the main hallway.

Admission: Free.

Open: Early June–late Aug daily 9am–8pm (tours every half hour from 9:15am);
the rest of the year Mon–Fri 9am–4pm.

**BEAVERBROOK ART GALLERY, Queen St., at Saint John St. Tel. 506/
458-8545.**

Across Queen Street from the Legislative Assembly Building is the center of
Fredericton's artistic life, a gift from Lord Beaverbrook to the people of New
Brunswick. Don't miss this fine modern gallery and its impressive collection of
British paintings (Reynolds, Gainsborough, Constable, Turner, and other greats),

---

IMPRESSIONS

*What was the secret behind all the great men that this tiny, rather backward
corner of Canada had produced? In Fredericton, the capital of New Brunswick, I
asked this of a dynamic, one-eyed British ex-Brigadier named Mike Wardell.
"I can tell you exactly what makes them," he replied. "It's the challenge of
having to creep out to the outhouse every winter's day at 30° below zero!"*
—ALISTAIR HORNE, *CANADA AND THE CANADIANS*, 1961

Canadian and provincial works, and Salvador Dalí's *Santiago el Grande*. In 1983 the gallery opened a new exhibition wing composed of period rooms, with displays of paintings and decorative arts from the 14th through 19th centuries. There are also some contemporary exhibits.

Admission: $3 adults, $2 seniors, $1 students; children under 6 free; family rate $6.

Open: July–Aug Sun–Mon noon–8pm, Tues–Wed 10am–8pm, Thurs–Sat 10am–5pm; Sept–June Tues–Sat 10am–5pm, Sun–Mon noon–5pm.

FREDERICTON NATIONAL EXHIBITION CENTRE, 503 Queen St., at Carleton. Tel. 506/453-3747.

The changing exhibits on the ground floor of this Second Empire French Revivial-style building might be anything from a collection of Japanese kites or Canadian photographers' works, to a display of the latest in computer technology. The second floor houses the New Brunswick Sports Hall of Fame. The building is easily recognizable by its mansard roof.

Admission: Free.

Open: May–Labor Day Sun–Thurs and Sat 10am–5pm, Fri 10am–9pm; rest of the year Tues–Fri noon–4:30pm, Sat 10am–5pm, Sun 1–5pm.

ORGANIZED TOURS

The **Calithumpians Theatre Company** (tel. 506/457-1975) provides one-hour escorted walking tours of the city featuring historically costumed guides and dramatic commentary. Tours begin at City Hall on weekdays at 10am and 2, 4, and 7pm, and on weekends and holidays at noon, 4pm, and 7pm. The group also performs plays for free at Officers' Square weekdays at 12:15pm, and on weekends and holidays at 2pm.

NEARBY ATTRACTIONS

KING'S LANDING HISTORICAL SETTLEMENT, Exit 259 off the Trans Canada Hwy. (Hwy. 2 west). Tel. 506/363-5090, or 506/363-5805 for recorded information.

 King's Landing, on the bank of the Saint John River, is 21 miles (34km) and at least 150 years from Fredericton. The most authentic re-creation of a place and time I've ever encountered, it brings back to life the New Brunswick of 1790 to 1900, in 10 historic houses and nine other buildings saved from destruction by the flooding that resulted from the Mactaquac hydro project and relocated here. At King's Landing, every facet of pioneer life, from sheepshearing to milling to dying wool with onion-skin coloring, is revealed. The aroma of freshly baked bread mixes with the smell of horses and livestock, and the sound of the blacksmith's hammer alternates with that of the church bell. More than 100 early settlers ("interpreters" to us modern folk) in every house, field, and workshop will chat about their lives, but they're also content if you choose just to watch them at work and play.

In your explorations, don't overlook the Hagerman House (with furniture by Victorian cabinetmaker John Warren Moore), the Jones House (the only stone house, brought here stone by stone), the Ingraham House with its fine New Brunswick furniture and artesian spring, the Morehouse House (where you'll see a clock Benedict Arnold left behind), the Victorian Perley House, and the sawmill and gristmill.

Allow four hours to fully explore the 300 acres and the numerous buildings on them, and to commune with the cows, horses, oxen, sheep, pigs, and their offspring (all typical of the livestock that was here in the 1800s). If you get tired, you can hitch a ride in an oxcart, or if you work up an appetite, head for the King's Head Inn, which actually served up grub and grog to the hardy types who traveled along the Saint John River a century or more ago. Today the lemonade, chicken pie, and corn chowder come highly recommended.

Children may participate in the unique Visiting Cousins program, in which children live for five days as they would have 100 years ago. They dress in period costume, attend school, do chores like making butter or candles, and eat Loyalist-style meals with their "families."

King's Landing hosts fall harvest dinners and Christmas dinners. There is a large gift shop at the entrance.

Admission: $7.50 adults, $5.25 seniors and students, $4.25 youths 6–18, $15 family pass.

Open: July–Aug daily 10am–6pm; June and Sept–Oct daily 10am–5pm.

Closed: Canadian Thanksgiving (second Monday in Oct); Nov–May.

MACTAQUAC PROVINCIAL PARK, Rte. 105. Tel. 506/363-3011 (Mon–Fri 8am–5pm).

Only 15 miles (24km) west of Fredericton on Route 105, off the Trans Canada Highway, is the province's largest (1,400 acres) and most elaborate park. A spin-off of the Mactaquac Power Development, the park spreads along the shores of the dam's 50-mile-long "headpond," in which park visitors can swim, fish, sail, row, and waterski. There are several kilometers of self-guided nature walks and hiking trails, and nearly 300 campsites for tents and trailers set up in the park. At the 18-hole golf course you don't even have to bring your own clubs; rental sets, lessons, and electric carts are all yours for a reasonable fee. In Mactaquac Lodge, the "19th hole," you will find a licensed lounge and restaurant for golfers and anyone else who has worked up an appetite. The park maintains cross-country ski trails in winter.

Admission: $3.50 per car.

Open: Mid-May to mid-Oct daily 8am–dusk.

WOOLASTOOK PARK, off the Trans Canada Hwy. Tel. 506/363-5410.

This park, only a few miles west of Mactaquac Park, west of Fredericton, just off the Trans Canada Highway (follow the bear-shaped signs) provides a living lesson in Canadian fauna. Woolastook's 196 acres harbor deer, caribou, moose, seals, cougars, coyotes, raccoons, skunks, and muskrats. There's a nursery where orphaned baby animals—fawns, bear cubs, fox pups, and others—are cared for. For a different type of wild life, indulge in a ride on one of four water slides in the park, or a round on its deluxe mini-golf course. And if you're having too good a time to leave, there are 200 campsites, a canteen, licensed restaurant, and gift shop to convince you to stay.

Admission: Rates vary according to activity. Wildlife park, $5.50 adults, $4 children 6–15, family pass $17. Golf, $4.75 adults, $3.25 age 15 and under.

Open: July–Aug daily 9am–9pm; mid-May to June and Sept daily 9am–5pm.

WHERE TO STAY
HOTELS

LORD BEAVERBROOK HOTEL, 659 Queen St. (P.O. Box 545), Fredericton, NB, E3B 5A6. Tel. 506/455-3371, or toll free 800/561-1441 in Canada and the New England states. Fax 506/455-1441. 153 rms, 10 suites. A/C TV TEL
$ Rates: $89 single or double; $95 suite. Weekend specials and packages available. AE, DC, DISC, ER, MC, V. **Parking:** Free.

Named for Fredericton's benefactor and Britain's powerful press baron, the Lord Beaverbrook Hotel, at the corner of Saint John Street, is conveniently located, next door to the Beaverbrook Art Gallery, across the street from the Playhouse and the Legislative Assembly Building, and very near the SMT bus station. The hotel, on the Saint John River, has been a presence in the city since 1947. It has modern rooms—so modern, in fact that each unit has a computer jack. Those on the executive floor have hairdryers and pants press. The staff is friendly and helpful.

Dining/Entertainment: The Terrace Room, with tremendous windows overlooking the river, serves breakfast, lunch, and dinner (kids eat for 99¢). The more formal Governor's Room serves dinner only and specializes in steaks and seafood. The casual River Room Lounge, open from 2pm to 2am, serves food until 9pm and has entertainment nightly, anything from folk music to country rock. The Cabana Bar, by the pool, serves light fare. Occasionally the hotel offers dinner theater.

Services: Room service from 6:30am to 10:30pm, same-day dry cleaning and laundry, airport shuttle service ($6), business services.

Facilities: Large indoor swimming pool (8am to midnight), kiddie pool, large Jacuzzi, sauna, games room with Ping-Pong, video games, and big-screen TV; no-smoking floors, executive floor, meeting rooms, gift shop, beauty salon.

SHERATON INN, 225 Woodstock Rd., Fredericton, NB, E3B 2H8. Tel. 506/457-7000, or toll free 800/325-3535. Fax 506/457-4000. 208 rms, 15 suites. A/C MINIBAR TV TEL

$ Rates: Sun–Thurs $122 single or double, Fri–Sat $59 single or double; from $135 suite. Extra person $10. Children under 17 stay free with parents. Packages available. AE, CB, DC, ER, MC, V. **Parking:** Free.

On a bucolic bend in the Saint John River, the Sheraton Inn made quite a splash when it opened in 1993 and has become a social center for those who live here and an idyllic getaway for those who stay here. The focal point is the pool and the poolside café and bar, overlooking the river. The view from here is mesmerizing, especially at sunset. The rooms, some of which offer that same wonderful view, are pretty and decorated in restful colors; they have good reading light, too. Guests have use of a voice-mail system. The hotel may be fortresslike from the outside, but it's altogether inviting on the inside. It's a pleasant 10-minute walk along the river from the historic center of town, or a quick drive away, and on the road to King's Landing.

Dining/Entertainment: Bruno's family-style restaurant, with an antipasto bar, is open 6:30am to 11pm. D. J. Purdy's lounge has jazz Thursday through Saturday nights (it's open 11am to 1am, to 2am on Friday and Saturday). The Dip poolside bar and grill is open 11am to midnight daily in summer, weather permitting.

Services: 24-hour room service, same-day dry cleaning and laundry, business services, babysitting.

Facilities: Indoor and outdoor swimming pools, Jacuzzi, sauna, small but well-equipped exercise room with TV; meeting rooms.

A MOTEL

TOWN AND COUNTRY MOTEL, 967 Woodstock Rd. (R.R. 3), Fredericton, NB, E3B 4X4. Tel. 506/454-4223. 18 units (all with bath). A/C TV TEL

$ Rates: June–Sept $51–$56 single, $56–$66 double; Oct–May $40 single, $45 double. Extra person $5 or $10. MC, V.

There are several good motels in Fredericton, but I'm partial to this mom-and-pop place. Small and tidy, this motel has sat on a clover-covered bank of the Saint John River welcoming travelers for 25 years, and it's had the same owners, Sally and Francis Delmas, all that time. Each of the units has one or two double beds, full bath, remote-control cable television, and telephone, and 11 units have their own kitchenette. Rooms 12, 13, and 14 have great river views. The view, by the way, rivals that of the motel's near neighbor, the Sheraton Inn, but the trade-off is that you pay less money for fewer amenities and no pool. In 25 years, the Delmases have not lost their enthusiasm for welcoming guests or keeping the property neat and clean. There's a lot to be said for that.

BED-AND-BREAKFAST

CARRIAGE HOUSE BED AND BREAKFAST, 230 University Ave., Fredericton, NB, E3B 4H7. Tel. 506/454-6090. Fax 506/453-1971. 7 rms (2 with bath). TEL

$ Rates (including breakfast): $45–$55 single; $50–$60 double. Extra person 12 and older $15; children under 12 $5. MC, V.

Despite the many lovely turn-of-the-century homes sprinkled through Fredericton's residential areas, surprisingly few are guest homes. An exception is the Carriage House Bed and Breakfast. Joan and Frank Gorham have created a quiet retreat only five minutes from downtown. All seven rooms, some large, some small, are made homey with floral wallpaper and colorful throw rugs. Two of the rooms have private baths; the other five share three baths. Breakfast is served in the solarium. The Gorhams raised eight kids in this house, and they are obviously comfortable with people coming in and out. There's a coin-operated washer and dryer for guests' convenience, and, a block away, a market selling ice cream and much more.

DORMITORY & HOSTEL ROOMS

Want to stay, inexpensively, at the lovely **University of New Brunswick,** P.O. Box 4400, Fredericton, NB, E3B 5A3 (tel. 506/453-4891)? During the summer months the university rents some of its dormitory rooms, usually about 50 of them, to visitors, and you can find out what's available by calling. Singles are $28 and doubles are $40.

YORK HOUSE YOUTH HOSTEL, 193 York St., Fredericton, NB, E3B 5A6. Tel. 506/454-1233. 30 beds.

$ Rates: $9 AYH members; $12 nonmembers. No credit cards. **Closed:** Sept-June.

Fredericton's youth hostel is in an old brick schoolhouse. Its beds are arranged dormitory style, with 14 in the women's section and 16 in the men's. There's also a room for a family. Guests share a kitchen and large common room that has games, a piano, and a Ping-Pong table. Meals are available: breakfast, a packed lunch, and supper, all inexpensive. The hostel, near the Old Burial Ground and just a few blocks from the heart of downtown Fredericton, stands on the site of the New Brunswick Baptist Seminary, the first college in Canada to admit men and women on equal footing.

WHERE TO DINE

BAR B Q, 540 Queen St. Tel. 506/455-2742.
   Cuisine: BARBECUE. **Reservations:** Not needed.
$ Prices: Appetizers $3–$8; main courses $4–$12. AE, DC, ER, MC, V.
   Open: Lunch daily 11am–5pm; dinner daily 5–11pm.
The wooden booths and tables at the Bar B Q Barn are constantly filled with people clamoring for barbecue chicken and ribs. There's plenty more on the menu, though, including club sandwiches, chicken potpie, fish-and-chips, and pasta. Check out the blackboard specials, too.

THE DIP, in the Sheraton Inn, 225 Woodstock Rd. Tel. 506/457-7000.
   Cuisine: LIGHT FARE. **Reservations:** Not needed.
$ Prices: Most items $3–$16. AE, DC, ER, MC, V.
   Open: Daily 11am–midnight, weather permitting. **Closed:** Oct to mid-May.

 This bar and grill draws locals and hotel guests like a magnet for two good reasons: a view that goes on forever and good food. Popular items on the short-but-sweet menu include the pasta salad, club sandwich, and "mussels mania." Beer and mixed drinks are $3.75 (including tax), specialty drinks $5.75, but don't forget about happy hour; it's from 4:30 to 7pm. The atmosphere at the Dip is relaxed, and the service friendly (and pretty speedy, even when it's crowded). If you're staying downtown, you can follow the River Walk here; it takes about 10 minutes.

J, M & T DELI, 66 Regent St., near Queen St. Tel. 506/458-9068.
   Cuisine: DELI. **Reservations:** Not needed.
$ Prices: Most items $1–$5. No credit cards.
   Open: Mon–Fri 7:30am–5pm, Sat 7am–3pm.

S J, M & T Deli, a family operation, is a popular breakfast spot frequented by everybody from politicians to students. It's also a Montréal-style deli, with smoked-meat sandwiches with cheese, pickles, and the like. Homemade muffins, yogurt, BLTs, Dagwoods, quiche, lasagne, and desserts are also served. For your coffee or tea, choose a cup or mug from their eclectic assortment. The bulletin board announces local entertainment and festivals. Sit at a stool in the window or a small table with vinyl tablecloth in front; there's more seating in back.

LA VIE EN ROSE, 570 Queen St. Tel. 506/455-1319.
   Cuisine: INTERNATIONAL. **Reservations:** Recommended.
$ Prices: Lunch appetizers $4–$9, specialty sandwiches $4–$9, main courses $9–$12; dinner appetizers $4–$7, main courses $7–$19. CB, DC, MC, V.
   Open: Mon–Fri breakfast 9am–11:30am, lunch 11:30am–2pm, dinner 5pm–midnight; Sat 5pm–midnight; Sun brunch 11am–2pm, dinner 5pm–midnight.
Pretty, quiet, and informal, La Vie en Rose serves something for every taste: sandwiches, barbecue spit-roasted chicken, teriyaki chicken brochette, beef or pork

Wellington, sirloin steak, baked stuffed garlic shrimp, bacon-wrapped scallops, sole amandine, and salmon. Breakfast is limited to muffins and coffee during the week, but Sunday brunch is an all-you-can-eat affair for $9 to $12. The daily lunch special costs about $6, and in the evening, you can add $9.95 to the price of any main course and get it as part of a four-course dinner. Specialty coffees and desserts, raspberry sour cream pie among them, are popular here. It's fully licensed. The kitchen closes at 10pm.

TRUMPERS, 349 King St., Piper Lane. Tel. 506/444-0819.
   Cuisine: VEGETARIAN. **Reservations:** Not needed.
$ **Prices:** Most items $2.50–$5.50. V.
   Open: Daily 8am–8pm (hours may be extended).
        This is a delightful, and tiny, family affair. Suzanne Giberson is the accomplished chef, and her husband and children (all of them hail from London) are her backup support. There are four tables inside and four more outside, so you may have to wait your turn—or settle for take-out. Popular items include lasagne and curry dishes, but you can get pita sandwiches, quiche, and salads. There are also four daily specials. They also serve herbal ice tea (a real find, since ice tea made from a mix is served throughout Atlantic Canada). The café takes its name from the Jeffrey Archer novel. The Exchange blues bar is upstairs in the same building.

EN ROUTE TO MONCTON

Traveling east toward Moncton from Fredericton or Saint John, the Trans Canada Highway meets Highway 114, the road to Fundy National Park. If you get an early start, there should be plenty of time to detour through the park, see "The Rocks," and arrive in Moncton, 56 miles (90km) away, at a decent hour.

FUNDY NATIONAL PARK, Hwy. 114. Tel. 506/887-2000.
        The area encompassing Fundy National Park was chosen—as were all the Canadian national parks—to preserve and make available to visitors various unique features of Canadian terrain. The park harbors forests and bogs resembling those found much farther north, in Newfoundland, not to mention the world-record Fundy tides. There is no tidal bore here; you'll have to catch that in Moncton, or Truro, Nova Scotia. But the rise and fall of the tides is astounding nonetheless. At low tide there's good beachcombing, and little marine creatures are everywhere. Besides 50 miles of hiking trails, Fundy park has a number of "auto trails," one-lane dirt roads kept in good condition for exploring by car. Civilized amusements compete with the call of the wild: a heated saltwater swimming pool, tennis courts, lawn-bowling green, and a nine-hole golf course, in addition to chalet accommodations and five campgrounds. To drive into the park you'll have to buy a one- or four-day permit, which entitles you to drive around, swim, picnic, and hike; other activities will require an extra fee.
        Admission: $5 per car per day (actually until noon the next day); four-day permit, $10. Canadian seniors free.
        Open: Year-round.

THE ROCKS, off Hwy. 114. Tel. 506/734-2026.
        Following Route 114 out of the park toward Moncton, watch for signs for the Rocks, perhaps the best place to appreciate the powerful force of the Fundy tides. The rich, red sandstone formations, some topped by trees, were formerly part of the nearby cliffs. Over time the tidal action has eroded and sculpted them into fantastical shapes of gigantic proportions. The Rocks are also known as "flowerpots" because at high tide all you see is the tops of the formations, crowned by the vegetation they support. During low tide you can descend the many flights of steps to get a closer look at nature's ongoing artistry. Be sure to ascend when the "giant clock" advises, or you'll find yourself in deep and dangerous trouble. Park interpreters are on hand in summer to answer your questions.

Admission: $3.50 per vehicle.
Open: Daily 8am–9pm. **Closed:** Nov–Apr.

WHERE TO STAY & DINE IN FUNDY PARK

FUNDY PARK CHALETS, Fundy National Park, P.O. Box 72, Alma, NB, E0A 1B0. Tel. 506/887-2808. 29 cabins. TV
$ Rates: Mid-June to Labor Day $62 one to four people; May to mid-June and early Sept to mid-Oct Sun–Thurs $47 one to four people, Fri–Sat $62. Extra person $3; crib or cot rental $2. No credit cards. **Closed:** Oct to mid-May.

Located in the headquarters area of the park, near the Alma entrance/exit, Fundy Park Chalets has 29 cabins, some with bay views. Clustered in a wooded area, they have a fully equipped kitchenette, private bath with shower, black-and-white TV, and a bed/living room with two double beds. For a bit of privacy, beds can be partitioned off from one another with a curtain. Management provides sheets, blankets, and towels. A dining room and pro shop are a few minutes' walk away, and there is a large children's playground across the road and a golf course and heated saltwater pool nearby. You can buy groceries in Alma. Off-season, write or call for reservations. They accept personal checks and traveler's checks and welcome pets on a leash.

6. MONCTON

121 miles (195km) NE of Fredericton, 94 miles (152km) NE of Saint John

GETTING THERE From Saint John, take Highway 1 to Sussex and pick up the Trans Canada Highway (Highway 2); the slow, scenic route follows Highway 2 to Penobsquis, picks up Route 114 through Fundy park and up the coast past Hopewell Rocks and then into Moncton. From Fredericton, the prettiest route is along the Trans Canada Highway all the way; the quickest way is via Coles Island and Route 112, through mostly wooded, scantly populated areas; no trucks are allowed on this route.

ESSENTIALS   Information The Public Relations and Tourism Office at City Hall, 774 Main St. (tel. 506/853-3596), will answer your questions and hand out free visitor guides and maps from 8am to 5pm Monday through Friday year-round. In addition, from mid-May to Labor Day two tourist information centers are in operation, one on Main Street (the address varies from year to year, but it's easy to find) and the other at Magnetic Hill on Highway 2 (the Trans Canada) at the intersection with Highway 126. The latter has a lookout with a view of the city.

Parking Securing a parking place can be tough in downtown Moncton. No parking is allowed on Main Street, but you can find some meters and two-hour zones, as well as the occasional lot, on some of the side streets.

To New Brunswickers, Moncton is the brash young town on the Atlantic coast, lacking the sense of history found in Saint John, perhaps, or the gentility of Fredericton, but with business savvy and eyes on the future. Coming into the city, you'll see the Telephone Tower (no longer in use) poking at the sky like some technological minaret.

It marks the spot of the fast-growing city in the province. Some 54,750 people live here—112,000 if you count greater Moncton. Location is everything, and Moncton is ideally situated near Maine, Nova Scotia, and Prince Edward Island.

Moncton is 30% francophone and is home to the sprawling campus of the French-language Université de Moncton, which occupies a large area north of the center of town. It has about 6,000 students, and there is an Acadian museum on the campus (see "What to See and Do," below). Drive out for a look. The university sponsors a hostel from May through August for about $20 a night (tel. 506/858-4008).

Although the city's name was given to honor Lt. Robert Monckton, commander of the British force that took nearby Fort Beauséjour in 1795, it was actually some legal clerk who gave the name its spelling. By inadvertently leaving out the "k," he blessed the town with its moniker.

WHAT TO SEE & DO

The big news in Moncton is the $3.5 million restoration and reopening of the **Capitol Theatre,** 811 Main St. (tel. 506/856-4377). The luxurious 875-seat theater, complete with box seats, first opened in 1922, and is now the cultural center for this region. It hosts Canadian and international artists, including the New Brunswick Symphony and Les Grands Ballets Canadiens; recent productions staged here have included *Brigadoon* and *The Nutcracker.* In the elegant lobby, theatergoers are greeted by the original chandelier and changing artwork; a bar/lounge is on the balcony level. The building also houses the 250-seat **Empress** (1908), which was a movie theater for many years. Ticket prices range from $8 to $35.

The **Moncton Coliseum** hosts big-name performers and seats 9,000 fans (tel. 506/859-2689).

Bore View Park, in the center of town off Main Street, is the best spot to watch the rippling waters of the tidal bore (or current) rush up the Petitcodiac River from the Bay of Fundy, more than 20 miles away. Bleachers are set up for onlookers, and lights for night viewing, and a large signboard lists the times for the action. The bore is highest in spring and autumn; in summer, it ranges from a few inches to six feet. The initial wave is less impressive than the flood that follows it.

The city's 450-acre **Centennial Park** has lawn bowling, tennis courts, paddleboat and canoe rentals, an English garden, a large playground, a couple of canteens, and washrooms. The 2.5-mile dirt road around the park is popular with walkers and joggers. There are sleigh rides and ice skating here in winter. The park is patrolled by police on horseback. Look for the Voodoo jet and Sherman tank at the entrance.

If you're a golfer, you'll be happy to know there are six courses within the city limits of Moncton.

Visit the local **Farmers Market,** at 132 Robinson St., on Saturday morning from 7am to 1pm or on Wednesday from noon to 4pm. Here you'll find flowers, herbs, Kurt's famous sausages, homemade butter, cider, breads, beeswax from Honey Tree Farm, and even baklava. The market is down the hill from Main Street (tel. 506/383-6876).

There's a small indoor **amusement park** out at the Champlain Mall. Parents ride free with children on certain rides. You buy a book of tickets and "spend" them as you go; one ride is one to three tickets.

Moncton is within an hour's drive of two national parks; Fundy, with its rugged cliffs, and Kouchibouguac, with its sand dunes and lowland marshes.

The city hosts a **Crafts Fair** the first Saturday in August. There's a good bookstore in town, **Friends Forever,** 569A Main St. (tel. 506/389-2437), with a large selection of books for children, as well as nonfiction for adults.

MAGNETIC HILL, Magnetic Hill exit off the Trans Canada Hwy. No phone.

Moncton's claim to fame, more than its two museums or the Petitcodiac's tidal bore, is unquestionably Magnetic Hill. Drive east out of town on Route 15, then take Highway 126 north to the intersection with Highway 2, the Trans Canada, and Magnetic Hill signs will guide you the distance to the site, actually part of Magnetic Hill Park.

Magnetic Hill is fun, but it's also confusing, and to enjoy the sensation of "coasting uphill," you must follow directions. (If you're not in a car, you can't really get the feel of the hill.) As you approach the hill, signs will instruct you to drive down the slope. At the bottom, cross to the left side of the roadway and stop your car by the white post. Put it in neutral, let off the brakes, and *voilà*—back you go up the gentle slope to the top where you started. How?

It really does seem like your car's gliding smoothly up the gentle slope. But now that you've had the fun, drive or walk to the top of the hill past the white post, near the turnaround area for cars with trailers, and all will become clear. Although anyone would swear that Magnetic Hill slopes upward from the white post, from any spot higher up it's evident that the slope is downward. What could cause so baffling an optical illusion? That's still a mystery to me, and whether the experience, which takes about three minutes, is worth $2 is a toss-up.

Admission: $2 per car.
Open: May–Nov daily dawn–dusk (approximately).

MAGIC MOUNTAIN WATER PARK, Magnetic Hill exit off Trans Canada Hwy.

Water, water everywhere. That's what you'll find at Magic Mountain, along with a replica of a Mississippi paddle wheeler and a 40-m.p.h. Kamikaze water slide.

Admission: Free to enter; you only pay for rides.
Open: Mid- to late June and last half Aug daily 10am–6pm; late June to mid-Aug daily 10am–8pm. **Closed:** Sept–early June.

MAGNETIC HILL ZOO. Tel. 506/384-9381.

There are about 100 species of native and exotic animals in the zoo, as well as a nursery and petting zoo. Beside the entrance, you can hop aboard a train for unlimited rides throughout the park; the fare is $4.

Admission: $3.75 adults, $2.75 seniors and youths 12–17, $2.25 children 6–11.
Open: Mid-May to Oct., daily 10am–dusk.

MONCTON MUSEUM/FREE MEETING HOUSE, 20 Mountain Rd., near the corner of Belleview. Tel. 506/853-3003.

You'll be into the realm of Old Moncton even before you enter the museum building: The entry was once part of the facade of Moncton's old City Hall. When it was razed, its front was preserved and re-erected as part of the facade of the modern museum. Inside you'll find a permanent exhibit on the history of Moncton (upstairs), as well as changing exhibits, often imported from Montréal's Museum of Fine Arts. Ask to see Moncton's Free Meeting House, the oldest building in the city, built in 1821 and restored in 1990, and right next door. Over the years it has been used by a dozen different congregations in the city, Protestant, Catholic, and Jewish among them.

Admission: Free.
Open: Summer daily 10am–5pm; winter Tues–Fri and Sun 1–5pm, Sat 10am–5pm.

THOMAS WILLIAMS HOUSE, 103 Park St., at the corner of Highfield. Tel. 506/857-0590.

Built in 1852, this home was in the Williams family for 100 years before it was deeded to the city of Moncton and subsequently opened to the public. Many of the furnishings belonged to the family. This unusual place actually invites visitors to make themselves at home—to sit on the furniture and browse through the photo albums. Drop by the Verandah Tea Room, on the premises, for muffins, ice cream (in summer), tea, coffee, ice tea, or lemonade. There is also an art gallery in the house that has changing exhibits.

Admission: Free.
Open: June and Sept Tues–Sat 9am–5pm, Sun 1–5pm; July–Aug Mon–Sat 9am–5pm, Sun 1–5pm; tearoom hours are slightly more restricted.

MUSEE ACADIEN [ACADIAN MUSEUM], Clement Cormier Building, Université de Moncton. Tel. 506/858-4088.

New Brunswick absorbed large numbers of the Acadian settlers driven from Nova Scotia by British troops, and the modern Acadian Museum's collection provides a visual history of almost every phase of daily life of this displaced people. It offers bilingual tours and also has an art gallery. To get to the university, head north on Archibald Street, which leads right to it. You can also take Wheeler Boulevard to the Archibald exit.

Admission: Free.
Open: Summer Mon–Fri 10am–5pm, Sat–Sun 1–5pm; rest of the year Tues–Fri 1–4:30pm, Sat–Sun 1–4pm.

WHERE TO STAY

EXPENSIVE

HOTEL BEAUSEJOUR, 750 Main St., Moncton, NB, E1C 1E6. Tel. **506/854-4344,** or toll free 800/828-7447 in the U.S., 800/268-9411 in Canada. Fax 506/854-4344. 301 rms, 13 suites. A/C TV TEL

$ Rates: $100 single; $112 double. Rates drop 15% to 20% in summer and on weekends the rest of the year. AE, DC, ER, MC, V. **Parking:** Free.

⭐ Business travelers gravitate to the Hotel Beauséjour, a CP hotel, which dominates the downtown area and is near restaurants, nightclubs, and the Capitol Theatre. The guest rooms are modern (ask for one with a city view); those on the business-class floor are particularly comfortable. There is a rooftop pool with a lifeguard and sun deck. The hotel also offers 24-hour room service, dry cleaning, in-room movies, and no-smoking wings. As for dining and entertainment, you'll find Caesar's piano bar, the Auberge café (for three meals a day), and the upscale Windjammer restaurant, which is intimate, serves continental cuisine with tableside cooking, and is open only for dinner.

MODERATE

HOTEL CANADIANA, 46 Archibald St., at Queen, Moncton, NB, E1C 5H9. Tel. 506/382-1054. 14 rms, 2 suites (all with bath). TV

$ Rates: $60–$70 single; $80–$90 double; from $85 suite. Extra person $10. Special family rates available for those with children. MC, V. **Parking:** Free. **Closed:** Dec–Jan.

You'll find the Hotel Canadiana at the corner of Queen Street, just a short stroll from Main Street. Here, another fine old Moncton mansion (1887) has been lovingly converted to an inn with hardwood floors, two parlors (among six public rooms), graceful verandas, and a pretty dining room with a mural painted by a guest almost 20 years ago. As you might expect, each room is different (guests get to pick the one they want), but all are blessedly quiet. No. 12 is a pretty double. Under the cheerful direction of bilingual hosts Alice and Roland Leger, the Hotel Canadiana provides a memorable stopover on any journey. A full breakfast is available in the dining room, for an additional charge, and they'll provide overnight laundry service for $3. If you don't feel like eating out, gather picnic fixings and eat on the inside or outside porch. And if you come in the autumn, you can go out and raid the grapevine at the side of the house.

BUDGET

YWCA, 35 Highfield St., Moncton, NB, E1C 5S8. Tel. 506/855-4349. Fax 506/855-3320. 3 rms (none with bath), 6 beds in dorm.

$ Rates: Hostel, May–Sept only, $8 using your own sleeping bag, $12 using their sheets; year-round, $20 single or $30 ($15 per person) double for a semiprivate room with two beds. Weekly and monthly rates available. No credit cards. **Parking:** Free.

Just across the street from the Colonial Inns is Moncton's YWCA, in a tower-topped, genteel old mansion, the Alfred Peters House, converted to accept female guests. There are no private baths; three showers and one tub are shared. Frankly, the accommodations are not top-notch by hostel standards, but the location is good. Three private rooms each have one twin bed. The YWCA serves inexpensive, simple meals: $3 for breakfast, $7.50 for a full-fledged meal at noon (reserve it at 9am), and $4 for supper. A laundry and TV room have been provided for guests' use.

BED-AND-BREAKFAST

BONACCORD HOUSE, 250 Bonaccord St., at Mountain Rd., Moncton, NB, E1C 5M6. Tel. 506/388-1535. Fax 506/853-7191. 4 rms (2 with bath), 1 suite.

$ Rates (including full breakfast): $35 single; $45–$48 double. Private bath $8 extra. From $53 suite. Extra person $8. V. **Parking:** Free, on site and on street.

✪ Bed-and-breakfast fans will be charmed by the special touches at the Bonaccord House: special toiletries, fresh flowers, and chilled springwater in each of the rooms, turndown service with chocolates on the pillow, and a separate telephone line and fax for guests. The four rooms, most with queen-size beds and pretty floral sheets, share three baths (two of which can be designated private for an additional $8 charge). There is also a family suite with a queen-size bed, two twin beds, a couch, and a full bath. Husband-and-wife team Patricia Townsend and Jeremy Martin are the warm, welcoming hosts. Their pretty yellow house with a picket fence in front, built around 1889, is a 10-minute walk from downtown Moncton. No smoking or pets, please.

WHERE TO DINE

Get a breakfast of pancakes or eggs for $3 at the counter inside the Farmers Market, Saturday mornings from 7am to noon. In summer it's at the end of Robinson Street, down the hill from Main Street. For an elegant, intimate dinner, go to the Windjammer at the Hotel Beauséjour.

JOE MOKA, 187 Robinson St. at Main St. Tel. 506/852-3070.
   Cuisine: LIGHT FARE. **Reservations:** Not needed.
$ Prices: Most items $1–$10. No credit cards.
   Open: Mon–Fri 9am–5:30pm, Sat 9am–5pm, Sun 10am–5pm.
Small, busy, and bilingual, this café and espresso bar serves breakfast, light lunches, and desserts, and has indoor and outdoor seating. Food—be it muffins, croissants, croque-monsieurs, quiche, or vegetarian pâte—is served in baskets. Coffees run the gamut from café au lait to espresso to cappuccino. Order at the counter. The owners, Pierre Dussault and Marc Belliveau, are from Québec. The café is around the corner from the Capitol Theatre.

7. SHEDIAC & SACKVILLE

Should you head east to Shediac or south to Sackville? It's a toss-up, really. Both are nearby, and both are special. Choose Shediac if you love the beach and lobster dinners, and you want to hang out in New Brunswick a little longer. Choose Sackville if marshlands, birdwatching, and a historic fort appeal more, or if you're ready to plunge headlong into Nova Scotia or Prince Edward Island.

SHEDIAC

A beach town that welcomes half a million visitors each year, Shediac (pop. 4,300) is the town nearest New Brunswick's balmy, warm Northumberland Strait beaches. Special conditions—low sandbars and shallow waters—allow the sun to warm up the chilly waters of the strait to bath temperatures.
   Parlee Beach, east of Shediac, is the most popular (and the most crowded during high season), but other beaches north and east of Shediac are almost as warm and less populated. On your beach search, get off Highway 15 at Exit 31B and wander the shorefront roads: 133, 134, 950, and 530.
   Seafood, Acadian, and French cuisine are featured in local restaurants, to make your stay even more enjoyable, and in the middle of July the town hosts an annual **Lobster Festival.**
   If you need more information about the area, drop by the Shediac information center. It'll be on your right as you drive into town. You can't miss it—just look for the 35-foot-long, 55-ton lobster in front! The center is open from 9am to 9pm June

through September. Next door, there's a popular gift shop, where you can buy local crafts and souvenirs.

At night the town twinkles with a "corridor of lights," thousands of small white lights in the shape of sea gulls decorating the buildings along rue Main (Main Street).

WHERE TO STAY

AUBERGE BELCOURT INN, 112 rue Main, (C.P. 631), Shediac, NB, E0A 3G0. Tel. 506/532-6098. 7 rms (5 with bath).

$ Rates (including full breakfast): $60–$75 single or double. Extra person $10. AE, DC, ER, MC, V.

Built in 1912 for Shediac's first dentist, the Auberge Belcourt is now an inviting inn with seven bedrooms, five with private baths with showers. (The large shared bath still has the original sink, tub, and beveled mirror.) The pretty, summery rooms are well lit and have ceiling fans and homemade quilts; many feature brass beds. One room has a queen-size bed. The library (my favorite room) has three overstuffed chairs and a rocker, and there's cable TV in the den. Rates include a full breakfast with fruit salad, eggs, and croissants served in a pretty dining room. Helpful hosts Thérèse and Alcide Arsenault keep a collection of local menus on hand for guests' perusal. The inn is open year-round; be sure to reserve ahead.

CHEZ FRANÇOISE, 93 rue Main, Shediac, NB, E0A 3G0. Tel. 506/532-4233. 19 rms (10 with bath).

$ Rates (including continental breakfast): $40–$55 single; $45–$65 double. Extra person $10. Packages available. AE, ER, MC, V. **Closed:** Jan–Apr.

Across the street from the Auberge Belcourt Inn, Chez Françoise is a country inn that is particularly popular with French-speaking travelers. The late-19th-century house, surrounded by elms, has an elaborate leaded-glass entry, five fireplaces, heavy wooden doors, and guest rooms with some furnishings original to the house. Continental breakfast is included, and the croissants are great. Owners Hélène and Jacques Cadieux Johanny offer an additional 10 rooms in another house across the street.

Dining at Chez Françoise is a Shediac tradition, in three pretty rooms decorated with lace curtains, fresh flowers, and hanging plants. The menu features meat and seafood dishes, prepared with French flair, as well as daily specials. Appetizers range in price from $3 to $6, main courses from $13 to $20. Dinner is served from 5 to 10pm, Sunday brunch from 11am to 3pm.

WHERE TO DINE

Lunch or dinner in Shediac is for seafood-lovers, especially during the Lobster Festival, when the delicious denizens of New Brunswick's waters are offered in greater quantity and at lower prices than normal.

FISHERMAN'S PARADISE, Main St. Tel. 506/532-6811.
   Cuisine: SEAFOOD. **Reservations:** Not needed.
$ Prices: Appetizers $3.50–$8.50; main courses $7–$25. AE, DC, ER, MC, V.
   Open: Daily 11:30am–11pm. **Closed:** Mid-Sept to mid-Apr.

Fisherman's Paradise is on the outskirts of town, not far from the intersection with Highway 15 (Exit 37). The inviting interior, with ship replicas and jaunty blue-and-white table linens, will put you in the mood for some serious seafood sampling, and their Fisherman's Paradise special will put you in the heavyweight seafood-eater's class: Half a lobster, fried clams, scallops, stuffed shrimp, and several kinds of fish are the usual ingredients, for $22. There's seafood chowder, and lobster dishes from live boiled to the fancier stuffed and salad items. Drinks are served, and there's a limited wine list.

HOTEL SHEDIAC, 279 Main St. Tel. 506/532-4405.
   Cuisine: HOME COOKING. **Reservations:** Not needed.
$ Prices: Most items $4–$10. AE, DC, ER, MC, V.
   Open: Breakfast daily 7–10am; lunch daily 11am–2pm.

The café in this old hotel is a casual, inexpensive place to eat lunch (it's where the locals go), with daily specials from $7 to $9, and sandwiches for less. It's a good place to come with kids because it has a large, fenced-in yard with picnic tables, grass, and trees, but also a pool, so keep a watchful eye. The hotel, which still lets rooms, uses its original operator-assisted "plug-in" phone system.

PATUREL SHORE HOUSE, Cape Bimet Rd., Rte. 133. Tel. 506/532-4774.

   Cuisine: SEAFOOD. **Reservations:** Recommended, especially on summer weekends.

$ **Prices:** Appetizers $5–$7; main course $7–$26. AE, ER, MC, V.

   Open: Daily 4–10pm. **Closed:** Oct–Apr.

The Paturel Shore House is the quintessential seafood restaurant, a simple white house right on the shore with a fine ocean view, and right next to a fish-packing plant. Take Route 133 about three miles east from Shediac, and turn left onto Cape Bimet Road (you should see a yellow sign on your left). As you come down to the water, the Paturel Seafood Ltd. plant will be on your right, the Paturel Shore House on your left, in a colony of summer beach houses. Arrive with a good appetite, and start with the hearty lobster stew, which can be a meal in itself. The mammoth seafood platter is a mini re-creation of the myriad products put up by the plant next door. All lobster is caught locally and will be served any way you like. If all this is too much to eat, a fish steak or seafood casserole might be more manageable.

AN EXCURSION FROM SHEDIAC

Kouchibouguac National Park has a daunting name but inviting beaches. At Kelly's Beach, lifeguards are on duty to watch children and adults; other beaches—by far the less crowded ones—have no lifeguards but lots more elbow room. Even if you don't want to swim or sunbathe, take the boardwalk out to Kelly's Beach; the 10-minute walk takes you across tidal pools, inlets, and dunes. The water all along the coast is incredibly warm, but the beaches also tend to be shallow—can't have everything! Hiking trails interlace the park. Canoe and boat rentals can be had at the rental center (call 506/876-2443, or ask the park warden). Although the number of campsites in Kouchibouguac Park is large and growing, the number of campers who vie for them in July and August—particularly on weekends—is even larger, and growing even faster. Get there early; camping fees drop off-season.

SACKVILLE

To get to Sackville from Moncton, you can either follow the Trans Canada Highway (Highway 2) all the way, or take the more scenic route—Highway 2 to St. Joseph to Route 106 east—which is only 15 minutes longer. It passes through pretty farmland and small French communities. In Dorchester, you may want to stop at **Keillor House** (1813), with period furnishings and, in its carriage house, a unique exhibit on the local maximum-security penitentiary, complete with confiscated knives and a bedsheet made into a rope. It's free (donations appreciated); open June to mid-September only, Monday through Saturday from 10am to 5pm and Sunday from 1 to 5pm. Also in Dorchester, the **Bell Inn** (1811), the oldest stone building in New Brunswick, serves home cooking Tuesday through Sunday 10am to 7pm, June to mid-September.

Sackville is home to 6,000 people and to Mount Albion University, which has 2,200 students. But just before you arrive, you'll pass signs for historic Fort Beauséjour.

The Sackville Information Center, on East Main Street, is open June through October (tel. 506/364-0431; 506/364-0400 November to May).

WHAT TO SEE & DO

FORT BEAUSÉJOUR NATIONAL HISTORIC PARK, near Aulac. Tel. 506/536-0720.

Just down the road from Sackville, near the hamlet of Aulac and almost at the Nova Scotia border, stands Fort Beauséjour (1751–55), commanding the sprawling Tantramar marshes and the head of the Bay of Fundy. The French built it because the

British had built a fort nearby the previous year. New England militia forces, under British command, captured the fort in June 1755, and their leader, young Colonel Monckton, renamed it Fort Cumberland. Visit the impressive earthworks and talk with park staff, who will gladly tell you about the great fort and its history. Indoor and outdoor picnic facilities are available, all with a view. A visitor center and a gift shop are on site.

Admission: Free.
Open: Daily 9am–5pm. **Closed:** Late Oct–May.

SACKVILLE WATERFOWL PARK, beside the Anglican Church.

Park across from the brown-shingled Anglican Church and pick up the path behind the church leading into the waterfowl park, to its mile-long boardwalk. Bring your binoculars and be on the lookout for warblers, yellow throats, red-wing blackbirds, ducks, and more feathered friends. There's an observation tower.

Admission: Free.
Open: Daily 5am–half an hour after sunset.

WHERE TO STAY

THE DIFFERENT DRUMMER BED AND BREAKFAST, 82 W. Main St. (P.O. Box 188), Sackville, NB, E0B 3C0. Tel. 506/536-1291. 8 rms (all with bath).

$ Rates (including breakfast): $40 single; $48–$51 double. Extra person $9. MC, V.
This restored Victorian home (1899) offers lovely rooms with individual heat controls and period furnishings. The double parlor and an expanded continental breakfast are just two of the many extra touches provided by hosts Georgette and Richard Hanrahan, who keep the menus of local restaurants for their guests. The beds are covered with handmade quilts. This no-smoking inn is a five-minute walk into town, and golfing, hiking, and swimming opportunities are nearby.

WHERE TO DINE

If you haven't brought a picnic to Fort Beauséjour, don't despair. There's always **Mel's,** and it's open long hours.

For fine dining, the **Drury Lane Restuarant** and the **Marshlands Inn** come recommended, though I have not had the opportunity to eat in either one.

MEL'S TEA ROOM, 27 Bridge St. Tel. 506/536-1251.

Cuisine: LIGHT FARE. **Reservations:** Not needed.
$ Prices: Most items $1–$8. No credit cards.
Open: Mon–Sat 7:30am–midnight, Sun 10am–11pm.

I love to happen upon this kind of place on a trip. Founded by Mel in 1945, and now run by his grandson, it's still got a soda fountain. You can get a cup of coffee, a slice of pie, or a grilled cheese sandwich, or play the jukebox, before you hit the road again. It's also got a megaselection of magazines, as well as yesterday's *USA Today* and *New York Times.*

8. THE ACADIAN PENINSULA

Acadian settlers, forced from their homelands farther south, have lived for centuries along the coast of New Brunswick, between the Gulf of St. Lawrence and the Baie de Chaleur. Fishing, farming, and the production of peat and peat moss are the region's main occupations, with lumbering also prominent.

The Acadian peninsula stretches from Neguac, on the east coast, all the way around to Bathurst, on the northern coast. Depending on where you're coming from, you can get to the Acadian peninsula by taking Highway 11 north from Shediac, Highway 126 north from Moncton, or Highway 8 from Fredericton. Some people approach the peninsula from Campbellton, and Highway 11 east, in the north of the province, after a tour of Québec's Gaspé Peninsula. Your goal is the town of Caraquet and a visit to a re-created village of the region as it was two centuries ago.

CARAQUET

Caraquet (pop. 4,500), on Highway 11, is 97% French-speaking and the center for Acadian culture in New Brunswick. Founded in 1758, it hosts an annual Acadian festival in August, and has an Acadian museum, a re-created Acadian village, and a small pilgrimage shrine (see "What to See and Do," below). The only fisheries school in New Brunswick is located here, along with a large commercial fishing fleet.

In Caraquet, Highway 11 becomes boulevard St-Pierre, and the hostelries and major points of interest are stretched along the west end of it, where you'll also find the **tourist information center,** open daily from 10am to 8pm in summer.

WHAT TO SEE & DO

For a pleasant day trip out of Caraquet, explore the fishing communities and beaches on the islands of Lamèque and Miscou, at the tip of the Acadian peninsula.

VILLAGE HISTORIQUE ACADIEN, six miles (10km) west of Caraquet. Tel. 506/727-3467.

Caraquet is famous for its Historic Acadian Village, a "living museum" of 42 buildings, a 15-minute drive west of Caraquet. Here "interpreters" in period costumes work at the trades and the daily chores, as well as play the traditional games, that made up the fabric of town and home life in Acadia 100 or 200 years ago.

Admission: June–early Sept $7.50 adults, $4.25 children, $15 family (less than half price early Sept–early Oct).

Open: June–early Sept daily 10am–6pm; early Sept–early Oct daily 10am–5pm. **Closed:** Mid-Oct to May.

MUSEE ACADIEN, 15 bd. St-Pierre est. Tel. 506/727-3269.

If you don't have time to drive out to the Historic Acadian Village described above, you can still get a good sense of Acadian life by visiting the Acadian Museum in Caraquet. Its two floors of exhibits ably display the trappings of the daily lives of Acadians in the area from the late 1700s to the early 1900s, much of it donated by their families, from clothing to fishing equipment to religious artifacts. There's even a bicycle with wooden wheels built in 1926. Don't miss the old-timey boudoir items upstairs.

Admission: $3 adults, $2 seniors, $1 students; children free.

Open: Sun–Fri noon–5pm, Sat 10am–5pm. **Closed:** Oct–May.

CHAPEL OF SAINT ANNE, west of Caraquet on Rte. 11. No phone.

If you savor serene spots, don't miss the tiny Chapel of Saint Anne, founded in memory of the area's Acadian settlers. Besides the small wooden chapel with only six short pews, there's a monument and "the Source," a fountain from which local folks come for a drink at sunset. The water may or may not have curative powers, but it's cold and refreshing, and the view of the sunset over the water from it will hold you enthralled. If you look inside the chapel, notice the crutches left behind by those who were cured and the words of thanks in the book to the right.

Open: Daily 9am–9pm.

WHERE TO STAY & DINE

HOTEL PAULIN, 143 bd. St-Pierre ouest, Caraquet, NB, E0B 1K0. Tel. 506/727-9981. 9 rms (2 with bath).

$ Rates: $44 single with bath, $31 single without bath; $65 double with bath, $51–$55 double without bath. MC, V. **Closed:** Nov–May.

Run by the Paulin family for three generations, this is a friendly place, its rooms simply furnished with old-fashioned decor. All the rooms are on the second floor; seven of the nine share baths, but most have sinks. You can't beat the price.

The hotel's country-style dining room, with only eight tables, wins kudos from locals and visitors alike. Hotelier and chef Gerard Paulin claims it's just simple cooking. Simply delicious, that is: meat and fish dishes accompanied by vegetables and potatoes—an Acadian version of nouvelle cuisine with the emphasis on substance, not sauces. Appetizers range in price from $2 to $4.50; main courses, $8 to $14. Breakfast is served daily from 7:30 to 10am, dinner from 5:30 to 10pm.

MAISON TOURISTIQUE DUGAS, 683 bd. St-Pierre ouest (R.R. 2, Site 8, BTE 11), Caraquet, NB, E0B 1K0. Tel. 506/727-3195. 6 rms (none with bath), 2 suites, 5 cabins.

$ Rates: Main house $22 single, $29 double; suite $40–$50 single or double; cabin $40 single, $40–$50 double; camping $6–$8 tent, $10–$16 camper. Breakfast about $3.50. No credit cards.

The Maison Touristique Dugas, run by Martina and Camillien Landry, offers something for most every vacation style. In the main house, six rooms share two baths, and there is a small sun room and lounge. In another building are two suites with a large kitchen and living room. For more rustic accommodation, there are five cabins, with kitchen. You're also welcome to camp, in tent or RV. The property's well-tended grounds are filled with clover, lupine, and pansy beds; it has picnic tables, as well as a private beach at the end of a dirt road through woods sprinkled with wild roses.

A YOUTH HOSTEL

AUBERGE DE JEUNESSE, 577 bd. St-Pierre ouest, Caraquet, NB, E0B 1K0. Tel. 506/727-2345. 15 beds.

$ Rates: July–Aug only, $12 adults, $7 children 12–18; younger children stay free. No credit cards.

The town's Auberge de Jeunesse (Youth Hostel) is small, clean, and in a picturesque spot near the Chapel of Saint Anne. It has picnic tables, a bright kitchen, one room with 10 bunk beds and another with five, two showers, and one toilet. Lockers are available. This is a good place to know about if you're camping and get caught in the rain.

ALONG THE NORTH COAST

The drive from Caraquet along the northern coast of the Acadian peninsula on Highway 11 to Bathurst is a wonderful experience. The roadway is bordered with brilliant wildflowers, even in late summer; the farms and fields are just waiting for an Andrew Wyeth or Ansel Adams to capture them. Driving west, you'll come to **Grande-Anse** (pop. 830), with **St. Simon Church,** with row after row of tombstones marching dramatically to the sea, and a tourist information center, with a children's playground beside it. The **Musée de Papes (Popes Museum),** housed in a big, modern building right on the highway, chronicles the history of the Roman Catholic religion and displays portraits of all the popes and a large model of St. Peter's Basilica in Rome. It's open from June to September.

Just down the road is the tiny village of **Pokeshaw** and its desolate beach. **Pokeshaw Provincial Park** is open 9am to 9pm daily; from the lookout here you can see clusters of cormorants on "sea stacks" in the bay and, on a clear day, Québec's Gaspé Peninsula.

Bathurst, in a pretty setting on the Bathurst Basin, is an industrial town of 15,700 souls, many of whom make their living at the city's large pulp-paper mill. In recent years, other industries have moved nearby, and when important strikes of minerals and metals were discovered in the region, the result was a mining boom.

While the towns on the Acadian peninsula are 95% French-speaking, Bathurst is bilingual.

WHERE TO STAY & DINE

If you decide to stay the night, there's a large Best Western property with a pool, tennis courts, playground, and dining room with fairly extensive menu. It's **Danny's Inn & Conference Centre** (tel. 506/546-6621; P.O. Box 180, Bathurst, NB, E2A 3Z2), on Highway 134 north of downtown Bathurst (you can take exit 318 off Highway 11 and turn right onto Highway 134).

Farther north, at Exit 321, there's a bed-and-breakfast/gourmet dining room called **La Fine Grobe-sur-Mer** (tel. 506/783-3138; P.O. Box 219, Nigadoo, NB, E0B 2A0), open daily from 11:30am to 10pm. Appetizers cost $2.50 to $12.90, main dishes $15 to $36, and there are some fixed-price choices. Owner/chef/innkeeper Georges Frachon gathers herbs from the garden and bakes bread in a clay oven behind the restaurant, which overlooks Nepisiguit Bay. The wine list is long, the coffee good and strong, and you're free to keep your table the whole evening. Turn left when you reach Nigadoo after exiting Highway 11; then turn right immediately after you cross the bridge over the Nigadoo River.

ONWARD TO THE GASPE

From Bathurst, Highway 11 skirts the shore of the Baie de Chaleur to Dalhousie and Campbellton. Past Campbellton is the city of Matapédia, Québec, on the road across the Gaspé to Mont-Joli. A much more scenic route, however, is around the tip of the peninsula. For this, you can save a considerable number of miles (or kilometers) by taking the bridge from Campbellton to Pointe-à-la-Croix, or the ferry at Dalhousie for $15. For full information on the Gaspé Peninsula, see Chapter 10.

WHERE TO STAY   Should you need to stay the night in Campbellton, there's a **Journey's End** at 3 Sugarloaf St. West, Campbellton, NB, E3N 3G9 (tel. 506/753-4121, or toll free 800/668-4200). Take Exit 415 off Highway 11, pass the Sugarloaf Mall, and the motel is on the right. Rates for the rooms are about $55 single, $63 double.

PRINCE EDWARD ISLAND

Atlantic Canada's "million-acre farm" in the Gulf of St. Lawrence can be described in two words: simply beautiful. The pastoral beauty and rural simplicity are carefully preserved by an island people proud of their land and their traditions. Each summer season, visitors come from all over North America to experience the island's charm: country roads bordered by swaths of wildflower color; tidy farms raising potatoes (the island's principal crop), broccoli, tomatoes, strawberries, grains, or dairy cattle; and thousands of kilometers of sinuous coastline bordered by beaches of red or white sand. Offshore waters teem with lobster, giant tuna, clams, and scallops; Malpeque Bay oysters are world-famous. And island streams and lakes yield trout and salmon.

Harvesting the island's natural wealth is the prime industry here, but tourism is a close second. The two are very carefully matched to one another: A large number of island farms supplement their incomes by renting rooms to visitors. In fact, there are many more tourist homes, housekeeping cottages, and farmhouse rooms than there are hotels and motels. Most people who come to Prince Edward Island (usually referred to simply as P.E.I.) are looking for a week or two of peace and quiet, simple living, pretty scenery, and excellent beaches—and they find them all.

For all its beauty, Prince Edward Island is Canada's smallest and most densely populated province, which may surprise you when you see the miles of rolling farmland and the small-scale cities and towns. But P.E.I. has no vast northern expanse as does, say, Québec or Ontario. In fact, the island province is a mere 140 miles (224km) from end to end, and only about 40 miles (64km) wide at its widest point. Although the population grows markedly during the warm summer months, year-round islanders only number 130,400.

As one impressed transplanted American described this talented, hardworking lot: "Everyone on the island either sings, dances, farms, or is a carpenter."

P.E.I.'S MULTINATIONAL HERITAGE The French first laid claim to the island in 1523, even before Jacques Cartier had sailed up the St. Lawrence. When Cartier came across the island in 1534, he was enchanted by it and wrote glowing reports to Paris. Samuel de Champlain, the great French colonizer who founded Québec City, named the island after St. John, and the name Ile St-Jean stuck for almost two centuries.

The French came here to settle in 1663, with larger groups coming a half century later. The great French fortress of Louisbourg on Cape Breton Island fell to British troops in 1758, and many French colonists fled to the Ile St-Jean to escape British domination. It did them little good, for the island was in British hands soon after the fall of Louisbourg—called St. John's Island by its new British owners. Some French

WHAT'S SPECIAL ABOUT PRINCE EDWARD ISLAND

Theater
- ☐ The Charlottetown Festival and Confederation Centre for the Arts productions, including the long-lived *Anne of Green Gables.*
- ☐ Repertory theater in Victoria.
- ☐ Dinner theater in Summerside.

"The Land of Anne"
- ☐ Green Gables House, part of Prince Edward Island National Park.
- ☐ Anne of Green Gables House at Silver Bush.

- ☐ The Lucy Maud Montgomery Birthplace.

Scenic Drives
- ☐ Blue Heron Drive in Central P.E.I.
- ☐ Lady Slipper Drive in Western P.E.I.
- ☐ King's Byway Drive in Eastern P.E.I.

Top-Notch Golf Courses
- ☐ The Links at Crowbush Cove.
- ☐ Brudenell Provincial Golf Course.

settlers managed to remain on the island, although settlers whose loyalty to the British Crown was in question were being deported throughout British North America.

In 1763 the island was part of Nova Scotia, but in 1769 it was named a colony in its own right, with Charlottetown as its capital, named after King George III's wife. Loyalists from the rebellious American colonies escaped the strife by coming to the island, and 1803 saw the beginning of a large influx of impoverished Scottish settlers, led by Lord Selkirk, seeking a better life in the New World. (Today Prince Edward Island boasts the highest percentage of Celtic descendants of all the Canadian provinces.) In 1798 the island was renamed for Queen Victoria's father, Edward, duke of Kent. Prince Edward Island was well on its way to possessing the rich national mix it enjoys today: Micmac, Acadian French settlers, Scots, and English.

By 1851 the island colony was self-governing, and in 1864 it had the honor of hosting the famous talks that would lead to Canada's confederation. Throughout its history, the fertile red soil has provided richly for anyone willing to till and plant it, and the fantastic riches of the "Garden of the Gulf" and its offshore waters attract visitors from thousands of miles away.

SEEING PRINCE EDWARD ISLAND

The beaches and the quiet country life are what visitors seek in P.E.I. The best beaches are those on the northern side of the island between New London Bay and Tracadie Bay. Each summer the towns and villages along Route 6 between New London and Mill Cove are busy with visitors looking for lodgings or on their way to the beaches of Prince Edward Island National Park. Beaches along the rest of the island's coast are pleasantly uncrowded, since in general they are farther from the concentrations of hotels and tourist homes. But all the beaches are warmed by the Gulf Stream, and are pleasantly warm in summer. If you're driving along Highway 16 on the northeast coast, be sure to visit lovely Basin Head and Bothwell beaches.

The Department of Tourism has mapped out three scenic drives, which roughly correspond to the three counties that constitute the island: Prince (western P.E.I.), Queens (central P.E.I.), and Kings (eastern P.E.I.), and marked the highways with signs that are easy to follow.

Lady Slipper Drive (180 miles, 288km) circles the western reaches of the island, sparsely populated and unspoiled. **Blue Heron Drive** (120 miles, 190km) circles the central portion of the island, through Charlottetown, past Summerside, and along the northern beach route. **King's Byway Drive** (234 miles, 375km) completes the map by winding along the sinuous coasts of the eastern portion. No matter where you go in P.E.I., you'll never be more than 10 miles (16km) from the water.

INFORMATION For toll-free information about P.E.I. and the free 160-page *Visitors Guide,* call 800/463-4PEI (tel. 902/368-4444 outside North America), or write to Visitor Services, Box 940E, Charlottetown, PEI, C1A 7M5.

GETTING THERE   By Plane   Air Nova, the commuter partner of Air Canada (tel. toll free 800/776-3000 in the U.S., 800/565-3940 in Maritime Canada, or 800/563-5151 in Newfoundland), and **Air Atlantic,** the commuter partner of Canadian Airlines International (tel. toll free 800/426-7000 in the U.S., 800/665-1177 in Canada), both serve Charlottetown from other points in Atlantic Canada. Call for schedules and fare information.

By Rail/Bus The closest you can get to Charlottetown by train is Moncton, N.B., which is served by Canada's VIA Rail network. From the train station in Moncton, two buses a day make the run to Cape Tormentine for the ferry crossing, then continue on to Charlottetown. The Moncton Charlottetown trip takes a little over four hours and costs $23 for adults, half price for children. For rail and bus information, call toll free 800/561-3952 in the Maritime Provinces, 800/561-3949 in most of the U.S.

By Car and Car-Ferry Most people come to P.E.I. by car-ferry from either Cape Tormentine, N.B., or Caribou, N.S.
   From Cape Tormentine, N.B., **Marine Atlantic** (121 Eden St., Bar Harbor, ME 04609) operates huge two-level car-ferries to Borden, P.E.I. Boats leave every hour on the half hour in summer between 6:30am and 8:30pm, with extra night sailings at 9:45 and 11:30pm and 1am. Extra sailings are made at peak times during busy midday hours. The ferry runs quite efficiently. You pay nothing to get onto the island—just drive down the wharf and right onto the boat—but pay a round-trip fare on your return. Prices are $7 for adults, $4.50 for seniors, $3 for children 5 to 12, and $18 for a car. You can't make reservations—indeed, none are necessary—but if you want to know how they're running, listen to a local radio station or call 506/538-7654 in Cape Tormentine, N.B.; 902/855-2030 in Borden, P.E.I.; or toll free 800/341-7981 in the U.S. The trip takes about 45 minutes.
   From Caribou, N.S., to Wood Islands, P.E.I., four ferries are operated by **Northumberland Ferries Ltd.,** P.O. Box 634, Charlottetown, PEI, C1A 7L3 (tel. 902/566-3838, or toll free 800/565-0201 in P.E.I. and Nova Scotia; fax 902/566-1550). Service is seasonal, from May 1 to December 20, and the sailing schedule varies, depending on time of year, but generally commences at 6am and runs to about 9pm. Sailings are approximately every 50 minutes, and crossing time is one hour and 15 minutes. A cafeteria is on board the boat. Rates, paid only when exiting P.E.I. (if you fly out you've beat the system), are $8.25 per adult, $6 senior, $4 children 5 to 12, and $26.50 per car. Call or write for a printed schedule. They don't take reservations.
   Finally, there is car-ferry service between Souris, P.E.I., and Grindstone, Magdalen Islands, Québec.

GETTING AROUND Prince Edward Island is best seen by private car, but those without a car won't be left stranded. **MacQueen's,** 430 Queen St., Charlottetown (tel. and fax 902/368-2453), offers seven half- and full-day specialized tours of the island, focusing on crafts, gardening, seal-watching, bicycling, and fishing. Rates range from $60 to $90, depending on the tour, often including a meal. The company also rents bicycles on a daily ($20) or a weekly ($75) basis.
   Abegweit Sightseeing Tours, 157 Nassau St., Charlottetown, PEI, C1A 2X3 (tel. 902/894-9966), operates from a booth on the corner of Queen and Grafton Streets and will take you aboard a double-decker London Transport bus for an hour-long tour of Charlottetown (adults pay $6; kids, $1), a 100-mile (160km) tour of the North Shore beaches and attractions ($27 for adults, $14 for children), or an 80-mile (129km) South Shore tour for the same rate. Their seven-hour Anne of Green Gables tour, also $27, includes admission fees.
   The company also runs buses from the Charlottetown Hotel out to the beaches at Dalvay, Stanhope, Brackley, Rustico, and Cavendish, returning in the early evening. Round-trip is about $9 or $10, depending on which beach you visit.
   A second beach shuttle (tel. 902/566-3243), which runs between Charlottetown

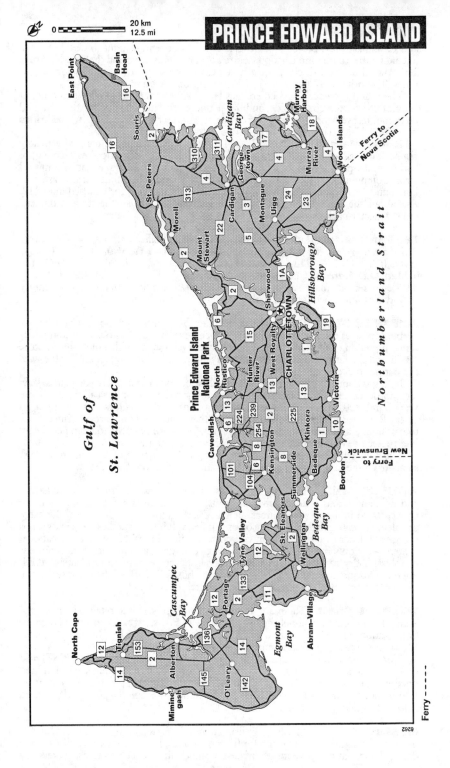

PRINCE EDWARD ISLAND

0 — 20 km
— 12.5 mi

Gulf of

St. Lawrence

Prince Edward Island
National Park

Northumberland Strait

Cascumpec Bay

Egmont Bay

Bedeque Bay

Hillsborough Bay

Cardigan Bay

North Cape

Tignish

Mimine-
gash

Alberton

O'Leary

Portage

Tyne Valley

Abram-Village

Wellington

St. Eleanors

Summerside

Kensington

Bedeque

Kinkora

Borden

Victoria

Cavendish

North Rustico

Hunter River

West Royalty

CHARLOTTETOWN

Sherwood

Mount Stewart

Morell

St. Peters

Souris

Basin Head

East Point

Cardigan

George-
town

Montague

Uigg

Murray River

Murray Harbour

Wood Islands

Ferry to
Nova Scotia

Ferry to
New Brunswick

Ferry – – – – –

6282

and Cavendish only, picks up passengers at half a dozen locations in Charlottetown (including the Tourist Information Centre at University Avenue and the Dundee Arms, 200 Pownal St.) and discharges them at the Cavendish boardwalk. Call for current times. The price is $7 one way, $12 round-trip on the same day.

The island province's taxi companies have banded together to offer taxi tours of Charlottetown, the countryside, and the seashore. You hire the taxi for the tour, and up to four or five people get to go for one price. For reservations, call **Ed's Taxi Tours** (tel. 902/892-6561) or **Star Taxi Tours** (tel. 902/892-6581).

Cruise Manada (tel. 902/838-3444), out of Montague, offers seal-watching cruises three times a day aboard the MV *Manada I*. The boat passes a colony of harbor seals, plies the Montague and Brudenell rivers, and pays a visit to a mussel farm. Complimentary iced tea and lemonade are served. This unique cruise lasts two hours and 15 minutes and costs $12.50 for adults and $6.50 for children under 12. Ask about the champagne and mussels cruise and the cruise/theater and dinner/cruise/theater packages.

Car Rentals   Charlottetown has several car-rental offices, among them **Budget,** 215 University Ave. (tel. 902/892-8333); **Discount Car Rental,** 30 Trans Canada Hwy. (tel. 902/566-3213); **Hertz,** 47A St. Peter's Rd. (tel. 902/566-5566); and **Tilden Car Rental,** Charlottetown Airport or 21 St. Peter's Rd. (tel. 902/894-8311). To rent a small car for a week with 434 free miles (700km) and insurance should cost about $350, more with gas (figure $35 to fill the tank).

WHERE TO STAY   Tourist homes, bed-and-breakfasts, farmhouses, and house-keeping cottages make up a large part of Prince Edward Island's stock of accommodations, preserving the scenic beauty from overdevelopment with hotels and motels. You'll find the latter in Charlottetown and Summerside, for sure, and along the way, the perfect tucked-away inn or resort.

It's a good idea to call in advance for reservations no matter where you plan to stay: farmhouse, cottage, or motel. You can write to the tourism office or call them toll free year-round: 800/463-4PEI. But if you do arrive on the island without a reservation, go to any P.E.I. Visitor Information Centre and they'll help you find a room. Since many tourist homes and farmhouses have only a few rooms to rent, the tourism people are in a better position to locate the vacant ones than you are.

The somewhat tight room situation during the peak time of late July to August stems from the fact that the island is a summer destination. Call ahead.

WHERE TO DINE   Tourism is strictly a seasonal business on Prince Edward Island, and as many island residents live on farms, city-style restaurants are rare and are concentrated in major tourist areas such as Charlottetown and Cavendish. But there are plenty of cafés, and in high season and at festival times, churches and civic groups sponsor "lobster suppers," held in church basements, Lions' Clubs, and recreational centers—the only buildings on the island large enough to accommodate the hundreds of folks hungry for lobsters. In a very real sense, the year-round residents of P.E.I. open their doors to summer visitors to provide hospitality. Don't be surprised if one of your favorite meals is served in a local church or social club.

WHERE TO SHOP   There are more than 100 highly visible retail outlets on the island. For information about them, contact the **P.E.I. Crafts Council,** a nonprofit organization, at 156 Richmond St., Charlottetown, PEI, C1A 1H9 (tel. 902/892-5152), or contact the Visitor Information Centre (address above).

Nonresidents are eligible for a refund on the 7% government sales tax (GST) paid on goods you are taking home (also on your accommodations). Claims are submitted once you get back home, so save those receipts and pick up a rebate form at an Information Centre (call 613/991-3346 to be walked through the process if you need help or forget to get a form).

FISHING   Nonresident fishing licenses are required, except for those going tuna or deep-sea fishing. Families may fish for trout on a single license for two weeks from the date of issue, but everyone must purchase a salmon license. For specifics, contact any

Visitor Information Centre, or the Department of the Environment, P.O. Box 2000, Charlottetown, PEI, C1A 7N8 (tel. 902/368-4683).

1. CHARLOTTETOWN
24 miles (39km) SE of Cavendish, 44 miles (71km) E of Summerside

GETTING THERE   See "Getting There" earlier in this chapter. If you're arriving by plane, the Charlottetown Airport is 5 miles (8km) from the center of the city. Allow 15 to 20 minutes' travel time and $7 per person for the taxi ride downtown.

ESSENTIALS Information   The Provincial Tourism Information Centre is on University Avenue at Summer Street, which is also Highway 1, the Trans Canada Highway (P.O. Box 940E, Charlottetown, PEI, C1A 7M5). If you come into town from the Borden ferry dock, you'll pass it on your right, in a shopping center. If you arrive after hours during July and August, telephone 902/368-4444 for help, 24 hours a day.

For local information in Charlottetown, go to the city tourism booth at the corner of Queen and Kent Streets, or to the tourist bureau at City Hall on Queen Street (tel. 902/566-5548).

Orientation   It's virtually impossible to get lost for long in Charlottetown's small downtown section. Using the Confederation Centre of the Arts, bordered by Queen, Grafton, Prince, and Richmond Streets, as your point of orientation, you'll find that most of the best hotels are within easy walking distance of the center.

Getting Around   Taxis may be dispatched or hired from the stands around town. Companies maintaining convenient stands on lower University Avenue are City Cab (tel. 902/892-6567) and Ed's Taxi (tel. 902/892-6561).

For tours of the island, see "Getting Around" earlier in this chapter. The City of Charlottetown sponsors a free guided hour-long walking tour from 10am to 5pm daily in July and August. Tours begin on the corner of Queen and Kent Streets. For more information, call 902/566-5548.

Downtown parking is a problem. Metered spaces (if you can find them) cost 25¢ for 30 minutes but are free weekdays after 6pm and on weekends. The Pownal Parkade, on Pownal Street between Grafton and Richmond, charges 60¢ an hour, $4 maximum a day, from 6:30am to midnight (tel. 902/368-3653). For details on car rentals, see "Getting Around" earlier in this chapter.

SPECIAL EVENTS   Confederation Centre is the focus of the annual Charlottetown Festival, held from late June to mid-September. Guest performers, special shows, and a list of musical performances are highlights, and a lively musical based on Prince Edward Island's own *Anne of Green Gables* is always part of the showbill; it lasts 2¾ hours, with one intermission. Schedules and tickets are at the box office near the corner of Queen and Grafton Streets. For reservations, call 902/566-1267 (toll free 800/565-0278 in the Atlantic Provinces, May to September; fax 902/566-4648), or stop for tickets between 9am and 9pm Monday through Saturday and 1 to 5pm on Sunday from mid-June through September. Prices generally range from $16.50 to $30. There's children's theater, too.

In July and August 1993, the Canadian government and others sponsored "Spirit of a Nation," a rousing and inspiring outdoor production in music and dance at Confederation Centre for the Arts, featuring an ethnic and geographical mix of talented young Canadians. Check with the tourist office to see if a similar program will be held this year. If so, it's free and well worth seeing. Grab a bag lunch and go, at noon Monday through Saturday.

The capital of Prince Edward Island is a lovely old town of 15,000 citizens (33,000 in the greater area), with many fine colonial and Victorian buildings and the new, ultramodern Confederation Centre of the Arts. "Confederation" is a word much bandied about in Charlottetown since it was here, in P.E.I.'s Province House, that the first discussions on the subject of Canada's confederation were held in 1864. At first it seems odd that the island province did not join the confederation until 1873, but the delay was entirely reasonable. Islanders had nothing against joining—they simply wanted the details to be worked out first, particularly those dealing with communications between P.E.I. and the rest of Canada. No doubt the marvelously easy access to the island today is the result of that prudence of a century ago.

WHAT TO SEE & DO

Take a tour on land or sea. **Abegweit Sightseeing Tours,** 157 Nassau St., Charlottetown, PEI, C1A 2X3 (tel. 902/894-9966), operates from a booth on the corner of Queen and Grafton Streets and will take you aboard a double-decker London Transport bus for an hour-long tour of Charlottetown (adults pay $6; kids, $1).

Charlottetown Harbour Cruises, at the Prince Street Wharf (tel. 902/368-2628), offers Little Ferryboat Tours of the harbor at 3pm for $8 ($5 children under 12); the 90-minute 6pm cruise includes a shared pot of freshly steamed mussels; the price is $16.

Gosbee Brother Tours, at Peake's Wharf, has morning and sunset harbor tours for $11 for adults, $5.50 for children under 12; seniors get a 10% discount (tel. 902/892-5083).

THE TOP ATTRACTIONS

CONFEDERATION CENTRE ART GALLERY AND MUSEUM, Queen and Grafton Sts. Tel. 902/628-1864.

Built in 1964 and the impetus for the city's downtown revitalization, the Confederation Centre for the Arts houses a library, three theaters (see "Special Events," above), an art gallery, a museum, and a gift shop. The art gallery, on the second level, exhibits notable works by Canadian artists, and one room has numerous paintings and portraits by Robert Harris, one of Canada's most renowned painters from the turn of the century (his equally talented brother, William, designed Province House; see below). Be sure to see the scrapbook of Lucy Maud Montgomery and her tidy 716-page manuscript for *Anne of Green Gables*, handwritten on both sides, as well as the new contemporary gallery, which has permanent and traveling exhibitions.

Admission: Museum and gallery, $1 adults, 50¢ children, $2 families. Free on Sun.

Open: July–Sept daily 10am–8pm; Oct–June Tues–Sun 10am–5pm.

PROVINCE HOUSE NATIONAL HISTORIC SITE, 165 Richmond St. Tel. 902/566-7626.

Next door to Confederation Centre stands the "birthplace of Canada." The three-story sandstone building was built (1843–47) as the colonial Government House, and with a market, office, and post office buildings, it framed Queen's Square Gardens. The other buildings were torn down in 1963 to make way for Confederation Centre, but by visiting the exhibit on Province House's second floor you can get a good idea of what it must have been like when the 26 delegates walked up Great George Street to discuss the idea of a union. The garden, with its circular drive and manicured lawns, must have been a delightful place. Province House is the seat of P.E.I.'s legislature, but visitors are welcome. A 15-minute film about the building and what went on inside it is shown continuously throughout the day.

On the ground floor are four realistically restored offices, those of the commissioner of Crown lands, the lieutenant governor, the registrar of deeds, and the colonial secretary. Also on this floor, to your right, is the room where Canada's confederate life was first discussed in 1864. Upstairs, exhibits of photographs and documents bring those momentous days to life. Take a look at Dusan Kadlec's painting of the public ball, one of the big social events of the Charlottetown Conference of 1864. Do you agree that everyone appears angry or unhappy or is gossiping? On the third floor are the legislative chambers, also open to visitors (same hours as above). When the House is in session you'll get to see the Speaker in ceremonial black robes, and the formally clad pages, as well as the attending members.

Those folks in period dress you see walking the streets of Charlottetown and nodding or tipping their hats to you are students with unusual summer work, portraying the fathers (and a couple of mothers) of the confederacy. Not only are they in costume, they're also in character. Ask them who they are and be prepared to learn some Canadian history.

Admission: Free.

Open: July–Aug daily 9am–8pm; June Mon–Fri 9am–5pm; Sept–early Oct daily 9am–5pm. **Closed:** Mid-Oct to May.

MORE ATTRACTIONS

BEACONSFIELD, 2 Kent St. Tel. 902/892-9127.

This 25-room Victorian mansion was designed in 1877 by William Harris, brother of the painter Robert Harris, whose work hangs in Confederation Centre. It was in the hands of one family, the Cundalls, from 1888 to 1916, when it became a "home for friendless young women" and offered them training in "useful arts." Today tour guides lead visitors through the restored Beaconsfield, which houses the Prince Edward Island Museum and Heritage Foundation. A small bookstore in back of the house sells books about the island.

Admission: $2.50; children under 12 free.

Open: Mon–Fri 8am–4pm.

ST. PAUL'S ANGLICAN CATHEDRAL, Church St. Tel. 902/892-1691.

East of Province House on Church Street, the landmark red sandstone building, the oldest Protestant church on the island, dates from 1777. The red sandstone, by the way, is typical of that quarried in P.E.I.; the sandstone from Nova Scotia, by contrast, is yellow. In summer, a tour guide is available at no charge.

Open: July–Aug only, Mon–Fri 10am–4pm; services only, Sat–Sun 8am–noon.

ST. PETER'S ANGLICAN CATHEDRAL, at the corner of Rochford and Fitzroy Sts. Tel. 902/566-2102.

Founded in 1869, St. Peter's is perhaps Canada's smallest cathedral. Its pretty All Soul's Chapel was a collaborative effort of the Harris brothers: William, the architect, and Robert, the artist, some of whose paintings hang inside. Evensong is held daily at 5pm, and there are special concerts in summer, and often a tour guide who will show you around at no charge.

Open: Daily 8am–5pm.

ST. DUNSTAN'S BASILICA, corner of Great George and Richmond Sts. Tel. 902/894-3486.

This Roman Catholic church is in Gothic style with 250-foot-high twin spires and an elaborate interior, including a nave and altar with handsome Italianate carved work. Above the altar rises a magnificent medallion stained-glass window. This is the fourth Catholic church to stand on this site; the first chapel was built in 1816.

Open: Mon–Fri 8am–4pm, Sat–Sun 9am–5pm.

VICTORIA PARK, Old Battery Point. No phone.

This well-used city park has walking trails, an outdoor pool, tennis courts, a baseball field, and a large children's playground. The striking white mansion in it is Government House (also known as the Legislative Building), since 1835 the official residence of the lieutenant governor of Prince Edward Island. The house is not open for visits, although you're free to park your car outside and stroll through the grounds and enjoy the garden. To get here, follow Kent or Euston Streets west.

SHOPPING

If you've got a little shopping in mind, Richmond Street is a treasure trove, with three outstanding gift shops in the block opposite Confederation Centre: The wonderful **Island Crafts Shop,** 156 Richmond St. (tel. 902/892-5152); the equally browsable **Two Sisters,** 150 Richmond St. (tel. 902/894-3407); and the **Anne of Green**

Gables Store, 110 Queen St. (tel. 902/368-2663), for well-heeled Anne fans. The latter sells first editions of L. M. Montgomery's books, books by and about the author, and *Your Guide to Finding Anne.* A number of shops are clustered in Peake's Wharf, at the water, between Queen and Great George Streets.

WHERE TO STAY

You won't find it difficult to locate the lodging or meal of your choice in Charlottetown. The small downtown area contains most of them, so walking to the city's major attractions is a given.

EXPENSIVE

CP PRINCE EDWARD HOTEL, 18 Queen St., Charlottetown, PEI, C1A 8B9. Tel. 902/566-2222, or toll free 800/828-7447 in the U.S., 800/268-9411 in Atlantic Canada. Fax 904/566-1745. 213 rms, 34 suites. A/C MINIBAR TV TEL

$ Rates: Mid-June to mid-Oct $115–$155 single, $135–$175 double; mid-Oct to mid-June $66–$113 single, $106–$133 double. From $250 suite ($190 off-season). Extra person $15. Children under 16 stay free in parents' room. Special rates and packages. AE, DC, DISC, ER, MC, V. **Parking:** $5.

The largest Charlottetown hostelry is the downtown Prince Edward Hotel, a Canadian Pacific property. It boasts all the things you'd expect in a modern luxury hotel: modern rooms, including no-smoking rooms, in-room movies, room service, same-day dry cleaning and laundry, an outdoor patio for barbecues, an indoor swimming pool, Jacuzzi, sauna, fitness center, masseuse, shops, two dining rooms, and a lounge. Add to that a waterfront park and marina and, in summer, a popular cabaret. Three meals a day are served in the Garden of the Gulf family dining room, dinner only in the elegant Lord Selkirk dining room, which has live piano music some evenings.

MODERATE

BEST WESTERN MACLAUCHLAN'S MOTOR INN, 238 Grafton St. (at Hillsborough), Charlottetown, PEI, C1A 1L5. Tel. 902/892-2461, or toll free 800/528-1234 in North America, 800/463-2378 in Atlantic Canada. Fax 902/566-2979. 146 rms, 46 suites. A/C TV TEL

$ Rates: $87–$111 single; $94–$118 double; from $98 housekeeping unit; from $117 suite. Theater package July–Aug. AE, CB, DC, DISC, ER, MV, V. **Parking:** Free.

Rooms at the Best Western, whether located in the main building or in the annex across the street (148 North Court), are comfortable, with tub-shower bathrooms, and decorated in shades of blue and dusty rose. There's an indoor pool and a sauna, along with a restaurant downstairs. As with other places in town, bus tours may take many of the rooms, so reserve in advance.

DUNDEE ARMS INN, 200 Pownal St. (at Fitzroy), Charlottetown, PEI, C1A 3W8. Tel. 902/892-2496. Fax 902/368-8532. 6 inn rms, 2 suites, 10 motel rms. TV TEL

$ Rates (all including continental breakfast): Inn rooms, mid-June to mid-Oct $95 single, $110 double, $135 suite; off-season $95 single, $100 double, $110 suite. Motel rooms, mid-June to mid-Oct $85 single, $95 double; off-season $70 single, $80 double; extra adult $10. Packages and senior discounts available. No children under 12 in the inn; children under 12 stay free in motel section. AE, MC, V. **Parking:** Free, in back of inn.

This Queen Anne Revival–style mansion, built in 1903, is evocative of another era, with rooms that are filled with period decor and old-fashioned charm. Happily for today's wayfarer, they also have modern conveniences such as private baths. All the

AN IMPORTANT NOTE ON PRICES

Unless stated otherwise, **the prices cited in this guide are given in Canadian dollars,** which is good news for U.S. travelers because the Canadian dollar is worth 25% less than the American dollar, but buys nearly as much. As we go to press, $1 Canadian is worth 75¢ U.S., which means that your $100-a-night hotel room will cost only U.S. $75, and your $6 breakfast costs only U.S. $4.50.

Here's a quick table of equivalents:

Canadian $	U.S. $
$ 1	$ 0.75
5	3.75
10	7.50
20	15.00
50	37.50
80	60.00
100	75.00
200	150.00

inn rooms have air conditioning. The Dundee also has a block of motel-style rooms (not air-conditioned) next to the original inn, all with two double beds, bath-shower combinations and cable color television sets. Don Clinton, whom you're likely to meet, has owned the inn since 1972.

The Dundee is well known as one of Charlottetown's best places to have a cocktail or a fine dinner. The pine-paneled Hearth and Cricket Pub has a huge fireplace, antiques and old guns hung here and there, and a clientele of the town's young professional set. It's open from noon to 1am Monday through Friday and 11:30am to 1am on Saturday; closed Sunday. Across the hall, the Griffon Room, done in colonial style with cupboards filled with antiques, serves outstanding fare, with an emphasis on seafood. Figure about $40 per person for dinner, $12 for lunch. The Griffon Room is open for lunch Monday through Friday from 11:30am to 3pm and for dinner every evening during the summer from 5:30 to 10pm. In winter it's closed Sunday, but open from noon to 2:30pm and 6 to 9pm other days. Dinner reservations are recommended, and inn or motel guests get a 10% discount.

ISLANDER MOTOR LODGE, 146–148 Pownal St. (P.O. Box 1712), Charlottetown, PEI, C1A 7N4. Tel. 902/892-1217, or toll free 800/268-6261. Fax 902/566-1623. 47 rms, 3 apts. A/C TV TEL

$ **Rates:** $69 single; $78 double; $85–$95 housekeeping unit for two. Extra person $8. Lower rates off-season. Senior rates and packages available. AE, ER, MC, V. **Parking:** Free.

Only two blocks from the main square of Charlottetown, this friendly two-story motel, whose rooms were renovated and upgraded in 1992–93, has a variety of rooms with full bath and either two doubles, a queen, or king-size bed. No-smoking rooms are available, as are convenient drive-up rooms, where you can park right outside your door. Three units are actually housekeeping apartments. The Islander's coffee shop is off the lobby-reception area; it also has a licensed dining room, and both specialize in P.E.I. home cooking. There's also a lounge. The mural in the lobby is of the Charlottetown Driving Park, which is still going strong.

BED-AND-BREAKFAST

EDWARDIAN, 50 Mount Edward Rd. (at Confederation St.), Charlottetown, PEI, C1A 5S3. Tel. 902/368-1905. 3 rms (all with bath). **Directions:** Across from Ardgowan National Historic Park; Mount Edward Road is one block east of University Avenue.

$ Rates (including continental breakfast): $85–$95 single or double. Extra person $15. No credit cards. **Parking:** Free.

The Edwardian (which I have not yet visited personally but several Frommer travelers have written me about) is the restored east wing (1850s) of the country estate of William Henry Pope, a father of Confederation. Owners Judy and Jordan Hill call it "la maison aux mille petits soins," which means "the home of 1,000 small treasures," referring to the many historic whatnots scattered about the place, along with artwork, period antiques, family quilts, and flowers from the garden. Two of the three guest rooms have queen-size beds, while one has a four-poster, hand-carved double bed. The large Loft room, overlooking the garden, has a sitting area, a kitchenette stocked with homemade granola "for midnight snacking," and a bath with a clawfoot tub. Besides scones and muffins at breakfast, there's a complimentary beverage in the afternoon on the back patio or under the linden tree. Guests have use of the living room and sun porch. The Hills are happy to suggest activities during your stay; they have a particular interest in biking since their daughter is an avid cyclist. When one guest had to catch a 5am flight, Judy provided her with "breakfast to go" in a peach basket. The house is a five-minute drive or 20-minute walk from downtown Charlottetown.

THE ELMWOOD, 121 North River Rd. (P.O. Box 3128), Charlottetown, PEI, C1A 7N8. Tel. 902/368-3310. 1 rm, 2 suites (all with bath). A/C TEL **Directions:** The driveway to the inn is on North River Road opposite Green Street.

$ Rates (including breakfast): May–Oct $85 single or double, $110 suite; Nov–Apr $60 single or double, $85 suite. Extra person $12. CB, DC, ER, MC, V. **Parking:** Free.

The Elmwood was built in 1889 by Charlottetown's famous architect William Harris. Today, owners Carol and Jay Macdonald, both originally from New York State, have turned it into a memorable home-away-from-home, with three guest units, each with a queen-size bed and full bath. Guests use a private entrance and share a sitting room with fireplace, balcony, refrigerator, books, and games. The two suites have fireplaces and one has a kitchen. The third unit, the Victorian Room, features a bed alcove, wingback chairs, and an old-fashioned tub and shower. Carol made the quilts on all the beds. The Elmwood, set on an acre filled with 36 elm trees, is at the end of a tree-lined drive in a residential neighborhood. It's a 15- to 20-minute walk into town, and Victoria Park and a swimming pool are just down the street. The "continental-plus" breakfast can be modified for special diets. They book up fast, so call ahead.

WHERE TO DINE

MODERATE TO EXPENSIVE

THE CLADDAGH ROOM, 131 Sydney St. Tel. 902/892-9661.
Cuisine: SEAFOOD/INTERNATIONAL. **Reservations:** Recommended.
$ Prices: Appetizers $6–$7; main courses $6.50–$19. AE, DC, ER, MC, V.
Open: Lunch daily 11:30am–2pm; dinner daily 5–10pm.

Small and congenial, the Claddagh Room serves primarily seafood, but you can also find vegetarian fettuccine and steak and chicken dishes on its menu. When you've finished dinner, go upstairs to hear Irish music in the Olde Dublin Pub.

OFF BROADWAY CAFE, 125 Sydney St. Tel. 902/566-4620.
Cuisine: INTERNATIONAL. **Reservations:** Recommended.
$ Prices: Appetizers $5–$7.50; main courses $7–$23. AE, DC, ER, MC, V.
Open: Lunch Mon–Sat 11:30am–2pm; dinner Sun–Thurs 5–10pm, Fri–Sat 5–11pm.

People like the Off Broadway Café because it's small, quiet, and tucked away from the bustle of downtown Charlottetown. The inviting decor includes a beamed wood ceiling, brick walls, and pine booths upholstered with a pretty floral print, and the menu tempts with dishes like crêpes (Florentine or beef Stroganoff), cheese and broccoli pie, and seafood linguine, all served with Caesar salad, and "desserts to die for." Wine is available by the glass or the bottle.

PAT'S ROSE AND GREY ROOM, 132 Richmond. Tel. 902/892-222⌐.
   Cuisine: INTERNATIONAL. **Reservations:** Recommended.
$ **Prices:** Lunch specials $6; special pasta dinners $10–$12; main dinner courses $13.50–$17.50; Sun brunch $4–$7. AE, MC, V.
   Open: Lunch Mon–Sat 11am–3pm; dinner Mon–Sat 5pm–midnight (bar until 1am); brunch Sun 10am–2pm.

High ceilings, dark woodwork, and a touch of stained glass contribute to the mellow Edwardian atmosphere at Pat's, across from the stage door of Confederation Centre. (Not surprisingly, a lot of actors and stagehands eat and drink here.) Even with the adjacent pub just behind the divider, diners are not distracted. Noontime specials include a rich seafood chowder, and the hot breadsticks are a treat. Dinner, for example, could be a pasta special, or a more expensive meat or seafood dish. There are half a dozen selections at Sunday brunch, from blueberry pancakes to eggs Benedict; drinks, be they coffee, Bloody Marys, or mimosas, cost extra.

INEXPENSIVE

CEDAR'S EATERY, 81 University, between Fitzroy and Kent. Tel. 902/892-7377.
   Cuisine: LEBANESE/CANADIAN. **Reservations:** Not needed.
$ **Prices:** Lunch specials $4; dinner specials (served Mon–Wed) $5; main courses $6–$13. MC, V.
   Open: Mon–Thurs 11am–midnight, Fri–Sat 11am–1am, Sun 4–10:30pm.

Cedar's delivers hearty portions at low prices. It's an unassuming place, with rustic atmosphere and wooden tables and booths, but it has nevertheless won kudos for its cooking. Filling soup-and-sandwich specials are offered at lunch. To sample Lebanese fare, you might try kibbe, falafel, hummus, stuffed vine leaves, kebab, tabbouleh, shwarma, or "shish taouk," which is boneless chicken on two skewers, served with Greek salad and Lebanese-style rice.

ICE CREAM & PICNIC SUPPLIES

Got a hankering for ice cream? **☼ Cow's Homemade Ice Cream,** strategically located opposite Confederation Centre at the corner of Queen and Grafton, will take care of you. Consider chocolate mud, bubblegum, grapenut, Oreo cookie, peppermint, heifermint, and many other flavors served in waffle cones (dipped in chocolate, if you like), and don't be daunted by the lines. They move quickly. Cow's, housed in an old pharmacy (1810) with a beautiful tin ceiling and woodwork, also sells clothing and other merchandise with cow motifs.

   If you want to stock up on food to munch on or take with you in the car, visit the **Root Cellar,** 34 Queen St. (tel. 902/892-6227), for trail mix, raisins, almonds, yogurt, baked goods, fresh fruit and vegetables, a large selection of cheeses, and frozen dinners. They have vitamins, too. The store is open Monday through Thursday from 9am to 5:30pm, Friday to 6pm, and Saturday to 5pm.

EVENING ENTERTAINMENT

Dispensing traditional Irish folk music is the **Olde Dublin Pub,** 131 Sydney St. (tel. 902/892-6992). This is not a pub in the traditional sense: You walk up a flight of stairs to the second floor instead of down into the depths of a dark cellar. Light meals are served with a variety of brews to satisfy most appetites, but most people come for an evening of conversation and toe-tapping. An informal threesome often jams on Wednesday afternoons from 5 to 8pm and professional players take the stage from mid-June to mid-September, Monday through Saturday from 9:30pm to 1:45am. Depending on the group, there may be a small cover charge at night.

   Bar- and disco-hop along Kent Street. Combine a relaxed atmosphere, pub food, a dash of trendiness, and occasional live music, and you've got **Myron's,** 151 Kent St. (tel. 902/892-4375), with a modern interior—sleek counters, booths, and tables—lit by low-hanging lamps. Hours are 11am to 2am daily, with music from 9:30pm.

Tradewinds, at 189 Kent (tel. 902/894-4291), is a DJ/rock bar with inexpensive food. It's a party place, with popular theme nights and food and drink specials. The dance floor is upstairs, where the restaurant is; the bar downstairs also serves food. The bar is open from 11am to 2am Monday to Saturday.

Between Tradewinds and Myron's, at 187½ Kent St., there's **Doc's,** where professionals meet after work to booze and schmooze (tel. 902/566-1069).

---

2. SUMMERSIDE

22 miles (36km) SW of Cavendish, 44 miles (71km) W of Charlottetown

GETTING THERE   By Car   From Charlottetown, take the Trans Canada Highway west to Highway 1A, then pick up Route 11 at Reads Corner to go into Summerside.

ESSENTIALS   The Lady Slipper Drive Visitor Centre is located one mile (2km) east of Summerside, on Route 11 in Wilmot (tel. 902/888-8364). It's open 9am to 9pm in July and August, 9am to 6pm in June and September. Either here or at one of the inns in Summerside, request the excellent pamphlet "Of Merchant, Fox, and Sail: A Walking Tour of Summerside." It gives the best possible orientation to the town.

SPECIAL EVENTS   Summerside is famous for its annual Lobster Carnival, which occupies everyone in town for a week in mid-July. Lobster feasts are held nightly in the civic stadium, while baseball games, fiddling contests, and other good-time events fill the days and nights.

Summerside, the province's second-largest city, is the commercial center for western P.E.I., with 10,000 people living in its environs. It's also on the "summer side of the island" to which Charlottetown residents used to move in good weather.

WHAT TO SEE & DO

Using the pamphlet "Of Merchant, Fox, and Sail: A Walking Tour of Summerside," available from any of the hotels or the visitor center in Wilmot, walk or drive around Summerside. The walk takes about an hour and incorporates many of the beautiful homes here. If you're pressed for time, do a smaller walking or driving loop, following Granville Street to Church Street to Summer Street and back to Granville via Water Street.

While you're here, drop in at the national exhibition center, called **EPTEK** (a Micmac word for "hot spot"), near the shopping center on the waterfront at 130 Water St. (tel. 902/888-8373). The small gallery has traveling shows of works by Canadian artists, and there's a Sports Hall of Fame as well. Admission to EPTEK is free, and it's open from 8:30am to 5pm weekdays, 10am to 5pm on Saturday, and 1 to 5pm on Sunday.

The **International Fox Museum,** in the Holman Homestead, at Fitzroy Street between Central and Summer Streets, traces the history of the fox-farming industry, which began on the island in 1894 and was concentrated in the west in the Summerside area. (In its heyday, between 1915 and 1920, a pair of silver foxes sold for as much as $35,000.) The museum is open May through September from 9am to 6pm (tel. 902/436-2400).

Head out to Industrial Crescent (to no. 149B, to be precise; look for the blue-sided building) for a tour through **Cavendish Figurines,** which makes figurines that bring to life moments from *Anne of Green Gables*. The figurines are made from island red clay and hand-painted; each year, an original figurine is added to the Anne Collection; the first 2,000 are signed and numbered. The figurines start at about $200, but the company also sells moderately priced "Anne" souvenirs.

In summer, dinner theater is offered at **Brothers Two** restaurant, beside the

Quality Inn–Garden on the Gulf, on Water Street East. It requires reservations and costs $25; for that price you get a set dinner with a choice of three main courses (tel. 902/436-9654 for reservations and ticket information). Dinner is served by a staff dressed in costumes and apt to break into song and dance at any given moment.

WHERE TO STAY

Prices tend to be well below those of Charlottetown, and here the pleasures of the northern beaches and of pretty Lady Slipper Drive are only a short drive away.

LOYALIST COUNTRY INN, 195 Harbour Dr., Summerside, PEI, C1N 5R1. Tel. 902/436-3333. Fax 902/436-4304. 50 rms. TV TEL

$ Rates: June–Sept $94–$104 single or double. Rates $10 less off-season. Golf and other packages available. AE, ER, MC, V.

Since opening its doors in 1991, the Rodd-affiliated Loyalist Country Inn, across the street from the marina and Spinnaker's Landing shopping and dining complex, has made a splash in Summerside. The stylish property, run by Jo-Anne Schurman and her conscientious staff, has an atrium lobby with Mexican tiles and a sparkling chandelier. The rooms are tastefully decorated in shades of green and rose, with cherry furniture and quilted bedspreads. Most have two double beds, though you'll find some with king-size beds, Jacuzzi, minibar, or housekeeping facilities. Twelve rooms are no-smoking.

Dining/Entertainment: The outstanding dining room serves three meals a day, with a focus on healthy eating, with specials from $8 to $20; the tavern, with a mural depicting Summerside in olden times, is open Monday to Saturday from 11am to midnight, with entertainment and the occasional sing-along on Friday and Saturday nights.

Facilities: Guests enjoy the indoor pool, sauna, tennis court, garden, and handcrafts shop.

QUALITY INN–GARDEN OF THE GULF, 618 Water St. East (P.O. Box 1627), Summerside, PEI, C1N 2V5. Tel. 902/436-2295, or toll free 800/228-5151 in the U.S. and Canada. Fax 902/436-6277. 85 rms. TV TEL

$ Rates: $74 single; $84 double. Extra person $7. Children under 18 free. Rates drop Nov–May. AE, DC, ER, MC, V.

This vacation complex, less than a mile from the center of town, focuses on outdoor activities, and since it's a big complex, you should ask for a poolside room (beside the pool and golf course) if sports is your focus. The rooms have one or two double beds; some have king-size beds; no-smoking and Jacuzzi rooms are available.

Dining/Entertainment: Coffee shop for breakfast only; Moby Dick poolside lounge in summer. Popular Brothers Two Restaurant, next door, serves plenty of seafood ($6 to $15), but you can also get sandwiches, burgers, and steaks; it features dinner theater (see "What to See and Do," above), and there's karaoke several nights a week in Friday's Pub, in the same building.

Facilities: A heated outdoor pool, a new indoor pool, a beach down on the bay, shuffleboard, and even a nine-hole golf course; gift shop.

SILVER FOX INN, 61 Granville St., Summerside, PEI, C1N 2Z3. Tel. 902/436-4033. 6 rms.

$ Rates (including continental breakfast): $55–$65 single; $60–$70 double. Extra adult $10, child $5 (no children under 10, please). Dinner-theater package July–Aug. AE, MC, V.

For a truly delightful bed-and-breakfast stay, book yourself into the Silver Fox Inn. Julie Simmons, the innkeeper, has tastefully retained the distinctive qualities of this vintage home, while providing all the expected modern comforts. Upstairs, each of the spacious double rooms has a private bath, while the first floor features a sitting room with a fireplace and breakfast area. It's difficult to decide between the most expensive "Blue Fox" master bedroom or a smaller room with a fireplace. This slate-gray beauty (1891) is situated on the quiet corner of Granville and Belmont. Ms. Simmons is knowledgeable about the area and happy to help you organize your days.

SUNNY ISLE MOTEL, 720 Water St., Summerside, PEI, C1N 4J1. Tel. 902/436-5665. 21 rms. TV

$ Rates: $36 single or double with one bed; $41 double with two beds. MC, V.

The Sunny Isle Motel is on the highway just two miles from the center of town, surrounded by fine lawns with plots of flowers here and there. Each room has radio, cable color TV, and tub-shower bathroom, but if you get a room numbered from 8 to 22, you'll have a quieter place to stay and also a view of the lawns and trees. There are picnic tables for your pleasure. Prices are superreasonable. Owners Phyllis and Brad Clark will give you a warm welcome.

WHERE TO DINE

Tops is the dining room at the **Loyalist Country Inn,** 195 Harbour Dr., where the food is healthily prepared and you're assured fresh vegetables al dente (tel. 902/436-3333). **Brothers Two Restaurant,** 618 Water St. East, is also a good choice (tel. 902/436-9654).

For light, flavorful fare, a popular local spot is the **Dominion Square Café,** downtown in Dominion Square, the converted department store building (1857) at 250 Water St. Walk through the store to the back to find the café, which serves muffins, biscuits, soups, sandwiches, and desserts, all homemade, even the salad dressing and mayonnaise. The café is open year-round Monday to Friday from 9am to 4pm, and Saturday 9am to 3:30pm (tel. 902/436-2229).

---

3. CAVENDISH & "THE LAND OF ANNE"

22 miles (36km) NE of Summerside,
24 miles (39km) NW of Charlottetown

GETTING THERE From Summerside, pick up Highway 1A, and at Travellers Rest, take the Blue Heron Drive (Highways 2 and 6) to Cavendish, on the North Shore. If you are traveling from Charlottetown, follow Highway 2 to Hunter River, and pick up Route 13 to Cavendish.

ESSENTIALS Information The large Cavendish Visitor Centre is open daily from 9am to 10pm in July and August, and 9am to 6pm June and September to early October (tel. 902/368-4444). It has some exhibits of local crafts, others devoted to Lucy Maud Montgomery, along with books and an audiovisual presentation about her. If you're shopping for gifts, they're here too, though the area has some good gift shops as well (see below and "Central P.E.I")

Getting Around You can drive, of course, but you don't have to. All the attractions are within about 6 miles (10km) of each other, a bit too far to walk but there are a couple of other options. The Cavendish Trolley stops at the Visitor Centre, as it makes its rounds of the area's attractions from 9am to 9pm in peak summer season. A full tour costs about $3.50, a partial tour $2. The town of Cavendish is a busy tourist mecca with its own fast-food-filled boardwalk, but it is surrounded by pastoral beauty and is just outside the national park.

Rent A Bike (tel. 902/566-2295) is located in the Cavendish Petro Canada station at the junction of Routes 6 and 13 in Cavendish. Bike rentals are $5 an hour and $17 a day for adults, about $1 less for kids. It's open daily 8am to 8am in May, June, September, and October, and 7am to midnight in July and August.

When you enter Cavendish, you are literally driving into a storybook setting, for it was here that many of the scenes were set for author Lucy Maud Montgomery's books, including the home that inspired Green Gables (now managed by the Canadian Parks Service), the Haunted Wood, and Lover's Lane.

Cavendish itself is a bustling tourist town, with its share of shops, fast-food eateries, and vacation cottages, but travel a couple of miles in either direction from the town, and once again you're in "The Land of Anne," a serene landscape and the final resting place of the person who immortalized it, Lucy Maud Montgomery, who was buried in the Cavendish Cemetery in 1942.

WHAT TO SEE & DO

GREEN GABLES HOUSE, Rte. 6, 1 mile west of Cavendish. Tel. 902/672-2211.

⭐ Green Gables House is a re-creation of the fictional farmhouse where orphan Anne Shirley was taken in by Matthew and Marilla Cuthbert, and it has been lovingly restored with many of the details from Montgomery's books. Anne's room is upstairs on the left; downstairs are photographs of the author at age 6, 21, 33, and 60. A 10-minute history of Green Gables, given in the front yard every half hour from 10am to 4pm from July to mid-August, will refresh your memory of the story and enhance your tour of the house. The house is part of the national park. The best time to go to avoid the crowds of "Anne with an E" fans is before 11am or after 3pm. A small tearoom, large gift shop, picnic area, and recreational facilities nearby are part of the park as well.

Admission: Free.
Open: Mid-June to Labor Day daily 9am–8pm; May–early June and Sept–Oct daily 9am–5pm. **Closed:** Nov–Apr.

"ANNE" LANDMARKS NEAR CAVENDISH

The listings below are strictly related to "Anne" activities. For information about other things to do in the Cavendish area and along Blue Heron Drive, see the next section, on "Central P.E.I."

ANNE OF GREEN GABLES MUSEUM AT SILVER BUSH, on Rte. 20 near Park Corner. Tel. 902/436-7329.

⭐ A location rich in Anne Shirley lore, the Anne of Green Gables Museum is less than five miles north of the intersection of Routes 20 and 6. The house, built in 1872 by John Campbell, was the home of John and his wife, Annie Laura MacNeill. Annie was Lucy Maud Montgomery's aunt, and young Maud (she hated the name Lucy) spent a good deal of time here collecting, as it turned out, material for stories she was later to write. It was, she wrote, "a spacious old house built in the days when wood was cheap and large families were to be housed." (The house is still in the family, and the museum is run by her great-great-nephew.) Maud had her wedding here on July 5, 1911, and visitors today can see the organ on which the wedding music was played, as well as the author's childhood room. Young people who have read the "Anne" books will be thrilled to see so many objects and places that became parts of the romantic stories. The Lake of Shining Waters, which Montgomery wrote about, is across the road. A tearoom and craft shop are on the premises. The 10 windows in the craft shop used to be in Maud's church, Clifton Presbyterian; besides excellent crafts, you can buy *Kindred Spirits*, a quarterly magazine for Anne fans.

Admission: $2.50 adults, 75¢ children under 16.
Open: June and Sept–Oct daily 9am–6pm; July–Aug daily 9am–dark. **Closed:** Nov–May.

LUCY MAUD MONTGOMERY BIRTHPLACE, at the intersection of Rtes. 6, 20, and 8, in New London. Tel. 902/886-2099.

The author was born in 1874 in this unassuming house, 7 miles (11km) west of Cavendish, in New London. Here you'll see her scrapbook and wedding dress. Books by and about her are for sale. (The excellent Memories gift shop is across the road.)

Admission: $1 adults, 50¢ children.
Open: Summer daily 9am–7pm. **Closed:** Fall–spring.

WHERE TO STAY

KINDRED SPIRITS COUNTRY INN AND COTTAGES, Rte. 6, Cavendish, PEI, C0A 1N0. Tel. and fax 902/963-2434. 10 rms (all with bath), 3 suites, 14 cottages. TV **Directions:** On Route 6, just west of the Cavendish intersection.

$ Rates: Inn rooms, $55 single, $65–$85 double (including continental breakfast buffet); $100–$110 suite; $70–$135 cottage. Extra person $10. Off-season rates available. MC, V.

⭐ Kindred Spirits Country Inn and Cottages, on six acres next door to the Anne of Green Gables House, is the prettiest place to stay in Cavendish. It manages to stay completely removed from the hubbub next door by a golf course and tree barrier. Along with friendly "down East" hospitality, you'll find nicely furnished inn rooms with private baths, toiletries, and hairdryers, one- and two-bedroom housekeeping cottages, three suites with living room and hardwood floors, a large, heated outdoor swimming pool, and a family-size whirlpool. Definitely family-oriented, it provides movies, books, toys, special activities, and a playground for kids. Adults get attention, too: afternoon tea served in front of the fireplace. Kindred Spirits is run and beautifully maintained by the James family.

SHINING WATERS COUNTRY INN, Rte. 13, Cavendish, PEI, C0A 1N0. Tel. 902/963-2251. Fax 902/963-2251. 10 rms, 20 housekeeping cottages. TV
$ Rates: $55–$64 double in the inn with full breakfast buffet; $86–$94 two-bedroom housekeeping cottage. Weekly rates available. MC, V. **Closed:** Mid-Oct to mid-May.

Near the national park entrance, this was once the real home of Rachel McNeel, and the fictional home of Rachel Lynn in *Anne of Green Gables*. It offers inn guests an airy breakfast room overlooking the Gulf of St. Lawrence and a large sitting room and library with a stone fireplace and copies of *Canadian Geographic* and *The Island* to peruse. The Shining Waters compound of pine-paneled cottages is built around a small children's playground and includes an outdoor pool surrounded by a wooden fence, and, beside it, two enclosed indoor whirlpools. The 10 newer cottages have high ceilings and sleep two to six people. The 10 cottages from the 1940s are popular for nostalgic reasons. All have front decks. Only adults may stay in the inn; families have full reign of the cabins. Basketball, shuffleboard, and Ping-Pong are available. Expect a warm welcome from owners Linda and Peter Steele, who have the enviable lifestyle of living in Cavendish, Charlottetown, and Naples, Florida.

WHERE TO DINE NEAR CAVENDISH

Enjoy good home cooking, even if only coffee and rhubarb crisp or a lemon square, at the tearoom at Anne of Green Gables at Silver Bush. There is also a tearoom at Green Gables House. The boardwalk in Cavendish is chockablock with eateries (shops, too), including a branch of Charlottetown's famous Cow's, for ice cream.

FIDDLES 'N' VITTLES, Hwy. 6. Tel. 902/963-3003 (summer), 902/566-3407 (winter). Fax 902/566-3407.
Cuisine: SEAFOOD. **Reservations:** Not needed.
$ Prices: Light lunch $3–$7; lunch or dinner appetizers $4–$8; main courses $10–$14; lobster supper $20. AE, MC, V.
Open: Breakfast daily 8–11:30am; lunch daily 11:30am–4:30pm; dinner daily 4:30–9pm. **Closed:** Labor Day–May.

Several miles west of the Cavendish intersection on Highway 6, Fiddles 'n' Vittles mixes a good time with good food. A raised level surrounds a square-dance floor—at one time fiddlers played for Saturday dancing here, but now the floor is crowded with dining tables. The staff is made up of local young people, and in the background there's the sound of country-style violins or "bingo while you eat." Three nights a week a "Sing for Your Supper" contest is held. The lobster dinner includes various vegetables, potato salad or coleslaw, rolls and lots of butter, plus a lobster—for what you get it's almost the same as in the famous "lobster supper" places. Seafood-lovers will find they can come back and try the other items such as scallops, fried clams, and fish, while meat eaters can always get steak or hamburgers. Children's plates are available.

If you decide to stay the night, they've got eight efficiency units ($39 to $69 single or double; off-season, make a reservation through Shirley Chappell, R.R. 1, Breadalbane, PEI, C0A 1E0); ask for a unit overlooking the Hope River.

READERS RECOMMEND

"In the Cavendish area, I stayed at Gulf Breeze Cottages & Farm Tourist Home (tel. 902/886-2678), about one mile east of the intersection of Route 6, on Route 224. The Simpsons were lovely. I paid $23 for a room in the main house. Morning coffee was free, breakfast extra." — Kenneth E. Kaplan, Washington, D.C. [*Author's note:* Inn rates now start at about $25, housekeeping cottages for one to four people are $70; VISA accepted.]

4. CENTRAL P.E.I.

The heart of Prince Edward Island is home to much of the Anne of Green Gables lore but also magnificent beaches, vacation hideaways, tasty island cooking, and charming little towns.

THE NORTH SHORE

It seems that everyone who comes to the island comes, at least in part, for the beaches, and the very best ones are on the north coast in Prince Edward Island National Park, reachable from Charlottetown by Route 15, which goes northwest to join Route 6, which skirts the northern shore.

PRINCE EDWARD ISLAND NATIONAL PARK

Noted for its spectacular sand dunes and beaches, Prince Edward Island Park stretches for 25 miles (40km) along the north shore of the island. The shallow waters of the Gulf of St. Lawrence are the warmest in Atlantic Canada, and there are several supervised beaches — Brackley, Stanhope, and Dalvay — where you can test them out.

Other park activities include hiking along one of six easy trails, cycling along Gulf Shore Parkway, picnicking, or attending one of the many interpretive events offered daily during the summer. In winter, the park offers cross-country skiing, snowshoeing, and ice skating. Green Gables House, on Route 6 in Cavendish (see separate listing, below), and Stanhope Cape Lighthouse, the site of a disaster at sea, are in the park.

Camping is available at several locations, with fees from about $9 to $19. You'll need a national park motor vehicle license, which costs $5 a day, $10 for four days, to drive in the park. For more information, contact the Cavendish Information Centre or the P.E.I. National Park at 2 Palmer's Lane, Charlottetown, PEI, C1A 5V6 (tel. 902/963-2391 in summer, otherwise 902/672-6350).

Note: Near the eastern edge of the park, near Lakeside in Kings County, a mile off Route 2, is the **Links at Crowbush Cove** (tel. 902/652-2356), which opened in 1993 and has been proclaimed one of Canada's top courses. Sprawled around the north shore dunes, it offers panoramic vistas and a challenging round of golf, including eight holes surrounded by dunes.

Where to Stay in or Near the Park

DALVAY-BY-THE-SEA, P.O. Box 8, Little York, PEI, C0A 1P0. Tel. 902/672-2048. Tel. and fax in winter 902/672-3315. 26 rms, 1 cottage.
Directions: Take Highway 6 to national park exit.
$ Rates (including breakfast and four-course dinner): $120–$135 single; $170–$270 double. Extra adult $60, child 4–12 $50, child 1–3 $20. $240 cottage (add $80 for a third person). Minimum stay of two nights in summer. AE, ER, MC, V.

In 1895 a graceful mansion rose on the north shore of Prince Edward Island. Its owner was Alexander MacDonald, a partner with John D. Rockefeller in the Standard Oil Company. As you can imagine, no expense was spared in building Mr. MacDonald's magnificent "summer cottage." Now a genteel hotel, Dalvay-by-the-Sea is off Route 25 in the national park grounds just before you come to Dalvay Beach. Rooms in the mansion all have private baths. Some rooms have ocean views; pretty no. 24 overlooks Lake Dalvay. And with no television or telephone, they are blessedly quiet. Besides tranquillity, grandeur, good food, a commanding stone fireplace in the lobby, and Dalvay Beach, the mansion has lovely grounds. Dalvay-by-the-Sea has only 26 bedrooms (some are wallpapered; some have wood paneling), and demand for this northern Shangri-La is great, so reserve far in advance. The park permit is waived for Dalvay guests.

Dining/Entertainment: If you can't stay the night but still want to experience a bit of Dalvay, dine here on local foods prepared with a twist—like Cajun spiced salmon with tomato coriander salsa and roasted seaweed. You'll pay $14 to $18 for main courses at dinner, double that with an appetizer, dessert, tax, and tip included. The lovely dining room is open from 8 to 9:30am for breakfast, noon to 2pm for lunch, and 6 to 9pm for dinner. Reservations recommended.

Facilities: Two tennis courts, a croquet green, a children's playground, a driving range, table tennis, canoeing, and boating; mountain bike rentals. Near the outstanding Links at Crowbush Cove golf course.

SHAW'S HOTEL, Brackley Beach, PEI, C0A 2H0. Tel. 902/672-2022. Fax 902/672-3000. 17 rms (14 with bath), 18 cottages (all with bath). **Directions:** Look for the signs on Route 15 near Brackley Beach.

$ Rates (including breakfast and dinner): $80–$105 single hotel room without bath, $130 single room with bath; $105–$120 double hotel room without bath, $140–$180 double hotel room with bath; $175–$215 double cottage unit with bath. AE, MC, V. **Closed:** Mid-Oct to May.

Brackley Beach has a gracious old resort hotel and cottages tucked away down a long drive. The immaculately kept hotel is small and Victorian, its white-and-red exterior looking as it did when it was built, in 1860, by the great grandfather of the present innkeeper, Robbie Shaw. Public rooms and guest rooms have been modernized to make them comfortable, but not enough to remove their charm. The beach is only a five-minute walk away. The cottages don't have housekeeping facilities, since occupants dine in the hotel dining room, which is licensed. The staff at Shaw's is young and congenial, and the Sunday supper buffet is an island event. Kids love the hayrides held just for them, and the resident dogs, Clancy and Duff.

Where to Dine

CAFE ST. JEAN, Rte. 6, Oyster Bed Bridge. Tel. 902/963-3133.
Cuisine: SEAFOOD/INTERNATIONAL. **Reservations:** Recommended for dinner.
$ Prices: Lunch appetizers $3.50–$9, main courses $5–$9; dinner appetizers $5–$9, main courses $16–$21. AE, MC, V.
Open: Lunch daily 11:30am–5pm; dinner daily 5–9pm. **Closed:** Oct to mid-June.

Pretty, intimate Café St. Jean is on Route 6 between Brackley Beach and South Rustico, overlooking the Wheatley River. The interior, awash with light wood, features plants and high-backed booths with brocade cushions. Salads, soups, and the house pâté are always available; at lunch, you can get sandwiches, burgers, quiche, and fish dishes; for dinner, chicken, pork, steak, and fish dishes, including the catch of the day. There's also vegetarian linguine, and half portions for kids. It's licensed. The owners sawed and milled every piece of wood you see on the premises. With that kind of care and pride in construction, imagine the care they take with your food. Check out The Loft craft shop upstairs.

DUNES CAFE, Rte. 15, just south of the national park gate. Tel. 902/672-2586.
Cuisine: SEAFOOD/LOCAL. **Reservations:** Recommended at night.
$ Prices: Lunch items $3.50–$10; dinner appetizers $4–$9, main courses $6–$17. AE, MC, V.
Open: Summer only. Hours vary, so call ahead.

Part of the exciting Dunes complex, with a gallery and shop showcasing the extraordinary pottery of Peter Jansons (see "What to See and Do Along the Drive," below), the café has special ambience, especially on nights when there's live jazz. At lunch, light fare includes soup of the day with beer and Cheddar bread, pasta of the day, and grilled lambburger. For dinner, you might start with grilled skewered shrimp with steamed greens and peanut-lime dipping sauce, or island mussels steamed in ginger-sesame broth with scallions, tomatoes, and steamed greens. Then move on to a main course of pan-seared sea scallops with spinach and roasted sweet potatoes; grilled chicken breast with asparagus, mashed potatoes, and grilled tomatoes; or roasted island lamb. Finish up with chocolate checkered cake. The gorgeous plates you dine on are made right here. Whether your interest is in fine dining, art, or architecture, or all three, expect a pleasurable sensory overload here. Even the bathrooms are memorable. No smoking, please.

WHAT TO SEE & DO ALONG THE DRIVE

In Brackley Beach, on Route 15 a mile from the national park gate, stands an architectural and artistic highlight of the island: **The Dunes** studio and gallery, which represents 40 artists (tel. 902/672-2586). Stop by to see the exquisite pottery of Dunes owner and designer Peter Jansons (you may recognize his work from shops in Charlottetown), the clean lines of the architecture so perfectly suited to its setting, and the view of Brackley Bay from the upper gallery. Be sure to see the "The Head." The shop sells candleholders, lamp bases, glasses, bowls, and conversation-piece vases, as well as cassettes and books about the island. There's a popular jazz café on the premises (see above).

The tiny **Gouda Cheese Shop,** a five-minute drive off Route 6 near Brackley Beach (watch for the sign), sells tasty cheese from a starter brought from Holland. Sample the product, then choose between plain, onion and red pepper, or herb and garlic. The shop also has homemade biscuits, jams, honey, marmalade, and chutney, and you can watch a video on how the Gouda is made. Open Monday through Saturday from 10am to 6pm.

Continuing west along Highway 6, you'll come to **South Rustico,** a bilingual pocket of P.E.I. and proof that small is beautiful. It's little more than a cluster of houses, a church, a museum, an inviting bed-and-breakfast, and plunderable gift shop.

The **Farmer's Bank of Rustico** (1864), in South Rustico, the oldest bank building in P.E.I., is now a museum. Built of island sandstone with three-foot-thick walls and founded by innovative Fr. Georges Belcourt from Québec, it printed its own currency until 1894. Farm artifacts, belongings of Belcourt, and some bank paraphernalia are displayed. The museum is open Monday through Saturday from 9:30am to 5pm and on Sunday from 11:30am to 4pm, and a guide will show you around. Adults pay $2 to enter; children under 12 are free (tel. 902/963-2505).

Just down the road, the wooden **St. Augustine's** parish church is beautiful in its simplicity. The doors are probably open, so go in for a look.

At the corner of Highway 6 and Highway 243 stands the **Old Forge Pottery,** a studio and shop showcasing and selling the graceful, functional, and affordable pottery of owner-potters Carol and Ken Downe. Visitors may get to see a work in progress when they drop by. Along with the stoneware and porcelain, the work of other island craftspeople is also for sale—sweaters, quilts, toys, and gift items. It's open late May to late September (tel. 902/963-2878).

Where to Stay in South Rustico

BARACHOIS INN, Rte. 243, South Rustico (mailing address: P.O. Box 1022, Charlottetown, PEI, C1A 7M4). Tel. 902/963-2194. 2 rms, 2 suites (all with bath).

$ Rates (including full breakfast): $75 single or double; $85 suite. Extra person $18. No credit cards. **Closed:** Nov–Apr.

Ten miniature Canadian flags flutter in welcome at the door of the Barachois Inn. This yellow house with cedar-shingled mansard roof and rockers on the porch has beautiful rooms with country decor and original board floors. No. 1 is particularly pretty, with a gorgeous four-poster bed. The suites have a separate sitting room. To add to its appeal, the owners have displayed their collection of contemporary art throughout the house. Not suitable for very young children.

Where to Dine in North Rustico

FISHERMAN'S WHARF, on the harbor in North Rustico. Tel. 902/963-2669.

    Cuisine: SEAFOOD. **Reservations:** Not needed.
$ Prices: Lobster (or steak) supper $22; "seafood extravaganza" $56 for two; most items $3–$23. AE, DC, MC, V.
    Open: Mid-May to June and Sept to mid-Oct daily 11am–9pm; July–Aug daily 8am–10pm; lobster supper served 4–9pm only. **Closed:** Late Oct–early May.
Ever wonder what kind of shape your lobster was in when it arrived at the restaurant? Head for Fisherman's Wharf to find out. Here, living under strictly controlled conditions and segregated according to weight, are 20,000 pounds of crawling crustaceans. Fisherman's Wharf does everything in a big way, from all those lobsters to gallons of chowder to seating for 400 to a 50-foot salad and dessert bar. And it's all part of their famed lobster supper. If this is too overwhelming, you can retreat to the smaller dining room with a full menu, from sandwiches to the "seafood extravaganza," which includes chowder, lobsters, scallops, shrimp, clams, and an array of fish, a bottle of wine with the Fisherman's Wharf label, and finally, dessert and coffee. There's also a children's menu.

Continuing Along the Drive

The drive along Highway 6 from North Rustico to Cavendish passes many of the tourist attractions and amusement parks on the island. The places that draw the most interest, of course, are those associated with P.E.I.'s famous author, Lucy Maud Montgomery, and with her storybook heroine Anne Shirley, of Green Gables. These two made "the Land of Anne" a reality to many people around the world—long before they set foot on the island or into adulthood. (The "Anne" attractions are described in depth in Section 3 of this chapter.)

    One non-"Anne" attraction, **Rainbow Valley** (tel. 902/963-2221 in summer, 902/836-3610 off-season), is a large amusement area just outside Cavendish on Route 6, a quarter mile from Green Gables House. The 37-acre park has pretty landscaped grounds, castle turrets peeking over trees, three island-dotted lakes and a variety of boats to enjoy them, six water slides, exhibits and displays, live animals, live and animated shows, gift shops, and more. The price of admission covers rides and entertainment (except the Shooting Gallery). Don't let the kids have all the fun! It's open June to Labor Day (sometimes later) from Monday through Saturday from 9am to 7pm and on Sunday from 1 to 7pm. Admission is $8.50 for adults, $7.50 for seniors, $7 for children; preschoolers free.

    Also on Route 6, **Sandspit** (tel. 902/963-2626), easy to spot with the bright yellow and red flags out front, draws kids like a magnet with its Ferris wheel, carousel, kiddie cars, Tilt-a-Whirl, bumper boats, and miniature golf. It's open from mid-June through Labor Day. Rides are priced individually, from $1.20, or you can get a day package.

    The unassuming **Lucy Maud Montgomery Birthplace** is at the intersection of Routes 6, 20, and 8, in New London, seven miles west of Cavendish (tel. 902/886-2099). See "What to See and Do" in Cavendish, above, for more information.

    Right across the road, **Memories** gift shop (tel. 902/886-2020) is filled with many items for children and their rooms; go upstairs and admire the nimbleness of local fingers in the handmade quilts, rugs, and afghans.

    You can do more shopping in **Memory Lane Antiques & Crafts,** in an old school (1832) on Route 234, 6½ miles from New London and 1½ miles from Route 20. Here you'll find outstanding gift items and sweaters at good prices. Under the same roof, the **Kitchen Witch,** a country café (see below), combines good home cooking with tea-leaf reading by the "resident witch." The café and shop are open daily in summer from 8am to 8pm, and the tea-leaf reader comes 'round daily from 10am to 6pm (tel. 902/886-2294 for shop and café).

    Also on Route 234, in Burlington, is a one-of-a-kind place called **Woodleigh** (tel. 902/836-3401). This unique, highly recommendable place is filled with detailed large-scale reproductions of some of Great Britain's most famous landmarks, including the Tower of London, York Minster Cathedral, Robert Burns's cottage, Shakespeare's birthplace, Anne Hathaway's cottage, and Dunvegan Castle (large enough to enter). Woodleigh was the dream of Lt. Col. E. W. Johnstone, who created the amazing models (he died in 1984). Eighty percent of the visitors to Woodleigh are adults, charmed by the buildings, the grounds, and the outdoor concerts, held here in July and August. It's open from 9am to 8pm in July and August, from 9am to 5pm in late May, June, September, and the first half of October. Admission is $6.25 for adults, $5.75 for seniors over 65, and $3.50 for children 6 to 15; younger kids free.

The outstanding (and authentic) **Anne of Green Gables Museum** at Silver Bush (near Park Corner) is less than five miles north of the intersection of Routes 20 and 6. The house was the home of John and his wife, Annie Laura MacNeill, who was Lucy Maud Montgomery's aunt. The author spent a good deal of time here and was married here in 1911 (young Japanese couples reserve the house a year in advance for their own marriages). A tearoom and excellent gift shop are on the grounds. For more information about the museum, see Section 3 of this chapter.

Where to Dine

THE KITCHEN WITCH, Rte. 234, 6½ miles from New London and 1½ miles from Rte. 20. Tel. 902/886-2294.
   Cuisine: HOME COOKING. **Reservations:** Not needed.
$ **Prices:** Most items $3–$10.
   Open: Daily 8am–8pm; tea-leaf readings 10am–6pm. **Closed:** Fall–Spring.

This country café combines good home cooking with tea-leaf reading by a "resident witch," who's on duty from 10am to 6pm. Who knows what fate lies your teacup, but in the kitchen there's bound to be soup and sandwiches (peanut butter, roast beef, ham and cheese) on thick homemade bread for lunch; at dinner, consider grilled ham steak, spaghetti, or sirloin strip. Makes me hungry just thinking about it. There's a small shop on the premises.

PRINCE EDWARD ISLAND PRESERVE CO., R.R. 2, New Glasgow, PEI, C0A 1N0. Tel. 902/964-2524. Fax 902/566-5565.
   Cuisine: LIGHT FARE. **Reservations:** Not needed.
$ **Prices:** Breakfast and lunch items $1–$7; dinner appetizers $3.50–$5.50, main courses $8.50–$14. AE, DC, MC, V.
   Open: July–Aug, breakfast daily 8–11:30am, lunch daily 11:30am–5pm, dinner daily 5:30–9:30pm; June and Sept daily 9am–5pm. **Closed:** Oct–May.

If you're in the mood for something light, or a food gift item, don't miss the Prince Edward Island Preserve Co., and pray there are no more than two buses there when you arrive. Founded by Bruce MacNaughton (the fetching fellow in the kilt), this place makes all manner of preserves and lines them up—more than 20 open jars—for you to taste. They've also got maple syrup, honey, and teas. Expect to be greeted by an orgasmic smell at the door.

For more in-depth food sampling, try the Preserve Co.'s café, overlooking the gentle River Clyde. Here the light fare includes homemade breakfast foods, sandwiches, soups, and salads, or more substantial items like cold lemon chicken with rice salad or a smoked fish plate. After 5pm in summer only, the menu expands to include poached salmon, mussels provençale, and lemon-and-thyme chicken. Lobster is available, but only in the pasta. It's licensed.

Lobster Suppers

Prince Edward Island is famous for its lobster suppers, not so much because of what is eaten—lots of places throughout Atlantic Canada and New England serve lobster—but because of how it's eaten. No doubt the idea began as a fund-raising plan for a local church, when members of the congregation were invited to bring a covered dish of something to be shared and the church would provide the lobsters. Everyone would pay a nominal amount, the church would make some money for charitable causes, and all would go home well fed.

Things have changed a bit from this original plan, but not much. Some of the proceeds from these dinners still go to fund the groups' charitable work in the surrounding communities. Diners have their lobster supper in the church hall or basement—each gets a lobster and other fixings such as potato salad, tossed salad, rolls, corn on the cob, steamed clams, vegetables, coleslaw, french fries or baked potato, and dessert. For children and others who don't like lobster, roast beef (hot or cold) is often served as a second choice. The atmosphere is simple but very convivial, and the food is plentiful and good. Prices these days run about $25 for the entire evening, with variations up to a few dollars more or less.

New Glasgow Lobster Suppers (tel. 902/964-2870) is one of the best known. Service is in the town recreation center, where the lobster is served hot, but virtually everything else from the roast beef alternative to the vegetables is cold. Tour buses abound. If you go, go early. The suppers are served in the tiny town of New Glasgow on Route 224 from early June to mid-October, with July and August the very busy months. The lobster dinner is $19 to $26, depending on the size of the lobster. It's served from 4 to 8:30pm.

St. Ann's Church Lobster Suppers (tel. 902/964-2385), not far from New Glasgow at St. Ann's on Route 224 between Hunter River and Stanley Bridge, originated the lobster suppers in P.E.I. and is very popular and crowded in July and August. It has the advantage of being licensed (cocktails, wine, and beer are served), and for those who don't want lobster the alternative is steak, scallops, sole, or pork chops ($14 to $19). There's a children's menu, and live entertainment. Dinners are served from 11:30am to 2pm and 4 to 9pm from the last Monday in May to the first Saturday in October; closed Sunday.

At the **New London Lions' Club** (tel. 902/886-2599), five miles west of Cavendish, on Route 6 not far from the center of New London, you dine on lobster and fixings in the cozy hall of the club. Have a drink in the lounge beforehand if you wish. Early June to mid-September is the season; 4 to 8:30pm nightly is the time for the lobster supper. The Lions' Club also has a hot and cold smörgåsbord where you can eat all you want (no lobsters, though) at a reasonable price from noon to 3pm. If you can't wait, breakfast begins at 8am in July and August.

THE SOUTH SHORE

Along the southern parts of the Blue Heron Trail lie several provincial parks with beaches, campgrounds and picnic areas, and the turnoff for Borden, 31 miles (50km) from Charlottetown and the departure point for car-ferries to Cape Tormentine, New Brunswick.

On your right, soon after leaving the ferry landing, as you head toward Charlottetown on Highway 1, you'll see the sign for **Tea Cups & Roses** on your right. Open in summer only, this mother-daughter operation serves an all-you-can-eat (and drink) afternoon tea, with a bottomless basket of scones, served with cruets of preserves and clotted cream; you can also get desserts, made from scratch (tel. 902/658-2463).

Near the intersection of Highway 1 and Route 10 is one of the most charming towns on the island, the seaside community of Victoria.

VICTORIA

The Trans Canada Highway bypasses Victoria, and in its way, so has time. On an island where everything seems small, slow-moving, and tranquil, this 19th-century seaport town (pop. 176) is even more so. Take Route 116 off Highway 1, and see for yourself.

The focal point of the town, the **Victoria Playhouse** (1918), at Howard and Main Streets, has a busy summer season, with repertory theater and concerts. Anne Murray sang here in the sixties; recent productions have included *Shirley Valentine* and *Sleuth,* and ticket prices are a reasonable $12 for adults, $10 for seniors and students, $6 for children under 12 (tel. 902/565-2025); you can get tickets in Charlottetown at Confederation Centre Ticketworks (tel. toll free 800/565-0278).

Visit the **Studio Gallery** (tel. 902/658-2733), across from the Victoria Playhouse, where you may see artist-in-residence Doreen Foster at work on one of her etchings. The work of others artists is also displayed and sold here, notably the stained glass of Mae Bain and the glass sculptures of Kate Poole, which depict Foster's art (nice cross-pollination). The gallery is open Tuesday to Sunday from 10am to 5pm or by appointment.

The small **Victoria Seaport Museum,** in a relocated lighthouse, is open from 11am to 5pm, Tuesday through Sunday in July and August.

The crafts shop in the **Landmark Café** (see below) sells maritime items, books, local music, T-shirts, and gift items. Other specialty shops and a used-book store line Main Street.

Walk down by the wharf and gaze out to sea. It's hard to imagine three busy wharves here 100 years ago, bustling with fishing and trade activities.

Where to Stay

THE ORIENT HOTEL, Main St., Victoria, PEI, C1A 7K4. Tel. 902/658-2503. 4 rms, 2 suites (all with bath).

$ Rates: Mid-June to mid-Sept, $50–$60 single, $70–$80 double; suite $75 single, $95 double. May to mid-June and mid-Sept to Oct, $10 less. Extra person $10. Weekly rates available. Rates drop off-season. AE, ER, MC, V.

At the turn of the century, the Orient Hotel welcomed sea captains, schoolteachers, traveling salesmen, bankers, and vaudeville troupes. The clientele has changed, the old-fashioned ambience remains. Despite its name, this looks like a place right out of Dodge City. Rooms are comfortable, with private baths; Room 7 has a nice view of the river and fields (the bath has shower only), and Room 8 in the front of the house has a queen-size bed and full bath. Guests may have a breakfast of muffins, cereal, fruit, and bacon and eggs. Owners Lee Joliffe and Darrell Tschirhart, originally from Toronto, are enthusiastic champions of Victoria's charms.

Mrs. Profitt's Tea Room, in the original lobby of the hotel, serves breakfast for guests and is open to the public for lunch and dinner in July and August, Tuesday through Sunday from noon to 8pm (dinner by request only, off-season). The tearoom takes its name from Jessie Profitt, daughter of the original hotel owner.

Where to Dine

LANDMARK CAFE, Main St. Tel. 902/658-2286.
Cuisine: LIGHT FARE. **Reservations:** On request.
$ Prices: Most items $8–$13. No credit cards.
Open: Daily 10am–11pm. **Closed:** Oct–May.

A popular place pre- or posttheater, or anytime, it serves light fare and desserts, like hot Gouda with crackers, cream cheese quiche, meat pies, salads, and praline cheesecake—all homemade. The owners are full of information about Victoria and love having people drop in. It's licensed, air-conditioned, and also sells local artwork, music, and gift items.

5. WESTERN P.E.I.

Like most of Prince Edward Island, the western region, which is encircled by Lady Slipper Drive, is agricultural. The farms are meticulously cared for, with neat and sometimes surprisingly brightly colored farmhouses. You'll pass field after field of potatoes, the green-leafed plants topping long mounds, a few white flowers at the top of each plant. Tomatoes, tobacco, wheat, corn, and other crops grow well on the island, too, but this is predominantly spud country.

Expanses of tilled fields end at patches of clover, or hills covered in wildflowers, or down in cattail-lined bottoms. Here and there you'll spot a herd of Holsteins, which provide the basis of the island's dairy-farming and beef industry. And nearby, a handsome weathered-shingle barn or a steep-gabled farmhouse. Western Prince Edward Island contains some of the prettiest farm country in all North America.

It is an area where the Acadian culture is still entrenched. Of the 15,000 Acadians still on P.E.I. today, about 6,000 still speak French as their first language.

WHAT TO SEE & DO ALONG LADY SLIPPER DRIVE

Following Route 1A from Summerside, go to St. Eleanors, then take Route 2 west to Miscouche.

ACADIAN MUSEUM, Rte. 2 west, Miscouche. Tel. 902/436-6237.

This museum, established in 1991 in a small log cabin five miles west of Summerside, has moved into modern new quarters. In the main gallery, dioramas and texts present Acadian history after 1720, while other exhibits depict the lifestyle before and during deportation and the difficulties following resettlement in 1760. There is a 15-minute audiovisual presentation. Note the photo gallery of the serious-minded faces of pioneer Acadian families—Arsenaults, Gallants, Gaudets, Doirons. They were hardworking, peace-loving homebodies, who lived in friendship with the Micmac, as shown by traces of intermarriage in the photos, although other settlers battled with them constantly. The Acadian flag that flies in front of the museum was designed here at the second national Acadian convention in 1884. Symbolizing the cultural unity of the Acadian people, it combines the French tricolor with a yellow "star of the sea."

Admission: $2.75 adults, $1.50 students, children under 6 free, $7 families.
Open: Mid-June to early Sept Mon–Sat 9:30am–5pm, Sun 1–5pm; the rest of the year Mon–Fri 9am–5pm.

GREEN PARK PROVINCIAL HISTORIC PARK, Port Hill. Tel. 902/831-2206 for the museum, 902/831-2370 for the park; off-season 902/859-8790.

From Miscouche, take Route 12 northwest toward Grand River, a bucolic village highlighted by its pale yellow church with white trim. North of Grand River the road follows the curve of Malpeque Bay, famed for its delicate-tasting oysters. Farther north you'll reach Port Hill.

In this historical park, you can visit the home of 19th-century shipbuilding magnate James Yeo, Jr., furnished with period pieces and peopled with guides in period costume. The house was built in 1865, and you can wander as you like through its three floors, even clambering up to the cupola for the panoramic view. Look for such oddities as the green glass "lusters" on the mantelpiece in one room, the old foot bath, the marble occasional tables, the four-poster beds, and the intriguing gadgets in the kitchen, laundry room, and pantry. The park also has a modern exhibition area with displays outlining the history of shipbuilding in P.E.I., and a re-created 19th-century shipyard down by the water. Buy your tickets, good for all the sights in the park, at the modern building next to the parking lot. Besides being a historical park, Green Park is a provincial park with areas for camping, picnicking, hiking, and swimming in Malpeque Bay.

Admission: House, $2.50 per person, $1.25 seniors; children under 12, free. The park itself is free; there is a charge for camping.
Open: Late June–Labor Day.

TYNE VALLEY STUDIO AND SHORELINE SWEATERS, Rte. 12. Tel. 902/831-2950.

In this delightful studio, owned by talented designer Lesley Dubey, striking sweaters are produced using local wool yarn. The designs are original, and the most popular is the Fair-Isle Lobster pattern. The sweaters may be ordered year-round from the studio, which also sells local handcrafts, at P.O. Box 99, Tyne Valley, PEI, C0B 2C0.

Open: June–Sept daily 9:30am–5pm; May and Oct by appointment or chance.
Closed: Nov–Apr.

LENNOX ISLAND MICMAC NATION, Rte. 163, off Rte. 12. Tel. 902/831-2653.

In the settlement, there is a small museum outlining the history of the tribe, right across the street from the church. Nearby is a craft shop operated by Ray Sark (tel. 902/831-2027), a Micmac whose father and grandfather were both chiefs of the island tribe. Ray is devoted to the promotion of craftwork, and his shop is stuffed with all types of pottery, beadwork, wood carving, leather items, and curiosities such as sweet grass baskets, as well as many collector's items and museum-quality pieces. The crafts represent many tribes in Canada, not just the Micmac, and his whole stock is of genuine Canadian handmade pieces. Ring the bell at the yellow house if the shop appears to be closed.

Open: July–Aug 10am–7pm; the rest of the year by appointment.

ALBERTON MUSEUM, corner of Church and Howlan Sts., Alberton. Tel. 902/853-4048.

This little museum, a century-old courthouse, holds a collection of genealogical files, community histories, and photos, as well as antiques, mementos, and furnishings used by the pioneers of P.E.I.

Admission: $2 adults, $1 children; families of more than four, $1 each.

Open: End of June–Labor Day Mon–Sat 10am–5pm.

ON TO CAPE NORTH

If you still have plenty of time left in your day, you can continue along Route 12 north to Tignish, a town rich in Acadian heritage, and on to Cape North at the very tip of the island. Only the persistent wind, flocks of gulls, and a few playful seals greet those who stand on the cliffs at the end of the road. You'll receive a ribbon of recognition for having made it this far; then if or when you get to East Point, just show your ribbon and you'll get a certificate proclaiming that you've traveled P.E.I. from tip to tip.

Near here, the Canadian government operates the **Atlantic Wind Test Site** (tel. 902/882-2746); you can get a close look at the large windmills and watch an audiovisual presentation daily in July and August from 10am to 8pm, but the laboratories are not open to the public.

Along the North Cape area of Lady Slipper Drive one may, by chance, catch a glimpse of a mighty workhorse wading along the shore pulling a scoop. This is one of the techniques used to harvest Irish moss after it has formed a thick carpet over rocks and ledges. Carrageenan, the substance extracted from the sun-dried moss, is used in ice cream, chocolate milk, insect repellent, toothpaste, and even beer.

To head back, take Route 14, the slow road, or if the day is wearing on, Route 2 south and east will zip you back toward Summerside, but in your hurry don't miss one of the most interesting places to stay, dine on home cooking, or simply explore for a nominal admission.

NEAR CEDAR DUNES PROVINCIAL PARK

By all means, visit the West Point Lighthouse, in Cedar Dunes Provincial Park (see below). After you tour through it, you could easily decide to stay for a meal—or for a night or two.

PRINCE EDWARD ISLAND POTATO MUSEUM, Rte. 142, O'Leary. Tel. 902/859-2039.

Finally, a museum that honors the lowly spud. This one opened in summer 1993, and is actually a small complex that also contains a community museum, chapel, school, and log barn housing a snack bar.

Admission: $2 adults, $5 families.

Open: Mon–Fri 10am–5pm, Sat 11am–4pm, Sun 2–4pm. **Closed:** Oct–May. **Directions:** Take Route 142 off Highway 2 and drive about 3 miles (5km); turn left on Darkview Drive, and left again into the museum complex.

Where to Stay and Dine

WEST POINT LIGHTHOUSE, Rte. 14, R.R. 2, O'Leary, West Point, PEI, C0B 1V0. Tel. 902/859-3605, or 902/859-3117 off-season. 7 rms, 1 tower rm, 1 suite (all with bath). **Directions:** Follow the beacon or take Route 14 through the entrance to Cedar Dunes Provincial Park at the southwestern tip of the island.

$ Rates (including full breakfast): July–Aug $65–$70 single or double. Mid-May to June and Sept–early Oct $55–$60 single or double. $110 ($100 off-season) Tower Room or Keeper's Quarters suite. Extra person $5. MC, V. **Closed:** Late Sept to mid-May.

At the West Point Lighthouse, lodging reaches new heights, and you can actually spend the night in an operating lighthouse, in the wonderful Tower Room, the only guest room in the original 1875 structure. The room, which encompasses the complete (angular) second floor of the lighthouse and features a whirlpool bath, gives you the feeling of being a live-in lighthouse keeper. The suite, called the Keeper's Quarters, is large with a slope roof, sea view, Jacuzzi, and living room with a queen-size sofa bed. All the rooms are furnished in P.E.I. antiques. The popular dining room serves home-style meals three times a day, at reasonable prices. Nature trails and hints of buried treasure are added attractions.

For $1.95 per adult, $1.75 for seniors, and $1 for children you can visit the lighthouse museum and climb to the top for the panorama of Northumberland Strait, a bit of a climb but wonderful if you're up to it.

AT THE END OF LADY SLIPPER DRIVE

For another look at the P.E.I.'s Acadian heritage, make one last stop along Lady Slipper Drive before returning to Summerside. Just after Route 2 crosses Grand River, turn right onto Route 124 (which becomes Route 177) and head for Mont-Carmel at the southern tip of Prince County.

LE VILLAGE PIONNIER ACADIEN, near the junction of Rtes. 177 and 11. Tel. 902/854-2227.
The village, a faithful reproduction of an early 19th-century settlement from the early days of Acadian life here, has a school, store, church, and all the other necessities of civilized town life. There are modern amenities, too: L'Etoile de Mer restaurant, which serves traditional Acadian cuisine; the 20-unit Motel du Village ($45 single, $49 double); and the new L'Auberge du Village, with 30 guest rooms, many of which look out to sea ($64 single, $74 double); rates drop off-season. Bicycle rental is available.
Admission: $2 adults, 50¢ children; preschoolers free.
Open: Mid-June to mid-Sept daily 9:30am–7pm. **Closed:** Late Sept–early June.

6. EASTERN P.E.I.

If western P.E.I. is traditionally Acadian French, the island's eastern reaches are still predominantly peopled by the descendants of early Scottish settlers, as a quick look at place-names on the map will show. Farming and fishing are the prime occupations here, with tourism adding a healthy boost to the local economy. King's Byway Drive begins in Charlottetown, then wanders east and south along the coast past numerous beaches and pretty provincial parks, most notable of which is Lord Selkirk Provincial Park, named for the man who brought a large group of Scottish settlers to the island in 1803.

Many travelers arrive in P.E.I. on the ferry to Wood Islands from Nova Scotia. Nearby is one of the most unusual and idyllically situated bed-and-breakfasts in Atlantic Canada.

WHERE TO STAY IN WOOD ISLANDS

MEADOW LODGE MOTEL, Trans Canada Hwy. (P.O. Belle River), Wood Islands, PEI, C0A 1B0. Tel. 902/962-2022. 19 rms. TV
$ Rates: $49–$71 single or double. Extra person $5. Prices lower off-season. MC, V. **Closed:** Early Oct to mid-May.
The nearest hostelry to the car-ferry dock is the Meadow Lodge Motel, only a mile from the dock and the beaches. The motel units are grouped in a U shape around a grassy lawn; one room is no-smoking; one has kitchen facilities. Prices vary, depending on the number of beds and bedrooms in your unit, or whether you take the unit with kitchen facilities, which sleeps up to four people.

The motel's restaurant, Pier 9, is not on the grounds, but down by the ferry docks; it's open conveniently early, from 5:30am to 9:30pm daily in the summer.

WHERE TO STAY IN UIGG

Though I haven't yet visited it, I hear from travelers, especially bicyclists, that **McLeod's Farm Home & Cottages** (tel. 902/651-2303), on Route 24, is a reasonably priced place to stay (about $40 double for a room, $60 for a housekeeping cottage) and a real farm experience, complete with kittens and Newfoundland dog.

DUNVEGAN FARM TOURIST HOME & MOTEL, Hwy. 24, (R.R. 2), Uigg, PEI, C0A 2E0. Tel. 902/651-2833. 3 farmhouse rms (none with bath), 6 motel units.

$ Rates: Farmhouse rooms $20–$25 single, $30–$35 double; extra person $5. Motel rooms $45–$50 single or double; extra person $6. Breakfast $3 extra, $2 for children under 10. V.

Two miles off Route 1 in Uigg (pronounced *You*-ig), the Dunvegan Farm, set on 170 picturesque acres, provides a central location for exploring Kings County. It's a working farm, producing beef cattle, hay, and grain. A red-and-white barn and assorted cats, dog, flowers, and playground equipment are part of the scene. The pretty farmhouse, built in 1906, has three guest rooms sharing one full bath; one room has a half bath. The motel units on the property have housekeeping facilities. Hosts Dorothy and Harold MacLeod obviously enjoy visiting with their guests. The farm has been in his family since 1829.

WHERE TO STAY & DINE IN LITTLE SAND

BAYBERRY CLIFF INN, R.R. 4, Little Sands, PEI, C0A 1W0. Tel. 902/962-3395. 8 rms (1 with bath). **Directions:** Five miles (8km) east of Wood Islands on Route 4.

$ Rates (including full breakfast): $35 single without bath, $35–$57 double without bath; $75 single or double with bath. Extra person $8. MC, V.

The Bayberry Cliff Inn offers a bed-and-breakfast alternative in a lovely, secluded multilevel home with an open post-and-beam design. Four double rooms, some with lofts tucked in for children, share a bath and overlook the ocean. Three more rooms, also with shared bath, are located upstairs in the renovated barn, which also houses a small art gallery and the Seacliff Room, a little hideaway with a private bath and a balcony. As the name implies, the inn is on a cliff, and steps lead from the lush backyard down to a rocky, sheltered cove, a popular spot for swimming, snorkeling, and inner-tubing. Owners Don and Nancy Perkins relocated here from Massachusetts. He's a retired teacher, and she's an artist who has designed some of the house's unique features, like the four-foot-high "step-up" beds and the perch in a nearby tree for watching the sunset.

In May, June, and July, the inn serves family-style lobster suppers for guests only. Ham or chicken is also an option, and the hearty meal includes soup, salad, rolls, and baked potato, choice of three desserts, and beverage. The cost is only $15, and the lobster are fresh from the waters in front of the inn.

EN ROUTE TO MONTAGUE

In Murray River, there is a crafts shop that's sure to separate you from some of the money in your wallet, the **Old General Store** (tel. 902/962-2459). The three rooms are filled with unabashedly romantic Victoriana, such as old-fashioned cotton nightgowns, aprons, stools with embroidered cushions, quilts, bedspreads, and stuffed animals. There are also sweaters, sweatshirts, jewelry, and much more. It's open from Monday through Saturday, June 10 to 30 and September 7 to 19 from 10am to 4pm, and from July to September 7 from 9:30am to 6pm. It's closed Sunday.

In nearby Murray Harbour, an equally fine craft studio, the **Compass Rose** (tel. 902/962-3881 or 902/962-3925), specializes in folk art, authentic country items, and art objects at reasonable prices. Be sure to see (and perhaps start to collect) the miniatures, paintings, and pottery of local artist Cynthia Gallant-Simpson.

Not far from Murray River, your kids may want to make a detour to **King's Castle Provincial Park** (tel. 902/962-2401), an outdoor amusement area for children and their parents established and operated by the provincial government. Statues of fairy-tale characters people the wooded grounds, picnic tables provide just the place for an outdoor lunch, and a nearby beach is just right for a cooling dip. Entrance to the park is free. It's open May 20 to September 10, from 9am to 9pm.

North of Murray River, King's Byway Drive follows Route 17 north and east, although many people turn left onto Route 4 instead, so as not to miss **Buffaloland** (tel. 902/652-2356) and its small herd of American bison. Open year-round; admission is free. Just a short drive north and you're at **Moore's Migratory Bird Sanctuary** (tel. 902/838-4834), only a few miles from Montague. Bird-lover Harvey Moore founded the sanctuary years ago, and his benevolent attitude allowed dozens of different species of waterfowl to thrive here, as they still do. Stop for a look at the Canada geese—often the tiny goslings will be here, too—and perhaps a blue goose plus various types of ducks. Free pamphlets will guide you on a nature trail in the sanctuary. Several years ago the provincial authorities bought the land from Mr. Moore's widow, and founded the Harvey Moore Wildlife Management Area (as the sanctuary is now called), open free to the public from June to mid-September.

MONTAGUE

Montague, a country town, with a bakery, an ice-cream kiosk, and well-tended homes, is also the commercial center for the eastern coast of P.E.I. Here you'll find several recommendable places to stay and eat.

Golfers will enjoy the 18-hole, par-72 **Brudenell River Provincial Golf Course,** one of Canada's best, just north of Montague, off Route 3 to Georgetown. It has a pro shop, two practice greens, and a driving range (tel. 902/652-2342).

WHERE TO STAY

FRASER'S HOUSEKEEPING COTTAGES, R.R. 2, Montague, PEI, C0A 1R0. Tel. 902/838-2453. 13 cottages. TV **Directions:** One mile (2km) from Highway 4, down a dirt road off of Robertson Road; follow the signs.

$ Rates: $50–$60 double; $310–$350 weekly for two to four people. Off-season rates before June 15 and after Sept 7. MC, V.

At Fraser's the cottages are sparkling white, comfortable, clean, and extra-large, with either two or three bedrooms, full bath, electric heat, cable television, and fully equipped with housekeeping facilities. And they look out over the river and birch trees. There are picnic tables on the grounds, and cream separators recycled as flower pots.

LANE'S COTTAGES, 33 Brook St. (P.O. Box 548), Montague, PEI, C0A 1R0. Tel. 902/838-2433. 18 cottages. TEL

$ Rates: $35 double; $49–$65 double with housekeeping facilities. MC, V.

If you'd like to have a little cottage all to yourself, try Lane's Cottages, in Montague down Brook Street: Just follow the signs. Although you're only a five-minute drive from Montague here, you're certainly in a quiet, bucolic hideaway far from anything that could be called frantic. Each cottage has a shower, good views of the water and the forest, and 14 have housekeeping facilities. There's a children's playground, picnic tables overlooking the water, a gazebo on the river bank, mini-golf, and a Laundromat. The location, in a birch thicket, is undeniably peaceful. The owner puts fresh flowers in the cottages as a special welcome for guests.

WHERE TO DINE

GALLERY CAFE, 30 Main St. North. Tel. 902/838-3700.

Cuisine: LIGHT FARE. **Reservations:** Not needed.

$ Prices: Most items $4–$11. MC, V.

Open: Café, June–Dec Mon–Tues 11am–9pm, Wed–Fri 11am–10pm, Sat noon–10pm, Sun noon–9pm; Jan–May Wed–Sun 11am–9pm, Mon–Tues 11am–7pm. Lounge, Mon 11am–10pm, Tues–Sat 11am–2pm.

A country café with booths and tables, a red-and-white tile floor, and green and floral fabric on the wall, it serves hefty portions of home cooking for lunch and dinner—breads, quiches, salads, pizza, and chowders, for which it is especially well known. The quiche (I had a spicy sausage and pepper one) is light and fluffy and comes with a large salad. After 9pm Monday through Saturday, the café metamorphoses into a lounge (except for the small room in back, which doubles as a gallery), featuring live jazz, blues, or reggae six nights a week. It's fully licensed.

THE GILLIS DRIVE-IN RESTAURANT, Hwy. 4, Montague. Tel. 902/583-2031.
   Cuisine: FAST FOOD.
$ Prices: Most items $2–$8. No credit cards.
   Open: Daily 11am–midnight. **Closed:** Nov–Mar.

S Just north of downtown Montague, the Gillis Drive-In Restaurant—you can't miss its bright blue siding—harks back to another era. Waitresses come to your car to take your order for hot sandwiches, burgers, fries, homemade pies, sundaes, or root beer, and then bring them out to you.

EN ROUTE TO SOURIS

North of Brudenell resort, King's Byway follows the sinuous coastline past beaches and through fishing areas up to Souris. Or you can travel along Highway 4 and then Highway 2 to get to Souris (pronounced *Soo*-ree).

WHERE TO STAY & DINE

THE INN AT BAY FORTUNE, Rte. 310 (R.R. 4), Souris, PEI, C0A 2B0. Tel. 902/687-3745 in summer, or 203/633-4930 off-season. Fax 902/687-3540. 11 rms (all with bath). TEL
$ Rates: Summer $95–$145 single, $105–$155 double; off-season $65–$100 single or double. Extra person $25. MC, V. **Closed:** Mid-Oct to late May.

On Route 310 near Highway 2, the Inn at Bay Fortune is the place to go to get away from it all. Built in 1910, the former summer home of the late actress Colleen Dewhurst is now an elegant country inn, with two rooms in the main house, two in the tower, and seven around the courtyard. The rooms have wood floors, radios, cassette players, cards and cribbage games, and a full tiled bath with hairdryer. Guests share a library/TV room in the top of the tower, overlooking the bay. Guests may rent bicycles and a canoe. Innkeeper David Wilmer hails from Connecticut.

The inn's outstanding dining room serves nouvelle cuisine from 5 to 9pm; it also offers a "tasting menu." Dinner will cost $30 to $35, without wine, tax, or tip, and reservations are recommended. It's licensed.

SOURIS

You can stay overnight in Souris should that fit in with your tour of the King's Byway Drive. The name is French for "mice," and the animals used to be a problem back when the French lived in these parts. The only staffed lighthouse left on the island is in Souris.

If you follow Highway 16 east from Souris to Bothwell and turn right onto the dirt road just before the Esso station, you'll soon come to a beautiful fantasy beach, almost too good to be true—or mention in a guidebook.

WHERE TO STAY & DINE

MATTHEW HOUSE INN, 15 Breakwater St. (P.O. Box 151), Souris, PEI, C0A 2B0. Tel. 902/687-3461. 8 rms (all with bath). TEL
$ Rates (including full breakfast): $59 single; $69–$125 double. Extra person $20. Romance, birdwatching, and lobster-fishing packages available. AE, MC, V.

One of the most memorable bed-and-breakfasts on P.E.I., for its beauty, history, and hospitality, is the Matthew House Inn, named for Uriah Matthew, a dashing local shipbuilder, whose photograph hangs in the parlor. Linda Anderson and Emma Cappelluzzo (a former anthropology professor and hospital administrator from Massachusetts) fell in love with the house, bought it from Uriah's great-granddaughter, Babe, and restored it to its 19th-century grandeur, leaving the original fixtures and winning an award for architectural preservation along the way. Every room has furniture that belonged to the Matthew family. These are appointed with toiletries and terrycloth robes for guests; there is also a parlor, library with cable TV and 50 videos, and books for travelers to swap, three working fireplaces, and, out in the restored barn, a hot tub. If you smoke, you'll have to retire to one of the three porches or stroll out under the linden trees.

Prices include a healthy, hearty breakfast, and lunch and dinner are available to Matthew House guests by arrangement. Gourmet box lunches for a beach outing are $5, and a five-course dinner with wine is $25. The inn rents mountain bikes and fishing equipment; it has an antique shop and a gift shop sells specially selected items, such as Micmac baskets, jewelry, and rugs. A deserted, windswept beach is minutes away.

BASIN HEAD

If you have time, continue six miles (10km) along Route 16 north of Souris to the **Basin Head Fisheries Museum** (tel. 902/357-2966), a complex of four buildings overlooking pretty Basin Head Beach. The day-to-day equipment and artifacts of an in-shore fisherman's life are displayed here, along with old photographs, a reconstructed fish shack, a fish-box factory, and a lobster cannery. There's also a gift shop. The admission is $2.50 for adults, free for children under 12.

Basin Head Beach, which you can walk down to from the museum, is known for its "singing sand," It supposedly whistles or shooshes when you walk on it, but it did neither for me. The beach is lovely and nearly deserted.

The **East Point lighthouse** is 10 miles (16km) farther out, at the tip of the island. They'll give you a ribbon to signify your getting to the far eastern reaches of the island (or a "Tip to Tip" certificate if you've also been to the West Point and can prove it with a ribbon). You can climb to the top of the East Point lighthouse (1867) and peruse the small craft shop. It's open daily in summer from 10am to 6pm. Tours are $2.50 for adults, $2 for seniors, $1 for children 6 and older; a family pass is $6.

ELMIRA

From Souris, you can double back and cut due west across to St. Peter's on Route 2 if time is short, or you can continue north on King's Byway Drive. After Basin Head, take a detour by turning left at South Lake onto Route 16A to reach the tiny hamlet of Elmira, the terminus of P.E.I.'s railroad line. Passenger trains are a thing of the past on the island, and the station has been turned into the **Elmira Railway Museum** (tel. 902/892-9127). Memorabilia of the great age of steam revives the days of chugging locomotives and happy excursionists. Open July to Labor Day, Tuesday to Sunday from 10am to 6pm. Admission is $1 for adults, children under 12 free.

North Lake Harbour, a short distance from Elmira or East Point, is a center for deep-sea tuna fishing, one of P.E.I.'s most famous sports. While hauling in one of the tremendous denizens after an exhausting fight of an hour or more is the thrill of a lifetime, not every boat that goes out comes back with a tuna. Boats put out daily at breakfast time with amateurs aboard, all equipped by the captain, with fees in the range of about $350 per boat. (Those who want to go out for just a few hours pay about $25 per person.) Note especially that if you hook a tuna—it may weigh up to half a ton!—you carry away with you only a photograph and the memory of the struggle, because the captain of the boat legally owns the fish no matter who catches it, and will probably sell it to an outfit that will ship it to Japan.

7. MAGDALEN ISLANDS (ILES DE LA MADELEINE)

The Magdalen Islands, settled in the mid-1700s by displaced Acadians and annexed to Québec from Newfoundland in 1774, bask in the Gulf of St. Lawrence, accessible from Prince Edward Island by ferry (or plane from Québec City). The dozen islands, with their colorful fishing villages and tranquil farming communities, are linked to one another by long sand spits, creating 186 miles of marvelous beaches and blue and green lagoons, as hordes of young Québecois have discovered. Soaking up sun, savoring seafood, windsurfing, skin diving, and swimming are just some of the activities *du jour*. Because the islands are isolated, accommodations and services are limited, and demand usually outstrips supply.

For information on lodging, restaurants, and activities in the Magdalen Islands, request the English-language version of the *Iles-de-la-Madeleine Tourist Guide* from **Québec Government House,** Rockefeller Center, 17 W. 50th St., New York, NY 10020-2201 (tel. 212/397-0220, or toll-free 800/363-7777).

GETTING THERE FROM P.E.I. The ferry ride from Souris to Cap-aux-Meules takes five hours, with frequent service aboard the MV *Lucy Maud Montgomery,* operated by the Coopérative de Transport Maritime, or C.T.M.A. (tel. 902/687-2181). The C.T.M.A. also operates a weekly boat from Montréal to Cap-aux-Meules, called *C.T.M.A.-Voyageur.* The *Lucy* can take up to 95 cars and 400 passengers, for one-way fares of $30 adult, $23 senior, $15 child, $55 for a car. Reservations, which are recommended, may be made by calling Cap-aux-Meules at 418/986-3278. During the busy summer months, the *Lucy* makes about nine trips per week. For an up-to-date schedule and rates, write to C.T.M.A. Traversier, C.P. 245, Cap-aux-Meules, Iles de la Madeleine, PQ, G0B 1B0.

CHAPTER 6

NEWFOUNDLAND & LABRADOR

- **WHAT'S SPECIAL ABOUT NEWFOUNDLAND & LABRADOR**
1. **PORT AUX BASQUES TO DEER LAKE**
2. **GROS MORNE & THE VIKING TRAIL**
3. **GRAND FALLS– WINDSOR & GANDER**
4. **THE BONAVISTA PENINSULA**
5. **ST-PIERRE & MIQUELON**
6. **ST. JOHN'S**
7. **LABRADOR**

Dramatic scenery and a sense of adventure fill any journey to Newfoundland. Although the island was one of the first European landfalls in the New World (John Cabot touched here in 1497, the Vikings even earlier), Newfoundland is sparsely populated. Labrador, almost three times as large, has fewer people still.

All this land, with so few people, makes the province perfect for outdoor adventures. The glacial lakes and streams are full of fish from trout to salmon; moose, caribou, and smaller game roam freely over the vast forests and bogs; seabirds cluster on islands; and whales frolic along the rugged coasts. Those interested in hunting and fishing in the province should get a copy of the *Newfoundland & Labrador Hunting and Fishing Guide,* published annually and distributed free by the Tourism Branch of the Department of Development, P.O. Box 8700, St. John's, NF, A1C 5R8 (tel. 709/576-2830, or toll free 800/563-6353 in Newfoundland). You will usually find the brochure at tourism information offices.

A LITTLE BACKGROUND Until 1949 Newfoundland—or "the Rock," as its inhabitants lovingly refer to it—was a separate British colony, unrelated to Canada except by friendliness and physical proximity. In that year the people (actually only 51% of them) decided that union with Canada was in their interests; World War II, with important Allied air bases providing a vital link between North America and Europe, was over. Economic stagnation had begun to set in, but confederation with Canada brought a shot of new vigor. And though they're loyal citizens, these hearty folk will always be Newfoundlanders first and Canadians second.

As a reminder of its long and colorful colonial period, Newfoundland retained the British Union Jack as its provincial flag until 1980. Though you'll still occasionally see the Union Jack displayed at legion halls and such, the province's stylish new flag represents both Labrador and the island of Newfoundland. By the way, the province is officially referred to as Newfoundland and Labrador. Though distinct geographically, the two territories make up one province.

The English first set foot on the island at the end of the 1400s, attracted by the incredible marine wealth of the Grand Banks off the coast. Other European nations were not long in discovering the seemingly inexhaustible supplies of nourishing codfish to be had from the Grand Banks, and soon Newfoundland was hotly disputed by the English, French, and Dutch as the base for Grand Banks fishing. Challenged in their ownership for centuries, the British finally gained undisputed control of the island with the victory of Col. William Amherst in St. John's, in 1762. Pirates—Americans and others—raided thereafter, but rule of the island was never in doubt.

Remote from the mainlands of Europe and North America, Newfoundland developed a lively and colorful folk culture of its own, based on life in the interior wilds and fishing along the coasts. Newfoundlander talk was—and delightfully still

✔

WHAT'S SPECIAL ABOUT
NEWFOUNDLAND & LABRADOR

Fauna
☐ Moose, whales, puffins, and king cod.
☐ Those wonderful Newfoundland dogs and their cousins, Labrador retrievers.

Nature
☐ Gros Morne and Terra Nova parks in Newfoundland.
☐ The aurora borealis, or northern lights, visible more than 200 nights a year.

Travel Adventures
☐ The train ride from Sept-Iles, Québec to Labrador City.
☐ A two-week ferry ride along the Labrador coast.
☐ Driving the Viking Trail in Newfoundland.
☐ Whale-watching expeditions.

Unique Food and Drink
☐ Cod tongues, fish and brewis, scrunchions, and bakeapples.
☐ Screech.

is—salted with unusual expressions and not a small dose of folk wisdom. "We speak neither of the official languages of Canada," one native explained. The good humor (despite 18% unemployment) and the warmth of the people, along with their strong family ties, are as unforgettable as the land they inhabit.

Odd place-names given by early explorers continue to delight anyone who studies a map of the island: Blow Me Down, Tickle Cove, Little Heart's Ease, Sitdown Pond, Cape Onion, and Joe Batts Arm (that's the name of a town). Speaking of names, "Newfoundland" is pronounced "New-fun-*land*," with the same emphasis as "un-der-*stand*."

Share in the folklore by doing what Newfoundlanders do. The favorite sport is "cod-jigging." Just take a length of fishing line, a hook, and a bit of bait, and plop it into the sea. Before you know it, you've got a cod on the line. Cod tongues are a local delicacy throughout Newfoundland, with a flavor and texture somewhere between scallops and fried clams. If prepared well, they are a treat.

Then there's "fish and brewis" (pronounced "brooze"): salt codfish soaked overnight to get out the brine, cooked with boiled hardtack (thick unleavened bread—today stale bread is often used), and topped with fried bits of pork, called "scrunchions." Some Newfoundlanders can even do without the brewis, in which case the dish is "cod and scrunchions." For dessert, sample some bakeapples, a locally found cousin of the raspberry which, with some sugar, tastes amazingly like baked apples but with the consistency of passion fruit. If all this is too exotic, fall back on other, more familiar, Newfoundland treats: fresh brook trout, Atlantic salmon, herring, or halibut. If this is your first visit, you'll have to be "screeched in" (initiated) with the local 40% proof rum called "screech."

More than its food or drink, however, Newfoundland is famous for that most wonderful of creatures, the Newfoundland dog. This big, black, shaggy animal, a cousin to the Labrador retriever, was around when the Beothuks inhabited the land before the European onslaught. Newfoundland dogs have been known to rescue drowning men and children and pull 100-pound sleighs for many miles. Having a strong neck and webbed toes helps. A Newfoundland dog accompanied Lewis and Clark's 1804 expedition to explore the Missouri River to its source. Proud owners of the dogs have included George Washington, Queen Victoria, and Robert Kennedy.

Some final figures: The Province of Newfoundland and Labrador has a population of close to 600,000 people, almost a quarter of whom live in or near St. John's. In Newfoundland, there are 6,000 miles of roads, and almost 11,000 miles of coastline. Temperatures along the east coast are moderate year-round due to the warm Gulf Stream currents—but when this flow meets the chilly Arctic Stream coming from the north, there's bound to be fog.

SEEING NEWFOUNDLAND & LABRADOR

INFORMATION   For printed tourist information on Newfoundland and Labrador, contact the **Department of Tourism and Culture,** P.O. Box 8730, St. John's, NF, A1C 5R8 (tel. 709/576-2830, or toll free 800/563-6353). You can also get information specifically on Labrador through **Destination Labrador,** 118 Humphrey Rd., Bruno Plaza, Labrador City, NF, A2V 2J8 (tel. 709/944-7788, or toll free 800/563-6353); request the excellent booklet *Labrador—Awaken your Heart and Soul.*

Before you plunge into your Newfoundland adventure, note: Newfoundland and Labrador are on "Newfoundland time," half an hour ahead of Atlantic time. So when you board the ferryboat at North Sydney, or the plane at Halifax, set your watch ahead 30 minutes.

A NOTE ON TAXES   Rooms and meals in the province are subject to a whopping 12% tax (PST), plus an additional federal 7% goods and services tax (GST). Both are refundable to visitors (with the exception of hotel rooms for the PST), and both require purchases of $100 or more and the submission of original receipts and an official claim form. File for the GST rebate first, because all receipts will be returned to you. Then file for the provincial rebate; these receipts will not be returned to you.

For the GST rebate, mail the form to **Revenue Canada,** Customs and Excise, Visitors' Rebate Program, Ottawa, ON, K1A 1J5. For more information, call 613/991-3346 outside Canada, or toll free 800/66-VISIT in Canada.

For the provincial tax rebate submit receipts and forms to the **Tax Administration Branch,** Office of the Comptroller General, Department of Finance, P.O. Box 8720, St. John's, NF, A1B 4K1 (tel. 709/729-3831).

GETTING TO NEWFOUNDLAND   Two ways exist to get to Newfoundland year-round: by air or by ferry, the latter being the continuation of any car or bus trip. Ferries go from Newfoundland to Labrador, and all along its coast, from June through November.

By Plane to Newfoundland   Newfoundland's place in aviation history is almost as thrilling as its Viking past. The early transatlantic air routes all passed through Gander, and during World War II it was the western jumping-off point for the transports that ran a virtual airborne pipeline of supplies to the Allied armies in Europe.

In most cases, a visitor (or a CFA, "come from away" in Newfoundland lingo) will have to change planes in Montréal, Toronto, or Halifax before continuing to Newfoundland. The major carriers serving Newfoundland from Maritime Canada are **Air Nova,** the commuter partner of Air Canada (tel. toll free 800/776-3000 in the U.S., 800/565-3940 in Maritime Canada, or 800/563-5151 in Newfoundland), and **Air Atlantic,** the commuter partner of Canadian Airlines International (tel. toll free 800/426-7000 in the U.S., 800/665-1177 in Canada). Air Nova has destinations in St. John's, Deer Lake/Corner Brook, Gander, and St. Anthony. Air Atlantic flies into St. John's, Deer Lake/Corner Brook, Stephenville, and Gander. Call to compare schedules and fares.

By Ferry to Newfoundland   The Trans Canada Highway reaches across the sea from North Sydney, Nova Scotia, to Port aux Basques, Newfoundland—on paper at least. By the terms of the 1949 agreement whereby Newfoundland became part of Canada, the ferry across the Cabot Strait is legally part of the highway. In fact, the ferry operation is so big that it is indeed almost like a highway across the water.

The terminal for ferries to Port aux Basques on the west coast (about five hours away) and Argentia on the east coast (14 hours away) is at North Sydney, N.S. Marine Atlantic's mammoth oceangoing ferries depart North Sydney daily all year round, several times a day in the summer. Between North Sydney and Argentia, ferries operate only a couple of times a week from June to late October. Fares to Port aux Basques are reasonable: Figure about $17 per adult, $13 per senior, $8.50 per child 5 through 12, and $52 one way for a car.

It costs more, of course, to travel between North Sydney and Argentia, especially if you rent a cabin for the overnight voyage; a reclining seat is inexpensive. Fares are about $47 per adult, $35 per senior, $24 per child 5 through 12; cars cost about $105;

0 300 km
   186 mi

N

Cape Chidley

Ungava
Bay

Hebron

QUEBEC

Atlantic

Ocean

Nain

Davis
Inlet

Lobstick
Lake

LABRADOR

Makkovik

502

Michikamau
Lake

Lake
Melville

Rigolet

Cartwright

Esker

501

Churchill Falls

520

Labrador
City

500

Happy Valley–
Goose Bay

500

Wabush

389

510

Battle Harbour

Red Bay

Blanc Sablon

St. Anthony

Harrington
Harbour

Gros
Morne
National
Park

430

Englee

Sept-Îles

Anticosti
Island

Baie Verte

Twillingate

Terra
Nova
National
Park

330

Corner
Brook

Deer
Lake

1

Gander

Bonavista

Gulf of
St. Lawrence

Stephenville

Grand
Falls

235

NEW FOUNDLAND

230

80

St.
John's

480

360

70

New
Brunswick

Prince
Edward
Island

Havre–
Aubert

Channel
Port aux
Basques

Grand Bank

210

100

Argentia

10

St-Pierre

90

Summerside

Charlottetown

Fredericton

Moncton

North Sydney

Saint
John

NOVA SCOTIA

Halifax

Atlantic

Yarmouth

Ocean

Ferry – – – –

e263

cabins, from $100 to $125; a "Daynighter" reclining chair, $12. For a couple, with a car and a normal, two-berth cabin, plus dinner and breakfast in the ship's cafeteria, the total cost exceeds $300, one way. Cabin and car space on the North Sydney–Argentia run is always heavily booked well in advance, which brings me to the topic of reservations.

Marine Atlantic recommends that all passengers on its two Newfoundland ferry runs make advance reservations. Furthermore, you must arrive one hour prior to departure to guarantee that reservation. Making the reservation is not always easy. In summer, the lines are often busy, but keep trying. The reservations numbers are as follows: in the U.S., toll free 800/341-7981; in North Sydney, 902/564-7480; in St. John's, 709/772-7701; in Argentia, 709/227-2413; in Port aux Basques, 709/695-4209.

If you don't succeed in getting through and you arrive without a car or cabin reservation, here's the best way to approach the situation: If you're in a car, try hard to arrive the night before the day you want to sail; get your tickets, get a waiting-line number, and park your car in line. You can sleep in your car, using the facilities (open 24 hours a day) of the terminal waiting room. If you can't get there the night before, get to the docks as early as possible in the morning—5 or 6am is not necessarily too early. If you're in line the night before, in almost every case you will be able to get on the first boat in the morning; even if that fails you'll get over, as you will have priority on the second boat of the day.

The procedure for getting to Argentia is somewhat different. There are only two sailings a week, on Tuesday and Friday, and they take only 20 names on the waiting list for cabins. If yours isn't one of those names, you won't get a cabin, but don't despair. You can book a reclining chair in a quiet area of the boat; it will be yours for the duration of the 14-hour voyage and will enable you to get some rest. The boat leaves at 7am, and cars begin to line up after midnight. To save anxiety over the trip, make reservations for car and/or cabin well in advance, and then arrive at the dock at least one hour before scheduled sailing time to retrieve them and buy your tickets. If you're later than one hour, you'll lose the reservations.

Note: Marine Atlantic requires that all vehicle fuel tanks be no more than three-quarters full.

If you get reservations and later decide not to use them, call and cancel, or send a card to Marine Atlantic Reservations Bureau, P.O. Box 250, North Sydney, NS, B2A 3M3 (tel. 902/562-9470; fax 902/564-3439). Think of all those people waiting in line.

All this dauntingly detailed inside information will speed your trip, but don't get the idea that a ferry trip to Newfoundland is difficult or exhausting: It's not. It's just that running the Trans Canada Highway across the Cabot Strait takes a bit of organization.

GETTING AROUND   From Port aux Basques by Bus   Bus service is provided by **Terra Transport** along the Trans Canada Highway to St. John's, with stops along the way (tel. 709/737-5916).

From the ferry terminal in Argentia, a van link to St. John's is provided by **Newhooks Transportation Ltd.** (tel. 709/227-2552) and **G & J Transportation** (tel. 709/682-6245).

If for some reason there is no bus running from Argentia when you arrive, you could overnight in the area and take the bus the next day, or get to St. John's by taxi. Find others to share the cost, then call 709/726-4400—**Bugden's Taxi** in St. John's.

There is no passenger train service in Newfoundland.

Car Rentals   While transportation does exist between the major towns, you'll need a car to strike out on your own into the countryside. Rental agencies can be found in St. John's, Corner Brook, and Deer Lake. In Labrador, you can rent a car in Labrador City and Goose Bay, as well as in Blanc Sablon, Québec, a few kilometers from L'Anse au Clair in Labrador.

You can rent a car in Newfoundland if you haven't brought your own, but be sure to reserve the car you want well in advance. Cars go quickly because public transportation in Newfoundland is so limited. Reserve your car by calling any of the

AN IMPORTANT NOTE ON PRICES

Unless stated otherwise, **the prices cited in this guide are given in Canadian dollars,** which is good news for U.S. travelers because the Canadian dollar is worth 25% less than the American dollar, but buys nearly as much. As we go to press, $1 Canadian is worth 75¢ U.S., which means that your $100-a-night hotel room will cost only U.S. $75, and your $6 breakfast costs only U.S. $4.50.

Here's a quick table of equivalents:

Canadian $	U.S. $
$ 1	$ 0.75
5	3.75
10	7.50
20	15.00
50	37.50
80	60.00
100	75.00
200	150.00

following (the toll-free numbers are operative within Canada): **Avis,** 800/879-2847; **Budget,** 800/268-8900; **Hertz,** 800/263-0600; **Thrifty,** 800/367-2277; and **Tilden,** 800/387-4747.

In Newfoundland and Labrador, you have to buckle seat belts in the front and back seats of the car. Always be on the lookout for moose crossing the road; most accidents with these bulky animals occur during the summer months at night. If there's fog, drive with your low beams on. And don't stash leftover food in trash bins along the highway; it attracts bears.

With insurance, 12% provincial tax, 7% GST, gas, 700 free kilometers (420 miles), and incidental charges, a week's car rental in Newfoundland might cost approximately $570.

GETTING TO LABRADOR   Goose Bay, Churchill Falls, and Wabush have airports served by daily flights from outside Labrador, most originating in Newfoundland.

By Plane   Labrador Airways Limited, P.O. Box 310, Station A, Happy Valley–Goose Bay, Labrador, A0P 1S0 (tel. 709/896-3387, or toll free 800/563-3042 in Newfoundland), has scheduled air service from St. Anthony to and from the Labrador coast and Goose Bay. The company also offers charter air service using float, ski, and wheel aircraft (tel. 709/896-3658). **Provincial Airlines** (tel. 709/576-1800; 709/576-1666 for reservations) also flies into Labrador.

Air Nova (tel. toll free 800/776-3000 in the U.S., 800/565-9513 in Maritime Canada, or 800/563-5151 in Newfoundland) and **Air Atlantic** (tel. toll free 800/426-7000 in the U.S. or 800/565-1800 in Maritime Canada, or 709/576-0274 in Newfoundland) both fly into Goose Bay and Wabush. Air Atlantic also has flights to Churchill Falls, and Air Nova flies into Blanc Sablon, Québec, where you can rent a car and drive the short distance into Labrador to L'Anse au Clair and beyond.

By Ferry   Marine Atlantic operates a ferry service from Lewisporte, Newfoundland, to Goose Bay, Labrador, either nonstop or via Cartwright, Labrador, a couple of times a week from mid-June to Labor Day. The nonstop trip to Goose Bay takes about 35 hours, and the fare is $80 adult, $60 seniors, and $40 children 5 to 12 years old; a car costs $130. For more information and reservations, contact the Marine Atlantic Reservations Bureau, P.O. Box 250, North Sydney, NF, B2A 3M3 (tel. toll free 800/341-7981 in the U.S., 709/772-7701 in Newfoundland).

The Strait of Belle Isle ferry crosses from St. Barbe, near the northern tip of Newfoundland, to Blanc Sablon, Québec, 3 miles (5km) from L'Anse au Clair, in the Labrador Straits (tel. 709/931-2309 in Labrador, 418/481-2056 in Québec).

By Train   Rail service is provided between Sept-Isles, Québec, and Labrador City by the Québec, North Shore, and Labrador Railway (tel. 418/968-7805 in Québec, 709/944-8205 in Newfoundland or Labrador).

By Car   There is a paved road, Route 510, from Blanc Sablon, Québec, to Red Bay, in the Labrador Straits. Route 389, a combination paved and gravel road, connects Baie Comeau, Québec, to Labrador City, in Labrador West; the road is open year round.

1. PORT AUX BASQUES TO DEER LAKE

PORT AUX BASQUES

As you cruise into Port aux Basques aboard the ferry, your first impression is of rocks. Under a gray sky, the rocky coast is crowned by treeless hills covered by a thick carpet of brilliant green grass, ferns, and moss. No large plants or tall buildings obscure anything in the town. It's stark, but not barren.

Port aux Basques (pop. 8,000), named in honor of early Basque fishermen-explorers thought to have set foot on these shores even before the intrepid Vikings, makes its living working on the ferry and railroad freight terminus, and in a fish-packing plant. It's a hometown of the old sort, where everyone knows everyone else, and close-knit community spirit prevails.

There are a couple of guesthouses in Port aux Basques should you decide to rest up for the explorations ahead.

All sorts of information, including festivals and crafts directories, are available at the **Port aux Basques Information Centre,** a couple of miles out of town on the Trans Canada Highway. The center is open from mid-May until the end of October (tel. 709/695-2262).

EN ROUTE TO CORNER BROOK

For the first-time visitor to Newfoundland setting out on the road north, the sense of adventure is almost as intense as what the early explorers to this place must have felt.

Dramatic scenery rolls out before you as you drive: volcanic cones, blankets of mist and fog, copses of evergreen trees. The rushing streams have got to be full of salmon—they just look that way. Near the shore, sea chimneys jut upward from the chilly waters.

North of Port aux Basques, you'll see signs for **Stephenville** (take Route 490 to Route 460). It is known for its exciting regional theater, some of the best in Canada, and every summer, usually from mid-July to early August, it gets its due during the three-week **Stephenville Festival,** which has been held every year since 1978 (tel. 709/643-4982).

CORNER BROOK

The first city north along the Trans Canada Highway is Newfoundland's second largest (pop. 30,000), Corner Brook, situated on the fjordlike Humber Arm in the Bay of Islands, named by Capt. James Cook in 1767. The backdrop of the Blow Me Down Mountains adds to the city's charm. A couple of scenic drives set them off to best advantage.

Corner Brook is home to the Bowater Newfoundland Pulp and Paper Mills, one of the largest paper mills in the world and the city's major employer (the mill is a major downtown landmark).

For information about the area, visit the helpful **Tourist Chalet** just off the Trans Canada Highway, on West Valley Road, opposite the Journey's End; it also sells crafts and gift items and is open daily from 8am to 10pm (tel. 709/639-9792).

WHAT TO SEE & DO

To view or invest in outstanding local artwork, visit the **Franklin Gallery,** 98 West St. (tel. 709/639-7100), and the **Ewing Gallery,** in the Glynmill Inn, 1 Cobb Lane (tel. 709/634-4577).

In summer, head out on the waters of the fjordlike Humber Arm aboard the **Humber Princess;** the four-hour cruise costs $25 for adults, $12 for children, and there is a family rate (tel. 709/785-2599). Or you can knock a golf ball around the 18-hole **Blomidon Golf Course.**

In winter, go skiing at **Marble Mountain,** 5 miles (8km) east of Corner Brook, in neighboring Steady Brook. It has 26 ski trails, a 1,600-foot vertical drop, numerous quad lifts, more than 16 feet of snow a year, and one of the longest ski seasons in eastern Canada (tel. 709/639-8531). Add to that reasonable prices. Other seasons, go up to the top of the mountain just to take in the panoramic view.

MARGARET BOWATER PARK, O'Connell Dr.

This pretty city park, not too far from the Tourist Chalet, has two playgrounds, a pool created from a natural stream, a waterfall, and a canteen. Take West Valley Road to O'Connell Drive. It's on both sides of the road, and you can get from one side to the other via an underground pedestrian tunnel.

Admission: Free.

Open: Daily sunup–10pm.

STICKS AND BONES HOUSE, 12 Farnell's Lane. Tel. 709/634-3275.

This attraction definitely ranks as an oddity. That makes it memorable, but it's curiously touching at the same time. Over 25 years, Clyde Farnell totally redecorated his modest house, built in 1955, with small stones and some 53,540 popsicle sticks that he and the neighborhood children collected. In his grand design, he also incorporated such disparate items as jar lids, hubcaps, car lights, mirrors, ashtrays, the foil around cigarette packages, and snail shells. Farnell was blind in one eye from the age of 5 (his brother poked him in the eye with a popsicle stick). He died of lung cancer in 1986.

Admission: $2 adults, $1 seniors and youth 13 and older, 50¢ children 12 and under.

Open: July–Aug daily 11am–7pm; or by appointment. **Directions:** Take Lewin Parkway or Main Street to Humber Road and follow it to Farnell's Lane, just past the gypsum plant; you'll see the signs.

WHERE TO STAY & DINE

GLYNMILL INN, 1 Cobb Lane (P.O. Box 550), Corner Brook, NF, A2H 6E6. Tel. 709/634-5181, or toll free 800/563-4400 in Canada. Fax 709/634-5106. 81 rms, 9 suites. TV TEL

$ Rates: $60–$80 single; $61–$90 double; from $95 suite. Weekend rates and senior discounts available. AE, DC, ER, MC, V.

The distinctive, ivy-covered Tudor-style Glynmill Inn opened in 1924 to house the construction crews that built the local paper mill. Attractive landscaped grounds surround the modern rooms, all of which have cable color TVs; 30 have air conditioning. Those in the original inn, where the hallways are lined with exposed steam pipes from the early days, have ash furniture; in the new wing, rooms have standard heating, air conditioning, and more contemporary furnishings. The more expensive rooms are larger and some offer a view over Glynmill Pond complete with Glynmill swans. Off the lobby, the Ewing Gallery sells outstanding local artwork in a variety of styles. Bowater Park is a 10-minute walk away.

Partridgeberry tarts, a not-to-be-missed local specialty, are offered fresh daily in the Carriage Room Restaurant just off the hotel lobby. The restaurant serves good home cooking three meals a day, from 7am to 9pm (8am to 9pm Sunday). For dinner in a more intimate setting, reserve a table in The Wine Cellar, a cozy, circular room with lamps on the tables. Steaks are the big draw here. One drawback: All the food in The Wine Cellar is fried because of limited kitchen equipment and space.

MAMATEEK INN, Rte. 1 (P.O. Box 787), Corner Brook, NF, A2H 6G7. Tel. 709/639-8901, or toll free 800/563-8600. Fax 709/639-7567. 55 rms. A/C TV TEL

$ Rates: $59–$75 single; $69–$83 double. Extra person $7. Children under 18 stay free in parents' room. AE, DC, ER, MC, V.

★ The large Mamateek Inn, a Best Western property, is on the Trans Canada Highway, opposite the Tourist Chalet. It has quiet rooms in restful hues of blue, rose, and beige, with two double beds or a queen-size bed and good area lighting. Some rooms have a desk and recliner, others a sofa bed and coffee table. The dining room is dramatically situated, overlooking the mountains, the city, and the Blomidon golf course. The view is beautiful at night; the food is good anytime. The hotel also offers room service (7am to 11pm) and same-day dry cleaning, and it allows pets.

HEADING NORTH EN ROUTE TO DEER LAKE

As you head out of Corner Brook, you should pass a local phenomenon called the Man in the Mountain; I'd say more, but I've only seen the etched rockface in postcards. Can't seem to spot it from the road.

Midway between Corner Brook and Deer Lake is **Pasadena Beach Park,** a lovely spot with a sandy beach, picnic tables, and outhouses. It's free for day use until 10pm (no camping).

The Irving Station in Pasadena, right on the highway, has a snack bar and restrooms, sells groceries and fruit, and is open from 7am to 11pm.

DEER LAKE

Northeast of Corner Brook, the Trans Canada Highway skirts the eastern shore of Deer Lake. At the northern end of the lake, 45 minutes away, stands the little town of Deer Lake, at the junction of the Trans Canada and Highway 430, the road to Gros Morne National Park and the Great Northern Peninsula.

Deer Lake (pop. 5,500) is dominated by the Bowaters Power Company's hydro-electric generating plant, which supplies the current needed at the Corner Brook pulp-and-paper mill.

In 1991 a small airport opened here, with flights arriving from Halifax on **Air Nova** (flight time is 1½ hours); rental cars are available at the airport. A local taxi into town costs about $7.

The **Tourist Information Chalet,** on the Trans Canada Highway, is open daily June through August from 9am to 9pm, and May and September from 10am to 5pm (tel. 709/635-2202).

Campers and those who've been on the road for a while will want to know that Deer Lake has its own coin-operated laundry facilities at the far end of Main Street. It also has a craft shop called **Valley Crafts** (tel. 709/635-5633 or 709/635-3861), on the Trans Canada Highway, near the tourist information office and the Deer Lake Motel. Open conveniently long hours in summer (9am to 9pm), it sells sweaters, blankets, quilts, jackets, pottery, Christmas ornaments, dolls, and carved wood items. There is a small, free **Humber Valley Heritage Museum** on the lower level.

Down the road toward Corner Brook, you'll happen upon the **Old Time General Store,** on Route 430, just north of Cormack, the dream child of Derick Tucker. Tucker has been collecting memorabilia since he was 19, and finally his rec room couldn't hold it anymore. Farm tools, clothing, kitchen utensils, kerosene flat irons, a three-legged bedroom stove, sausage press, tobacco cutter, gum boots, and much more—just what you'd expect to find in an old store in a small Newfoundland community. Admission is $2.50 for adults; $1 for children 10 and older; children under 10 free (tel. 709/635-7088). Next door you'll find an ice-cream parlor and tearoom, serving old-timey snacks. Open spring, summer, and autumn.

WHERE TO STAY

DEER LAKE MOTEL, P.O. Box 820, Deer Lake, NF, A0K 2E0. Tel. 709/635-2108, or toll free 800/563-2144 in Newfoundland. Fax 709/635-3842. 56 rms and suites. TV TEL
$ Rates: $59–$71 single; $65–$77 double; from $96 suite. AE, DC, ER, MC, V.
Easily spotted from the Trans Canada Highway, the Deer Lake Motel is an oasis of city-style services in a small town. It has a car-rental agency, room service,

no-smoking rooms, large two-room suites, in-room movies, a small shop, and food take-out service (for those zooming through town). For those with more time, there's the licensed Cormack Dining Room, the Flight Deck Lounge, and the Humber Café, with filling home cooking. The modern motel units all have fans and coffee makers. Rooms in the newer section are equipped with hairdryers.

DRIFTWOOD INN, near the intersection of Main St. and Nicholsville Rd. (P.O. Box 58), Deer Lake, NF, A0K 2E0. Tel. 709/635-5115. Fax 709/635-5901. 24 rms. TV TEL **Directions:** From the Trans Canada Highway, turn at the Esso station (next to the tourist information kiosk) onto Nicholsville Road. You'll see the sign.

$ Rates: $52 single; $58 double. Extra person $6. Senior discounts available. AE, DC, ER, MC, V.

In town, the Driftwood Inn has a pseudo-Tudor green-and-white facade. The rooms are comfortable; those upstairs have seen recent painting and recarpeting and are quieter. The popular country-style dining room is open from 7am to 10pm. The inn also has a licensed lounge and, in the basement, live entertainment on the weekends.

2. GROS MORNE & THE VIKING TRAIL

Newfoundland's great northern peninsula, the Viking Trail and Gros Morne National Park, suggest parallels with Nova Scotia's Highlands, the Cabot Trail, and the Cape Breton Highlands National Park. Both regions are exquisite and entrench themselves in your memory long after your visit has ended. The main difference is that fewer people know about Gros Morne and the Viking Trail. In the throes of the tourist season, maybe that's a blessing.

GROS MORNE NATIONAL PARK

Canada's collection of national parks includes many with breathtaking scenery, and Gros Morne, a UNESCO World Heritage Park, has got to be in the first rank of these. Eons ago, glaciers gouged and ground out the Long Range Mountains, and left fjords and lakes scattered among them. The vistas, the rock and land formations, and the waterways are spectacular.

As you come to Wiltondale on Highway 430, watch for the park sign that points the way. Highway 430, also known as the Viking Trail because it stretches all the way to L'Anse aux Meadows National Historic Site, where the Vikings established the first European settlement in North America, about 1,000 years ago. If the ferry is running, you can also get into the park via Highway 431, which goes south to the small fishing villages of Glenburnie, Woody Point, and Trout River. As you come into Trout River, turn left to cross the little bridge and head to the end of the short road. From here you'll get a seagull's-eye view of the daily fish catch being unloaded. A visit to the Tablelands, which tower over Bonne Bay, near Woody Point, offers you an intriguing glimpse of continental drift. The exhibit at the Tablelands Lookout describes the wonders of this area and the process that created it.

The modern **Gros Morne Visitor's Centre,** on Highway 430 just before Rocky Harbour, can supply any information you might need. Be sure to see the 17-minute film entitled *A Wonderful Fine Coast.* It's well worth seeing, and gives a good introduction to the park's geological history, flora, and fauna. The visitor's center has a compelling exhibit of photographs taken from 1900 to 1985 of people living and working in this region.

During the summer, park naturalists are on hand to suggest activities, lead interpretive walks, give evening lectures with slides, and organize campfires. Check the monthly schedule of activities at the information center, which is open daily from 9am to 10pm late June to early August, and 9am to 4pm daily the rest of the year (tel. 709/458-2066).

The 1½-mile (3km) walk in to **Western Brook Pond,** which is surrounded by some of the oldest rocks in North America, takes about 45 minutes, through forests and along boardwalks over the bog. Bakeapples can be spotted along the trail, and in the bogs watch for the insect-eating pitcher plant, Newfoundland's provincial flower. At the end of the trail is the fjordlike "pond," bordered by towering rock cliffs over 2,000 feet high. It's simply spectacular, a "must see" for anyone in Gros Morne—but only if the weather is good.

A two-hour **boat tour** of Western Brook Pond is a highlight of a visit to Gros Morne. The vessels *Western Brook I* and *Western Brook II* travel the length of the 10-mile (16km) freshwater fjord, past hanging valleys and waterfalls, to its spectacular terminus. Don't forget your wide-angle lens, and bring plenty of film, a sweater, and a snack (no food is sold on board). Several trips a day are planned, weather permitting, from late May to early October; they go if it's raining but not if it's foggy. Hikers may disembark at the end of the lake and be retrieved by a later tour, but be certain to make firm arrangements and double-check them with the skipper. For reservations and information, call the **Ocean View Motel** in Rocky Harbour (tel. 709/458-2730). Fares are $23 for adults, $6 for children 8 to 16. Allow time for the 45-minute walk to the boat.

North of the national park, pretty **River of Ponds Provincial Park** has picnic and swimming areas. If you prefer swimming indoors in a big pool, you'll find one just north of Rocky Harbour (watch for the signs); adults pay about $3, children 17 and younger, about $2.

WOODY POINT

The half-hour drive to Woody Point from the turnoff in Wiltondale is gorgeous, snaking through the park. There used to be a ferry from Woody Point to Norris Point; if it's back in service when you visit, be sure to take it for a thrilling ride. Allow time for tea and wheat buns in the local café opposite the ferry dock or to browse the one-room museum and adjoining craft store, where you'll find a small selection of handcrafted items. There is also a bed-and-breakfast here (see below).

WHERE TO STAY & DINE

VICTORIAN MANOR, Main St. (P.O. Box 165), Woody Point, NF, A0K 1P0. Tel. 709/453-2485 or 709/451-3461. 4 rms (none with bath), 3 efficiency units, 1 guesthouse.
$ Rates: Guest room (including breakfast) $40–$50 single or double; $55 or $70 one- or two-bedroom efficiency unit; $85 guesthouse. MC, V.

Hosts Jenny and Stan Parsons lovingly maintain this house, with its tree-filled yard overlooking the harbor. Built in the 1920s, it belonged to Stan's great-grandfather. Three of the four pretty guest rooms have double beds (one has a twin), and one room has a bay window. They share one full bath. On the property there also are three two-bedroom efficiency units with kitchen, television, and telephone service, and a guesthouse with its own Jacuzzi. The Victorian Manor is no-smoking.

The Parsons own and run the Seaside Restaurant in nearby Trout River, which specializes in seafood and traditional Newfoundland dishes (tel. 709/451-3461).

NORRIS POINT

Norris Point, about 4 miles (7km) from the Gros Morne Visitor's Centre and from Rocky Harbour, is a photogenic fishing village, but in recent years its claim to fame has been as the home of one of the best inns—certainly the most upscale and unique—in Newfoundland, with a cuisine that matches the level of accommodation.

WHERE TO STAY & DINE

SUGAR HILL INN, P.O. Box 100, Norris Point, NF, A0K 3B0. Tel. 709/458-2147. 4 rms (all with bath). TV
$ Rates: $58–$88 single or double, depending on the room. Extra person $10. Packages available. AE, MC, V. **Closed:** One month a year—Nov, Dec, or Apr; call ahead.

On a hill on the left side of the road as you drive into Norris Point, the two-story, green-shingled Sugar Hill Inn is a showplace of pine, cedar, birch, and oak, starting with a living room with a cathedral ceiling, overlooking the hills. Each guest room is different but with a queen-size bed and private bath: Nos. 1 and 2 are large with private entrances, no. 3 has a skylight. Guests may use the hot tub, under a skylight, and adjacent sauna free of charge.

If you book dinner in the licensed dining room, expect to linger two or three hours over a four- to six-course meal, accompanied by fine wine. Breakfast, not included in the room rate, costs $6 to $8; dinner, $25 to $35. The house is on an artesian well, so the water is wonderful.

Husband-and-wife team Vince McCarthy (also the chef) and Marina Sexton, who is a dentist, get all the credit for creating this little bit of paradise. They are happy to provide wine tastings, in-room meals, and laundry service for guests, as well as help them plan their activities in the park.

ROCKY HARBOUR

Rocky Harbour (pop. 1,300), the activity center of Gros Morne, has a motel with a good dining room, cabins, a campground, a couple of convenience stores, an art gallery, some shops, and an indoor swimming pool nearby. From here, it's easy to explore the park.

WHERE TO STAY

GROS MORNE CABINS, P.O. Box 151, Rocky Harbour, NF, A0K 4N0. Tel. 709/458-2020. 22 cabins. TV

$ Rates: $55 one-bedroom cabin; $75 two-bedroom cabin; $99 honeymoon cabin with Jacuzzi, champagne, and flowers. One child stays free. Extra person $5. Special rates available off-season. AE, MC, V.

Gros Morne Cabins, next door to Endicott's store, provide comfortable lodging in the park, with carpeted bedrooms, cable color TVs, full kitchens and baths, lots of room, and ocean views. Made of Newfoundland spruce, the cabins, which are close together, are surrounded by a lawn with picnic tables, swings, sandboxes, a seesaw, and a barbecue. There are two cabins for the disabled and a laundry on the premises. Coyley Endicott started out with three cabins in 1979 and has done an admirable expansion job. Pay at Endicott's Store, which is open daily from 9am to 11pm (call if you'll arrive later and they'll leave the key for you). Pets are welcome.

OCEAN VIEW MOTEL, P.O. Box 129, Rocky Harbour, NF, A0K 4N0. Tel. 709/458-2730. Fax 709/458-2841. 37 rms. TV

$ Rates: $54 single; $59 double ($5 extra for rooms in front). Extra person $5. AE, ER, MC, V.

The two-story, blue-and-white Ocean View Motel is another possibility if you want to spend the night in the park. The rooms are modern but dimly lit, and noise from neighboring rooms is sometimes inescapable. On the other hand, the motel has a good dining room, is an information center for activities in the area, and accepts your pet. The constantly busy Ocean Room dining room serves three meals a day, from 7am to 9:30pm. The food's good, and the service is friendly but can be slow. Reception sells handmade sweaters and cassettes of local music, and dances with live bands are held some evenings in winter in the bar downstairs.

Camping

North of the national park, **River of Ponds Provincial Park** has wooded campsites (with outhouses, no showers) from June through early September. In Rocky Harbour itself, at **Juniper Campground** (tel. 709/458-2917), there are 54 campsites with hot showers and flush toilets. Rates are $11 a day (semihookup) or $9 (no hookup). It's open from late May to mid-September.

PICNIC SUPPLIES & TAKEOUT

Across the road from Endicott's store, **Pizza Plus** (tel. 709/458-2577) has small, medium, and large pizzas for $7.25, $9.75, and $11.55, respectively, take-out only.

They're good and filling, and you get your choice of toppings. You can also get homemade baked goods, including bread, pies, and muffins, and pick up anything you might need from **Earle's Video & Convenience Store,** on the premises. This place is popular with local teenagers, who come in regularly for videos and pizzas to go.

HEADING NORTH ALONG THE VIKING TRAIL

The scenery doesn't get any more dramatic than it does in Gros Morne, but if you're one who likes to go where few have gone or you have a strong interest in Vikings, head north up the western shore of the Great Northern Peninsula. It's 284 miles (443km) from Deer Lake to the tip of the peninsula at St. Anthony (pop. 4,000). Tourist services and motels along the way can provide for your needs.

Just south of St. Paul there's a short circular drive that looks onto a rocky beach; it's unmarked but worth the stop for the view, so keep an eye out for it. The drive along here passes desolate areas and a striking interplay of rivers, coast, forest, and scrub. Long, straight stretches make for easy driving except for some potholes along the way.

At **Port aux Choix** is a small national historic site on the site of excavations into Newfoundland's aboriginal past. Artifacts dating from the time of the Maritime Archaic people, over 4,000 years ago, have been found aplenty at Port aux Choix, along with much later remains from the Dorset and Groswater Paleo Eskimo cultures. The most southerly evidence of Eskimos in North America has been discovered here. The **information center** is open daily from 8:30am to 6pm mid-June to Labor Day, and admission is free (tel. 709/861-3522).

At the very tip of the Great Northern Peninsula is **L'Anse aux Meadows National Historic Site** (tel. 709/623-2608), harboring one of the most thrilling archeological discoveries in modern times. Guided by the verses of the 12th-century *Greenlanders' Saga,* Norwegian explorer Helge Ingstad and an international team of archeologists in 1960 discovered unmistakable evidence of a Viking settlement at L'Anse aux Meadows, dating from A.D. 1000. The only known Viking settlement in North America, it is believed to be that of Leif Eriksson. The park, with its re-created sod houses and interpretive center, was designated a World Heritage Site by UNESCO in 1978. It is open daily from mid-June to Labor Day, from 9am to 8pm (off-season, by appointment; call 709/623-2608); free admission.

St. Anthony, the largest town on the Northern Peninsula, and the final stop along the Viking Trail, lies another 29 miles (48km) north, at the very tip of Newfoundland. Here you'll find **Grenfell House Museum** (tel. 709/454-3333), built in the 1900s and the former home of Sir Wilfred Thomason Grenfell, who founded the Grenfell Mission to northern Newfoundland and Labrador to raise money for hospitals, nursing stations, and children's homes. The house is open to the public daily from late May to early September, from 10am to 8pm (to 6pm until late June); admission is $2 for adults, $1 for seniors and students; children under 5 enter free. You may buy the hand-embroidered parkas and other unique items for which the area is known at Grenfell Handicrafts store, a short walk away.

From St. Anthony you can get the ferry to Red Bay in the Labrador Straits or to Lewisporte, which is near Gander. Or you can make your way back along the Viking Trail to Deer Lake to link up once again with the Trans Canada Highway.

WHERE TO STAY & DINE NEAR ST. ANTHONY

TICKLE INN, R.R. 1 (Box 62), Cape Onion, NF, A0K 4J0. Tel. 709/452-4321 (June–Sept) or 709/739-5503 (Oct–May). 4 rms (none with bath).
$ Rates (including continental breakfast): $40 single; $45–$50 double. Extra person $10. MC, V. **Closed:** Oct–May.

The Tickle Inn, a beachfront property set on nine acres, sits at the top of the world that is Newfoundland. From here you can hike, go cod-jigging or whale-watching, or just relax and visit with hosts Barbara and David Adams. Three of the rooms have a double bed; one has two twins. They share two full baths. If you want to have lunch or dinner here, book it ahead of time. The inn is half an hour's drive from St. Anthony and L'Anse aux Meadows. (Isn't it fun to stay in a place with "AOK" as part of its postal code?)

3. GRAND FALLS–WINDSOR & GANDER

The Trans Canada Highway weaves its way westward through the glacial lakes and rivers that fill the Newfoundland interior. Watch for moose along the way; they tend to come out to the side of the road early and late in the day.

GRAND FALLS–WINDSOR

The amalgamated town of Grand Falls–Windsor (pop. 16,000), on the banks of the Exploits River, was founded in 1904 by Lord Northcliffe and the Anglo-Newfoundland Development Company to produce paper for his British newspaper empire.

The **tourist information** chalet, on the Trans Canada Highway, is open daily from 9am to 9pm June through August, from 9am to 5pm in September (tel. 709/489-6332).

WHAT TO SEE & DO

MARY MARCH REGIONAL MUSEUM, on Cromer Ave. and St. Catherine St. Tel. 709/489-7331.

This octagonal museum, practically at the intersection with the Trans Canada Highway, is dedicated to the memory of Mary March and the Beothuk people (pronounced "Bee-*aw*-thuk"), who inhabited this region and much of Newfoundland's interior when the first European settlers of the 1600s came ashore. In winter they retired inland, built teepee-shaped shelters called "mamateeks," and hunted caribou. In spring they would migrate to the coast to live on seals and salmon. Early contacts were friendly, but not for long. Continued settlement of the island by outsiders kept the Beothuk from living according to their centuries-old annual rhythm. By 1829 they had become extinct, the victims of hostilities with the newcomers, disease (especially tuberculosis), and starvation—symbols, as the museum suggests, of "the cost of cultural replacement."

Mary March, a Beothuk whose real name was Demasduit, was captured by white furriers on Red Indian Lake in 1819, and she died of tuberculosis almost a year later, before being reunited with her people. (Her obituary ran in the London *Times*). Much of the understanding of Beothuk culture and traditions comes from Mary March's niece, Shanawdithit, who surrendered to white furriers in 1823 when she was close to starvation. Shanawdithit, who died in 1829, was the last known surviving Beothuk. The museum has a number of films and audiovisual presentations; request *Lost Race,* a 12-minute film about the Beothuks.

Admission: Free.

Open: Mon–Fri 9am–noon and 1–5pm, Sat–Sun 2–5pm. **Closed:** Holidays.

BEOTHUK VILLAGE, behind the Mary March Museum. Tel. 709/489-3559.

Behind, but not an official part of, the Mary March Museum, the Beothuk Village has reconstructed several tents used by the extinct "Red Indians." The guides here are quite knowledgeable about the Beothuks and their lifestyle, making a visit quite worthwhile. The village is small and easy to circumnavigate.

Admission: Free.

Open: July–early Sept.

LOGGING VILLAGE AT BEOTHUK PARK.

The interpretive exhibits trace the history of logging in this part of Newfoundland. The province's first sawmill was built in 1610, and lumber has been produced for human consumption here ever since (for export since the 19th century). You'll visit a reconstructed logging camp from the early 19th century, including the cookhouse, grub shed (like a pantry), bunkhouse, and foreman's quarters; among the clothing on display are handy "piss quick" boots. In those days, 50 to 90 men lived at the camps and did their work with the help of 25 to 30 workhorses. You'll learn a lot about how nonmechanized logging was carried out from 1915 to 1925. There are plans to create exhibits devoted to mechanized logging from the mid-1920s to the present.

Admission: Free.

Open: June–Labor Day.

SALMONID INTERPRETATION CENTRE, Exploits River. Tel. 709/489-7350.

Located on the bank of the Exploits River a mile from town, this center gives you a fish-eye view of the king of fish as it migrates upstream to spawn. Outside there is an observation deck overlooking the Grand Falls, for which the town is named.

Admission: Free.

Open: Daily 9:30am–8:30pm. **Closed:** Oct–early June.

WHERE TO STAY & DINE

CARRIAGE HOUSE, 181 Grenfell Heights, Grand Falls–Windsor, NF, A2A 2J2. Tel. 709/489-7185. 4 rms (none with bath). **Directions:** Take the Grenfell Heights exit and turn right onto Grenfell; the house will be on the left.

$ Rates (including full breakfast): $49 single; $59 double. DC, ER, V.

Not far from downtown Grand Falls–Windsor, the trim, gray Carriage House with the red barn and stable out back is run by friendly horse woman Paula Flood and her family—and Woody, their Newfoundland dog, of course. Flood also runs a riding school, so if you have an interest in or love for horses, you'll be doubly happy here. You might even do some horseback riding. The bedrooms, a couple of which have brass beds, share two baths, one with a Jacuzzi, another with a shower. A sitting room and library are on the second floor.

MOUNT PEYTON HOTEL AND MOTEL, 214 Lincoln Rd., Grand Falls, NF, A2A 1P8. Tel. 709/489-2251, or toll free 800/563-4894 in the Atlantic Provinces. Fax 709/489-6365. 134 hotel rms, 32 motel rms, 16 efficiency units. TV TEL

$ Rates: Hotel and housekeeping units $75 single; $81 double; motel units $64 single, $70 double. Extra person $6. Children under 12 free. AE, DC, ER, MC, V. **Closed:** Motel, Oct–Apr.

The lobby and lounge of the Mount Peyton Hotel give it the feel of a western lodge. This is a welcoming, comfortable place, with an outstanding staff and a variety of rooms from which to choose—hotel, motel, or efficiency units—all carefully maintained. In the hotel, which has no-smoking rooms, ask for a room in the new section, added in 1977 but still called the "new section." The motel units are pleasant, with paneled ceilings and big baths. Free in-room movies are available in the hotel, but not the motel. If you stay in the latter, you still have to register at the hotel, on the opposite side of the road. Three meals a day are served in Clem's, the quiet dining room, and dinner only in the pretty Peyton Corral steakhouse (6 to 11pm Monday through Saturday). The Millroom lounge, with its big-screen TV, often has entertainment on weekends.

GANDER

From Grand Falls and Windsor it's 60 miles (94km) to Gander (pop. 14,000), Newfoundland's most famous town after St. John's. In the 1930s Gander was chosen as the western station for the first regular transatlantic flights. It was almost the closest point to the British Isles, and it was noted for being fog free. Little did these early planners know how important it would become during World War II, when literally thousands of aircraft flew to Gander from all parts of Canada and the United States, and from Gander made the leap to Europe. The air link was crucial to the Allied victory.

Gander's primacy survived the war, but not the commercial jet's invention. When long-range cargo and passenger jets took over command of the airways, Gander lost some of its importance, since these big planes could fly directly from New York, Montréal, or even Chicago to European cities. But Gander, still as fog free as ever, continues to be an important touchdown point, particularly for around-the-world flights.

Today at least two vintage airplanes are displayed in Gander in summer and fall, visible reminders of the town's air link to the world: a Beech 18, a Voodoo CF101, and sometimes a Consolidated Canso. Eventually, the planes will be housed in a museum, to be built near the airport.

The **Gander Tourist Information Chalet** (tel. 709/256-7110), on the Trans Canada Highway between the Hotel Gander and the Albatross Hotel, can provide information about the region, as well as some on other Canadian provinces.

WHAT TO SEE & DO

The town is trying to raise money to build an aviation museum. In the meantime, the **airport**—which is colorful and reminiscent of a cruise-ship terminal—acts as a pseudomuseum. It has exhibits in the domestic area, along with a tremendous mural and more exhibits in the international waiting area. If you aren't taking an international flight but still want to see the mural, follow the stairs and the signs at the back of the domestic waiting area. There's also a children's play area. It's only about half a mile from the center of town.

The best craft shop west of St. John's, the **Gander Craft Studio,** is in the same building as the tourist office, so avail yourself of the opportunity (tel. 709/256-2944).

Adjacent to the same building, you can pick up half-mile-long **Gill's Trail,** leading through the woods to Gander Lake. It takes half an hour to walk down, 45 minutes to come back up.

A one-mile boardwalk surrounds **Cobb's Pond,** where there is also a children's playground. Follow Gander Bay Road to get there.

SILENT WITNESS MEMORIAL, 4 miles (6km) east of Gander on the Trans Canada Hwy.

In Peace Keeper Park, the Silent Witness Memorial stands watch over Gander Lake at the tragic scene of the December 12, 1985, crash of the U.S. military chartered jet that killed all 258 of the 101st Airborne Division "Screaming Eagles" on board. Grass now covers the swath the plane cleared through the woods. A statue of a young American soldier with two children, a boy and a girl each holding an olive branch, depicts the peacekeeping work of the "Screaming Eagles" on the Sinai Peninsula. It was designed by Lorne Rostotski of St. John's and sculpted by Stephen Shields, from Kentucky. A list of the victims of the crash is beside the statue.

Admission: Free.

Open: Daily sunup–sundown. **Directions:** Drive 3.3 miles (5.5km) east on the Trans Canada Highway, then half a mile (1km) down the hill; it's well marked.

WHERE TO STAY

Gander has a number of hotels and motels, most of them lined up along the Trans Canada Highway.

ALBATROSS MOTEL, Trans Canada Hwy. (P.O. Box 450), Gander, NF, A1V 1W8. Tel. 709/256-3956, or toll free 800/563-4900 in the Atlantic Provinces. Fax 709/651-2692. 102 rms, 4 suites. TV TEL

$ Rates: $70 single; $79 double; from $100 suite. Extra person $6. Children free. Ask about special rates. AE, DC, ER, MC, V.

The Albatross Motel is easy to spot, with its modern, chalet-style facade. On the inside, it's comfortable, with mauve- and sand-colored rooms, in-room movies, dry cleaning and laundry (except Sunday), a dining room (7am to 10pm), room service (7am to midnight), and a quiet lounge open from 4pm to midnight. Half the rooms have air conditioning, and of the nine floors, two are no-smoking.

HOLIDAY INN, 1 Caldwell St., Gander, NF, A1V 1T6. Tel. 709/256-3981, or toll free 800/465-4329. Fax 709/651-3297. 63 rms, 1 suite. TV TEL

$ Rates: $80 single; $90 double. Extra person free. Children under 12 eat free. Senior and AAA discounts. AE, DC, DISC, ER, MC, V.

Just off the Trans Canada Highway, the Holiday Inn provides all the comforts of the road: modern rooms with coffee makers, hairdryers, and balconies; no-smoking rooms; a licensed dining room open from 7am to 10pm; a small, pleasant lounge; an outdoor swimming pool; a coin-operated laundry; and indoor and outdoor parking. Rooms, some of which have minibars, are decorated in dark browns, coral, and sand; baths have separate sinks. The quietest rooms face the Trans Canada Highway. There is room service and dry cleaning. Pets are allowed. There is no elevator in the hotel. The hotel plans to do some refurbishing as soon as a legal snag with the Newfoundland government is resolved.

HOTEL GANDER, Gander, NF, A1V 1P5. Tel. 709/256-3931. Fax 709/651-2641. 148 rms, 5 suites. TV TEL

$ Rates: $55–$82 single or double; from $95 suite. AE, DC, ER, MC, V.

The Hotel Gander is the first hotel you come to on your entry to Gander, and it gets lots of repeat travelers—pilots, businesspeople, flight crews—who enjoy its small indoor pool and exercise area. The modern rooms are decorated in soft colors and have one or two double beds, good reading lights, in-room movies, and a desk and table; some have air conditioning. The helpful staff can arrange babysitting. Dry cleaning is available. The dining room is open from 7am to 10pm, and room service is available during these hours; the lounge, which has live bands, is open from 4pm to 2am. Guests may use the fitness equipment or take aerobics classes at the Gander Body Works (in the nearby Fox Moth Hotel) for $3.

PICNIC SUPPLIES

As you pass through, stop at the **Bread Shoppe,** 136 Bennett Dr., opposite Sinbad's Motel. The assortment of freshly baked breads, rolls, pastries, and buns is truly astounding. It's all made fresh, right here. It's open Monday, Tuesday, and Saturday from 8am to 6pm, and Wednesday through Friday from 8am to 9pm (tel. 709/651-2738).

ICEBERG TERRITORY

Memorable side-trip possibilities abound at each intersection of Highway 1. In search of the elusive free-floating iceberg, you may wander up to **Farewell,** no more than a two-hour drive following Route 330 out of Gander, then onto Routes 331 and 335, and settle in for a berg-watch at **Change Islands,** a tiny dot on the ocean of my map. Getting there is an adventure, beginning with the chance to mingle with locals and tourists lining up for the ferry that leaves from Farewell four times daily (less during off-season). You can't beat the price: The 20-minute voyage costs $2 for a automobile and driver, 50¢ for adults, 25¢ for seniors and children. For up-to-date ferry times, call 709/627-3448 or 709/627-3256. The Change Islands are home to several hardy families who fish for a living, but for the visitor they represent a serene reprieve from the road.

Another great lookout point for icebergs is from the headland lighthouse at **Crow Head.** From Route 331, take Route 340 past innumerable photo opportunities toward Twillingate and keep heading in a northerly direction. To avoid disappointment and increase your chances of a sighting, stop at the information center at the junction of the Trans Canada Highway and Route 330. They should be able to tell you where bergs have been reported most recently.

TERRA NOVA NATIONAL PARK

Some 46 miles (74km) past Gander, heading east, lies beautiful Terra Nova National Park (tel. 709/533-2801). The highway runs right through the middle of the vast reserve, bringing drivers conveniently close to the beaches, boat ramp, camping areas, trailheads—and moose, so keep an eye out, especially early and late in the day. The park's natural beauty exemplifies Newfoundland's east coast scenery, with jutting headlands and deeply indented bays and coves.

The park's developed campground at Newman Sound has 387 sites, showers, laundry facilities, and a store. A full schedule of interpretive talks and shows will acquaint you with Newfoundland's natural beauties. Although Terra Nova is the national park nearest to St. John's, campgrounds are sufficiently large to handle the volume of summer traffic. You may find one or two of the campgrounds full if you arrive late in the afternoon, but unless you come in very late indeed, you should be able to secure a spot for yourself.

4. THE BONAVISTA PENINSULA

Heading south from Terra Nova National Park on the Trans Canada Highway you'll soon come to Route 230, which leads to the Bonavista Peninsula; the colorful Discovery Trail, which threads through its harbors and fishing villages; and historic Trinity, the prettiest town in Newfoundland.

TRINITY

On Trinity Bay, Trinity is a village of firsts: It was here in 1615 that the first English court of justice was held outside of England, convened to settle squabbles among fishermen. The first Church of England school was built here in 1722, and in 1796, the smallpox vaccine was introduced in North America for the first time. Trinity boomed as a center for trade and commerce until the early 1900s and the advent of the railroad.

Trinity Roman Catholic Church, the oldest standing church in Newfoundland, was built here in 1833. And picturesque St. Paul's Church, built in 1892 and perhaps the finest wooden church in Newfoundland, wasn't far behind.

Be sure to visit the **Hiscock House,** unique because it honors an "ordinary" hardworking woman, Emma Hiscock, who kept her family of six children afloat after her 39-year-old husband drowned, in 1893 (a not-uncommon occurrence in those days). The house, restored to 1910, is filled with items used by the Hiscock family. Note the interesting way the pictures are hung. A guide will show you around daily from 10am to 5:30pm from June to Labor Day (tel. 709/729-2460). It's free.

You may also visit the **Green Family Forge,** which operated here for 200 years; the Interpretation Centre, to learn about Trinity's fascinating history; and the reconstructed **Ryan's General Store,** which served this community from the early 1900s to 1952. All are free. Just park your car and walk everywhere. It's an added pleasure of a trip to Trinity.

In nearby Trinity East, visit **Trinity Loop Fun Park and Railway Village,** a well-done amusement park for families, with a popular 1.6-mile miniature train ride, a little museum in a railcar, paddleboats, kayaks, canoes, bumper boats, miniature golf, horse and pony rides, and a Ferris wheel. The **Conductor's Choice Diner,** also in a railway car, serves a variety of fare, including great ice cream. The park is open daily from 10am to 7pm; the museum, which is free, opens at noon; the diner is open daily from 10am to midnight (tel. 709/464-2171). Admission to the park is $2.50 adults, $2 for seniors over 65 and children under 12. There's entertainment on Sunday and sometimes on Saturday.

WHERE TO STAY

CAMPBELL HOUSE, Trinity (mailing address: 24 Circular Rd., St. John's, NF, A1C 2Z1). Tel. 709/464-3377 (off-season, 709/753-8945, in St. John's). 4 rms (1 with bath). TEL

$ Rates (including full breakfast): $50–$65 single or double. Extra person $10. MC, V. **Closed:** Mid-Oct to late May.

Campbell House, built in 1840, has been lovingly restored (1991–92) and filled with period pieces by Dutch-born Tineke Gow, your host. The beds are covered with duvets and cotton blankets, and a radio and bathrobe are provided in the rooms, all of which overlook the sea and have lockable doors. One room has a queen-size bed; another, a particularly beautiful room, a double bed and a day bed; the two rooms with single beds also have sinks in them. There's a refrigerator for guests' use, and mountain bikes are available for rent. A flagstone patio, picnic table, and nearby heritage garden with plants from 1840 overlook the harbor. Mrs. Gow, who greets wayfarers with muffins and coffee or tea, and invites them to come and "park" for a while, plans to open up a housekeeping unit down the hill. No smoking, pets, or children younger than 7.

PEACE COVE INN, Trinity East, NF, A0C 2H0. Tel. 709/454-3738 or 709/464-3419 (off-season 709/781-2255, in St. John's). 5 rms (1 with bath, 2 with half bath). **Directions:** Take Route 230 to Port Rexton and turn right (at the Ultramar station) for Trinity East, 2 miles (3km) away.

$ Rates (including continental breakfast): $42 single or double with shared bath; $44 single or double with half bath; $48 single or double with full bath. Extra person $12. V. **Closed:** Mid-Oct to late May.

Don't look for this turn-of-the-century house in Trinity, because it's 10 miles (16km) away, in Trinity East (it's easy to confuse the two). The spirits of former owners, Aunt Lizzie and Skipper Dick, seem to linger in the house, which has the cozy feel of a farmhouse, complete with a big kitchen, good country cooking, a sitting room with a freestanding fireplace, and functional bedrooms. Guests share two baths, though two of the five rooms have toilet and sink, and one has a full bath and private entrance. The real lure here is hosts Louise and Art Andrews and the family-style meals. A full breakfast costs $3.50 (continental breakfast is included in the price of the room), lunch $7.50, and dinner $15 for three courses. No smoking, please. If you want to explore Trinity Harbour or other fishing villages in the vicinity, book a tour or charter (from $25 per person) with Art, who'll take you out on his 46-foot motorsailer.

AROUND THE PENINSULA

En route to Bonavista and the tip of the peninsula, swing by **Mabley,** 5 miles (8km) from Route 230, for dramatic cliff and sea views. The area around Summerville is pretty and fjordlike.

In Bonavista, see **Mockbeggar estate,** the former home of F. Gordon Bradley, one of Newfoundland's first representatives in the Canadian Senate (tel. 709/468-7300), and the photogenic, candy-cane-colored **Cape Bonavista Lighthouse** (tel. 709/468-7444). You can tour both attractions for free. A statue of John Cabot stands near the lighthouse nearby.

ONWARD TO AVALON

Past the Bonavista Peninsula, the Trans Canada Highway heads due south to the isthmus that joins the main part of Newfoundland to the Avalon Peninsula, a fragment of the African plate left behind as a result of continental drift 200 billion years ago. Framed by Trinity Bay to the north and Placentia Bay to the south, the isthmus has unusual weather conditions. While Gander, not all that far away, remains virtually fogless year-round, the isthmus always seems to be fogged in. Highway signs will warn you of this, but you hardly need them: The dense misty clouds rushing dramatically over the roadway speak for themselves. When the fog interferes with visibility, use low beams and keep your eye on the white or yellow line along the highway.

Once off the isthmus and into Avalon, watch for the junction of the Trans Canada and Highway 100. South along 100 is Argentia, terminus for Marine Atlantic's car-ferry. (See "Getting to Newfoundland," earlier in this chapter, for details about ferries to North Sydney, N.S.) Just south of Argentia is Placentia, today a small town, but the capital city of French Newfoundland in the 1600s. In August 1941, Winston Churchill and Franklin D. Roosevelt hammered out the agreement called the Atlantic Charter while moored on a warship in Placentia Bay. The shape of the world was changed here, as the charter dealt with what was to happen when the Allied armies were victorious. In 1941 that was an optimistic thing to be doing, as the Allied armies at that time were in quite a fix, but history ultimately vindicated these long-range planners.

Deep into the Avalon Peninsula on the Trans Canada Highway, Highway 90 leaves the main road to go south along the Salmonier River. Seven miles (12km) from the main road along Highway 90 is one of Newfoundland's most fascinating attractions, a "must see" for any visitor interested in the province's natural beauties. Whoever conceived of **Salmonier Nature Park,** P.O. Box 190, Holyrood, NF, A0A 2R0 (tel. 709/729-6974), should be heartily applauded, for this zoo-with-a-difference gives visitors the best possible introduction to the many species of wildlife that live in the province. Open between noon and 8pm Thursday through Monday (closed Tuesday and Wednesday) from early June to Labor Day, Salmonier Nature Park has moose, snowy owls, beavers, red foxes, caribou, bald eagle, the rare peregrine falcon, spruce grouse, ducks and geese, otter and hare, all living in natural mini-environments rather than cages. Roomy enclosures keep the animals and some of the birds from roaming outside the park without cramping them as cages would do. Visitors circulate among the enclosures on a self-explanatory one-mile (2km) boardwalk and wood-chip nature trail through the forest and bog. The trail walk can take anywhere between one and two hours to complete, depending on how long you want to linger, watching the moose doze, or the red fox dart about its habitat, or the beavers slap the pond's surface with their broad tails.

As the Trans Canada Highway turns northeast toward St. John's (see Section 6), 22 miles (36km) away, a sign will come into view marking the entrance to **Butter Pot Provincial Park,** one of the province's nicest—and certainly its most crowded. Hiking trails transport you through forests of black spruce, balsam fir, and white birch, fields of wildflowers, and barrens to striking lookouts. The park also has more than 140 campsites, playgrounds, two swimming areas, trout ponds, and even a wooded 18-hole mini-golf course set with a Newfoundland theme. A "butter pot" is a Newfoundland term for a rounded hill.

Along the highway you may notice cars parked here and there. Many of the occupants are circulating through the fields and hills beside the road, gathering bakeapples (*Rubus chamaemorus,* also called cloudberries). The plants flower in June, and by late July the amber-colored fruit is ready to pick. Bakeapples are related to raspberries, and they look it, but the taste—with a spoonful of sugar—is distinctly and surprisingly like baked apples. If you see one of the enthusiastic berrypickers holding up a few jars of the red-orange fruit as you speed by, that's an invitation to buy. Take them up on it if you're at all curious, as bakeapple berries are more of a home delicacy, rarely appearing on restaurant menus.

5. ST-PIERRE & MIQUELON

Ready for a side trip to France? No, this travel writer doesn't need a geography lesson. Instead of heading south to the Avalon Peninsula from the Bonavista Peninsula, take Route 210 off the Trans Canada Highway, south of Clarenville. This route takes you through the Burin Peninsula. From Clarenville, it's 145 miles (245km) to Grand Bank, near the tip of the peninsula. Once you've driven that distance, you'll be surprisingly close to . . . France.

On a map, the boot-shaped Burin Peninsula seems about to punt three small islands, named Grande Miquelon, Petite Miquelon, and St-Pierre. Believe it or not, these tiny bits of turf belong to—and are looked upon as an integral part of—the French Republic. Gendarmes, French wines and perfumes, and baguettes are all here, in the chilly waters off Fortune Bar.

Jacques Cartier, on one of his cruises of exploration in the 1500s, touched ashore at St-Pierre and Miquelon and claimed them for the king of France. The king is long gone, but the islands remain French.

The town and island of St-Pierre, named for the patron saint of fishermen, boasts 6,000 citizens and over 20 miles (32km) of roads, a museum, and shops in which to buy French goods. Besides tourism, St-Pierre is engaged in supplying fishing and cargo boats that touch port here; some of the people have small farms. The island saw its share of rum-running earlier in the century; Al Capone and Bill McCoy were only a couple of the "entrepreneurs" who came here.

There is no car-ferry service from Newfoundland to St-Pierre and Miquelon, but on the islands you can rent mopeds and bikes, use taxi services, or hop aboard an excursion bus.

The **Newfoundland Department of Tourism and Culture** can provide information about transportation to and on the islands, as well as lodging information. If you need further help, contact the Tourist Office on St-Pierre (tel. St-Pierre 011-508/41-22-224; fax 011-508/41-33-55) at 14 place du Général-de-Gaulle (B.P. 4274), 97500 St-Pierre et Miquelon, France. If there's a French Government Tourist Office near you, they may be able to help as well.

TRANSPORTATION   The daily ferry, the MV *Eugene 5,* departs from the town of Fortune, a few miles southwest of Grand Bank, on the 12-mile (19km), 55-minute voyage to St-Pierre.

Between late June and late September, contact **Lloyd G. Lake Ltd.,** P.O. Box 70, Fortune, NF, A0E 1PO (tel. 709/832-1955, 709/832-2791 after hours; fax 709/832-2529). Ferries leave Fortune each afternoon at 2:15pm and cost $29 one-way and $48 round-trip for adults, about half that for children 2 to 16. Round-trip excursion fares of $43 for adults and $20 for children are available on certain dates. Service from St-Pierre to Miquelon is also available.

Pick up your reservation at least an hour before the boat's departure, and reconfirm your returning reservation as soon as you arrive on St-Pierre. *Important:* Remember that you're going to France, and *you must have some documentation to prove your identity.* Passport, birth certificate, or voter's registration is preferred, but a driver's license or other such ID will probably serve as well.

You can also fly to St-Pierre. **Provincial Airlines Limited** operates year-round air service from St. John's on Monday through Friday; for more information about it, call 709/576-1666 or toll free 800/563-2800. **Air St-Pierre** provides service between St-Pierre and Sydney and Halifax, Nova Scotia, and Montréal, Québec (tel. 902/562-3140 in Sydney, N.S., or 902/873-3566 in Enfield, N.S.). You can also book these flights through **Canadian Airlines Reservations** (tel. toll free 800/426-7000 in the U.S., 800/665-1177 in Canada).

PACKAGE TOURS   For many visitors to St-Pierre and Miquelon, it's easier to book a vacation package. Several are offered through **S.P.M. Tours Ltd.,** 38 Gear St., St. John's, NF, A1C 2J5 (tel. 709/722-3892 year-round). The company has day packages that trundle you down to the ferry by bus or self-drive rental car. They also include ferry passage from Fortune; accommodations for one or more nights in a hotel, motel, or bed-and-breakfast; welcome drink; information session; and return passage all for about $90 to $160 per person, based on double occupancy.

If you have a car, you can save $60 by driving yourself to Fortune and joining S.P.M. there. The company operates its own ferry, the MV *Arethusa,* from mid-June to late September, and the trip takes one hour and 45 minutes. Fares are about $30 one-way and $50 round-trip for adults; children under 16 travel free with parents. Reservations may be made only through the **Newfoundland/St-Pierre Ferry Service** at 709/738-1357 in St. John's or 709/832-0429 in Fortune.

Make an advance reservation 30 days ahead, if possible, for the *Arethusa;* reservations will be canceled if you are not at the ferry dock an hour before sailing.

6. ST. JOHN'S

118 miles (189km) SE of Clarenville, 207 miles (331km) SE of Gander

GETTING THERE   Continue traveling south along the Trans Canada Highway through the Avalon Peninsula. The highway dead-ends in St. John's. But it's actually the other way around. St. John's marks the beginning of the Trans Canada Highway, the longest national artery in the world. Mile 0 is at City Hall in St. John's, and the highway ends in Victoria, B.C., 4,976 miles (7,775km) away.

ESSENTIALS Information   For tourist information, contact the St. John's Economic Development and Tourism Division, in City Hall on Gower Street (P.O.

Box 908), St. John's, NF, A1C 5M2 (tel. 709/576-8106; fax 709/576-8246), open from 9am until 4:30pm weekdays.

Getting Around   Except for the downtown section of St. John's, it's good to have a car for sightseeing. If you are carless, contact Bugden's Taxi, 266 Blackmarsh Rd., St. John's, NF, A1E 1T2 (tel. 709/726-4400; fax 709/722-3600), and they'll be glad to arrange a cab tour for you for up to five people. Along Marine Drive to Torbay and back costs $40; to Cape Spear and Petty Harbour, $75.

No place in Newfoundland has a more fascinating and romantic history than St. John's (pop. 157,440). Its location as the North American point closest to Europe was the prime factor in shaping its history; second came its beautiful, safe, rockbound natural harbor. No wonder the earliest Renaissance explorers from Europe chose to put in here.

First of these swashbuckling commodores was John Cabot, who is said to have sailed into the harbor on St. John's Day in 1497. Documents show for certain that Capt. John Rut, aboard the *Mary of Guildford,* came to the harbor 30 years later. He wrote home to his sovereign, Henry VIII, to recommend that a permanent settlement be established here, no doubt for the benefit of the cod fishermen as much as for military purposes. A year later, in 1528, this was done, and today the citizens of St. John's take this date for the city's founding.

From its founding, St. John's went on to a series of attacks, defenses, pirate raids, celebrations, great fires, and great feasts unmatched in North America. Today, quaint town houses with brightly colored facades line the streets in the old downtown section of St. John's while modern suburbs sprawl on the outskirts. You can't miss the city's connection with the sea: Flags from any nation may be flying from the ships in port, menus are filled with seafood, and reminders of a nautical past are everywhere, including local songs.

The city is filled with beautiful homes. The stateliest ones line Circular Road and King's Bridge Road, while downtown, along eastern Gower Street, for instance, you'll find colorful old row houses, their clapboards sporting pastel hues and some bold colors.

WHAT TO SEE & DO

St. John's grew up around its harbor, so the first thing to do is take a walk along **Harbour Drive** for a look at the ships. They fly flags from all over the world, and sailors of half a dozen different nationalities abound.

Water Street, a block north of Harbour Drive, is said to be "the oldest main street on the continent" because it served as a pathway for the earliest explorers here, and later for the settlers. On Water Street, between Holloway and Cochrane, stands the **War Memorial,** for Newfoundlanders who fell in World War I. The War Memorial stands on the spot where, in 1583, Sir Humphrey Gilbert proclaimed that Newfoundland was a territory under the British Crown.

A few blocks east of the basilica on Military Road, **Bannerman Park** is a delightful place to rest your feet and boost your spirits. Across Bannerman Road stands **Government House,** the official residence of Newfoundland's lieutenant governor. The elegant mansion is not open to the public.

One block farther along Military Road is **St. Thomas Church,** which opened its doors to worshipers in 1836, making it today the second-oldest place of worship still standing in the province. St. Thomas was the garrison church for the British forces until they were withdrawn in the late 1800s.

St. John's has a vibrant **Arts and Culture Centre** at the corner of Allandale Road and Prince Philip Drive, a mile or so from downtown. It houses the Gallery, which mounts traveling exhibitions that provide a look at the best of modern Canadian painting and sculpture. Windows in the gallery are inhabited by tremendous banana plants, giving a splash of green to the white walls and lending an air of the tropics to this northern climate. The Gallery is open year-round, Tuesday through Sunday from noon to 5pm and 7 to 10pm; admission is free. The Arts and Culture

Centre also houses a library, the 1,000-seat Main Theatre, and the 100-seat Basement Theatre (for information, call 709/729-3901; for ticket reservations, call 709/729-3900).

The arts center is part of the large **Municipal University of Newfoundland (MUN),** a cluster of buildings off Prince Philip Drive. All but one of them are connected by underground tunnels, so students, almost 20,000 of them, can go in as freshmen and leave as seniors without ever seeing the light of day. Besides the usual undergraduate degrees, the university offers one in Newfoundland folklore.

In 1,343-acre **Pippy Park,** across the street from the university, there is a 32-acre reserve of plants and wildlife, the Memorial University Botanical Garden. Naturalist-led walks are available.

The **Confederation Building,** seat of Newfoundland and Labrador's provincial government, rises above Prince Philip Drive east of the Arts and Culture Centre. You can visit the building free of charge during weekday business hours.

Take Highway 10 west (Waterford Bridge Road) from downtown to reach **Bowring Park,** the city's favorite green spot, a few miles from the center. Given to the city by the Bowring family, the park was opened by the duke of Connaught in 1914. Look for the statues: *The Fighting Newfoundlander, Peter Pan* (a copy of the one in London's Kensington Park), and *The Caribou,* in loving memory of the 710 out of 800 members of the Royal Newfoundland Regiment who died in the battle of Beaumont Hamel during World War I (the original statue stands in Beaumont Hamel Park in France).

Shopping anyone? The **Newfoundland Weavery,** 177 Water St. (tel. 709/753-0496), sells all manner of traditional and contemporary Newfoundland crafts, including striking wool sweaters and pottery. **Wordplay,** 221 Duckworth St. (tel. 709/726-4723), is an excellent bookstore with an art gallery upstairs. If you're taken with Newfoundland music, take some with you, from **Fred's** music store, 198 Duckworth St. (tel. 709/753-9191; fax 709/739-4849); they offer mail order.

CATHEDRAL OF ST. JOHN THE BAPTIST, 22 Church Hill. Tel. 709/726-5677.

⭐ Begun in 1843, finished in 1885 under the supervision of Sir Gilbert Scott, the Anglican cathedral was gutted by fire in 1892, but restoration work done in 1905 has given it the look it has today. The Gothic nave, carved-wood pews, Scottish sandstone, rough-hewn Newfoundland stone, and the 36 stained-glass windows (particularly the 16 Kempe windows made in London; there are only 20 in North America) are very handsome. In the small museum in back are photographs of the cathedral after the fire. Inside the entry is a schedule (which changes frequently) of when the church is open. Volunteer guides are on hand to show you around (call ahead to arrange a walk-through).

Admission: Free.

Open: Tours late May to mid-Oct 10:30am–4:30pm.

COMMISSARIAT HOUSE, King's Bridge Rd. Tel. 709/729-6730.

Commissariat House, a beautiful Georgian structure, depicts what life was like when Newfoundland was a vital link in the defense chain of the young British Empire. The first floor, which dates from 1818, was for offices, archives, and messengers on commissary business. The officers lived on the second floor. The military stores were kept for Forts Townsend and William. When the British forces withdrew in 1870, Commissariat House was used as the rectory for St. Thomas Church, and later as a children's hospital, among other things. The house, restored by the Canadian government and the Newfoundland Historic Resources Division, is now filled with beautiful Brussels carpets, English china, silver, lace, and fine paintings. Guides in period costume are on hand to show you around.

Admission: Free.

Open: Summer daily 10am–6pm.

NEWFOUNDLAND MUSEUM, 285 Duckworth St. Tel. 709/729-2329.

The permanent exhibits, on the second and third floors, focus on the native peoples of Newfoundland and on 19th-century daily life. They include rural furnishings, toys, a schoolroom, cooperage, fishery stage, grocery, and stoves manufactured in St. John's. Exhibits are devoted to the Inuits, who have been on the Labrador coast since 1400 A.D., Dorset, Naskapi, and Montagnais Indians, and most poignantly, the Beothuks (pronounced "Bee-*aw*-thuks"), called the "Red Indians" because they covered their bodies in red ocher. The story of the Beothuk's extinction is a sad part of Newfoundland history. Guides are available to tour you through at 11am and 2pm.

A branch of the Newfoundland Museum at the historic Murray Premises, downtown off Harbour Drive, traces the development of sea trade in the province from the 16th century to the present, as well as its military history, and there is a comprehensive display on Newfoundland's natural history. It keeps the same hours as the main museum.

Admission: Free.

Open: July–Aug daily 9am–4:30pm; other months Mon–Fri 9am–5pm, Sat–Sun 9–4:30pm.

ROMAN CATHOLIC BASILICA, Military Rd. Tel. 709/754-2170.

The two towers of the city's impressive Roman Catholic Basilica of St. John the Baptist dominate the city. The basilica, built of limestone and granite from 1841 to 1851, is in the shape of a Latin cross. Beyond the large granite entrance gate, the marble foyer opens into a nave of clean lines and a ceiling with a gilded relief of scrolls and leaves. The statue of Christ at the foot of the altar, by John Hogan, has twins in Dublin and Edinburgh. Around the basilica are the Academy of Our Lady of Mercy and the Mercy Convent, St. Patrick's Hall, and St. Bonaventure College.

Tours: Guided tours available on request.

SIGNAL HILL, at the entrance to St. John's Harbour. Tel. 709/772-5367.

The view from the hill at Signal National Historic Park (when it's not socked in by fog) is magnificent, and the breezes are cool even on the hottest day in summer. Midway up the slope is the park's visitor center, with attractive exhibits explaining the history and importance of Signal Hill and the harbor and town it protected. Drop in and ask about free guided tours in summer.

About two-thirds of the way uphill from the visitor center is the **Queen's Battery,** established in 1796 by the British and enlarged during the War of 1812. Originally an elaborate complex of barracks, blockhouses, and furnaces, the battery was left to deterioration by the elements until 1969, when restoration began. Several of the great old cannons are still at the battery, mounted on carriages with small wheels that ran on a semicircular track for ease of aiming.

Across the Narrows from Queen's Battery is **Fort Amherst,** named for Col. William Amherst, who captured St. John's from the French in 1762. The lighthouse on the point was built in 1813. Together with a chain that stretched across the Narrows, Queen's Battery and Fort Amherst were very effective in closing the harbor of St. John's to enemy attack until larger guns and ironclad vessels rendered such defenses obsolete. Past Fort Amherst, to the south, you should be able to see Cape Spear, the most easterly point in North America, jutting into the Atlantic.

Atop Signal Hill, **Cabot Tower** was begun in 1897 in commemoration of Queen Victoria's jubilee, and John Cabot's landing on Newfoundland's shores in 1497, four centuries earlier. It was opened in 1900, and served as a lookout and signal tower until 1958. It was from this tower that Guglielmo Marconi received the first transatlantic wireless broadcast from a village in Cornwall, England, in 1901. The broadcast consisted of the Morse code for the letter "S," three short signals that made communications history. Cabot Tower maintains communications with the world through the branch post office on its ground floor (open during the summer months); the tower also holds displays that recount the early experiments of Sir Home Popham and the great Marconi in electromagnetic wave transmission. On the tower's top level is an observation deck with the finest of panoramic views.

In summer, the **Signal Hill Tattoo** reenacts military exercises from the 1800s. It's a great pageant, performed at 3 and 7pm on Wednesday, Thursday, Saturday, and Sunday from mid-July to mid-August.

Admission: Free.

Open: Mid-June to Labor Day daily 9am–8pm; the rest of the year daily

8:30am–4:30pm; tower daily 9am–5pm year-round. **Directions:** City buses don't run to Signal Hill, but you can walk, take a taxi, or drive by following Duckworth Street east to Signal Hill Road.

QUIDI VIDI LAKE & BATTERY

Pronounced "Kitty Vitty," this odd name refers to the pretty lake east of downtown, and to the battery that protected its narrow entrance channel, known as "The Gut." The battery was constructed in 1762 by the French troops who held St. John's for a short period that year. Within three months it was in British hands. The American Revolution caused the British to reinforce this strongpoint against American privateers, and again in 1812 it was spruced up for action. Totally restored in 1967 during Canada's centennial, the battery's little building houses a small, free museum explaining the era of its activity. Quidi Vidi Battery is open free of charge, daily from 9am to 6pm mid-June to mid-September (tel. 709/576-2460).

Take time to stroll through Quidi Vidi, a truly picturesque and photogenic spot. Walk along the banks of the lake, as so many St. John's residents do late in the day; the entire circuit takes about 45 minutes. You may see scullers practicing here for the St. John's Regatta, a popular all-day event for fixed-seat boat races held here (as it has been since 1826) the first Wednesday in August.

You can get to the lake (and then continue on to Quidi Vidi) by following Signal Hill Road to Quidi Vidi Road; turn right onto Forest Road, and at Lakeview Avenue, turn left and proceed down the hill. You'll pass some striking houses along the way. Turn right when you reach the lake.

SHORT DRIVES FROM ST. JOHN'S

No visitor to St. John's should leave it without having taken the ride along **Marine Drive,** north of the city. Past Logy Bay to Outer Cove and Torbay is some of the area's prettiest scenery, not to mention a good spot for spying on puffins and whales. On his first visit to Torbay, a traveler was captivated by the sight of a single whale rolling through the sea, and then an old-timer sunning nearby pointed out an entire school of the monster denizens rolling and spouting farther out to sea. Near the base of the cliffs, puffins dive and swim deep below the surface to catch the little fish they live on.

Marine Drive goes all the way through Flat Rock to Pouch (pronounced "Pooch") Cove. Past this quaint town the paved road ends, but a rough road of dirt and crushed stone climbs into the hills, past some marvelous views, to a lighthouse at Cape St. Francis.

Seven miles (11km) south and east of downtown St. John's is **Cape Spear National Historic Site** (tel. 709/772-5367). The lighthouse (1836), perched on a rocky cliff, is at the most easterly point in North America. There's also a World War II gun battery, with underground passages connecting two gun sites with magazines and equipment rooms. The Visitor Reception Centre tells you all about Cape Spear. Guides are on hand in the lighthouse from mid-June to early September. And there are hiking trails to explore year-round.

ORGANIZED TOURS

McCarthy's Party, Topsail, Conception Bay, St. John's, NF, A0A 3Y0 (tel. 709/781-2244; fax 709/781-2233), offers a 2½-hour tour of St. John's and environs from $25, where the beauty and history of the area are rivaled only by the knowledge and humor of the McCarthys. There's Regina, the mom and brains behind the outfit, with able backup support and guide service provided by her four sons, who help out during their summers off from the university. Catch this outstanding family-run show on wheels if you can. (The McCarthys also offer eight- and 14-day guided motorcoach tours of Newfoundland; the latter includes Labrador.)

City & Outpost Adventures, P.O. Box 1211, St. John's, NF, A1C 5M9 (tel. 709/747-8687), also offers local and far-flung Newfoundland adventures. Besides hitting the high points of the city, the company also takes visitors to the outports near

St. John's and farther away, among them Cape Spear National Historic Park, Petty Harbour, Bay Bulls, Witless Bay, and Tors Cove. It will organize ski, golf, scuba, horseback riding, fishing, and hunting outings, as well.

The O'Brien family runs **Bird Island Charters and Humpback Whale Tours,** which takes one or two boats of 48 people to commune with whales and puffins. The whales are usually in these waters from early July to early August, and the boats get quite close to them. The tour also takes you to the largest puffin colony on the east coast of North America—in fact, one of the largest puffin sanctuaries in the world. There's rousing local music and sometimes even a spontaneous jig. A shuttle bus is provided from major hotels in St. John's to Bay Bulls, 19 miles (30km) to the south, for $10; the tour, which costs $25, has daily departures at 9:30 and 11am, and 2 and 5pm. Contact the company at 150 Old Topsail Rd., St. John's, NF, A1E 2B1 (tel. 709/753-4850).

WHERE TO STAY

EXPENSIVE

HOTEL NEWFOUNDLAND, Cavendish Sq. (P.O. Box 5637), St. John's, NF, A1C 5W8. Tel. 709/726-4980, or toll free 800/268-9411 in Canada, 800/828-7447 in the U.S. Fax 709/726-2025. 288 rms, 14 suites. A/C TV TEL

$ Rates: $160 single; $170 double; from $200 suite. AE, CB, DC, DISC, ER, MC, V.

When people say "fish" in St. John's, they mean cod, and when they say "the hotel," they mean the Hotel Newfoundland, a CP Hotels property. This posh luxury hotel, which opened in 1926, was later demolished, and completely rebuilt in 1982 (the only item saved was the brass mailbox to the right of the entry), features many no-smoking and handicapped-access rooms. The unique mini-suites have a round window in the bedroom, which is separated from the large sitting area by a screen. The standard rooms are cozy, with queen-size bed, desk and lamp, TV, upholstered chairs, and hairdryer.

Dining/Entertainment: A waterfall, the highlight of the atrium lobby, is also the centerpiece for the Court Garden. The hotel's upscale restaurant, the Cabot Club, as well as its family eatery, change menus often and host special evenings, such as Newfoundland night.

Facilities: Indoor swimming pool, sauna, whirlpool, and squash courts. Outstanding among the hotel shops is Images of Newfoundland, with evocative photos by Don Lane.

RADISSON PLAZA HOTEL, 120 New Gower St., St. John's, NF, A1C 1J3. Tel. 709/739-6404, or toll free 800/333-3333. Fax 709/739-4154. 267 rms, 9 suites. A/C MINIBAR TV TEL

$ Rates: $110–$140 single; $125–$155 double; from $230 suite. Summer rates about 25% lower; weekend rates available. AE, CB, DC, DISC, ER, MC, V.

Parking: Free to hotel guests.

At the opposite end of town from the Hotel Newfoundland stands the equally elegant Radisson Plaza Hotel, with large scale models of a three-masted wooden steamship and a two-masted schooner in the lobby. The immense marble lobby is punctuated with plants and half a dozen conversation areas. The rooms have a restful decor, tables and chairs or couches, and hairdryers; they feature prints by Newfoundland artists. Two floors are no-smoking, and there's a friendly staff to welcome you.

Dining/Entertainment: There's Newman's legendary dining room for dinner only (see "Where to Dine," below) plus two more informal eateries, Brazil Square, which is buffet-oriented serving three meals a day, and the Cat & Fiddle Pub, with live entertainment Thursday through Saturday. For drinks, there's the Blue Puttee, the hotel's lovely piano bar, which draws a lively business crowd on Friday night.

Services: Room service from 6:30am to 11pm; dry cleaning and laundry; complimentary airport pickup and drop-off for guests on the business floor, who also have a concierge and private lounge.

Facilities: Indoor heated pool (good-sized, but with a low ceiling above it), sauna,

Jacuzzi, weight room, two squash courts (you supply the racket); business floor, gift shop.

MODERATE

JOURNEY'S END, 2 Hill O'Chips, St. John's, NF, A1C 6B1. Tel. 709/ 754-7788, or toll free 800/668-4200. Fax 709/754-5209. 161 rms. A/C TV TEL
$ Rates: $85–$99 single; $95–$99 double. Extra person $4. AE, DC, ER, MC, V.
Parking: Free.
Near the Hotel Newfoundland and overlooking the harbor, the Journey's End has rooms with in-room movies, modern decor, a table and chairs, windows that open, and two double beds or a queen-size bed with a sofa bed. Request a room with a harbor view. Guests get complimentary newspapers and coffee, and can make local calls for free. There's also same-day dry cleaning and laundry service Monday through Saturday, 1½ floors of no-smoking rooms, and an independent restaurant on the premises.

TRAVELLER'S INN, 199 Kenmount Rd., St. John's, NF, A1B 3P9. Tel. 709/722-5540, or toll free 800/528-1234. Fax 709/722-1025. 88 rms. TV TEL
$ Rates: $61–$70 single; $68–$77 double. Extra person $7. Children under 18 free with parents. Weekend rates and packages available. AE, CB, DC, DISC, ER, MC, V.
Renovated in 1992, the family-owned and -operated Traveller's Inn, a Best Western property, has an airy lobby. Rooms have double, twin, or queen-size beds, cable TV, and full baths. Those in the back section are particularly quiet with views of a pretty hillside (you'd never know there's a city nearby). Baths are a little on the small side except in the twin rooms, but they have good counter space. There's an outdoor pool and picnic area. Pretty Abigayle's dining room serves three meals daily, including an inexpensive breakfast buffet. The inn offers room service (9am to 9pm), same-day dry cleaning and laundry (except Sunday), and no-smoking rooms, and it rents VCRs and videos. BB's Lounge is open from noon to 1am (to midnight Sunday).

BED-AND-BREAKFAST

FORT WILLIAM BED & BREAKFAST, 5 Gower St., St. John's, NF, A1C 1M9. Tel. 709/726-3161. Fax 709/576-0849. 3 rms (1 with shower), 1 apt. TV TEL
$ Rates (including breakfast): $46 single; $62 double; suite $66 single, $76 double. Extra person $15 (child under 8, $10 in suite only). MC, V. **Parking:** On street.
Almost right across the street from the Hotel Newfoundland stands the welcoming Fort William Bed & Breakfast. One room has a private bath with shower only. Two rooms on the third floor share a full bath, and there is a beautiful, self-contained apartment with kitchen and patio deck on the ground floor. All units are carpeted and terrycloth robes are provided for guests' use. It's easy to feel at home in this house, where guests make their own breakfast in the large country kitchen that is fully stocked with bread, muffins, bagels, cereal, milk, yogurt, fruit, eggs, and bacon. Coffee has been readied and all you have to do is push a button. The kitchen is filled with brochures and books about the area. There is a live-in house manager, and the owners live right next door.

KINCORA HOSPITALITY HOME, 36 King's Bridge Rd., at Empire Ave., St. John's, NF, A1C 3K6. Tel. 709/576-7415. 5 rms (all with bath). TV
Directions: Follow King's Bridge Road from the airport.
$ Rates (including breakfast): $50–$60 single; $70 double. Extra person $10. No credit cards. **Parking:** Free, on premises.
In this, the showpiece of St. John's bed-and-breakfasts, antiques and plush carpets are the norm, except in the baths, which are thoroughly modern. The guest rooms have fireplaces and beds covered with cuddly duvets. In Room 3, for instance, you are greeted by burgundy drapes and carpets, a bay window, a bed with a carved wooden headboard, and a marble fireplace with a copy of *Memoirs of Winston Churchill* on the mantel. Breakfast, served in a formal dining room, includes homemade muffins and breads. Owner June Dillon is well traveled and many of the

lovely belongings in the house have been collected from her trips. The house (1871) is surrounded by a white picket fence. You can walk to Quidi Vidi from here.

PRESCOTT INN BED AND BREAKFAST, 19 Military Rd., St. John's, NF, A1C 2C3. Tel. 709/753-6036. 6 rms (none with bath), 2 suites (with bath). TV TEL

$ Rates (including breakfast): $46 single; $56 double; $66 or $76 suite. Extra person $15. Off-season discount of 10%. MC, V. **Parking:** On street.

Each of the large bedrooms in this stylish row house (actually two row houses, side by side) is painted a bold, solid color, and contains original plaster ceilings, a fireplace, and period furniture. Rooms are supplied with bathrobes, fluffy towels, and helpful tourist information. I'm partial to no. 4 and no. 6. The two shared baths have been beautifully renovated with wood and tiles. The two suites have a bedroom, living room with sofa bed, kitchen, and full bath; one also has a deck and a freestanding stove. Some of the striking original artwork in the bedrooms, library, and kitchen is for sale. Coffee, tea, and cocoa are available for guests all day long, and they also have the use of a refrigerator. Breakfast here is an event, and conducive to getting to know the other guests. Owners Janet Peters, a fifth-generation Newfoundlander, and her husband, Peter Koop, originally from New York, can help you plan activities during your stay. This is a no-smoking abode.

WHERE TO DINE

EXPENSIVE

NEWMAN'S, in the Radisson Plaza Hotel, 120 New Gower St. Tel. 709/739-6404.
Cuisine: INTERNATIONAL. **Reservations:** Recommended.
$ Prices: Appetizers $5–$9 ($75 for the Russian caviar for two with chilled vodka); main courses $17–$28. AE, CB, DC, DISC, ER, MC, V.
Open: Dinner Mon–Sat 6–11pm.

The elegant, intimate dining room at the Radisson takes its name from the port that has been aged in Newfoundland for almost 200 years and provides the perfect backdrop for sipping it. Its menu features seafood and game, including Labrador caribou, venison, rabbit, and pheasant. Popular dishes include the flambé items (known for their dramatically high flames), the chateaubriand, and New York pepper steak. They make the Caesar salad right at your table. For dessert, consider cherries jubilee, bananas Foster, or crêpes Suzettes. There is a large wine list, as well as 15 to 20 wines available by the glass. It's perfectly acceptable to come here just for appetizers or desserts. You can park at the hotel for free if you dine in the restaurant.

STONE HOUSE, 8 Kennas Hill. Tel. 709/753-2380.
Cuisine: SEAFOOD/GAME. **Reservations:** Recommended.
$ Prices: Lunch appetizers $4–$7, main courses $8.50–$14.50, two-course meal $13–$15; dinner appetizers $7–$9, main courses $18–$28; fixed-price dinner $25. AE, DC, DISC, ER, MC, V.
Open: Lunch Mon–Fri 11:30am–2:30pm; dinner daily 5–10:30pm.

The elegant Stone House, built in 1834 for the Keough family, has three-foot-thick walls and is one of the few stone houses in Newfoundland. With wide-board pine floors and four intimate dining rooms, it provides an undeniably beautiful backdrop for dining. Choose from the Map, Rose, Library or Keough rooms—all appealing, but the Rose Room is the prettiest. The menu features Newfoundland cuisine, highlighting the fresh produce, seafood, and game. Consider appetizers of gravlax, cod tongues, cod au gratin, or steamed mussels, and main courses of pork tenderloin, duck breast, rack of lamb filet mignon, partridge, pheasant, and more exotic offerings like wild boar, caribou, moose, and alligator (how local can the latter be!). The wine cellar is dependably well stocked. Any meal here is a special occasion.

MODERATE

STELLA'S, 183 Duckworth St. Tel. 709/753-9625.

Cuisine: VEGETARIAN/SEAFOOD. **Reservations:** Accepted for dinner until 7pm; if you plan to come later, call 15 minutes prior to arrival, and they'll hold a table for you if possible.

$ Prices: Appetizers $3.50–$8; lunch main courses $3–$8; dinner main courses $10–$14. MC, V.

Open: Mon–Tues 11:30am–3:30pm, Wed–Thurs 11:30am–9:30pm, Fri–Sat 11:30am–10pm, Sun 11:30am–9pm. Kitchen closes half an hour earlier.

Stella's represents great value for great victuals. Pretty, small, and always crowded, it serves tasty vegetarian and seafood dishes, and specializes in nondairy main courses and desserts. Favorites on the dinner menu include basil pesto fettuccine, black bean or (organic) chicken burrito, spanakopita, daily fish special, assorted cheesecakes, and nondairy pies and chocolate cake. The tables get snapped up quickly; if there are two of you, request one by the window in front. They do offer take-out. The original Stella, by the way, was owner Irene Taylor's dog. Licensed.

VICTORIA STATION, 288/290 Duckworth St. Tel. 709/722-1290.

Cuisine: CONTINENTAL. **Reservations:** Recommended.

$ Prices: Lunch items $3–$7.50; dinner appetizers $3–$5, main courses $6–$15; Sun brunch $3–$8. AE, DC, ER, MC, V.

Open: Lunch daily 11:30am–5pm; dinner daily 5pm–midnight; brunch Sat–Sun 11am–4pm.

In an inn (yes, you can stay here, too) downtown across the street from the Newfoundland Museum, Victoria Station has charm, good food, and friendly service. Who could ask for more? The restaurant is known for its homemade pastas, and the fettuccine Alfredo is the richest you'll ever taste (the dinner portion's a killer). You can get Caesar and Greek salads, crêpes, seafood linguine, stir-fry chicken or beef, and shepherd's pie. The dinner menu expands to include more fish and meat dishes, including pan-fried cod, grilled halibut, and chicken dijonaisse or Cordon Bleu. Among almost a dozen desserts are chocolate yogurt cheesecake (the "ultimate chocolate dessert") and "the best crème caramel east of Montréal." Classical guitar music accompanies Sunday brunch, and Sunday evenings there is special entertainment ($4 cover). In nice weather, you can eat in the patio in back. Happy hour is on Friday from 4 to 7pm. This is an inn, so if you want to be near this excellent kitchen, you can also book one of the 10 rooms on the third and fourth floors (from $65).

BUDGET

There are a number of economical Chinese, Mexican, and fish-and-chips restaurants in downtown St. John's, all good and all with devotees who swear they're the best in town.

THE SHIP INN, 265 Duckworth St. Tel. 709/753-3870.

Cuisine: LIGHT FARE. **Reservations:** Not needed.

$ Prices: Most items $3–$8. ER, MC, V.

Open: Mon–Thurs and Sat 11am–1am, Fri 11am–2am, Sun 11am–midnight. Lunch served Mon–Fri noon–2pm; happy hour Mon–Sat 11am–7pm, Sun noon–7pm.

My favorite pub in Newfoundland is the Ship Inn, a second home to writers, musicians, actors, and artists of all ages. Students congregate here as well, and women on their own feel quite comfortable. Enter the bar by going down the steps at 271 Duckworth and immersing yourself in the cozy, congenial atmosphere. Sandwiches, meat pies, and salads ($3 to $6) are served at lunchtime, when the place fills up uncharacteristically with a business crowd. Beer is the specialty here: Guinness, Harp, and Smithwick's on tap for about $5 a pint (ha' pints available). Most of the day is devoted to happy hour.

PICNIC SUPPLIES

At **Mary Jane's,** in a large, two-story building at 377 Duckworth St. (tel. 709/753-8466), you can get all manner of healthy foods. The multifaceted store also sells jewelry, T-shirts and other clothing, household items, and publications that include the *Utne Reader* and *Fit for Life*. There's an in-store snack bar.

At **Robert Caines Grocery,** 104 Duckworth St., near Hotel Newfoundland, you can get sandwiches (ready-made, or the fixings for your own), fruits, vegetables, snack foods, and soft ice cream. It's open from 7:30am to midnight daily (tel. 709/753-7543).

EVENING ENTERTAINMENT

For a small place, St. John's has a thriving nightlife; just stroll down Duckworth Street and you'll see. It's centered mostly around music, and the bars and clubs get "blocked" (that's Newfoundland talk for crowded) early. Listen to Irish music at **Erin's Pub,** 184 Water St. (tel. 709/722-1916), and **Bridgett's Pub,** 29 Cookstown Rd, where Wednesday is folk music night and fish-and-chips are half price with beer (tel. 709/753-9992); blues at Bridgett's and the **Fat Cat Blues Bar,** 5 George St. (tel. 709/722-6409); and alternative music in **The Loft,** on the third floor at Haymarket Square. If there is a charge to listen to music at the bars, it's no more than $3.

The **LSPU (Longshoremen's Protective Union) Hall,** 3 Victoria St. (tel. 709/753-4531), also has live entertainment; check the newspaper for a schedule of its upcoming events.

Two of the most popular bars in the city are **Nautical Nellies** (and the small and quieter Nelly's Belly, downstairs), 201 Water St. (tel. 709/726-0460), where popcorn is served free after 4pm; and, at the university, the **Breezeway Bar,** in the Thompson Student Centre (tel. 709/737-7464). Run by the student union, it's a nonprofit bar (beer and mixed drinks run a mere $2). There's taped music and a dance floor. A good place to meet students and young professionals, it gets crowded on Thursday and Friday nights.

Theatrical productions are mounted at the **Arts and Culture Centre** at the university (tel. 709/729-3900).

7. LABRADOR

Labrador may be sparsely inhabited but it has been home to human beings for thousands of years. The Innu (Indian) culture in Labrador goes back 8,000 years, and the Inuit (Eskimo) culture, 4,000 years.

The Vikings sighted Labrador but did not stop in 986 A.D.; they came ashore first in 1010 A.D. Traces of them remain in the shape of "fairy holes," deep, cylindrical holes in the rocks, at an angle away from the sea, where they were thought to have moored their boats.

The 1540s to the 1620s was the period of the Basque whalers. As many as 2,000 of them arrived in 20 galleons, and returned to Europe with 20,000 barrels of oil from whale blubber. It has been said that the whale oil of Newfoundland and Labrador was as valuable to the Europeans as the gold of South America. Vestiges of a whaling station from the 16th century remain on Saddle Island, off the coast of Red Bay.

Next came the British and French fishermen, fur traders, and merchants. They began summering or settling in Labrador in the 1700s. In 1850 as many as 1,000 men came for the summer cod fishing, but by 1870 most of the fishermen were local, and many of their supplies came from St. John's or Halifax rather than from across the Atlantic.

Many of the Europeans intermarried with the Innu and Inuit women. The present-day Naskapi and Montagnais Indians got their names from the Europeans. The Inuit whalers had conflicts with the "settlers" along the south coast, and removed themselves to the far north, where they remain today.

In the late 1800s, Dr. Wilfred Grenfell, a medical missionary from England, brought much-needed medical services to the isolated regions of Labrador and northern Newfoundland. In numerous ways he improved their social and economic lot in life, and books by and about this local hero proliferate.

Today 30,345 people inhabit the "Big Land," 13,000 in western Labrador, 8,000 in Happy Valley–Goose Bay, and the remaining people along the coast. Some 80% to 85% of those who were born here remain here, and not surprisingly, ties to family and neighbors are strong. Yet the people are not closed to strangers, as one might imagine, but are warm and welcoming.

The dog of choice for pet owners here is obvious: the Labrador retriever. Besides having a fetching personality, the "Lab" is an excellent bird dog, which comes in handy in these parts.

Labrador is almost three times the size of Newfoundland, yet it is a place where small is still beautiful: small villages, small homes, small roads, even small foliage, as evidenced in the dwarf Labrador black spruce, indigenous to the whole province. The white, green, and blue striped Labrador flag represents the connection of the people to the land: the white bar, with a spruce twig in one corner, represents the snow; the green bar represents the land, and the blue bar, the waters of the sea, rivers, and lakes.

Many come here for the sport fishing, for brook trout, Atlantic salmon, arctic char, ouananiche, lake trout, white fish, and northern pike. Others come for wilderness adventure, hiking, and camping under the undulating northern lights; still others simply curious about a remote part of the world and want to meet the warm people who call it home.

For most visitors to the "Big Land," there are three major destinations: Labrador West, including Labrador City and Wabush, reachable by train from Sept-Iles, Québec (pronounced Set-*teel*); the Labrador Straits, with tiny fishing villages and the rushing Pinware River, reachable by plane or ferry; and Central Labrador, the commercial and industrial center of Labrador, where most of its inhabitants live.

Those who yearn to venture still farther afield can take the coastal ferry along the Labrador coast, known as "Iceberg Alley" because of the many icebergs that float past it in spring and summer, propelled by the strong Labrador Current. The South Coast is an excellent place to view the dislodged ice boulders; the North Coast, more remote and filled with rugged mountains, is the home of the indigenous peoples of Labrador, the Innu and Inuit (Indian and Eskimo).

There is no highway link on the Atlantic coast of Labrador; the Marine Atlantic ferry is the only means of transportation and it takes two weeks to make the entire round-trip from Red Bay to Nain, or 16 days if you start out from Lewisporte in Newfoundland and return there.

Some 46 fishing camps in Labrador, operated by 26 outfitters, are scattered throughout Labrador, and Destination Labrador can supply a list (see "Seeing Newfoundland and Labrador" at the beginning of this chapter).

It can also supply a list of the many tour operators who bring motorcoach and other tours into Labrador, among them **Globus Gateway** (motorcoach), 53011 S. Federal Circle, Littleton, CO 80123 (tel. 303/797-6000; fax 303/795-0962); **Maineline Tours,** 184 Main St., South Portland, ME 04106 (tel. 207/799-8527; fax 207/799-5656); **Vermont Transit Tours,** 135 St. Paul's St., Burlington, VT 05401 (tel. 802/862-9671; fax 802/862-7812); and **McCarthy's Party,** Topsail, Conception Bay, NF, A0A 3Y0 (tel. 707/781-2244; fax 707/781-2233).

Of these regions, I have explored the straits and will describe the area more in depth below. On my next trip to Labrador, I plan to take the train from Sept-Iles to Wabush on the Québec North Shore and Labrador Railway (the QNS&R), but if you do it first, drop me a note and tell me all about it.

The world's largest barren-ground caribou herd roams across Labrador and the fantastically old Laurentian Shield, which has apparently remained unchanged since long before any hooves set foot on this planet. It's possible that Labrador is the only such spot in the world, and that alone might make it worth a visit: to see what the world was like when life began.

Details on obtaining advance-planning information, getting there, and getting around are found at the beginning of this chapter.

THE LABRADOR STRAITS

To get here, I flew in to Blanc Sablon, rented a car at the airport, and drove the 3 miles (5km) into Labrador to L'Anse au Clair, the gateway to the straits. This region, to me, is reminiscent of the terrain around Barrow, Alaska, another remote and appealing part of the world. There's only one two-way road through the area, linking eight outport villages from L'Anse au Clair, which means "Clear Water Cove," to Red Bay. It's a mere 50 miles (80km) long, so you can get to know the straits well in a couple of days.

The straits presents a rugged terrain with muted colors except for a vibrant stretch of green along the Pinware River. The area is sparsely populated, like most of Labrador, with small houses clustered close together, an anomaly to me since there is so much space here, and often brightened up with "yard art"—replicas of windmills, wells, churches, and such. In Capstan Island (pop. 74, and not really an island, though there is an island you can walk to at low tide), you'll see some attractive houses with larger yards, but not necessarily larger yard art. There is a greenhouse here, filled with flowers, seedlings, and vegetables, that travelers are welcome to visit.

In summer, some 2,000 icebergs float by the coast and whales cavort offshore. The landscape is covered with cotton grass, clover, partridgeberries, fireweed, buttercups, and bog laurel. The fog rolls in easily and stays a while or just as easily rolls out again (and this can affect flights in and out of Blanc Sablon). The caplin roll, too. The tiny migrating fish crash-land on the shore by the thousands during a week in late June or early July. So many come in that it looks like a dark wave approaching. Local folks crowd the beach to scoop up the six- to eight-inch-long fish and take them home to cook up for supper.

The **tourist office** for the region, in small, restored **St. Andrews Church** in L'Anse au Clair, is open from June to August (tel. 709/931-2013). Note the quilt that is the size of and shaped after the church's original stained-glass window.

The **Red Bay Visitor Centre,** in Red Bay, is open mid-June through September, Monday to Saturday 8am to 8pm, and Sunday noon to 8pm (tel. 709/920-2197).

The tourist association plans to mark some of the footpaths and trails in the area, so be sure to inquire; also ask about the "fairy holes." If you come in mid-August, you get to attend the annual **Bakeapple Festival,** celebrating the tiny fruit with the baked-apple taste that's the star of many a dessert in Newfoundland and Labrador.

WHAT TO SEE & DO

Drive the "slow road" that connects the villages of the Labrador Straits. Traveling west to east, here is some of what you'll find along the way.

In L'Anse au Clair (pop. 267), there's a good handcrafts shop, **Moore's Handicrafts,** 8 Country Rd. (tel. 709/931-2022), which sells summer and winter coats, traditional cossacks, moccasins, knitted items, handmade jewelry, and other crafts. It's open daily, often until late.

Just outside L'Anse Amour (pop. 25), 12 miles (19km) from L'Anse au Clair, be sure to stop by the **Labrador Straits Museum,** with two rooms of exhibits. My favorite is the series of photographs of an Irish and two German pilots who flew off course in April 1928 and landed on Greely Island (Québec), off the Labrador/Québec coast. They were the first to fly the North Atlantic east to west nonstop, and photos show them talking with local children and holding Labrador puppies, then being greeted in New York City by crowds in front of the public library. Their plane, the *Bremen,* was purchased by Henry Ford and is now displayed in the Henry Ford Museum & Greenfield Village in Dearborn, Michigan (tel. 313/271-1620).

The oldest **burial mound** in North America is in L'Anse Amour (it means "Love Cove"), on the road to the lighthouse. You'll see a monument. Here the remains of a Maritime Archaic Indian child (about 12 years old) who died around 6,906 B.C. were discovered, lying face down with a rock on his back. No one has been able to come up with an explanation.

Continue down this road to the **Point Amour Lighthouse** (1857), at the western entrance to the Strait of Belle Isle, which at 109 feet is the tallest lighthouse in Atlantic Canada and the second tallest in Canada (the tallest one is on the Gaspé Peninsula in Québec). The walls of the slightly tapered, circular tower are 6½ feet thick at the base. Climb the 122 steps to the top if you're up to the challenge. The dioptric lens was imported from Europe at a cost of $10,000, quite a sum for 1870.

The lighthouse, which kept watch for submarines for the Canadian government during World War II, is still in use and has a live-in lightkeeper. The lighthouse is being restored to its original condition, with an interpretation center added. In the meantime, the lighthouse keeper is happy to share his stories with you. It's open to the public in summer from 8am to 5pm.

The L'Anse Amour Lighthouse is a two-mile drive from the main road.

In L'Anse au Loup (pop. 600), 9 miles (14km) from L'Anse au Clair and 2.5 miles (4km) from the turnoff for the lighthouse, there's a fish plant where tours are given on request. There's also a modest little café overlooking the water called **Beryl's Place.** The name L'Anse au Loup means "Wolf Cove."

After you pass West St. Modeste (pop. 272), where food (and a bakery) and lodging are available, the landscape becomes quite scenic where the road follows the Pinware River. Along this stretch of road, you'll see some "erratics," boulders deposited on the tops of mountains, in fields or meadows. Closer to the shore, you're bound to see icebergs drifting by, and, the greatest delight of all, an occasional whale.

At **Pinware Provincial Park,** 27 miles (43km) from L'Anse au Clair, you'll find a pretty beach, a picnic area, campsites, and outhouses. Where the road follows the Pinware River, the trees are noticeably taller. The 50-mile long Pinware River is known for salmon fishing. The town of Pinware is home to 201 people.

The highway ends in **Red Bay** (pop. 316). Besides the Visitor Centre here, there's a restaurant, cabins, a craft shop, and an Interpretation Centre for Saddle Island, the scene of Basque whaling stations from the 16th century. Free transportation to archeological sites on the island is available in summer Monday through Saturday from 9am to 4pm. Whether or not you take the boat over to it, see the exhibits that tell the story of the Basque fishermen, who were the first whalers in North America, arriving as early as the 11th century.

It's said that at its peak, some 2,000 men in 20 galleons came to Red Bay and returned to Europe with 20,000 barrels of oil. They would go out in crews of seven men in a boat to pit themselves against the mighty sea animals.

In the **Interpretation Centre,** read the exhibited last will and testament of one of the men, dated June 22, 1577. There is a model of a cooperage and the tryworks, where blubber was made into oil. You can see Saddle Island from the observation level on the third floor.

In the Red Bay area, you're likely to see "komatiks"—long, low wooden sleds used for transportation in winter. In the late 19th century and early 20th century they were pulled by teams of huskies and were used to carry the mail. Today they are used to transport people (behind dogsleds or snowmobiles) and for hauling wood, cargo, and supplies, and on caribou hunts.

WHERE TO STAY & DINE IN L'ANSE AU CLAIR

BEACHSIDE HOSPITALITY HOME, L'Anse au Clair, Labrador, A0K 3K0. Tel. 709/831-2662. 3 rms (none with bath). **Directions:** Follow the red, white, and blue signs in the area.

$ Rates: $32–$38 single or double. Extra person $5. No credit cards.

Gloria and Norman Letto obviously love opening their home up to new friends (I say that purposefully; I don't think they've ever met a stranger). A stay here is your best opportunity to know a local family and learn firsthand from them about life in this region of Labrador. Yet there is privacy, as well. The three bedrooms have a separate entrance and share two full baths. One room has a double bed; one, two doubles; and one, a double and a twin. Access to telephone. Delicious home-cooked meals are available by arrangement.

NORTHERN LIGHT INN, L'Anse au Clair, Labrador, A0K 3K0. Tel. 709/931-2332. Fax 709/931-2708. 28 rms, 1 suite, 5 housekeeping units. TV TEL

$ Rates: $60–$65 single; $68–$75 double. Extra person $5. AE, DC, ER, MC, V.

The largest accommodation in the area and here since 1974, the Northern Light Inn is well set up for guests, with comfortable, well-maintained rooms, a gift shop with wonderful sweaters, a friendly staff, and good home cooking. The coffee shop, open from 8am to 11pm, serves strong coffee, soups, sandwiches, baskets of scallops, fried chicken, and pizza, from $2 to $9. In the adjacent Basque Dining Room, which comes highly recommended, seafood is the specialty, with prices ranging from $2 to $5 for appetizers and $11 to $14 for main courses. The coffee shop doubles as a lounge.

WHERE TO DINE IN FORTEAU

SEA-VIEW RESTAURANT, 35 Main St. Tel. 709/931-2840.
  Cuisine: HOME COOKING.
$ Prices: Most items $2–$13. AE, MC.
  Open: Summer daily 9am–11:30pm; the rest of the year Mon–Sat 9am–11:30pm, Sun noon–10pm.
This family-style restaurant in Forteau (pop. 536), 8 miles from L'Anse au Clair, offers eat-in or take-out meals, home cooking, of course. Seafood dishes are the specialty, and the seafood basket ($13) is particularly popular. The pretty dining room, with photographs of local scenes on the walls, is fully licensed.

Adjacent to it is a grocery store and bakery where you can buy homemade bread, peanut butter cookies, and much more. Across the road, the same management has four motel rooms, with television and telephone jack, two of which are efficiency units ($55 single, $65 double). It's 12 miles (19km) from Blanc Sablon.

WHERE TO STAY IN L'ANSE AMOUR

DAVIS HOSPITALITY HOME, L'Anse Amour, Labrador, A0K 3J0. Tel. 709/927-5690. 2 rms (none with bath).
$ Rates: $32 single; $36 double. No credit cards.
L'Anse Amour calls itself "the smallest community with the most to offer," and one of the best things it has to offer is the warmth of this hospitality home with a serene setting, overlooking the rocks, water, and beach. Rita and Cecil Davis, your hosts, have lived here for 40 years, so they can tell you all about the place. In fact, through a special grant, only members of the Davis family live along this road (they can tell you all about that, too). The two guest rooms, which are side by side and near the hosts' bedroom, share a full bath; one of the rooms has a double bed, one a three-quarter bed. Breakfast and seafood supper are available on request, at an extra charge; you really should try Mrs. Davis's rhubarb relish. From here, you can walk along a footpath to Point Amour Lighthouse.

LABRADOR WEST

The most affluent and industrialized part of Labrador, Labrador West, lies on the Québec border and is home to the twin cities of Wabush and Labrador City, 4 miles (7km) apart. The two share many attractions, activities, and services. This region offers top-notch cross-country skiing, and has hosted two World Cup cross-country skiing events. Labrador West is also home to the largest open-pit iron ore mine in North America, which produces almost half of Canada's iron ore.

For indoor activities, go to the **Labrador West Arts and Culture Centre,** which draws performers from throughout North America.

Labrador City or Wabush makes a good base from which to go hiking, canoeing, and birdwatching. You can also play 18 holes at the **Tamarack Golf Course,** or go windsurfing, scuba diving, or sailing on one of the many surrounding lakes. And don't forget about cross-country skiing.

The annual **Labrador 400 Sled Dog Race,** held here in March, draws about 25 teams from Canada and the United States who match skills on 400 miles of challenging terrain.

Labrador City is the northern terminus of the **Québec North Shore and Labrador Railway (the QNS&R),** which departs from Sept-Iles, Québec, and is the only passenger train service in the entire province of Newfoundland and Labrador. The railway was carved out in the wilderness over a five-year period (1950 to 1954) to access Labrador's huge iron ore deposits. The eight- to 10-hour trip covers 260 miles, across 19 bridges, 11 tunnels, along riverbanks, through forests, and past rapids, mountains, and waterfalls, and finally through subarctic vegetation. In summer a highlight is the vintage dome car (1958) with sofa seats that was once part of the Wabash Cannonball (tel. 418/968-7805 in Québec, 709/944-8205 in Newfoundland and Labrador).

CENTRAL LABRADOR

From the North West River and Mud Lake to the Mealy Mountains, a visit to the interior of Labrador is filled with vivid images of water and spruce forests that seem to go on forever. Some people believe that Lake Melville is "Markland, the land of forests" in the Viking sagas.

Outdoor activities include berry-picking from August to the first snowfall of November, excellent sportfishing, canoeing the Churchill River, kayaking the rapid-filled Kanamou River, and snowmobiling.

Fur traders were the first settlers in Central Labrador, in the 1700s, but the area is better known for more recent developments: the establishment, in the 1940s, of a military base for NATO forces in Happy Valley–Goose Bay, and in the 1960s for a mammoth hydroelectric project set up in Churchill Falls, the largest such complex in the western hemisphere.

The Montagnais band of Innu live near Happy Valley–Goose Bay, in North West River and Sheshatshit, along with the descendants of English, French, and Scottish settlers.

Them Days quarterly magazine, which chronicles the stories and memories of Labrador's people, is published in Happy Valley–Goose Bay. Pick up a copy during your Labrador stay. It's sold everywhere.

To take a little bit of Labrador home with you, stop by **Labrador Handicrafts,** 367 Hamilton River Rd., in Happy Valley–Goose Bay. The largest craft store in Labrador, it sells Innu tea dolls, grasswork, soapstone carvings, labradorite jewelry, hooked rugs, and parkas.

The **Labrador Winter Games** are held here every three years; mark your calendar for February 1995.

THE SOUTH COAST

Along Labrador's southern coastline, you can visit several coastal communities by ferry, including **Battle Harbour,** where Dr. Wilfred Grenfell established Labrador's first hospital in 1893.

From Cartwright, visit the **Gannet Island Seabird Ecological Reserve,** home to almost 95,000 seabirds, including the largest razorbill population in North America; or the 35-mile sandy beach that the Vikings labeled "Wonderstrands."

The South Coast lends itself to salmon fishing, hiking, and canoeing; and in winter, to iceberg- and whale-watching, as well as snowmobiling along groomed trails that link Cartwright and Red Bay, in the Labrador Straits.

THE NORTH COAST

Take the Marine Atlantic coastal ferry northward to enjoy the remote beauty of Labrador's North Coast, its magnificent fjords, Innu and Inuit culture and crafts. The ferry calls on sparse communities here as far north at Nain.

Beginning in 1771, Moravian missionaries arrived, bringing with them prefabricated buildings from Germany, some of which are still standing. The **Hopedale Mission** (1782) is the oldest wooden-frame building east of Québec and a National Historic Site. In **Nain,** the community museum, called Piulimatsivik, displays Moravian and Inuit artifacts.

The Inuit live along the North Coast, in Makkovik, Rigolet, Hopedale, and Nain, while the Naskapi band of Innu are in Davis Inlet and in central Labrador, in North West River and Sheshatshit. They continue to fish, hunt, and carry on many aspects of their traditional culture. Friendly but shy peoples, they interact with visitors.

Skilled outdoor enthusiasts love the North Coast for hiking, sea kayaking, camping, climbing in the Torngat Mountains, skiing, ice climbing, snowmobiling, and dogsledding.

CHAPTER 7
SETTLING INTO MONTREAL

Montréal, an island city, floats serenely in the St. Lawrence River. It covers a bit more than 30 percent of its island home, sharing the rest with 28 other municipalities, to comprise a metropolitan area of three million people, almost half the population of the entire province of Québec.

The port of Montréal, with almost 16 miles (25km) of waterfront, is second only to New York as the Atlantic seaboard's largest port. In warm weather, the revitalized, mile-long Old Port provides myriad water and land activities for visitors and Montréalers alike.

An international phenomenon, Montréal is the largest French-speaking city outside of France, yet it's thoroughly bilingual, and a portion of its diverse population speaks neither English nor French as a first language. The city has its own Chinatown and Little Italy, along with Greek, Portuguese, Jewish, and other ethnic enclaves, and its Botanical Garden contains the largest Chinese garden outside of Asia.

Consider the yin and yang of this unique North American city. It encompasses both a picturesque old town and a modern skyline punctuated with needle-nose skyscrapers. There's fine French cuisine and inexpensive ethnic fare; a world-class symphony and down-and-dirty jazz; haute couture and a Just for Laughs festival devoted to comedy; 65 metro (subway) stops and 149 miles of bicycle lanes; Canada's oldest museum and its largest casino; some of the nation's prettiest churches and its feistiest hockey team.

This is one smart city: home to four universities, two French-speaking and two English-speaking, including the highly regarded McGill University. The Canadian Center for Architecture houses the largest collection of documents on architecture anywhere in the world.

Added to all this, Montréal is clean, safe, and easy to explore—the urban vacationer's dream come true.

1. ORIENTATION

For a city of more than one million inhabitants (more than three million if you count the greater area), Montréal is easy to maneuver. The two airports that serve it are nearby, one only 14 miles away, and, once you get to town, the Metro system is fast and efficient. For those with the time, walking is the best way to get to know this fun, fascinating city, neighborhood by neighborhood.

WHAT'S SPECIAL ABOUT MONTREAL

Old Montréal
☐ Place Jacques-Cartier, the most enchanting of the old city's squares.
☐ Notre-Dame Basilica, big enough to hold 3,500 worshipers.

Dining
☐ French cuisine in fine restaurants and local bistros.
☐ More ethnic restaurants than you ever imagined.

Special Events
☐ International Jazz Festival in July.
☐ Just for Laughs Festival in July.
☐ World Film Festival in August.
☐ Benson & Hedges International Fireworks Competition every summer.
☐ International Festival of New Dance in September.

Architecture
☐ Row houses from the 1920s and 1930s with gracefully curving exterior iron stairways, especially around St-Louis Square.

☐ Soaring skyscrapers, such as the IBM Marathon building and cathedrallike 1000 de la Gauchetière.
☐ The Canadian Center of Architecture, a mix of modern and classical.

Museums
☐ The Museum of Fine Arts with its modern new annex.
☐ McCord Museum of Canadian History.

Parks and Gardens
☐ Parc Mont-Royal, right in the middle of the city, enjoyed by joggers, cyclists, sun-bathers, picnickers, cross-country skiers, and ice skaters.
☐ Botanical Garden, which spreads across 180 acres.

Shopping
☐ Fine department stores and boutiques.
☐ World-class designers, from the up-and-coming to the well established.

ARRIVING

BY PLANE   The **Aéroport de Dorval** (tel. 514/633-3105, or toll free 800/465-1213) is 14 miles (22km) southwest of downtown, and it handles all flights from North American cities. The ride into town takes 30 minutes if the traffic is not badly tied up, and costs about $27, tip included, by taxi. **Autocar Connaisseur/Gray Line** runs between Dorval and downtown hotels for $8.50 one way (tel. 514/934-1222).

Montréal's **Aéroport Mirabel** (tel. 514/476-3010, or toll free 800/465-1213), 34 miles (55km) northwest of the city, is the world's largest in terms of surface area. If you're flying in from Europe, Africa, South America (including the West Indies), or Asia, you'll land here. The ride into the city takes about 45 minutes in normal traffic, and costs about $60, tip included, if you go by taxi. Autocar Connaisseur/Gray Line runs between Mirabel and Dorval airports and from Mirabel to downtown hotels for $13 one way (tel. 514/934-1222). The fare between Mirabel and Dorval airports is $11.

BY TRAIN   Montréal has one intercity rail terminus, **Central Station,** situated directly beneath the Queen Elizabeth Hotel at the corner of boulevard René-Lévesque and rue Mansfield. Central Station is part of the Underground City, and is thus connected to the Metro (Bonaventure station), and to Windsor Station, the terminus for commuter and suburban trains (tel. toll free 800/426-8725 for Amtrak information, 514/871-1331 for VIA Rail information).

BY BUS   In the **Terminus Voyageur,** bd. 505 de Maisonneuve est (tel. 514/842-2281), you'll find a bar, cafeteria, tourism-information booth, car-rental desk, and a travel agency selling tours, air tickets, and last-minute travel bargains. The Terminus Voyageur is also the terminus for the airport buses that go to Mirabel and Dorval airports throughout the day.

From here, you're virtually on top of the Berri-UQAM Métro station, the junction of several important Métro lines and the starting point for a quick trip to any quarter of the city. If you'd rather take a taxi, expect to find some waiting outside the terminal building.

BY CAR The Trans Canada Highway runs right through Montréal, connecting it with both ends of the country. Interstate 87 runs due north from New York City to link up with Canada's Highway 15 at the border, making the entire 377-mile (608km) journey entirely on expressways. From Boston, I-93 north joins I-89 just south of Concord, N.H. At White River Junction you have two choices: continue on I-89 to Lake Champlain, then follow various smaller roads to join I-87 and Canada Highway 15 north; or link up with I-91 at White River Junction to go due north toward Sherbrooke, P.Q. At the border I-91 becomes Canada Highway 55, and joins Canada Highway 10 (the Estrie, or Eastern Townships, autoroute) to Montréal. The trip from Boston to Montréal is about 317 miles (512km); from Toronto it's 339 miles (546km); from Ottawa, 118 miles (190km). Remember that highway distances and speed limits are given in kilometers (km) in Canada.

TOURIST INFORMATION

The main information center for visitors in Montréal is the large and impressively organized **Infotouriste,** at 1001 rue du Square-Dorchester, between rues Peel and Metcalfe in the downtown hotel and business district; take the Métro to Peel to get there. The local number is 514/873-2015, but you can call toll free from anywhere in Canada and the U.S., 800/363-7777. Employed by the Québec Ministry of Tourism, staff workers are extremely knowledgeable—and bilingual—and the center is an invaluable information resource regarding dining, accommodations, and attractions in Montréal and throughout the province. It can provide currency exchange, hotel bookings, and car rentals. The city has an information center that is convenient to Old Montréal and place Jacques-Cartier. It's at 174 rue Notre-Dame est, at the corner of rue Notre-Dame and place Jacques-Cartier, near the monument to Lord Nelson.

CITY LAYOUT

At the risk of confusing my readers, I'll point out that Montréal is laid out oddly and that Mark Twain was right when he said this is the only city where the sun sets in the north. Scrutinize a map of the city and you'll see that the streets labeled east or west, such as Ste-Catherine or René-Lévesque, in reality run north and south (well, northeast and southwest). To simplify things, I'll break with tradition, too, and refer to directions as the Montréalers do.

MAIN ARTERIES & STREETS In downtown Montréal, the principal streets running east-west include boulevard René-Lévesque, rue Ste-Catherine, boulevard de Maisonneuve, and rue Sherbrooke, and the north-south arteries include rue Crescent, rue McGill, rue St-Denis, and boulevard St-Laurent, the line of demarcation between east and west Montréal (most of the downtown area you probably will visit lies in the west). Near Mont-Royal Park, north of the downtown area, major streets are avenue du Mont-Royal and avenue Laurier. In Old Montréal, rue St-Jacques (home to many banks), rue Notre-Dame, and rue St-Paul are the major streets, along with rue de la Commune, which hugs the St. Lawrence River.

FINDING AN ADDRESS Boulevard St-Laurent is the dividing point between east and west (*est* and *ouest*) in Montréal; there's no equivalent division for north and south; the numbers start at the river and climb from there, just as the topography does. For instance, if you're driving along boulevard St-Laurent and pass no. 500, you'd be in Old Montréal, near rue Notre-Dame; no. 1100 would be near boulevard René-Lévesque, no. 1500 near boulevard de Maisonneuve, and no. 3400 near rue Sherbrooke. You'll find even numbers on the west side of north-south-bound streets and the south side of east-west-bound streets; odd numbers are on the east and north sides, respectively. For more help, check the handy "Address Locator" map in the free *Montréal Tourist Guide,* available everywhere.

Note: In earlier days Montréal was split ethnically between those who spoke

English, living in the city's western regions, and those who spoke French, concentrated to the east. And things do sound more French as you walk east: Street names and Metro station names change from Peel and Atwater to St-Laurent and Beaudry. While the east-west dividing line for the city's street-numbering system is boulevard St-Laurent, the "spiritual split" comes farther west, at avenue de Bleury/avenue du Parc.

MAPS Happily, good ones are inside the handy, free *Tourist Guide* supplied by the Greater Montréal Convention and Tourism Bureau and distributed widely throughout the city. The bureau also provides a large, foldout city map for free.

NEIGHBORHOODS IN BRIEF

Downtown Bounded (loosely) by rue Sherbrooke to the north, boulevard René-Lévesque to the south, rue Berri to the east, and rue Guy to the west, Montréal's vibrant downtown area is filled with elegant hotels, museums, chic shops and department stores, and soaring skyscrapers that lend distinction to the city's modern skyline. McGill University, with its pretty urban campus, is also in the downtown area.

Crescent Street One of downtown Montréal's major restaurant districts, it holds hundreds of eateries of all styles. Most are on Crescent Street, between Sherbrooke and René-Lévesque, but others are on neighboring streets. From east to west, the streets in this district are Stanley, Drummond, de la Montagne, Crescent, Bishop, and MacKay.

Old Montréal The city was born here in 1642, down by the river at Pointe-à-Callière, and today life centers around place Jacques-Cartier, especially in summer, when the café tables line narrow terraces, and the flower sellers, itinerant artists, and strolling locals and tourists congregate here. The area is bounded on the north by rue St-Jacques, once the "Wall Street" of Montréal and still home to many banks; to the south by the river, the Old Port, and rue de la Commune; to the east by rue Berri; and to the west by rue McGill. The shops, cafés, churches, and waterfront park will keep you enthralled for hours.

St-Denis Rue St-Denis, from rue Ste-Catherine est to avenue du Mont-Royal, running from downtown to the Plateau Mont-Royal section, is the heart of Montréal's Latin Quarter, thick with cafés, bistros, and a few posh places. The café prices here are moderate to cheap—it's still a student area.

Plateau Mont-Royal Due north of the downtown area, this may be the part of Montréal where Montréalers feel most at home—away from the bustle of downtown and the heavy foot traffic of Old Montréal. Bounded by boulevard St-Joseph to the north, rue Sherbrooke to the south, avenue Papineau to the east, and rue St-Dominique to the west, it has a lively ethnic mix and an abundance of shops and restaurants converted from former warehouses.

Prince Arthur Between square St-Louis and boulevard St-Laurent to the west, and part of Plateau Mont-Royal, the five short blocks of rue Prince-Arthur est are a pedestrian street lined with Greek, Portuguese, and Vietnamese restaurants, street performers, trees, and benches. On boulevard St-Laurent you'll find more ethnic restaurants as well.

Duluth Four blocks north of rue Prince-Arthur and boulevard St-Laurent, avenue Duluth is packed with restaurants, the greatest concentration being three blocks on either side (east and west) of rue St-Denis. The mix of cuisines here is much like that on Prince Arthur.

IMPRESSIONS

While [Montréal] has a European flair which charms Americans, her carefree American attitude astonishes Europeans.
—JEAN-CLAUDE MARSAN, PREFACE TO *DISCOVER MONTREAL*, BY JOSHUA WOLFE AND CECILE GRENIER

Mont-Royal Park   Not many cities have a mountain at their core, but Montréal does; in fact, it's named for it. And you can drive, walk, or take a horse-drawn calèche to the top for a view of the city, the island, and the St. Lawrence River. The park, which encompasses the mountain, was designed by the famous American landscape architect Frederick Law Olmsted.

Chinatown   Just north of Old Montréal, south of boulevard René-Lévesque, and centered on pedestrian rues de la Gauchetière and Clark, Montréal's small Chinatown appears to be mostly restaurants and a small park, with the occasional grocery, laundry, church, and small business. For the benefit of "outsiders," most (but not all) notices are in French or English as well as Chinese. Community spirit is strong, as it's had to be to resist the bulldozers and builders of urban redevelopment, and Chinatown's inhabitants remain faithful to their ancient traditions despite the encroaching modernism all around them. The area is colorful and deserves a look, but the best Chinese restaurants are actually in other parts of the city.

The Gay Village   The Gay Village runs east along rue Ste-Catherine from rue St-Hubert to rue Papineau. A small but lively area, it is filled with clothing stores, small eateries, a bar/disco complex in a former post office building, and the Gay and Lesbian Community Centre, at 1355 rue Ste-Catherine est.

Ile Ste-Hélène/Ile Notre-Dame   Ile Ste-Hélène (St. Helen's Island) in the St. Lawrence River changed completely to become the site of Terre des Hommes for Expo '67. In the four years before Expo opened, construction crews reshaped the island and doubled its surface area, then went on to create a brand-new island right next to it, Ile Notre-Dame, since 1993 home to the Montréal Casino. Much of the earth needed to do this was dredged up from the bed of the St. Lawrence River, and 15 million tons of rock from the excavation of the Metro and the Décarie Expressway was brought in by truck. Bridges were built and 83 pavilions constructed. When Expo closed, the city government preserved the site; parts were used for Olympic Games events in 1976, and today it is home to Montréal's lively amusement park, La Ronde, which is open in the summer.

The Underground City   You can find a hotel or restaurant, do business, see a movie, attend a concert, go shopping or swimming in Montréal—all without ever setting foot outdoors. Major building complexes in the downtown area such as Place Ville-Marie, Place Bonaventure, Place Montréal Trust, Promenades de la Cathedral, Complexe Desjardins, Palais des Congrès, and Place des Arts have several underground levels, and are connected to one another or to the Metro, so you ride the long distances and walk the shorter ones. The term "Underground City" is not completely true since some complexes, such as Place Bonaventure or Complexe Desjardins, define their own spatial levels, which may have nothing to do with "ground level." Still, the "enclosed city" has obvious advantages but it covers a vast area, without the convenience of a logical street grid, and can be confusing. You'll see plenty of signs, but still expect to get lost.

2. GETTING AROUND

BY PUBLIC TRANSPORTATION

BY METRO   For speed and economy, nothing beats Montréal's Metro system. Long, modern, speedy trains whisk you through an ever-expanding network of underground tunnels for $1.75 a ride (90¢ for children). A strip of six tickets is only $7 ($3.25 for children), or only about $1.15 a ride, but with no discount passes or reduced fares for children. Buy your tickets at the ticket window of any station, then slip one into the slot in the turnstile to enter the system. Take a transfer (*correspondance*) from the machine just inside the turnstiles of every station, and this allows you to catch a bus at any other Metro station for no extra fare. But remember to take your transfer at the station where you enter the system. (If you're starting your trip by bus and plan to continue on the Metro, ask the bus driver for a transfer when you board.) Most transfers from one Metro line to another can be made at the

Berri-UQAM, Jean-Talon, and Snowdon stations. The Metro runs from about 5:30am to midnight on weekdays and until 1:30am on Friday and Saturday.

BY BUS   Buses cost the same as Metro trains, and Metro tickets are good on buses, too. If you pay the bus fare in cash, you'll need exact change. Though riding the buses is pleasant, and they run throughout the city, they aren't as frequent or as efficient as the Metro. Whenever I've waited for a bus in Montréal, I've *waited* for a bus.

BY TAXI

If you don't want to take public transportation, there are plenty of taxis representing a variety of private companies and charging $2.25 at the flag drop. Most short rides from one point to another downtown cost about $5. Tip about 15%, as in the United States. Your hotel staff can call a cab for you, or you can walk to any large hotel entry or transport terminal to get one.

BY CAR

RENTALS   Terms, cars, and prices are much like those in the United States. The large, well-known companies operate here, or have affiliates (National is represented in Canada by Tilden). Basic rates are about the same from company to company. If you don't return the car to the city where you rented it, you will probably have to pay a delivery charge.

    Budget has a convenient car-rental location in Montréal, in Central Station, 895 rue de la Gauchetière ouest (tel. 514/866-7675, or toll free 800/268-8900). Other car-rental companies include **Avis,** 1225 rue Metcalfe (tel. 514/866-7906, or toll free 800/879-2847); **Hertz,** 1475 rue Aylmer (tel. 514/842-8537, or toll free 800/263-0600); **Thrifty,** 1600 rue Berri, Suite 9 (tel. 514/845-5954, or toll free 800/367-2277); and **Tilden,** 1200 rue Stanley (tel. 514/878-2771, or toll free 800/387-4747).

GASOLINE   Gasoline and diesel fuel are sold by the gallon or the liter at prices somewhat higher than those in the U.S. If sales are by the gallon, it's the Imperial gallon that's used. One Imperial gallon equals 1.2 U.S. gallons, or 4.546 liters. Gas in Canada is expensive; it costs more than $25 to fill a tank with regular unleaded gasoline. Really. To figure the cost of Canadian gas by U.S. standards, multiply the cost per liter in Canadian dollars by 4 (I'm rounding off from the 3.78 liters that equal a U.S. gallon). Then convert the price to U.S. dollars.

PARKING   It can be tough in downtown Montréal, which gets its share of heavy traffic. There are plenty of parking meters, with varying hourly rates. Most downtown shopping complexes have underground parking lots, as do the big downtown hotels. Some of the hotels don't charge you extra to take your car in and out of the lot during the day, which can save you money if you plan to do a lot of sightseeing by car.

DRIVING RULES   The expressways in Québec are called autoroutes, and speed limits and distances are given in kilometers. Some highway signs are in French only, although Montréal's autoroutes and bridges bear lots of dual-language signs.

    It is required by law that you wear your seat belt while driving or riding in a car in Québec, and you can be fined if you disobey.

FAST MONTREAL

    American Express   Offices of the American Express Travel Service are at 1141 rue de Maisonneuve ouest (tel. 514/384-3640), and at La Baie (The Bay), 585 rue Ste-Catherine ouest, fifth floor (tel. 514/281-4777). For lost or stolen cards, call toll free 800/268-9824.

    Area Code   Montréal's area code is 514.

    Babysitters   Large hotels offer babysitting, *garderie enfants* (the Delta Montréal particularly comes to mind) as a service. In the smaller hotels and guesthouses, the management may know of someone dependable to call. Give as

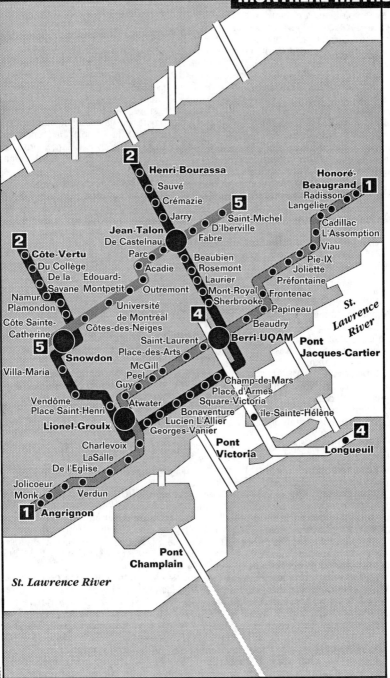

MONTREAL METRO

2 Henri-Bourassa
Sauvé
Crémazie
Jarry
5 Saint-Michel
D'Iberville
Jean-Talon
De Castelnau
Fabre
Beaubien
Parc
Rosemont
Acadie
Laurier
Edouard-
Mont-Royal
Montpetit
Sherbrooke
Outremont
Beaudry
Université
de Montréal
4
Côtes-des-Neiges

2 Côte-Vertu
Du Collège
De la
Savane
Namur
Plamondon
Côte Sainte-
Catherine
5
Villa-Maria
Snowdon
Saint-Laurent
Place-des-Arts
Berri-UQAM
McGill
Peel
Guy
Champ-de-Mars
Vendôme
Atwater
Place d'Armes
Place Saint-Henri
Square-Victoria
Bonaventure
île-Sainte-Hélène
Lionel-Groulx
Lucien L'Allier
Georges-Vanier
4 Longueuil
Charlevoix
LaSalle
De l'Eglise
Jolicoeur
Monk
Verdun
1 Angrignon

Honoré-
Beaugrand 1
Radisson
Langelier
Cadillac
L'Assomption
Viau
Pie-IX
Joliette
Préfontaine
Frontenac
Papineau

St.
Lawrence
River

Pont
Jacques-Cartier

Pont
Victoria

Pont
Champlain

St. Lawrence River

6264

much notice as possible, and be clear about rates and extra charges, such as carfare, before you make a commitment.

Bookstores Montréal has many bilingual bookstores. W. H. Smith has a store in Central Station, beneath the Queen Elizabeth Hotel (tel. 514/861-5567), with many others scattered throughout the city. Coles is centrally located downtown at 1171 St-Catherine ouest (tel. 514/849-8825), and in many other locations. For travel-related books, guidebooks, maps, and travel accessories, the place to go is Ulysses, in the Latin Quarter at 4176 rue St-Denis near Duluth (tel. 514/289-9875); near the Delta Montréal Hotel at 560 av. du Président-Kennedy (tel. 514/843-7222); and on the lower level of Ogilvy department store, on Ste-Catherine at de la Montagne (tel. 514/842-7711, ext. 362). L'Androgyne, the gay, lesbian, and feminist bookstore at 3636 bd. St-Laurent (tel. 514/842-4765), has books in French and English. Champigny, 4380 rue St-Denis (tel. 514/844-2587), is a large, primarily French-language bookstore, with a vast selection—great for French teachers and students.

Business Hours Store hours are 9am to 6pm Monday through Wednesday; 9am to 9pm on Thursday and Friday; and 9am to 5pm on Saturday. Many stores now open on Sunday from noon to 5pm. Banks are usually open weekdays from 8 or 9am to 4pm. Bars tend to open around 11:30am and go late, many until 3am.

Car Rentals See "Getting Around" in this chapter.

Climate See "When to Go" in Chapter 2.

Consulates The American Consulate-General is at 1155 Ste-Alexandre (tel. 514/398-9695). The Consulate-General of the U.K. is at 1155 University, Suite 901 (tel. 514/866-5863). Other English-speaking countries have their embassies in Ottawa.

Currency Exchange There are currency exchange offices just where you're likely to need them most: at the airport, in the train station, on place Jacques-Cartier in Old Montréal, in Infotouriste at Dorchester Square, and near Notre-Dame cathedral at 86 rue Notre-Dame. The Bank of America Canada, 1230 Peel, also offers foreign exchange services, Monday to Friday from 8:30am to 5:30pm, and Saturday from 9am to 5pm.

Doctors and Dentists Your hotel can contact a doctor quickly. If you have more time, call your consulate and ask for a recommendation. Consulates don't "guarantee" or "certify" local doctors, but consular staff may list the ones they have used with good results. Even if the consulate is closed, a duty officer should be on call to help you. For dental information, call the 24-hour hotline at 514/342-4444. In an emergency, dial 911.

Electricity Canada uses the same current as the United States and Mexico (110–120 volts, 60 cycles), with the same flat-prong plugs and sockets.

Emergencies Dial 911 for the police, firefighters, or an ambulance; for a dental emergency, call 514/342-4444.

Etiquette The magic words—excusez-moi, s'il vous plaît, and merci—work wonders here, as they do in any country. The Québécois are a polite, gracious lot; you'll hear excusez (short for excusez-moi) on the street all the time.

Hairdressers and Barbers Try Alain Charbonneau Coiffure & Maquillage, 2086 rue Drummond (tel. 514/288-5275), and ask for Silvain Limoges. Other possibilities include Institut Lise Watier, 392 Laurier ouest (tel. 514/270-9296), and Eclectic, 5133 bd. St-Laurent (tel. 514/270-9144).

Hospitals If you must contact a hospital, your hotel or consulate will undoubtedly help you out; or call Jewish General (tel. 514/340-8222), Montréal Children's (tel. 514/934-4400), Montréal General (tel. 514/937-6011), Royal Victoria (tel. 514/842-1231), or St. Mary's (tel. 514/345-3511).

Hotlines In a crisis, you can call the Sexual Assault Center 24-hour crisis line, 514/934-4604; the suicide action line, 514/723-4000; or Tel-Aide, 514/935-1101.

Information See "Tourist Information" earlier in this chapter.

Laundry and Dry Cleaning The term for dry-cleaning in French is nettoyage à sec; for laundry, it's blanchissage; and for ironing, repassage. Try T Brilotti in Central Station (tel. 514/875-5799), where you can get same-day service if you bring in your laundry by 9:30am. Tailoring is also available.

Libraries The Québec National Library (La Bibliothèque Nationale du Québec), a research facility in a striking building with stained-glass windows at 1700 rue St-Denis in the Latin Quarter, is open June to August, Monday to Friday from 9am to 5pm, September to May, Tuesday through Saturday from 9am to 5pm. It's a quiet place to read or riffle through the genealogy section if you have (or have had) relatives in this part of the world (tel. 514/873-1100).

Liquor Laws All hard liquor in Québec is sold through official government stores operated by the Québec Société des Alcools; wine and beer can be bought in grocery stores and supermarkets. The legal drinking age in the province is 18.

Lost Property If you lose something in the Metro, call 514/280-4637. If you leave something in a taxi, call the company and tell them when and where the driver picked you up.

Luggage Storage and Lockers You may check your luggage at Central Station. Most hotels and guesthouses will store luggage for you if you go on a short excursion for a day or two and don't want to carry all your belongings with you.

Mail To receive mail in Montréal, have it addressed to you, c/o Poste Restante, Station "A," Montréal, PQ, Canada; you'll go to the main post office (mentioned below) to claim it; bring valid identification.

Newspapers and Magazines Montréal's prime English-language newspaper is the *Montréal Gazette.* Most large newsstands and those in the larger hotels also carry the *Wall Street Journal,* the *New York Times, USA Today,* and the *International Herald Tribune,* as does the large bookstore Champigny, 4380 rue St-Denis. For information about current happenings in Montréal, pick up the *Gazette,* or the free monthly booklet called *Montréal Scope,* available in some shops and hotel lobbies.

Photographic Needs Always take as much film with you as you think you'll need, but if you run low, you can get more at a reasonable price at Photo Service Ltée., 222 rue Notre-Dame ouest (tel. 514/849-2291). The store, which is in Old Montréal, also carries batteries, equipment, and accessories. They do not make repairs on premises, but will send cameras out.

Police Dial 911 for the police. You'll see three types of officers in Québec: local city police in Montréal, Québec City, and other towns; Sûreté de Québec officers, like state police or rangers in the United States, patrolling the highways and countryside; and RCMP (Royal Canadian Mounted Police), who, like U.S. marshals or the FBI, handle cases involving infraction of federal laws. RCMP officers (you'll run into few of these) speak English and French. Other officers are not required to know English, though they might anyway.

Post Office Remember that all mail posted in Canada must bear Canadian (not American) stamps. The main post office is at 1250 rue University, near Ste-Catherine (tel. 514/395-4539). Hours are 8am to 6pm on weekdays. A convenient post office is in Old Montréal at 155 rue St-Jacques at Rue St-François-Xavier.

Radio For English-language FM radio, tune to CFQR (92.5), CBM (93.5), CJFM (95.9), or CHOM (97.7); a French station that plays classical music is 100.7 FM. AM stations broadcasting in English are CFCF (600), CJAD (800), CBC (940), and CKGM (980). You'll be able to pick up some American AM and FM stations.

Religious Services Most hotels, especially the larger ones, have full directories of services. Services are held at Notre-Dame Basilica, 116 Notre-Dame ouest (tel. 514/849-1070), St. Joseph's Oratory, 3800 chemin Queen Mary (tel. 514/733-8211); and Christ Church Cathedral (Anglican), 1444 av. Union (tel. 514/286-6421), among many others.

Restrooms With so many shopping complexes throughout the city, you're never far from a bathroom. If you're stuck, go into a café and buy a cup of coffee (or ask if there is a pay telephone; a toilet is usually nearby).

Safety Montréal is a safe city, but whenever you're traveling in an unfamiliar place, it pays to stay alert. Be aware of your immediate surroundings. Wear a moneybelt and keep a close eye on your possessions. Be particularly careful with cameras, purses, and wallets, all favorite targets of thieves and pickpockets.

Taxes Most goods and services in Canada are taxed 7% by the federal government. On top of that, the Province of Québec adds an additional 8% tax on goods and services, and, since summer 1992, a 4% tax on hotels. In Québec, the federal tax is called—and appears on the bill as—the TPS (in other parts of Canada, it's called the GST), and the provincial tax is known as the TVQ. Tourists may receive a rebate on both the federal and provincial tax on items they have purchased but not used in Québec, as well as on lodging. To take advantage of this, you have to fill out necessary forms (ask for them at duty-free shops and hotels) and submit them, with the original receipts, within a year of the purchase. Contact the Canadian consulate or Québec tourism office for up-to-the-minute information about taxes and rebates. And save those receipts.

Telephones and Telegrams   The telephone system, operated by Bell Canada, resembles the American system. All operators (dial "0") speak French and English, and will respond in your language as soon as you speak to them. Pay phones in Québec require 25¢ for a three-minute local call. Directory information calls (dial 411) are free. If you're having any problems, dial "0"—that's zero ("Operator"). From hotels, calls usually cost more, be they local or long distance. Directories (*annuaires des téléphones*) come in white pages (residential) and yellow pages (commercial). To send a telegram, call the 24-hour number, 514/861-7311.

Television   Montréal has two English-language channels, 6 and 12, and you can also receive some American stations with network affiliations, including CBS from Burlington, Vt. (Channel 3); NBC from Plattsburgh, N.Y. (Channel 5); and ABC from Burlington, Vt. (Channel 22).

Transit Info   Dial "AUTOBUS" (tel. 514/288-6287) for information about the Métro and city buses. For airport transportation to Dorval or Mirabel, call Autocar Connaisseur/Gray Line (tel. 514/934-1222). For the Aqua-Taxi, making stops at the Old Port, Ile Notre-Dame, Ile Ste-Hélène, and the Longueil Yacht Club, call 514/891-6533.

Useful Telephone Numbers   Alcoholics Anonymous, 514/376-9230; 24-hour pharmacy, 514/842-4915; Sexual Assault Center, 514/934-4504; Gay and Lesbian Association of UQAM, 514/987-3039; lost or stolen VISA cards, toll free 800/361-0152 (for American Express, see above); Canada Customs, 514/283-2953; U.S. Customs, 514/636-3875.

Weather   For a weather report in English, call 514/283-4005 (outside Montréal 514/636-3284). See also "When to Go" in Chapter 2.

3. NETWORKS & RESOURCES

FOR STUDENTS   You're in luck because this is a university town. You can be assured of someone with whom to speak English on the McGill campus; French-speaking and bilingual students are more likely found in the cafés along rue St-Denis. A lot of students congregate in Le St-Sulpice, 1682 rue St-Denis (tel. 514/844-9458); the Shed Café, 3515 bd. St-Laurent (tel. 514/842-0220); and Café Ciné-Lumière, 5163 bd. St-Laurent (tel. 514/495-1796). Activities of interest to students are likely to be noted in the free weeklies *Mirror* and *Hour,* both in English, and *Voir,* in French.

FOR GAY MEN & LESBIANS   There are several ways to plug into Montréal's gay scene, which is alive and well. Wander through the Gay Village along rue Ste-Catherine between rue St-Hubert and rue Papineau, where you'll pass shops, bars, a disco, restaurants, and a upscale strip joint called Campus where Monday is ladies' night (to watch). The **Gay and Lesbian Community Centre** is at 1355 rue Ste-Catherine est. Montréal's gay neighborhood used to be along upper boulevard St-Laurent, and the excellent gay, lesbian, and feminist bookstore **L'Androgyne,**

established in 1973, is still there, at 3636 bd. St-Laurent (tel. 514/842-4765); books are in French and English, and they are happy to answer travelers' questions.

FOR WOMEN The **McGill Women's Union,** in Room 423, 3480 McTavish, has drop-in hours from 10am to 4pm daily during the school year; call otherwise to see if they're open (tel. 514/398-6823). The union has a large library, information about women's services, and a space where you can share coffee with some of the women students at McGill University.

4. ACCOMMODATIONS

In Montréal's downtown hotels, you can almost always count on special discounts and package deals, especially on weekends, when the hotels' business clientele has packed their bags and gone home. If you think smaller and opt for a B&B, expect to get to know a Montréaler or two better (your hosts), to pay very little for that privilege, and to start each day with a home-cooked meal.

I've recommended my favorite B&Bs below, but if you'd like information about others, contact **Relais Montréal Hospitalité,** 3977 av. Laval, Montréal, PQ, H2W 2H9 (tel. 514/287-9635; fax 514/287-1007), or **Downtown Provincial Network Bed & Breakfast,** 2670 bd. Pie-IX, Suite 06, Montréal, PQ, H1V 2E7 (tel. 514/256-7847; fax 514/256-0543).

Happily for monolingual travelers (those firmly entrenched in the English language, that is), the staff at all the hotels and the friendly folks at the smaller hostelries are reassuringly bilingual.

In mid-July and August and during any holidays (Canadian or American), "no vacancy" signs spring up like mushrooms after a rain, so reserve in advance, especially if special rates or packages are involved. Most other times, expect to find plenty of rooms at your disposal.

Expect to pay $195 to $250 for a two people per night in a hotel designated very expensive; $145 to $195 expensive; $100 to $145 moderate; $60 to $100 inexpensive; and less than $60 budget.

Since July 1992, the provincial government has imposed a 4% tax (PST) on accommodations; add to that a 7% federal goods and services tax (GST/TPS). Unless specifically noted, *prices given here do not include federal or provincial taxes.*

DOWNTOWN
VERY EXPENSIVE

BONAVENTURE HILTON INTERNATIONAL, 1 place Bonaventure, Montréal, PQ, H5A 1E4. Tel. 514/878-2332, or toll free 800/445-8667 in the U.S., 800/268-9275 in Canada. Fax 514/878-0028. 375 rms, 18 suites. A/C MINIBAR TV TEL **Metro:** Bonaventure.

$ Rates: $155–$210 single; $179–$234 double. Weekend package $109 single or double Apr–Oct. Children of any age stay free in parents' room. AE, CB, DC, ER, MC, V. **Parking:** $12 self-parking, $19.50 valet parking.

This three-story penthouse hotel atop place Bonaventure exhibition center is particularly convenient for those attending meetings or shows in the complex. But the central location, next to Central Station and place du Canada, makes it a good choice for any visitor. The Bonaventure's lobby and reception area are on the 17th floor, along with its 2½-acre rooftop garden and outdoor pool, heated year-round. The guest rooms are modern and comfortable, with views of the garden and pool, or of the city. All the rooms have large color television sets in the bedrooms and smaller black-and-white sets in the baths. The outdoor pool is deliciously cool in summer, warm as a bath in winter. The hotel's main entrance is at de la Gauchetière and Mansfield.

Dining/Entertainment: Le Castillon is the hotel's French restaurant, open for lunch Monday through Friday and dinner nightly; its outdoor garden terrace is open during the summer. La Bourgade, a family restaurant, is open from 6:30am to 11:30pm daily; its terrace is open for dining in summer. Le Belvédère, the lobby bar and lounge, serves cocktails and light lunch, while Le Bar Soleil serves light fare and drinks poolside during the summer.

Services: In-room movies, babysitters available.

Facilities: No-smoking rooms, executive lounge and rooms, rooftop garden with heated outdoor pool; passes to a nearby downtown health club; meeting rooms.

HOTEL VOGUE, 1425 rue de la Montagne, between Maisonneuve and Ste-Catherine, Montréal, PQ, H3G 1G3. Tel. 514/285-5555, or toll free 800/465-6654. Fax 514/849-8903. 134 rms, 20 suites. A/C MINIBAR TV TEL **Metro:** Peel.

$ Rates: $175 single; $195 double; from $350 suite. Extra person $20. Children under 16 stay free. Weekend rate $125 per night ($20 more with continental breakfast), single or double, on availability. AE, CB, DC, ER, MC, V. **Parking:** Indoor, valet, $15.

The Hôtel Vogue has been creating a stir since it opened in late 1990. For starters, it's stunning, from the lobby to the guest rooms. The elegant rooms feature king- or queen-size beds with feather pillows and duvets, fresh flowers, umbrella, furniture made of cherrywood, a fax, a briefcase-size safe, and a large bath with Mexican marble, separate shower, Jacuzzi, telephone, and TV.

Dining/Entertainment: Société Café serves international cuisine and three meals a day; there's piano music Thursday through Saturday in the lobby bar, L'Opéra, as well as in the restaurant.

Services: In-room movies, large electronic in-room safe, robes, hairdryer, bathroom scale, 24-hour room service, babysitters available, fax machine in each room.

Facilities: Small exercise room, meeting facilities.

WESTIN MONT-ROYAL, 1050 Sherbrooke ouest, Montréal, PQ, H3A 2R6. Tel. 514/284-1110, or toll free 800/268-6282 in Canada, 800/332-3442 in the U.S. Fax 514/845-3025. 300 rms, 27 suites. A/C MINIBAR TV TEL **Metro:** Peel.

$ Rates: $180–$225 single; $205–$250 double; from $360 suite. Extra person $25; children under 18 stay free with parents or in an adjoining room for $75. Upgrade to a suite $25 on availability. Weekend rates and special packages. AE, CB, DC, ER, MC, V. **Parking:** $11 self-park, $19 valet.

AN IMPORTANT NOTE ON PRICES

Unless stated otherwise, **the prices cited in this guide are given in Canadian dollars,** which is good news for you because the Canadian dollar is worth 25% less than the American dollar, but buys nearly as much. As we go to press, $1 Canadian is worth 75¢ U.S., which means that your $100-a-night hotel room will cost only U.S. $75, and your $6 breakfast costs only U.S. $4.50. Here's a quick table of equivalents:

Canadian $	U.S. $
$ 1	$ 0.75
5	3.75
10	7.50
20	15.00
50	37.50
80	60.00
100	75.00
200	150.00

The Westin Mont-Royal, in the heart of downtown at Sherbrooke and Peel, provides a quality of service unsurpassed in the city, with a staff that simply dotes on its guests. Add to that important plus an inviting lobby and a proliferation of plants and flowers, and large, well-lit rooms (the furnishings are a tad dated), with terrycloth robes for guests' use and an in-room safe-deposit box. Bathrooms feature a hairdryer, a retractable clothesline over the tub, and incandescent lighting. The most comfortable bed I've ever slept on was in my room at the Four Seasons. Particularly impressive, the extensive health club serves coffee and juice in the morning and even supplies workout clothes or a swimsuit free of charge if you've forgotten yours. The heated outdoor lap pool is open year-round.

Dining/Entertainment: The pleasant Le Cercle features French cuisine, with some bows to Italy and California, and serves three meals a day, including Saturday brunch and an alternative low-calorie, low-cholesterol menu. Zen, the hotel's upscale Chinese restaurant, offers lunch, dinner, and the perennially popular "Zen Experience," where you can order anything from a 40-item sampler for only $19.95. In the lobby, hot and cold buffet breakfasts and lunches are served in the piano bar, L'Apéro, which features music in the evenings.

Services: 24-hour concierge and room service, housekeeping twice a day, valet parking, in-room movies, complimentary overnight shoeshine, massage, car and limo rentals, business services.

Facilities: Health club with exercise classes, whirlpool, sauna, and outdoor heated lap pool; 12 no-smoking floors; meeting rooms; boutiques.

RITZ-CARLTON KEMPINSKI MONTREAL, 1228 Sherbrooke ouest (at the corner of Drummond), Montréal, PQ, H3G 1H6. Tel. 514/842-4212, or toll free 800/363-0366. Fax 514/842-3383. 185 rms, 45 suites. A/C MINIBAR TV TEL **Metro:** Peel.

$ Rates: $185–$215 single; $220–$250 double; from $350 suite. Children under 14 stay free in parents' room. Packages available. AE, CB, DC, ER, MC, V.
Parking: $15 self or valet, with in/out privileges.

In 1912, the Ritz-Carlton opened its doors to the carriage trade, and over the years the clientele has remained faithful. Carriages gave way to Pierce-Arrows, and those in turn gave way to Rolls-Royces and Lamborghinis. You'll always see a few of these (or at least a Cadillac limo or custom-built Lincoln) parked in readiness near the front door. Svelte beauties and silver-haired tycoons move easily through the classic elegance of gilt trim and crystal-and-brass sconces of the Palm Court, reminiscent of Victoria's reign, and in fine weather, in the garden complete with duck pond. Rooms are elegantly decorated, with bathrobes and umbrellas supplied for guests during their visit. Baths are equipped with hairdryers and makeup mirrors. The Ritz is only a few blocks from the boutiques of Crescent and Sherbrooke Streets and the big downtown department stores. A bit of trivia: Elizabeth Taylor and Richard Burton married at the Ritz in 1964, recruiting a staff member to be a witness. The management also fitted out the Royal Suite so that Sophia Loren could cook her own pasta here.

Dining/Entertainment: The Ritz's Café de Paris is well known for its Sunday brunch, power breakfasts during the week, and a wine cellar that has been building its stock for three-quarters of a century. Meals are served in Le Jardin du Ritz garden restaurant in summer. There's piano music nightly in the pleasant Ritz Bar adjacent to Café de Paris. Le Grand Prix bar also has piano music, with dancing nightly.

Services: Concierge; 24-hour room service; free in-room movies; hairdryer, makeup mirror and scale in rooms; overnight shoeshine; laundry and valet; babysitting.

Facilities: Newsstand, gift shop, barbershop, meeting rooms; access to tennis and golf.

EXPENSIVE

LE CENTRE SHERATON, 1201 bd. René-Lévesque ouest (between Drummond and Stanley), Montréal, PQ, H3B 2L7. Tel. 514/878-2000, or toll free 800/325-3535. Fax 514/878-2305. 826 rms, 22 suites. A/C TV TEL **Metro:** Bonaventure or Peel.

FROMMER'S SMART TRAVELER: HOTELS

VALUE-CONSCIOUS TRAVELERS SHOULD TAKE ADVANTAGE OF THE FOLLOWING:

1. Special rates and packages. Very few people staying in a large, moderately priced or high-priced hotel pay the so-called rack rates (the prices charged someone who just walks in off the street and asks for a room). Always ask about discounts.
2. Lower weekend rates. Many of the larger hotels drop their rates on weekends—usually Friday, Saturday, and Sunday nights—when their business clientele have gone home.
3. Business discounts. Even if you're on vacation, show your business card and see if you can get a corporate rate.
4. Family rates. In some hotels, a family of four is given a room at the normal double-room price; that is, kids stay for free. Age limits vary from up to 12 years to about 18 years old.
5. If you plan to use hotel parking but need to take your car in and out of the garage a lot during the day, choose a hotel that will not charge you extra to do so.
6. A bed-and-breakfast accommodation. Montréal has some inviting ones, including one in Old Montréal, where rooms have private baths.
7. If you're really strapped for cash, don't overlook the YWCA and the YMCA; both are centrally located and reasonably priced.

QUESTIONS TO ASK IF YOU'RE ON A BUDGET:

1. Is there a surcharge for local or long-distance telephone calls made from the room?
2. Is breakfast included in the price? If so, is it buffet style, so that you can eat as much as you like?
3. Are complimentary services such as airport pickup or parking included in the price?

$ Rates: $155 single or double; from $275 suite. Extra person $20. Children under 17 stay free. Weekend rates available. AE, CB, DC, DISC, ER, MC, V. **Parking:** $9, with in/out privileges; $10 valet.

Altogether a pleasant place, from the reception area to the lounges to the rooms, Le Centre Sheraton rises to lofty heights near Central Station, a few steps off Dorchester Square. Despite the central location, it manages to be a quiet place, and the lobby's high glass wall transforms it into an immense greenhouse, big enough to shelter two royal palm trees and plenty of plants. And whichever room you choose, you'll find a bath with ample counter space, which is always a plus. Half the rooms have minibars.

Dining/Entertainment: The hotel has two restaurants; the Boulevard serves three meals a day; the Musette, breakfast and lunch only. Traditional and light jazz and blues are performed Tuesday through Saturday evenings in the Impromptu Bar. La Croisette Lounge, in the plant-filled lobby, makes a pleasant meeting spot.

Services: 24-hour room service, coffee- and tea-making facilities, in-room movies.

Facilities: No-smoking floors, pool, gym, sauna, executive (32nd) floor, meeting rooms.

HOTEL MERIDIEN, 4 Complexe Desjardins, C.P. 130, Montréal, PQ, H5B 1E5. Tel. 514/285-1450, or toll free 800/543-4300. Fax 514/285-1243. 550 rms, 50 suites. A/C MINIBAR TV TEL **Metro:** Place des Arts.

$ Rates: $150–$170 single during the week; $170–$190 double during the week;

from $285 suite. Extra person $25. Children under 18 stay free in parents' room. Packages available. AE, DC, DISC, ER, MC, V. **Parking:** Self, $9; valet, $15.

Air France's Montréal hostelry, the Hotel Méridien, is an integral part of the striking the Complexe Desjardins, with its gray rough brick facade with plants spilling over the sides. Rooms, decorated in tones of mauve, sand, sea green, and gray, are comfortable, though baths are on the small side. A glass-enclosed elevator glides from the foyer down to the various levels of the complex while others whiz up and down the dozen floors. From its foyer you can gaze down on the complex's active plaza. For diversion, Place des Arts and the Montréal Museum of Contemporary Art are right across the street. The haunts of Montréal's Chinatown are on the next block, and the downtown shopping district, Old Montréal, and the ethnic neighborhoods are each about a 15-minute walk away. The hotel's entrance is at Jeanne Mance at Ste-Catherine.

Dining/Entertainment: Café Fleuri brasserie serves three meals a day and Sunday brunch. Le Club, a French gourmet restaurant, serves lunch and dinner. L'Eté des Indiem is a café on the lower level open for lunch only. Le Bar is a piano bar overlooking Complexe Desjardins with entertainment nightly.

Services: In-room movies, massage.

Facilities: Glass-enclosed swimming pool and sun deck; Jacuzzi; no-smoking rooms; public sitting areas on each floor.

QUEEN ELIZABETH, 900 bd. René-Lévesque ouest (corner of Mansfield), Montréal, PQ, H3B 4A5. Tel. 514/861-3511, or toll free 800/828-7447 in the U.S., 800/268-9411 in Canada. Fax 514/954-2256. 1,046 rms, 60 suites. A/C MINIBAR TV TEL **Metro:** Bonaventure.

$ Rates: $140–$161 single; $166–$187 double; concierge-level rates, about $50 higher; from $310 suite. Various discounts, and weekend and excursion packages available. Children 18 and under stay free in parents' room. AE, CB, DC, DISC, ER, MC, V. **Parking:** Indoor, $12.

Montréal's largest hotel, which stands beside another queen (Mary Queen of the World cathedral), has been providing quality accommodations and impressive service since 1958. Popular with conventiongoers, business folk, and vacationers alike, the recently renovated 21-floor hotel has an enviable location on top of VIA Rail's Central Station, with place Ville-Marie, place Bonaventure, place du Canada, and the Métro all accessible by underground arcades, and Dorchester Square a short stroll away. The Queen Elizabeth has hosted its share of celebrities, among them Nat King Cole, Carol Channing, and John Lennon and Yoko Ono. Lennon taped "Give Peace a Chance" in Suite 1742, as the photographs on the wall attest. Request a room with a view of the cathedral.

Dining/Entertainment: The hotel claims one of Montréal's most venerable restaurants, the Beaver Club, which serves lunch, dinner, and Sunday brunch, and features a three-piece orchestra on Saturday nights. The Montréalais bistro/bar also serves three meals a day, including a table d'hôte lunch, and Sunday brunch; it's the setting for a fashion show with high tea the first Tuesday of the month from 3:30 to 5pm. Les Voyageurs bar, adjacent to the Beaver Club, serves lunch Monday through Friday and has live piano music nightly from 5pm to midnight. Le Golden Hind serves curry specials Monday through Friday for lunch and dinner.

Services: Concierge, 24-hour room service, in-room movies, outstanding executive floor with a warm, accommodating staff and a beautiful lounge with a fireplace and incredible views of the city.

Facilities: No-smoking floors; small health club; lobby shops; business center, business and executive floors, meeting rooms; video checkout.

MODERATE

LE CANTLIE SHERBROOKE, 1110 rue Sherbrooke ouest (at Peel), Montréal, PQ, H3A 1G9. Tel. 514/842-2000, or toll free 800/567-1110. Fax 514/844-7808. 95 rms, 82 suites. A/C TV TEL **Metro:** Peel.

$ Rates: $89–$99 single; $99 double; from $99 suite. Extra person $25. Children under 12 stay free. Weekly and monthly rates available. AE, CB, DC, ER, MC, V. **Parking:** $8 per day, much less per month.

A neighbor to the Ritz-Carlton, this apartment-building-turned-hotel with its discreet green awning offers a prime location at lower-than-expected prices. Furnishings are restful, and the rooftop pool (open in summer only) offers a glorious view; the hotel opened a fitness center in spring 1993. The lobby is welcoming, and there's a terrace café in spring and summer. The standard studio has plenty of room, and the accommodations get even bigger as the prices go up. For stays of a few days only, there is daily housekeeping; for longer stays, on weekdays only, which keeps the prices down.

HOLIDAY INN CROWNE PLAZA DOWNTOWN, 420 Sherbrooke ouest (at av. du Parc), Montréal, PQ, H3A 1B4. Tel. 514/842-6111, or toll free 800/HOLIDAY. Fax 514/842-9381. 486 rms. A/C MINIBAR TV TEL **Metro:** Place des Arts, one block south.

$ Rates: $89–$130 single; $104–$145 double. Spouses free. Children under 19 stay free with parents. Extra person $15. Summer and family packages represent savings of $20–$50. AE, CB, DC, ER, MC, V. **Parking:** Underground, $10.

With a good central location, this hotel (don't confuse it with the similarly named Holiday Inn Crowne Plaza Métro Centre) could easily represent the city's best bargain: Spouses stay for free, as do two children under age 18. Kids younger than 12 get to eat for free, too, and there's no charge for in-room movies. The guest rooms all have city views, attractive furnishings, and a king-size or two double beds. The sink is separate from the bath, which is small.

Dining/Entertainment: Les Verriers restaurant serves lunch weekdays and dinner nightly (continental cuisine), and Café Les Verriers serves a buffet brunch on weekends. The hotel has two bars, one with a pool table.

Services: Room service 7am to 11pm, free in-room movies, washers and dryers for guests' use (for a small charge), dry cleaning, hairdresser.

Facilities: No-smoking floors, a large indoor pool, saunas, whirlpool, and exercise facilities; shops; executive floors, meeting rooms.

HOTEL CHATEAU VERSAILLES, 1659 rue Sherbrooke ouest (at St-Mathieu), Montréal, PQ, H3H 1E3. Tel. 514/933-3611, or toll free 800/361-7199 in Canada, 800/361-3664 in the continental U.S. Fax 514/933-7102. 70 rms. A/C TV TEL **Metro:** Guy, two blocks away. **Bus:** No. 24, half a block away.

$ Rates: $95 single; $145 double. Extra person $15; children 16 and under, no charge. Special weekend rates Nov–May, and summer packages. AE, CB, DC, ER, MC, V. **Parking:** Valet, $8.50.

Montréal's Hôtel Château Versailles has a unique reputation among the city's fine hostelries. For many years it has been the place to stay for visitors who wanted dignified accommodations and service at rates just at the top of the moderate price scale. Although its owners, the Villeneuve family, began the establishment as a European-style pension in 1958, it has grown and absorbed four fine old stone houses with comfortably furnished guest rooms, some with minibars. Expect high-class hotel amenities: bellhop, color TV, private bath—but with personalized treatment. Breakfast and afternoon tea are served in a small dining room with a fireplace displaying the original Delft tiles and handmade quilts on the walls (Madame Villeneuve is a quilter). And there's a bulletin board to keep you up-to-date on what's happening in the city. The Château Versailles is one-of-a-kind in Montréal, so reserve a month in advance to be assured of getting a room. If you prefer a modern hotel with more upscale rooms, they also offer La Tour Versailles at the same prices, right across the street. Here, the rooms have sea-foam green and mauve decor with curtains and bedspreads in a grape-arbor motif, Shaker furniture, desks, Italian marble bathrooms, minibars, and safes. There are two no-smoking floors and a French restaurant, and laptops and fax are available on request.

HOTEL DELTA MONTREAL, 450 Sherbrooke ouest, Montréal, PQ, H3A 2T4. Tel. 514/286-1986, or toll free 800/877-1133. Fax 514/284-4306. 483 rms, 6 suites. A/C MINIBAR TV TEL **Metro:** Place des Arts.

$ Rates: $115 single or double; from $250 suite. Weekend rates from $99. Children under 18 stay free in parents' room, and children under 6 eat for free. AE, ER, MC, V. **Parking:** $9.50.

⭐ One thing guests who stay here all seem to have in common is that they all look like they're having a good time. What you'll find in the Delta is a fun hotel with a young staff that goes out of their way to make you feel welcome. Part of a Canadian hotel chain, the Delta represents comfort, value-for-money, and style (dark wood, gleaming brass, and glinting crystal greet you in the lobby). Rooms are handsomely appointed and airy, with interesting angles, one king-size bed or two double beds, and Milton Avery prints; most have a small balcony. The bathrooms are well lit and have good counter space. Enter the 23-story tower from Sherbrooke or avenue du Président-Kennedy (the sole entrance after 10:30pm), at rue City Councillors.

Dining/Entertainment: The Bouquet café serves breakfast, lunch, and dinner, while Le Cordial lounge serves a buffet lunch and has piano music nightly. Opposite Le Bouquet is a comfortable nook for guests with several desks and lots of newspapers.

Services: Shoeshine, complimentary coffee and tea; 24-hour room service.

Facilities: A fitness club with exercise room, whirlpool, sauna, lap pool, outdoor pool, and two squash courts; massage; aerobics classes; a bright and cheerful Children's Creative and Activity Centre, a supervised play area equipped with games, toys, and things to make and do; electronic-games room.

L'APPARTEMENT, 455 Sherbrooke ouest, Montréal, PQ, H3A 1B7. Tel. 514/284-3634, or toll free 800/363-3010. Fax 514/287-1431. 126 apts. A/C TV TEL **Metro:** Place des Arts.

$ Rates: $82.50–$129.50 apartment by the day, depending upon size. By the week, prices are 25% lower; by the month, 44% lower. AE, CB, DC, ER, MC, V. **Parking:** Indoor, $11.50; for a week to 27 days, $8 a day.

 As you might have guessed, L'Appartement is an apartment hotel. Accommodations range in size from small one-room studios to spacious three-room apartments, each with kitchenette, full bath, and balcony. Guests may use the hotel's glass-enclosed rooftop swimming pool, washer and dryer, and sauna. Housekeeping service is provided Monday through Friday, and same-day dry cleaning is available. The rooms are pleasant, but the small lobby is almost an afterthought. A handy, large drugstore is on the ground floor. It represents great savings if you stay a week.

MANOIR LE MOYNE APARTMENT HOTEL, 2100 Maisonneuve ouest, Montréal, PQ, H3H 1K6. Tel. 514/931-8861, or toll free 800/361-7191. Fax 514/931-7726. 42 studios, 220 suites. A/C TV TEL **Metro:** Atwater.

$ Rates: $72–$115 single; $80–$125 double. Weekend rates $59–$85 single or double, subject to availability. Two children under 18 stay free with parents. Weekly and monthly rates available. AE, DC, DISC, ER, MC, V. **Parking:** Indoor or outdoor, $8, on availability.

The unprepossessing Manoir Le Moyne is two blocks from Montréal's Forum concert and sports hall, and a cab ride or short drive west of the center of town. The accommodations, most with balconies, offer pleasant furnishings in mauve and gray, cable color television with sports and cable-news networks, complimentary coffee- and tea-making facilities, and refrigerators in fully equipped kitchenettes. Most rooms have queen-size beds. The studios are comfortable for one person, the suites (either mid-size or large) better for two people. There's also a pub-style restaurant with a summer terrace, exercise room, a large whirlpool, men's and women's saunas, and daily housekeeping. This is a good choice for families and for anyone else longing for the comforts of home. It does help to have a car if you stay here, even though parking is limited. Reserve ahead: It often serves as a home-away-from-home for business travelers.

INEXPENSIVE

HOTEL ARCADE, 50 bd. René-Lévesque ouest (at Clark), Montréal, PQ, H2Z 1A2. Tel. 514/874-9090, or toll free 800/363-6535. Fax 514/874-0907. 242 rms. A/C TV TEL **Metro:** Place d'Armes.

$ Rates: $72 single or double. Extra person $7. Children under 12 stay free. AE, CB, DC, DISC, ER, MC, V. **Parking:** $10 per day.

Ⓕ FROMMER'S COOL FOR KIDS: HOTELS

Delta Montréal *(see p. 226)* The Activity Centre for supervised play and crafts-making is a big draw for small kids, along with the swimming pool and (for bigger kids) an electronic-games room.

Holiday Inn Crowne Plaza Downtown *(see p. 226)* Two kids under 18 stay free with parents, kids under 12 get to eat for free, and everyone gets to enjoy free in-room movies and the big swimming pool; special packages for families.

Jardin d'Antoine *(see p. 228)* Some rooms open onto the pleasant patio garden, where kids are welcome to play; all rooms have private baths, and breakfast is included in the price. The live-in owners have a child, too.

L'Appartement *(see p. 227)* The glass-enclosed rooftop pool is the big attraction here, and the kitchenette in the room comes in handy.

Manoir Le Moyne *(see p. 227)* Kids and their folks have to flip a coin to see who gets the loft bed and who sleeps downstairs in these split-level accommodations. There's also cable TV and free in-room movies.

YMCA *(see p. 229)* It has three family rooms, a cafeteria that serves three meals a day, and a big indoor pool that guests may use.

Ⓢ First on the list of the New Wave budget hotels is the attractive and quite modern Hôtel Arcade, part of a successful European chain. Catercorner to the Complexe Desjardins, around the corner from the Palais des Congrès, and midway between east and west Montréal, the hotel has a convenient location. Its guest rooms are small but clean and bright, with single or twin beds (some rooms have up to four beds), cable color TV with remote control, and a tiled shower with convenient counter space. Plastic card-keys unlock the doors. Hallways are cheerful, and the attractive lobby has a small bar with kites hanging from the ceiling. The little restaurant one flight up serves lunch and dinner daily, and the lobby bar is open from 10am to 2pm. There are two no-smoking floors. The hotel is around the corner from Chinatown and a 10-minute stroll from Old Montréal.

HOTEL LORD BERRI, 1199 rue Berri, Montréal, PQ, H2L 4C6. Tel. 514/845-9236, or toll free 800/363-0363. Fax 514/849-9855. 148 rms, 6 junior suites. A/C TV TEL **Metro:** Berri-UQAM.
$ Rates: May to mid-Oct $82.50 single or double, $129.50 suite; off-season $75.50 single or double, $109.50 suite. Extra person $7. AE, CB, DC, DISC, ER, MC, V.
Parking: Next door, outdoor, $10 per day, with unlimited access.

★ A congenial place that is popular with Americans, the Hôtel Lord Berri, located between boulevard René-Lévesque and rue Ste-Catherine, is just a few blocks from the lively cafés of St-Denis and a five-minute walk from Old Montréal. It has a friendly staff, a pretty little lobby, and an Italian restaurant with a sidewalk terrace. Rooms have full baths and are equipped with color television sets connected for in-room movies. The decor and lighting in the rooms are on the dull side, but the location, staff, and ambience make up for it. Several floors are set aside for nonsmokers.

LE JARDIN D'ANTOINE, 2024 rue St-Denis, Montréal, PQ, H2X 3K7. Tel. 514/843-4506. Fax 514/281-1491. 14 rms. A/C TV TEL **Metro:** Berri-UQAM or Sherbrooke.

$ Rates (including full breakfast): May–Oct $64–$74 single, $69–$79 double; about $10 less off-season. Extra person $10. AE, MC, V. **Parking:** Not available. In the heart of the Latin Quarter near some wonderful restaurants, and more upscale than the other small inns you'll find along rue St-Denis, this bed-and-breakfast has no two rooms alike. Most have brick walls, a brass or oak bed, and old-fashioned ambience. All the rooms have a private bath, and the larger (more expensive) ones have a tub. There's a patio garden for guests' use. Pierre Giardina and his wife, Francine Gaudreault, are the friendly hosts. They have a daughter and welcome children here.

BUDGET

CASTEL ST-DENIS, 2099 rue St-Denis, Montréal, PQ, H2X 3K8. Tel. 514/842-9719. Fax 514/281-0065. 18 rms (about half with shower). A/C TV **Metro:** Berri-UQAM or Sherbrooke.

$ Rates: $45 single; $50 double; $10 less without private shower. Extra person $10. MC, V. **Parking:** Not available.

Among the inexpensive tourist lodges in Montréal's Latin Quarter, the Castel St-Denis is among the best. It's midway between square St-Louis and the café-filled lower reaches of the street, and two long blocks from the Terminus Voyageur. Most of the rooms are fairly quiet, and all are tidy and simply decorated. The higher-priced rooms have private shower, air conditioning, and cable color television. Friendly, bilingual owner Anne Marie Imam, originally from France, is knowledgeable about local restaurants and attractions. The Castel St-Denis is just about equidistant from the Berri-UQAM and Sherbrooke Metro stations, but if you get off at Sherbrooke you'll be walking downhill to get to the Castel—an important consideration if you are carrying luggage.

YMCA, 1450 rue Stanley (between de Maisonneuve and Ste-Catherine), Montréal, PQ, H3A 2W6. Tel. 514/849-8393. Fax 514/849-8017. 331 rms (4 with shower). TV TEL **Metro:** Peel.

$ Rates: $30–$33 single without bath, $44 single with bath and telephone; $48 double without bath, $54 double with bath and telephone; $66 quad. Students with ID and seniors over 60 get a $2 reduction. AE, MC, V. **Parking:** Not available.

The centrally located YMCA has rooms in an assortment of configurations, all with color TV. It has three rooms that accommodate four people, perfect for families. The cafeteria serves breakfast, lunch, and dinner. Guests may use the 82-foot indoor pool and jogging track for free. Reserve ahead. There's no curfew.

YWCA, 1355 bd. René-Lévesque ouest (at rue Crescent), Montréal, PQ, H3G 1T3. Tel. 514/866-9941. Fax 514/866-4866. 150 rms (3 with bath). **Metro:** Lucien-L'Allier.

$ Rates: $30 single without bath, $40 single with semiprivate bath, $45 single with private bath; $50 double without bath, $54 double with semiprivate bath. Weekly rates available. MC, V. **Parking:** A lot across the street gives discounts.

Rooms at the attractive YWCA provide comfortable lodging for women only, and their children (boys to about age 8). Guests may use the recreation room, pool, sauna, and fitness classes at no additional charge. There is a thrift shop on the ground floor. Reservations are accepted, but be aware that many of this Y's rooms are rented to students during the school year. Concordia University is in this area, and its Fine Arts Building is right across the street. There's no curfew. The popular restaurants along Crescent Street are within walking distance.

OLD MONTREAL

EXPENSIVE

HOTEL INTER-CONTINENTAL, 360 rue St-Antoine ouest, Montréal, PQ, H2Y 3X4. Tel. 514/987-9900, or toll free 800/327-0200. Fax 514/987-9904. 336 rms, 23 suites. A/C MINIBAR TV TEL **Metro:** Square Victoria.

$ Rates: $170–$185 single or double; from $325 suite. Packages available. AE, CB, DC, ER, MC, V. **Parking:** indoor valet, $15.

★ This striking new addition to the downtown hotel scene and an integral part of Montréal's new World Trade Centre opened in mid-1991. A commingling of old and new, its new hotel tower houses the sleek reception area and guest rooms, while the restored annex, the Nordheimer building (1888), houses meeting rooms and some of the hotel's restaurants and bars. Guest rooms—the prettiest in the city, I think—are quiet, well lit, and decorated in soft greens, cream, and sienna. Local art, including photographs and lithographs, graces the walls. The turret suites are particularly fun, with round bedrooms with wraparound windows. Baths are of gray and green marble, with a separate glass-enclosed shower. All rooms have two or three telephones. Some of the architectural touches in the new tower discreetly echo those from the elaborate Nordheimer building, with its extensive use of tiles and its early-19th-century vaults. The Inter-Continental is only a few minutes' walk from Notre-Dame cathedral.

Dining/Entertainment: In the new tower is the main dining room, Les Continents, which serves breakfast, lunch, and dinner, and international cuisine; and Chrystallin, a popular lobby-level piano bar, with music nightly. In the Nordheimer building, on street level, is congenial Chez Plume, popular for lunch and after work with Montréalers and out-of-towners alike.

Services: Concierge on duty 24 hours, 24-hour room service, robes and umbrellas supplied for guests, same-day laundry/valet Monday through Friday, overnight shoeshine, weekday complimentary newspaper, in-room movies, seamstress, massage, hairdresser, express checkout.

Facilities: Four no-smoking floors, health club with small, enclosed rooftop pool, sauna and steamrooms, massage, weight and aerobics room; rooftop garden; business center, executive floor and lounge, meeting rooms.

INEXPENSIVE

LES PASSANTS DU SANS SOUCY, 171 rue St-Paul ouest, Montréal, PQ, H2Y 1Z5. Tel. 514/842-2634. Fax 514/842-2912. 9 rms (all with bath). A/C TV TEL **Metro:** Place d'Armes.

$ Rates (including full breakfast): $85–$100 single or double; $100 suite. Extra person $10. AE, ER, MC, V. **Parking:** Outdoor, free on weekends, $7.50 Mon–Fri.

★ Even if Les Passants du Sans Soucy weren't the only bed-and-breakfast in Old Montréal, it would still be the best. The elegant entry, an unusual combination of marble floors and exposed brick and beams, doubles as gallery, displaying the works of local artists. Behind the entry lies a sitting area and a cozy breakfast nook with a skylight. Nine pretty guest rooms are upstairs, and each has stucco-and-rock walls, fresh flowers, lace curtains, and wrought-iron or brass beds. Room 203 is a quiet double in the back of the house; no. 102, in the front, is a little larger with a couch. Bilingual owners Daniel Soucy and Michael Banks have lovingly converted the 1723 building, and they go to great lengths to make your stay in it memorable. The hospitality and the location, eight blocks from place Jacques-Cartier, not to mention the hearty breakfasts, particularly the chocolate croissants and café au lait, can't be beat.

PLATEAU MONT-ROYAL

MODERATE

AUBERGE DE LA FONTAINE, 1301 rue Rachel est (at Chambord), Montreal, PQ, H2J 2K1. Tel. 514/597-0166, or toll free 800/565-5455, ext. 100. Fax 514/597-0496. 21 rms. A/C TV TEL **Metro:** Mont-Royal or Sherbrooke.

$ Rates (including buffet breakfast): $89–$125 single; $105–$140 double; $175 suite with whirlpool bath. Extra person, children included, charged $15. AE, ER, MC, V. **Parking:** Free, in back of the inn or on the street.

For those who like to be in a city but not be reminded of it, Auberge de la Fontaine is idyllically situated opposite pretty Lafontaine Park, where you may jog, bike, play tennis, stroll the promenade, and enjoy free concerts in summer. The inn has modern rooms, all with private bath, toiletries, hairdryers, brick walls, and restful decor. Those in the new section are roomier; units in back are quieter. A bulletin board near the dining room/TV lounge fills you in on what's happening in Montréal. Guests may use the terrace on the third floor, as well as a small kitchen that's kept stocked with complimentary cookies, tea, and juice just for them and a microwave they can use.

INEXPENSIVE

MAISON DE GRAND-PRE, 4660 rue de Grand-Pré, Montréal, PQ, H2T 2H7. Tel. 514/843-6458. 5 rms (none with bath), 1 apt. **Metro:** Laurier, two blocks away (St. Joseph exit; last car of train).
$ Rates (including full breakfast): $45 single; $65 double; 10% off for stays over five days. No credit cards. **Parking:** On street only.

Tucked a block off rue St-Denis, the Maison de Grand-Pré is a memorable stop on any traveler's journey, thanks to the efforts of owner Jean-Paul Lauzon. The house, built around 1865, is set back from the street and has dormer windows, two balconies, and a small frontyard with maples in it. There's a small park in back. Inside, you'll find painted wood floors and five bedrooms: four double (the Blue Room is my favorite) and one single. They share two large baths with old-fashioned tubs. Guests have the use of a small reading room upstairs, and downstairs, a large lounge with a freestanding fireplace and a TV; they may use the telephone for local calls at no charge. M. Lauzon also has an apartment with a kitchen and bath available for families. Rates include a big breakfast with hot bread from nearby bakeries, fresh fruit, homemade crêpes with maple syrup, and (if you like) French toast, omelets, and espresso. The congenial bilingual host makes a point of getting to know his guests, serving them afternoon tea and cookies in the lounge and recommending local restaurants, which he visits twice a year. He also rents bicycles. The house is between rue Mont-Royal and rue St-Joseph.

4. DINING

No one's done an exact count, but Montréal is thought to have at least 5,000 restaurants, large and small, representing 75 international cuisines. No wonder the city's citizens love to dine out.

For a visitor, finding your way through this culinary kaleidoscope can be exhilarating, bewildering, and exhausting, not to mention fattening. So here are some suggestions, by no means complete or inclusive, of some of the places I like best. As an added resource, pick up a copy of the Greater Montréal Convention and Tourism Bureau's helpful *Restaurant Guide*.

Happily, many good restaurants are often clustered in one neighborhood or along one street, such as rue Crescent, St-Denis, or St-Laurent. Eating out can be expensive in Québec, since a hefty 15% tax is added to the bill (7% federal tax and 8% provincial tax), and then there's the tip, another 15% or so. All have menus posted outside, so do some culinary and budgetary comparison shopping before deciding.

It's a good idea, and in Montréal an expected courtesy, to make a reservation if you want to dine at one of the city's top restaurants. If your hotel has a concierge, that person will be happy to make the reservation for you. It's looked upon as bad form to come late or not at all, so if you can't make it, call and cancel. Proper dress is required in the top establishments, even at lunchtime.

What about those times when "cuisine" is the last thing on your mind and all you want is a good, quick meal that will barely make a dent in your pocketbook? Montréal won't disappoint in this respect, either. The traditional French quick-lunch *casse-croûte* (it means "break a crust") establishments are actually short-order places, complete with lunch counter and rows of chrome-plated stools, and they're all over town (I counted 75 in the Montréal telephone directory). Steamed hot dogs (also called chiens chauds) are a staple here, along with plates of feves au lard (pork and beans), and frites (french fries, served with cider vinegar or ketchup). Prices are low—figure less than $5 for a hot dog, trimmings, and a soft drink—and service is quick. You'll also find plenty of places that serve sandwiches for only a few dollars and a lunch special for $8 or less.

For your convenience, the restaurants recommended below have been categorized by neighborhood and then by price. The category is determined by the price range of the main courses served at dinner: $25 to $35, very expensive; $20 to $25, expensive; $12 to $20, moderate; $8 to $12, inexpensive; and less than $8, budget.

Prices do not include the tax (food that you buy in a market or grocery store is not taxed).

Since parking space is at a premium in Montréal, take the Metro to the restaurant (most are within a block or two of a Metro station), or a bus or taxi, to allow more time for dining—and to ensure that you arrive in a good mood.

DOWNTOWN
VERY EXPENSIVE

LES HALLES, 1450 rue Crescent between Ste-Catherine and de Maisonneuve. Tel. 514/844-2328.
   Cuisine: FRENCH. **Reservations:** Recommended. **Metro:** Guy-Concordia or Peel. **Parking:** Next door.
   $ Prices: Appetizers $2.50–$6.50 at lunch, $9.75–$14.75 at dinner; main courses $9–$14 at lunch, $20–$32 at dinner; three-course table d'hôte $27.50, four-course table d'hôte $39.95. AE, MC, V.
   Open: Lunch Tues–Fri 11:45am–2:30pm; dinner Mon–Sat 6–11pm.

Les Halles, which opened in 1971 and was completely redecorated in 1992, is consistently recommended by concierges in the city's top hotels. Three-course lunches can feature omelets, beef Stroganoff, or a seafood salad, while dinner menus follow the classic tradition, but with fascinating digressions: Consider frogs' legs in garlic with a splash of Pernod added in the cooking, or duck cooked in a wine sauce accompanied by sliced pears.

EXPENSIVE

LES MIGNARDISES, 2035–2037 rue St-Denis. Tel. 514/842-1151.
   Cuisine: FRENCH. **Reservations:** Recommended. **Metro:** Sherbrooke.
   $ Prices: Lunch appetizers $7–$13, main courses $17–$27; dinner appetizers $9–$15, main courses $20–$29; two-course table d'hôte lunch $11–$18; three-course table d'hôte dinner $27–$40. AE, MC, V.
   Open: Lunch Tues–Fri 11:45am–2pm, dinner Mon–Sat 6–10pm.

⭐ Upstairs and to the right after you enter, you'll find the main dining room, simply and tastefully decorated—understated, in fact, for one of Montréal's best restaurants. The service is impeccable, and there are little extras that make a visit here memorable, like pâté brought to the table when you sit down and some cookies, even if you don't order dessert. The food is well prepared and beautifully presented. If you buy a bottle of wine, expect to pay at least $35 to $40.

MODERATE

BACI, 2095 av. McGill College, at Sherbrooke. Tel. 514/288-7901.
   Cuisine: ITALIAN. **Reservations:** Recommended. **Metro:** McGill.
   $ Prices: Lunch and dinner appetizers $5.50–$10, main courses $12–$26; three-course lunch table d'hôte $14–$7.50; salad and pasta of the day $10.50; two-course dinner specials $16–$25. AE, CB, DC, ER, MC, V.
   Open: Lunch Mon–Fri noon–3pm; dinner Mon–Sat 5:30–11pm. Music nightly 7–11pm.

Ask anyone who spends any time in downtown Montréal to recommend a good Italian restaurant and the name Baci usually comes up. It's got upbeat ambience; a contemporary triple-level design (no Chianti bottles to be seen); efficient service; soft piano music in the evening; and, last but most importantly, stellar cuisine, mostly northern Italian, with a creative spin. Consider Italian sausages with grilled rabbit; tortellini in walnut sauce; homemade gnocchi, linguine, and fettuccine; and penne Baci, with cream, mushrooms, bacon, and curry. You'll also find plenty of grilled fish, veal, and beef dishes, and they'll even prepare risotto at night, if you're willing to wait 45 minutes for it. This is one of the prettiest parts of downtown, with McGill University campus right across the street.

BUKHARA, 2100 rue Crescent. Tel. 514/289-9808.
   Cuisine: INDIAN. **Reservations:** Recommended. **Metro:** Peel.
$ **Prices:** Appetizers $3.50–$7; main courses $7.50–$18.50. AE, MC, V.
   Open: Lunch Mon–Fri noon–2:30pm; dinner daily 5:30–10:30pm.

My most memorable Indian meal—and I'm a devotee of Indian food—was at Bukhara, a quiet, sleek, and serene space where carpets embellish walls and modernity is tempered with brick and wood. Menu items include tandoori chicken; leg of lamb for two; fish, chicken, lamb, and prawn kebabs; vegetarian dishes; and a savory dish called murgh mukhani, chicken cooked with tomatoes, cream butter, cashew paste, ginger, and garlic. By all means, try the dhal, unlike any other I've tasted—made with a secret recipe with a tomato base. They encourage you to eat with your hands and offer aprons to catch any spills (if you protest, cutlery is forthcoming), and provide finger bowls before and after the meal. You'll dine on copper plates and goblets. Portions are large, even the salads, so order one and share, if you're with a friend. The glass-enclosed kitchen showcases the chef at work. Bukhara was founded in New Delhi and has moved east and west from there.

KATSURA, 2170 rue de la Montagne, between Maisonneuve and Sherbrooke. Tel. 514/849-1172.
   Cuisine: JAPANESE. **Reservations:** Recommended. **Metro:** Peel.
$ **Prices:** Lunch or dinner appetizers $4–$8; main courses $13–$25; three-course lunch specials $7.50–$18.50; nine-course dinner specials $26–$35. AE, DC, ER, MC, V.
   Open: Lunch Mon–Fri 11:30am–2:30pm; dinner Mon–Thurs 5:30–10pm, Fri–Sat 5:30–11:30pm, Sun 5:30–9:30pm.

Katsura manages to be poshly appointed and moderately priced at the same time. A tuxedo-clad maître d' welcomes you at the door and seats you in a dusky dining room with plush chairs, or on the traditional tatami mats at a low Japanese table. Waitresses in kimonos move quickly but quietly, hardly heard above the soft Japanese music. The house special dinner is a nine-course parade—from baked clams and sashimi (raw fish) through shrimp tempura, salad, egg-flower soup, sirloin teriyaki, all the way to ice cream with mandarin oranges. For lighter, quicker meals, head for the sushi bar in the rear. The lunch specials are particularly good value.

LA SILA, 2040 rue St-Denis, just north of rue Ontario. Tel. 514/844-5083.
   Cuisine: ITALIAN. **Reservations:** Recommended. **Metro:** Sherbrooke.
$ **Prices:** Appetizers $5.50–$12; pasta courses $8–$9; meat and seafood courses $13–$15; three-course table d'hôte $17–$30. DC, ER, MC, V.
   Open: Dinner Mon–Sat 5:30–11pm.

In the Latin Quarter, located on a pretty block, La Sila serves all manner of pasta, from Alfredo to al pesto, and meat dishes from piccata to marsala. The menu changes seasonally, but you might start with mussels in white wine or fresh asparagus, move to fresh salmon or veal scaloppine, and finish up with tiramisu, cassata, or crème caramel. This is a small, intimate place, where you're likely to linger. Look for the gray and white awning. There's free parking in back.

INEXPENSIVE

BOMBAY PALACE, 2051 Ste-Catherine ouest, at rue du Fort. Tel. 514/932-7141.
   Cuisine: INDIAN. **Reservations:** Not needed. **Metro:** Atwater, then walk about three blocks east.

FROMMER'S SMART TRAVELER: RESTAURANTS

VALUE-CONSCIOUS DINERS SHOULD TAKE ADVANTAGE OF THE FOLLOWING:

1. Table d'hôte (fixed-price) menus are widely available for lunch or dinner. You get two to four courses at reasonable prices compared to ordering similar fare à la carte.
2. Have lunch instead of dinner at expensive restaurants that you really want to try. The food is often the same, but the prices are noticeably lower.
3. There are half a dozen dining complexes throughout the city—fast-food heaven if you're in the market for a quick meal.
4. Have a picnic lunch on a pretty day at place Jacques-Cartier or Dorchester Square.
5. Stay in a hotel or bed-and-breakfast where breakfast (ideally a big, filling one) is included in the cost of the room.
6. Choose lodging that includes a kitchenette. Several downtown hotels offer this, as well as a few apartment hotels (apartment buildings that have been converted into hotels). You can have breakfast and some dinners in the room, then splurge when you want to.
7. Go ethnic. Montréal has its share of diverse cuisines, from Indian to Vietnamese, along with several deli-restaurants, where the prices are reasonable.
8. Choose a main dish that comes with a vegetable and bread.
9. Go easy on the booze. Alcohol is expensive.

$ Prices: Appetizers $2–$6; main courses $6–$16; lunch buffet $8. AE, DC, ER, MC.

Open: Lunch daily 11:30am–5pm (lunch buffet until 3pm); dinner daily 5:30–11pm.

Off the beaten tourist track, the Bombay Palace (formerly Pique Assiette) has an excellent lunch buffet from 11:30am to 3pm. A la carte, start with dhal, the savory lentil dish; go on to an assorted platter of appetizers and tandoori (barbecue) chicken or shrimp, which come with rice or nan bread; finish up with mango ice cream, the house specialty. The curries and vegetarian platter cost a few dollars less, and curries and house specials come with rice or bread. This pretty restaurant, with linen tablecloths and napkins and shadowboxes displaying Indian figures, also has a popular neighborhood bar, and it offers take-out.

MAGNAN, 2602 St-Patrick at rue Charlevoix. Tel. 514/935-9647.

Cuisine: STEAK. **Reservations:** Not accepted. **Metro:** Lionel-Groulx, then a 10-minute walk. **Directions:** If you're driving, follow Notre-Dame west to rue Charlevoix.

$ Prices: Most items $4–$14. MC, V.

Open: Daily upstairs in the tavern 6:30am–midnight, downstairs in the restaurant 11am–11pm.

This well-loved tavern and restaurant, founded in 1932, is known for its filling food and unbelievably low prices. Magnan has its own butcher shop, which goes through 1,000 pounds of meat a week. Rib steaks start at $10.50, and for the same price you can get *two* lobsters in season (spring). Other popular menu items include homemade sausage, meat and salmon pies, and, for dessert, sugar pie, all of which may be ordered as take-out. Magnan seats 650 people, mostly upstairs in the cavernous, freewheeling tavern area, with three large screen TVs, that was off-limits to women until about 10 years ago. The downstairs area, which was always open to women, is quieter and more refined—with linen napkins and tablecloths, no less—and has a salad bar, but most folks opt for the more casual tavern scene upstairs. Magnan is five minutes from the Atwater Market, where you can fish for your own trout in spring and summer.

LE 9e, 677 rue Ste-Catherine ouest. Tel. 514/284-8421.
   Cuisine: LIGHT FARE. **Reservations:** Not accepted. **Metro:** McGill.
$ **Prices:** Appetizers $2–$5; main courses $8–$16; daily special $10.50. AE, MC, V.
   Open: Lunch Mon–Sat 11:30am–3pm; afternoon tea Mon–Sat 2:30–4:30pm; dinner Thurs–Fri 4:30–7pm.

   Opened in 1931, this restaurant, on the ninth floor of Eaton's department store, is a replica of a dining room aboard the ocean liner *Ile de France,* complete with murals, marble columns, and giant alabaster vases. Menu items include soups, sandwiches, and salads, and daily specials include soups, dessert, and coffee. The waiters and waitresses, some of whom have worked here for many years, wear starched black-and-white uniforms. Kitschy, unique, and noisy.

LES PRES, 902 Ste-Catherine, between McGill and Mansfield. Tel. 514/876-1096.
   Cuisine: LIGHT FARE. **Reservations:** Not needed. **Metro:** McGill.
$ **Prices:** Appetizers $2–$4; main courses $5.50–$13; two-course table d'hôte lunch $6–$8; three-course table d'hôte dinner $10–$15. AE, ER, MC, V.
   Open: Mon–Thurs 11am–11:30pm, Fri–Sat 11am–midnight, Sun noon–11pm.

   This coffee shop, whose name means "the meadows," comes highly recommended by Montréalers as a place that will fill you up without flattening your wallet. The lunch special, which includes soup, a main course, and coffee, is a particularly good value, and any main course—be it pasta, chicken, or sausages—comes with fries and a vegetable. They've also got beer on tap. Lunch is served until 2pm.

BUDGET

CAFE VIA CRESCENT, 1418 rue Crescent. Tel. 514/843-3890.
   Cuisine: ITALIAN/LIGHT FARE. **Reservations:** Not accepted. **Metro:** Peel.
$ **Prices:** Most items $2–$8. No credit cards.
   Open: Daily 7am–1:30am.
Quieter and less trendy than most of the places along Crescent Street, this little café, nothing more than a glass box grafted onto the facade of a modern building, is popular with local folks and easy on the pocketbook. It offers an unobstructed view of the Crescent Street bustle, both winter and summer, and offers outdoor seating in warm weather. The menu here is Italian, with authentic Italian desserts (including some tasty cookies with an unpronounceable name that means "ugly but good"); you can also get light-meal fare including pizzas, Italian salads, sandwiches, coffees, and soft drinks. Fixed-price breakfasts cost about $4, and a light lunch or dinner is yours for $6 to $10.

LE COMMENSAL, 1204 av. McGill College, at Ste-Catherine. Tel. 514/871-1480.
   Cuisine: VEGETARIAN. **Reservations:** Not accepted. **Metro:** McGill.
$ **Prices:** Dishes priced by weight $1.40 per 100 grams (about 3½ ounces), $1.50 for desserts; after 3pm, $1.25; after 9pm, $1.10. AE, MC, V.
   Open: Daily 11am–11:30pm.

   Le Commensal serves fresh, superb vegetarian fare—soups, salads, hot and cold main dishes, hot side dishes, tofu prepared several ways, and a bevy of desserts. It's cafeteria-style, so help yourself, then pay by weight. My only complaint is that the hot dishes aren't always piping hot. The second-floor location affords a lovely view. Le Commensal has other locations, including a convenient one at 2115 St-Denis and Sherbrooke (tel. 514/845-2627).

SIR WINSTON CHURCHILL PUB, 1459 rue Crescent, between Maisonneuve and Ste-Catherine. Tel. 514/288-0623.
   Cuisine: LIGHT FARE. **Reservations:** Not needed. **Metro:** Guy-Concordia or Peel.

$ Prices: Most items $5–$11; lunch buffet or Sun brunch $10. AE, DC, ER, MC, V.
Open: Lunch daily 11:30am–4pm; dinner daily 5–11pm. **Closed:** Sun–Mon in winter.

Sitting at a sidewalk table here on a sunny day, if you're lucky enough to snag one, to munch burgers, sandwiches, salads, or cheeses and sip a beer is a long-standing Montréal tradition. It has one of the city's longest terraces.

OLD MONTREAL

VERY EXPENSIVE

LA MAREE, 404 place Jacques-Cartier. Tel. 514/861-8126.
   Cuisine: SEAFOOD. **Reservations:** Required. **Metro:** Champ-de-Mars.
$ Prices: Appetizers $5–$17 ($29 if you order the Russian caviar); lunch main courses $15–$16.50, dinner main courses $23–$29. AE, CB, DC, DISC, ER, MC, V.
   Open: Lunch Mon–Fri 11:30am–3pm; dinner daily 6–11pm. **Closed:** Dec 25–Jan 1.

In Old Montréal sits La Marée, in the historic del Vecchio house (the one with the blue awnings). The restaurant oozes elegance, with delicate wallpaper; burgundy velvet curtains; striking paintings of fish, fowl, and game; and stately stone walls and fireplaces. It is well known for its refined cuisine and presentation, and painstaking service. Though the restaurant is lauded for fish dishes such as stuffed trout with salmon and lobster mousse or lobster with tomato and fresh basil with a white wine sauce, pheasant and chateaubriand are also popular. In summer, there is lighter fare such as seafood salad with endive and oak-leaf lettuce or a pancake with scallops and lobster. Half a dozen specials are offered. While you don't have to dress as elegantly as the waiters, leave your shorts or jeans back at the hotel. La Marée shares its kitchen with St. Amable restaurant, which is next door.

EXPENSIVE

CLAUDE POSTEL, 443 rue St-Vincent. Tel. 514/875-5067.
   Cuisine: FRENCH. **Reservations:** Recommended. **Metro:** Place d'Armes.
$ Prices: Appetizers $6.50–$16 ($35 for beluga caviar); main courses $12.50–$28.50; three-course lunch table d'hôte menu $14–$20, three-course dinner table d'hôte $18–$26. AE, CB, DC, DISC, ER, MC, V.
   Open: Lunch Mon–Fri 11:30am–3pm; dinner daily 5:30–11pm.

One of the most upbeat places for a memorable meal in Old Montréal, Claude Postel takes its name from its animated French owner and chef. When the building, which dates from 1862, was a hotel, Sarah Bernhardt stayed in it; as a restaurant, it has hosted Gérard Depardieu, Madonna, Jean-Paul Belmondo, and Donald Sutherland, among others. They come for the lobster specialties, the roasted rack of lamb in venison sauce, the médaillons of veal in a bacon and mustard-seed cream sauce, the fresh salmon, the steamed scampi "Sarah Bernhardt," and the ambience. The foie gras and smoked salmon are popular appetizers.

MODERATE

LE BOURLINGUEUR, 363 St-François-Xavier, near St-Paul. Tel. 514/845-3646.
   Cuisine: FRENCH. **Reservations:** Recommended. **Metro:** Place d'Armes.
$ Prices: Four-course lunch or dinner $8.50–$15. AE, ER, MC, V.
   Open: Lunch Mon–Sat 11:30am–3pm; dinner Mon–Sat 4–9pm.

Le Bourlingueur is a real find in Montréal—a licensed restaurant with café prices. For $8.50 to $15, you get a four-course meal from a menu that changes almost daily. The specialties of the house are seafood (especially poached salmon) and roast beef. This place is small and pretty, with stone walls and plants hanging in oversize windows. It tends to be crowded and noisy with faithful business folk at lunchtime, so try to come for dinner, if possible.

CASA DE MATEO II, 440 rue St-François-Xavier. Tel. 514/844-7448.

Cuisine: MEXICAN. **Reservations:** Not needed. **Metro:** Place d'Armes.
$ **Prices:** Appetizers $6–$14; main courses $14–$18; daily midday special $8–$10. AE, MC, V.
Open: Mon–Sat 11:30am–11pm, Sun 11:30am–10pm, later in summer.

For Mexican fare, head to Old Montréal and Casa de Mateo II, with its welcoming green awnings and lantern-trimmed doorway. The staff and ambience are Latin, the service attentive. Main dishes include vegetarian enchiladas and regional specialties such as pescado veracruzano and burritos oaxaqueños. The chips here are homemade, light, and crisp. If you choose the plato mexicano, you'll share half a dozen appetizers. The restaurant has two dining areas and a large bar, and there's rousing mariachi music Friday and Saturday nights.

LE PETIT MOULINSART, 139 rue St-Paul ouest, at place Royale. Tel. 514/843-7432.
Cuisine: BELGIAN. **Reservations:** Not accepted. **Metro:** Place d'Armes.
$ **Prices:** Appetizers $8–$10; main courses $12–$16; fixed-price three-course lunch $10–$16. ER, MC, V.
Open: Mon–Thurs 11:30am–10pm, Fri 11:30am–midnight, Sat 4–10pm, Sun 2pm–midnight (dinner from 6pm daily).

 This is a good place to get away from the tourist crowds any day of the week. Stroll seven short blocks west along rue St-Paul to this delightful corner café with wood-paneled walls and ceiling. Menu highlights include mussels with fries and mayo, black and white blood pudding, waterzooi (a Belgian dish of steamed fish or chicken with white wine and cream), bavette de cheval (horse steak), and, for dessert, Brussels waffles. The place is known for its imported beers, more than 70 brands, not to mention some tasty ones on tap that come from local microbreweries. There's a terrace for outside dining. The only live entertainment here is games and books of cartoons.

INEXPENSIVE

IL ETAIT UNE FOIS . . . , 600 rue d'Youville, at rue McGill. Tel. 514/842-6783.
Cuisine: LIGHT FARE. **Reservations:** Not accepted. **Metro:** Victoria.
$ **Prices:** Most items $2–$9.50. MC, V.
Open: Daily 11am–9pm.

In the far-western reaches of Old Montréal, two blocks from the Centre d'Histoire de Montréal, you'll find a one-of-a-kind place, whose name means "Once Upon a Time . . ." The name refers to the small brick building that houses the café—it was a train terminal from 1909 to 1955—and to the collectibles inside the restaurant itself, including its potbellied stove, gumball machines, and vintage signs from a bygone era. The burgers, including a veggie burger, are big and come with a variety of trimmings. Hot dogs are equally memorable, including one called the Big Foot. Fish (or scallops) and chips, lobster rolls, and salads are also on the menu. Not surprisingly, you may order malteds, sundaes, apple pie à la mode, and strawberry-rhubarb pie. For grown-ups with a taste for something harder, there's beer, wine, and mixed drinks. It's a short walk to get here but worth it.

LA MAISON CARTIER/LE JARDIN NELSON, 407 place Jacques-Cartier, Old Montréal. Tel. 514/861-5731.
Cuisine: FRENCH/LIGHT FARE. **Reservations:** Not accepted. **Metro:** Place d'Armes.
$ **Prices:** Appetizers $2.50–$5; main courses $5–$9.50. ER, MC, V.
Open: May–Oct Sun–Thurs 11:30am–midnight, Fri–Sat 11am–2am. Nov–Apr Sat–Sun 11:30am–5pm.

On the east side of place Jacques-Cartier, near the foot of the hill, it specializes in crêpes, though you can get soups, omelets, salads, and sandwiches. The restaurant's garden, Le Jardin Nelson, has a pretty crab-apple tree and features the same menu as its indoor counterpart, plus classical music at lunchtime and usually on Sunday through Thursday evenings; from May to October, there's jazz on Friday and Saturday nights.

**STASH'S, 200 rue St-Paul ouest, at rue St-François-Xavier. Tel. 514/
845-6611.**
   Cuisine: POLISH. **Reservations:** Not accepted. **Metro:** Place d'Armes.
$ Prices: Appetizers $4–$12; main courses $9–$13; four-course meal $18.50. AE,
   MC, V.
   Open: Mon–Fri 11am–10:30pm, Sat–Sun noon–10:30pm.
It's moved from its former spot beside Notre-Dame cathedral, but still draws
enthusiastic crowds for its hearty food and low prices. The pretty, new setting features
brick and stone walls, exposed beams, colorful hanging lamps, and blond-wood
furniture. The larger tables are actually refectory tables and pews from an old
convent. Choose from pirogies, potato pancakes, borscht with sour cream, roast
duck, beef Stroganoff, and much more. The place is named after the original owner,
now in Europe, and you'll find a stash of good food and friendly ambience here, along
with a library of newspapers and secondhand books to peruse.

PLATEAU MONT-ROYAL
EXPENSIVE

WITLOOF, 3619 rue St-Denis. Tel. 514/281-0100.
   Cuisine: BELGIAN. **Reservations:** Recommended. **Metro:** Sherbrooke.
$ Prices: Appetizers $5.50–$7.50; main courses $13.50–$18.50; table d'hôte
   $13–$22. AE, DC, ER, MC, V.
   Open: Mon–Wed 11:30am–11pm, Thurs–Fri 11:30am–midnight, Sat 5pm–
   midnight, Sun 5–11pm.
Its name is Flemish for "endive," and Witloof is an elegant place, with pale
yellow walls, white linen tablecloths, and a burgundy bar. Lunch and dinner
specialties include soup or two appetizers, a main course of seafood or beef
(including horse), and coffee or tea. The restaurant has a large selection of desserts,
from crème caramel to praline crêpes, as well as its own bottled wine and assorted
Belgian beers. Tell the maître d' or waiter you've come at Frommer's suggestion; he's
always curious to know how people find out about Witloof.

MODERATE

**AU COIN BERBERE, 73 rue Duluth est, between St-Laurent and av.
Coloniale. Tel. 514/844-7405.**
   Cuisine: ALGERIAN/NORTH AFRICAN. **Reservations:** Not needed. **Metro:**
   Mont-Royal or Sherbrooke.
$ Prices: Appetizers $3–$5; main courses $9–$17. MC, V.
   Open: Dinner daily 5–11pm.
A good choice—and change of pace—for anyone ready for something different
foodwise, but it's particularly appealing for vegetarians hungry for something other
than salad. Check out the couscous specialties. Au Coin Berbère is small, quiet, and
altogether pleasant. It's licensed, too.

L'EXPRESS, 3927 rue St-Denis. Tel. 514/845-5333.
   Cuisine: FRENCH. **Reservations:** Recommended. **Metro:** Sherbrooke.
$ Prices: Appetizers $4–$8 ($18 for foie gras); main courses $9–$16. AE, CB, DC,
   ER, MC, V.
   Open: Mon–Fri 8am–3am, Sat 10am–3am, Sun 2pm–1am.
There is no sign hanging outside or emblazoned on the front here—only the name of
the restaurant discreetly inscribed in white tiles in the sidewalk. But L'Express has no
need to call attention to itself, since it is one of the "in" places of the Latin Quarter.
That media types and politicians, as well as writers, actors, and artists, congregate here
has certainly added to the restaurant's cachet. Physically, it is a long, narrow space,
with lots of mirrors, plain black café tables and chairs, black-and-white tile floor, and
a shiny, modern bar. But what really counts here is the solid, delicious, and reasonably
priced French food, prepared with imagination and a nod toward nouvelle cuisine.
You might try the octopus salad, chicken liver mousse with pistachios, fresh salmon,
or the ravioli maison. Service is impressively good and quick.

INEXPENSIVE

CAFE CINE-LUMIERE, 5163 bd. St-Laurent, north of Laurier. Tel. 514/495-1796.

Cuisine: FRENCH. **Reservations:** Not needed. **Metro:** Laurier.

$ **Prices:** Appetizers $3–$8; main courses $7–$10; two-course table d'hôte lunch $6–$13; table d'hôte dinner $7–$14; Sat–Sun brunch $9 adults, $5 children 12 and younger. AE, MC, V.

Open: Mon–Thurs and Sun 11am–1am, Fri–Sat 11am–2am (the kitchen closes about an hour earlier); brunch Sat–Sun 10am–3pm.

If you love old films, you'll love this 1930's-style place, where standards from the golden age of film are shown from 3:30pm on; headsets are provided free of charge so that you have your own private sound (it'll be in French if the film is a talkie). The French bistro food is memorable (I can recommend the mussels), and the table d'hôte offerings can't be beat for value. Check the blackboard for specials. The rustic decor includes board floors, and pictures of film stars like James Dean, Elizabeth Taylor, and Anthony Quinn grace the walls. Fully licensed.

MAISON DE CARI GOLDEN, 5210 bd. St-Laurent. Tel. 514/270-2561.

Cuisine: INDIAN. **Reservations:** Not accepted. **Metro:** Laurier.

$ **Prices:** Appetizers $2–$4; main courses $9–$15; lunch specials $6–$7. AE, MC, V.

Open: Lunch Mon–Sat 11:30am–2pm; dinner daily 5–10:30pm.

The real value at the pleasant and popular Maison de Cari Golden (Golden Curry House) is the lunch special. The large menu offers 15 curries and delectable Indian breads. Popular choices include the tandoori chicken liver appetizer, followed by chicken, lamb, or shrimp tandoori, or the mild butter chicken, a cross between tandoori and curry.

RESTAURANT DELTA-BA, 131 Prince-Arthur est, at the corner of Bullion. Tel. 514/843-7147.

Cuisine: VIETNAMESE. **Reservations:** Not needed. **Metro:** Sherbrooke.

$ **Prices:** Lunch items, including salad and rice, $5–$8; dinner items $8–$12; dinner combination plates $12.50–$18. AE, MC, V.

Open: Mon 4:30–11pm, Tues–Thurs noon–11pm, Fri–Sat noon–11:30, Sun 4–11pm.

The Restaurant Delta-Ba is a fairly fancy Vietnamese place, where the choice of courses is simplified by the set menus: asparagus soup with crabmeat, an "imperial" egg roll, beef brochettes marinated in honey, brochettes of chicken flavored with ginger, rice, and fragrant tea. Or have the same five-course meal with seafood sizzling in saké and oyster sauce. Low, dramatic lighting, tropical plants, and Vietnamese lanterns will help you get in the Asian mood.

BUDGET

GALAXIE DINER, 4801 rue St-Denis, at rue Gilford. Tel. 514/499-9711.

Cuisine: LIGHT FARE. **Reservations:** Not accepted. **Metro:** Mont-Royal; turn left at the Métro, right at St-Denis, and walk four blocks.

$ **Prices:** Most items $3.50–$7.50 (breakfast $2–$6). MC, V.

Open: Sun–Wed 7am–midnight, Thurs–Sat 7am–1am.

Some things about this diner are undeniably American—its origin, for one. It started out in 1952 as Uncle Will's Diner on Route 23 near Newark, New Jersey (the French Canadian owner found it on a scrap heap near Boston, rebuilt it, and added a terrace). It still looks and sounds American, with neon out front; jukebox selections that include the Doors, Dion and the Belmonts, the Big Bopper, Aretha, and the Mamas and Papas; and food like Rice Krispies, burgers, hot dogs, Heinz ketchup, root beer, and cherry Cokes. But you can also get oeufs au choix, poutine, and sugar pie. And the waitresses, who carry money changers at their waists, have a French allure notably absent in diners Stateside.

PIZZEDELIC, 3509 bd. St-Laurent. Tel. 514/282-6784.

Cuisine: ITALIAN. **Reservations:** Not accepted. **Metro:** St-Laurent.

$ Prices: Most items $3.50–$5. MC, V.
Open: Mon–Tues 11:30am–midnight, Wed–Fri 11:30am–1am, Sat noon–1am, Sun noon–midnight.

As the name suggests, pizza's the fare of choice here—as traditional or as farfetched as you want, from feta cheese with olives to fresh basil to vegetarian to escargots to artichokes to pesto—all on a thin crust. Just peruse the list on the wall and stake your claim. A second Pizzedelic is downtown at 1329 Ste-Catherine (tel. 514/526-6001).

SCHWARTZ'S MONTREAL HEBREW DELICATESSEN, 3895 bd. St-Laurent. Tel. 514/842-4813.
   Cuisine: DELI. **Reservations:** Not accepted. **Metro:** St-Laurent.
$ Prices: Most items $4–$12. No credit cards.
   Open: Sun–Thurs 9am–1am, Fri 9am–2am, Sat 9am–3am.
Fanatically loyal fans crowd Schwartz's Montréal Hebrew Delicatessen, a long, narrow space with a lunch counter and a collection of simple tables and chairs, for the smoked meat, served in a huge sandwich, a small plate, or a large plate. You might want to add a side order of french fries and one of two mammoth garlicky specimens of pickles. Schwartz's has no liquor license.

SPECIALTY DINING
PATISSERIES

The word means "pastry shop" in French, and Montréal has some delightful ones. They also serve light fare, but I usually head straight for the sweets.

LA BRIOCHE LYONNAISE, 1593 rue St-Denis. Tel. 514/842-7017.
   Cuisine: LIGHT FARE/PASTRIES. **Metro:** Berri-UQAM.
$ Prices: Most items $3–$8. MC.
   Open: Mon–Sat 8:30am–midnight, Sun 10am–midnight.
Every dessert in the display case—from the chocolate-filled triangles to the Marie Claires to the megameringues—epitomizes the word "yummy" with a French accent, so much so that I drop in to sample something different every time I come to town. Deliberate carefully, then sit down in one of several seating areas, and someone will

---

FROMMER'S COOL FOR KIDS:
RESTAURANTS

Faubourg Ste-Catherine   (see p. 242) This fast-food complex blends tempting foods and aromas from many countries and is a great place to buy picnic fare. If kids are shy about trying exotic dishes, they'll be able to find something familiar.

Il Etait Une Fois . . .   (see p. 237) The name means "Once Upon a Time . . . ," and kids will think this restaurant, in an old train station, is a big playhouse just for them. Besides the fun memorabilia, there are ice-cream sundaes, all manner of hamburgers, and a hot dog called the Big Foot. It's the perfect place to celebrate a birthday.

Kilo   (see p. 241) Just inside the entrance are jars crammed with candies that hold children enthralled, much as the pies and cakes in the showcase do their adult sidekicks.

Le 9e   (see p. 235) A ship's dining room has escaped to the ninth (9e) floor of Eaton's department store. It's only a replica but kids can pretend they're on a fantasy voyage, and since this is a noisy place, they can be as enthusiastic as they like.

take your order. The café is across the street from the St-Denis Theatre and is the perfect spot pre- or post-show time.

KILO, 5206 bd. St-Laurent, between Maguire and Fairmount. Tel. 514/ 277-5039.

Cuisine: LIGHT FARE/DESSERTS. **Reservations:** Not accepted. **Metro:** Mont-Royal.

$ Prices: Most items $3–$6. MC, V.

Open: Sun–Thurs 10:30am–midnight, Fri 10:30am–4:30am, Sat 11am–4:30am.

Jewels in a display case never shone as enticingly as the mousses and pies displayed and sold here. Desserts, in fact, are the main order of the day—or night—at Kilo. Some serious food is served, and some refreshing juices, but given the sheer scrumptiousness of the sweets, why bother? There's hard candy, too, and some tart desserts for those partial to them. Go a decadent step further and complement your choice with strong coffee laced with cognac, amaretto, or Grand Marnier.

HOTEL DINING

THE BEAVER CLUB, in the Queen Elizabeth Hotel, 900 René-Lévesque ouest. Tel. 514/861-3511.

Cuisine: FRENCH. **Reservations:** Recommended. **Metro:** Bonaventure.

$ Prices: Appetizers $5–$12 at lunch, $12–$15.50 at dinner; main courses $16–$21 at lunch, $30–$35 at dinner; two-course table d'hôte lunch $16–$23; three-course table d'hôte dinner $30–$35; Sun brunch buffet $23 per person, half price for children under 10. AE, CB, DC, ER, MC, V.

Open: Lunch daily noon–3pm; dinner daily 6–11pm; brunch Sun 11am and 1:30pm.

★ At this, one of Montréal's most revered restaurants, don't be surprised to dine under the solemn gaze of a stuffed polar bear, musk-ox, or bison, for the restaurant takes its name from a hardy and socially prominent group of explorers and trappers established in 1785, who held regular banquets to socialize, boast of their latest adventures, and dine splendidly. Two panels hark back to those days: a stained-glass one by the artist Plamondon, represents the fur trade, on which the early economy of the region was based, as well as the French joie de vivre, while a carved wood panel, by Alphonse Pare, depicts the trapper's life and the animals indigenous to this part of Canada. Lunch here is as much a tradition among the financial movers and shakers of the city as those gatherings of the city fathers used to be. (To spot the heads of corporations, just check out the back corner of this large restaurant, which seats 225.) The Beaver Club's menu changes twice a year, in spring/summer and autumn/winter, but whatever the season, the dish of choice here is roast beef. You can also expect to find temptations such as stuffed paupiette of chicken with green asparagus for starters, followed by grilled noisettes of veal with a fresh garden herb sauce or lobster risotto with parmesan cheese. The lunch table d'hôte main course might be pork loin with a creamy garlic sauce or radicchio and wild rice salad with tuna and oil; at lunch only, calorie, salt, and fat content of each dish is given. The Beaver Club hosts a popular dinner dance on Saturday, with a trio playing from 7:30pm. The restaurant's charming maître d', Charles Ploem, who is Dutch, has been here since 1962, and is an important part of what makes this such a special place.

DINING WITH A VIEW

TOUR DE VILLE, in the Radisson Gouverneurs Hotel, 777 rue University, 32nd floor. Tel. 514/879-1370.

Cuisine: CONTINENTAL. **Reservations:** Required. **Metro:** Square Victoria; there is direct access to the hotel from here.

$ Prices: Appetizers $4–$9.50; main courses $24–$37; buffet $26 Sun–Thurs, $32 Fri–Sat; Sun brunch $22, children under 12 $9.50. AE, CB, DC, DISC, ER, MC, V.

Open: A la carte dinner daily 6–11pm; buffet Sun–Fri 6–10pm, Sat 6–11pm; brunch Sun 10am–2pm.

Romantic. Memorable. Breathtaking. These are a few words to describe the setting—and the view from Montréal's only revolving restaurant. The best time to come in summer is between 7 and 8:30pm, when the sun is setting and the city lights are beginning to twinkle. The restaurant is known mainly for its buffets (which may have a theme, such as foods from Spain, the south of France, Italy, or California) and its lamb and sirloin menu selections. If you don't want to have a meal, go one flight down to the bar, which has the same wonderful view, along with a dance floor, and a band five nights a week (Wednesday through Sunday from 9pm to 1am, 2am on Saturday); there's no cover, but drinks are steep, from $5.50 to $9. The bar opens at 6pm.

DINING COMPLEXES

The open dining areas surrounded by stands selling take-away Chinese, Greek, Italian, Mexican, and North American cuisine are especially appealing in Montréal, a city in the throes of a long-term love affair with food. These two dining complexes stand out.

The French word *faubourg* means "suburb" or "section of town." On rue Ste-Catherine ouest, between Guy and St-Mathieu, a large old brick building has been renovated and is now called **Le Faubourg Ste-Catherine.** The restored building is now a lively space filled with eateries and food shops of every kind, and it's where many food-loving Montréalers come on weekends to do their shopping. Here's a sampling of the variety and diversity of edibles to be found at Le Faubourg: burgers, crêpes, souvlaki, kebabs, sushi, empanadas, teriyaki, submarine sandwiches, pastries, frozen yogurt, breads. On street level are food shops selling fresh fruits and vegetables, fish and meat, baked goods, candies, snacks, and ice cream, along with a selection of international magazines and newspapers, writing pads, and envelopes (you can get stamps on the second floor). Below street level you'll find the cinemas. The mezzanine level is given over to boutiques and pushcarts selling clothing, personal accessories, art objects, and similar browsable items. The third level, with a seating area, is devoted to prepared food. Restrooms are on the premises. Le Faubourg is open Monday through Saturday from 7am to 10pm and Sunday from 10am to 10pm, and the Guy-Concordia Metro will get you there.

Place Ville-Marie complex, the first segment of Montréal's famous Underground City (1962), with its landmark cruciform office tower, has open-air plazas with grass and trees and huge skylights that let natural sunlight flood into the underground shopping mall below. Circular marble café tables stand bright and ready beneath a glass canopy, and nearby is another seating area where booths and tables gleam with polished brass and marble. Called **Les Cours de la Place,** it features food shops surrounding the dining area that serve crêpes, quiches, muffins, ice cream, souvlaki, hot dogs and french fries, fried chicken, Chinese food, burgers, Italian dishes, and deli delights—mainly to executives and office workers from the skyscrapers surrounding Place Ville-Marie, and on weekends, to shoppers. A quick coffee break, lunch, snack, or light supper here need cost no more than $8, and it is quite difficult to spend more than $10. The food shops are open daily, with several opening early on weekdays to provide for office workers in need of a quick muffin and coffee.

LATE-NIGHT/24-HOUR EATERIES

BEN'S DELICATESSEN AND RESTAURANT, 990 Maisonneuve, at the intersection of Metcalfe and Maisonneuve. Tel. 514/844-1000.
   Cuisine: DELI. **Metro:** Peel.
$ **Prices:** Most items $2–$9. MC, V. **Closed:** Dec 25.
   Open: Sun–Thurs 7am–4am, Fri–Sat 7am–5am.
Ben's Delicatessen and Restaurant is where Montréal's famous smoked-meat (pastrami) sandwich originated, and it is still where hundreds of breakfasts, lunches, and suppers originate daily. Besides the inevitable smoked-meat sandwich, called the Big Ben, the rambling menu features cheese blintzes, potato latkes, chicken potpie, corned beef and cabbage, and much more. This deli-restaurant was founded by Ben and Fanny Kravitz in 1908 and is still in the family.

LUX, 5220 bd. St-Laurent. Tel. 514/271-9277.

Cuisine: LIGHT FARE. **Metro:** Laurier.
$ Prices: Most items $3.25–$8.95. AE, MC, V.
Open: Daily 24 hours.

This is the one place in Montréal where you can buy jawbreakers, pick up a copy of *Vanity Fair*, the *Atlantic*, or the *New York Times*, shop for T-shirts, and have a Bloody Mary and an omelet in the same space—all at 3am. Lux is a combination café, shop, newsstand, and bar—a 24-hour mini-mall for Montréal night owls. The interior of this converted textile mill looks like a cross between a New Wave Left Bank club and a space-age industrial loft: a grand circular main room with a steel floor and two stainless-steel staircases spiraling up to a glass-domed second floor. But the centerpiece of this expanse of shiny chrome and steel is the café, surrounded by racks holding more than 1,000 magazines. Lux is known more for its late hours and unique ambience than its food.

PICNIC FARE & WHERE TO EAT IT

Want to make your own picnic, or pick up supplies for a dinner in your room? Consider a stop at **La Vieille Europe,** 3855 St-Laurent near St-Cuthbert, a storehouse of culinary sights and smells (tel. 514/842-5773). Choose from cheeses, salamis, sausages, pâtés, cashews, sunflower seeds, pistachios, honey, fresh peanut butter, or dried fruits. You can watch coffee beans being roasted in the back. A big grocery store, **Warshaw,** is next door, should you need more supplies. From here you're not far from Mont-Royal Park, so head there to enjoy your bounty.

If you happen to be in Old Montréal, pick up supplies at the dépanneur (small market) at 8 rue St-Paul, at rue St-Jean-Baptiste, which keeps late hours, and then take them to place Jacques-Cartier or the Old Port, both only steps away.

Dépanneurs also sell wine but you'll find a bigger selection at the **Maison Des Vins,** 505 av. du Président-Kennedy at Aylmer, near the Delta hotel (tel. 514/873-2274), or at Faubourg Ste-Catherine, on Ste-Catherine ouest between Guy and St-Mathieu (tel. 514/935-5127).

CHAPTER 8

WHAT TO SEE & DO IN MONTREAL

1. ATTRACTIONS
- **FROMMER'S FAVORITE MONTREAL EXPERIENCES**

2. SPORTS/RECREATION

3. SAVVY SHOPPING

4. EVENING ENTERTAINMENT

Greater Montréal is home to more than three million people—half the population of the province of Québec—yet it is surprisingly easy to explore. The wondrous Metro system, a fairly logical street grid, wide boulevards, and the interwoven Underground City all aid in the swift, uncomplicated movement of people from one inviting place to another.

So whether you choose to hike up the mountain in the middle of the city, bike through the Old Port and out along the Lachine Canal, visit a museum or a Chinese garden, or watch a hockey game, rest assured you can do it easily and enjoyably. In Montréal, getting there is part of the fun.

SUGGESTED ITINERARIES

IF YOU HAVE ONE DAY Explore Vieux-Montréal (Old Montréal), dating from the 1700s; don't miss stunning Notre-Dame Basilica and the exciting Pointe-à-Callière Museum of Archeology and History, which opened in 1992 and provides a clever and engaging orientation to the city (kids and adults alike are enthralled). Then, for contrast, stroll through the downtown sections of the modern city, including its tiny Chinatown section, and visit the new pavilion of the Museum of Fine Arts, which has a big bookstore and gift shop. Then have a table d'hôte dinner in one of the city's fine downtown restaurants.

IF YOU HAVE TWO DAYS **Day 1** Spend Day 1 as outlined above.

Day 2 Take the Metro to the architecturally daring Olympic Complex with its inclined tower and observation deck. Across the street is the Botanical Garden, where you can spend hours of peaceful meditation; while there, see the new Chinese garden and take the pleasant, open-air train tour. If you visit in summer and your timing is good, go to La Ronde, Montréal's amusement park, in the evening to watch the fireworks, or head to Old Montréal to take in a performance of the English-language Centaur Theatre or to listen to jazz in one of several lively clubs.

IF YOU HAVE THREE DAYS **Days 1–2** Spend these days as outlined above.

Day 3 In the morning, take an exhilarating jet boat ride through the Lachine Rapids, or a calmer harbor cruise aboard the sleek Bateau Mouche. Get to know the Montréal of the Montréalers, by wandering along boulevard St-Laurent, the axis of the city's ethnic neighborhoods, then through carré St-Louis (St. Louis Square) to the Latin Quarter, the center of the French-speaking student part of town. In the evening, listen to music or dine in one of the fine restaurants in the quarter.

IF YOU HAVE FIVE DAYS OR MORE **Days 1–3** Spend these days as outlined above.

Day 4 If you're feeling athletic, climb up Mont-Royal from rue Peel and admire the view of the city and river from the lookout, then relax in this verdant spot for as long as you like (if you're not feeling athletic, take the Metro to Guy, then bus No. 165).

In the afternoon take in a specialized museum, such as the Canadian Center for Architecture or the McCord Museum of Canadian History.

Day 5 Visit St. Joseph's Oratory, one of the city's most noteworthy shrines, which will give you a glimpse of Montréalers' religious life. If the weather's glorious, rent a bike and follow the Lachine Canal 7 miles (11km) to Lake St-Louis. Or if the weather turns dicey, descend to the climate-controlled world of Montréal's Underground City, a labyrinth of passages, subway tunnels, and building complexes where you can amuse yourself without ever stepping outdoors.

1. ATTRACTIONS

THE TOP ATTRACTIONS
DOWNTOWN

McCORD MUSEUM OF CANADIAN HISTORY, 690 rue Sherbrooke ouest, at Victoria. Tel. 514/398-7100.

To learn about things Canadian—primarily English Canadian and, to some extent, Amerindian—seek out this private museum, which showcases on a revolving basis the eclectic (sometimes eccentric) 80,000-artifact collection of the museum's founder, David Ross McCord (1844-1930), a merchant whose family immigrated first to Québec from Northern Ireland in 1760. Furniture, clothing, china, silver, paintings, photographs, and folk art reveal middle- and upper-class, mostly English-speaking European-immigrant city life, as well as rural life, mostly from the 18th through 20th centuries. The Amerindians are represented by exhibits of Micmac clothing, jewelry, and beautiful beadwork purses, pouches, sashes, and moccasins. A weathered totem pole from British Columbia spans the museum's three floors, and don't overlook the immense carved mahogany mantel with a copper and iron hood crowned with a clock set in a slate and jasper case (1901) or the large painted-wood cross (1946), topped with a rooster (the symbol of St. Peter's denial of Christ). Exhibit texts are in English and French. The McCord opened in 1921 and underwent extensive expansion and reopened in 1992. Exhibits fill the first and second floors; a library is on the third; the museum also has a gift shop and tearoom. Outside is the imposing Inuit sculpture, *Inukskuk,* created with more than 300 stones.

Admission: $5 adults, $3 seniors, $2 students, children under 12 free; families $8.

Open: Tues–Wed, Fri–Sun, and holidays 10am–5pm; Thurs 10am–9pm. Library hours Tues–Sun 1–4pm (ask for an access card at the front desk). **Closed:** Mon, except holidays. **Metro:** McGill.

MUSEE DES BEAUX-ARTS [MUSEUM OF FINE ARTS], 1379–1380 rue Sherbrooke ouest. Tel. 514/285-1600.

Near the corner of rues Crescent and Sherbrooke is Montréal's finest, and Canada's oldest, museum, with its extensive collection of more than 25,000 items. The original Greek Revival building (1912), the Benaiah Gibb Pavilion, on the north side of Sherbrooke, is devoted to art of the Americas: Canadian art before 1960, Mesoamerican art, Inuit art, and Amerindian art. An ultramodern annex, the Jean-Noël Desmarais Pavilion, on the south side of Sherbrooke, opened in late 1991, is devoted to contemporary international art and Canadian art after 1960, and to European paintings, sculpture, and decorative arts from the Middle Ages to the 19th century. The two pavilions are connected by an underground tunnel that is actually a large gallery devoted to the art of ancient cultures. Texts are in French and English, and the special exhibits in both pavilions are dependably noteworthy. The new annex more than doubled the museum's exhibit space, with galleries on six levels (four above ground and two below); its surprisingly placed windows and angles reveal the city when you least suspect it. The architect, Boston-based Moshe Safdie, incorporated into his design the facade of a 1902 apartment building that the city did not want torn down. Both the original museum and its sleek annex are made of

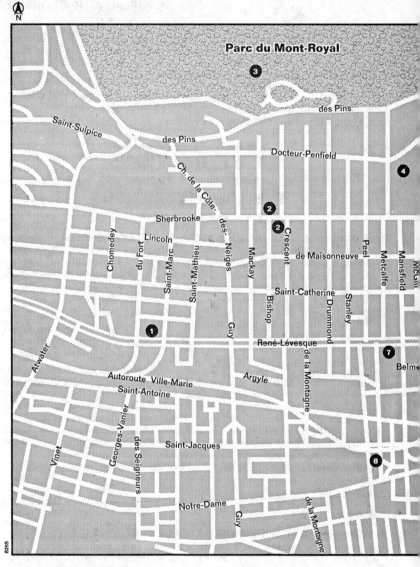

N

Parc du Mont-Royal ❸

des Pins

Saint-Sulpice

des Pins

Docteur-Penfield ❹

Ch. de la Côte-des-Neiges

Sherbrooke

Lincoln

Chomedey

du Fort

Saint-Marc

Saint-Mathieu

❷
❷ Crescent

de Maisonneuve

Mackay

Peel

Metcalfe

Mansfield

McGill

Saint-Catherine

Bishop

Guy

Stanley

Drummond

René-Lévesque

❼

Belmo

Atwater

Autoroute Ville-Marie

Saint-Antoine

Argyle

de la Montagne

Georges-Vanier

des Seigneurs

Vinet

Saint-Jacques

❽

Notre-Dame

Guy

de la Montagne

6265

Canadian Center for
   Architecture ❶
Christ Church Cathedral ❻
Dow Planetarium ❽
International Museum of
   Humour ❿

Mary Queen of the
   World Cathedral ❼
McCord Museum of
   Canadian History ❺
Museum of Contemporary Art ❾
Museum of Fine Arts ❷

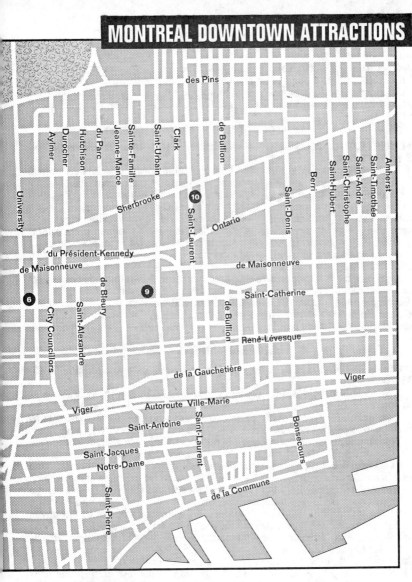

Mont-Royal Park ❸
Redpath Museum ❹

Vermont marble. A large gift shop, bookstore, and museum café are located in the annex.

Admission: Permanent collection only $4.75 adults, $3 students and children 12 and under, $1 seniors 65 and older and children 12 and under, $9.50 families; free Wed 5:50–9pm. Special temporary exhibitions and the permanent collection $9.50 adults, $4.75 students and seniors 65 and older, $2 children 12 and under, $19 families.

Open: Tues–Sun 11am–6pm, to 9pm Wed. **Metro:** Peel or Guy-Concordia.

INTERNATIONAL MUSEUM OF HUMOR, 2111 bd. St-Laurent. Tel. 514/845-4000.

This engaging museum, dedicated to humor in all its forms, opened in Montréal on April Fool's Day 1993, and is reminiscent, in layout and approach, of the Museum of the Moving Image in London. Mammoth shows with lavish exhibits are mounted for six to eight months at a time. You're likely to see clips of world-famous clowns, cartoons, sitcoms, and comic shorts. Videos and historic film clips hold museumgoers, many of them students, enthralled for hours. Though the museum is international in scope, a lot of American humor is represented. The museum closes for two months while another multifaceted exhibition filling three floors is put together, so call before you go to make sure it's open. It also houses a 250-seat cabaret-theater, a humor hall of fame, a shop, a café, and more. If you're drawn to unique places, set aside at least two hours to come here and laugh your cares away.

Admission: $11 adults; $8 seniors, students, and children 5–12; $25 families.

Open: Tues–Sat 1–10pm (arrive by 8:30pm), Sun 1–7pm (arrive by 5:30pm). **Metro:** St-Laurent. **Bus:** No. 55.

OLD MONTREAL

NOTRE-DAME BASILICA, 116 rue Notre-Dame ouest. Tel. 514/849-1070.

Big enough to hold 3,500 worshipers, and breathtaking in the richness of its interior furnishings, this magnificent structure was designed in 1829 by an American architect named James O'Donnell, who, the story goes, was so inspired by his work that he converted to Roman Catholicism after it was done. (He is one of only a few persons actually buried in the crypt.) The main altar, a hand-carved linden tree, and pulpit were the work of Victor Bourgeau; the church's oversize bell, called Le Gros Bourdon, weighs over 12 tons, its ring a deep, low vibration. Go around behind the main altar to the Chapel of the Sacred Heart, much of it destroyed by a deranged arsonist in 1978 but rebuilt and rededicated in 1982. The chapel is a popular place for weddings, though couples have to book it a year and a half in advance; its altar, 32 panels cast in bronze, by Charles Daudelin of Montréal, represents birth, life, and death. Next to the chapel is a small museum (open only on Saturday and Sunday for a small admission) displaying some of the stunning artifacts from the church.

Admission: Basilica, free; museum, $1 adults, 50¢ students.

Open: Basilica, June 25–Labor Day daily 7am–8pm; rest of the year daily 7am–6pm; tours mid-May to June 24 and Labor Day to mid-Oct Mon–Fri 9am–4pm (4:30pm in summer). Museum, Sat–Sun 9:30am–4pm. **Metro:** Place d'Armes.

PLACE JACQUES-CARTIER, between rue Notre-Dame and rue de la Commune.

Just over the hill from City Hall is the focus of summer activity in Old Montréal—place Jacques-Cartier. Without doubt the most enchanting of the old city's squares, its cobbled streets and ancient buildings instantly transport you back to the 1700s, while its outdoor cafés, street musicians, flower sellers, and

IMPRESSIONS

You can't throw a stone in Montréal without hitting stained glass.
—Attributed to Mark Twain

horse-drawn carriages tug you forward at least to the Montréal of a century ago. Young, old, hang-loose, and upwardly mobile Montréalers all mingle with the crowds of visitors on nice days, each enjoying the circus of activity in the square. Soak up the square's carnival atmosphere, then take a closer look at the ancient buildings that surround it.

Metro: Place d'Armes.

POINTE-A-CALLIERE (MUSEUM OF ARCHEOLOGY AND HISTORY), 350 place Royale. Tel. 514/872-9150.

Built on the site where Montréal was established in 1642 (Pointe-à-Callière), the modern Museum of Archeology and History engages visitors in ways other museums can only aspire to. A visit to Montréal can best begin here. Go first to the eight-minute show, "Mystery of Montréal," a tongue-in-cheek bilingual, three-dimensional experience. Pointe-à-Callière, archeologists discovered, was also the site of the city's first Catholic cemetery, the resting place of 38 people; you'll see part of it, along with other unearthed treasures. Display cases where each glass shelf represents a particular century reveal some of the findings from the digging that went on here for more than 10 years; the bottom shelf is for items "before 1600," and there's a shelf for each consecutive century. The complex incorporates the dynamic new building, which architecturally hints at the triangular Royal Insurance building (1861), which stood here for many years, a lookout tower with L'Arrivage café and an exquisite view of Old Montréal and the Old Port, an underground exhibition area (be sure to say hello to Stanley and his pals), and the old Custom House (1838), where you'll find more exhibits and a well-stocked gift shop. Allow at least two hours for a visit.

Admission: $6 adults, $5 seniors, $4 students, $12 families, children 12 and under free; free Wed 5–8pm.

Open: Tues and Thurs–Sun 10am–5pm, Wed 10–8pm. **Metro:** Place d'Armes.

OLD PORT (VIEUX-PORT), 333 rue de la Commune ouest, at McGill. Tel. 514/496-7678.

Since 1992, Montréal's commercial wharves area has metamorphosed into an appealing 1.2-mile-long (2km), 133-acre promenade and park with public spaces, exhibition halls, family activities, bike paths, a tall ship called the *Pelican* to explore, and a big, browsable flea market. Cyclists, joggers, walkers, strollers, lovers, sitters, and sunbathers come here to do their thing in good weather—or to attend scheduled outdoor events or take a boat ride. To get an idea of all there is to see and do here, hop aboard the small Balade tram that travels throughout the port ($2 adults, $1 children 3 to 11). During even-numbered years in spring, the internationally acclaimed Cirque du Soleil wows 'em at the port under its bright yellow-and-blue big top. There's also a large-scale, wraparound IMAX theater. The Old Port stretches along the waterfront from rue McGill to rue Berri. You can rent quadricycles and bicycles and explore on your own.

Admission: Port and interpretation center, free. Charges vary for other attractions.

Open: Interpretation Center, mid-May to early Sept daily 10am–9pm; for hours of specific attractions, check the *Montréal Tourist Guide.* **Metro:** Champ-de-Mars, Place d'Armes, or Square Victoria.

ELSEWHERE IN THE CITY

BOTANICAL GARDEN (JARDIN BOTANIQUE), 4101 rue Sherbrooke est. Tel. 514/872-1400.

Right next to the Olympic Sports Complex, Montréal's lovely Botanical Garden spreads out across 180 acres of Maisonneuve Park. Begun in 1931, it has grown to include an astounding 26,000 different types of plants in 31 specialized gardens, ensuring something beautiful for the eye year round. Ten huge conservatory greenhouses shelter tropical and desert plants and bonsai from the cold weather, so taking a stroll here is fun any time of year. One greenhouse, called the Wizard of Oz, is especially fun for kids. Roses bloom here from mid-June to the first frost; May is the month for lilacs, and June for the flowering hawthorn trees.

Inaugurated in summer 1991, the six-acre Chinese Garden, a joint project of Montréal and Shanghai, is the largest of its kind ever built outside Asia. You may think for a moment that you are gazing at a classic garden along the Yangtze River, but the pavilions, inner courtyards, ponds, and myriad plants indigenous to China are no mirage. The serene Japanese Garden has a cultural pavilion with an art gallery, a tearoom where the ancient tea ceremony is observed, and a Zen garden; it fills almost 15 acres. The striking green stone that dominates the landscape, peridotite, actually comes from Québec's Estrie region. The Botanical Garden's grounds are also home to the creepy, crawly Montréal Insectarium, displaying some of the world's most beautiful insects, and some of its homelier ones (see "Cool for Kids," below). If you're a birder, be sure to bring your binoculars to spot some of the more than 130 species of birds that spend at least part of the year in the Botanical Garden. In summer, an outdoor aviary is filled with Québec's most beautiful butterflies. Year-round, a free shuttle bus links the Botanical Garden and Olympic Park; a small train runs regularly through the gardens and is worth the small fee charged to ride it.

Admission: For the outside gardens, 10 greenhouses, and Insectarium, $7 adults, $5 seniors over 65, $3.50 children 6–17. A ticket for the Botanical Garden, Insectarium, and Biodome, good for two consecutive days, costs $12.50 adults, $9.50 seniors, and $6.25 children.

Open: Daily 9am–6pm. **Metro:** Pie-IX; walk up the hill to the gardens or take the shuttle bus from Olympic Park.

OLYMPIC PARK, 4545 av. Pierre-de-Coubertin. Tel. 514/252-8687.

Site of the Olympic Games in 1976, Montréal's outspokenly modern Olympic Park, punctuated by a bold inclined tower, has been thoughtfully recycled by the city for its citizens and guests. It now incorporates a stadium, a swimming center, and, most recently, an environmental Biodome (see "Cool for Kids," below). The swimming center has six different pools: a competition Olympic pool with an adjustable bottom, a training pool, warm-up pool, children's wading pool, diving pool, and an amazing 50-foot-deep scuba-diving pool. The stadium seats an astounding 60,000 to 80,000 spectators, who come here to see the Expos' baseball games, rock concerts, motorcycle shows, football games—you name it. The east-side scoreboard is as large as a hockey rink, and Rome's Colosseum could fit through the stadium's roof opening without even touching the edges. The stadium's 4½-acre, 65-ton retractable Kevlar roof, is suspended by 125 tons of steel cables, and the 626-foot inclined tower, the tallest in the world, is essential to its operation of the roof (to raise or lower the roof takes about 45 minutes, as 45 computer-controlled winches slowly pull it up—or let it down—in perfect synchrony) and serves as an observation deck. Most of the tower's 183,000-ton mass is near the base in order to make the breathtaking incline possible; on a clear day, all of Montréal is laid out at your feet, and you can see into the neighboring Laurentians for a distance of 50 miles. From mid-May to mid-September, a free shuttle bus links the Olympic Park and the Botanical Garden.

Admission: Round-trip cable-car ride, $7 adults, $6 seniors, $5.50 children 5–12. Guided tours, same prices as cable car. Recorded-tour train, $3. Public swim periods are scheduled at various times, with low admission rates.

Open: Cable car, May–Aug, Mon noon–11pm, Tues–Sun 10am–11pm; Sept to mid-Jan and mid-Feb to Apr daily Mon noon–6pm, Tues–Sun 10am–6pm. Guided tours in English, daily 12:40 and 3:40pm (sometimes more in summer). **Closed:** Mid-Jan to mid-Feb (for maintenance). Recorded-tour train, June to mid Sept daily 10am–6pm. **Metro:** Pie-IX or Viau (choose the Viau station if you're headed for the guided tour).

PARC MONT-ROYAL. Tel. 514/844-6559 (information) or 514/872-3911 (special events).

Not many cities can boast a mountain right in the center of town. But Montréal can—the city takes its name from it, in fact—and it's all one huge and delightful park that rises to a height of 761 feet (232m) above sea level. Joggers, cyclists, dogwalkers, lovers, and everyone else in search of a little peace and quiet head here in summer. On Sundays hundreds of folks congregate around the statue of George-Etienne Cartier to listen and sometimes dance to improvised music, and Lac des Castors (Beaver Lake) is surrounded by sunbathers and picnickers in summer (no swimming). In wintertime, cross-country skiers follow the miles of paths and snowshoers tramp and crunch along other trails laid out especially for them. In the cold months before the snow sets in, the lake becomes an ice-skater's paradise. The large, refurbished Chalet Lookout provides a splendid view of the city and an opportunity for a snack. The five mountains you see rising from the St. Lawrence plains, along with Mont-Royal itself, make up the Monteriegiennes chain. Up the hill behind the chalet is the spot where, tradition has it, de Maisonneuve erected his wooden cross in 1642 (in 1535, Jacques Cartier had given the mountain its name, which in ancient French was spelled Mont-Real). Today the cross is a 100-foot-high steel structure rigged for illumination at night and visible from all over the city. Park security is enforced by mounted police (the only ones you'll see in Montréal). If you love to poke around old cemeteries, as I do, you'll find three on the mountain: Catholic, Protestant, and Jewish.

Admission: Free.

Open: Daily 6am–midnight; stables daily 9am–5pm. **Metro:** Mont-Royal. **Bus:** No. 11; hop off at Lac des Castors. **Walk:** From downtown, go north on rue Peel to connect with a stairway and a switchback bridle path, called Le Serpent, that leads to the Chalet Lookout and beyond.

MORE ATTRACTIONS
DOWNTOWN

CHRIST CHURCH CATHEDRAL, 1444 av. Union (Ste-Catherine and University). Tel. 514/288-6421.

 ## FROMMER'S FAVORITE MONTREAL EXPERIENCES

Experiencing a Thoroughly Bilingual Culture Listening to French in the streets, in the shops, in hotel elevators (and vowing to practice more).

Exploring Old Montréal Meandering through the cobblestone streets of the oldest part of the city or lingering over café au lait at a table in an outdoor café on a sunny afternoon.

Listening to Jazz Downtown, old town, all around the town, this is a favorite activity, especially in June during the Montréal Jazz Festival, when music spills into the streets.

Shopping Browsing the designer shops, department stores, dazzling multi-level complexes, well-stocked bookstores, gourmet food shops, or the string of antique stores along rue Notre-Dame between rue Guy and rue des Seigneurs.

Eating Savoring French haute cuisine, an inexpensive meal at a small ethnic café, or something sweet in an old world–style pâtisserie.

Ethnic Diversity After the French and the English, the major ethnic groups in Montréal are the Italian, Jewish, and Greek communities, though in the past few decades, the city has also seen an influx of people from the Caribbean, mainly Haiti, and from Southeast Asia, mainly Vietnam. Boulevard St-Laurent has always been a major district for immigrants; wander along it to find a rich ethnic diversity. There is a small Chinatown at rues de la Gauchetière and Clark.

Riding the Metro It's clean; it's efficient; it's economical; and they pipe music into the stations to make the experience relaxing as well.

This fine Gothic building, which holds its own just fine amid the city's downtown skyscrapers, was built in 1859 and is the seat of the Anglican bishop of Montréal. The cathedral hosts concerts throughout the year, notably from June through August on Wednesday at 12:30pm (for concert information, call 514/843-6577).

Admission: Free; donations accepted.
Open: Daily 8am–6pm; services Sun 8am, 10am, 4pm. **Metro:** McGill.

MARY QUEEN OF THE WORLD CATHEDRAL (MARIE-REINE-DU-MONDE), bd. René-Lévesque at Mansfield. Tel. 514/866-1661.

No, it's not St. Peter's Basilica in Rome, but a faithful replica constructed on a smaller scale over a 24-year period, from 1870 to 1894. The striking statues atop it represent the patron saints of the archdiocese when the cathedral was built. It's more impressive outside than in.

Admission: Free; donations accepted.
Open: Summer daily 7am–7:30pm; rest of the year Sat 8am–8:30pm, Sun 9:30am–7:30pm. **Metro:** Bonaventure.

MUSEUM OF CONTEMPORARY ART (MUSEE D'ART CONTEMPORAIN DE MONTREAL), Place des Arts, 185 rue Ste-Catherine ouest. Tel. 514/873-2878.

Here you'll find eight large galleries, one leading to another, showcasing the works of local Québec and Canadian contemporary artists, as well as international artists, creating from 1940 to the present in a range of media and styles. The museum's permanent collection includes more than 3,400 works of art, including those by Jean Dubuffet, Max Ernst, Jean Arp, Ansel Adams, Lisette Modoel, Robert Mapplethorpe, and Montréal photographer Michel Campeau. A shop and restaurant are on the premises. As you stand in front of the Place des Arts complex, it will be to your left.

Admission: $5 adults, $4 seniors, $3 students; children 12 and under free; free to all Wed 6–9pm.
Open: Tues and Thurs–Sun 11am–6pm, Wed 11am–9pm. **Metro:** Place des Arts.

REDPATH MUSEUM, McGill University, 859 rue Sherbrooke ouest. Tel. 514/398-4088.

The Redpath Museum, housed in a building dating from 1882, is part of McGill University. The main draw here is the Egyptian antiquities, the second-largest collection in Canada.

Admission: Free.
Open: Sept–June Mon–Fri 9am–5pm; rest of the year Mon–Thurs 9am–5pm. **Metro:** McGill.

OLD MONTREAL

BANK OF MONTREAL BUILDING AND MUSEUM, 119 and 129 rue St-Jacques. Tel. 514/877-7373 (bank) or 514/877-6892 (museum).

Facing place d'Armes is Montréal's oldest bank building, with a classic facade with a graceful dome, carved pediment, and six Corinthian columns, mostly unchanged since its completion in 1847 (the pediment was uncarved until 1867). The interior was renovated in 1901–05 by the famed U.S. firm McKim, Mead, and White to become "probably the largest, and architecturally the most monumental, bank building in the world" at that time. By all means go inside to admire the Ionic and Corinthian columns of syenite granite from Vermont; the walls and piers of pink marble from Knoxville, Tennessee; and the counter of Levanto marble. The bank contains a small museum with a replica of its first office (and its first bank teller, Henry Stone from Boston), gold nuggets from the Yukon, a $3 bill (one of two in Canada), and a collection of 100-year-old banks with movable parts. A bilingual guide is available to answer questions.

Admission: Free.
Open: Bank, Mon–Fri 10am–4pm; museum, Mon–Fri 10am–4pm. **Closed:** Banking holidays. **Metro:** Place d'Armes.

CHATEAU DE RAMEZAY, 280 rue Notre-Dame est. Tel. 514/861-3708.
Built by Gov. Claude de Ramezay in 1705, the château was the home of the city's royal French governors for four decades, before being taken over and used for the same purpose by the British conquerors. In 1775 an army of American rebels invaded and held Montréal, using the château as their headquarters. Benjamin Franklin, sent to persuade Montréalers to rise with the colonists against British rule, stayed in the château and no doubt enjoyed his stay even though he failed to persuade the city's people to join his cause. After the short American interlude, the house was used as a courthouse, government office building, teachers' college, and headquarters for Laval University before being converted into a museum in 1895 almost 100 years ago. Old coins, furnishings, tools, and other memorabilia related to the economic and social activities of the 18th century and first half of the 19th century fill the main floor. In the cellar, you'll see the original vaults of the house, which is across rue Notre-Dame from City Hall.
Admission: $5 adults, $3 seniors and students, $10 families, children under 6 free.
Open: Mid-June to early Sept daily 10am–4:30pm; rest of the year Tues–Sun 10am–4:30pm. **Metro:** Champ-de-Mars.

CITY HALL, 275 rue Notre-Dame est. Tel. 514/872-3355.
This is a modern building by Old Montréal standards, having been finished in 1878; the Renaissance French design makes it look as though Maisonneuve brought it with him, stone by stone. It was from the balcony above the awning that Charles de Gaulle proclaimed, "Vive le Québec Libre!" in 1967. Free 15-minute guided tours are given throughout the day on weekdays May through October. Or go in on your own to admire the architectural handiwork, including statues at the entry of a sower and his wife by Alfred Laliberte. Inside, the bust to the left is of Jacques Viger, Montréal's first mayor; the one to the right of Peter McGill, the city's first anglophone mayor. The Hall of Honour is made of green marble from Campagna, Italy, with art deco lamps from Paris and a bronze and glass chandelier, also from France, that weighs a metric ton. In the display cabinet to the left by the elevator are gifts from mayors of other cities from around the world. Council Chamber meetings, on the first floor, are open to the public. Go in for a look at the striking room, with a hand-carved ceiling and five stained-glass windows representing religion, the port, industry and commerce, finance, and transportation. The mayor's office is on the fourth floor.
Admission: Free.
Open: Daily 8:30am–4:30pm. **Metro:** Champ-de-Mars.

EGLISE NOTRE-DAME-DE-BON-SECOURS (NOTRE-DAME-DE-BON-SECOURS CHAPEL), 400 rue St-Paul est. Tel. 514/845-9991.
Just past Marché Bonsecours, this is called the Sailors' Church because of the wooden ship models hanging inside, given as votive offerings by sailors. The first church building, the project of an energetic teacher named Marguerite Bourgeois, was built in 1657; the one you see today dates from 1771–73. Mme Bourgeois did a lot to educate the children of rough-and-ready Montréal in the latter half of the 17th century. She and several sister teachers founded a nuns' order called the Congregation of Notre-Dame. The church has a small museum downstairs with 58 dioramas dedicated to her life and work. This pioneer of education was recognized as a saint in 1982. There's a fine view of the harbor and Old Montréal from the church's tower.
Admission: Chapel, free; museum, $2 adults, 50¢ children.
Open: Chapel, May–Oct daily 9am–5pm, Nov–Apr daily 10am–3pm. Museum, May–Oct Tues–Sun 9am–4:30pm; Nov–Apr Tues–Sun 10:30am–2:30pm. **Metro:** Champ-de-Mars.

MARCHE BONSECOURS (BONSECOURS MARKET), 330 rue St-Paul est. No phone.
This imposing building with a colonnaded facade and a handsome dome was built in the mid-1800s and first used as Montréal's City Hall, then for many years as the central market. After restoration in 1964, it housed city government offices, and in 1992 became the information and exhibition center for the grand celebration of the

city's 350th birthday. Today it continues to be used as exhibition space. The dome is a landmark in Old Montréal; the inside has been modernized.
Metro: Champ-de-Mars.

MUSEE MARC-AURELE FORTIN, 118 rue St-Pierre. Tel. 514/845-6108.

✪ This is Montréal's only museum dedicated to the work of a single Canadian artist. In his work, innovative landscape painter Marc-Aurèle Fortin, who died in 1970, captured the special beauty of the Québec countryside, such as the Laurentians and Charlevoix. His work is on the ground floor, while temporary exhibits, mounted downstairs, feature primarily the work of other Québec painters.
Admission: $3 adults, $1 students and seniors, children under 12 free.
Open: Tues–Sun 11am–5pm. **Metro:** Place d'Armes.

SIR GEORGE-ETIENNE CARTIER NATIONAL HISTORIC SITE, 458 rue Notre-Dame est, at Berri. Tel. 514/283-2282.

Operated by the Canadian Parks Service, this is actually two houses: one, which has been reconstructed to represent the year 1860, was a Victorian-style residence of Sir George-Etienne Cartier, one of Canada's fathers of confederation (1814–73), and his wife; the adjacent house is devoted to Cartier's career and work. During the summer, the site has costumed guides, and hosts concerts and other activities.
Admission: Free.
Open: Mid-May to Labor Day daily 10am–6pm; rest of the year Wed–Sun 10am–noon and 1–5pm; guided tour with reservation. **Closed:** Jan. **Metro:** Champ-des-Mar.

PLATEAU MONT-ROYAL

HOTEL-DIEU HOSPITAL MUSEUM, 201 av. des Pins ouest. Tel. 514/849-2919.

Opened in 1992 to coincide with the city's 350th birthday, this unique museum, in the former Hôtel-Dieu Hospital, traces the history of Montréal from 1659 to the present, and focuses on the hospital itself, including an exhibit of medical instruments, and on the founder of the first hospital in Montréal, the missionary nurse Jeanne Mance, who arrived in 1642, the only woman among the first settlers who left France with Sieur de Maisonneuve. The museum's three floors are filled with memorabilia, and its architectural highpoint is a marvelous staircase brought to the New World in 1634 from the Maison-Dieu hospital in La Flèche, France. The original Hôtel-Dieu was built in 1645 in what is now Old Montréal; the building that houses the museum, in 1860.
Admission: $5 adults, $3 seniors and students 12 and over.
Open: Mid-June to mid-Oct Tues–Fri 10am–5pm, Sat–Sun 1–5pm. Mid-Oct to mid-June Wed–Sun 1–5pm. **Metro:** Sherbrooke. **Bus:** No. 129 or 80.

PARC LAFONTAINE, Plateau Mont-Royal. Tel. 514/872-2644.

The pretty European-style park near downtown has a lake that is used for paddle-boating in summer and ice-skating in winter. Its amphitheater is the setting for outdoor theater and movies in summer. It's popular with joggers, bikers, picnickers, and tennis buffs (there are 14 courts). Look for the statue of Félix LeClerc, renowned French Canadian poet and songwriter, near the esplanade.
Admission: Free; small fee for use of tennis courts.
Open: Park always open; tennis courts, 9am–10pm. **Metro:** Sherbrooke.

ST. JOSEPH'S ORATORY, 3800 chemin Queen Mary. Tel. 514/733-8211.

✪ This impressive shrine, with its great dome, was built by Montréal's Catholics to honor St. Joseph, patron saint of Canada, and in memory of the city's beloved Brother André, who was beatified in 1982. When Brother André, a friar of the Congregation of Holy Cross, built a small wooden chapel on the slope of Mont-Royal in 1904, he already had a reputation as a healer who had obtained hundreds of cures. The fame of his powers attracted supplicants from all around, and Brother André performed his benevolent work faithfully until his death in 1937. His dream of building a magnificent shrine to his patron saint became a reality only after his death; in 1966 the magnificent Italian Renaissance-style basilica was completed. Take a look at the museum dedicated to Brother André (his heart is on display here), the exhibition on St. Joseph's life, and the pretty outdoor Way of the Cross (where scenes from the film *Jesus of Montréal* were shot). The original wooden chapel, with Father André's tiny bedroom, are on the grounds and open to the public. Pilgrims, some ill, come to seek intercession from the saint and Brother André, and usually climb the middle set of steps on their knees. At 862 feet (263m), the shrine is the highest point in Montréal. (Can you guess how they cut the grass?) Plan to spend at least an hour here. A cafeteria and snack bar are on the premises; guided tours are offered at 10am and 2pm daily in summer and on weekends in September and October (donation only). It's also possible to stay inexpensively.

Admission: Free; donations are requested at the museum.

Open: Daily 8am-10pm; museum daily 10am-5pm. The 56-bell carillon plays Wed-Fri noon-3pm, Sat-Sun noon-2:30pm. **Metro:** Côtes-des-Neiges.

ELSEWHERE IN THE CITY

MUSEE DES ARTS DECORATIFS DE MONTREAL [DECORATIVE ARTS MUSEUM], 2929 Jeanne-d'Arc; enter on Pie-IX. Tel. 514/259-2575.

In 1916 Oscar and Marius Dufresne began construction of a harmonious Beaux Arts-style mansion across boulevard Pie-IX from the Botanical Garden and Olympic Park. The two brothers, one an industrialist and one an engineer, divided the house down the middle and then proceeded to fill it with silver, porcelain, paintings, sculpture, furniture, and textiles of the period, in order to live in style. Besides the lavish use of Italian marble and African mahogany, and Dufresnes' original furnishings, the museum displays religious sculptures from the 1700s and 1800s, a collection devoted to the Hébert family of artists from Québec, and another collection from the museum of the School for Interior Decoration. The house holds the largest Canadian collection of furnishings in the International style of the 1940s and 1950s. Just consider it *House Beautiful,* Canadian style. And don't overlook the nymphs on the ceilings and walls.

Admission: $3 adults, $2 seniors, $1.50 students 13-25; free to children 12 or younger.

Open: Wed-Sun 11am-5pm. **Metro:** Pie-IX.

LA RONDE, Parc des Iles, Ile Ste-Hélène. Tel. 514/872-6222, or toll free 800/361-8020.

Montréal's delightful amusement park, called La Ronde, fills the northern reaches of the island Ile Ste-Hélène with 35 rides, family entertainment, an international circus, and fireworks. Thrillseekers will love the Monster, the tallest double-track roller coaster in the world, which reaches heights of 132 feet and speeds in excess of 60 m.p.h. A big attraction every year is the International Fireworks Competition, which begins in late May or early June and continues until early August. (Some Montréalers choose to watch them from the Jacques Cartier Bridge, which is closed to traffic then; they take a Walkman to listen to the accompanying music.)

Admission: Unlimited all-day pass $17.30 for those 12 and older, $9 under 12, $40 family pass. Reserved seating for fireworks, $21 including all rides. Ground admission only, $9.50; parking $6.50.

Open: Mid- to late May and early Sept, Sat-Sat 11am-1am; June-Aug Sun-Thurs 11am-midnight, Fri-Sat 11am-1am. **Metro:** Papineau, or Ile Ste-Hélène and bus no. 169.

ST. LAWRENCE SEAWAY [ST. LAMBERT LOCKS], St-Lambert, under Victoria Bridge. Tel. 514/672-4110.

The St. Lawrence Seaway was inaugurated by Queen Elizabeth II and President Eisenhower in 1959, after a century of planning and years of construction. The system of locks and canals now meant that oceangoing vessels could sail right into the heartland of North America, 1,300 miles (2,100km) from the Atlantic. To learn more about the seaway, visit the observation deck and exhibition space overlooking St. Lambert Lock. In the mammoth lock, 860 feet long by 80 feet wide, tremendous ships are raised about 50 feet, and then the upriver gates are opened for them to

continue the journey via the Great Lakes to the center of the continent. In January, February, and March, ice on the river prevents ships from sailing, so they sit out the cold weather, waiting for the spring thaw.
Admission: Free.
Open: Mid-Apr to mid-Nov Mon–Fri 8am–7pm; call to verify times. For a guided tour, make a reservation two weeks in advance. **Directions:** Drive or take a taxi across Victoria Bridge to the observation deck overlooking St. Lambert Lock.

COOL FOR KIDS

BIODOME, 4777 av. Pierre-de-Coubertin. Tel. 514/868-3000.
Near the Viau Metro station entrance, this major new attraction, the former Olympic velodrome, re-creates four different ecosystems under a huge transparent roof, complete with the appropriate flora and fauna: a polar environment, a tropical rain forest, a boreal (Laurentian) forest, and marine life of the St. Lawrence River. The Biodome, which opened in June 1992, absorbed the Montréal zoo and aquarium. It has a games room for kids called Naturalia, a shop, and a café on the premises.
Admission: $8.50 adults, $6 seniors 65 and older, $4.25 children 6–17.
Open: Daily 9am–8pm in summer (to 6pm the rest of the year). **Metro:** Viau.

DOW PLANETARIUM, 1000 rue St-Jacques ouest, in Chaboillez Sq. Tel. 514/872-4530.
Montréal's planetarium is right downtown, only two blocks from Windsor Station. Shows under the 65.6-foot (20m) dome dazzle and delight kids while managing to inform them at the same time. Alternating shows in French and English feature a lecturer. Plan to spend at least 1½ hours.
Admission: $4 adults, $2.50 children and seniors.
Open: Late June–Labor Day daily; other months Tues–Sun; call for times.
Metro: Bonaventure—Windsor Station exit.

IMAX THEATER, corner of de la Commune and St-Laurent, Old Port. Tel. 514/496-4629 (shows and times).
Fasten your (imaginary) seat belts and get ready to see the world from a bird's-eye view—or a helicopter's, or satellite's. The images and special effects are larger-than-life, in true IMAX fashion on a seven-story screen. If your mind isn't blown, it'll certainly be expanded. Arrive for shows at least 10 minutes early, earlier on weekends and evenings.
Admission: $11.50 adults, $9.50 students, $7 seniors and children 10 and under.
Open: Year round; call for current schedule of shows in English. **Metro:** Place d'Armes.

INSECTARIUM, 4581 rue Sherbrooke est. Tel. 514/872-8573.
A creepy, crawly addition (purposefully so) to the Botanical Garden, this airy, two-level complex exhibits the collections of two avid entomologists, Georges Brossad (whose brainchild the place is) and Fr. Firmia Liberté. Scorpions, scarabs, maggots, locusts, beetles (including one named Goliath), tarantulas, and giraffe weevils—some 3,000 in all—are displayed, and live exhibits feature crickets, cockroaches, and praying mantises.
Admission (including the Botanic Garden): May–Oct $7 adults, $5 seniors over 65, $3.50 children 6–17. Nov–Apr $5 adults, $3.50 seniors, $2.50 children.
Open: Summer daily 9am–7pm; rest of year daily 9am–4:30pm. **Metro:** Pie-IX; walk up the hill to the gardens or in summer take the shuttle bus from Olympic Park.

S.O.S. LABYRINTINE, Old Port, King Edward Pier, at bd. St-Laurent. Tel. 514/982-9660.
True to its name, it offers a little over a mile (2km) of indoor twisting paneled paths, obstacles, and challenges, including a tunnel and a secret passage, all connected by a maze of corridors. The course changes weekly and incorporates a treasure hunt. Kids, up to teen age, love it. Guides on in-line skates are on duty, in case you can't find your way out.
Admission: $7 adults, $6 students, $5.50 children under 12; $18 families.
Open: June–early Sept. **Metro:** Champ-de-Mars.

THEATRE BISCUIT, 221 rue St-Paul ouest. Tel. 514/845-7306.
Montréal's only permanent puppet theater has shows on weekends; reservations are required. Visitors may explore its small puppet museum. This is good family fun, and understanding French is not a prerequisite.
Admission: $9.50 adults, $7.50 children.
Open: Sat–Sun only; performances at 3pm. Pick up tickets at 2:30pm. **Metro:** Place d'Armes.

SPECIAL-INTEREST SIGHTSEEING
FOR THE ARCHITECTURE ENTHUSIAST

CENTRE CANADIEN D'ARCHITECTURE, 1920 rue Baile. Tel. 514/939-7000.

⭐ The bold Canadian Centre for Architecture (CCA) building fills a city block and melds a modern structure with an existing older building (the Shaughnessy House, 1875), both of gray limestone. Founded in 1979 by architect Phyllis Lambert, the CCA doubles as a study center and a museum with changing exhibits devoted to the art of architecture and its history. Its collection is international in scope and encompasses architecture, urban planning, and landscape design. Texts are in French and English. The large bookstore on the premises features books on architecture, with a special section on Canadian architecture with emphasis on Montréal and Québec City, landscape and garden history, photography, preservation, conservation, design, and city planning, as well as posters, postcards, and children's books (tel. 514/939-7028). Be sure to visit the CCA's unique sculpture garden across the Ville-Marie autoroute, designed by artist/architect Melvin Charney.
Admission: $5 adults, $3 students and seniors, children 12 and under free.
Open: Wed and Fri 11am–6pm, Thurs 11am–8pm, Sat–Sun 11am–5pm. **Metro:** Atwater, Guy-Concordia, or Georges-Vanier.

FOR THE HISTORY BUFF

CENTRE D'HISTOIRE DE MONTREAL, 335 place d'Youville. Tel. 514/872-3207.
Built in 1903 as Montréal's Central Fire Station, the red-brick and sandstone building is now the Montréal History Center, which traces the history of the city from its first occupants, the Amerindians, to the European settlers who arrived in 1642, to the present day. The city fathers and mothers are duly noted, and the railroad, Metro, and generic row house given their just due in the form of imaginative exhibits, videos, and slide shows. On the second floor (a spiral stair leads to it) you'll find memorabilia from the early 20th century. Ask at the front desk for a visitor's guide in English.
Admission: $4.50 adults, $3 students, children 6–17, and seniors.
Open: Early Jan–early May and early Sept to mid-Dec Tues–Sun 10am–5pm; early May–early July daily 9am–5pm; early July–early Sept daily 10am–6pm.
Closed: Mid-Dec to end of Dec. **Metro:** Champ-de-Mars.

DAVID M. STEWART MUSEUM, Old Fort, Ile Ste-Hélène. Tel. 514/861-6701.
Islands are wonderful points for defense, Ile Ste-Hélène particularly so. The British built a fortified arsenal here in 1822, and the local inhabitants dubbed it Le Vieux Fort (the Old Fort) sometime thereafter. Today the volcanic stone buildings house a museum where you can browse through navigational and scientific instruments and maps that helped European explorers discover the New World, military and naval artifacts and maps, uniforms, and paraphernalia, re-creating the mood of Canada from the time of Jacques Cartier (1535) through the end of the colonial period. From late June through late August, the Old Fort comes to life with reenactments of military parades by La Compagnie Franche de la Marine and the 78th Fraser Highlanders, at 11am, 2:30pm, and 5pm.
Admission: $5 adults, $3 seniors (65 or older) and children (6–17); slightly less off-season.
Open: Summer Wed–Mon 10am–6pm; rest of the year Wed–Mon 10am–5pm.
Metro: Ile Ste-Hélène.

ORGANIZED TOURS

I'm a firm believer in starting out a visit to any new city—or one you haven't seen in five years or so—with a guided tour. That way, you get an idea of the lay of the land, the history, the top attractions, and most important, what you'd like to go back and visit in depth on your own. Montréal spruced itself up, expanded and added many attractions for its 350th birthday in 1992. You'll be pleased with the changes.

GUIDED TOURS For a complete listing of tours and tour operators, check under "Sightseeing Tours" in the *Montréal Tourist Guide*, or at Infotouriste (tel. 514/873-2015, or toll free 800/363-7777). Many of the land tours leave from Dorchester Square downtown; boat tours depart from the Old Port in Old Montréal. You can park free at the dock, or take the Métro to the Champ-de-Mars station and walk six blocks to the dock.

BOAT TOURS Numerous opportunities for experiencing Montréal and environs by water are laid out under "Cruises" in the *Montréal Tourist Guide*. Among them: ✪ **Le Bateau-Mouche,** sleek air-conditioned, glass-enclosed boats (reminiscent of those in Amsterdam), ply the St. Lawrence River on 90-minute daytime cruises or a three-hour dinner cruise. They depart from the Jacques-Cartier Pier (tel. 514/849-9952).

Croisières du Port de Montréal (Montréal Harbor Cruises) (tel. 514/842-3871) plies the waters of Montréal harbor and the St. Lawrence, giving voyagers a stunning skyline view of the city from the water. The boats depart up to five times a day from May to mid-October from the Clock Tower Pier at the foot of rue Berri in Old Montréal, for tours, dinner and dancing, or extended sightseeing for one to nine hours.

The **Croisières Nouvelle-Orléns,** a replica of a paddle wheeler, plies the St. Lawrence regularly, departing from the Jacques Cartier Pier at the Old Port (tel. 514/842-7655).

For a wonderful, wild, and wet experience, try ✪ **jet-boating** in a saute-moutons (wave-jumper) powerboat on the dicey Lachine Rapids of the St. Lawrence River. The modern, streamlined boat makes the 1½-hour trip every two hours from 10am to 5pm daily May through September. After a half-hour cruise upstream you arrive at the rapids; another half hour is spent splashing and storming up the river, before the half-hour return to dock at Victoria Pier in the Old Port. Arrive 45 minutes early to get your rain gear and life jacket (wearing a sweater is a good idea; so is bringing a change of clothes, as you may get wet). For more information, call 514/284-9607.

BUS TOURS Now for something a little different: An amphibious bus tours Old Montréal much like any other bus—until it plunges into the waters of the Old Port for a dramatic finish. Is it a boat, or is it a bus? It's both. Inventor/driver Jacques Tourigny originally designed the bus, called Kamada, for his family to tour the Amazon in, but as he progressed, his plans changed. Since launching the "amphibus" in 1985, he's proud to say he's never had an accident. The one-hour, now-you've-done-it-all excursion is offered daily from 10am to 11pm from May through October. Kids will love reporting on this during "What I did on my family vacation" at school. The point of debarkation is place Jacques-Cartier (tel. 514/386-1298).

Commercial guided tours in air-conditioned buses are offered daily year round by **Gray Line,** 1001 Dorchester Sq. (tel. 514/934-1222). The basic city tour takes three hours, or sign up for the deluxe, five-hour city tour, which includes an hour-long stop at the Botanical Garden. Other tours take you to Ile Ste-Hélène, the St. Lawrence Seaway, the Laurentians, and Québec City.

HORSE-DRAWN CARRIAGE TOURS Montréal's romantic **calèches** (tel. 514/653-0751) are horse-drawn open carriages that take visitors clip-clopping through the city's streets and sights. In winter the drivers hitch their steeds to old-fashioned sleighs for the ride around the top of Mont-Royal, the horses puffing steam, the passengers bundled in sleigh rugs. Prices run about $40 for an hour's tour in the carriage or sleigh, which can seat four comfortably, five if one sits with the driver. In addition to Mont-Royal, calèches depart from Dorchester Square and in Old Montréal at Jacques-Cartier Square and rue de la Commune, rue Notre-Dame opposite rue St-Vincent, and place d'Armes opposite Notre-Dame Basilica.

WALKING TOURS You can arrange walking tours of Old Montréal, the Underground City, or anywhere else your heart and feet desire, through **Guidatour** (tel. 514/844-4021) or **Visites de Montréal** (tel. 514/933-6674).

Guided tours of **McGill University** and its beautiful campus on the slope of Mont Royal are also available and free, but you must call at least 24 hours in advance (tel. 514/398-6555). Should you decide to look around the university on your own, note the large stone inside the fence just to the left of the McGill Gate (at the corner of Sherbrooke and McGill). It designates the spot—well, nearly so—of the Hochelaga settlement that existed here before the first Europeans dropped anchor. The Amerindian community consisted of 50 houses, with several families living in each, and the people farmed and fished for a living.

2. SPORTS/RECREATION

SPORTS

Montréal's got plenty of muscle, and it's flexed regularly. Depending on the season, check the newspaper schedules for hockey with the **Canadiens,** who have won the Stanley Cup 24 times since 1929 (tel. 514/932-2582), baseball with the **Expos** (tel. 514/522-3434), and soccer with the **Impact** (tel. 514/328-3668), or basketball with the **Dragons** (tel. 514/725-9164). There is harness-racing regularly at the **Blue Bonnets Racetrack** (tel. 514/739-2741).

Add to that several special sporting events, such as the **Molson Grand Prix** in June, the **Player's Ltd. International** men's tennis championship in late July, and the **Montréal Marathon** in September.

RECREATION

BICYCLING Montréal is unusual for its 149-mile (240km) network of cycling paths. Popular outings include the 6.8-mile (11km) path along the Lachine Canal that leads to Lake St-Louis; the 10-mile (16km) path west from the Lambert Locks to the city of Côte Ste-Catherine; and Angrignon Park, with its four-mile cycling path interspersed with inviting picnic areas (take the Metro, which accepts bikes in the last two doors of the last car, to Angrignon station). You can rent bikes or the popular four-wheel "Q Cycles" at the Old Port at the place Jacques-Cartier entrance.

CROSS-COUNTRY SKIING You don't have to go far from downtown Montréal to enjoy a 1.3-mile (2.1km) cross-country course. It's right in Mount Royal Park. The Botanical Garden has an ecology trail. The problem for either is, you have to supply the skis. Just an hour from the city is one of the finest centers for cross-country skiing in North America, the Far Hills Inn and Ski Centre, where you can rent equipment.

HIKING The most popular (and obvious) hike in Montréal is up to the top of Mont-Royal, the city's geographical *pièce de résistance.* Start downtown on rue Peel, which leads north to a stairway, which in turn leads to a half-mile (800m) path of switchbacks called Le Serpent, or you could opt for the 200 steps that deposit you at the Chalet Lookout. Your reward for having exerted the effort is a panoramic view of the city—and a snack bar in the chalet. Figure on 1.25 miles one way.

JOGGING For a flat surface, jog along the **Lachine Canal,** where you can go for miles. Or for an up-and-down workout that beats the Stairmaster, follow rue Peel north to Le Serpent switchback path on Mont-Royal; jog (uphill) on it for half a mile (800m) until it runs out; turn right and continue (2km) to the monument of

George-Etienne Cartier, one of Canada's fathers of confederation. From here you can get a bus back downtown—or jog back the way you came, or along avenue du Parc and avenue des Pins (turn right when you get to it).

SWIMMING   Plage de l'Ile Notre-Dame is the former Regatta Lake from Expo '67. The water is drawn from the Lachine Rapids and treated by a mostly natural filtration system of sand, aquatic plants, and ultraviolet light (and a bit of chlorine) to make it safe for swimming. To get there, take the Metro to the Ile Ste-Hélène station (tel. 514/872-6093).

If you prefer a pool and your hotel doesn't have one, take the Metro to Viau station and **Olympic Park,** 4141 Pierre-de-Coubertin, which has indoor six pools, open from about 9:30am to 9pm Monday through Friday and 1 to 4pm on Saturday and Sunday. Call ahead to confirm swim schedules, which are affected by holidays and swim competitions (tel. 514/252-4622).

The **City of Montréal Department of Sports and Leisure** can give you more information about other city pools, indoor or outdoor (tel. 514/872-6211); admission varies from free to about $4, with the exception of the artificial beach, Plage de l'Ile Notre-Dame, which is $6 for adults, seniors, and students; $2 for children 5 to 18.

3. SAVVY SHOPPING

THE SHOPPING SCENE U.S. readers of this book have the advantage of markdowns on all prices encountered in Montréal shops due to the 10% to 12% difference in exchange rates between the Canadian and U.S. dollars. If you're traveling with U.S. dollars, be sure to take the trouble to go to a bank to exchange your U.S. cash for Canadian. Banks will give you the best rate, and the transaction takes only a few minutes. If you spend U.S. money, in dollars or traveler's checks, in the stores, you'll probably get about 5% less for your money than if you had exchanged it in a bank for its Canadian equivalent.

Note that if you're buying with a credit card, the charges will automatically be converted at the favorable bank rate before appearing on your monthly credit-card statement.

BEST BUYS What causes shoppers to part with their money in Montréal? Plenty. Chic clothing, for sure, and the most beautiful men's ties in the world, along with paintings, sculpture, Inuit art, crafts, books, gourmet foods, country antiques, and much more. When buying crafts, it's sometimes hard to tell the difference between crafts and art objects. Careful workmanship and inspiration goes into making Inuit drawings and carvings, or quaint Québec wood-carved figures and patchwork quilts. Prices are a good index, the beauty of the piece matched by a suitably lofty price.

STORE HOURS Most stores are open Monday through Wednesday from 9am to 6pm, Thursday and Friday from 9am to 9pm, and Saturday and Sunday from 11am to 5pm. Department stores downtown tend to open a little later, 10am, and are closed on Sunday, but many shops and boutiques, especially in heavily touristed areas, stay open.

TAXES & REFUNDS Save your receipts any time you shop in a duty-free store in Montréal (indeed, anywhere in Québec or Canada), and ask the shopkeeper for a duty-free form. When you return home mail them to the specified address with the filled-in form, then wait a few months for your refund on the tax you paid to come back to you. A small service fee will have been taken out. The money will not be returned to you at the airport.

GREAT SHOPPING AREAS One of Montréal's prime boutique collections is on rue Crescent between Sherbrooke and Maisonneuve, while haute couture is around the corner, on Sherbrooke. If you are looking for antiques, you'll find them on rue Sherbrooke near the Musée des Beaux-Arts, and along the little side streets near the museum. For more antiques and collectibles, one tempting shop after another, check out the two-block section of rue Notre-Dame between Guy and Atwater.

More boutiques can be found near place Jacques-Cartier and along rue St-Paul in Old Montréal, where many of the shops are open on Sunday. A couple of good art galleries (La Guild Graphique at no. 9 and L'Empreinte at no. 272) are on rue St-Paul, and artists themselves display and sell their works along compact rue St-Amable, just off place Jacques-Cartier; from it, meander into a walkway called Le Jardin Amable, a courtyard filled with kiosks stocked with eye-catching costume jewelry and items crafted in silver and gold. Rue St-Denis north of Sherbrooke has a string of shops where you're assured of finding something fun or funky.

You may also find something noteworthy in the vast accumulation of collectibles in the large flea market (Marché aux Puces) at the Old Port.

As in many cities, some of the best shops in Montréal are in its museums, tops among them the Museum of Fine Arts, Pointe-à-Callière, and the McCord Museum of Canadian History.

DEPARTMENT STORES   Most of Montréal's great and dazzling emporia stretch along rue Ste-Catherine (except for Holt Renfrew), from Guy Street eastward to Phillips Square at rue Aylmer: Eaton's, Ogilvy, La Baie, and Henry Birks. A walk along this 12-block stretch can keep a serious shopper busy for quite some time. Another fine store, Holt Renfrew, is at 1300 rue Sherbrooke ouest, at the corner of rue de la Montagne.

SHOPPING COMPLEXES   A unique facet of Montréal, its Underground City is a warren of hidden passageways connecting 1,600 shops in 10 shopping complexes, one more modern and chic than the next. Consider the possibilities: **Centre Eaton,** 705 Ste-Catherine ouest, next door to Eaton's department store; **Complexe Desjardins,** bounded by rues Jeanne-Mance, Ste-Catherine, St-Urbain, and boulevard René-Lévesque, with waterfalls and fountains, trees and hanging vines, music, and lanes of shops going off in every direction, and elevators whisking people up to one of the four tall office towers or the Méridien Hotel; **Les Cours Mont-Royal,** 1455 Peel, a modern restoration and architectural recycling of the old Mount Royal Hotel; **Place Alexis-Nihon,** rue Atwater at rue Ste-Catherine, a shopping center/apartment complex facing the Montréal Forum; **Place Bonaventure,** at de la Gauchetière and University, perhaps the city's largest shopping complex, with 125 boutiques (and the Bonaventure Hilton International); **Place Montréal Trust,** 1500 McGill College, a five-story shopping complex; Place Ville-Marie, opposite the Queen Elizabeth Hotel on René-Lévesque, between boulevard René-Lévesque and Cathcart, Montréal's first great shopping complex and called simply "PVM"; **Promenades de la Cathédrale,** at the corner of rue University and rue Ste-Catherine, with 255 shops; the new **Ruelle des Fortifications,** in the World Trade Center, on rue St-Pierre between rues St-Antoine and St-Jacques, with 80 upscale boutiques in a quiet setting, the centerpiece of which is two fountains, one modern and one traditional; and **Westmount Square,** at rue Wood and rue Ste-Catherine, a shopping center/office complex/condominium designed by Mies van der Rohe.

Besides shops, the **Underground City** is home to (at last count) 200 restaurants, 45 bank branches, 34 theaters and cinemas, two exhibition halls, and numerous hotels.

4. EVENING ENTERTAINMENT

Montréal's reputation for lively nightlife stretches back to Prohibition times (the U.S.'s), and though bar-hopping still remains a popular activity, most Montréalers' nocturnal pursuits are as cultural as they are social: they enjoy the symphony, the opera, the theater, the cinema. The city boasts its own outstanding symphony, French- and English-speaking theater companies, and the incomparable Cirque du Soleil (Sun Circus); it is also on the concert circuit that includes Chicago, Boston, and New York, so rock singers, orchestra conductors and virtuosos, ballet and modern dance companies, and internationally known entertainers pass through frequently.

In summer, the city becomes livelier than usual with several particularly fun events: the **Montréal Jazz Festival,** the **Just for Laughs Festival,** and the flashy **International Fireworks Competition.** Every even year (in 1994 and 1996, say) the **Cirque du Soleil** presents a circus par excellence.

Every autumn, at the end of September and the beginning of October, the exciting **Festival International de Nouvelle Danse** attracts modern dance troupes and choreographers from around the world, along with enthusiastic audiences.

Montréal's daily newspapers, both French and English—check *La Presse* or the *Gazette*—carry listings of films, clubs, and performances in their Friday and Saturday editions. Also check listings in the free weekly newspapers *Mirror* (in English) or *Voir* (in French), available in many Montréal cafés.

If you simply want to pub-crawl, listen to some music (or jokes), head for rue Crescent, rue Bishop, or rue de la Montagne, north of rue Ste-Catherine; all three streets are near each other and parallel to each other. To do a little dancing, choose rue Ste-Catherine, the address for several popular discos. For jazz and blues, go to Old Montréal and meander along rue St-Paul, where the music floats into the street and lures you inside, or go to the Latin Quarter, where students cluster in the clubs along lower rue St-Denis.

When they graduate and become young professionals, they gravitate slightly uptown to the more sophisticated nightspots along upper rue St-Denis. In the Plateau Mont-Royal area, boulevard St-Laurent, known locally as "the Main," has become an outpost of chic restaurants and late-night clubs; this lively stretch runs for several miles, roughly from avenue Viger to St-Viateur. St-Laurent is a good place to end up in the wee hours; you'll always find a welcome mat out.

THE PERFORMING ARTS

THEATER

CENTAUR THEATER, 453 rue St-François-Xavier. Tel. 514/288-3161.

The Old Stock Exchange building (1903) is now home to Montréal's primary English-language theater; the 1993 season included *Uncle Vanya, Dancing at Lughnasa, Someone Who'll Watch over Me, La Bête,* and *Cabaret.* Off-season, the theater is rented out to other groups, French- and English-speaking. The Centaur complex includes two theaters, a lounge, and bar, which is open during intermission and after the show. Box office open usually Monday to Wednesday from 10am to 5pm, Thursday to Saturday from 10am to 8:30pm, Sunday from noon to 5pm; performances, October to June, Tuesday to Saturday at 8pm, Sunday at 7pm, Saturday (and most Sunday) matinees at 2pm. Metro: Place d'Armes.

Prices: Tickets $20–$30, students $16, seniors $12.

SAIDYE BRONFMAN CENTRE, 5170 chemin de la Côte-Ste-Catherine. Tel. 514/739-2301 (information) or 514/739-7944 (box office).

Not far from St. Joseph's Oratory, the Saidye Bronfman Centre stages two plays a year in Yiddish. They run for three to four weeks, usually in June and November. Other times during the year, the 300-seat theater hosts dance, music, children's, and other theatrical programs, and an occasional lecture or forum. There's also an art gallery on the premises, with changing exhibits almost monthly, and across the street, in the Edifice Cummings House, a small Holocaust Museum and the Jewish Public Library. The center takes it name from Saidye Bronfman, wife of Samuel Bronfman, a founder (with his brother) of Seagram Company Ltd. Box office open usually Monday to Thursday from 11am to 8pm, Friday from 10am to 4pm, Sunday from noon to 7pm—call ahead; performances Tuesday to Thursday at 8pm, Saturday at 8pm, Sunday at 1:30 and 7pm. Metro: Côte-Ste-Catherine. Bus: No. 129 ouest (west).

Prices: Tickets $18, seniors $15.

MAJOR PERFORMANCE ARTS COMPANIES

ENSEMBLE NATIONAL DE FOLKLORE, LES SORTILEGES. Tel. 514/274-5655.

This folkloric company, whose name means "magic spell," has been around for 25 years and is the best known of its kind in Canada. Its 20 dancers, representing almost as many different countries, dazzle audiences with their colorful costumes and multiethnic, including québecois folk dances and lore. They perform in various halls in Montréal; watch for announcements in local papers, particularly in summer.

Price: Tickets free–$15, depending on the show.

LES GRANDS BALLETS CANADIENS, Salle Wilfrid-Pelletier, Place des Arts, 260 de Maisonneuve ouest. Tel. 514/849-8681.

The Grand Canadian Ballet has had a large following for more than 35 years, performing both a classical and a modern repertory and bringing to prominence new Canadian choreographers and composers in the process. It has toured internationally and was the first Canadian ballet company to be invited to the People's Republic of China. Its production of *The Nutcracker Suite* the last couple of weeks in December is always a big event in Montréal. Box office open Monday to Saturday from noon to 8pm; performances, late October to early May at 8pm. Metro: Place des Arts.

Prices: Tickets $12–$40.

METROPOLITAN ORCHESTRA OF MONTREAL, Maisonneuve Theatre, Place des Arts, 260 de Maisonneuve ouest. Tel. 514/598-0870.

This orchestra, whose conductor is Agnes Grossman, has a regular season at Place des Arts but also performs in St-Jean-Baptiste church and tours regionally. It's a young assemblage age-wise; most of the musicians are in their mid-thirties. Box office open Monday to Saturday from noon to 8pm; performances, mid-October to early April, usually at 8pm. Metro: Place des Arts.

Prices: Tickets $15–$30.

MONTREAL SYMPHONY ORCHESTRA, Salle Wilfrid-Pelletier, Place des Arts, 260 de Maisonneuve ouest. Tel. 514/842-3402.

The world-famous orchestra, under the baton of Swiss conductor Charles Dutoit (and Zubin Mehta before him), performs at Place des Arts and the Notre-Dame Basilica, as well as around the world, and may be heard on numerous recordings. Box office open Monday to Saturday from noon to 8pm; performances, usually at 8pm. Metro: Place des Arts.

Prices: Tickets $10–$50.

OPERA DE MONTREAL, Salle Wilfrid-Pelletier, Place des Arts, 260 de Maisonneuve ouest. Tel. 514/985-2222 (information) or 514/985-2258 (tickets).

Founded in 1980, this outstanding opera company mounts about seven productions a year in Montréal, with talented performers from Québec and abroad participating in productions such as *Romeo and Juliet, Madama Butterfly,* and *Die Fledermaus.* Video translations from the original language into French and English keep the audience clued in to what's going on. Box office open Monday to Friday from 9am to 5pm; performances, September to June, usually at 8pm. Metro: Place des Arts.

Prices: Tickets $18–$76; 15% discount for students.

CONCERT HALLS & ALL-PURPOSE AUDITORIUMS

MONTREAL FORUM, 2313 rue Ste-Catherine, at Atwater. Tel. 514/932-2582.

Big-name stars and groups are booked into Montréal's Forum, which is perhaps best known as home to the Montréal Canadiens hockey team. If a concert is scheduled, rest assured flyers, radio and TV ads, and general informational osmosis will let you know. It seats up to 16,500 for hockey. The Forum will move to a more central location in spring 1996. Box office open Monday to Friday from 10am to 6pm, to 9pm days of events; performances, 7:30 or 8pm. Metro: Atwater.

Prices: Tickets $15–$40.

MONTREAL SPECTRUM, 318 rue Ste-Catherine ouest. Tel. 514/861-5851.

True to its name, it hosts a spectrum of entertainers from pop singers to comedians and is host to part of the city's annual jazz festival. All seats are available on a first-come, first served basis, so arrive early. Box office open Monday to Saturday from 10am to 9pm, Sunday from noon to 5pm; performances, 8:30 or 9pm. Metro: Place des Arts, Bleury exit.

Prices: Tickets $20–$40.

PLACE DES ARTS, 260 bd. de Maisonneuve ouest. Tel. 514/285-4200 (information), 514/842-2112 (tickets), or 514/844-1211 (guided tours).

Founded in 1963 and in its striking new home since 1992, Place des Arts mounts performances of musical concerts, opera, dance, and theater in five halls: Salle Wilfrid-Pelletier (2,982 seats), where the Montréal Symphony Orchestra performs; the Maisonneuve Theatre (1,460 seats), where the Metropolitan Orchestra of Montréal and the McGill Chamber Orchestra perform; Jean-Duceppe Theatre (755 seats); the new Cinquième Salle, which opened in 1992 (350 seats), and the small Café de la Place Theatre (138 seats). Noontime performances are often scheduled. The Museum of Contemporary Art, which moved here in 1992, also has concerts and lectures on a regular basis. Box office open Monday to Saturday from noon to 8pm; performances, usually at 8pm. Metro: Place des Arts.

Prices: Ticket prices vary according to hall and performance.

POLLACK CONCERT HALL, McGill University, 555 rue Sherbrooke ouest. Tel. 514/398-4547.

This hall, in a landmark building dating from 1899 and fronted by a statue of Queen Victoria, constantly bustles with activity, especially during the school year. You can attend a concert or recital by professionals, students, or soloists from McGill's music faculty. Some of the most memorable concerts are available on the university's own label, McGill Records. Concerts are also given in the campus's smaller Redpath Hall, 3461 rue McTavish, with an entrance at McTavish Gate (tel. 514/398-4547). Performances, 8pm. Metro: McGill.

Prices: Tickets almost always free.

THEATRE DE VERDURE, Lafontaine Park. Tel. 514/872-2644.

Nestled in a quiet city park, the open-air theater presents free music and dance concerts and theater, often with well-known artists and performers. Sometimes they even show outdoor movies; instead of a drive-in, it's a "walk-in." Pack a picnic. Performances: June to August; call for days and times. Metro: Sherbrooke. Bus: No. 24.

Prices: Free.

THEATRE ST-DENIS, 1594 rue St-Denis. Tel. 514/849-4211.

Recently refurbished, this theater in the heart of lively St-Denis, hosts a variety of shows, including pop singers and groups and comedians, as well as the popular "Just for Laughs Festival" in summer. It houses two theaters, one seating more than 2,000 people, one almost 1,000. Box office open daily from noon to 9pm; performances, usually 8pm. Metro: Berri-UQAM.

Prices: Tickets $25–$40.

A CIRCUS *EXTRAORDINAIRE*

CIRQUE DU SOLEIL, 1217 rue Notre-Dame est. Tel. 514/522-2324.

See it, and it will become the circus by which you will gauge all others. At a Cirque du Soleil (Sun Circus) performance, you don't have to worry that the animals are being mistreated—because there are no animals. What you do see and experience is pure magic, pure skill, pure theater, and pure fun, with plenty of clowns, trapeze artists, tightrope walkers, and contortionists. Performances are held in the Old Port, on quai Jacques-Cartier. Open late April to early June in even-numbered years; the show goes on the road throughout North America during odd-numbered years. Box office, late April to June, Tuesday to Sunday from 9am to 9pm; performances, Monday to Friday 8pm, Saturday 4 and 8pm, Sunday 1 and 5pm. Metro: Champ-de-Mar.

Prices: Tickets $14–$35 adults, $7–$22 children.

THE CLUB & MUSIC SCENE

For up-to-date information on who's performing where and when, check the entertainment section of the Saturday edition of the *Gazette*.

COMEDY CLUBS   The city has two comedy clubs: the **Comedy Nest,** 1459 rue Crescent, third floor (tel. 514/849-NEST), upstairs from the popular Sir Winston Churchill Pub, and the **Comedy Works,** 1238 rue Bishop, upstairs (tel. 514/398-9661), which often features top local comedians as well as headliners from Toronto, New York, or Boston.

FOLK, JAZZ, BLUES & ROCK   For folk music, head to Old Montréal and **Aux Deux Pierrots,** 104 rue St-Paul est (tel. 514/861-1270); in summer the Pierrots' terrace area next door, Pierrot-la-Bire, is open.

Also in Old Montréal is a long-standing favorite for jazz, **L'Air du Temps,** 191 rue St-Paul ouest at rue St-François-Xavier (tel. 514/842-2003), which has occupied this corner for a long *temps*. Downtown, jazz can be heard at **Biddle's,** 2060 rue Aylmer (tel. 514/842-8656).

Deep in the Latin Quarter is a lively jazz bar, the **Grand Café,** 1720 rue St-Denis (tel. 514/849-6955), with the stage upstairs, a pool table downstairs, and sometimes blues or rock for a change of pace. When it's chilly out, they stoke up the fireplace.

If your heart is set on hearing blues, head for the Latin Quarter and **Les Beaux Esprits,** 2073 rue St-Denis, just down the hill from rue Sherbrooke (tel. 514/844-0882). Simple and unpretentious, it attracts young, artsy, avid fans who come to hear local musicians.

Le Quai des Brumes, 4481 rue St-Denis (tel. 514/499-0467), is a good choice for jazz, blues, and rock. Jazz gets lots of play upstairs in the Central bar. Loosely translated the name means "foggy dock," and the crowd has been described as "a fairly uniform group of postsixties francophone smokers."

In the Hôtel Château Champlain, 1050 rue de la Gauchetière ouest (tel. 514/878-9000), there's the **Caf' Conc.** The name is an abbreviated version of "Café Concert," and it presents reviews of music and dance four nights a week. Call for current schedule. Tickets run about $30.

DANCE CLUBS/DISCOS   Among the most popular discos in Montréal at this writing are three conveniently strung out along rue Ste-Catherine: **Metropolis,** 59 rue Ste-Catherine est (tel. 514/288-5559), in a handsome old building dating from the 1890s, which can accommodate 2,200 gyrating bodies at once; **Les Foufounes Electriques,** 87 rue Ste-Catherine est (tel. 514/845-5485); and **Le Royal,** at 251 rue Ste-Catherine est (tel. 514/848-0302).

A pleasant enough place where a homesick American would feel at home, the **Hard Rock Café,** 1458 rue Crescent (tel. 514/987-1420), like so many Montréal nightspots, gets crowded on weekends.

The most popular gay disco in Montréal is **Le K.O.X.,** 1182 rue Montcalm (tel. 514/523-0064). With a modern interior with stainless-steel drums stacked one on the other, it draws an enthusiastic mixed crowd of men and women.

THE BAR SCENE

A remarkable concentration of restaurants, bars, and cafés with European character peppers boulevard St-Laurent and rue St-Denis, while more of an Anglo atmosphere permeates the establishments along rue Crescent.

On rue St-Denis, the most popular bar in the summer is **Le St-Sulpice,** 1682 rue St-Denis (tel. 514/844-9458), because of its large courtyard; the crowd is a young crowd and it's often crowded. The noisily upbeat **Le Continental Bistro Américain,** 4169 rue St-Denis (tel. 514/845-6842), draws the after-theater crowd from Théâtre Saint-Denis.

On boulevard St-Laurent, **Lux,** 5220 bd. St-Laurent (tel. 514/271-9277), known for its late hours and unique ambience, is a favorite gathering spot for young Montréalers. The converted textile mill has a grand circular main room with steel floor and two stainless-steel staircases spiraling up to a glass-domed second floor. The bar's on the ground floor, behind the café, which is surrounded by racks displaying more than 1,000 magazines. If you don't want to talk to anyone, you can always read.

At the **Shed Café,** 3515 bd. St-Laurent (tel. 514/842-0220), it looks like the ceiling is caving in on the bar, but that's just part of the decor; they sell good local beers.

If you like whisky, particularly imports like Glenfiddich, make the trip farther uptown to the **Whisky Café,** 5800 bd. St-Laurent at Bernard (tel. 514/278-2646). There are 30 different labels to sample here. Trouble is, you pay stiffly for the privilege. Most patrons stick to beer, and nurse it. The decor is sophisticated, with handmade tiled tables and large wood-enclosed columns, but the real lure is the men's urinal, with a waterfall for a *pissoir.* Women are welcome to tour it.

Young professionals crowd into the **Lutècia Bar** in the lobby of L'Hôtel de la Montagne, 1430 rue de la Montagne (tel. 514/288-5656), as kitschy and as popular as they come. Expect a standing-room-only crowd weeknights after 5:30pm, when there's often live piano music and jazz.

An older crowd seeks out the quiet **Ritz Bar** in the Ritz-Carlton Hotel, 1228 rue Sherbrooke ouest (tel. 514/842-4212), which is adjacent to the Ritz's Café de Paris restaurant and shares its piano player. It's off the hotel lobby, to your right.

Nearby, **Sir Winston Churchill Pub,** 1459 rue Crescent (tel. 514/288-0623), is a landmark on rue Crescent, with its English-pub decor (and grub) and sidewalk tables on the ground level. The pub is frequented by a mixed crowd, with upscale young professionals predominating. **Thursday's,** 1441–1449 rue Crescent (tel. 514/288-5656), is a prime watering place for Montréal's young, upwardly mobile professional set. A pub and disco connected to Les Beaux Jeudis restaurant in the same building, Thursday's may take its name from ancient custom of prowling the nightspots on Thursday evening in search of the perfect date for Friday night.

BARS WITH A VIEW **La Tour de Ville,** on the 32nd floor of the Hôtel Radisson Gouverneurs Montréal, 777 rue University (tel. 514/879-1370), has what is probably the best view of Montréal, and directly above it, the city's only revolving restaurant, with the same name (see "Dining" in Chapter 7). The bar has a dance floor and a band five nights a week (Wednesday through Sunday from 9pm to 1am, 2am on Saturday); there's no cover, but drinks are steep, from $5.50 to $9. The bar opens daily at 6pm; on Monday and Tuesday, when there is no band, it closes around midnight.

The bar in the restaurant **l'Escapade,** on the 36th floor of the Hôtel Château Champlain, 1050 rue de la Gauchetière (tel. 514/878-9000), also provides a fine view of the city.

In warm weather only, the **Sunset Terrasse** atop the Hôtel de la Montagne, 1430 rue de la Montagne (tel. 514/288-5656), draws imbibers like bees to honey to the 20th floor to enjoy the bar, which is built on two levels, rooftop pool, dance floor, and two gazebos.

GAY BARS Gay bars come and go, but one with staying power is **Kache,** 1450 rue Ste-Catherine est (tel. 514/523-0064), on the ground level of Complexe Gai in the Gay Village. It resembles a hotel lobby bar (the inviting kind) and is popular with both men and women. Once you've had a drink or two here, you can dance the night away at K.O.X. disco (see above), on the same premises.

L'Exit II, 4297 rue St-Denis, is a lesbian bar popular with women of all ages. It has pool tables and a dance floor that's put to good use on Fridays and Saturdays, and is a good center for information about gay goings-on in the city (tel. 514/843-8696).

MORE ENTERTAINMENT

A CASINO In autumn 1993, the **Montréal Casino,** Québec's first casino, opened on Ile Notre-Dame in the modern French Pavilion from the days of Expo '67. The casino has 65 gaming tables, including roulette, blackjack, and mini-baccarat, and 1,200 one-armed bandits. It can accommodate 5,300 people, who've come to try their luck, have a meal, or simply survey the scene. Gaming hours are 11am to 3am daily (tel. 514/282-8000). You can take the Metro to the Ile Ste-Hélène stop, which is adjacent to Ile Notre-Dame, and walk or take the shuttle bus from there. No shorts or jeans are allowed.

CINEMA   In Montréal, English-language films are usually presented with subtitles in French. However, if the initials VF follow a movie title, that means it's *version française* and it has been dubbed. Besides the many first-run movie houses that advertise in the daily newspapers, Montréal is rich in "ciné-clubs," which tend to be slightly older and show second-run, foreign, and art films at reduced prices. A downtown ciné-club that shows English-language films is the **Conservatoire d'Art Cinématographique,** at 1400 bd. de Maisonneuve ouest; the price of admission is $4 per screening (tel. 514/848-3878). Old movies are also shown at no charge at the unique eatery, **Café Ciné-Lumière,** 5163 St-Laurent, where headsets are provided for individual listening while dining (tel. 514/495-1796).

In first-run movie houses, admission is $8 for adults in the evening, $5 for adults in the afternoon, and $4.50 for children all the time. At Odeon Cineplex theaters, on Tuesday tickets are $4.25 day and evening. The **Centre Eaton,** 705 rue Ste-Catherine ouest, near the corner of McGill, has a complement of six modern cinemas. And I must commend the **Palace** cinema, at 698 Ste-Catherine ouest (tel. 514/866-6991), for providing 14 stalls in the women's restroom; admission here is $4 all the time.

The **National Film Board of Cinema (Cinema ONF),** 1564 rue St-Denis (tel. 514/796-6895), shows Canadian and international films, primarily in English and French, particularly film classics. Showings are Tuesday through Sunday; call for times.

Awesome images surround you on the seven-story screen in the **IMAX theater** in the Old Port, at de la Commune and St-Laurent (tel. 514/496-4629). This is fun entertainment for the whole family.

POOL   A nondescript entry and a stairway that smells of stale beer lead to a surprisingly trendy pool hall that attracts as many men and women who come to drink and socialize as to play pool. **Le Swimming** (get it?), 3643 bd. St-Laurent (tel. 514/282-POOL), has 12 pool tables, piped-in music, and six TV monitors. **Sharx,** 1606 rue Ste-Catherine ouest (tel. 514/934-3105), in the Faubourg Ste-Catherine, is considered by some to be the city's best pool hall.

CHAPTER 9

THE LAURENTIANS & THE ESTRIE REGION

1. **THE LAURENTIANS**
- **WHAT'S SPECIAL ABOUT THE LAURENTIANS & THE ESTRIE REGION**
2. **THE ESTRIE REGION**

To "go up north," a favorite pastime in Québec, you only have to drive one hour north of Montréal to find yourself in the heart of the Laurentian mountains, home to impressive year-round resorts and ski centers, including Mont Tremblant, the highest peak in eastern Canada. Or head east from Montréal, travel for an hour, and you'll come to the idyllic Estrie Region, also called the Eastern Townships, blessed with picturesque lakes and villages, and unforgettable country inns.

SEEING THE LAURENTIANS & THE ESTRIE REGION

INFORMATION For tourist information on the entire province, contact **Tourisme Québec,** Case postale 20,000, Québec, PQ, G1K 7X2 (tel. 873-2015 in the Montréal area, or toll free 800/363-7777 from Québec, elsewhere in Canada, and the U.S.).

In Section 1 of this chapter you'll find specifics on the Laurentians, including how to get there and where to find regional tourist information. Section 2 contains similar information on the Estrie region.

A NOTE ON TAXES Most goods and services in Canada are taxed 7% by the federal government. On top of that, the Province of Québec adds an additional 8% tax on goods and services, and, since summer 1992, a 4% tax on hotels. In Québec, the federal tax is called—and appears on the bill as—the TPS (in other parts of Canada, it's called the GST), and the provincial tax is known as the TVQ. Tourists may receive a rebate on both the federal and provincial tax on items they have purchased but not used in Québec, as well as on lodging. To take advantage of this, you have to fill out necessary forms (ask for them at duty-free shops and hotels) and submit them, with the original receipts, within a year of the purchase. Contact the Canadian consulate or Québec tourism office for up-to-the-minute information about taxes and rebates. And save those receipts.

---

1. THE LAURENTIANS

37 miles (60km) N of Montréal

GETTING THERE By Car The fast and scenic Autoroute des Laurentides (Laurentian Autoroute), also known as Highway 15, goes straight from Montréal to the Laurentian mountains. Just follow the signs to St-Jérôme. The exit numbers are actually the distance in kilometers the village is from Montréal (your first stop, for

WHAT'S SPECIAL ABOUT THE LAURENTIANS & THE ESTRIE REGION

The Sporting Life in the Laurentians

☐ Nineteen ski centers, several ski schools, and slopes that are skiable, day and night, from mid-November to mid-April.

☐ Fifty-six miles of cross-country trails, and a cross-country ski school.

☐ Other sports—mountain biking, hiking, boating, golf, and fall-foliage forays.

Cool for Kids in the Laurentians

☐ Séraphin Village, near Ste-Adèle, the recreation of a 19th-century Laurentian village.

☐ Village du Père Noël, in Val-David, the summer residence of Santa Claus.

☐ Mont St-Sauveur, Canada's largest water park, with a wave pool and water slide.

☐ The "Superglissoire," a half-mile-long superslide on Mont-Gabriel, for summer fun.

The Laurentians' Accommodations par Excellence

☐ Year-round resorts like L'Esterel, Tremblant, Gray Rocks, and Far Hills.

☐ Chalets and cottages, for a true alpine experience.

☐ Intimate inns with memorable dining rooms.

☐ B&Bs and motels with personality.

The Picturesque Villages of Estrie

☐ North Hatley, the jewel of Lake Massawippi, in an idyllic setting, with excellent inns.

☐ Sutton, reminiscent of New England, with cafés, a good bookstore, and an old Quaker cemetery.

☐ Stanstead Plain, with gorgeous Victorian houses.

The Undiscovered Resorts of Estrie

☐ Orford, the centerpiece of a recreational park and an alpine ski center.

☐ Sutton, with popular alpine and glade skiing in winter and hiking and mountain biking trails in summer.

☐ Owl's Head, a popular family ski center.

☐ Bromont, with downhill and cross-country skiing, 43 miles of mountain biking trails, and an aquatic park.

Fine Cuisine

☐ The French tradition of fine dining.

---

instance, will probably be at the Laurentian Tourism House at Exit 39 in St-Jérôme, and St-Jérôme is 39km, or 24 miles, from Montréal). This is a pretty drive, once you've invested half an hour to get past the tangle of expressways surrounding Montréal. The Laurentian Autoroute gives a sweeping, panoramic introduction to the area, from the rolling hills and forests of the Lower Laurentians to the mountain drama of the Upper Laurentians.

If you prefer smaller, slower roads, at St-Jérôme you can pick up the older, parallel Highway 117, along which the region's towns (and motels) are strung. As you approach each town, signs will direct you to the local tourism information office for tips on lodging, restaurants, and things to do. North of Ste-Agathe, Highway 117 actually becomes the major artery for the region, continuing deep into Québec's north country and finally ending at the Ontario border hundreds of miles from Montréal.

Be forewarned that Québec's equivalent of the Highway Patrol keeps a careful lookout for speeders along the stretch of Highway 15 between St-Faustin and Ste-Adèle.

By Bus Limocar Laurentides buses depart Montréal's Terminus Voyageur, 505 bd. de Maisonneuve est, stopping in most Laurentian towns, including Ste-Agathe, Ste-Adèle, St-Jovite; call for schedules (tel. 514/842-2281). An express bus can make the run to St-Jovite and Mont Tremblant in less than two hours, while a local bus, making all the stops, takes almost three. From Montréal to Ste-Adèle takes about 1½ hours, 15 minutes more to Val-Morin and Val-David. Some of the major resorts provide their own bus service at an additional charge.

By Limousine Taxis and limousines await your arrival at both Dorval and Mirabel airports in Montréal, and will gladly whisk you off to any Laurentian hideaway—for a price. To pay for the one-hour trip by limo from Dorval is pretty steep, but four or five people sharing the cost brings the price down considerably. Mirabel is actually in the Laurentians, five minutes south of St-Antoine and 35 minutes from the slopes. Ask the standard fare to your inn or lodge when you call for reservations. In most cases the inn will take the responsibility for seeing that a taxi or limo is indeed waiting for you, and they may even help you find other guests arriving at the same time to share the cost.

ESSENTIALS For an orientation to the entire region, make your first stop La Maison du Tourisme des Laurentides, 14142 rue de la Chapelle, R.R. 1, St-Jérôme, PQ, J7Z 5T4 (tel. 514/436-8532; fax 514/436-5309), a regional tourist information and reservations office located in St-Jérôme at Exit 39 off the Laurentian Highway 15. The red-roofed cottage is just to the east off the highway; take Highway 158 and follow the signs. In summer, it's open from 8:30am to 8:30pm daily.

The soft, rounded mountains making up the Laurentian Shield are among the oldest in the world, worn down by wind, water, fire, and ice over the eons, while titanic upheavals were forming jagged mountain ranges elsewhere in the world.

A half century ago the first ski schools, rope tows, and trails were established in these mountains, and today there are 19 ski centers in a 40-mile radius, and cross-country skiing has as enthusiastic a following as downhill (the best cross-country trails are at Far Hills in Val-Morin and L'Esterel in Ville d'Esterel, and on the grounds of a monastery called Domaine du St. Bernard near Villa Bellevue in Mont Tremblant). Posh Laurentian resorts and modest lodges and inns are packed each winter with skiers, some of them through April.

But skiing is only half the Laurentians' story. As transportation improved, people saw the alluring opportunities for water sports, golf (courses in the area now number 30), tennis, mountain biking, hiking, and every other kind of summer sport. Before long the region gained a far-flung reputation for good dining, refined service, and genteel atmosphere that survives to this day.

Winter or summer, a visit to any of the little villages and luxurious resorts in the Laurentians is sure to yield unforgettable memories. Keep in mind that the busiest times are in July and August, during the Christmas–New Year's holiday period, and in February and March. Other times of the year, reservations are easier to get, prices of virtually everything are lower, and crowds less dense. Some of the resorts, inns, and lodges close down for a couple of weeks in the spring and the fall.

If you visit during March or April, you're in for a treat, for this is the season when the maple trees are tapped, and "sugar shacks" spring up everywhere to serve delighted customers eggs with ham and maple syrup, crêpes with maple syrup, or sugarie.

In May and June, the black flies can be bad in the region, so come prepared for them with Cutters or Avon Skin So Soft. You can get "Off" in local shops. In June, the region's major event, its annual **Wine Festival,** is held for about a week, with the emphasis on gastronomy and wine tasting; a dozen restaurants in the area take part.

July and August usher in glorious summer days in the Laurentians, and the last two weeks in September the leaves put on an unrivaled show of autumnal color. Skiers can usually expect reliable snow from mid-December to mid-April.

As for prices, they can be difficult to pin down: The large resorts have so many various types of rooms, cottages, meal plans, discounts, and packages that you may need a travel agent (who will be glad to help you at no charge) to work your way

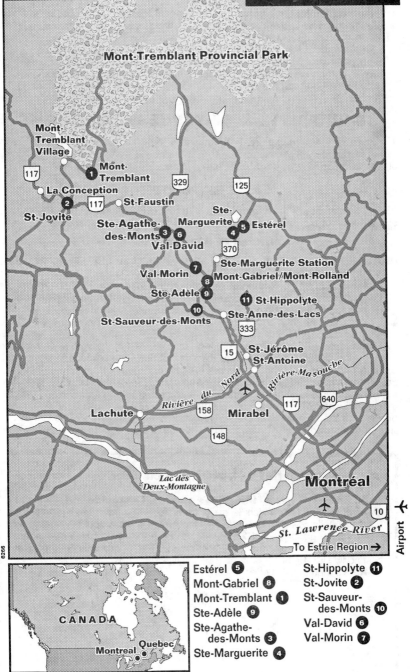

THE LAURENTIANS

Mont-Tremblant Provincial Park

Mont-Tremblant Village

117

1 Mont-Tremblant

La Conception

329

125

2 117 St-Faustin

St-Jovite

Ste-Agathe-des-Monts **3** **6**
Val-David

Ste-Marguerite **4** **5** Estérel

370

Ste-Marguerite Station

7 Val-Morin

8 Mont-Gabriel/Mont-Rolland

Ste-Adèle **9**

11 St-Hippolyte

10

St-Sauveur-des-Monts

Ste-Anne-des-Lacs

333

15 St-Jérôme
St-Antoine

Rivière du Nord

Rivière-Masouche

158

117

640

Lachute

Mirabel

148

Lac des Deux-Montagne

Montréal

10

St. Lawrence River

To Estrie Region →

Airport

6266

CANADA

Montreal Quebec

Estérel **5**	St-Hippolyte **11**
Mont-Gabriel **8**	St-Jovite **2**
Mont-Tremblant **1**	St-Sauveur-des-Monts **10**
Ste-Adèle **9**	
Ste-Agathe-des-Monts **3**	Val-David **6**
Ste-Marguerite **4**	Val-Morin **7**

through the thicket. But knowing about all the details is important if you are out to have the most fun for the least money. The regional tourism association, **La Maison du Tourisme des Laurentides,** rue de la Chapelle, R.R. 1, St-Antoine, PQ, J7X 5T4, has a central reservation service that can make reservations for you at no charge (tel. 514/436-8532).

Remember that Montréalers crowd the highways when they "go up north" on weekends, particularly during the good skiing months of February and March, so plan ahead when making reservations.

A final note: Pet lovers, despair. Few Laurentian resorts accept animals.

ST-HIPPOLYTE & ST-SAUVEUR-DES-MONTS

The first two towns to explore, both known for their haute cuisine, are so close to Montréal they may be visited on a day trip. St-Hippolyte is only 34 miles (55km) north of Montréal; St-Sauveur-des-Monts, only 37 miles (60km) north of Montréal.

ST-HIPPOLYTE

It's less than an hour's drive from Montréal to the village of Lac L'Achigan, which is officially part of the town of St-Hippolyte, and an outstanding restaurant.

Where to Stay and Dine

AUBERGE DES CEDRES, no. 26, 305th Ave., Lac L'Achigan, PQ, J0R 1P0. Tel. 514/563-2083. Fax 514/563-1663.
  Cuisine: FRENCH. **Reservations:** Recommended. **Directions:** Follow the Laurentian Autoroute to Exit 45 (Lafontaine–St-Hippolyte). At the first traffic light, make a left turn onto Route 333 north for about nine miles (15km).
  $ Prices: Appetizers $6–$22; main courses $20–$32; four-course table d'hôte $35. AE, CB, DC, ER, MC, V.
  Open: July–Aug lunch Tues–Fri noon–2pm; the rest of the year lunch Mon–Fri noon–2pm; year round dinner Tues–Sun 6–9:30pm. **Closed:** Mon for dinner year round; Mon for lunch and dinner July–Aug.

Proprietors Thérèse and Jean Duval moved here from Normandy many years ago, and have been serving some of the region's best cuisine ever since. Mme Duval is the chef de cuisine, while M. Duval is the welcoming host. A typical dinner at the auberge begins with an apéritif in the parlor. You survey the menu, with explanations and suggestions provided by M. Duval. The wine list features good, moderately priced

---

AN IMPORTANT NOTE ON PRICES

Unless stated otherwise, **the prices cited in this guide are given in Canadian dollars,** which is good news for U.S. travelers because the Canadian dollar is worth 25% less than the American dollar, but buys nearly as much. As we go to press, $1 Canadian is worth 75¢ U.S., which means that your $100-a-night hotel room will cost only U.S. $75, and your $6 breakfast costs only U.S. $4.50.

Here's a quick table of equivalents:

Canadian $	U.S. $
$ 1	$ 0.75
5	3.75
10	7.50
20	15.00
50	37.50
80	60.00
100	75.00
200	150.00

wines, as well as rare vintages. When the first course is ready, M. Duval escorts you to your table overlooking the lake. Then the fun begins. Choicest of appetizers is the foie gras frais de canard (fresh duck liver pâté), but there's also smoked salmon or numerous other starters. Fish include trout stuffed with foie gras and served with morel sauce, Dover sole, and filet of doré. Among the meats is the incredible magret de canard à la framboise (sliced breast of wild duck with a mild, tart raspberry sauce), but there are also tournedos, veal, rabbit, and lamb. The desserts are all made at the inn.

Many city people come just for dinner, though you may in fact rent rooms for $75 double or $60 single, or $170 including breakfast and dinner for two—but the real draw is the food.

ST-SAUVEUR-DES-MONTS

Mont St-Sauveur bustles with activity most of the time, so be prepared to have difficulty finding a parking place in season. Dining and snacking are popular activities here, and you can find everything from French food to fast food, crêpes to hot dogs. Pick up some bread or pastries at **Page,** on the town square, as do the locals and Montréalers who have weekend cottages in the area. In season, there's a tourist kiosk on the town square.

The area is well-known for its **night skiing**—23 well-lit trails, only three fewer than those available during the day. The mountain is wide, with a 700-foot vertical drop and a variety of well-groomed trails, making it a good choice for families. In summer, Mont St-Sauveur becomes Canada's largest **water park,** with a wave pool and a mountain slide where you go up in chair lifts and come down in tubes.

Where to Stay

AUBERGE ST-DENIS, 61 rue St-Denis, St-Sauveur-des-Monts, PQ, J0R 1R4. Tel. 514/227-4602, or toll free 800/361-5724. Fax 514/227-8504. 42 rms. A/C MINIBAR TV TEL
$ Rates: $84 single; $94 double; $123 suite. Extra person $10. Meal plans with breakfast and/or dinner available. AE, DC, ER, MC, V.
Set back from the road and surrounded by birch, maples, and evergreens, Auberge St-Denis looks much like a country club, complete with an outdoor pool. Rooms in the old section are modern and comfortable, with fireplace (where you may burn fake logs) and large bath. Those in the new wing are larger and more elegant, with a queen-size bed, fireplace, TV, minibar, and whirlpool. Reception is in the building with the green awning.

L'AUBERGE VICTORIENNE, 119 rue Principale, St-Sauveur-des-Monts, PQ, J0R 1R0. Tel. 514/227-2328 or 514/667-9985. 5 rms.
$ Rates (including full breakfast): $45–$65 single; $60–$70 double. No credit cards. **Parking:** Free; five spaces in front of house.
From the street, it looks like a Victorian doll's house, narrow and made of brick, with a roof more pointed than any mountains in these parts. Inside, it's romantic, with lots of floral touches. I prefer the downstairs bedrooms. The five bedrooms share four full baths, which is almost as good as having a private bath. The 1937 house has been fully renovated, and there's a patio at the side for guests' use. The hearty breakfast may include muesli, lemon bread, muffins, waffles, eggs. The cordial owners are Odette and Karam Guindi; she's French Canadian and a teacher; he's Egyptian, a former banker, and a retired teacher.

MANOIR ST-SAUVEUR, 246 chemin du Lac Millette, St-Sauveur-des-Monts, PQ, J0R 1R3. Tel. 514/227-1811, or toll free 800/361-0505. Fax 514/227-8512. 225 rms. A/C MINIBAR TV TEL **Directions:** Take Exit 60 off Highway 15.
$ Rates: Mid-June to mid-Oct $99–$118 single or double; $10 less the rest of the year. Extra person $10. Children under 18 free. Suite from $180 ($160 off-season). Condos and weekend packages available. AE, DC, ER, MC, V. **Parking:** Free, condos; $5 hotel.
Everything is on a large scale at Manoir St-Sauveur. The hotel itself is big, as are the

grounds, the facilities, the outdoor pool, the rooms, and even the bathrooms. It has a green roof with distinctive dormer windows (you can't miss it from the road), a gym, sauna, indoor pool, outdoor pool, racquetball, squash, tennis, in-house movies, and a shop. The rooms are modern with light-wood furniture.

Where to Dine

LES BERGES, 129 rue Principale. Tel. 514/227-3695.
  Cuisine: FONDUES. **Reservations:** Recommended.
  $ Prices: Appetizers $3.50–$7.50; main courses $11.50–$19.50; daily special $8.50.
  Open: Dinner daily 6–10pm.
It's only open for dinner, and the specialty is fondues: cheese, beef, chicken, seafood. You name it, you can dip it at Les Berges. The filling, reasonably priced special includes a Swiss fondue entrée with a salad (or choose a different fondue and pay the difference). The restaurant, in a house a bit out of town, has linen tablecloths, a terrace café, and a glass-enclosed porch. It's particularly popular in winter as a place to stop in and take the chill off. Licensed.

LES PRES, 231 rue Principale. Tel. 514/227-8580.
  Cuisine: LIGHT FARE. **Reservations:** Not needed.
  $ Prices: Appetizers $2–$4; main courses $5.50–$13.
  Open: Mon–Thurs 11am–9pm, Fri 11am–2am, Sat 9am–11pm, Sun 9am–10pm.
In a striking three-story Victorian house in the middle of town, Les Prés is a good choice if you're just passing through and need a quick bite. Part of the Montréal chain whose name means "the meadows," it has daily lunch specials with soup, a main course, and coffee; à la carte, all main courses come with a vegetable and fries. You can eat out on the porch in summer.

RESTAURANT MARIE-PHILIP, 352 rue Principale. Tel. 514/227-2171.
  Cuisine: FRENCH. **Reservations:** Required.
  $ Prices: Appetizers $7–$13; main courses $22–$29; four-course table d'hôte $27; seven-course table d'hôte $50. AE, DC, ER, MC, V.
  Open: Late June–early Sept dinner Tues–Sun 5–10:30pm; the rest of the year dinner Tues–Sat 5–10:30pm.
The place to try is the award-winning Restaurant Marie-Philip, on the main street but a little removed from the clutch of the action. Look for the little chalet-style place of white stucco, dark wood, and bay windows trimmed with lace curtains. The menu features such items as cassoulet, breast of duck with a pepper-vinegar sauce, or lamb with fresh tarragon sauce and, as an appetizer, lobster lasagne with a saffron-cream sauce.

MONT-GABRIEL

Mont-Gabriel is only 2.5 miles (4km) from Mont St-Sauveur; to get there follow Highway 15 to Exit 64, and turn right at the stop sign. There is no tourist office in Mont-Gabriel, but the staff at Auberge Mont-Gabriel and at nearby tourist bureaus can answer your questions.

Popular as a resort destination and convention spot in summer, Mont-Gabriel truly comes into its own each winter when guests schuss down its 21 trails and slopes and then slide back up again on the seven T-bar lifts, the triple-chair, or the quadruple-chair lift. Snowmaking equipment keeps the slopes slippery, and eight of them are lit for nighttime skiing. Cross-country trails girdle the mountain and range through the surrounding countryside. When you tire of the Mont-Gabriel's trails, you can take a short drive to reach any of several other mountains in the region.

WHERE TO STAY & DINE

STATION TOURISTIQUE MONT-GABRIEL, Mont-Rolland, PQ, J0R 1G0.
  Tel. 514/229-3547, or 514/861-2852 in Montréal, or toll free 800/668-5253 in Canada. Fax 514/229-7034. 126 rms. A/C TV TEL **Directions:** Coming north on the Laurentian Autoroute, take Exit 64.

$ Rates (including breakfast): $92 per person single; $50 per person double; $40 per person triple. Children 6–12 $7.50, under 5 free. Packages available. AE, ER, MC, V.

Perched atop Mont-Gabriel, commanding the highways and the valley and looking like an overgrown log cabin, is the Auberge Mont-Gabriel. Set on a 1,200-acre forest estate, the auberge is a full-fledged resort complex featuring golf/tennis-week programs in summer, ski packages in winter, and comfortable accommodations and fun year-round. I particularly like the rooms in the Tyrol section, because they are spacious and have soft colors and a nice bath (no. 192 also has a great view of the mountains). Those in the Old Lodge are more rustic. Some rooms in the resort have air conditioning and a minibar, but you'll have to request them specially. With the Club Package, you get three meals and unlimited access to all their sports facilities (golf, tennis, mountain biking, Super Slide, and more), and prices include tax and service charge; rates drop if you stay two to five nights.

Dining/Entertainment: Meals are served in the resort's main dining rooms, and in the evenings there's dancing in the main lodge.

Services: In July and August, there are special activity programs for children.

Facilities: Indoor facilities include a pool, sauna, whirlpool, and exercise room. The outdoor swimming pool (summer only) is heated, and there is an 18-hole golf course, volleyball, and basketball. For summer skilike thrills the Mont-Gabriel has its own "Superglissoire" (Super Slide), a half-mile-long track down the mountainside that you descend on a little one-person "sled," shooting down the straightaways and leaning into the corners as fast or as slowly as you wish—don't brake in the curves!

STE-ADELE

Highway 117 goes directly into Ste-Adèle to become its main street, the boulevard Ste-Adèle; or you can take Exit 67 off Highway 15 north.

The village of Ste-Adèle, only 42 miles (67km) north of Montréal, is a near-metropolis compared to the other Laurentian villages that line the upper reaches of Highway 117. What makes it "big" is not so much its population as its services: police, doctors, ambulances, a shopping center, art galleries, and a larger collection of places to stay and dine than you'll find most anywhere else in the Laurentians.

As rue Morin mounts the hill to Lac Rond, Ste-Adèle's resort lake, you'll see why the town is divided into a lower part ("en bas") and an upper part ("en haut"). But once you arrive at the shores of the lake and gaze across its placid surface, you'll understand what makes Ste-Adèle such a popular summer resort.

The **Bureau Touristique de Sainte-Adèle**, at 301 bd. Ste-Adèle (tel. 514/229-2921), is open year-round daily from 9am to 5pm.

WHAT TO SEE & DO

The main street of Ste-Adèle, rue Valiquette, is a busy, narrow, one-way thoroughfare lined with cafés, galleries, and bakeries. But **Lac Rond** is the center of activities during a Ste-Adèle summer. Canoes, sailboats, and "pédalos" (pedal-powered watercraft), rented from several docks, glide here and there, while swimmers splash and play near shoreside beaches.

In winter the surrounding green hills are swathed in white, and the **ski trails** come right down to the frozen lake. You can rent downhill ski equipment and sign up for lessons at Le Chantecler resort, which has 22 trails served by six chair lifts and two T-bars. Some of the trails end right by the main hotel. At the town's **Centre Municipal,** Côtes 40/80, 1400 rue Rolland (tel. 514/229-2921), the trails are good for beginners: Three T-bar lifts will slide you up the slopes for the run down five different trails.

Year-round it's possible to see English-language movies in Ste-Adèle.

SÉRAPHIN VILLAGE, Montée à Séraphin, off Hwy. 177 (Exit 72), Ste-Adèle. Tel. 514/229-4777.

For an excursion into the past, visit this re-creation of the sort of village found throughout the Laurentians almost 100 years ago. Rude log cabins and slightly more refined public buildings set within the forest on crude dirt streets allow you to imagine what life was like during the period of large-scale settlement in the region. The amusement park takes its name from a novel by Claude Henri Grignon entitled *Un homme et son Péché* (A Man and His Sins), which depicts the demanding life of the Laurentian frontier and how one man—Séraphin Poudrier—failed to meet its challenge, responding to its demands with greed rather than generosity. Children will love the park's old-time atmosphere, and for a thrill they can have a ride on "Le Petit Train du Nord," a miniature train that chugs under a covered bridge and sets out for a 20-minute run through the village and the forest. In Bar Chez Ti-Père, you can taste Québec old-time favorites like "caribou," "ti-blanc" (highly alcoholic), and cider.

Admission: $8.50 adults; $6.50 children 12–17; $5 children 5–11.

Open: Mid-May to mid-June and mid-Sept to mid-Oct, Sat–Sun 10am–5pm; mid-June to mid-Sept, daily 10am–5pm. **Directions:** Drive one mile north of Ste-Adèle on Highway 117.

WHERE TO STAY

AUBERGE CHAMPÊTRE, 1435 bd. Ste-Adèle (Hwy. 117), Ste-Adèle, PQ, J0R 1L0. Tel. 514/229-3533, or toll free 800/363-2466. Fax 514/229-3534. 48 rms. A/C TEL TV

$ Rates (including European breakfast): $66–$94 single or double. Extra person $10. Children 12 and younger $6. Lower rate and breakfast included if you stay longer than one night; off-season rates with breakfast included spring and fall; packages available. Discounts and full breakfast available for stays longer than two nights. AE, DC, ER, MC, V.

Considerable savings can be worked into your holiday budget if you choose a place offering accommodations alone, without the extras such as sports possibilities and meals, which are all nearby. Ste-Adèle's Auberge Champêtre is somewhere between a resort motel and a condominium block, boasting several different kinds of modern, rustic-decor accommodations, the most appealing of which are the mid-price-range rooms called "Chalet Nest" and "Whirlpool Nest." The least expensive for two people are the "Champêtre" rooms equipped with a double bed or two twin beds, cable color TV, and AM/FM radio. Besides the Franklin fireplace (with firewood) in each room, the auberge has a pretty breakfast room, its own little pool surrounded by a hedge, as well as lawn furniture, and a walkway beside a stream. Denis Gelinas is the helpful owner.

AUBERGE SPA EXCELSIOR (incorporating Auberge Altitude Days Inn), 3655 bd. Ste-Adèle, Ste-Adèle, PQ, J0R 1L0. Tel. 514/229-7676, or toll free 800/363-2483. Fax 514/229-8310. 104 rms. A/C TV TEL **Directions:** Coming directly from Montréal, take Exit 67 from the autoroute.

$ Rates: $89 per person, double occupancy; $125 person, with breakfast and dinner. AE, MC, V.

A modern, fully equipped resort hostelry, the auberge is perched on a slope above Highway 117 about a mile north of town. Rooms are attractively furnished and spotlessly clean, and all share the luxuries of color TVs, modern bathrooms, and a little heated swimming pool surrounded by lounge chairs (open in summer only). Although you're not right in the town of Ste-Adèle, the place has advantages: indoor and outdoor pools, sauna, whirlpool, bar and restaurant, no-smoking rooms, and the amusements of the Séraphin Village are only a five-minute stroll up the road.

L'EAU A LA BOUCHE, 3003 bd. Ste-Adèle, PQ, J0R 1L0. Tel. 514/229-2991, or toll free 800/363-2582 from Montréal. Fax 514/229-7573. 23 rms, 2 suites. A/C TV TEL

$ Rates (including breakfast): $115 single; $135 double; $220 suite. Packages available. AE, DC, ER, MC, V.

L'Eau à la Bouche started as a restaurant (see "Where to Dine," below), and added a hotel, both of which draw raves. A member of Relais & Châteaux, and set against a mountain, facing the Chantecler ski trails and across the road from a golf course, the innlike hotel has a large living room with a brick fireplace and bar, and an outdoor heated pool. Its pretty guest rooms have queen- or king-size beds, air conditioning and ceiling fans, and full bath. The standard rooms feature a sitting area, while six rooms also have a fireplace and balcony or patio, along with hairdryers and bathrobes. The two suites offer sofa beds, fireplaces, and whirlpools. It's about two miles north of town.

LE CHANTECLER, 1474 chemin de Chantecler (C.P. 1048), Ste-Adèle, PQ, J0R 1L0. Tel. 514/229-3555, or toll free 800/363-2420. Fax 514/229-5593. 280 rms, 20 suites. MINIBAR TV TEL **Directions:** Take Exit 67 off Highway 15; turn left at the fourth traffic light onto Morin Street; then turn right at the top of the hill.

$ Rates: $99–$139 single; $159 double; from $225 suite. Extra person $19. Children 12 and under stay free in parents' room. Packages available. AE, CB, DC, ER, MC, V.

Sprawled enticingly across four mountains, Le Chantecler resort has 22 slopes for all levels of skiers and a ski school, making it a good family-vacation choice. The rooms are comfortable and decorated with pine furniture made locally; most have air conditioning. Many of the suites have fireplaces. The sumptuous buffet breakfast served in the glass-enclosed dining room will get your day off to a memorable start. The rooms and suites, most with whirlpool bath, overlook the active slopes.

Dining/Entertainment: Dining room, piano bar, disco (winter only), movies in the projection room, summer-stock theater.

Services: Babysitting, dry cleaning, ski lockers.

Facilities: Ski school; a 622-foot vertical drop; 22 runs on four mountains, including 13 night-lit runs; ski chalet with cafeteria, bistro, and bar; cross-country trails; ice skating; indoor sports complex with pool, sauna, Jacuzzi, squash, racquetball, badminton, and some fitness equipment; nine-hole lit golf course, six tennis courts, sandy beach, windsurfing, canoeing, paddleboats, rowboats, mountain bikes; gift shop, hairdresser, masseur; meeting rooms.

Bed-and-Breakfast

BONNE NUIT, BONJOUR, 1980 bd. Ste-Adèle (C.P. 2168), Ste-Adèle, PQ, J0R 1L0. Tel. 514/229-7500. 6 rms (4 with bath).

$ Rates (including breakfast): Mid-June to Sept, Sun–Thurs $45–$50 single, $65–$75 double; the rest of the year $40–$45 single, $50–$60 double. Prices are $5–$15 higher Fri–Sat and holidays. Packages available. MC, V.

Perched on a hill above Highway 117, in a thicket of cedar trees, stands this pretty B&B, a stone house with two dormer windows, pink shutters, and a stone walk. Inside, there's a sitting room with rock fireplace, a small TV room, and a solarium breakfast room, where guests are served restaurant-style, overlooking a garden with a stream running through it and a wishing well. (Birds dine at the feeders outside.) The rooms are simply decorated, but they have wonderfully plush carpet. Two rooms share a large tiled bath, while the others have private bath, including one with a tiled sunken tub. Room 5 has its own balcony (and a bath with shower but no tub). The large outdoor pool is 8½ feet deep—this beats most hotels. Says the engaging live-in owner, Colette Martineau, "The rooms start with number two; number one is mine." It's difficult to spot this house from the road; watch for the stone fence with the wrought-iron gate, and the white sign out front.

WHERE TO DINE

L'EAU A LA BOUCHE, 3003 bd. Ste-Adèle. Tel. 514/229-2991, or toll free 800/363-2582 from Montréal.

Cuisine: FRENCH. **Reservations:** Recommended.

$ Prices: Appetizers $7.50–$16; main courses $19.50–$29.50; three-course table d'hôte lunch $10–$16; four-course table d'hôte dinner $45; eight-course, no-holds-barred gastronomic dinner $65. AE, ER, MC, V.

Open: Lunch Sun–Fri 11:30am–1:30pm; dinner daily 6–9pm.

In the decade or so since Anne Desjardins opened this place with her husband, Pierre Audette, it has received prizes and superlative reviews. The small rooms and country-inn interior, a few yards from the inn of the same name, provide the perfect setting for a romantic dining experience. Anne studied with some of Europe's most revered chefs and has lovingly applied that training to an imaginative mating of traditional Québec dishes with nouvelle cuisine. Her varied and constantly changing menu lives up to the promise of the restaurant's name (*l'eau à la bouche* means "mouthwatering"). Pierre, a professional sommelier, makes a knowledgeable guide to the restaurant's formidable array of French wines. A typical dinner might include roast partridge stuffed with oyster mushrooms in a cream sauce; veal prepared with white ginger, vermouth, and fresh chives from the garden; or duck bathed in a raspberry, green pepper, and vinegar sauce. A meal here can be a memorable experience for those ready to splurge.

RESTAURANT LA BRUYERE, 173 rue Morin (at chemin de Chantecler). Tel. 514/229-4417.
   Cuisine: INTERNATIONAL. **Reservations:** Not required.
$ Prices: Lunch $8.50–$15; dinner $15–$25. AE, MC, V.
   Open: Dinner Tues–Sun 4:30–11pm; brunch Sat–Sun 11am–3pm.
The all-around favorite dining place in Ste-Adèle is the Restaurant La Bruyère. You'll spot the outdoor roadside patio bar as you approach, and if the weather's not good enough to have your lunch or dinner outside, there's plenty of room in the L-shaped dining room. The chefs, Michel Bruyère and Nathalie Charbonneau, are the owners here, so quality control comes from the top. The luncheon menu includes crêpes, quiche Lorraine, sandwiches, salads, and grilled sirloin, or you can take advantage of a full set-price meal. In the evening, the offerings are fancier, with chicken shish kebab, seafood linguine, rack of lamb provençale, surf-and-turf, and more. Table d'hôte dinners are the thrifty way to order.

STE-MARGUERITE & ESTEREL

To get to Ste-Marguerite or Esterel, only two miles apart, follow Highway 15 North to Exit 69. Or if you're driving from Ste-Adèle, look for a street heading northeast named chemin Ste-Marguerite. It becomes a little road that crosses the Laurentian Autoroute (at Exit 69), bridges the Rivière du Nord, and leads into a beautiful lake-sprinkled area punctuated with imposing holiday estates.

Ste-Marguerite and Esterel are 53 miles (85km) and 55 miles (88km) north of Montréal, respectively. In summer you can get information from about the area from **Pavillon du Parc,** 74 chemin Masson, in Ste-Marguerite (tel. 514/228-3525); year-round, pick up tourist information from the nearby tourist bureau in Sainte-Adèle (see above).

WHERE TO STAY & DINE IN ESTEREL

HOTEL L'ESTEREL, bd. Fridoolin-Simard (C.P. 38), Ville d'Esterel, PQ, JOT 1E0. Tel. 514/228-2571, or toll free 800/363-3623 in the U.S., the Maritimes, Ontario, and Québec (except Montréal). Fax 514/228-4977. 135 rms. A/C TV TEL **Transportation:** Transportation from Montréal can be arranged with advance notice. Or take a Limocar bus from Montréal into Ste-Adèle, and the hotel will pick you up from there.
$ Rates (including full breakfast, five-course dinner, and service): $159–$175 single; $252–$309 double. Lower rates Dec 23–May. Discounts for stays of three or five nights year-round. Golf, tennis, and downhill and cross-country–ski packages available. AE, DC, ER, MC, V.

One of the finest Laurentian resorts and almost a town in itself, the Hotel L'Esterel is a fabulous year-round holiday hideaway capable of accommodating 300 guests. On an immense 5,000-acre estate with three lakes, one linked to the other, it offers almost unlimited activities. Perched dramatically on the shore of Lac Dupuis, the modern hotel has rooms with private bath and color TV. Those with a view of the lake are more expensive than those with a forest view, and a block of economy (or Terrace) rooms is also available. Daily rates include the use of all indoor facilities and the tennis courts. All resort facilities except the indoor pool and gym are available to day guests.

Dining/Entertainment: Breakfast is served buffet-style in La Brioche, and the five-course table d'hôte dinner, served in two dining rooms overlooking the lake, La Bordelaise and Le Voilier, is more formal. In addition, there are two lounges, with dancing nightly to live music. Social gatherings, including beach parties, are planned a couple of times a week.

Services: Limo service from Dorval or Mirabel airports (extra charge); massage; room service 7:30am to midnight, next-day dry-cleaning and laundry.

Facilities: 48 miles of cross-country ski trails (guides available), an alpine ski school and nearby downhill skiing, ice skating on a rink surrounded by woods, snowmobile rentals, sleigh and dogsled rides, hot-air ballooning in winter, snowshoes available, a golf school and private 18-hole golf course, seven tennis courts (three of them floodlit), indoor sports center with two racquetball courts, jogging track, badminton, basketball, volleyball, a games room with Ping-Pong and pool, and indoor heated pool, with whirlpool and saunas; putting green, four hiking and walking trails, nearby horseback riding, sailing, parasailing, waterskiing, canoeing, paddleboats, and cruises on the lakes.

WHERE TO DINE IN STE-MARGUERITE

LE BISTRO A CHAMPLAIN, 75 chemin Masson. Tel. 514/228-4988. Fax 514/228-4893.

Cuisine: FRENCH. **Reservations:** Recommended.

$ Prices: Appetizers $4–$21; main courses $15–$25; three-course table d'hôte menu $20; gourmet menu dégustation $50. AE, ER, MC, V.

Open: Summer Tues–Sat 6–10pm, Sun noon–5pm; rest of the year Thurs–Sat 6–10pm, Sun noon–5pm.

In the town of Ste-Marguerite (pop. 3,000) on Lac Masson, you'll find one of the best restaurants in the Laurentians. The building that houses it dates from 1864 and used to be a general store. It still retains the rough-hewn board walls, exposed beams, wooden ceiling, and old cash register, but instead of sockets, dishes, and jeans, people now come here for gourmet dinners. Owner Champlain Charest claims "the best cuisine is what you make with what's available at the market because the ingredients are the freshest." The wines—and you may sample 20 of them by the glass or choose one of 35,000 bottles—are as outstanding as the food. Consider a main course of fresh lamb from the region, lightly smoked in the restaurant, accompanied by a California chardonnay. Delicious French bread, made at the restaurant, is served at every meal. The front windows are filled with corks and empty wine bottles, and wine-label collages appear under the glass-top tables (which can be noisy) and on the walls, along with bold paintings by well-known Québecois artist Riopelle. The jovial Charest will answer any question about wines you put to him; ask for a tour of the wine cellar.

VAL-MORIN & VAL-DAVID

Follow Autoroute 117 north to Exit 78 or 80, respectively, to arrive at Val-Morin or the bohemian enclave of Val-David.

To those who know it, Val-David, 50 miles (80km) north of Montréal, conjures up images of chalet and cabin hideaways; residents who paint, or carve, or write for a living; and a setting that hinges itself forever in the memory—abruptly rising hills, scatterings of ponds, creeks, and lakes, and a fragrant forest lushness.

Val-Morin has its own special lure: the Far Hills Inn. The neighboring villages, only two miles apart, both sponsor an annual **Arts Festival** the first two weeks of August.

There's no **tourist office** in Val-Morin, but in Val-David you'll find a seasonal one, open from mid-June to Labor Day, daily 10am to 6pm; it's on the main drag at 2265 rue de l'Eglise (tel. 819/322-1515). If it's closed, **La Maison du Village,** a two-story wooden building at 2495 rue de l'Eglise, can provide tourist information (tel. 819/322-2043).

Note that once you come this far north in your explorations of the Laurentians, the telephone area code changes to 819.

WHERE TO STAY & DINE IN VAL-MORIN

FAR HILLS INN, Val-Morin, PQ, J0T 2S0. Tel. 819/322-2014, or toll free 800/567-6636 from Montréal. Fax 819/322-1995. 73 rms (all with bath). TEL

Directions: Leave the autoroute at Exit 76, go through Val-Morin, and follow the signs up into the hills for almost three miles.

$ Rates (including breakfast and dinner): $99 per person. Children under 10 stay for half price in their parents' room. Packages available. AE, ER, MC, V.

This Laurentian hideaway is truly that—hidden away; even the name connotes serenity. The gracious stone-and-frame inn is set in the midst of a botanic garden, including a Japanese garden, that keeps two gardeners employed full-time. The inn has a large public room with picture windows and two sitting areas, and an outdoor pool beautifully situated on a hillside. The rooms are comfortable and well lit, but most of them are not fancy and do not come with amenities. Most have double, queen-, or king-size beds; and some have air conditioning and television, but not cable. Rooms in the inn and the 18-bedroom Cedar Lodge are particularly cozy; pretty no. 107, in the inn, has a fireplace, leather couch, exposed beams, and original artwork.

Dining/Entertainment: All the activities at Far Hills are enticing, but one of the biggest draws is the dining room, a pine-paneled room with beamed ceiling and picture windows, and meals that will leave you in raptures. The chef chooses and prepares the freshest local produce (consider shrimp with new potatoes, red peppers, cauliflower, and brussels sprouts) and presents it appealingly. The wine list reads like a Who's Who of French wines, and good wine-by-the-glass is readily available. When reserving a seat, ask for the corner table overlooking the grounds and hills; if you're not a guest at the inn, expect to pay about $35 for a five-course dinner. In addition, you'll enjoy patio brunches in summer, the Panorama Bar with piano music several nights a week (always on Saturday), and barbecues.

Facilities: A cross-country ski school and more than 62 miles of some of the Laurentians' best cross-country trails; indoor and outdoor pools; sauna; tennis, squash, and racquetball courts; Ping-Pong, championship snooker table, shuffleboard, and racquetball; hiking and mountain climbing; canoeing, sailing, and paddle-boating on the inn's motor-free lake; backgammon for the less athletically minded; shop.

WHAT TO SEE & DO IN VAL-DAVID

Val-David is small, so you can park anywhere and meander at leisure. A favorite activity here is visiting the studios of local artists, including the pottery workshop of **Kinya Ishikawa,** where you may admire or buy the engaging artist's work and chat with him, at 2435 rue de l'Eglise (tel. 819/322-6868).

Or have a picnic beside the North River at petite, pretty **Parc des Amoureax.** There are plenty of benches, and some parking spots just as you approach the park, which is 2.5 miles (4km) from the main road through town; watch for the sign "Site Pittoresque" and turn at chemin de la Rivière.

The first two weeks of August heralds Val-David's annual **Village d'Art festival,** when painters, sculptors, ceramists, jewelers, pewtersmiths, and others display their work. There are concerts and other outdoor activities.

LE VILLAGE DU PERE NOEL, Rte. 117, Val-David. Tel. 819/322-2146.
Kids may be excited to learn that the summer home of Santa Claus is in Val-David and has been since 1954. Besides Santa's house, set in an alpine village, there are animals, audiovisual shows, games, a room filled with 38,000 balls that kids may plunge into, boats, souvenirs, a picnic area, and good old fast food. Some surprises are in store, too.

Admission: $7 for those 13 and older; $5.50 for those 12 and under.

Open: Mid-May to mid-June, Sat–Sun 10am–6pm; mid-June to Labor Day, daily 10am–6pm. **Closed:** Labor Day–early May.

WHERE TO STAY IN VAL-DAVID

AUBERGE DU VIEUX FOYER, Val-David, PQ, J0T 2N0. Tel. 819/322-2686, or toll free 800/567-8327 in Canada. Fax 819/322-2687. 22 rms, 3 chalets.

Directions: Follow the signs through the town 1½ miles (3km) to the inn.

$ Rates (including breakfast and dinner): $89–$109 single; $65–$89 per person double; $118 single or double for a chalet. Extra person $55 in rooms, $70 in chalets. Weekend packages available. MC, V.

In the tidy living room of this Swiss-style inn, comfortable armchairs are drawn up to the big fireplace, and in the nearby dining room the predominance of honey-colored natural wood is soothing. The guest rooms are simply decorated and on the small side but pleasant; all have baths (a few with whirlpool) and fine views of the surrounding forested hills. There are also three chalets that hold up to eight people. The rates for all accommodations, including the chalets, include breakfast and dinner. The auberge is located on its own private little pond, suitable to swim in or sun by, and equipment for outdoor games is yours for the asking. You can count on lots of cross-country skiing in winter, and you'll discover that guests go in for chess in a big way. Val-David is so appealing, and the Auberge du Vieux Foyer so popular (but so small), that advance reservations are necessary most of the year, and at least two months in advance in winter.

Dining/Entertainment: The auberge's dining room offers brunch, a buffet, or dinner to guests and nonguests; the emphasis is always on fresh seasonal foods. A small bar provides a focus for après-ski conviviality.

Facilities: Pool, table tennis, and indoor shuffleboard; bicycles, paddleboats, and whirlpool; an outdoor pool; equipment for outdoor games; cross-country skiing, a skating rink.

LA MAISON DE BAVIERE, 1472 chemin de la Rivière, Val-David, PQ, JOT 2N0. Tel. 819/322-3528. 4 rms (all with bath and shower). **Directions:** Take Exit 76 off Highway 15; turn right at the first traffic light, then turn left at the first street. If you're driving from Val-David's main street, rue de l'Eglise, it's almost a mile.

$ Rates: $45 single; $100 double. No credit cards.

My happiest discovery during a recent visit to the Laurentians was La Maison de Bavière (the name means Bavarian House), a bed-and-breakfast on the bank of the North River. The care that husband-and-wife team André Lesage and Ute Schule have put into this place is evident everywhere, from the soft duvets on the beds, to the lamps by local artists, to Ute's hand-stenciled doors, reminiscent of her native Germany. Guests eat in the atrium dining nook under a skylight and share a cozy reading room with a wood-burning stove. The four guest rooms are named after Strauss, Haydn, Mozart, and Beethoven. The large Beethoven room has no fewer than five windows overlooking the river, a painted milk can, an old-fashioned freestanding bathtub in the bedroom, plus a separate toilet, shower, and sink, and a private deck.

WHERE TO DINE IN VAL-DAVID

AU PETIT POUCET, no. 1030, Hwy. 117. Tel. 819/322-2246.
Cuisine: QUEBECOIS.
$ Prices: Sandwiches $6–$10; main courses $6–$15; weekend buffet $15, half price for children 12 and younger. AE, MC, V.
Open: Daily 8am–10:30pm; Sat–Sun buffet 5–10pm.

Driving north on Highway 117 from Montréal, make your first contact with Val-David by stopping for a meal at the roadside restaurant named Au Petit Poucet, on the right-hand side just a short distance before the Val-David turnoff. With minimal formality, Au Petit Poucet still manages to be charming, particularly because of the large windows that expose a marvelous view of the Val-David region. Red-and-white-checked tablecloths, natural wood, and other homey touches set the scene for the house specialty: maple-smoked ham, the best in the region. Other menu items include meat-pie plates, roasted chicken, and ragoût (pigs' knuckles). A hot and cold dinner buffet is served on weekends. This is a good place to come for breakfast because there's lots to choose from, from simple to simply humongous.

STE-AGATHE-DES-MONTS

With a population approaching 10,000, Ste-Agathe-des-Monts, 53 miles (85km) from Montréal, is the largest town in the Laurentians. To get here, follow Highway 15 north to Exit 83 or 86. Ste-Agathe marks the end of Highway 15.

Early settlers and vacationers must have flocked here in search of precious lakefront footage on beautiful Lac des Sables, and local business and industry followed the crowds. Ste-Agathe's main street, rue Principale (Main Street), is the closest you'll come to citification in these timeless mountains, but don't be concerned by this touch of urbanity.

Many intersections in the village have four-way stops, so be prepared for them. If you follow rue Principale from the highway through town, you'll end up at the town dock on the Lac des Sables. For a night or two the motels near town on Highway 117 provide comfort and convenience, but for longer stays you may want to consider a lakeside lodge.

The **Bureau Touristique de Ste-Agathe-des-Monts,** 190 rue Principale est (tel. 819/326-0457), is open daily 9am to 8:30pm in summer, 9am to 5pm the rest of the year.

WHAT TO SEE & DO

The dock and surrounding waterfront park make Ste-Agathe a fine place to stop for the day (you can rent a bike from **Jacques Champoux Sports,** 74 rue St-Vincent, and ride around the lake, a three-mile circuit). But the summer waterskiing activities and lake cruises may lure you into lingering for a week.

Get your bearings by taking one of the **Alouette** cruises (tel. 819/326-3656), which depart the dock at the foot of rue Principale from mid-May to late October. After the 50-minute, 12-mile voyage on a boat equipped with a bar and running commentary of the sights, you'll know, among other things, that Ste-Agathe and the Lac des Sables are famous for waterski competitions and windsurfing. Cost for the Alouette cruise is $10 per adult, $9 seniors with ID, $5.50 for children 5 to 15. There are half a dozen departures a day; call for exact times.

WHERE TO STAY

AUBERGE DU COMTE DE WATEL, 250 St-Venant, Ste-Agathe, PQ, J8C 2Z7. Tel. 819/326-7016. Fax 819/326-7556. 21 rms. A/C TV TEL
$ Rates (including breakfast in high season): $120 double. Extra person $20. Children under 16 stay free in parents' room. AE, DISC, MC, V.
A stone's throw from the auberge listed below, the three-story Watel, across the road from the lake and boating, looks a bit like a wedding cake atop a hill. Some of the modern rooms have double whirlpool baths and refrigerators. The Watel has an outdoor swimming pool with a lovely deck, some exercise equipment, a TV lounge, and an excellent licensed dining room (try to have lunch or dinner here, even if you don't stay here).

AUBERGE DU LAC DES SABLES, 230 St-Venant (C.P. 151), Ste-Agathe, PQ, J8C 2Z7. Tel. and fax 819/326-3994. 19 rms. A/C TV
$ Rates (including breakfast): $80–$120 double. Extra person $20. AE, DISC, MC, V.

★ The pretty rooms in this small, modern lakefront bed-and-breakfast inn have soft colors and whirlpool baths. Rooms with a double whirlpool bath and a view of the lake are slightly more expensive. The auberge has a nice little terrace overlooking the lake, a great place to watch the sunset, and a whirlpool that has a bubble top in winter. Downstairs there's a games room with pool table and pinball machine. The living room is filled with plants and current magazines and has a fireplace and piano for your enjoyment. The Auberge du Lac des Sables is about 1½ miles from the village center, and within walking distance of the beach and boating. Your hosts are Lise and Claude Fleurent, who are bilingual and as engaging a couple as you're likely to meet. They also own the Auberge du Comte de Watel (see above).

AUBERGE LA SAUVAGINE, no. 1592, R.R. 2, Rte. 329 nord, Ste-Agathe, PQ, J8C 2Z8. Tel. 819/326-7673. 9 rms (6 with bath).
$ Rates: $60–$130 single; $75–$130 double. MC, V.

★ This pretty country inn is also an award-winning restaurant, housed in a former chapel. An order of nuns added the chapel when they bought the property and made it a retirement home. The rooms are filled with antiques. Six have private bath; one has its own bath outside the room; and two rooms share a bath. The house has a living room with television, a porch, and a patio for guests' enjoyment. The restaurant, open for dinner only, Wednesday through Sunday, offers a three-course table d'hôte with lots of choices for $37; the menu favors French cuisine and regional foods. Be sure to make reservations. Auberge la Sauvagine is 1.2 miles (2km) north of Ste-Agathe, on the road to St-Donat.

WHERE TO DINE

CHEZ GIRARD, 18 rue Principale ouest. Tel. 819/326-0922.
  Cuisine: FRENCH. **Reservations:** Recommended.
$ Prices: Appetizers $3–$9; main courses $14.50–$29.50; three-course table d'hôte lunch $7.50–$13, five-course table d'hôte dinner $18–$35. AE, ER, MC, V.
  Open: Summer lunch daily 11:30am–2pm; dinner Sun–Thurs 5–9pm, Fri–Sat 5:30–9:30pm. Off-season lunch Thurs–Fri and Sun 11:30am–2pm; dinner Sun–Thurs 5–9pm, Fri–Sat 5–9:30pm.
If you head to the town dock and scan the end of rue Principale, you spot a Québec-style house, the Restaurant and Auberge Chez Girard, where in good weather diners may sit on the terrace overlooking the lake. The menu here changes often, but you can usually expect to find fresh salmon, lobster, duck liver in a pastry shell, elk, and lamb dishes. A popular dish is Ly-Ann lobster, with cream, mandarin sauce, ginger, and shiitake mushrooms. In summer, there's a salad and dessert bar.
  Chez Girard also offers lodging in six rooms in two houses in the village for $50 to $70 single, $60 to $80 double.

CREPERIE LA QUIMPERLAISE, 11 Tour du Lac. Tel. 819/326-1776.
  Cuisine: CREPES/STEAKS.
$ Prices: Appetizers $3–$6; main courses $5–$15. MC, V.
  Open: Winter Sun–Thurs 10am–10pm, Fri–Sat 10am–11pm; summer Sun–Thurs 10am–11pm, Fri–Sat 10am–midnight.
If you are a crêpe lover, you're in luck, because Crêperie la Quimperlaise has myriad choices, including vegetarian, mussels in season, fresh fruit in summer, and avocado with shrimp and crabmeat. Servings are ample, and two people can easily share one crêpe, which comes with a cheese or béchamel sauce. They're flexible here, so you can mix and match ingredients if you've a mind to. The food is superfresh.

ST-FAUSTIN

St-Faustin, which lies 16 miles (25km) north of Ste-Agathe and 71 miles (115km) north of Montréal, is not a tourist town, just a peaceful mountain village with a pretty church spire (and there's a lot to be said for that).
  The big draw lies directly across the highway: Mont Blanc, the second-highest peak in the Laurentians after Mont Tremblant. To get here, follow Highway 117 north from Ste-Agathe. It's just south of St-Jovite.
  The **Bureau Touristique de St-Faustin,** 1535 Rte. 117 (tel. 819/688-3738), is open from 9am to 8pm in summer, 9am to 5pm the rest of the year.

WHERE TO STAY & DINE

HOTEL MONT BLANC, Rte. 117 (C.P. 122), St-Faustin, PQ, J0T 2G0.
  Tel. 819/688-2444, or toll free 800/567-6715 in Québec. Fax 819/688-6112. TV 23 rms, 3 suites, 15 condos.
$ Rates (including breakfast, dinner, and two lift tickets): Late Nov to mid-Feb and mid-Mar to early Apr, $85–$118 per person; mid-Feb to mid-Mar, $90–$125 per person; suites and condos from $105 low season, $113 high season. Rates drop significantly with stays of two or more days. Weekend specials and packages available. AE, MC, V.
Open only in winter, Mont Blanc ski resort, beside the highway, at the base of Mont Blanc, has 35 ski trails and eight ski lifts, including one quad chair lift, and snowmaking equipment to cover 80% of the trails. Each room in the lodge is different, and some of the furnishings are worn, given the heavy traffic the place gets. Opt for accommodations on the third floor, where the rooms have country antiques and

duvets on the beds. All rooms have a sofa bed. The suites have marble fireplaces and Jacuzzis; one, no. 227, has its own terrace. Check-in may be as late as 4:30pm.

Dining/Entertainment: Le Chamonix dining room; cafeteria, bar.

Services: Babysitting.

Facilities: Ski school, ski shop; indoor and outdoor pools, exercise room, Jacuzzis, steam baths, saunas; meeting rooms.

ST-JOVITE & MONT TREMBLANT

Follow Highway 117 some 23 miles (37km) north from Ste-Agathe to the St-Jovite exit. It's 76 miles (122km) north of Montréal.

To get to Mont Tremblant, turn right on Route 327, just before the church in St-Jovite; most vacationers make their base at one or another of the resorts or lodges scattered along Route 327. Mont Tremblant is 28 miles (45km) north of Ste-Agathe and 80 miles (130km) north of Montréal.

Tourist information, including maps of local ski trails, is available at the **Bureau Touristique de Mont-Tremblant,** rue du Couvent (tel. 819/425-2434), open daily in summer from 9am to 9pm, the rest of the year daily from 9am to 5pm; and from the **Tourist Bureau of Saint-Jovite/Mont-Tremblant,** 305 chemin Brebeuf (tel. 819/425-3300), open daily in summer from 9am to 7pm, the rest of the year daily from 9am to 5pm.

St-Jovite (pop. 6,888) is the commercial center for the most famous and popular of all Laurentian locales, the area surrounding Mont Tremblant, the highest peak in the Laurentians (2133 ft., or 650m). In 1894, the provincial government set aside almost 1,000 square miles of wilderness as Mont Tremblant Park, and the foresight of this early conservation effort has yielded unlimited outdoor enjoyment to vacationers past, present, and future.

In summer, water-sports lovers come to dip into the region's lakes and rivers; in winter, the ski centers of Mont Tremblant and Gray Rocks, along with miles of cross-country ski trails and snowmobile terrain lure snow bunnies here; and the colorful spectacle of autumn in the Laurentians is best seen from one of the multitude of chair lifts at Mont Tremblant.

The mountain's curious name comes from a legend of the area's first inhabitants: When the first Amerindians arrived here early in the 17th century, they named the peak after Manitou, their god of nature. When humans dared to disturb nature in any way, Manitou became enraged and made the great mountain tremble—*montagne tremblante.* So goes the legend. (Would that more gods like Manitou were around today to lend our endangered planet a hand.)

An appealing town in its own right, St-Jovite provides all the modern services, and its main street, rue Ouimet, is lined with inviting cafés, restaurants, and shops, including **Le Coq Rouge,** which sells folk art and country antiques. The village of Mont Tremblant, though several miles nearer the large resorts and the mountain itself, has only the most basic services, including a market and post office but no pharmacy.

WHAT TO SEE & DO

Water sports in summer are as popular as the ski slopes and trails in winter, because the base of Mont Tremblant is surrounded by no fewer than 10 lakes: Lac Tremblant, a gorgeous glacial stretch of water 10 miles long; and also Lac Ouimet, Lac Mercier, Lac Gelinas, Lac Desmarais, and five smaller bodies of water, not to mention rivers and streams. From mid-May to mid-October, **Grand Manitou Cruises,** 2513 chemin Principale, in Mont Tremblant, offers a 75-minute narrated tour of Lac Tremblant, focusing on its history, nature, and legends (tel. 819/425-8681).

Mont Tremblant, which has the same vertical drop as Mont Ste-Anne near Québec City, draws the biggest downhill ski crowds in the Laurentians. Founded in 1939 by Philadelphia millionaire Joe Ryan, **Station Mont Tremblant** is one of the oldest ski areas in North America, and the first to create trails on both sides of a mountain. It was the second in the world to install a chair lift. There may be higher mountains with longer runs and steeper pitches, but something about Mont Tremblant compels people to return time and again—a certain mountain magic, if you will.

By the late 1980s, the resort was in need of refurbishment, and under the new management of Ultrawest since 1991, it has gone beyond that and is on its way to becoming a world-class resort year-round. Today Mont Tremblant has extensive snowmaking capability to cover 328 acres, making skiing possible from early November to late May, with more than 30 trails open at Christmastime (as opposed to nine in 1992). Station Mont Tremblant now has 43 downhill runs and trails, including the newly opened Dynamite and Verige trails, with 245-meter (810-ft.) and 225-meter (745-ft.) drops, respectively, and the Edge, a peak with two gladed trails. By 1996, thanks to a $413 million investment, it could easily become the largest four-season destination resort in North America. You can stay in the new digs at the base of the mountain or elsewhere in the immediate area.

On nearby Lac Ouimet stands Gray Rocks resort, the first resort built in the Laurentians. It actually was first established, by George Wheeler of Chazy, New York, as a sawmill, in 1896, but by 1906, and a quirk of destiny, had become better known as an inn. Its low mountain slopes make it particularly popular with families.

The Laurentians region, however, is known for more than its downhill skiing. It also sees plenty of cross-country action on 56 miles (90km) of maintained trails. And in summer, there's no lack of things to do. Choose from championship golf, tennis, horseback riding, boating, swimming, biking, and hiking—for starters. And you can always just relax and do nothing, sometimes the most difficult activity of all.

WHERE TO STAY

The area is known for its large resorts, but there are smaller, equally convivial establishments that offer their own warm welcome at lower prices. Of course, you may have to drive to Gray Rocks or Mont Tremblant for a golf game, seaplane ride, or ski lift, but that's little enough to ask.

Resorts

CLUB TREMBLANT, av. Cuttle, Mont Tremblant, PQ, J0T 1Z0. Tel. and fax 819/425-2731, or toll free 800/363-2413 in the U.S., 800/567-8341 in Canada. 87 rms. TV TEL

$ Rates (including breakfast, dinner, and use of all sports facilities): Summer $110–$195 per person; winter per person. From $120 per person suite. Rates drop with stays of two days or more. Packages available. AE, DC, ER, MC, V.

Nestled into a hillside just up from the shores of Lac Tremblant, this attractive alpine lodge, a Canadian Pacific property, is well away from busy roads and vacation bustle, yet very accessible. For the lowest price, you get a twin-bedded room in the main building; most of the accommodations consist of a deluxe suite with private bath, sitting room, and fireplace. The bar, with its inviting stone fireplace, is a popular spot on chilly evenings, and there's usually piano music Thursday through Saturday nights. The bar and dining room both overlook the lake. The resort also has an indoor pool, Jacuzzi, and exercise room. It's less than a mile off Highway 327; turn near the Auberge Sauvignon and follow the signs.

GRAY ROCKS, on Lac Ouimet (P.O. Box 1000), St-Jovite, PQ, J0T 2H0. Tel. 819/425-2771, or toll free 800/567-6767. Fax 514/425-3006. 198 rms, 116 condos. A/C TEL

$ Rates (including breakfast, lunch, and dinner): $130–$180 single; $89–$142 per person double. Children 11–16 stay in parents' room at 40% discount; children 5–10, 50% discount. Ski-school packages available. AE, DC, ER, MC, V.

At Gray Rocks, the area's dowager resort, under new management since 1993, accommodations—rooms and condos—are in a huge rambling main lodge, in cozier Le Château lodge, or in one of the resort's four-person cottages. Only the condos have television. The resort not only has its own airport for guests who fly in, but also its own seaplane base on Lac Ouimet. Activities are nonstop. There's the ski school. And

Gray Rocks has lots of tennis courts, but would you have guessed 22 of them? For the kids, there is a complete playground with attendants to provide child care, as well as a program of free swimming lessons.

Dining/Entertainment: Dining room serving three meals a day, bar with piano and other music.

Services: Child care, same-day dry cleaning and laundry, room service.

Facilities: Par-72 golf course, indoor pool and fitness center, horseback riding, sailboat rentals, shuffleboard, croquet; skiing, lifts, ski school, and access to 56 miles (90km) of cross-country skiing.

TREMBLANT, 3005 chemin Principal, Mont Tremblant, PQ, J0T 1Z0. Tel. 819/425-8711, or toll free 800/461-8711. Fax 819/425-8862. 50 lodge rms, 193 condos, 10 chalets. TV TEL **Directions:** Drive three miles north of St-Jovite on Highway 117; then take Montée Ryan and follow the blue signs for about 6 miles. **Transportation:** Limocar Laurentides bus from Montréal stops at the front door. Door-to-door transport from Dorval and Mirabel Fri–Sun.

$ Rates (including breakfast, dinner, and lift ticket): Two-night minimum, $208–$357 single occupancy; $186–$307 per person, double occupancy. From $137 per person, condo and chalet. Children 6–12 $77–$80 (meals only), children 3–5 $44 (meals only). Special packages, two-night-minimum rates without meals, and occasional one-night specials available. AE, MC, V.

This is an exciting time to visit or stay at Tremblant, the resort that takes its name from Mont Tremblant, the highest vertical drop in eastern Canada. Since 1993, this French Canadian mountain village, stretching from the mountain's skirts to the shores of 10-mile-long Lac Tremblant, has been in the throes of a giant metamorphosis. The two-story Le Saint-Bernard, at the base of the mountain, is a new but historic-looking condominium hotel, with 193 condos with one, two, or three bedrooms, underground parking for 200 cars, and boutiques. The building is the creation of Cote, Leahy & Associates, the architectural firm that successfully restored the Hotel Victoria and the Quartier Petit Champlain in Québec City. A 300-room Canadian Pacific hotel and a recreation center are slated for completion in 1996. When the snow is deep (as it usually is), skiers here like to follow the sun around the mountain, making the run down slopes with an eastern exposure in the morning and the western-facing ones in the afternoon.

Dining/Entertainment: At the base of the South Side, Bistro La Catalogne for light fare and snacks, Chalet des Voyageurs cafeteria; the more upscale La Canadienne, open for three meals a day, including a lunch buffet; and the Octo Bar for après-ski. At the base of the North Side, short orders from Fourchette de la Diable and Pizzatinni. On the summit of the mountain, Le Rendez-vous café, with a circular fireplace, far-flung view, chili, smoked-meat sandwiches, cappuccino, espresso, and hot chocolate; and the new, 1,000-seat Le Grand Manitou restaurant, with a dining room, bistro, and cafeteria.

Services: Supervision for children 2 to 6 at Kids' Kamp, ski rentals and repair, a gondola to take visitors and residents from the parking lot to the village (planned for the 1994–95 season).

Facilities: In winter, 39 slopes and trails in all, served by 10 ski lifts, including two base-to-summit high-speed quads, triple-chair lifts, double-chair lifts, a T-bar, and a surface tow; ski school; ski shop; access to cross-country ski trails. In summer, pool or lake swimming, boat cruise (extra fee), chair-lift rides to the top of Mont Tremblant (extra fee), six lighted Har-Tru tennis courts, 18-hole golf course (to open in 1995), and a dozen other indoor and outdoor amusements.

VILLA BELLEVUE, Mont Tremblant, PQ, J0T 1Z0. Tel. and fax 819/425- 2734, or toll free 800/567-6763 in Quebec, the Maritimes, and the U.S. 119 rms. TV TEL

$ Rates: $72–$114 double without meals; $128–$256 double with breakfast and dinner. Condos for four to eight people available. Children 17 and under stay free in parents' room. Weekly rates and ski weekend packages available. DC, ER, MC, V.

The two-level, shingled Villa Bellevue is adapted to the shores of Lac Ouimet, and guests profit from the efficiently designed, cheerfully decorated but somewhat worn modern rooms, all of which have large, sunny windows. Some have air conditioning.

You have a choice from those in the lodge to deluxe units in a newer building. A few rooms even have kitchenettes, of particular interest to families. The resort also has an indoor swimming pool and spa. In summer, staff will take care of your children during the afternoon and evening at an extra charge, so you can relax completely. Villa Bellevue has been run by the Dubois family for three generations. Cross-country skiing is nearby.

A Laurentian Inn

CHATEAU BEAUVALLON, 616 Montée Ryan (Box 138), Mont Tremblant, PQ, J0T 1Z0. Tel. 819/425-7275. 12 rms (3 with bath).
$ Rates (including full breakfast): $30 per person. Children 12 and under stay for half price in parent's room. Dinner available in winter. No credit cards. **Parking:** Free.

Prettiest of Mont Tremblant's inns is the Château Beauvallon, a white gambrel-roofed and gabled structure with yellow shutters set in a swath of emerald lawn and bordered by a log fence. The château's own lake beach is a short stroll away on Lac Beauvallon, and its boats are moored nearby. Built in 1942 as part of the Mont Tremblant Lodge resort, the château was later sold—perhaps because it is some distance from the rest of the resort. Today this seclusion is a major attraction, and hardly anything happens to disturb the tranquility of life here.

The rustic and comfortable rooms are done in Québec country style. The cozy dining room seats only 30 guests, and the tiny honor bar vies with the pine-paneled lounge (with fireplace) in attracting before- and after-dinner conversation groups. Hosts Judy and Alex Riddell provide a warm welcome and memorable stay.

Motellike Inns

Several motels near Mont Tremblant and St-Jovite offer the undeniable advantages of modernity, reasonable prices, and predictable comforts. Bonuses may include kitchenettes—great money-savers for groups of skiers willing to do their own cooking—and private swimming pools open in the summer months. They may lack the spacious grounds, comfy lounges, or long lists of activities found at larger Laurentian hostelries, but these amenities are easily accessible nearby.

AUBERGE DU COQ DE MONTAGNE, 2151 chemin Principal (C.P. 208), Mont Tremblant, PQ, J0T 1Z0. Tel. 819/425-3380. Fax 819/425-7846. 14 rms (13 with bath), 2 suites.
$ Rates: $45 single; $55 double; $80 suite. Weekend packages and meal plan available. AE, MC, V. **Parking:** Free.
A petit lodging in a rustic setting on the shores of Lac Moore, the auberge is less than a mile from the center of Mont Tremblant village. The rooms here are complemented by a comfortable dining room and bar. Two suites each come with two double beds, a sofa, color TV, and private bath.

AUBERGE LA PORTE ROUGE, rue Principale, Mont Tremblant, PQ, J0T 1Z0. Tel. 819/425-3505. 14 rms (all with bath). A/C TV
$ Rates (including breakfast and dinner): $55 per person, double occupancy; $47 per person, triple occupancy; $43 per person, quad. Rates without meals are about 25% less. Five-night ski or summer packages available. MC, V.
The closest motel to everything is the Auberge La Porte Rouge, in the village right across the road from the Hôtel de Ville (City Hall). Here, you'll wake to a panoramic view of Lake Mercier through your room's picture window, or from your own little private balcony. For breakfast, wander down to the motel's small dining room, and later in the day relax in the cocktail lounge or on the terrace facing the lake. Chalets, with kitchen and fireplace, are available for three to 10 people. In summer, guests may enjoy the pool, nicely positioned by the lake; the motel provides rowboats and paddleboats for lake outings. Its name means "The Red Door Inn," and with two red doors, it's easy to spot; the St. Louis family has run it for three generations.

AUBERGE MOUNTAIN VIEW, Rte. 327 (C.P. 817), St-Jovite, PQ, J0T 2H0. Tel. 819/425-3429, or toll free 800/561-5122. Fax 819/425-9109. 44 rms. A/C TV TEL

$ Rates: $75 double with fireplace, $71 double without fireplace, $71 double without kitchenette. Extra person $14. Packages and off-season discounts available. AE, MC, V.

Just over a mile from the center of St-Jovite stands the Auberge Mountain View. The landscaped inn is set perpendicular to the highway, minimizing any noise from traffic. All the rooms have modern private baths; some have fireplaces and refrigerators. There's a nice little outdoor heated pool for summer use. In the slack off-season, when most other Laurentian lodgings are closed, it lowers its rates substantially, by 20% to 40%, depending on the dates and the number of people sharing the room. This comfortable, easygoing place is operated by the Leroy family. They also rent snowmobiles.

WHERE TO DINE

Although most Laurentian lodgings have their own dining facilities, and—at least in wintertime—require or prefer that you use them, anyone exploring the surroundings of Mont Tremblant should know of a few other possibilities for the odd night out, lunchtime snack, or stop en route. Here are some local favorites.

ABBE DU NORD, 15 rue des Lauriers. Tel. 819/425-8394.
   Cuisine: CONTINENTAL. **Reservations:** Recommended, especially on weekends.
$ Prices: Appetizers $3.50–$5.50; main courses $15–$25; table d'hôte $15–$25. AE, MC, V.
   Open: Winter Tues–Sat and holidays 6–9pm; the rest of the year Wed–Sat and holidays 6–9pm.

The Abbé du Nord, in a historic house on the top of a hill in the middle of the village, is particularly popular in winter because of its hearty fare, generous servings, and cozy decor, with dark paneling, antiques, and stained glass. The specialties of the house, prepared by chef Louise Stafford and her son, sous-chef Bruce Stafford, are ribs and rack of lamb; fish is also on the menu. All the breads, sauces, and desserts are homemade, and no one leaves hungry, Bruce promises.

ANTIPASTO, 855 Ouimet. Tel. 819/425-7580.
   Cuisine: ITALIAN.
$ Prices: Appetizers $3–$10; main courses $8–$18. MC, V.
   Open: Dinner daily 4–11pm.

Housed in an old train station moved to this site, Antipasto supplies a charming backdrop for dinner: wood floor and paneling, old photos and illustrations of trains, an outdoor café and bar. You're assured of getting minestrone, gazpacho, a variety of pastas and pizzas, and spumoni here. Specials include arrabiata, seafood dishes, and pasta primavera. You'll see the restaurant's sign hanging from a recycled train signal. All aboard.

CHARCUTERIE PETITE EUROPE, 804 Ouimet. Tel. 819/425-3141.
   Cuisine: DELI.
$ Prices: Most items $2.50–$10. MC, V.
   Open: Summer daily 8am–11pm; winter daily 8am–6pm.

In French a charcuterie once meant a pork butcher's shop, but today it signifies a delicatessen. Besides selling uncounted delicacies—all sorts of cold meats, cheeses, pastries, and coffee beans—the casual Petite Europe has a few small booths and tables and a patio where you can have sandwiches made from any of these good things, or assorted salads, pâtés, omelets, pasta dishes, or daily specials, not to mention fresh coffee, especially the café au lait, and bières en fût (beer on tap). Petite Europe is, much to hungry travelers' delight, conveniently located downtown, on the town's main street.

LA TABLE ENCHANTEE, Hwy. 117, just north of St-Jovite. Tel. 819/425-7113.

Cuisine: FRENCH/QUEBECOIS. **Reservations:** Required. **Directions:** Head 1.8 miles (2.9km) northwest of the steel river bridge in St-Jovite, on Highway 117.
$ Prices: Appetizers $6.50–$9; main courses $14.50–$21; three-course table d'hôte $18.50–$24.50. AE, MC, V.
Open: Dinner Tues–Sun 5–10pm.

This tiny restaurant doesn't look like much from the outside, and first-timers here might think they were in for fish-and-chips. Not so. On the small neatly set tables are served some of the most carefully prepared and tasty dishes in the region. Owners Ghislaine and Leopold Handfield stick to traditional and authentic Québec cuisine, with the occasional excursion into the realms of the French (*cuisses de grenouilles,* frogs' legs) or the Anglo-Saxons (steak). A full traditional dinner might start with fiddlehead greens (fresh, in season) or clam chowder. Then comes the Québec pâté called cretons, followed by authentic cipaille, a many-layered potpie made with pheasant, guinea hen, rabbit, veal, reindeer, and pork—but too often these days (in other restaurants) consisting of chicken, beef, and pork. Dessert might be any of three homemade ice creams, or grand-pères au sirop d'érable (dumplings in maple syrup). Or you could choose the prix-fixe meal offered daily. La Table Enchantée is near the settlement of Lac Duhamel.

---

2. THE ESTRIE REGION

48 miles (80km) SE of Montréal

GETTING THERE   By Car   Leave the island of Montréal by the Champlain Bridge, which leads to Autoroute 10, heading for Sherbrooke. You can remain on the autoroute, which is a lovely drive, or take the slower road through small villages by turning off the autoroute at Exit 37 and going north a short distance to link up with Highway 112.

By Bus   Local buses leave Montréal to follow Highway 112 numerous times a day, arriving in Sherbrooke, 99 miles (160km) away, 3¼ hours later, and stopping in Bromont, Granby, and Magog along the way. Beyond Sherbrooke, it stops in Sutton Junction.

ESSENTIALS   For information about the Estrie Region, contact Tourisme Estrie, 25 rue Bocage, Sherbrooke, PQ, J1L 2J4 (tel. 819/820-2020, or toll free 800/263-1068; fax 819/566-4445).

Southeast of Montréal lies Québec's breadbasket, a flat and fertile region broken by rolling hills and by the 2,600-foot (792m) peak of Mont Orford, centerpiece of an enchantingly beautiful provincial park and ski area. Only a short distance from Mont Orford stands Sherbrooke, the industrial and commercial capital of the Estrie Region (also known as the Eastern Townships), and throughout the Mont Orford–Sherbrooke area are serene glacial lakes that attract summer fishing enthusiasts, sailors, and swimmers from all around. Touristically speaking, the Estrie Region is Québec's best-kept secret, so it's mostly Montréalers and Québecois who come here to rent summer houses or to launch their boats or to ski.

Follow their lead: The restful drive (once you get out of Montréal) east along Highway 10 passes silos and fields, clusters of cows, and dandelion-strewn meadows. When you crest the hill at kilometer 100, you'll see what the excitement is all about, as an enchanting view of mountains and countryside stretches out before you.

Unlike the Laurentians, which virtually close down in "mud time" when spring warmth thaws the ground, the Estrie Region fairly bustles with activity as crews penetrate every "sugar bush" (stand of sugar maples) to tap the sap and "sugar off." Autumn, likewise, has its special attraction here, for in addition to the glorious autumn colors (best from mid-September to mid-October), the Estrie Region brims to overflowing with apples of every variety, and the cider mills hum day and night to produce the "wine" of Québec. It's not unusual for visitors to help with the autumn apple harvest, paying a low price for the basketful they collect themselves. And the cider mills throw open their doors for tours and tastings.

As for maple-sugar time, local towns and villages often have maple-sugar festivals, and numerous farms host "sugaring parties" at which guests partake of a gargantuan country repast, and claim their dessert out by the sugar house. Boiling maple sugar is poured on the fast-melting winter snow and cooled instantly to produce a unique maple-sugar candy. Montréal newspapers and local tourist offices and chambers of commerce keep current lists of what's happening where and when.

For extended stays in the region, consider basing yourself in Magog, or if you prefer a small village, North Hatley, and take day trips from there.

Although town names such as Granby, Knowlton, and Sherbrooke are obviously English, the Estrie Region is now overwhelmingly French-speaking. Tidy little towns along the road through apple country are filled with houses kept neat as a pin, and surrounded by carefully tended orchards and farmland.

Rougemont is a major apple orchard and cider-mill town, and at all times of the year the main street is dotted with little stands selling various sorts of apples, apple products, vegetables, and homemade bread. To get there, take Exit 37 off Autoroute 10 and travel 13½ miles (22km) along Highway 112. At St-Césaire, a few kilometers farther along the highway, small stands and shops specialize in handcraft items made locally. The next town, St-Paul-d'Abbotsford, was founded in the late 1700s by Scottish settlers. Abbotsford became the name of the town in 1829, the "St-Paul" being added later by the French inhabitants. It was here in 1896 that the local apple-growers cooperative, Société de Pomologie du Québec, was founded.

MYSTIC

Yes, Virginia, there is a Mystic, Québec (as pretty as Mystic, Connecticut, too), and it's worth the 17-mile (27km) detour from Autoroute 10; take Exit 55 and pick up Highway 233 sud to Highway 104 est (briefly) to Highway 235 sud, which soon becomes the main street of Mystic.

Sixty-four people live in this little town, 48 miles (80km) from Montréal, which enjoyed a short-lived prosperity from 1868 to 1880, when an ironworks was located here and the railroad passed through town. Highlights on a visit include the Gothic-inspired brick church (1882) in the center of town, an old school with a bell tower (a white building that's easy to spot) on the north side of town, and an unusual 12-sided barn on the south side of town.

Mystic is also home to a special little place called L'Oeuf, or Egg—a combination B&B, restaurant, chocolatier, and gift and food shop. Even if you don't plan to stay the night in Mystic, give L'Oeuf a look.

WHERE TO STAY & DINE

L'OEUF, 229 chemin Mystic, Mystic, PQ, J0J 1Y0. Tel. 514/248-7529.
    5 rms (all with sink; none with private bath).
    $ Rates (including breakfast): $35 single; $50 double; $67.50 three people; $80 four people. MC, V. **Parking:** Free.
It's easy to spot—unmistakably pink and right across the street from the church. The house, built in 1860 and formerly a general store and family home, has changed little architecturally (except for the entry), with wide-board floors and tongue-in-groove paneling. The five upstairs bedrooms are furnished with wonderful old wooden beds (doubles only) and old-fashioned bureaus; they share two baths (one with shower, one with tub) and two toilets. Downstairs, guests may read, chat, or sip coffee in the parlor; peruse the items in the shop; or dine memorably in the restaurant, with floral tablecloths and wildflowers on the tables.

Owner Pier Normandeau is a talented, intuitive chef and chocolatier who makes his jams, desserts, ice creams, and sorbets with fruits from the regions. The cuisine is French and Québecois, and features crusty French bread, fish steamed and served with lemon or white-wine sauce, rabbit crème estragon or mustard, and pork médaillons with mustard; you may also order omelets or crêpes. L'Oeuf, which is fully licensed, is open for dinner Wednesday through Sunday from 5 to 10pm, and for lunch on weekends from noon to 2pm. The store is open Wednesday through Sunday from noon "until the last customer leaves."

A SHORT DRIVE FROM MYSTIC

From Mystic, it's a short drive south to **Stanbridge East,** a pretty town with the Aux Brochets River flowing through it. The regional **Missiquoi Museum,** open in summer only, is beside the river, in the photogenic old Cornell Mill with a waterwheel (1860). There's a picnic area beside it.

From Stanbridge East, follow Highway 202 est to Dunham and several local vineyards, whose wines and vines are still maturing. The family-owned and -run **Les Blancs Coteaux,** at 1046 Rte. 202, which opened in 1990, serves lunch and gives tours in summer, but you can visit anytime from June to November. The vineyard's shop sells its white wines, an interesting hard cider with an oak flavor, apple syrup, wine syrup with rose petals, strawberry vinegar, relish, cider jelly, and striking dried wreaths and wildflower arrangements made with straw, wheat, roses, and grapevines. The area's oldest vineyard, **l'Orpailleur,** 1086 Rte. 202, opened in 1982.

GRANBY

Granby (pop. 40,000), at Exit 68 (actually the first exit in the Estrie Region as you travel from Montréal), is an industrial town with a surprising attraction—the most important zoological garden in the Province of Québec. The **Granby Zoo** (Société Zoologique de Granby), at 347 rue Bourget, at Parc (tel. 514/372-9113), is 70 wooded acres harboring more than 1,000 mammals, exotic birds, reptiles, and amphibians from all over the world. Founded in 1953, the zoo has an active educational program and offers numerous activities. It is open daily from the end of May to mid-September from 10am to 5pm. Admission, including rides, is $15 for adults, $13 for seniors, $8 for students 5 to 17, $4 for children 1 to 4. Parking is $2. Take Exit 68 off the Estrie Region Highway 10; you'll see signs for the zoo.

Granby also has **Yamaska Park,** with a two-miles (3km) hiking trail and 25 miles (40km) of cross-country ski trails, 13½ miles (22km) of cycling trails along an old railroad track between the city, Bromont, and Waterloo. And be sure to see **Boivin Fountain,** with its 150-foot plume of water in Lake Boivin.

Tourisme Granby, is at 650 rue Principale, Granby, PQ, J2G 8L4 (tel. 514/372-7273; fax 514/372-7782). It's open daily in summer from 10am to 6pm, the rest of the year from 8am to 5pm.

BROMONT

If you take Exit 78 off Highway 10, you'll come to Bromont (pop. 30,000), a popular area for skiing (including night skiing), mountain biking (rent bikes at the entrance to the town opposite the tourist office), golf, horseback riding, hiking, zipping down alpine and water slides, and shopping in the two largest factory outlets in Canada— **Versants de Bromont** and **Les Manufacturiers de Bromont**—and at the area's largest flea market, 350 stalls set up in the local drive-in from 9am to 5pm the first Sunday in May to the second Sunday in November.

The **Bureau Touristique de Bromont,** 83 bd. Bromont (C.P. 666), Bromont, PQ, J0E 1L0 (tel. 514/534-2006; fax 514/534-4827), is open daily in summer from 10am to 6pm, the rest of the year from 8am to 5pm.

WHERE TO STAY & DINE

CHATEAU BROMONT, 90 rue Stanstead, Bromont, PQ, J0E 1L0. Tel. 514/534-3433, or toll free 800/363-0363. Fax 514/534-0514. 154 rms. A/C MINIBAR TV TEL

$ Rates: $100–$135 per person, double occupancy. Extra person $10. Spa, ski, and other packages available. AE, DC, ER, DISC, MC, V. **Parking:** Free.

At the base of Mont Bromont stands the striking Château Bromont, where all the rooms have rocking chairs, a loft bedroom with adjustable lamps, in-room movies, and toiletries in the bathrooms; half the rooms have fireplaces. That sets the tone for the hotel: one of comfort and relaxation. A landscaped terrace and two hot tubs overlook the mountain. Spa facilities (see below) cost extra. The staff is young and bilingual.

Dining/Entertainment: Les Quatre Canards restaurant serves lunch and dinner, and there is a bistro bar, L'Equestre, and the Château Terrasse Bar-BBQ.

Services: Babysitting, same-day dry cleaning and laundry, hairdresser.

Facilities: No-smoking rooms, indoor and outdoor pools and Jacuzzis, a sauna, a small gym, squash, racquetball, badminton, volleyball, mountain-bike rentals, games room and playground for kids, a large shop with local handcrafts and gift items from around the world, and a European spa featuring mud and algae baths, an immersion tub, and massage; equestrian center 10 minutes away.

KNOWLTON

If Estrie is the New England of Canada, then Knowlton is its Rockport, Maine—chockablock with shops, outlets, and tourists. So if your idea of a good vacation includes a shopping spree, make this one of your destinations. Knowlton is compact, with only two main shopping streets, so you can easily come for lunch and a few hours of shopping—in good company with Liz Claiborne, Ralph Lauren, Ben & Jerry, and others.

Knowlton is on the southeast corner of Lake Brome, and is part of the five-village municipality known as Lac Brome. The first settler here, Paul Holland Knowlton, a Loyalist from Vermont, arrived in 1815 and established a farm where the golf course is now. By 1834, he had added a sawmill, a gristmill, a blacksmith shop, and a store. He also founded the first high school.

Another Knowlton resident, Reginald Aubrey Fessenden, invented a wireless radio in 1906, a year ahead of Marconi, and relayed a message from Brant Rock, Massachusetts, to ships in the Caribbean.

Large mansions overhang the lake on either side of town (you might be tempted to drive around the lake, but other routes are prettier). If you decide to stay the night, you'll find a number of hotels and motels, and an outstanding bed-and-breakfast.

The town hosts a **Blue Grass Festival** in June, and the **Brome Fair** is held over Labor Day weekend.

The **tourist information office** is in the local museum (see below).

WHAT TO SEE & DO

MUSEE HISTORIQUE DU COMTE DE BROME (BROME COUNTY HISTORICAL MUSEUM), 130 Lakeside St. (Rte. 243). Tel. 514/243-6782.

This museum fills five historic buildings, including the town's first school, established by Paul Holland Knowlton. Exhibits focus on the various aspects of town life, with re-creations of a schoolroom, bedroom, parlor, and kitchen. The Martin Annex (1921) is dominated by the 1917 Fokker single-seat biplane, the finest example of German aircraft in World War I. It also houses a gun collection from the 18th to the early 20th century. There is also a collection of old radios. The museum sells books about the area.

Admission: $2.50 adults, $2 seniors, $1 students.

Open: Mon–Sat 10am–4:30pm, Sun 11am–4:30pm. **Closed:** Late Sept–early May.

WHERE TO STAY

L'ABRICOT, 562 Knowlton Rd. (Rte. 104 ouest), Knowlton, PQ, J0E 1V0. Tel. 514/243-5532. 4 rms (2 with private bath).

$ Rates (including full breakfast): $40–$60 single; $60–$80 double. Discounts if you stay two nights. No credit cards. **Parking:** Free.

Set in a pine grove 1½ miles west of town on Route 104, L'Abricot, built in 1889, has a light, airy downstairs, with wide-board spruce floors, comfortable furniture, a sun room, breakfast room, patio, and living room with a stone fireplace. The bedrooms, each named for an animal, are upstairs. The Cat Room, with a skylight in the bath, and the Duck Room are particularly appealing. Two smaller, wallpapered rooms share a large bath with a clawfoot tub. Outside, there's a large swimming pool and even a totem pole in the backyard. Besides being a delightful hostess, Denise Boyer is an excellent guide to the area. And she's likely to spoil you with cheese, pâté, fruit, or sherry—and, of course, a big breakfast—while you're there.

SUTTON

A delightful outing from Knowlton (or anywhere in the vicinity), Sutton (pop. 1,587) is a quiet, pretty town with little cafés and a great bookstore. Nearby Mont Sutton is known in summer for its 33 miles (54km) of hiking trails that link up with the Appalachian Trail, and for its glade skiing in winter. The surrounding country roads are popular with bikers.

There are several old cemeteries in or near the town, including a small 19th-century Quaker resting place, on a hill 2.5 miles (4km) from Sutton, off Route 139 on Mudget Road; park by the side of the road.

For more information about the town and the area, drop by the **Sutton Tourist Association,** beside the bookstore, and chat with Lucie Bellehumeur (tel. 514/538-2646).

MONT ORFORD

Mont Orford Provincial Park is among Québec's loveliest and most popular for camping and hiking. In high summer season, campsites fill up quickly, especially on weekends. From mid-September to mid-October it blazes with autumn splendor, and in winter, visitors come for the more than 20 miles of ski trails and slopes, with a vertical drop of 1,500 feet, or for the extensive network of cross-country ski and snowshoe trails.

Mont Orford is an old-timer of a ski area compared to Mont Bromont (see above), and has long provided the slopes of choice for the monied families of Magog and Montréal. The other two mountains in the area, Owl's Head and Mont Sutton, are less glitzy than these two and more family-oriented. These four ski centers have banded together to form Ski East, enabling skiers to purchase an all-inclusive five-day ticket good at all four anytime. Similarly economical lesson plans are available.

Orford has its own special claim to fame in the **Centre d'Arts Orford** (tel. 819/843-3981), set on a 222-acre estate within the park and providing master music classes for advanced students and young professionals during the summer. A series of concerts is also given in connection with the Orford Festival. Prices are usually $20 to $30, less $7 to $11 for student performances, which are held on Sunday mornings. The center is the starting point for some of the park's walking trails.

The **Bureau d'Information Touristique Magog-Orford** is at 55 rue Cabana (via Route 112), Magog, PQ, J1X 2C4 (tel. 819/843-2744, or toll free 800/267-2744.

WHERE TO STAY

CHERIBOURG, no. 2603, Rte. 141 North (C.P. 337), Orford, PQ, J1X 3W9. Tel. 819/843-3308, or toll free 800/567-6132 in Québec. Fax 819/843-2639. 97 rms, 90 chalets. A/C MINIBAR TV TEL **Directions:** Take Exit 118 from Autoroute 10.

$ Rates: $82 single; $92 double. Extra adult $12. Children under 12 free. From $435 per week, chalet. Discounts and packages available. AE, DC, DISC, ER, MC, V.

The Cheribourg is a collection of up-to-date mountain chalets and hotel rooms very near Mont Orford, Lac Memphremagog, and the Orford Arts Centre road to the Lac Stukely Campground. Founded in 1971, it is one of the area's oldest resorts, set on 200 acres in Mont Orford Park. Guests may enjoy clay tennis courts, indoor and outdoor volleyball, badminton, two outdoor pools, an exercise room, sauna, Jacuzzi, mountain bikes, a children's playground, a gift shop, and a disco in summer. The rooms, most of which have two queen-size beds, are decorated with white-pine furniture. If you're with a small group of friends, you might choose one of their boldly designed, brightly colored two- or three-room chalets for a week (for two or three days, depending on availability, if you reserve a week in advance). The chalets sleep up to six people in varying degrees of luxury, and all are equipped with a fireplace, kitchenette, and utensils. The Cheribourg is open year-round.

MAGOG & LAKE MEPHREMAGOG

Orford is where the people go, but Magog is where the people live. But how did a nice little town at the northern tip of a beautiful lake get such a name? Certainly this isn't the place inhabited by the nations of Gog and Magog who, according to the Book of Revelation in the New Testament, will follow Satan into battle against the Kingdom of God in the Last Days. As with countless other spots with incredible Canadian and American place-names, Magog (pop. 14,500) came by its handle through corruption of a Native Canadian (Amerindian) name. The Abenaki name Memrobagak ("Great Expanse of Water") somehow became Mephremagog, which was eventually short-ened to Magog, pronounced *May*-gog. The name of the lake is pronounced *Mem*-phree-*may*-gog.

WHAT TO SEE & DO

Magog has a vibrant waterfront, and in July each year the **International Crossing** of Lake Memphremagog creates quite a splash here. Participants start out in Newport, Vermont, at 6am and swim 24 miles to Magog, arriving midafternoon around 3:30 to 4pm. If you prefer to experience the lake without getting wet, take a 1¾-hour **cruise** aboard the *Aventure I* or *II* (tel. 819/843-8068); the cost is $10.50 for adults, $5.25 for children under 12; a day-long tour cruise is $38.50. The boats leave from Point Merry Park, the focal point for many of the town's outdoor activities.

BENEDICTINE ABBEY OF SAINT-BENOIT-DU-LAC, 12 miles (19km) southwest of Magog. Tel. 819/843-4080.

Although Saint-Benoît-du-Lac dates only from 1912, the serenity of its monks and of their way of life is timeless. The abbey is a beautiful spot where the ancient art of Gregorian chant is kept alive by the 40 monks in their liturgy. For the 45-minute service (see times below), walk to the rear of the abbey and down the stairs; follow signs for "Oratoire," and sit in back if you prefer not to do a lot of standing and sitting. The abbey receives 7,000 pilgrims a year—interestingly, 60% between the ages of 16 and 25—and a hostel for men and a separate one nearby for women is provided. (Make arrangements in advance; figure $35 or so per person.) The Canadian blue cheese known as L'Ermite, among Québec's most famous, and a tasty Swiss-type cheese, are produced at the monastery, and are for sale in a little shop, open 9 to 10:15am and 2 to 4:30pm Monday through Saturday. It also sells chocolate from Oka, honey, a tasty nonalcoholic cider, and tapes of religious chants. Should you bump into friendly Pére Bolduc while you're there, you're in for a treat. He will surely tell you about the large new church being built from local granite. And do visit the tiny stone chapel to your left at the entrance to the property, opposite the small cemetery. If you come the last two weeks of September or the first two weeks of October, there's the added pleasure of picking apples in the orchard.

Admission: Free; donations accepted.

Open: Daily 6am–8pm; mass with Gregorian chant at 11am, vespers with Gregorian chant at 5pm (7pm on Thurs)—no vespers on Tues in July–Aug; compline at 7:30pm. Shop, Mon–Sat 9–10:45am and 2–4:30pm.

WHERE TO STAY

AUBERGE L'ETOILE SUR LE LAC, 1150 rue Principale ouest, Magog, PQ, J1X 2B8. Tel. 819/843-6521, or toll free 800/567-2727 in Québec. Fax 819/843-5007. 26 rms. A/C TEL TV **Directions:** Take Exit 115 from Autoroute 10 and follow Highway 112 into Magog; you'll see the hotel soon after you pass the Tourist Information Bureau.

$ Rates: $78–$109 single; $88–$119 double. Golf, sailing, biking, and other packages available. AE, CB, DC, DISC, ER, MC, V.

Its name means "star on the lake," and this "star" gets a star for its friendly staff and location (right in town, right on the lake, and only 3½ miles, or 6km, from Mont Orford). The property was built in 1933 and renovated in 1990. All the rooms overlook Lake Memphremagog and the lakeside park and have a private patio or balcony. The standard rooms have one or two double beds; the pretty superior rooms, in the new section, are slightly bigger, with queen-size beds, bigger baths, and a closet for skis. Upstairs, there's a TV room with a fireplace, a rustic lounge, and a glass-enclosed Jacuzzi overlooking the lake. The hotel rents bicycles and ice skates; in winter the park just outside its door becomes a three-mile-long rink. This is a wonderful place to stay if you like to take walks or bike rides when you're on a trip.

Dining/Entertainment: L'Eau à la Bouche dining room and bar; terrace dining in summer.

Services: Massage; meeting rooms.

Facilities: Small outdoor pool in a garden setting, Jacuzzi, exercise room.

LA SAUVAGINE, 925 rue Merry nord, Magog, PQ, J1X 2G9. Tel. 819/843-9779. 5 rms (none with bath). **Directions:** Take Exit 118 off Highway 10.

$ Rates (including breakfast): $60–$90 single; $70–$90 double. Extra person $10. No credit cards.

If the area casts its spell over you and you decide to stay, consider La Sauvagine, a hospitable bed-and-breakfast whose name means "The Wild Bird." You'll arrive at a tidy white house with burgundy roof and shutters and a stone chimney, with a maple tree out front. Guests have breakfast on the terrace overlooking a sloping yard that leads to an apple orchard. There is an outdoor pool and, in winter, ski trails. The rooms, which have country decor and queen-size or twin beds, share two baths (one with a tub). Two have ceiling fans, three have sinks. The large "honeymoon suite" on the second floor features a rock fireplace and TV. The house also has a TV room and an art gallery with changing exhibits. Congenial André Poupart, with his wife, Louise Malepart, is your host. An artist, he has created the unique lamps for the rooms and the whimsical sculpture out front.

GEORGEVILLE

So tiny and picturesque it could be a mirage, Georgeville, established in 1797 on the eastern shore of Lake Memphremagog, was once a stop (along with Knowlton) along the stagecoach route from Montréal to Brome, then a five-day trip. Today the town has just enough houses to shelter 845 residents, an old-timey general store, a little church, a gracious country inn, and a nine-hole golf course with views of the lake. It is also a summer home of the actor Donald Sutherland, and the ideal getaway for those who like to mix simplicity and nature with fine dining.

The 14-mile (22km) drive along Highway 247 south from Georgeville to Beebe (see below) is lovely and highly recommended. You'll see Owl's Head mountain off to your right, and just before you enter Beebe Plain, watch for Claude Dupont's whimsical wood carvings of bears, in a yard to your left.

WHERE TO STAY & DINE

AUBERGE GEORGEVILLE, 71 chemin Channel, Rte. 247, Georgeville, PQ, J0B 1T0. Tel. 819/843-8683. 12 rms (all with sink, 4 with bath, 1 with toilet). **Directions:** Take Highway 247 10 miles south from Magog.

$ Rates (including full breakfast): $56–$61 single; $86–$91 double. Rates including dinner available. MC, V. **Parking:** Free. **Closed:** Oct 31–Dec 10 and Dec 24–25.

Built in 1890 as an inn to serve the stagecoach traffic, the Auberge Georgeville is particularly known for its dining room, where a five-course table d'hôte featuring fish or filet mignon is served each evening for about $30; call ahead if you prefer vegetarian. The three dining areas have board floors and fresh daisies, handmade pottery and handwoven placemats on the table. A two-sided fireplace warms the sitting room and the dining room. Owner and chef, Monique Morissette, keeps her regional cuisine healthy and flavorful, with a touch of fruit in almost everything, and loves to swap cooking tips and recipes with her guests. "People call me Grandma who are older than me," she admits, "but if I don't chat with people this feels like a job." Of the inn's dozen rooms, no. 11, with a bath and a view of the lake and mountains, is particularly restful. All the rooms with bath (small, with shower, no tub) face the lake. There is a shared bath on each floor. The inn, a pink house with white shutters, has a wraparound porch and lawn chairs, picnic tables, and a swing in the front yard.

LAKE MASSAWIPPI

Southeast of Magog, reachable by Highway 141 or 55, is 10-mile-long Lake Massawippi. Set among rolling hills and rich farm country, the scenic lake with its jagged shoreline was discovered long ago by those in search of a beautiful place to retreat. Men of wealth and power built grand "summer cottages" in prime locations along the lakeshore, some of which have been converted to inns. For a few days' relaxation from the rigors of travel, you won't do better than Lake Massawippi.

In winter, the lake has 35 miles (56km) of cross-country ski trails, and a special three- or six-night package, called **Skiwippi,** allows any takers to ski from the Ripplecove Inn to Hovey Manor to the Hatley Inn (see below), enjoying the accommodations, hospitality, and cuisine at each. For the less athletically inclined, a similar package (sans skis), called A Moveable Feast, is also available. You may book the package through any of the inns.

NORTH HATLEY

The jewel of Lake Massawippi, this town of 725, only half an hour from the Vermont (U.S.) border and 85.5 miles (138km) from Montréal, has a river meandering through it and is the dream retirement home for this writer (a summer home here immediately would be even better). Besides its beauty, including phenomenal sunsets over the lake, it has a variety of lodgings and places to dine, shops, golf, horseback riding, a marina, post office, Laundromat, and a general store. The English-language **Piggery Theatre,** on a country road outside of town, presents plays during the summer (tel. 819/842-2431).

Where to Stay

AUBERGE HATLEY INN, 325 chemin Virgin (P.O. Box 330), North Hatley, PQ, J0B 2C0. Tel. 819/842-2451. Fax 819/842-2907. 25 rms. A/C TEL **Directions:** Take Exit 29 from Highway 55, and follow Highway 108 east, looking for signs.

$ Rates (including breakfast and dinner): $200 double weekdays; $225 double Fri–Sat. AE, MC, V.

North Hatley's famous "relais gastronomique" (dining resort) is the stately Auberge Hatley Inn, up on a hill overlooking the lake. All rooms have a private bath or shower, some with sauna or Jacuzzi or fireplace and Jacuzzi; most have lake views. Linger on the back porch, by the pool, or in the gazebo beside the pool, and soak up the tranquillity all around you. Hosts Liliane and Robert Gagnon will fill you in on what there is to do nearby: riding, hiking, fishing, water (or snow) skiing, hunting—and of course, dining. The inn is a member of Relais & Châteaux.

AUBERGE L'ENTRE 2 COTES, Rte. 108, Grand Rue, Ste-Catherine-de-Hatley, PQ, J0B 1W0. Tel. 819/843-6824. 7 rms (1 with bath).

$ Rates (including full breakfast): Sun–Thurs $59 single, $99 double; Fri–Sat $69 single, $109 double (with dinner included, $79 single, $119 double). Packages available. MC, V.

This country inn, a white house with red geraniums spilling over everywhere, a mere four miles (6km) south of North Hatley, has a hypnotic view overlooking Mont Orford, the Appalachian Mountains, and Lake Magog. The rooms are pretty; Room 5 is particularly spacious, with a big bath, and Room 6, small but cozy and quiet because it's in the back of the house. Guests are provided with essentials such as a hairdryer and chocolates. The public rooms, one with a Franklin stove, are appealing and conducive to losing oneself in a good book or a game of chess. The dining room serves home cooking for breakfast, lunch, and dinner. Right beside the highway, the inn gets a little noise from passing cars. Renée Constantin is your host.

HOVEY MANOR, chemin Hovey (P.O. Box 60), North Hatley, PQ, J0B 2C0. Tel. 819/842-2421. Fax 819/842-2248. 35 rms. A/C TEL

$ Rates (including full breakfast, dinner, gratuities, and most of the recreational facilities): $105–$160 single; $160–$270 double. Extra person $65. Children under 13 half price when sharing room with two parents. AE, DC, ER, MC, V. **Parking:** Free.

Hovey Manor is named for Capt. Ebenezer Hovey, a Connecticut Yankee, "discoverer" of the lake (1793), and first white settler in North Hatley. The grand manor itself, part of the Auberges Romantiks chain, has towering, vine-covered columns and lakeside English gardens, and was built in 1900 to resemble George Washington's estate at Mount Vernon. Set on a hill and encompassing 20 acres and 1,600 feet of lakefront property, it is one of Canada's most romantic inns. Many of the guest rooms have fireplaces, balconies, and whirlpool baths. All the public rooms have fireplaces, and the library adjoining the reception area is one of the prettiest rooms I've ever seen, decorated in deep reds and greens, with a stone fireplace and floor-to-ceiling bookshelves. A lighted tennis court, heated outdoor pool, two beaches, water sports, and, above all, old-world ambience add to the inn's appeal.

The outstanding dining room serves French cuisine, with a menu that changes with the seasons and features herbs, vegetables and edible flowers from the kitchen garden. I enjoyed a memorable dinner that started with pâté and a warm salad of goat cheese, wild mushrooms, and greens, followed by tender pheasant with apricot sauce and a complement of cauliflower, carrots, and puréed beets; then a dessert of maple mousse served in a barley-sugar tulip.

The quietness at Hovey Manor is broken only by the chirping of birds during the day and crickets at night, and the view of the moonrise is unforgettable. Steve and Kathy Stafford are the gracious hosts.

LA RAVEAUDIERE, 11 rue Hatley, North Hatley, PQ, J0B 2C0. Tel. 819/842-2554. 8 rms (3 with bath). A/C
$ Rates (including breakfast): $70–$115 single; $85–$130 double. MC, V.
La Raveaudière, opposite Massawippi Golf Club, combines the elegance and refined service of a five-star hotel with the tranquillity of a country inn, and it must be experienced to be believed, from the *House Beautiful* decor to the breakfast (in bed, if you choose), complete with peeled grapes and your own plunger pot of coffee. An optional Sunday brunch October through May features eggs Benedict or eggs Romanoff with caviar, dessert, and coffee. The former Loyalist farmhouse (1826), now graced by rich, dark colors on the walls and plush fabrics everywhere, is carefully tended by owner Serge Raveau. The bedrooms, two with private bath (one has a large tub), are filled with interesting architectural angles, beds with padded headboards, striking area rugs on wood floors, and antiques and other collectibles. The room in the back of the house gets the least noise from the road. Call before you arrive.

Where to Dine

PILSEN, 55 rue Principale. Tel. 819/842-2971.
Cuisine: INTERNATIONAL. **Reservations:** Recommended on weekends.
$ Prices: Appetizers $2.25–$8.50; main courses $7–$22.50. MC, V.
Open: Wed–Thurs and Sun 11:30am–9pm, Fri–Sat 11:30am–9:30pm. The bar stays open until 3am.
Ask anybody where to have a casual meal in North Hatley and they'll point you in the direction of the Pilsen, a local pub and restaurant in the center of town. Specialties include chicken and seafood dishes, souvlaki brochette, and lobster bisque, but you can get everything from nachos to burgers to pasta to vegetarian dishes. There's an extensive choice of beers, imported and local, including Massawippi Blonde and nonalcoholic. You can park behind the restaurant.

WHERE TO STAY & DINE IN AYER'S CLIFF

RIPPLECOVE INN, 700 Ripplecove St. (P.O. Box 246), Ayer's Cliff, PQ, J0B 1C0. Tel. 819/838-4296. Fax 819/838-5584. 25 units. TEL **Directions:** Take Highway 55 to Exit 21.
$ Rates: $80–$140 single; $90–$175 double; package with breakfast, dinner,

activities, and tips for two people, $99–$158 per person (less if you stay longer than one night). AE, MC, V.

Some 22 miles (35km) from North Hatley, the country-mansion-style Ripplecove Inn sits on the shore of Lake Massawippi in Ayer's Cliff. The original installations in the inn, located on 12 private acres, date from 1945, with a lobby and dining room redecorated in Victorian style in 1992. The rooms are quite modern, with deluxe rooms, suites, and cottages. All have private baths, and many have fireplaces, private balconies, and whirlpool tubs. The property has a private beach, a landscaped heated outdoor swimming pool, a school for sailing and sailboarding, facilities for waterskiing, canoes for guests' use, and cross-country skiing. Golf courses and horseback-riding stables are only a short ride away. Its award-winning lakeside dining room serves lunch and dinner daily.

SHERBROOKE

Seat of an archbishopric, university town, and home to 90,000 people and about 150 different manufacturing firms, Sherbrooke is the "metropolis" of Québec's Estrie Region, where some of eastern Canada's elusive trains actually still stop.

It's a hilly city, built where the Magog and Saint-François rivers meet. Just before the Magog River flows into the Saint-François, it widens to form the Lac des Nations right in the center of town. Sherbrooke is 16 miles (26km) northeast of North Hatley, and 99 miles (160km) east of Montréal.

Rue King, the city's main artery, is 7½ miles (12km) long, and most of the hotels, restaurants, bars, and shops line it. The center of town is King and Wellington. The **tourist office** is nearby, in the old train station, at 48 rue Depot, Sherbrooke, PQ, J1H 5G1 (tel. 819/564-8331).

The city has a **Fine Arts Museum** (Musée des Beaux-Arts de Sherbrooke), downtown at 174 du Palais, and a **Natural Sciences Museum,** at 195 Marquette. In **Parc Jacques Cartier,** there are 12½ miles (20km) of bike trails.

The French-speaking **University of Sherbrooke,** with 10,000 students, is here, and its English counterpart, **Bishop's University,** built by one of the architects of Oxford University in England, is a few miles south, in Lennoxville.

Every year in mid-May, Sherbrooke, which despite its name, is 90% French-speaking, hosts the **Festival des Harmonies du Québec,** a popular music festival, followed by the **Fête du Lac des Nations** (Environmental Festival) in July and an **Exposition Agricole** (Agricultural Fair) in August.

WHERE TO STAY

LE MITCHELL, 219 rue Moore, Sherbrooke, PQ, J1H 1C1. Tel. 819/ 563-8636. Fax 819/562-8779. 4 rms (1 with bath). TEL
$ **Rates** (including breakfast): $75 single without bath, $90 single with bath; $85 double without bath, $100 double with bath. AE, MC, V.

If you prefer to stay in bed-and-breakfasts, you're in luck in Sherbrooke. The Tudor-style Le Mitchell, which opened in 1991, has four spacious rooms, one with a private bath. The other rooms share a large bath with a cathedral ceiling. Guests may use the den/TV room, living room, and sun room, and grow mellow in front of three different fireplaces. There's some noise from the street, and the room in the back of the house is quietest. Host Lise Couture spoils her guests with afternoon and evening refreshments, not to mention breakfast. A bit of trivia: The house was featured in *Homes & Garden* magazine in February 1932. Le Mitchell is a five-minute walk from downtown. A fax and photocopier are available for business travelers.

WHERE TO DINE

LE DEVINIERE, 17 Peel St., at King St. Tel. 819/822-4177.
Cuisine: FRENCH. **Reservations:** Recommended.
$ **Prices:** Appetizers $3.50–$8; main courses $16–$22. MC, V.
Open: Lunch Tues–Fri 11am–2pm; dinner Tues–Sat 5–10pm.

This centrally located, upscale restaurant promises a delicious meal in tranquil surroundings. The cuisine is thoroughly French, and the specialty is lamb (*agneau* on the menu). The restaurant is not licensed to serve alcohol, but you're welcome—encouraged, in fact—to bring your own.

STANDSTEAD PLAIN, ROCK ISLAND & BEEBE PLAIN

For a unique day or half-day trip from North Hatley, follow Highway 143 south as far as you can go without actually crossing the United States border and explore three winsome French villages. If you should cross the border accidentally, which is easy to do, just report yourself to the inspectors and come back across.

The first town you'll come to is Stanstead Plain (pop. 1,059), some 30 miles (49km) south of North Hatley and only nine miles (15km) north of Newport, Vermont. Known for the striking architecture of its buildings, Stanstead Plain offers such points of interest as **Centenary United Church,** with a unique clock face that bears the name of the person who donated the granite to build the church; the lovely **Butler House** (1866), at 10 rue Dufferin; and the Renaissance-style **Colby Curtis—Carroll Croft Museum,** 35 rue Dufferin, filled with Victorian and American furnishings and outstanding portraits by Québec artist Orson Wheeler. It is open Tuesday through Sunday from 10am to 5pm, with an admission of $3 for adults, $1.50 for seniors, and 50¢ for children (tel. 819/876-7322).

Stanstead East runs into the village of Rock Island (pop. 1,067), which is the commercial center of the area. Doctors still make house calls, and you can show up in their waiting room without an appointment. Imagine.

Follow Stevens Street (uphill) as you enter Rock Island; it's a cul-de-sac, but you'll be rewarded by a great view. If you continue straight through the town without turning left or right, you'll find yourself in Vermont.

The **Haskell Opera House** (1901) is literally and logistically half Canadian and half American: The stage and performers are in Canada, and the audience is in the United States.

About 2½ miles (4km) west of Rock Island, Beebe Plain (pop. 975) is a center for quarrying granite. The Catholic church here (enter through the side door) has outstanding wood sculptures, and the portrait of St. Teresa behind the altar appears to watch your every move. But what makes this town most unique is half-mile-long Canusa Street, the north side of which is in Canada, the south side in the United States (thus, its name). If you don't believe me, just check the car plates. Here, it's long-distance to call your neighbor across the street, and while you're free to walk across the street for a visit, you have to report to the authorities if you decide to drive.

QUEBEC CITY & THE GASPE PENINSULA

Québec City has always been the soul of New France. It was the first settlement, and today is the capital of the huge and fiercely independent province of Québec. The Old City, a jumble of ancient, picturesque houses clustered around a "castle" (actually, a hotel—the fairy-tale Château Frontenac), is every bit as romantic as you could imagine. For its history, its beauty, and its unique status as North America's only walled city, it was named a UNESCO World Heritage city in 1985.

Québec City is almost solidly French in feeling, in spirit, and in language; 95% of its population speaks French. But many of its 464,900 citizens speak some English, especially those who work in hotels, restaurants, and shops, where they deal with English-speaking people every day. It may be more difficult in Québec City than in Montréal to understand and be understood, but rest assured, a Québécois will go out of his or her way to communicate in English or listen attentively to your halting efforts at French. The Québécois are a gracious and charming lot, and it is a pleasure to spend time in their company and in their city.

After exploring Québec City, consider a trip to the gardenlike Ile d'Orléans, the popular shrine of Ste-Anne-de-Beaupré, the provincial park and ski resort at Mont Ste-Anne, or the picturesque southern bank of the mighty St. Lawrence, where riverside villages, like St-Jean-Port-Joli, nationally known for its wood-carvers and other artisans, beckon you to linger.

1. ORIENTATION

Believe it or not, you could spend almost all your visit to Québec in the Old City, as most accommodations, restaurants, and tourist-oriented services are based here. The colonial city was first built right down by the St. Lawrence at the foot of Cap Diamant. It was here that merchants, traders, and boatmen earned their livelihoods, but due to unfriendly fire in the 1700s, this Lower Town became merely a wharf and warehouse area, and residents moved to safer houses atop Cap Diamant.

The Upper Town, the Québécois later discovered, was not immune from

WHAT'S SPECIAL ABOUT QUEBEC CITY

The Layout
- ☐ Twice the fun—an Upper Town and a Lower Town, joined by numerous stairs and a funicular.
- ☐ Compact, with narrow streets and pedestrian walkways, and no way to get lost.
- ☐ Dufferin Terrace, on a cliff high above the Lower Town, overlooking the St. Lawrence River and backed by the Château Frontenac.

Architecture
- ☐ Ancient city walls and gates.
- ☐ The star-shaped Citadel, atop Cap Diamant.
- ☐ The Château Frontenac, the city's literal and architectural high point.

Festivals
- ☐ Festival d'Eté International (International Summer Festival), the largest French-speaking cultural event in North America, in July.
- ☐ Winter Carnival, in February, with a fun-loving mascot named Bonhomme, a parade, an ice palace, an ice sculpture competition, and a stiff drink called *caribou*.

Museums
- ☐ The Museum of Civilization, a pocket of modernity in an ancient city.
- ☐ The Québec Museum, with exhibition space in a recycled prison.

cannonade either, as General Wolfe was to prove. Nevertheless, the division into Upper and Lower Towns persisted for obvious topographical reasons. The Upper Town remains enclosed by the old city's fortification walls, and several ramplike streets and a cliffside elevator (*funiculaire*) connect it to the Lower Town.

For a panoramic look at the city, seek out the Québec government's office building, called Edifice "G," 1037 rue de la Chevrotière, off the Grande-Allée and near the Parliament building (tel. 418/644-9841). Enter the tower at the corner of de la Chevrotière and St-Cyrille, and look for signs and special elevators labeled "Anima G, 31e Etage." On the 31st floor a plush observatory, with an information desk, is open from 10am to 4pm weekdays, 1 to 5pm on Saturday, Sunday, and holidays.

Another good place for an overall view is L'Astral, the revolving restaurant atop Loews Le Concorde Hotel, where you could drop in for a drink. Nothing ties it all together like being able to take in the entire city at once.

ARRIVING

BY PLANE   Québec City's airport is small and pleasant. From it, you can take a bus into town operated by **Maple Leaf Sightseeing Tours, Inc.** (tel. 418/649-9226). The trip costs $7.50, and buses leave at least every hour, except on Saturday and Sunday, when they run less frequently. A taxi into town costs about $25.

BY TRAIN   The train station in Québec City, though more beautiful than Montréal's (it was designed by Bruce Price, who designed the city's fabled Château Frontenac), is not as centrally located as its counterpart. Figure on an uphill hike or a $6 cab ride to the Old City—that's $6 per ride, not per passenger, and don't let the occasional entrepreneurial cabbie convince you otherwise.

BY BUS   The bus station, **Terminus Voyageur,** in Québec City, 225 bd. Charest est (tel. 418/524-4692), is near the train station, both of which are an uphill climb (or quick cab ride) to Château Frontenac and the Old Town. A taxi should cost about $6, same as from the train station. You can save money by taking a bus; walk out the front door of the bus station, turn right, and walk to the end of the block. Turn right again and you'll be on Dorchester/Côte d'Abraham, at some bus stops. The no. 3 bus heads up the hill to the Haute Ville (Upper Town) every 15 minutes (but it usually makes more sense and saves time to spring for a taxi), and goes directly to the Château Frontenac; fare is $1.80 in exact change.

BY CAR   From New York, follow I-87 to Autoroute 15 to Montréal, where you'll pick up Autoroute 20 to Québec City (take 73 Nord and exit onto Champlain Boulevard immediately after crossing the bridge; turn left at Battlefields Park and right onto the Grande-Allée); for a slower but more scenic route, follow Highway 132 from Montréal along the south shore of the St. Lawrence River to Québec City. You may also follow the north shore from Montréal, along Autoroute 40. From Boston, you can take I-89 to I-93 to I-91 in Montpelier, which connects with Autoroute 55 in Québec to link up with Autoroute 20. You can also follow I-90 up the Atlantic coast, through Portland, Maine, to Highway 201 west of Bangor, then Highway 173 to Lévis, where there is a car-ferry to Québec City, which is directly across the St. Lawrence River and a 10-minute ride away; the ferry runs every hour on the hour during the day from Lévis (slightly less often at night), and costs $3 for the car and $1 per person.

TOURIST INFORMATION

The **Greater Québec Area Tourism and Convention Bureau** operates two well-staffed provincial tourist information centers, open year-round. One is in the old part of Québec City at 60 rue d'Auteuil (tel. 418/692-2471). The other is in suburban Ste-Foy, at 3005 bd. Laurier, which is near the Québec and Pierre-Laporte bridges (tel. 418/651-2882). Hours for both centers are 8:30am to 8pm daily June to early September; daily 8:30am to 5:30pm early September to mid-October; 9am to 5pm Monday through Friday mid-October to mid-April; and 8:30am to 5:30pm mid-April through June.

The Québec Government's Tourism Department operates a **city information office** on place d'Armes, down the hill from the Château Frontenac, at 12 rue Ste-Anne (tel. 418/873-2015, a local call from Montréal, or toll free 800/363-7777 from other parts of Québec, Canada, and the United States). It's open from June 10 to early September from 8:30am to 7:30pm, the rest of the year from 9am to 5pm; closed Christmas, New Year's Day, and Easter. The office has brochures for the entire province, as well as handy toilets. Across the hall in the same building are travel and car-rental agencies, cruise and bus tour operators, a 24-hour instant teller, a currency-exchange office, and a free accommodations reservation service. In summer only, a small tourist office is open in the Lower Town near place Royale.

Parks Canada operates an information kiosk in front of the Château Frontenac; it's open daily in summer from 9am to noon, and 1 to 5pm.

CITY LAYOUT

MAIN ARTERIES & STREETS   In the Old City, the main streets of the Upper Town are St-Louis, which fronts the Château Frontenac (it becomes the Grande-Allée outside the city walls and leads to the Plains of Abraham), Ste-Anne, and St-Jean, and the Dufferin Terrasse, which overlooks the river and is for pedestrians only. In the Lower Town, major streets are St-Pierre, Dalhousie, St-Paul and, parallel to it, St-André.

IMPRESSIONS

Is there any city in the world that stands so nobly as Québec?
—RUPERT BROOKE, *LETTERS FROM AMERICA, 1913,* 1916

NEIGHBORHOODS IN BRIEF The Upper Town Part of the walled Old City, it lies on the crest of Cap Diamant overlooking the St. Lawrence River and includes many sites for which the city is famous, among them the Château Frontenac, place d'Armes, the Basilica of Notre-Dame, Québec Seminary and museum, Dufferin Terrace, and the UNESCO World Heritage monument. (Unfortunately, at place d'Armes, the city powers-that-be allow large tour buses to glut what would be an otherwise perfectly picturesque and quiet spot.)

The Lower Town Linked to the Upper Town by the funicular on Dufferin Terrace and numerous stairways, including one near the entrance to the funiculaire, it features place Royale, the quartier du Petit-Champlain, including the pedestrians-only rue du Petit-Champlain, the small Notre-Dame-des-Victoires church, and nearby, the impressive Museum of Civilization.

The Grande-Allée This, the eastern end of this impressive boulevard from the city walls and St-Louis Gate to avenue Taché, encompasses some of the city's most popular spots: the stately Parliament building, in front of which Winter Carnival takes place every year (the ice sculptures pop up across the street), numerous cafés, fine restaurants, a popular disco, the Museum of Fine Arts, and the Citadelle and the Plains of Abraham. The city's large hotels are also on or near the Grande-Allée. Avenue Cartier, off the Grande-Allée and near the museum, is a popular café street.

STREET MAPS You'll find good ones of the Upper and Lower Towns in the Greater Québec Area tourist guide, provided by any tourist office, along with a large map of the greater Québec area.

2. GETTING AROUND

It's simple: Walk. Once you've reached the center of town, virtually no place of interest, hotel, or restaurant is out of walking distance.

BY PUBLIC TRANSPORTATION Although you can walk between the Château Frontenac (top of the cliff) and place Royale (bottom of the cliff), you can also allow yourself the luxury of a ride on the funicular, which operates up the cliff face between those two points along a 210-foot track. The cost for the short trip is $1, and the car operates daily from 8am to midnight in summer; it closes at 11:30pm in winter. The upper station is just off Dufferin Terrace near the front of the Château Frontenac and place d'Armes; the lower station is in Maison Louis-Jolliet on rue Petit-Champlain, a block or two from place Royale. Local buses run quite often (something Québec City has over Montréal) and charge $1.80 in exact change; no. 7 travels up and down rue St-Jean; no. 11, Grande-Allée/rue St-Louis (this bus, along with nos. 7 and 8, also goes to Ste-Foy, in case you want to visit the shopping centers there). One-day bus passes are available for $3.50.

BY TAXI They're everywhere—cruising and parked in front of the big hotels outside the city gates—and they're expensive. If you need to call a cab, try **Taxi Coop** (tel. 418/525-5191) or **Taxi Québec** (tel. 418/522-2001).

BY CAR Rentals Car-rental companies in Québec City include **Avis,** at the airport (tel. 418/872-2861) and in the Old City (tel. 418/523-1075); **Budget,** at the airport (tel. 418/872-9885) and in the Old City (tel. 418/692-3660); **Hertz Canada,** at the airport (tel. 418/871-1571) and in the Old City (tel. 418/694-1224); and **Thrifty,** at the airport (tel. 418/877-2870) and in the Old City (tel. 418/683-1542).

Parking On-street parking is a problem in the cramped quarters of Old Québec. Should you be so lucky as to find a space on the street, check the signs for hours that parking is permissible; where meters are concerned, you pay 25¢ per 15 minutes up to

120 minutes. You may park free in a metered spot on Sunday *but not Saturday,* before 9am and after 6pm Monday through Wednesday and on Saturday, and before 9am and after 9pm Thursday and Friday.

Many of the smaller hotels have special arrangements with local lots, which results in a discount for their guests, who pay about $6 per day instead of the standard $10 or so (so check in at your hotel before you stick your car in a lot).

If your particular hotel or inn does not have access to a lot, don't despair. There are plenty of parking lots (clearly marked on the foldout city map available at tourist offices) that cost about $10 a day; several convenient ones include the Hôtel de Ville (City Hall), where parking is free in the evening and on weekends; Complexe G, off the Grande-Allée on rue St-Cyrille, where you can take your car in and out of the lot twice a day at no extra charge; and in the Lower Town across the street from the Museum of Civilization, on rue Dalhousie, where discounts are often offered on weekends.

BY BICYCLE My first impulse is to say, "Forget it," given the up-and-down (sometimes straight up-and-down) geographical layout of the city, but you can actually rent a pedal bicycle if you're so inclined, or a motorized bike, from a little place in the Lower Town at 94 rue du Petit-Champlain, near the lighthouse. Bikes are about $6 an hour, $30 a day; mopeds, $20 for the first hour, $6 for each additional hour, $50 per day. The shop, **Location Petit-Champlain,** also rents strollers, and it's open daily from 9am to 11pm (tel. 418/692-2817). You may also rent bikes on nearby (and highly recommended) Ile d'Orléans, right across the bridge at the gas station (tel. 418/828-9215).

FAST FACTS QUEBEC CITY

American Express There is no office right in town, but for lost traveler's checks, call toll free 800/221-7282.

Area Code Québec City's area code is 418.

Bookstores Most of Québec City's bookstores cater to the solidly French-speaking citizenry, but a few shops carry some English books for the tourist trade, such as Librairie Garneau, 24 côte de la Fabrique (tel. 418/692-4262). Librairie du Nouveau Monde, 103 rue St-Pierre in Old Québec (tel. 418/694-9475), features a wide range of titles dealing with Québec history and culture, including books in English. Librairie Pantoute, 1100 rue St-Jean, a large, well-lit space, sometimes carries copies of *French for Travellers,* and is open Monday through Saturday from 10am to 10pm and Sunday from noon to 10pm (tel. 418/694-9748). For travel books, visit **Ulysses,** 4 bd. St-Cyrille est (tel. 418/529-5349).

Business Hours Banks are open from 10am to 3pm, with most also having hours on Thursday and Friday evenings. Several banks have Saturday hours, but the ones that do are mostly located outside of Old Québec.

Car Rentals See "Getting Around" in this chapter.

Consulates The U.S. Consulate is near the Château Frontenac, facing Jardin des Gouverneurs at 2 place Terrasse-Dufferin (tel. 418/692-2095).

Currency Exchange Conveniently located near the Château Frontenac, the Bureau de Change at 19 rue Ste-Anne and rue des Jardins, is open Monday, Tuesday, and Friday from 10am to 3pm, and Wednesday and Thursday from 10am to 6pm.

Dentist Call 418/653-5412 Monday and Tuesday 8am to 8pm, Wednesday and Thursday 8am to 5pm, and Friday 8am to 4pm; for weekend emergencies, call 418/656-6060.

Doctor For emergency treatment, call Info-Santé 24 hours a day (tel. 418/648-2626).

Drugstores Go to Caron & Bernier, in the Upper Town, 38 côte du Palais, at rue Charlevoix; it's open from 8:15am to 8pm Monday through Friday, and 9am to 3pm on Saturday (tel. 692-4252). In an emergency, you'll have to travel to the suburbs to Pharmacie Lippens-Brunet, in Les Galeries Charlesbourg, 4266 Première Avenue (1ère or First Avenue), in Charlesbourg (tel. 623-1571), open daily until midnight.

Electricity   Happily, what works in the U.S. works in Québec.

Emergencies   For police, call 418/691-6911; fire, 418/691-6911; Marine Search and Rescue (Canadian Coast Guard), 24 hours a day, 418/648-3599 (Greater Québec Area) or toll free 800/463-4393 (St. Lawrence River); Poison Control Center, 418/656-8090; for pets, Vet-Medic (tel. 418/647-2000—24 hours a day).

Information   See "Tourist Information" earlier in this chapter.

Lost Property   Go to (or call) the place where you think you left it, or call the police (tel. 418/691-6911).

Luggage Storage and Lockers   Luggage storage is available in both the train station, Gare du Palais, 450 rue de la Gare-du-Palais, and in the bus station, Terminus d'Autobus Voyageur, 225 bd. Charest est. Both are in the Lower Town.

Newspapers and Magazines   Québec City's English-language newspaper, the *Chronicle-Telegraph,* is the equivalent of a small-town newspaper, published weekly on Wednesday. The content is local news and advertisements. Founded in 1764, it claims to be North America's oldest newspaper. Broader-scope Canadian and American English-language newspapers and magazines are available in the newsstands of the large hotels.

Photographic Needs   You can buy film or get it developed at Librairie Garneau, 24 côte de la Fabrique (tel. 418/692-4262).

Police   For the Québec City police, call 418/691-6911.

Post Office   The main post office (Bureau de Poste) is in the Lower Town, at 300 rue St-Paul near rue Abraham-Martin, not far from Parent Square by the port; hours are 8am to 5:45pm Monday through Friday (tel. 418/648-3340). A convenient branch in the Upper Town, half a block down the hill from the Château Frontenac at 3 rue Buade, keeps about the same hours (tel. 418/648-4686).

Radio   In Québec City, most broadcasts are in French; however, FM 104.7 is in English.

Restrooms   You'll find them in the tourist offices and on the ground floor of the commercial complex at 41 rue Couillard, in the Upper Town just off rue St-Jean (it's wheelchair accessible). In the Lower Town, one of the souvenir shops at place Royale makes its restroom available for 25¢; look for the sign out front. Also remember that many cafés situate their restrooms near the telephone, just like in the States.

Safety   Whenever you're traveling in an unfamiliar city or country, even one as "docile" as Québec, stay alert. Be aware of your immediate surroundings. Wear a moneybelt and keep a close eye on your possessions. Be particularly careful with cameras, purses, and wallets, all favorite targets of thieves and pickpockets.

Shoe Repairs   Down at heel? Go to Bottier le Cosaque, 29 rue d'Auteuil, in the Upper Town (tel. 418/529-9272).

Taxes   Except for crafts made in Canada, you'll be paying 15% tax—7% federal tax and 8% provincial tax—on the items you buy. Since 1992, there's also been a 4% tax on hotels. To get most of that tax money back, be sure to ask for your receipt and special duty-free form when you shop in a duty-free store. (The duty-free form is usually available at the front desk of hotels, as well.) When you return home, mail your receipts with the filled-in form to the address specified on the form, then wait a few months for the refund, minus a small service charge, to arrive. No money will be returned to you at the airport.

Telegrams   The telegram office in Québec City is at 25 place Marché-Champlain (tel. 692-3994), or call toll free 800/361-7657. The number is also good for sending money orders.

Television   Most programming is in French. In the large hotels, you'll be plugged into cable and can get some English-language stations. Channel 5 has English-language programming.

Time   Québec City is on the same time as New York, Boston, Montréal, and Toronto; it's an hour behind Halifax.

Transit Info   Call 418/627-2511.

Weather For the weather forecast, call 418/872-6088, 24 hours a day; for road conditions, call 418/643-6830, 24 hours a day, November 1 to April 19.

3. ACCOMMODATIONS

Staying in one of the small hotels or guesthouses within the old city walls is one of Québec City's memorable experiences. In many of these places each room is unique, and the standards of comfort, amenities, and prices vary so much from one small hotel to another that it is truly difficult to imagine that you couldn't find just what you want. From rooms with private bath and color TV down to plain and simple budget accommodation, the old city has everything, even a modern motor inn hidden away on a quiet street. It's always a good idea to check out the room first, to be sure it meets your requirements for comfort.

The Château Frontenac offers the services of a modern hotel behind a fairy-tale facade; a Hilton and a Radisson wait just outside the ancient walls and a ritzy Loews stands a little farther away. These high-rise hostelries are easily within walking distance of the attractions in the old city (10 to 20 minutes, depending on where you're going), or are only a quick bus or taxi ride away, if your energy flags.

In the listings below, expensive properties are those that charge $125 to $185 for a double room in summer; moderate, $80 to $120; inexpensive, $45 to $75; and budget, $40 or less. Prices often drop significantly in winter (November through April).

In line with policies at luxury digs throughout the world, Québec City's top hotels have rate structures that only a computer can understand: peak-period rates, slump-period discounts, special packages. So if you're not coming for Christmas or New Year's or during Winter Carnival, and if you ask for specifics on weekend stays, honeymoon specials, or discounts for extended stays, you can bring the price of luxury down to more affordable levels. Remember also that for families, luxury hotels can prove to be surprisingly moderate because most rooms have two double beds, and if your children use one bed and you use the other, there should be no extra charge above the normal price for a double room with two double beds.

Don't forget that you'll be faced with federal, provincial, and accommodations taxes on top of your bill. Ask your hotel for refund forms and save your receipts, because non-Canadians can file for tax refunds once they've returned home.

UPPER TOWN

EXPENSIVE

CHATEAU FRONTENAC, 1 rue des Carrières, Québec, PQ, G1R 4P5. Tel. 418/692-3861, or toll-free reservations through CP Hotels at 800/441-1414. Fax 418/692-1751. 544 rms, 24 suites. A/C MINIBAR TV TEL
$ Rates: Summer $129–$205 single, $154–$230 double; winter $109–$185 single, $134–$220 double. Special packages and senior-citizen discounts available. AE, CB, DC, DISC, ER, MC, V. **Parking:** Indoor, $12.25 per day.

Québec's castlelike and undeniably magical Château Frontenac turned 100 years old in 1993, and added a new, 66-room wing, a stunning indoor pool, and an extensive gym overlooking Governor's Park to celebrate. During its illustrious past, the hotel has hosted Queen Elizabeth and Prince Philip, a half-dozen other British and foreign monarchs, and Madame Chiang Kai-shek. During World War II, Churchill and Roosevelt held a conference here; because of wartime security measures, they had the entire place to themselves. The hotel, now in an A configuration, was built in phases, following the landline, so don't be surprised by the crooked (and wonderfully wide) hallways. The price of your room will depend on its size, location, views, and on how recently it was renovated. The greatest disadvantage of staying at the Frontenac is that you can't gaze at its stunning architecture when you're inside it!

Dining/Entertainment: In addition to the upscale Le Champlain, with its high painted ceiling and brocade drapes, there's the more casual Café de la Terrasse for a buffet dinner and dancing on Saturday nights. The circular Veranda Bar overlooks place Dufferin, but tends to get smokey; the adjacent St-Laurent Bar has the same view but less smoke.

Services: Concierge, room service, laundry/valet service, babysitting, hairdresser, limo services within three miles, secretarial services.

Facilities: Large indoor pool, kiddie pool, gym, shops (one that sells stamps), meeting rooms, Jacuzzi.

MODERATE

CAP DIAMANT MAISON DE TOURISTES, 39 av. Ste-Geneviève, Québec, PQ, G1R 4B3. Tel. 418/694-0313. 9 rms. A/C TV

$ Rates (including morning coffee and orange juice): Summer $54–$100 single or double; winter $45–$70 single or double. Extra person $10. MC, V. **Parking:** $5 in nearby lot.

Besides being a charming and comfortable place to stay, the Cap Diamant Maison de Touristes is almost a bona fide "museum of domestic decoration." The rooms, each one different, hold an astounding assortment of furniture: brass beds, Victorian memorabilia from grandma's attic, pieces from the '30s, and especially nice lighting fixtures (and light, period). Several rooms have small refrigerators; all have full baths. Behind the house, which dates from 1826, there's an enclosed veranda and a garden for guests' enjoyment, not to mention a "special surprise" from thoughtful host Florence Guillot. The Cap Diamant is only 2½ blocks from the Jardin des Gouverneurs. The grassy lawns of the Plains of Abraham are right behind it, and the rooms overlook the rooftops of the old city (the view from room no. 2 is sure to captivate).

CHATEAU BELLEVUE, 16 rue Laporte, Québec, PQ, G1R 4M9. Tel. 418/692-2573, or toll free 800/463-2617. Fax 418/692-4876. 55 rms. A/C TV TEL

$ Rates: $89 single; $94 double. Extra person $10. AE, CB, DC, ER, MC, V. **Parking:** Free.

Don't let the antique facade of the Château Bellevue fool you, for behind it lurks a modern mini-hotel with central air conditioning, a pleasant lobby with leather couches and chairs, and a friendly, helpful staff. Vending machines off the lobby provide sandwiches, soda, and coffee, and there's a microwave for guests' use. While the rooms suffer from some unfortunate decorating choices, they are quiet and each has a private bath; some (the higher-priced units) look onto the Jardin des Gouverneurs and the Château Frontenac. In summer the hotel's valet, for no extra charge, will park your car in the private lot behind the hotel after your luggage has been unloaded.

CHATEAU DE PIERRE, 17 av. Ste-Geneviève (just off the Jardin des Gouverneurs), Québec, PQ, G1R 4A8. Tel. 418/694-0429. 15 rms. TV

$ Rates: $89 single; $92–$105 double, less in winter. Extra person $10. MC, V. **Parking:** $5 a day in nearby lot.

Immaculate, tastefully decorated rooms greet you at Le Château de Pierre, where marble fireplaces, sconces with crystal prisms, pretty wallpaper and carpets, and other elegant touches highlight the fine decor. But modern conveniences aren't forgotten: The lighting is terrific; most rooms are air-conditioned; and in the larger rooms, you may find two sinks in the roomy bathroom (useful if a family or group of four share the same room). The house, built in 1853, is the only one on the street with balconies (you may request those two rooms specifically). Room no. 1 has a bow window (no balcony) and overlooks the Jardin des Gouverneurs and the river. The host, Mme. Lily Couturier, speaks English, French, and Spanish, and prefers personal checks to credit cards.

HOTELLERIE FLEUR-DE-LYS, 115 rue Ste-Anne, Québec, PQ, G1R 3X6. Tel. 418/694-0106, or toll free 800/567-2106. Fax 418/692-1959. 35 rms. A/C TEL TV
$ Rates: $80–$110 single or double. Extra person 16 and older $12; children 6–15 $6. Continental breakfast in the room $4. AE, DISC, MC, V. **Parking:** $7.25 in the inn's street-level lot.
This modern motor inn in the midst of Québec City's quaint antiquity may come as a bit of a shock—or a pleasant surprise for those who'll be happy to find a 24-hour laundry on the premises ($1 to wash, $1 to dry, and the friendly management provides the soap). Each of the rooms displays bright colors and decorator touches and has a full bath, refrigerator, and table and chairs. Some rooms have kitchenettes and TVs. It's near the corner of rue Ste-Ursule.

L'HOTEL DU VIEUX QUEBEC, 1190 rue St-Jean (at rue Collins), Québec, PQ, G1R 4J2. Tel. 418/692-1850. Fax 418/692-5637. 42 rms. A/C TV TEL
$ Rates: Summer $99 single or double; winter $69 single or double. Kitchenette $10 extra. Extra person $10. AE, MC, V. **Parking:** $5.
Just off busy rue St-Jean near the intersection with rue de la Fabrique is L'Hôtel du Vieux Québec, a century-old brick building that has been carefully renovated and modernized. Tidy, modern guest rooms are decorated in pastels and earth tones and come with sofas, double beds, cable color TVs, and modern bathrooms. Some rooms are on the small side; 24 have kitchenettes. The hotel is particularly popular with families and visiting high-school groups and is a good location for exploring the Upper or Lower Towns.

MANOIR STE-GENEVIEVE, 13 av. Ste-Geneviève (at the corner of Laporte), Québec, PQ, G1R 4A7. Tel. and fax 418/694-1666. 9 rms. A/C TV
$ Rates: May–Oct $85 single, $87–$100 double; Nov–Apr rates drop 30%. Extra person $10. No credit cards, but they accept personal checks and traveler's checks. **Parking:** $6.
The front of the Manoir Ste-Geneviève, on the Jardin des Governeurs, hints at the

---

AN IMPORTANT NOTE ON PRICES

Unless stated otherwise, **the prices cited in this guide are given in Canadian dollars,** which is good news for U.S. travelers because the Canadian dollar is worth 25% less than the American dollar, but buys nearly as much. As we go to press, $1 Canadian is worth 75¢ U.S., which means that your $100-a-night hotel room will cost only U.S. $75, and your $6 breakfast costs only U.S. $4.50.
Here's a quick table of equivalents:

Canadian $	U.S. $
$ 1	$ 0.75
5	3.75
10	7.50
20	15.00
50	37.50
80	60.00
100	75.00
200	150.00

gentility that awaits you inside: a tasteful light-gray facade, a leaded-glass doorway, the name of the hotel scripted in wrought-iron lettering, and flower boxes in the windows in summer. The rooms are decorated in a comfortable, slightly formal style; six have full bath, while three have shower only; a few have kitchenettes. Room no. 4 is particularly old-fashioned, with beautiful wallpaper. From the bay window in room no. 6 you get a fantastic view of the garden and Château Frontenac. The second-story terrace is for guests' use.

INEXPENSIVE

AUBERGE DE LA CHOUETTE, 71 rue d'Auteuil, Québec, PQ, G1R 4C3. Tel. 418/694-0232. 10 rms (all with bath). A/C TV TEL

$ Rates: Summer $50–$55 single, $60–$65 double; winter $45 single, $50 double. AE, MC, V. **Parking:** $6 a day.

 The Auberge de la Chouette, across the street from Esplanade Park and near the Porte St-Louis, combines an outstanding Asian restaurant—Apsara—and lodging in an elegant town house. The rooms, all with full baths, have walls embellished with Renoir prints, and a spiral stairway leads to them. Complimentary English-language magazines are provided for guests, and they won't charge you for any local calls you make. The tourist office, Citadelle, and Winter Carnival or the Québec Summer Festival activities are only minutes away.

AUBERGE ST-LOUIS, 48 rue St-Louis, Québec, PQ, G1R 3Z3. Tel. 418/692-2424, or toll free 800/663-7878. Fax 418/622-3797. 22 rms (9 with bath). TV

$ Rates: May–Oct $39–$85 single or double; Nov–Apr $35–$73 single or double. Extra person $10; children under 5 free. Winter packages available. MC, V. **Parking:** $5, across the street.

The Auberge St-Louis, renovated in 1989, contains a number of guest rooms in a variety of shapes and sizes, decorated in soft colors and flower prints, with soothing touches of natural wood and the occasional antique piece or feature to add visual interest: a carved-wood fireplace or a stained-glass window. But modernity prevails, particularly in the tiled bathrooms with showers (some with small tubs). Some rooms only have a sink; others have a sink and shower, but no toilet. A number of rooms have color or black-and-white TVs. Only two units have air conditioning; the rest have fans.

CHATEAU DE LERY, 8 rue Laporte, Québec, PQ, G1R 4M9. Tel. 418/692-2692, or toll free 800/363-0036 from eastern Québec. 19 rms (17 with bath). A/C TV

$ Rates: $62–$68 single or double; one room is $80. Continental breakfast $3.50. AE, MC, V. **Parking:** Nearby, $5 a day.

Small but sweet—tidy, too, and not cramped at all—the Château de Léry faces the Jardin des Gouverneurs. Most of the rooms have small, neat showers, although a few have bathtubs. Fresh wallpaper and paint give it an inviting look; the simple furnishings provide adequate comfort; and the location is great.

HOTEL LE CLOS SAINT-LOUIS, 71 rue St-Louis, Québec, PQ, G1R 3Z2. Tel. 418/694-1311, or toll free in Canada 800/461-1311. Fax 418/694-9411. 30 rms (13 with bath).

$ Rates: Summer $55 single or double with shared bath, $75 single with private bath, $75–$95 double with private bath. Winter $45 single or double with shared bath, $56 single with private bath, $56–$65 double with private bath. Special packages from $60 per person. MC, V. **Parking:** Nearby, $5.

✪ The Hotel Le Clos Saint-Louis, between the Château Frontenac and Battlefields Park, is actually two adjoining historic houses near the corner of rue Ste-Ursule. Both houses have many fine old touches, though the guest rooms at no. 71 (built in 1834 and very Victorian) are more elegant. Most of the rooms have TV, and the larger rooms have marble fireplaces, but just for looks. While no. 69 is not one of the prettiest rooms, it is restful because it looks out onto the tree-filled garden; no. 3 is a sweet, tiny room for a lone traveler. Rates include morning croissants and coffee served in the old-fashioned parlor and depend on the size of the room and its amenities. The location is convenient, and the staff, headed by Mme. Ghislaine Donais, friendly and helpful.

LA MAISON DEMERS, 68 rue Ste-Ursule (at rue St-Louis), Québec, PQ, G1R 4E6. Tel. 418/692-2487. 8 rms (4 with bath). TV
$ Rates (including continental breakfast): $30–$35 single; $45–$65 double. Extra person $5–$10. MC, V. **Parking:** Free.
La Maison Demers has simple, clean rooms, four with tiled baths, some with balconies and refrigerators, and one with an air conditioner. There's a telephone for guests' use in the hall. Friendly host Jennine Demers obviously enjoys opening her home to people (she's done so for 30 years), and she makes sure her guests get toiletries in their rooms, chocolate on their pillows, and complimentary croissants, coffee, tea, or juice in the morning. She supplies kids with lollipops and games and can arrange for babysitting. She and her husband and son also arrange local tours for guests. Coming here is like visiting the home of a favorite aunt.

LA MAISON DOYON, 109 rue Ste-Anne, Québec, PQ, G1R 3X6. Tel. 418/694-1720, or toll free 800/267-1720. 19 rms (12 with bath). TV
$ Rates (including continental breakfast): $40 single without bath, $45 single with bath; $45–$60 double without bath, $45–$75 double with bath; $85 triple with bath; $95 quad with bath. Rates drop about 40% in winter. MC, V. **Parking:** Nearby, $5.
Maison Doyon is an informal guesthouse—more like a small hostel—spare though quite clean and presentable. Rooms tend to be small, but all have ceiling fans and cable TV. No. 23 is a cozy single attic room, and no. 25 an equally cozy double. The breakfast room, where you'll enjoy croissants and coffee, has a map of the city on the wall, and the backyard is open to guests. The house is a five-minute stroll from most of the attractions in Old Québec.

BUDGET

YOUTH HOSTEL (AUBERGE DE JEUNESSE), 31 rue Couillard, Québec, PQ, G1R 3T4. Tel. 418/694-0735. 56 beds.
$ Rates (including breakfast): $15 per person. Sheets $2. **Parking:** Nearby, $5 per day.
An "unofficial" youth hostel smack in the middle of the Upper Town is as welcoming as it is well situated. Twelve rooms have 56 beds in configurations of three to eight beds per room, along with three rooms for couples. There's also a kitchen, lounge, tree-filled interior courtyard and picnic area, and a closet in the office where you may lock valuables. The hostel is impressively clean; men and women share toilets and showers, and nobody seems to mind. It's open from 8am to 2am, and there's no limit to the number of days you can stay. They only take 15 reservations a day; the rest are walk-ins.

YOUTH HOSTEL (AUBERGE DE JEUNESSE), 19 Ste-Ursule, at rue Dauphin, Québec, PQ, G1R 4E1. Tel. 418/694-0755, or toll free 800/461-8585 from elsewhere in the province except Montréal, or 514/252-3117 from Montréal or outside the province. Fax 418/694-2278 or 514/251-8038 from Montréal and outside the province. 281 beds.
$ Rates: $15.75–$17.75 room with two beds, $13.75–$15.75 room with four to six beds, $10.75–$12.75 dorm with 10–12 beds. Children pay half price. Membership is compulsory but cards are available at the hostel. AE, MC, V. **Parking:** Nearby.
This larger, "official" hostel, in a two-story brick building up the hill from rue St-Jean, has lockers for luggage, skis, and bicycles; a laundry; a lounge with a pool table; a cafeteria where breakfast runs about $3.50; public telephones; and a backyard with picnic tables. There are plans to add a kitchen for guests' use. You can reserve a bed in advance with a credit card Monday through Friday during the day. There's a food market and parking nearby. No curfew.

ON OR NEAR THE GRANDE-ALLEE
EXPENSIVE

HILTON INTERNATIONAL QUEBEC, 3 place Québec, Québec, PQ, G1K 7M9. Tel. 418/647-2411, or toll free 800/HILTONS. Fax 418/647-6488. 499 rms, 63 suites. A/C MINIBAR TV TEL **Directions:** If you're heading into town along the Grande-Allée, turn left on Dufferin and take the first left, passing the Parliament building, then drive one block to the hotel.

$ Rates: $118–$158 single; $140–$180 double; from $350 suite. Extra person $22. Children stay free in parents' room. Special rates and packages available. AE, CB, DC, DISC, ER, MC, V. **Parking:** $12.50.

The location of the Hilton International Québec is excellent, considering that the hotel is right across the street from the city walls. It's also near the Québec National Assembly and the Radisson, and is connected to the place Québec shopping complex, where there are two cinemas. And, best of all, you're only about 10 minutes from the heart of the old city.

The rooms look a little outdated, with dark furniture and uninspired decor; most have a king-size bed, which cramps the space a little, or two single beds. On the plus side, the views are great and the staff couldn't be more congenial.

Dining/Entertainment: Le Croquembroche, specializes in French cuisine and seafood dishes, serving dinner nightly (it also serves lunch in winter). At Caucus restaurant and bar, you can get a buffet breakfast, lunch, or dinner, as well as order à la carte. There's live piano music in Caucus bar nightly except Monday.

Services: 24-hour room service, car-rental desk, business support services; babysitting.

Facilities: Heated outdoor pool (summer only), health club with sauna, whirlpool, and massage; lobby shop; no-smoking floors, executive floors, meeting rooms.

LOEWS LE CONCORDE, 1225 place Montcalm (at the Grande-Allée), Québec, PQ, G1R 4W6. Tel. 418/647-2222, or toll free 800/223-0888. Fax 418/647-4710. 400 rms, 22 suites. A/C MINIBAR TV TEL

$ Rates: $105–$155 single; $175–$250 double; from $475 suite. Extra person $20, children under 10 free. Special off-season rates available, along with weekend and ski packages. AE, DC, ER, MC, V. **Parking:** Indoor, $12.

Québec City's most attention-getting hotel is Loews Le Concorde, off the Grande-Allée next to the Plains of Abraham. The reason for its prominence is its great hulk, towering above the battlefields where Wolfe and Montcalm fought to the death. Standard rooms feature desert tones, marble bathrooms, prints of Québec City street scenes, in-room movies, and three telephones; they offer gorgeous views of the old city, even from the lower floors. Although you're still within walking distance of the old city here, it's about a five-minute walk to the walls and then another five minutes to the center of the Upper Town (this is the most distant of the hotels mentioned in this book, so that's not bad). It's seven blocks from the Québec Museum.

Dining/Entertainment: L'Astral is the city's only revolving rooftop restaurant, and it also has a bar and piano music nightly except Monday. There's dancing 9pm to 3am Wednesday through Saturday in Le Dancing disco. Those who want a light lunch or dinner can head to to Le Café; for a buffet or à la carte breakfast served until 11:30am (noon on weekends), there's La Place Montcalm.

Services: Concierge, room service 6am to midnight; same-day laundry and dry cleaning.

Facilities: Five no-smoking floors; small health facility with sauna, whirlpool, and some equipment; outdoor heated pool (April through November; access to pool in private club the rest of the year); five executive floors; meeting rooms.

RADISSON, 690 bd. St-Cyrille est, Québec, PQ, G1R 5A8. Tel. 418/ 647-1717, or toll free 800/463-2820. Fax 418/647-2146. 365 rms, 12 suites. A/C TV TEL **Directions:** From the Grande-Allée, turn left onto Dufferin, passing the Parliament building, then take the first left and drive two blocks to the hotel.

$ Rates: $135 single; $155 double; from $195 suite. Extra person $15. Ask about summer rates. AE, DC, DISC, ER, MC, V. **Parking:** $10 (with in/out privileges).

This modern tower is reminiscent of Montréal's multilevel building complexes. And indeed the hotel is part of Québec City's first such complex, place Québec, and is also connected to the city's convention center. The atmosphere is relaxed and refined, and the location good, a block from the Hilton, two blocks from the old city walls and Porte (Gate) Kent, not far from the Québec National Assembly. While the decor of the hotel is outspoken and ultramodern, it is the most successful and tasteful of Québec City's large hostelries. The renovated rooms and suites are decorated in soft colors and feature full baths with plenty of counter space. Most overlook the Lower Town and have a queen or two double beds. Some rooms have minibars, and all have in-room movies. The unique outdoor swimming pool, with an indoor waterway leading to it, is heated and open year-round, even when it's surrounded by snow. If you're strolling back to the hotel from the old city, remember it's an uphill climb. Reception is two levels up; take the escalator to it, passing the giant froufrou chandelier.

Dining/Entertainment: Le Vignoble restaurant serves buffet and à la carte meals; l'Imprévu piano bar is in the lobby.

Services: Room service.

Facilities: Three no-smoking floors; two executive floors called "L'Exclusif"; health club with sauna, Jacuzzi, and large workout room, including exercise bikes; outdoor heated pool (year-round); meeting rooms.

LOWER TOWN

EXPENSIVE

AUBERGE ST-ANTOINE, 10 rue St-Antoine, Québec, PQ, G1K 4C9. Tel. 418/692-2211. Fax 418/692-1177. 22 rms, 1 suite. A/C TV TEL **Directions:** In the Lower Town, follow rue Dalhousie to rue St-Antoine; it's beside the Museum of Civilization.

$ Rates (including breakfast): $100–$230 single or double; suite $400. Extra person $10. Children under 12 free. AE, MC, V. **Parking:** Free.

One of the city's newest hostelries, and its most unique, in a converted warehouse built in 1830, the Auberge St-Antoine is startlingly beautiful. It has retained the original dark beams and stone floor (but with new mortar), and added replicas of the old windows and doors, antique furniture, sisal rugs from England in the public areas, and dramatic colors throughout. The country modern rooms are spacious (the size of a studio apartment), each with a big bath and separate shower and two stainless-steel sinks, robes, special amenities, and a clock radio. Most have two double beds; three have private terraces. In the airy lobby, complimentary cookies, fruit, and coffee are left out on a sideboard for guests. The filling breakfast, included in the room rate, offers everything short of bacon and eggs. By summer 1994, they plan to have eight suites with kitchens; they'll fill the refrigerators for guests. Two of the suites will be furnished in period style in collaboration with the Museum of Civilization, one with a bow to the French regime, the other to the English, and modern amenities will be hidden from view.

LE PRIORI, 15 rue Sault-au-Matelot, Québec, PQ, G1K 3Y7. Tel. 418/692-3992. Fax 418/692-0883. 20 rms, 5 suites. TV TEL
$ Rates: $65–$90 single; $80–$110 double; from $125 suite. AE, MC, V. **Parking:** $8 a day.

A second newcomer to the emerging Lower Town hotel scene, Le Priori provides postmodern ambience, behind the 1766 facade of a house that started out as an architect's home. The architecture and the furniture are sleek and bold in both the lobby and the rooms, which have queen-size beds with black tubular frames and soft duvets, cone-shaped stainless steel sinks, and lighting that could be brighter. In several rooms, a clawfoot tub sits beside the bed. Suites each have a living room with wood-burning fireplace, bedroom, kitchen, and bath with Jacuzzi. The hotel houses the popular Laurie Raphael restaurant, which serves three meals a day and focuses on *nouvelle cuisine québécoise.* The Martin family owns and runs the hotel, which, despite the age of the building, has an elevator.

MODERATE

AUBERGE LOUIS HEBERT, 668 Grande-Allée est, Québec, PQ, G1R 2K5. Tel. 418/525-7812. Fax 418/525-6294. 10 rms. TV TEL

$ Rates (including breakfast and parking): May–Sept $60 single, $80 double; $10 less the rest of the year. AE, DC, ER, MC, V. **Parking:** Free.

Named after the area's first French settler, the renovated Auberge Louis Hébert (1781) has 10 rooms, all with large tiled baths. The rooms in back are smaller but quieter, and they have air conditioning. The larger rooms in front, which get the noise from the busy Grande-Allée, have fans. Antiques punctuate each landing, and the inn's pretty ground-floor restaurant deserves sampling (see Section 4 of this chapter for details).

HOTEL CHATEAU LAURIER, 695 Grand-Allée est (at Georges V), Québec, PQ, G1R 2K4. Tel. 418/522-8108, or toll free 800/463-4453. Fax 418/524-8768. 110 rms. A/C TV TEL

$ Rates: Summer $59–$74 single; $64–$89 double; winter $49–$54 single, $54–$75 double. AE, DC, ER, MC, V. **Parking:** Free.

Across the street from Auberge Louis Hébert and just a few blocks outside the Porte St-Louis is the Hôtel Château Laurier. This sturdy, well-maintained stone structure, which is over a century old, has a Victorian lobby (parlor) with a grandfather clock, and comfortable guest rooms, all with private bath with shower. Rates depend on your room's size, accoutrements, and view (of the National Assembly, the Plains of Abraham, or the old city walls). An elevator serves the several floors, and a restaurant, Le Patrimoine, occupies the ground floor and is open almost around the clock.

If they're booked up, ask about rooms at their sister property, the popular 69-room Hôtel Manoir Lafayette, five doors down, at 665 Grande-Allée, where the newer, larger rooms are recommended. It has a pleasant lobby with a fireplace, but steep stairs up three flights to reach rooms; the rates and amenities are similar to the Hôtel Château Laurier. The Château Frontenac is a 15-minute walk away.

INEXPENSIVE

MANOIR DE L'ESPLANADE, 83 rue d'Auteuil (at rue St-Louis), Québec, PQ, G1R 4C3. Tel. 418/694-0834. Fax 418/692-0456. 37 rms. A/C TV TEL

$ Rates (including continental breakfast): Summer $60–$90 single or double; winter $40–$80 single or double. Extra person $15. AE, MC, V. **Parking:** $5–$6 a day.

Though not as well appointed as some of the other places around the Grande-Allée, this selection is clean and comfortable and has the most convenient location for Winter Carnival. You can easily scurry back to your room from the ice palace or ice sculptures, warm up, then head back for more frolicking with Bonhomme. All the rooms have private baths (some with tubs). I prefer the ones facing the street, like no. 22 with one double bed or no. 26 with two double beds. The seating area off the lobby is a convenient spot for meeting friends. Students particularly like this place, which used to be a nunnery. Book as early as possible for Winter Carnival. The tourist office is right across the street.

4. DINING

Even if Québec City did not have other delights, chances are it would still be filled with people coming here just to sample the culinary pleasures. The dining is outstanding for several good reasons. First, the people involved in running a restaurant look upon it as their profession, not merely a job. Second, the Québec countryside—its rivers, woods, and streams—produces bountiful and high-quality edibles to inspire good chefs. (If quail is on the menu, it probably came from nearby Ile d'Orléans.) Finally, the French tradition of haute cuisine—of food prepared with exceptional care, of attentive service—is the legacy of both restaurateurs and diners.

A few pointers: Make reservations for busy periods like weekends and holidays and if you can't keep them, cancel them promptly. Dress well (jacket-and-tie is the custom at finer restaurants; "presentable" will do elsewhere). It helps to remember that for the French "dinner" means lunch, and "supper" means dinner (just as it does for my family down in Georgia).

The restaurants recommended below are arranged by price category and location. Those listed as expensive charge $20 to $30 à la carte for most of their main courses at dinner (supper); moderate, $10 to $20; and budget, $10 or less. When figuring costs, remember to add in the 8% provincial sales tax, the 7% federal government sales tax, and a 15% tip.

THE UPPER TOWN

EXPENSIVE

CAFE DE LA PAIX, 44 rue Desjardins, off rue St-Louis. Tel. 418/692-1430.
   Cuisine: FRENCH. **Reservations:** Recommended.
$ Prices: Appetizers $8–$10; main courses $17–$22; three-course table d'hôte lunch $10–$13; three-course table d'hôte dinner $20–$28. AE, CB, MC, V.
   Open: Lunch daily 11:30am–2:30pm; dinner daily 5–11pm.
Very near the Château Frontenac, Café de la Paix has been around for a long time and shows every sign of being around a lot longer. Pass by this small and cozy place and you won't be able to resist pausing to look at the sumptuous desserts displayed in the front window. Diners do not live by dessert alone, of course, so to precede those irresistible cakes, pies, and mousses, there are seafood specialties, filet of veal with morels, sweetbreads with truffle sauce, and much more. The list is long and varied, with table d'hôte choices to save you money without cramping your gustatory style. They offer free valet parking.

CAFE D'EUROPE, 27 Ste-Angele, off rue St-Jean. Tel. 418/692-3835.
   Cuisine: CONTINENTAL. **Reservations:** Recommended.
$ Prices: Appetizers $7; main courses $18–$20; pizza $11; table d'hôte dinner $23–$26. AE, CB, DC, ER, MC, V.
   Open: Lunch daily 11:30am–2pm; dinner daily 5–11:30pm.
The Café d'Europe is among this city's oldest and most established restaurants. Having started out almost 30 years ago serving delicious pizzas, it now has a more eclectic menu: veal piccata with lemon butter, Dover sole, rabbit with mustard and tarragon sauce, and quails with foie gras, plus a table d'hôte menu to keep prices down. In season there's even wild game, but you can also still get one of the famous pizzas. Wood paneling, mirrors, linen tablecloths, fresh flowers, and experienced waiters preserve a European ambience, and there's free valet parking.

CAFE DE PARIS, 66 rue St-Louis. Tel. 418/694-9626.
   Cuisine: FRENCH/ITALIAN/QUEBECOIS. **Reservations:** Recommended.
$ Prices: Appetizers $5–$11; main courses $16–$27; three-course dinner $20–$30. AE, CB, DC, ER, MC, V.
   Open: Lunch daily 11am–3pm; dinner daily 3–11pm.
A small knot of people is often clustered at the entrance to the Café de Paris, poring over the specialties on the menu, and peering in the doorway for a glimpse of the strolling musician (there's a singer every night). The decor is *très* old world, if not blatantly Parisian, but as the owners are named Jos and Franco, the ambience is more Italian than Parisian. Still, you can order canard à l'orange, coq au vin, steak au poivre, rack of lamb, or chateaubriand bouquetière, as well as veal scaloppine with lemon sauce, baked cannelloni, lasagne, or fettuccine. For something strictly québecois, try

the meat pie called tourtière, or salmon pâté. The dessert menu is fully international. Children's portions are available. And the service is attentive.

LA RIPAILLE, 9 rue Buade at rue du Fort. Tel. 418/692-2450.
  Cuisine: FRENCH. **Reservations:** Recommended.
$ **Prices:** Appetizers $4.50–$9; lunch main courses $8–$13, dinner main courses $18–$19; table d'hôte dinners $23–$27. AE, DISC, ER, MC, V.
  Open: Lunch 11:30am–2:30pm; dinner daily 5–11pm.
Experienced service, plush but not overly formal ambience, and good food keep people coming back to La Ripaille. Last time I was there, the table d'hôte included veal, salmon, and rack of lamb. Add a glass of wine, the tax, and the tip, and the bill comes to $32 or so. This is an old and dependable standard for either lunch or dinner. The lunch special, by the way, is a reasonable $8 to $14. La Ripaille has been around since 1970.

LE SAINT-AMOUR, 48 rue Ste-Ursule. Tel. 418/694-0667.
  Cuisine: FRENCH. **Reservations:** Recommended.
$ **Prices:** Appetizers $9.50–$13.50; soups $3.50–$5; main courses $20–$25; three-course lunch table d'hôte $9.50; three-course dinner table d'hôte $25–$28; gastronomic dinner $48. AE, CB, DC, ER, MC, V.
  Open: Lunch Tues–Fri noon–2:30pm; dinner daily 6–10:30pm.
⭐ At Le Saint-Amour, an array of hanging plants, a skylight, and the wicker dining chairs provide a pastoral, almost gazebolike atmosphere in the pretty dining areas, including a year-round garden (a special treat during slushy winter days). For an appetizer, consider escargots with herbs and spices in a cream sauce or frogs' legs served with a vegetable sauce, followed by a main course of salmon filets topped with a light chive mousse, lobster, filet mignon with a red pepper sauce and spinach flan, or stuffed boneless quails in a port sauce. Sweetbreads is a favorite here. Complement your meal with a selection from the long wine list. A no-holds-barred gastronomic dinner is served nightly except on Saturday evenings in summer. Chef and co-owner Jean-Luc Boulay is a master chocolatier, so save some room to test his expertise. The service is smoothly efficient, while the candlelit tables and the classical music add to the pleasure of having a meal here. The house, built in the 1820s, is a little off the well-worn tourist track.

RESTAURANT CONTINENTAL, 26 rue St-Louis, at the intersection with Haldimand. Tel. 418/694-9995.
  Cuisine: FRENCH. **Reservations:** Recommended.
$ **Prices:** Appetizers $5–$9 (foie gras $20, caviar $25), main courses $17–$25.50; two-course lunch special $8.25–$13; four-course table d'hôte $23.50–$26.50. AE, CB, DC, DISC, ER, MC, V.
  Open: Lunch Mon–Sat 11:30am–3pm; dinner Mon–Sat (and Sun in Oct–Nov) 6–11pm.
The Restaurant Continental has been successfully serving Québec City since 1956 in a house built in 1845. In a traditional setting with white tablecloths, attentive waiters, and old-fashioned furnishings, you can order lobster bisque or onion soup gratiné, Dover sole or frogs' legs, filet mignon, or rack of lamb, and finish off with champagne sherbet or crêpes Suzette—in short, the classics in a classic setting. The menu changes monthly, and the restaurant provides free valet parking.

MODERATE

APSARA, 71 rue d'Auteuil. Tel. 418/694-0232.
  Cuisine: INDOCHINESE. **Reservations:** Not needed.
$ **Prices:** Appetizers $3–$4; main courses $9–$13. AE, MC, V.
  Open: Lunch Mon–Fri 11:30am–2pm; dinner daily 5:30–11pm.
 Near the tourism office and the city walls, this pretty restaurant is in a fine old town house. The unlikely setting doesn't bother diners who come for breaded shrimp in a spicy sauce, roast Thai beef with spices, and similar delicacies. The

best deal is to order one of the set-price dinners: seven courses *for two people* for about $35.

FLEUR DE LOTUS, 38 Côte de la Fabrique. Tel. 418/692-4286.
  Cuisine: INDOCHINESE. **Reservations:** Not needed.
$ Prices: Appetizers $3–$5.50; main courses $8–$14. MC, V.
  Open: Mon–Wed 11:30am–10:30pm, Thurs–Fri 1–11pm, Sat 5–11pm, Sun 5–10:30pm.

The one tiny dining room at Fleur de Lotus, across from City Hall (Hôtel de Ville), is busy each noontime and evening for all the right reasons: fine food, nice service, low prices. It serves Cambodian, Thai, and Vietnamese food such as chicken in ginger, pork in sweet sauce, and shrimp in soya purée. Each weekday from 11:30am to 3pm there's a filling, delicious business lunch for about $8, and each evening table d'hôte meals are priced at $16, $18, or $25. The à la carte menu opens up many more possibilities.

RESTAURANT AU PARMESAN, 38 rue St-Louis, near Haldimand. Tel. 418/692-0341.
  Cuisine: ITALIAN. **Reservations:** Recommended in summer.
$ Prices: Appetizers $5–$11.50; main courses $9.50–$25; three-course table d'hôte lunch $9–$13; three-course table d'hôte dinner $18.50–$25.50. AE, CB, DC, ER, MC, V.
  Open: Daily 11:30am–11:30pm; lunch served until 2:30pm.

The friendly folks at Restaurant au Parmesan believe that some things are best done at home—like smoking the salmon, curing the ham (for two years at least), and making the pasta. And those who dine here choose from Italian specialties and international dishes. The table d'hôte menu features pasta, meat, or fish dishes. Large portions are the rule, and Italian and French wine, beer, and cocktails are served. The restaurant's unique bottle collection creates an unusual decor. In wine racks, on shelves along the walls, on the tables as wax-bedripped candleholders, all shapes and sizes of bottles fill two narrow dining rooms and a small bar. A guitarist or accordionist contributes to the "dolce vita" feeling in the evening. Free valet parking is available.

BUDGET

CASSE-CREPE BRETON, 1136 rue St-Jean. Tel. 418/692-0438.
  Cuisine: CREPES. **Reservations:** Not needed.
$ Prices: Crepes $3–$6.50; lunch specials Mon–Fri $4.50. No credit cards.
  Open: Mon–Wed 7:30am–midnight, Thurs–Sun 7:30am–2am.

At this crowded crêperie, you can eat at the bar and watch the crêpes being made, or attempt to snag one of the five tables in the place (good luck). Main-course crêpes come with two to five ingredients, which you select, and you can also order salads and sandwiches, which are as inexpensive as the crêpes. The name of the café is a play on the word *casse-croûte*, which means "snack." You can't beat the long hours here, and breakfast is served all day, but when it gets busy, the service moves at an escargot's pace. Beer is served in bottles or on tap.

LE PETIT COIN LATIN, 8½ rue Ste-Ursule. Tel. 418/692-0919.
  Cuisine: INTERNATIONAL. **Reservations:** Not needed.
$ Prices: Most items $1.50–$7; three-course lunch $5.50–$7; three-course dinner $8–$9. MC, V.
  Open: Breakfast daily 8am–11am; lunch daily noon–2pm; dinner daily 6–11pm. The café closes at 1am (later in summer).

This is the kind of place that you pass by and before you know it, you're seated inside. It's small, with two seating levels, multipaned windows trimmed with lace curtains, hanging plants, old-fashioned lamps, brick floors, and ceiling fans rotate lazily overhead. The amount and quality of the food you get for the price is unbelievable: Consider cream of turnip soup with a choice of quiche Lorraine, chicken potpie, or a beef kebab, with salad, dessert, and tea or coffee for $8.50. There are always vegetarian dishes, like spinach lasagne, and the signature dessert is *tarte au sirop d'érable* (maple syrup pie). The café, which has been here 20 years, is tucked away, on quiet rue Ste-Ursule, just uphill from lively rue St-Jean. Even when it's full, it's quiet, and it never seems crowded. Though it looks like strictly a coffee and herbal tea type of place, wine (not great), beer, and the hard stuff are all served. In summer, its large patio, Côte Jardin, is open.

ON OR NEAR THE GRANDE-ALLEE

EXPENSIVE

LE PARIS-BREST, 590 Grande-Allée est at de la Chevrotière. Tel. 418/529-2243.

Cuisine: FRENCH. **Reservations:** Recommended.

$ **Prices:** Appetizers $5.50–$8.50; main courses $17.50–$28; table d'hôte lunch $9–$14; table d'hôte dinner $23. AE, DC, ER, MC, V.

Open: Lunch Mon–Fri 11:30am–2:30pm; dinner Mon–Sat 6–11:30pm, Sun 5:30–11:30pm.

Named for two cities in France and for a well-known French dessert, Le Paris-Brest is a fashionable restaurant with a solid reputation for fine dining. The interior features mahogany paneling, soft lighting, lush flowers, unique three-legged chairs from France, and a walk-in wine depository. You can expect polished service and memorable cuisine: escargots provençales or au Pernod, lamb noisettes, seafood cassoulette, caribou, Atlantic salmon, steak tartare, and beef Wellington. The wine list is long. There's a small patio for outdoor dining, and free valet parking is available from 5:30pm.

RESTAURANT LOUIS HEBERT, 668 Grande-Allée est. Tel. 418/525-7812.

Cuisine: FRENCH. **Reservations:** Recommended in summer.

$ **Prices:** Appetizers $3.50–$11; main courses $13–$30; three-course table d'hôte $18.50, four-course table d'hôte $24.50–$26.50. AE, DC, ER, MC, V.

Open: Lunch daily 11:30am–2:30pm; dinner daily 5:30–11pm.

On the ground floor of a 10-room inn, this pretty restaurant serves French fare, and its menu changes often. Consider starting with a warm salad with scallops and almonds, followed by a main course of shrimp and seafood in ginger sauce, linguine with scallops, trout ravioli in lobster coulis, a filet of beef with pine nuts and Roquefort, or rack of lamb. You may sit outside or inside, where exposed brick walls and a greenhouse with hanging plants and two skylights add to the restaurant's charm.

BUDGET

AU PETIT COIN BRETON, 655 Grande-Allée est. Tel. 418/525-6904.

Cuisine: CREPES. **Reservations:** Not needed.

$ **Prices:** Dinner crêpes $2–$10; dessert crêpes $3–$5.50. AE, MC, V.

Open: Summer daily 10am–midnight; winter daily 10am–11pm.

At Au Petit Coin Breton (Little Brittany Corner), the crêpe's the thing, be it for breakfast, brunch, a light lunch, a snack, or dessert. Stone, brick, and wood in the decor set the mood, and when the waitress approaches your table dressed in her traditional costume of lace cap, long dress, and apron, you really begin to think in Breton terms. Choose one (or several) of the 87 varieties of the savory dinner crêpes and sweet dessert crêpes. Drinks are served. Au Petit Coin Breton is often packed with people, especially its terrace on a sunny day, and service can be slow.

A second location, at 1029 rue St-Jean, rue Ste-Ursule (tel. 418/694-0758), has similar hours, menu, and prices.

THE LOWER TOWN

LE CAFE DU MONDE, 57 rue Dalhousie, at rue de la Montagne, Old Port. Tel. 418/692-4455.

Cuisine: FRENCH. **Reservations:** Recommended.

$ **Prices:** Appetizers $2.50–$8; main courses $6.50–$15; three-course table d'hôte lunch $8–$12; three-course table d'hôte dinner (after 5pm) $18–$21; brunch $7–$11. AE, MC, V.

Open: Daily 11:30am–11pm (dinner from 3pm); brunch Sat–Sun 9:30am–3pm.

★ Beside the Old Port is a fairly new kid on the block, enjoying its share of popularity. It's known for its large portions of mussels, its imported beers, and its large assortment of wines by the glass. The chef, who hails from Brittany, creates a five-course evening meal called "Le Ciel, La Terre, La Mer"—"Sky, Earth, Sea"—each of which will be represented on your plate. The restaurant is a couple of doors down from the Musée de la Civilisation. Look for the crisp striped awnings and bright neon sign out front.

LE COCHON DINGUE, 46 bd. Champlain. Tel. 418/692-2013.
   Cuisine: INTERNATIONAL. **Reservations:** Not needed.
$ **Prices:** Appetizers $3–$9; main courses $6–$12.50; table d'hôte lunch $7–$11; table d'hôte dinner $15–$19; Sat–Sun brunch $7–$9.50. AE, MC, V.
   Open: Daily 7:30am–midnight.

Le Cochon Dingue (The Crazy Pig) is a big restaurant-café-pastry shop under the same ownership as the equally oddly named Le Lapin Sauté (Jumping Rabbit; see below). It faces the ferry dock and lighthouse and offers some sidewalk tables and several indoor dining areas with rough fieldstone walls, black-and-white checkerboard floor tiles, black tables and chairs, and white tablecloths. All the food is prepared fresh on the premises, and most items on the menu will cost under $10. Choose from among fettuccine Oscar in a cream sauce with seafood and asparagus, hefty plates of french fries with mayonnaise, chicken liver pâté with pistachios, smoked salmon, half a dozen salads, onion soup, quiches, sandwiches, grilled meats, and more than 20 homemade desserts, including apple pie with a maple sugar–crumb crust. Wine is sold by the glass, quarter liter, half liter, or bottle, at reasonable prices, and there is a children's menu for kids 10 and under.

LE LAPIN SAUTE, 52 rue Petit-Champlain. Tel. 418/692-5325.
   Cuisine: INTERNATIONAL. **Reservations:** Not needed.
$ **Prices:** Appetizers $2–$5; main courses $6–$12; three-course lunch table d'hôte lunch $6–$9; three-course table d'hôte dinner $16–$20; Sat–Sun brunch $4–$9. AE, ER, MC, V.
   Open: Daily 8am–11pm in summer, 9am–9 or 10pm in winter; brunch Sat–Sun 9am–2pm.

⑤ One of the most convenient and congenial places for brunch, lunch, a snack, or supper in the Lower Town is Le Lapin Sauté (The Jumping Rabbit). The small café, with its fieldstone terrace, looks onto a little park and the busy pedestrian shopping street. Its menu is perfect for the discriminating grazer: Provence chowder, several rabbit dishes including pâté and cassoulet, European-style sausages, burgers, sandwiches, salads—everything from croque-monsieur (a slice of bread topped with ham and cheese) to filet mignon. It's inviting, with a rustic interior, low lights, a friendly staff, some outdoor seating, and long hours, and is a favorite spot for brunch among the local Québecois.

SPECIALTY DINING

FOR PETIT DEJEUNER

CAFE CHEZ TEMPOREL, 25 rue Couillard. Tel. 418/694-1813.
   Cuisine: LIGHT FARE. **Reservations:** Not needed.
$ **Prices:** Most items $1.50–$5.25. No credit cards.
   Open: Sun–Thurs 7:30am–1:30am, Fri–Sat 7:30am–2:30am.

★ A Bohemian café with tile floor and wooden tables, half a block off rues St-Jean and Côte de la Fabrique in the city's Latin Quarter, it attracts early-morning newspaper readers and students in earnest conversation. To relive fond moments spent in Paris, or to have the quintessential French breakfast of croissants, jam, butter, and strong French coffee, or cappuccino (for about $4), no place beats this one. Later in the day, drop by for a sandwich, quiche, salad, or glass of wine or beer, but breakfast is best because it's so typically French. The café seats only 20 people downstairs, and 26 more upstairs, where there are some beautiful stained-glass windows.

A CAFE STREET

Québec's equivalent of the boulevard St-Germain is undoubtedly the Grande-Allée between the Porte St-Louis and Loews Le Concorde. As you walk out of the old city through the gate, you'll pass Québec's parliament on your right, and soon see a row of cafés with small terraces along the sidewalk, on both sides of the street. When traffic is not too heavy, it's fun to sit and watch, sip and munch, and then stroll to see what's going on at the other cafés—the québécois version of musical chairs.

DINING WITH A VIEW

Revolving restaurants rarely make any gourmet's short list of favorite places, and **L'Astral,** in Loews Le Concorde hotel, 1225 place Montcalm (tel. 418/647-2222), may be a case in point. Still it does provide breathtaking views as it rotates high above Battlefields Park and the Old City, taking in a vista that stretches many miles. At night, the experience is undeniably romantic. To cut down on the cost of that experience, opt for a buffet lunch or Sunday brunch (children under 12 eat at a reduced price), or come just for drinks after 10:30pm. The bar closes at 3am.

PICNIC SUPPLIES

Pick up picnic supplies—cheese, sandwiches, crackers, cold cuts, chips, ice cream (even Häagen-Dazs), fruit, vegetables, wine, and beer—from **Epicerie Gaboury,** 27 rue Couillard (tel. 418/692-3748), beside the youth hostel; it's open daily from 10am to 11pm. You'll enjoy talking with the friendly proprietor, Monsieur Gaboury, whose family also owns the Christmas shop in town. A larger selection of wines (2,000, in fact) is available at **Maison des Vins,** in the Lower Town, at 1 place Royale (tel. 418/643-1214). While you're there, be sure to visit the downstairs cellars.

Off the Grande-Allée on avenue Cartier, there's a wonderful bakery in a small shopping gallery called **Place Cartier,** where you can stock up on everything from baguettes to nine-grain bread to sugar pie. In the same complex, you'll find sandwiches, cheeses, cold cuts, fruit, vegetables, chocolates, and ground coffee (tel. 418/688-1630 for general information).

5. ATTRACTIONS

Just being in the Old City of Québec, wandering the narrow streets to happen upon an ancient convent, gabled house, or cozy café, is one of the simple pleasures of traveling. This is such a compact city that you hardly need to plan sightseeing itineraries —it's much better to stumble upon the funicular (elevator) that descends to the Lower Town; or the Plains of Abraham, where Wolfe and Montcalm fought to the death; or the mighty Citadel, in which brilliantly uniformed soldiers still troop the colors.

Most of what you'll want to see is right here within the city walls, or at the base of Cap Diamant in the Lower Town. It's all easy walking, but if rain or fallen arches discourage you from exploring Québec on foot, you can always hop a horse-drawn calèche or a tour bus.

THE TOP ATTRACTIONS

THE UPPER TOWN

CHATEAU FRONTENAC, 1 rue de Carrières, place d'Armes. Tel. 418/ 692-3861.
Perched atop Cap Diamant, the Château Frontenac, which looks more like a fairy-tale castle than a hotel, was built in 1893, with additions added in 1925 and just recently in 1992. It's the city's most recognizable landmark, and you're

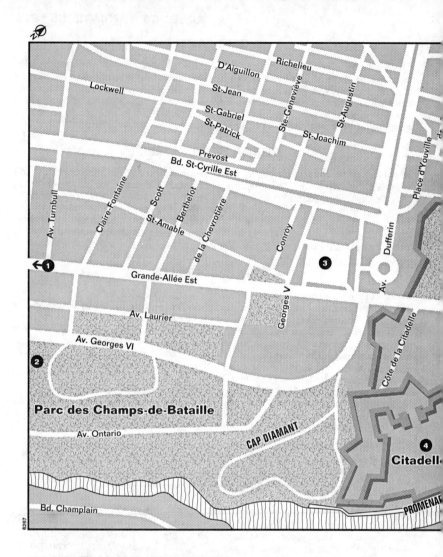

Battlefields Park ②
Château Frontenac ⑥
Chevalier House ⑫
The Citadel ④
Fort Museum ⑪
Museum of Civilization ⑭
Notre-Dame Basilica ⑨

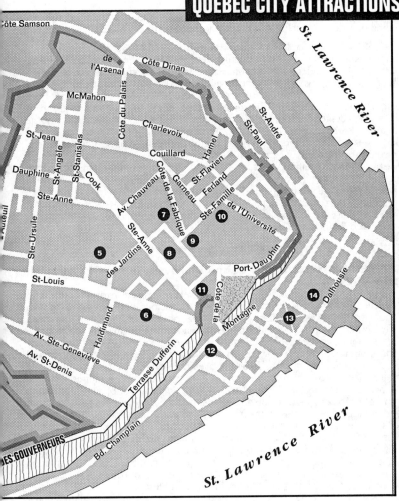

Côte Samson
de l'Arsenal
Côte Dinan
McMahon
Côte du Palais
Charlevoix
St-Jean
St-Angèle
St-Stanislas
Couillard
Dauphine
Cook
Côte de la Fabrique
Garneau
St-Flavien
Ferland
Av. Chauveau
St-André
St-Paul
Hamel
Ste-Famille
de l'Université
Ste-Anne
Ste-Ursule
des Jardins
St-Louis
Port-Dauphin
Haldimand
Côte de la Montagne
Dalhousie
Av. Ste-Geneviève
Av. St-Denis
Terrasse Dufferin
DES GOUVERNEURS
Bd. Champlain
St. Lawrence River
St. Lawrence River

Parliament Building ❸
Place Royale ⓭
Québec Museum ❶
Seminary Museum ❿
Urban Life Interpretation Center ❼
Ursuline Chapel and Museum ❺
Wax Museum ❽

welcome to wander inside and look around the lobby and shops. The real joy, though, is standing outside the hotel and gazing up at the magnificent facade.

LA CITADELLE, 1 côte de la Citadelle. Tel. 418/648-3563.

The star-shaped Citadel keeps a usually silent vigil from the tip of Cap Diamant, except for occasional ceremonial cannonfire. Construction of the great fortress, now a national historic site, was begun by the French in 1820, continued by the British, and took 30 years to complete. Soon afterward it was obsolete. Since 1920 it has been home to Québec's Royal 22nd Regiment, making it the largest fortified group of buildings still occupied by troops in North America. As part of a guided tour only, the public may visit the Citadel, including the regimental museum in the former powderhouse and prison, and watch the changing of the guard or beating the retreat.

Admission: $4 adults, $2 children 7–17.

Open: Guided 55-minute tours, mid-Mar to Apr daily 10am–3pm; May–June and early Sept–Oct daily 9am–4pm. Nov to mid-Mar, group reservations only. Changing of the guard (40 min.), mid-June to early Sept daily 10am (cancelled in case of rain); beating the retreat (30 min.) July–Aug Tues, Thurs, and Sat–Sun after the last tour at 6pm (cancelled in case of rain). Cannonfire, from Prince-de-Galles bastion, daily noon and 9:30pm.

THE LOWER TOWN

MUSEE DE LA CIVILISATION, 85 rue Dalhousie, in the Old Port. Tel. 418/643-2158.

Designed by Boston-based, McGill University-trained Moshe Safdie and opened in 1988, this museum is a modern, spacious, and innovative (though nonintrusive) presence in a compact, historic part of the city. Suspended walkways, waterfalls, and a large atriumlike main floor with the massive sculpture *La Débâcle*, symbolizing the ice breakup in the spring, greet visitors. What's particularly engaging about the museum is the clever use of "hands-on" exhibits, computers, and videos. The exhibits—as many as 10 at any given time, all relating to the evolution of civilization—appeal equally to children and adults, particularly "Mémoires" (Memories), a permanent time capsule filled with vivid reminiscences of Québec history, from the province's roots as a fur-trading colony to the present. Furnishings from frontier homes, tools of the trappers' trade, old farm implements, 19th-century religious garments, old campaign posters, a re-created classroom from the past, mementos from historic events, and television footage envelop the visitor with a rich sense of Québec's daily life, generation to generation. The special exhibit "Survival of the Planet" will be on display from July 1994 to March 1995. Exhibit texts are in French, but English-speaking guides are available to take visitors through the galleries. A café and well-stocked gift shop are on the ground floor.

Admission: $5 adults, $4 seniors, $3 students. Free to all on Tues; children under 16 free all the time.

Open: Late June–early Sept 15 daily 10am–7pm; early Sept–late June Tues–Sun 10am–5pm (to 9pm on Wed).

PLACE ROYALE, Lower Town. Tel. 418/643-6631 for the interpretation center.

Picturesque place Royale is the literal and spiritual heart of the Lower Town, and you shouldn't make the trip down the cliff from the Upper Town without seeing it. (It's a short walk from the lower terminus of the funicular, or Breakneck Stairs, via rue Sous-le-Fort.) In the 17th and 18th centuries, it was the town marketplace and the

---

IMPRESSIONS

The old world rises in the midst of the new in the manner of a change of scene on the stage . . . on its rocky promontory sits the ancient town, belted with its hoary wall and crowned with its granite citadel . . .
—HENRY JAMES, "QUÉBEC," 1871, IN *PORTRAITS OF PLACES*, 1883

center of business and industry. Folk dances, impromptu concerts, and other festive gatherings are often held near the bust of Louis XIV (the "Roy," or king, in place Royale).

ON OR NEAR THE GRANDE-ALLEE

MUSEE DU QUEBEC (QUEBEC MUSEUM), 1 av. Wolfe-Montcalm. Tel. 418/643-2150.

In the southern reaches of Battlefields Park, just off the Grande-Allée, the museum now occupies two buildings, one a former prison, linked together by a modern structure housing the reception area, a stylish cafeteria, and shop. The original building houses the permanent collection, the largest collection of Québec art in North America, filling eight galleries with works from the beginning of the colony to the present. The new addition to the museum is in a former prison, which later became a youth hostel nicknamed the "Petite Bastille"; one cellblock has been left intact as an exhibit. In this building, six galleries house temporary shows, and the tower (which you shouldn't miss—for the art and the view) contains a provocative sculpture called *Le Plongeur* (The Diver) by David Moore, an Irish artist who lives in Montréal. The museum is just off the Grande-Allée, at the intersection of rue George VI and avenue Wolfe-Montcalm—a half hour's walk or a bus ride from the Upper Town. You'll recognize it by the needle-nose roof of the entry and the monument to Wolfe outside.

Admission: $4.75 adults, $2.75 students 16 and older; free for everyone on Wed.

Open: Mid-June to early Sept daily 10am–5:45pm (to 9:45pm Wed); early Sept to mid-June Tues–Sun 10am–5:45pm (to 9:45pm Wed). **Closed:** Christmas Day, New Year's Day. **Bus:** 11.

PARC DES CHAMPS DE BATAILLE (BATTLEFIELDS PARK), just outside the city walls, off the Grande-Allée. Tel. 418/648-4071.

⭐ Covering more than 250 acres of grassy knolls, sunken gardens, monuments, fountains, and trees, Québec's Battlefields Park stretches over the half-mile-wide Plains of Abraham, where Wolfe and Montcalm fought to the death, and is a favorite place for all Québécois when they want some sunshine and fresh air, a jog, or a bike ride. Be sure to see Jardin Jeanne d'Arc (Joan of Arc Garden), with 500 kinds of flowers, just off avenue Laurier between Loews Le Concorde Hôtel and the Ministry of Justice. The statue was a gift from some anonymous Americans. It was here that "O Canada," the country's national anthem, was sung for the first time; it was originally written in French. Within the park are two martello towers, cylindrical stone defensive structures built between 1808 and 1812, when Québec feared an invasion from the United States. This sort of tower, which became popular during the Napoleonic Wars, housed supplies on the first floor and troops on the second.

Admission: Free.

Open: Park never closes; park interpretation center, 390 av. de Bernières, open late May–Labor Day, daily 10am–5:45pm (to 9:45pm Wed), the rest of the year Tues–Sun 10am–5:45pm (to 9:45pm Wed).

MORE ATTRACTIONS
THE UPPER TOWN

BASILICA OF NOTRE-DAME, 16 rue Buade, at côte de la Fabrique. Tel. 418/692-2533.

The oldest Christian parish (1647) in North America north of Mexico has seen a tumultuous history of bombardment, reconstruction, and restoration. The interior is ornate, the air rich with the scent of burning candles, and many valuable old paintings and ecclesiastical treasures still remain from the time of the French regime, including a chancel lamp given by Louis XIV. Here you'll find the tomb of Monseigneur Laval, North America's first bishop. Finished in 1948, the tomb displays yellow marble, a gilt mosaic ceiling, and bronze croziers surrounding a recumbent marble sculpture of Laval. The basilica is actually connected to the complex of old buildings that makes up Québec Seminary, but to enter that complex, you must go to rue de l'Université.

Admission: Free.
Open: Daily 6:30am–8pm; guided tours available May–Nov 9am–5pm.

CENTRE D'INTERPRETATION DE LA VIE URBAINE (URBAN LIFE INTERPRETATION CENTER), 43 côte de la Fabrique. Tel. 418/691-4606.

It's in the basement of City Hall, and you'll probably pass it a number of times on jaunts between place d'Armes and the lively activity of rue St-Jean. Do drop in. It's interesting; it's small, so it won't take much time to visit; and it's free. The main attraction is the big model of Québec City as it was in 1975 (that's about the same as much of it was in 1875 or 1775). It will give you a good idea of the topographical layout of things. Other exhibits focus on urban planning in one way or another.
Admission: Free.
Open: Late June–early Sept daily 10am–8pm; early Sept–late June Tues–Sun 10am–5pm.

MUSEE DU FORT, 10 rue Ste-Anne. Tel. 418/692-2175.

You can't miss this place if you're standing in place d'Armes. Inside, there's a sound-and-light diorama, on a 400-square-foot model of the city and surrounding areas, that outlines the six sieges of Québec, including the famous battle on the Plains of Abraham, which occurred on a Friday the 13th. I find it expensive, but a history buff might not. The complement to the diorama is Explore, in the Lower Town, which looks at the French exploration of North America from 1492 to 1608 and the founding of Québec.
Admission: $4.25 adults, $2.75 students and seniors.
Open: Summer daily 10am–6pm; fall and spring Mon–Sat 10am–5pm, Sun noon–5pm; winter Mon–Fri 11am–5pm, Sat 10am–5pm, Sun 1–5pm. **Closed:** Dec 1–26.

MUSEE DE CIRE (WAX MUSEUM), 22 rue Ste-Anne. Tel. 418/692-2289.

In a 17th-century house, this bigger-than-it-looks Wax Museum provides one of the most pleasurable ways to learn about Québec's (and America's) history and heroes; Wolfe and Montcalm are portrayed, of course, in two of the 16 exhibits that fill three floors. Detailed texts are in French and English.
Admission: $3 adults, $1.50 children.
Open: Summer daily 9am–11pm; winter daily 10am–5pm.

MUSEE DU SEMINAIRE, 9 rue de l'Université. Tel. 418/692-2843.

Within this museum, the collections of artistic and scientific works, acquired throughout Québec Seminary's more than three centuries of existence (1663), are on display. To add spice, there's even an Egyptian mummy. If you visit in summer, be sure to see the seminary chapel and the adjoining funeral chapel, which is dedicated to Monseigneur Laval, founder of the seminary and North America's first bishop. Small and quite lovely, it once housed Laval's tomb, which was moved to the Basilica of Notre-Dame in 1993. Free guided tours of the seminary grounds and the chapels depart from 2 côte de la Fabrique; while walking on the grounds you're likely to see a quadrangle surrounded by stark-white buildings on three sides. A sundial on one of the buildings dates back to 1773, and here American officers, having failed in their attempt to capture Québec in 1775–76, were held prisoner.
Admission: Museum, $2 adults, $1 students and seniors, 50¢ children under 12.
Open: June–Sept Tues–Sun 10:30am–5:30pm; Oct–May Tues–Sun 10:30am–5pm. Guided tours of chapels in summer only.

URSULINE CHAPEL AND MUSEUM, 12 rue Donnacona. Tel. 418/694-0694.

The interior of the chapel, which shelters the remains of the city's beloved Montcalm, has been restored to its Louis XIV brilliance and is open only from May through October. The museum, open year-round, displays many of the accoutrements of the daily and spiritual life of the Ursulines. Don't overlook the third-floor exhibits of fine vestments woven with gold thread by the Ursulines, and the 17th-century cape made from the drapes from the bedroom of Anne of Austria and given to Marie de l'Incarnation, the reverend mother and one of the two founders of the convent, when she left France for New France in 1639. There are also musical instruments—harps, lyres, concertinas, guitars, a zither, and a viola—and Amerindian crafts, including the flèche, or arrow sash, still worn during Winter Carnival. The Ursuline convent was built originally as a girls' school in 1639, and is the oldest one in North America.

Admission: Museum, $2.50 adults, $1.25 students and seniors, 75¢ children, $5.75 families; chapel, free.

Open: Museum, Jan 3–Nov 24 Tues–Sat 9:30am–noon and 1:30–4:45pm, Sun 12:30–5:15pm; chapel, May–Oct, same hours as museum.

THE LOWER TOWN

EXPLORE SOUND AND LIGHT SHOW, 63 rue Dalhousie. Tel. 418/692-2063.

Relive the heyday of the Age of Exploration through the impressions, adventures, and hardships of Columbus, Vespucci, Verrazano, Cartier, and Champlain, as depicted in this 20-minute sound-and-light show. The theater is shaped like an early sailing vessel, complete with rigging. The show depicts the difficulties of Champlain and his crew of 28 who came here in 1608; 20 men died during the first winter, mainly of scurvy and dysentery (one was hanged for mutiny). (They lived in the Habitation, which you can visit near Annapolis Royal, in Nova Scotia, then part of French territory in North America.) Some good books about the founding of Québec are sold here; the map on the back wall depicts the world of 1608.

Admission: $4.25 adults, $2.75 students and seniors.

Open: Summer daily 10am–6pm; fall and spring Mon–Sat 10am–5pm, Sun noon–5pm; winter Mon–Fri 11am–5pm, Sat 10am–5pm, Sun 1–5pm. **Closed:** Dec 1–26.

MAISON CHEVALIER, 60 rue du Marché-Champlain, at rue Notre-Dame. Tel. 418/643-9689.

The Maison Chevalier was originally built as three houses—two from 1675 and 1695, and a third from 1752—for shipowner Jean-Baptiste Chevalier. Inside, you'll find wood beams, wide-board floors, stone fireplaces, and changing exhibits on Québec history and civilization. The house is managed by the Museum of Civilization.

Admission: Free.

Open: Daily 10am–5pm.

ON OR NEAR THE GRANDE-ALLEE

PARLIAMENT BUILDING, Grande-Allée est and av. Dufferin. Tel. 418/643-7239.

Since 1968, the legislature has occupied the imposing Hôtel du Parlement, a Second Empire castle constructed in 1886 that is the center of the Cité Parlementaire, Québec's government complex. Twenty-two bronze statues of the most illustrious figures in Québec's colorful, tumultuous history gaze out from the facade, which is dramatically backlit at night. The fountain in front, called "La Halte dans la Forêt," the work of Philippe Hébert (1890), was dedicated to Québec's original Native

---

IMPRESSIONS

Québec is the most interesting thing by much that I have seen on the Continent, and I think I would sooner be a poor priest in Québec than a rich hog-merchant in Chicago.
—MATTHEW ARNOLD, LETTER TO WALTER ARNOLD, 1884

Québec . . . ranks by herself among those Mother-cities of whom none can say, 'This reminds me.'
—RUDYARD KIPLING, LETTERS TO THE FAMILY, 1907

American inhabitants. You may tour the gilded and sumptuous rooms of the building with a guide for no charge. Highlights include the magnificent National Assembly Chamber, where the assembly sits, and the former Legislative Council Room. Throughout the building, symbols of the fleur-de-lys, the initials "VR" (for Victoria Regina), and the maple leaf remind visitors of Québec's tri-national heritage. When the assembly is in session, the crown in the center tower of the building is lit.

Admission: Free.

Open: Guided tours, Sept–May Mon–Fri 9am–4:30pm; June 24–early Sept daily 9am–4:30pm. **Closed:** June 1–23.

COOL FOR KIDS

Québec is such a storybook town that children will probably be delighted just walking around. But if you need some goals, head for **Dufferin Terrace** (Terrasse Dufferin), which has those coin-operated telescopes kids love so much. A few steps away in place d'Armes are the **calèches,** and even if you don't hire one, the children will love to look at the horses. Or they'll gaze at lifelike historical figures dramatically crafted in wax at the **Musée du Cire (Wax Museum),** on place d'Armes at 22 rue Ste-Anne.

Also at place d'Armes is the **funicular** to the Lower Town; its glass walls allow a splendid view of the river, and its precipitous (if slow and careful) drop is a sure thrill. In the Lower Town, at 86 rue Dalhousie, the playful **Musée de la Civilisation (Museum of Civilization)** will keep kids occupied for hours—in the exhibits, shop, and café.

Kids also get a charge out of the monstrous cannon ranged along the battlements on **rue des Remparts.** The gun carriages are impervious to the assaults of small humans, so kids can scramble over them to their hearts' content. Other military sites are usually a hit. Go to the **Citadel** for the changing of the guard, or a tour of all the grounds and military paraphernalia.

The **ferry** to Lévis across the St. Lawrence is inexpensive, convenient from the Lower Town, pleasant, and exciting for kids. The crossing, over and back, takes less than an hour.

Do they need to run off some excess energy? Head for the **Plains of Abraham,** which is also Québec National Battlefields Park. You can get there by the Grande-Allée, or by the walkway along Dufferin Terrace and the promenade des Gouverneurs. Acres of grassy lawn will give children room to roam and provide the perfect spot for a family picnic. You can see the Appalachian Mountains from here.

If there's time for a short excursion, drive out to impressive **Montmorency Falls,** which dwarf small-fry and adults (see Section 9 of this chapter).

ORGANIZED TOURS

Québec City is small enough so that you can acquaint yourself with it quickly on your own, but a tour is always helpful to get some background information on the fascinating history of the city and to see a few of the attractions that are a bit farther afield. Here are some possibilities should you decide to put yourself in someone else's hands.

HORSE-DRAWN CARRIAGE TOURS A delightful and romantic way to tour this wonderful city is in a horse-drawn carriage, called a **calèche.** You can hire one at place d'Armes or on rue d'Auteuil, just within the city walls near the tourist information office. The guided tour in either French or English costs about $50 for 30 minutes; the carriages operate all summer, rain or shine.

WALKING TOURS Points of departure for walking tours change, so to get up-to-date information, check at the conveniently located kiosk on Dufferin Terrace beside the Château Frontenac and the funicular entrance. There may even be a tour leaving from here; if not, it's bound to be nearby. Parks rangers lead free one-hour walking tours to the Citadel most every day.

At the Musée du Fort on the place d'Armes opposite the Château Frontenac, you can make a reservation for a walking tour of the Upper and Lower Towns with **Baillairge Cultural Tours, Inc.** (tel. 418/658-4799), which operates "Québec by Foot" tours.

In the Lower Town, the tourist information center, in the old Thibodeau warehouse in place Royale, offers free tours in English and French. They're given by enthusiastic student guides from 10am to 5pm, daily June through September only. Each of the half-dozen volunteer guides can handle only about two dozen tourists at once, and in peak season demand may exceed supply. You can reserve in advance, though (tel. 418/643-6631).

Stroll around parts of scenic Ile d'Orléans (see Section 9 of this chapter) by linking up with **Beau Temps, Mauvais Temps** (Rain or Shine) tours (tel. 418/828-2275).

BUS TOURS   Buses are obviously convenient if you're low on leg power, especially in a city that has more ups and downs than a roller coaster. My only complaint is that, because of their size, they tend to glut place d'Armes and spoil an otherwise picturesque spot.

Maple Leaf Sightseeing Tours (tel. 418/649-9226) will pick you up at your hotel in a 25-passenger "trolley bus" and give you a comprehensive tour of Québec, old and new, Upper and Lower Towns, for $19.95 per adult, half price for children under 12 (this tour may be incorporated with a river cruise). You can get on and off the trolley as often as you like and tour at your own pace. The company also offers half- or full-day (lunch included) tours to Ste-Anne-de-Beaupré, Montmorency Falls, and Ile d'Orléans, and a popular whale-watching tour.

Gray Line (tel. 418/622-7420) also offers city and regional tours and a river cruise, which range from two hours to a full day, and cost $19.50 to $110 for adults.

Tours are also offered by **Visite Touristique de Quebec (VTQ)** (tel. 418/563-9722) and **Old Quebec Tours** (tel. 418/624-0460).

For more information about bus tours of the city, check the "Tour" section of the guide supplied by the tourist office.

RIVER CRUISES   The days of the rugged wilderness may be over, but you can still sail up the St. Lawrence and gaze in wonder at the "Gibraltar of the New World." The MV *Louis Jolliet* can supply that experience. Weighing in at 900 tons, it will take you on a motor-cruise up the St. Lawrence past Ste-Foy, or down the St. Lawrence around the tip of Ile d'Orléans. Sailing season is from mid-June to September (with additional cruises before or after depending on demand); cruises last one to 1½ hours in the afternoon, two to three hours in the evening; fares are $12 to $20 in the afternoon, $12 to $24 at night, less for children. For more information or tickets, drop by the kiosk beside the funicular on Dufferin Terrace, or call the operator, **Croisières AML** (tel. 418/692-1159). Board the boat at quai Chouinard, 10 rue Dalhousie, near place Royale in the Lower Town.

To cruise around Ile d'Orléans, stopping at a farm and a crafts shop along the way, contact **Beau Temps, Mauvais Temps** (Rain or Shine) tours (tel. 418/828-2275).

6. SPORTS/RECREATION

The **Québec Nordiques,** the city's professional hockey team, play in the autumn, winter, and early spring at the Québec Coliseum, 2205 av. due Colisée, parc de l'Exposition (tel. 418/529-8441, or toll free 800/463-3333 outside Québec). The team, which has a strong following in Québec, belongs to the National Hockey League. To get to the coliseum, take the no. 5 or 12 bus to Exposition Park.

Another popular spectator sport that has been around since 1916 is harness racing, held at the **Hippodrome de Québec,** 2205 av. du Colisée, parc de l'Exposition (tel. 525-8268). Le Cavallo clubhouse is open year-round, with races Thursday, Saturday, and Sunday at 7:30pm June through August, and Thursday at 7:30pm and Saturday and Sunday at 1:30pm January through March, November, and December. Admission to the clubhouse is $4.50; otherwise, $2.25 for adults, $1 for children and seniors.

Most of your recreation will be walking from the Upper Town to the Lower Town, and vice versa (unless you cheat and take the funicular), or from the Upper Town to the Plains of Abraham or the Québec Museum. Don't complain; after all the exercise you won't feel so guilty ordering a four-course table d'hôte meal, complete with sugar pie and crème anglaise.

7. SAVVY SHOPPING

Québec City's small size makes it especially conducive to shopping and browsing. Happily, there is a surprising number of art galleries in the city, including an outdoor one in the heart of the Old City's Upper Town.

In the Upper Town, wander along rue St-Jean, both within and outside the city walls, and nearby rue Garneau and côte de la Fabrique. There's a shopping concourse on the lower level of the Château Frontenac. For T-shirts, postcards, and other souvenirs, myriad shops line rue St-Louis. On narrow rue du Trésor between rue Ste-Anne and rue Buade near place d'Armes, local artists sell their watercolors, paintings, prints, and caricatures in an open-air gallery, much like the artists on Saint Amable Lane in Old Montréal. Expect to see at least one illustrator doing a good business drawing caricatures.

Côte de la Montagne, which leads from the Upper Town to the Lower Town as an alternative to the funicular, has an interesting art gallery. The Lower Town itself, particularly the Quartier Petit-Champlain, just off place Royale and encompassing rue Petit-Champlain, boulevard Champlain, and rue Sous-le-Fort (opposite the funicular entrance), is rich in shopping possibilities: clothing for men and women, gifts, household items, and unique collectibles, from jewelry to dolls. Place Royal itself is filled with souvenir shops.

Dealers in antiques have gravitated to rue St-Paul in the Lower Town (follow rue St-Pierre or rue Sault-au-Matelot from the place Royale, then walk away from the river on rue St-Paul), lined with close to a dozen shops, filled with old brass beds, colonial furnishings and knickknacks, Québec furniture, candlesticks, old clocks, even Victoriana and art deco kitsch. Besides antiques, the area is filled with the troubled ghosts of defeated soldiers, for it was along here that Benedict Arnold and his misguided band of American troops marched to their defeat at the hands of Québec's defenders (at the corner of rues St-Pierre and St-Jacques, to be exact).

BEST BUYS Like Montréal, Québec City provides numerous opportunities to purchase crafts, handmade sweaters, wood carvings, and Inuit and other art. You can tell if it's original Inuit (Eskimo) art, and not mass-produced, by the official igloo trademark. Except for a couple of shops, Québec City does not have the high-profile designer clothing so often showcased in Montréal.

SHOPPING COMPLEXES In the Upper Town there's a small complex filled with upscale shops called **Les Promenades du Vieux Québec,** at 43 rue Buade; here you'll find a perfumery, clothing for men and women, and soapstone carvings. Just outside the city walls at Porte Kent, **place Québec** incorporates dozens of shops, a cinema, restaurants, and the Hilton hotel, an easy-to-spot landmark. Place Québec also houses the city's convention center, so it's a particularly busy place. If large shopping malls are what you're after, you won't find them in Québec City but in the neighboring municipality, Ste-Foy, where most of the people who live in Québec City do their shopping; **place Laurier,** at 2700 bd. Laurier, has 350 stores.

STORE HOURS Stores in Québec City all tend to keep similar hours, opening and closing in tandem. You can usually expect to find their welcome mats out Monday through Wednesday from 9:30am to 5:30pm, Thursday and Friday from 9:30am to 9pm, and Saturday from 9:30am to 5pm. Many shops—but not Simon's department store—stay open on Sunday from noon to 5pm. In the busy summer months, it's not unusual for stores to keep much longer hours—from 9am to 9pm daily.

SHOPPING A TO Z

ART At **Abaca,** 38 rue Garneau (tel. 418/694-9761), owners Dinneu Koo and Patrice Blouin travel the globe in search of the hand-picked items in their shop/

gallery, and it shows. They've collected (and are selling) masks, sculpture, and other pieces from Africa, India, Afghanistan, Asia, Japan, Korea, and China, among the 35 countries represented. Some jewelry and handcrafts by Québec artists are also sold here. The store takes its name from a multipurpose tree that grows in Africa.

The **Galerie aux Multiples,** opposite the Hôtel de Ville at 69 rue Ste-Anne (tel. 418/692-1230), sells Eskimo, folk, and modern Canadian art. The most striking items are the carved wood and stone. The shop ships.

Galerie Zanettin, 28 côte de la Montagne (tel. 418/692-1055), is an excellent place to view and invest in the works of established Québécois artists, as well as some artists from the Maritime Provinces and Alberta. While the artists are contemporary, their work isn't necessarily. Various styles are represented here, primitive included, as well as Japanese-influenced sculpture.

BOOKS   Strictly a travel bookstore, **Ulysses,** 4 bd. St-Cyrille est (tel. 418/529-5349), specializes in travel books, guidebooks, and travel accessories. It also has a smaller shop in the same building as the tourist information office, 12 rue Ste-Anne, at place d'Armes.

The English-language books in **Librairie Garneau,** 24 côte de la Fabrique (tel. 418/692-4262), are in a small section to the right just after you enter the store. It actually sells much more than books, by the way, so you can do some one-stop shopping if you're in the mood and also pick up cards, stationery, gift items, coloring books, and film.

CHRISTMAS ITEMS   It's Christmas year-round at **La Boutique de Noël de Québec,** 42 rue Garneau (tel. 418/692-2457), just off rue St-Jean. The shop is filled with ornaments and decorations from around the world, Nativity sets, cards, Santas and angels galore, and holiday music—plenty of collectibles. The Gaboury family, who run the place, are so nice they must have been hand-picked by Saint Nick himself.

CLOTHING   For Women   The fashions at **Oke,** 40 côte de la Fabrique (tel. 418/692-0102), come close to rivaling those ever-so-stylish ones of the up-and-coming designers in Montréal. A shop showcasing primarily the fashions of Québecois designers is **Zazou,** 31 Petit Champlain (tel. 418/694-9990).

For clothing that is more comfortable than stylish, or stylish in an ethnic way, head to **La Maison du Hamac,** 91 rue Ste-Anne (tel. 418/692-1109), for hats, shirts, belts, vests, colorful bags, and jewelry from Mexico, Guatemala, and Brazil. The shop, as its name implies, also sells hammocks, which start at $35.

For Men   A link in the popular chain, **America,** at 1147 rue St-Jean (tel. 418/692-5254), offers dependably good quality and style in casual and dress clothes for men. The clothing in the upscale **François Côté,** 35 rue Buade (tel. 418/692-6016), couldn't be more eye-catching. You'll find suits, jackets, shirts, and great ties.

For Children   Shopping with your kids, or looking for the perfect gift to bring home to them? Then you'll want to browse through the **Boutique Le Fou du Roy,** 57, rue Petit-Champlain (tel. 418/692-4439), which carries an array of children's clothing and games.

A Department Store   **Simon's,** 20 côte de la Fabrique (tel. 418/692-3630), the only department store in the old city, opened here in 1840 and has expanded to two other locations. Small by modern standards, it has two floors for men and women's clothing and for household goods. Women's clothing and accessories are on the ground and second floors; men's clothing is on the ground level; and sheets and towels are on the mezzanine. The styles are conservative.

Accessories   If you've a propensity for gemstones—jade, onyx, malacite, and more—set in gold or silver, visit **Geomania,** 59 rue Dalhousie (tel. 418/692-2773). Quality leather, including bags, briefcases, shoes, jackets, and hats, are sold at **Atelier de Cuir Ibiza,** 49 Petit-Champlain (tel. 418/692-2103).

GIFT ITEMS **Adrien Racine,** 30 côte de la Fabrique (tel. 418/692-2109), is a large, well-stocked store selling quality crafts and other items. All are a little on the expensive side but competitive with other shops in the city. You'll find wood carvings, sweaters for adults and kids, and plenty of gift possibilities. Nearby, **Claude Berry,** 6 côte de la Fabrique (tel. 418/692-2628), is a great little shop to find inexpensive but clever whatnots or expensive French country porcelain.

La Dentellière, 56 rue Cul-de-Sac, sells some of the beautiful lace you've admired hanging from so many house and restaurant windows in Québec City.

At **Galerie le Fil du Temps,** 88 rue Petit-Champlain (tel. 418/692-5867), the dolls with elegant clothing are astounding. More are probably bought for collectors than for children because of the price and workmanship.

For a bottle or two of wine, visit **La Maison des Vins,** 1 place Royale (tel. 418/643-1214), really a tourist attraction in itself. You'll find about 2,000 labels here. Be sure to visit the cellar, if only on a sightseeing mission.

If you need to buy an obligatory T-shirt or two before you go back home, you won't have any trouble finding souvenir shops anywhere in Québec City. One of them, **Place Royale Souvenirs,** 11 Notre-Dame, near place Royale (tel. 418/692-2201), has a good selection of T-shirts, sweatshirts, postcards, and crests. Keep an eye out for sale items.

8. EVENING ENTERTAINMENT

Dignified, traditional-minded Québec City doesn't try to compete with exuberant Montréal in the realm of nightlife, but neither does it roll up its sidewalks at 9pm.

Some people's idea of a night on the town is to sit and gaze for an hour or more at the view from **Dufferin Terrace** (it's beautiful and free as the crisp night air). Others soak up the ambience in the cafés along lively **rue St-Jean, rue Ste-Anne, rue Petit-Champlain,** and the **Grande-Allée.** During the Summer Festival the upper portion of rue St-Jean is closed to cars to become a pedestrian promenade.

Drop in at the tourism information office in place d'Armes or on rue d'Auteuil for a list of summertime or wintertime events, such as the annual **Festival d'Eté** (Summer Festival) in July, when free concerts and shows are staged all over town in the evenings. The same holds true for the **Carnival d'Hiver** (Winter Carnival) in February, when the city salutes this chilly time of year with a magnificent ice palace, ice sculptures, and parades.

THE PERFORMING ARTS

PERFORMING ARTS COMPANIES The Québec Symphony Orchestra, Canada's oldest, performs at the Grand Théâtre de Québec September to May; the Québec Opera mounts performances in the spring and fall, at the Grand Théâtre. The Trident Theatre troupe performs in the Salle Octave-Crémazie in the Grand Théâter. Danse-Partout is also at the Grand Théâter.

CONCERTS Many of the city's churches host sacred and secular music concerts, as well as special Christmas festivities; among them, the Cathedral of the Holy Trinity, église St-Jean-Baptiste, historic chapelle Bon-Pasteur, the Chalmers-Wesley United Church, and, on Ile d'Orléans, église Ste-Pétronille.

THEATERS At the **Grand Théâtre de Québec,** near the Québec Museum, at 269 bd. René-Levesque est (tel. 418/643-8131), classical music concerts, theater and dance productions, and other shows are performed in two halls, one of them housing the largest stage in Canada. Visiting conductors, orchestras, and companies often perform here. Québec's Conservatory of Music is underneath the theater. The mural in the theater is by Jordi Bonet. The box office is open Monday to Friday from noon to 6pm; performances start at 7:30 or 8pm year-round but primarily September to May. Prices range from $20 to $45; students sometimes get discounts. Take bus no. 5, 8, 11, or 25.

In the Lower Town, the **Théâtre du Petit-Champlain** 68 rue Petit-Champlain (tel. 418/692-2631), sits in the shadow of the Château Frontenac, towering from the cliff above. Québecois and French singers fill this roomy café theater with cabarets and revues. Buy your ticket down the street at 76 rue Petit-Champlain, and have a drink on the patio before the show. The shows are in French. The box office, at 76 rue Petit-Champlain, is open Monday to Friday from 1 to 5pm, to 7pm the night of a show (doors open at 7:30pm). Prices are $20 to $24. Take bus no. 1.

OUTDOOR THEATERS   Québec City blossoms in summer, with outdoor performances outside City Hall in the Jardins de l'Hôtel-de-Ville; in the Pigeonnier at Parliament Hill, on the Grande-Allée; and at place d'Youville.

The **Agora,** 120 rue Dalhousie (tel. 418/692-4540), a 5,800-seat amphitheater at the Old Port, is the scene of classical and contemporary music concerts and a variety of other shows in the summer. The city makes a dramatic backdrop. Box office hours are daily from 9am to 6pm; performance times vary. Prices are around $25. Take Bus no. 1.

THE CLUB & MUSIC SCENE

NIGHTCLUBS   Tucked at the end of an alleyway off rue St-Jean (that's where the ½ in the address comes from), **Les Yeux Bleus,** 1117½ rue St-Jean (tel. 418/694-9118), looks like a shanty from the outside, but is altogether inviting on the inside. The music is 75% Québecois and 25% American. It's open nightly from 8pm to 3am. Prices are $3 to $5.50. Admission is free.

For folk music, head to the venerable **Chez Son Père,** in the Upper Town, at 24 St-Stanislas (tel. 418/692-5308). A musical institution in Québec since 1960, Chez Son Père is the place where French Canadian folksingers get their start. Climb the stairs to the second floor, where you'll find brick walls, sparse decor, a stage in one corner, and a young, friendly crowd. It's a few steps uphill from bustling rue St-Jean, open nightly from 10pm to 2:30am. Drink prices are $2.75 to $7.50; admission is free.

Rock concerts are generally held in the **Colisée de Québec (Québec Coliseum),** 2205 av. du Colisée (tel. 418/691-7211); hockey games are also held here. In summer, the box office is open Monday to Friday from 9am to 4pm, and in the winter, from 10am to 5pm and in the evening prior to a show. The prices for tickets range from $25 to $35.

For jazz, you have to go no farther than **L'Emprise Bar,** in the Hôtel Clarendon, 57 rue Ste-Anne, at the corner of Desjardins (tel. 418/692-2480). Listening to good jazz in this pleasant, mellow place is a long-standing Québec City tradition. The bar, on the ground level of the once-elegant hotel, has beamed ceilings, large windows, etched glass, art deco touches, and seating at tables and on bar stools. There's no admission, but the drink prices ($4.50 to $6.25) make up for it. It's open from 4pm to 3am, with music Sunday through Wednesday from 9:30pm, and Thursday through Saturday from 10:15pm. Admission is free.

DISCOS/DANCE CLUBS   Chez Dagobert, 590 Grande-Allée (tel. 418/522-0393), a huge, three-story club, draws crowds and raves with an elaborate lighting system and a catwalk for observing the mass of dancers driven by the thundering beat of the music. It attracts both casually dressed students and more fashionably attired young professionals, all of whom claim it's a good place to meet people. It's open nightly 9pm to 3am. Drink prices are $4 to $6, and admission is free.

Across the street, there's **Le Dancing,** the disco in Loew's Le Concorde, 1225 place Montcalm, at the Grande-Allée (tel. 418/647-2222). The dance floor is slightly sunken, the crowd young and enthusiastic. There's a small sitting area behind the disco, should you decide to attempt a conversation. With Chez Dagobert across the street, disco-hopping is as easy as changing a CD. It's open 9pm to 3am Wednesday to Saturday. Drink prices are $4.25 to $6.75, and admission is free.

THE BAR SCENE

PUBS/WINE BARS   A favorite with the local after-work crowd, the **Aviatuc Club,** Gare-du-Palais (Train Station), Lower Town (tel. 418/522-3555), is in the city's pretty train station. The theme here is aviation, with two miniature planes hanging from the ceiling. Bar food and meals are served, along with local and imported beers.

The bar is to your immediate left after you enter the train station. It's open Monday to Saturday from noon to 2am, Sunday from noon to midnight. Prices are $3.50 to $6.50.

Cozy **Le Pape-Georges,** 8 rue Cul-de-Sac, in the Lower Town (tel. 418/692-1320), features jazz or a French singer on Thursday through Sunday at 10pm. Light fare is served during the day. Hours are daily from 9:30am to 2:30am. Prices are $3.75 to $5.57, admission is free.

Le Pub Saint-Alexandre, 1987 rue St-Jean (tel. 418/694-0015), manages to be big and sophisticated but intimate at the same time. It's also Québec City's prettiest bar. The specialty here is beer, 175 kinds, 19 of them on tap, and there's light fare to accompany the brews. The large front windows provide a pleasant berth for observing the busy street life on rue St-Jean. It's open daily from 11am to 12:30am. Prices are $3.75 to $17.50 (for rare imported labels).

A SIDEWALK CAFE   Au Café Suisse, 26 rue Ste-Anne (tel. 418/694-1321), promises the perfect aisle seat—outdoors, of course. The congenial sidewalk café faces off against the Château Frontenac across place d'Armes, and is beside the colorful artist alleyway, rue du Trésor. The easygoing atmosphere makes it easy to meet people or just to relax with a coffee or a drink, anytime, day or night. It's open daily from 11am to midnight, later in summer. Prices are $3.75 to $7.50.

A BAR WITH A VIEW   Spinning slowly above a fairy-tale city and a silent plain, **L'Astral** bar and restaurant, at Loew's Le Concorde, 1225 place Montcalm, at the Grande-Allée (tel. 418/647-2222), has a view that is nothing less than breathtaking. Many people come for dinner, but it's acceptable to come just for drinks and sit at the bar after 10:30pm. The bar seats 36; the restaurant, 200. It's open Monday to Friday from 3:30pm to midnight, Saturday from 10:30pm to 2:30am, and Sunday from 3:30pm to 1am. Drink prices are $4 to $7.

GAY BARS   The gay scene in Québec City is a small one, centered in the Upper Town on rue St-Jean at rue d'Agustine. A long-entrenched, popular bar and disco, frequented by both men and women (and by men who look like women) is **Le Ballon Rouge (the Red Balloon),** at 811 rue St-Jean (tel. 418/647-0227).

MORE ENTERTAINMENT

AN EVENING CRUISE   Dancing and cruising are the focal point for those aboard the MV *Louis Jolliet*'s evening cruise from the Old Port. The boat also has a complete bar and snack bar. The price is $24 (tel. 418/692-1159).

MOVIES   First-run English-language films are shown with French subtitles at the **Cinéma Place Québec,** in the place Québec shopping mall, under the Hilton hotel (tel. 418/525-4524), or the **Cinéma Galeries de la Capitale,** in the Galeries de la Capitale shopping mall (tel. 418/628-2455).

9. EASY EXCURSIONS FROM QUEBEC CITY

Québec City is perfectly situated for day trips, because a number of places of interest are nearby, and it's easy to get to them, whether or not you drive or leave that to a tour operator.

Montmorency Falls are just outside the city limits, and the famous Shrine of Ste-Anne-de-Beaupré is only a half hour from the city by car, as is bucolic Ile d'Orléans.

And if you've time for exploration of the St. Lawrence's southern bank, you won't be disappointed. Make your goal the wood-carvers' village of St-Jean-Port-Joli; you can return to Québec by crossing the river by ferry at Rivière-du-Loup to St-Siméon and driving through the picturesque Charlevoix region.

Maple Leaf Sightseeing Tours (tel. 418/687-9226) and **VTQ** (tel. 418/653-9722) offer tours to the falls, the shrine, and Ile d'Orléans. In winter the Québec City Skibus brings skiers from city hotels to the Laurentian slopes.

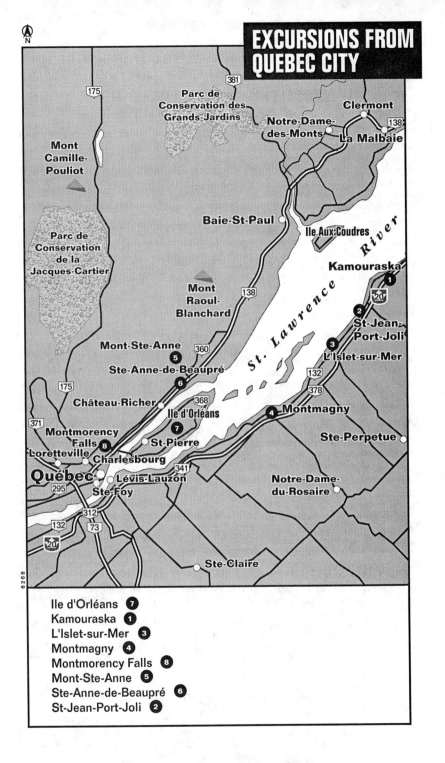

EXCURSIONS FROM QUEBEC CITY

N

Parc de Conservation des Grands-Jardins

Clermont

Notre-Dame-des-Monts

La Malbaie

138

381

175

Mont Camille-Pouliot

Parc de Conservation de la Jacques-Cartier

Baie-St-Paul

Ile Aux Coudres

St. Lawrence River

Kamouraska ❶

20

St-Jean-Port-Joli ❷

Mont Raoul-Blanchard

138

L'Islet-sur-Mer ❸

Mont-Ste-Anne ❺

360

Ste-Anne-de-Beaupré ❻

132

Château-Richer

368

378

Ile d'Orléans

St-Pierre ❼

Montmagny ❹

175

371

Montmorency Falls ❽

Loretteville

Charlesbourg

341

Ste-Perpetue

Québec

Lévis-Lauzon

295

Ste-Foy

Notre-Dame-du-Rosaire

312

132

73

20

Ste-Claire

6268

Ile d'Orléans ❼
Kamouraska ❶
L'Islet-sur-Mer ❸
Montmagny ❹
Montmorency Falls ❽
Mont-Ste-Anne ❺
Ste-Anne-de-Beaupré ❻
St-Jean-Port-Joli ❷

Should you want to rent a car to explore the countryside around Québec City, contact **Tilden Car Rentals,** 295 St-Paul (tel. 418/687-3322; from the U.S. toll free 800/227-7368). Check other listings in the free *Greater Québec Area Tourist Guide.*

MONTMORENCY FALLS & STE-ANNE-DE-BEAUPRE

Legend has it that French mariners were sailing up the St. Lawrence River in the 1650s when they ran into a terrifying storm. Up against the Ultimate Cruise, they prayed to their patroness, Saint Anne, to intercede for their deliverance. Surviving the storm, they dedicated a wooden votive chapel to Saint Anne near the site of their perils, on the north shore of the St. Lawrence, 22 miles northeast of Québec City. Not long afterward, a pilgrim to the spot was cured of an affliction while praying there, and since that time pilgrims have come to pay their respects to Saint Anne, the mother of the Virgin Mary.

If you're driving, get on Autoroute 40, north of Québec City, going east. At the end of the autoroute, where it intersects with Highway 360, is Montmorency Falls. From here, it's a 20-minute drive along Highway 360 east to the small town of Ste-Anne-de-Beaupré—you can't miss it as the highway goes right past the magnificent basilica. It's 22 miles (35km) northeast of Québec City, and 15 miles (24km) northeast of Montmorency Falls.

The tourist office in Québec City can supply all you need to know about Ste-Anne-de-Beaupré.

WHAT TO SEE & DO

At the intersection of Autoroute 40 and Highway 360, 15 miles southwest of Ste-Anne-de-Beaupré, is **Montmorency Falls,** surrounded by a provincial park where you can stop for the view and a picnic. You'll hear the proud boast that the falls, named by Samuel de Champlain for Charles de Montmorency, governor of New France, are well over the height of Niagara. The falls are an impressive sight in summer, but even more so in wintertime, when the freezing spray sent up by the plunging torrent builds a huge mountain of white ice at the base.

Opposite the falls is the bridge to the Ile d'Orléans, described below.

In the town of Ste-Anne-de-Beaupré is the **basilica,** which is the most recent building raised in Saint Anne's honor. After the sailors' first modest wooden chapel was swept away by the flooded St. Lawrence in the 1600s, another chapel was built in a safer place. Floods, fires, and the ravages of time dealt with later buildings, until a tremendous and impressive structure was put up in 1887. In 1926 it too lay in ruins, gutted by fire. The present basilica was begun shortly after that disastrous fire—of stone this time, and in a streamlined and altogether beautiful variation of the traditional Romanesque design. It combines modern art and traditional grandeur, using the best of materials: marble, granite, cut stone, mosaic, stained glass, and hand-carved wood. No sterile monument, the basilica exhibits the craftsmanship of Québec's master artisans. The pews, for instance, are of wood with hand-carved medallions at the ends, each portraying a different animal in God's creation; the realism is surprising, and goes so far as to portray the monkey hanging upside-down—its natural pose.

Behind the main altar are eight side chapels and altars, each different, each excellent in its artistic harmony. Be sure not to miss the very fine ceiling mosaics in the nave, surely an outstanding achievement of 20th-century art. Whether you come to pay your respects to Saint Anne or just out of curiosity, the magnificent artistry of the basilica will make your visit worthwhile.

Note that the church, and in fact the whole town of Ste-Anne-de-Beaupré, is particularly busy on days of significance to the saint: first Sunday in May, mid- to late July, fourth Sunday in August, and early in September.

Besides the basilica, the Fountain of Saint Anne, Scala Santa Chapel, and the Old Chapel, other attractions in town include the **Historial,** a wax museum celebrating the worship of Saint Anne in North America, and the **Cyclorama,** a 360° painting of Jerusalem—but these you must pay to see.

PARC DU MONT STE-ANNE

Just as Montréal has its Laurentian Mountain resorts at Val-David and Mont Tremblant, Québec City has its Laurentian hideaways. But there are differences. The Laurentians sweep down very close to the St. Lawrence, and so Québecois need drive only 30 minutes or less to be in the woods. And as Québec City is much smaller than Montréal, the Québec resorts are more modest in size and fewer in number, but they are equally inviting.

Twenty-five miles northeast of Québec City, Parc du Mont Ste-Anne (tel. 418/817-4561) surrounds a 2,625-foot-high Laurentian peak that has become Québec City's best skiing area. Some 15 lifts (gondola included) take downhill skiers to the starting points of 35 trails and slopes. Miles of cross-country trails lace the park, dotted with 10 heated rest huts, all yours for free.

The Québec City Skibus network serves the slopes at Mont Ste-Anne, so you can stay downtown and ski at the mountain with no trouble. Or you can stay in a hotel or condo at the park.

In summer there's camping and golf, and the gondola to the top of the mountain operates any day (late June through August) when it's not too windy. Tickets cost $6 for adults, half price for children, and the view is worth many times the price.

ILE D'ORLEANS

Until 1935, the only way to get to Ile d'Orléans, 10 miles (16km) northeast of Québec City, was by boat in summer or by tromping over the ice in winter. The building of the highway bridge has allowed the fertile fields of Ile d'Orléans to become Québec City's market-garden district; the fruits and vegetables are picked fresh on the farms and trucked into the city daily. If you take a drive out here in mid-July, you'll notice many handpainted signs announcing "Fraises: cueillir vous-même" (Strawberries: pick 'em yourself). Don't pass up the invitation; that goes for raspberries and apples, too. The farmer will hand you a basket and quote a figure, which you pay when the basket's full. Bring along a bag or box to carry away your bounty, and possibly some heavy cream.

Three stone churches on the island date back to the days when the French ruled this part of the world. There are only seven such churches left in all of Québec, so this is an accomplishment for Ile d'Orléans, due in part to its isolation until the bridge linked it to the mainland in 1935. This is also the reason the island has remained so undeveloped, with so many of its old houses intact—and the good folks who live here are determined to keep it that way. They've got plans to put in a bike lane to cut down on car traffic and to bury their telephone lines. Maybe they'll even go back to wooden sidewalks, which the villages had until the late 1930s.

A coast-hugging road circles Ile d'Orléans, which is 21 miles long and 5 miles wide, and another couple of roads bisect it; one of them, Route du Mitan, is particularly pretty and worth a short detour. On the east side of the island, you'll see a lot of farms and picturesque houses; on the west side, an abundance of apple orchards. If you visit in May or October, you will be blessed with the sight of migrating Canada geese, which are temporary residents these times of year.

There are six tiny villages on Ile d'Orléans, each with a church as its focal point. It's possible to do a quick circuit of the island in half a day, but I'd suggest taking a full day and rambling to your heart's content; better still, stay the night. If you're strapped for time, drive as far as St-Jean, then take Route du Mitan across the island, and return to the bridge, and Québec City, via Highway 368 west.

GETTING THERE   **By Bus**   There are no local buses. To link up with a bus tour, contact **Visite Touristique de Québec** (VTQ; tel. 418/563-9722), **Old Québec Tours** (tel. 418/624-0460), or **Maple Leaf Sightseeing Tours** (tel. 418/649-9226).

By Car   It's a snap from Québec City to get to the island. Follow rue Dufferin (in front of the Parliament building) to connect with Highway 440 east, in the direction of Ste-Anne-de-Beaupré. In 15 minutes you'll be at the Ile d'Orléans bridge.

Essentials   The **area code** is 418. Once you're on the island, turn right on

Highway 368 east (toward Ste-Pétronille); the **tourist information office** will be in the house on your immediate right, and it can supply you with an excellent tourist guide of the island (tel. 828-9411). It's open daily 8:30am to 7pm in summer; off-season, Monday through Friday only, from 8:30am to noon and 1 to 4:30pm. A good backup if you can't get the Ile d'Orléans guide is the Québec City tourist guide, which has a short tour of Ile d'Orléans.

You can rent or buy a **driving-tour cassette** from the tourist office or Auberge La Goéliche (see "Where to Stay and Dine," below).

If you want to rent **bikes,** you can do so from the gas station/grocery store, Depanneur Godbout, right across the road from the bridge (tel. 418/828-9215); if none is available, check at Le Vieux Presbytère bed and breakfast in St-Pierre (tel. 418/828-9723). The tourist office can supply you with a bike map.

If you'd like to go on a **guided walking tour** of several of the island's historical villages, or a nearly two-hour **boat tour** visiting an apple orchard and the church in St-Pierre and its craft-filled gift shop, contact Beau Temps, Mauvais Temps (Rain or Shine) tours (tel. 418/828-2275).

STE-PETRONILLE

The first village you come to is Ste-Pétronille, which is two miles from the bridge. With 1,050 inhabitants, it's best known for its Victorian inn, La Goéliche (see below), and also claims the northernmost stand of red oaks in North America, which is stunning in autumn. Its church dates from 1871, and its houses were once the summer homes of wealthy English in the 1800s. Even if you don't stay at the inn, drive down to the water's edge to see it (there's a small public area with benches there, as well). Also stroll or drive down the picturesque rue Laflamme; the cul-de-sac rue Horatio Walker provides a nice view of Montmorency Falls.

From Ste-Petronille, continue on Highway 368 east and do a complete loop of the island.

Where to Stay and Dine

AUBERGE LA GOELICHE, 22 chemin du Quai, Ste-Pétronille, PQ G0A 4C0. Tel. 418/828-2248. Fax 418/828-2745. 22 rms (all with bath).
$ Rates: $70–$100 single, $90–$160 double. Extra person $25–$50, less for children to age 10. AE, MC, V. **Parking:** Free. **Closed:** Nov.

On a rocky point of land at the western tip of the island stands La Goéliche, a country house in a dramatic setting, with a wraparound porch, a glass-enclosed terrace dining room used from April through October (a grand spot to watch cruise ships and Canada geese drift by), and an aquariumlike swimming pool. The inn (1880) takes its name from the small cargo boat once used in these parts; each room is named for a ship that used to ply these waters. All are light and airy, with board floors, soft colors, and private bath (two baths are across the hall from the room). In summer, the river provides the air conditioning. The dining room of La Goéliche is well known in these parts, so make a reservation if you plan to eat here. The cuisine is French, and the dishes are prepared with a delicate touch. When I dined here, I enjoyed escargots aux fines herbes and almonds, filet of pork in Calvados sauce, dessert, and tea. For a main course, I could have chosen entrecôte, quails, seafood, or veal médaillons. The dessert specialty is the Goéliche cake, soaked in pear liqueur and topped with crème anglaise, yet still surprisingly light. When ordering dinner à la carte, expect to pay $3 to $5 for appetizers and $14 to $17 for main courses; a four-course table d'hôte meal will run $20 to $23. Lunch ranges from $7 to $12. In summer, you can eat on the outdoor terrace. Meals are served daily from 11am to 4pm and from 5:30 to 9:30pm. Off-season, only table d'hôte meals are served. The inn and restaurant are both closed in November.

ST-LAURENT

Four miles from Ste-Pétronille is St-Laurent. In its heyday, St-Laurent, with a population of 1,462, was a center of boat building, turning out more than 400 boats a year. To learn more about this activity, visit the **St-Laurent Maritime Park,** which was a bustling wooden-boat yard from 1908 to 1967; before the bridge was built, it provided islanders the wherewithal to get across the river to Québec City, and you can still see the drydocks. The Maritime Park, which incorporates the old Godbout Boatworks and tools, offers a boat-building demonstration; it's open in summer only, daily 9:30am to 5:30pm (tel. 418/828-2322).

The town's church was erected in 1860, and there are a couple of picturesque roadside chapels as well. (I once peeked into one and found a coffin inside; the locals can't bury their dead until the spring thaw.) You can get a great view of the local farms and the river from the St-Laurent golf course; just follow the signs from the main road (look for a dirt road off to the left). Since the island is mound-shaped, you get more spectacular vistas by going inland. Fortunately it's not very wide, so you don't have to go far.

Where to Stay

LA MAISON SUR LES ARBRES, 1415 chemin Royal, St-Laurent, IO, G0A 3Z0. Tel. 418/828-9442. 3 rms (1 with bath).

$ Rates (including full breakfast): $45 single; $55 double. Extra person $20, child $10. No credit cards.

The name means "the house under the trees," a line taken from a popular French song, and this lovely house—surprisingly modern for this old-fashioned island—is actually tucked back behind the trees, at the water's edge. The comfortable rooms have their own private entrance, and the two that share one large bath are conveniently close to it. One large room with private bath also has a fireplace and can accommodate up to six people. You'll relish a breakfast of cereal, homemade bread, fruit, cheeses and pâtés, eggs, French toast, and more in the glass-enclosed breakfast room overlooking the river, the pool (which you may use after 5pm), and the landscaped terrace. Hosts Germaine and Louis Dumas have been welcoming guests since 1983 to their home, the island's first B&B. She's a freelance writer (and an enthusiastic cook) who has created cassettes and a video about the Ile d'Orléans. The house is closed to guests from 10:30am to 5pm.

Where to Dine

LE MOULIN DE SAINT-LAURENT, 754 chemin Royal. Tel. 418/829-3888.
Cuisine: FRENCH. **Reservations:** Recommended.
$ Prices: Lunch items $4–$11, three-course lunch specials $10–$17; four-course table d'hôte dinners $23–$35. DC, MC, V.
Open: Lunch daily 11:30am–2:30pm; dinner daily 5–9pm. **Closed:** Mid-Oct to mid-May.

✪ The old flour mill in St-Laurent, which operated from 1720 to 1928, has been transformed into one of the island's best and most romantic restaurants. On a warm day, sit on the terrace beside the waterfall, and be sure to wander upstairs to see the Québécois antiques displayed for your enjoyment. At lunch, you might go light with a salad or cheese plate, or wild game or liver pâté; if you're hungry you can opt for a three-course lunch, starting with soup and ending with one of the restaurant's fine desserts. There are half a dozen main courses to choose from, including filet of pork with mustard sauce, rolled filet of sole with spinach, vegetable quiche, and stuffed rabbit with nut sauce. At dinner, you'll add a pâté course. On weekends, a small combo plays in the evenings. One of the three owners, vivacious Elise Premont, is the baby of a large island family of 19 children.

ST-JEAN

St-Jean—four miles from St-Laurent—was home to sea captains, and the homes tend to be more prosperous. A sign of that is the yellow-brick facades of some of the houses; the bricks were ballast in boats that came over from Europe. The houses in St-Jean are the only ones on the island whose porches are ornamented with wrought iron. While you're here, be sure to visit the **Mauvide-Genest Manor** (tel. 418/829-2630) and museum, to your left as you come into town (if you pass the quai, you've gone too far). It's the best-preserved manor house (1734–1752) on the island and is filled with period furnishings, including an ornate American chest (1850) with carved flowers and an impressive eagle, and a "Beggar's Bench," where a homeless person who appeared at the door late in the day would be offered a bed for the evening (otherwise, he might cast a spell on the house). A small chapel was added in 1930; the altar was made by Huron Indians. If you're not squeamish, ask what was used to stain the beams in the house. If the dining room is open to the public, avail yourself of the good country cooking, which promises plenty of fresh vegetables and bread.

Beside the Mauvide-Genest Manor, there's a theater where productions are staged in summer. The church was built in 1732 and in front, the walled cemetery overlooking the river was the resting place for many a seafarer (a great spot for a photo). If you drive by at high tide, you might notice that the church appears to float on the water. St-Jean was considered the "capital" of the island until the bridge and St-Pierre, now the most accessible village, took prominence.

If you're pressed for time, pick up Route du Mitan, which crosses Ile d'Orléans here (it'll be to your left) and links up with St-Famille on the west side of the island. (Route du Mitan, not so easy to spot, is on the left just after you pass the church in St-Jean.) For only 10 minutes of your time, it's a gorgeous drive through farmland and forest. If you're not in a hurry, drive this road anyway, then come back to St-Jean and proceed on Highway 368 east to St-François.

ST-FRANÇOIS

The 5½-mile drive from St-Jean to St-François is filled with vistas of the Laurentian Mountains off to the left; just past the town center of St-Jean you'll see ski-trail-etched Mont Ste-Anne. At St-François, home to about 500 people, the St. Lawrence, a constant and mighty presence, is 10 times wider than in Québec City. The town's original church (1734) burned in 1988.

At St-François, which is 15 miles (24km) from the bridge, the road becomes Highway 368 *west*.

Where to Dine

AUBERGE CHAUMONOT, 425 av. Royale, St-François. Tel. 418/829-2735.
   Cuisine: QUEBECOIS. **Reservations:** Recommended.
$ **Prices:** Appetizers $6–$13; main courses $18–$27; fixed-price three-course lunch $10–$15; fixed-price four-course dinner $19–$24, fixed-price five-course dinner $25–$32. AE, MC, V.
   Open: lunch daily 11am–3pm (4pm if you're lucky); dinner daily 5–9pm (10pm in summer). **Closed:** Nov–Apr.
In the midst of your sightseeing, take time out to sample some regional cooking amid country decor in a riverside inn. The dishes, with memorable French twists, are reminiscent of what farmers must have eaten on this island for generations: pork chops, lamb, salmon (they serve it in lemon butter), *tourtière* (meat pie), tomato-and-onion relish, and plenty of warm bread. The farmers probably didn't eat—but you will—dishes like cream of broccoli soup, quiche Lorraine, and shrimp and duck liver pâté. The restaurant's picture windows give ample opportunity for gazing out to sea. The inn's eight rooms aren't as memorable as the view or the food, but the latter two are ample reason to follow the winding dirt road to this tranquil spot. By the way, the inn takes its name from the Jesuit priest Pierre Chaumonot, who led the Hurons to the island in 1651 to protect them from the attacking Algonquins.

STE-FAMILLE

The oldest parish on the island, Ste-Famille was founded at the northern tip of the island in 1661. With around 1,660 inhabitants, it is 5 miles (8km) from St-François and 12 miles (19km) from the bridge. The triple-spired church dates from 1743; across the road from it stands the convent of Notre-Dame Congregation, founded by Marguerite Bourgeoys (if you have visited Montréal, you've heard of her) in 1685. In this area, you'll find dairy and cattle farms and apple orchards, where you can pick your own *pommes* (apples) in autumn. As you drive out of town, notice the picturesque house with the red trim off to your left. From here, there is a striking view of the town.

While you're in town, visit the **Blouin Bakery** for a sweet treat (the Blouin family, by the way, has lived on this island for 300 years) and a little shop called **Le Mitan** to buy crafts, souvenirs, or books about the island. Just out of town, swing by **Ferme Piscicole Richard Boily,** 4739 chemin Royal (tel. 418/829-2874), where you can fish for speckled or rainbow trout (or watch others do it) in a well-stocked pond, daily from 9am to sunset; the Boilys supply the pole and bait (no permit necessary), and you only pay for what you catch—about 30¢ per inch, and the fish run 9 to 12 inches. They'll clean, cut, and pack the fish for you, and some local restaurants will even cook it for you. If you opt for a more passive activity, buy a handful of fish pellets for 25¢, toss them on the water, and watch the greedy trout jump.

Where to Dine

L'ATRE, 4403 chemin Royal, Ste-Famille. Tel. 418/829-2474.

Cuisine: QUEBECOIS. **Reservations:** Required off-season; recommended for dinner and on weekends July–Aug.

$ Prices: $16 minimum per person at lunch, $26 at dinner; fixed-price meals $28.50–$38. AE, MC, V.

Open: July–Aug, lunch daily noon–3pm; dinner daily 5:30–10pm. Sept–June, usually dinner daily 5:30–9:30pm by reservation only.

If you'd like to have someone reap and prepare the bucolic wealth of Ile d'Orléans for you, go to L'Atre (the name means Fireplace)—or rather, let L'Atre come to you. Park in the lot marked by a sign, then wait for the horse-drawn carriage to come from the restaurant. The short carriage ride is free, although you may want to tip the driver. You'll be deposited at a charming old Québécois house with rough board floors, rustic decorations, and a marvelous view of the river and the northern shore, with the Laurentians in the distance. The menu is short but to the point, touting good Québécois cooking such as *soupe aux légumes et fines herbes* (vegetable soup flavored with herbs), or perhaps *cretons* (Québécois pork pâté) or *pâté de foie gras* (goose liver pâté); then there's *boeuf en cocotte* (beef stewed in red wine), *tourtière* (Québécois meat-and-game pie), or roasted Cornish game hen with fresh asparagus. For dessert you can have maple-sugar pie, or island-grown fresh fruit. Wine and beer are served. There is a minimum of $16 to dine here at lunch, $26 at dinner—well worth the investment. Half portions are available for children.

ST-PIERRE

A "big city" by Ile d'Orléans standards, St-Pierre, 12 miles (20km) from Ste-Famille and only a mile from the bridge, has grown to a population of 2,000 (location is everything, it's said, and this village is closest to the bridge). It is best known for having the island's oldest church (1717) and for sheltering thousands of migrating snow geese, Canada geese, and ducks in the spring. They produce quite a sight—and sound. If you visit the church, be sure to visit the large handcraft shop in the back, open from May through October. It's behind the altar, which is even older than the church (1695), and sells pottery, beeswax candles, dolls, scarves, woven rugs, blankets, "scuffies," and much more. Services are no longer held in the church.

When you head back to Québec City, you'll have a fine view of Montmorency Falls from the Ile d'Orléans bridge.

Where to Stay

LE VIEUX PRESBYTERE, 1247 place Mgr. D'Esgly, St-Pierre, PQ G0A 4E0. Tel. 418/828-9723. 5 rms (1 with bath).

$ Rates: $40–$60 single; $47–$69 double. Extra person $15. Children 8–15 $10; younger than 8, free. MC, V. **Parking:** Free.

Down the hill from the historic church, Le Vieux Presbytère, which once served as its rectory, has a row of five dormer windows framed by a chimney at each end, country ambience and decor, a cozy sitting room (with a TV), a sun porch overlooking the St. Lawrence River and Beaupré coast, and picnic tables in the backyard. The rooms are comfortable (no. 2 is particularly so), and one has its own bath, while the other four share 1½ baths. The owners love animals, so don't be surprised to see goats, chickens, and the occasional buffalo (not in the house, of course). The inn, which has a gift shop and rents bicycles, is open year-round. Mont Ste-Anne is 25 minutes away.

THE SOUTHERN BANK

Several towns on the southern bank of the St. Lawrence are within easy range of a day's excursion, and in good weather the beautiful views of the river and its islands are by themselves worth the drive. Road-tripper that I am, however, I highly recommend overnighting in the area. There are some memorable inns, a couple with outstanding dining rooms (read on). You might want to make your final destination the artisans' village of St-Jean-Port-Joli, or, if you have time, Kamouraska, one of the southern shore's oldest settlements.

For the first 20 miles of the drive, Ile d'Orléans will be off to the left—a fertile garden in midstream, with the Laurentian Mountains on the north bank as a compelling backdrop.

GETTING THERE By Car I recommend taking Autoroute 20 as far as St-Michel (or Beaumont, if you want to see a picturesque old mill), then pick up Highway 132 east for the slightly slower scenic drive. You can return by the faster autoroute if you choose. Both roads follow the riverbank fairly closely.

ESSENTIALS The **area code** is 418. The **Montmagny Tourist Office,** in the historic Manoir Couillard-Dupuis, 301 bd. Taché est (tel. 418/248-9196; fax 418/248-1436), is open Monday through Friday 8:30am to 4:30pm. It's in a little park with a pleasant walkway beside the river. The **St-Jean-Port-Joli Tourist Office,** in the center of town at 7 av. Gaspé est (tel. 598-3747), is open in summer daily 9am to 8pm, in May and early September daily 9am to 5pm; it's closed the rest of the year. There is also a **seasonal tourist office** (summer only) in the town of St-Pascal-de-Kamouraska (tel. 492-9552), adjacent to Kamouraska.

MONTMAGNY

The first big town you'll come to is Montmagny, a farming and industrial center, with a population of about 12,000. From here in summer, you can fly or take a boat out to **Grosse Isle,** the Ellis Island of Canada. Parks Canada is in the process of transforming it into a powerful reminder of one period in the country's history, when 4.5 million people immigrated to Canada via Québec. Thousands with cholera or typhoid fever were quarantined on the island from 1832 to 1937; 4,000 were buried here. Some 300,000 Irish immigrants alone came through here in 1847 and 1848. A small train with a guide carries visitors through the island and makes stops along the way.

Offshore from Montmagny lie the **South Shore Islands,** known best as a wildfowl hunter's paradise. There are six islands in all, the largest being two islands joined by an isthmus: Ile aux Grues (Cranes' Island) and Ile aux Oies (Geese Island). A ferry goes out to the Ile aux Grues from Montmagny.

You can get excellent background information on both the immigrants and the birds by visiting the new **interpretation center** in Montmagny, which houses numerous exhibits and a theater.

If shopping ranks high on your list of things to do, Montmagny has an elegant but not outrageously priced shop called **Boutique Jean Grenier,** at 61 St-Jean-Baptiste ouest, near Café Renoir, which sells clothing, jewelry, and some gift items.

Where to Stay and Dine

CAFE L'EXPRESS, 11 rue St-Jean-Baptiste est. Tel. 418/248-8158.
   Cuisine: FRENCH/MODERN. **Reservations:** Required.
$ Prices: Four-course table d'hôte dinner $20–$30.
   Open: Summer and winter, dinner Tues–Sun 6–10pm; spring and fall, dinner Wed–Sat 6–10pm.

Owner/chef François Morin and his wife Lucie have created a tiny pocket of culinary perfection and exploration in Montmagny. Morin calls his food "petite moderne cuisine," but the quantity you'll consume by the time the last course comes around will be grande, and it's not so modern as to be questionable. You'll start off with an assortment of appetizers (chicken pâté and pork routlette with crackers and candied carrots and onions perhaps), then continue with a choice of soup (I had cream of fiddlehead fern), a main course (mine was salmon), dessert (three perfect balls of homemade ice cream with butter cookies), followed by chocolate truffles. There are only six booths in the whole ingenious little place, so you have to reserve a seat. Blues and jazz play softly in the background. It's licensed, and there are magazines for solitary diners to read.

CAFE RENOIR, 43 St-Jean-Baptiste ouest. Tel. 418/248-3343.
  Cuisine: FRENCH/QUEBECOIS. **Reservations:** Not required.
  $ Prices: Appetizers $3.50–$8.75; main courses $6.50–$18; fixed-price four-course dinner $19–$27. AE, MC, V.
  Open: Lunch Tues–Sat 11am–2pm; dinner Tues–Sun 5–10pm; brunch Sun 11am–2pm (May–Aug only).

Café Renoir offers large servings of tasty dishes at reasonable prices in intimate surroundings. For lunch, consider quiche Lorraine, a ham-and-cheese croissant, a bagel with smoked salmon and cream cheese, or pasta. For dinner, order a mussels casserole or chef salad to start, followed by the soup of the day and filet of sole with asparagus, a seafood crêpe, or chicken pâté with a cream sauce—and save room for dessert. Sunday brunch, available May through August only, features enormous omelets and crêpes. There's something to suit every taste here. Owner Jean Grenier (who also owns the boutique mentioned above) admits that the café got its name because "the works of Renoir give me goose bumps"; prints of works by the master are prominently displayed.

Next door to the café and under the same ownership is modern and somewhat kitschy Le Tandem bed and breakfast (tel. 418/248-7132; on Monday, 418/248-5511).

MANOIR DES ERABLES, 220 bd. Taché est (Rte. 132), Montmagny, PQ G5V 1G5. Tel. 418/248-0100; fax 418/248-9507.
  Cuisine: FRENCH. **Reservations:** Recommended.
  $ Prices: Breakfast $3–$7.50; lunch appetizers $3–$6, main courses $7.50–$18; four-course dinner $30–$39, eight-course (three-hour) dinner $54. AE, DC, DISC, MC, V.
  Open: Breakfast daily 7:30–10am; lunch daily 11:30am–2pm; dinner daily 6–8:30pm. **Closed:** Sun lunch Nov to mid-Apr.

Since 1975, Lorraine and Renaud Cyr and now their children, Jean and Johanne, have welcomed guests to their stately inn (1812) and splendid dining room lit by sparkling chandeliers. Here, sumptuous meals are served on sterling silver. The menu changes daily and the choice is vast: Appetizers include smoked trout, mussels with anise, and asparagus spears with hollandaise sauce; and main courses include filet of beef in pink pepper sauce, duck with rum and raisin sauce, salmon with shrimp sauce, and ragoût with lobster and scallops. Wines range in price from $20 to $960 (the 1973 Château Pétrus). The full French breakfast includes crêpes or eggs.

Manoir des Erables, part of the Relais & Châteaux chain, is equally well known as an elegant inn, with 19 rooms and five suites (all with bath). Unfortunately, only a few of the large Victorian bedrooms remain due to a fire in 1982; the rest are modern. Suites have fireplaces and whirlpool baths, and there are nine hotel-style units behind the main house. Eight rooms in a stone house on the property, the Pavillon Collin (1867), are air conditioned. Rooms start at $60, single or double May through October ($50 off-season), and these are a particularly good value; suites cost $135 or $175 ($114 or $148 off-season). Packages are available on a double-occupancy basis and include breakfast, dinner, and golf, or a visit to Grosse Isle National Park.

L'ISLET-SUR-MER

About 10.5 miles (17km) east of Montmagny, this fishing village is a good spot to see the migrating geese. In years past, it produced sailors who roamed the world, among them an Arctic explorer named Joseph-Elzéar Bernier, who claimed the Arctic islands for Canada. Bernier, who became a captain at the tender age of 17, made 269 voyages and crossed the Atlantic 45 times. In 1874, he did it in 15 days and 16 hours—quite a feat in those days.

What to See and Do

NOTRE-DAME-DE-BONSECOURS, rue des Pionniers est, in the heart of town. No phone.

The pretty church in the center of town, half a block from the museum, was built in 1768 and beautifully restored in the 1940s. The pristine white interior gleams with gold-leaf trim. Pews and floor are of naturally finished wood, and the stations of the cross are bas-relief wood carvings done by Médard Bourgault.

Admission: Free.
Open: Usually daily 9am–6pm.

MUSEE MARITIME BERNIER, 55 rue des Pionniers est. Tel. 418/247-5001.

⭐ Dedicated to the town's favorite son, Capt. Joseph-Elzéar Bernier, the museum relives the area's nautical history from the 17th century forward. The museum, housed in a former 19th-century convent, has three floors of exhibits—my favorites deal with catastrophes at sea—and a shop. Behind it, you can also admire a hydrofoil and tour through the icebreaker *Ernest Lapointe,* which was built in Canada before World War II and used until 1978. There are several tours of the museum a day during summer; if you don't take one, ask at the front desk for English translations for the exhibits. The monument in front of the museum shows Bernier's explorations on a globe, above which is the aurora borealis.

Admission: $3.25 adults, $1.50 children, $7.50 families.
Open: May 20–Sept 29, daily 9am–6pm; Sept 30–May 19, Tues–Fri 9am–noon and 1:30–5pm.

Where to Stay

LA MARGUERITE, 88 rue des Pionniers est., L'Islet-sur-Mer G0R 2B0. Tel. 418/247-5454. 5 rms. A/C

$ Rates (including full breakfast): $45–$85 single; $53–$95 double. MC, V.
Parking: Free.

When you drive through town, you're bound to notice the striking white house with multiple dormer windows with yellow trim and black wrought iron on the porch. It's just down and across the street from the Bernier Maritime Museum, and is named for one of the owners, Marguerite Caron. She and her husband, Denis, who speaks English (she doesn't but communicates animatedly without it) are happy to help you plot out activities, suggest places to eat, or provide two bikes or cross-country skis. The rooms are modern and comfortable, with good reading lights and lots of built-ins; three rooms have queen-size beds, and the others have two twins. Guests share a refrigerator. The house, which dates from 1808 and is strictly no-smoking, has a TV room and a sitting room with a fireplace, where you can mix with other guests or chat with the hosts. There's a pretty garden out back.

ST-JEAN-PORT-JOLI

St-Jean-Port-Joli is famous throughout Québec for the quality of wood carving that has been done here for generations. It started in the early days when much of the decoration for local churches was done in carved wood. But in the 1930s, three brothers—Médard, André, and Jean-Julien Bourgault—began carving other things as well: bas-reliefs, statues, figurines, even portraits. The fame of the Bourgault brothers spread and attracted dozens of students. A wood-sculpture school was established, and the town became the heart of Québec's wood-carving artistry. Today the town has about 100 working artists and is filled with their shops and galleries; besides carved wood, you'll find sculpture in stone, textiles, and pottery.

Of all the towns along the southern bank, St-Jean-Port-Joli is well organized to welcome travelers and help them find their way around. Drop by the tourist information office to see the realistic reproduction of the town, which will help you get your bearings.

What to See and Do

Once you've marveled at the masterpieces in the museum and the church (see below), wander into some of the wood-carving shops in town for a look at what's being done today. The artists are usually happy to talk with you and to show you their studios. Most work on commission, and you're welcome to order a piece from them. Among others, visit sculptors Benoi Deschênes (tel. 418/598-3707) and Maurice Harvey (tel. 418/598-3846), both of whom speak English, as well as Mme Edmond Chamard and her school of weavers. Madame Chamard sells examples of the best weaving in the region, and other crafts, at her shop on the way out of town to the east (tel. 418/598-3425).

MUSEE DES ANCIENS CANADIENS, 332 av. de Gaspé ouest. Tel. 418/598-3392.

This is the place to start to learn about and see the works of the Bourgault brothers (Médard's religious sculptures and nudes, André's country folk, and Jean-Julien's religious sculptures and furniture) and of other artisans in the village. Look for the work of Nicole Deschênes Duval, Jean Leclerc, and Pierre Cloutier (a talented student of Jean-Julien Bourgault, he died tragically at age 39 of a brain tumor), and the boats carved by members of the Leclerc family. There's a craft shop on the premises.

Admission: $3.50 adults, $1.50 children 6–12.

Open: May–June, daily 9am–6pm; July–Aug, daily 9am–9pm; Sept–Oct, daily 9am–5pm; Nov–Apr, by reservation only.

CHURCH OF ST-JEAN-PORT-JOLI, 2 av. de Gaspé ouest. Tel. 418/598-3023.

Another place to admire the artistry of the town's citizens is in its church, built in 1779–81 and decorated by the early wood-carvers, including the Bourgaults, who created the pulpit in 1937. A more recent artistic addition is the 17-piece crèche, each piece carved by a different local artist and presented to the church in 1987. Buried in the church under the seigneurial pew is the author of *Anciens Canadiens,* Philippe-Aubert de Gaspé, who was the last in a line of lords of the manor (*seigneurs*) who had owned and governed St-Jean since 1633. Look for the nearby plaque that lists all of the town's seigneurs, back to the time when the original land grant was made by the king of France.

Admission: Free.

Open: June 27–Labor Day, daily 9am–5pm; Labor Day–June 26, Mon–Fri 9am–5pm (or by reservation).

SEIGNEURIE DES AULNAIES, 525 de la Seigneurie, St-Roch-des-Aulnaies. Tel. 418/354-2800.

If you'd like nothing better than to spend a couple of hours in a scenic spot, drift this way. You can stroll and admire the wonders of both nature and human beings. Thanks to a micro climate, the grounds are filled with chestnuts, black locusts, and redwoods—trees not ordinarily found in this area. The working flour mill dates from 1842, the victorian manor house from 1850. You can tour both (the guides at the house portray the lord and lady of the manor), or just bask in the beauty of this spot by the Ferrée River. The fresh-ground flour is for sale. The seigneurie is 9 miles (14km) east of St-Jean-Port-Joli.

Admission (including tours): $3.50 adults, $1.25 children under 12.

Open: Late June–early Sept, daily 9am–6pm. Six tours of mill and manor house given daily starting at 9:30am.

Where to Stay

AUBERGE DES GLACIS, 46 route Tortue, C.P. 102, St-Eugène, PQ, G0R 1X0. Tel. 418/247-7486. 10 rms (all with bath).

$ Rates: $60 single; $70 double. Extra person $10. Package for two, including supper, $113.50. AE, MC, V. **Parking:** Free.

About 7½ miles (12km) west of St-Jean-Port-Joli, this stone mill-turned-inn is a little piece of heaven beside a stream in the woods and dates from 1841. The only noise you'll hear is the sound of crickets and gurgling water. Each room has special touches—a spinning wheel or walking stick, for instance—that hark back to another century, but has all the modern comforts. One room has a television; another is perfect for families, with a bedroom, separate sitting area, and loft with two single beds and a ladder leading to it. Baths in three rooms have both tub and shower (otherwise you get a shower). The innkeepers, Gilbert Rainville and Lina Bourgault, make a stay here special; they rent cross-country skis, and they have plans to rent bikes. Horseback riding is available a couple of miles away. Gilbert is bilingual, and Lina, who speaks only French, is the excellent chef who has transformed the inn's dining room into one of the best in the region. The menu changes daily, but includes such dishes as house pâté de foie gras, asparagus soup with sherry, filet of sole with capers, and crabmeat salad. And you can usually get some homemade mustard and relish. A three-course lunch is $7 to $9; a three-course dinner, $18 to $21.

AUBERGE DU FAUBOURG, Rte. 32, St-Jean-Port-Joli, PQ, G0R 3G0. Tel. 418/598-6455, or toll free 800/463-7045. Fax 418/598-3302. TV TEL 100 rms (all with bath), 8 cottages.

$ Rates: Late June–early Sept, $47–$82 single or double; $84 cottage. May–late June and early Sept to mid-Oct, $46–$61 single or double; $84 cottage. AE, MC, V. **Closed:** Mid-Oct to Apr. **Parking:** Free.

The last time I stopped by the Auberge du Faubourg, I met an American couple on their honeymoon. They loved the place. Even from the highway, it looks delightful, with white A-frame units with jaunty red roofs, and well-maintained grounds with picnic tables and a landscaped pool, all set dramatically against the river. The standard rooms are large with a picture window; and though there's no air conditioning, you can count on a steady breeze from the river. Each room has a full bath, and each cottage, which accommodates two to five people, has a deck facing the river. The cottages and rooms beside the river are the most expensive. The inn has a restaurant, coffee shop, bar, and shop. The reception desk is open daily from 7am to 11pm.

Where to Dine

CAFE LA COUREUSE DES GREVES, 300 rue de l'Eglise (Hwy. 204). Tel. 418/598-9111.
   Cuisine: CONTINENTAL/QUEBECOIS. **Reservations:** Not required.
$ Prices: Appetizers $2–$6; main courses $3.50–$13.25; fixed-price three-course meal $5–$10. AE, MC, V.
   Open: Daily 8am–midnight.

A popular place for lunch, supper, or coffee and pastries is the Café La Coureuse des Grèves, a block along Highway 204 from the junction with 132. The café's strange name comes from a legend, which tells of a beautiful maiden who would run ("la coureuse") along the river's shores ("des grèves"), tempting fishermen and mariners. She might be caught in a net, but no man could hold on to her for more than a single evening. The café is a magnet for local artists and crafts workers (and everybody else, for that matter), and so the decor of carved-wood tables and stained-glass lamps is appropriate. The portions here are plentiful, and menu items include pastas, chicken, steak, seafood, vegetarian dishes, kebabs, a cheese plate with fresh fruit, soup and fish chowder, and the house special—a spinach, rice, and cheese square. Every month there are changing exhibitions of the works of local artists, and the upstairs bar gets lively with local musicians on Thursday evenings.

LA BOUSTIFAILLE, 547 av. Gaspé est. Tel. 418/598-3061.
   Cuisine: QUEBECOIS. **Reservations:** Recommended.
$ Prices: Appetizers $3–$5; main courses $5–$10; fixed-price four-course lunch or dinner $8–$19; dinner and theater (including tax and tip) $35; breakfast $3–$10.
   Open: Mon–Sat 8am–midnight, Sun 7:30am–midnight. **Closed:** Mid-Sept to mid-May.

There's home cooking galore at La Boustifaille, which provides the "dinner" part of La Roche à Veillon summer theater, both operated by the Tourist Commission of Port-Joli. The large menu (ask for the English version) tempts with homemade pea, cabbage, vegetable, or barley soup; Québec-style meat pie; quiche; fresh salmon pie with egg sauce; seafood casserole; meatballs and pork stew in a brown sauce; chicken pot pie; and homemade breads and pies. Breakfast includes bran and raisin muffins, homemade breads, French toast, pancakes, eggs, toast, bacon, and sausage. If you arrive after 8am, expect to wait on line. Theater productions are comedies, in French.

KAMOURASKA

Travel a bit farther up the coast along Highway 132 to the picture-postcard village of Kamouraska, 40 miles (65km) east of St-Jean-Port-Joli. One of the southern shore's oldest settlements, it has a fine local museum with a small handcrafts shop, lots of charming old houses, riverbank panoramas, photographic angles to discover, and a couple of bed-and-breakfasts should you choose to linger here.

RIVIERE-DU-LOUP

The commercial, governmental, and educational center for the surrounding region, Rivière-du-Loup is also known for its colorful sunsets and its health spas. The **tourist information office,** at 189 bd. Hôtel-de-Ville (tel. 418/867-3015), is open daily from late June to early September, from 8:30am to 7pm; other times of the year, Monday through Friday from 8:30am until 5pm.

Should you need a diversion, the best place is the **Château de Reve,** an amusement park with fun for the whole family: miniature golf, bumper cars, a restaurant, and more. It's on the river near the ferry dock: Follow Highway 132 through town until you see signs for the ferry operated by Clarke Transport Canada. But instead of following the ferry road, take the road down the hill just to the right of it. This'll take you to the park, and if you keep on going, to the ferry as well.

THE FERRY TO ST-SIMEON

The car-ferry across the St. Lawrence, run by Clarke Transport Canada, operates between late March and early January, weather permitting, with eight sailings a day in high season in each direction. Fares are $7.50 for adults, $3.55 for children 5 to 11, $19.20 for a car, one-way. The larger boat takes 100 cars and 450 passengers on the 1½-hour voyage. Arrive half an hour before departure. For the latest information, call 418/862-5094 or 418/862-9545 (418/867-1410 after hours) in Rivière-du-Loup, or 418/638-2856 in St-Siméon, on the northern shore. (*Note:* If you're staying the night in Rivière-du-Loup and you just want a chug on the river, take the "sunset cruise," across and back for only $9, offered on a sailing late in the day from mid-June to the end of August.)

At the Yacht Club near the ferry dock, **La Societé Duvetnor** (tel. 418/862-1660) offers three-hour guided tours to the Lower St. Lawrence Islands, known principally for birdwatching. It's possible to stay on one of the islands in a converted lighthouse.

CHARLEVOIX

If you're headed back to Québec City instead of continuing on the Gaspé Peninsula (see below), rather than retrace your steps, follow the road that hugs the northern bank of the St. Lawrence River and takes you through the Charlevoix region, a favorite getaway for Québec City residents, who enjoy the wonderful inns and dining rooms there.

Consider an overnight at **Auberge des Peuplers (the Poplar Inn),** 381 St-Raphaël, Cap-à-l'Aighe (tel. 418/665-4423, fax 418/665-3179); or a meal at **Auberge des Trois Canards,** on the highway in Pointe-au-Pic (tel. 418/665-3761), or **Auberge des Sablons,** 223 Chemin les Bains, St-Irénée (tel. 418/452-3594).

10. TO THE GASPE

The southern bank of the St. Lawrence sweeps north and then eastward toward the Atlantic. At the river's mouth the tongue of land called the Gaspé Peninsula juts into the Gulf of St. Lawrence. The Gaspé is a region of rugged hills, forests blanketing hundreds of square miles, and a dramatic rocky coastline. It's pointless to compare the Gaspé to the Maine coast or Big Sur, for nowhere else will you find the same tidy fishing villages nestled in coves cut from the rocky coast, or lumber towns at the mouths of rivers brimming with salmon. It's a land for hikers, hunters, fishers, bicyclists, campers, and anyone who loves the outdoor life. You don't need much equipment to enjoy the Gaspé, however, as almost every little town has a modest but clean and comfortable motel and a restaurant to match. As for things to do, the breathtaking scenery will absorb your interest every minute of the way, and the picturesque villages, each with its church spire towering over a cluster of simple houses, provide interesting variations to the scene.

Coming from Québec City, you can plunge right into the outdoor life by taking a short detour from Highway 20 on Highway 289 to the **Wilderness Center** at Pohenegamook, by the beautiful lake of the same name. It's about a 30-mile detour, one-way. On Highway 289 you'll pass through the Parke Game Reserve (camping and picnicking) and then the town of St-Eleuthère. In Estcourt, at the end of the road, turn left and follow the road that starts beside the church to get to the center. Children's camps, nature walks, sailing, canoeing, and fishing are on the program here, and you can enjoy them even if you have no camping equipment. There are family chalets for rent, and camping. To reserve a chalet or to get more information, phone 418/859-2405, or toll free 800/463-1364 in Québec, or write to: Base de Plein-Air-de Pohenegamook, Ville Pohenegamook, PQ, G0L 2T0. Ask about the new health resort, which offers aquatic relaxation, easy gymnastics, and soothing baths in peat moss, algae, and oils.

FROM RIVIERE-DU-LOUP TO MATANE

Past Rivière-du-Loup along Highway 132, the country slowly grows more typically Gaspésien. Peat bogs on the river side of the road yield bales and bales of famous Canadian peat moss, shipped to gardeners throughout the continent. Past the town of Trois-Pistoles (the name comes from a French coin, the pistole, and not from firearms) are miles of lush wood-post-fenced fields and low rolling hills. Along the roadside, hand-painted signs advertise *pain de ménage* (homemade bread) and other baked goods for sale. If you're lucky, you can pick up some homemade cretons, Québec country pork pâté, to go with the fresh bread.

Approaching **Bic,** prepare for a photogenic scene. As you come over the hill to the town, the view of the settlement, bay, and islands is a bewitching sight. The **Parc du Bic,** encompasses 14 square miles of bays, caves, capes, rocky points, and hardy alpine plants. The park office is at 365 bd. Ste-Anne, Pointe-au-Père, PQ, G5M 1E8 (tel. 418/722-3779).

Rimouski (pop. 40,000) is the largest city in the region, boasting regional business and governmental headquarters. One gets the feeling of a boomtown, with lots of new buildings going up. The highway skirts the center of town along the riverbank. Hunters and campers pass through Rimouski on their way to the 300-square-mile **Rimouski Reserve,** filled with moose, deer, fish, and small game. It's about 30 miles southeast along Highway 232.

Past Rimouski is the **Musée de la Mer,** 1034 rue du Phare, Pointe-au-Père (tel. 418/724-6214), with exhibitions and interpretation of the region's history, most notably the sinking of the *Empress of Ireland* in 1914, when 1,012 people died. The museum is in the keeper's house at Pointe-au-Père National Historic Site, and the **lighthouse** itself is one of the highest in Canada; 128 steps lead to the top. The museum is open from mid-June to early September daily from 9am to 6pm.

Once you've passed Rimouski, the Gaspé begins in earnest. Some say the highway between Matapédia and Mont-Joli actually marks the boundary of the peninsula proper. The highway's number is 132—the tail end of the road that loops all the way around the peninsula to join itself again at Mont-Joli. Thus the confusing signs: 132 *est* (east) and 132 *ouest* (west). If you choose 132 ouest, go to the end of this section and read backward. Otherwise, on 132 est, read on.

METIS GARDEN

Near Grand Métis is the former Reford estate, now **Jardin Métis** (tel. 418/775-2221), last owned by a lady with such a passion for gardening that even in the relatively severe climate of Gaspé she was able to cultivate a fabulous botanical wonderland: 100,000 plants of 2,500 varieties. It all started in 1886 when the first president of Canadian Pacific bought the land and built the mansion so he could angle for salmon in the Métis River nearby. His niece, Mrs. Reford, inherited it in 1919. By 1929 her army of gardeners had produced, under her guidance, a garden fine enough to get her admitted to the Royal Horticultural Society in London. The provincial government took over in 1962, and you can visit the park June through mid-September daily from 8:30am to 8pm. Admission is $4.25 for adults, $3 for seniors, 50¢ for children not accompanied by their parents, and 50¢ for disabled visitors. A family ticket is $8. Visit the mansion while you're here and learn about Mrs. Reford and the period in which she lived. You can even stay for supper: Meals are served during park open hours.

As you approach Matane, the foothills off to the right of the highway get larger and larger, and roadside communities are farther apart. When you reach Matane, you'll know you're well into the Gaspé.

MATANE

At first Matane can fool you: The highway enters town and passes spick-and-span gas stations and a new shopping center reminiscent of the bustle in Rimouski. But turn right and head up avenue St-Jérôme along the Matane River, and this small city on a salmon river reveals itself. Before you get that far, however, you may want to stop at the **phare** (lighthouse) a short distance before the aforementioned shopping center. The town maintains an **information bureau** here, open daily from 9am to 8pm. The bilingual person at the desk will give you a map of the town, answer your questions, and tell you about the small museum in the next room.

WHAT TO SEE & DO

Matane is a fishing and logging town. If you're here in mid- to late June you may get to participate in the **Shrimp Festival:** Shrimp of excellent quality are caught out in the St. Lawrence. (If you miss the festival, no matter.) Wander up avenue St-Jérôme to the bridge across the Matane River. The modern architecture of the **Hôtel de Ville (City Hall)** is an unmissable landmark. Behind it, on an island in the river, is a beautiful **municipal park** with an open-air theater for summertime evening entertainments, as well as a playground and picnic grove. There's a footbridge to the island near the City Hall.

But even before the island park, right next to City Hall and the river dam, is a fascinating, very Gaspésien sight you won't want to miss. Starting in June and continuing through September, **Atlantic salmon** swim up the Matane River to get to their spawning grounds. The dam, built in the early 1970s, would have blocked their way were it not for the ingenious construction of a "migratory passage," a sort of backdoor through which the salmon could swim. The passage, right beside the dam, simulates the rushing channels a salmon might have to battle when swimming upstream between huge boulders—only here the rushing waters swirl among wood-and-concrete stalls. In the little building at the top of the passage, a plate-glass window in one stall lets you watch the salmon—sometimes up to three feet long and weighing 25 pounds—shoot themselves up the rapids with a single powerful push from the tail. Push the button marked "Anglais" (English) for a short explanation of the whole marvelous phenomenon.

The authorities in Matane monitor the number of salmon that pass through the migratory passage. Their number can vary from 334 to 2,881 in any given year. Some are caught and banded so their movements can be traced. You can fish for salmon below the dam, but you need a license, available in the fisheries bureau across the street from the dam. Otherwise, the fish-packing plant on St-Pierre, at the intersection with avenue Fraser, will sell you some fresh-caught salmon if there's any available the day you're in town. Even if there's no salmon, there will be delicious cod filets (morue) and smoked cod (morue fumé), halibut (flétan), and shrimp (crevettes). For a picnic, take your fixings down to the mouth of the river, on the eastern bank, where there's a nice picnic area right on the St. Lawrence shore.

THE CAR-FERRY

This is your last chance to ferry across the St. Lawrence to the northern shore. After Matane, the river widens to become virtually a sea. The ferry over to Baie-Comeau or Godbout is operated by the **Société des Traversiers du Québec,** takes just under 2½ hours, and costs $8.25 per adult, $4.25 per child 5 to 11, $8.75 for a motorcycle, and $21.50 for a car. You can go across and back the same day for only $12.50 per person. People over 65 years old are charged a child's passenger fare—have identification ready. From mid-June to early September there are two or three daily sailings in each direction, one or two at other times of the year. For reservations, call: in Matane, 418/562-2500; in Baie-Comeau, 418/296-2593; in Godbout, 418/568-7575; or toll free in Québec, 800/463-2420.

WHERE TO STAY & DINE

HOTEL DES GOUVERNEURS, 250 av. du Phare est, Matane, PQ, G4W 3N4. Tel. 418/566-2651, or toll free 800/463-2820. Fax 418/562-7365. 72 rms and suites. A/C TV TEL

$ Rates: $69–$89 single; $79–$99 double; $150 suite. Packages and off-season (Sept–May) discounts available. AE, CB, DC, DISC, ER, MC, V. **Parking:** Free.
The Hôtel des Gouverneurs is on the water and near the harbor. Half the modern rooms have ocean views, and the executive rooms have minibars. The licensed, award-winning dining room serves all meals, with dinner entrées in the $14 to $20 range. The hotel, which is a few minutes from downtown, also has a piano bar called Amadeus, a heated pool, sauna, exercise room, lighted tennis court, windsurfing, volleyball on the beach, a marina, salmon fishing, and a private golf course about a mile away.

MOTEL & HOTEL BELLE PLAGE, 1310 Matane-sur-Mer, Matane, PQ, G4W 3M6. Tel. 418/562-2323. Fax 418/562-3562. 44 rms. TV TEL
$ Rates: $50–$60 single; $65–$75 double. Extra person $10. Children under 12 free. AE, MC, V.
Matane has several motels in the higher price range, the most delightful of which is the Motel & Hotel Belle Plage, not far from the car-ferry dock. The rooms offer private baths and color TVs. Volleyball and games are available, and a beach and hiking are nearby. The combination hotel-motel is on a quiet road; vines cover the porch and climb the walls. Look for the two red spinning wheels at the entrance.

The property has its own salmon smokehouse (you can visit it), the products of which are served in the dining room for lunch or dinner. The menu is table d'hôte, including soup, dessert, and coffee with whatever main course you select: The salmon, at $20 if available, is right up there with boiled live lobster at $24; grilled or poached scallops are less expensive at $19. The dining room has walls of glass overlooking the river, and at first glance you'll think you're actually floating just above the water. After lunch or dinner, wander into the lounge to a seat near the crackling wood fire, lit on any day when there's the slightest suggestion of a chilly breeze.

PICNIC ITEMS

As dining places in Matane are limited, you may want to find picnic fixings. The shopping center mentioned above has a well-stocked supermarket with many exotic items, and wine, beer, and cider. Get your baked goods at the Boulangerie Pelletier, on the avenue des Amours, two blocks from the bridge in the center of town.

STE-ANNE-DES-MONTS

Ste-Anne (pop. 6,000), like Matane, is a fishing town, and if you missed buying fresh salmon there, you might be able to get it here. Try the **Poisonnerie Ste-Anne,** opposite the church and right next to the fishing-boat docks in the center of town. If you have cooking facilities, buy some fresh salmon steaks and poach or grill them yourself.

In Ste-Anne, you'll find a local tourism information booth on Route 132, half a mile past the bridge, and also stores, garages, gas stations, and the other necessary services. Architecture lovers stop at **La Maison Lamontagne,** 707 bd. du Rivage (tel. 418/722-4038), to see the distinctive Regency house, one of the few remaining examples of its style in Québec. There are 45-minute guided tours. Adults pay $2; families, $4.

PARC DE LA GASPESIE

The enormous parks of Matane and Gaspésie, Cap-Chat and Chic-Chocs, cover much of the mountainous land south of Highway 132 from Matane to Anse-Pleureuse, 60 miles up the road. You can spend a day picnicking, hiking, or camping in the Parc de la Gaspésie by turning onto Highway 299 in Ste-Anne-des-Monts and heading for the Gîte du Mont-Albert, 25 miles inland.

The road climbs into the steep mountains called the **Chic-Chocs** (that's "sheek-shocks"), some of which are naked rock at the summits. Back in the mountains, the rivers brim with baby salmon and speckled trout, and the forests hold large herds of moose, caribou, and deer. The **Gîte du Mont-Albert,** Parc de la Gaspésie, C.P. 1150, Ste-Anne-des-Monts, Comté de Matane, PQ, G0E 2G0 (tel. 418/763-2288), has a hotel, cottages, restaurant, and nature center as well as camping and picnicking areas. Trails start from here. Get maps and regulations from the information office on the road before coming to the gîte.

Should you want to stay overnight or even to have a meal, reservations are almost essential as the Gîte du Mont-Albert has acquired an excellent reputation both for the quality of its cuisine and the tranquillity of its accommodations. The large main lodge, white with a black roof, is right in the valley up against the mountains. Rooms for two persons start at $54 in the lodge, at $57 in the cabins ("chalets") next to the lodge. There are a few twin-bedded rooms with shared bath $32. Telephone to hold your room.

The restaurant here is surprisingly elegant for being deep in the forest, and it has cuisine to match this elegance. Breakfast is served between 7:30 and 9:30am. Lunch, from noon to 2pm, is table d'hôte. For about $12 to $15 you can have, say, the soup of the day, ham smoked in the chef's own smokehouse, vegetables, dessert, and coffee. At dinner the table d'hôte still reigns, although your choice of entrée determines the price: Everyone starts with lobster bisque (who wouldn't?) and ends with peach shortcake and coffee. As a main course you can choose among poached cod filet, coq au vin, or grilled salmon with béarnaise sauce, priced from $18 to $23. For reservations, call the same number for rooms, above.

BACK ON HIGHWAY 132

From Ste-Anne, the highway becomes a narrow band of asphalt at the base of a sheer rock wall. Offshore, seabirds perch on rocks, pecking at tidbits in the water. High above the shore, don't miss the many waterfalls that spill from the cliffs beside the highway. Each Gaspésien village resembles the last: a pretty church with a graceful spire, white houses with black roofs that catch the heat of the sun. The setting of each village is unique, though, and gives each a special charm. It's all reminiscent of other northerly areas: Iceland, Norway, British Columbia, or even Alaska.

MONT-ST-PIERRE

Around a rocky point and down a slope, Mont-St-Pierre is much like other Gaspésian villages except for the eye-catching striations in the rock of the mountain east of town.

As you look at the elliptical patterns in the rock, you may notice a strange flying object soaring in the currents that sweep in from the river and up the mountainside. It's a human with wings: The tiny village is one of the most popular hang-glider spots on the continent because of the perfect updrafts. Each year in late July and early August the town holds its two-week **Fête du Vol-Libre (Hang-Gliding Festival)**, when the sky is filled with birdmen and birdwomen who take their ungainly nylon-and-aluminum contraptions up the steep road just east of town to the cross at the top of the mountain. A few minutes of assembly, a harness hookup, the right moment, and they're in flight hundreds of feet above the town, looping and curving as they like for as long as they like, then finally coming down to a belly-landing in the sports grounds behind city hall. For more information, contact the Corporation Vol Libre, C.P. 82, Mont-St-Pierre, Gaspésie (tel. 418/797-2222; fax 418/797-2558).

A batlike metal sculpture near the mouth of the small Pierre River commemorates the town's popularity with winged humans.

FORILLON NATIONAL PARK

At Gros Morne the colored banding in the rocks is spectacular. Soon the road winds into the mountains, up to a rise, down into the valley, and again up to the next. Settlements get smaller, but still there are roadside stands advertising fresh-baked homemade bread and fresh fish. At Petite-Rivière-au-Renard, Highway 197 heads southwest toward the town of Gaspé while Highway 132 continues eastward to the tip of the peninsula. Motels, restaurants, and services line the roadside in Rivière-au-Renard, Anse-au-Griffon, Jersey Cove, and Cap-des-Rosiers before the highway enters Forillon National Park (tel. 418/368-5505).

Chosen because of its representative terrain, the park's 92 square miles capture a surprising number of the features characteristic of eastern Canada. A rugged coastline, dense forests, and rich flora and fauna attract hikers and campers from all North America. On the northern shore are sheer rock cliffs carved by the sea from the mountains. On the south, the Bay of Gaspé has warmer waters than you'd normally find at this latitude because of temperate ocean currents. The park has a full program of nature walks, trails for hiking, cross-country skiing and snowshoeing, beaches, picnic spots, and campgrounds. You must pay a fee to enter and drive in the park ($5.20 per day, $10.40 for a four-day pass, $36.20 for a year-long pass to all the Canadian national parks). Camping fees are $11.45 to $15 per night. As you enter the park, the bilingual attendant will give you maps and information, including a map of the park's trails.

With the approval of the park officials, **Forillon Tours** operates deep-sea fishing trips and boat cruises (tel. 418/892-5629 in summer, otherwise 418/368-2448) from Cap-des-Rosiers harbor seven days a week in the warm months. A guide comes aboard to describe the flora and fauna observed on the cruise. A cruise costs about $12 per adult, $11 per child; a fishing trip (tackle included), $16 and $10, respectively. Reserve in advance.

WHERE TO STAY

Of the park's three camping grounds, the heavily wooded one at **Petit-Gaspé** is the most popular. The one at **Des-Rosiers,** the only one with electricity, is subject to a gentle but persistent breeze from the sea. **Cap-Bon-Ami** is for tents only. For swimming, the beach at Penouille is best because of the warm water in the Bay of Gaspé.

The appeal of Forillon is so strong that you may want to plant yourself as close to it as possible for as long as possible. If that's the case, there are two good possibilities.

HOTEL-MOTEL LE PHARILLON [THE LIGHTHOUSE], 1293 bd. Cap-des-Rosiers, Cap-des-Rosiers, PQ, G0E 1E0. Tel. 418/892-5200. Fax 418/892-5832. 29 rms. TV
$ Rates: $50–$55 single; $65–$70 double. MC, V. **Parking:** Free. **Closed:** Late Oct–early May.
A few miles outside the park, Hotel-Motel Le Pharillon (the Lighthouse) is run by a friendly host, Leopold Gleeton, of Irish ancestry, who has rooms with full baths and one or two double beds. The dining room serves breakfast, lunch, and dinner. Cap-des-Rosiers, by the way, was named by Champlain, who marveled at the wild rose bushes growing here (maybe then, but not now).

LES PETITES MAISONS DU PARC, 910 bd. Forillon, Gaspé Peninsula, PQ, G0E 1H0. Tel. 418/892-5873 in Gaspé, 418/562-8195 in Matane. 28 cottages (all with bath). A/C

$ Rates: Late June–late Aug $480–$580 for six nights for two adults and two children; May–late June and late Aug to mid-Oct $56–$80 per day for two adults and two children. MC, V. **Parking:** Free. **Closed:** Mid-Oct to Apr.

⭐ Tops, if you're willing to spend a week in one place, is Les Petites Maisons du Parc, on Route 132 at Penouille, run by Wellie Gauthier, an impeccably charming host, and his teenage son, Louis François. The well-maintained chalets, with one, two, or four bedrooms and full kitchen and bath with either shower or tub, are actually at two sites about a mile apart. Some are right at a swimming beach (and from it you can walk through shallow water to Forillon's Penouille Beach), and others (the larger ones) on a hillside with decks overlooking the bay. Linens are provided.

GASPE

The town of Gaspé has a momentous place in Canadian history, for it was here that Jacques Cartier stepped ashore in 1534 to claim the land for the king of France. He erected a wooden cross to mark the spot. Today Gaspé is the seat of a bishopric (you can look inside its modernistic wood cathedral, built in 1969), and it is important because of the three salmon rivers whose mouths are here, for the government fish hatchery, and for its deep-water port. It's an important but unprepossessing town with subtle charms.

The large, modern **Gaspésie Museum,** at Jacques Cartier Point on Highway 132 (tel. 418/368-5710), tells the story of Cartier's landing, and the granite dolmens out front are reminiscent of the explorer's native Brittany. You shouldn't miss any of its four galleries (the first on your right houses the permanent exhibits); ask for the English translation of the texts. In the exhibit on women of the region, look for the photo of one with 17 children (seven more came along after the shot was taken!). An old guest register boasts the name of a young visitor named Shirley Temple, dated August 1942. Admission is $3.50 for adults, $2.50 for seniors, and $1.50 for children; children under 11 enter free, and it's $7.50 for a family. In summer it's free for students and seniors. The museum is open late June to Labor Day, daily from 8:30am to 9:30pm; Labor Day to late June, Monday to Friday from 9am to noon and 1 to 5pm, Saturday and Sunday from 1 to 5pm.

WHERE TO STAY & DINE

Word has it that one of the region's best restaurants, **La Belle Hélène,** 135A rue de la Reine (tel. 418/368-1455), just happens to be in downtown Gaspé, not far from the hostelries mentioned below.

AUBERGE DES COMMANDANTS, 178 rue de la Reine (C.P. 479), Gaspé, PQ, G0C 1R0. Tel. 418/368-3355. Fax 418/368-1702. 56 rms. TV TEL

$ Rates: $57 motel single, $64 hotel single; $67 motel double, $74 hotel double. Children under 18 stay free in parents' room. AE, DC, ER, MC, V. **Parking:** Free.

The Auberge des Commandants has 44 hotel rooms and 12 motel units, all with TVs and radios; the motel rooms have no air conditioning. The auberge, which has a dining room and offers dry-cleaning service, looks onto the cathedral in one direction and over the bay in the other. The staff gets high marks for friendliness.

MAISON CARTER, 146 rue de la Reine (C.P. 2261), Gaspé, PQ, G0C 1R0. Tel. 418/368-5332. Fax 418/368-2382. 6 rms (none with bath), 1 apt.

$ Rates (including breakfast): $45–$55 single; $50–$60 double; $80 apt. **Parking:** Free.

I'm a bed-and-breakfast fan, and am particularly happy I found Maison Carter sequestered at the top of a hill, 50 long steps from the street (happily, there's a back entrance). In fact, once you find it, it may become your own secret hideaway. Six pretty rooms share two baths, and an apartment is also available, in which two adults can share a bedroom, living room, and kitchen. The house was built in 1870; the artwork in it is by local artists. Alain Bernatchez is the friendly live-in manager. You can park on the street, just below the cathedral, behind the house.

PERCE

As you wind through the hills and along the water toward Percé, you'll be greeted by the dramatic view of the **Pic de l'Aurore (Peak of the Dawn),** which dominates the northern reaches of the town. Over the hill from the Pic, famous **Percé Rock** and the bird sanctuary of **Ile Bonaventure** come into view. The rock is Percé's most famous landmark and most dramatic accent, and it's especially beautiful when the golden sunlight of late afternoon warms up all its colors.

The town of Percé is not large, and except for a few quiet, well-groomed inland residential streets, it's confined to the highway that winds along the shore. Little private museums, cafés, snack bars, gift shops, restaurants, and motels line both sides of the highway, and young people in bathing suits or shorts and T-shirts give it all a beach-party ambience.

The **information center,** which is right in town at 142 Rte. 132, is open daily from 8am to 8pm in summer (more restricted hours off-season).

WHAT TO SEE & DO

Enjoy the scenery, first thing. Take a picnic up to the roadside rest just north of the Pic de l'Aurore for the view, then take in different views of Percé Rock. At low tide you can walk out to the fossil-filled rock without getting your feet wet by going along a sandbar.

Board a unique glass-bottom catamaran, the ***Capitaine Duval,*** for an underwater view of the fish and marine vegetation in these waters. The cat has a heated lounge, large windows, padded seats, bar service, lavatories, and bilingual crew who are graduates of the Marine Institute. Tours go to Percé Rock, Bonaventure Island (see below), and even Forillon National Park. It departs from the Percé Quai (tel. 418/782-5401 or 418/782-5355).

Marine transportation to Ile Bonaventure is also provided by **Les Bateliers de Percé** (tel. 418/782-2974); disabled access is provided. The excursion motors near Percé Rock, then lands on Ile Bonaventure. A ferry departs the Percé wharf hourly from 8am until 5pm. Admission is $11 for adults, $4.50 for children under 12.

For underwater exploration of the area, contact the **Club Nautique de Percé** (tel. 418/782-5403 in summer, 418/782-5222 in winter; fax 418/782-5624), which can take you to one of a dozen or more dive sites in Percé's submarine park. The water is about 50°F to 64°F (10°C to 18°C) from June through August, and about 57°F (14°C) until mid-October.

Art collectors and nature lovers alike flock to the **gallery** of artist John Wiseman, 4.3 miles (7km) south of town in a gray house with a red roof set off the road. His work pays homage mainly to the feathered creatures of the Gaspé—loons, puffins, owls, morning doves, sparrows, ducks. Summer hours are 9am to 9pm. Call ahead off-season.

The low, green island beyond Percé Rock, **Ile Bonaventure** is a provincial park and bird sanctuary, and its lure is the 25,000 nesting pairs of gannets on it. For a photographic exhibit of the history of the island, visit the **Information Centre** (tel. 418/782-2721), in the Cold Storage Building at the foot of the Percé wharf. Naturalists are on the island to answer questions. Transportation is provided from Percé wharf.

In the center of town, at 145 rue Principale, **Le Chafaud Museum** (tel. 418/782-5100), is in the distinctive warehouse with the sloping roof, almost directly across the street from the tourist information center. Exhibits depict aspects of Percé. If you take a deep breath, you'll get a hint that this used to be a fish warehouse. Admission is $2 for adults, $1.50 for seniors and students, $1 for children 8 to 12. It's open June through September, daily from 10am to 10pm.

The **Parc de l'Ile-Bonaventure-et-du-Rocher-Percé Interpretation Centre,** on l'Irlande Road (tel. 418/782-2240), focuses on the ecology of the Gulf of St.

Lawrence and the natural features of Ile Bonaventure. A 10-minute film of the gannet colonies is shown, and there's a nice bookstore. The unique Lichen Trail in the environs of the center redirects attention earthward. Photographers, note there's a great view of the rock, Bonaventure Island, and the town from here. It's open 9am to 5pm daily from late June through August; there are restricted hours the rest of the year.

WHERE TO STAY
Moderate

HOTEL-MOTEL LA NORMANDIE, C.P. 129, Percé, PQ, G0C 2L0. Tel. 418/782-2112, or toll free 800/463-0820. Fax 418/782-2337. 45 rms. A/C TV TEL

$ Rates: $49–$79 single; $68–$98 double. Packages available. AE, CB, DC, DISC, ER, MC, V. **Parking:** Free. **Closed:** Late Oct–Apr.

Percé's most elegant place to stay is the Hotel-Motel La Normandie, right in the middle of town on the water. The building is of tasteful weathered wood in a simple attractive traditional design. The rooms are all modern, with generous use of light natural wood; 13 oceanfront units were added in 1991. All rooms have bath-shower combination, color TV, and a little sitting area. Rooms on the water side have decks for sitting and taking in the view, and cost more than those on the land side. There is an exercise room and sauna for guests' use.

The Normandie's dining room, open for breakfast and dinner, is well respected for both its food and its tasteful decor. Bentwood wicker chairs and black circular tables keep to the mood of simplicity. The menu is table d'hôte; that is, you order your main course and you get soup, dessert, and coffee included in the price. Both the sautéed scallops, a favorite in these nautical parts, and the salmon, fresh from nearby Gaspé rivers, cost $27, and come with appetizer, soup, dessert, and beverage. Most popular is the lobster in puff pastry au champagne. The view of the water and Percé Rock is very fine. The lounge is open from noon to midnight.

MOTEL MIRAGE DU ROCHER, 288 Rte. 132 ouest, Percé, PQ, G0C 2L0. Tel. 418/782-5151, or toll free 800/463-9011. Fax 418/364-6165. 60 rms. TV TEL

$ Rates: $72 single; $90 double; $102 triple; $112 quad. AE, DISC, MC, V. **Parking:** Free.

Slightly removed from the traffic and activity of downtown Percé, the Motel Mirage du Rocher has its own distinctive style. First off, the rooms are so richly appointed, you'll swear you're in a hotel. Each has restful green colors, a full bath, a balcony or patio, and a view. From the deck, where there is a small outdoor pool, you can see the town, Percé Rock, and the Percé Cathedral. Cocktails are served in the modern, spacious lobby.

LES TROIS SOEURS MOTEL, Percé, PQ, G0C 2I0. Tel. 418/782-2183. Fax 418/782-2610. 57 rms, 2 apts, 1 three-bedroom cottage. A/C MINIBAR TV TEL

$ Rates: $52–$85 single; $69–$125 double. AE, DC, MC, V. **Parking:** Free.

The unpretentious Les Trois Soeurs Motel is a five-minute walk along Route 132 to downtown. The rows of rooms, with the road on one side and the sea on the other, seem to be holding them apart. Several thoughtful conveniences are available, including an inexpensive Laundromat, housekeeping appliances and utensils in some units, and provisions for babysitting. Coffee, juice, and croissants are served in the lobby. From one of the picnic tables on the lawn, you can gaze at the dramatic Pic de l'Aurore (Peak of Dawn), then saunter down to the beach, which is right out front.

Budget

AUBERGE LE COIN DU BANC, Percé, PQ, G0C 2L0. Tel. 418/645-2907. 11 rms (5 with bath), 7 cottages.

$ Rates: $35 single; $45–$50 double; $65–$80 cottage. V. **Parking:** Free.

Five miles north of Percé on Route 132, the Auberge Le Coin du Banc has the feel of a mountain lodge, albeit from a location a few feet away from seven miles of beach.

There are 11 rooms in the inn, five with private bath. The other six rooms share three baths. The decor is country inspired; room no. 5 is particularly nice, with a four-poster bed. There are also cottages on the property, some with fireplaces and all with TVs ("bring as many people as you want"). The rustic dining room, complete with wagon wheels, an upright piano, and two wood-burning stoves, specializes in seafood; the table d'hôte fare is $16 to $28.

L'EXTRA, 222 Rte. 132 (C.P. 373), Percé, PQ, G0C 2L0. Tel. 418/782-5347. 4 rms (none with bath).

$ Rates: $30 single; $40 double. Children 7–10 pay $8, children under 7 $5. No credit cards. **Parking:** Free.

This bed-and-breakfast is filled with whimsical touches: a year-round soft-sculpture Christmas tree, dreamlike masks, and teapots with faces. The upstairs guest rooms share two baths (one with a tub). This is a freewheeling household with a lively breakfast table. Husband-and-wife team, artist Danielle Gagne and Denis Harbour, create an ambience of joie de vivre that you won't want to miss. It's a no-smoking house.

MAISON AVENUE HOUSE, 38 av. de l'Eglise, Percé, PQ, G0C 2L0. Tel. 418/782-2954. 5 rms (one with shower).

$ Rates: $15–$18 single; $20–$24 double. Extra person $4. No credit cards. **Parking:** Free.

On Church Avenue, only a few steps from the church itself, has fine rooms all done in narrow strips of wood—floor, walls, ceiling—back when pretty wood and honey-colored lacquer could be had at a better price. All are very clean, and equipped with washbasins. Bathrooms are in the hall. It's quiet back by the church as all the traffic is on the main highway. Sit out on the porch and soak up the tranquillity. Your host, Ethel Cass, a rare native English speaker from the Gaspé, has been welcoming people here for 50 years.

WHERE TO DINE

LA MAISON DU PECHEUR, place du Quai. Tel. 418/782-5331.

Cuisine: SEAFOOD. **Reservations:** Recommended.

$ Prices: Appetizers $4–$7; main courses $9–$20; table d'hôte $20 or $39. AE, DC, DISC, ER, MC, V.

Open: Late June to mid-Sept daily 11:30am–9pm; crêpes and steaks served in the bar until midnight.

La Maison du Pêcheur makes good use of its location at the end of the wharf. The seaside walls are lined with windows offering views of the bustling wharf activity and, of course, the rock. The decor is subdued nautical with open-beam ceiling, rough-pine walls, and kerosene/electric lights on each table. (Who'd guess this is a former youth hostel?) I recommend the reasonable midday luncheon, a complete meal with a choice of meat or fish entrée for about $10. The table d'hôte meal may include fish soup, seafood crêpe, salmon steak, and a selection of desserts. Wines and liquors are available. The lower-level bar-café, open from 8am to 3am, is a convenient stop for a drink or espresso after a busy day of enjoying the sights.

HEADING EAST & SOUTH

Leaving Percé, Highway 132 heads southeast. The southern shore of the Gaspé, on the Baie de Chaleur, is distinct from the north, with much more farming and commercial activity, fields of wildflowers, and small houses flanked by the day's wash flapping in the breeze. The air is warmer here, and more humid.

WHERE TO STAY & DINE IN PORT-DANIEL

MAISON ENRIGHT, 504 Rte. 132 (C.P. 207), Port-Daniel, PQ, G0C 2N0. Tel. 418/396-2254. 5 rms (none with bath).

$ Rates (including hearty breakfast): $30 single; $45 double. Extra adult $15, child under 12 $10. Guests receive 10% discount starting the third night of their stay. No credit cards. **Parking:** Free.

In Port-Daniel (pop. 2,000), you'll encounter a bed-and-breakfast that makes stopping just for the sake of stopping worthwhile. Maison Enright is a country house (1904) and café, run by the cordial Hamel family. Its five upstairs guest rooms share a large full bath and an additional toilet on the first floor. Two rooms have twin beds, two have a double bed, and one has two double beds. Part of the house's appeal is the enclosed porch, rock fireplace in the living room, and local art (for sale) on the walls. A three-course dinner here costs $13 to $15. The area, particularly pretty in autumn, is popular for trout and cod fishing.

FROM BONAVENTURE TO NEW RICHMOND

Continue east along Route 132 to Bonaventure (pop. 3,000) and the fine **Musée Acadien du Québec à Bonaventure** (Acadian Museum of Québec at Bonaventure), 95 av. Port-Royal (C.P. 730), Bonaventure, PQ, G0C 1E0 (tel. 418/534-4000); it'll be on the right. The museum pays homage to Québec's Acadian forebears and to outstanding Acadians of the present day. Exhibits are sophisticated and well worth a look. Ask for the text in English. It's open late June to Labor Day daily 9am to 8pm; the rest of the year, weekdays 9am to noon and 1 to 5pm and weekends 1 to 5pm. Admission is $3.50 for adults, $2.50 for students and seniors; families, $7.50; children under 6, free.

Almost directly across the street from the museum is a most unique craft shop, **Les Cuirs Fins de la Mer** (tel. 418/534-3821). The name means Fine Leathers from the Sea, and, indeed, every item—skirts, belts, ties, wallets, bags, earrings—is made from fish skin. Quality items; nothing fishy about them.

Farther east, just outside New Richmond (pop. 4,100), is another outstanding museum, one that pays homage to Québec's British heritage. **The British Heritage Centre,** 351 bd. Perron ouest (C.P. 395), New Richmond, PQ, G0C 2B0 (tel. 418/392-4487), with Union Jacks fluttering out front, seems an anachronism in this resolutely French region. Yet it is an impressive tribute, with 20 buildings from the late 1700s to the early 1900s. The Loyalists, the Scots, and the Irish are all represented. Guided tours are available in summer, and the 80 acres and many trails are conducive to strolling. There's a restaurant on the property, along with a children's playground and a beach. Make a day of it. Admission is $3.50 per person, $2.50 for seniors and students, $7.50 for families. It's open mid-June to Labor Day only, daily from 9am to 6pm.

CARLETON

After passing through New Richmond, Highway 299 heads north in Gaspésie Provincial Park to the Gîte du Mont-Albert (see above), and then to Ste-Anne-des-Monts on the St. Lawrence shore. Highway 132, though, continues southeastward as far as Matapédia, where it turns northeastward to take you back to the St. Lawrence at Mont-Joli. Long before Matapédia, but after passing through New Richmond, you'll come to Carleton (pop. 2,650), a pretty port and resort town.

Where to Stay

HOTEL-MOTEL BAIE BLEUE, Rte. 132 (C.P. 150), Carleton, PQ, G0C 1J0. Tel. 418/364-3355, or toll free 800/463-9099. Fax 418/364-6165. 95 rms, 3 suites. TV TEL

$ Rates: $77 single; $90 double; from $100 suite. Extra person $12. Half price for children 2–12. AE, DISC, ER, MC, V. **Parking:** Free.

If upscale accommodation suits you, you'll find it along Route 132 at the Hotel-Motel Baie Bleue. The pleasant rooms have plush carpeting, remote-control TV, good lighting, and firm mattresses. Comfort is foremost here, and with it comes room service. The restaurant, where you can get breakfast and dinner, has fast, personable service; the menu changes daily. The staff at the Baie Bleu is bilingual and helpful. There is an outdoor pool and tennis court on the premises.

Where to Dine

CAFE L'INDEPENDENTE, 215 rte. du Quai, Carleton. Tel. 418/364-7602.

Cuisine: LIGHT FARE. **Reservations:** Not needed.
$ **Prices:** Most items $2.50–$19. AE, MC, V.
Open: Daily 7am–10pm. **Closed:** Oct 11–early May.

Ⓢ For dining in a casual setting that draws a young crowd, head out to the quay in Carleton to Café l'Independente. Its daily three-course table d'hôte menu ranges from $14 to $19. You may order soups, salads, and casse-croûtes quite reasonably. It's licensed.

EN ROUTE TO NEW BRUNSWICK

If you're headed south to New Brunswick, you'll want to cross the western end of the Baie de Chaleur at Pointe-à-la-Croix, where a bridge will take you across to Campbellton, New Brunswick.

Don't make your way to the New Brunswick side, however, without seeing at least one of the top-notch attractions on the Gaspé side of the bay, all within a few miles of the bridge. One is a natural site; another, historic; the third, cultural—an abundance of riches for the visitor.

You can stop first at the Gaspé tourist information center (tel. 418/788-5670) in the Young House (1830) in Pointe-à-la-Croix; there's a gallery upstairs and restrooms in the modern building adjacent to it.

WHAT TO SEE & DO

On Route 132, due east of Pointe-à-la-Croix, you'll first come to **Miguasha Park** (270 Miguasha ouest, Box 183, Nouvelle, PQ, G0C 2E0) in Nouvelle (tel. 418/794-2475), the site of fish and plant fossils 370 million years old, discovered in the cliffs here in 1842; some of the ancient ferns were 100 feet (9m) tall! There is an interpretation center, but because of the fragility of the area, access to the fossils themselves is by guided 1½-hour tour only. They're free, and the park is open June through September from 9am to 6pm.

From Miguasha, there is regular ferry service to Dalhousie, New Brunswick; it costs $12 one-way and can shave half an hour off your trip, especially in summer traffic. I also enjoy the drive around to Campbellton, which is scenic and rural; granted, you risk getting behind a slow-moving truck or car on the winding roads—choose the route that best suits your temperament.

The town of Listuguj is home to the largest Micmac reservation in the Gaspé and of the **Micmac Culture Interpretation Centre,** a private museum in a former monastery that details the way of life of the Micmacs before the Europeans arrived. The boutique sells handcrafts of the Micmacs, Navajos, and other tribes. The center is open daily from 9am to 6pm (tel. 418/788-5034). Admission is $3 for adults, $2 for students and seniors, and $5 for families.

Continuing east on Route 132, you'll quickly arrive at **Battle of Restigouche National Historic Site,** in Pointe-à-la-Croix (tel. 418/788-5676), which commemorates the April 1760 aborted attempt by French troops from Bordeaux to get to Québec City and save the area for France. They were aided by the Micmacs and the Acadians, but the British attacked them in a battle that lasted several hours in the estuary of the Restigouche River, and thus was history written. It was the end of New France in Canada. The modern interpretive center displays parts of the actual hull with still-intact contents of one of the three ships that was sunk (by the French themselves) and lay buried in the river until its excavation from 1969 to 1972. The exhibits bring that daring time realistically back to life. The historic site is open from late June to Labor Day daily from 9am to 5pm. Admission is $3 for adults, $1.50 for students, free for seniors over 65 and children under 6; families, $6.

CHAPTER 11

OTTAWA

It would be silly to compare Ottawa (pop. over 800,000) with such lively and cosmopolitan capitals as London and Paris, but this city certainly possesses a unique and strangely alluring beauty of its own.

First, it has been blessed with a striking natural physical beauty, set high on a bluff above the confluence of the Ottawa, Gatineau, and Rideau rivers, with the gently rolling contours of the Gatineau Hills as a northern backdrop.

On top of such natural assets, the Gothic Parliament buildings brood romantically above the city, reminiscent of a Turner painting; the Rideau Canal cuts a vibrant swath through the city, worthy of any Dutch palette in summer or winter; and Wordsworth would surely have sung of the daffodils in Rockcliffe Park had he seen them.

In short, Ottawa has not yet really been visited by choked downtown streets and that imprisoned feeling so often the hallmark of modern North American cities. You can still see the hills and rivers from downtown.

Where else in North America can you see sentries in scarlet and busby changing guard just as they do at Buckingham Palace, skate and boat on a canal reminiscent of Amsterdam, and wonder at the three million tulips that blaze and sway throughout the city in early May? Where else can visitors ski, fish, and hike through wilderness only 12 minutes away from downtown; watch the dramatic debates and pomp of parliamentary proceedings; and then visit a rustic French inn across the river in Québec? Well, you can do all these things—and more—in Ottawa.

A BIT OF HISTORY From the time European explorer Samuel de Champlain discovered the Ottawa River in the 17th century, the waterway was used by the French and their allies for transporting furs from Michigan to Montréal. The first European settlement was established in 1800 by Philemon Wright, who had migrated from Massachusetts, pioneering the log route to Québec City in the early 1800s.

The Ottawa side of the river didn't really develop until 1826, when it was chosen as the site for the development of a canal to safeguard the transport of troops and communications between Kingston and Montréal as an alternative route to the St. Lawrence, then so vulnerable to American attack. When Colonel By came to construct the canal, the town took the name Bytown. During and after the construction, it grew into a reckless backwoods lumber town where many a raucous brawl broke out among the lumberjack and navy population, especially between the French and the Irish.

In the mid-19th century the two Canadian provinces of Upper Canada (Ontario) and Lower Canada (Québec) were fused into the United Provinces of Canada, but the fierceness of their rivalry continued to such an extent that the legislature had to meet alternately in Toronto and Montréal. Casting around for an acceptable site for the new capital, Queen Victoria selected the brawling village in 1855, probably hoping that its location, right on the Ontario-Québec border, would resolve French-speaking and English-speaking differences.

Her choice was not exactly praised: Essayist Goldwin Smith commented tersely,

WHAT'S SPECIAL ABOUT OTTAWA

The Houses of Parliament
☐ The glorious Gothic buildings where Parliament debates are what makes the city Canada's capital.

The Changing of the Guard
☐ Where else outside of the United Kingdom can you see such a pageant?

Museums
☐ The National Gallery of Art, which provides a walk-through history of Canadian art and spectacular architectural gems like the Rideau Convent Chapel.

The Byward Market
☐ Because it's real—farmers bring their wares and Ottawans shop there for the freshest produce and plants.

Events/Festivals
☐ Canada Day can only really be celebrated in the capital.
☐ The Tulip Festival—an event that can only be matched by a visit to Holland.
☐ Winterlude, when the ice on the canal, the ice sculptures, and the outdoor events put a positive sheen on the whole city.

The RCMP Stables
☐ The training stables for the famous Musical Ride.

Sports Galore
☐ Skiing in the Gatineau.
☐ Cycling along the towpath.
☐ Skating and boating along the canal.

"A sub-Arctic lumber village, converted by royal mandate into a political cockpit," while the American press merely remarked that it was an excellent choice because any soldiers who tried to capture it would get lost in the woods trying to find it.

Certainly, for nearly a century the city languished in provincialism as dull as its gray-flanneled denizens and developed a reputation for sobriety and propriety. Nightlife, then, was something you indulged in across the river in Hull—and even today Ottawa is not exactly the nightlife capital of the world. (It has changed considerably, though; just go to the Byward Market area any night of the week.) Still, even during its early days it managed to throw up some colorful characters, not the least of whom was Mackenzie King (who conducted World War II with the help of his dog, his deceased mother, and frequent spiritual consultations with former prime minister Sir Wilfrid Laurier), and later Charlotte Whitton, Ottawa's mayor in the '50s and early '60s, about whom I have this favorite tale. When she met the Lord Mayor of London, both formally decked out in their chains of office, he bent down and asked permission to smell the rose pinned to her shoulder, saying, "If I smell your rose, will you blush?" To which she replied: "If I pull your chain, will you flush?"

In the 1960s, perhaps because of Canada's newly expressed nationalism and independence of spirit, or perhaps because the government wished to create a real capital, Ottawa changed. The National Arts Centre was built (Hull also underwent, and is still undergoing, a massive transformation), ethnic restaurants multiplied, the Byward Market area and other old buildings were renovated, and public parks and recreation areas were created. And still the process continues with the recent opening of the spectacular new building for the National Gallery of Art and the equally fabulous Museum of Civilization.

1. ORIENTATION

ARRIVING Located about 20 minutes south of the city, the airport has been expanded and revamped. Airport bus service to and from major downtown hotels is operated by **Pars Transport** (tel. 613/523-8880); fare is $9. **Air Canada** (tel.

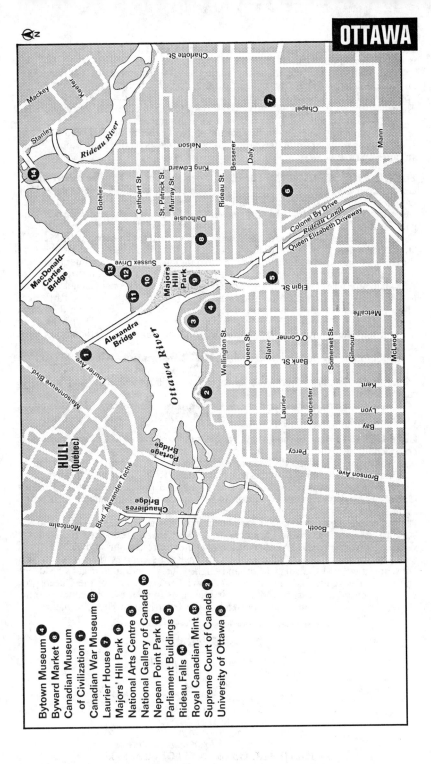

OTTAWA

Bytown Museum ❹
Byward Market ❻
Canadian Museum
  of Civilization ❶
Canadian War Museum ⓬
Laurier House ❼
Majors' Hill Park ❾
National Arts Centre ❺
National Gallery of Canada ❿
Nepean Point Park ⓫
Parliament Buildings ❸
Rideau Falls ⓮
Royal Canadian Mint ⓭
Supreme Court of Canada ❷
University of Ottawa ❻

HULL
(Quebec)

Rideau River
Ottawa River
Rideau Canal

MacDonald-
Cartier
Bridge

Alexandra
Bridge

Portage
Bridge

Chaudières
Bridge

Majors'
Hill
Park

Charlotte St.

Chapel
Mann
Nelson
Besserer
Daly
King Edward
Rideau St.
St. Patrick St.
Murray St.
Dalhousie
Cathcart St.
Boteler

Colonel By Drive
Queen Elizabeth Driveway

Sussex Drive
Laurier Ave.
Wellington St.

Elgin St.
Metcalfe
Queen St.
O'Connor
Bank St.
Slater
Somerset St.
Gilmour
McLeod
Laurier
Gloucester
Kent
Lyon
Bay
Percy
Bronson Ave.
Booth

Mackey
Keefer
Stanley

Maisonneuve Blvd.
Blvd. Alexander Taché
Montcalm

❶ ❷ ❸ ❹ ❺ ❻ ❼ ❽ ❾ ❿ ⓫ ⓬ ⓭ ⓮

613/247-5000) and **Canadian Airlines International** (tel. 613/237-1380) are the main airlines serving Ottawa.

VIA Rail trains come in at the station at 200 Tremblay Rd., at boulevard St-Laurent in the southeastern area of the city. From here buses connect to downtown. For VIA Rail information, contact VIA Rail Canada, Ottawa Station, 200 Tremblay Rd., Ottawa, ON, K1G 3H5 (tel. 613/238-8289 for reservations or 613/238-4706 for schedules), or call your local Amtrak office.

Buses come into the Central Bus Station at 265 Catherine St., between Kent and Lyon. **Voyageur Colonial** (tel. 613/238-5900) provides service from other Canadian cities and the U.S.

TOURIST INFORMATION   The friendly personnel at the **Tourist Information Centre** in the National Arts Centre, at 65 Elgin St. (tel. 613/237-5158 or 237-5159), will answer all your queries daily from 9am to 9pm from May 1 to Labor Day, and weekdays 9am to 5pm (10am to 4pm on weekends), the rest of the year. Free half-hour parking is available to visitors. Parking stubs must be validated at the center.

The **National Capital Commission's Information Centre,** at 14 Metcalfe St. at Wellington, opposite Parliament Hill (tel. 613/239-5000), is also an excellent source of information on Ottawa and the surrounding area. Open in winter from 9am to 5pm Monday through Saturday and 10am to 4pm on Sunday, and from 9am to 9pm daily during the summer. For current events in the National Capital area, call 613/232-1234. The commission also runs the "Info-tent" on the lawn of Parliament Hill, where visitors book free tours of Parliament. It's open in July from 8:30am to 9pm weekdays, 8:30am to 6pm weekends; in August (to Labor Day) 8:30am to 8:30pm weekdays, until 6pm on weekends; and from mid-May to the end of June from 8:30am to 5pm daily.

For information about Hull, contact **Hull Information Kiosk,** Maison du Citoyen, 25 Laurier St., Hull (tel. 819/778-2222), open from 9am to 5pm weekdays in winter, from 8:30am to 8pm Monday to Friday, until 5pm Saturday and Sunday in summer.

Canada's **Ottawa Tourism and Convention Authority,** 111 Lisgar St. (second floor), Ottawa, ON, K2P 2L7 (tel. 613/237-5158), can also be of help.

CITY LAYOUT   One of the great advantages that any visitor to Ottawa enjoys is its compactness. All the major attractions, with one or two exceptions, are clustered downtown within walking distance of each other.

Ottawa is located on the south side of the Ottawa River, which arcs above the city. The downtown area is divided into Centre Town and Lower Town by the **Rideau Canal,** which comes up from Kingston and sweeps past the National Arts Centre and eventually out into the Ottawa River.

In **Centre Town** you'll find Parliament Hill and the Supreme Court, and the National Museum of Natural Sciences. In **Lower Town** are located the National Gallery of Art, the Byward Market (a vibrant center for restaurants and nightlife), and along Sussex Drive (which follows the Ottawa River's course), the Canadian War Museum, the Royal Canadian Mint, and farther out, the prime minister's residence and finally Rockcliffe Park and diplomats' row. The area south of the Queensway, west to Bronson and east to the canal, is known as the **Glebe** and contains some interesting restaurants and clubs, on Bank Street from First to Fifth Avenues.

IMPRESSIONS

Canada could have enjoyed:
English government,
French culture,
and American know-how.
Instead it ended up with:
English know-how,
French government,
and American culture.
—JOHN ROBERT COLOMBO, *OH CANADA,* 1965

North across the river, in Québec, lies **Hull,** reached by the Macdonald-Cartier and Alexandra bridges from the east end of town, and the Portage and Chaudière bridges from the west end. At the end of the Alexandra Bridge stands the curvaceous Museum of Civilization and nearby are some of the city's very best French restaurants and the most lively nightlife action (which continues until 3am). North of Hull stretch the Gatineau Hills and ski country.

Getting around can be a mystifying experience for the visitor. Streets have a habit of disappearing and reappearing a few blocks farther on, while some streets change their names several times. For example, the main street starts in the west as Scott Street, changes to Wellington Street as it passes through downtown west in front of the Parliament buildings, changes again to Rideau Street in downtown east, and finally to Montréal Road on the eastern fringes of town. So carry a map unless you know Ottawa well.

Just a few pointers: The main east-west streets going south from the river are Wellington, Laurier, and Somerset; the Rideau Canal demarcates the east from the west; the main north-south streets starting in the west are Bronson, Bank, and Elgin.

FAST FACTS

Area Code   The telephone area code for Ottawa is 613. The area code for Hull is 819, but it is not needed if you're calling from Ottawa to Hull.

Embassy   The U.S. embassy is located at 100 Wellington St. (tel. 613/238-4470). It's open Monday through Friday from 8:30am to 5pm.

Emergencies   For all life-threatening emergencies (police, fire, and medical), call 911.

Liquor   For conveniently located liquor stores and beer outlets, check the yellow pages. Hours at liquor stores are 10am to 6pm Monday through Wednesday and on Saturday, until 9pm on Thursday and Friday. Hours for beer outlets are noon to 8pm Monday through Wednesday and on Saturday, until 9pm on Thursday and Friday. The legal drinking age is 19.

Post Office   The most conveniently located post office is at 59 Sparks St., at Confederation Square (tel. 613/844-1545), open Monday through Friday from 8am to 6pm.

Taxes   In Ontario there's an 8% provincial sales tax plus a 5% accommodations tax and the national 7% GST.

2. GETTING AROUND

BY BUS   The city is served by about 130 bus routes operated by the **Ottawa-Carleton Regional Transit Commission (OC Transpo).** Pick up a system map at their downtown office at 294 Albert St. (at Kent), between 8:30am and 5pm weekdays. For daily information about schedules, where to buy tickets, etc., call 613/741-4390 from 6am to 11pm. Fares change by time of day and by type of route. The fare for each route is displayed in the front window of the bus. As of 1993, from 6 to 8:30am and 3 to 5:30pm on weekdays green routes numbered 1 to 119 are $2.60; red and black routes numbered 1 to 119 are $2; and all other routes are $1.30. At other times including weekends all routes are $1.30. Tickets can be bought at certain outlets (newsstands, etc.); otherwise you need the exact fare. The transit company also offers a special $3 one-day mini-pass valid after 9am. Ask at their office about where to buy it. All routes in downtown meet at the Rideau Centre.

Bus stops are color coded to indicate the type of route: black for regular routes, red and green for rush-hour routes. Routes start closing down at midnight and there's no service after 1am.

In Hull, buses are operated by the **Société de Transport l'Outaouais (STO)** (tel. 819/770-3242). Transfers between the two systems are obtainable when you pay your fare on the bus.

BY TAXI Taxis as usual are expensive: $2 when you step in and $1.90 for each mile thereafter plus 10¢ per bag. Call **Blue Line** (tel. 613/238-1111).

BY CAR Car-rental prices vary so much that it's impossible to keep track, so always ask about special promotions, weekend rates or advance reservation discounts. Here, just to give you some idea, are Tilden's rates for a compact: $30 daily with 250 free kilometers (150 miles; plus 12¢ for each additional kilometer) and $180 weekly including 1,500 free kilometers (900 miles). There are **Tilden** offices at 226 Queen St. at Bank (tel. 613/232-3536), the airport (tel. 613/737-7023), 1859 Carling Ave. (tel. 613/729-2068), 1150 Cyrville Rd. (tel. 613/745-0408), and in Hull at 531 St. Joseph Blvd. (tel. 819/771-1222).

   Thrifty Car Rental, at Ottawa International Airport (tel. 613/737-4510) and downtown at 328 Kent St. (tel. 613/238-8000), has compacts for $43 a day including 200 free kilometers (120 miles), and $190 per week with 1,400 free kilometers (840 miles). Additional kilometers are 12¢ each. For toll-free information call 800/367-2277.

   Budget Rent-a-Car, 443 Somerset St. West, at Kent Street (tel. 613/232-1526), has compacts for $50 per day including 200 free kilometers (120 miles), or $250 per week including 1,400 free kilometers (840 miles). Additional kilometers are 12¢. There are additional offices at the airport (tel. 613/521-0608) and at the Minto Place Hotel, 407 Laurier Ave. West, Unit 130 (tel. 613/230-0770). Budget's toll-free number is 800/268-8900.

   When driving, remember that Ontario has a **compulsory seat-belt requirement.** Be warned also that you can spend considerable time trying to extricate yourself from the maze of one-way streets, which can make arriving on time at a destination difficult. The **Queensway** (Highway 417) cuts right across the city, also adding to the confusion. It makes the journey from hotels in the west and east ends to downtown quick and easy. The downtown entrance to the highway is at O'Connor Street. Exit the highway at Kent Street for downtown.

   Parking will cost about $3 per half hour, with about a $9 maximum at most local garages. Your best parking bets are the municipal parking lots at 210 Gloucester St., 70 Clarence St., and 21 Daly St.

3. ACCOMMODATIONS

Ottawa accommodations do not come cheap. Luxury and expensive hotels there are aplenty; downtown there are a few moderately priced establishments and apartment hotels where you can get a double for about $75, but there's no real downtown budget hotel. In summer, check in at the university; otherwise it's the YMCA or the youth hostel.

   On the outskirts some full-facility hotels still manage to charge over $100 for a double, and quite frankly, many of the motels are no longer cheap—$60 double for a basic motel room.

   In the section that follows I have picked out as many moderately priced establishments as possible. If it's nightlife and gourmet dining you're after, stay over in Hull or near the Byward Market.

   Note: Add 5% hotel tax and 7% GST to the rates quoted here.

DOWNTOWN

VERY EXPENSIVE

CHATEAU LAURIER, 1 Rideau St. (P.O. Box 474, Station A), Ottawa, ON, K1N 8S7. Tel. 613/232-6411. Fax 613/786-8031. 449 rms. A/C MINIBAR TV TEL

$ Rates: $120–$165 single or double standard room. Weekend rates as low as $99. Summer specials available. AE, DC, DISC, ER, MC, V. **Parking:** $14.

A fairy-tale castle—that's the Château Laurier, one of those venerable hotels, which has attracted kings, queens, potentates, and such celebrities as Marlene Dietrich, Duke Ellington, and Nana Mouskouri. Opened in 1912, this granite-and-sandstone replica of a French château, with its copper roof and cylindrical turrets, is ideally situated at the bottom of Parliament Hill, with many rooms offering views over the Ottawa River to the Gatineaus.

The hotel recently completed a full renovation—all the spacious rooms, with high ceilings and moldings, have been redecorated in mauve and gray or blue and gray with French-style reproductions, including elegant desks, TVs tucked away in armoires, and glass table lamps. The executive Gold Floor has its own concierge and such extras as complimentary bathrobes and wine and cheese.

Dining/Entertainment: Here, you may rub shoulders with the mandarins, most likely in Wildrid's Grill, a small fine dining room on the upper level of Wilfrid's, which has an excellent view of the Parliament buildings. Wilfrid's à la carte menu lists many dishes that combine classic Canadian ingredients with Asian flavors—lamb Musaman curry, stir-fried chicken and tiger shrimp, or fresh Atlantic salmon satay with an orange and chive sauce. Prices range from $11 to $16. In the grill, prices range from $19 for a baked red snapper filet with a light paprika cream sauce to $23.50 for the rack of lamb with mint and herb crust, served on a red currant and green peppercorn sauce. Zoe's Lounge, an atrium-lit room with soaring columns, delicate stucco, and brilliant chandeliers, and accented by elegant plant-filled urns, is a lovely place for afternoon tea, cocktails, and, on Friday and Saturday, for dancing.

Facilities: For recreation, there's a large indoor swimming pool, sauna, steamroom, massage salon, and exercise room.

OTTAWA HILTON, 150 Albert St. (at O'Connor), Ottawa, ON, K1P 5G2. Tel. 613/238-1500, or toll free 800/HILTONS. Fax 613/235-2723. 223 rms. A/C MINIBAR TV TEL

$ Rates: $134–$155 single; $175 double. Extra person $20. Weekend packages available. AE, DC, ER, MC, V. **Parking:** $12.

The Hilton is a lavishly appointed accommodation that emphasizes personal service. The lobby, with its Oriental rugs, rich wood and brass accents, and fluid spiral staircase, provides a dramatic yet gracious welcome.

The rooms, spread over 17 floors, are tastefully furnished with marble-top desks, color-coordinated blue-and-rose decor, remote-control color TV, AM/FM clock radio, and individual climate control. Bathrooms contain hairdryers and full amenities.

Dining/Entertainment: The Carleton Room, exquisitely elegant with its embroidered wallpaper and French provincial decor, offers fine continental cuisine, while the lounge of the same name makes for a pleasant gathering spot.

Services: Same-day laundry and overnight dry cleaning, one-hour pressing, and 24-hour room service and concierge.

Facilities: Indoor heated swimming pool, saunas, exercise room, and games room.

THE WESTIN HOTEL, 11 Colonel By Dr., Ottawa, ON, K1N 9H4. Tel. 613/560-7000. Fax 613/560-7359. 478 rms. A/C MINIBAR TV TEL

$ Rates: $189–$229 single; $199–$239 double. AE, CB, DC, ER, MC, V. **Parking:** $8.50 per day.

Located right in the heart of downtown Ottawa, the Westin has views over the canal and connecting walkways to both the Rideau Centre and the Ottawa Congress Centre.

The rooms are all furnished elegantly in beige and rust, with light oak furniture, brass lamps, and half-poster beds. Ten are specially equipped for the disabled.

Dining/Entertainment: From the oak-and-marble atrium-capped lobby, escalators lead to the two upper floors where the restaurant and other public spaces are located. Daly's is a popular dining spot commanding a close-up view onto the canal and serving three meals a day. Hartwell's, just off the lobby, has a central square bar and is a popular dance spot Monday to Saturday.

Services: 24-hour room service, shoeshine, valet, and concierge.

Facilities: The sixth-floor health club houses an indoor pool, three squash courts, a hot tub, and saunas.

EXPENSIVE

THE ALBERT AT BAY SUITE HOTEL, 435 Albert St. (at Bay), Ottawa, ON, K1R 7X4. Tel. 613/238-8858. Fax 613/238-1433. 130 suites. A/C TV TEL

$ Rates: $125–$145 single; $135–$155 one-bedroom unit for two; $150 two-bedroom unit for two, $160 two-bedroom unit for three. Weekend rates $85 single or double. AE, DC, ER, MC, V. **Parking:** $8 per day.

This conveniently located hostelry is one of Ottawa's best buys, especially for triples or quads. Originally built as apartments, all units are suites with living/dining rooms, fully equipped kitchens and bathrooms, bedrooms with ample storage space, and balconies.

One- and two-bedroom units are available. The smallest is a one bedroom (with a den off the living room), with a sofa bed; a fully furnished living room that opens onto a terrace; two bathrooms; and a kitchen equipped for four, with an electric stove, refrigerator, dishwasher, toaster, coffee maker, kettle, silverware, and dishes. Each bedroom has a push-button phone and a clock radio. Deluxe rooms have microwaves and brass beds. Facilities include an exercise room with a whirlpool and a spacious terrace, laundry facilities, daily valet, and a convenience store open 24 hours. VCRs are available for rent.

CARTIER PLACE AND CARTIER TOWERS HOTEL, 180 Cooper St., Ottawa, ON, K2P 2L5. Tel. 613/236-5000. Fax 613/238-3842. 207 suites. A/C TV TEL

$ Rates: $92–$102 bachelor suite; $102–$112 one-bedroom suite; $133–$143 two-bedroom suite. Children under 14 stay free in parents' room. Weekend and monthly rates available. AE, DC, ER, MC, V. **Parking:** $7.

One of Ottawa's best buys, the Cartier Place and Cartier Towers Hotel offers bachelor (studio) and one- and two-bedroom suites done in gray-pink decor, with large closets. Each unit comes complete with private bathroom, AM/FM radio, and color TV. The kitchens are fully equipped with stove, fridge, dishwasher, linen, dishes, cutlery, and microwave; there's also a laundry conveniently located on every other floor. All units have a separate living area furnished with sofa bed, coffee table, desk, and dining table. Guests also have access to the heated indoor pool with outdoor patio, sauna, and exercise room. An Italian restaurant with an outdoor patio is located off the lobby. The hotel provides daily maid service, dry cleaning, and babysitting.

CITADEL INN OTTAWA, 101 Lyon St., Ottawa, ON, K1R 5T9. Tel. 613/237-3600, or toll free 800/268-1332. Fax 613/237-2351. 450 rms. A/C TV TEL

$ Rates: $90 single; $100 double. Extra person $10. Children under 16 stay free in parents' room. Weekend packages available. AE, DC, DISC, ER, MC, V. **Parking:** $10.

The Citadel has undergone extensive renovations. The lobby has been redone with rock pools, red and mauve wall tapestries, and some interesting chandeliers that look rather akin to sea urchins.

Off the lobby you'll find two very different dining rooms: Le Trianon for nouvelle cuisine in elegant surroundings, and Charlie's for light casual fare every night of the week. At lunch traditional English items feature strongly on the menu. The Rendezvous Lounge provides comfortable surroundings for unwinding, and there's also another restaurant and bar.

The rooms have also been upgraded and include all the facilities expected of a large hotel—color TV, radio, and modern furnishings. For recreation there's an indoor swimming pool.

THE CLARION HOTEL, OTTAWA, 123 Metcalfe St. (at Laurier), Ottawa, ON, K1P 5L9. Tel. 613/237-5171, or toll free 800/4-CHOICE. Fax 613/237-0733. 146 rms. A/C TV TEL
$ Rates: $110 single or double. Extra person $15. Children 18 and under stay free in parents' room. AE, DC, ER, MC. **Parking:** Valet, $10 per day.

Simple, tasteful accommodations and personal service are the hallmarks of the small, six-story Clarion Hotel. The lobby is small and elegant, with burnished brass columns and accents of mahogany and rose marble, while the rooms are decorated in sage green with modern appointments. Most have minibars.

Lily's serves moderately priced continental cuisine, and there's a cozy bar as well. Newspaper and a breakfast of croissants or muffins, fresh fruit, juice, and coffee are included in the price of most rooms.

DELTA OTTAWA, 361 Queen St., Ottawa, ON, K1R 7S9. Tel. 613/238-6000, or toll free 800/268-1133. Fax 613/238-2290. 329 rms. A/C MINIBAR TV TEL
$ Rates: $145–$160 single; $160–$185 double. Weekend packages available. AE, CB, DC, ER, MC, V. **Parking:** $11.

There are two things that you will notice immediately at the Delta Ottawa: first, the skylit lobby filled with trees, flowers, and street-lamp–style lighting, which has obviously been carefully designed to blend with the Sparks Street Mall outside; and second, the friendliness that pervades the atmosphere.

All the rooms are spacious and modern; over half of them have balconies and kitchenettes. The decor is primarily in earth tones. Two squash courts add cachet to the usual recreational facilities of indoor swimming pool, saunas, and exercise room.

Perriers Restaurant-Lounge changes moods with the passing day. It's open from 7am to 1am. During the day in summer the patio is filled with people, and on winter eves the fire is warming. The menu also changes, offering an array of sandwiches, omelets, salads, steaks, and other continental dishes.

MINTO PLACE SUITE HOTEL, 433 Laurier Ave. West (at Lyon St.), Ottawa, ON, K1R 7Y1. Tel. 613/232-2200. Fax 613/232-6962. 418 suites. A/C TV TEL
$ Rates: $125–$140 one-room suite; $155–$170 two-room suite; $225–$240 three-room suite. Children under 18 stay free in parents' room. Weekend rates available. AE, DC, ER, MC, V. **Parking:** $10.

ⓕ FROMMER'S SMART TRAVELER: HOTELS

1. Always ask about special discount rates for particular groups of people, such as corporate personnel, government employees, the military, seniors, students, etc.
2. In Ottawa, always ask about summer discounts and weekend packages, especially during the government recess.
3. The rates quoted here are so-called "rack rates"—the rates quoted to an individual who walks in off the street. No smart traveler today will pay these rates unless business in the city is so brisk that rooms are not available. Always ask about discounted rates. If you don't ask, these rates will not be offered to you. If it's late in the day or there's not much business, quote the price that you're willing to pay. You'll be surprised at how often your quote will be accepted—after all, hotel rooms are perishable commodities insofar as if the room isn't rented it provides no income to the hotel at all.

The Minto Place has more than 400 one- and two-bedroom suites, each very well equipped and attractively furnished. Those units on the upper floors have magnificent views. Each suite's kitchen contains a microwave, electric stove, dishwasher, toaster, coffee maker, and coffee, tea, milk, and sugar, as well as silverware and pots and pans. The spacious living rooms have comfortable couches and chairs, coffee tables, desks, computer-compatible multiline telephones, and dining tables. Bedrooms contain large closets, beds with floral comforters, and chests of drawers. Your bathroom will also have a push-button phone; and there's an additional half bath. Facilities include a fitness spa and pool. Shops and restaurants are conveniently located at the base of the tower.

RADISSON OTTAWA CENTER, 100 Kent St. (at Queen and Kent), Ottawa, ON, K1P 5R7. Tel. 613/238-1122. Fax 613/783-4229. 504 rms. A/C MINIBAR TV TEL

$ Rates: $110 single; $160 double. Extra person $15. AE, DC, ER, MC, V. **Parking:** $6.50.

Just down the street from the Delta Ottawa, the Radisson offers rooms with all the usual appurtenances associated with the chain, plus vanity sinks and mirrors. The decor is color coordinated in blue/beige or brown.

The hotel boasts Ottawa's only revolving rooftop restaurant, La Ronde, on the 29th floor, which affords fabulous views of the Ottawa River and the Parliament buildings. The chef and his food are also celebrated. At dinner, prices range from $20 to $25 for rack of lamb with garlic-and-mint sauce, pheasant filled with truffled goose pâté and served with riesling sauce, or whole Dover sole. The luncheon buffet is a good value at $13.50. So, too, is the brunch buffet at $16.50. Closed Saturday for lunch and Monday for dinner.

Other facilities include Lautrec's, a comfortable piano bar with dancing, and Café Toulouse, a pleasant coffee shop with a very inviting outdoor patio, trimmed with flower boxes, where tables are arranged under a colorful awning. There's also an indoor pool, and a cabana-style bar outside, plus a games room for family entertainment.

Near the Byward Market

LES SUITES, 130 Besserer St., Ottawa, ON, K1N 9M9. Tel. 613/232-2000. Fax 613/232-1242. 241 suites. A/C TV TEL

$ Rates: $140 single; $150 double. Special weekends and promotional packages available. AE, DC, ER, MC, V. **Parking:** $10.

Conveniently located for the Byward Market, Les Suites does indeed have lovely bachelor, one- and two-bedroom suites with fully equipped kitchens, dining alcoves, spacious sitting rooms, attractively furnished bedrooms, and full baths. Microwave ovens are available upon request. Facilities include a heated indoor pool, whirlpool and exercise room. Local telephone calls are free. Other services include valet, concierge, and business center.

NOVOTEL, 33 Nicholas St. (between Besserer and Daly), Ottawa, ON, K1N 7B7. Tel. 613/230-3033. Fax 613/230-4186. 283 rms. A/C MINIBAR TV TEL

$ Rates: $145 single; $155 double. Weekend packages available. AE, DC, DISC, ER, MC, V. **Parking:** $10.

Well located for the Byward Market and Rideau Canal, the Novotel offers rooms decorated in gray/mauve, with light-oak furnishings and such little extras as hairdryers in the bathrooms. Other facilities include an indoor swimming pool, whirlpool, fitness area and a bar/dining room called Café Nicole.

MODERATE

ARISTOCRAT APARTMENT HOTEL, 131 Cooper St., Ottawa, ON, K2P 0E6. Tel. 613/232-9471. Fax 613/563-2836. 36 studios, 162 one-bedroom suites, 10 two-bedroom suites. A/C TV TEL

$ Rates: $90 one-bedroom suite; $140 two-bedroom suite. Special rates available July–Aug and weekends. Children under 12 stay free, except in two-bedroom suites. AE, DC, ER, MC, V. **Parking:** Free.

For a really great bargain—a home away from home—head straight to the Aristocrat Apartment Hotel, and the **Westbury**, at 141 Cooper St. (same mail address and phone), which are linked together and share the same management and same facilities. Between them they offer 208 bachelor (studios) and one- and two-bedroom rose-colored suites with fully equipped kitchens. All the suites have plenty of closet space and all the conveniences, including daily chamber service.

The Westbury has bachelor studios available for $80 single, $85 double, and one-bedroom suites for $105 (extra person $5) (maximum four persons). The Aristocrat contains one- and two-bedroom suites (the latter for six persons maximum), and its rates, noted above, include chamber service and free local calls. Washers and dryers are available. The public spaces have recently been renovated and the two hotels now share a spiffy new marble-and-oak lobby, a restaurant-bar-lounge, and a health club with sauna, whirlpool, and exercise room. Call collect for reservations.

BEST WESTERN VICTORIA PARK SUITES, 377 O'Connor St. (at Gladstone), Ottawa, ON, K2P 2M2. Tel. 613/567-7275, or toll free 800/465-7275. Fax 613/567-1161. 100 suites. A/C TV TEL

$ Rates (including continental breakfast): $80–$95 studio suite; $90–$105 one-bedroom suite. Extra person $10. Special weekend rates available. AE, DC, ER, MC, V. **Parking:** $6 per day.

An apartment-style property, Victoria Park Suites is similar to the Albert at Bay Suite Hotel. The smallest unit offered is a studio-suite with a nicely furnished bedroom/living room, and a kitchenette equipped with fridge/bar, microwave, and china for four. The bathroom has a hairdryer and nonfoggable mirrors. The one-bedroom has a queen-size sofa in the living room, two TVs, two telephones, and full bathroom. Prices include a continental breakfast (muffins, danish, and croissants) to which you help yourself in an attractively furnished room. Other facilities include sauna and fitness room with equipment and a convenience store selling microwavable meals, soft drinks, and the like. Local calls are free.

CAPITAL HILL HOTEL & SUITES, 88 Albert St., Ottawa, ON, K1P 5E9. Tel. 613/235-1413, or toll free 800/463-7705. Fax 613/235-6047. 150 rms and suites. A/C TV TEL

$ Rates: $80 single; $85 double; $90 suite. Extra person $10. Children under 18 stay free in parents' room. AE, CB, DC, ER, MC, V. **Parking:** $8 per day.

Right downtown, the old Beacon Arms Hotel has recently undergone a spanking renovation and been renamed. The lobby now glows with polished wood and the large rooms all have free pay TV, private bathrooms, and pleasant modern furnishings, including a table and chairs. Kitchenettes contain an electric stove, and if you stay a week or more they'll be fully equipped. Some of the rooms are suites containing one bedroom plus a room with a hideaway and a kitchenette. Single rooms are small, but compared to those in most other hotels, extraordinarily spacious.

Facilities include a coffee shop, restaurant, and lounge. At the back of the property, La Bibliothèque, complete with stone fireplace and books as decor, warms to the tones of a piano player on Friday nights. Livingstone's is also the home of Yuk Yuk's Komedy Kabaret from Thursday to Saturday evening.

DORAL INN, 486–488 Albert St., Ottawa, ON, K1R 5B5. Tel. 613/230-8055, or toll free 800/263-6725. Fax 613/237-9660. 37 rms. A/C MINIBAR TV TEL

$ Rates (including full breakfast): $64 single; $74 double. Extra person $10. Children under 12 stay free in parents' room. AE, DC, DISC, ER, MC, V. **Parking:** $4 per day.

The Doral Inn occupies a conveniently located and handsome Victorian brick town house. Its rooms are all equipped with private baths and clock radios; the comfortable furnishings include modern brass beds, desk/drawers, and armchairs. On the ground floor, two handsome bay-windowed rooms serve as a comfortable lounge/sitting room and a breakfast room. Guests also have use of a nearby pool and health club. A great choice for the price.

The restaurant, Costa Brava, serves Spanish/Catalan cuisine with such dishes as pork with figs, paella valenciana, and cod, priced from $13 to $20. At lunch there's a selection of sandwiches, omelets, and pasta.

EMBASSY APARTMENT HOTEL, 25 Cartier St. (at Cooper), Ottawa, ON, K2P 1J2. Tel. 613/237-2111. Fax 613/563-1353. 140 rms. A/C TV TEL

$ Rates: Bachelor studios $73 single, $80 double; one-bedroom apt $81 single, $90 double. Extra person $8. AE, DC, ER, MC, V. **Parking:** $4.

Decorated in color-coordinated earth tones, the sizable and really very lovely rooms offered here come with large double closets and balconies. Bachelor rooms (studios) have separate, fully equipped kitchens and bed-sitting areas. For the price, these accommodations are excellent. On the premises you'll find a study-lounge, dining room for breakfast and lunch, laundry, and fitness room.

LORD ELGIN, 100 Elgin St., Ottawa, ON, K1P 5K8. Tel. 613/235-3333, or toll free 800/267-4298. Fax 613/235-3223. 312 rms. A/C TV TEL

$ Rates: $90 single; $95 double. Extra person $6. Children 18 and under stay free in parents' room. AE, CB, DC, ER, MC. **Parking:** $10 per day.

Only three blocks south of Parliament Hill and across from the National Arts Centre, the Lord Elgin offers one of the city's top values—not surprising, given its sturdy Scottish flavor and demeanor. This dignified stone edifice with its green copper roof was built in 1940 and named after the eighth earl of Elgin, who was governor-general of Canada. The lobby has a quiet, respectful air about it. The place has always attracted guests of substance—Sir Michael Redgrave and Sir John Mills, for example.

The hotel has recently completed an $11 million renovation that has enlarged the rooms and softened the decor throughout. All rooms are spacious, furnished in pastels and fully equipped with color TVs, clock radios, and full-length mirrors. Many of the tile and faux granite bathrooms have windows—a benefit bestowed by the age of the building, which dates back to a more gracious time when windows could be opened. About half of the rooms also have fridges.

The lobby bar is comfortably furnished with wingbacks and club chairs; the Connaught dining room is a light and airy galleria famous among Ottawans for its liver, although obviously it serves other fare.

VENTURE INN, 480 Metcalfe St., Ottawa, ON, K1S 3N6. Tel. 613/237-5500, or toll free 800/387-3933. Fax 613/237-6705. 156 rms. A/C TV TEL

$ Rates: $68 single or double. Extra person $10. Children 19 and under stay free in parents' room. AE, DC, DISC, ER, MC, V. **Parking:** Free.

In the southern part of the city, behind the Museum of Natural Sciences, you'll find the Venture Inn. It's a member of the chain that features country-style Canadian ambience, created by utilizing pine furnishings and brass accents throughout. The accommodations have pine beds, with blue-and-rust patchwork quilts, side tables, Windsor-style chairs, and TV sets housed in pine cabinets. Facilities include an indoor pool.

Two Ottawa Inns

AUBERGE MCGEE'S INN, 185 Daly Ave., Sandy Hill, Ottawa, ON, K1N 6E8. Tel. 613/237-6089. Fax 613/237-6201. 14 rms (10 with private bath, 4 sharing 2 baths). A/C TV TEL **Directions:** From downtown, take Laurier Avenue East and turn left at Nelson Street.

$ Rates: $53–$63 single with shared bath, $60–$70 double with shared bath; $73–$93 single with private bath, $80–$100 double with private bath; $110–$120 deluxe room with Jacuzzi. MC, V. **Parking:** Free.

AN IMPORTANT NOTE ON PRICES

Unless stated otherwise, **the prices cited in this guide are given in Canadian dollars,** which is good news for American travelers because the Canadian dollar is worth 25% less than the American dollar, but buys nearly as much. As we go to press, $1 Canadian is worth 75¢ U.S., which means that your $100-a-night hotel room will cost only U.S. $75, and your $6 breakfast costs only U.S. $4.50.

Here's a quick table of equivalents:

Canadian $	U.S. $
$ 1	$ 0.75
5	3.75
10	7.50
20	15.00
50	37.50
80	60.00
100	75.00
200	150.00

On a quiet street only blocks from the University of Ottawa, McGee's Inn occupies a handsome Victorian home with steep dormer roof. The proprietor, Anne Schutte, has decorated each of the rooms in a distinctive way, often with Peruvian touches reflective of her Anglo-Peruvian upbringing. Room 6 has a brass bed, couch, and desk in a room with carved-wood fireplace. In Suite 10 there's a king-size bed with a pretty lace canopy and a double Jacuzzi. All the queen-size rooms have minibars. Some have Jacuzzis. A breakfast of prunes, fruit, yogurt, muffins, eggs, and cereal is served in an elegant room with a carved cherrywood fireplace, Empire-style sideboard and Oriental-style rugs. No smoking.

CARTIER HOUSE INN, 46 Cartier St. (at Somerset), Ottawa, ON, K2P 1J3. Tel. 613/236-4667. Fax 613/563-7529. 10 rms. A/C TV TEL
$ Rates (including breakfast): $99–$134 single; $15 for each extra person. AE, DISC, ER, MC, V. **Parking:** Free.

Steps away from the canal, the Cartier House Inn has served variously as a Supreme Court judge's residence, a convent, and a senior citizens' home before it became an inn in recent years. All the rooms in this old Victorian house have modern conveniences (such as clock radios), and each is furnished differently with a mixture of authentic antiques and reproductions. For example, in Room 202 there stands a fine bed with marquetry inlay alongside a couple of period-style side tables, a desk, a chest of drawers, and a couple of wing chairs. Room 204 is particularly attractive, with its bay window, large armoire, and marble-top coffee table.

At breakfast, croissants, muffins, melon, tea, and coffee are served at a large table that seats eight. In the adjoining lounge, two comfortable couches are placed invitingly in front of the marble fireplace—perfect relaxing places to sit while reading one of the many books or watching the TV. In summer you can retreat out onto the veranda and laze in one of the Adirondack-style chairs. Service includes nightly turndown service and a fine chocolate to relish. The inn is ideally located, only a few blocks from the Parliament buildings.

BUDGET

Bed-and-Breakfast

Certainly, the best deal for the budget traveler (and also the most interesting option) is to take advantage of **Ottawa Bed and Breakfast,** an organization that represents about 10 homes, which rent for $55 double, $45 single, with breakfast. For information, contact Robert Rivoire, 488 Cooper St., Ottawa, ON, K1R 5H9 (tel. 613/563-0161).

For more bed-and-breakfast possibilities in the Ottawa area, write or phone the **Ottawa Tourism and Convention Authority,** 2nd floor, 111 Lisgar St., Ottawa, ON, K2P 2L7 (tel. 613/237-5158), and ask for their accommodations booklet.

AUSTRALIS, 35 Marlborough Ave., Ottawa, ON, K1N 8E6. Tel. 613/ 235-8461. 3 rms (1 with private bath).

$ Rates (including breakfast): $52 single; $55 double; $65 triple or the room with private bath. No credit cards.

Located in a residential district, this typical Ottawan home offers three rooms—one large room with private bath, a room with a double and cot, and an extra-large family room with a Queen-size bed and two singles. Brian and Carol, the owners, hail from England and Australia, and they provide a relaxing atmosphere for international guests. Carol serves a full breakfast of fresh fruit like kiwi, strawberries, and bananas, followed by a baked egg dish and croissants. The sitting room has a TV, piano, and fireplace, all available for the comfort of the guests.

GASTHAUS SWITZERLAND, 89 Daly Ave., Ottawa, ON, K1N 6E6. Tel. 613/237-0335. Fax 613/594-3327. 25 rms (21 with private bath, 4 with shared bath, 1 Jacuzzi suite). A/C TV TEL

$ Rates (including breakfast): $68 single; $78 double; $110 Jacuzzi suite. AE, DC, ER, MC, V. **Parking:** Free.

Located in an old stone building in downtown Ottawa, the Gasthaus Switzerland has the familiar hallmarks of red gingham and country pine associated with typical rustic Swiss hospitality. Red gingham covers the futons and hangs at the windows; in the dining room it covers the pine tables. All units have cable TV, and one room boasts a Jacuzzi. There's a comfortable sitting room with cable TV, and free use of a garden barbecue in summer. A breakfast of fruit, cheese, eggs, muesli, and more is included in the price. The Gasthaus is at the corner of Cumberland and Daly, across the canal, and near the market area just south of Rideau.

HAYDON HOUSE, 18 The Driveway, Ottawa, ON, K2P 1C6. Tel. 613/ 230-2697. 3 rms (with shared bath). A/C

$ Rates (including breakfast): $55 single; $70 double. **Parking:** Free.

Pleasantly situated on the Queen Elizabeth Driveway at Somerset, only steps from the canal, Haydon House occupies a red-brick Victorian house with pine interior and stained-glass accents. The three rooms (two doubles and a twin) are furnished Canadian style and share 2½ bathrooms. The book-lined and art-filled living room is comfortably inviting.

O'CONNOR HOUSE, 172 O'Connor St., Ottawa, ON, K2P 1T5. Tel. 613/236-4221. Fax 613/236-4232. 34 rms (4 with bath), 3 suites. A/C TEL

$ Rates (including hot buffet breakfast): From $60 single, $65 double. AE, DC, ER, MC, V. **Parking:** $7 Mon–Fri 8am–3:30pm; free overnight and weekends.

Among the city's best buys is O'Connor House, a bed-and-breakfast with 34 rooms, and three two-bedroom family suites. Guests also have use of a comfortable lounge with TV and fireplace where they can meet fellow travelers. Snacks are also available, along with coffee and tea. Laundry facilities are offered, too.

Hostels, Ys, and Dorms

NICHOLAS GAOL INTERNATIONAL HOSTEL, 75 Nicholas St., Ottawa, ON, K1N 7B9. Tel. 613/235-2595. Fax 613/569-2131. 155 beds.

$ Rates: $16 members, $21 nonmembers. MC, V. **Parking:** $5.35 flat rate for stay.

If you like, while you're in the city you can stay in jail at the Nicholas Gaol International Hostel—a gray stone building opened in 1862 as a model prison. Gradually it became outmoded as a jail facility, and was taken over and opened as a hostel in 1973. The old chapel is now used as a dining room, and the walls between cells have been removed to create small dorms housing anywhere from four to ten beds per room. Attractive lounges, skate rentals, games, meals, laundry facilities, and heritage tours are all available. Reservations are recommended from May to September. The hostel is conveniently located for the Byward Market and Parliament Hill.

UNIVERSITY OF OTTAWA RESIDENCES, 100 University Private (mailing address: University of Ottawa, University Centre, Conventions and Reservations Sector, Room 339, Ottawa, ON, K1N 6N5). Tel. 613/564-3463. Fax 613/564-9534. 865 rms (none with bath).
$ Rates: $32 single; $43 twin. MC, V. **Parking:** $9 per day.
Between May and the end of August, the University of Ottawa Residences in Stanton Hall offers economical accommodations. Rooms consist of singles and twins with shared bathroom down the hall. There are telephones on each floor, and the rooms are not air-conditioned.

There are several options for dining—a cafeteria, licensed dining room, coffee shop, and terrace. An average three-course meal in the dining room will cost between $6 and $8, while in the cafeteria breakfast goes for $5, lunch for $7, and dinner for $8. The indoor pool, saunas, and games room are also open to guests.

YM-YWCA, 180 Argyle St., Ottawa, ON, K2P 1B7. Tel. 613/237-1320. Fax 613/788-5095. 264 rms (26 with bath). A/C TEL
$ Rates: $42 single without bath, $48 single with bath; $52 double without bath. Children under 12 stay free when accompanied by an adult. MC, V. **Parking:** $2.75.
At the corner of Argyle and O'Connor there rises a five-star, luxury 15-story YM-YWCA. Most rooms are singles with shared washroom facilities, although a few have private bath; some doubles are available. All rooms have telephones with free local calls. There are TV lounges and laundry facilities, plus the added attractions of an indoor pool, gym, exercise rooms, handball and squash courts, cafeteria, and residence counselors available 24 hours a day. And, of course, the price is right.

OTTAWA WEST

BEST WESTERN MACIES OTTAWAN, 1274 Carling Ave. (at Merivale Rd.), Ottawa, ON, K1Z 7K8. Tel. 613/728-1951. Fax 613/728-1955. 121 rms. A/C TV TEL
$ Rates: $86–$95 single; $90–$100 double. Extra person $4. Children under 14 stay free in parents' room. AE, CB, DC, DISC, ER, MC, V. **Parking:** Free.
The Best Western has nicely decorated rooms, all fully equipped with color TVs and phones (local calls are free). There's a pleasantly secluded outdoor pool, plus an indoor sauna, whirlpool, and exercise area, as well as a dining lounge.

OTTAWA EAST

EXPENSIVE

CHIMO HOTEL, 1199 Joseph Cyr St., Ottawa, ON, K1J 7T4. Tel. 613/744-1060. Fax 613/744-7845. 271 rms. A/C MINIBAR TV TEL
$ Rates: $109 single or double. Extra person $10. Children under 18 stay free in parents' room. Weekend rates from $80. AE, DC, MC, V. **Parking:** Free.
Out near the Museum of Science and Technology, the Chimo Hotel, located at St. Laurent Boulevard and the Queensway, offers modern accommodations at reasonable prices. Its rooms are spacious, well equipped, and furnished in russet colors. Other facilities include the airy, plant-filled coffee shop, Quincy's, the jolly Clancy's pub, the lobby lounge, an atrium-style pool and whirlpool, games room and weight room.

MODERATE

WELCOM INN, 1220 Michael St., Ottawa, ON, K1J 7T1. Tel. 613/748-7800, or toll free 800/387-4381. Fax 613/748-0499. 110 rms. A/C TV TEL
$ Rates (including continental breakfast): $67 single; $77 double. Children under 18 stay free in parents' room. AE, DC, ER, MC, V. **Parking:** Free.
Right around the corner from the Chimo Hotel, the Welcom Inn has pleasant modern rooms decked out in gray and pastel colors with striped bedspreads and oak

furnishings. All rooms have refrigerators. Other facilities include a whirlpool, sauna, and exercise room. A complimentary continental breakfast is served in the lobby.

BUDGET

CARLETON UNIVERSITY, 1125 Colonel By Dr. (contact the Tour and Conference Centre), Ottawa, ON, K1S 5B6. Tel. 613/788-5609. Fax 613/788-3952. 800–1,000 rms available.

$ Rates (including all-you-can-eat breakfast): $32 single; $60 double. MC, V. **Parking:** $3.25 (free on weekends).

Carleton University, four miles southwest of the city, has summertime single and double accommodations in several residences. Only two of the buildings are air-conditioned. A snack bar, cafeteria, lounge, and some sports facilities are available.

HULL

HOTEL RAMADA, 35 rue Laurier, Hull, PQ, J8X 4E9. Tel. 819/778-6111, or toll free 800/567-9607. Fax 819/778-8548. 202 rms. A/C TV TEL

$ Rates: $100 single; $110 double. Extra person $10. Children under 16 stay free in parents' room. AE, CB, DC, DISC, ER, MC, V. **Parking:** $5 per day.

Just across from the Museum of Civilization, the Hotel Ramada offers attractively decorated rooms, featuring modern furnishings with teak finish. There's also an indoor swimming pool, and restaurant/bar off the lobby, as well as the Restaurant Renaissance.

QUALITY INN, 131 rue Laurier, Hull, PQ, J8X 3W3. Tel. 819/770-8550. Fax 819/770-9705. 131 rms. A/C TV TEL

$ Rates: $85 single; $95 double. Extra person $10. Children under 18 stay free in parents' room. AE, CB, DC, ER, MC, V. **Parking:** Free.

Five minutes across the river just off the Alexandra Bridge, the Quality Inn provides moderately priced accommodations near the Museum of Civilization. The rooms are large with modern furniture, and are tastefully decorated. There's a dining room, plus a piano bar that's open seven days a week (remember, we're over the border here) until 3am. An indoor pool completes the facilities.

IN THE GATINEAU HILLS

THE CHATEAU CARTIER SHERATON, 1170 Aylmer Rd., Aylmer, PQ, J9H 5E1. Tel. 819/777-1088. Fax 819/777-7161. 129 rms (6 suites). A/C TV TEL

$ Rates: $140 single or double. AE, DC, DISC, ER, MC, V. **Parking:** Free.

Across the river in the Gatineau Hills, the Château Cartier Sheraton, set on 152 acres, provides a resort experience only 20 minutes' drive from Ottawa. Everything has been designed with the comfort and needs of the visitor in mind, from the welcoming pink-marble lobby tastefully furnished with Persian rugs, chandelier, and wood-burning fireplace to the extra-large Nautilus room overlooking the golf course.

The rooms are all very spacious, well designed and fully equipped with TVs, clock radios, and full-length mirrors. The bathrooms are tile and marble, and equipped with hairdryers and personal toiletry amenities; all rooms have couch and well-lit desks. Most of the rooms are king- or queen-size suites with parlor and bedroom separated by French doors. They also have two TVs and two telephones. In addition, there are four suites with fireplaces, and two with Jacuzzis.

Dining/Entertainment: The stylish dining room, with French windows that open onto the patio, overlooks the golf course. There's also a lounge that features a pianist on weekends; it has a circular bar, club chairs, and a small dance floor.

Services: Valet, room service until 1am.

Facilities: The sports facilities are extensive. The 18-hole golf course provides cross-country skiing in the winter. There's one racquetball and one squash court, and two tennis courts. The indoor pool with a wraparound terrace is perfect for catching rays. There's also a health club, aerobics room, and the aforementioned Nautilus room.

4. DINING

Not too long ago it was difficult to find a good meal in Ottawa. Most people dined at home, so there were few, if any, exciting restaurants—and they were over the river in Hull. It's still true that most of the best French restaurants are in Hull, but downtown Ottawa has been sprouting many continental and ethnic restaurants—Chinese, Mexican, Italian, Greek, Turkish—of its own, so that now you can find whatever your palate desires.

CENTRE TOWN
MODERATE

FAIROUZ, 343 Somerset St. West. Tel. 613/233-1536.
   Cuisine: LEBANESE/MIDDLE EASTERN. **Reservations:** Recommended.
 $ **Prices:** Appetizers $4–$8; main courses $8.50–$15. AE, ER, MC, V.
   Open: Mon–Fri 11:30am–11pm, Sat–Sun 5–10pm.
An elegant Lebanese restaurant, Fairouz consists of several rooms each with well-set tables and Chippendale-style chairs and art and photographs of Lebanon. The well-flavored food includes kafta mashwi (lamb minced with parsley, onions, and spices and broiled on a skewer), roast leg of lamb, and couscous with lamb or chicken. To start, there's hummus, tabbouleh, and other traditional Middle Eastern dishes.

FIORI'S, 239 Nepean St. Tel. 613/232-1377.
   Cuisine: ITALIAN. **Reservations:** Recommended.
 $ **Prices:** Pasta courses $11–$14; main courses $13–$17. AE, ER, MC, V.
   Open: Lunch Mon–Fri 11:30am–2:30pm; dinner Mon–Sat 4:30–11pm.
Diagonally across the street from Ritz 3, Fiori's is a small one-room restaurant in a town house. It serves some carefully prepared Italian favorites like veal marsala, veal parmigiana, and pasta alla vongole. The true specialty of the house, though, is the veal Fiori, prepared in a cognac sauce with shrimp, spinach, and fontina cheese. The atmosphere is intimate.

FLIPPERS, 823 Bank St. Tel. 613/232-2703.
   Cuisine: SEAFOOD. **Reservations:** Accepted only for parties of eight or more.
 $ **Prices:** Main courses $12–$16. AE, ER, MC, V.
   Open: Lunch Mon–Fri 11:30am–3pm; dinner daily 5–10pm.
Flippers is a cozy jovial fish house where the tables sport checkered tablecloths. The raw bar features oysters, littlenecks, and other varieties of shellfish while the main course specials run to Cajun fish, salmon, and many other varieties of seafood. A popular place with Ottawans seeking good values.

LE CAFE, in the National Arts Centre. Tel. 613/594-5127.
   Cuisine: CANADIAN. **Reservations:** Recommended.
 $ **Prices:** Main courses $12–$21. AE, MC, V.
   Open: Mon–Sat noon–11pm, Sun (in summer only) noon–8pm.
The National Arts Centre's Le Café commands a marvelous view across the canal from its summertime terrace and offers fine food year-round in a relaxing setting. The menu features imaginatively prepared dishes that use prime Canadian ingredients like New Brunswick salmon, Petrie Island mussels, Nova Scotia scallops, venison, and lamb. You might start with the mussels steamed in Okanagan Valley Chenin Blanc with leeks, garlic, and chili peppers, and follow with médaillons of fallow deer with fresh honey mushrooms and Newfoundland partridge berries or the salmon broiled with teriyaki and ginger glaze. Among the desserts the Canadian specialty is Newfoundland screech cake (a rum-flavored cake) or maple syrup mousse in a chocolate tartlet.

MAMMA TERESA'S, 300 Somerset St. West. Tel. 613/236-3023.
   Cuisine: ITALIAN. **Reservations:** Recommended.
 $ **Prices:** Pasta around $9; veal and other main courses $12–$18. AE, ER, MC, V.
   Open: Mon–Fri noon–11pm, Sat 5–11pm, Sun 4–10pm.

Mamma Teresa's continues as an Ottawa tradition. You need shoulder pads to get into this red-brick town house where Mamma's portrait hangs in the hall. It's no wonder, when you look at the menu and see that for $14.50 you can get a full dinner that includes antipasti, minestrone soup, chicken parmigiana with spaghetti, spumoni, and coffee or tea. There are several such set menus, plus a whole host of antipasti, pastas, and main dishes to tempt the palate as well as the wallet. The oak-columned bar is a pleasant waiting room for a table in the ever-crowded series of dining rooms furnished with red and black tablecloths and pictures of Italian scenes.

The veal dishes—with ham and cheese, vermouth sauce and olives, parmigiana, marsala, pizzaiola—are all under $14, most under $11. Most of the pastas are around $9, while there are some more expensive items, such as the sirloin steak pizzaiola. For dessert, take the smooth zabaglione or the delicious Mamma cake. You should by this time be fully satisfied.

THE MILL, 555 Ottawa River Pkwy. Tel. 613/237-1311.
   Cuisine: CANADIAN. **Reservations:** Required even at lunch.
$ **Prices:** Appetizers $2–$6; main courses $9–$16. AE, ER, MC, V.
   Open: Lunch Mon–Fri 11:30am–2:30pm; dinner Mon–Fri 4:30–11pm, Sat 4:30–11:30pm; Sun 10:30am–10:30pm.
On the Ottawa River, the Mill offers a delightful setting for a selection of beef cuts, steak, and seafood dishes. Erected in the 1840s, when Ottawa was a lusty, hell-raising lumber town, it now provides a glass-enclosed atrium dining room, and several other dining areas upstairs and down with a magnificent view over the river. The fare is definitely traditional—prime rib plus rack of lamb, veal, chicken, lobster, and filet of sole amandine.

RITZ UPTOWN, 226 Nepean St. Tel. 613/238-8752.
   Cuisine: ITALIAN. **Reservations:** Recommended.
$ **Prices:** Pasta courses $6–$9; main courses $10.50–$14. AE, DC, ER, MC, V.
   Open: Mon–Fri 11:30am–midnight, Sat–Sun 5pm–midnight.
Ritz Uptown is the latest Ritz success. Located in a town house, the dining room has a bistro look with its red-checked tablecloths and modern Canadian art. There's a wine bar in the back. The food consists of a variety of pastas, including gnocchi and linguine, cooked in several ways—pomodoro, Alfredo, etc.—as well as such specials as chicken piccata and beef tenderloin with red wine and mushrooms. Great desserts, all under $5, include Italian trifle and apricot and apple crêpe cake.

SILK ROADS, 300 Sparks St. Mall. Tel. 613/236-4352.
   Cuisine: AFGHAN. **Reservations:** Recommended at lunch and weekends at dinner.
$ **Prices:** Appetizers $4–$7; main courses $10–$16. AE, DC, MC, V.
   Open: Mon–Fri 11:30am–10:30pm, Sat 5–10:30pm.
An Ottawan favorite serving exotic Afghan cuisine, Silk Roads features succulent kebabs, mahi, lamb, beef, and chicken. Start with a tangy bouranee banjan (eggplant simmered in a spicy sauce served on a minted yogurt) or bolanee (pastry filled with spinach, leeks, and green onions, and cooked on a taba grill). Finish with jelabi (rings of fried pastry dipped in syrup) or firni (milk pudding topped with pistachios). There's also a daily luncheon buffet for $12.

BUDGET

CICCIO'S, 330 Preston St. Tel. 613/232-1675.
   Cuisine: ITALIAN. **Reservations:** Recommended on weekends.
$ **Prices:** Pasta courses under $9; main courses under $13. AE, DC, ER, MC, V.
   Open: Mon–Sat 11:30am–11pm.
West of downtown you'll find Little Italy and such local favorites as Ciccio's, a tiny down-home neighborhood place with red tablecloths, where Italian men gather in the afternoons to sip a glass of wine and exchange their opinions with much gesticulation.

The decor is typical home-style Italian: a map of Italy and a few vistas of the old country. In the back there's a small room with wine-bottle candles on the tables. One young man left his wedding reception and brought his still-dressed-in-white bride here to dine—such loyalties and sentiment does this warm, friendly place conjure.

The prices help—specials change daily but will read "Pollo alla Ciccio," the chef's version of chicken cacciatore served with bread and butter for $10—and the same goes for gnocchi, osso buco, stuffed peppers, or Italian sausages. There are two terraces for summer dining.

SALVATORE, 388 Booth St. Tel. 613/233-4731.
   Cuisine: ITALIAN. **Reservations:** Recommended on weekends.
$ Prices: Pasta courses around $8; main courses $11–$17. AE, ER, MC, V.
   Open: Lunch Mon–Fri 11:30am–2pm; dinner Sun–Fri 5–10pm, Sat 5–11pm.
If you can't get into Ciccio's, then try another Little Italy favorite, Salvatore, another small spot usually crowded with families. Veal and pasta are the main items here, all served in spicy, delicious sauces for reasonable prices. Veal pizzaiola and marsala, lasagne, spaghetti matriciana, and lobster tails are just a few of the items.

SHANGHAI, 651 Somerset St. West, near Bronson. Tel. 613/233-4001.
   Cuisine: CHINESE. **Reservations:** Recommended on weekends.
$ Prices: Main courses $7–$15. AE, MC, V.
   Open: Mon–Fri 11am–1am, Sat 4pm–1am, Sun 4–10pm.
Shanghai offers comfort, attractive decor, and some very fine Chinese cuisine—Szechuan, Shanghai, and regional—which may be why it's popular with many prominent government figures.
   Soups include Chinese melon and Chinese greens, which you might follow with such tempting specialties as gee bow guy (breast of chicken rolled around sweet ham, green onions, and almonds, covered with rice paper, and deep-fried in peanut oil), steamed pickerel served with green onions and their own sauce, or beef or barbecued pork with bean curd and oyster sauce. Regular dishes like beef with broccoli (between $7 and $10), round out the menu.

LOWER TOWN
MODERATE

CANAL CAFE, 221 Echo Dr. Tel. 613/238-1296.
   Cuisine: CONTINENTAL/ITALIAN. **Reservations:** Recommended.
$ Prices: Main courses $8–$19. AE, ER, MC, V.
   Open: Lunch daily 11:30am–2:30pm; dinner Sun–Thurs 5–10pm, Fri–Sat 5–11pm.
The Canal Café is all its name implies. It sits alongside the Pretoria Bridge, which arches over the canal. The interior is sleek, with glass-brick walls, black bar, and tables sporting coral-pink and gray tablecloths. In summer the outdoor patio is popular. The specialty of the restaurant is mussels, plus such pastas as linguine with clam or pesto, fettuccine Alfredo, and spaghetti carbonara. For dessert, any one of a selection of cheesecakes or such tempting delights as chocolate-raspberry torte finishes it all off very nicely.

SITAR, 417A Rideau St. Tel. 613/789-7979.
   Cuisine: INDIAN. **Reservations:** Recommended.
$ Prices: Curries $6–$10; other main courses $8–$11. AE, ER, MC, V.
   Open: Lunch Mon–Sat 11am–2:30pm; dinner daily 5–11pm.
Sitar has the reputation of serving the finest Indian food in Ottawa. Here, in a large room softened only with Indian wall hangings, you can feast on a selection of curries, biryanis, tandoori, and vegetarian dishes. Various combination dishes are available; for example, a vegetarian dish combining onion bhaji, vegetable curry, dhal, and breads, is priced at $13.

BUDGET

NATES, 316 Rideau St. Tel. 613/789-9191.
   Cuisine: DELI. **Reservations:** Not accepted.
$ Prices: Sandwiches and other items $5–$7. AE, DC, ER, MC, V.
   Open: Mon–Fri 7am–2am, Sat 7am–2am, Sun 8am–midnight.
An Ottawa institution—that's Nates, where you can get really good (and fattening) cheese blintzes, cheese bagels, potato latkes, meat kreplach, boiled potato vareniki

with stuffed kishke, plus a whole host of sandwiches (pastrami included, of course) and a bagel and nova with cream cheese. Just as the sign says, "You don't have to be Jewish to enjoy Nates." And you don't have to have low lights and tablecloths to fress well (that's Yiddish for eat well, in case you were wondering). Good for breakfast under $2.

THE BYWARD MARKET AREA
EXPENSIVE

LE JARDIN, 127 York St. Tel. 613/238-1828.
Cuisine: FRENCH. **Reservations:** Recommended.
$ Prices: Appetizers $5–$50 (highest price for caviar); main courses $17–$31. AE, DC, ER, MC, V.
Open: Dinner daily 5:30–11pm.

The atmosphere is formal at Le Jardin, as befits its setting in a beautiful old Victorian gingerbread house. In summer you'll find a small terrace in front with tables topped by bright umbrellas; inside you'll find two small tastefully decorated rooms with chintz fabric-covered walls (one with a fireplace), highlighted by antiques, greenery and fresh flowers, and among other things, a magnificent Gaspé quilt. Upstairs the atmosphere is more sophisticated and romantic, created by large bouquets of fresh flowers, low lights, heavy burgundy drapes with valances, and elegant French-style chairs. It's a lovely room in which to dine.

The restaurant selects the freshest ingredients possible. At dinner you might choose from six or so hors d'oeuvres like pheasant pâté with goose liver and truffle, shrimp flambéed with Pernod and tarragon, or Persian caviar. Main courses feature a variety: chicken breast with raspberry vinegar sauce, noisettes of veal with onion stew, rabbit with a Dijon mustard sauce, saddle of lamb in a pastry dough, stuffed trout with Meursault, or lobster blanquette with morels and vegetables. Among the desserts there's lemon and raspberry mousse, almond cheesecake, and most tempting of all, chocolate sublime with Armagnac and Corinthian grapes.

MODERATE

BISTRO 115, 110 Murray St. Tel. 613/562-7244.
Cuisine: FRENCH. **Reservations:** Recommended.
$ Prices: Main courses $14–$18; three-course prix fixe $24.95. AE, ER, MC, V.
Open: Daily 11:30am–11:30pm.

This place affects a very French atmosphere with lace tablecloths, floral banquettes, and a trellis-covered dining terrace in the back. The prix fixe is an excellent deal and might offer such appetizers as chicken liver and brandy pâté or shrimps and mango salad with yogurt, to be followed by poached salmon with a beurre blanc of red pepper or loin of lamb with mint or another two choices. A la carte choices might include cioppino or filet mignon with Roquefort butter. For dessert there's often a fine white chocolate raspberry tart.

BLUE CACTUS, 2 Byward Market. Tel. 613/238-7061.
Cuisine: SOUTHWESTERN. **Reservations:** Accepted only for parties of eight or more.
$ Prices: Main courses $6–$15. AE, MC, V.
Open: Sun–Thurs 11:30am–11pm, Fri–Sat 11:30am–1am.

The ambience at the Blue Cactus is created by desert colors (sienna and orange) and the cactus emblem, along with wildly painted chairs and stools. The food is typical—fajitas, quesadillas, nachos, lime-grilled chicken, and some fine pizzas. There's a roof terrace in summer.

CAFE SPIGA, 271 Dalhousie, at the corner of Murray. Tel. 613/567-4381.
Cuisine: ITALIAN. **Reservations:** Recommended.
$ Prices: Pasta $9–$12; main courses $12–$16. AE, MC, V.
Open: Lunch Mon–Fri 11:30am–3pm; dinner daily 5–11pm.

There's very little ornament except for mirrors, sparkling white tablecloths, and

Italian food ingredients and condiments at this Italian winner in the market. A variety of pasta is offered, including fusilli with warm pancetta, crushed chilies, olive oil and asiago, and such subtly flavored dishes as orecchiette with shrimp and ginger as well as the more traditional gnocchi. Typical main courses might be breast of chicken with spinach and gorgonzola cream sauce, médaillons of beef with glazed onions and barolo wine sauce, or salmon with red and yellow pepper sauce.

CAFE VIENNA, 11 George St. Tel. 613/594-8758.
   Cuisine: CONTINENTAL. **Reservations:** Not accepted.
$ Prices: Sandwiches, light fare, and desserts $4–$6. AE, MC, V.
   Open: Sun–Thurs 11am–11pm, Fri–Sat 11am–midnight.
A fabulous dessert display case up front at the Café Vienna is filled with Mozart nougat cake, chocolate-raspberry zuccotto, Sachertorte, and many other tantalizing specialties. The room itself is attractive, with its draped round tables, each with a sprig of fresh flowers; the ambience is further enhanced by background classical music. The menu also features such items (served until 8pm) as seafood quiche, poached salmon with hollandaise, and such sandwiches as smoked turkey with Emmenthaler or Reuben. Special coffees and teas are available.

CLAIR DE LUNE, 81B Clarence St. Tel. 613/230-0022.
   Cuisine: FRENCH. **Reservations:** Recommended.
$ Prices: Main courses $11–$19; fixed-price dinner $22. AE, ER, MC, V.
   Open: Lunch daily 11:30am–2:30pm; dinner Sun–Wed 6–11pm, Thurs–Sat 6pm–midnight.
   Here in the market area there are an astounding number of restaurants and cafés. Among the many, Clair de Lune is one of my special favorites. It's a little French bistro where you can obtain a reasonable two-course lunch, featuring such items as cod grenobloise or rabbit chasseur. At dinner the fixed-price menu will offer three or so appetizer and main course choices, like the grillade of quail or halibut with sun-dried tomatoes, all capped off with a dessert like the chocolate tulip with yogurt and brandy. The à la carte menu is also reasonably priced, and features about 10 meat, fish, and pasta dishes.
   Moreover, Clair de Lune is a snappily decorated spot with a handsome glass-block bar, gray decor, and marble-top tables that make for a pleasant dining experience. During the summer, climb to the very popular rooftop terrace and enjoy a few spicy tropical snacks ranging in price from $2.50 to $6; they're supplemented by such items as grilled fish and brochettes.

THE COURTYARD RESTAURANT, 21 George St. Tel. 613/238-4623.
   Cuisine: CONTINENTAL. **Reservations:** Recommended.
$ Prices: Appetizers $4–$8; main courses $14–$21. AE, DC, ER, MC, V.
   Open: Lunch Mon–Sat 11:30am–2pm, Sun 11am–2pm; dinner Mon–Sat 5:30–9:30pm, Sun 5–9pm.
With a distinct flavor of Old Montréal, the Courtyard Restaurant is set in a gray stone building that possesses a high-ceilinged stone-walled dining room and an outdoor café with colorful parasols—it's only a dream away from Vieux Montréal. The menu is rather predictable—filet mignon with béarnaise, sole amandine, veal Oscar. The Sunday brunch is accompanied by live classical music. The Outdoor Café is a popular meeting spot. At lunch, grilled halibut, chicken teriyaki, seafood crêpes, and more are priced from $8 to $10.

HAVELI, 87 George St. Tel. 613/230-3566.
   Cuisine: INDIAN. **Reservations:** Recommended.
$ Prices: Appetizers $3–$6; main courses $9–$16. AE, MC, V.
   Open: Lunch Sun–Fri 11:45am–2:15pm; dinner Mon–Sat 5–10pm.
Popular Indian stars like Jagjit & Chitra, Anup Jalota, and Chanchal have all headed upstairs in the Market Mall to dine in this comfortable restaurant decorated Indian style. The menu is quite broad, offering a wide selection of vegetarian dishes—aloo gobi, senza jalfraize, Gandhi's delight—and meat and fish preparations. Special dishes include Bhuna shrimp and Bombay bahar scallops in batter, deep-fried with a cream sauce, and of course, items from the tandoor, including the most expensive dish on the menu, lobster tails marinated in Indian spices and broiled in the tandoor. The best

deals are the buffets offered at lunch and on Sunday (when South Indian specialties like dhosa are also served).

ICHO JAPAN, 87 George St., in Market Mall. Tel. 613/230-6857.
  Cuisine: JAPANESE. **Reservations:** Recommended.
$ Prices: Sushi $3–$6; other main courses $11–$18. AE, DC, MC, V.
  Open: Dinner Tues–Fri 5:30–10pm, Sat 5–10pm, Sun 5–9:30pm.
A pleasant Japanese restaurant, this place sports a small sushi bar and one or two Japanese-style tables. The food is finely cooked and presented—dishes like broiled eel, tonkatsu dishes, chicken teriyaki, tempura, and assorted sushi.

MAXWELL'S BISTRO, 33 Clarence St. Tel. 613/567-4677.
  Cuisine: BISTRO FARE. **Reservations:** Recommended.
$ Prices: Sandwiches and pizzas $5–$9; main courses $11–$14. AE, MC, V.
  Open: Mon–Thurs 11am–11pm, Fri–Sat 11am–midnight, Sun 10am–midnight.
A popular Market Mall spot, Maxwell's offers reasonably priced fare in a pleasant ambience. Tables are set with red-and-white gingham cloths, and there's a pleasant outdoor terrace under an awning. The menu features assorted sandwiches and wood-fired pizzas (including Szechuan, with shrimp and vegetables). There are also more substantial dishes, like jumbo shrimp with curry sauce and breast of chicken with lemon, black pepper, and cream. On Saturday there's a luncheon buffet; brunch is served on Sunday. There's also a dance-bar adjacent to the restaurant.

THE OLD FISH MARKET, 54 York St., at William. Tel. 613/563-4954.
  Cuisine: SEAFOOD. **Reservations:** Accepted only for parties of 10 or more.
$ Prices: Appetizers $4–$8; main courses $10–$37. AE, DC, DISC, ER, MC, V.
  Open: Lunch daily 11:30am–2:30pm; dinner Mon–Sat 4:30–11pm, Sun 4:30–10pm. Sun lunch served only in summer.
The Old Fish Market seems to have found the magic formula for serving fresh fish in a simple way to the delight of the crowds who pack this place daily. The original Old Fish Market is in Toronto; Ottawa's is smaller but along the same lines.
  Downstairs, the two rooms bedecked with rope decoration, lobster pots, and other nautical regalia feature fresh fish, ranging from halibut fish and chips to a whole Dover sole, with swordfish, snapper, mackerel, and rainbow trout in between. The most expensive dishes include surf-and-turf and the mixed grill of baked oysters, half a lobster, shrimp, queen crab legs, scallops, and smoked salmon. There's also a selection of chowders and seafood appetizers. Cheesecake and ice-cream choices complete the dessert menu. Coaster's, upstairs, features a lighter menu—mussels, oysters, shrimp, crab, and herring appetizers.

SANTE, 45 Rideau St. Tel. 613/232-7113.
  Cuisine: INTERNATIONAL/ECLECTIC. **Reservations:** Recommended.
$ Prices: Main courses $14–$18. AE, DC, ER, MC, V.
  Open: Mon–Sat 11:30am–10pm.
Originally attached to a spa, this restaurant specializes in healthy fresh food that can be enjoyed in comfort. The tables are graced with fresh flowers, the walls with botanical prints, and if you're lucky, you'll be seated at one of the tables with armchairs. Start with the delicious callaloo soup, chicken satay, or Bali spring rolls. Follow with a sizzling hot plate like the seafood with basil coconut cream sauce, or with the Thai spicy shrimp stir-fried in tamarind, garlic, lemon grass, and chilies. Other specialties include chicken escabeche (in raspberry vinegar, sweet pepper, red onion, and chilies), veal tropicale sautéed with capers and garlic and served with mango lemon and rum sauce, and several vegetarian dishes.

BUDGET

CAFE BOHEMIAN, 89 Clarence St. Tel. 613/238-7182.
  Cuisine: INTERNATIONAL. **Reservations:** Accepted only for parties of six or more.
$ Prices: Main courses under $11. AE, DC, MC, V.
  Open: Lunch Mon–Fri 11:30am–4pm; Sat–Sun 10am–3:30pm; dinner Sun–Thurs 5–11pm, Fri–Sat 5pm–midnight.

A simple setting of oak and tile serves as the background for a variety of very reasonably priced fare at the Café Bohemian—burgers, croissants, pita-bread sandwiches, salads, spanokopita, moussaka, and more. Every day there are also luncheon and dinner specials—tournedos, seafood gratin, and spiced pork chops, for example.

15 CLARENCE, 15 Clarence St. Tel. 613/562-0705.
   Cuisine: PIZZA. **Reservations:** Not accepted.
   $ Prices: Pizzas $8–$11. AE, ER, MC, V.
   Open: Sun–Tues 11:30am–11pm, Wed–Sat 11:30am–midnight. Shorter hours in winter.

15 Clarence gets rave reviews and draws a large crowd to its two patios (back and front) and its small dining room with gray marble tables and gray carpet set against exposed brick walls. The front outdoor patio sports super scarlet-and-gray fringed umbrellas, while the back patio has an awning. The kitchen turns out innovative food—one-person pizzas (from the wood-burning oven) featuring, for example, artichoke, zucchini, sweet pepper, and fontina, or pesto, mozzarella, and plum tomatoes, along with such calzones as curried lamb with fontina cheese. Salads and daily specials are also available, and so, too, are some divine desserts—apricot and apple crêpe cake or chocolate sabayon cake, for example.

LA CREPERIE, 47 York St., at Byward. Tel. 613/232-8805.
   Cuisine: CREPES. **Reservations:** Recommended.
   $ Prices: Main-course crêpes $7–$9. AE, ER, MC, V.
   Open: Mon–Fri 11am–11pm, Sat 9am–12:30am, Sun 9am–10pm.

A stylish art deco bentwood-cane-and-posters spot, La Crêperie specializes in crêpes, of course—such savory delights as chicken Florentine, Atlantic crêpe with tender shrimp, and filet of sole with mushrooms in a white wine cream sauce. Then there are other, even more enticing, sweet temptations. Who could resist the Hungarian chocolate-nut crêpe filled with chopped walnuts, raisins, and grated orange peel in dark-chocolate sauce for a mere $6? Fully licensed.

LAS PALMAS, 111 Parent St. Tel. 613/238-3738.
   Cuisine: MEXICAN. **Reservations:** Recommended on weekends.
   $ Prices: Main courses $7–$12. AE, ER, MC, V.
   Open: Daily 11am–11pm.

Offering a less frantic and more pleasing experience than most Mexican places, Las Palmas sports the usual brilliant colors—yellow, pink, and turquoise—yet manages to retain a certain restrained, comfortable air. Prices are moderate for the traditional Mexican fare: nachos, guacamole, enchiladas, chili relleno.

MEMORIES, 7 Clarence St. Tel. 613/232-1882.
   Cuisine: BISTRO. **Reservations:** Not accepted.
   $ Prices: Sandwiches and light fare $4–$9. AE, MC, V.
   Open: Mon 11:30am–11pm, Tues–Fri 11:30am–midnight, Sat 10:30am–midnight, Sun 10am–11pm.

Next door to 15 Clarence, Memories is another very attractive and well-frequented café that offers a light menu and is particularly hailed for its desserts. Among the menu items you might find sandwiches (such as avocado and tomato on rye, or ham and cheese on croissant), a variety of salads, soups, and pâtés, and raclette served as an appetizer. Saturday and Sunday brunch offers the usual croissants, quiches, and eggs as well as luscious waffles served with your choice of fruit toppings. The tables out front fill up quickly.

THE TEA PARTY, 119 York St. Tel. 613/562-0352.
   Cuisine: TEA. **Reservations:** Not accepted.
   $ Prices: Most items $4–$9. MC, V.
   Open: Mon–Fri 10am–5pm, Sat 9:30am–5pm, Sun 11am–4pm. (Shop remains open half an hour later.)

Stop by this Victorian house for a delicious afternoon Devonshire cream tea. Afterwards you can browse among the whimsically designed tea pots, tea towels, assorted teas and coffees, and other gourmet items.

WILLIAM STREET CAFE, 47 William St. Tel. 613/235-4254.

Cuisine: BURGERS. **Reservations:** Accepted only for parties of six or more.
$ Prices: Burgers $5–$7; daily special under $9. AE, MC, V.
Open: Mon–Fri 11am–midnight, Sat 10am–midnight, Sun 10am–11pm.

The William Street Café is the kind of place that's always crowded with young and not-so-young people devouring really good burgers, salads, and other wholesome fare in two small but light and airy rooms with the current plants-and-brick look.

Daily specials are chalked on a blackboard, while the regular fare consists of a selection of esoteric burgers, including a teriyaki specimen and a pecan burger made with a rich filling of pecans, almonds, and vegetables, topped with Mornay sauce. Salads are a little less unusual. For dessert there's good old-fashioned hot apple crumble or a supersoft frozen-yogurt sundae with seasonal fresh fruits. On Saturday or Sunday, stop in for brunch—eggs Benedict, quiches, with juice and coffee or tea, for under $7.

ZAKS DINER, 14 Byward Market. Tel. 613/233-0433.
Cuisine: DINER. **Reservations:** Accepted only for parties of 12 or more.
$ Prices: Main dishes $6–$10. AE, MC, V.
Open: Mon–Wed 8am–midnight, Thurs–Sat 8am–1am, Sun 8am–11pm.

The latest trendsetter, Zaks is a brand-new '50s-style diner complete with turquoise stools and booths, plenty of chrome, an equal amount of glass brick, and music from the '50s. Classic diner fare—burgers, hot dogs, meat loaf, nachos, and chicken dishes plus milk shakes and sundaes—is offered for those who desire retro.

IN VANIER

IL VAGABONDO, 186 Barrette St. Tel. 613/749-4877.
Cuisine: ITALIAN. **Reservations:** Recommended.
$ Prices: Pasta courses around $10; main courses $10–$17. AE, DC, ER, MC, V.
Open: Lunch Tues–Fri noon–3pm; dinner Mon–Sat 5–11pm, Sun 5–10pm.

If you're prepared to travel a little off the beaten track across the bridge into Vanier, you'll discover this much-recommended little Italian bistro in a corner house. The bi-level dining room is cozy with its wooden oak bar, colorful tablecloths, and tiled floor. The specials are written on a blackboard and you'll have to come early to ensure your choice, for they soon disappear. The two specials the night I was there were pollo a basilico and fettuccine con erbe, both served with salad. The à la carte menu lists médaillons of veal either limone, marsala, or paiarda (with rosemary), and pasta dishes like cannelloni fiorentina with tomato sauce. The veal is indeed supertender and of a very high quality. Meat portions are large, but vegetables are more of a garnish. The parmesan is freshly grated at your table.

OTTAWA SOUTH

This arbitrary designation refers to an area that stretches from Wellington Street to the Queensway, along Bank and Elgin Streets in particular. It's the kind of area where you find cafés that carry free literature like the *Peace Information News,* and a medley of food stores and other neighborhood services and vendors. A budget haven.

MODERATE

LE METRO, 315 Somerset St. West (between Bank and O'Connor). Tel. 613/230-8123.
Cuisine: FRENCH. **Reservations:** Strongly recommended.
$ Prices: Appetizers $6–$8; main courses $17–$20. AE, ER, MC, V.
Open: Lunch Mon–Fri 11:30am–2:30pm; dinner Mon–Sat 6–10:30pm.

A romantic Paris bistro—that's Le Métro. In a town house setting you'll find rooms accented dramatically with gilded statuary and lavish flower arrangements. Silver candelabra set off the tables, which are covered with rich burgundy colored cloths and handsome table settings. French songs add to the atmosphere. The menu changes daily and reflects whatever is really fresh and outstanding at the local markets. To start, you might begin with a shrimp bisque or a pheasant terrine with prunes, and follow with a selection from the 10 or so entrées. Breast of duck à l'orange, filet mignon béarnaise, or salmon feuilleté with a beurre blanc might appear on the menu.

BUDGET

CHAHAYA MALAYSIA, 749 Bank St. Tel. 613/237-4304.
   Cuisine: MALAYSIAN. **Reservations:** Recommended on weekends.
$ **Prices:** Main courses $9–$13. AE, MC, V.
   Open: Lunch Mon–Fri 11:30am–2:30pm; dinner Mon–Sat 5–11pm, Sun 5–10pm.

A simple restaurant, Chahaya Malaysia specializes in the fragrant and sometimes spicy cuisine from Southeast Asia. Start with either some satay or rojak, a sweet hot concoction accompanied by apple, pineapple, cucumber, bean sprouts, and lightly fried bean curd in a spicy sauce. Then follow with a fish or chicken curry, or chili shrimp, and top it all off with kek har heart cake. The decor is very simple, with brown cloths on the tables and a few artifacts. If they ask you if you want things spicy, be careful—the chili sauce on the table will take your breath away.

SAVANA CAFE, 431 Gilmour, between Bank and Kent. Tel. 613/233-9159.
   Cuisine: CARIBBEAN. **Reservations:** Recommended.
$ **Prices:** Appetizers $3–$5; main courses $10–$15. AE, ER, MC, V.
   Open: Lunch Tues–Fri 11:30am–3pm; dinner Mon–Sat 5–10pm.

With its tropical flavor, the Savana Café has caught Ottawans' imaginations. Past the small bar up front are a couple of rooms hung with brilliantly colored Caribbean art. The food is equally spicy, like the fabulous kalaloo (or callaloo) soup made Caribbean style with okra, spinach, thyme, Congo peppers, and lime. Other appetizers include satay, spring rolls, and Jamaican patties. Among the favorites are spicy Thai noodles, tiger prawns with coriander pesto, and escabeche of chicken served spicy hot with crisp onions, peppers, and pimientos. The chef is always adding new exotic items, like the chicken breast stuffed with banana cream cheese and banana ketchup! Most of the dishes can be ordered mild, medium, or hot. To my taste, the hot is just fine—anything less wouldn't do, which suggests that Ottawans prefer less spice. In winter, the fire adds a welcome touch; in summer, so does the patio.

THE GLEBE

The Glebe refers to the southern part of Ottawa, an area stretching from just south of the Queensway to the Rideau Canal and from Bronson Avenue to Rideau.

CANAL RITZ, 375 Queen Elizabeth Dr. Tel. 613/238-8998.
   Cuisine: INTERNATIONAL. **Reservations:** Recommended.
$ **Prices:** Pizzas and pasta courses $6–$8; fish courses about $12. AE, ER, MC, V.
   Open: Mon–Sat 11:30am–11pm, Sun 10:30am–11pm. Summer hours are extended.

The Canal Ritz occupies a fabulous old boathouse right on the canal. In summer, outside tables are distinctly attractive perching spots, while inside, the light and airy two-story interior with water views is also welcoming. Pizzas are the real specialty here, fresh from the wood-burning oven. There's a delightful choice: pears and Brie on braised onions; scallops in mustard, watercress, and sesame seed; pesto, mozzarella, and plum tomato; and many others. Pasta—a variety of fettuccine—charcoal-grilled fish, and a selection of brochettes are among the other specialties. The place is also known for desserts, like the mocha or amaretto cheesecake, or zuccotto (consisting of sponge cake, hazelnut cream, and chocolate mousse iced in white chocolate and glazed in dark). In fact, this is a chocoholic's paradise. Kids' books and coloring pads make it a great place for families too.

OTTAWA WEST

It's a bit off the beaten path, but there are several worthwhile restaurants out here.

OPUS BISTRO, 1331 Wellington St. Tel. 613/722-9549.
   Cuisine: CONTEMPORARY. **Reservations:** Required.
$ **Prices:** Appetizers $2.50–$6; main courses $8–$18. MC, V.
   Open: Dinner Tues–Sat 5–11pm.

A small West End restaurant, the Opus Bistro is worth visiting to savor the finely prepared, continentally inspired food. The restaurant is one room, with a clean and simple decor and a small bar up front. The reasonably priced main dishes might include duck with raspberry sauce or calves' liver with Calvados. The menu changes daily—but if the crabcakes en filo are among the appetizers, try them.

SIAM BISTRO, 1268 Wellington St. Tel. 613/728-3111.
   Cuisine: THAI. **Reservations:** Recommended.
$ **Prices:** Main courses $7–$13. AE, DC, ER, MC, V.
   Open: Lunch Mon–Fri noon–2pm; dinner daily 5:30–10pm.

It's worth a trek out to the west end if you enjoy Thai food. This intimate room is long and narrow and furnished with one or two artifacts. The cuisine is fragrant and spicy. Try the tom yum gai (chicken soup) or tom yum kung (shrimp soup) and follow with pad Thai noodles, chicken or beef with basil, or one of the delicious curries. Fried banana or mango ice cream makes for a refreshing ending.

TETE A TETE, 9 Richmond Rd. Tel. 613/722-6082.
   Cuisine: FRENCH/CONTINENTAL. **Reservations:** Recommended.
$ **Prices:** Main courses $11–$18. MC, V.
   Open: Lunch Tues–Fri 11:30am–2pm; dinner Mon–Sat 5–10pm.

Last summer, Tête à Tête, located in a town house in the West End, was being talked about by many Ottawans for the quality of its food and dining experience. It certainly serves some fine dishes, such as breast of chicken stuffed with chèvre and sun-dried tomatos in roasted pepper coulis; beef with Armagnac, fresh herbs, and demiglaze; salmon with capers, tarragon, lemon, and cream; and duck with pearl onions, maple syrup, and allspice. To start, try the gravlax with a Pommery dill sauce, the deep-fried cantaloupe with prosciutto, or the steamed mussels with Gorgonzola, pears, pine nuts, and cream—all winners.

HULL

CAFE HENRI BURGER, 69 rue Laurier. Tel. 819/777-5646.
   Cuisine: FRENCH. **Reservations:** Recommended.
$ **Prices:** Main courses $18–$30; three-course luncheon prix fixe $15; four-course dinner prix fixe $36. AE, ER, MC, V.
   Open: Lunch Mon–Fri noon–2:30pm; dinner Mon–Sat 6–10pm. The Terrace open daily in summer noon–11pm.

"Let's go to Burger's" used to be a byword in Ottawa in the early '20s when Henri Burger, chef at the Château Laurier, founded his restaurant, Café Henri Burger. Although he died in 1936, the name still attracted people to this landmark brick building with its Italianate windows, side porch, and finialed entrance overlooking the Museum of Civilization and beyond across the river to Parliament Hill.

The café continues to excel. The lunch menu still offers a prix fixe, plus à la carte dishes priced from $14 to $18. At night, the prix fixe includes appetizer, soup, entrée, dessert, and coffee. Or you can select from such specialties as paupiettes of Dover sole with red butter sauce, saddle of lamb with ginger-and-curry sauce, and veal loin with onion-and-gewürztraminer sauce. For dessert the classic tarte au citron is a must.

LE RAJ, 151 rue Wellington. Tel. 819/777-7277.
   Cuisine: INDIAN. **Reservations:** Recommended.
$ **Prices:** Main courses $9–$14. AE, DC, ER, MC, V.

Open: Lunch Mon–Fri 11:30am–2pm; dinner Tues–Sat 5–10pm.

A lovely Indian restaurant located in a town house, Le Raj is a series of handsomely decorated dining rooms, each with plush banquettes. In the back dining room you can observe the chefs working at the tandoor and turning out subtly spiced dishes like shrimp in coriander-and-mint sauce, along with more usual tandoori items.

LE PIED DE COCHON, 248 rue Montcalm. Tel. 819/777-5808.
   Cuisine: FRENCH. **Reservations:** Recommended.
$ Prices: Main courses $14–$17; three-course prix fixe $26. AE, DC, ER, MC, V.
   Open: Lunch Tues–Fri noon–2pm; dinner Tues–Fri 6–10pm, Sat 6–11pm.

 When people need a reliable spot offering classically good cuisine, they often head for Le Pied de Cochon, a small, unpretentious place. There's no awning outside, and if you didn't know about it you'd probably walk on by.

The food is fresh and good, the atmosphere casual, and the welcome gracious. There's also a certain joie de vivre about the place, which is always filled with local Québecois, especially at lunchtime. The decor is simple and rustic—stucco walls and burgundy tablecloths—but what really counts is the food. The menu is limited. For example, at lunch there might be three choices of entrée: salmon in puff pastry, lamb tarragon, and wild boar with pepper sauce, priced from $10 to $13. To start there might be mussels, oysters, snails, or a salad like endive, radicchio, and escarole. At dinner, a similar table d'hôte, priced at $26, will offer additional entrées like escalope de veau or mignonettes de boeuf Henri IV.

ONCLE TOM, 138 rue Wellington. Tel. 819/771-1689.
   Cuisine: FRENCH. **Reservations:** Required.
$ Prices: Main courses $15–$18; three-course prix fixe $20; four-course prix fixe $24. AE, DC, ER, MC, V.
   Open: Lunch Mon–Fri noon–2:30pm; dinner Mon–Fri 5:30–10:30pm, Sat 6–10:30pm.

Set in a Victorian house, Oncle Tom is an intimate dining spot decorated with stained glass, art works by local artists, and French provincial chests. Upstairs, you can settle into a cozy little alcove amid a warm rose-and-russet decor.

The cooking is as classic as the decor: rack of lamb or filet mignon; for starters, the terrine du chef and the escargots au parfum d'ail are both excellent choices. The table d'hôte is good value at $20. It includes soup, salad, appetizer, main course, and dessert, and among the selections there might be lamb stuffed and glazed with honey-mustard or monkfish. Luncheon prices run $9 to $12.

TWO NEARBY PLACES TO DINE IN QUEBEC

L'ECHELLE DE JACOB, 27 bd. Lucerne, Aylmer, Québec. Tel. 819/684-1040.
   Cuisine: FRENCH. **Reservations:** Required well in advance.
$ Prices: Appetizers $4–$7; main courses $15–$20; prix fixe $25–$28. AE, MC, V.
   Open: Dinner Wed–Mon 6:30–10pm.

This is one of the most popular Ottawa area restaurants. And that's not surprising, for it's truly a delightful spot. Ex-teachers Peter Brice and Daniel Lepage, who journeyed to Paris to learn the art of cooking, have created an authentic French inn filled with antiques that they brought back with them.

The small upstairs dining room, with only 16 tables, has a warm, rustic air, created by beamed ceiling, natural stone walls, and candlelight burnishing the oak chairs and china-filled breakfronts. Simplicity is the keynote here—even the menu is handwritten. It might contain such appetizers as mushroom charlotte made with oyster mushrooms and served with green peppercorn sauce or a warm duckling salad on a bed of watercress in a raspberry sauce. The specialty of the house is roast suckling pig, which is served every Saturday evening. Or there's a selection of such dishes as chicken with coriander and hazelnuts; crown roast of lamb with garlic, basil, oregano, and thyme; or duckling with lemon and ginger. The best value is the four-course prix fixe. Among the dessert treats there's an extra special chocolate mousse cake called Jacob's Dream, fresh cheesecakes, parfaits, and crème caramel.

It's a little difficult to find, but worth it. From Ottawa, drive over the Champlain Bridge and make a sharp left immediately off the bridge. Drive about 2½ miles (4km) to the first cluster of buildings and pull into the parking lot on the left. The restaurant (there's a tiny hanging inn sign) is in the old stone building farthest from the road. From Hull, take boulevard Taché and turn left on Vanier Road and follow the previous instructions.

L'OREE DU BOIS, Chemin Kingsmere, P.O. Box 756, Old Chelsea, PQ J0X 1N0. Tel. 819/827-0332.
Cuisine: FRENCH. **Reservations:** Required.
$ Prices: Appetizers $4–$8; main courses $14–$18; prix fixe $22. AE, ER, MC, V.
Open: Dinner Tues–Sat 5:30–10pm.

In the heart of the Gatineau, this traditional French restaurant offers excellent value, especially if you choose the prix fixe. From Hull, take Autoroute 5 north to Old Chelsea Exit 12.

TWO REAL PUBS OUTSIDE OTTAWA

THE CHESHIRE CAT, 2193 Richardson Side Rd. Carp. Tel. 613/831-2183.
Cuisine: ENGLISH. **Reservations:** Not needed.
$ Prices: Main courses $7–$10. MC, V.
Open: Mon–Wed 11:30am–11pm, Thurs–Sat 11:30am–1am, Sun noon–11pm.

Located in a stone cottage that formerly housed a school, this English-style pub with wood-burning stove, decorative horse brasses, and good pub food is as authentic as you're likely to find outside England. There's a variety of sandwiches available, plus such main courses as liver and bacon; mixed grill; sausage, eggs, and chips; and shepherd's pie. An afternoon tea of scones, jam, and whipped cream is also served. On summer days the garden is a lovely spot to relax and imagine yourself back in England's green and pleasant land.

THE SWAN AT CARP, Falldown Lane, Carp. Tel. 613/839-SWAN.
Cuisine: ENGLISH. **Reservations:** Not needed.
$ Prices: Most items $4–$7. AE, MC, V.
Open: Mon–Sat 11am–1am, Sun noon–11pm.

Another corner of England waits here at the Swan, a more Victorian-style English pub, located in a brick house complete with separate public bar as well as lounge bar. Originally a Presbyterian manse built in 1902, the Dugdale/Nadeau families opened it as a pub in 1987, naming it after a pub they ran in Stoke, England. There are no videos, no TV. Instead you'll find good conversation, beer at cellar temperature, Brit-inspired events like the Dambusters Anniversary celebration, and honest pub fare like bangers and mash, Lancashire hot pot, fish and chips, and "afters" like sherry trifle.

SPECIALTY DINING

BEAVER TAILS For a real Ottawa tradition, stop at **Hooker's** stand in the center of the Byward Market and purchase a beaver tail. This local specialty is in fact a very tasty deep-fried whole-wheat pastry served either with cinnamon, sugar, and lemon, or with garlic butter and cheese, or with raspberry jam. Delicious. And dirt cheap!

LIGHT, CASUAL FARE & ICE CREAM Across from the Byward Market, the shopping mall, the Rideau Centre, spans Rideau Street and has several fast-food spots including the **Baguette** (tel. 613/237-6366), great for breakfast pastries.

For ice cream, Ottawans flock to **Lois 'n' Frimas,** 361 Elgin St. (tel. 613/230-7013), a small parlor at which you can actually watch them make the ice cream complete with rock salt and ice freezer. A sign boasts that the ice cream uses no artificial stabilizers or preservatives, and contains only 25% air as opposed to other traditional brands that pump in much more. In other words, it tastes darn good! And it does. Try a regular or large cone (they're also made on the premises), or better yet, buy a monster waffle. Prices run $2 to $3, and Lois 'n' Frimas is open from 11am to 11pm Sunday through Thursday, until midnight on Friday and Saturday.

5. ATTRACTIONS

Most of Ottawa's major sights are clustered together downtown, so you can easily walk from one to another—from Parliament Hill to the Byward Market, from the National Gallery to the Museum of Civilization.

Your first stop should be the Parliament buildings and the Changing the Guard ceremony. From there you can either explore the canal or river by taking a boat trip, or walk over to the Byward Market to enjoy the colorful displays of fruits and vegetables along with the many lively restaurants/cafés in the area. A cycle ride or a jog along the canal is also great fun—you can go all the way down to Dow's Lake Pavilion and stop there for lunch, drinks, or some other refreshment. Then you can choose among the many museums listed below for more activities. At night, see the sound-and-light show on Parliament Hill and catch a show or concert at the National Arts Centre. If you have an extra day, why not try rafting down the Ottawa River from Beachburg, Ontario, courtesy of Wilderness Tours?

ORGANIZED TOURS   A fun way to introduce yourself to Ottawa is to ride the red double-decker buses operated by **Piccadilly Bus Tours** (tel. 613/235-7674). Tickets are $12 for adults, $10 for students and seniors, $6 for children under 12; call for current schedules. Other bus tours are operated by OC Transpo's **Gray Line** (tel. 613/741-4391).

PARLIAMENT HILL

Standing on a bluff jutting into the Ottawa River, the Parliament buildings, with their high, pitched copper roofs, are truly spectacular. In 1860 Prince Edward, later Edward VII, laid the cornerstone of the **Parliament buildings,** which were finished in time to host the inaugural session of the first Parliament of the new Dominion of Canada in 1867. If you enter through the south gate you will pass the **Centennial Flame,** lit by Lester Pearson on New Year's Eve 1966–67 to mark the passing of 100 years since this historic event.

The Parliament buildings (especially the Centre Block) represent the heart of Canadian political life, housing the Senate and **House of Commons.** You may attend the House of Commons sessions and observe the 295 elected members debating in the handsome green chamber with its tall stained-glass windows. Parliament is usually in recess from the end of June to early September, and on occasion between September and June including the Easter and Christmas holidays. Otherwise, the House usually sits from 11am to 6:30pm on Monday, 10am to 6:30pm on Tuesday and Thursday, 2pm to 8pm on Wednesday, and 10am to 4pm on Friday. The Senate is housed in an opulent red chamber with murals depicting Canadians fighting in World War I. The 104 notables from all regions of the country are appointed and sit until age 75. They initiate and refine legislation.

The great 302-foot tower rising from the Centre Block—the **Peace Tower**— houses a 53-bell carillon, a huge clock, an observation deck, and the **Memorial Chamber,** which commemorates Canada's war dead, most notably the 66,650 who lost their lives in World War I. Stones from the battlefields are lodged in the walls and floors of the chamber. Atop the tower rises a bronze mast, 35 feet high, flying a Canadian flag. The tower is lit when Parliament is in session.

When you go up to the tower, see if you notice anything strange about the elevator.

IMPRESSIONS

The national voice in Canada is muted. To quote Hugh Hood . . . there cannot be an Uncanadian Activities Committee because 'Uncanadianism is almost the very definition of Canadianism.'
—GEORGE WOODSTOCK, *CANADA AND THE CANADIANS*, 1970

Does it travel vertically as practically every other elevator does? Not quite. For the first 98 feet of your journey it travels on a 10° angle. This special elevator was recently installed; previously you had to take two elevators to reach the observatory.

The original Centre Block was destroyed by fire in 1916. Only the **Library** at the rear was saved. A glorious 16-sided dome, supported outside by huge flying buttresses and beautifully paneled inside with Canadian white pine, features a marble statue of the young Queen Victoria and magnificent carvings—gorgons, crests, masks, and hundreds of rosettes. The original floor was an intricate pattern of oak, cherry, walnut, and ash.

The Centre Block is flanked by the **East and West blocks.** The latter is closed to the public and contains parliamentary offices. The East Block, which formerly contained the offices of prime ministers, governors-general, and the Privy Council, contains four historic rooms that are open to the public: the original governor-general's Office, which has been restored to the period of Lord Dufferin (1872–78); the offices of Sir John A. MacDonald and Sir Georges-Etienne Cartier (the principal Fathers of Confederation); and the Privy Council Chamber with anteroom.

Stroll the grounds, which are dotted with statues honoring such political figures as William Lyon Mackenzie King, Sir Wilfrid Laurier, and pre-Confederation figures such as Robert Baldwin and Louis Hippolyte Lafontaine, the architects of responsible government during the ministry of 1848–51.

Behind the Centre Block stretches a promenade with great views of the river. Here, too, you will find the old Centre Block's bell, which crashed to the ground shortly after tolling midnight on the night of the fire in 1916. At the bottom of the cliff behind the Parliament buildings (accessible from the entrance locks on the Rideau Canal) is a pleasant path leading along the Ottawa River.

TOURS   Free tours of the Centre Block and library are given daily year round, except on Christmas, New Year's Day, and Canada Day (July 1). Although the precise tour times for 1994 are not available, they should be very similar to the 1993, tour times which were as follows: Canadian Thanksgiving to late May, every 30 minutes from 9am to 4pm (9pm on Tuesday); June to Labor Day, every 10 minutes weekdays from 9am to 8pm and weekends from 9am to 4pm; Labor Day to Canadian Thanksgiving, every 30 minutes from 9am to 4pm (8pm on Tuesday). The last tour excludes a visit to the Peace Tower. From Victoria Day to Labor Day you need to make same-day reservations for tours at the Info Tent (east of Centre Block). For more information on tour hours, call 613/992-4793.

Tours of the East Block historic offices are usually given daily from May to Labor Day and on weekends from September to May. For more information, call 613/992-1149.

Discover the Hill Walking Tours, exploring the events and personalities that shaped the Hill and the nation, are also given daily from the end of June to September 1. Make reservations at the Info Tent.

CHANGING THE GUARD   From late June to late August a colorful half-hour ceremony is held on the lawn of Parliament Hill daily (weather permitting). The Ceremonial Guard is made up of two historic regiments: the Governor-General's Foot Guards (red plumes) and the Canadian Grenadier Guards (white plumes). The parade of 125 soldiers in busbies and scarlet jackets (guard, Colour party, and band) assembles at Cartier Square Drill Hall (by the canal at Laurier Avenue) at 9:30am and marches up Elgin Street to reach the Hill at 10am. Upon arrival on the Hill, the Ceremonial Guard splits into two groups, one division of the old guard positioned on the west side of the Parliament Hill lawn and two divisions of the new guard, or "duties," on the east side of the lawn. The ceremony includes the inspection of dress and weapons of both groups to ensure that the new guard is appropriately turned out and to determine if the old guard is still properly regaled and has no deficiencies in the equipment after their tour of duty. The Colours are then marched before the troops and are saluted. The guards also compliment each other by presenting arms. Finally the outgoing guard commander gives the key to the guard room to the incoming guard commander, signifying that the guard has been changed.

SOUND & LIGHT SHOW   From May through August, Canada's history unfolds

✪ in a dazzling half-hour display of sound and light against the dramatic backdrop of the Parliament buildings. Weather permitting, there are two performances per night, one in English, the other in French. Bleacher seating. Admission is free. For more information, contact the National Capital Commission at 613/239-5000. If you can understand what some of those sergeant-majors yell, you're a natural-born soldier.

THE RIDEAU CANAL

✪ Built to avoid using the St. Lawrence River (which was once so vulnerable to American attack) for transporting troops and supplies to the interior of Canada should another war like that of 1812 break out between the United States and Britain, the canal is one of Ottawa's greatest assets. In summer you can either walk or cycle along the canal paths, or else canoe or boat your way along before stopping in at the canalside beer garden at the National Arts Centre. In winter it's turned into a glorious skating rink worthy of any Dutch artist's palette as people come and go to work, skating with their briefcases, and families take to the ice with children perched atop their backs or drawn upon sleighs. For daily information on the state of the ice, call 613/992-1234.

The construction of the canal began under the direction of Lieutenant-Colonel By of the Royal Engineers in 1826. The 123-mile engineering feat was completed in 1832. For many years Parliament Hill served as the barracks site for the regimental soldiers involved.

Starting in Ottawa, the canal follows the course of the Rideau River to its summit on Upper Rideau Lake, which is connected to Newboro Lake, where the canal descends the Cataraqui River (through a series of lakes controlled by dams) to Kingston. In Ottawa there's a flight of eight locks that carry boats the 80-foot difference between the artificially constructed portion of the canal and the Ottawa River—a sight not to be missed, between Parliament Hill and the Château Laurier Hotel.

OTHER TOP ATTRACTIONS

THE BYWARD MARKET, Sussex, Rideau, St. Patrick, and King Edward Sts.

Here in the old market area of the city there's still a colorful traditional farmer's market selling all kinds of local food and vegetable products. The market building now houses two floors of interesting boutiques displaying a wide variety of wares and crafts. During market season you can enjoy the outdoor cafés and watch life drift by over a cold beer or glass of wine.

Take some time to wander past the stalls, piled high with fresh, shining locally grown produce. Pick up some fruit, some cheese from the International Cheese shop, some desserts from Aux Délices, and take your picnic back down to the canal.

Explore, too, the Sussex courtyards, which extend from George to St. Patrick Streets along Sussex Drive.

Open: May 1–Nov 1 Mon–Sat 9am–6pm, Sun 10am–6pm. Winter daily 10am–6pm.

CANADIAN MUSEUM OF CIVILIZATION, 100 Laurier St., in Hull. Tel. 819/776-7000.

The Canadian Museum of Civilization is housed in a spectacular building designed by Albertan architect Douglas Cardinal that rises from the banks of the Ottawa River as if its curvaceous form had been sculpted by wind, water, and glacier. Suggesting the relationship between the earth and its inhabitants, Cardinal used Tyndall stone that contained fossils and designed a main entrance resembling the shape of a Kwakiutl mask. The exhibits within this magnificent building tell the history of Canada and its various ethnic peoples, but the exhibits don't live up somehow to the promise of the building itself. The **Grand Hall** is devoted to six Native Canadian tribes of the West Coast, featuring an impressive collection of huge totem poles. In the **History Hall** 900 years of Canadian history unfold from the arrival of the Vikings to the turn of this century, captured in tableaux and audiovisual shows. In its temporary exhibition halls the museum presents exhibitions featuring the arts and crafts of ethnic peoples like **Contemporary Indian and Inuit Art.** The **Children's Museum** invites the kids to discover other cultures and the excitement of such disciplines as archeology. **CINEPLUS,** the only one of its kind in the world, is a theater containing an IMAX and an OMNIMAX (dome-shaped) screen that propels the viewer giddily into the action of any film.

Admission: $4.50 adults, $3 seniors and youths 16–21, free for children under 15. Free to all Thurs after 5pm. Tickets to CINEPLUS $7 adults, $5 youths, seniors, and children.

Open: Apr–June Fri–Wed 9am–5pm, Thurs 9am–8pm. July–Aug Fri–Wed 9am–6pm, Thurs 9am–8pm. Sept–Mar Thurs–Wed 9am–8pm.

CENTRAL EXPERIMENTAL FARM, The Driveway and Carling Ave. Tel. 613/993-5222 or 993-4802 for the museum only.

There are numerous parks in the city, but the biggest and possibly the most attractive isn't a park at all—it's the Central Experimental Farm—1,200 acres of green open space, now completely surrounded by Ottawa suburbia.

Its greenhouses are famous, and every November a spectacular chrysanthemum show is held. The farm itself has tree-shaded roads, barns, and fields with lots of farm animals that the kids will love to see. There's also a flower garden, plus an arboretum with clusters of trees and shrubs from all over the world. During the summer, from May to early October, you can take rides in wagons drawn by Clydesdales, weather permitting, from 10 to 11:30am and 2 to 3:30pm Monday through Friday. This is a lovely place to relax and have a picnic.

Admission: Free.

Open: Agricultural Museum daily 9:30am–5pm. Barns and tropical greenhouse daily 9am–4pm. **Closed:** Christmas and New Year's days.

NATIONAL AVIATION MUSEUM, Rockcliffe Airport. Tel. 613/993-2010.

This collection of more than 115 aircraft is one of the best of its kind in the world. The main exhibit hall features a "Walkway of Time," tracing aviation history from the turn of the century through two world wars to the present. Among the aircraft on display are the Lancaster bomber, the Supermarine Spitfire (which helped win World War II), the Vickers Viscount (the first turbine-powered plane to be used for passenger service), and the Star Fighter, with its rapierlike nose. Many are still being flown.

You can also see a replica of the Silver Dart, which rose from the ice of Baddeck Bay, Nova Scotia, in February 1909, performing the first powered flight in Canada. It flew for nine minutes—not bad, considering it looks as though it were built out of bicycle parts and kites. Films and videos of historical aviation events are also shown, and displays too, detailing the lives and exploits of Canada's flying aces.

Admission: $5 adults, $4 seniors and students, $1.75 children 6–15. Free to all Thurs 5–9pm.

Open: May 1–Labor Day Fri–Wed 9am–5pm, Thurs 9am–9pm. Rest of year Tues–Wed and Fri–Sun 9am–5pm, Thurs 9am–9pm. **Directions:** From Sussex Drive, take Rockcliffe Parkway and exit at the National Aviation Museum.

NATIONAL GALLERY OF CANADA, 380 Sussex Dr., at St. Patrick St. Tel. 613/990-1985.

The National Gallery, a rose-granite crystal palace, shines as architect Moshe Safdie intended, like a candelabra on a promontory overlooking the Ottawa River and Parliament Hill. A dramatic long glass concourse leads to the Grand Hall commanding glorious views of Parliament Hill. The galleries themselves are also filled with natural light thanks to ingeniously designed shafts with reflective panels.

Inside is a great collection of Canadian art from the 17th century to the present. Among the highlights, don't miss the fabulous Rideau Convent Chapel (1888), a rhapsody of wooden fan vaulting, cast-iron columns, and intricate carving created by architect-priest Georges Bouillon; the works of such early québecois artists as Antoine Plamondon, Joseph Legare, Abbé Jean Guyon, and Frère Luc; works by Paul Kane, Canada's chronicler of the west, or snow scenes by Cornelius Krieghoff; turn-of-the-century talents Homer Watson and Ozias Leduc; Tom Thomson and the Group of

Seven; Emily Carr and David Milne; the Montréal Automatistes Paul-Emile Borduas and Jean-Paul Riopelle. The European masters are also represented—Rembrandt, Cézanne, van Gogh, El Greco, Monet, Renoir, Canaletto, Courbet, Matisse, and Braque.

The contemporary galleries exhibit the work of pop artists Warhol, Oldenburg, and Lichtenstein, and of the minimalists, and later abstract works, both Canadian and American. Facilities include three restaurants, a bookstore, and auditorium.

Tours: Guided tours daily at 11am and 2pm. Register at the information desk.
Admission: Free. Fees charged for special exhibits.
Open: Summer Fri–Wed 10am–6pm, Thurs 10am–8pm. Winter Tues–Wed and Fri–Sun 10am–6pm, Thurs 10am–8pm. **Closed:** Holidays.

NATIONAL MUSEUM OF NATURE, at the corner of Metcalfe and McLeod Sts. Tel. 613/996-3102.

Located in the impressive stone Victoria Memorial Building, this museum focuses on nature. The dinosaur hall is one of its popular highlights and so, too, are the mineral galleries. Other displays focus on Canadian birds and animals and their evolution and relationships with each other and with the environment. A huge tree of life traces the evolutionary threads of life from 500 million years ago to the present. Additional themes include plant and ocean life and space. Kids will enjoy the activity area called the Discovery Den. On the third floor kids can also trade their "natural" treasures.

Admission: $4 adults, $3 students, $2 children 6–16 and seniors, $12 for families. Half price on Thurs 9:30am–5pm; free 5–8pm.
Open: May 1–Labor Day Tues–Wed and Fri–Sat 9:30am–5pm, Sun–Mon and Thurs 9:30am–8pm. Rest of year Fri–Wed 10am–5pm, Thurs 10am–8pm.

NATIONAL MUSEUM OF SCIENCE AND TECHNOLOGY, 1867 bd. St-Laurent, at Lancaster Rd. Tel. 613/991-3044.

This museum offers fun and learning through involvement. You can pull levers to demonstrate physical principles such as viscosity, climb aboard a steam locomotive, observe the heavens through Canada's largest refracting telescope, watch what's going on in the adjacent parking lot through a couple of periscopes, see chicks hatching, and try to walk through the Crazy Kitchen, where everything looks normal but the floor is tilted at a sharp angle. Displays relate to agriculture, communications, space, computer technology, transportation, graphic arts, and physics.

The museum also houses a collection of antique trains, streetcars, fire engines, and autos, including the Bricklin, "the safest car on the road," which was produced in Canada in 1974 and 1975.

Admission: $4.50 adults, $3.50 seniors and students, $1.50 children 6–15; $9 family maximum. Free to all on Thurs after 5pm.
Open: May 1–Labor Day Fri–Wed 9am–5pm, Thurs 9am–9pm. Winter Tues–Wed and Fri–Sun 9am–5pm, Thurs 9am–9pm. Appointments are necessary to enter the observatory (call 613/991-9219 8am–4pm).

RCMP, THE CANADIAN POLICE COLLEGE, 8900 St. Laurent Blvd. North. Tel. 613/993-3751.

The Musical Ride military pageant was first produced in Regina in 1878. Horses and riders practice at the Canadian Police College and the public is welcome to attend the practice ride. Check before you go, though, because the ride is often on tour.

Admission: Free.
Directions: At St. Laurent Boulevard North, take Sussex Drive east past Rideau Hall and pick up Rockville Driveway; turn left at Sandridge Road and continue to the corner of St. Laurent.

THE SUPREME COURT, Wellington St., at Kent. Tel. 613/995-4330, or 613/995-5361 for tour information.

Although the Supreme Court was created in 1875, cases were appealed to the Judicial Committee of the Privy Council until 1949, when the court finally became Canada's highest court of appeal. The lofty art deco building houses three courtrooms—one for the Supreme Court, two for the Federal Court.

Three sessions are held during the year: The first session begins on the fourth Tuesday in January and ends just before Easter, the second begins on the fourth Tuesday in April and continues to the end of June, and the third begins on the first Tuesday in October and ends just before Christmas. The court does not normally sit during July, August, and September. While in session, the court usually hears appeals on Monday, Tuesday, Wednesday, and Thursday from 10:30am to 1pm and 2:30 to 4pm. The first and third Mondays in each month are usually reserved for the hearing of motions for leave to appeal.

Tours: Thirty-minute tours given May–Sept Mon–Fri 9am–5pm (weekends also, in July).

MORE ATTRACTIONS

BILLINGS ESTATE MUSEUM, 2100 Cabot St. Tel. 613/564-1363.

This house, set on eight acres, affords an opportunity to look into the early-1800s lifestyle of one of Ottawa's more prosperous pioneer families.

Admission: $2.25 adults, $1.60 seniors, $1 children.

Open: May 1–Aug 31 Sun–Wed noon–5pm, Thurs noon–5pm and 6pm–8pm. Sept 1–Oct 31 Sun–Wed noon–5pm. **Directions:** Go south on Bank Street, cross the Rideau River at Billings Bridge and take Riverside East; turn right on Pleasant Part and right on Cabot.

BYTOWN MUSEUM, 540 Wellington St., at Commissioner. Tel. 613/ 234-4570.

Housed in the oldest stone building (1827) in Ottawa, which served originally as the Commissariat for food and material during the building of the Rideau Canal, the museum displays possessions of Lieutenant-Colonel By, the builder of the canal, as well as artifacts that reflect the social history of early Bytown/Ottawa. There are three period rooms and some changing exhibits. The museum is located beside the Ottawa Locks, between Parliament Hill and the Château Laurier Hotel.

Admission: $2.25 adults, $1.10 seniors and students, 50¢ children, $5.50 families.

Open: Apr to mid-May and mid-Oct to Nov Mon–Fri 10am–4pm. Mid-May to mid-Oct Mon and Wed–Sat 10am–4pm, Sun 2–5pm.

CANADIAN WAR MUSEUM, 330 Sussex Dr. Tel. 613/992-2774.

Kids love to clamber over the tanks that are stationed outside the War Museum, and they seem to love almost as much imagining themselves in battle in the life-size replica of a World War I trench.

The collection, which traces Canadian military history, contains airplanes, cars (Adolf Hitler's Mercedes, for example), guns, torpedoes, mines, uniforms (including that of Canadian air ace Billy Bishop), and tools, plus several large displays complete with sound effects showing famous battles such as the Normandy D-day landings.

Admission: $2.50 adults, $1.25 seniors, free for children under 6. Free for everyone on Thurs 5–8pm.

Open: Fri–Wed 9:30am–5pm, Thurs 9:30am–8pm. **Closed:** Christmas Day.

THE CURRENCY MUSEUM, 245 Sparks St. Tel. 613/782-8914.

At the Bank of Canada, this museum will set you thinking creatively about money. It houses the most complete collection of Canadian notes and coins in the world, and traces the history of money—beads, wampum, and whale teeth—from early China to the modern era.

Admission: $2 adults, children 7 and under free.

Open: May–Sept Mon–Sat 10:30am–5pm, Sun 1–5pm. Oct–Apr Tues–Sat 10:30am–5pm, Sun 1–5pm.

LAURIER HOUSE, 335 Laurier Ave. East. Tel. 613/692-2581.

Outside this house there's a stone by the curb that was used as an aid for getting in

IMPRESSIONS

Geography has made us neighbors. History has made us friends. Economics has made us partners. And necessity has made us allies. Those whom nature has so joined together, let no man put asunder.
—JOHN F. KENNEDY, 1961

and out of carriages. From 1897 to 1919 this mansion was the home of Canada's seventh prime minister (and first French-Canadian PM), Sir Wilfrid Laurier. From 1923 to 1950 it was the residence of Mackenzie King, who served as prime minister for 21 years. The house is crammed with mementos of them both. In the library where King held seances you can see the crystal ball that King supposedly had seen and coveted in London but said he couldn't afford (an American bought it for him when he overheard King's remarks). You can also see the portrait of his mother in front of which he used to place a red rose daily, and also a copy of the program Abraham Lincoln held the night of his assassination, plus copies of the death mask (completed four years before his death) and hands of the president. Lester B. Pearson's library has also been re-created, and there you can see the Nobel Peace Prize medal he won for his role in the 1956 Arab-Israeli dispute.

Admission: Free.

Open: Oct–Mar Tues–Sat 10am–5pm, Sun 2–5pm. Apr–Sept Tues–Sat 9am–5pm, Sun 2–5pm.

ROYAL CANADIAN MINT, 320 Sussex Dr. Tel. 613/993-8990.

From an elevated walkway you can watch the transformation of gold and silver into special commemorative coins, medals, and investment tokens. Built as a branch of the Royal Mint in London, this mint struck its first coin in 1908. In 1931 it became an independent operation, but since 1976 circulating coinage has been made in Winnipeg.

Tours: May–Aug Mon–Fri at 15-minute intervals between 8:30 and 11am and again between 12:30 and 4:30pm. By appointment only.

ALONG THE PARKWAY & SUSSEX DRIVE

This makes for a very picturesque and interesting drive. The **Ottawa River Parkway** starts in the west end at Carling Avenue and runs along the river into Wellington Street, all the way offering glorious views over the islands in the river.

From Confederation Square, proceed along Sussex Drive to St. Patrick Street, where you can turn left into **Nepean Point Park.** Here, you and the statue of Samuel de Champlain can share a beautiful view over the river.

Across the road is **Major's Hill Park,** between the Château Laurier and the National Gallery, where the noonday gun is fired (at 10am on Sunday to avoid disturbing church services). You can, if you wish, watch the lighting of the cannon.

Just beyond the Macdonald-Cartier Bridge stands **Earnscliffe,** originally the home of Sir John A. Macdonald and now the impressive residence of the British high commissioner.

Farther along Sussex Drive you cross the Rideau River, whence you can look down upon the modern Ottawa City Hall pat in the middle of Green Island overlooking Rideau Falls, before proceeding past the prime minister's house, well sheltered by trees at 24 Sussex Dr., and on to **Government House,** at no. 1, still often referred to as Rideau Hall, the residence of the governor-general. For tours of the grounds, call 613/998-7113 or 613/998-7114.

On the 88-acre grounds there's a red oak tree that was planted by President Kennedy and also a sapling planted by President Nixon (which local wags note has grown rather crooked).

The grounds are closed only during state visits by world leaders.

The drive then becomes the National Capital Commission Driveway, a beautiful route along the Ottawa River and through **Rockcliffe Park.** Where the road forks in the park, follow the right fork to Acacia Avenue to reach the **Rockeries,** where carpets of daffodils and narcissus herald the spring in April.

GATINEAU PARK

Only two miles, about a 10-minute drive, from the House of Parliament lie 88,000 acres of woodland and lakes named after notary-turned-explorer Nicolas Gatineau of Trois-Rivières. The park began in 1938, when the federal government purchased some land in the Gatineau Hills to stop destruction of the forests brought on by the demand for cheap firewood during the depression. Now there are white-tailed deer, beaver, and more than 100 species of birds in the park. The black bear, timber wolf, otter, marten, and raccoon are regular residents. If you're lucky you might spy a moose, lynx, or wolverine.

Facilities in the park include 90 miles of **hiking trails** and supervised **swimming beaches** at Meech Lake, Lac Philippe, and Lac la Pêche. Vehicle access fees to beach areas are $5.50. Boats can be rented at Lac Philippe and Lac la Pêche. Motorboats are not permitted on park lakes except on Lac la Pêche, where motors up to 10 h.p. may be used for **fishing.** Most lakes can be fished (if it's not allowed, it's posted). A Québec license is required and can be obtained at many convenience stores around the park.

Camping facilities are at or near Lac Philippe, accessible by Highways 5, 105, and 366. For information on this and other camping facilities, call the Gatineau Park Visitor Centre, Meech Lake Road, Old Chelsea (tel. 819/827-2020), or write the National Capital Commission, 161 Laurier Ave. West, Ottawa, ON, K1P 6J6. Reservations are vital. Call 819/456-3016 after June 1 between 9am and 4pm. Fees are $16 per site per day ($8 for seniors).

In winter the hiking trails become cross-country ski trails, marked by numbers on blue plaques with chalets along the way. Winter camping is available at Lac Philippe.

While you're in the park, visit the summer retreat of Mackenzie King at **Kingsmere.** You can have tea in a summer cottage there and inspect the architectural fragments he dragged here from the parliamentary building after the 1916 fire and from London's House of Commons after the 1941 Blitz. The Moorside tearoom is open only in summer from 11am to 6:30pm. For reservations call 819/827-3405.

To get to the park you can take several routes: cross over to Hull and take boulevard Taché (Route 148) to the Gatineau Parkway, which will lead you to Kingsmere, Camp Fortune (a ski resort), and eventually to Meech Lake. Or come up Highway 5 north, take Exit 12 for Old Chelsea, turn left and proceed ¾ mile (1.2km) on Meech Lake Road to the Gatineau Park Visitor Centre. To reach Lac Philippe you should take Highway 105 north out of Hull up to Wakefield. Beyond Wakefield, take Route 366 west. Just before you reach Ste-Cecile-de-Masham you can turn off to Lac Philippe; to reach Lac la Pêche, keep going along the Masham road to St-Louis-de-Masham and enter the park just beyond.

SPECIAL EVENTS

For any of the events mentioned here the best source of information is the Convention and Tourist Bureau, 111 Lisgar St. (tel. 613/237-5150).

Ottawa's biggest event is the **Canadian Tulip Festival** in May, when the city is ablaze with 200 varieties of tulips stretching along the driveways, around public buildings, monuments, embassies, and private homes. (Probably the best viewing is to be had at Dow's Lake.) The festival began in 1945, when the people of the Netherlands sent 100,000 tulip bulbs to Canada in appreciation of the role Canadian troops played in liberating Holland. Queen Juliana of the Netherlands, who had spent the war years in Canada during the occupation, arranged for an annual presentation of bulbs to celebrate the birth of her daughter, Princess Margriet, in Ottawa in 1943 (to ensure that the princess was born a citizen of the Netherlands, the Canadian government proclaimed her room in the Ottawa Civic Hospital part of Holland).

Over the years the festival has grown, and now features a flurry of spectacular events: fireworks displays, parades, flotilla, craft show featuring over 120 artisans, marathon, daily lunchtime and evening entertainment on an outdoor stage, and a host of activities centered on Dow's Lake—waterski shows, boating events, a helicopter rescue demonstration.

For information on the Canadian Tulip Festival contact Canadian Tulip Festival, 275 Bay St., Ottawa, ON, K1R 5Z5 (tel. 613/567-5757).

At the National Museum of Natural Science, the **Children's Festival** is held in early June, with dance, mime, puppetry, and music, all for the kids.

On July 1, Canadians flock to the city to celebrate ✪ **Canada Day,** a huge birthday party complete with all kinds of entertainments, including fireworks.

When the ice hog comes up through the ice of the Rideau Canal, that means it's time for ✪ **Winterlude,** a snow and ice extravaganza that features parades, bands, floats, fireworks, speed-skating, snowshoe races, ice boating, curling, and more. One of the most colorful events is the bed race on the canal, while the most exciting is perhaps harness racing on ice. The carnival usually takes place the first or second week in February. For information, call 613/239-5000.

Other major events include: the **Franco-Ontarien Festival,** usually the third week in June or thereabouts, which celebrates French culture with musical entertainment, fashion shows, clowns and acrobats, and more; the 10-day **Ottawa International Jazz Festival** (tel. 613/594-3580), in mid-July; the 10-day **Super-Ex (Central Canada Exhibition)** (tel. 613/237-7222), in mid- to late August; and the **Gatineau Hot-Air Balloon Festival** on Labor Day weekend.

6. SPORTS/RECREATION

BOATING/CRUISING   You can rent boats on the Rideau Canal at the following locations.

Hog's Back Marina, on Hog's Back Road between Riverside Drive and Highway 16 (tel. 613/736-9893), rents canoes for $7 per hour or $25 a day.

The old Dow's Lake boathouse has been transformed into a $3-million glass-and-steel complex that from a distance looks, appropriately enough, like a cluster of sails. Here at **Dow's Lake Pavilion,** 1001 Queen Elizabeth Dr. (tel. 613/232-1001), you can rent bikes, paddleboats, and canoes at the marina (tel. 613/232-5278), and also relax and dine at several restaurants. It makes a great haven after a winter skate down the canal, or after a summer running or cycling jaunt alongside the canal. The city really does fade into oblivion as you sit on the lakeside terrace.

Paul's Boat Lines Ltd., 219 Colonnade Rd., in Nepean (tel. 613/225-6781), operates two cruises: the Ottawa River cruise, which takes you along Embassy Row to Rockcliffe Park, departing from the dock in Hull, east of Alexandra Bridge in Jacques Cartier Park; and the Rideau Canal cruise, which leaves from the docks opposite the Arts Centre and goes down the canal to the Experimental Farm and Carleton University.

River cruises leave at 11am, and 2, 4, and 7:30pm. Adults pay $9.50; seniors, $8; children $5. The trip lasts 1½ hours. The canal trip leaves at 10 and 11:30am, and 1:30, 3, 4:30, 7, and 8:30pm, and takes 1¼ hours. Adults are charged $9.50; seniors, $8; children, $5.

The *Sea Prince II* also cruises daily along the Ottawa River from both Ottawa and Hull docks. Adult fare is $10, students and seniors pay $8.50, and children under 12 $6. The boat also offers dinner-dance cruises, theme events, and day cruises to Château Montebello. For more information, contact the **Ottawa Riverboat Company,** 30 Murray St., Suite 100, Ottawa, ON, K1N 5M4 (tel. 613/562-4888).

CYCLING   In all, there are over 100 miles of bike paths along the Ottawa and Rideau rivers, the Rideau Canal, and in Gatineau Park, and more miles are being added. All bikeways are marked with a blue, black, and white cyclist logo.

From April to Canadian Thanksgiving you can rent cycles from **Rent a Bike** in the parking lot behind the Château Laurier Hotel (tel. 613/233-0268). Town bikes, sport bikes, mountain bikes, and touring bikes are all available, from $18 a day. The company will also provide maps of the best day trips around the city for you to follow on your own. For information, write P.O. Box 1204, Station B, Ottawa, ON, K1P 5R3.

ICE-SKATING/ROLLER-SKATING During the winter the **Rideau Canal** is flooded to a depth of three feet, becoming the longest and most romantic skating rink in the world—it stretches six miles from the National Arts Centre to Dow's Lake and Carleton University. (Every morning the state of the ice is reported on the radio news.) Skates can be rented at three places: at Dow's Lake, opposite the NAC, and at Fifth Avenue. Call ahead to make sure they have them, for supplies are limited. For daily ice-condition reports, call 613/232-1234.

The canal is fully serviced with heated huts, sleigh rentals, boot check and skate-sharpening services, food concessions, and restrooms. The season usually runs from late December to late February.

SKIING Mont Cascades, just 30 minutes north of Ottawa across the Gatineau River outside of Cantley on Highway 307 (tel. 819/827-0301), has 14 trails, one triple- and one double-chair lift, and three T-bars. The longest run is 2,500 feet. There are two day lodges with cafeteria and restaurant-bar at the hill. During the summer you can enjoy the thrill of coming down the superslide, careening around corners in real bobsled style at your own pace. Night skiing is available. Lift rates are now hourly: $7 for adults for one hour, $20 for seven hours or more; $5 and $18 respectively for children.

Eighteen miles from the city, **Edelweiss Valley,** Route 366, Wakefield (tel. 819/459-2328), has 24 runs, four lifts (including three double-chairs and one quad, ski school, night skiing, and a warm cozy lodge, plus overnight accommodations. You can also ice-skate and take sleigh rides through the snow. Lift rates for adults are $14 for two hours, $28 for eight hours. Tennis, golf, and a water slide are summer attractions.

Mont Ste-Marie, 55 miles north of Ottawa at Lac Ste-Marie (tel. 819/467-5200), is the most complete year-round resort in this area. Winter activities include skiing on twin peaks, with a 1,250-foot drop and the longest run at two miles. There are two quads and a Poma. Other facilities include cross-country skiing, skating, and tobogganing. Lift rates are $20 weekdays, $32 weekends for adults.

Summer facilities include four tennis courts, an 18-hole golf course, private lakes where you can swim and canoe, a stocked trout lake, and of course miles of hiking trails through the mountains.

WHITE-WATER RAFTING While you're in Ottawa, you really should take the opportunity to enjoy the thrills and spills of white-water rafting. Several companies operate such tours. **Wilderness Tours** has an outdoor center in Beachburg just 90 minutes west of Ottawa on the Ottawa River complete with large restaurant and bar, a beach, and such activities as sailing, canoeing, kayaking, and windsurfing. Their white-water rafting trips near Beachburg start at $70 per person per day during the week. For information, call 613/646-2241 or toll free 800/267-9166, or write Wilderness Tours, Route 21 (P.O. Box 89), Beachburg, ON, K0J 1C0.

Other companies operating similar trips and facilities include: **River Run,** P.O. Box 179, Beachburg, ON, K0J 1C0 (tel. 613/646-2501); and **Equinox Adventures,** 5334 Yonge St., no. 609, Toronto, ON, M2N 6M2 (tel. 416/222-2223).

7. EVENING ENTERTAINMENT

Ottawa's culture and nightlife pickings are somewhat meager, really only extending to the National Arts Centre, several bars, and one or two dance clubs, the raciest of which are concentrated in Hull.

For entertainment information, call **Chez Nightlife** (tel. 613/562-1111) for taped information, and secure copies of any of the following: *Where,* a free guide usually provided in your hotel; *Ottawa* magazine; the Friday edition of the *Ottawa Citizen;* or most au courant, *Metro.*

THE PERFORMING ARTS

THE NATIONAL ARTS CENTRE, 53 Elgin St., at Confederation Square. Tel. 613/996-5051.

A dazzling variety of Canadian and international musical, dance, and theater artists—including the resident National Arts Centre (NAC) Orchestra—perform at this marvelous center at 1 Confederation Sq. right in the heart of Ottawa alongside the Rideau Canal. Architect Fred Lebensold created three interlocking hexagons with terraces and spectacular view of the Canal and Ottawa.

There are four auditoriums: the European-style **Opera,** seating 2,300; the 950-seat **Theatre,** with its innovative apron stage; the 350-seat **Studio,** suitable for experimental works; and the pocket theater **Atelier,** seating 85.

The NAC offers a tremendous variety of programs, hosting such visiting companies and artists as the National Ballet of Canada, the Royal Winnipeg Ballet, and Les Grands Ballets Canadiens, Twyla Tharp, Yehudi Menuhin, and such variety artists as Nana Mouskouri, Tom Jones, B. B. King, Gilbert Bécaud, Andy Williams, José Feliciano, and so on.

The **National Arts Centre Orchestra** (tel. 613/996-5051), performs two main concert series and has featured such guest artists as Isaac Stern, James Galway, Philippe Entremont, and Barry Tuckwell.

The center also offers drama in English and French. In the past the English series has ranged from such classics as *Hamlet* to modern plays by Europeans and Canadians. The French ensemble has produced everything from Jean Genet's *Les Paravents* to Molière and Corneille classics.

Tickets at the center range in price from $10 to $65, depending on the presentation. For ticket reservations, call TicketMaster (tel. 613/755-1111) or visit the NAC box office, Monday and Thursday 10am to 9pm; Tuesday, Wednesday, Friday, and Saturday noon to 9pm; Sunday and holidays when performances are scheduled from noon to curtain time. Guided tours are available. A free monthly *Calendar of NAC Events* is available from the NAC Marketing and Communications Department, Box 1534, Station B, Ottawa, ON, K1P 5W1. For information call 613/996-5051. See also the restaurant listings for the center's canalside Le Café.

THEATER

Besides the ensemble at the National Arts Centre (where top-price tickets are $10.50), **Ottawa Little Theatre,** 400 King Edward Ave. (tel. 613/233-8948), offers good productions of such popular shows as Garson Kanin's *Born Yesterday* and Agatha Christie's *Murder at the Vicarage.* The company started in 1913 in an old church that burned down in 1970, but it now has a fully equipped, modern theater. Tickets are $9.

The **Great Canadian Theatre Company,** 910 Gladstone Ave. (tel. 613/236-5196), specializes in Canadian contemporary and experimental theater.

THE CLUB & MUSIC SCENE

FOLK, ROCK & JAZZ

As the guy who runs the place puts it, "everyone from politicians to truckdrivers" crams into **Patty's Place Pub,** 1070 Bank St. (tel. 613/730-1020), to raise a jug or two, tuck into some real fish-and-chips or Irish stew, and listen to the stirring Irish ballads rendered by a folksinger (resident Wednesday through Sunday). Small, it's the kind of place where you're tossed into the fray and wind up having a good old time playing darts, chatting, singing, and wassailing.

For a more rollicking scene, try **Molly McGuire's,** 130 George St. (tel. 613/235-1972), a cavernous pub where, on weekends only, the rock-and-roll and jazz bands belt out their sounds. For more local folk talent in a relaxed atmosphere, try **Rasputin's,** 696 Bronson Ave. (tel. 613/230-5102). The **Bytown Penguin,** 292 Elgin St. (tel. 613/233-0557), features a mixture of sounds—everything from Kris Kristofferson to rock and blues. The admission ranges from $5 to $18 depending on the act.

For jazz the best source of information is the **Jazz Ottawa Jazzline** at

613/730-7755. On Saturdays there's jazz from 4 to 7pm at **Hartwell's** in the Westin. **Vineyards,** 54 York St., in the market (tel. 613/563-4270), features a duo on Wednesday nights. Mainly blues action can be found upstairs at the **Rainbow Bistro,** 76 Murray St. (tel. 613/594-5123), with a special Sunday jam from 3 to 6pm and 9:30pm to 1am. Also check out what's playing at these clubs: **Café Van Gogh** (tel. 613/778-7199); **Sammy's Cellar** (tel. 613/232-0202); **Woody's** (tel. 613/567-1088); and **Creek Alley** (tel. 613/234-9942).

For rock, the latest crowd pleaser is **Grand Central,** 141 George St. (tel. 613/233-1435 or 613/233-1216), for dancing to live rock bands, weekends only.

DANCE CLUBS

Nightlife closes down at 1am (11pm on Sunday) in Ottawa, but across the river in Hull it continues until 3am every night of the week. The hottest discos/dance bars are found there. Note that recently the strip where most of the clubs are located has developed a reputation for late-night fights and muggings.

IN HULL   The current crowd pleaser is **Citi Club,** 179 Promenade du Portage (tel. 819/771-0396), which houses a multilevel disco-bar and attracts a fashionable crowd. Admission is $4 on weekends.

Tucked away behind Citi Club are several dance bars, **Le Bop** (tel. 819/777-3700) and **Le Bistro** (tel. 819/778-0968) among them.

Farther along the street, you'll find **Ozone,** 117 Promenade du Portage (tel. 819/771-6677), where the decor will transport you to Hawaii for the hula shuffle. It attracts a young crowd with its new rock sound. Open daily until 3am.

Shalimar, 100 Promenade du Portage (tel. 819/770-7486), is a disco-pub; **Broads** (tel. 819/772-1225) has a small dance floor and outdoor café.

IN OTTAWA   **Hartwell's,** in the Westin (tel. 613/560-7000), 11 Colonel By Dr., attracts an over-25 crowd for dancing to DJ top tunes Monday through Saturday (cover charged). On weekends there's also dancing in **Zoe's** piano bar in the Château Laurier, 1 Rideau St. (tel. 613/232-6411).

Stoney Mondays, 62 York St. (tel. 613/236-5548), is a dance bar with a popular outdoor patio in summer.

THE BAR SCENE

In the Byward Market area, **Vineyards,** 54 York St. (tel. 613/563-4270), is one of the city's coziest hangouts, with its downstairs cellarlike atmosphere, stone floors, and red checked tablecloths. Five different house wines are featured (from $5 a glass) plus over 150 different varieties. There's live jazz on Wednesday nights. Snacks are available too. Open Monday through Saturday from 4pm to 1am.

Another popular Byward Market spot is **Tramps,** on William Street.

For quiet drinking with a piano background, **Friday's Victorian Music Parlour,** 150 Elgin St. (tel. 613/237-5353), with its clubby atmosphere, old London engravings, and comfortable wingbacks, plus an inviting fire in winter, is a good choice, especially for single women who just want to have a quiet, dignified drink. The pianist entertains Tuesday to Saturday.

A similar parlor upstairs at the **Full House Restaurant,** 337 Somerset St. West (tel. 613/238-6734), provides piano entertainment and a jolly atmosphere Monday to Saturday nights.

Maxwell's, at 340 Elgin St., is an attractive contemporary-style bar where you can stop in and meet people.

For a truly relaxing ambience, where you can sink into the plush upholstery and enjoy the lilting piano strains, go to **Perriers,** at the Delta Ottawa Hotel, 361 Queen St. (tel. 613/238-6000); **Zoe's,** at the Château Laurier, 1 Rideau St. (tel. 613/232-6411); or **The Lounge,** at the Westin Hotel, 11 Colonel By Dr. (tel. 613/650-7000).

For pub-style conviviality, check out the **Brigadier's Pump,** in the Byward Market area at 23 York St. (tel. 613/230-6368), and the **Elephant & Castle,** at 50 Rideau St. (tel. 613/234-5544).

A QUEBECOIS BRASSERIE   For some real down-home québecois fun and atmosphere, visit **Les Raftsmen,** 60 rue St-Raymond, Hull (tel. 819/777-0924), a large tavern (brasserie) decked out in log-cabin style with cart wheels for decoration. At lunch or dinner you'll find plenty of joie de vivre here and reasonably priced traditional French Canadian cuisine—tourtière and pigs' feet as well as spaghetti, sandwiches, burgers, chicken, steak, and fish—all under $13 (most under $6 or $7). Dinner is served until 9pm, but the place is open Monday through Saturday from 7am to 3am. Entertainment every night.

MORE ENTERTAINMENT

FILM   The **ByTowne Cinema,** 325 Rideau St., shows old and new art films and other classics. A complete bimonthly calendar is available—call 613/789-4600.

The **Canadian Film Institute,** 2 Daly St. (tel. 613/232-6727), offers regular programs of Canadian and international art films. Screenings take place every Thursday, Friday, and Saturday at the Museum of Civilization, 100 Laurier St. in Hull.

SON ET LUMIERE   In summer don't miss the evening spectacular on Parliament Hill—a sound-and-light show relating the history and culture of Canada. There are two shows nightly (one in French and one in English), and admission is free. English performances are given first on Monday, Wednesday, Thursday, and Saturday at 9:30pm May through July, and at 9pm in August and September (9:30 and 10pm on other nights).

CHAPTER 12

SETTLING INTO TORONTO

Once lampooned as dull and ugly, a city whose inhabitants fled to Buffalo for a good time and where the blinds were drawn on Sunday at the main department store (Eaton's) to stop anyone from sinfully window-shopping, Toronto, now with a population of over three million, has burst forth during the last decade from its stodgy past and grabbed attention as one of the most exciting cities on the North American continent. It's already the subject of rave reviews by the media and visiting foreign experts, and I can only add two enthusiastic chapters.

How did it happen? Unlike most cities, Toronto got a second chance to change its image with a substantial blood transfusion from other cultures. Once a quiet, conservative community dominated by sedate Anglo-Saxons, who either entertained at home or in their clubs, Toronto was given a huge infusion of new energy by a post–World War II influx of 400,000 Italians, 80,000 Chinese, and 65,000 Portuguese, plus Germans, Jews, Hungarians, Greeks, Indians, West Indians, Vietnamese, Thais, and French Canadians. Now the place vibrates with street cafés, restaurants, cabarets, boutiques, theater, music, and life—ad infinitum.

And somehow, perhaps because of its past, it has become a model city where conservative traditions have tempered the often runaway impulse to destroy in order to create anew. When you see the old church and one of the oldest houses in the city standing proudly against the futuristic Eaton Centre, retained because the people wished it so, you know that certain values and a great deal of thoughtful debate have gone into the making of this city.

A model city. Indeed, Jane Jacobs, the urban planner, historian, and sociologist, chose to live here to watch her theories actually working on the downtown streets—where people walk to work from their restored Victorian town houses, where no developer can erect downtown commercial space without including living space, where the subway gleams and the streets are safe. In Toronto old buildings are saved and converted to other uses, the architects design around the contours of nature instead of just bulldozing the trees, 200 parks invite you to please walk on the grass, and over three million people live graciously in harmony, surrounded by a city created with flair and imagination but also a sense of traditional values.

A HISTORICAL NOTE In 1615 French explorer Etienne Brûlé was the first European to visit the site of Toronto, then referred to by the Native Canadians very

WHAT'S SPECIAL ABOUT TORONTO

Architectural Highlights

- [ ] The Royal Bank Tower (1972–76), a shimmering shaft of gold.
- [ ] City Hall (1965), by Viljo Revell, symbol of Toronto's rebirth.
- [ ] SkyDome (1989), the world's first stadium with a fully retractable roof.
- [ ] Roy Thomson Hall (1981), glass and mirrors outside, acoustic high-tech inside.
- [ ] Underground City, five miles of interconnecting tunnels lined with 1,000 stores.
- [ ] The Flatiron Building (1892), as photogenic as ever at Church and Front.
- [ ] The Provincial Parliament Buildings, great Romanesque architecture in pink sandstone.

Museums

- [ ] The Royal Ontario Museum, known for its Chinese and Canadiana collections.
- [ ] The Art Museum, with the world's largest collection of Henry Moore works.
- [ ] The Ontario Science Centre, with hundreds of engaging interactive exhibits that wow kids and adults alike.

Events/Festivals

- [ ] Canadian National Exhibition, the world's largest annual fair.
- [ ] Caribana, carnival Toronto style.
- [ ] The Royal Agricultural Show, a serious "State Fair" plus a horse show attended by royals.

For the Kids

- [ ] The Ontario Science Centre, Harbourfront, Ontario Place, and Metro Zoo are the top hits.

Shopping

- [ ] The Eaton Centre, 300-plus stores in attractive glass-domed marble-and-fountain ambience.
- [ ] Honest Ed's, the original launching pad for Ed Mirvish's meteoric rise to wealth and fame.

Streets/Neighborhoods

- [ ] Chinatown, a large bustling community with great shopping, browsing, and dining.
- [ ] Bloor/Yorkville, whose designer boutiques, art galleries, and cafés make it prime strolling territory.
- [ ] Queen Street West, youthful, funky, and fun with lots of reasonably priced, sophisticated dining.

A Zoo

- [ ] Metro Zoo, great for the animals and great for the visitors.

Natural Spectacles

- [ ] The Toronto Islands, a great escape from the urban landscape that's only a short ferry trip away.

After Dark

- [ ] 40-plus theaters make Toronto the second-largest theater center in North America.

---

simply as "a meeting place." Friction between the native population and the eastern colonists delayed the establishment of a settlement until 1749, when Fort Rouille was erected. The tiny fort was contested by the French and the English in the mid-1700s, and eventually became known as Fort York in 1793, and the capital of Upper Canada in 1797.

During the War of 1812, Fort York was occupied and set afire by American troops, in retaliation for which some Canadians went down and torched the American president's residence. (The Americans later whitewashed it to hide the charred wood—hence, the White House!) With the cessation of war in 1814 the town really began to grow. Yonge Street was opened as a public thoroughfare and military road, the Bank of Upper Canada was founded, and in 1834, with a population of 9,000, the city was incorporated and renamed Toronto.

Thereafter industrialization continued apace and Toronto boomed as lake travel increased and the railroads arrived. Between 1834 and 1884 the foundations of an industrial city were laid: waterworks, gas, and later electrical lighting were installed, public transportation organized, and the first telephone exchange established.

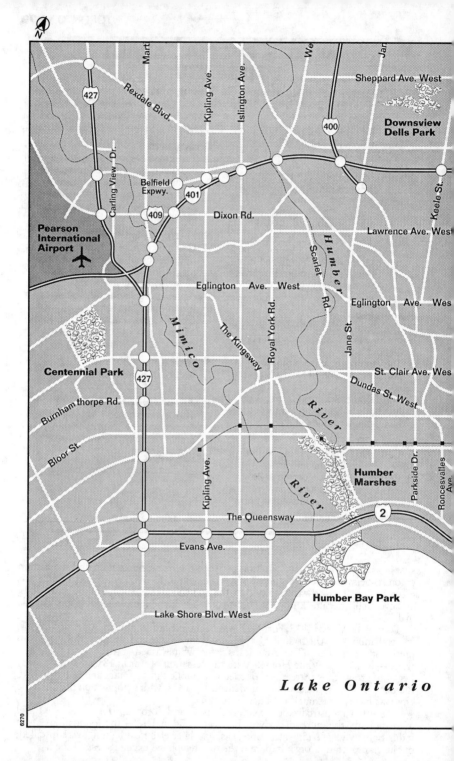

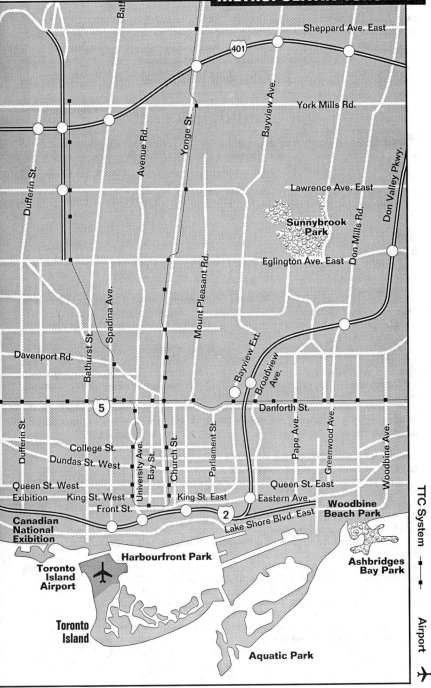

METROPOLITAN TORONTO

Sheppard Ave. East

401

York Mills Rd.

Bayview Ave.

Lawrence Ave. East

Don Mills Rd.

Don Valley Pkwy.

Sunnybrook Park

Eglington Ave. East

Avenue Rd.

Yonge St.

Dufferin St.

Mount Pleasant Rd.

Spadina Ave.

Bathurst St.

Davenport Rd.

Bayview Ext.

Broadview Ave.

Danforth St.

5

College St.

Dundas St. West

University Ave.

Bay St.

Church St.

Parliament St.

Pape Ave.

Greenwood Ave.

Woodbine Ave.

Queen St. East

Queen St. West

Exibition

King St. West

King St. East

Eastern Ave.

Woodbine Beach Park

Dufferin St.

Front St.

2

Lake Shore Blvd. East

Canadian National Exibition

Harbourfront Park

Ashbridges Bay Park

Toronto Island Airport

Toronto Island

Aquatic Park

TTC System

Airport ✈

By World War II, because of its prime location on Lake Ontario and its nearness to raw materials, power, and fuel, Toronto had become prosperous. After the war the tremendous European influx turned it into the exciting cosmopolitan city it is today.

1. ORIENTATION

ARRIVING

BY PLANE   More than 30 major airlines serve Toronto with regularly scheduled flights departing and arriving at **Pearson International Airport,** located in the northwest corner of Metro Toronto about 30 minutes (17 miles) from downtown. Three terminals, serviced by more than 60 airlines, cater to the traveler and offer the full services expected at international airports.

Most spectacular is the new Trillium Terminal 3 (tel. 416/612-5100) used by American, Canadian Airlines, British Airways, Japan Airlines, KLM, Lufthansa, Air France, United, and Varig, among others. This is a supermodern facility with moving walkways, a huge food court, and hundreds of stores, including North America's first branch of Harrods.

At Terminal Two, Air Canada has a Customer Care Centre, staffed full-time with representatives to assist the disabled, the elderly, unaccompanied children, and other inconvenienced passengers.

Other facilities at the airport include the exceptionally useful **Transport Canada Information Centres** in all terminals, where a staff fluent in 10 languages will answer queries about the airport, airline information, transportation services, and tourist attractions (tel. 416/676-3506).

Here are a few useful airline addresses: **Air Canada,** 130 Bloor St. West, at Avenue Road (tel. 416/925-2311); **USAir,** 100 Front St. West (tel. 416/361-1560); **American Airlines,** in the Royal York Hotel, Manulife Centre, and Toronto Dominion Centre (tel. toll free 800/433-7300); **Canadian Airlines International,** on the concourse level of Toronto Dominion Centre, 69 Yonge St. (tel. 416/798-2211); **Delta Airlines** 2 Bloor St. West (tel. 416/868-1717); **United Airlines,** at the airport (tel. 416/362-5000, or toll free 800/241-6522 for reservations); and **Northwest Airlines,** in the Royal York Hotel (tel. toll free 800/225-2525).

Getting to and from the Airport   The most convenient way, of course, is by **taxi,** which will cost about $32 to downtown.

Also very convenient is the **Airport Express,** which travels between the airport and downtown hotels—Harbour Castle Westin, the Royal York, Crown Plaza Toronto Centre, the Sheraton Centre, Holiday Inn, and the Delta Chelsea Inn—every 20 minutes all day. Fare is $10.75 ($18.50 round-trip) for adults, free for children under 11 accompanied by adult.

The cheapest way to go is by **subway and bus,** which will take about an hour. Buses travel between the Islington subway stop and the airport about every 40 minutes for a fare of $6 ($10 round-trip). Buses also travel between the Yorkdale and York Mills subway stations and the airport about every 40 minutes for a fare of $7.50 ($11.75 round-trip) from Yorkdale; $6.50 ($11.25 round-trip) from York Mills. On both routes children under 11 travel free if accompanied by an adult.

For information, call 416/594-3310.

In addition, most first-class hotels inside and outside the downtown area run their own **hotel limousine services,** so check when you make your reservation.

If you're driving to the airport, take the Gardiner Expressway West and Queen Elizabeth Way to Highway 427 north; then follow the airport expressway signs. From the airport take 427 south to the Gardiner Expressway East.

BY TRAIN   All **VIA Rail Canada** passenger trains pull into the massive classically proportioned **Union Station** on Front Street, one block west of Yonge opposite the Royal York Hotel. The station, of course, has direct access to the subway so that you can easily reach any Toronto destination from here. For VIA Rail information, call 416/366-8411; in the U.S., call your travel agent.

BY BUS   Out-of-town buses arrive and depart from the **Bus Terminal,** 610 Bay St., at Dundas Street, and provide fast, cheap, and efficient service to Canadian and American destinations. **Gray Coach Lines** (tel. 416/594-3310) services Niagara Falls; **Greyhound** (tel. 416/367-8747) services towns south and west of the city; **Voyageur** (tel. 416/393-7911) travels east and **Ontario Northland** (tel. 416/393-7911) services towns to the north.

BY CAR   From the U.S. you are most likely to enter Toronto via either Highway 401, or Highway 2 and the Queen Elizabeth Way if you come from the west. If you come from the east via Montréal, you'll use also Highways 401 and 2. Here are a few approximate driving distances to Toronto: from Atlanta, 977 miles; from Boston, 566; from Buffalo, 96; from Chicago, 534; from Cincinnati, 501; from Dallas, 1,452; from Detroit, 236; from Minneapolis, 972; and from New York, 495.

TOURIST INFORMATION

Contact the **Metro Toronto Convention & Visitors Association,** 207 Queen's Quay West, Suite 509, in the Queen's Quay Terminal at Harbourfront (P.O. Box 126), Toronto, ON, M5J 1A7 (tel. 416/203-2500), open in winter from 8:30am to 5pm Monday through Friday, 9am to 5pm Saturday and 9:30am to 5:30pm Sunday; in summer 8:30am to 10pm weekdays, 9am to 10pm Saturday and Sunday. Take the Harbourfront LRT down to the terminal building.
   More conveniently located, the **Visitor Information Centre,** outside the Eaton Centre on Yonge Street at Dundas, stays open from 9:30am to 5:30pm Tuesday to Saturday in winter, from 9am to 7pm daily in summer.
   Six summer-only centers are found at several locations. These locations vary from year to year but likely spots are at the Royal Ontario Museum on the southwest corner of Bloor Street and Avenue Road, at the Art Gallery on Dundas, Nathan Phillips Square, in front of City Hall at Queen West and Bay; the ferry docks, beside the Hilton Harbour Castle hotel; and at the CN Tower on Front Street West. These are open from 9am to 7pm daily.
   For information about Ontario, visit the **Ontario Ministry of Tourism and Recreation's Travel Centre** in the Eaton Centre, 220 Yonge St., level one, open Monday to Friday from 10am to 9pm, Saturday 9:30am to 6pm, and Sunday noon to 5pm, or write Ontario Travel, Queen's Park, Toronto, ON, M7A 2R9 (tel. 416/314-0944, or toll free 800/ONTARIO).

CITY LAYOUT

Toronto is laid out in a grid system. **Yonge Street** (pronounced Young) is the main south-north street, stretching from Lake Ontario in the south well beyond Highway 401 in the north; the main east-west artery is **Bloor Street,** which cuts right through

---

IMPRESSIONS

There is a Yankee look about the place . . . a pushing, thrusting, business-like, smart appearance.
—CHARLES MACKAY, *LIFE AND LIBERTY IN AMERICA,* 1857–8, 1859

Returning to Toronto was like finding a Jaguar parked in front of the vicarage and the padre inside with a pitcher of vodka martinis reading Lolita.
—ARTICLE IN *MACLEAN'S,* 1959

the heart of downtown. Yonge Street divides western cross streets from eastern cross streets.

"Downtown" usually refers to the area stretching south from Eglinton Avenue to the lake between Spadina Avenue in the west and Jarvis Street in the east. Because this is such a large area, for the purposes of this book I have divided it into **downtown** (from the lake to College/Carlton Streets), **midtown** (College/Carlton Streets to Davenport Road), and **uptown** (north from Davenport Road). In the first you will find all the lakeshore attractions—Harbourfront, Ontario Place, Fort York, Exhibition Place, the Toronto Islands—plus the CN Tower, City Hall, Skydome, Chinatown, the Art Gallery, and Eaton Centre. Midtown includes the Royal Ontario Museum, the University of Toronto, Markham Village, and chic Yorkville, a prime area for browsing and dining al fresco. Uptown is a fast-growing singles and young couples residential and entertainment area.

Because metropolitan Toronto is spread over 634 square kilometers (255 square miles) and includes East York and the cities of (from west to east) Etobicoke, York, North York, and Scarborough, some of its primary attractions exist outside the core, such as the Ontario Science Centre, the Metropolitan Zoo, and Canada's Wonderland—so be prepared to journey somewhat.

UNDERGROUND TORONTO It is not enough to know the streets of Toronto; you also need to know the warren of subterranean walkways that enable you to go from Union Station to City Hall. Currently, you can walk from Yonge and Queen Street Station west to the Sheraton Centre, then south through the Richmond-Adelaide Centre and First Canadian Place, all the way (through the dramatic Royal Bank Plaza) to Union Station. En route, branches lead off into the Toronto Dominion Centre and Stock Exchange. Other walkways also exist around Bloor and Yonge, and elsewhere in the city (ask for a map of these at the tourist information office). So if the weather's bad, you can eat, sleep, dance, and go to the theater without even donning a raincoat.

2. GETTING AROUND

BY PUBLIC TRANSPORTATION

Public transit is operated by the Toronto Transit Commission (TTC) (tel. 416/393-4636 from 7am to 11:30pm for information), which provides an overall interconnecting subway, bus, and streetcar system.

Fares (including transfers to buses or streetcars) for adults are $2 (or two for $3, five for $6.50 or 10 for $13), $1 for students and seniors (10 for $6.50), 50¢ for children 2 to 12 (eight for $2.50). You can purchase from any subway collector a special $5 pass good for unlimited travel after 9am weekdays, anytime Saturday and Sunday, which may be used by up to six people (maximum of two adults). On surface transportation you need a ticket, a token, or exact change. Tickets and tokens may be obtained at subway entrances or authorized stores that display the sign TTC TICKETS MAY BE PURCHASED HERE.

BY SUBWAY It's a joy to ride—fast, quiet, and sparkling clean. It's a very simple system to use, designed basically in the form of a cross: The **Bloor Street east-west line** runs from Kipling Avenue in the west to Kennedy Road in the east, where it connects with Scarborough Rapid Transit traveling from Scarborough Centre to McCowan. The **Yonge Street north-south line** runs from Finch Avenue in the north to Union Station (Front Street) in the south. From here, it loops north along University Avenue and connects with the Bloor line at the St. George Station. A **Spadina extension** runs north from St. George to Wilson.

A **Light Rapid Transit** connects downtown to Harbourfront. It operates from Union Station along Queen's Quay to Spadina, stopping at Queen's Quay ferry docks, York Street, Simcoe Street, and Rees Street. A transfer is not required as the LRT links up underground with the Yonge-University subway line.

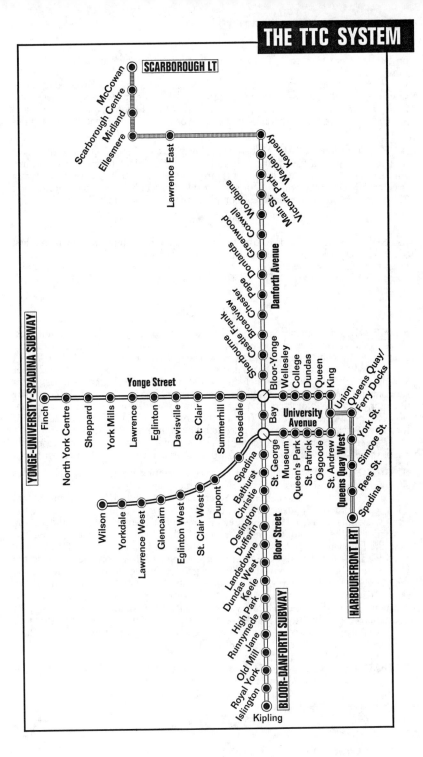

THE TTC SYSTEM

SCARBOROUGH LT

McCowan
Scarborough Centre
Midland
Ellesmere
Lawrence East
Kennedy
Warden
Victoria Park
Main St.
Woodbine
Coxwell
Greenwood
Donlands
Pape
Chester
Broadview
Castle Frank
Sherbourne
Danforth Avenue

YONGE-UNIVERSITY-SPADINA SUBWAY

Yonge Street

Finch
North York Centre
Sheppard
York Mills
Lawrence
Eglinton
Davisville
St. Clair
Summerhill
Rosedale
Bay
Bloor-Yonge
Wellesley
College
Dundas
Queen
King

University Avenue

Museum
Queen's Park
St. Patrick
Osgoode
St. Andrew
Union
Queens Quay/ Ferry Docks
York St.
Simcoe St.
Rees St.
Spadina

St. George

Spadina
Bathurst
Christie
Ossington
Dufferin
Landsdowne
Dundas West
Keele
High Park
Runnymede
Jane
Old Mill
Royal York
Islington
Kipling

Wilson
Yorkdale
Lawrence West
Glencairn
Eglinton West
St. Clair West
Dupont

Bloor Street

BLOOR-DANFORTH SUBWAY

Queens Quay West

HARBOURFRONT LRT

Note: The subway operates from 6am to 1:30am Monday through Saturday and on Sunday from 9am to 1:30am. For route information, pick up a Ride Guide at subway entrances or call 416/393-4636.

Smart commuters (and visitors!) park their cars for a low all-day parking fee at subway terminal stations—Kipling, Islington, Finch, Wilson, Warden, Kennedy, and McCowan; or at smaller lots at Sheppard, York Mills, Eglinton, Victoria Park, and Keele. You'll have to get there early, though. For GO train information about trains servicing the suburbs call 665-0022.

BY BUS & STREETCAR   Where the subway leaves off, buses and streetcars take over to carry you east-west or north-south along the city's arteries. When you buy your subway tickets, always pick up a transfer as well, so that if you want to board a streetcar or bus at the end of your subway ride you won't have to pay another fare (ditto when boarding the bus). For complete TTC information, call 416/393-4636.

BY TAXI

As usual, an expensive mode of transportation: $2.20 the minute you step in and then $1.35 for every kilometer. There's also a 20¢ charge for each bag. As you can see, cab fares can mount up, especially in rush hours. Nevertheless, here are the major companies: **Diamond** (tel. 416/366-6868), **Yellow** (tel. 416/363-4141), **Metro** (tel. 416/363-5611).

BY CAR

RENTALS   Prices change so frequently and vary so widely that probably your best bet is to shop around via the yellow pages. Still, just to give you some idea, here are a couple of companies and their rates: **Budget,** 141 Bay St. (tel. 416/364-7104), charges $50 (including 200 free kilometers, or 120 miles) per day plus 12¢ per kilometer, or $250 per week (including 1,400 free kilometers, or 840 miles), for a subcompact. **Tilden,** 930 Yonge St. (tel. 416/925-4551), charges $40 per day (including 200 free kilometers, or 120 miles) plus 15¢ per kilometer for a subcompact, or $195 per week with 1,400 free kilometers (840 miles). There are 20 Metro locations. Always ask about special weekend rates or other discounts.

Note: If you're under 25, check with the company—many will rent on a cash-only basis, some only if you have a credit card, and others will not rent to you at all.

DRIVING IN TORONTO   It can be very frustrating because the traffic moves slowly downtown and parking costs are extremely high.

Parking downtown runs about $2.50 per half hour, with $10 to $15 maximum. After 6pm and on Sunday, rates go down to $5 or thereabouts. Generally, the city-owned lots, marked with a big green P, are slightly cheaper. Observe the parking restrictions—the city will tow your car away. Still, if you can't do without your car, note the following:

You can turn right on a red light after coming to a full stop and checking the intersection, but watch out for those signs forbidding such turns at specific intersections. Watch carefully also for one-way streets and no-left- and no-right-turn signs. The driver and front-seat passenger must wear their seat belts or, if caught, pay a substantial fine. The speed limit within the city is 30 m.p.h. You must stop at pedestrian crosswalks. If you are following a streetcar and it stops, you must stop well back from the rear doors so that passengers can exit easily and safely. (Where there are concrete safety islands in the middle of the street for streetcar stops, this rule does not apply, but still exercise care.)

The **Canadian Automobile Association (CAA),** 2 Carlton St. (tel. 416/964-3111), provides aid to any driver who is a member of AAA.

 TORONTO

Area Code   Toronto's area code is 416.

Business Hours Banks are generally open Monday through Thursday from 10am to 3pm and Friday from 10am to 6pm. Most government and corporate offices are open Monday through Friday from 9am to 5pm. Stores are generally open Monday through Wednesday from 9:30 or 10am to 6pm and Saturday and Sunday from 10am to 5pm, with extended hours (until 8 to 9:30pm) on Thursday and usually Friday.

Car Rentals See "Getting Around," earlier in this chapter.

Climate As a general rule, you can say that spring runs from late March to mid-May (though occasionally there'll be snow in mid-April); summer, from mid-May to mid-September; fall, from mid-September to mid-November; and winter, from mid-November to late March. The highest recorded temperature was 105°F; the lowest, –27°F. The average date of first frost is October 29; the average date of last frost is April 20.

The blasts from Lake Ontario can sometimes be fierce, even in June. Bring a windbreaker or something similar.

Dentist The Royal College of Dental Surgeons (tel. 961-6555) offers emergency after-hours dental care. Otherwise, ask at the front desk or the concierge at your hotel.

Doctor The College of Physicians and Surgeons, 80 College St. (tel. 961-1711), operates a referral service from 9am to 5pm.

Drugstores Look under "Pharmacies" in the yellow pages. Shoppers Drug Mart, at 360 Bloor St. West, at Spadina Avenue, stays open Monday through Friday until midnight. They operate many other branches downtown. The other big chain is Pharma Plus, with a store at 68 Wellesley St., at Church Street (tel. 924-7760), which is open daily from 8am to midnight.

Electricity Same as in the United States—110 volts, 50 cycles, AC.

Embassies and Consulates All embassies are in Ottawa, the national capital. However, many nations maintain consulates in Toronto, including the following: Australian Consulate-General, 175 Bloor St. East (tel. 323-1155 or 323-3919); British Consulate-General, 777 Bay St. (tel. 593-1267); Irish Trade Board, 160 Bloor St. East (tel. 929-7394); and the United States Consulate, 360 University Ave. (tel. 595-1700).

Emergencies Call 911 for fire, police, and ambulance.

Hospitals Try Toronto General Hospital, 200 Elizabeth St. (emergency tel. 340-3948).

Hotlines Help is available from the following: rape crisis (tel. 597-8808), assault victims (tel. 863-0511), drug/alcohol crisis (tel. 595-6128), and suicide prevention (tel. 285-7779).

Information See "Orientation," earlier in this chapter.

Laundry and Dry Cleaning The following are conveniently located self-service Laundromats: Bloor Laundromat, 598 Bloor St. West, at Bathurst Street (tel. 588-6600); and Speedy Automatic Coin Wash, 568 Church St., at Wellesley Street (tel. 922-1147).

For one-hour dry cleaning, try Best Serve–One Hour Cleaners, 531 Yonge St., at Wellesley Street (tel. 416/921-9016), which gives this service until 10am. It's open from 7am to 6pm Monday through Saturday. One-hour dry cleaning is also available at Parliament One-Hour Cleaning, 436 Parliament St., at Spruce Street, near Carlton Street (tel. 923-5276).

Libraries Metro Library is at 789 Yonge St. (tel. 393-7000).

Liquor and Liquor Laws Liquor is sold at Liquor Control Board of Ontario (LCBO) stores, open Monday through Saturday. Most are open from 10am to 6pm (some stay open evenings). Call 365-5900 or 963-1915 for locations. These stores sell liquor, wine, and some beers. Check the white pages under "Liquor Control Board" for locations.

True wine lovers, though, will want to check out Vintages stores (also operated by the LCBO), which carry a more extensive and more specialized selection of wines. The most convenient downtown location is in the lower-level concourse of Hazelton Lanes (tel. 924-9463).

Beer is sold at Brewers Retail Stores, most of which are open Monday through

Friday from 10am to 10pm and Saturday from 10am to 8pm. Check the yellow pages under "Beer and Ale" for locations.

Some quiddities of the local law: Drinking hours are 11am to 1am Monday through Saturday and noon to 11pm Sunday (cocktail lounges are not usually licensed to sell liquor on Sunday; dining lounges are). The minimum drinking age is 19.

Lost Property The TTC Lost Articles Office is at the Bay Street subway station (tel. 416/393-4100), open Monday through Friday from 8am to 5:30pm.

Post Office There is no main post office. One convenient downtown branch is at 36 Adelaide St. East. For a full list of postal stations, look in the white pages under "Government of Canada" or call 416/973-2433 to find out which is closest to you. Hours are generally 8am to 5:45pm Monday through Friday. For basic services you can also go to such retail stores as Shopper's Drugmart, which are open on Saturday.

Taxes The provincial retail sales tax is 8%. In general, visitors may apply for a refund of this tax once they have accumulated $100 worth of receipts for nondisposable merchandise that will be used outside Ontario. The 5% accommodations tax can also be refunded.

For an application form and full information, write or call: Retail Sales Tax District Office, 2300 Yonge St., 10th floor, Toronto, ON, M4P 1H6 (tel. 416/487-1361); or Ontario Travel, Queen's Park, Toronto, ON, M7A 2R9 (tel. 416/314-0944, or toll free 800/268-3735).

Note: These taxes are in addition to the 7% national GST.

3. ACCOMMODATIONS

Although Toronto has many fine hotels, it's not easy to find good-value accommodations downtown. The city is expensive. Most of the top hotels are pricey and cater to a business clientele; at even the more moderate establishments you can expect to pay $80 to $100 a day. Budget hotels, which are few, charge less than $80, while nonhotel accommodations like university dorms start at $45 to $50 a night. Bed-and-breakfasts are a good budget bet, but even they are creeping upward in price.

The situation is not helped by a 5% Ontario accommodations tax and the national 7% GST.

Note: When these room rates were researched, Canada was still in a severe recession—worse than that in the U.S. I was astonished to find that some hotel prices had actually dropped below those listed in the previous edition of this book. I have changed the prices to reflect that but if the economic situation improves substantially, expect the prices to zoom back up.

In the pages that follow I have categorized my favorites according to location and price. Downtown runs from the lakeshore to College/Carlton Streets between Spadina and Jarvis. Midtown refers to the area north of College/Carlton Streets to where Dupont crosses Yonge, also between Spadina and Jarvis. Uptown, west, and east simply designate areas outside the city core. I have also included one or two airport hotels.

The financial categories for a double room are roughly as follows: very expensive, $175 and up per day; expensive, from $100 to $175; moderate, from $70 to $100; budget, under $65. I emphasize that these are only very rough categories, and subtle distinctions of taste, clientele, and reputation must also be taken into account.

BED-AND-BREAKFAST For interesting, truly personal accommodations, contact **Toronto Bed & Breakfast** for their list of homes offering bed-and-breakfast accommodations within the city for an average $55 to $65 a night, double. The association will reserve for you. Contact 253 College St. (Box 269), Toronto, ON,

M5T 1R5 (tel. 416/588-8800 from 9am to noon and 2 to 7pm Monday to Friday). Or you can also try **Metropolitan Bed and Breakfast,** which lists about 30 lovely bed-and-breakfast accommodations, ranging from $40 to $60 single and $55 to $80 double. Include $2 for postage and handling when you request their booklet; write to Metropolitan Bed and Breakfast, Suite 269, 615 Mount Pleasant Rd., Toronto, ON, M4S 3C5 (tel. 416/964-2566). They will make reservations for you.

Other organizations to try include the **Downtown Toronto Association of Bed and Breakfast Guesthouses,** P.O. Box 190, Station B, Toronto, ON, M5T 2W1 (tel. 416/690-1724). This association represents about 30 B&Bs and is operated by Susan Oppenheim, an enthusiastic B&B host herself who has a spacious Victorian home where she welcomes guests into her large country kitchen. Best time to call is between 9am and 7pm. Most homes are no-smoking. Room prices range from $45 to $65 single, and $55 to $75 double.

Bed and Breakfast Homes of Toronto, Box 46093, College Park Post Office, 444 Yonge St., Toronto, ON, M5B 2L8 (tel. 416/363-6362), is a cooperative of about 15 independent B&B operators offering rooms from $35 single and from $45 to $95 double.

Bed & Breakfast Accommodators, 223 Strathmore Blvd., Toronto, ON, M4J 1P4 (tel. 416/461-7095), offers six rooms, sharing three baths. Facilities include a kitchen and daily maid service. Breakfast is included. It's located off Greenwood Avenue, convenient to the Greenwood subway stop. Rates are $40 single, $50 double for small rooms; $50 and $60, respectively, for large rooms.

DOWNTOWN

The downtown area runs from the lakefront to College/Carlton Streets between Spadina and Jarvis.

VERY EXPENSIVE

KING EDWARD HOTEL, 37 King St. East, Toronto, ON, M5C 2E9. Tel. 416/863-9700. Fax 416/367-5515. 315 rms and suites. A/C MINIBAR TV TEL
   Subway: King.
$ Rates: $210–$245 single or double; from $360 suite. Weekend packages available for $150–$170 per night, including free parking. AE, CB, DC, ER, MC, V.
   Parking: $24.

During the 1970s, the King Edward Hotel was a fading relic that was trying to survive with dignity, but without too much success. Happily, the King Eddie (as it was fondly known), built in 1903, did not succumb to the bulldozer, but underwent a $40-million refurbishment instead, and reopened in 1981.

In its heyday it welcomed the Prince of Wales (later Edward VIII); hosted a dinner for Cecil B. deMille that transformed the Crystal Ballroom into a 15th-century castle complete with moat; and attracted such notables as Rudolph Valentino, Charles de Gaulle, Olivia de Havilland, Richard and Liz, the Beatles, and anybody who was anybody in Toronto.

Today the original elements of the hotel, such as imported marble Corinthian columns and sculpted ceilings, have been restored to their former elegance. The lobby soars 40 feet to a glass dome that lets the sun stream in.

The small number of rooms guarantees very personal service. All units are extremely spacious, beautifully decorated with mahogany antique reproductions and floral prints, and come fully equipped with telephones in the bedroom and bathroom, clock radios, and such niceties as bathrobes, superfluffy towels sans monogram, shampoo, perfume, and marble bathtubs.

Dining/Entertainment: Off the lobby you'll find the Lobby Lounge, a focal point for the hotel's social life, offering afternoon tea and cocktails. The famous old Victorian Room, a refuge for the well-to-do, has been turned into the Café Victoria, where the baroque plasterwork is complemented with a light, airy feel imparted by many tall shrubs. The Consort Bar, also on the main floor, has eight-foot-high windows looking out onto King Street.

For formal dining, Chiaro's, decorated in stunning gray lacquer with etched-glass panels and French-style chairs, specializes in fine continental cuisine, with dinner entrées priced from $18 to $28.

Services: If you wish, the staff will clean your shoes, provide 24-hour room and concierge service, and deliver your newspaper.

Facilities: Health club.

THE ROYAL YORK, 100 Front St. West, Toronto, ON, M5J 1E3. Tel. 416/863-6333, or toll-free 800/828-7447 in the U.S., 800/268-9411 elsewhere. 1,408 rms, 71 suites. A/C MINIBAR TV TEL **Subway:** Union.
$ Rates: $210 single; $225 double. Add $20 for business class service. Many special packages available. AE, MC, V. **Parking:** $17.

To many citizens and regular visitors, the Royal York *is* Toronto, because in its 35 banquet and meeting rooms many of the city's historical and social events have taken place. It is by any measure a huge enterprise—a major convention hotel, and as such, not to everyone's taste. Still, there is a magnificence to this hotel, which opened in 1929 and has hosted a raft of royalty, heads of state, and celebrities. The lobby itself is vast, impressive, and crowned by an incredible inlay coffered ceiling, which is lit by large cast-bronze chandeliers.

The hotel has recently undergone and is still undergoing major renovations. Rooms vary in size but a standard room will have a king-size bed. The decor varies but tends to staid beiges, golds, and ochres or else a combination of jade and rose with antique reproduction furnishings that will always include an armchair and a well-lit desk. Nice features are solid wood doors, windows that open, and wall mouldings. Handicapped rooms are exceptionally well-equipped for wheelchair guests and for the deaf and blind.

Dining/Entertainment: An incredible 12 restaurants and lounges. The Imperial Room is perhaps the best known, with its full stage and floor to ceiling drapes and classical accents. Once the cabaret venue of the city, it's only used for functions today. The Acadian Room offers continental cuisine in an elegant atmosphere; for a show of Japanese finesse there's a Benihana steakhouse; the Gazebo affords a garden-like setting for lunch and afternoon tea; Lytes is also a luncheon spot. The Lobby Bar features a sports screen; the Library Bar is a more intimate and cozy meeting spot, while downstairs you'll find Piper's Bar and Grill, York's Deli and York's Kitchen.

Services: Room service from 7am to 1am; concierge. Business class provides a superior room on a private floor with private lounge, complimentary breakfast and newspaper, and nightly turndown.

Facilities: Skylit indoor lap pool with hand-painted trompe l'oeil murals and potted palms, exercise room, saunas, steam rooms and whirlpool, barbershop and beauty salon, shopping arcade, business center.

On the Lakefront

RADISSON PLAZA HOTEL ADMIRAL, 249 Queen's Quay West, Toronto, ON, M5J 2N5. Tel. 416/203-3333, or toll free 800/387-1626. Fax 416/203-3100. 157 rms. A/C MINIBAR TV TEL **Subway:** Union.
$ Rates: $160–$190 single; $180–$210 double. Extra person $20. Weekend packages available. AE, DC, ER, MC, V. **Parking:** $12.50.

As the name and the harborfront location suggest, the Hotel Admiral has a strong nautical flavor. The lobby combines polished woods and brass with nautical paintings. The rooms are elegantly furnished with campaign-style chests of drawers with brass trimmings, marble-top side tables, and desks, all set on jade carpets. Extra amenities include two push-button phones, real hangers, hairdryer and clothesline in the bathroom, and clock radios. The hotel is on the LRT route.

Dining/Entertainment: The Commodores Dining Room looks out onto Lake Ontario and the waterfront. The dining room serves classic continental cuisine ranging in price from $20 to $28 for such dishes as sautéed quails with lime sauce or salmon scallops with tarragon sabayon. The Galley serves a more modest menu featuring such items as calves' liver with onions and bacon, prime rib, or filet of salmon with eggplant, priced from $8 to $15. The adjacent bosun's bar also offers light snacks.

Services: 24-hour room service, complimentary newspaper, concierge.
Facilities: On the horseshoe-shaped roofdeck is a pool and cabana-style bar-terrace.

WESTIN HARBOUR CASTLE, 1 Harbour Sq., Toronto, ON, M5J 1A6. Tel. 416/869-1600. Fax 416/361-7448. 978 rms. A/C MINIBAR TV TEL **Subway:** Union, then take the LRT.
$ Rates: $160 single; $180 double. Extra person $20. Children stay free in parents' room. Special weekend packages (double occupancy) available. AE, DC, ER, MC, V. **Parking:** $16.

Located right on the lakefront, the Westin is ideally situated for visiting Harbourfront and is linked to downtown by a Light Rapid Transit system.

Guest rooms, all with a view of the lake, are located in two towers joined at the base by a five-story podium. Marble, oak, and crystal gild the spacious lobby, which commands a great harbor view. The hotel recently underwent a $50-million facelift. All are equipped with remote-control color TVs with in-room movies and bathroom telephones; they're furnished with marble-top desks and night tables, table and floor lamps, and color-coordinated fabrics. No-smoking rooms total 442.

Dining/Entertainment: The Regatta and Terrace, overlooking the harbor, is open 24 hours a day. The Lighthouse, a revolving restaurant on the 37th floor that's reached via a glass-walled elevator, provides fabulous views during lunch, brunch, or dinner. Dinner entrées run $21 to $34. Tea is served in the Lobby Lounge, in the center lobby, along with cocktails and a continental breakfast. Off the main lobby, the Chartroom offers a quiet haven for a drink, with piano entertainment in the evenings.
Services: 24-hour room service.
Facilities: The fitness center has an indoor pool, whirlpool, sauna, steamroom, tennis court, and massage clinic. Several shops are also available.

Near the Convention Centre

CAMBRIDGE SUITES HOTEL, 15 Richmond St. East, Toronto, ON, M5C 1N2. Tel. 416/368-1990, or toll free 800/463-1990. Fax 416/601-3751. 231 suites. A/C MINIBAR TV TEL **Subway:** Queen.
$ Rates (including continental breakfast): $250 single or double. AE, DC, DISC, ER, MC, V. **Parking:** $14.
The suites offered here are extremely comfortable and make all the difference to the regular traveler. Each large, 550-square-foot unit has a refrigerator, microwave, and

---

AN IMPORTANT NOTE ON PRICES

Unless stated otherwise, **the prices cited in this guide are given in Canadian dollars,** which is good news for American travelers because the Canadian dollar is worth 25% less than the American dollar, but buys nearly as much. As we go to press, $1 Canadian is worth 75¢ U.S., which means that your $100-a-night hotel room will cost only U.S. $75, and your $6 breakfast costs only U.S. $4.50.
Here's a quick table of equivalents:

Canadian $	U.S. $
$ 1	$ 0.75
5	3.75
10	7.50
20	15.00
50	37.50
80	60.00
100	75.00
200	150.00

dishes, and is stocked with coffee, tea, and cookies. The furnishings are extremely comfortable and include couches, armchairs, and coffee tables. There are two TVs and two telephones in each suite, with hookups for conference calls and computers. In some cases, French doors separate the living area from the bedroom. There's also a dressing area with full-length mirror and marble bathroom equipped with hairdryer and full complement of amenities. Some luxury suites are duplexes and have Jacuzzis.

Dining/Entertainment: There's a restaurant and bar, and the rates include a continental breakfast to which you help yourself.

Services: If you like, you can leave a list and your grocery shopping will be done. Daily maid service, valet, concierge.

Facilities: Fitness area with a fine view of the city, whirlpool, sauna, convenience store, washers, and dryers.

CROWN PLAZA TORONTO CENTRE, 225 Front St. West, Toronto, ON, M5V 2X3. Tel. 416/597-1400, or toll free 800/828-7447. Fax 416/597-8128. 587 rms. A/C MINIBAR TV TEL **Subway:** Union.

$ Rates: $160–$200 single; $180–$280 double. Children 18 and under stay free in parents' room. Weekend packages available. AE, DC, DISC, ER, MC, V. **Parking:** $19.

Formerly L'Hôtel, this hotel is ideally located near the CN Tower, SkyDome, Roy Thomson Hall, the theater district, and the Convention Centre (to which it is in fact attached).

The rooms, decorated in dusky rose or muted green, are finely appointed with marble bathroom counters, writing desks, and elegant table lamps, and feature such residential touches as draped tables and matching window valances. All feature color TVs, clock radios, and two telephone lines. No-smoking rooms are available.

Dining/Entertainment: Rose marble, cherry, and polished bronze are used throughout the lobby. The 25-story tower slopes back and upward from the main entrance, creating a garden court, which accommodates the Trellis Bistro and Lounge. The first, decorated with trees and plants, is well known for its Sunday brunch and after-theater menu.

In the elegant Chanterelles, dinner entrées range from $20 for suprême of chicken grilled with rice vinegar and sesame to $32 for lobster ragoût with linguine and truffle juice. Luncheon prices range from $10 to $16. A special pretheater fixed-price menu is offered at $24.

Services: Room service available 6am to 2am.

Facilities: Indoor pool, whirlpool, saunas, well-equipped exercise room, squash courts, and sun deck.

HILTON INTERNATIONAL, 145 Richmond St. West, Toronto, ON, M5H 3M6. Tel. 416/869-3456, or toll free 800/445-8667. Fax 416/869-3187. 600 rms. A/C MINIBAR TV TEL **Subway:** Osgoode.

$ Rates: $175 single or double. Extra person $20. One child under 18 may stay free in parents' room. Weekend packages available. AE, DC, ER, MC, V. **Parking:** $16.

If you approach the Hilton International from the rear you'll see the steam rising from this plush hotel's show pool, just one of the luxury facilities available at this stylish, personalized, 32-story, $40-million member of the Hilton hotels chain.

If you wish, you can take the glass-enclosed elevators to your room, which will be large and impeccably decorated, with all the expected conveniences—color TV, AM/FM radio, and individual temperature control—plus scales and alarm clocks. Rooms are currently furnished in white French provincial or dark-wood contemporary with blue-green or melon and gold color schemes.

Dining/Entertainment: Twenty-foot-tall trees separate the comfortable lobby from the Garden Court restaurant, an open garden-landscaped dining room, created by an atrium that allows daylight to filter down from louvered windows two levels above. To complete the light atmosphere, a fountain plays, green filaments drift down from the plants placed around the balcony above, and a filigree light curtain consisting of seven panels, each with 2,200 lights, sparkles over all. Here you can enjoy breakfast, lunch, afternoon tea, and dinner while seated on cushioned rattan chairs.

Besides the Garden Court, the hotel houses the renowned Trader Vic's, featuring

Polynesian fare and decor; the adjacent lounge offers over 90 potent, exotic drinks such as the Scorpion (with a fresh gardenia floating in the glass). Barristers, as might be expected, has a clubby atmosphere with wonderful leather armchairs and couches to sink into, and even comfy armchairs at the bar itself, which is sunken to accommodate self-indulgent tipplers. Leather-bound legal volumes abound. Barristers also has a Sunday sports spectacular during which you can watch your favorite sport on a seven-foot TV screen.

Services: 24-hour room service.
Facilities: Indoor/outdoor pool.

SHERATON CENTRE, 123 Queen St. West, Toronto, ON, M5H 2M9. Tel. 416/361-1000, or toll free 800/325-3535. Fax 416/947-4854. 1,393 rms. A/C TV TEL **Subway:** Osgoode.

$ Rates: $120–$200 single; $120–$230 double. Extra person $20. Two children under 18 can stay free in parents' room. Special packages available. AE, DC, ER, MC, V. **Parking:** Available in underground City Hall parkade, which connects to the hotel, for $20 per day. Additional charge for valet parking.

A city in itself, the Sheraton Centre contains dozens of shops in the Plaza, eight restaurants and bars, and two movie theaters. It's conveniently located at the heart of the city's underground passageways, right across from City Hall. At the back of the lobby, you'll even find two acres of landscaped gardens with a waterfall and summer terrace.

In this 43-story complex there are spacious rooms, all attractively furnished and well equipped. The Towers rooms, which are more expensive, offer additional amenities—bathrobes, additional telephones in the bathrooms, and a separate reception area.

Dining/Entertainment: The hotel has a bevy of restaurants and lounges. In the shopping concourse you'll find a very authentic English pub (shipped from England in sections), Good Queen Bess, complete with toby jugs and cozy fireplaces; it's one of the few places around where you can enjoy a mug of Newcastle brown. Off the lobby, Reunion is a lively bar, with several videos, a pool table, and upbeat music, while on the second floor the Long Bar provides a spectacular view of City Hall. There are two cafeteria-style restaurants. On the ground floor, Bites Café offers assorted salads, sandwiches, and other light fare; downstairs, the Brown Bag has breakfast croissants, subs, and similar items.

The premier restaurant is Postcards, which features cuisines from around the world and offers daily buffet breakfasts and lunches and moderately priced dinners.

Services: 24-hour room service, valet, concierge.
Facilities: Indoor/outdoor pool (20 feet inside, 60 feet outside), sauna, games room, hot tub, and health clinic.

TORONTO MARRIOTT EATON CENTRE, 525 Bay St., Toronto, ON, M5G 2L2. Tel. 416/597-9200. Fax 416/597-9211. 459 rms. A/C TV TEL **Subway:** Dundas.

$ Rates: $194 single; $204 double. If you book 21 days in advance, a special rate of $98 is available; also reduced rates for booking 7 or 14 days in advance. AE, CB, DC, ER, MC, V. **Parking:** $12.

Overlooking Holy Trinity Church, the Marriott has all the chain's hallmark amenities. In addition to the features listed above, rooms contain clock radios and attractive modern furnishings. No-smoking rooms and rooms for the disabled are available.

Dining/Entertainment: Dining facilities include a family-style restaurant, the Parkside atrium, which is open for all-day dining, and the more formal J. W.'s, which is only open on weekends. Characters bar features billiards and table games as well as music and sporting events; the lobby bar is more relaxing.

Services: 24-hour room service, concierge, babysitting.
Facilities: Indoor swimming pool and a complete health club.

Near the St. Lawrence/O'Keefe Centres

BEST WESTERN CHESTNUT PARK HOTEL, 108 Chestnut St., Toronto, ON, M5G 1R3. Tel. 416/977-5000. Fax 416/977-9513. 522 rms. A/C MINIBAR TV TEL **Subway:** St. Patrick.

$ Rates: $160 single; $180 double. Children under 16 stay free in parents' room. AE, DC, ER, MC, V. **Parking:** $15.

Conveniently located two blocks from the Eaton Centre on Chestnut, just off Dundas between Bay and University, the Chestnut Park offers a modern ambience, with many Oriental decorative furnishings in the lobby and throughout. The rooms are spiffily furnished and equipped with telephones with computer- and fax-compatible jacks, safes, and bathrobes. Four of the floors are also occupied by the Museum for Textiles.

Dining/Entertainment: Tapestries is open for breakfast, lunch, and dinner. Among the offerings are Chinese specialties, pasta, and continental cuisine (from $10 to $20 at dinner). The Gallery Lounge overlooks the lobby.

Services: 24-hour room service, concierge, and valet.

Facilities: An indoor swimming pool, whirlpool, sauna, health club, and business center complete the facilities.

EXPENSIVE

CLARION ESSEX PARK HOTEL, 300 Jarvis St. (just south of Carlton), Toronto, ON, M5B 2C5. Tel. 416/977-2233, or toll free 800/567-2233. Fax 416/977-4830. 102 rms. A/C TV TEL **Subway:** College.

$ Rates: $110–$135 single; $120–$150 double. Children under 18 stay free in parents' room. Extra person $15. AE, CB, DC, DISC, ER, MC, V. **Parking:** $10.

The Clarion Essex Park Hotel has undergone a total renovation—everything has been transformed. The lobby is sheathed in marble and accented with Asian screens and fresh flowers, and the whole place has been turned into a very comfortable moderately priced facility. All the rooms are queens or kings, nicely furnished with sofas, desks, and coffee tables, and fully equipped with color cable TVs housed in cabinets, full-tile bathrooms with hairdryers and all the amenities, and large closets. There's a restaurant/bistro with a bar, an indoor pool, and a fitness center. Room service is available from 7am to 11pm.

DELTA CHELSEA INN, 33 Gerrard St. West (between Yonge and Bay), Toronto, ON, M5G 1Z4. Tel. 416/595-1975, or toll free 800/268-1133. Fax 416/585-4362. 1,586 rms and suites. A/C TV TEL **Subway:** College.

$ Rates: $170–$180 single or double; from $200 suite. Extra person $15. Children under 18 stay free in parents' room. Weekend and other packages available, like

---

Ⓕ FROMMER'S SMART TRAVELER: HOTELS

1. Try quoting the price you're willing to pay. Hotel rates move up and down depending on the traffic. If a room goes unsold, the revenue is lost forever. The management would much prefer to sell a room than not, so don't be ashamed to ask. State what you're prepared to pay and see what happens. If business is slow, it will work; if it's not, it won't.

2. Always ask about special discounts for corporate personnel, government employees, military, seniors, or students—whatever group to which you legitimately belong.

3. Ask, too, about seasonal discounts, especially summer discounts and weekend packages, when you can secure some great bargains even at the most luxurious establishments.

4. Always ask about parking charges and surcharges on local and long-distance phone calls. Both can make a big difference to your bill.

5. Remember that the prices quoted here are so-called rack rates—the prices quoted to walk-ins. These can be as much as 40% higher than other discounted rates—government, corporate, etc. No smart traveler pays the rack rate today.

the Summer '93 rate, which was $96. Seniors Plan offers substantial discounts. AE, DC, ER, MC, V. **Parking:** $14 per day.

The Delta Chelsea Inn is still one of Toronto's best buys—particularly for families and on weekends—although prices have risen considerably in recent years.

All rooms have color TVs, in-room movies, and bright, modern furnishings. Four hundred rooms have minibars and some rooms have kitchenettes. Rooms in the south tower feature dual phones with data jacks, call waiting, and conference-call features.

Dining/Entertainment: Currently, the hotel has two restaurants, Wittles for casual but elegant dining, and the Market Garden, a self-service cafeteria with very reasonable prices. Both serve all three meals. The children's menu offers good value, and children 6 and under eat free. At the series of counters in the Market Garden you can find grilled items, salads, burgers, bagels, and such items as breaded veal, all priced under $6. The food can then be taken out to the large pleasant outdoor courtyard or eaten inside. The Chelsea Bun offers live entertainment daily and Dixieland jazz on Saturday afternoons (lunch buffets and Sunday brunch are also served here); for a relaxing drink there's the Elm Street Lounge or Deck 27 on the 27th floor, which offers writing desks and telephones for the final wrap-up at the end of the day.

Services: Babysitting is available for a fee, plus there's 24-hour room service and valet pickup.

Facilities: Hotel facilities include two swimming pools, whirlpool, sauna, fitness room, lounge, and games room (with three pool tables), and—a blessing for parents—a children's creative center where 3- to 8-year-olds can play under close and expert supervision. It's open until 10pm on Friday and Saturday. The new tower also features a second-floor business center.

HOLIDAY INN CITY HALL, 89 Chestnut St., Toronto, ON, M5G 1R1. Tel. 416/977-0707. Fax 416/977-1136. 715 rms. A/C MINIBAR TV TEL **Subway:** Dundas or University.

$ Rates: $130 single; $145 double. Extra person $15. Children under 19 stay free in parents' room. AE, DC, ER, MC, V. **Parking:** $13.

Right behind City Hall, the Holiday Inn Downtown has all the earmarks of the chain, plus a little extra. The rooms have recently been upgraded, with such nice amenities as pants pressers and hairdryers added. All rooms are large and well furnished, and have console control panels by the bed for the color TV and radio, and vanity mirrors or sinks outside the bathroom.

Dining/Entertainment: In the Dewey Secombe and Howe Bar there's piano entertainment and drinks; the Chestnut Tree restaurant on the main floor offers all-day dining.

Services: Room service from 6am to 11pm.

Facilities: Indoor and outdoor swimming pools, sauna, exercise room, games area, and sun terrace.

HOLIDAY INN ON KING, 370 King St. West, Toronto, ON, M5V 1J9. Tel. 416/599-4000. Fax 416/599-7394. 426 rms. A/C TV TEL **Subway:** St. Andrew.

$ Rates: From $100 single; from $120 double. Extra person $15. AE, CB, DC, DISC, ER, MC, V. **Parking:** $10.

Located in an odd-looking Miami-style building, the Holiday Inn on King is well located for the theater district and the CN Tower. The rooms are pleasantly furnished in pastels with sage-green carpeting and floral bedspreads and are fully equipped with clock radios, TVs on stands, and decently lit desks. Many have balconies. The bathrooms have hairdryers and other amenities. There are two restaurants and a lounge; facilities include an indoor pool, sauna, and fitness center.

NOVOTEL, 45 The Esplanade, Toronto, ON, M5E 1W2. Tel. 416/367-8900, or toll free 800/221-4542. Fax 416/360-8285. 266 rms. A/C MINIBAR TV TEL **Subway:** Union.

$ Rates: $110 single; $125 double. Special weekend rates available. Up to 2 children under 16 stay free in parents' room. AE, CB, DC, DISC, ER, MC, V. **Parking:** $10.

Just off Yonge, the Novotel is an ultramodern hotel, built in Renaissance style with a

Palladian entrance arcade leading into a marble lobby with oak and Oriental decorative accents. The rooms are nicely appointed with all the expected conveniences, including remote-control TVs, two telephones in each room, hairdryers, radio/TV speakers in the bathrooms, and skirt hangers.

Dining/Entertainment: The restaurant/lounge, the Café Nicole, serves breakfast, lunch, and dinner. A quick buffet breakfast is available and free morning coffee is provided.

Services: Room service from 6am to midnight, concierge, laundry/valet.

Facilities: Indoor pool, sauna, whirlpool, and exercise room.

MODERATE

BEST WESTERN PRIMROSE HOTEL, 111 Carlton St. (near Jarvis), Toronto, ON, M5B 2G3. Tel. 416/977-8000, or toll free 800/268-8082 in Canada and the U.S. Fax 416/977-6323. 350 rms. A/C TV TEL **Subway:** College.
$ Rates: $85 single; $95 double. Up to 2 children under 16 stay free in parents' room. Extra person $15. Weekend packages available (except July–Sept). AE, DC, DISC, ER, MC, V. **Parking:** $9.

The spacious rooms at the Best Western all come with wall-to-wall carpeting and color-coordinated furnishings. About 25% contain king-size beds and sofas; the rest have two double beds.

The downstairs coffee shop charmingly evokes the atmosphere of a Viennese café with its painted wood decor. For relaxing there's the One Eleven lounge with nightly live entertainment, and also an outdoor heated pool and saunas.

BOND PLACE HOTEL, 65 Dundas St. East, Toronto, ON, M5B 2G8. Tel. 416/362-6061. Fax 416/360-6406. 286 rms. A/C TV TEL **Subway:** Dundas.
$ Rates: $75–$100 single; $75–$125 double. Children 14 and under stay free in parents' room. AE, DC, DISC, ER, MC, V. **Parking:** $10.

Ideally located just one block from Yonge Street and the Eaton Centre, the Bond Place Hotel is an independently owned, medium-size modern place offering all the appurtenances of a first-class hotel at reasonable prices. The small triangular lobby is welcoming, with its natural oak reception desk. The rooms, all pleasantly decorated in autumnal colors with floral bedspreads and curtains, cane headboards, Scandinavian-style furniture, and wall-to-wall carpeting, contain color TVs with in-house movies available.

Off the lobby, the Garden Café serves reasonably priced fare from 7am to 11:30pm daily. Downstairs, Freddy's serves a weekday buffet lunch and complimentary hors d'oeuvres from 5:30 to 6:30pm.

DAYS INN TORONTO DOWNTOWN, 30 Carlton St., Toronto, ON, M5B 2E9. Tel. 416/977-6655, or toll free 800/325-2525. Fax 416/977-0502. 535 rms. A/C TV TEL **Subway:** College.
$ Rates: $100 single or double. Extra person $10. Children under 12 stay free in parents' room. AE, CB, DC, DISC, ER, MC, V. **Parking:** $10.

Nicely furnished rooms with modern conveniences at fair prices are the hallmark of the former Carlton Inn, a modern high-rise. All rooms contain color TVs with in-house movies, and refrigerators are available on request.

During a recent renovation two lounges and a restaurant were added. The inn also features an indoor/outdoor pool and saunas. Besides the reasonably priced (for Toronto) accommodations, the inn is well located, only a few steps from Yonge Street, right next door to Maple Leaf Gardens.

HOTEL VICTORIA, 56 Yonge St. (at Wellington), Toronto, ON, M5E 1G5. Tel. 416/363-1666. Fax 416/363-7327. 48 rms. A/C TV TEL **Subway:** King.
$ Rates: $80–$115 single or double. Extra person $15. Children under 12 stay free in parents' room. Special weekend rates available. AE, ER, MC, V.

In search of a small, personal hotel? Try the six-floor Hotel Victoria, only two blocks from the O'Keefe Centre. The rooms are either standard or select (the latter are larger). Furnishings are modern, with a gray-and-burgundy decor, color TVs, private baths, and clock radios. The lobby is small and elegant, and the renovation has retained the marble columns, staircase, and decorative moldings of an earlier era. A complimentary *Globe and Mail* is included in the price of a room. There's an attractive restaurant and lounge, as well as a lobby bar.

JOURNEY'S END, 111 Lombard St. (between Adelaide and Richmond), Toronto, ON, M5B 2E9. Tel. 416/367-5555. Fax 416/367-3470. 130 rms. A/C TV TEL **Subway:** King or Queen.
$ Rates: $88 single; $100 double. AE, MC, V. **Parking:** $9.
The modern rooms at the Journey's End are fully appointed with color TVs and jade-and-rose or gray-blue decor.

THE STRATHCONA, 60 York St., Toronto, ON, M5J 1S8. Tel. 416/363-3321. Fax 416/363-4679. 193 rms. A/C TV TEL **Subway:** Union.
$ Rates: May 1–Oct 30 $70 single or double; Nov 1–Apr 30, $50 single or double. AE, CB, DC, ER, MC, V. **Parking:** $12.

 Currently one of the city's best buys, the Strathcona is located right across from the Royal York Hotel, within easy reach of all downtown attractions. Although the rooms are small, they have recently been refurbished and furnished with modern blond-wood furniture, gray carpeting, brass floor lamps, and private baths.

BUDGET

NEIL WYCIK COLLEGE HOTEL, 96 Gerrard St. East (between Church and Jarvis), Toronto, ON, M5B 1G7. Tel. 416/977-2320, or toll free 800/268-4358. Fax 416/977-2809. 300 rms (none with bath). **Subway:** College.
$ Rates: $30–$37 single; $40–$46 double; $49 family room (two adults plus children). MC, V. **Parking:** $8. **Closed:** Sept–early May.
From mid-May to late August the Neil Wycik College Hotel has basic accommodations available to tourists and families at extremely reasonable rates. Since these are primarily student accommodations, rooms contain only the most essential furniture—beds, chairs, and desks. Family rooms have two single beds and room for two cots. Bathrooms and kitchen facilities are down the corridor. If you wish to cook, you have to furnish your own utensils. Other facilities in the building include a TV lounge, rooftop sun deck, sauna, a laundry room on the 22nd floor, and a cafeteria.

TORONTO INTERNATIONAL HOSTEL, 223 Church St. (between Queen and Dundas), Toronto, ON, M5B 1Y7. Tel. 416/368-0207. Fax 416/368-6499. 180 beds. **Subway:** Dundas.
$ Rates: $15 for dormitory accommodations; $21.30 for semiprivate; add $4 for nonmembers. Membership $25. MC, V. **Parking:** $12 in nearby lot.
The hostel, which incorporates four buildings, contains about 180 beds, providing both dormitory-style and semiprivate accommodation. Two of the buildings are air-conditioned; the other two are cooled by fans. There's a restaurant/bar, a comfortable common room with couch, kitchen, and laundry facilities. The reception is open 24 hours.

MIDTOWN

The midtown area runs north from College/Carlton Streets between Spadina and Jarvis, to where Dupont crosses Yonge.

VERY EXPENSIVE

FOUR SEASONS HOTEL, 21 Avenue Rd., Toronto, ON, M5R 2G1. Tel. 416/964-0411, or toll free 800/268-6282 in Canada, 800/332-3442 in the U.S. Fax 416/964-2301. 381 rms and suites. A/C MINIBAR TV TEL **Subway:** Bay.
$ Rates: $275–$335 single; $300–$335 double; from $350 suite. Children under 18 stay free in parents' room. Extra person $20. Weekend rates available. AE, CB, DC, ER, MC, V. **Parking:** $16.

 In the heart of the Bloor-Yorkville area, the Four Seasons has a well-deserved reputation for highly personal service, quiet but unimpeachable style, and total comfort. The lobby, with its marble-and-granite floors, Savonnerie carpets, and stunning fresh flower arrangements, expresses the style.
The extra-large rooms are furnished with king-size, queen-size, or twin beds, and

supplemented with dressing rooms and marble bathrooms. The table lamps are porcelain, the furnishings elegant, and the fabrics plush. All units have remote-control color TVs, AM/FM radios, and terrycloth bathrobes. Extra amenities include hairdryers, makeup and full-length mirrors, tiebars, and closet safes. Corner rooms have balconies. Four Seasons rooms have additional seating areas, two televisions, and deluxe telephone with two lines and conference-call capability. No-smoking rooms are available.

Dining/Entertainment: The hotel has two restaurants and two lounges. Truffles, on the second floor, provides a lavish setting of fine woods, fabric, and furnishings for extraordinary French-California cuisine. The main courses, priced from $27 to $37, might include lobster with two sauces and winter-vegetable mousse, grilled duckling with orange-ginger sauce, or braised chicken and forest mushrooms in a red wine stock. The crab soup is amazing—Oriental style and full of flavor. The Studio Café serves meals all day. The room is airy and beautifully decorated with modern Italian fabrics and furniture, tables covered with Gianni Versace fabrics and display cases filled with original modern art glass. A luncheon buffet, evening hors d'oeuvres, and Sunday brunch are served in La Serre, where a pianist entertains in the evening. The lobby bar is a pleasant area for afternoon tea and cocktails. Special kids' menus are available.

Services: 24-hour concierge, 24-hour room service and valet pickup, one-hour pressing, complimentary shoeshine, and twice-daily maid service, babysitting, doctor on call, courtesy limo to downtown, complimentary newspaper.

Facilities: There's a business center, health club with an indoor/outdoor pool, whirlpool, Universal equipment, and massage. Bicycles and video games are also available for kids.

INTERCONTINENTAL, 220 Bloor St. W., Toronto, ON, M5S 1T8. Tel. 416/960-5200. Fax 416/960-8269. 213 rms. A/C MINIBAR TV TEL **Subway:** St. George.

$ Rates: $190–$235 single; $210–$260 double. **Parking:** $22.

The Intercontinental, conveniently located on Bloor Street at St. George, is small enough to provide excellent, very personal service from the minute you enter the small but rich-looking marble lobby. The rooms are spacious and well furnished with comfortable French-style armchairs and love seats. The marble bathrooms, with separate showers, are large and equipped with every kind of amenity—each has a telephone; a clothesline; large fluffy towels; a bathrobe; scales; and a full range of soaps, lotions, and more. Extra-special room features include closet lights, a large desk-table, a clock-radio, a full-length mirror, and a telephone with two lines.

Dining/Entertainment: Signatures offers fine dining with dinner entrées priced from $18 to $25. It also offers one of the best brunches in town, accompanied by harp music. The attractive, comfortable Harmony Lounge, with its marble bar, fireplace, and cherry paneling, is a pleasant retreat for cocktails or afternoon tea. From here, french doors lead out to an inviting patio.

Services: 24-hour room service, laundry/valet, twice-daily maid service, nightly turndown, concierge, complimentary shoeshine and newspaper, video check-out in four languages (English, French, Spanish, and Japanese).

Facilities: Lap pool with adjacent patio; fitness room with treadmill, bikes, Stepmaster, and Paramount equipment.

PARK PLAZA, 4 Avenue Rd. (at Bloor), Toronto, ON, M5R 2E8. Tel. 416/924-5471, or toll free 800/268-4927 Fax 416/924-4933. 244 rms. A/C MINIBAR TV TEL **Subway:** Museum.

$ Rates: $255 double in the Plaza Tower; $165 single, $185 double in the Prince Arthur Tower. Extra person $20. Children under 18 stay free in parents' room. AE, ER, MC, V. **Parking:** $15.

The Park Plaza is still being renovated. So far the 64 rooms in the Plaza Tower or southern tower have been completely renovated and redecorated, and the results are very fine indeed. The rooms are very tastefully furnished in a candystripe style, with brass and glass accents. They're fully equipped with the latest conveniences including clock radios, two push-button phones (one in the bathroom), louver closets, and full-length mirrors. Each marble bathroom has a hairdryer, makeup mirror, bathrobe, and full amenities. These rooms are more expensive than the 180 rooms in the Prince Arthur or north tower because they are more lavish, though the latter rooms are large and well furnished.

Dining/Entertainment: The Prince Arthur Dining Room is a popular city breakfast and lunch spot. Chandeliers ring the room and there's always a brilliant floral centerpiece. The main dining room, the Roof Restaurant, though, is on the 18th floor, adjacent to the lounge, which has attracted so many Toronto literati. Their books and portraits are on display in this comfortable room, with its inviting couches in front of the fireplace, and marble-top tables. In summertime the outdoor terrace affords a spectacular downtown view. Prices of main dishes in the dining room range from $17 to $23.

Services: Twice-daily maid service, nightly turndown, complimentary newspaper and shoeshine, 24-hour room service, and concierge

Facilities: Business center.

SUTTON PLACE GRANDE LE MERIDIEN, 955 Bay St., Toronto, ON, M5S 2A2. Tel. 416/924-9221, or toll free 800/268-3790. Fax 416/924-1778. 208 rms, 72 suites. A/C MINIBAR TV TEL **Subway:** Museum or Wellesley.

$ Rates: $200 single; $230 double; from $260 suite. Extra person $20. Children under 18 stay free in parents' room. Extra person $20. Weekend rates available. AE, DC, ER, MC. **Parking:** $19.

A small luxury hotel, the Sutton Place attracts a celebrity/entertainer and business clientele. It has a luxury European flair that is exhibited in the decor and the service. Throughout the public areas you will find authentic antiques, old-master paintings, 18th-century Gobelins, Oriental carpets, and crystal chandeliers. The very spacious rooms are luxuriously furnished in a French style and each is spacious enough for a couch and desk. All have remote-control color TVs, two telephones—allowing hookup to a fax or PC via a modem—bathrobes, and hairdryers.

Dining/Entertainment: The Sanssouci is one of the city's most beautiful dining rooms with its Gobelins, fresh azaleas, silver, and crystal. Breakfast, lunch, and dinner is served here, and a spectacular brunch on Sunday ($31.95 per person). At dinner the best value is the four-course $33.50 table d'hôte; otherwise the à la carte menu features such entrées as bouillabaisse, swordfish steamed with chives and shallots, organic chicken breast with couscous, or herb-crusted breast of pheasant. Among the appetizers there might be a savarin of hardwood-smoked salmon with shrimp or carpaccio of veal with salsa sorbet. Desserts are also suitably extravagant. Prices range from $18 to $24. The wine list is expansive, and dinner is served to piano accompaniment and candlelight.

Alexandra's is a comfortable piano lounge, where light lunches are also served and you can dance in the evening. It's open from 11am to 1am daily.

Services: 24-hour room service, valet pickup, complimentary shoeshine, twice-daily maid service, and concierge.

Facilities: Indoor pool with sun deck, sauna, massage, fully equipped fitness center, and business center.

MODERATE

COMFORT HOTEL, 15 Charles St. East, Toronto, ON, M4Y 1S1. Tel. 416/924-7381, or toll free 800/263-7142 in the U.S. and Canada. Fax 416/927-1369. 113 rms. A/C MINIBAR TV TEL **Subway:** Bloor.

$ Rates: $94 single or double. Weekend rates available. AE, DC, DISC, ER, MC, V. **Parking:** $4.

The Comfort Hotel is a pleasant small place. The rooms are large, furnished with light-oak pieces and all major extras, including complimentary newspapers. Each bathroom is equipped with a dryer and an amenity package.

The restaurant, which is plushly comfortable day or night, serves a continental dinner menu. Prices begin at $11.50. Piano entertainment is provided at both lunch and dinner. The hotel is ideally situated less than 100 yards off Yonge Street and only two blocks south of Bloor. A fully equipped health club is nearby and open to hotel guests.

JOURNEY'S END, 280 Bloor St. West, Toronto, ON, N5S 1V8. Tel. 416/968-0010. Fax 416/968-7765. 212 rms. A/C TV TEL **Subway:** St. George.
$ Rates: $100 single; $110 double. AE, DC, ER, MC, V. **Parking:** $12.
The budget chain Journey's End has a hotel several blocks west of the Inter-Continental, a great value for the location. Rooms are modern, well equipped with remote-control cable TVs and modern light furnishings, including useful well-lit worktables.

VENTURE INN, 89 Avenue Rd., Toronto, ON, M5R 2G3. Tel. 416/964-1220, or toll free 800/387-3933. Fax 416/964-8692. 71 rms. A/C TV TEL **Subway:** Bay or Museum.
$ Rates (including continental breakfast): $85 single; $95 double. Children under 12 stay free in parents' room. AE, MC, V. **Parking:** $5.50.
Though the Venture Inn has a high-priced location in Yorkville, it charges moderate prices for its modern rooms, which are decorated with pine accents.

BUDGET

AMSTERDAM GUEST HOUSE, 209 Carlton St., Toronto, ON, M5A 2K9. Tel. 416/921-9797. 14 rms (none with bath). A/C **Subway:** College.
$ Rates: $55 double with bathroom on another floor; $65 double for other units. AE, V. **Parking:** Free.
The Amsterdam Guest House is a brightly painted Victorian in Cabbagetown at Parliament owned by Adrian and Doreen Verpaalen. Among the rooms there's a couple of large doubles with TV. Most of the units are on a different floor from the bathrooms. In summer a continental breakfast of fruits, croissants, cheese, and cold meats is served; in winter there's more likely a cooked breakfast. Guests have use of a comfortable living room.

HOTEL SELBY, 592 Sherbourne St., Toronto, ON, M4X 1L4. Tel. 416/921-3142, or toll free 800/387-4788. Fax 416/923-3177. 62 rms, 5 suites. A/C TV TEL **Subway:** Sherbourne.
$ Rates (including continental breakfast): From $60 single or double; from $100 suite. MC, V. **Parking:** Free.
Representing a great bargain, the Hotel Selby is located in a large heritage Victorian. Downstairs at the front desk there's a comfortable lobby sitting area with chandelier and fireplace. The rooms are all different and individually decorated with an eclectic mix of furniture. Ceilings are high, making the rooms airy and dramatic; many units have stucco decoration and moldings. In several the old bathroom fixtures have been retained. Room 303, for example, the Gooderham Suite, is very large with a fireplace. There's a large walk-in closet and the bathroom has a clawfoot tub and pedestal sink. The Hemingway suite has a brass-hooded fireplace, an oak dresser, a couple of wingbacks, and a small tub with shower in the bathroom. Room 401 has an old-fashioned burled wood bed, angled ceilings, track lighting, and a pair of leatherette wingbacks. Facilities include a restaurant, piano bar, and access to a nearby health club for a small charge.

VICTORIA UNIVERSITY, 140 Charles St. West, Toronto, ON, M5S 1K9. Tel. 416/585-4524. Fax 416/585-4530. 425 rms (none with bath). **Subway:** Museum.
$ Rates (including breakfast): $45 single; $62 double. Discounts for seniors and students. MC, V. **Parking:** $11. **Closed:** Sept–early May.
For a great summer bargain downtown, stay at Victoria University, across from the Royal Ontario Museum. Rooms in the university residence are available from mid-May to late August. Each is furnished as a study/bedroom and supplied with

fresh linen, towels, and soap. Bathrooms are down the hall. Guests enjoy free local calls and use of laundry facilities, as well as access to the dining and athletic facilities (including tennis courts).

UPTOWN

BRADGATE ARMS, 54 Foxbar Rd., Toronto, ON, M4V 2G6. Tel. 416/ 968-1331, or toll free 800/268-7171. Fax 416/968-3743. 109 rms. A/C MINIBAR TV TEL **Subway:** St. Clair.
$ **Rates:** $110–$120 single or double. Weekend rates available. AE, DC, DISC, ER, MC, V. **Parking:** Free.

The Bradgate Arms has a tranquil secluded air, tucked away as it is on a side street off Avenue Road at St. Clair. It was created by joining two apartment houses, which are now linked by a pink marble atrium lobby filled with trees and a fountain. The rooms are large and well furnished with solid pieces, and feature mini-refrigerators and wet bars. Avenues, the dining room, has a good reputation, and there's also a cozy piano lounge. Facilities include a whirlpool at an affiliated health club and a library.

AT THE AIRPORT

There are many airport hotels, most bearing the famous hotel chain names—Best Western, Comfort Inn, Days Inn, Holiday Inn, Howard Johnson, Journey's End, Ramada, Hilton, Marriott, and Venture Inn. For information about them call their 800 numbers. There are however two extra-special airport hotels.

BRISTOL PLACE, 950 Dixon Rd., Rexdale, ON, M9W 5N4. Tel. 416/675-9444, or toll free 800/268-4927. Fax 416/675-4426. 285 rms. A/C MINIBAR TV TEL **Subway:** Kipling.
$ **Rates:** $180 single; $195 double; from $325 suite. Extra person $15. Children under 18 stay free in parents' room. Many special packages available. AE, DC, ER, MC, V. **Parking:** Free.

For really personal service—the kind that caters to the idiosyncrasies of each guest—and ultra-chic surroundings, the spot out here is the Bristol Place, a select hotel where contemporary architecture and facilities blend with old-fashioned attention to detail and service. Outside, the red-brick building is striking enough, looking like a concertina from a distance—but step into the lobby and it's stunning. It soars three stories to a skylit ceiling, through which the sun dances on the trees, sculptures, mosaics, and contemporary wall hangings. The sound of the waterfall alone makes me want to stay.

And now the rooms. If you can't afford to stay in the Prime Minister's Suite—usually reserved only for the Aga Khan and duke of Kent, a $3,000-a-day triplex furnished with a baby grand, antiques (many of them Chinese), a skylit bathroom with Jacuzzi whirlpool, and a private sun deck—don't despair, for the regular rooms are beautifully designed, decorated, and appointed. Each room has custom-made contemporary furniture, double or king-size beds, geometric design throws, two telephones, bedside console, alarm clock, and large parlor lights in the bathroom.

Dining/Entertainment: Le Café, raised slightly to overlook the lobby, is a plush coffee shop with comfortable banquettes and handmade ceramic tiles. Also overlooking the lobby, the quiet lounge just happens to have a coromandel screen by which you can relax on really comfy chairs.

Zachary's dining room, specializing in nouvelle cuisine, is delightfully contemporary and graced with a kaleidoscopic tapestry hung over white tile.

Services: Room service from 6:30am to midnight, laundry/valet, concierge.
Facilities: Indoor pool and sun deck. The health club has an exercise room, sun room, and sauna.

SHERATON GATEWAY AT TERMINAL THREE, Toronto AMF, Box 3000, Toronto, ON, L5P 1C4. Tel. 416/672-7000, or toll free 800/565-0010. Fax 416/672-7100. 500 rms. A/C MINIBAR TV TEL
$ **Rates:** $129–$139 single or double. AE, CB, DC, ER, MC, V. **Parking:** Free.
Connected by skywalk to Terminal 3, this is the most convenient place to stay at the

airport. All rooms are soundproofed, luxuriously decorated and contain all the amenities including hairdryers. For travelers it's also convenient to be able to view flight departure and arrival times on your own personal TV.

Dining/Entertainment: Three buffets daily are served in the Café Suisse, while the Mahogany Grill is reserved for fine dining. There's also a bar/lounge featuring nightly piano entertainment.

Services: Room service from 7am to 1:30am, hair salon.

Facilities: Indoor pool, whirlpool, and exercise center.

METRO EAST

VERY EXPENSIVE

INN ON THE PARK, 1100 Eglinton Ave. East, Don Mills, ON, M3C 1H8. **Tel.** 416/444-2561, or toll free 800/332-3442 in the U.S., 800/268-6282 in Canada. Fax 416/446-3308. 568 rms, 27 suites. A/C MINIBAR TV TEL

$ Rates: $125–$185 single; $145–$205 double. Extra person $20. Two children under 18 stay free in parents' room. Weekend packages available. AE, DC, ER, MC, V. **Parking:** Free parking for 800 cars.

The Four Seasons' Inn on the Park is a luxury hotel-resort only 15 minutes from downtown via the Don Valley Parkway. It's conveniently located for the Ontario Science Centre, which is not something to be sneered at, since to enjoy this sight fully you have to get there at opening time and beat the crowds.

Set at the top of a ravine on 600 acres of parkland, the inn takes advantage of its natural setting: A lounge faces west to capture the magnificent sunsets and a landscaped two-acre courtyard has Douglas firs, silver birches, a rock garden, and duck pond, all crisscrossed by walkways and dotted with benches.

The rooms, located in a 14-story low-rise and a 21-story tower, have beautiful views (those facing west have balconies). All are superbly decorated with contemporary pieces and have those extra little features like alarm clocks, hairdryers, and bathrobes, as well as the usual color TV with in-house movies.

Dining/Entertainment: The Terrace Lounge, a piano bar, features lunch, plus wine and cheese during the cocktail hours. During the summer months the Cabana, the poolside restaurant, is open for pleasant outdoor dining.

A stylish garden atmosphere is the backdrop for sophisticated continental cuisine in Seasons, the hotel's premier dining room. Start with maple smoked salmon, crisp rye toast and lemon cream, or green asparagus with slivers of sprintz cheese and balsamic vinaigrette, and follow with a selection from a dozen or so entrees: broiled filets of red snapper and sea bass with mint and basil, duckling with hoisin sauce, or beef tenderloin with Côte du Rhône sauce and oyster mushrooms. Prices range from $20 to $25. For casual dining, there's the Harvest Room. All the restaurants feature "alternative cuisine" for the health-conscious.

Services: The hotel has particular appeal to families. It offers Inn Kidz, a supervised recreational program for children ages 5 to 12. In summer the program is offered daily from 9:30am to 4:30pm; in winter, on weekends and holidays only. The hotel also offers all the services associated with a Four Seasons hotel—24-hour room service, complimentary shoeshine, 24-hour valet, one-hour pressing, 24-hour concierge, twice-daily maid service.

Facilities: Facilities include a fully equipped business center; an indoor pool; an outdoor pool and diving pool; a games room with pinball, badminton, shuffleboard, indoor tennis; a children's play area; and a health club with saunas and gym. A racquet club with squash and racquetball courts, a lounge, and a gym is also available. Meanwhile, to help you take advantage of the 600 acres of park across the road, bicycles are available in the summer, and in winter you can ski cross-country and toboggan. And if you want to get your nose (or anything else) fixed, there's even a plastic and cosmetic surgeon on the premises!

PRINCE HOTEL, 900 York Mills Rd., Don Mills, ON, M3B 3H2. **Tel.** 416/444-2511, or toll free 800/268-7677 in Canada, 800/323-7500 in the U.S. Fax 416/444-9597. 406 rms. A/C TV TEL **Subway:** York Mills.

Ⓕ **FROMMER'S COOL FOR KIDS:**
HOTELS

Delta Chelsea Inn *(see p. 414)* The Chelsea Chum Club for kids aged 3 to 12 sponsors special activities in the Children's Creative Centre and throughout the hotel. When they check in at the life-size gingerbread house they get a registration card and passport. Children under 6 eat free; there are special menus for the older set. All this goes a long way toward creating a smooth family stay.

Inn on the Park *(see p. 422)* Swings, ice skating, bicycles, and a video room make this a miniparadise for kids of all ages. The hotel operates an Inn Kidz supervised recreational program for those aged 5 to 12 and even sponsors special themed weekends for them.

The Four Seasons *(see p. 417)* Free bicycles, video games, and the pool should keep them occupied. The meals served in Animal World wicker baskets or on Sesame Street plates, and the complimentary room-service cookies and milk on arrival will make them feel special.

$ **Rates:** $150–$175 single; $170–$195 double; from $300 suite. Children under 18 stay free in parents' room. Extra person $15. AE, DC, ER, MC, V. **Parking:** Free outdoor parking.

The other luxury resort hotel in this area is much quieter, having an almost ethereal serenity, which may derive from its Japanese connections. The Prince Hotel is located 20 minutes from downtown and set in 15 acres of private parkland where you can wander nature trails.

A warm and soft decor will greet you in your room, which may have a beautiful bay window or balcony. Each of the oversize rooms has a marble bathroom, a color TV with in-house movies, a refrigerator, and a hairdryer.

Dining/Entertainment: Velvet-covered booths and copper-colored walls create a certain "je ne sais quoi" ambience in Le Continental, a restaurant for haute cuisine and dancing, but really unique dining awaits you in Katsura, which houses four separate dining experiences: a tempura counter and sushi bar, tatami-style dining, teppanyaki-style cuisine, and a robata bar.

The blending of indoors and outdoors is well accomplished in the Coffee Garden by an earth-tone color scheme. The restaurant overlooks a grove of 30-foot-tall trees, as does the Brandy Tree, a sophisticated piano bar, restfully decorated in gray and plum, which, in summer, overflows onto an outside patio where you can sip under blue parasols while seated on wide garden furniture.

Services: 24-hour room service.

Facilities: Indoor-outdoor pool, sauna, and tennis courts, fitness center with Nautilus, table tennis, billiards, putting green, and nature trails.

EXPENSIVE

GUILD INN, 201 Guildwood Pkwy., Scarborough, ON, M1E 1P6. Tel. 416/261-3331. Fax 416/261-5675. 96 rms. TV TEL **Subway:** Kennedy.

$ **Rates:** Main inn $109 single or double; new wing $125 single or double. Extra person $10. Children under 14 stay free in parents' room. AE, DC, DISC, ER, MC, V. **Parking:** Free.

If you want to stay only 10 miles outside the city (25 minutes from downtown) in a unique and beautiful setting, then try the Guild Inn. Enter through the broad iron gates forged in England in 1839, which used to serve as the entrance to Toronto's main military fortification, the Stanley Barracks, until they were brought here. Follow the circular drive, which is shaded by trees and bordered with flowers, and walk into the original entrance hall, which retains the character of an English manor, with its broad staircase, oak beams, and wrought-iron chandeliers.

As you may have guessed, besides serving as an inn, the place has become a repository for art and architecture. The 90-acre grounds are dotted with historic architectural fragments—limestone Ionic columns rescued from Toronto's Banker Bond Building, torn down to make way for the futuristic Canadian Place, for instance. Inside you'll also find other wonderful collections.

Part of the reason for this plethora of art lies in the fact that the property was occupied from 1932 by the Guild of All Arts, which established art and craft workshops here. So many visitors were attracted that dining facilities were added and guest rooms soon followed, until the Guild became a flourishing country inn. During these halcyon years many notables visited, including Queen Juliana, Dorothy and Lillian Gish, Moira Shearer, Rex Harrison, Sir John Gielgud, and Lilli Palmer, to name just a few.

The gardens at the rear sweep down to the Scarborough Bluffs rising 200 feet above Lake Ontario, and for a room with this view you'll pay a little extra. The original central section of the inn was built in 1914 and the rooms here have no air conditioning. Rooms in the newer wing have air conditioning, AM/FM radio, color TV, and private balconies.

Dining/Entertainment: The dining room is still a popular gathering place for Sunday brunch, and serves primarily grills, roasts, and seafood, priced from $15 for steamed vegetables served with pasta or potato to $22 for rack of lamb with minted red wine and mustard seed. Try some smoked salmon, smoked on the premises after it has been marinated in rum. In summer, tea is served outdoors in the garden; there's a lovely veranda for cocktails.

Services: Room service from 7am to 10pm.

Facilities: For recreation there's an outdoor swimming pool, tennis court, and nature trails.

MODERATE

RELAX INN–TORONTO EAST, 20 Milner Business Court, Scarborough, ON, M1B 3C6. Tel. 416/299-9500, or toll free 800/667-3529. Fax 416/299-6172. 160 rms. A/C TV TEL **Subway:** Scarborough Town Center.
$ Rates: $69 single; $75 double. Children under 19 stay free in parents' room. AE, DC, DISC, ER, MC, V. **Parking:** Free.
The Relax Inn has rooms with color TV and in-room movies, individual climate control, and attractive furnishings. Facilities include an indoor pool, a whirlpool, and a restaurant and lounge.

VENTURE INN, 50 Estate Dr., Scarborough, ON, M1H 2Z1. Tel. 416/439-9666, or toll free 800/387-3933. Fax 416/439-4295. 136 rms. A/C TV TEL **Subway:** McCowan.
$ Rates (including continental breakfast): $75 single; $85 double. Children under 19 stay free in parents' room. AE, DC, DISC, ER, MC, V. **Parking:** Free.
The Venture Inn has pleasantly decorated rooms with the chain's pine look. Facilities include a restaurant/bar and whirlpool and sauna.

BUDGET

UNIVERSITY OF TORONTO IN SCARBOROUGH, Student Village, 1265 Military Trail, Scarborough, ON, M1C 1A4. Tel. 416/287-7369. Fax 416/287-7667. **Directions:** Take the subway to Kennedy, then the Scarborough Rapid Transit to Ellesmere, then bus 95 or 95B to the college entrance.
$ Rates: $135 for two nights; each additional night $65, to a maximum of $385 per week. MC, V. **Parking:** Free. **Closed:** End of Aug–early May.
From mid-May to the third week in August the University of Toronto in Scarborough has accommodations available in town houses for families (two adults and children

under 17) that sleep four to six people and contain equipped kitchens. There's a cafeteria, pub, and recreation center. *Note:* Accommodations are available for a minimum stay of two nights.

4. DINING

Dining is a delight in Toronto. There are, in fact, more than 5,000 restaurants, catering to every taste and every price range. In the section that follows I have selected about 75 of my favorites, categorizing them by location and price. The locations are as follows: **Downtown** refers roughly to streets from the waterfront to and including College/Carlton Streets between Spadina Avenue and Jarvis Street; **midtown** refers to the area north of College/Carlton Streets to Davenport and Yonge Streets, and also between Spadina and Jarvis. I have also further subdivided both of these sections into west and east. **Uptown** covers Yonge-Davenport and north.

Prices are rather broad categories: At very expensive establishments expect to pay $110 and up for dinner for two without wine; expensive, $80 to $110; moderate, $40 to $80; and budget, under $40. These, I stress, are only rough guidelines, and at many of the moderately priced and budget-priced establishments you can pay much less by choosing carefully.

SOME DINING NOTES   Food prices are high and dining in Toronto can be rather expensive. First, there's an 8% provincial sales tax. Then there's the 7% GST.

And then, if you enjoy wine with your meal, the cost will increase dramatically: The government places a 100+% tax on all imported wines, primarily to protect and promote the Canadian wine industry in British Columbia and Ontario. Thus you may pay as much as $6 for a glass of house wine in the better restaurants, and $18 or more for a one-liter carafe. There's also a 10% tax on all alcohol—keep in mind that the prices quoted often do not reflect that tax.

At lunch, do what the Torontonians do. Get some take-out and sit outside in one of the many squares or plazas. Great sources for this can be found in First Canadian Place, Eaton Centre, Queen's Quay, and many other downtown office buildings. Just head for the concourse.

DOWNTOWN WEST

EXPENSIVE

BARBERIAN'S, 7 Elm St. Tel. 416/597-0225 or 416/597-0335.
   Cuisine: STEAK. **Reservations:** Required.
$ Prices: Appetizers $4.25–$9; main courses $18–$30. AE, DC, ER, MC, V.
   Open: Lunch Mon–Fri noon–2:30pm; dinner Mon–Sat 5pm–midnight, Sun 5–11pm.

Steakhouses, in my opinion, are usually rather dull establishments, but Barberian's is a cozy comforting retreat, filled with Canadiana including several paintings by the Group of Seven, a bust of Canada's first prime minister (Sir John A. Macdonald), an early Canadian grandfather clock, coal-oil lamps, and firearms.

Despite the traditional air, the friendliness and humor of the management are reflected in the irreverent attitude expressed toward the dreaded dress code. A note reads: "In the beginning, the Lord created Light, Heaven, Earth and, among other things, the Fig Leaf. He never created the Jacket. The Tie. . . . Not being one to mess with Divine Wisdom, Barberian's wishes to announce the following dress restriction—you must wear something."

This nonchalance does not extend to the food, however, which focuses on 10 or so steak and seafood dishes that run the gamut from the fish of the day to a thick and juicy New York sirloin. The food is well worth the price. After 10pm a fondue and dessert menu awaits the after-theater or late diner.

LE BISTINGO, 349 Queen St. West. Tel. 416/598-3490.
Cuisine: FRENCH. **Reservations:** Recommended.
$ Prices: Appetizers $5–$9; main courses $14–$28. AE, MC, V.
Open: Lunch Mon–Fri noon–2:30pm; dinner Mon–Sat 5:30–10pm.

Simple and sleek, Le Bistingo is a small place with plain-white cloths on tables set with fresh sprigs of flowers. The atmosphere is intimate and comfortable, and the walls are hung with art. The food takes full advantage of the freshest ingredients and is well prepared and well served.

The dinner menu features a dozen or so entrées—for example, grilled salmon with olive oil, red wine vinegar and green lentils, breast of chicken with five spices and Chinese noodles, or a Provimi veal chop with chives jus. To start there's a selection of oysters, and terrines or a salad of duck confit, green asparagus, field mushrooms, and baby greens. Make sure to save room for the delicious warm apple tart with Calvados ice cream or the marquise au chocolat with coffee bean sauce and chocolate ice. The wine list is reasonable and also offers several varieties by the glass.

LOTUS, 96 Tecumseh St. Tel. 416/368-7620.
Cuisine: ASIAN/EUROPEAN. **Reservations:** Imperative—at least two weeks in advance.
$ Prices: Appetizers $8–$15; Main courses $25–$30. AE, MC, V.
Open: Dinner Tues–Sat 6–10pm.

Located off King, west of Bathurst, Lotus focuses on the food and the dining clientele, for the storefront's decor is plain, with a tiny bar, a blush of color on one wall, and some herbed vinegars for decorative accent. That's all. But the word, though, is out and the place is well-booked in advance. Chef Su Sur Lee hails from Hong Kong and he creatively combines European and Asian styles and flavors to produce such thrilling dishes as quick-sautéed large shrimps in a Thai green curry sauce with fresh mango, chop suey vegetables, and an orange pepper rice noodle cake or organic crispy skin duck breast with raspberry wildflower honey and lavender glaze, roasted squash, and young potato and hazelnut homefries.

The menu changes daily. Among appetizers you might find such delicately flavored dishes as sautéed wild chanterelle and red lobster mushrooms with green garlic butter and spinach spaetzle or seared foie gras with beet-and-apple compote with carrot vinaigrette and mustard oil. The desserts, which currently cost $8, range from a classic baked raspberry tart in a light custard with white chocolate ice cream to Peking-style fig fritters with caramel ice cream, mango purée, and hot chocolate sauce.

MODERATE

AVOCADO CLUB, 165 John St. Tel. 416/598-4656.
Cuisine: INTERNATIONAL. **Reservations:** Recommended on weekends.
$ Prices: Main courses $9–$14. AE, DC, ER, MC, V.
Open: Lunch Mon–Fri noon–2pm; dinner Mon–Sat 6–10pm.

The Avocado Club features hot hues with its yellow, fuchsia, and turquoise floor and ceiling and its vaguely Mediterranean murals, and hot flavors with its Vietnamese-, Mexican-, Thai-, and Indian-inspired cuisine. The space affords views of the CN Tower and the downtown skyline at night. Ingredients are fresh and seasonal and very international. For example, you might find kick-ass lamb chili, roll-your-own tacos, herb-seared filet of Atlantic salmon, and Thai noodle stir-fry. Ditto among the appetizers, which might include Vietnamese grilled pork sticks, avocado salad with salsa, or soba noodle salad with sushi. Finish with one of the fresh seasonal fruit pies.

BANGKOK GARDEN, 18 Elm St. Tel. 416/977-6748.
Cuisine: THAI. **Reservations:** Recommended.
$ Prices: Appetizers $6–$7; main courses $17–$20. AE, DC, ER, MC, V.
Open: Lunch Mon–Fri 11:30am–2:30pm; dinner daily 5–10pm.

Bangkok Garden offers Thai cuisine in a lush dining room fashioned out of teak. Those who are unfamiliar with the flavors of Thai cuisine might try one of the special dinners for $37 and up, so that you can sample an appetizer assortment, lemon mussel soup, steamed ginger fish, tamarind curry, and stir-fried green vegetables with shrimp, rice, fruit, and Thai sweets, for example. A la carte dishes include smooth curries made with chili, lime, and coconut milk; chicken richly flavored with tamarind; and my favorite fish, crispy-fried in a tamarind sauce. At lunch an all-you-can-eat buffet is offered for $9.95. For dessert, try sticky rice and fresh mangoes.

You may dine either in the lushly tropical Garden, which is complete with a flowing river stocked with fish, or on the Verandah, where Somerset Maugham would feel at home. A spirit house, bronze nagas, and porcelain jardinières add to the exotic ambience throughout. The Brass Flamingo bar also offers light lunches and other snacks from 11:30am to midnight Monday through Saturday. Try something from the noodle bar, seasoning choices to your own particular taste with spring onions, fresh coriander leaves, salted turnip, chili vinegar, and many other exotic flavors.

FRED'S NOT HERE SMOKEHOUSE AND GRILL, 321 King St. Tel. 416/ 971-9155.

Cuisine: CONTINENTAL. **Reservations:** Recommended.
$ Prices: Appetizers $6–$8; main courses $11–$20. AE, DC, ER, MC, V.
Open: Lunch Mon–Fri 11:30am–2:30pm; dinner Sun–Wed 5–10pm, Thurs 5–11pm, Fri–Sat 5–11:30pm.

Upstairs at Fred's Not Here Smokehouse and Grill, the atmosphere is more sedate than what you'll find downstairs but the food is equally fun. To start you might opt for any one of the tempting seafood morsels—steamed mussels in Pernod, or fried coconut shrimp with Thai dipping sauce to name only two. To follow there's a raft of choices, from the simple but tasty gnocchi with hot Italian sausage, tomato basil cream and Gorgonzola to the venison with an orange-pear Madeira sauce. It's hard to single out one of the dozen desserts but banana fritters with caramel ice cream and chocolate sauce hits my spot.

LA BODEGA, 30 Baldwin St. Tel. 416/977-1287.

Cuisine: FRENCH. **Reservations:** Recommended for dinner.
$ Prices: Main courses $17–$26; prix fixe $19. AE, DC, ER, MC, V.
Open: Lunch Mon–Fri noon–2:30pm; dinner Mon–Sat 5–11pm.

Ensconced in an elegant town house, La Bodega, two blocks south of College and two west of University Avenue, is still a favorite because it serves fine fresh food at moderate prices in a very comfortable atmosphere. Every day, usually inspired by the freshest produce at the market, the menu specials are written on the blackboard menu. There's usually a dozen or so interesting choices, including several fresh fish dishes. For example, on my last visit the chef was offering blackened mahimahi garnished with shrimp, breast of duck with raspberry sauce, and venison au genièvre. The best bet of all, though, is the prix fixe for $19, offering a choice of two set menus—one meat, the other fish—with soup or salad and tea or coffee. In summer the patio, with tables covered in red gingham and bearing multicolored umbrellas, is a popular dining spot.

At lunchtime, when the restaurant is especially popular, there's lighter fare with such things as coq au vin, tourtière, and salade niçoise, priced from $8 to $12.

The dining rooms are quite fetching. The walls are graced with French tapestries and the windows with lace curtains. French music adds a definite Gallic air. There's a definite glow about the place.

LA FENICE, 319 King St. West. Tel. 416/585-2377.

Cuisine: ITALIAN. **Reservations:** Required.
$ Prices: Main courses $15–$24. AE, CB, DC, ER, MC, V.
Open: Lunch Mon–Fri noon–2:30pm; dinner Mon–Sat 5:30–11pm.

La Fenice is an Italian outpost that's convenient for the theater. Really fresh ingredients and authentic fine olive oil are the hallmarks of the cuisine here, where a plate of assorted appetizers will include pungent roasted peppers, crisp-fried zucchini, squid, and a roast veal in tuna sauce (vitello tonnato). There are 18 or more pasta dishes to choose from—tagliatelle burro and basilico with a fragrant basil sauce, seafood risotto—along with a fine selection of Provimi veal, chicken, and fresh fish dishes. Dessert offerings include a refreshing raspberry sherbet, zabaglione, and fresh strawberries and other fruits in season.

La Fenice also has an attractive downstairs pasta bar that is open all day for light fare. It's decked out with marble, glass tables, and Milanese-style stools and chairs.

MASA, 205 Richmond St. Tel. 416/977-9519.
   Cuisine: JAPANESE. **Reservations:** Recommended.
$ **Prices:** Appetizers $3.50–$5.50; sushi $2–$3; fixed-price dinner $12–$20. AE, DC, MC, V.
   Open: Lunch Mon–Fri noon–2:30pm; dinner Mon–Sat 5–11pm, Sun 5–10pm.

At Masa you can seat yourself at the sushi bar (and choose from a whole assortment), or dine Western style or tatami style. Saké containers, Japanese prints, fans, and screens and a rock garden make for a serene atmosphere.

There's a full range of appetizers—sliced fishcake, oysters in rice vinegar, seaweed pasted crab leg, to name only a few. Or you can preface your dinner with soup—soybean with clams, for instance. The best deal, though, is to opt for one of the prix-fixe dinners, which will include vinegared fishcake, miso soup, a small appetizer, rice, and such main courses as salmon teriyaki, raw tuna sashimi, or garlic beef yakiniku. Don't miss the mitsu mame dessert—jelly made from seaweed with black peas.

Masa is frequented by many Japanese customers—a good sign to aficionados of Japanese cuisine.

OLE MALACCA, 49 Baldwin St. Tel. 416/340-1208.
   Cuisine: MALAYSIAN. **Reservations:** Not needed.
$ **Prices:** Appetizers $3–$6; main courses $10–$16; all-you-can-eat luncheon $6.95. AE, MC, V.
   Open: Lunch Mon–Fri 11:30am–2:30pm; dinner Mon–Sat 5–11pm.

A very appealing restaurant, Ole Malacca is comfortable, welcoming, and furnished with bamboo, rattan, and paper lanterns. It's full of Southeast Asian atmosphere. So is the spicy food—tiger prawns with garlic, ginger, and chili with brandy; filet of sole in a hot curry sauce with coconut; or chicken in a dry curry with garlic, ginger, spices, and lemongrass. Try one of the sambals (based on shrimp paste) or the satays (cooked on a hibachi at the table). The gado gado Bali (slivers of cucumber, bean sprouts, hard-boiled egg, and slivers of chicken topped with spicy peanut sauce) is enough for three.

ORSO, 106 John St. Tel. 416/596-1989.
   Cuisine: ITALIAN. **Reservations:** Recommended.
$ **Prices:** Appetizers $8–$11; pizzas $11.50; pasta courses $13.50; main courses $16.50–$23. AE, ER, V.
   Open: Mon–Sat 11:30am–midnight, Sun 11:30am–10:30pm.

Orso is a cozy Italian bistro located in a brick town house in the theater district. Pink marble floors, low ceilings, and framed paintings make for an intimate ambience, with an elegant small bar up front. The menu is the same at lunch and dinner. At lunch you might opt for one of the 10 or so appetizers, such as grilled smoked salmon with black beans or warm arugula salad with roasted goat cheese and balsamic vinegar. Or try one of the half-dozen delicious crisp crusted pizzas, topped variously with Gorgonzola, prosciutto, and sun-dried tomatoes, or smoked chicken, mushrooms, onion, and mozzarella, to name only two. At dinner you could do the same, or choose a pasta dish or an entrée such as red snapper grilled with tomato and black olives; capon breast with peppers, lemon, and rosemary; or grilled lamb chops with red wine and polenta.

RED TOMATO, 321 King St. Tel. 416/971-6626.
   Cuisine: INTERNATIONAL. **Reservations:** Not needed.
$ **Prices:** Appetizers $4–$6; main courses $9–$15. AE, DC, MC, V.
   Open: Upstairs lunch Mon–Fri 11:30am–2:30pm; dinner Sun–Tues 5–10pm, Wed 5–10:30pm, Thurs 5–11pm, Fri–Sat 5–11:30pm. Downstairs Mon–Fri 11:30am–12:30am, Sat noon–1am, Sun 4:30–10pm. Bar open daily until 1am.

Red Tomato is famous for its hot rocks cuisine—Korean beef, Jamaican jerk chicken, chicken with mango-chili salsa—all cooked the way it sounds. At night the downstairs space, with large central bar, video screens, exposed plumbing, and wild murals, is filled with the young and not-so-young feasting on an array of small dishes like the great spicy Yucatán shrimp, the nachos, or the satay. More substantial dishes, like broiled lobster in garlic butter with pasta with smoked jalapeño sauce or stir-fried chicken with garlic, chilies, and lemongrass served over noodles, are also available. Happy hour is Monday to Saturday from 2:30 to 6pm, Sunday 4:30 to 10pm.

TIDAL WAVE, 100 Simcoe St., at Adelaide. Tel. 416/597-0016.
   Cuisine: JAPANESE. **Reservations:** Recommended.
   $ Prices: Main courses $9–$14; weekday luncheon buffet $15.95; dinner buffet Sun–Tues $25.95. AE, DC, ER, MC, V.
   Open: Mon–Fri noon–1am, Sat–Sun 5pm–1am.

The fun and focal point of the dining room at Tidal Wave is the 40-seat sushi bar in which an endless procession of small barges laden with freshly made sushi and sashimi float round an oval water-filled canal. There is also a selection of udon dishes and familiar favorites like tonkatsu, tempura, and teriyaki (including soup and rice). Every night from 9:30pm to 1:30am you can join the karaoke crowd.

Along Queen Street

This continues to be one of the city's liveliest neighborhoods, where moderately priced bistros and clubs are crowded with young artists and professionals and where avant-garde boutiques stand beside quaint junk-turned-antiques stores and second-hand book emporiums.

LE SELECT, 328 Queen St. West. Tel. 416/596-6406.
   Cuisine: FRENCH. **Reservations:** Recommended.
   $ Prices: Appetizers $6–$8; main courses $13–$18; prix fixe $16. AE, DC, MC, V.
   Open: Mon–Thurs noon–midnight, Fri–Sat noon–1am, Sun 5:30–11pm.

People throng the entrance of Le Select, a real French-style bistro decorated in Paris Left Bank style, complete with authentic zinc bar. Breakfronts, fringed fabric lampshades over the tables, tollware, French posters, and a jazz background set the scene.

What draws the young artistic crowd here is the chance to dine on moderately priced but good French food—from mussels steamed in white wine and shallots to filet with green peppercorn sauce, with most dishes averaging under $10 (filet of salmon with dill and Pernod, for example). There's also a $16 prix-fixe dinner that includes appetizer, entrée, and dessert. The day I visited they were offering beef tongue with capers and gherkins in a warm vinaigrette, and a turkey drumstick with braised cabbage among the selections. For dessert there was fruit tart and chocolate mousse. At lunch, dishes average $9.

PETER PAN, 373 Queen St. West. Tel. 416/593-0917.
   Cuisine: CONTINENTAL. **Reservations:** Recommended for parties of six or more.
   $ Prices: Main courses $10–$14. AE, MC, V.
   Open: Lunch Mon–Sat noon–2:30pm; dinner Sun–Wed 6pm–midnight, Thurs–Sat 6pm–1am; brunch Sun noon–4pm.

Peter Pan still remains a favorite of many who know this budget gourmet row intimately. A bare-bones '30s look with tin ceilings and high booths lit by art deco sconces provides the background. On the menu you'll find about a dozen appetizers, several pastas, and about eight main courses. The cuisine is imaginative, and often flavored with au courant Asian accents. For example, you might start with Thai rolls with a spicy peanut sauce or a Cantonese noodle salad, and follow with shrimp curry with coriander, coconut milk, and garlic, grilled chicken with rosemary tomato and roasted shallots, or baked rabbit with sliced almonds and roasted garlic. Desserts are always enticing, like the pear tart with almond cream or the Brazilian fig tart with kirsch sabayon.

QUEEN MOTHER CAFE, 208 Queen St. West. Tel. 416/598-4719.
   Cuisine: INTERNATIONAL. **Reservations:** Recommended.
   $ Prices: Appetizers $3–$6; main courses $6–$10. AE, MC, V.
   Open: Lunch Mon–Sat 1:30am–4:30pm; dinner Mon–Sat 5:30–midnight.

Another longtime favorite here is the Queen Mother Café, a simply adorned restaurant with polished wood tables and bentwood chairs. Food is displayed in the counter at back and the menu will offer such Laotian- and Thai-inspired items as pad Thai (noodles with seafood and meat), stir-fried chicken with Thai spices, and shrimp curry, as well as daily specials and the famous QM burger—a patty of grains, nuts, mushrooms, herbs topped with cheese and served in a whole-wheat pita.

ZAIDY'S, 275 Queen St. West. Tel. 416/977-7222.

Cuisine: CAJUN. **Reservations:** Recommended, especially at lunch.

$ Prices: Appetizers $4–$6; main courses $12–$16. AE, ER, MC, V.

Open: Lunch Mon–Fri noon–2:30pm; dinner Mon–Thurs 5–10pm, Fri–Sat 5–11pm.

Just west of Simcoe Street is another popular spot where the desserts are everyone's downfall—bourbon chocolate fudge cake, pecan tart, peanut butter pie with hot fudge sauce, and great sorbets, all freshly made. Start with a zesty Cajun shrimp or a thick gumbo, and follow with blackened loin of lamb, shrimp Créole, or Jack Daniels pepper steak. There's always a pasta of the day along with a seasonal game or fowl dish. The atmosphere is light, modern, and informal—brick, poster art, and maple bar. Prices run around $7 for a selection of po'boys (open-face sandwiches) at lunch.

BUDGET

THE BAGEL, 285 College St. Tel. 416/923-0171.

Cuisine: DELI. **Reservations:** Not accepted.

$ Prices: Most items $3.50–$11. MC, V.

Open: Daily 7am–9:30pm.

You have to be a member of the "clean plate club" if you want to eat at the Bagel; otherwise the waitresses will get after you with "C'mon, eat already." Blintzes, bagels, lox, and cream cheese are the tops at this really characterful spot. Everything is under $9—sweet-and-sour meatballs, cabbage rolls—except for the breaded veal chop and one or two other dinner plates.

EATING COUNTER, 21–23 Baldwin St., near McCaul and Dundas. Tel. 416/977-7028.

Cuisine: CHINESE. **Reservations:** Not needed except for large parties.

$ Prices: Most items $5–$11. MC, V.

Open: Daily 11am–11pm.

Lines extend out onto the street from the Eating Counter. Most of the eager patrons here are Chinese, who relish the perfectly cooked Cantonese fare—crisp fresh vegetables, noodles, barbecue specialties, and, a particular favorite, fresh lobster with ginger and green onions. A blackboard lists the daily specialties in Chinese characters, which are not listed on the English menu. Ask the waiter about the freshest items of the day. Prices are low, running from $5 and up (you can even enjoy two lobsters for $17). Decor is nonexistent but the food is good.

FILET OF SOLE, 11 Duncan St. Tel. 416/598-3256.

Cuisine: SEAFOOD. **Reservations:** Recommended.

$ Prices: Most main courses $12–$18. AE, CB, DC, ER, MC, V.

Open: Lunch Mon–Fri noon–2:30pm; dinner Sun–Wed 5–10pm, Thurs–Sat 5–11pm.

Conveniently located near the CN Tower is the Filet of Sole, where you'll find an up-to-the-minute oyster bar and an extensive seafood menu that also features daily specials. The restaurant serves everything from fish-and-chips to a two-pound lobster with rice and vegetable. Most of the dishes are in the $12 to $18 range—mahimahi with a soy-ginger vinaigrette and green onion coulis, poached salmon with a sauce of ginger, cilantro, lemongrass, basil and coconut milk, arctic char, yellowfin tuna, and many other varieties. An Alaskan crab leg platter will cost $24. For non-fish lovers there are steak and chicken.

Downstairs the **Whistling Oyster Seafood Café** (tel. 416/598-7707) has a happy oyster hour and a happy dim sum hour on Sunday from 4:30 to 10pm. Enjoy 20 or so appetizers including a variety of fresh clams and oysters and such dishes as steamed clams in wine, tomato and garlic, blackened tiger shrimp with mangoes and Thai coleslaw, conch fritters and many more. Most items are under $3; everything is under $5. At other times there's an extensive shellfish and fish menu featuring items

FROMMER'S SMART TRAVELER: RESTAURANTS

1. Go ethnic—Toronto has some great inexpensive ethnic dining.
2. Eat your main meal at lunch, when prices are lower—and you can taste the cuisine at the gourmet hot spots for a fraction of the dinner prices.
3. Picnic or grab a sandwich at a take-out spot and head for one of the parks, gardens, or plazas downtown.
4. Watch the booze—it can add greatly to the cost of any meal because it's not cheap.

from $10 for a coquille maison to $20 for Alaskan king crab legs. The Whistling Oyster is open Monday to Saturday from 11am to 1am and Sunday from 4 to 11pm.

KENSINGTON PATTY PALACE, 172 Baldwin St. Tel. 416/596-6667.
   Cuisine: CARIBBEAN. **Reservations:** Not accepted.
$ Prices: Most items $2.50–$5. No credit cards.
   Open: Mon–Sat 10am–6pm.
Folks line up at Kensington Patty Palace, in the heart of the market, and with good reason, because, for a few dollars, you can secure some satisfying tasty food, which you can enjoy if you can find space on the bench out front. The beef, chicken, and goat rôtis ($4.20) are famous; so too are the potato and chickpea rôtis, which are even cheaper. Beef, chicken, and vegetable patties are also available for $1 or less. For a real Jamaican experience try the salted codfish and callaloo (a strong-flavored spinach). To round out your feast take away some totoes (coconut cookies) or gizzadas (coconut tarts). This one's a real Toronto tradition.

LEE GARDEN, 358 Spadina Ave., at Nassau St. Tel. 416/593-9524.
   Cuisine: CHINESE. **Reservations:** Not accepted.
$ Prices: Main courses $8–$10. MC, V.
   Open: Dinner daily 4–11pm.
Lee Garden is known for its seafood specialties, like abalone with sliced chicken and Chinese vegetables; fresh oyster, clam, abalone, and crab cooked with green onion and ginger; or shrimp with hot-pepper sauce Hakka style. The menu also features beef hot pot and chicken dishes. The duck with onion-lemon sauce is also popular.

THE MOGHUL, 33 Elm St. Tel. 416/597-0522.
   Cuisine: INDIAN. **Reservations:** Recommended.
$ Prices: Main courses $8–$10. AE, DC, ER, MC, V.
   Open: Lunch Mon–Fri 11:30am–2:30pm; dinner Mon–Fri 5–11pm, Sat 5pm–midnight, Sun 5–10pm.
The Moghul is a very comfortable Indian restaurant serving superb curries. Try the hot vindaloo or a rogan josh, or any of the other chicken, shrimp, and beef specialties. For those who prefer subtlety, the biryanis are also excellent. At lunch there's a 20 hot and cold dish buffet available.
   There's another branch of this restaurant at 563 Bloor St. West (tel. 416/535-3315).

PEKING RESTAURANT, 257 College St. Tel. 416/979-2422.
   Cuisine: CHINESE. **Reservations:** Recommended for large parties.
$ Prices: Main courses $8–$12. AE, MC, V.
   Open: Mon–Fri 11:30am–10:30pm, Sat 11:30am–11pm, Sun noon–10pm.
The Peking Restaurant specializes in Szechuan, Cantonese, and Mandarin food. Try their Peking duck, which is served in three courses—there's enough for four and the price is only $27.

THE RIVOLI, 332 Queen St. West. Tel. 416/597-0794.
   Cuisine: CONTINENTAL. **Reservations:** Not accepted.

$ Prices: Appetizers $4.50–$8; main courses $9–$12. MC, V.
Open: Mon–Sat 11:30am–1am.

The Rivoli attracts an avant-garde crowd and offers some good light fare—crabmeat with melted cheese sandwich, or curried tuna with pineapple, for example. The dinner menu features half a dozen Lao-Thai specialties like pad Thai and Siam curry (shrimp with hot chili and fresh basil) as well as a burger and chicken potpie. Three or so daily specials supplement the menu, usually a pasta, a meat, and a fish dish. The lunch menu continues the theme with special light-lunch sandwiches, like the grilled cheese made with challah or the pita stuffed with crabmeat salad. In summer the sidewalk patio is jammed. There's nightly avant-garde entertainment, and the decor is appropriately basic black.

SAIGON PALACE, 454 Spadina Ave. Tel. 416/968-1623.
Cuisine: CHINESE/VIETNAMESE. **Reservations:** Not needed.
$ Prices: Most items under $5. No credit cards.
Open: Lunch daily 11am–3pm; dinner daily 6–10pm.

Saigon Palace is a superbudget eatery—a Vietnamese-style café with minimal decor. Hardly anything on the menu is over $5. There's a fine beef with noodle soup, pork chop, and curry chicken and steamed egg, all three going for $3.75. The place is filled with Chinese and Vietnamese residents.

VANIPHA, 193 Augusta Ave. Tel. 416/340-0491.
Cuisine: THAI/LAO. **Reservations:** Accepted only for parties of six or more.
$ Prices: Appetizers $2.25–$6.25; main courses $7.25–$10. V.
Open: Mon–Sat 4pm–midnight.

Serving some really fine cuisine, Vanipha is housed in a plain but comfortable step-down storefront. Try the pad Thai, mango salad, grilled fish with tamarind sauce, chicken red curry, and of course, the special treat—sticky rice.

WAH SING, 41 Baldwin St. Tel. 416/596-1628.
Cuisine: CHINESE. **Reservations:** Accepted only for large parties.
$ Prices: Most items $8–$11. AE, MC, V.
Open: Sun–Thurs 11:30am–11pm, Fri–Sat 11:30am–midnight.

People come to Wah Sing to enjoy terrific seafood at reasonable prices, especially the lobster special, which is $15.95—plus one free! There's plenty of other shellfish on the menu, such as mussels with black bean sauce or oysters with ginger sauce. Duck, pork, noodles, and other traditional Chinese fare are offered, too. The decor is minimal, but the food makes for crowds. Expect to wait.

Village by the Grange

GINSBERG AND WONG, 71 McCaul St. Tel. 416/979-3458.
Cuisine: DELI/CHINESE. **Reservations:** Recommended.
$ Prices: Appetizers $3–$4; deli items and sandwiches $7–$9; Chinese dishes $7–$12. AE, DC, MC, V.
Open: Mon–Thurs 11:30am–11pm, Fri 11:30am–12:30am, Sat noon–12:30am, Sun noon–10pm.

Ginsberg and Wong packs people in for what have to be two of the most popular food styles in the world—deli and Chinese. Here you can choose from the vast menu either your favorite deli-style sandwich, ribs and barbecue chicken (burgers, hot dogs, and salads also), or else switch to the Chinese side of the menu, which features such all-time favorites as sweet-and-sour chicken, Szechuan scallops, or orange beef. Kids love watching the cooks in the open kitchen, and on their special days, receiving a giant fortune cookie, accompanied by a sing-along from the staff.

YOUNG LOK GARDENS, 122 St. Patrick St. Tel. 416/593-9819.
Cuisine: CHINESE. **Reservations:** Accepted only for parties of six or more.
$ Prices: Main courses $8–$11. AE, MC, V.
Open: Mon–Sat noon–11pm, Sun noon–10pm.

One of Toronto's most highly rated and popular restaurants serves good Peking and Szechuan cuisine and tasty barbecue from the Mongolian grill. The latest addition is a fresh fish market where you can select a fish and either have it steamed Chinese style in black bean sauce or with ginger and scallion or else grilled on the barbecue. Kick off with hot-and-sour soup, and follow with orange-spiced duck, Szechuan shrimp sautéed with cashew nuts, or the Mongolian barbecue beef marinated in mustard, chili, wine, ginger, and plenty of garlic. At lunch the $8 prix fixe offers soup, spring roll, rice or noodles, and a selection from six or so dishes. On weekends there's a 50-item dim sum brunch.

DOWNTOWN EAST

MODERATE

BIAGGIO, 155 King St. East. Tel. 416/366-4040.
   Cuisine: ITALIAN. **Reservations:** Recommended.
   $ Prices: Appetizers $5–$10; main courses $13–$25. AE, DC, DISC, ER, MC, V.
   Open: Lunch Mon–Fri noon–2:30pm; dinner Mon–Sat 5:45–10:30pm.
Biaggio is a large comfortable restaurant with a separate bar to the left of the entrance. Each of the restaurant's rooms has high ceilings making for an extremely elegant ambience. At the back there's one of the nicest secluded brick patios in the city complete with fountain and antique gaslights. The menu features a selection of about 20 tempting pastas and risottos, like the crab-filled tortellini in a light green onion sauce, the angel hair with black olives and capers, and risotto with wild mushrooms or the classic with saffron. Among the entrées try the mixed grill Biaggio style, a veal chop with wine butter and sage, or one of the fresh fish dishes. Round the whole meal off with tiramisu, fresh berries, or some Italian ice cream.

BRASSERIE LES ARTISTES, 243 Carlton St., at Parliament. Tel. 416/ 963-9433.
   Cuisine: FRENCH. **Reservations:** Recommended on weekends.
   $ Prices: Main courses $9–$13; prix fixe $16. AE, MC, V.
   Open: Lunch Mon–Fri noon–2:30pm; dinner Mon–Wed 6–10:30pm, Thurs–Sat 6–11pm.
For a modest bistro-style meal, try Cabbagetown's Brasserie Les Artistes. The atmosphere is casual and friendly, the wall art evokes Paris in the '90s, and the tables are marble—a suitable setting for the traditional moules marinières, steak and frites, escalope of veal aux fines herbes, and rack of lamb with fresh mint.

FLORENTINE COURT, 97 Church St. Tel. 416/364-3687.
   Cuisine: ITALIAN. **Reservations:** Recommended.
   $ Prices: Main courses $13–$23. AE, ER, MC, V.
   Open: Lunch Mon–Fri noon–2pm; dinner Mon–Sat 5:30–10pm.
At Florentine Court, one of the city's old traditions, you can enjoy a fine bargain—a seven-course dinner from soup through pasta, salad, main course, Florentine trifle, and beverage. Just add $10 to the price of your chosen main course. For example, if you choose the most expensive dish—a combination of veal with shrimp—you'll pay $33. Choose the chicken Florentine and the price goes down to $23.

LA MAQUETTE, 111 King St. East. Tel. 416/366-8191.

Ⓕ **FROMMER'S COOL FOR KIDS:
RESTAURANTS**

Ginsberg and Wong (see p. 432) Serves the perennial junior favorites—Chinese and burgers, barbecue, and hot dogs.

Toby's Goodeats (see p. 440) Enough kid-appealing items to satisfy even the fussiest child. Lots of locations.

The Organ Grinder (see p. 435) The organ, the pizza, and the rest of the kid crowd will keep them marvelously entertained.

Cuisine: CONTINENTAL. **Reservations:** Recommended.
$ Prices: Appetizers $4–$8; main courses $15–$24. AE, MC, V.
Open: Lunch Mon–Fri noon–2:30pm; dinner Mon–Sat 5:30–10:30pm.

You'll make a grand entrance through the lobby and up the staircase to reach La Maquette. The best option is the $18 prix fixe, which brings appetizer, entrée, dessert, and tea or coffee. The kind of dishes you might discover are grilled salmon with beurre blanc; beef tenderloin with wild mushroom sauce; or a seafood risotto. To start, try the scallops wrapped in nori and rice paper served with wasabi and tomato coulis, or the asparagus in orange-tarragon butter. The menu, though, changes frequently.

MONTREAL, 65 Sherbourne St., at Adelaide and Sherbourne. Tel. 416/363-0179.
Cuisine: QUEBECOIS. **Reservations:** Recommended, especially on weekends.
$ Prices: Appetizers $3.50–$6; main courses $14–$16. AE, DC, ER, MC, V.
Open: Lunch Mon–Fri 11:30am–3pm; dinner Mon–Sat 5–11pm.

Montréal is the place to try québecois specialties, such as the famous pea soup and the tourtière, a really tasty meat pie. The food here is excellent and very reasonably priced. A table d'hôte lunch, including soup or salad and veal roast with wild mushrooms or lemon-pepper linguine with chicken and vegetables, will come to $7.95. At night such specialties as rack of lamb with rosemary, braised rabbit, and linguine take center stage. For dessert, try the really special deep-fried ice cream with hot raspberry sauce.

To the left of the entrance you'll find one of the more comfortable and also one of the hottest Toronto jazz clubs in the city. You can enjoy the same food here, too.

NAMI JAPANESE SEAFOOD, 55 Adelaide St. East. Tel. 416/362-7373.
Cuisine: JAPANESE. **Reservations:** Recommended Thurs–Sat.
$ Prices: Sushi $4–$6; main courses $14–$25. AE, DC, MC, V.
Open: Lunch Mon–Fri noon–2:30pm; dinner Mon–Sat 6–10:30pm.

This is high-class Tokyo come to Toronto. The restaurant is very atmospheric and low lit at night. Up front there's a grilling bar/sushi bar, and behind, attractive booth seating or traditional tatami-style dining. Offerings range from beef kushikatsu (kebabs) to a sashimi assortment. The place attracts many Japanese, both businesspeople and families.

THE OLD FISH MARKET, 12 Market St. Tel. 416/363-0334.
Cuisine: SEAFOOD. **Reservations:** Recommended.
$ Prices: Main courses $10–$16. AE, CB, DC, DISC, ER, MC, V.
Open: Lunch Mon–Fri noon–2:30pm, Sat 11am–3pm, Sun noon–3pm; dinner Mon–Thurs 5–10pm, Fri–Sat 5–11pm, Sun 4–10pm.

The seafood place that packs them in lies across town by the St. Lawrence Market, and is the original in a chain of similarly named establishments that are popping up throughout eastern Canada. The Old Fish Market, set in a converted warehouse now topped by a boat with a red-and-white funnel, is a cavernous place. Downstairs on the ground floor there's a small oyster bar and a large restaurant with comfortable booths and wooden tables, decorated with numerous photographs of old salts and fishing scenes, plus such nautical regalia as lobster traps and foghorns.

Upstairs you'll find Coasters, a black arborite shellfish bar where you can relax and eat while seated on low sofas, if you prefer that to a table. Here the decor consists of exposed brick and painted plumbing warmed by a huge fire blazing in the back during the winter. Coasters features daily specials, an oyster bar, cold and hot seafood appetizers, and specializes in imported beers. It's open Monday through Saturday from noon to 1am and on Sunday from noon to 10pm.

Downstairs you'll get a selection of the freshest fish, usually pan-fried, broiled, or barbecued. Start with one of the chowders, and then choose from the night's fresh fish offerings: rainbow trout, snapper, halibut filet, Pacific shark, or tilefish, for example, all served with sourdough roll and butter, mackerel pâté, house salad, and boiled or french-fried potatoes.

TAKESUSHI, 22 Front St. Tel. 416/862-1891.

Cuisine: JAPANESE. **Reservations:** Recommended.
$ **Prices:** Appetizers $2.50–$9; sushi/sashimi $12–$29; donburi noodle and other dishes $7–$15. AE, DC, MC, V.
Open: Lunch Mon–Fri noon–2:30pm; dinner Mon–Sat 5:30–10:30pm. Also open Sun in summer.

Takesushi is a fashionable, plush Japanese restaurant specializing in sushi. For novices there's even a beginner's sushi offered: salmon marinated in vinegar and salt, and ebi or cooked shrimp sushi. Otherwise, you can order eight nigiri and one makimono for $16, or a special deluxe sushi that includes 10 nigiri and one makimono for $29. Other sushi thrills include uni (sea urchin gonads) and kazunoko, which is herring roe soaked in saké, soy, and broth. Traditional tempura, teriyaki, and sukiyaki dinners also available.

BUDGET

GROANING BOARD, 131 Jarvis St., at Richmond. Tel. 416/363-0265.
Cuisine: VEGETARIAN. **Reservations:** Recommended on weekends.
$ **Prices:** Most items $3–$9. AE, DC, ER, MC, V.
Open: Sun–Thurs 11:30am–midnight, Fri–Sat 11:30am–1am.

One of the best buys in entertainment in Toronto awaits you at the Groaning Board. Every night a selection of international award-winning commercials is shown from the Cannes and Venice festivals.

The food is 50% vegetarian, 50% meat. There's a gigantic 74-item salad bar, four soups, steamed vegetables, and a build-your-own sandwich and sundae area as well as such items as eggplant parmesan, vegetarian lasagne, and rice pilaf, all priced under $9 (under $5 for sandwiches or salad bar). A '60s-style coffeehouse atmosphere prevails. Ninety-minute screenings of award-winning international cinema and TV commercials add to the fun weekdays at 7 and 9pm and weekends at 7, 9:30, and 11pm. There's a $3 cover charge. Live jazz Saturday and Sunday from 1 to 3pm.

MOVENPICK MARCHE, Galleria of the BCE Building, Front St. East. Tel. 416/366-8986.
Cuisine: CONTINENTAL. **Reservations:** Not accepted.
$ **Prices:** Most items $5–$8. AE, DC, MC, V.
Open: Mon–Fri 11:30am–2am; Sat–Sun 7:30am–2am.

This large restaurant with a variety of different seating areas is the latest innovation in food merchandising. Pick up a tab at the entrance and stroll through the bustling market—where various stands and carts are set up displaying fresh foods and ingredients—selecting and purchasing as you go. Stop at the rosticceria and select a meat for the chef to cook or at the seafood and raw bar and pick out a fish for the grill. Then wander over to the bistro de vin and check out the cases of wine or enjoy a boccalino of one of the open wines. The chefs and staff are easily identifiable by their boaters as they stand behind counters heaped with fresh salads, fish, meats, and pizzas. Ask and it will be made before your very eyes—Cornish hens, roasti with salmon, steak, sausages, and more. A fun place for breakfast, lunch, or dinner.

THE ORGAN GRINDER, 58 The Esplanade. Tel. 416/364-6517.
Cuisine: ITALIAN. **Reservations:** Accepted only for parties of 10 or more.
$ **Prices:** Pizzas and main courses $7–$12. AE, DC, ER, MC, V.
Open: Sun–Thurs 11am–11pm, Fri–Sat 11am–1am.

The Organ Grinder is a vast musical pizza parlor where an organist bashes out popular tunes on the theater pipe organ, which has a fascinating array of gadgets—submarine sirens, sleigh bells, bird whistles, horse hooves, all kinds of drums, chimes, cymbals, and a glockenspiel—and over 1,000 pipes made of wood, zinc, lead, and tin.

To the tunes of this rare monstrosity you and the kids can chew any one of nine pizzas or the lasagne, veal parmigiana, and other Italian dishes.

SHOPSY'S, 33 Yonge St. Tel. 416/365-3333.
Cuisine: DELI. **Reservations:** Not needed.
$ **Prices:** Sandwiches $7–$10. AE, MC, V.
Open: Mon–Fri 7am–midnight, Sat 8am–midnight, Sun 8am–11pm.

Right across from the O'Keefe Centre, Shopsy's occupies spiffy quarters sporting an outdoor patio arrayed with brilliant yellow umbrellas. They still serve stuffed deli sandwiches. For a real feast try the Deli Platter, consisting of your choice of two meats (brisket, chopped liver, smoked turkey, or pastrami) served with coleslaw and potato pancakes—all for $11. Look for Shopsy's carts on the streets.

MIDTOWN WEST

This section of the city includes the well-heeled and well-touristed area known as Yorkville. Dining in Yorkville is not always a pleasant experience. Rents are high and consequently prices are also high, and the quality sometimes just doesn't match. That said, I have included in this section one or two selections that can be relied upon to deliver quality at a decent price.

EXPENSIVE

ACROBAT, 60 Bloor St. West (entrance at 1221 Bay St.). Tel. 416/920-2323.
   Cuisine: ITALIAN. **Reservations:** Recommended.
$ Prices: Pasta and pizza $12–$16; main courses $18–$23. AE, MC, V.
   Open: Mon–Sat 4:30pm–1am.
Acrobat is dramatic indeed. To the right you'll find a sinuous bar of dark and blond wood, which attracts a fashionable city crowd. Behind and above it the eye is drawn to the brilliant tile mosaic of bottles and a cascading waterfall. The dining area is equally striking, with high-backed, brilliant turquoise banquettes and eccentrically sculpted flower holders. The food is equally interesting, showing a definite Oriental influence— as in the spring rolls and tempura with tamarind cream and honey mustard dipping sauce, or the Thai seafood soup, among the ten or so appetizers. The pizza and pasta choices, however, run, respectively, to lamb sausage, rosemary mozzarella, roasted peppers, and Bermuda onions or penne with smoked salmon and an vodka tomato cream sauce. Among main courses the Oriental reappears with a spicy swordfish with citrus-fruit relish, or a Atlantic salmon with a black bean butter and baby bok choy.

BISTRO 990, 990 Bay St., at St. Joseph. Tel. 416/921-9990.
   Cuisine: FRENCH. **Reservations:** Required.
$ Prices: Appetizers $6–$12; main courses $16–$26. AE, ER, MC, V.
   Open: Lunch Mon–Fri noon–3pm; dinner Mon–Sat 6–11pm.
   ★ Bistro 990 could have been airlifted from the French provinces with its French doors, lace curtains, and outdoor café tables. The cuisine ranges from such traditional dishes as rack of lamb provençale, steak bordelaise, and half a roast chicken with garlic mash to shrimp mango curry. Among the appetizers the tartare of salmon is fresh tasting, and the confit of duck a tasty dish. Desserts change daily but might include a lemon tart, tarte Tatin, raspberry cheesecake, and a selection of sorbets.

SPLENDIDO BAR AND GRILL, 88 Harbord St. Tel. 416/929-7788.
   Cuisine: ITALIAN. **Reservations:** Recommended well in advance.
$ Prices: Pizzas and pasta courses $8–$12; main courses $15–$25. AE, DC, ER, MC, V.
   Open: Dinner Mon–Sat 5–11pm, Sun 5–10pm.
The Splendido Bar and Grill is the city's current scene-stealer, and steal the scene it does. It's an absolutely stunning dining room. Up front there's a black-gray granite bar. Behind stretches the dining room—a riot of brilliant yellow lit by a host of tiny, almost fairylike track lights, while the walls are hung with huge flower canvases by Helen Lucas. The food is Italian with international inspirations, and the menu changes monthly. Start with the unique antipasto of bacon-wrapped shrimp, coppa, peperonata, bocconcini, with tomatoes and tapenade crostini, or the pistacchio-crust sea scallops baked in a brick oven and served with mango chutney and fermented black bean sauce. Follow with either pasta, pizza, or a main course—for example, the pizza with goat cheese, roasted ricotta, sun-dried tomatoes, olives, eggplant, and oregano or the pasta ribbons with pancetta, mushroom, and peppered vodka cream. Among the main courses the corn-fried salmon with mashed potatoes, sweet corn

relish, and arugula with a citrus dressing is a special treat, and so too is the beef tenderloin with mushroom duxelles, artichokes, fried ravioli and barbecue butter sauce. It's a loud, lively place, not for that romantic dinner.

MODERATE

ARLEQUIN, 134 Avenue Rd. Tel. 416/928-9521.

Cuisine: CONTINENTAL. **Reservations:** Recommended.
$ Prices: Appetizers $4–$8; pastas $12.50; main courses $14–$16. MC, V.
Open: Lunch Mon–Fri 11:30am–3pm; dinner Mon–Sat 5:30–11pm.

Arlequin is a handsome small restaurant with a counter display of fabulous pâté, cheeses, salads, and baked goods up front. The menu is keyed to market-fresh ingredients and might list quails with tomato and rosemary, lamb with a garlic and thyme glaze, or veal pavette with mushrooms and balsamic vinegar. Luncheon items are priced from $6 to $8. Brunch also stretches to such dishes as lumache with scallops, shrimp, peppers, tomato, and basil pesto. The current excitement is understandable.

BOULEVARD CAFE, 161 Harbord St., between Spadina and Bathurst. Tel. 416/961-7676.

Cuisine: PERUVIAN. **Reservations:** Recommended for upstairs dining.
$ Prices: Appetizers $3–$6; main courses $10–$16. AE, MC, V.
Open: Lunch daily 11:30am–3:30pm; dinner daily 5:30–11:30pm.

A favorite gathering spot of young creative types, the Boulevard Café is somehow reminiscent of Kathmandu in the '60s, although the inspiration is Peru. Upstairs there's a dining room furnished with wooden banquettes softened by the addition of Peruvian cushions and South American wall hangings. The outside summer café is strung with colored lights and attracts an evening and late-night crowd. The menu features empanadas (spicy chicken or beef pastry); tangy shrimp in a spiced garlic, pimiento, and wine sauce; and tamal verde (spicy corn, coriander, and chicken pâté) to start. For the main course the major choice is anticuchos, marinated and charbroiled brochettes of your own choosing: sea bass, shrimp, pork tenderloin, beef, or chicken. Burgers, lamb chops, and steamed mussels are some of the other selections.

CHIADO, 864 College St., at Concord Ave. Tel. 416/538-1910.

Cuisine: PORTUGUESE. **Reservations:** Recommended.
$ Prices: Main courses $14–$18. AE, DC, MC, V.
Open: Lunch daily noon–3pm; dinner daily 5pm–midnight.

Chiado refers to the district in Lisbon, which is filled with small bistrettos like this one. Beyond the appetizing display at the front of the room you'll discover a long, narrow dining room decorated with elegant French-style pink chairs and colorful art on the walls. In summer the storefront opens entirely onto the street, adding to the atmosphere. Among the appetizers the pinheta of salted cod or the marinated sardines with lemon and parsley will appeal to the true Portuguese; others might prefer the tiger shrimp served with a sweet pepper coulis. On the main menu a Portuguese might pine for the poached filet of cod or the bistretto style steak with fried egg and fries, while a friend might go for the roast rack of lamb with a red Douro wine sauce or the braised rabbit in a Madeira wine sauce. To top it all off, choose from the peach coconut flan, chocolate mousse, or pecan pie or any of the other tempting desserts.

IL POSTO, 148 Yorkville Ave. Tel. 416/968-0469.

Cuisine: ITALIAN. **Reservations:** Recommended.
$ Prices: Appetizers $5–$9; pasta $8–$11; main courses $16–$24. AE, MC, V.
Open: Lunch Mon–Sat noon–2:30pm; dinner Mon–Sat 6–10:30pm.

Right in the heart of high-rent Yorkville, where restaurants are constantly opening and closing, Il Posto, tucked away in York Square, has thrived for many years and still offers a very attractive setting, both inside and outside on the brick terrace under a spreading maple tree. The dessert spread at the entrance is tempting enough—fresh raspberry tarts with kiwi, fresh strawberry and blueberry tarts, fresh oranges, and other delights. The menu features such Italian specialties as pollo alla marsala (chicken in a marsala wine sauce), scaloppine pizzaiola (veal cooked in a spicy tomato garlic sauce), beef with green peppercorns served with a brandy-flavored sauce, linguine with seafood or (even more delicious) with Gorgonzola. There are also fish dishes, salads like arugula and endive and a special vitello tonnato. For dessert, besides the very special pastries you might discover poached pears in chocolate, or of course the smooth, creamy zabaglione. The restaurant's beige walls, Italian prints, and classical music create a serene dining atmosphere made even more so by the handsome bouquets of fresh flowers.

JACQUES' BISTRO DU PARC, 126A Cumberland St. Tel. 416/961-1893.
Cuisine: CONTINENTAL. **Reservations:** Not needed.
$ Prices: Omelets $8–$11; other main courses $15–$18; prix fixe $15. AE, MC, V.
Open: Lunch Mon–Sat 11:30am–3pm; dinner daily 5–10:30pm.

Upstairs above a boutique in the heart of Yorkville, this spot specializes in omelets and bistro fare. Everything about the small room is tasteful—the fresh flowers on the bar and the French prints and pictures of Paris. But the patrons come for the omelets—18 selections—from simple fines herbes to lobster, cheese, and herbs. Salads, quiches, cheeses, soups, and a small selection of hors d'oeuvres, plus veal, chicken, and fish entrées make this a good dining spot. You don't have to pay through the nose for well-prepared food, not even in Yorkville.

JOSO'S, 202 Davenport Rd., just east of Avenue Rd. Tel. 416/925-1903.
Cuisine: SEAFOOD. **Reservations:** Recommended.
$ Prices: Appetizers $4–$9; pasta $9–$14; main courses $14–$27. AE, MC, V.
Open: Lunch Mon–Sat 11:30am–3pm; dinner Mon–Sat 5:30–11pm.

Yugoslav Joseph Spralja of Malka and Joso has appeared on the "Johnny Carson Show" and performed at Carnegie Hall, but since he gave up folk singing and playing the guitar because of an ulcer, he has taken to combing the fish markets for his restaurant, Joso's. Besides having a fascinating owner, this place has some interesting seafood and also a rather idiosyncratic decor (which might offend some, so I have to mention the erotic ceramic sculptures of golf-ball–bosomed females).

If you don't care a fig about such indelicate matters, but you do care about fresh seafood prepared to retain its flavor, then stop by Joso's. At dinner a selection of fresh fish will be presented to you, from which you can choose the specimen that appeals to you. It will then be grilled and served with a salad (such dishes are priced by the pound). Or you can have octopus steamed in garlic and parsley sauce, deep-fried squid with salad, or spaghetti with an octopus, clam, and squid tomato sauce. A selection of exotic coffees is available, along with a special homemade baklava, and Italian ice creams and sorbets. Bentwood cane chairs and pale-lemon tablecloths complete the decor of the tiny downstairs room. A larger room upstairs is similarly appointed. Remember, this cosmopolitan bistro makes a very personal statement: You can either take it or leave it, but you should know about it.

LE RENDEZ-VOUS, 14 Prince Arthur Ave. Tel. 416/961-6111.
Cuisine: FRENCH. **Reservations:** Recommended.
$ Prices: Appetizers $5–$9; main courses $16–$22. AE, CB, MC, V.
Open: Lunch Mon–Fri noon–2:30pm; dinner daily 5:30–10pm.

At Le Rendez-Vous you'll find a variety of dining and decor in the classic French style. In summer the outdoor dining area is filled, along with the comfortable plant-filled atrium dining area. Rattan chairs, burgundy upholstery, and classical music provide atmosphere to the interior. Dining choices are very appealing: salmon with basil sauce, rack of lamb provençale, Dover sole in a variety of ways, duck with five spices, veal with pesto and artichokes, duck with pepper peaches, and tiger shrimp with shallot and lemon. At lunch choices might include mushrooms stuffed with crab and topped with hollandaise, and egg and pasta dishes. For before- or after-dinner tippling, go downstairs to the wine cellar.

SOUTHERN ACCENT, 595 Markham St. Tel. 416/536-3211.
Cuisine: CAJUN/CREOLE. **Reservations:** Recommended.
$ Prices: Appetizers $3–$8; main courses $14–$20. AE, ER, MC, V.
Open: Dinner daily 5–10:30pm; brunch Sun 11am–3pm. **Closed:** Mon in winter.

Southern Accent has a real down-home feel. The background music is cool, the art interesting, and the floral tablecloths somehow funky. There are three areas to dine in—upstairs in the dining room, downstairs on the bar level, or out on the brick patio. The menu features the goods—gumbo, jambalaya, shrimp étouffée, and blackened fish with lemon. At brunch the theme continues with beignets, Cajun pain perdu (the New Orleans version of French toast) and po'boy sandwiches. Oh, and don't miss the bread pudding.

TRATTORIA GIANCARLO, 41-43 Clinton St., at College. Tel. 416/533-9619.
   Cuisine: ITALIAN. **Reservations:** Highly recommended.
$ Prices: Pasta and rice $10–$13; main courses $16–$19. AE, MC, V.
   Open: Dinner Mon–Sat 5:30–11pm.

This restaurant is one of my all-time favorite spots in Little Italy, if not in the whole city, and I find myself returning here time after time. It's small and cozy and thoroughly Italian, with an outside dining area in summer. The tablecloths are covered with butcher paper; the floor is black-and-white tile, and the background music is opera or jazz. For a real treat start with the fresh wild mushrooms brushed with herbs, garlic, and oil or the carpaccio of salmon. Follow with any one of six pasta dishes—spaghettini with shrimps and fra diavolo sauce or the risotto of the day. Good grilled fresh fish and meats are also part of the attraction like the tender lamb brushed with lemon, rosemary and fresh mint or the red snapper marinated in fresh thyme and bay, olive oil and lemon. For dessert try the tiramisu, crème caramel, or the delicious chocolate-raspberry tartufo. The evening somehow is always memorable and the welcome real.

YVES BISTRO, 36A Prince Arthur Ave. Tel. 416/972-1010.
   Cuisine: FRENCH. **Reservations:** Recommended.
$ Prices: Prix fixe $15 for main course and appetizer. MC, V.
   Open: Lunch Mon–Fri noon–2pm; dinner daily 6–10pm.

Comfortable, gracious, and made cozy by its mullioned windows, small serving bar, and brilliant sunflower mirrors, this bistro also delivers good, well-priced food. Start with asparagus with crumbled blue cheese and a raspberry vinaigrette or the mussels steamed in white wine, mushrooms, tomatoes, and tarragon. Among the ten or so entrées you will find pasta, fish, and meat—such as fusilli with hazelnut pesto, artichokes, and black olives; salmon steamed with leeks, tomato, spinach, and Pernod; and lamb chops grilled with mustard and herbs and served with mint sauce.

BUDGET

ANNAPURNA RESTAURANT, 1085 Bathurst, just south of Dupont. Tel. 416/537-8513.
   Cuisine: VEGETARIAN/HEALTH FOOD. **Reservations:** Not needed.
$ Prices: All items under $7.50. No credit cards.
   Open: Mon–Sat noon–9pm.

Some 17 years ago at the request of his spiritual leader, Sri Chinmoy, Shivaram Trichur opened the Annapurna Restaurant. A bell announces your arrival. At the front counter you can purchase various goodies, including Ayurvedic tonics, carob balls, books on yoga, and copies of *Meditation at the U.N.* Just beyond you'll find a room with no particular decor to speak of but with some fine low-priced food.

   Nothing on the menu is over $7.50 and for that amount you'll receive a veritable vegetarian feast—raita, bonda (gingery potato-and-vegetable balls dipped in chickpea batter and deep-fried), bhajia, samosas, pappadum, sagu (spinach and mixed-vegetable curry), potato masala, and rice or puris. Salads and vegetarian sandwiches, including tofu burgers, supplement the South Indian dishes.

   Enjoy the smoke-free peaceful atmosphere and the meditational background music along with the young and rather intellectual, interesting crowd that gathers here.

BLOOR STREET DINER, 50 Bloor St. West. Tel. 416/928-3105.
   Cuisine: LIGHT FARE. **Reservations:** Not needed.
$ Prices: Main courses $7–$13. AE, ER, MC, V.
   Open: Daily 11am–3am.

This is a convenient place to stop for a wide selection of reasonably priced food—from a grilled cheese sandwich or chicken wings to veal parmigiana, pasta, and fajitas.

INDIAN RICE FACTORY, 414 Dupont St. Tel. 416/961-3472.

Cuisine: INDIAN. **Reservations:** Not needed.

$ **Prices:** Main courses $8–$12. AE, ER, MC, V.

Open: Mon–Sat 11am–11pm, Sun 4–10pm.

A friend of mine who was raised in India swears by the Indian Rice Factory, operated by Mrs. Patel, who was born in the Punjab. It is an elegant place, with comfortable plush booths, light-oak wooden bar, and Indian artifacts for decoration. The food is good and the prices are right. All the curries—chicken, beef, shrimp—are under $11. The restaurant also serves a wide selection of Indian vegetarian dishes, including aloo gobi (a curried mixture of potato and cauliflower), matar paneer (peas and cheese cooked with spices), aloo palak (spinach with potatoes), and a complete thali for $11 that includes a meat or vegetable entrée, vegetable of the day, dhal, rice, chapati, raita, pappadum, and kachumber.

KENSINGTON KITCHEN, 124 Harbord St. Tel. 416/961-3404.

Cuisine: MIDDLE EASTERN. **Reservations:** Not accepted.

$ **Prices:** Main courses $7–$12. DC, ER, MC, V.

Open: Daily 11:30am–11pm.

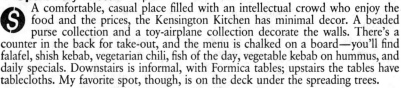 A comfortable, casual place filled with an intellectual crowd who enjoy the food and the prices, the Kensington Kitchen has minimal decor. A beaded purse collection and a toy-airplane collection decorate the walls. There's a counter in the back for take-out, and the menu is chalked on a board—you'll find falafel, shish kebab, vegetarian chili, fish of the day, vegetable kebab on hummus, and daily specials. Downstairs is informal, with Formica tables; upstairs the tables have tablecloths. My favorite spot, though, is on the deck under the spreading trees.

MORI, 1280 Bay St. Tel. 416/961-1094.

Cuisine: JAPANESE. **Reservations:** Recommended at dinner.

$ **Prices:** Main courses $7.50–$12. AE, MC, V.

Open: Lunch Mon–Sat noon–4pm; dinner Mon–Fri 4–10pm, Sat 4–11pm.

For budget dining, Mori is great to know about. It's a tiny Japanese café furnished with wrought-iron tables covered with deep-blue tablecloths. The attraction here is the sushi and other Japanese dishes like salmon teriyaki or chicken teriyaki, served with soup, oshitashi, and green tea. The variety of vegetarian sushi (spinach, carrot, etc.) is notable. So, too, is the vegetarian sukiyaki.

TOBY'S GOODEATS, 93 Bloor St. Tel. 416/925-2171.

Cuisine: BURGERS PLUS. **Reservations:** Not needed.

$ **Prices:** Burgers $4–$7.50. AE, MC, V.

Open: Sun–Thurs 11:30am–1am, Fri–Sat 11:30am–3am.

Capture those childhood dreams of milk shakes, Coke floats, and a good burger along with the rest of the crowd at this '50s-flavor hamburger joint. The decor suits: an eclectic combination of Formica tables, cookie jars, funky posters, and the traditional brick-and-plant look. It's very crowded at lunchtime. About a dozen burgers are offered in addition to salads, sandwiches, pizza, and pasta.

Toby's Goodeats can also be found at: 1502 Yonge St. (tel. 416/921-1062), 2293 Yonge St. (tel. 416/481-9183), 725 Yonge St. (tel. 416/925-9908), in the Eaton Centre (tel. 416/591-6114), and First Canadian Place (tel. 416/366-3953).

VIVA, 459 Bloor St. West. Tel. 416/922-8482.

Cuisine: MEXICAN. **Reservations:** Accepted only for large parties.

$ **Prices:** Main courses $6–$11. AE, DC, MC, V.

Open: Daily 10am–1am.

 Viva is a large restaurant filled with happy folks slurping down sangría at long family-style tables while the Mexican music group performs in the back and the tamale machine chugs along upfront with dough being churned in a large bowl.

Colorful paper decorations hang from the ceiling and a few masks and other artifacts decorate the long bar area. The food can be ordered and shared or enjoyed individually. The choices are wide. You can roll your own fajitas using any of nine ingredients—from beef and chorizo to eggplant and peppers. There's a number of barbecue dishes like chicken with mole, or with achiote and pineapple and several dinners like salmon with basil, garlic, and lime or chorizo with mustard and honey. All tasty and washed down well with a pitcher of sangría.

MIDTOWN EAST/THE EAST END

In the East End along Danforth Avenue you'll find yourself in a veritable Little Greece. Streets are lined with tavernas; bouzouki music spills out onto the sidewalk, and restaurant after restaurant bears a Greek name.

BUDGET

ASTORIA, 390 Danforth Ave. Tel. 416/463-2838.
   Cuisine: GREEK. **Reservations:** Not needed.
 $ Prices: Main courses $8–$11. AE, MC, V.
   Open: Mon–Wed and Fri–Sat 11am–1am, Sun and Thurs 11am–midnight.
Astoria is a little fancier than most of the Greek restaurants in the neighborhood, with its outdoor patio complete with fountain. The offerings include shish kebab, quails over charcoal, and a 12-ounce New York steak.

OMONIA, 426 Danforth Ave., at Chester. Tel. 416/465-2129.
   Cuisine: GREEK. **Reservations:** Not needed.
 $ Prices: Main courses $9–$12. AE, DC, ER, MC.
   Open: Daily 11am–1am.
One of the most popular local Greek restaurants, Omonia has a large outdoor dining area and up front, in the window, you can watch the lamb turning on a spit. Barbecued specialties, souvlaki, chicken, and pork selections are the main features. The Greek pictures, the patio, and the blue tablecloths provide an authentic ambience.

OUZERI, 500A Danforth Ave. Tel. 416/778-0500.
   Cuisine: GREEK. **Reservations:** Not accepted.
 $ Prices: Main courses $6–$10. AE, DISC, ER, MC, V.
   Open: Daily noon–3am; lunch served until 3pm, dips and appetizers only served 4–5pm.
Ouzeri is the hot place out here—it's spirited, casual, and fun. People either jam the few small circular tables outside or occupy the tables inside, drinking one of the numerous international beers or wines by the glass. It's all très Athens, with tile floors, sun-drenched pastel hues, and eclectic art objects and art. The food is good and cheap. It runs the gamut from all kinds of seafood (prawns with feta and wine, sardines with mustard, calamari, broiled octopus) and all kinds of meat (pork, lamb, and beef kebabs) to rice, pasta, and phyllo pie dishes. Various snacks, too, complete the menu, like hummus, taramosalata, mushrooms à la grecque, and dolmades.
   At lunch Ouzeri dishes out its version of dim sum, "meze sum"—hot and cold appetizers that are proffered on trays or wheeled by on carts. Sunday brunch is a filling repast that begins with a buffet spread of appetizers and proceeds through cooked-to-order main courses. A frenetic scene, especially at night.

UPTOWN

EXPENSIVE

SCARAMOUCHE, 1 Benvenuto Place. Tel. 416/961-8011.
   Cuisine: CONTINENTAL. **Reservations:** Required.
 $ Prices: Appetizers $8–$13; main courses $24–$30. AE, DC, ER, MC, V.
   Open: Lunch Mon–Fri noon–2:30pm; dinner Tues–Sat 6–10:30pm. Pasta bar open Tues–Fri 6–10pm, Sat 6pm–midnight.
Scaramouche has a reputation as one of Toronto's top-class restaurants. A little

difficult to find (it's located in the basement of an apartment building, about four blocks south of St. Clair Avenue and Yonge Street, off Edmund Street), it's certainly worth seeking out. Try to get a window seat, which grants a vista all the way to the downtown city skyline. The decor, the large flower arrangements, and the careful presentation of the food make it special.

Although the menu changes frequently, it may well have dishes similar to the following. To begin there'll be a selection of hot and cold appetizers and at least three soups. For example, there might be warm buckwheat pancakes with smoked salmon, sweet-and-sour red onions, capers, and crème fraîche, or gnocchi with tomato sauce and Gorgonzola cream. Among the half dozen or so main courses there might be crisped red snapper on a saffron and fresh shellfish sauce or pepper roasted rack of lamb with roasted eggplant, sweet pepper, and chèvre couscous. If you don't feel like eating so much, then you can always select from the pasta bar menu, which offers similar appetizers and a selection of fettuccine, linguine, lasagne, and cannelloni, all done in excitingly different ways. Similarly, the desserts always have an original spin like the raspberry crème brûlée.

MODERATE

BIFFI'S BISTRO, 699 Mount Pleasant Rd. Tel. 416/484-1142.
   Cuisine: CONTINENTAL. **Reservations:** Recommended.
$ **Prices:** Appetizers $5–$8; pasta courses $9–$11; main courses $11–$16. AE, DC, DISC, ER, MC, V.
   Open: Mon–Thurs 11:30am–10pm, Fri 11:30am–11:30pm, Sat 5–11:30pm downstairs, noon–1am upstairs.
A meal at Biffi's might start with the salmon carpaccio or fresh oysters, and follow with a choice of a dozen such entrées as grilled salmon with a maple syrup glaze, breast of chicken served on mixed organic greens topped with a warm sesame oil vinaigrette, or cioppino alla livornese, an assortment of seafood and with calamato olives in a Pernod-scented broth. Among the mouthwatering desserts, check out the chocolate-raspberry tartufo filled with raspberry ice and topped with Strega or the chocolate-and-amaretto pie with toasted almonds. At lunchtime, look for calves' liver with onion and parsley butter, cannelloni, and the like.

BROWNES BISTRO, 1251 Yonge St., just south of St. Clair. Tel. 416/924-8132.
   Cuisine: CONTINENTAL. **Reservations:** Recommended.
$ **Prices:** Pizza and pasta courses $12–$13; main courses $13–$17. AE, MC, V.
   Open: Lunch Tues–Fri noon–2:30pm; dinner Mon–Sat 6–10:30pm.
The decor at Brownes is rather nondescript, but the clientele is well-heeled and the food is typical, well-flavored bistro fare, plus five or so choices of pizzas and pastas. The menu might list lamb sausage with roasted garlic, mashed potatoes and brown sauce, Provimi liver with onion jam, roasted rack of lamb with lentils, and roasted puréed sweet potatoes. The wine list is excellent and includes a selection of 35 wines by the glass.

CENTRO, 2472 Yonge St., north of Eglinton. Tel. 416/483-2211.
   Cuisine: ITALIAN. **Reservations:** Recommended.
$ **Prices:** Main courses $18–$25. AE, DC, ER, MC, V.
   Open: Dinner Mon–Sat 5–11:30pm.
   Occupying a huge space with a mezzanine and a downstairs wine and pasta bar, Centro exhibits grand Italian style—dramatic classical columns, brilliant murals, and ultra-moderne Milan-style furnishings—and attracts a chic, animated crowd.

The cuisine is northern Italian with a California accent. The menu changes monthly, but among the dishes might be lamb in a honey mustard crust with thyme, rosemary, and garlic jus; Jamaican jerk swordfish; or Oriental-style shrimp with julienne of yellow peppers, Enoki mushrooms, and bean sprouts in a saffron garlic butter. There are four or so pasta dishes—angel hair, penne, and fusilli—all with flavorsome sauces, and gourmet pizzas, too. Desserts are worth waiting for—lemon mascarpone tart with blackberry sauce, chocolate pecan napoleon with a Southern

Comfort sauce being only two examples. Retire for a relaxing nightcap in the downstairs piano bar.

LOBSTER TRAP, 1962 Avenue Rd., just north of Lawrence. Tel. 416/ 787-3211.
   Cuisine: SEAFOOD. **Reservations:** Not accepted. Expect a line on Saturday.
   $ Prices: Lobsters $15–$35. AE, DC, ER, MC, V.
   Open: Dinner daily 5–10pm.
People wend their way north to the Lobster Trap for one reason only. And that really should be stressed—it's the only place in the city where you can still pick out a one- to four-pound live lobster for an honest and fair price. Look around, you may even be sitting next to a celebrity in this room, where the tables have brown gingham tablecloths, and most are sheltered under a shingled construction to evoke that maritime province atmosphere.

For a dinner that includes clam chowder or lobster bisque, salad, rolls and butter, french fries or rice, and beverage, and a one-pound lobster, steamed or broiled and served with drawn butter, you will pay $25. Other fish dinners are available, but I'd stick to the lobster if I were you.

N 44, 2537 Yonge St., just south of Sherwood Ave. Tel. 416/487-4897.
   Cuisine: CONTINENTAL. **Reservations:** Recommended.
   $ Prices: Appetizers $7–$12; main courses $20–$26. AE, DC, MC, V.
   Open: Lunch Mon–Fri noon–3pm; dinner Mon–Sat 5–10:30pm.
At the back of a dramatic space with soaring ceilings, the glassed-in kitchen is etched with the restaurant's compass logo (North 44 is Toronto's latitude). The atmosphere is enhanced by mirrors that sparkle and reflect the flowers that are displayed in the attached floral holders. The food is equally à la mode. On the dinner menu you might find grilled teriyaki salmon with miso lime sauce; a Caribbean seafood stew with tomato-squash broth, thyme, and lemon; crackling roast chicken with grilled vegetable risotto; and roasted apple and sage sauce. Pizzas and pastas are also featured. Besides an extensive wine list, there's also a number of wines by the glass. There's even a wine bar upstairs.

PRONTO, 692 Mount Pleasant Rd., just south of Eglinton. Tel. 416/486-1111.
   Cuisine: ITALIAN. **Reservations:** Recommended well in advance.
   $ Prices: Appetizers $7–$9; main courses $16–$25. AE, ER, MC, V.
   Open: Dinner daily 5pm–midnight.
Behind its austere black tile facade, Pronto occupies a handsome, inviting low-ceilinged room that is alive and vibrant. In the back behind a tiled counter you can see the chefs in their crisp white toques preparing the cuisine. At the center of the room there's always a lavish fresh flower arrangement.

The cuisine has a reputation to match the room. Among the long list of appetizers and pastas (any of which can be ordered as a main course), there's a buckwheat crêpe with smoked salmon tartare; pan-fried Portobello mushrooms on red oak and frizze with white truffle oil; or steamed blue mussels in white wine with leeks and garlic. For your main course, select from the 10 or so carefully prepared entrées, like crispy chicken with shallot-lemon spaetzle, grilled tiger shrimp with a jade lime butter, or roasted rack of lamb with maple-glazed pecans, fresh herbs, and natural juices.

THAI MAGIC, 1118 Yonge St. Tel. 416/968-7366.
   Cuisine: THAI/SEAFOOD. **Reservations:** Recommended.
   $ Prices: Appetizers $4–$6; main courses $8–$14. AE, ER, MC, V.
   Open: Lunch Mon–Fri 11:30am–3pm; dinner Mon–Sat 5:30–11pm.
Magical indeed is Thai Magic. Orchids, Thai statuary, and artifacts decorate the long, narrow room with a bar in the center. Warm mauves and greens make it even more inviting—a perfect backdrop for the sophisticated cuisine. Start with tom yum kai, a really spicy soup flavored with lemongrass and containing succulent shrimp, or the familiar satay or a combination plate of appetizers. For main courses there are stir-fries and curries (like the flavorsome chicken green curry or shrimp red curry with okra) as well as tamarind fish and coriander lobster. Fresh fruit, sherbet, ice creams, and of course sticky rice make up the dessert menu.

BUDGET

GRANO, 2035 Yonge St. Tel. 416/440-1986.

Cuisine: ITALIAN. **Reservations:** Accepted for parties of six or more only.
$ **Prices:** Main courses $9–$18. AE, DC, MC, V.
Open: Mon–Fri 10am–10:30pm; Sat 9:30am–11pm.

Grano is a wild Italian celebration. But it's a celebration of the down-to-earth food of the Italians served in an atmosphere of washed Mediterranean pastels. It's casual and fun. The wine is served in tumblers; there's a courtyard out back; the tables are painted in brilliant colors of mustard and cherry; the latest Italian art/posters decorate the walls and large colorful majolica vessels abound. At the entrance the display counters are filled with a variety of antipasti and any three (piccolo) or seven (grande) of these can be ordered, ranging in price from $9 for a small all-vegetable plate to a large plate of salmon carpaccio for $18. In addition there are several pasta dishes like the rigatoni siracusa with eggplant, peppers, olives, anchovies, and capers in a spicy tomato sauce, or gnocchi with a pink sauce. The meat or fish entrées change daily. To finish there's tiramisu, biscotti, and a variety of Italian custard cream desserts.

JERUSALEM, 955 Eglinton Ave. West, just west of Bathurst. Tel. 416/783-6494.

Cuisine: MIDDLE EASTERN. **Reservations:** Not accepted.
$ **Prices:** Appetizers under $4; main courses $9–$13. AE, DC, ER, MC, V.
Open: Mon–Thurs noon–11pm, Fri–Sat noon–midnight, Sun noon–10pm.

At Jerusalem it's the food and prices that count. All the appetizers are under $4—falafel, koubeh (a cracked-wheat roll stuffed with ground meat, onions, and pine nuts), various styles of hummus, tahina, and tabbouleh (a delicious blend of cracked wheat with chopped tomatoes, onions, parsley, mint, lemon, and olive oil).

You can follow them with liver fried in garlic and hot pepper sauce, and siniyeh (mixed ground lamb and beef with onions, parsley, and pine nuts, and oven-baked with tahina sauce), lamb or beef shish kebab, or any other dish.

The decor is simple—just some hammered brass tabletops on the walls—but the atmosphere is extremely warm, the service friendly and unhurried.

SPECIALTY DINING

HOTEL DINING

Currently considered the top haute-cuisine rooms are **Truffles,** at the Four Seasons, 21 Avenue Rd. (tel. 416/964-0411); **Chiaro's,** at the King Edward, 37 King St. East (tel. 416/863-9700); **Sanssouci,** at the Sutton Place, 955 Bay St. (tel. 416/924-9221); **Seasons,** at the Inn on the Park, 1100 Eglinton Ave. East (tel. 416/444-2561) and the **Roof Restaurant** at the Park Plaza, 4 Avenue Rd., at Bloor (tel. 416/924-5471).

For the above dining choices, see the hotel recommendations, earlier in this chapter.

DINING CLUSTERS/COMPLEXES

MOVENPICK A veritable Swiss complex has been created at Movenpick, 165 York St., between Richmond and Adelaide (tel. 416/366-5234).

The **Veranda Delicatessen** is a fine place to stop during the day for a tempting array of pastries, ice cream, truffles, cheeses, soup of the day, and sandwiches. Homemade breads, pastries, and Swiss chocolate truffles are available for take-out. Open Monday through Friday from 7:30am to 6pm, on Saturday from 10am to 6pm, and on Sunday from 10am to 4pm.

The tiled **Belle Terrasse,** filled with colorful potted plants, looks like an outdoor café and serves a variety of Swiss specialties, priced from $10 to $15, including several Rösti potato dishes, Rahmschnitzel (pork schnitzel covered with a creamy mushroom sauce), Swiss bratwurst with Rösti, or tender veal liver sautéed in butter. Seafood, steaks, salads, curries, and burgers complete the menu. Breakfast is served here from 7:30 to 11am. In the evenings specials are featured. Monday and Tuesday are pasta nights, all you can eat for $13; on Wednesday and Thursday a gourmet buffet ($20) is served; while on Friday and Saturday there's a fisherman's feast (from $25). On Sunday a brunch buffet is served ($20). Open daily 7:30am to midnight.

The wood-paneled **Rossli Restaurant,** decorated with horse saddlery (the name, in fact, means little horse), is for more formal dining. Start your meal with risotto with boletus mushrooms or air-dried beef and follow with one of the specialties, which run from $14 to $20—chicken breast served with spinach, hazelnut sauce, and Rösti; veal in a white wine sauce with mushrooms; rack of lamb provençale; or sautéed beef tenderloin in Pinot Noir sauce. Seafood and steaks complete the menu. Save room for the tempting Swiss chocolate truffle cake. Open daily 11:30am to 2pm and from 6pm except on Sunday.

And finally, there's the **Grape 'n' Cheese Wine Bar,** serving the complete menu and Swiss cheese fondue and raclette.

DRAGON CITY   In the basement of Dragon City, the Asian shopping complex on Spadina Avenue at Dundas Street, you'll find tables surrounded by a series of counters frequented by the local Chinatown residents. You could be anywhere in Asia. The food offered is Indonesian, Japanese, Chinese, Taiwanese, noodles, and seafood. A real Toronto experience.

HARBOURFRONT DINING   A great variety and some decent budget dining can be found in **Queen's Quay,** particularly upstairs with most items priced between $4 and $8. Croûtes and pita sandwiches can be found at **La Bouchée.** At **Sbarro's** (tel. 416/364-3036) you can choose among pizza (vegetarian even), spaghetti with all kinds of sauces, veal cutlet, lasagne, sausages, and a salad bar. All the items are under $8. The **Coyote Grill** (tel. 416/203-0504) has burritos and nachos priced from $7 to $12.

Downstairs there are several restaurants, each one also operating an outdoor terrace/café from which you can watch the sailboats and other craft plying the harbor. **Fruiteria** (tel. 416/203-0274) offers soups, salads, and fresh fruits of all sorts, with most items under $5. **Spinnakers** (tel. 416/203-0559) has an inside dining room as well, and a cocktail bar, too. Here you can enjoy fish-and-chips, baked halibut, salads, and more, priced from $8 to $17. **Baguette** (tel. 416/203-0287) has chocolate-almond croissants, and makes tuna melts and other fare, all under $5.

Also on the Harbourfront on Pier 4 are **Wallymagoo's** (tel. 416/203-6248), a nautical-theme restaurant known for its seafood pizza and finger foods, and live entertainment; **Pier 4 Storehouse** (tel. 416/863-1440), which features a raw bar and serves steak, seafood, and pasta priced from $15 to $27; **Tony's Fish and Lobster,** (tel. 416/203-5865), featuring seafood from a $10 catch of the day to $20 lobster. Open Monday through Saturday from noon to 2:30pm and 5 to 11:30pm daily.

The **Water's Edge Patio and Bar** (tel. 416/203-0717) overlooks Lake Ontario, has a huge outdoor bar and serves fresh salads and grilled and barbecue items. It's jam-packed on weekends. Open 11am to 1am. On weekends live entertainment goes on all day.

VILLAGE BY THE GRANGE   Conveniently located south of the Art Gallery, Village by the Grange, at 71 McCaul St., contains the **International Food Market,** where you'll find everything from Chinese, Middle Eastern, Japanese, and Mexican fast food to Coney Island hot dogs and a booth specializing in schnitzels. Salads, burgers, Japanese specialties, meat pies, and more are also readily available. All the fare is around $5.

BREAKFAST/BRUNCH

Nearly every restaurant in Toronto offers Saturday and Sunday brunch. Here are just a few of my favorites: **Le Rendez-Vous,** 14 Prince Arthur Ave. (tel. 416/961-6111); **Sanssouci,** at the Sutton Place, 955 Bay St. (tel. 416/924-9221); and the **Boulevard Café,** 161 Harbord St. (tel. 416/961-7676). Most major hotels also offer splendid buffet-style brunches.

At 3 Charles St. East, **Chez Cappuccino** (tel. 416/925-6142), just off Yonge, is a good way to start the day with a melt-in-the-mouth croissant, banana bread, or a bagel sandwich washed down with a smooth frothy cappuccino. Most items are priced from $4 to $7. It's open 24 hours.

LIGHT, CASUAL & FAST FOOD

Hughie's Burgers, 22 Front St. West (tel. 416/364-2242), offers a variety of burgers, sandwiches, and salads. There's even a 10-ouncer for $8.50. A popular, pleasant hangout, especially in early evening. It's open on Monday and Tuesday from 11:30am to 11:30pm, Wednesday through Saturday until 1am, and on Sunday from 4:30 to 10pm.

Il Fornello, 214 King St. West (tel. 416/977-2855), is famous for its pizzas (50 varieties available) cooked in a wood-fired clay oven and a variety of popular Italian dishes. Open Monday through Thursday from noon to 11pm, Friday and Saturday from noon to midnight and Sunday from 5 to 10pm.

FOR DESSERT

Diet books, Optifast, and Weight Watchers may be ubiquitous, but bold enough to buck the trend, **Just Desserts,** 306 Davenport Rd. (tel. 416/922-6824), is open practically around the clock on weekends for those in need of that sugar fix. Around 50 desserts are available—as many as 14 different cheesecakes, 10 or so assorted pies, plus a whole array of gâteaux, tortes, meringues, etc. (all $4 to $5). I don't need to describe them—just go, order with a cappuccino or coffee, savor every bite, and feel bad afterward.

Enjoy them in a nostalgic atmosphere created by oak swivel chairs, black tiled tables, and the old-movie/Broadway melodies. While you're here you might like to purchase one of the many whimsical cookie jars.

Open from 8:30am to 3am on weekdays, to 5am on weekends.

CHAPTER 13

WHAT TO SEE & DO IN TORONTO

1. ATTRACTIONS
- **FROMMER'S FAVORITE TORONTO EXPERIENCES**

2. SPORTS/RECREATION

3. EVENING ENTERTAINMENT

It takes five or six days to really see Toronto's highlights. Although some of the major sights are centrally located, there are also several favorites outside the downtown core, and these take extra time and effort to reach. Ideally, you should spend one day each at Ontario Place, the Ontario Science Centre, Canada's Wonderland, and Harbourfront. In fact, that's what the kids will definitely want to do.

Then there's also the zoo, which could take a whole day complete with a picnic.

The Art Gallery of Ontario, Chinatown, and the Royal Ontario Museum could be combined in a pinch, but the day might be too museum-oriented for some. Ontario Place could conceivably be combined with Fort York and Exhibition Place. En route to Canada's Wonderland, you could stop in at Black Creek Pioneer Village, but I don't recommend that since it will cut into your time at Canada's Wonderland, which really requires a day.

As you can see, there are numerous major attractions in Toronto worthy of a whole day's visit. There are also many other downtown sights—the CN Tower, the Eaton Centre, Yorkville, Queen Street, City Hall, and Casa Loma—that any visitor will want to explore. Depending on your interests and whether you have children, there's enough to keep you going for several weeks in Toronto. But that said, below are a few suggestions.

SUGGESTED ITINERARIES

IF YOU HAVE TWO DAYS   Get to the Ontario Science Centre the minute it opens on Day 1 and then come back into town to spend the late afternoon/early evening at Harbourfront or Ontario Place.

Start early at the Kensington Market on Day 2 and from there walk up to College Street and through the university area to the Royal Ontario Museum. Leave enough time to wander through Yorkville and browse in some of the stores and galleries before they close.

IF YOU HAVE THREE DAYS   Spend the first two days as outlined above. On Day 3, explore Chinatown and stop at the Art Gallery. Then pop over to the Eaton Centre and head down to Queen Street to explore Queen Street Village in the early evening.

IF YOU HAVE FIVE DAYS   Spend Days 1–3 as discussed above. On Day 4, visit either Canada's Wonderland (if the family's in tow) or the McMichael Collection in Kleinburg. Black Creek Pioneer Village could be squeezed in, too. Take a trip to the Toronto Islands and while away Day 5 among the lagoons, picnicking, relaxing, or bicycling.

1. ATTRACTIONS

THE TOP ATTRACTIONS
ON THE LAKEFRONT

ONTARIO PLACE, 955 **Lakeshore Blvd. West. Tel. 416/314-9811,** or 416/314-9900 for a recording.

When this 96-acre recreation complex on Lake Ontario opened in 1971, it seemed futuristic, and over 20 years later it still does (although, admittedly, it was revamped in 1989).

From a distance you'll see five steel-and-glass pods suspended 105 feet up on columns above the lake, three artificial islands, and alongside, a huge geodesic dome that looks like a golf ball magnified several thousand times. The five pods contain a multimedia theater, live children's theater, a high-technology exhibit, and other displays that tell the story of Ontario in vivid kaleidoscopic detail. The dome houses **Cinesphere,** where a 60- by 80-foot screen shows specially made IMAX movies.

Located under an enormous orange canopy, the **Children's Village** provides a well-supervised area where children aged 12 and under can scramble over rope bridges, bounce on an enormous trampoline, and slide down a twisting chute, or most popular of all, squirt water pistols, garden hoses, swim, and generally drench one another in the water-play section. Afterward, parents can just pop them in the conveniently available dryers before moving on to three specialty children's theaters.

A stroll around the complex reveals two marinas full of yachts and other craft, the HMCS *Haida* (a destroyer, open for touring, that served in both World War II and the Korean War), a miniature 18-hole golf course, plenty of grassland for picnicking and general cavorting, and a wide variety of restaurants and snack bars serving everything from Chinese, Irish, German, and Canadian food to hot dogs and hamburgers. And don't miss the wildest ride in town—the Wilderness Canoe Ride, the Water Slide, and bumper boats. Or for something more peaceful, the pedal or remote-control boats. The latest attraction is **The Amazing Maze,** a three-dimensional labyrinth that presents quite a challenge.

At night the **Forum,** an outdoor amphitheater that accommodates 10,000 under the copper canopy and outside on the grassy slopes, comes alive. During the summer all manner of entertainments are held here, from the Toronto Symphony and National Ballet of Canada, to Tony Bennett, Dionne Warwick, and Bruce Cockburn. For tickets call 416/870-8000.

Admission: Free, with some exceptions. IMAX movies $5 adults, $2.50 seniors and children 12 and under.

Open: Mid-May to Labor Day Mon–Sat 10:30am–midnight, Sun 10:30am–11pm. **Subway and Bus:** Located west of downtown, Ontario Place can be reached by taking the subway to Bathurst or Dufferin and buses south from there to Exhibition. Call TTC Information (tel. 416/393-4636) for special bus service details. **Parking:** $9.

HARBOURFRONT CENTRE, Queen's Quay West. Tel. 416/973-3000 for information on special events, or 416/973-4000 for box office.

The federal government took over a 96-acre strip of prime waterfront land in 1972 to preserve the waterfront vista—and since then Torontonians have rediscovered their lakeshore. Abandoned warehouses, shabby depots, and crumbling factories have been refurbished, and a tremendous urban park now stretches on and around the old piers.

The resulting Harbourfront is one of Toronto's most exciting happenings. Sailboats, motorboats, houseboats, ferries, and other craft ply the water or sit at anchor dockside, their happy denizens dining or drinking in one of the many waterside cafés, shopping, or attending one of the entertainment events that are very much part of the waterfront scene. It's a great place to spend the whole day.

Queen's Quay, at the foot of York Street, is the closest quay to town, and it's the first point you'll encounter as you approach from the Harbour Castle Westin. From here, boats depart for tours of the harbor and islands. An old warehouse, it now houses the Premiere Dance Theatre, plus two floors of shops, restaurants, and waterfront cafés.

After exploring Queen's Quay, walk west along the glorious waterfront promenade to **York Quay.** To get there you'll pass the **Power Plant,** a contemporary gallery, and behind it, the **Du Maurier Theatre Centre.** At **York Quay Centre** you can secure a lot of information on programming as well as instruct yourself in several galleries, including **The Craft Studio,** where you can watch artisans blow glass, throw pots, and make silk-screen prints. On the other side of the center you can attend one of the free Molson Dry Front Music outdoor concerts, held all summer long at **Molson Place.** Also on the quay in the center is the **Water's Edge Café,** overlooking a small pond for electric model boats and a children's play area. The **Lookout** is home to Kaleidoscope, an active arts program for families, where you might find youngsters having a jubilant time painting one another's faces with finger paints.

From here, take the footbridge to John Quay crossing over the sailboats moored below, to the stores and restaurants on Pier 4—**Wallymagoo's** marine bar, and the **Pier 4 Storehouse.** Beyond on **Maple Leaf Quay** lies the **Nautical Center,** home of the **Harbourfront Sailing School.**

The **Harbourfront Antiques Market,** at 390 Queen's Quay West, at the foot of Spadina Avenue (tel. 416/260-2626), will keep antiques-lovers busy browsing for hours. More than 100 antiques dealers spread out their wares—jewelry, china, furniture, toys, and books. Indoor parking is adjacent to the market, and there's also a cafeteria that serves fresh salads, sandwiches, and desserts for that oft-needed rest stop. Open May through October, Tuesday through Friday from 11am to 6pm, Saturday from 10am to 6pm, and Sunday from 8 to 6pm; November through April, Tuesday through Friday from 11am to 5pm, Saturday 10am to 5pm, and Sunday from 8am to 6pm.

At the west end of the park stands **Bathurst Pier,** which most resembles a park. Here you'll find a large sports field for romping around, plus two adventure playgrounds, one for older kids and the other (supervised) for 3- to 7-year-olds.

More than 4,000 events take place annually at Harbourfront, including a **Harbourfront Reading Festival,** held every Tuesday on York Quay, and attracting some very eminent writers. Other happenings include films, dance, theater, music, children's events, multicultural festivals, marine events, and other exciting programs. Two of the most important events are the annual **Children's Festival** and the **International Festival of Authors.** Most of the activities are free.

Train: Take the LRT from Union Station. **Bus:** Take the no. 77B bus from Union Station or the Spadina subway station; or the no. 6 or 6A bus to the foot of Bay Street and walk west.

THE TORONTO ISLANDS

A stolid little ferry will take you across to 612 acres of island park crisscrossed by shady paths and quiet waterways—a glorious spot to walk, play tennis, cycle, feed the ducks, putter around in boats, picnic, or just sit.

Children will find **Centreville** (tel. 416/363-0405), a 19-acre old-time amusement park, built and designed especially for them. But you won't find the usual neon signs, shrill hawkers, and the aroma of greasy hot-dog stands. Instead you'll find a turn-of-the-century village complete with Main Street, tiny shops, a firehouse, and even a small working farm where the kids can pet lambs and chicks and enjoy pony rides. They'll also love trying out the miniature antique cars, fire engines, old-fashioned train, the authentic 1890s carousel, the flume ride, and the aerial cars.

IMPRESSIONS

Canada is really two countries held together by three nation-saving bywords—conservatism, caution, and compromise—bequeathed to us by Britain.
—WILLIAM TOYE, *A BOOK OF CANADA,* 1962

TORONTO

Downtown Toronto

Allan Gardens ❷
Art Gallery of Toronto ❹
Bus Station ❸
Campbell House ❻
City Hall ❼
CN Tower ⓱
Convention Centre ⓲
Toronto Dominion Centre ⓬
Eaton Centre ❾
The Grange ❺
Harbourfront Antiques Market ⓴
Maple Leaf Gardens ❶
O'Keefe Centre ⓮
Old City Hall ❽
Royal Alexandra Theatre ❿
Royal Bank Plaza ⓭
Roy Thomson Hall ⓫
St. Lawrence Market ⓯
SkyDome ⓳
Union Station ⓰

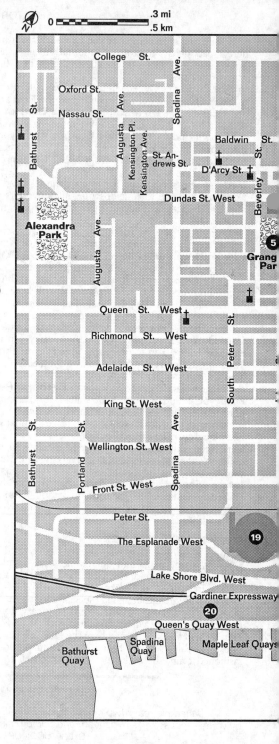

.3 mi
.5 km

College St.

Oxford St.
Nassau St.
Spadina Ave.

Augusta Ave.
Kensington Pl.
Kensington Ave.

Baldwin St.

St. Andrews St.
D'Arcy St.

Bathurst St.

Dundas St. West

Beverley St.

Alexandra Park

Augusta Ave.

❺
Grange Par

Queen St. West

Richmond St. West

Adelaide St. West

Peter St.

King St. West

South Ave.

Spadina Ave.

St.

Bathurst St.

Portland St.

Wellington St. West

Front St. West

Peter St.

The Esplanade West

⓳

Lake Shore Blvd. West

Gardiner Expressway

⓴

Queen's Quay West

Bathurst Quay

Spadina Quay

Maple Leaf Quays

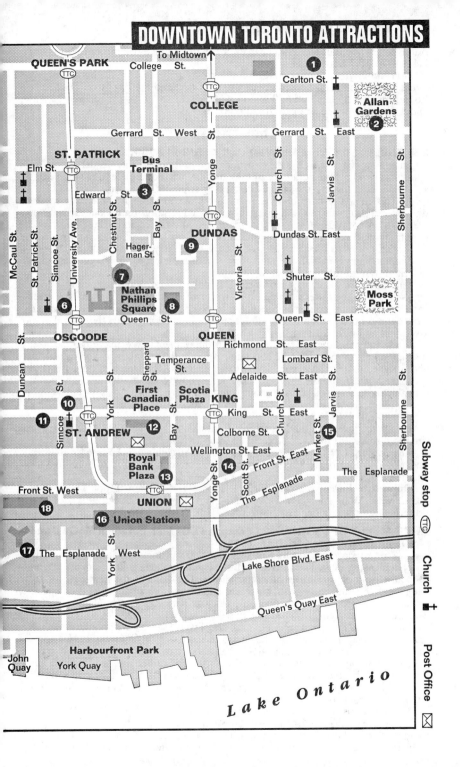

DOWNTOWN TORONTO ATTRACTIONS

QUEEN'S PARK
TTC

To Midtown
College St.

Carlton St.

COLLEGE

Allan
Gardens

Gerrard St. West

Gerrard St. East

ST. PATRICK
TTC

Bus
Terminal

Elm St.

Edward St. 3

Church St.

Jarvis St.

Sherbourne St.

McCaul St.
St. Patrick St.
Simcoe St.
University Ave.
Chestnut St.

Hager-
man St.

Bay St.

DUNDAS 9

Dundas St. East

Victoria St.

Shuter St.

Moss
Park

Nathan
Phillips
Square 8

7

6

Queen St.
TTC

OSGOODE

QUEEN
TTC

Queen St. East

Duncan St.

Sheppard St.

Richmond St. East

Temperance St.

Lombard St.

Adelaide St. East

York St.

First
Canadian
Place

Scotia
Plaza KING
TTC

Simcoe St.
Bay St.
Church St.
Jarvis St.
Sherbourne St.

10
11
ST. ANDREW

12

King St. East

Colborne St.

15

Royal
Bank
Plaza 13

UNION
TTC

Wellington St. East

14

Front St. East
Market St.

Scott St.

The Esplanade

Front St. West

18

16 Union Station

The Esplanade

17 The Esplanade West

York St.
Yonge St.

Lake Shore Blvd. East

Queen's Quay East

Harbourfront Park

John
Quay
York Quay

Lake Ontario

Subway stop TTC

Church ✝

Post Office ✉

Admission is free, but there is a charge for the rides. Open daily from mid-May to Labor Day, 10:30am to 6pm.

Ferries: Ferries, which operate all day, leave from the docks at the bottom of Bay Street. To get there, take a subway to Union Station and the Bay Street bus south. Round-trip fare $3 adults, $1.50 seniors and ages 15 to 19, $1 for children 14 and under. For ferry schedules, call 416/392-8193.

DOWNTOWN

CN TOWER, 301 Front St. West. Tel. 416/360-8500.

As you approach the city, the first thing you will note is this slender needlelike structure. Tiny colored elevators that look like jumping beans glide to the top of this 1,815-foot-high tower—the tallest freestanding structure in the world.

As you enter the base of the tower, just look up through the atrium to the top . . . yes, that's where you're going. Glass-walled elevators on the outside walls of the tower whisk you to the 1,136-foot-high seven-level sky pod in just under one minute. From here, on a clear day you can't quite see forever, but you *can* see, I'm told, all the way to Niagara Falls, or even Buffalo, if you wish. One of the two observation levels is partially open to allow you to experience that dizzying sensation of height (vertigo sufferers beware).

The pod also contains broadcasting facilities, a revolving restaurant, and a nightclub. Atop the tower sits a 335-foot antenna mast that took 3½ weeks to erect with the aid of a giant Sikorsky helicopter. It took 55 lifts to complete the operation. Above the sky pod is the world's highest public observation gallery, the Space Deck, 1,465 feet above the ground.

While you're up there, don't worry about the elements sweeping it into the lake: It's built of contoured reinforced concrete covered with thick glass-reinforced plastic, and designed to keep ice accumulation to a minimum. The structure can withstand the highest winds, and the effects of snow, ice, lightning, and earth tremors, which is probably more than you can say about your own house.

For lunch, dinner, or Sunday brunch reservations at the Top of Toronto revolving restaurant, call 416/362-5411.

Also at the tower you'll find a futuristic attraction, "The Tour of the Universe," a simulated spaceport that will project you into the year 2019.

Admission: CN Tower $12 adults, $8 seniors, $6 children 5–12, free for children under 5. The Tour of the Universe $8 adults, $7 seniors, $6 children 5–12, free for children under 5.

Open: CN Tower Mon–Thurs 10am–10pm, Fri–Sat 10am–11pm. The Tour of the Universe Mon–Thurs 11am–7pm, Fri–Sat 10am–10pm. **Subway:** Union Station, then walk west along Front Street.

ART GALLERY OF ONTARIO, 317 Dundas St. West, between McCaul and Beverley Sts. Tel. 416/977-0414.

The exterior gives no hint of the light and openness inside this beautifully designed gallery. The newly refurbished and expanded gallery is dramatic and the paintings are imaginatively displayed. The walls of the new galleries are stunning colors and throughout there are audiovisual presentations and computer terminals that provide information on particular paintings or schools of painters. There are several highlights not to be missed.

Although the European collections are fine, I would concentrate on the Canadian galleries. The galleries displaying the Group of Seven—Tom Thomson, F. H. Varley, Lawren Harris, and Emily Carr, et al.—are extraordinary. In addition, there are other galleries showing the genesis of Canadian art from earlier artists like Cornelius Krieghoff, Paul Kane, and Paul Peel, to such moderns as Harold Town, Kenneth Lochhead, Jock MacDonals, Jack Bush, Michael Snow, and the Montréal Automatistes Riopelle and Borduas.

Also don't miss the galleries featuring Inuit art.

The **Henry Moore Sculpture Centre**, possessing more than 800 pieces (original plasters, bronzes, maquettes, woodcuts, lithographs, etchings, and drawings), is the largest public collection of his works. They were given to Toronto by the artist, supposedly because he was so moved by the citizens' enthusiasm for his work (remember, public donations bought the sculpture that decorates Nathan Phillips Square at City Hall). In one room, under a glass ceiling, 20 or so of his large works stand like silent prehistoric rock formations. Along the walls flanking a ramp are color photographs showing Moore's major sculptures in their natural locations, which fully reveal their magnificent dimensions.

The collection of European old masters ranges from the 14th century to the French impressionists and beyond. An octagonal room is filled with works by Pissarro, Monet, Boudin, Sisley, and Renoir. De Kooning's *Two Women on a Wharf* and Karel Appel's *Black Landscape* are just two of the more modern examples. Among the sculpture you'll find Picasso's *Poupée* and Brancusi's *First Cry*, two beauties.

Behind the gallery and connected by an arcade stands **The Grange** (1817), Toronto's oldest surviving brick house. It was in fact the gallery's first permanent home. Originally the home of the Boulton family, it was a gathering place for many of the city's social and political leaders as well as for such eminent guests as Matthew Arnold, Prince Kropotkin, and Winston Churchill. Today it's a living museum of mid-19th-century Toronto life, having been meticulously restored and furnished to reflect the 1830s. Entrance is free with admission to the art gallery.

The gallery has an attractive restaurant/atrium bar open for lunch and dinner as well as a cafeteria, a gallery shop, plus a full program of films, concerts, and lectures.

Admission: $7.50 adults, $15 families (two adults plus children), $4 students and seniors, free for children under 12. Free on Wed 5–10pm.

Open: Wed and Fri 10am–10pm, Thurs and Sat–Sun 10am–5:30pm. The Grange House is open Wed and Fri noon–9pm, Thurs and Sat–Sun noon–4pm. **Closed:** Christmas Day and New Year's Day. **Subway:** St. Patrick on the University line; or take the subway to Dundas and the streetcar west.

MIDTOWN

ROYAL ONTARIO MUSEUM, 100 Queen's Park, at Avenue Rd. and Bloor St. Tel. 416/586-5549.

The ROM, as it's affectionately called, has recently undergone a $55-million renovation. Among the museum's highlights are the Roman gallery (the most extensive collection in Canada), the world-class textile collection, nine life science galleries (devoted to evolution, mammals, reptiles, and botany), and the Discovery Gallery, which is in fact a mini-museum where kids and adults can touch authentic artifacts from Egyptian scarabs to English military helmets. The Bat Cave Gallery is a miniature replica of the St. Clair bat cave in Jamaica, complete with more than 4,000 very authentic-looking bat models. The Chinese collection is numbered among the top 10 in the world, and includes the Bishop White Gallery, which displays three impressive wall paintings of Buddhist and Daoist deities (ca. 1300) and 14 monumental wooden Buddhist sculptures dating from the 12th to 16th centuries. The Ming Tomb Gallery features elements from a Ming tomb—a series of gateways and guardian figures arranged in typical funerary order. Galleries are also devoted to Ontario and Canadiana, and to many other subjects. A favorite with the kids is the Dinosaur Gallery.

Admission (including admission to the George R. Gardiner Museum of Ceramic Art and the Astrocentre of the McLaughlin Planetarium): $7 adults, $4 seniors and students, $3.50 children 5–14, $15 families, free for children under 5; free for seniors all day on Tues, free for all Tues 4:30–8pm.

Open: Wed and Fri–Mon 10am–6pm, Tues and Thurs 10am–8pm. **Closed:** Mon during winter season (first Mon in Oct to last Mon in May). **Subway:** Museum or St. George.

GEORGE R. GARDINER MUSEUM OF CERAMIC ART, 111 Queen's Park. Tel. 416/586-8080.

Across the street from the ROM, the George R. Gardiner Museum houses a diverse display of porcelain and pottery. There are four galleries. The pre-Columbian

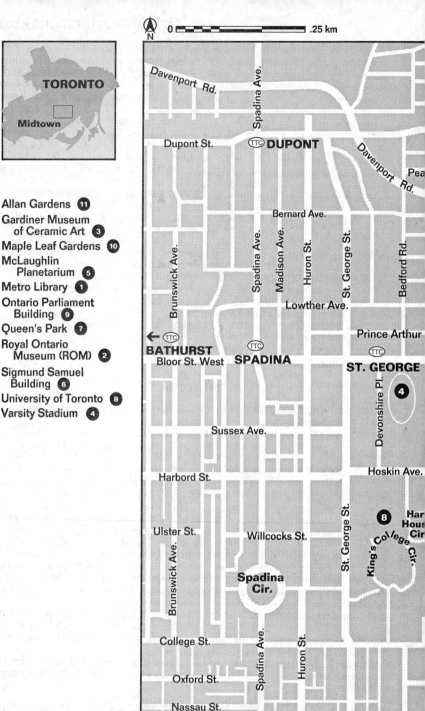

TORONTO

Midtown

Allan Gardens ⑪
Gardiner Museum
  of Ceramic Art ③
Maple Leaf Gardens ⑩
McLaughlin
  Planetarium ⑤
Metro Library ①
Ontario Parliament
  Building ⑨
Queen's Park ⑦
Royal Ontario
  Museum (ROM) ②
Sigmund Samuel
  Building ⑥
University of Toronto ⑧
Varsity Stadium ④

0 ▬▬▬▬▬▬ .25 km
N

Davenport Rd.
Spadina Ave.
Dupont St.   TTC DUPONT
Davenport Rd.
Pea

Bernard Ave.

Brunswick Ave.
Spadina Ave.
Madison Ave.
Huron St.
St. George St.
Bedford Rd.

Lowther Ave.

Prince Arthur

← TTC
BATHURST   TTC
Bloor St. West   SPADINA   TTC
                                ST. GEORGE

Devonshire Pl.
④

Sussex Ave.

Hoskin Ave.

Harbord St.

St. George St.

Ulster St.
Willcocks St.
⑧ Har
    Hous
    Cir
King's College Cir.

Brunswick Ave.

Spadina
Cir.

College St.

Spadina Ave.
Huron St.

Oxford St.

Nassau St.
↓ To Downtown Toronto

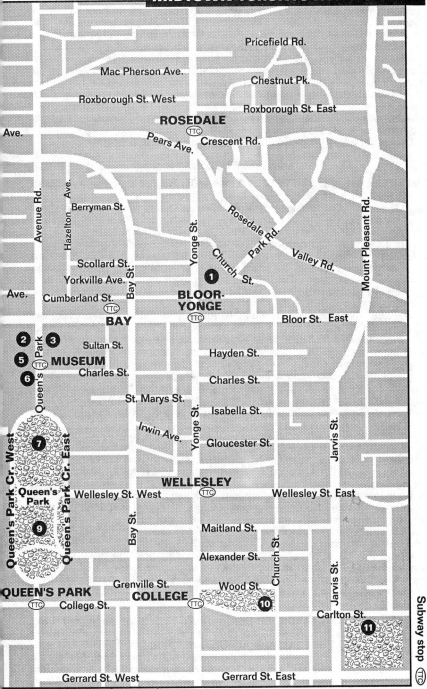

Pricefield Rd.

Mac Pherson Ave.

Chestnut Pk.

Roxborough St. West

Roxborough St. East

ROSEDALE (TTC)

Crescent Rd.

Pears Ave.

Ave.

Rosedale Rd.

Berryman St.

Park Rd.

Valley Rd.

Mount Pleasant Rd.

Avenue Rd.

Hazelton Ave.

Bay St.

Yonge St.

Church St.

Scollard St.

Yorkville Ave.

Cumberland St. (TTC)

1

Ave.

BLOOR-YONGE

BAY (TTC)

Bloor St. East

2 **3**

Queen's Park

Sultan St.

Hayden St.

5 (TTC) **MUSEUM**

Charles St.

Charles St.

6

St. Marys St.

Isabella St.

Irwin Ave.

Yonge St.

Gloucester St.

Jarvis St.

7

WELLESLEY

Queen's Park Cr. West

Queen's Park

Wellesley St. West (TTC)

Wellesley St. East

Queen's Park Cr. East

9

Maitland St.

Bay St.

Alexander St.

Church St.

Jarvis St.

QUEEN'S PARK

Grenville St.

Wood St.

(TTC)

COLLEGE

College St. (TTC)

10

Carlton St.

11

Gerrard St. West

Gerrard St. East

Subway stop (TTC)

contains fantastic Olmec and Mayan figures, and other objects from cultures in Ecuador, Colombia, and Peru. The majolica gallery displays both modern and spectacular 16th- and 17th-century pieces from Florence, Faenza, and Venice. There's also a Delftware section displaying 17th-century chargers and other examples.

Upstairs the galleries are given over to porcelain—Meissen, Sèvres, Worcester, Chelsea, Derby, and other great names. All are spectacular. Among the highlights are the pieces from the Swan Service—a 2,200-piece set that took four years (1737–41) to make. There's one oddity—a very prettily molded and painted bourdaloe (portable urinal).

Admission (including admission to the ROM): $7 adults, $4 seniors and students, $3.50 children 5–14, $15 families.
Open: Tues–Sun 10am–5pm. **Subway:** Museum or St. George.

ON THE OUTSKIRTS

ONTARIO SCIENCE CENTRE, 770 Don Mills Rd., at Eglinton Ave. East. Tel. 416/429-4100.

Described as everything from the world's most technical fun fair to a hands-on museum of the 21st century, the Science Centre really does hold a series of wonders for adult and child—650 hands-on experiments, no less.

The building itself is another one of architect Raymond Moriyama's miracles. Instead of flattening the ravine and bulldozing the trees on the site, Moriyama designed to the contours of the ravine so that a series of glass-enclosed escalators providing views of the natural surroundings take you down an escarpment to the main exhibition halls. Supposedly Moriyama built penalty clauses into the subcontractors' contracts for each and every tree destroyed!

Wherever you look there are things to touch, push, pull, or crank. Test your reflexes, balance, heart rate, and grip strength; play with computers and binary-system games and puzzles; and shunt slides of butterfly wings, bedbugs, fish scales, or feathers under the microscope. Tease your brain with a variety of optical illusions; learn from simple demonstrations the rules of physics and mathematics; or land a spaceship on the moon. Watch bees making honey; try to lift sponge building blocks with a mechanical grip; or see how many lights you can light or how high you can elevate a balloon with your own pedal power. The fun goes on and on as you explore more than 650 participational exhibits in 10 themed exhibit halls. It's a wonder I ever made it home.

Throughout, there are small theaters showing film and slide shows on various topics, while at regular times demonstrators present 20-minute expositions on such subjects as lasers, metal casting, and high-voltage electricity (watch your friend's hair stand on end). Facilities include a licensed restaurant and lounge, cafeteria, and science shop.

When one million people visit every year, you know that the best time to get to the museum is promptly at 10am—that way you'll be able to play without too much interference and negotiation.

Admission: $6.25 adults, $5 youths 13–17, $2.25 children 12 and under, $15.75 families; free for senior citizens and children under 5. Parking $2.
Open: Sat–Thurs 10am–6pm, Fri 10am–9pm. **Closed:** Christmas Day. **Subway and Bus:** Take the Yonge Street subway to Eglinton, then the Eglinton bus going east, and get off at Don Mills Road. **Directions:** If you're driving from downtown, take the Don Valley Parkway and follow the signs from Don Mills Road north.

THE METROPOLITAN ZOO, Meadowvale Rd., north of Sheppard Ave., Scarborough. Tel. 416/392-5900. For zoo information, contact Metro Toronto Zoo, P.O. Box 280, West Hill, ON, M1E 4R5.

Covering 710 acres of parkland in Scarborough is a unique zoological garden containing some 4,000 animals, plus an extensive botanical collection. The plants and animals are housed either in the eight pavilions—including Africa, Indo-Malaya, Australasia, and the Americas—or in outdoor paddocks. A photographer's dream.

Six miles of walkways offer the visitor access to any area of the zoo, or two modes of transportation can be used. During the warmer months the Zoomobile takes the zoogoer around the major walkways, viewing the animals contained in outdoor facilities. The monorail, which runs year-round, travels through the beautiful Rouge River Valley where animals native to Canada are displayed.

Facilities include restaurants, gift shop, first aid, and family center; strollers and wheelchairs are also available. The zoo is equipped with ramps and washrooms for the disabled. The Africa pavilion is also equipped with an elevator for strollers and wheelchairs. There is ample parking at the zoo, and for picnickers there are plenty of picnic areas with tables.

Admission: $9 adults, $6 seniors and children 12–17, $4 children 5–11; free for children under 5.

Open: Winter daily 9:30am–4:30pm; summer daily 9am–7:30pm. **Closed:** Christmas Day. **Subway and Bus:** Take the subway all the way to Kennedy on the Bloor-Danforth line. Then take bus no. 86A from there north. Check with the TTC for schedules (tel. 416/393-4636). **Directions:** From downtown, take the Don Valley Parkway to Highway 401 east and exit on Meadowvale Road.

MCMICHAEL CANADIAN ART COLLECTION, Islington Ave., Kleinburg. Tel. 416/893-1121.

Located 25 miles north of the city, this collection of Canadian, Inuit, and native art is worth a visit for the setting alone.

You'll approach the two-level gallery through quiet stands of pine trees to a log-and-stone building specially designed to house the Canadian landscapes within. The lobby itself is a work of art: A pitched roof soars to a height of 27 feet on massive rafters of Douglas fir and throughout the gallery panoramic windows look south over white pine, cedar, ash, and birch.

The gallery houses works by Canada's famous group of landscape painters, the "Group of Seven"—Arthur Lismer, Frederick Varley, and Lawren Harris, among others—as well as Tom Thomson, David Milne, Emily Carr, and their contemporaries. These devoted painters, inspired by the Canadian wilderness early in this century, particularly that of Algonquin Park and northern Ontario, recorded its rugged landscape in highly individualistic styles.

An impressive collection of Inuit and contemporary Native Canadian art and sculpture is also on display.

Founded by Robert and Signe McMichael, the gallery began in 1965 when they donated their property, home, and collection of close to 200 works to the Province of Ontario. Since 1965 the collection has expanded and now contains over 5,000 works. Still, its unique atmosphere has been preserved—with log and barnwood walls, fieldstone fireplaces, and such decorative touches as hooked rugs and earthenware urns filled with flowers.

Admission: $6 adults, $3 seniors and students, $13 families, free for children under 5.

Open: June 1–Oct 31 daily 10am–5pm; Nov 1–May 31 Tues–Sun 10am–4pm. **Directions:** It's tough to get there by public transportation. Best bet is to take the subway to Islington and call for a taxi at 416/738-6611.

CANADA'S WONDERLAND, 9580 Jane St., Vaughan. Tel. 416/832-7000, or 416/832-2205 for a recording, 416/832-8131 for concert information at the Kingswood Music Theatre. For information, write P.O. Box 624, Vaughan, ON, L6A 1S6.

Nineteen miles (or 30 minutes) north of Toronto, Canada now has its answer to Disneyland: a smaller theme park, Canada's Wonderland.

The 370-acre park is divided into eight themed areas, boasting more than 130 attractions including 50 rides. New for 1993 was the opening of Kids Kingdom, an interactive playland for kids complete with secret tunnels, slides, ball crawls, a foam forest, dragon bones to climb on, a cast of costumed characters, and family shows at the Woodland Theatre and the Shady Grove Playhouse. Also new is the 18-hole championship mini-golf course and also major league batting cages. The Grande World Exposition of 1890 recaptures the atmosphere of a Victorian-era world's fair, while in Medieval Faire, you are transported back to the age of chivalry, with a castle, a pirate's galleon anchored in a bay, and the Canterbury Theatre, which featured a dazzling ice show and a laser light and music spectacular in 1993. Hanna Barbera Land springs to life for kids, who can encounter Fred Flintstone, Yogi Bear, and Scooby Doo. International Street unfolds before you with boutiques and wares from around the world. Here you'll be greeted by the Heritage Kids, a troupe of friendly characters representing different nations. International Festival features 150-foot-high Wonder Mountain, from which daredevil divers leap out over the cascading waterfalls, and a groovy video rock show at the International Showplace. White Water Canyon is the name of a thrilling raft ride and also offers a five-story plunge down Timberwolf Falls, the closest you'll come to experiencing what it must be like to go over Niagara Falls. Water thrills continue at Splashworks, a 10-acre water playground with 16 slide and tube rides.

You can also test your daring against a variety of roller coasters, from stand-up, backwards, looping, wooden to the Vortex, a suspended version that plunges off Wonder Mountain at 85kmph (140 m.p.h.). All are guaranteed to receive standing ovations from seasoned roller-coaster fans. Top-name entertainment appears at the Kingswood Theatre for an extra charge.

You'll probably need eight hours to see everything. If you picnic on the grounds, forgo souvenirs, and avoid the video games, a family of four can do the park for about $108. *Note:* Watch out for the extra added attractions that are not included in the admission pass, particularly the many "games of skill," which the kids love but the purse hates.

Admission: Pay One Price Passport, for the day, including unlimited use of all rides and shows (excludes food, games, merchandise, parking, special attractions, and the Kingswood Music Theatre), $26.95 adults, $13.45 seniors and children 3–6, free for children under 2. Grounds admission only is $16.95 (no rides). Parking is $6.

Open: May and Labor Day–early Oct weekends only 10am–8pm; June 1–25 Mon–Fri 10am–8pm, Sat–Sun 10am–10pm; June 26–Labor Day daily 10am–10pm. Hanna Barbera Land and Kids Kingdom close daily at 8pm. "Splashworks" is generally open 11am–7pm, depending on weather and lighting. **Bus:** GO Express Bus from Yorkdale or York Mills subway directly to Wonderland. **Directions:** Take Yonge Street north to Highway 401 and travel west to Highway 400 north. Take the Rutherford Road exit off Highway 400 and follow the signs. Exit at Major Mackenzie if heading south on Highway 400.

MORE ATTRACTIONS

ARCHITECTURAL HIGHLIGHTS

CASA LOMA, 1 Austin Terrace. Tel. 416/923-1171.

Every city has its folly and Toronto has a charming one, complete with Elizabethan-style chimneys, Rhineland turrets, secret panels, passageways, and a mellifluous-sounding name: Casa Loma.

Sir Henry Pellatt, who built it between 1911 and 1914 at a cost of $3.5 million, had a lifelong and incurably romantic fascination with medieval castles—so he decided to build his own. He studied European medieval castles, gathered materials and furnishings, bringing marble, glass, and paneling from Europe, teak from Asia, and oak and walnut from prime areas of North America. He imported Scottish stone-masons to build the massive walls that surround the six-acre site.

It's a fascinating place to explore: the majestic Great Hall with its 60-foot ceiling; the Oak Room, where three artisans worked for three years to fashion the paneling; the Conservatory, with its elegant bronze doors and stained-glass dome; the battlements and towers; Sir Henry's suite, containing a shower with an 18-inch-diameter shower head; the 1,700-bottle wine cellar; and the 800-foot tunnel to the stables, where horses were quartered amid the luxury of Spanish tile and mahogany. As you go through the house, a tape recording in each room explains what you are seeing.

Admission: $8 adults, $4.50 seniors and children 6–16.
Open: Daily 10am–4pm. **Subway:** Dupont; then walk two blocks north.

CITY HALL, Queen St. West. Tel. 416/392-7341.

Another architectural spectacle houses the Mayor's Office and the city's administrative offices. Daringly designed in the early 1960s by Finnish architect Viljo Revell, it consists of a low podium topped by the flying-saucer-shaped Council Chamber, which is enfolded between two curved towers. In front stretches Nathan Phillips Square (named after the mayor who initiated the project), where in summer you can sit and contemplate the flower gardens, fountains, and reflecting pool (which doubles as a skating rink in winter), as well as listen to concerts. Here also stands Henry Moore's *Three-Way Piece No. 2*, locally referred to as *The Archer*, purchased through a public subscription fund.

The interior is as dramatic as the exterior, and a cafeteria and dining room are located in the basement. In contrast, to the east stands the Old City Hall, a green-copper-roofed Victorian Romanesque-style building.

Tours: Free tours conducted Mon–Fri at 3:15pm.
Subway: Queen Street. **Streetcar:** Take the Queen streetcar west.

THE EATON CENTRE, stretching from Dundas and Yonge Sts. south to Queen St.

Buttressed at both ends by 30-plus-story skyscrapers, this high-tech center, which cost over $250 million, encompasses six million square feet. Eaton's Department Store takes up one million square feet, and the rest is filled with 300+ stores and restaurants, and three garages.

Inside, the structure opens into the impressive Galleria, a long glass-domed arcade with marble floors dotted with benches, orchids, palm trees, and fountains where light flows in colorful waves. Three tiers rise above, reached by escalator and glass elevators, giving glorious views over this Crystal Palace/Milan-modern-flavored masterpiece designed by Eb Zeidler (who also designed Ontario Place). Here, no matter what the weather does, you can enjoy the sights, sounds, and aromas in comfort—and don't be surprised by the twittering of the sparrows, some of which have decided that this new facility is as pleasant as the outdoors.

One more amazing fact stands out about this new construction: It was built around two of Toronto's oldest landmarks—**Trinity Church** (1847) and the **Scadding House** (home of the rector, Dr. Scadding)—because the public demanded that the developers allow the sun to continue to shine on the church's twin towers. It does.

Subway: Dundas or Queen.

ONTARIO LEGISLATURE, Queen's Park. Tel. 416/325-7500.

East of the university, at the top of University Avenue, lies Queen's Park, surrounding the rose-tinted sandstone and granite Ontario Parliament buildings, which are profusely carved, with stately domes, arches, and porte cochères. Drop in between 2 and 3pm when the legislature is in session (in fall, winter, and spring) for some pithy comments during the Question Period.

Tours: Given Mon–Fri Labor Day–Victoria Day; daily Victoria Day–Labor Day. Call ahead to check times.
Subway: Queen's Park.

ROYAL BANK PLAZA, at the corner of Front and Bay Sts.

Shimmering in the sun, the Royal Bank Plaza looks like a pillar of gold—and in a way it is. More importantly, it is a masterpiece of design and architectural drama. Two triangular towers of bronze mirror glass flank a 130-foot-high glass-walled banking hall. The external walls of the towers are built in a serrated configuration so that they reflect a phenomenal mosaic of color from the skies and surrounding buildings.

In the banking hall, hundreds of aluminum cylinders hang from the ceiling—the work of Venezuelan sculptor Jesus Raphael Soto, while two levels below there's a waterfall and pine tree setting naturally illuminated from the hall above.

If you want to see modern architecture at its most imaginative, then don't miss Royal Bank Plaza. It's a free visual inspiration.

Subway: Union.

SKYDOME, 1 Blue Jays Way. Tel. 416/341-2770.

A gala event in 1989 was the opening of the downtown 53,000-seat SkyDome, new home to the Toronto Blue Jays baseball team and the Toronto Argonauts football team. The stadium itself represents an engineering feat, featuring the world's first fully retractable roof, which spans more than eight acres, and a gigantic video scoreboard. So large is it that you could fit a 31-story building inside the complex when the roof is closed. Indeed, there's already an 11-story hotel with 70 rooms facing directly onto the field.

Tours: One-hour tours begin most days at 10am; cost is $8 adults, $5.50 seniors and children.

Subway: Union.

COLLEGES & UNIVERSITIES

UNIVERSITY OF TORONTO, 21 King's College Circle. Tel. 416/978-5000 for summer tour information.

Just south of the Royal Ontario Museum sprawls the main campus of the University of Toronto, with its quiet wooded pathways, ivy-covered buildings, and spreading lawns used by students and staff. Insulin was discovered here, the first heart pacemaker was built here, and baby's pabulum was developed here.

Wander through and note the architecturally interesting buildings, such as the Gothic-inspired Hart House.

Tours: June–Aug, tours leave from the map room at Hart House on Wellesley St. Mon–Fri at 10:30am, 1pm, and 2:30pm.

Subway: Queen's Park or St. George.

HISTORIC BUILDINGS

CAMPBELL HOUSE, 160 Queen St. West. Tel. 416/597-0227.

Just across the street from Osgoode Hall, on the opposite corner of University and Queen, sits Sir William Campbell's mansion, built in 1822 by this Loyalist and subsequent chief justice of Upper Canada. He retired to his mansion in 1829 where he resided until he died in 1834 despite a diet of snipe prescribed by his physician.

Admission: $2.50 adults; $1.25 seniors, students, and children.

Open: Mon–Fri 9:30–11:30am and 2:30–4:30pm. Also open Sat–Sun noon–4:30pm May 24 weekend–end of December. **Subway:** Osgoode.

FORT YORK, Fleet St., between Bathurst St. and Strachan Ave. Tel. 416/392-6907.

Established by Lieutenant-Governor Simcoe in 1793 to defend "little muddy York," as Toronto was then known, Fort York was sacked by Americans in 1813. At the fort you can see the soldiers' and officers' quarters, clamber over the ramparts, and view demonstrations and exhibits.

Admission: $4.75 adults, $2.75 children 6–10, $3 seniors and youths 11–17; free for children 5 and under.

Open: Winter Mon–Sat 9:30am–5pm, Sun noon–5pm; summer daily 9:30am–5pm. **Streetcar:** Bathurst streetcar south to the gate.

OSGOODE HALL, 130 Queen St. West. Tel. 416/947-3300.

To the west of City Hall extends an impressive, elegant wrought-iron fence in front of an equally gracious mansion, Osgoode Hall, currently the home of the Law Society of Upper Canada. The fence was originally built to prevent the cows from getting in and trampling the flower beds. On a conducted tour you can see the splendor of the grand staircase, the rotunda, the Great Library, and the fine portrait and sculpture collection. Building began in 1829 on this structure, troops were billeted here during the Rebellion of 1837, and the buildings now house the headquarters of Ontario's legal profession and several magnificent courtrooms—including one using materials from London's Old Bailey. The courts are open to the public.

Tours: By appointment, except in summer when daily tours are given Mon–Fri at 1 and 1:20pm.

Subway: Osgoode.

MARKETS

Toronto has a colorful and lively tapestry that should not be missed—the **Kensington Market**, between Spadina Avenue and Bathurst Street just south of College Street. If you can struggle out of bed to get there around 5am, you'll see the squawking chickens being carried from their trucks to the stalls. Here, in what used to be primarily a Jewish market in the heart of the then garment center, you'll hear the accents of Portuguese, Italians, and others, stallowners who spread their wares before them—squid and crabs in pails, chickens, pigeons, bread, cheese, apples, pears, peppers, ginger, and mangoes from the West Indies, salted fish from Portuguese dories, lace, fabrics, and other colorful remnants. The place seethes with crowds on its narrow streets, a cacophony of bargaining and shrieking—a veritable bazaar.

As I said, if you want to capture the essence of the market, then go in the early morning; if you're a bargain seeker, go later in the day when the vendors are anxious to be rid of their wares (I should know—I once lived that way, carping and bargaining with these merchants, buying shiny smelts and other wonders for half the price). There's no market on Sunday.

The other market has a far more staid atmosphere. The accents are clearly English at the daily (except Sunday and Monday) ✪ **St. Lawrence Market,** held from 7am to 5pm (Saturday is the day). Ontario farmers gather here to offer meat and produce for sale, and you can capture the aroma of cheese, meat, and fish mingled with the scent of flowers and freshly made candies and pastries. It's a good place to pick up your picnic fare for a day at the Islands.

While you're here, seek out the restored St. Lawrence Hall, 157 King St. East (tel. 416/392-7120). In the 19th century it used to be the focal point for Toronto's social life—everything from Jenny Lind performances to temperance and antislavery meetings—a glorious building designed in the Renaissance style.

MUSEUMS

THE BATA SHOE MUSEUM, 131 Bloor St. West. Tel. 416/924-7463.
For Imelda Marcos or anyone interested in shoes, this museum, the personal collection of the Bata family, displays decorative/functional shoes, national and international shoes and modern and historical shoes. It makes for a fascinating history. *Note:* The museum will move in Spring '95.
Admission: $3 adults, $1 students.
Open: Tues–Sun 11am–6pm.

BLACK CREEK PIONEER VILLAGE, Steeles Ave. and Jane St. Tel. 416/736-1733.
Life here moves at the gentle pace of rural Ontario as it was 100 years ago. You can watch the authentically garbed villagers as they go about their chores—harrowing, seeding, rail splitting, sheepshearing, and threshing. Enjoy the fruits of their cooking, wander through the cozily furnished homesteads, visit the working mill, shop at the general store, and rumble past the farm animals in a horse-drawn wagon. There are over 30 restored buildings to explore in a beautifully landscaped village.
Admission: $7 adults, $4.50 seniors, $3 children 5–14; free for children under 5.
Open: Mar and Nov–Dec daily 10am–4:30pm; Apr–June Sat–Sun 10am–5:30pm; May–Sept Mon–Fri 10am–5pm; July–Aug Sat–Sun 10am–6pm. **Closed:** Jan to mid-Mar. **Subway and Bus:** Take the Yonge Street subway north to Finch and transfer to the no. 60 bus that runs along Steeles Avenue West to Jane Street.

CANADIAN DECORATIVE ARTS COLLECTION, in the Sigmund Samuel Building, 14 Queen's Park Crescent West. Tel. 416/586-5549.
The ROM's Canadian Decorative Arts collection, in the Sigmund Samuel Building, a 10-minute walk south of the museum, is a showcase for early Canadian artists and artisans. The collection displays examples of artistry from eastern Canada in thematic room settings featuring 18th- and 19th-century Canadian furnishings. Glass, silver, woodenware, and ceramics as well as toys, weathervanes, and paintings are on view. The famed McCrea models of buildings, farm implements, and tools provide a miniature representation of early rural Ontario.
Admission: Free.
Open: Mon–Sat 10am–5pm, Sun 1–5pm. **Closed:** Christmas and New Year's days. **Subway:** Queen's Park. Please note that the collection will be moving to the ROM in spring '94. Currently it is closed.

HOCKEY HALL OF FAME, 30 Yonge St., at Front in BCE Place. Tel. 416/360-7735.

Ice-hockey fans will thrill to see the original Stanley Cup (donated in 1893 by Lord Stanley of Preston), a replica of the Montréal Canadiens' dressing room, Terry Sawchuck's goalie gear, Newsy Lalonde's skates, and the stick that Max Bentley used, along with photographs of the personalities and great moments in ice hockey history. Interactive displays and videos make it fun for all.

Admission: Hockey Hall of Fame $7.50 adults, $5.50 seniors and children 13 and under.

Open: Mon–Wed 9am–6pm, Thurs–Fri 9am–9:30pm, Sat 9am–6pm, Sun 10am–6pm.

MARINE MUSEUM, Exhibition Place. Tel. 416/392-1765.

This museum interprets the history of Toronto Harbour and its relation to the Great Lakes. From May to October, visitors can also board the fully restored 1932 *Ned Hanlan*, the last steam tugboat to sail on Lake Ontario.

Admission: $3.25 adults, $2.50 children 13–18 and seniors, $2.25 children under 13, free for children 5 and under.

Open: Tues–Fri 9:30am–5pm, Sat–Sun and holidays noon–5pm. **Directions:** Take 511 streetcar southbound from Bathurst.

MCLAUGHLIN PLANETARIUM, 100 Queen's Park. Tel. 416/586-5736.

The McLaughlin Planetarium, located beside the Royal Ontario Museum, offers exhibits and three or four new audiovisual presentations in its Theatre of the Stars throughout the year. The animated Astrocentre gallery on the second floor explores and displays the development of astronomy. One of the gallery's chief attractions is the solar telescope, which actually allows the visitor to observe the sun, "live," as it appears at that very moment.

Admission: $5.50 adults, $3.50 seniors and students, $2.75 children 14 and under. $8.50 for special laser shows.

Open: Hours vary. Call ahead for show times. **Closed:** Mon in winter. **Subway:** Museum or St. George.

MUSEUM FOR TEXTILES, 55 Centre Ave. Tel. 416/599-5515.

This fascinating museum displays not only what you'd expect—fine Oriental rugs—but also tapestries from all over the world including African story-telling cloth.

Admission: $2.50.

Open: Mon–Fri 11am–5pm, Sat–Sun noon–5pm.

NEIGHBORHOODS

CHINATOWN Stretching along Dundas Street from Bay Street to Spadina Avenue, and north and south along Spadina, Chinatown, home to many of Toronto's 350,000 Chinese, is a great area for browsing in fascinating shops and eating. Even the street signs are in Chinese here.

If you're interested in things Asian, then do go into **Dragon City,** a large shopping mall on Spadina that's staffed and shopped by Chinese. Here you'll find all kinds of stores, some selling exotic Chinese preserves like cuttlefish, lemon ginger, whole mango, ginseng, and antler, and others specializing in Asian books, tapes, and records, as well as fashions and foods. Downstairs, a whole court is given over to a number of Korean, Indonesian, Chinese, and Japanese fast-food restaurants.

As you stroll through Chinatown, stop at the **Kim Moon Bakery** on Dundas Street West (tel. 416/977-1933) and pick up some Chinese pastries and/or a pork bun. Or go to one of the tea stores. A walk through Chinatown at night is especially exciting. The sidewalks are filled with people, families, and youths, and neon lights shimmer everywhere. You'll pass windows where ducks hang gleaming, noodle houses, record stores selling the top 10 in Chinese, and trading companies filled with all kinds of Asian produce. Another stopping place might be the **New Asia Supermarket** (tel. 416/591-9314) around the corner from Dundas at 293–299 Spadina Ave.

QUEEN STREET WEST This is a great street to wander along. There's a marvelous collection of small avant-garde restaurants, entertainment spots, and bars along its sidewalks. Browse in the few art galleries; the one or two surviving

> ## ⭐ FROMMER'S FAVORITE TORONTO EXPERIENCES
>
> **A Picnic on the Toronto Islands** A short ferry ride will transport you to another world of lagoons and rush-lined backwaters, miles away from the urban tarmac—a world of houseboats and bicycles, a place to stroll beside the weeping willows.
>
> **A Day at Harbourfront** Bring a model boat; watch artisans blowing glass; take a sailing lesson; tour the harbor; shop the quay and the antique mart—and this is just a beginning.
>
> **A Day at the Beaches** Stroll along the boardwalk, picnic in the adjacent parkland and gardens, and browse the stores one block from the beach.
>
> **An Afternoon at Kleinburg** A unique Canadian and Toronto experience—the Group of Seven landscape artists' work displayed in an idyllic setting.

antiquarian and secondhand bookstores; nostalgia record stores selling hundreds of 45s and other records from the '50s, '60s, and '70s; the outright junk shops; the kitchen supply stores; and all kinds of fascinating emporiums.

YORKVILLE This is the name given to the area that stretches north of Bloor Street, between Avenue Road and Bay Street. In 1853 Yorkville became a village, surrounded then by trees and meadows; in the 1960s it became Toronto's Haight Ashbury, the mecca for young suburban runaways; and in the 1980s it became the focus of the chic, who shopped at the famous-name boutiques (Hermès, Courrèges, Fabiani, Cartier, Turnbull & Asser, names with more than simply cachet), and occupied the restored town houses, as well as the art galleries, cafés, and restaurants.

Stroll around and browse; sit out and have an iced coffee in the sun at one of the cafés on Yorkville Avenue and watch the parade go by.

Some good vantage points can be had at Hemingway's or any one of many cafés along Yorkville Avenue, all on the south side of the street. Most of these cafés have happy hours from 4 to 7 or 8pm.

Make sure you wander through the labyrinths of Hazelton Lanes between Avenue Road and Hazelton Avenue, where you'll find a maze of shops and offices clustered around an outdoor court in the center of a building that's topped with apartments—the most sought-after in the city.

And while you're in the neighborhood (especially if you're an architecture buff), take a look at the red-brick building on Bloor Street at the end of Yorkville Avenue, which houses the Metro Library. If more libraries had been built like this one in the past, then perhaps study and learning would have come out of the dim and musty closets and into the world where they belong. Step inside—a pool and a waterfall gently screen out the street noise and pine fencelike partitions undulate through the area like those you find along the sand dunes. Step farther inside and the space opens dramatically to the sky. Every corner is flooded with light and air. I envy the citizens of Toronto their designer-architect Raymond Moriyama.

MIRVISH VILLAGE One of Toronto's most famous characters is Honest Ed Mirvish, who originally started his career in the '50s with his no-frills shopping at the store at the corner of Markham Street (one block west of Bathurst) and Bloor Street, where signs screaming bargains leap at you from everywhere. Among other things, Ed Mirvish rose to save the Royal Alexandra Theatre from demolition, established a whole row of adjacent restaurants for theater patrons, and finally created this block-long complex with numerous art galleries and restaurants. His latest triumph was, of course, the purchase and renovation of London's Old Vic.

Stop by and browse, and don't forget to step into Honest Ed's on the corner.

ORGANIZED TOURS

One easy way to see four of Toronto's major attractions is to ride the double-decker buses operated by **Grayline Tours,** 610 Bay St. (tel. 416/351-3311). One- ($10) and two-hour ($18) tours are given with on/off privileges at two places along the route.

    Gray Line Boat Tours, 5 Queen's Quay West (tel. 416/364-2412), offers 60-minute cruises of the harbor and islands in glass-covered boats modeled after Amsterdam's canal cruisers. Tours leave hourly (late April to late October) from either the foot of Yonge Street right beside the Harbour Castle Westin or from the foot of York and Queen's Quay (Harbourfront). You can cruise in and out of the lagoons spying Canada geese and other wild fowl during the day, or at night (9 and 10pm) when the star-spangled skyline unfurls before you. Adults pay $10; seniors and students, $8; children 4 to 14, $6; families of 4, $22; under-4s, free.

    Similar harbor tours are also operated by **Toronto Tours Ltd.,** 134 Jarvis St. Boats depart from 145 Queen's Quay West (tel. 416/869-1372), from May to October. Adults pay $11.95; seniors, $9.95; children, $5.95.

SPECIAL EVENTS

Call the Metro Toronto Convention & Visitors Association at 416/203-2600 for additional information on festivals and events. The prime events and dates to remember when planning a visit to Toronto are the following:

    The big event in May is the nine-day **Children's Festival,** featuring more than 30 international entertainment troupes—acrobats, mimes, comedians, storytellers, theater companies, and puppeteers.

    In June, the ✪ **Metro Caravan** (tel. 416/977-0466) celebrates the ethnic life of the city for nine days. The food and cultural life and entertainments of the many different communities—from Armenian to Vietnamese—are featured in more than 50 pavilions around town.

    In late June or early July, the **Queen's Plate** is run at Woodbine Racetrack. Begun in 1859, it is the oldest stakes race in North America.

    Other big June events include the **duMaurier Jazz Festival** and the **Mariposa Music Festival** featuring more than 200 top performers of folk, R & B, and blues. Also in late June/early July the **Fringe Theater Festival** lets anyone enjoy a broad variety of experimental and new drama for 10 days.

    In July the **Molson Indy** is run at the Exhibition Place circuit on the third weekend usually.

    At the end of July or the beginning of August, Toronto's Caribbean community celebrates with ✪ **Caribana,** which features moonlight cruises, carnival balls, music, dancing, picnics, and tropical fun. High point of the celebrations is the Saturday grand parade, when the city throbs to the beat of steel drums, as the colorful befeathered and sequined retinue snakes its way downtown, singing and dancing in best Mardi Gras fashion.

    In August the big 20-day event is the **Canadian National Exhibition,** at Exhibition Place, featuring midway rides, display buildings, free shows, and grandstand performers. It was first staged, by the way, in 1878. For information contact Canadian National Exhibition, Exhibition Place, Toronto, ON, M6K 3C3 (tel. 416/393-6000). On Labor Day the **Canadian Air Show** is spectacular; the Snowbirds, the Canadian Air Force Performance Team, performs. Good vantage points are from the islands or Ontario Place.

    Also in August, the **World of Music, Art and Dance (WOMAD)** brings a host of international cultural performances to Harbourfront.

    In September the ✪ **Festival of Festivals** is a major film festival, which is followed in October by the **International Festival of Authors** at Harbourfront.

    In November the ✪ **Royal Agricultural Winter Fair** is a major event that has been held since 1929. At this sort of huge state fair the largest fruits and vegetables are on display, along with crafts, farm machinery, and livestock. The royal event is the accompanying horse show traditionally attended by a member of the British royal family.

COOL FOR KIDS
TOP CITY ATTRACTIONS

Look under "The Top Attractions" and "More Attractions," above, for the following Toronto-area attractions that have major appeal to kids of all ages. I've summarized them here in what I think is the most logical order, at least from a kid's point of view (the first five, though, really belong in a dead heat).

Ontario Science Centre *(see p. 456)* Kids race to be the first at this paradise of fun hands-on games, experiments, and push-button demonstrations—700 of 'em.

Canada's Wonderland *(see p. 457)* The kids love the rides in the theme park. But watch out for those video games, which they also love—an unanticipated extra cost.

Harbourfront *(see p. 448)* Kaleidoscope is an ongoing program of creative crafts, active games, and special events on weekends and holidays. There is also a summer pond, winter ice skating, and a crafts studio.

Ontario Place *(see p. 448)* Waterslides, a huge Cinesphere, a futuristic pod, and other entertainments are the big hits at this recreational/cultural park on three artificial islands on the edge of Lake Ontario.

Metro Zoo *(see p. 456)* One of the best in the world, modeled after San Diego's—the animals in this 710-acre park really do live in a natural environment.

Toronto Islands–Centreville *(see p. 449)* Riding a ferry to this turn-of-the-century amusement park is part of the fun.

CN Tower *(see p. 452)* Especially for the "Tour of the Universe."

Royal Ontario Museum *(see p. 453)* The top hit is always the dinosaurs.

McLaughlin Planetarium *(see p. 462)* For special shows and stargazing.

Fort York *(see p. 460)* For its reenactments of battle drills, musket and cannon firing, and musical marches with fife and drum.

Hockey Hall of Fame *(see p. 461)* Especially the interactive video displays.

Black Creek Pioneer Village *(see p. 461)* For craft and other demonstrations.

Casa Loma *(see p. 458)* For the stables and the fantasy rooms.

Art Gallery of Ontario *(see p. 452)* For its hands-on exhibit.

A ZOO & FARM

RIVERDALE FARM, 201 Winchester St., east of Parliament, north of Gerrard. Tel. 416/392-6794.

Idyllically situated on the edge of the Don Valley ravine, this early 19th-century farm is a favorite with small tots, who enjoy watching the cows and pigs and petting the other farm animals. Historic buildings, gardens, implement displays, and a large variety of livestock make for a surprising visit to the country in the heart of the city.

Admission: Free.

Open: Daily 9am–4, 5, or 6pm, depending on the season.

OUT-OF-TOWN ATTRACTIONS

AFRICAN LION SAFARI, R.R. No. 1, Cambridge, ON. Tel. 519/623-2620.

Kids enjoy driving through this 500-acre wildlife park, sighting lions and other game. The entrance fee entitles visitors to drive through the park, ride the *African Queen*, take the scenic railway, and see animal performances. There are playgrounds, too, for toddlers, as well as a water playground. Bring bathing suits.

Admission: $14 adults, $12 seniors and youths, $10 children 3–12.

Open: Apr 1–Oct 31 daily 9am–5:30pm. **Directions:** Take Highway 401 to Highway 6 south.

CHUDLEIGH'S, P.O. Box 176 (Hwy. 25 north of Hwy. 401), Milton, ON. Tel. 416/826-1252.

A day here will introduce the kids to life on a farm. They'll enjoy the hay rides; pony rides; sleigh rides; and, in season, the apple picking and sugaring off of the maple trees. All of the produce is on sale, too, in the bake shop and fruit-and-vegetable markets.
Admission: Free.
Open: July 1–Oct daily 9am–7pm; Nov–June daily 10am–5pm.

CULLEN GARDENS AND MINIATURE VILLAGE, Taunton Rd., Whitby, ON. Tel. 416/294-7965.
The miniature village (made to one-half scale) has great appeal. The 27 acres of gardens and the shopping and live entertainment add to the fun.
Admission: $9.50 adults, $6.95 seniors, $3.95 children.
Open: Daily 9am–8pm. **Closed:** Mid-Jan to early Apr.

WILD WATER KINGDOM, Finch Ave., 1 mile west of Hwy. 427, Brampton, ON. Tel. 416/369-9453 or 416/794-0565.
Kids love this huge water theme park complete with a 20,000-square-foot wave pool, tube slides, speed slides, giant hot tubs, and this year's thriller, the Cyclone water ride. In between they can use the batting cages or practice on the mini-golf circuit.
Admission: $15 adults, $13 children 4–9 and seniors.
Open: May to mid-June Sat–Sun 10am–6:30pm; mid-June to Labor Day daily 10am–11pm (water rides, to 8pm).

ENTERTAINMENT

ROY THOMSON HALL CUSHION CONCERTS, 60 Simcoe St. Tel. 416/ 593-4828.
Music is presented in the lobby of one of Toronto's premier concert halls. Kids love to settle down into the cushions and tuck into the doughnuts and meet the artists after the performance. Concerts are usually given for 4- to 6-year-olds and 9- to 11-year-olds. October to April only. Call for information.
Admission: $8.
Subway: St. Andrews.

YOUNG PEOPLE'S THEATRE, 165 Front St. East, at Sherbourne St. Tel. 416/862-2222 (box office) or 416/363-5131 (administration).
Devoted to the entertainment of young people. The season runs from November to May. Call for information.
Subway: Union.

2. SPORTS/RECREATION

Some wag once said that there's only one really religious place in Toronto and that's **Maple Leaf Gardens,** 60 Carlton St. (tel. 416/977-1641), where the city's ice hockey team, the Maple Leafs, wield their sticks to the delight and screaming enthusiasm of fans. Tickets are nigh impossible to attain because many are sold by subscription and as soon as the remainder go on sale, there are lines around the block. Your only hope is to find a scalper.

SkyDome, on Front Street beside the CN Tower, is the home of the Blue Jays baseball team, World Series champs in 1992 and 1993; the Toronto Argonauts football team; and the Toronto Blizzard soccer team. For information, write to the Toronto Blue Jays Baseball Club, P.O. Box 7777, Adelaide Street Post Office, Toronto, ON, M5C 2K7 (tel. 416/341-1000; for ticket information 416/341-1111.)

Racing takes place at **Woodbine Racetrack,** at Rexdale Boulevard at Highway 427, Etobicoke (tel. 416/675-6110), famous for the Queen's Plate (contested in July) and the Rothman's Ltd. International, a world classic turf race, contested in October.

For information on golf courses, tennis, swimming pools, beaches, and picnic areas, call **Metro Parks** (tel. 416/392-6641 or 416/392-8186 Monday through Friday).

3. EVENING ENTERTAINMENT

Toronto has the National Ballet of Canada, the Canadian Opera Company, and the Toronto Symphony, two large arts centers, a concert hall, theaters galore (with a second-only-to-Broadway reputation), plus enough bars, clubs, cabarets, and other entertainment to keep anyone spinning. For local happenings, check *Where Toronto* and *Toronto Life,* as well as the *Globe and Mail,* the *Toronto Star,* and the *Toronto Sun.*

There are half-price tickets available at **Five Star ticket outlets** for many plays and dinner theater performances. There is a Five Star booth at Yonge and Dundas, right on the sidewalk. Tickets are cash only, and sold on the day of performance.

THE PERFORMING ARTS
MAJOR MULTI-PURPOSE PERFORMANCE VENUES

MASSEY HALL, 178 Victoria St. Tel. 416/363-7301, or 416/872-4255 for tickets and information.

A Canadian musical landmark, Massey Hall is a 2,757-seat auditorium that today hosts a variety of programming, including classical, rock, ethnic, and theatrical presentations.

Prices: Tickets $20–$75.

O'KEEFE CENTRE, 1 Front St. East, Toronto, ON, M5E 1B2. Tel. 416/393-7469, or 416/872-2262 for ticket sales.

With its 60- by 130-foot stage and 3,223-seat theater, O'Keefe Centre is home to the Canadian Opera Company and the National Ballet of Canada. It also presents the very best in live entertainment with hit Broadway musicals, variety and family shows, international superstars, comedians, and dance companies. Tickets may be purchased at the box office or by phone for which there is a service charge.

Prelude, the O'Keefe Centre café, is available for pretheater dining. Call 416/393-7478 for reservations.

Prices: Opera and ballet tickets $10–$88; other shows $17–$60, depending on the attraction.

ROY THOMSON HALL, 60 Simcoe St. Tel. 416/593-4822, or 416/593-4828 for tickets and information.

Toronto's premier concert hall presents top international performers of classical music, jazz, big bands, and comedy. It is also home to the Toronto Symphony Orchestra, which performs here September through June (the group plays at Ontario Place in July).

Designed to give the audience extraordinary intimacy with every performer, no seat in this 2,812-seat hall is more than 107 feet from the stage. The exterior of the building itself is spectacular—rose-colored, petal-shaped, and enveloped in a huge glass canopy that's reflective by day and transparent by night.

Prices: Tickets $18–$75.

ST. LAWRENCE CENTRE, 27 Front St. East. Tel. 416/366-7723.

Other classical music concerts, recitals, and chamber music featuring internationally famous artists are given at the St. Lawrence Centre, most often in the Jane Mallett Theatre.

Prices: Tickets $20–$60.

OPERA, DANCE & SYMPHONY

CANADIAN OPERA COMPANY, 227 Front St. East, Toronto, ON, M5A 1E8. Tel. 416/363-6671 (administration), or 416/872-2262 for tickets.

The Canadian Opera Company began life in 1950 with 10 performances of three operas. It now stages eight different operas a season at the O'Keefe Centre and the Elgin Theatre from September to June.

Prices: Tickets $25–$95.

NATIONAL BALLET OF CANADA, 157 King St. East, Toronto, ON, M5C 1G9. Tel. 416/362-1041, or 416/366-4846 for information on programs and prices.

Most famous of all Toronto's cultural contributions is perhaps the National Ballet of Canada. It was launched at Eaton Auditorium in Toronto on November 12, 1951, by English ballerina Celia Franca, who served initially as director, dancer, choreographer, and teacher. Over the years the company has achieved great renown, and among the highlights of its history have been the invitation to perform at Expo '70 in Osaka, Japan, its 1973 New York debut (which featured Nureyev's full-length *Sleeping Beauty*), and Baryshnikov's appearance with the company soon after his defection in 1974.

Besides its tours of Canada and its annual summer season at the Metropolitan Opera House in New York, the company performs its regular seasons in Toronto at O'Keefe Centre in the fall, winter, and spring, as well as summer appearances before enormous crowds at the open-air theater at Ontario Place.

Included in their repertoire are such classics as *Swan Lake* and *Napoli,* a variety of modern works including Glen Tetley's *Sphinx* and Kenneth MacMillan's *Elite Syncopations,* together with a growing number of works especially choreographed for the company.

Prices: Tickets $14–$90.

PREMIERE DANCE THEATRE, 207 Queen's Quay West. Tel. 416/973-4000.

Toronto has a theater specifically designed for dance at Queen's Quay West. For information on productions and the dance series, phone the Harbourfront box office, at the number given above, from 11am daily.

The leading contemporary dance company is Toronto Dance Theatre (tel. 416/967-1365). Tickets are usually $23 to $26.

Prices: Tickets $20–$30.

TAFELMUSIK BAROQUE ORCHESTRA, 427 Bloor St. West. Tel. 416/964-6337 for tickets, or 416/964-9562 for administration.

This group plays baroque music on authentic historic instruments, giving a series of concerts at Trinity United Church.

Prices: Call for dates, programs, and ticket prices.

TORONTO MENDELSSOHN CHOIR, 60 Simcoe St. Tel. 416/598-0422.

A world-renowned choir, this group first performed in Massey Hall in 1895.

Prices: Call for dates, programs, and ticket prices.

TORONTO SYMPHONY ORCHESTRA, 60 Simcoe St. Tel. 416/593-4828 for tickets, 593-7769 for administrative offices.

The symphony performs at Roy Thomson Hall from September through June. The repertoire ranges from classics to pop and new Canadian works. In June and July, concerts are also given at outdoor venues throughout the city.

Prices: Call for dates, programs, and ticket prices.

THEATER

Toronto has a very active theater scene.

The city's big theaters include the O'Keefe Centre, the St. Lawrence Centre for the Arts, the Royal Alexandra Theatre, fondly referred to as the Royal Alex, the Princess of Wales Theatre, and the Elgin and the Pantages theaters. Small theater groups also thrive in the city producing exciting offbeat drama—a burgeoning Toronto equivalent to Off-Broadway. As there are a great number of these smaller companies, I have picked out only the few whose reputations have been established.

BAYVIEW PLAYHOUSE, 1605 Bayview Ave. Tel. 416/481-6191.

The Bayview Playhouse has a 500-seat theater presenting a wide variety of entertainment. One of its most successful productions was *Godspell,* as well as the more recent *Cloud 9.*

Prices: Tickets $15–$40.

CANADIAN STAGE COMPANY, 26 Berkeley St. Tel. 416/366-7723 for tickets, or 416/367-8243 for administration.

The Canadian Stage Company performs comedy, drama, and musicals in the St. Lawrence Centre, and also presents free summer Shakespeare performances in High Park. Call for dates and programs.

Prices: Tickets $18–$40; discount tickets for seniors and students sometimes available 30 minutes before the performance.

THE ELGIN AND WINTER GARDEN THEATRES, 189 Yonge St. Tel. 416/872-5555.

Two other old theaters now vie with the Alex for attention. The Elgin and Winter Garden Theatres, which opened their doors in 1913, were recently restored to their original gilded glory at a cost of $29 million and are the only double-decker theaters functioning today.

The downstairs Elgin is the larger, seating 1,500 and featuring lavish gilded and domed ceiling and boxes. The Winter Garden is smaller and decorated to resemble a garden even to the beech-bough ceiling. The Royal Shakespeare Company has performed here and several major Broadway shows have opened in both.

Prices: Tickets $15–$75.

FACTORY THEATRE, 125 Bathurst St. Tel. 416/864-9971.

Started in 1970, the experimental Factory Theatre is the home of Canadian playwriting, where promising new authors get the chance to develop and showcase their works. In the past it has presented festivals of Canadian plays in London and New York.

Prices: Tickets $10–$20.

O'KEEFE CENTRE, 1 Front St. East. Tel. 416/393-7469.

O'Keefe Centre presents such musicals as *Man of La Mancha* and *Anne of Green Gables* when it's not showcasing diverse artists such as Joan Armatrading and Phoebe Snow.

Prices: Tickets $19–$75, depending on the star or the show.

PANTAGES THEATRE, 244 Victoria St. Tel. 416/872-2222.

The Pantages Theatre opened shortly after the Elgin and Winter Garden in 1920 and it too has been restored to the tune of $18 million. Another historic gem, it hosted *Phantom of the Opera* when it opened.

Prices: Tickets $60–$95.

THE MAJOR CONCERT & PERFORMANCE HALL BOX OFFICES

For TicketMaster's telecharge service, call 416/872-1111.

Elgin and Winter Garden Theatres, 189–191 Yonge St. (near Queen Street; tel. 416/872-5555).
Massey Hall, 178 Victoria St. (at Shuter Street; tel. 416/593-4828 or 416/872-4255).
O'Keefe Centre, 1 Front St. East (tel. 416/872-2262).
Pantages Theatre, 244 Victoria St. (near Shuter Street; tel. 416/872-2222).
Premier Dance Theatre, in the York Quay Centre, 207 Queen's Quay West (tel. 416/973-4000).
Royal Alexandra Theatre, 260 King St. West (tel. 416/872-3333).
Roy Thomson Hall, 60 Simcoe St. (tel. 416/593-4828).
SkyDome, 1 Blue Jays Way West (tel. 416/341-3663).
St. Lawrence Centre for the Arts, 27 Front St. East (tel. 416/366-7723).
Young People's Theatre, 165 Front St. East (tel. 416/862-2222).

PRINCESS OF WALES THEATRE, 300 King St. West. Tel. 416/872-1212 for tickets and information.
This brand-new theatre built by the father-and-son team of David and Ed Mirvish opened in May 1993 with *Miss Saigon*. The theater itself is remarkable, featuring more than 10,000 square feet of original artwork created by Frank Stella. It seats 2,000 and boasts one of the largest stages in existence.

ROYAL ALEXANDRA THEATRE, 260 King St. West, Toronto, ON, M5V 1H9. Tel. 416/593-4211, or 416/872-3333 for tickets and information.
Shows from Broadway migrate to the Royal Alexandra Theatre. Tickets are often snapped up by subscription buyers, so your best bet is to write ahead to the theater at the above address.
The theater itself is quite a spectacle. Constructed in 1907, it owes its current lease on life to owner Ed Mirvish, who refurbished it in the 1960s (as well as the surrounding area). Inside it's a riot of plush reds, gold brocade, and baroque ornamentation, with a seating capacity of 1,493. Apparently, you're wise to avoid the second balcony and also sitting under the circle.
Prices: Tickets $40–$90.

ST. LAWRENCE CENTRE FOR THE ARTS, 27 Front St. East. Tel. 416/366-7723.
There are two prime tenants of the St. Lawrence Centre for the Arts—the Canadian Stage Company (tel. 416/368-3110) and Theatre Plus. Both present a season of drama including both classics and Canadian plays.
Prices: Tickets $33–$50. For many shows, remaining seats are available to seniors and students 30 minutes before curtain at discounted prices.

TARRAGON THEATRE, 30 Bridgman Ave. Tel. 416/536-5018.
Located near Dupont and Bathurst, the Tarragon Theatre opened in the early '70s and continues to produce original works by Canadian playwrights—John Murrell, Mavis Gallant, Judith Thompson, and Michael Ondaatje, for example—and an occasional classic like Chekhov's *Uncle Vanya* or a Broadway play like Marsha Norman's *'night, Mother*. It's a small, intimate theater where you can get coffee and cookies in the foyer.
Prices: Tickets $13–$22. On Sun you pay what you can afford.

THEATRE PASSE MURAILLE, 16 Ryerson Ave. Tel. 416/363-2416.
Theatre Passe Muraille started in the late '60s when a pool of actors began experimenting and improvising original Canadian material. Set in another warehouse, there's a main space seating 270, and a back space for 70. Take the Queen Street streetcar to Bathurst.
Prices: Pay what you can afford to $25.

TORONTO TRUCK THEATRE, 94 Belmont St. Tel. 416/922-0084.
The attraction here is Agatha Christie's *The Mousetrap*, now in its 17th year. It's Canada's longest-running show.
Prices: Tickets $15–$20.

THE CLUB & MUSIC SCENE
DINNER THEATER, CABARET & COMEDY

In addition to the offerings listed below, other comedy clubs include the **Big City Improv,** at 534 Queen St. West (tel. 416/867-8707), and the **Laugh Resort,** 26 Lombard St. (tel. 416/364-5233), which also has dinner packages.
At **Harper's Dinner Theatre,** 26 Lombard St. (tel. 416/863-6223), it's a combination magic/music and comedy show plus dinner.
For the art of female impersonation there's **La Cage Dinner Theatre,** 278 Yonge St. (tel. 416/364-5200). For an Elizabethan feast head out to **His Majesty's Feast** at the Lakeshore Inn, 1926 Lakeshore Blvd. (tel. 416/769-1165).
Musicals are the specialty at the **Limelight Theatre,** 2026 Yonge St. (tel. 416/482-5200); tickets are $50 weekdays and Sunday, $55 Friday, and $60 on Saturday for dinner and show.

SECOND CITY, 110 Lombard St. Tel. 416/863-1162.

One of Toronto's zaniest theater groups, specializing in improvisational comedy, this is the company that nurtured Dan Aykroyd and Bill Murray, and continues to turn out talented young comedians. The skits are always funny and topical. Its home is an old firehall that now houses a theater seating 200 and a restaurant. Second City has had a marked impact on Canadian entertainment with its various workshops, touring company, seasoned resident company, and internationally syndicated TV series.

Admission: Dinner and show $35 Mon–Thurs, $38 Fri, $42 Sat. Show only $14 Mon–Thurs, $18 Fri, $20 Sat.

UKRAINIAN CARAVAN, 5245 Dundas St. West, at Kipling. Tel. 416/ 231-7447.

For an evening of Cossack dance, song, and comic repartee, head for the Ukrainian Caravan. Dinner might consist of such Ukrainian specialties as chicken Kiev, kielbasa, and pirogies.

Admission: Dinner and show $22–$35.

MARK BRESLIN'S YUK-YUK'S KOMEDY KABARET, 1280 Bay St. Tel. 416/967-6425.

Situated in the heart of Yorkville, Yuk-Yuk's occupies an ideal location for amateur and professional stand-up comics to puncture a few contemporary social pretensions in a stream of totally unpredictable monologue. Comic Mark Breslin founded the place following the trend of New York's Catch a Rising Star and Los Angeles's The Comedy Store. Besides the comics, other bizarre and hilariously grotesque troupes find their way to this spotlight. There's another Yuk-Yuk's uptown at 2335 Yonge (tel. 416/967-6425).

Admission: $8 weeknights, $13 Fri, $15 Sat. Dinner and show Fri $33, Sat $35. Reservations needed.

JAZZ

The city is really big on jazz—especially on Saturday afternoons when many a hotel lounge or restaurant lays on an afternoon of rip-roaring rhythm.

ALBERT'S HALL, upstairs at the Brunswick House, 481 Bloor St. West. Tel. 416/964-2242.

There's always a good smörgåsbord of '30s, '40s, Chicago-, and New Orleans-style jazz here, nightly from 9pm. It also has the funkiest blues in the city—from names like Buddy Guy and Junior Wells, and John Lee Hooker.

Admission: $6 weekends, $3 Thurs.

BEN WICKS, 424 Parliament. Tel. 416/961-9425.

At Ben Wicks, there's jazz, folk, and blues on Saturday from 8pm to midnight.

Admission: Free.

CHELSEA BUN, at the Delta Chelsea Inn, 33 Gerrard St. West. Tel. 416/595-1975.

The Chelsea Bun is a good spot for Saturday-afternoon jazz. Open Monday to Saturday from 5pm to 1am.

Admission: $5 Fri–Sat.

GEORGE'S SPAGHETTI HOUSE, 290 Dundas St. East, at Sherbourne. Tel. 416/923-9887.

George's Spaghetti House features local jazz groups, including Moe Koffman and his quintet. There's no cover if you sit at the bar.

Admission: $5 weekends, $4 Tues–Thurs.

MONTREAL BISTRO/JAZZ CLUB, 65 Sherbourne St. Tel. 416/363-0179.

A cool atmosphere for an array of jazz artists—Ray Bryant, Arlene Smith, Joe Sealy, and Velvet Glove have all appeared here. Entertainment begins at 9pm. Great, too, because the bistro is next door and you can select from its menu. Open 5pm to 1am Monday to Saturday.

Admission: Depends on the band.

TOP O' THE SENATOR, 249 Victoria. Tel. 416/364-7517.

Toronto's swankiest jazz club. A long and narrow room with a bar down one side and a distinct '30s look, it's a great place to hear fine jazz, including local favorite Moe Koffman. The atmosphere is enhanced by the funky old movie-theater seats set around tables, the couches alongside the performance area, and portraits of band leaders and artists on the walls. Open Tuesday to Saturday.

Admission: $10 Fri–Sat, $8 Thurs.

COUNTRY, FOLK, ROCK & REGGAE

BAMBOO, 312 Queen St. West. Tel. 416/593-5771.

Bamboo, decked out in Caribbean style and colors, offers an exciting assortment of reggae, calypso, salsa, and world beat sounds. The club takes up one side of the space, while a small restaurant decorated with masks from New Guinea occupies a small side area.

The menu mixes Caribbean, Indonesian, and Thai specialties. Thai spicy noodles are really popular, blending shrimp, chicken, tofu, and egg. Lamb and potato rôti, and Caribbean curry chicken served with gado gado, banana, and steamed rice are other examples. Music starts at 10pm. Drinks run $4 to $5. Subway: Osgoode or Queen; then a streetcar west.

Admission: $5 Mon–Wed, $7 Thurs, $10 Fri–Sat.

BERLIN, 2335 Yonge St. Tel. 416/489-7777.

One of the more sophisticated clubs in the city, Berlin attracts a well-heeled crowd ranging from 25 to 50 years old. Things get started at 9pm and spin until 3:30am Tuesday and Thursday to Saturday.

Admission: $7 Tues, $3 Thurs, $8 Fri, $10 Sat.

BIRCHMOUNT TAVERN, 462 Birchmount. Tel. 416/698-4115.

The city's longtime country venue attracts a broad range of Canadian and American artists. The music goes on Thursday to Sunday from 9pm to 1am.

Admission: $3 weekends.

CHICK 'N' DELI, 744 Mount Pleasant Rd. Tel. 416/489-3363.

At Chick 'n' Deli, south of Eglinton Avenue, Tiffany-style lamps and oak set the background for Top 40 or rhythm and blues every night. The dance floor is always packed.

Chicken wings and barbecue are the specialties, along with nachos, salads, and a selection of sandwiches—club, corned beef, etc. On Saturday afternoon the sounds are Dixieland. Entertainment begins at 9pm on Monday to Friday (from 5 to 7pm and 9pm to 1am on Sunday and from 3:45 to 7pm and 9pm to 1am on Saturday).

Admission: Free.

EL MOCAMBO, 464 Spadina Ave. Tel. 416/922-1570.

El Mocambo is the famous bar where the Stones chose to do their gig back in the '70s. It's still a rock-and-roll landmark.

Admission: Varies, depending on the band.

FREE TIMES CAFE, 320 College St. Tel. 416/967-1078.

The Free Times Café has a back room that functions as one of the city's regular folk venues. The music usually starts at 9:30pm daily.

Admission: $2–$10.

HORIZONS, 301 Front St. West. Tel. 416/601-4721.

What must be one of the world's highest nightclubs swings atop the CN Tower. Horizons is open daily from 8:30pm.

Admission: No cover, but admission to the tower is $12.

HORSESHOE TAVERN, 368 Queen St. West. Tel. 416/598-4753.

An old traditional Toronto venue, the Horseshoe Tavern attracts a cross section of people from age 20 to 60. Rock-and-roll daily attracts a hard-driving crowd. Bands go on at 10pm.

Admission: $4–$10.

LOOSE MOOSE, 220 Adelaide St. West (between Simcoe and Duncan Sts). Tel. 416/971-5252.
This is a crowd-pleaser for a younger set who like the multilevel dance floors, the DJ, and the booze and schmooze. Starts every night at 9pm.
Admission: Free.

OPERA HOUSE, 735 Queen St. East, at Broadview. Tel. 416/466-0313.
This club offers a variety of sounds from hip-hop and retro to rock, metal, and even disco. DJ and live entertainment. Call for programming.

STILIFE, 217 Richmond St. West. Tel. 416/593-6116.
Stilife occupies a weird cavelike space, with a somewhat spooky atmosphere, where the young, avant-garde, fashion-conscious crowd dances or gathers in the quiet back room. Thursday and Friday, according to Torontonians, are the best nights. Saturday is Scarborough night. Action starts around 11pm.
Admission: $6 Tues–Wed, $7 Thurs, $10 Fri, $12 Sat.

THE BAR/PUB SCENE

First, let me repeat some of my favorite hotel bars. The fairly formal **Chartroom,** at the Harbour Castle Westin, 1 Harbour Sq. (tel. 416/869-1600), has a good view of the lake and the islands ferry. For a cozy fireside conversation in winter, or a summer cocktail with a view, I like the **Roof Lounge** at the Park Plaza, 4 Avenue Rd. (tel. 416/924-5471). The **Consort Bar** at the King Edward Hotel, 37 King St. East (tel. 416/863-9700), is also comfortable, as is **La Serre,** at the Four Seasons, 21 Avenue Rd. (tel. 416/964-0411). The **Chelsea Bun,** at the Delta Chelsea Inn, 33 Gerrard St. West (tel. 416/595-1975), has a fine selection of single-malt whiskies and good musical entertainment. If you prefer a pubby atmosphere, there's **Dick Turpin's,** at the Royal York, 100 Front St. West (tel. 416/368-2511), or the **Good Queen Bess,** in the Sheraton Centre, 123 Queen St. West (tel. 416/361-1000).
And now for the independents.

ALICE FAZOOLI'S, 294 Adelaide St. West. Tel. 416/979-1910.
Baseball art and memorabilia, including a full-scale model of an outfielder making a wall catch, fills this large bar and dining room. It's always jam-packed with an older business crowd either quaffing in the bar or feasting in the back on crabs cooked in many different styles, pizza, pasta, and raw-bar specialties.

AMSTERDAM, 133 John St. Tel. 416/595-8201.
This is the downtown spot where young professionals and the financial crowd make the scene at the end of the day. In winter they jam into the huge warehouse space, with its exposed plumbing, and in summer they cluster around the tables on the large outdoor terrace. It's crowded, with a lot of networking going on. Drinks are $4 and up.

BELLAIR CAFE, 100 Cumberland St. Tel. 416/964-2222.
With a sleek suede ambience, this place attracts a fashion-conscious and celebrity crowd. It really gets jammed every night and on weekends, both inside at the square bar and outside on the terrace.

BEMELMAN'S, 83 Bloor St. West. Tel. 416/960-0306.
With its mirrors, marble, gleaming brass rails, and plants, Bemelman's has a certain slice-of-Manhattan air about it, and the characters that inhabit it are dramatic and definitely trendy, too. A long stand-up marble-top bar is the focus for the action; in the back you can get a decent meal, choosing from a large menu offering soups, salads, sandwiches, pastas, and egg dishes as well as fish, chicken, pork, and beef entrées. Everything is under $12. Weather permitting there's an outdoor patio open April to October. The bar is well known for its luscious fresh-fruit daiquiris. This is also a popular place for brunch from 11am to 3pm on Sunday. Open from 11:30am to 10:30pm Sunday and Monday, until 11pm Tuesday, until midnight Wednesday and until 1am Thursday to Saturday.

BRUNSWICK HOUSE, 481 Bloor St. West. Tel. 416/964-2242.

For a unique experience, go to the Brunswick House, a cross between a German beer hall and an English north-country workingmen's club. Waitresses move through the Formica tables in this cavernous room carrying high trays of frothy suds to a largely student crowd. And while everyone's quaffing or playing bar shuffleboard, they're entertained by Rockin' Irene, who's been here for years belting out three rollicking sets on Friday and Saturday nights. An inexpensive place to down some beer.

Upstairs, there's a good jazz, blues, and R & B spot, Albert's Hall (see above).

CENTRO, 2472 Yonge St. Tel. 416/483-2211.

Centro has a well-patronized bar downstairs at the restaurant. It's a comfortable relaxing place to listen to the pianist and get to know the sophisticated mid-30s-and-up crowd.

C'EST WHAT?, 67 Front St. East. Tel. 416/867-9499.

Downstairs in a historic warehouse building, C'est What? sports rough-hewn walls and a cellarlike atmosphere reminiscent of a Paris *cave*. Casual and comfortable, it attracts a young, politically conscious crowd. Board games are available.

JACK RUSSELL PUB, 27 Wellesley St. East. Tel. 416/967-9442.

A comfortable local, the Jack Russell attracts a mixed crowd—families, professionals, students. It's located in an old heritage house. The main pub, complete with dart board, is on the main floor; upstairs on the third floor there's a large tavern with games room. It's a friendly place to go and chat. It sells eight different types of draft.

THE MADISON, 14 Madison. Tel. 416/927-1722.

The Madison is always jam-packed with people crowding into the bars on each floor of this town house and out onto the outdoor porches. Everyone seems to know everyone.

THE QUEENS HEAD, 263 Gerrard St. East, at Berkeley. Tel. 416/929-0940.

In this friendly freethinking bar, you're likely to meet locals and enjoy some controversial Canadian commentary.

PEPINELLO, 180 Pearl St. (between Duncan and John Sts.). Tel. 416/599-6699.

Pepinello attracts crowds to its downstairs bar for vino bianco and vino rosso and to its upstairs dining area, which offers separate serving counters for pizza, pasta, and risotto—the latest in sophisticated group dining experience.

THE REAL JERK, 709 Queen St. East, at Broadview. Tel. 416/463-6906.

Originally small and located out east, the Real Jerk became so popular that it moved to a larger space. The hip crowd digs the moderately priced superspiced Caribbean food—jerk chicken, curries, shrimp Créole, and rôtis and patties—and the lively crowd and hot background music. No reservations are accepted. Open Monday through Saturday from 11:30am to 1am and on Sunday from 2 to 10pm.

THE ROTTERDAM, 600 King St. West, at Portland. Tel. 416/868-6882.

A beer-drinker's heaven, the Rotterdam serves 370 different labels—more than one for each day of the year—as well as 45 different types on draft. It's not so much an after-work crowd that gathers here, but by 8pm the tables in the back are filled and the long bar is jammed. In summer the patio is fun, too.

SANTA FE, 129 Peter St. Tel. 416/345-9345.

At Santa Fe the southwest hits Toronto. Snakes are painted on the walls, iguanas float down from the ceiling, and coyotes bay at the moon. In the early evening the bar is jammed with financial downtown types; the crowd gets younger as the night goes on.

SQUEEZE CLUB, 817 Queen St. West, west of Bathurst. Tel. 416/365-9020.

A laid-back bar/restaurant and pool hall attracting a mixed crowd ranging from

18 to 50, the Squeeze Club has been the chosen venue for rock-celebrity parties. The music background is whatever tape is playing. It's the place to go on Queen if you don't want to dance or be entertained.

THE WHEATSHEAF TAVERN, 667 King St. West. Tel. 416/364-3996.
Toronto's oldest tavern, dating from 1849, the Wheatsheaf Tavern has been designated a landmark.

WINE BARS

A couple of other fun wine bars? In addition to those listed below, **Le Rendez-Vous Cellar,** 14 Prince Arthur Ave. (tel. 416/961-6111), has daily choices available by the glass. **Montréal,** 65 Sherbourne St. (tel. 416/363-0179), also has a pleasant bar/lounge.

THE HOP AND GRAPE, 14 College St. Tel. 416/923-2818.
The Hop and Grape provides, not surprisingly, beer on one level and wine on another, and is one of the most popular wine bars in the city. On the ground floor the pub offers 60 types of beer with 11 varieties on draft (imported beers are $5 and up). Upstairs, the wine bar offers a selection of 100 wines, some by the glass and some by the bottle.

RACLETTE, 361 Queen St. West. Tel. 416/593-0934.
Along Queen Street, go to Raclette, which stocks more than 100 wines, including 24 that are available by the glass; the bar also offers raclette. It's open Monday through Saturday from noon to 1am, on Sunday until 11pm.

VINES, downstairs at 38 Wellington St. East. Tel. 416/869-0744.
Vines provides a pleasant atmosphere to sample a glass of champagne or any of 54 wines, priced between $4 and $10 for a four-ounce glass. Salads, cheeses, and light meals (from $7 to $10), are available.

COCKTAILS IN THE SKY

AQUARIUS 51 LOUNGE, 55 Bloor St. West. Tel. 416/967-5525.
Go for the lit skyline view available from this comfortable bar atop the Manulife Centre.

HORIZONS, 301 Front St. West. Tel. 416/601-4721.
For obvious reasons, Horizons, perched on the CN Tower, can be difficult to get into because of the crowds. But it's worth the wait to sip that drink and gaze at the panoply of Toronto's lights. It's open from 11am to 2am Monday through Saturday and from noon to 11pm on Sunday. No jeans are allowed on Friday and Saturday nights. At 9 or 10pm it converts from a cocktail bar to a dance club. There's a $12 charge for the elevator.

FILM

Although it's easy enough to find a movie theater either from the yellow pages or the local daily newspapers, you should know about Toronto's exceptional film buffs' heaven—**Cineplex,** in Eaton Centre (tel. 416/593-4536). Always chary of describing any animal, vegetable, or mineral as the biggest, let me just say that the film complex houses 17 theaters with seating capacities ranging from 57 to 137.

Located in Eaton Centre, the Cineplex has exterior screens over the entrance displaying ongoing slide presentations; an annunciator board in the lobby lists all movies and starting times. By staggering the starting times and selling tickets in advance, this celluloid wonderland avoids the modern filmgoers' bugaboo of standing on line. Furthermore, the complex can respond to lulls and swells in the crowd flow because it has the ability to show the same movie in anywhere from one to 10 screening rooms, depending on demand.

Recent releases are the staples; tickets are $8.

Cinemathèque Ontario, 70 Carlton St. (tel. 416/967-7371), features the best in contemporary cinema, directors' retrospectives, and seasons of new international films. The films are shown at the Art Gallery of Ontario. Admission is $6.

CHAPTER 14

THE GOLDEN HORSESHOE & EAST ALONG THE ST. LAWRENCE

"**G**olden" because the communities along the lake are wealthy, "horseshoe" because of its shape, this stretch of the Ontario lakefront from Niagara-on-the-Lake to Oshawa offers the visitor some golden opportunities: Niagara Falls itself; Niagara-on-the-Lake, home of the famous Shaw Festival; the engineering wonder, the Welland Canal; Niagara wineries; and Dundurn Castle and Royal Botanical Gardens in Canada's steel town of Hamilton.

East from Port Hope, a worthy antiques center, stretches the Bay of Quinte and Quinte's Isle, a tranquil region of farms and orchards that was largely settled by the Loyalists. It's still little-trafficked today—except by those in the know who come to explore the pretty small towns, to go antiquing, or to enjoy the beaches, dunes, and waterfront activities. Kingston is a very appealing lakefront town with its own weekly market, and is architecturally and historically full of interest. It's also the gateway to the mighty St. Lawrence River and the Thousand Islands.

SEEING THE GOLDEN HORSESHOE

INFORMATION For information about Ontario, contact the **Ontario Ministry of Culture, Tourism, and Recreation,** 77 Bloor St. West, 9th floor, Toronto, ON, M7A 2R9 (tel. 416/314-0944, or toll free 800/ONTARIO from 9am to 8pm). The offices are open from 8:30am to 5pm Monday through Friday (daily from mid-May to mid-September).

A NOTE ON TAXES As you travel, keep in mind that Ontario has a provincial sales tax of 8%, plus a 5% accommodations tax—in addition to the national 7% GST.

ONTARIO PARKS There are 260 provincial parks in Ontario, offering ample opportunities for outdoor recreation. The daily in-season entry fee for a vehicle is $6; campsites cost anywhere from $13 to $18. For more information, contact the **Ontario Ministry of Natural Resources** (tel. 416/314-2000).

SPECIAL ONTARIO VACATIONS Ontario has an extensive network of canals ideal for **cruising/boating vacations.** You can cruise up the Rideau Canal to Ottawa or through the Thousand Islands or along the Trent-Severn waterway. For information about houseboat holidays and rentals, contact either of the following: **Big Rideau Boats,** 56 Meadowbank Dr., Ottawa, ON, K2G ON9 (tel. 613/828-0138);

WHAT'S SPECIAL ABOUT THE GOLDEN HORSESHOE

Natural Spectacles

☐ Niagara Falls, a thundering beauty that triumphs over all the artificial surroundings.

☐ The Niagara Parkway, a veritable 35-mile-long garden trail lined with fruit trees and wineries—ideal for biking, hiking, and picnicking.

☐ St. Lawrence Islands National Park, more than 1,800 islands surrounded by boat-filled waters and home to heron and other fascinating waterfowl.

☐ The 80-feet-high freshwater dunes at Sandbanks and North Beach Provincial Park.

Events/Festivals

☐ The Shaw Festival, celebrating GBS and his contemporaries and held in a 19th-century village, Niagara-on-the-Lake.

Activities

☐ Viewing the Falls from the *Maid of the Mist* or from a helicopter.

☐ Tasting wines at the many vineyards—wines that are winning awards today for Ontario.

☐ Renting a houseboat and traveling up the Trent-Severn waterway from Kingston to Ottawa.

Historic Monuments/Museums

☐ Fort George National Historic Site, where you can vividly imagine playing the part of a Canadian soldier during the War of 1812.

☐ Upper Canada Village, Ontario's answer to Williamsburg, where Canadian pioneer life is reenacted.

☐ Quinte's Isle. Largely settled by Loyalists, this bucolic corner takes you back to an earlier, more colonial Canada.

Gardens

☐ The Royal Botanical Gardens in Hamilton—3,000 acres of spring bulbs, rhododendrons, chrysanthemums, roses, and the largest display of lilacs you're ever likely to see.

Architectural Highlights

☐ The Welland Canal, a 19th-century engineering feat—27 feet deep and 26 miles long, with seven locks that lift vessels an average of 47 feet.

Houseboat Holidays, R.R. 3, Gananoque, ON, K7G 2V5 (tel. 613/382-2842). Most boats sleep up to six and have fully equipped kitchen, hot and cold running water, and a propane system for heat and light. Weekly rentals in summer average $1,000.

One way to really experience Ontario is to **stay on a farm.** Enjoy the home-produced and home-cooked meals, the peace of the countryside, and the working rhythms of a dairy or mixed farm. There are all kinds of farms and locations to choose from. Rates average $35 to $60 double per night, $220 a week, all meals included. For information contact the **Ontario Vacation Farm Association,** R.R. 2, Alma, ON, N0B 1A0; or contact **Ontario Travel,** Ministry of Culture, Tourism, and Recreation, 77 Bloor St. West, 9th floor, Toronto, ON, M7A 2R9 (tel. 416/314-0944), where you can obtain a free "Farm Vacation Guide."

1. NIAGARA FALLS

81 miles (130km) S of Toronto, 131 miles (210km) E of London, 244 miles (390km) SW of Kingston, 18 miles (30km) N of Buffalo, N.Y.

GETTING THERE   By Train   Amtrak and VIA Rail operate trains between

Toronto (tel. 416/366-8411) and New York, stopping in St. Catharines and Niagara Falls. Call toll free 800/361-1235 in Canada or 800/USA-RAIL in the U.S.

By Bus   Gray Coach (a Greyhound company) operates about 10 or so buses a day from Toronto to Niagara Falls and also from major cities in upstate New York. Call Toronto 416/594-3310 or your local Greyhound office for info.

By Car   From Toronto take the QEW Niagara. From the U.S. take the Rainbow Bridge directly into Niagara Falls (ON).

ESSENTIALS   Information   For travel information in and around the falls, contact the Niagara Falls Visitor and Convention Bureau, 5433 Victoria Ave., Niagara Falls, ON, L2G 3L1 (tel. 905/356-6061); or the Niagara Parks Commission, 7400 Portage Rd. South (P.O. Box 150), Niagara Falls, ON, L2E 6T2 (tel. 905/356-2241 or 905/354-6266).

Summer information centers are open at Table Rock House, Maid of the Mist Plaza, Rapids View Parking Lot, and Niagara-on-the-Lake.

Getting Around   You used to be able to park along the main street/parkway in Niagara Falls, but now that is forbidden; instead the way to get around is to travel aboard the People Movers (tel. 905/357-9340). Park your car at Rapid View several kilometers away from the falls, or else at the so-called Preferred Parking (overlooking the falls—it costs more), and then take the People Mover, an attraction in itself. People Movers travel a loop making nine stops from Rapid View to Spanish Aero Car. Shuttles to the falls also operate from downtown and Lundy's Lane. An all-day pass costs $3 for adults, $1.50 for children 6 to 12. In-season only.

Niagara Falls, with its gimmicks, amusement parks, wax museums, daredevil feats, and a million motels, each with a honeymoon suite complete with Jacuzzi and heart-shaped bed, may seem rather ticky-tacky and certainly overcommercialized. But somehow the falls still steal the show, and on the Canadian side, with its parks and gardens, nature manages to survive with grace.

WHAT TO SEE & DO

Ever since the falls were first seen by Fr. Louis Hennepin, a Jesuit priest, in December 1678, people have flocked to see the seventh natural wonder of the world. More than 12 million visit annually. Many are honeymooners, although how the trend got started no one quite knows—legend has it that Napoléon's brother started it when he came on his honeymoon, traveling all the way from New Orleans by stagecoach. One way to see many of the town's highlights is to purchase an Explorer's Passport, which secures admission to Table Rock Scenic Tunnels, Great Gorge Adventure, and the Niagara Spanish Aero Car. It costs $12.60 for adults, and $6.35 for children 6 to 12.

VIEWING THE FALLS

Still, whoever started it all, people do come to see the falls, and that can be done from many vantage points above, below, and in the middle, when you take a trip on the *Maid of the Mist*, 5920 River Rd. (tel. 905/358-5781). It takes you practically into the maelstrom through the turbulent waters around the American Falls, past the Rock of Ages, to the foot of the Horseshoe Falls where the 34.5 million Imperial gallons fall per minute over the 176-foot-high cataract. Your nose will probably drip, your sunglasses mist, but that will not detract from the thrill of the experience.

Boats leave from the dock on the parkway just down from the Rainbow Bridge. Trips begin in mid-May and operate daily as follows: mid-May to May 21, 9:45am to 4:45pm weekdays, until 5:45pm weekends; Victoria Day weekend (late May), 9:45am

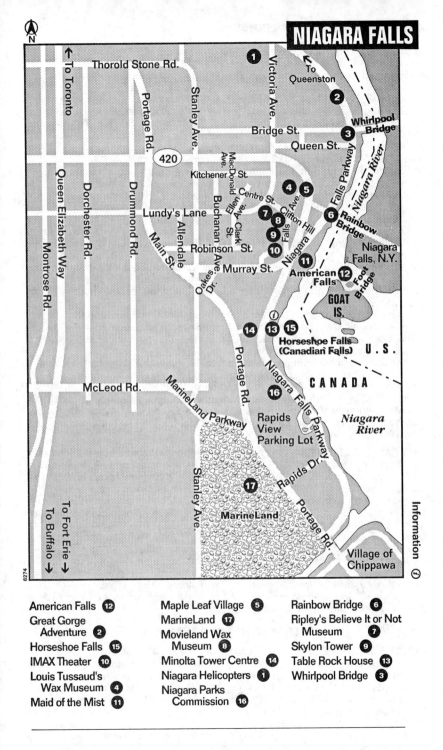

NIAGARA FALLS

To Toronto →

Thorold Stone Rd.

To Queenston

Victoria Ave.

Stanley Ave.

Portage Rd.

Whirlpool Bridge

Bridge St.

Queen St.

Falls Parkway

Niagara River

420

Kitchener St.

MacDonald Ave.

Centre St.

Ellen Ave.

Buchanan Ave.

Clark St.

Lundy's Lane

Allendale

Main St.

Robinson St.

Murray St.

Oakes Dr.

Clifton Hill

Falls Ave.

Niagara

Rainbow Bridge

Niagara Falls, N.Y.

American Falls

Foot Bridge

GOAT IS.

Horseshoe Falls (Canadian Falls)

U.S.

Drummond Rd.

Dorchester Rd.

Queen Elizabeth Way

Montrose Rd.

McLeod Rd.

MarineLand Parkway

Portage Rd.

Niagara Falls Parkway

CANADA

Rapids View Parking Lot

Rapids Dr.

Niagara River

Stanley Ave.

MarineLand

To Fort Erie →
To Buffalo →

Portage Rd.

Village of Chippawa

Information ⓘ

Queen St.

① ② ③ ④ ⑤ ⑥ ⑦ ⑧ ⑨ ⑩ ⑪ ⑫ ⑬ ⑭ ⑮ ⑯ ⑰

V4C9

American Falls ⑫	Maple Leaf Village ⑤	Rainbow Bridge ⑥
Great Gorge Adventure ②	MarineLand ⑰	Ripley's Believe It or Not Museum ⑦
Horseshoe Falls ⑮	Movieland Wax Museum ⑧	Skylon Tower ⑨
IMAX Theater ⑩	Minolta Tower Centre ⑭	Table Rock House ⑬
Louis Tussaud's Wax Museum ④	Niagara Helicopters ①	Whirlpool Bridge ③
Maid of the Mist ⑪	Niagara Parks Commission ⑯	

to 7:45pm; Memorial Day weekend, 9am to 7:45pm; Memorial Day to June 18, 9:45am to 5:45pm; June 19 to July 2, 9:45am to 7:45pm; July to mid-August, 9am to 7:45pm; mid-August to Labor Day, 9am to 7:15pm; Labor Day, 9am to 4:45pm; September to mid-October, 9:45am to 4:45pm weekdays, until 5:45pm weekends. Fares are $8.65 for adults, $5 for children 6 to 12; children 5 and under, free.

Go down under the falls via the elevator at Table Rock House, which drops you 150 feet down through solid rock to the **Table Rock Scenic Tunnels** (tel. 905/358-3268) and viewing portals. Do put on the black oilskin mackintosh and rubber boots. The tunnels are open all year, and the admission charge is $5.25 for adults, $2.65 for children 6 to 12; children under 6, free.

To view the falls from above most spectacularly, take an eight-minute spin in a chopper over the whole Niagara area. Helicopters leave from the **Heliport,** adjacent to the Whirlpool at the junction of Victoria Avenue and Niagara Parkway, from 9am to dusk, weather permitting, daily. Contact **Niagara Helicopters,** 3731 Victoria Ave. (tel. 905/357-5672).

Or else you can ride up in the external glass-fronted elevators 520 feet to the top of the **Skylon Tower** observation deck at 5200 Robinson St. (tel. 905/356-2651). At the base of the tower there are 40 boutiques and stores to browse in, and an indoor amusement park with a Ferris wheel, several carousels, and appropriate vending outlets. The observation deck is open from 10am to 9pm daily, from 8am to 1am June through Labor Day. Adults pay $6 for admission; seniors, $5; and children 12 and under, $3.50.

A similar perspective can be gained from the observation floors atop the 325-foot **Minolta Tower Centre and Marine Aquarium,** 6732 Oakes Dr. (tel. 905/356-1501). On-site attractions include a Minolta exhibit on the 30th floor and gift shops, arcades, and snack bars at the base.

The tower is open in summer from 9am to 11:30pm, and in winter from 9am to 9pm (closed December 24 and 25). Admission to the tower is $5.95 for adults, $4.95 for students and seniors; free for children under 10.

For a thrilling introduction to the experience of Niagara Falls, stop by the **IMAX Theater** and view the raging, swirling waters in *Niagara: Miracles, Myths and Magic,* which is shown on a six-story-high screen. It's at 6170 Buchanan Ave. (tel. 905/374-IMAX).

THE FALLS BY NIGHT Jean François Gravelet (or Blondin, as he was known), the famed tightrope walker, is believed to have inspired the first effort to light the falls in 1859 when he walked across the river on his rope at night, setting off fireworks that illuminated the gorge. Various installations have been run since then.

Today, don't miss the vision of the falls lit by 22 xenon gas spotlights (each producing 250 million candlepower of light), in shades of rose pink, red magenta, amber, blue, and green. You can see it any night of the year as follows: January 3 to February 28, 6:30 to 9pm; March 1 to April 3, 7 to 10pm; April 4 to April 30, 8:30 to 10pm; in May, 9pm to midnight; in June, 9:15pm to midnight; in July, 9:15pm to 12:30am; in August, 9pm to 12:30am; September 1 to Labor Day, 8pm to 12:30am; September 7 to September 30, 8 to 11pm, in October 7 to 10pm; November 1 to November 19, 6:30 to 9pm; November 20 to January 2, 5 to 10pm.

In addition, from July to early September, free fireworks are set off every Friday night at 11pm illuminating the falls, too.

OTHER TOP ATTRACTIONS

WHITE WATER, 7430 Lundy's Lane. Tel. 905/357-3380.

Everyone loves White Water, where you can don your bathing suit and swoop around the curlicues and corkscrew turns of the five slides all the way from the top to the heated pools at the bottom. The wave pool is also lots of fun for the family. If you prefer to just wallow in the hot tub, you can do that, too. The little 'uns can also ride three small slides designed specially for them. Take a picnic and spend a greater part of the day (there's also a snack bar).

Admission: $13.95 adults, $10.95 children 3–7, which allows you to stay all day and return evenings, when the lights go on.

Open: Daily 10am–8pm. **Closed:** Winter.

MARINELAND, 7657 Portage Rd. Tel. 905/356-8250, or 905/356-9565 for taped information.

This is not to be missed on your trip to the falls. At the aquarium, King Waldorf, Marineland's sea lion mascot, presides over the performances of killer whales and sea lions. The indoor aquarium features a display of freshwater fish and a show starring harbor seals and dolphins. At the game farm wildlife roams freely—deer, bears, and Canadian elk. You can pet and feed the deer. There are three restaurants available or you can spread your picnic lunch on one of the many tables provided.

Marineland also has theme-park rides, including a roller coaster, Tivoli wheel, Dragon Boat rides, and a fully equipped children's playground. The big thriller is Dragon Mountain, a roller coaster that loops, double-loops, and spirals its way through 1,000 feet of tunnels.

Admission: Summer $20 adults, $17 children and seniors; free for children under 4. Admission lower in other seasons.

Open: July–Aug daily 9am–6pm; call ahead for operating hours during the rest of the year. Park closes at dusk. Rides open Victoria Day–first Mon in Oct. **Directions:** Drive south on Stanley Street and follow the signs.

ATTRACTIONS ALONG THE NIAGARA PARKWAY

The Niagara Parkway was conceived in 1867 by a group of Americans that included Frederick Law Olmsted, designer of New York City's Central Park, who had become outraged at the peddlers, hawkers, and barkers of freak sideshows who preyed upon Niagara's tourists. Today it provides a 35-mile stretch of parkland and gardens that are exquisitely kept and a delectable sight.

You can drive all the way to Niagara-on-the-Lake, taking in the attractions en route. The first attraction you'll come to is the **Great Gorge Adventure and Daredevil Exhibit,** 4330 River Rd. (tel. 905/374-1221), where you can learn about Niagara's daredevil history, who died and who survived, and examine several of the actual barrels used to ride over the falls. Then you can stroll along the scenic boardwalk beside the raging white waters of the Great Gorge Rapids and wonder how it must have felt to challenge this mighty torrent, where the river rushes through the narrow channel at an average speed of 30 m.p.h. Admission is $4.25 for adults, $2.50 for children, free for kids under 6.

Half a mile farther north and you'll arrive at the **Niagara Spanish Aero Car** (tel. 905/354-5711), a red-and-yellow cable-car contraption that will whisk you on a 3,600-foot jaunt between two points in Canada, high above the whirlpool, providing excellent views of the surrounding landscape. Open daily May 1 to the third Sunday in October: from 9am to 6pm in May, until 8pm in June, until 9pm in July and August, from 10am to 7:30pm in September, and 9am to 5pm in October. Admission is $4.50 for adults, $2.25 for children 6 to 12; children under 6, free.

From here you'll pass the **Whirlpool Golf Club** (tel. 905/356-1140), an outstanding public course. Greens fees are $30 for 18 holes, $20 for nine holes.

Next stop is the **School of Horticulture,** and a free view of the vast gardens there, before you go on to look at the Floral Clock, which contains 25,000 plants in its 40-foot-diameter face.

From here you can drive to **Queenston Heights Park,** site of the battle of that name during the War of 1812. Shortly after daybreak on October 13, 1812, an American force invaded Canada at Queenston and a small company captured the strategic Redan Battery. British General Brock led a charge to recapture it but was killed. Later his aide-de-camp, MacDonnell, fell leading a second unsuccessful charge. Despite these reverses and the loss of their leaders the British forces won the Battle of Queenston Heights. Brock and his aide-de-camp are buried here. You can take a walking tour of the battlefield. Picnic or play tennis ($5 an hour) in this shaded arbor before moving to the **Laura Secord Homestead,** Partition Street in Queenston (tel. 905/262-4851), home of this redoubtable woman. It contains a fine collection of Upper Canada furniture from the 1812 period as well as artifacts recovered from an archeological dig. Stop at the candy shop and ice-cream parlor. It's open from Victoria Day weekend (late May) to Labor Day, daily 10am to 5pm. Tours are given every half hour. Admission is $1.

Also worth viewing just off the parkway in Queenston is the **Samuel Weir Collection and Library of Art,** R.R. 1, Niagara-on-the-Lake (tel. 905/262-4510), a small personal collection that is displayed as it was originally when the house was occupied by Samuel Weir himself. Mr. Weir (1898–1981) was a lawyer from London, Ontario, who was an enthusiastic collector of Canadian, American, and European art as well as of rare books. The displays are changed frequently but among the items you might see works by Cornelius Krieghoff, Homer Watson, Paul Kane, Tom Thomson, Fred Varley, George Romney, and Jacob Epstein, to name only a few of the more famous names. Open from Victoria Day to Canadian Thanksgiving Wednesday to Saturday from 11am to 5pm, and Sunday from 1 to 5pm.

Next stop is the Georgian-style **McFarland House** (tel. 905/468-3322 or 905/356-2241), built in 1800 and home to John McFarland, "His Majesty's [George III] Boat Builder." It's open daily June 26 to Labor Day from 11am to 5pm, and Tuesday to Sunday late May to June 25 from 1 to 4pm; off-season group tours by appointment only. Admission is $1.25 for adults, 75¢ for children.

From here the parkway continues into Niagara-on-the-Lake. It is lined with fruit farms like **Kurtz Orchards** (tel. 905/468-2937), and wineries, notably the **Inniskillin Winery,** Line 3, Service Road 56 (tel. 905/468-3554 or 905/468-2187), and **Reif Winery** (tel. 905/468-7738). Inniskillin is open daily from 10am to 6pm June to October and Monday through Saturday from 10am to 5pm November to May. Tours are given daily at 10:30am and 2:30pm from June to September (Saturday and Sunday at 2:30pm only in May and October). At Reif Winery, tours are given daily at 1:30pm from June to August.

A trip south along the parkway will take you by the Table Rock complex to a stop at the **Park Greenhouse,** which is a year-round free attraction (open daily from 9:30am to 7pm during July and August, until 4:15pm at other times).

Farther along, visit **Dufferin Islands,** where the children can swim, rent a paddleboat, and explore the surrounding woodland areas. Or else you can play a round of golf on the illuminated nine-hole par-three course. Open the second Sunday in April to the last Sunday in October.

A little farther on, stop for a picnic in **King's Bridge Park** and relax on the beaches before driving on to **Fort Erie** (tel. 905/871-0540), a reconstruction of the fort that was seized by the Americans in July 1814, besieged later by the British, and finally blown up as the Americans retreated across the river to Buffalo. You will be conducted through the museum and display rooms by guards in 1812–14 period uniforms of the British Eighth Regiment. These guards also stand sentry duty, fire the cannons, and demonstrate drill and musket practice. Open the first Saturday in May to September 12 (and weekends until October 3), Monday through Thursday from 10am to 3:30pm, Friday through Sunday 10am to 5:30pm. Admission is $3.50 for adults, $2 for children 6 to 16.

MORE ATTRACTIONS

The **Niagara Falls Museum,** 5651 River Rd. (tel. 905/356-2151), was founded in 1827. Its exhibits range from Egyptian mummies to some of the original barrels that traveled over the falls in Niagara's Daredevil Hall of Fame. Other exhibits range from Indian and Asian artifacts, shells, fossils, and minerals, to the Freaks of Nature display. Open in summer daily from 8:30am to 11pm; in winter hours are irregular, usually weekends only, from 10am to 5pm. Admission costs $6 for adults, $5 for seniors, $3.75 for students 11 to 18, $2.75 for children under 11; under 5, free.

There's a whole slew of sideshows on Clifton Hill ranging from **Ripley's Believe It or Not, Castle Dracula, Houdini Museum, Movieland Wax Museum,** and **Louis Tussaud's Wax Museum**—all of them charging about $5 for adults, $2.50 for children.

CROSS-COUNTRY SKIING

Niagara Falls is a four-season resort with most of the attractions open all year. The falls' ice formations and the ice bridge formed in winter are quite remarkable (you'll know how remarkable if you've ever seen a building in winter after the firemen have put out the fire). At the **Whirlpool Golf Course** you can ski cross-country on the three trails: one for beginners, one for intermediates, and a five-miler for advanced skiers. Use of the ski trails is free, and there's tobogganing also.

WINERY TOURS

Niagara is set in the fruit- and wine-producing area of the Niagara escarpment. The Niagara peninsula has over 25,000 acres of select vineyards cultivating some 45 varieties of wine grapes. There are a number of wineries in the region: Barnes, Château Gai, Inniskillin House, Andrés, and Brights. At **Brights,** 4887 Dorchester Rd. (tel. 905/357-2400), the largest winery in Canada, you can see champagne processed in the European way by fermenting the wine in the bottle, and at any of the wineries you can view the winemaking process from the moment the grapes enter the crush house to the fermentation, bottling, and packaging stages. And then comes the fun part—the wine tasting.

Probably the best time to visit is during vendange or harvest season, from the first week in September to the end of October. At Brights, free one-hour tours are offered year-round Monday through Friday at 10:30am, 2pm, and 3:30pm; and 2 and 3:30pm Saturday and Sunday. Call 905/357-2400, or write: Brights Winery Tours, P.O. Box 510, Niagara Falls, ON, L2E 6V4. For other winery tours and tastings, write to: Andrés Wines, P.O. Box 10550, Winona, ON, L8E 5S4 (tel. 905/643-TOUR, or toll free 800/263-2170). See also "Attractions along the Niagara Parkway," above.

WHERE TO STAY

Every other sign in Niagara Falls advertises a motel. In summer, rates tend to go up and down according to what the market will bear, and some proprietors will not even quote rates ahead of time. So be warned. What follows is a very small selection of favorites.

I cannot emphasize enough how much the room market in Niagara Falls depends on the daily traffic. You can secure a reasonably priced room if you're lucky enough to arrive on a "down night." For example, in June at a very fine hotel, I was offered a room for $55 when the official rates were posted as $89 and up. So push a little. Keep requesting a lower rate. Don't take no for an answer.

EXPENSIVE

CLARION OLD STONE INN, 5425 Robinson St., Niagara Falls, ON, L2G 7L6. Tel. 905/357-1234, or toll free 800/663-1144. Fax 905/357-9299. 114 rms. A/C TV TEL
$ Rates: May–Sept 30 $95–$135 single or double; Oct–May $60–$100. Special packages available. AE, CB, DC, ER, MC, V. **Parking:** Free.
The Clarion Old Stone Inn, right across from the Skylon Tower and Pyramid Place, was built 14 years ago and retains some vestige of character. It was designed to re-create the atmosphere of a country inn by using natural rough-hewn stone, heavy crossbeam supports, and barn-style paneling. The rooms set in a three-story L-shaped configuration are spacious, furnished in shades of peach and green, and contain the usual conveniences. Three rooms have fireplaces and double sunken showers; 36 ground-floor rooms face the outdoor heated pool.

The lounge, with its wingbacks and love seats, leads right to the indoor pool while the dining room, with its huge fireplace, brass chandelier, bookcases, and high cathedral-style ceiling, provides a cozy atmosphere for such specialties as blackened shark or prime rib.

NIAGARA FALLS RENAISSANCE HOTEL, 6455 Buchanan Ave., Niagara Falls, ON, L2G 3V9. Tel. 905/357-5200, or toll free 800/363-FALLS. Fax 905/357-3422. 262 rms. A/C MINIBAR TV TEL
$ Rates: Summer $145–$200 single or double, $200–$230 whirlpool room; winter $70–$115 single or double, $130–$180 whirlpool room; spring and fall $90–$165 single or double, $180–$210 whirlpool room. AE, DC, DISC, ER, MC, V. **Parking:** Free.
Opened in the summer of 1985, originally as a Ramada, the Renaissance offers rooms that are tastefully furnished with oak furniture, and equipped with two telephones

and remote-control TVs. Bathrooms have double sinks, hairdryers, and all the rest of the modern accoutrements. Each of the Renaissance Club rooms has three telephones, a whirlpool tub, and access to a special lounge with concierge. Facilities include an indoor pool, a whirlpool, and a health club featuring saunas, squash and racquetball courts, and a fitness and weight room. There's also a rooftop café overlooking the falls.

SKYLINE BROCK, 5705 Falls Ave., Niagara Falls, ON, L2E 6W7. Tel. 905/374-4444 or 905/357-3090, or toll free 800/648-7200. Fax 905/374-0885. 233 rms. A/C TV TEL

$ Rates: June 1–Oct 1 $115–$220 single or double; Oct and Apr–May $95–$175 single or double; winter $75–$145 single or double. Prices based on room and view. Extra person $10. Children under 18 stay free in parents' room. Special packages available. AE, DC, DISC, ER, MC, V. **Parking:** $4.25.

Right next door to the Skyline Foxhead, with only Maple Leaf Village between, the Skyline Brock has been hosting honeymooners and falls visitors since 1929. It still has a certain air of splendor—a huge chandelier and marble walls in the lobby. The management has completed a major renovation and offers elegantly appointed rooms, some furnished with antique reproductions. One hundred and fifty of the 232 rooms face the falls. City-view rooms are slightly smaller and less expensive. New furnishings and decor include corridors of burgundy and gray and rooms in beige, highlighted by wall hangings, drapes, and bedspreads featuring a blend of Japanese prints in greens, blues, and dusty rose.

For dining there's the Rainbow Room on the 10th floor, with a lovely view over the falls, serving a popular menu of such entrées as half a roast chicken with cranberry sauce, salmon hollandaise, or prime rib, from $16 to $24. Isaac's lounge is available on the lobby level.

SKYLINE FOXHEAD, 5705 Falls Ave., Niagara Falls, ON, L2E 6W7. Tel. 905/374-4444 or 905/357-3090, or toll free 800/263-7135. 399 rms. A/C MINIBAR TV TEL

$ Rates: June 1–Oct 1 $145–$210 single or double; Oct and Apr–May $120–$175 single or double; winter $80–$125 single or double. Prices depend on whether the room has a view of the falls, gardens, village, or city. Extra person $10. Children under 18 stay free in parents' room. AE, DC, DISC, ER, MC, V. **Parking:** $5.50.

For an unblemished view of the falls, you have a choice of either the Skyline Brock or the Skyline Foxhead. The Foxhead, which has recently undergone an extensive renovation, offers rooms spread over 14 floors, all with private baths or showers and color TVs with in-room movies. Half of the units have balconies.

The 14th-floor Penthouse Dining Room takes fair advantage of the view with its large glass windows, and serves a daily buffet for breakfast, lunch, and dinner with nightly dancing to a live band (in season). Or there's the Steak and Burger for reasonably priced fare and the Japanese-style Yakatori restaurant. Recreation facilities include an outdoor rooftop pool.

MODERATE

THE CANUCK, 5334 Kitchener St., Niagara Falls, ON, L2G 1B5. Tel. 905/374-7666. Fax 905/374-6270. 75 rms. A/C TV TEL

$ Rates: High season $85 single or double. Rates about 40% less off-season. Extra person $5. Special packages available. AE, CB, DC, DISC, MC, V. **Parking:** Free.

The Canuck has fairly reasonably priced rooms (at least for Niagara Falls), which are pleasantly furnished and well kept. All the spacious units have contemporary furnishings. Honeymoon suites are available, and so are efficiencies with two-ring electric hotplates, sinks, and refrigerators. Facilities include a pleasantly landscaped pool, a restaurant that serves breakfast and dinner, laundry equipment, and a babysitting service.

DAYS INN LUNDY'S LANE, 7280 Lundy's Lane, Niagara Falls, ON, L2G 1W2. Tel. 905/358-3621. Fax 905/358-0277. 136 rms. A/C TV TEL

$ Rates: High season $80–$100 double. Rates about 30% less off-season. Extra person $5. Children under 12 stay free in parents' room. AE, DC, DISC, MC, V. **Parking:** Free.

The Days Inn offers decent motel rooms decorated with matching drapes and spreads and modern furniture. There's an indoor pool and an adjacent Denny's restaurant.

MICHAEL'S INN, 5599 River Rd., Niagara Falls, ON, L2E 3H3. Tel. 905/354-2727, or toll free 800/263-9390. Fax 905/374-7706. 130 rms. A/C TV TEL

$ Rates: June 16–Sept 15 $70–$165 double, $200–$450 bridal suite; Mar 16–June 15 and Sept 16–Oct 31 $50–$150 double, $200–$300 bridal suite; Nov 1–Mar 15 $45–$100 double, $100–$200 bridal suite. Rollaway bed $10; crib $5. AE, CB, DC, ER, MC, V. **Parking:** Free.

Long and fine traditions of hospitality stretch back for Michael's Inn, a four-story white building overlooking the Niagara River gorge. The rooms are large, have all the modern conveniences, and are nicely decorated. Many have heart-shaped tubs and Jacuzzis. There's a solarium pool out back. The Embers Open Hearth Dining Room is just that—the charcoal pit is enclosed behind glass so you can see all the cooking action. There's a lounge, too.

RED CARPET INN, 4943 Clifton Hill, Niagara Falls, ON, L2G 3N5. Tel. 905/357-4330, or toll free 800/668-8840. Fax 905/357-0423. 71 rms, 6 suites. A/C TV TEL

$ Rates: Mid-May to June $68.50 single or double; July–Sept $86.50 single or double; Oct–Dec $68.50 single or double; Jan to mid-May $66.50 single or double. Extra person $5. Children under 12 stay free in parents' room. AE, DISC, MC, V. **Parking:** Free.

Just up Clifton Hill, around the corner from the Foxhead, window boxes with geraniums draw the eye to the Red Carpet Inn. The units on two floors are set around a courtyard with an outdoor heated pool; six of the rooms are honeymoon suites with canopied beds and extra-plush decor, while the other rooms have colonial-style furniture and pink walls, clock radios, and full bathrooms. Rooms 54 through 58 have a direct view of the falls; 12 rooms have private balconies. Convenient facilities include a washer-dryer, gift shop, and an outdoor beer garden.

VILLAGE INN, 5705 Falls Ave., Niagara Falls, ON, L2E 6W7. Tel. 905/374-4444 or 905/357-3090, or toll free 800/263-7135. 205 rms. A/C TV TEL

AN IMPORTANT NOTE ON PRICES

Unless stated otherwise, **the prices cited in this guide are given in Canadian dollars,** which is good news for American travelers because the Canadian dollar is worth 25% less than the American dollar, but buys nearly as much. As we go to press, $1 Canadian is worth 75¢ U.S., which means that your $100-a-night hotel room will cost only U.S. $75, and your $6 breakfast costs only U.S. $4.50.

Here's a quick table of equivalents:

Canadian $	U.S. $
$ 1	$ 0.75
5	3.75
10	7.50
20	15.00
50	37.50
80	60.00
100	75.00
200	150.00

$ Rates: June 1–Oct 1 $75 single or double; Oct and Apr–May $55 single or double. Special packages available. AE, DC, DISC, MC, V. **Parking:** $4. **Closed:** Winter.

Located behind the two Skyline hotels, the Village Inn is ideal for families—all the rooms are large. Some family suites have 700 square feet that includes a bedroom with two double beds and a living room. There's an outdoor heated swimming pool and a restaurant.

BUDGET

THE AMERICANA, 8444 Lundy's Lane, Niagara Falls, ON, L2H 1H4. Tel. 905/356-8444. Fax 905/356-8576. 120 rms. A/C TV TEL
$ Rates: Late June–late Aug $70–$120 single or double; Sept–June $50–$90 single or double. AE, DISC, ER, MC, V. **Parking:** Free.

One of the nicer moderately priced motels on this motel strip is set in 25 acres of grounds with a pleasant tree-shaded area for picnicking right across from the office. Sports facilities include tennis, squash, two pools, sauna, and fitness room, and an outdoor swimming pool. The very large rooms are fully equipped with color TVs, vanity sinks, and full bathrooms. A dining room, lounge, and coffee shop are on the premises.

NELSON MOTEL, 10655 Niagara River Pkwy., Niagara Falls, ON, L2E 6S6. Tel. 905/295-4754. 25 rms. A/C TV TEL
$ Rates: June 16–Sept 12 $55–$90 single or double; Sept 13 to mid-Nov and mid-Mar to June 15 $35–$55 single or double. Rollaways and cribs extra. MC, V. **Parking:** Free. **Closed:** Mid-Nov to mid-Mar.

For budget accommodations try the Nelson Motel, run by John and Dawn Pavlakovich, who live in the large house adjacent to the motel units. The units have character, especially the family units with a double bedroom adjoined by a twin-bedded room for the kids. Regular units have modern furniture, some with color and some with black-and-white TV. Singles have shower only. All units face the fenced-in pool and neatly trimmed lawn with umbrellaed tables and shrubs (none has a telephone). It's located a short drive from the falls overlooking the Niagara River, away from the hustle and bustle of Niagara itself.

SURFSIDE INN, 3665 Macklem St., Niagara Falls, ON, L2G 6C8. Tel. 905/295-4354, or toll free 800/263-0713. 32 rms and suites. A/C TV TEL
$ Rates: Summer $65.50–$85.50 single or double, $150 deluxe Jacuzzi suite; off-season $50–$60 single or double, $125 deluxe Jacuzzi suite. AE, MC, V. **Parking:** Free. **Closed:** Jan–Mar.

Another budget place is the Surfside Inn, where the units have been completely and nicely redecorated in French provincial, Italian provincial, and Chinese black-lacquered style. The pastel-patterned bedspreads are color coordinated with the rugs and curtains; baths are fully tiled. A few rooms in the secluded area at the back are furnished with water beds and Jacuzzis. All rooms are individually heated and air-conditioned. There's a public beach across the street in Kings Bridge Park. To get there, follow the Niagara Parkway south.

A NEARBY PLACE TO STAY IN QUEENSTON

SOUTH LANDING INN, at the corner of Kent and Front Sts. (P.O. Box 269), Queenston, ON, L0S 1L0. Tel. 905/262-4634. 23 rms. A/C TV
$ Rates: Mid-Apr to end of Oct $90–$110 double; Nov to mid-Apr $60–$70 double. AE, MC, V. **Parking:** Free.

In the nearby village of Queenston, the South Landing Inn has rooms with bath and color TV. Five units are in the old original inn built in the early 1800s and their early Canadian furnishings, including poster beds, reflect this era. The rest are in the modern annex. There's a distant view of the river from the inn's balcony. In the original inn you'll also find a cozy dining room with red gingham covered tables, where breakfast is served for $4.

CAMPING

There's a **Niagara Falls KOA** at 8625 Lundy's Lane, Niagara Falls, ON, L2H 1H5 (tel. 905/354-6472), which has 365 sites (some with electricity, water, and sewage) plus three dumping stations. Facilities include water, flush toilets, showers, fireplaces, store, ice, three pools (one indoor), sauna, and games room. Fees are $23 minimum for two; each additional adult, $5; each additional child 4 to 17, $3; hookups range from $3 for electricity, $4 for water and electricity, and $6 for water, electricity, and sewage. Open April 1 to November 1.

WHERE TO DINE

EXPENSIVE

CASA D'ORO, 5875 Victoria Ave. Tel. 905/356-5646.
　Cuisine: ITALIAN. **Reservations:** Recommended.
$ Prices: Main courses $12–$18. AE, DC, DISC, ER, MC, V.
　Open: Lunch Mon–Fri noon–3pm; dinner Mon–Fri 4–11pm, Sat 4pm–1am, Sun 4–10pm.
For fine dining amid opulent surroundings one goes to Casa d'Oro to savor Italian delights amid an overwhelming array of gilt busts of Caesar, Venetian-style lamps, statues of Roman gladiators, Roman columns, and murals of Roman and Venetian scenes. Taste the splendors of clams casino or the brodetto Antonio (a giant crouton topped with poached eggs and floated on savory broth garnished with parsley and accompanied by grated cheese). Follow with specialties like saltimbocca alla romana, pollo cacciatore, or sole basilica (flavored with lime juice, paprika, and basil). Then, if you can bear it, choose from the dessert wagon or really spoil yourself with cherries jubilee or bananas flambé and an espresso.
　At the back of the Casa d'Oro, stroll over the Bridge of Sighs and onto the disco floor of the Rialto Room, where you can dance from 9pm to the wee hours to Top 40 music, except on Sunday, Monday, Wednesday, and Thursday, which are karaoke nights.

HAPPY WANDERER, 6405 Stanley Ave. Tel. 905/354-9825.
　Cuisine: GERMAN. **Reservations:** Not accepted.
$ Prices: Main courses $16–$25. AE, MC, V.
　Open: Daily 8am–11pm.
Real gemütlichkeit greets you at the chalet-style Happy Wanderer, where you can lay your knapsack down and tuck into a host of schnitzels, wursts, and other German specialties. Transport yourself back to the Black Forest among the beer steins and the game trophies on the walls. The several rooms include the Black Forest Room, with a huge, intricately carved sideboard and cuckoo clock, and the Jage Stube, with solid wood benches and woven tablecloths. At lunch there are omelets, cold platters, sandwiches, and burgers. Dinner might start with goulash soup, proceed with bratwurst, knackwurst, rauchwurst (served with sauerkraut and potato salad) or a schnitzel—wiener, Holstein, or jaeger. All entrées include potatoes, salad, and rye bread. Desserts include, naturally, Black Forest cake and apple strudel (under $5).

ROLF'S, 3840 Main St., Chippawa. Tel. 905/295-3472.
　Cuisine: CONTINENTAL. **Reservations:** Recommended, especially on weekends.
$ Prices: Appetizers $6–$10; main courses $12–$32. MC, V.
　Open: Dinner Tues–Sun 5–9pm.

Perhaps the best dining in Niagara Falls can be found at Rolf's, in Chippawa. Rolf hails from Germany, trained and worked in Zurich, and later at several Niagara establishments, before opening his own restaurant in a secluded town house complete with a front porch with room for two tables. The dining-room tables sport crisp white linen, Rosenthal china, and fresh flowers. The menu might feature orange roughy meunière, wienerschnitzel, chateaubriand, or filet of lamb provençale. There's also a four-course prix fixe for $17. Take the Niagara Parkway south all the way to Chippawa.

MODERATE

BETTY'S RESTAURANT & TAVERN, 8911 Sodom Rd. Tel. 905/295-4436.
   Cuisine: CANADIAN. **Reservations:** Accepted only for parties of eight or more.
$ Prices: Burgers and sandwiches under $5; main courses $6–$16.50. AE, MC, V.
   Open: Mon–Sat 7am–10pm, Sun 9am–10pm.
A local favorite for honest food at fair prices is Betty's Restaurant & Tavern. It's a family dining room where the art and generosity surface in the food—massive platters of fish-and-chips, breaded pork chops, chicken cutlet, all including soup or juice, vegetable, and potato. There are burgers and sandwiches, too. If you can, save room for dessert, for the pies are home-baked and the portions are enormous.
   Breakfast and lunch also offer superb low, low-budget eating and there's an $8.50 brunch on Sunday from October to May.

HUNGARIAN VILLAGE RESTAURANT, 5329 Ferry St. Tel. 905/356-2429.
   Cuisine: HUNGARIAN. **Reservations:** Required on weekends.
$ Prices: Main courses $10–$18. AE, MC, V.
   Open: Summer weekdays 4pm–midnight, weekends noon–1am; other seasons Tues–Fri 4pm–1am, Sat–Sun noon–1am.
Restaurateur Frank Kovalec, who comes from Budapest, has gone to great lengths to create a really authentic Hungarian atmosphere at his Hungarian Village Restaurant. The front room is designed to resemble a village inn complete with courtyard garden and pleasant grape arbors. Another room suggests a roadside inn with handwoven placemats and tokaj (rustic paintings on canvas, all with a wine-and-grape theme). At the rear the more formal Franz Liszt Room is studded with a few prime Hungarian tapestries and a cimbalom stands in the center. Here, you can sample Hungarian specialties: chicken paprikas, veal goulash, cabbage rolls "Kolozavar style" (served with pork chop and potatoes), gypsy steak, or the Transylvanian wooden platter (beef tenderloin, pork chop, veal cutlet, cabbage roll, and sausage, piled high on a bed of rice and served with french fries and sweet-and-sour cabbage; $30 for two). For dessert, there's palacsinta or Viennese pastries, of course. Continental dishes are also available.

NIAGARA PARKWAY COMMISSION RESTAURANTS

The Niagara Parkway Commission has commandeered the most spectacular scenic spots and there operates some reasonably priced dining outlets.

QUEENSTON HEIGHTS, Niagara Pkwy. Tel. 905/262-4274.
   Cuisine: CANADIAN. **Reservations:** Recommended.
$ Prices: Main courses $16–$19. AE, DISC, MC, V.
   Open: Lunch daily 11:30am–3pm; dinner Sun–Fri 5–9pm, Sat 5–10pm.
   Closed: Jan to mid-Mar.
The star of the commission's eateries stands dramatically atop Queenston Heights, and that's its name. Set in the park among fir, cypress, silver birch, and maple, the open-air balcony affords a magnificent view of the lower Niagara River and the rich fruitland through which it flows. Or you can sit under the cathedral ceiling with its heavy crossbeams where the flue of the stone fireplace reaches to the roof. At lunchtime, light entrées, seafood, pizza, pasta, salads, and lamb burgers (from $9 to $12) are offered. At dinner, among the selections might be filet of Atlantic salmon with strawberry champagne hollandaise, roast pork with an apricot peppercorn glaze, and prime rib. Afternoon tea is also served from 3 to 5pm in summer season.
   Go for a drink on the deck. There's a terrific view.

TABLE ROCK RESTAURANT, Niagara Pkwy. Tel. 905/354-3631.
   Cuisine: CANADIAN/INTERNATIONAL. **Reservations:** Recommended.
$ **Prices:** Main courses $13–$17. AE, DISC, MC, V.
   Open: Summer Sun–Thurs 9am–10pm, Fri–Sat 9am–11pm.
Located only a few yards from the Canadian Horseshoe Falls, the Table Rock Restaurant offers such dinner choices as prime rib; grilled tiger shrimp marinated with tomato, onion, garlic, olive oil, and rum; or chicken schnitzel with mushrooms and cheese sauce. Pizza, pasta, ribs, and light entrées are the luncheon choices. Breakfast is also a good bet here.

VICTORIA PARK RESTAURANT, Niagara Pkwy. Tel. 905/356-2217.
   Cuisine: CANADIAN. **Reservations:** Recommended.
$ **Prices:** Main courses $12–$19. AE, DISC, MC, V.
   Open: Mid-May to mid-Oct Sat–Thurs 11:30am–10pm, Fri 11:30am–11pm.
   Closed: Canadian Thanksgiving in Oct–early May.
Within spitting distance of both the Canadian and American falls, the Victoria Park Restaurant offers not only a terrace with an awning where you can sit and dine, but an inside dining room warmed by its burnt-orange tablecloths and globe lights, a downstairs cafeteria, plus a fast-food outlet pushing hot dogs and ice cream. Here, at least in the dining room and terrace, you'll find quite an elaborate menu with a whole range of appetizers (shrimp cocktail, smoked goose breast, gravlax), and entrées that include steaks, coconut fried shrimp, and fettuccine with shrimp and okra. Pasta, sandwiches, and stir fries are available at lunch.

WHIRLPOOL RESTAURANT, Niagara Pkwy. Tel. 905/356-7221.
   Cuisine: CANADIAN. **Reservations:** Recommended.
$ **Prices:** Main courses $6–$12. AE, DISC, MC, V.
   Open: Daily 6am–8pm. **Closed:** Oct 31–Mar.
Along the parkway toward Queenston lies the rather delightful Whirlpool Restaurant, at the commission's 18-hole golf course. It has a fine view of the first tee, the 18th green, and the 6,945-yard championship course, and serves a hearty breakfast and eminently reasonable lunch as well as dinner.

DINING WITH A VIEW

PINNACLE, 6732 Oakes Dr. Tel. 905/356-1501.
   Cuisine: CANADIAN/CONTINENTAL. **Reservations:** Recommended.
$ **Prices:** Main courses $16–$37. AE, DC, DISC, ER, MC, V.
   Open: Lunch daily 11am–4pm; dinner daily 5–10pm.
You can dine atop the Minolta Tower in the Pinnacle Dining Room, on typical North American/continental favorites—steak, salmon, grilled chicken, plus daily specials.

SKYLON TOWER RESTAURANTS, 5200 Robinson St. Tel. 905/356-2651, ext. 271.
   Cuisine: CONTINENTAL. **Reservations:** Recommended.
$ **Prices:** Main courses $26–$38. AE, CB, DC, DISC, MC, V.
   Open: Lunch daily 11:30am–2:30pm; dinner daily 5–10:30pm. Dinner hours shorter in the off-season.
Besides the view from atop the 520-foot tower at the Skylon Tower Restaurants, you can enjoy breakfast, lunch, or dinner buffets ($12, $18 or $28 respectively) in the Summit Suite dining room, or lunch or dinner in the Revolving Restaurant, where typical favorites like chicken Cordon Bleu, prime rib, and fresh salmon are served.

2. NIAGARA-ON-THE-LAKE

80 miles (128km) S of Toronto, 35 miles (56km) N of Buffalo, N.Y.

GETTING THERE   By Train   Amtrak and VIA operate trains between Toronto (tel. 416/366-8411) and New York stopping in St. Catharines and Niagara Falls. Call toll free 800/361-1235 in Canada or 800/USA-RAIL in the U.S.

By Bus Gray Coach lines stop in St. Catharines and Niagara Falls. From either town, your best bet is a cab, although buses operate from St. Catharines' bus terminal on Tuesday, Thursday, and Saturday (one in the morning and one in the afternoon).

By Car From Toronto take the QEW Niagara via Hamilton and St. Catharines and exit at Highway 55. From the U.S. cross from Buffalo to Fort Erie via the Peace Bridge or from Niagara Falls, N.Y., via the Rainbow Bridge and then take the QEW to Highway 55. Or cross at the Queenston-Lewiston bridge and follow the signs along the Niagara Parkway into Niagara-on-the-Lake. Allow plenty of time for crossing the border.

ESSENTIALS The Niagara-on-the-Lake Chamber of Commerce & Visitor & Convention Bureau, 153 King St. (P.O. Box 1043), Niagara-on-the-Lake, ON, L0S 1J0 (tel. 905/468-4263), will provide extensive information and also help you find accommodations at one of 55 bed-and-breakfasts licensed in the town. Open in summer, Monday through Wednesday from 9am to 5pm, Thursday through Saturday from 9am to 7pm, Sunday from 10am to 5pm; in winter, Monday through Friday from 9am to 5pm, Saturday from 11am to 5pm.

SPECIAL EVENTS The major event and the primary reason for visiting is to enjoy the ✪ **Shaw Festival.** Brian Doherty, a local lawyer, founded the theater festival here with eight weekend performances of *Don Juan in Hell* in the summer of 1962.

Devoted to the works of George Bernard Shaw and his contemporaries, the festival is housed in three theaters: the historic Court House, the Edwardian Royal George, and the exquisite Festival Theatre, where intermissions can be spent near the reflecting pools and gardens. Gourmet snacks are served at the Parasol Café on the terrace 1½ hours before curtain time. The season includes drama, musicals, comedy, and a lunchtime performance at the Royal George Theatre. Ticket prices for all three theaters range from $12 for lunchtime performances to $50.

The Shaw Festival opens in mid-April and runs to November, offering a wide selection of plays. Some recent performances have included Shaw's *Saint Joan,* Noël Coward's *Blithe Spirit,* and Agatha Christie's *And Then There Were None.*

For more information, write or phone the Shaw Festival, P.O. Box 774, Niagara-on-the-Lake, ON, L0S 1J0 (tel. 905/468-2172).

Only 1½ hours from Toronto, Niagara-on-the-Lake claims a lot of firsts: first capital of Upper Canada (1792), first gristmill (1782), first census taken (1792), and the first newspaper (1792). It's also one of the best-preserved and prettiest 19th-century villages in North America, with its lakeside location and tree-lined streets bordered by handsome clapboard and brick period houses. Such is the setting for one of Canada's most famous events, the Shaw Festival.

WHAT TO SEE & DO

In addition to visiting the sights mentioned below, taking a stroll along Queen Street will take you to some entertaining shopping stops. At the 1866 **Niagara Apothecary Shop** (tel. 905/468-3845), with its original black-walnut counters and the contents of the drawers marked in gold-leaf script, the original glass and ceramic apothecary ware is on display. **Niagara Fudge,** 92 Picton St. (tel. 905/468-7835), offers 35 varieties that you can watch being made on marble slabs. **Greaves Jam** offers the wares of fourth-generation jam makers. **Loyalist Village,** at no. 12 (tel. 905/468-7331), has distinctively Canadian clothes and crafts, including Inuit art, Native Canadian decoys, and sheepskins. The **Shaw Shop,** next to the Royal George, has GBS memorabilia and more. There's also a Dansk outlet and several

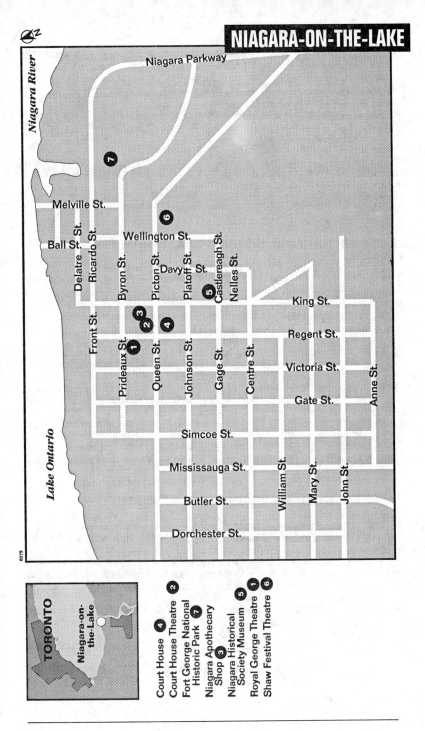

NIAGARA-ON-THE-LAKE

Niagara River

Lake Ontario

Niagara Parkway

Melville St.

Ball St.

Delatre St.

Ricardo St.

Wellington St.

Byron St.

Picton St.

Davy St.

Platoff St.

Castlereagh St.

Nelles St.

King St.

Front St.

Prideaux St.

Queen St.

Johnson St.

Gage St.

Centre St.

Regent St.

Victoria St.

Gate St.

Anne St.

Simcoe St.

Mississauga St.

William St.

Mary St.

John St.

Butler St.

Dorchester St.

TORONTO

Niagara-on-the-Lake

Court House ❹

Court House Theatre ❷

Fort George National Historic Park ❼

Niagara Apothecary Shop ❸

Niagara Historical Society Museum ❺

Royal George Theatre ❶

Shaw Festival Theatre ❻

galleries selling contemporary Canadian or other ethnic crafts, and a charming toy store, **The Owl and the Pussy Cat,** 16 Queen St. (tel. 905/468-3081).

NIAGARA HISTORICAL SOCIETY MUSEUM, 43 Castlereagh St., at Davy. Tel. 905/468-3912.

One of the oldest and largest of its kind in Canada, this museum houses over 20,000 artifacts pertaining to local history, including comprehensive collections from a number of families dating back to the late 18th and early 19th centuries. There are a number of unique items in the collection, such as a hat belonging to Gen. Sir Isaac Brock, who was killed in the War of 1812, and many possessions of United Empire Loyalists who first settled the area at the end of the American Revolution, plus many other exciting exhibits.

Admission: $2.50 adults, $1 students, $1.50 seniors, 50¢ children under 12.

Open: May 1–Oct 31 daily 10am–5pm; Nov 1–Dec 31 and Mar–Apr daily 1–5pm; Jan–Feb Sat–Sun 1–5pm.

FORT GEORGE NATIONAL HISTORIC SITE, Niagara Pkwy. Tel. 905/ 468-4257.

South along the Niagara Parkway, Fort George National Historic Park is really impressive. It's easy to imagine taking shelter behind the stockade fence and watching for the enemy from across the river, even though today there are only condominiums staring back from the opposite riverbank. The fort played a key role in the War of 1812 when the Americans invaded and it was destroyed by American artillery in May 1813. Although rebuilt by 1815, because it did not dominate the mouth of the Niagara River it was abandoned in 1828 and not reconstructed until the 1930s. View the guard room with its hard plank beds, the officers' quarters, the enlisted men's quarters, and the sentry posts. In the gunpowder-storage area no metal fitments are used, for a stray spark could ignite the lot. The floor boards are secured with wooden pegs and the soldiers working in the magazine wore special smocks and wooden clogs. The self-guided tour includes interpretive films and occasionally performances by the Fort George Fife and Drum Corps.

Admission: $2.75 adults, $1.25 children 6 and over, free for children under 5 and senior citizens, family rate $7.

Open: Mid-May to June 30 daily 9:30am–4:30pm; July 1–Labor Day daily 10:30am–5:30pm; Labor Day–Oct 31 daily 9:30am–4:30pm; Nov 1 to mid-May, open weekdays by appointment only.

NIAGARA-ON-THE-LAKE WINERIES

If you take Highway 55 (Niagara Stone Road) out of Niagara-on-the-Lake you will come to **Hillebrand Estates Winery** (tel. 905/468-7123), just outside Virgil. It's open year-round; tours are given daily at 11am and 1, 3, and 4pm.

If you turn off Highway 55 before reaching Hillebrand and go down Four Mile Creek Road to Line 7, you'll reach **Château des Charmes,** in St. Davids (tel. 905/262-4219). Tours are given Tuesday through Saturday at 11am, 1:30pm, and 3pm from May to September; by appointment at other times.

The **Konzelmann Winery,** Lakeshore Road (tel. 905/935-2866), can be reached by driving out Mary Street. Tours are given June to late August Wednesday to Saturday at 2pm, in September every Saturday at 2pm.

For other wineries in the region, see the "Winery Tours" section in Niagara Falls.

WHERE TO STAY

During the summer season it can be hard to find accommodations in this small popular town. Don't despair if you're having trouble nailing down a room somewhere—contact the chamber of commerce, which provides an accommodations reservation service.

A good bet is always one of the many bed-and-breakfast accommodations in the area. For more information, contact the **Niagara-on-the-Lake Chamber of**

Commerce & Visitor & Convention Bureau, 153 King St. (P.O. Box 1043), Niagara-on-the-Lake, ON, L0S 1J0 (tel. 905/468-4263).

Please note that the Oban Inn, the oldest and dearest inn and the one most frequented by theater people, burned down in December 1992. It was scheduled to reopen as this book was being prepared, so do inquire about its status before making your trip.

INNS

GATE HOUSE HOTEL, 142 Queen St. (P.O. Box 1364), Niagara-on-the-Lake, ON, L0S 1J0. Tel. 905/468-3263. Fax 905/468-7400. 9 rms. A/C MINIBAR TV TEL
$ Rates: June 1–Sept 30 $155 double; Oct 1–May 31 $135 double. AE, ER, MC, V. **Parking:** Free. **Closed:** Jan.

The accommodations at the Gate House Hotel are strikingly different from other accommodations in the town. They are not country Canadian, but rather are decorated in cool, up-to-the-minute Milan style. Each has a turquoise marbleized look accented with ultramodern basic black lamps, block marble tables, leatherette couches, and bathrooms with sleek Italian fitments and hairdryers.

GEORGE III, 61 Melville St., Niagara-on-the-Lake, ON, L0S 1J0. Tel. 905/468-4800. Fax 905/468-7004. 8 rms. A/C TV
$ Rates (including continental breakfast): $90–$105 double; $115 room with balcony. MC, V. **Parking:** Free.

Down by the harbor, the George III offers attractive rooms that have pretty wallpaper treatments, quilts and flounce pillows on the beds, and clock radios and TVs. Room 8 has a large balcony. The inn is operated by the Pillar & Post Inn, so call there for reservations.

KIELY HOUSE HERITAGE INN, 209 W. Queen St. (P.O. Box 1642), Niagara-on-the-Lake, ON, L0S 1J0. Tel. 905/468-4588. 13 rms. A/C TEL
$ Rates (including breakfast): $90–$110 double; $175 room with fireplace. Extra person $15. AE, MC, V. **Parking:** Free.

Ideally situated in a fine stately summer home that was built in 1832, Kiely House offers rooms that are graciously decorated with fine antiques. Some have canopy beds and some have fireplaces. The sitting and breakfast rooms have carved walnut fireplaces and comfortable furnishings that make them appealing places for afternoon tea and your complimentary morning muffins and fresh fruit. The inn also has a pleasant garden out back. Bicycles are available in summer and fall, cross-country skis in winter.

MOFFAT INN, 60 Picton St., Niagara-on-the-Lake, ON, L0S 1J0. Tel. 905/468-4116. Fax 905/468-4747. 22 rms. A/C TV TEL
$ Rates: May 1 to mid-Oct and Christmas/New Year holiday period $85–$105 double; mid-Oct to Apr $65–$95 double. Extra person $10. AE, MC, V. **Parking:** Free.

Niagara-on-the-Lake has a fine accommodation at the Moffat Inn. Seven of the rooms offer fireplaces, and all the units are quite comfortable. Most are furnished with either brass or cannonball beds, and wicker and bamboo pieces, and feature built-in closets. A nice touch is the tea kettle and appropriate supplies in every room. Free coffee is available in the lobby.

OLD BANK HOUSE, 10 Front St. (P.O. Box 1708), Niagara-on-the-Lake, ON, L0S 1J0. Tel. 905/468-7136. 4 rms (none with bath), 4 suites (all with bath). A/C
$ Rates (including full English breakfast): $90 room without bath; $110 room with private bath; $130 suite; $225 two-bedroom suite for up to four. Lower rates in winter. AE. **Parking:** Free.

 Beautifully situated down by the river, the Old Bank House, a two-story Georgian, was built in 1817 and was in fact the first branch of the Bank of Canada. The inn is operated by Marjorie Ironmonger and her husband. It has four rooms, each with a washbasin, sharing a full bathroom plus an extra toilet. In addition there is a room with private bath, two suites with private bath and separate entrances, and a two-bedroom suite with sitting room and bathroom. All rooms are tastefully decorated, and all but one have fridge and coffee or tea supplies. The sitting room with fireplace is very comfortable and furnished with Sheraton and Hepplewhite.

PILLAR & POST INN, 48 John St. (at King St.), Niagara-on-the-Lake, ON, L0S 1J0. Tel. 905/468-2123. Fax 905/468-3551. 84 rms, 7 suites. A/C MINIBAR TV TEL

$ Rates: $145 double; $155 fireplace room; $205 suite. AE, DC, ER, MC, V. **Parking:** Free.

Rustic to every last inch of barn board, the Pillar & Post Inn has 91 lovely rooms, 48 of them with wood-burning fireplaces. Although each room is decorated slightly differently, any room will certainly contain early Canadian-style furniture, Windsor-style chairs, and a color TV tucked into a pine cabinet, historical engravings, plus the usual modern conveniences. The suites all come with cathedral ceilings, red-brick wood-burning fireplaces, pine settles with cushions, four-poster beds, and Jacuzzis. Some rooms facing the pool on the ground level have bay windows and window boxes. The brick-and-pine lobby sets the tone and opens onto a tiny courtyard with tubs of flowers.

Dining/Entertainment: The dining room occupies a former canning factory that preserved the peaches and tomatoes brought in by local farmers. The last can came down the line in 1957, and it became a basket-manufacturing plant until assuming its present role as a restaurant in 1970. A craft shop adjoins the restaurant and is worth shopping for country quilts, kitchenware, pine furniture, dolls, toys, and more. The menu features continental cuisine—filet mignon and shrimp brochette with garlic parsley and a white wine sauce; or rack of lamb with almond, walnut and pine nut crust, for example. Prices range from $16 to $24. There's also a comfortable lounge to relax in.

Services: Room service from 7:30am to 9pm; laundry/valet.

Facilities: In the back there's a secluded grass-surrounded pool, a sauna, and a whirlpool. Bike rentals available.

PRINCE OF WALES HOTEL, 6 Picton St., Niagara-on-the-Lake, ON, L0S 1J0. Tel. 905/468-3246. Fax 905/468-5521. 104 rms. A/C TV TEL

$ Rates: May 1–Oct 31 $110–$178 single, $115–$188 double, from $200 suite. Extra person $12. Rates slightly less at other times. AE, MC, V. **Parking:** Free.

For a more lively atmosphere that still retains the elegance and charm of a Victorian inn, the Prince of Wales Hotel has it all: full recreational facilities; lounges, bars, and restaurants; and attractive rooms, some with colonial-style furniture, others with brass bedsteads. All units are beautifully decorated with antiques or reproductions and color-coordinated carpeting, drapes, and spreads. The large bathrooms are equipped with bidets.

The original section of the hotel was built in 1864 and contains the room where the Prince of Wales supposedly slept (hence the Prince of Wales feathers carved on the headboard). In the Prince of Wales Court, rooms are larger, huge wardrobes house the TVs, and botanical prints on the walls set the tone. The newer wing has been extremely well designed to match as closely as possible the original red-brick and cream exterior with its slate dormer roof.

Dining/Entertainment: An impressive old oak bar that came from Pennsylvania dominates the quiet bar off the lobby. Royals, the main dining room, is an elegant room decorated in French style, with the Greenhouse patio overlooking Simcoe Park. Here breakfast, lunch, and dinner are served. The dinner menu offers a dozen entrées, from rack of lamb packed with herbs and Dijon mustard to salmon and scallops with ginger butter. Prices range from $17 to $24. At lunch, lighter dishes are featured, like ratatouille and mozzarella in phyllo pastry and pan-fried trout with sautéed leeks, priced from $9 to $12. Three Feathers Café is light and airy for breakfast, lunch, or tea. The Queen's Royal lounge, furnished with wingbacks and armchairs, is a pleasant drinking spot.

Services: Room service from 7:30am to midnight; laundry/valet.

Facilities: Indoor pool, sauna, whirlpool, sun and exercise room, and platform tennis court.

QUEEN'S LANDING, Byron St. (P.O. Box 1180), Niagara-on-the-Lake, ON, L0S 1J0. Tel. 905/468-2195. Fax 905/468-2227. 137 rms. A/C MINIBAR TV TEL

$ Rates: $145 double; $155 fireplace room; $195 deluxe room with fireplace and Jacuzzi. Extra person $20. Children under 12 stay free in parents' room. Special packages available. AE, DC, ER, MC, V. **Parking:** Free.

Overlooking the river, but also within walking distance of the theater, the Queen's Landing is a fine establishment. Seventy of the rooms have fireplaces and 32 have Jacuzzis. Rooms are spacious and comfortably furnished with pine furnishings, half-canopy or brass beds, wingback chairs, and large desks, and equipped with color cable TVs and clock radios.

Dining/Entertainment: The lounge, with its fieldstone fireplace, is cozy; and the dining room looks out over the yacht-filled dock. At dinner about a dozen or so fish and meat dishes are offered, priced from $17 to $28 for such dishes as filet of grilled Atlantic salmon in tamarind and ginger sauce or médaillons of veal basted with a roasted shallot and garlic jus. Breakfast and lunch are served here, too.

Services: Room service from 7am to 11pm; laundry/valet.

Facilities: Indoor pool, whirlpool and sauna, exercise room, lap pool, and bicycle rentals.

A RACQUET-SPORTS ENTHUSIAST'S PARADISE

WHITE OAKS INN AND RACQUET CLUB, Taylor Rd., Niagara-on-the-Lake, ON, L0S 1J0. Tel. 905/688-2550. Fax 905/688-2220. 90 rms. A/C TV TEL

$ Rates: July–Aug $104–$114 single or double, $160–$180 suite; off-season $100–$104 single, from $140 suite. AE, DC, ER, MC, V. **Parking:** Free.

Not far from Niagara-on-the-Lake, the White Oaks Inn and Racquet Club is a fantastic facility for the fitness freak or the interested athlete. Anyone can come here, spend the whole weekend, and not stir outside the resort.

The rooms are as good as the facilities, featuring oak beds and furniture, gray-blue or blue-rose decor, vanity sinks, and those additional niceties like a phone in the bathroom and complimentary shampoo, cologne, and toothbrush. The Executive Suites, as they're called, also have brick fireplaces, marble-top desks, Jacuzzi tub (some are heart-shaped), and a bidet. Deluxe suites also have sitting rooms and the ultimate in furnishings.

Dining/Entertainment: While you enjoy the resort's activities you can also take a break and enjoy the lounge area, the outdoor terrace café, a formal restaurant, and a pleasantly furnished café/coffee shop.

Services: Room service from 7am to 11pm; valet.

Facilities: On the premises are four outside tennis courts, six squash courts, two racquetball courts, and eight air-conditioned indoor tennis courts with indirect lighting systems. There's also a fully equipped fitness/aerobics room, jogging trails, massage therapist, sauna, suntan beds, and a terrific day-care center staffed with fully qualified personnel.

WHERE TO DINE
EXPENSIVE

THE BUTTERY, 19 Queen St. Tel. 905/468-2564.

Cuisine: CANADIAN/ENGLISH/CONTINENTAL. **Reservations:** Required for Henry VIII feast.

$ Prices: Main courses $17–$21. AE, MC, V.

Open: Summer daily 11am–12:30am; other months daily noon–8pm, except on Fri–Sat when the Henry VIII feast takes place. Afternoon tea served 2–5pm; after-theater menu served 10pm–12:30am.

With its terrace brightened by hanging geraniums, the Buttery has been a main-street dining landmark for years. It's particularly known for its weekend Henry VIII feasts

(9pm upstairs, 9:30pm downstairs), when serving wenches will "cosset" you with food and wine, "and being most amiable call your attention to the jongleurs, musickers and those who have been summoned expressly for your entertainment." You will in fact receive "four removes"—broth, chicken, roast lamb, roast pig, sherry trifle, syllabub, and cheese, washed down with a goodly amount of wine, ale, and mead. This will take 2½ hours and cost you $40, including tax and gratuity for Henry VIII.

At other times a full tavern menu is served during the day from 11am to 5:30pm, featuring traditional favorites like spareribs, filet mignon, and shrimp in garlic sauce, along with such English specialties as Cornish pasty (worthy of the name, by the way), steak, kidney, and mushroom pie, and Welsh rarebit. Prices run $7 to $16 (most under $9).

At dinner the menu lists eight or so choices, from breast of chicken with a lemon-chardonnay sauce to lobster Newburg (with cream and brandy). Highly recommended is the leg of lamb served with a real garden mint sauce. Finish with key lime pie or mud pie. If you're wise, you'll take home some of the fresh baked goods available—pies, strudels, dumplings, cream puffs, and scones.

RISTORANTE GIARDINO, on the ground floor of the Gate House Hotel, 142 Queen St. Tel. 905/468-3263.
   Cuisine: ITALIAN. **Reservations:** Recommended.
$ **Prices:** Main courses $19–$26. AE, CB, ER, MC, V.
   Open: Summer lunch daily noon–2pm, dinner daily 5:30–9pm; winter dinner daily 5:30–9pm.

The Ristorante Giardino is a sleek, ultramodern restaurant with gleaming marble-top bar and glass and brass accents throughout. The food is classic northern Italian. The dinner menu lists a dozen or so main courses—scallops in saffron-chardonnay cream sauce, steamed salmon with red pepper and basil sauce, grilled filet mignon in green peppercorn deglazed with Barolo red wine. Appetizers, pasta, and soup round out the menu. Desserts include tiramisu—lady fingers soaked in marsala and espresso, buried in sweet cream cheese and topped with cocoa. Lunch prices range from $7 to $14.

MODERATE

FANS COURT, 135 Queen St. Tel. 905/468-4511.
   Cuisine: CHINESE. **Reservations:** Recommended.
$ **Prices:** Main courses $8–$16. AE, MC, V.
   Open: Summer Mon noon–9pm, Tues–Sun noon–10pm; winter Tues–Sun noon–10pm. **Closed:** Jan.
Some of the best food in town can be found at Fans Court, a comfortable Chinese restaurant. Fans decorate the entrance, while inside there are comfortable cushioned bamboo chairs and round tables spread with golden tablecloths. In summer, the courtyard also has tables for dining. The cuisine ranges from Cantonese and Beijing to Szechuan. Singapore beef, moo shu pork, Szechuan scallops, and lemon chicken are just a few of the dishes available. If you wish, you can order Peking duck 24 hours in advance.

BUDGET

GEORGE III, 61 Melville St. Tel. 905/468-4207.
   Cuisine: CANADIAN. **Reservations:** Not accepted.
$ **Prices:** Main courses $7–$15. MC, V.
   Open: Daily 11am–9pm. **Closed:** Dec–Mar.
Down by the harbor, Georgie's is a good budget dining choice serving burgers by design—with a choice of meats and toppings ranging from guacamole to Cajun spice—plus chicken, ribs, stir-fries, and salads. There's a publike atmosphere, and a pleasant outdoor patio, too.

SPECIALTY DINING

The **Niagara Home Bakery,** 66 Queen St. (tel. 905/468-3431), is the place to stop for chocolate-date squares, cherry squares, croissants, cookies, and individual quiches.

For breakfast, go to the **Stagecoach Family Restaurant,** 45 Queen St. (tel. 905/468-3133), for a down-home budget-priced meal.

3. ST. CATHARINES TO PORT COLBORNE

GETTING TO THE AREA

BY TRAIN   Amtrak and VIA operate trains between Toronto (tel. 416/366-8411) and New York, stopping in St. Catharines and Niagara Falls. Call toll free 800/361-1235 in Canada or 800/USA-RAIL in the U.S.

BY BUS   Gray Coach (a Greyhound company) operates daily buses from Toronto (tel. 416/594-3310) and from Buffalo (tel. 716/852-1750) to St. Catharines. The closest stop for Port Colborne is Fort Erie.

BY CAR   From Toronto, take the QEW Niagara to the St. Catharines exit; for Port Colborne the easiest way is to take the QEW Niagara to Highway 3 east.

If you take Mary Street from Niagara-on-the-Lake, you'll be heading out along Lakeshore Road past the **Konzelmann Winery** (tel. 905/935-2866)—tours by appointment only.

Just before you enter St. Catharines, there's a sign on the right for the **Happy Rolph Bird Sanctuary and Children's Petting Farm** (tel. 905/935-1484), which the kids will love. Open daily from late May to mid-October from 10am to dusk. Admission is free.

Back on Lakeshore Road you'll come to the junction of Lake Street. Turn left for downtown St. Catharines. In the heart of the wine country and the Niagara fruit belt, St. Catharines is a historic city that is home to two major events: the **Royal Canadian Henley Regatta** in early August and the 10-day **Niagara Grape and Wine Festival** held in late September.

THE WELLAND CANAL

The Welland Canal was built to circumvent Niagara Falls and to connect Lake Ontario to Lake Erie, which is 327 feet higher than Lake Ontario. Some 27 feet deep, the canal enables ocean vessels to navigate into the heart of the continent via the Great Lakes. The canal is 26 miles long and has seven locks, each with an average lift of 46.5 feet. The average transit time for any vessel is 12 hours. More than a thousand oceangoing vessels travel through in a year, the most common cargoes being wheat and iron ore.

The first canal opened in 1829 in St. Catharines, where today remnants of the first three canals (1829, 1845, and 1887) have been preserved. At **Port Dalhousie,** where the canals entered Lake Ontario, the locks, lighthouses, and 19th-century warehouses and architecture are reminders of a once-thriving waterway.

Best places to observe the canal are at the **Welland Canal Viewing and Information Centres,** at Lock 3 in St. Catharines and at Lock 8 in Port Colborne. At the first, from a raised platform you can watch ships from over 50 countries passing between Lake Erie and Lake Ontario and being raised or lowered at the lock. It's exciting. If you walk along the road from the lock, you can look up above the bank and see just the ship funnels passing by. It's on Canal Road north of Glendale Avenue, right off the QEW. At the second, Lock 8, there's also an observation stand overlooking one of the longest locks anywhere.

At Locks 4, 5, and 6—the twin flight locks—ships can be locked simultaneously in both directions. They're in **Thorold,** on Canal Road, south of Glendale Avenue.

In **Welland,** a section of the fourth canal, which is no longer trafficked, is now used for recreational purposes—waterskiing, boating, and picnicking.

For vessel information and estimated arrival times, call 905/688-6462 for a recorded message.

OTHER REGIONAL ATTRACTIONS

Welland is known for its two-week **Rose Festival** in early June, when the city bursts out with sports events, art shows, rose-growing contests, a military band tattoo, ethnic foods, and a parade.

ST. CATHARINES MUSEUM, Lock 3, 1932 Canal Rd., St. Catharines. Tel. 905/984-8880.

The Historical Museum features displays illustrating the construction of the Welland Canal as well as pioneer and War of 1812 memorabilia. Check ahead, as the museum is scheduled to move to a building at Lock 3.

Admission: $3 adults, $2 students and seniors, $1 children 5-12.

Open: Labor Day–Victoria Day Mon–Fri 9am–5pm, Sat–Sun 1–5pm; Victoria Day–Labor Day daily 9:30am–7pm. **Closed:** Good Friday, Dec 25–26, and New Year's Day.

PRUDHOMME'S LANDING—WET 'N' WILD, off Victoria Ave., Vineland. Tel. 905/562-7304.

This entertainment complex features water slides, a wave pool, go-karts, kids' rides, and miniature golf.

Admission: All-day pass $14.95 adults, $11.17 children 5-12.

Open: Mid-June to Labor Day daily 10am–9pm.

TIVOLI MINIATURE WORLD, off Prudhomme Blvd., Vineland. Tel. 905/685-9012.

Here visitors see famous buildings like St. Peter's Basilica and the Kremlin built on a scale of one-fiftieth actual size.

Admission: $9 adults, $8 students and seniors, $4.25 children 5-12.

Open: Mon–Thurs 9am–10pm, Fri and Sun 9am–11pm, Sat 9am–midnight.

Directions: Take the Victoria Avenue exit off the QEW, near Vineland Station.

PORT COLBORNE HISTORICAL AND MARINE MUSEUM, 280 King St. Tel. 905/834-7604.

The southern end of the canal opens into Lake Erie at Port Colborne. A good sense of the history and development of the area can be gained at the Port Colborne Historical and Marine Museum, a six-building complex downtown, where there's a fully operational blacksmith shop and also a tearoom.

Admission: Free.

Open: May–Dec daily noon–5pm.

WHERE TO DINE

IN THE PORT DALHOUSIE HARBOR AREA

MURPHY'S, Lakeport Rd. Tel. 905/934-1913.

Cuisine: CANADIAN. **Reservations:** Recommended for large parties.

$ Prices: Main courses $10–$30. AE, MC, V.

Open: Sun–Thurs 11:30am–10pm, Fri–Sat 11:30am–11:30pm.

Murphy's has a polished, nautical look, with prints on the walls relating to the Welland Canal. There's a profusion of healthy plants, and the place is a popular dining and drinking spot, attracting a mid-30s/40s professional crowd. Offerings run from steak, pasta, seafood, and chicken wings to sandwiches. Prices top out with the lobster tail dinner.

THE PORT MANSION, 12 Lakeport Rd. Tel. 905/934-0575.

Cuisine: CANADIAN. **Reservations:** Recommended, especially on weekends.

$ Prices: Main courses $15–$28. AE, DC, MC, V.

Open: Lunch Mon–Sat 11am–3pm, Sun 10:30am–3pm; dinner daily 4–10pm.

The Port Mansion has a kitschy Victorian atmosphere—stained-glass lamps and bamboo furniture mixed with the more classic look of wing chairs and reading material. There's a pleasant outdoor patio for dining while overlooking the boat traffic in the harbor. Prime rib, surf-and-turf, pasta, shrimp and scallop fettuccine, chicken stir-fry, and similar fare are the specialties here.

IN ST. CATHARINES

ISEYA, 22 James St., between St. Paul and King Sts. Tel. 905/688-1141.
   Cuisine: JAPANESE. **Reservations:** Recommended for dinner.
$ **Prices:** Main courses $9–$16. AE, MC, V.
   Open: Lunch Tues–Fri 11:30am–2:30pm; dinner Tues–Sun 5:30–10pm.
Iseya is one of the few traditional Japanese restaurants in the region, serving sushi as well as teriyaki, tempura, and sukiyaki dishes.

WELLINGTON COURT CAFE, 11 Wellington St. Tel. 905/682-5518.
   Cuisine: CONTINENTAL. **Reservations:** Recommended.
$ **Prices:** Main courses $10–$20. MC, V.
   Open: Lunch Mon–Sat 11:30am–2:30pm, dinner Tues–Sat 5–9:30pm.
⭐ In downtown St. Catharines, the Wellington Court Café is a pleasant café-restaurant in a town house with a flower trellis. Inside the decor is contemporary with modern lithographs and photographs. The menu features daily specials—fish and pasta of the day, for example—along with such items as veal chop in pecan crust with port, stuffed breast of chicken with black currant cream sauce, or salmon in various sauces. At lunch, soups, salads, and sandwiches are the staples, priced from $6 to $8.

IN DOWNTOWN WELLAND

RINDALIN'S, 24 Burgar St. Tel. 905/735-4411.
   Cuisine: FRENCH. **Reservations:** Recommended.
$ **Prices:** Main courses $15–$26. AE, MC, V.
   Open: Lunch Tues–Fri noon–2:30pm; dinner Tues–Fri 6–9pm, Sat 5:30–9pm.
⭐ An intimate town house dining spot, Rindalin's has a very good reputation locally for traditional French cuisine. On the dinner menu you might find veal citron or veal with morels in a cream sauce or veal with white wine, sage, and prosciutto, as well as Dover sole, rack of lamb, and venison with wild mushrooms and game sauce. Desserts are seasonal.

4. HAMILTON

42 miles (63km) SW of Toronto

GETTING THERE   By Bus   Greyhound operates six or so buses a day from London (tel. 519/434-3245) and from Toronto (tel. 416/393-7911).

By Car   From Toronto take the QEW Niagara to the Hamilton exit.

ESSENTIALS   For information, stop in at the Tourist Information Centre, at the corner of King and Catherine Streets (tel. 905/546-2666), or contact Greater Hamilton Tourism and Convention Services, 1 James St. South, 3rd floor, Hamilton, ON, L8P 4R5 (tel. 905/546-4222).

Situated on a landlocked harbor spanned at its entrance by the dramatic sweep of the Burlington Skyway, Hamilton (pop. 312,000) has long been known as "Steeltown." Although it certainly has steel mills and smoke-belching chimneys, it has recently received an extensive facelift, the most remarkable results being Hamilton Place, a huge cultural center, Lloyd D. Jackson Square, a new City Hall with splashing fountains out front, and many an urban-renewal project, the most notable being Hess Village. Such a renaissance has also spawned restaurants and other facilities that a cultured city naturally possesses.

WHAT TO SEE & DO

ROYAL BOTANICAL GARDENS, Hwy. 6. Tel. 905/527-1158.

On the northern approaches to the city, these gardens provide almost 3,000 acres of stunning horticultural exhibits. The Rock Garden features spring bulbs in May, summer flowers from June to September, and chrysanthemums in October. The Laking Garden blazes during June and July with iris, peonies, and lilies. The arboretum fills with the heady scent of lilac from the end of May to early June, and the exquisite color bursts of rhododendrons and azaleas thereafter. The Centennial Rose Garden is at its best from late June to mid-September.

Twenty-five miles of nature trails crisscross the area inviting exploration, while nearby, and still part of the gardens, is **Cootes Paradise,** a natural wildlife sanctuary with trails leading through some 18,000 acres of water, marsh, and wooded ravines. For a trail-guide map, stop in at either the Nature Centre (open daily from 10am to 4pm) or at headquarters at 680 Plains Rd. West (Highway 2), Burlington.

Refreshments can be had at the Tea Houses: one overlooking the Rock Garden, the other the Rose Garden.

Admission: $4.25 adults, $3.25 seniors and children 5–12.

Open: Outdoor garden areas mid-Apr to Oct 11 9:30am–6pm; Mediterranean Garden daily 9am–5pm. **Directions:** From Hamilton, take Main Street West to Highway 403, and then Highway 403 north. Exit at Highway 6 and follow the signs.

DUNDURN CASTLE, Dundurn Park, York Blvd. Tel. 905/522-5313.

For a glimpse of the opulent life as it was lived in this part of southern Ontario in the mid-19th century, visit Dundurn Castle. It was built between 1832 and 1835 by Sir Alan Napier MacNab, prime minister of the United Provinces of Canada in the mid-1850s and a founder of the Great Western Railway, who was knighted by Queen Victoria for the part he played in the Rebellion of 1837. The 36-room mansion has been restored and furnished in the style of 1855. The cream exterior, with its classical Greek portico, is impressive enough, but inside from the grand and formal dining rooms to Lady MacNab's boudoir the furnishings are equally rich. The museum contains a fascinating collection of Victoriana.

Special displays and exhibits are featured throughout the year. In December the castle is decorated quite splendidly for a Victorian Christmas.

Admission: $4.50 adults, $2.75 seniors and students, $1.75 children under 14.

Open: June–Labor Day daily 10am–4pm; rest of the year Tues–Sun noon–4pm. **Closed:** Christmas and New Year's days. **Directions:** From downtown Hamilton, take King Street West to Dundurn Street, turn right, and Dundurn will run into York Boulevard.

DOWNTOWN

Don't forget to explore **Hess Village,** a four-block area of restored clapboard houses now containing boutiques, galleries, and restaurants.

Hamilton Farmer's Market is worth a visit to **Lloyd D. Jackson Square,** where you can also find a lot of good shopping, including such budget shoppers' paradises as Marks & Spencer.

CANADIAN FOOTBALL HALL OF FAME AND MUSEUM, 58 Jackson St. West. Tel. 905/528-7566.

Aside from steel, Hamilton is probably best known for its professional football team, the Hamilton Tiger Cats. It is fitting, therefore, to find the Canadian Football Hall of Fame and Museum located in Civic Square. Opened in 1972, this national shrine to Canadian professional and amateur football traces the last 130 years of football history; Petro Canada Theatre has run the Grey Cup game highlights from 1949 to the present.

Admission: $2 adults, $1 students and seniors, 50¢ children.
Open: June–Oct Mon–Sat 9:30am–4:30pm, Sun and holidays noon–4:30pm; Nov–May Mon–Sat 9:30am–4:30pm. **Closed:** Christmas and New Year's days.

ART GALLERY OF HAMILTON, 123 King St. West. Tel. 905/527-6610.

Aside from its excellent collection of Canadian and 20th-century American and British works, the art gallery offers special exhibitions.
Admission: $2 adults, $1 seniors and students; free for children under 12.
Open: Wed and Fri–Sat 10am–5pm, Thurs 1–9pm, Sun 1–5pm.

NEARBY ATTRACTIONS

AFRICAN LION SAFARI, off Hwy. 8 between Hamilton and Cambridge. Tel. 519/623-2620.

Just a half-hour drive northwest of Hamilton, you can drive or take the guided safari tram through the African Lion Safari, near Cambridge, keeping an eye out for rhinos, cheetahs, tigers, giraffes, zebras, and many, many more. Inside the park there's a cafeteria, souvenir shop, picnic areas, playground, and pets' corner.

Admission includes a tour of the six large game reserves; a cruise aboard the *African Queen* boat; a journey on the Nature Boy scenic railway; the Bird of Prey flying demonstrations; the elephant roundup; the Parrot Paradise show; and the Animals and Man show. The park's latest attractions are the Jungle Playground for toddlers and the Wet Play Area for cooling off. Bring swimsuits.
Admission: $14 adults, $12 seniors and youths 13–17, $10 children 3–12.
Open: Apr–Oct daily 10am–5:30pm. **Closed:** Winter.

MUSEUM OF STEAM AND TECHNOLOGY, 900 Woodward Ave. Tel. 905/549-5225.

Another Hamilton museum captures the aura of the industrial age. Here on operating days you can experience the sights and sounds of the old 1859 pumping station as it goes into action.
Admission: $2.25 adults, $1.75 seniors and students, $1.50 children 5–13; free for children under 5.
Open: June 1–Labor Day daily 11am–4pm; Labor Day–June 1 daily noon–4pm.

WHERE TO STAY

About a dozen bed-and-breakfast homes, renting rooms for $40 single and $60 double, have joined together to advertise. To secure a brochure listing the individual homes, contact the **Hamilton Chamber of Commerce, 555** Bay St. North, Hamilton, ON, L8L 1H1 (tel. 905/522-1151).

ROYAL CONNAUGHT, 112 King St. East, Hamilton, ON, L8N 1A8. Tel. 905/527-5071. Fax 905/546-8144. 208 rms. A/C TV TEL

$ Rates: $95 single or double. Extra person $10. Children under 14 stay free in parents' room. AE, DC, ER, MC, V. **Parking:** $4.75.
A grand old hotel, the Royal Connaught has recently undergone a $3 million renovation. In the lobby, glass, marble, and hand-rubbed wood dramatically set off the huge crystal chandeliers, Corinthian columns, and a flying staircase. Note the gleaming old-style brass royal mailbox. Built in 1904, the hotel has undergone a series of renovations, the most recent in 1984, and the spacious rooms currently feature gray-blue decor and dark-toned furniture. The bathrooms are exceptionally large. The hotel has Fenton's bistro and grill for dining, and an indoor pool.

SHERATON HAMILTON, 116 King St. West, Hamilton, ON, L8P 4V3. Tel. 905/529-5515, or toll free 800/325-3535. Fax 905/529-8266. 302 rms. A/C TV TEL

$ Rates: $140 single; $150 double. AE, DC, ER, MC, V. **Parking:** $8.
The Sheraton offers spacious rooms appointed with remote-control color TVs, clock radios, extra telephones, hairdryers, and tasteful modern furnishings that include desks. There are two restaurants—Windows for burgers, omelets, and sandwiches; and Chagall's for classic continental dishes. Other facilities include a health club with sauna and hot tub, and an indoor pool with a landscaped sun deck. The hotel is

connected conveniently to the Convention Centre, Hamilton Place, Lloyd D. Jackson Square, and the Indoor Farmer's Market. There's valet service, and room service is available until 1am.

WHERE TO DINE
HESS VILLAGE

Among the many boutiques and restaurants here, only two or three stand out. My favorites follow.

CAFE VIENNA, 15 Hess St. South. Tel. 905/525-7607.
   Cuisine: CONTINENTAL. **Reservations:** Recommended.
$ Prices: Main courses $11–$17. AE, ER, MC, V.
   Open: Lunch 11am–3pm; dinner daily 5–11pm.
Light and airy inside, the Café Vienna also has three or four tables placed outside. Food runs from wienerschnitzel to sole amandine and chicken suprême. The decor is simple but elegant: burgundy tablecloths, a majolica chandelier, and classical music in the background.

MARIO'S, 20 Hess St. North. Tel. 905/528-8108.
   Cuisine: ITALIAN. **Reservations:** Not needed.
$ Prices: Main courses $7–$11. AE, MC, V.
   Open: Lunch Tues–Fri noon–3pm; dinner Tues–Fri 5–11pm, Sat–Mon 5pm–midnight.
A small budget dining place, Mario's features rigatoni with meatballs, lasagne, cannelloni, and chicken parmigiana. There's patio dining in summer.

DOWNTOWN

BLACK FOREST INN, 255 King St. East. Tel. 905/528-3538.
   Cuisine: GERMAN. **Reservations:** Not accepted.
$ Prices: Main courses $7–$14. AE, CB, DC, ER, MC, V.
   Open: Tues–Thurs 11:30am–10:30pm, Fri–Sat 11:30am–11pm, Sun noon–9:30pm.
The Black Forest Inn provides an eminently festive background for good budget dining. Here among the warm wood paneling and the painted wood furniture of southern Germany, served by waitresses in colorful dirndls, you can sample all manner of schnitzels—paprika, jaeger, wiener, à la Holstein—and various sausages including Bock, Bavarian white, Hungarian country, Thüringer, and farm sausage, all served with home fries and sauerkraut. Naturally, for dessert you'll have Black Forest cake or Dobostorte.

LE GANGES INDIAN RESTAURANT, 234 King St. East. Tel. 905/523-8812.
   Cuisine: INDIAN. **Reservations:** Recommended.
$ Prices: Main courses $6–$14. AE, DC, ER, MC, V.
   Open: Lunch Mon and Wed–Fri 11:30am–2pm; dinner Wed–Mon 5–10pm.
★ Some fine Indian cuisine can be had at Le Ganges. Besides the food, the decor is also very pleasant—Indian wood carvings, beige tablecloths and napkins, exposed brick walls, and Breuer-style cane chairs. The vegetable samosas and pakoras are served piping hot, and crisp, not greasy. At lunch the best choice is the thali. Other choices include a succulent rogan josh and delicious royal basmati rice with delicately flavored shrimp. The menu includes a variety of meat, fish, and vegetarian dishes—shrimp do piaz, murg vindaloo (chicken), aloo gobi, and navratan biryani.

PAPPAS' DINING, 309 Main St. East. Tel. 905/525-2455.
   Cuisine: GREEK. **Reservations:** Recommended.
$ Prices: Appetizers $3–$14; main courses $12–$25. AE, CB, DC, ER, MC, V.
   Open: Lunch Mon–Fri 11:30am–2:30pm; dinner Sun–Thurs 5–10pm, Fri–Sat 5–11pm.
The blue-and-white sign outside Pappas' Dining hints at the Greek delicacies to be

found within among the Corinthian columns, the blue wall friezes, and classical statues in the wall alcoves. Waitresses in white Grecian robes will serve you fried feta cheese or avgolemono soup to start, followed by souvlaki, moussaka, or kokinisto (tenderloin with peppers, onions, and rice, sautéed over a low flame with light Greek wine). Steaks and seafood are also available, and Greek feasts for two. The least expensive includes soup, salad, chicken riganato, spareribs kokinisto, fresh fruit bowl, and coffee for two ($40). Lunchtime finds a selection of omelets, sandwiches, and Greek dishes from $7 to $13.

SHAKESPEARE'S STEAK HOUSE AND TAVERN, 181 Main St. East. Tel. 905/528-0689.

Cuisine: CANADIAN. **Reservations:** Recommended.
$ **Prices:** Main courses $17–$28. AE, CB, DC, ER, MC, V.
Open: Lunch Mon–Fri noon–2:30pm; dinner Mon–Fri 5–10:30pm, Sat 5–11:30pm, Sun 5–9pm.

Shakespeare's has endured for almost 24 years as a Hamilton dining institution because it serves well-prepared steaks. The decor underlines the restaurant's name—beams, horse brasses, and portraits of the Bard and his characters. Select marinated Bismarck herring to start or consommé au sherry, and follow with a 6½-ounce filet or a 16-ounce New York sirloin, both of which will be served with garlic bread, kosher dills, and french fries or a baked potato. There's also a $19 three-course prix fixe. For dessert the apple beignets are irresistible. At the end of your meal you will be presented with a huge goblet of candies to rummage through—it even contains Liquorice Allsorts—Bassett's, of course, for all you Anglophiles. For lunch you'll find various sandwiches and a daily special, including soup or salad and coffee for $12.

ZURI, 236 King St. Tel. 905/528-7446.

Cuisine: SWISS. **Reservations:** Recommended.
$ **Prices:** Main courses $10–$18. AE, MC, V.
Open: Lunch Tues–Fri 11:30am–2pm; dinner Mon–Thurs 5–9:30pm, Fri–Sat 5–11pm.

Zuri features Swiss specialties in a comfortable atmosphere of wood and red woven cloths. House specialties include cheese fondue and venison chasseur, as well as such typical Swiss items as veal Zurich (with white wine and mushrooms), and wiener-schnitzel. At lunch, almost everything's under $8. Start with goulash soup and finish with crêpe normande or apple strudel.

A FRIENDLY PUB

THE WINKING JUDGE, 25 Augusta St. Tel. 905/527-1280.

Cuisine: PUB FARE. **Reservations:** Not accepted.
$ **Prices:** Most items $3–$7. AE, V.
Open: Mon–Thurs 11:30am–midnight, Fri–Sat 11:30am–2am, Sun noon–11pm.

You're guaranteed to find a convivial crowd at lunchtime or on weekends when the piano player swings and people sometimes sing along. Among the crowd you're bound to find one or two expatriate Britons, Australians, or New Zealanders, or Canadians whose forebears hailed from such places.

The fare caters to the palates of such denizens—Cornish pasties, steak-and-kidney and shepherd's pies, served all day in the downstairs bar.

A NEARBY PLACE TO DINE BETWEEN HAMILTON & BRANTFORD

ANCASTER OLD MILL INN, off Rte. 2, Ancaster. Tel. 905/648-1827.

Cuisine: CANADIAN. **Reservations:** Recommended.
$ **Prices:** Appetizers $5–$11; main courses $13–$28. AE, DC, MC, V.
Open: Lunch Mon–Sat 11:30am–2:30pm; brunch Sun 10am–2:30pm; dinner Mon–Thurs 4:30–9pm, Fri–Sat 4:30–11pm, Sun 4–9pm. Sun evening buffet served 5–8pm.

To reach the restaurant, you cross the mill race. You'll find dining rooms are pleasantly country with pine furnishings. One end overlooks the falls, the other the old mill built in 1792. The menu features traditional dishes made from flour without preservatives and fresh, not canned vegetables. Your appetizer might be bacon-wrapped scallops or oysters Rockefeller; main courses include such items as veal piccata, prime rib, and barbecue ribs. Choose the steak and lobster tail if you're feeling flush.

EVENING ENTERTAINMENT

For symphony concerts, top-class international entertainers, theater, and dance, go to **Hamilton Place,** a modern $11-million arts complex housing two theaters: the Great Hall, holding over 2,000, and the smaller, more intimate Studio seating 400. The **Hamilton Philharmonic Orchestra** and **Opera Hamilton** are prime tenants, along with visiting entertainers who have included Nana Mouskouri, Cleo Laine, Paul Anka, Tom Jones, and Harry Belafonte. Ticket prices range from $15 to $80, depending on the show (the top rate is for opera). Hamilton Place is at Main and MacNab Streets (tel. 905/546-3050), opposite City Hall.

5. FROM PORT HOPE TO TRENTON

GETTING TO THE AREA

Voyageur Colonial operates daily buses from Ottawa (tel. 613/238-5900), Kingston (tel. 613/547-4916), and Toronto (tel. 416/393-7911). If you're driving from Toronto, take the 401E; from Kingston, the 401W.

PORT HOPE

This is an attractive old lakefront town situated at the mouth of the Ganaraska River, 72 miles east of Toronto, where the prime attractions for visitors are the antiques stores that line the main street.

WHERE TO STAY

THE CARLYLE, 86 John St., Port Hope, ON, L1A 2Z2. Tel. 905/885-8686. 7 rms, 1 suite. A/C TV
$ Rates: $65 single; $80 double; $110 suite. AE, DC, ER, MC, V.
For a place to stay, try the Carlyle, which occupies the old 1857 Bank of Upper Canada building. The rooms, all with private baths, have iron and brass beds or cherrywood beds attractively combined with oak or pine furnishings. One honeymoon suite has a Jacuzzi. The dining room offers casual food—lasagne, burgers, chicken kiev, and seafood dishes, priced from $5 to $12. The restaurant is open Monday through Saturday for lunch and dinner.

BRIGHTON/PRESQU'ILE

Brighton, named after the English resort, is at the heart of apple country and is also the gateway town to **Presqu'ile Provincial Park,** a 2,000-acre area of marsh and woodland that offers superb birdwatching (attracting birds from both the Atlantic and Mississippi flyways), camping, and a mile-long beach. Major birdwatching weekends are organized in spring and fall. The visitor center is open from Victoria Day to Labor Day. For information, contact the Superintendent, Presque'ile Provincial Park, R.R. 4, Brighton, ON, K0K 1H0 (tel. 613/475-2204).

TRENTON

This historic waterfront town 40 miles east of Port Hope is the starting point for the **Trent-Severn Canal,** a 240-mile waterway that travels via 44 locks to Georgian Bay on Lake Huron. It is also the western entrance to the Loyalist Parkway (Highway 33), leading to Quinte's Isle.

6. QUINTE'S ISLE

130 miles (210km) E of Toronto, 22 miles (36km) S of Belleville, 52 miles (85km) W of Kingston

GETTING THERE **By Car** From Trenton, take Highway 33S; from Belleville, Highway 62S off the 401; and from Kingston, Highway 49S off the 401.

ESSENTIALS Contact Quinte's Isle Tourist Association, 116 Main St., Picton, ON, K0K 2T0 (tel. 613/476-2421).

Prince Edward County is an island surrounded by Lake Ontario and the Bay of Quinte. It's a place apart and so has retained much of its early character and its relaxed pace. It was settled by United Empire Loyalists in the 1780s, and many of their descendants still live, work, and farm here. The solid attachment to the past here shows in the quiet streets of such historic towns and villages as Picton, Bloomfield, and Wellington.

FROM CARRYING PLACE TO BLOOMFIELD

Carrying Place was indeed a portage place—at the narrow isthmus at the head of the Bay of Quinte. In fact, this former portage road is the oldest road in continuous use in Upper Canada. The road goes from the Bay of Quinte to Weller's Bay on Lake Ontario, and it was here that the Gunshot Treaty was signed in which the natives signed over land stretching as far west as Toronto.

Consecon is an old milling village with an attractive millpond and marsh and water views.

Drive through **Wellington** and you can't help but notice how clean and neat it is and how well kept the houses and their gardens are. You'll feel like you are suddenly standing in an English village.

Bloomfield was settled in the early 1800s and its history has been strongly influenced by two groups, the Methodists and the Quakers. The latter were harassed in their native New York for their pacifism during the American Revolution, and fled to Canada with the Loyalists. Two Quaker cemeteries in town are part of that legacy.

Today this pretty town has become a haven for retirees, artists, and craftspeople, and it now shelters several potteries, craftshops, and antique stores like the **Bloomfield Pottery,** at 54 Main St. (tel. 613/393-3258), and the **Village Gallery,** at 29 Main St. (tel. 613/393-2943), to name only two.

WHERE TO STAY

In Wellington

TARA HALL, 146 Main St., Wellington, ON, K0K 3L0. Tel. 613/399-2801. Fax 613/399-1104. 3 rms. A/C TV
$ Rates (including breakfast): $50 single; $65 double. Extra person $12. V. **Parking:** Free.
Tara Hall is a landmark home built by a wealthy local grain-shipping and dry-goods merchant. The entranceway has a curved ceiling and the front door is flanked by sidelights and topped with a fan transom. Throughout the house the wood paneling and decorative plasterwork is very fine. Originally the whole upper front floor served as a ballroom; today it has been divided into three guest rooms. Each room is furnished pleasantly with some antiques. A full and formal breakfast is served, the table set with linen. No smoking.

In Bloomfield

CORNELIUS WHITE HOUSE, 8 Wellington St., Bloomfield, ON, K0K 1G0. Tel. 613/393-2282. 3 rms (1 with bath), 1 suite (with bath). A/C
$ Rates (including breakfast): $55 double or twin without bath, $65 double with bath; $80 suite. Extra person in suite $10. MC, V. **Parking:** Free.
This 19th-century red-brick house offers a lovely view over meadows dotted with

Holsteins. There are two doubles, a twin, and a suite, each furnished differently. One has an iron-and-brass bed; another is furnished in pine (rocker, dresser, bed, and chest). A full breakfast (or continental, if you prefer) is served in the 1867 dining room with wide pine floors and brick fireplace. Cottage also available with small kitchen.

MALLORY HOUSE, R.R. 1, Box 10, Bloomfield, ON, K0K 1G0. Tel. 613/393-3458. 3 rms (none with bath).

$ Rates (including breakfast): $42 single; $55 double. No credit cards. **Parking:** Free.

Mallory House offers three really appealing accommodations sharing 1½ baths in an old 1810/1850 farmhouse. One is furnished with a brass bed and marble-top dresser, another has twin brass beds, and the third sports a pine bed and an old trunk among the furnishings. The bathroom features an old-fashioned tub. Two sitting rooms are available to guests, both very comfortably furnished with antiques, Oriental rugs, good books, and a marble fireplace. A complete breakfast of scones, muffins, cereals, and pancakes or bacon and eggs is served in the dining room adjacent to the country kitchen with a pine fireplace and harvest table. This is a really fine accommodation and a great value, watched over by Hobbes, the black mutt, and four resident cats. The grounds are also lovely.

WHERE TO DINE
In Consecon

THE SWORD, R.R. 1, Consecon, ON, K0K 1T0. Tel. 613/392-2143.
Cuisine: CONTINENTAL. **Reservations:** Recommended.
$ Prices: Main courses $12–$22. MC, V.
Open: Summer lunch daily 11am–2pm; dinner daily 4–9pm, Fri–Sat 4–9:30pm. Winter dinner Thurs–Sun 4–9pm.

Ignore the roadhouse exterior of the Sword, for inside you'll find a veritable little corner of England. The proprietors will greet you at the bar, which is hung about with horse brasses, and take you into the beamed lounge where you'd swear you were in a real English country pub. The food is highly recommended and the wine cellar excellent and extensive—2,500 bottles. Cajun dishes are among the specialties, as well as such Créole dishes as shrimp étouffée. Start with the Cajun seafood appetizer of shrimp, scallops, and lobster in a delicate cheese sauce or with the delicious house pâté. Follow with any of the Cajun/Créole dishes, or such items as chicken teriyaki, shrimp stuffed with lobster sautéed and flamed with brandy, or a prime rib steak. When I visited I enjoyed a superb loin of lamb that had been deboned and defatted and was served with an intense bordelaise sauce accompanied by roast potatoes.

A twin room that shares a bath is also available, as well as one suite with a sitting room and private bath. A real, hearty well-cooked Canadian breakfast will be supplied, too. Rates are $45 for a twin and $70 for a suite.

In Bloomfield

This area was once dotted with cheese factories. Today only one or two survive; the rest have been converted to other uses.

ANGELINES, in the Bloomfield Inn, 29 Stanley St. West (P.O. Box 16), Bloomfield, ON, K0K 1G0. Tel. 613/393-3301.
Cuisine: CONTINENTAL. **Reservations:** Recommended.
$ Prices: Appetizers $4–$7; main courses $17–$21. MC, V.
Open: July–Aug breakfast daily 8–11am, lunch daily noon–2pm, dinner daily 5:30–9pm. June and Sept breakfast Wed–Mon 8–11am, lunch Wed–Mon noon–2pm, dinner Wed–Mon 5:30–9pm. Winter lunch Thurs–Mon noon–2pm, dinner Thurs–Mon 5:30–9pm.

The Bloomfield Inn (formerly the Coachouse Motel) is mainly known for its restaurant, Angelines, which is operated by a young Austrian chef. The restaurant is located in an 1869 house with polished floors and casement windows. Umbrellaed tables are on the lawn out front. The cuisine is seasonal and the chef grows his own herbs. Dinner entrées might include beef médaillons with mustard sauce, chicken breast with tarragon and chives, rack of lamb with garlic confit and rosemary, or salmon niçoise. There's also a seven-course degustation menu for $33. Afternoon teas are also served; it's then that the chef, who specializes in pastries, really comes into his own, offering Sachertorte and other fine Austrian pastries and tortes.

FROM BLOOMFIELD TO PICTON-GLENORA

Picton is the hub and county town of Prince Edward County. East of the town lies the mysterious **Lake on the Mountain,** a small, clear lake 200 feet above Lake Ontario. From one side of the escarpment there's a fabulous view of the ferry crossing Picton Bay, water, and islands stretching into infinity, it seems. It's a great place for a picnic. Lake on the Mountain was called Lake of the Gods by the Mohawks, who worshiped the three sisters—corn, beans, and squash—here. Nobody has as yet discovered the source of this lake set atop a mountain. Is it an ancient volcanic crater, a meteorite hole, a sinkhole caused by rain, or what?

The other major attraction, 11 miles west of Picton, is ✪ **Sandbanks and North Beach Provincial Parks.** Sandbanks has some of the highest (more than 80 feet) freshwater dunes anywhere—a spectacular sight. The best swimming beach is at Sandbanks. Camping is available in four areas at Sandbanks for $15 per day. Entry to the park is $6 per vehicle. Park officials begin taking reservations April 1. Windsurfing is great here. Go to the Surf Shack (tel. 613/393-3410) for sailboat, kayak, and sailboard rentals and lessons. Open from May to October. For information, contact the Superintendent, Sandbanks Provincial Park, R.R. 1, Picton, ON, K0K 2T0 (tel. 613/393-3319).

The last remaining cheese factory (in the 1930s there were 16 on the island), the **Black River Cheese Company** is eight miles southeast of Picton outside Milford on County Road 13 (tel. 613/476-2575). Open daily from 9am to 5pm.

Waupoos Island is famous for its pheasant, and many hunters and anglers come to the **Waupoos Island Pheasant and Sheep Farm,** R.R. 4, Picton, ON, K0K 2T0 (tel. 613/476-3910), to enjoy farmhouse cooking and accommodation, pheasant and lamb dinners, as well as the rolling hills and secluded shores.

The best way off Quinte's Isle is to take the rewarding 15-minute ferry trip from Glenora across to Adolphustown. The ferry operates every 15 minutes in summer, less frequently in winter, and has been operating since settlement began.

WHERE TO STAY

ISAIAH TUBBS RESORT, R.R. 1, Picton, ON, K0K 2T0. Tel. 613/393-2090. Fax 613/393-1291. 57 rms. TV TEL
$ Rates: $90–$125 single; $100–$135 double; $145–$175 kitchenette suite; $185 Jacuzzi suite. Lakeside cabin $650–$775 per week. AE, ER, MC, V.

A mini-resort spread over 30 acres on West Lake, the Isaiah Tubbs Resort offers very attractive accommodations. The Carriage House rooms, located in the oldest part of the original building, have kitchenettes, comfy pine furnishings including rockers and tables, original beamed ceilings, brick fireplaces, and microwaves. Upstairs there's a sleeping loft furnished with bunk beds, TV, and shower. A standard room with sloping ceiling is furnished Ethan Allen country style with push-button phone, alarm clock, TV, and full bath. There are several cabin-lodges scattered around the property featuring a living room with fieldstone fireplace and two bedrooms, one upstairs with skylights and a Jacuzzi tub. Some have sun porches.

MERRILL INN, 343 Main St. East (P.O. Box 2310), Picton, ON, K0K 2T0. Tel. 613/476-7451. 14 rms. A/C TV TEL
$ Rates (including continental breakfast): July–Aug $90–$100 single; off-season $80–$90 single. Extra person $10. AE, ER, MC, V. **Parking:** Free.

A silver Rolls is parked outside the Merrill Inn, and inside, the rooms are individually decorated with antiques. Room 101, for example, features a high-back Victorian bed, wing chairs, and bay windows. One room has a Jacuzzi, another a fireplace. All have TVs tucked away in armoires. There's a comfortable sitting room, barbecue area, and sun porch for guests.

WHERE TO DINE

WARING HOUSE RESTAURANT, on Hwy. 33 just west of Picton. Tel. 613/476-7367.

   Cuisine: CONTINENTAL. **Reservations:** Recommended.

$ Prices: Main courses $17–$23. MC, V.

   Open: Summer daily Tues–Sun 11:30am–2pm; dinner daily 6–9:30pm. Winter lunch Tues–Sun 11:30am–2pm; dinner Tues–Sun 5–9pm.

The Waring House Restaurant is located in an old stone house surrounded by pretty shrubbery. Pine floors, pelmeted curtains, floral wallpaper, and Windsor chairs set the country ambience. The menu features sole amandine, rack of lamb with rosemary and port sauce, and veal schnitzel. The inviting lounge has a big brick-and-beam fireplace.

WHEELHOUSE VIEW CAFE, Picton. Tel. 613/476-7380.

   Cuisine: CANADIAN. **Reservations:** Recommended.

$ Prices: Main courses $8–$16. MC, V.

   Open: May–early Oct Mon–Wed 11am–8pm, Thurs–Sun 11am–9pm; other months Wed–Sun 11am–7pm.

The Wheelhouse View Café, down by the ferry to Adolphustown, offers good value. The decor is simple—Formica and aluminum. The menu includes fish-and-chips, veal parmigiana, chicken Kiev, roast turkey, sole, barbecued ribs, and sandwiches.

---

7. KINGSTON

103 miles (172km) SW of Ottawa, 153 miles (255km) NE of Toronto

GETTING THERE   **By Train**   There are several daily trains from Ottawa (tel. 613/244-8289), Toronto (tel. 416/366-8411), and Montréal (tel. 514/871-1331) to Kingston.

By Bus   From Toronto and from Ottawa, Voyageur Colonial (tel. 416/393-7911 in Toronto and 613/238-5900 in Ottawa) operates several express and local buses daily. Local stops include Port Hope, Trenton, and Belleville, and Brockville and Gananoque.

By Car   From Ottawa take Highway 16S to the 401W and drive to the Kingston Exits. Or you can take the more scenic Highway 2, instead of the 401. From Toronto take the 401E to the Kingston Exits.

ESSENTIALS   For information about the Kingston area, contact the Kingston Tourist Information Office, 209 Ontario St., Kingston, ON, K7L 2Z1 (tel. 613/548-4415).

About two hours' drive from Ottawa, and about three hours' drive from Toronto, Kingston has much to offer the visitor. First, there's the water. Kingston stands at the confluence of Lake Ontario, the Rideau Canal, and the St. Lawrence Seaway, and this affords splendid scenic possibilities, best viewed by taking a free ✪ **ferry trip to Wolfe Island,** largest of the Thousand Islands, about 22 miles long and 7 miles wide. Ferries leave at frequent intervals for this sparsely populated island that doubles as a marvelous, quiet rural retreat. A stroll along Kingston's waterfront, site of many of the city's hotels and restaurants as well as of the maritime museum and attractive gardens, is also a must.

    Then there's Kingston's history, more than 300 years of it, much of it retained in the fine old limestone public buildings and private residences that line the downtown streets and give the city a gracious air. Still more of that history can be found in the 8 of 16 remaining martello towers that once formed a string of defense works guarding the waterways along the U.S.-Canadian border.

    Other architectural highlights include the Wren-style St. Georges Church, which contains a Tiffany window at the back of the nave on the right as you face the altar. The columns are also encrusted with an unusual stucco decoration.

During the summer **Confederation Park** is the site for band concerts and other performances; during the winter you might catch a local ice-hockey contest. In **Market Square** on Tuesday, Thursday, and Saturday, a colorful market is held, and on Sunday an antiques market is held at the same location.

WHAT TO SEE & DO

The best way to explore Kingston is aboard the **tour train** that leaves from in front of the Greater Kingston Tourist Information Office, on the waterfront across from the City Hall, every hour on the hour between 10am and 7pm from May to September. The tour lasts 50 minutes and costs $7.50 for adults, $5.50 for seniors and youths.

FORT HENRY, on Hwy. 2 just east of Kingston. Tel. 613/542-7388.

History lives at Fort Henry, which broods above the town on a high promontory, eerily unchanged since it was rebuilt in the 1830s (it was originally built in 1812). Here, all summer long the Fort Henry Guard, complete with their goat mascot named David, perform 19th-century drills, musters, and parades, including the spectacular Sunset Ceremony every Saturday during July and August at 7pm (weather permitting). The ceremony includes a display of music and marching by the fife-and-drum band, an exhibition of infantry drill, and a mock battle with artillery support, all brought to a close with the firing of the garrison artillery and the lowering of the Union Jack. Part of the fort—officers' quarters, men's barracks, kitchens, artisans' shops, and a bakery—is restored to show the military way of life circa 1867. The fort also houses an extensive collection of British and Canadian military and naval artifacts.

Admission: Day or evening $9 adults (combination $13.50), $5 seniors (combination $7.50), $5.85 students (combination $8.95), $3.80 children 6–12 (combination $5.60). Tatoo only, $3.40 adults, $1.75 for students, seniors, and children.

Open: Mid-May to mid-June and Labor Day–early Oct daily 10am–5pm; mid-June to Labor Day daily 10am–6pm. **Closed:** Rest of year.

ROYAL MILITARY COLLEGE, On Point Frederick. Tel. 613/541-6652.

The Royal Military College, Canada's West Point, is also close to the fort. Located on Point Frederick, the campus occupies the site of a Royal Navy Dockyard, which played a key role in the War of 1812. Although you can tour the grounds, the only building open to the public is the museum, located in a large martello tower that houses displays about the college's history and Kingston's Royal Dockyard, plus the Douglas collection of small arms and weapons.

Admission: Free.

Open: Daily 10am–5pm. **Closed:** Labor Day to mid-June.

BELLEVUE HOUSE, 35 Centre St. Tel. 613/545-8666.

On July 1, 1867, the Canadian Confederation was proclaimed in Kingston's Market Square. The Confederation's chief architect, and Canada's first prime minister, Sir John A. Macdonald, is closely identified with the city of Kingston, his home for most of his life, and he is commemorated in several places. The most notable is Bellevue House, an Italianate villa, jokingly referred to as "Pekoe Pagoda" and "Tea Caddy Castle" by the local citizenry. It has been restored to the period 1848–49, when John A. lived there as a young lawyer and rising member of Parliament.

Admission: Free.

Open: June 1–Labor Day daily 9am–6pm; other months daily 10am–5pm. **Closed:** Statutory holidays Nov 11–Easter.

AGNES ETHERINGTON ART CENTRE, University Ave. at Queen's Crescent. Tel. 613/545-2190.

At Queen's University, a campus of 13,000 students, the Agnes Etherington Art Centre offers an eclectic collection ranging from medieval to African art. It combines the beautiful 18th-century home of benefactor Agnes Richardson Etherington (1880–1954) with period furnishings and seven exhibition galleries. The outstanding permanent collection includes historical and contemporary Canadian art, European old-master paintings, antique silver and glass, heritage quilts, and a renowned collection of African art.

Admission: $2 adults, $1 seniors and students.
Open: Tues–Fri 10am–5pm, Sat–Sun 1–5pm.

THE WATERFRONT

A great free 30-minute trip can be taken aboard the ferry to **Wolfe Island.**
Kingston is very much a waterfront defense town. Along the waterfront, **Confederation Park** stretches from the front of the old 19th-century hall down to the magnificent yacht basin (worth looking at). On the waterfront within walking distance of the marina is one of the finest martello towers, built during the Oregon Crisis of 1846 to withstand the severest of naval bombardments. The **Murney Tower** (tel. 613/544-9925) is now a museum where you can see the basement storage rooms, the barrack room, and the gun platform. Open daily from 10am to 5pm from mid-May to the end of October. Admission is $2 for adults; children under 6 free. Farther along the waterfront is **Portsmouth Olympic Harbour Park,** site of the 1976 Olympic sailing events, and now one of the most up-to-date marina facilities in Ontario. Open to local as well as transient boaters, it offers a safe harbor at reasonable rates. For more information on Confederation Basin Marina and Portsmouth Olympic Harbour, call 613/544-9842.

A little farther along the waterfront is **Lake Ontario Park,** providing the camping enthusiast with all the excellent services offered to boaters. The campground is operated by the city of Kingston; has electricity and water hookups, an amusement park, and fishing; and makes an ideal place to stay (three miles from City Hall). The rates are reasonable ($12 for campsite; $16 with electric and water, $18.75 with electric, water, and sewer), and reservations are accepted (tel. 613/542-6574). The season is mid-April to October.

While you're exploring downtown and along the waterfront, pop into the **City Hall,** 264 Ontario St. (tel. 613/546-4291). Thirty-minute tours are given of the magnificent domed building, but if you can't afford the time, at least view the stained-glass windows in Memorial Hall, each one commemorating a battle in World War I. The bell tower also contains a display of old bottles, locks, and other artifacts that were unearthed during renovation. You can also make rubbings of a couple of handsome brasses that stand just inside the entrance. Tours available weekdays only.

For an understanding of the great shipping days on the Great Lakes, visit the **Marine Museum of the Great Lakes,** 55 Ontario St. (tel. 613/542-2261), filled with galleries on sail, steam, and diesel that document the change from sail in the 17th century to steam in the early 19th century and from the days of the great schooners in the 1870s to today's bulk carriers that still ply the Great Lakes. Other exhibits recapture the area's boat- and shipbuilding industry. Open daily mid-April to mid-December from 10am to 5pm; January to March Monday to Friday from 10am to 4pm. Adults pay $5.25 to see the ship and the museum, and students and seniors pay $4.75; kids under 6 are free.

SEEING THE THOUSAND ISLANDS

✪ The famous Thousand Islands holiday area is right on the town's doorstep. Known to Native Canadians as Manitouana (Garden of the Great Spirit), it is alive with cruise boats in summer which meander through the more than 1,800 islands past such extraordinary sights as **Boldt's Castle,** built by millionaire George Boldt at the turn of the century as a gift for his wife. (When she died suddenly, the work was abandoned, and so it stands a relic to lost love.) The **cruise boats** leave from various points along the St. Lawrence. From Kingston Harbour at City Hall, you can take a three-hour cruise on the *Island Queen,* a whistle-blowing triple-deck paddle wheeler. Cost is $16 for adults, $6 for children 4 to 12. Or you may choose a 90-minute cruise aboard the *Island Bell* that takes in the Kingston Harbour and waterfront. It costs $10 for adults, $6 for children 4 to 12. For cruise information, write or phone the *Island Queen* Showboat, 6A Princess St., Kingston, ON, K7L 1A2 (tel. 613/549-5544 or 613/549-5545).

The nimble catamaran *Sea Fox II* also cruises the islands and the harbor from the

IMPRESSIONS

It may be said of Kingston, that one half of it appears to be burnt down, and the other half not to be built up.
—CHARLES DICKENS, *AMERICAN NOTES*, 1842

bottom of Brock Street in Kingston. The two-hour islands tour costs $12 for adults, $11 for seniors, and $6 for children 6 to 12. For information, call in season 613/542-4271.

COOL FOR KIDS

CELEBRITY SPORTSWORLD, 801 Development Dr., just off Hwy. 401. Tel. 613/384-1313.
The number-one Kingston attraction for kids is Celebrity Sportsworld, a 12-acre park featuring a huge roller-skating rink, 12 bowling lanes, mini-golf, the "Moonwalk" action ride and many other electric rides, two video and games arcades, and a golf driving range, plus a teen dance club. Refreshments are available, as well as a supervised play area for toddlers and preschoolers.
Admission: Bowling $5.95 adults, $4.95 children; roller-skating $4.50 adults, $3.50 children 11 and under; mini-golf $2.25 adults, $1.50 children; driving range $4.75 for small basket of balls.
Open: Daily noon–5pm and 6:30–9:30pm.

HOUSEBOAT & CANOE RENTALS

You can charter your own houseboat that sleeps up to eight people and cruise the islands independently. In August the cost starts at $700 for a weekend, and $1,150 per week. Prices are higher in July, less in May, June, and September, and also during the week. Boats are fully equipped—you need only bring sleeping bags and towels. For information, contact **St. Lawrence River Houseboat and Cruiser Rentals,** c/o Halliday Point, Wolfe Island, ON, K0H 2Y0 (tel. 613/385-2290).
Or try canoe camping in nearby Frontenac Provincial Park. A canoe/camp package that provides canoe, paddles, life jacket, car-top carrier, tent, sleeping bags, stove, and utensils costs a modest $22 per person per day. For information, contact **Frontenac Outfitters,** P.O. Box 377, Sydenham, ON, K0H 2T0 (tel. 613/376-6220 in season, 613/353-6867 off-season).

WHERE TO STAY

An alternative to staying in traditional hotel accommodations can be found through **Bed and Breakfast—Kingston** (tel. 613/542-0214), a reservation service for a fine selection of homes throughout the area. Rates are $40 to $45 single, $50 to $55 double; children 1 to 10 pay $10, children 11 and over, $15. Call or write to the organization at P.O. Box 37, Kingston, ON, K7L 4V6, Attention: Janet Borlase. Enclose $1 for their brochure.

EXPENSIVE

Two chains have commandeered the spectacular position overlooking the harbor—the **Holiday Inn,** 1 Princess St., Kingston, ON, K7L 1A1 (tel. 613/549-8400), charging $145 for a double in summer; and the **Howard Johnson's,** 237 Ontario St., Kingston, ON, K7L 2Z4 (tel. 613/549-6300), charging $120. Another possibility is the **Ramada Inn,** 1 Johnson St., Kingston, ON, K7L 5H7 (tel. 613/549-8100), also on the lakefront.

BEST WESTERN FIRESIDE, 1217 Princess St., Kingston, ON, K7M 3E1. Tel. 613/549-2211. Fax 613/549-4523. 75 rms. A/C TV TEL
$ Rates: $105 single; $120 double. Fantasy suites $205 weekdays, $255 Fri and Sun, $305 Sat. Extra person $10. Children under 18 stay free in parents' room. AE, CB, DC, DISC, ER, MC. **Parking:** Free.

The Best Western has a good restaurant, a comfortable lounge, rooms with fireplaces and some very popular, fun fantasy suites decorated in four different styles—English, Asian, futuristic, and one called Flights of Fantasy with a hot-air balloon theme.

MODERATE

FIRST CANADA INN, First Canada Court, Kingston, ON, K7K 6W2. Tel. 613/541-1111. Fax 613/549-5735. 75 rms. A/C TV TEL
$ Rates: $55–$65 single; $65–$75 double. Extra person $5. Children under 12 stay free in parents' room. AE, MC, V. **Parking:** Free.
It's hard to beat the price of the rooms at the First Canada Inn, located just off Highway 401 at Division Street and Weller Avenue. The rooms are fully appointed, and there's a lobby bar.

HOCHELAGA INN, 24 Sydenham St. South, Kingston, ON, K7L 3G9. Tel. 613/549-5534. Fax 613/549-5534 23 rms. TV TEL
$ Rates (including breakfast): $87–$133 single or double. Extra person $10. AE, DC, ER, MC, V. **Parking:** Free.
One of Kingston's choice accommodations is the Hochelaga Inn, an elegant Victorian home with a charming garden. Each room offers a private bath and is furnished with period pieces. My favorite is no. 301, an oddly shaped space where the carved bed is set on a diagonal while the rest of the room is taken up by a large armoire and a love seat. Three steps lead to a delightful 11-sided tower with windows. A stepladder leads to a tiny sitting area set with plants while atop the ladder you'll find a futon on which you can sleep under the Gothic windows. Many of the other rooms are furnished in oak pieces along with wing chairs, brass table lamps, and similar elements. A comfortable array of couches and armchairs grace the large sitting room, which is complete with a carved ebony fireplace. There's another fireplace in the large breakfast room. Wicker chairs are placed on the outdoor veranda overlooking the pleasant gardens, which are also home to a grill. In the adjacent cottages are found the smallest rooms, some with little porches. A breakfast of cereal, croissants, muffins, and the like is spread out in the mornings for you to help yourself.

HOTEL BELVEDERE, 141 King St. East, Kingston, ON, K7L 2Z9. Tel. 613/548-1565. Fax 613/546-4692. 20 rms. TV TEL
$ Rates (including breakfast): $99–$189 double. AE, DC, ER, MC, V. **Parking:** Free.
The place to stay in Kingston is the Hotel Belvedere, a mansard-roofed brick residence that has been lovingly restored and redecorated with great personal flair. Each of the rooms is furnished differently, taking advantage of the natural elements and contours of the original house. All have king- or queen-size beds with duvets and pleasant sitting areas; most are air-conditioned.
Just to give you some idea, Room 207 has an art deco flavor featuring a scalloped-style bed, Madame Récamier sofa, and sideboard, all set on marble floors. The white duvet is set off by a turquoise cushion. Room 205 sports a handsome brass bed and marble-and-brass side tables, a couple of wing chairs, and a closet tucked up a tiny staircase. It also has a kitchenette equipped with a small sink, fridge, and hotplate. In Room 204 there's a brilliant marine-blue tile fireplace, tasseled curtains, kneehole dresser, and a bed covered with an embroidered and lace coverlet, to name only a few of the items that make the room so charming. On the third floor, rooms derive their character from the sloping walls. One room here also has a skylit kitchenette and a red-tile bathroom.
Guests also may use the elegant sitting room that has a turquoise marble coal-burning fireplace and tall French windows that open onto a porch prettily decorated with flowers and plants in classical urns. A continental breakfast is served.

LA SALLE HOTEL, 2360 Princess St., Kingston, ON, K7M 3G4. Tel. 613/546-4233. Fax 613/546-4233. 110 rms. A/C TV TEL
$ Rates: New units $60–$70 single, $70–$90 double; motel section $38–$50 single, $46–$70 double. Winter rates drop 15%. AE, DC, DISC, ER, MC, V. **Parking:** Free.
The 70 pleasant newer units at the La Salle accented with cedar wall strips and

decorated in blue, fully appointed with a remote-control switch for the color TV, a double vanity with theatrical-style lighting, a massager, and sliding glass doors. The rest of the units consist of pleasantly decorated motel-style rooms. There's a dining room on the premises, outdoor and indoor pools, and a cocktail lounge with a mirrored cedar bar, comfortable couches, and working fireplace.

PEACHTREE MOTOR INN, Peachtree Plaza, 1187 Princess St., Kingston, ON, K7M 3E1. Tel. 613/546-4411. 79 rms. A/C TV TEL

$ Rates: $60 single; $80 double. Extra person $5. AE, DC, DISC, ER, MC, V. **Parking:** Free.

Each of the attractively decorated rooms at the Peachtree is furnished with two queen-size beds, a well-lit desk table and chairs, and all the modern conveniences, including cable TV with a sports channel, and a clock radio. Services are available in the plaza or nearby.

PRINCE GEORGE HOTEL, 200 Ontario St., Kingston, ON, K7L 2Y9. Tel. 613/549-5440. Fax 613/549-4998. 30 rms. A/C TV TEL

$ Rates: $55–$120 single; $80–$130 double. Extra person $10. Children under 18 stay free in parents' room. AE, DC, ER, MC, V. **Parking:** Free.

On the waterfront, the Prince George Hotel, originally built in 1809 and complete with a double balcony, has been renovated and offers pine-furnished rooms and an assortment of lounges and restaurants. In the hotel, Shaky's has a sports-bar atmosphere and Dollar Bill's, a video dance bar, packs them in six nights a week, closing at 1am. Needless to say, the rooms immediately above are less expensive. The Canoe Club doubles as a restaurant and bar, serving British beers on tap as well as typical light Canadian fare. Tables migrate outside in summer.

QUEEN'S INN, 125 Brock St., Kingston, ON, K7L 1S1. Tel. 613/546-0429. 17 rms. A/C TV TEL

$ Rates (including continental breakfast): $60 single; $90 double. AE, DC, ER, MC, V. **Parking:** Free.

Downtown, the Queen's Inn, in an old three-story stone building, offers nicely decorated rooms that sport light-oak furnishings. For me, the rooms with the most character are on the third floor tucked under the eaves. The Coppers dining room has an outdoor patio; there's also a sports bar with large-screen TV.

BUDGET

***ALEXANDER HENRY*, 55 Ontario St., Kingston, ON, K7L 2Y2. Tel. 613/542-2261.** Fax 613/542-0043. 19 cabins.

$ Rates (including continental buffet breakfast): $38 single; $42–$52 double; $60 Captain's Cabin. AE, MC, V. **Closed:** Labor Day to mid-May.

A unique bed-and-breakfast can be found at the Marine Museum aboard the 3,000-ton icebreaker *Alexander Henry*. The accommodations are not exactly roomy and you may think twice about drinking the water, but it's certainly different. The Captain's Cabin comes with double bed, a desk large enough to spread out navigational charts on, a sitting area with a table, and a bathroom with a shower. There are also two twin-bedded rooms aboard. Continental breakfast is served buffet style in the officers' mess.

DONALD GORDON CENTRE, 421 Union St., Kingston, ON, K7L 3N6. Tel. 613/545-2221. 75 rms. A/C TEL

$ Rates: $40 single; $45 double. AE, MC, V. **Parking:** Free.

Good reasonably priced accommodations can be found at the university's Donald Gordon Centre. Rooms consist of either two-bedroom suites with shared bathroom or twin-bedded rooms with private bath. The spaces are furnished in typical study-bedroom fashion. Other facilities in the building include a dining room, a lounge, and a basement bar and games room.

JOURNEY'S END, 1454 Princess St., Kingston, ON, K7M 3E5. Tel. 613/549-5550. Fax 613/549-1388. 58 rms. A/C TV TEL

$ Rates: $70 single; $75 double. AE, DC, ER, MC, V. **Parking:** Free.

One of the cheapest choices lies at Journey's End, in a two-story motel-style building.

Downstairs rooms have sliding glass doors, and all the units have up-to-the-minute decor, queen-size beds, love seats, and large well-lit writing tables. An added attraction: Local phone calls are free.

A NEARBY RETREAT ON WOLFE ISLAND

GENERAL WOLFE HOTEL, Wolfe Island, ON, K0H 2Y0. Tel. 613/385-2611. Fax 613/385-1038. 6 rms. A/C TV TEL

$ Rates: $30–$55 double; $95 suite for six. AE, MC, V. **Parking:** Free.

The General Wolfe Hotel has to be one of the most spectacular budget finds ever. Located on Wolfe Island near where the ferry docks, it's mainly known for its dining room but also rents six rooms that vary in size. A small room furnished with a double bed, side table, chair, and TV, and also with a private bath, rents for $30. A suite containing a double and single bed and a sitting room equipped with refrigerator goes for $55, while a two-room suite accommodating six tops out at $95. Besides the dining room, there's also a cocktail lounge with dancing on weekends.

The dining room, where the tables are covered in pink, affords views of the ferry landing and waterfront—great for sunset viewing. The food is continental—steak Diane, duck à l'orange, salmon steak béarnaise, and coquilles St-Jacques—priced from $15 to $25. There's always a special prix-fixe menu too, at $23 for soup, salad, main course, dessert, and coffee. Open mid-May to Labor Day daily for lunch from 11:30am to 5pm and for dinner from 5pm to midnight. At other times the restaurant closes Monday. In winter when the river is frozen (from January to early April), the owners operate a shuttle to Dawson's Point connecting to the mainland.

WHERE TO DINE

EXPENSIVE

Another top choice for dining is the General Wolfe Hotel (see "A Nearby Retreat on Wolfe Island," above).

CHEZ PIGGY, 68R Princess St. Tel. 613/549-7673.
   Cuisine: CONTINENTAL/ECLECTIC. **Reservations:** Recommended on weekends.
$ Prices: Main courses $17–$20. AE, MC, V.
   Open: Mon–Sat 11:30am–midnight, Sun 11am–9:30pm. Lunch served 11:30am–2pm; dinner served 6–9:30pm; Sun brunch served 11am–2:30pm.

Just off Princess Street, along a narrow passageway in what is known as the Old Stones, a complex of old buildings that have been renovated and now house interesting stores and boutiques, you'll find Chez Piggy occupying an 1820s building that probably served as a stable. In front there's a paved courtyard where you can sit outdoors. Inside, on the ground floor there's a long bar with brown high director's chairs, while in the loft, wood and cane furniture provides a classical setting where the only real decor consists of two glorious Tunisian rugs. The menu is small and might feature seven or so dinner entrées plus daily specials. Try the chicken breast marsala or roast leg of lamb after you've sampled either the hummus or the Stilton pâté. Salads, omelets, and sandwiches are offered at lunch, all under $7. Brunch dishes are interestingly different—lamb kidneys with scrambled eggs and home fries, smoked mackerel with eggs, Thai beef salad, along with the more typical brunch fare. All are under $8.

CLARK'S BY THE BAY, 4085 Bath Rd. Tel. 613/384-3551.
   Cuisine: CONTINENTAL. **Reservations:** Recommended.
$ Prices: Appetizers $8–$9; main courses $18–$22. MC, V.
   Open: Dinner Tues–Sat 5:30pm–midnight.
The premier dining place is Clark's By the Bay, west of Kingston proper. It's located in a stone house that is set well back from the road. Inside, a series of intimate dining rooms are decorated either with floral or striped wallpapers, and gilt-framed pictures. Tables are set with damask tablecloths and fresh flowers.
   The menu changes seasonally and the dishes will contain the freshest ingredients.

Specialties might include salmon with a mousse of scallops, orange roughy, and lobster, served with an américaine sauce; rabbit served with a cèpe, morel, and oyster mushroom sauce; or a rack of lamb coated with ground hazelnuts and Dijon mustard and served with garlic, port, and rosemary sauce; and several varieties of steaks. For a complete gourmet experience try the $40 table d'hôte, which includes carefully selected wines to accompany the dishes. On a recent evening it began with a consommé of chicken quenelles with peppers and peppercorns, which was followed by lobster amouraine and clams with hollandaise sauce. A kiwi sherbet with champagne came before the main course of filet mignon with a raspberry béarnaise and a mushroom cream sauce. Brie with crème fraîche and berries in phyllo with quadruple cheesecake completed the meal.

Owners Clark and Laurie Day also offer attractive accommodations to retire conveniently to after a satisfying meal.

GENCARELLI, 629 Princess St. Tel. 613/542-7976.
  Cuisine: ITALIAN. **Reservations:** Recommended.
  $ Prices: Pasta courses under $12; main courses $13–$17. AE, CB, DC, ER, MC, V.
  Open: Mon–Sat 11am–11pm, Sun 4–9pm.
Gencarelli has been a local favorite for years and it continues to serve fine cuisine in an intimate series of dining rooms with black-and-salmon table settings, brick archways, and brass-and-frosted-glass light fixtures. Pastas like fettuccine, tortellini, and rigatoni can be married to a sauce of your choice, or you can select such dishes as cannelloni parmigiana or lasagne al forno, all under $10, including a salad. Main courses include traditional Italian favorites like veal marsala and chicken parmigiana, along with more continental dishes like veal Oscar. The dessert specialty is the chocolate-amaretto cheesecake. At lunch prices range from $6 to $13.

MODERATE

THE LONE STAR CAFE, 251 Ontario St. Tel. 613/548-8888.
  Cuisine: TEX-MEX. **Reservations:** Recommended.
  $ Prices: Main courses $7–$15. AE, MC, V.
  Open: Daily 11:30am–11pm.
Located in a firehouse, the Lone Star consists of three very different rooms. Downstairs, stained-glass accents and historical prints set the tone; in summer the waterfront patio and bar is popular. The original metal red staircase leads up to Pumpers dance bar, where the hoses are still coiled. The menu in the main restaurant features fajitas, burritos, enchiladas as well as steaks, seafood, sandwiches, and burgers.

KINGSTON BREWING COMPANY, 34 Clarence St. Tel. 613/542-4978.
  Cuisine: LIGHT FARE. **Reservations:** Not needed.
  $ Prices: Burgers, sandwiches, and main courses under $10. AE, DC, ER, MC, V.
  Open: Mon–Sat 11am–1am, Sun 11:30am–1am.
At the Kingston Brewing Company, you can peer behind the bar and view the huge tanks in which the beer is brewed every few days, a fine real ale and a pleasant lager, both of which are brewed without the usual chemicals and other substances that adulterate modern mass-produced beers. Typical bar fare—burgers, sandwiches, and lamb chops—is also served at polished wood tables in a typical smoky bar atmosphere.

BUDGET

Along the waterfront, **Slices** (tel. 613/544-6250) is a comfortable pizza parlor serving pies from $2 and up.

The **Canoe Club** at the Prince George Hotel, 200 Ontario St., reputedly has the best burgers in town. **Brownies,** at the Best Western Fireside Inn, 1217 Princess St., also has a good reputation locally.

SUNFLOWER, 20 Montréal St. Tel. 613/542-4566.
  Cuisine: NATURAL FOODS. **Reservations:** Recommended on weekends.

$ Prices: All items under $10. DC, ER, MC, V.
Open: Tues–Sat 11:30am–midnight.

For really healthful, well-cooked food, head for Sunflower natural-foods restaurant. Whatever is fresh at the market will determine the daily hot specials.
The regular menu features a variety of salads, vegetarian entrées like chili and goulash, along with egg dishes, great pancakes, and sandwiches from hummus to soyburgers. No smoking; beer and wine are served.

EVENING ENTERTAINMENT

For some British pub fun, stop at the **Duke of Kingston** at 331 King St. East (tel. 613/542-2811). For evening bar entertainment, try **Tom's Place,** at the Best Western Fireside, 1217 Princess St. (tel. 613/549-2211); **Pumpers,** upstairs at the Lone Star, 251 Ontario St. (tel. 613/548-8888); or the **Silver Saddle,** the country and western bar at the Howard Johnson's Confederation Place Hotel, 237 Ontario St. (tel. 613/549-6300).

Cocamo's, 178 Ontario St. (tel. 613/544-6885), on the waterfront, is a multilevel dance bar with rock and roll, hip-hop, and other contemporary sounds. It attracts an under-40 crowd. Cover is usually $3 on weekends.

During the summer, check out what's on at the **Kingston Summer Festival,** at the Grand (tel. 613/530-2050). It might be a production of a recent Broadway play or musical, or a nostalgic revival. Tickets are $12 to $20.

8. ALONG THE ST. LAWRENCE

The mighty St. Lawrence River was the main route into Upper Canada from the 17th century to the mid-19th century, traveled first by explorers, fur traders, and missionaries and later by settlers en route to Ontario and the plains west. It led to the heart of Canada. In places as much as 12 miles wide, it is in itself a magnificent and humbling sight.

GETTING TO THE AREA

Voyageur Colonial operates daily buses from Toronto (tel. 416/393-7911), Kingston (tel. 613/547-4916), and Montréal (tel. 514/842-2281), stopping at all of the towns mentioned below. Buses also travel from Ottawa (tel. 613/238-5900) to Kingston via Brockville and Gananoque.

If you're driving, the 401 is the fastest route connecting these townships, or you can take the more scenic Highway 2.

THE THOUSAND ISLANDS

Today the St. Lawrence continues as a major shipping route into Canada and the Great Lakes. But for the visitor it is mainly known for the Thousand Islands. According to a Native Canadian legend, petals of heavenly flowers fell to earth and were scattered on the river, creating Manitouana, the Garden of the Great Spirit, or as we know it, the Thousand Islands.

The best way to savor the island-river landscape is aboard one of the many cruise boats that operate from such major cities Kingston and Gananoque. Or better yet, visit one of the islands in Canada's smallest national park, the St. Lawrence Islands. Camping is available on several islands. The flora and fauna on the islands are quite diverse and an interpretive program is given by the park rangers. The park's headquarters is at Mallorytown Landing, located between Gananoque and Brockville. Here, too, there are camping facilities (no electrical hookups or showers, though). There's also a day-use area with beach and picnic facilities. For more information, contact the Superintendent, **St. Lawrence Islands National Park,** 2 County Rd. 5, Mallorytown, ON, K0E 1R0 (tel. 613/923-5261).

VIEWING THE ISLANDS From May to mid-October boats leave from Gananoque on 1½ hour trips. **Thousand Island Boat Tours** (tel. 613/659-2293) offers cruises from Ivy Lea using smaller craft that can navigate into the narrow scenic channels between islands, and in fact stop at the islands. These boats leave from west of the International Bridge on the Thousand Islands Parkway. Prices are $11 for adults and $5.50 for children 4 to 12.

The **Thousand Islands Gananoque Boat Line** (tel. 613/382-2144 or 613/382-2146 for 24-hour information) operates cruises from May to October. Three-hour and one-hour cruises available. Call ahead for schedule. Boats leave from the waterfront in Gananoque.

For trips from Kingston, see the Kingston section, above.

For a dramatic view from above, climb the **Skydeck** on Hill Island near Ivy Lea, which soars 400 feet above the river. You'll be rewarded with a 40-mile panorama.

WHERE TO STAY
In Gananoque

ATHLONE INN, 250 King St. West, Gananoque, ON, K7G 2G6. Tel. 613/382-2440. 4 suites in the inn, 6 motel units. A/C TV

$ Rates: $100–$130 suite in the main inn; $60 motel room. MC, V. **Parking:** Free.

The Athlone Inn, located in a Victorian home built by a local industrialist, is known primarily for its food, which is served in a handsome dining room filled with lace-covered tables and wall tapestries. The food is classic continental—rack of lamb, chicken Kiev, sole meunière, shrimp with garlic and white wine, and veal Oscar— priced from $15 to $20.

The inn itself has four attractive suites. The windows are swagged and the furnishings include a love seat and gilt-framed pictures; the furniture itself is more Ethan Allen style. There are also some nicely kept motel units.

BRITTON HOUSE, 110 Clarence St., Gananoque, ON, K7G 2C7. Tel. 613/382-4361. 4 rms (1 with bath).

$ Rates (including breakfast): $65–$85 room without bath, $85 room with private bath. MC, V. **Parking:** Free.

⭐ This inviting bed-and-breakfast home was built in 1906. It's owned and operated by Mark and Nicole Bussières, who have four bedrooms available, one with private bath and balcony overlooking the river and three that share two bathrooms. Each room is nicely decorated, and each has an old-fashioned 1930s sink that seems to fit with the antique Eastlake or highboy dressers. There's a sitting room and dining room, both of which lead out onto a veranda with views of the river. Mark is a chef by profession and the breakfasts reflect that. The preserves are homemade and so too are the breads. Fresh herbs from the garden flavor the eggs or other hot dish that is always served.

CARRIAGE HOUSE MOTOR INN, King St. (P.O. Box 198), Gananoque, ON, K7G 2T9. Tel. 613/382-4781. Fax 613/382-1037. 67 rms.

$ Rates: June–Sept $70–$80 single, $85–$90 double; other months $45–$50 single, $50–$55 double. Higher rates are for weekends. Special packages available. **Parking:** Free.

The Carriage House Motor Inn has nicely furnished modern rooms. Facilities include a dining room, lounge, swimming pool, tennis court, and games room.

TRINITY HOUSE INN, 90 Stone St., Gananoque, ON, K7G 1Z8. Tel. 613/382-8383. 6 rms (5 with bath), 1 suite. A/C TV

$ Rates: Summer $80–$120 double. Labor Day–summer rates are about $30 less. DISC, MC, V. **Parking:** Free.

⭐ The Trinity House Inn is an impressive red-brick Victorian home built in 1859. All of the rooms come with bath, except for the smallest room, which has a bath down the hall. In addition there's a one-bedroom suite with kitchen in an adjacent building that was originally Gananoque's jail. Throughout, the period furnishings are fine and eclectic—Oriental rugs and screens, brass beds with flouncy pillows and skirts. There's a comfortable sitting room with marble fireplace and also an art gallery displaying local art in the basement. The owners also offer day sailing aboard their 30-foot yacht.

The Bistro has two dining rooms, a bar, a comfortable lounge, and an outside veranda. Among the specialties are a citrus chicken, shrimp bouillabaisse, a salad with an authentic Thousand Island dressing, and a French silk pie. Prices range from $10 to $17. Open Tuesday to Sunday from 6pm in summer.

WHERE TO DINE

In Gananoque

THE GOLDEN APPLE, 45 King St. West. Tel. 613/382-3300.
  Cuisine: CONTINENTAL. **Reservations:** Recommended.
$ **Prices:** Main courses $16–$36. MC, V.
  Open: May 1–Oct 31 lunch daily 11am–3pm, dinner daily 5–9pm; Nov 1–Dec 31 Thurs–Sun only. **Closed:** Jan 1–Apr 1.

Situated in an early 19th-century limestone farmhouse, the Golden Apple has an authentic country ambience with its pine accents. The cuisine ranges from chicken parmigiana to prime rib, veal normande, and sole amandine. In summer, the flagstone terrace is very pleasant.

In Brockville

ROBERT SHEPHARD GRIST MILL, on the waterfront. Tel. 613/345-2563.
  Cuisine: CONTINENTAL. **Reservations:** Recommended.
$ **Prices:** Appetizers $6–$7; main courses $15–$28. AE, MC, V.
  Open: Lunch Mon–Fri 11am–2pm; dinner daily 5–10pm.

At the Brockville waterfront you can practically reach out and touch the freighters and other vessels churning through the water. You can also dine in an atmospheric ambience at the Robert Shephard Grist Mill, on such dishes as stuffed sole, chicken Madeira, rack of lamb provençale, chicken Kiev, or surf-and-turf.

UPPER CANADA VILLAGE

Located 60 miles southeast of Ottawa, just east of Morrisburg, Upper Canada Village (tel. 613/543-3704), is Ontario's Williamsburg, illustrating pioneer history. All 35 structures and their contents have been restored with painstaking accuracy and devoted attention to detail—hand-forged nails and wooden dowel pegs, for instance, hold them together. The original buildings were scattered through eight village sites that bordered the St. Lawrence River; when the river's course was changed, they were all assembled here.

They appear as if still inhabited. In the wooden mill the waterwheel spins, the old machinery turns, and the wool is woven into soft blankets; the clang of hammer on anvil rings out from the blacksmith's shop, while a heady smell of fresh bread wafts from the bake shop near Willard's Hotel. Stop at the hotel for lunch or dinner. The village artisans, dressed in period costume, who operate the 19th-century machinery will explain any questions you may have. Meanwhile, you can ride a horse-drawn carryall or watch the horse ply the towpath pulling a barge along the canal.

Upper Canada Village is only open May to October. Hours are 9:30am to 5pm daily.

Admission is $9 for adults, $5.50 for seniors, $3.75 for children 6 to 12; free for children 5 and under.

SOUTHERN & MIDWESTERN ONTARIO

Part of the long sweep of the Niagara Escarpment, where the land is flat and eminently farmable, this is the pioneer country to which Canada's early settlers came. A landscape dotted with silos, barns, and dairy herds, and broken up by hedgerows, it attracted the Scottish to such towns as Elora, Fergus, and St. Mary's, the Germans to Kitchener-Waterloo; the Mennonites to Elmira and St. Jacobs; and the English Loyalists to Stratford and London. This ethnic heritage and the festivals that it nourishes—Oktoberfest, the Highland Games, the Mennonite quilt sale—are part of the attraction of the area, but so, too, are the world-famous theater festival at Stratford and the music festival in Elora.

SEEING SOUTHERN & MIDWESTERN ONTARIO

INFORMATION For information about Ontario, contact the **Ontario Ministry of Culture, Tourism, and Recreation,** 77 Bloor St. West, 9th floor, Toronto, ON, M7A 2R9 (tel. 416/314-0944, or toll free 800/ONTARIO from 9am to 8pm). The offices are open from 8:30am to 5pm Monday through Friday (daily from mid-May to mid-September).

A NOTE ON TAXES As you travel, keep in mind that Ontario has a provincial sales tax of 8%, plus a 5% accommodations tax—in addition to the national 7% GST.

ONTARIO PARKS There are 260 provincial parks in Ontario, offering ample opportunities for outdoor recreation. The daily in-season entry fee for a vehicle is $6; campsites cost anywhere from $13 to $18. For more information, contact the **Ontario Ministry of Natural Resources** (tel. 416/314-2000).

FARMSTAYS One way to really experience Ontario is to stay on a farm. Enjoy the home-cooked meals, the peace of the countryside, and the working rhythms of a dairy or mixed farm. There are all kinds of farms and locations to choose from. Rates average $35 to $60 double per night, $220 per week, all meals included. For information write the **Ontario Vacation Farm Association,** R.R. 2, Alma, ON, N0B 1A0; or contact **Ontario Travel,** Ministry of Culture, Tourism, and Recrea-

✓

WHAT'S SPECIAL ABOUT SOUTHERN & MIDWESTERN ONTARIO

Events/Festivals

☐ The Stratford Theatre Festival, one of North America's finest, held in a delightful town that also has some really fine dining.

☐ Oktoberfest, when Kitchener-Waterloo celebrates its German heritage.

☐ The Fergus Highland Games, where you can see an authentic version of this unique Scottish event.

Ethnic Heritage

☐ The Mennonite country around Stratford and Elmira.

Architectural Heritage

☐ The town of St. Mary's, filled with large, sturdy stone buildings dating from the 19th century.

Natural Spectacles

☐ Point Pelee National Park, an ornithologist's delight, where 100 species of birds have been spotted in a single day.

---

tion, 77 Bloor St. West, 9th floor, Toronto, ON, M7A 2R9 (tel. 416/314-0944, or toll free 800/ONTARIO), where you can obtain a free "Farm Vacation Guide."

1. WINDSOR & ENVIRONS

Right across the river from Detroit, Windsor is likewise an automobile and industrial center, but it makes a good base for visiting several all-time Canadian highlights. For information contact the **Convention & Visitors Bureau,** City Centre, 333 Riverside Dr. West, Suite 103, Windsor, ON, N9A 5K4 (tel. 519/255-6530).

Among the city's prime sights is the **Hiram Walker distillery,** 2072 Riverside Dr. East, Windsor, ON, N8Y 4S5 (tel. 519/254-5171), famous maker of Canadian Club whiskey. The view of the Detroit skyline from Dieppe gardens is also worth seeing. Outside the city, though, are several historical sites and natural spectacles that are not to be missed.

Windsor became a major destination for the slaves traveling the Underground Railroad and the **North American Black Historical Museum,** 277 King St., Amherstburg, ON, N9V 2C7 (tel. 519/736-5433), about 19 miles south on Lake Erie, will provide some of the fascinating historical background to that epic tale and the African-American history of the area. To get there from Windsor, take Riverside Drive West, which becomes Sandwich Street and then Highway 18.

Also in Amherstburg, see **Fort Malden National Historic Park,** Box 38, 100 Laird Ave., Amherstburg, ON N9V 2Z2 (tel. 519/736-5416), which was built by the British at the end of the 18th century, after they had abandoned Detroit to the Americans. The barracks have been restored and you can get a good sense of military life at the time. The fort played a major role in the 1812 war and also during the rebellion of 1837–38, which was led by William Lyon Mackenzie.

Just south of Amherstberg, families will enjoy a trip to **Boblo Island,** Box 39, Amherstburg, ON N9V 2Z2 (tel. 519/736-5442) for its rides and carnival atmosphere.

From Windsor, take Highway 3 east to reach one of the nation's great bird-watching areas, ✪ **Point Pelee National Park** (tel. 519/322-2371), on Pelee

Island. A sandspit at the junction of a couple of flyways, it is an ornithologist's delight. The spring and fall migrations are spectacular; as many as 100 different species have been spotted in a single day. In fall, it's also the gathering place for flocks of monarch butterflies, which cover the trees before taking off for their migratory flight. Located at the southernmost tip of Canada jutting down into Lake Erie, at the same latitude as Northern California, it features some of the same flora—white sassafras, sumac, black walnut, and cedar, for example. Take the ferry from Kingsville or Leamington, about 25 and 31 miles from Windsor, respectively. You'll need reservations in advance, so call **Pelee Island transportation** (tel. 519/724-2115).

On the island, visit the **Pelee Island Vineyards,** which have been producing some winning wines recently. Back on the mainland you can stop in at the **Pelee Island Winery,** 455 Hwy. 18 East, Kingsville, ON N9Y 2K5 (tel. 519/733-6551).

While you're in the area, also visit **Jack Miner's Bird Sanctuary,** Road 3 West, two miles north of Kingsville off Division Road (tel. 519/733-4034); it was established by the famed naturalist in Kingsville to protect migrating Canadian geese. The best time to visit is late March or late fall.

2. LONDON

118 miles (190km) SW of Toronto

GETTING THERE   By Plane   Canadian Airlines International (tel. 519/455-8385) flies to London. A taxi from the airport into town will cost about $17.

By Train   VIA operates a Toronto-Brantford-London-Windsor route and also, in conjunction with Amtrak, a Toronto-Kitchener-Stratford-London-Sarnia-Chicago route. Both offer several trains a day. The VIA Rail station in London is at 197 York St. (tel. 519/672-5722).

By Bus   Greyhound buses arrive at the terminal at 101 York St. (tel. 519/434-3245) from Buffalo, Hamilton, Toronto, Niagara Falls, Detroit, and Windsor.

By Car   London is about 120 miles (192km) from Detroit, 68 miles (110km) from Kitchener, 121 miles (195km) from Niagara Falls, and 40 miles (65km) from Stratford.

ESSENTIALS   Information   For information, contact the London Visitor's and Convention Bureau, 300 Dufferin Ave. (P.O. Box 5035), London, ON, N6A 4L9 (tel. 519/661-5000).

Getting Around   For bus schedules, contact the London Transit Commission (tel. 519/451-1347). Exact fare of $1.10 is required, 65¢ for children.

Taxis charge an initial $2.30 plus 10¢ each nine-tenths of a kilometer thereafter. There's an additional charge from 11pm to 6am. Taxi companies include Abouttown Taxi (tel. 519/432-2244) and U-Need-A-Cab (tel. 519/438-2121).

SPECIAL EVENTS   The London International Air Show, Canada's largest military air show, ushers in the summer season each June. It's followed by the Royal Canadian Big Band Festival, held over the July 1 weekend. The Home County Folk Festival, featuring folk arts, crafts, and music, is the third weekend in July.

The Great London Barbecue and Rib Cookoff and Hot Air Balloon Fiesta, is usually August 1 or thereabouts. Awards are given for the best barbecue sauce, among other things.

The 10-day Fair at the Western Fairgrounds is the seventh largest in Canada, held in September.

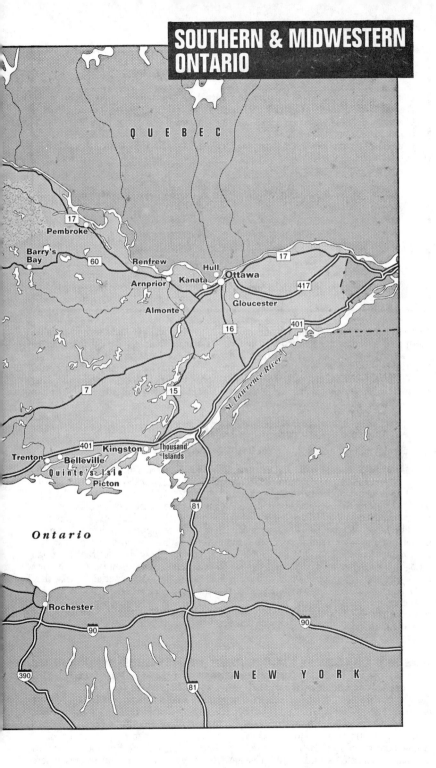

SOUTHERN & MIDWESTERN ONTARIO

AN IMPORTANT NOTE ON PRICES

Unless stated otherwise, **the prices cited in this guide are given in Canadian dollars,** which is good news for American travelers because the Canadian dollar is worth 25% less than the American dollar, but buys nearly as much. As we go to press, $1 Canadian is worth 75¢ U.S., which means that your $100-a-night hotel room will cost only U.S. $75, and your $6 breakfast costs only U.S. $4.50.

Here's a quick table of equivalents:

Canadian $	U.S. $
$ 1	$ 0.75
5	3.75
10	7.50
20	15.00
50	37.50
80	60.00
100	75.00
200	150.00

If you're driving into Canada from the U.S. Midwest, you certainly should plan on stopping in this pretty university town that sits on the Thames River (pronounced as it's spelled)—particularly if you have kids in tow, for London has several unique attractions that have special appeal to children. If nothing else, a family should stop at the Children's Museum and Storybook Gardens. Other stops include the Guy Lombardo Music Centre (a great favorite with grandparents), the Museum of Indian Archaeology, and Fanshawe Pioneer Village.

WHAT TO SEE & DO

If you enjoy antiquing, explore **Wortley Village,** one block west of Ridout.

CHILDREN'S MUSEUM, 21 Wharncliffe Rd. South. Tel. 519/434-5726.

The Children's Museum is an incredible place housed in an old school building. It occupies several floors, and a family could spend the whole day here exploring the various rooms and engaging in a myriad of activities. Every room allows children to explore, experiment, and engage their imaginations. For example, in "The Street Where You Live" kids can dress up in firefighters' uniforms, don the overalls of those who work under the streets, and assume the role of a dentist or a doctor or a construction worker. Some rooms contrast how people lived long ago with how they live today. A child can stand in a train station, send a Morse code message, shop in a general store, and sit in a schoolhouse—all experiences that they can share with their grandparents. More up-to-the-minute experiences can be enjoyed in the computer hall, at the photosensitive wall or the zoetrobe. And so on and on—fun for children and also for parents. I loved it.

Admission: $3.50 adults, $3 children.
Open: Daily 10am–5pm.

MUSEUM OF INDIAN ARCHAEOLOGY AND LAWSON PREHISTORIC INDIAN VILLAGE, 1600 Attawandaron Rd., off Wonderland Rd. North, just south of Hwy. 22. Tel. 519/473-1360.

The Museum of Indian Archaeology and Lawson Prehistoric Indian Village also should not be missed. The museum contains artifacts from various periods of Native Canadian history—projectiles, pottery shards, effigies, and such artifacts as turtle rattles. Most evocative, though, is the on-site reconstruction of an Attawandaron village. Behind the elm palisades, longhouses built according to original specifications and techniques have been erected on the five acres where archeological excavations are taking place. About 1,600 to 1,800 people once lived in the community, about 70 sharing one longhouse. The houses have been constructed of elmwood, sealed with the pitch from pine trees, and bound together with the sinew of deer hide. In an Attawandaron longhouse there were several fires with smokeholes.

Admission: $3.50 adults, $2.75 seniors and students, $1.50 children under 12, families $8.

Open: Tues–Sun 10am–5pm.

GUY LOMBARDO MUSIC CENTRE, 205 Wonderland Rd. South. Tel. 519/473-9003.

Nostalgia. That's what can be captured on Wonderland Road at the outdoor bandshell where bandleader Guy Lombardo began playing in the '30s before he hit the big time and became famous for bringing in the New Year at the Waldorf Astoria in New York. There's also a Guy Lombardo Music Centre filled with Lombardo memorabilia. Adjacent to the bandshell is a restaurant that will help take you on a trip down memory lane (see "Where to Dine," below).

Admission: $2 adults, free for children under 12.

Open: Late May–Labor Day Mon–Thurs 10am–5pm, Fri–Sun 11am–5pm. Limited hours in winter—call ahead.

SPRINGBANK PARK STORYBOOK GARDENS, off Commissioners Rd. West. Tel. 519/661-5770.

The Springbank Park Storybook Gardens is a children's zoo with a storybook theme. Special daily events include seal feeding at 3:30pm, a storytelling hour, and a juggler and other performers. There's also a maze and Playworld, with many activities for children.

Admission: $4.50 adults, $3 seniors, $2.50 children 3–14.

Open: May–Labor Day daily 10am–8pm; Labor Day–early Oct Mon–Fri 10am–5pm, Sat–Sun 10am–6pm. **Closed:** Oct–Apr.

LONDON REGIONAL ART AND HISTORICAL MUSEUMS, 421 Ridout North. Tel. 519/672-4580.

Here you'll view the historical and contemporary works of local, national, and international artists. The gallery also offers the opportunity to "Be a Sunday Artist" as well as providing a children's workshop. The building itself—six barrel vaults slotted together to accommodate domed skylights—is striking.

Admission: Free.

Open: Tues–Sun noon–5pm.

FANSHAWE PIONEER VILLAGE, Fanshawe Park. Tel. 519/457-1296.

In Fanshawe Park (tel. 519/451-2800) you can rent paddleboats, and there's also a large pool and beach at this four-mile-long lake. Here also is the Pioneer Village, a 20-plus building complex where you can see craft demonstrations, enjoy wagon rides, and imagine what life was like during the 18th century. It's east of the city off Clarke Side Road north of Huron.

Admission: Park $5.50 per vehicle. Pioneer Village $5 adults, $4 seniors and students, $3 children 12 and under, free for children under 5.

Open: Park, open all year. Village, May 1–Oct 31 daily 10am–4:30pm; Oct 31–Dec 20 Wed–Fri 1–4pm, Sat–Sun 10am–4:30pm.

ELDON HOUSE, 401 Ridout North. Tel. 519/661-5169.

Downtown there's a cluster of historic sights. Eldon House is the city's oldest remaining house (1834) and it houses a historic museum.

Nearby at nos. 435, 441, and 443 Ridout North are the original Labatt Brewery buildings.

Admission: $3 adults, $2 seniors, $1 children under 16, families $6.

Open: Tues–Sun noon–5pm. **Closed:** Christmas Day and New Year's.

ROYAL CANADIAN REGIMENT MUSEUM, at Oxford and Elizabeth Sts. Tel. 519/660-5102.

The Royal Canadian Regiment Museum, in historic Wolseley Hall, contains exhibits about regimental history and battles from the Northwest Rebellion to Korea.

Admission: Free.
Open: Tues–Fri 10am–4pm, Sat–Sun noon–4pm.

WHERE TO STAY

For bed-and-breakfast accommodations priced from $35 to $55 a night, contact the **London Area Bed and Breakfast Association,** 2 Normandy Gardens, London, ON, N6H 4A9 (tel. 519/641-0467).

EXPENSIVE

IDLEWYLD INN, 36 Grand Ave., London, ON, N6C 1K8. Tel. and fax 519/433-2891. 27 rms. A/C MINIBAR TV TEL
$ Rates (including continental breakfast): $89–$120 single or double; $120–$175 suite. AE, DC, ER, MC, V. **Parking:** Free.

The Idlewyld Inn is the town's top-choice accommodation. Located in a house that was built by a wealthy leather industrialist, it has much fine detail—eight-foot-tall windows, oak and cherry carved fireplaces, casement windows, oak-beamed ceilings, and a wallpaper crafted to look like tooled leather in the dining room.

Room 101 is the largest unit. The bathroom contains the original bathtub and toilet, and the bedroom, which boasts a comfortable chaise longue and a glazed tile fireplace, is separated from the sitting area by huge carved cherry columns. It has a TV and a telephone. All the rooms are furnished differently. Room 302 has a tiny Romeo and Juliet balcony. Room 105 has valanced windows. Room 202 has a marvelous fireplace of green cabbage leaf tiles, and a scallop-shell marble sink stand.

At breakfast guests help themselves to muffins, toast, cereal, and coffee in the large, comfortable kitchen equipped with toasters, coffee makers, and refrigerators. The breakfast can be taken out on the porch.

SHERATON ARMOURIES HOTEL, 325 Dundas St., London, ON, N6B 1T9. Tel. 519/679-6111. Fax 519/679-3957. 250 rms. A/C MINIBAR TV TEL
$ Rates: $130 single; $140 double; from $230 suite. Extra person $10. Children under 18 stay free in parents' room. Special weekend rates available. AE, CB, DC, DISC, ER, MC, V. **Parking:** $5.

The Sheraton, occupying the old armory, is a worthy example of architectural conservation and conversion. The main floor and base of the building is formed by the 12-foot-thick walls of the armory, and above the crenellated turrets and ramparts soars a modern glass tower. Inside the rooms are all well equipped with such niceties as hairdryer and makeup mirror, and antique reproductions, including wing chairs.

The Armouries is the main dining room while The Cantata lounge features entertainment on weekends. Facilities include a squash court and racquetball court, pool and an exercise area, both now occupying the former drill parade area.

MODERATE/BUDGET OPTIONS

London has several modest hotel chain options: **Best Western Lamplighter Inn,** 591 Wellington Rd. South, London, ON, N6C 4R3 (tel. 519/681-3271), charging $62 single, $72 to $88 double; **Ramada Inn** 401, 817 Exeter Rd., London, ON, N6E 1W1 (tel. 519/681-4900), charging $69 to $89 single and $79 to $95 double; **Comfort Inn,** 800 Exeter Rd., London, ON, N6E 1L5 (tel. 519/681-1200), with rates of $55 single, $63 double; and **Journey's End,** 1156 Wellington Rd. South, London, ON, N6E 1M3 (tel. 519/685-9300), charging $63 single, $72 double.

WHERE TO DINE

EXPENSIVE

ANTHONY'S, 434 Richmond St. Tel. 519/679-0960.
Cuisine: SEAFOOD. **Reservations:** Recommended.
$ Prices: Main courses $17–$20. AE, ER, MC, V.
Open: Lunch Mon–Fri 11:30am–2:30pm; dinner Mon–Sat 5–10pm.

Anthony's is a seafood specialty house where the ingredients are fresh and superb and the presentation itself is mouthwatering. As an example, the salmon with dill sauce might come with lime wedges cut into tiny petals placed around a center of caviar. The dinner menu might offer tuna tonnato or shrimp bisque with Calvados to start, followed by perch with pine nuts, paella valenciana, or beef tenderloin with tarragon and white wine sauce. The ambience is enhanced by the open kitchen hung with gleaming copper pots. The room is also brightened by a mural depicting tropical fish and faux aquariums. Desserts are all made on the premises, as are the handmade chocolates that conclude the meal. The desserts change daily, but you might be tempted by a lemon tart, a chocolate nocturne gâteau, or sorbet.

THE HORSE AND HOUND, Hyde Park. Tel. 519/472-6801.
 Cuisine: CONTINENTAL. **Reservations:** Recommended.
$ Prices: Appetizers $7–$9; main courses $16–$22. AE, DC, ER, MC, V.
 Open: Lunch daily 11:30am–2:30pm; dinner daily 5:30–10pm. A limited menu is served between meals and 10pm–1am.

A real local favorite is the Horse and Hound, located in a Victorian house where there are six intimate and elegant dining rooms. Start with warmed goat cheese wrapped in phyllo pastry on a raspberry coulis, or leek, corn, and Stilton soup. Follow with a selection from the 10 or so entrées that might include a classic chateaubriand, a hearty ragoût of venison with vegetables and spaetzle, or poached Atlantic salmon with basil pesto cream sauce. Luncheon prices range from $8 to $11. There's piano entertainment in the downstairs lounge on weekends.

MICHAELS ON THAMES, 1 York St. Tel. 519/672-0111.
 Cuisine: CONTINENTAL. **Reservations:** Recommended.
$ Prices: Appetizers $3–$8; main courses $13–$21. AE, DC, ER, MC, V.
 Open: Lunch Mon–Fri 11:30am–2:30pm; dinner daily 5–11pm.
Michaels on Thames is a local favorite overlooking the river. Downstairs, visitors can wait in the Captain's bar before entering the bi-level dining room, which in winter is made cozy by a blazing fire. The food is well prepared and nicely served. Among the entrées you might find chicken Camembert with lemon wine sauce, rabbit forestière, rack of lamb roasted with mint finished with demiglace and port wine, salmon with hollandaise, and steak Diane. Desserts include a flamboyant cherries jubilee along with a tray featuring many choices, including raspberry cheesecake.

MIESTRO'S, 352 Dundas St. Tel. 519/439-8983.
 Cuisine: ECLECTIC. **Reservations:** Recommended.
$ Prices: Main courses $15–$18. AE, ER, MC, V.
 Open: Lunch Tues–Sat 11:30am–2:30pm; dinner Tues–Sat 5:30–10pm.
A popular downtown place with an intimate atmosphere, Miestro's serves an eclectic selection of dishes. At lunch you could sample everything from a lemon-shrimp salad or an apricot-chicken terrine to nasi goreng and soba noodles sautéed in sesame oil with Oriental vegetables, seaweed, saké, tomatoes, and leeks, all priced from $7 to $9. A similar breadth of choice prevails at dinner, and, in fact, some dishes appear on both menus. At dinner the choices are likely to include veal sautéed with oyster mushrooms, and toasted almonds in a marsala cream sauce, or salmon wrapped in lotus leaf steamed with rice wine, sesame oil, and oyster sauce.

WONDERLAND RIVERVIEW DINING ROOM, 284 Wonderland Rd. South. Tel. 519/471-4662.
 Cuisine: CONTINENTAL. **Reservations:** Recommended.
$ Prices: Main courses $13–$23. AE, MC, V.
 Open: Lunch daily 11:30am–2:30pm; dinner daily 5–9pm.
Still a favorite venue for special family occasions, the Wonderland Riverview Dining Room offers such dishes as chicken breast with soya cream, perch with tartare sauce, or prime rib. Luncheon and brunch prices range from $7 to $9. Around the walls are framed clips of events that took place here in the '30s and '40s—dancing to Ozzie Williams, Shep Fields, and Mart Kenney. There's a lovely outdoor dining terrace under the trees and an outdoor dancing area overlooking the river.

MODERATE

JEWEL OF INDIA, 390 Richmond, between King and Dundas. Tel. 519/434-9268.
  Cuisine: INDIAN. **Reservations:** Recommended on weekends.
  $ Prices: Main courses $8–$13. AE, DC, ER, MC, V.
  Open: Lunch Mon–Sat 11:30am–2:30pm; dinner daily 5–11pm.

Local Indian food aficionados swear by the Jewel of India. Dishes include biryanis, tandoori chicken, and lamb tikka, as well as various vindaloos, Madras, bhuna, dansak, and dopiaz dishes.

JO KOOL'S, 595 Richmond, at Central. Tel. 519/663-5665.
  Cuisine: SNACKS. **Reservations:** Not needed.
  $ Prices: Most items $3–$6. AE, MC, V.
  Open: Mon–Sat 11am–1am, Sun 11am–midnight.

Jo Kool's is a university hangout. Nachos and kitchen-sink pizza are the specialties, and T-shirts are the primary decor. Some come solely to drink, others to eat.

POACHER'S ARMS RESTAURANT, 171 Queens Ave. Tel. 519/432-7888.
  Cuisine: CANADIAN. **Reservations:** Recommended, especially at lunch.
  $ Prices: Appetizers $3–$6; main courses $10–$15. AE, ER, MC, V.
  Open: Lunch daily 11:30am–4pm, dinner daily 4pm–12:45am.

The Poacher's Arms has typical pub grub at lunch—burgers and fries, fish-and-chips, plus pasta, nachos, barbecued chicken, and pizza—all under $7. At dinner prices are a bit higher, for such items as grilled calves' liver and onions, and grilled Thai chicken.

SAY CHEESE, 246 Dundas St. Tel. 519/434-0341.
  Cuisine: CONTINENTAL. **Reservations:** Accepted.
  $ Prices: Most items $9–$13. AE, ER, MC, V.
  Open: Lunch Mon–Sat 11am–3pm; dinner Mon–Sat 5–10pm.

You'll feel you can relax and commune over a bottle of wine with strangers-turned-friends at the next table in the casual, comfortable ambience that prevails at Say Cheese. Cheese inspires the cuisine. The traditional menu, which hasn't changed in 24 years, features such all-time favorites as cheese soup, quiches, sandwiches, and assorted cheese platters. The supplemental "seasonal" menu changes frequently and might feature such dishes as cauliflower cheeses, oyster and Cheddar pie, and braised chicken with onions, pimiento, and sage and a potato Gruyère gratin. There's a good selection of wines by the glass and the bottle. Ideal for breakfast, lunch, or dinner—and afternoon tea, too. While you're here browse in the downstairs cheese shop.

EVENING ENTERTAINMENT

The **Grand Theatre,** 471 Richmond St. (tel. 519/672-8800), features drama, comedy, and musicals from mid-October to May. The theater itself, built in 1901, is worth viewing.

Harness racing takes place from October to June at the Western Fairgrounds track (tel. 519/438-7203).

London also has a few bars and clubs: **Barneys,** 671 Richmond St. (tel. 519/432-1232) attracts a young professional crowd; and **Dr. Rockits American Bandstand,** 60 Wharncliffe Rd. North (tel. 519/432-1191), is a dance club with large '50s-style checkered dance floor.

3. GODERICH & BAYFIELD

For Goderich information, call 519/524-6600 or call the visitor centre (tel. 519/524-2513), which is open daily in summer. Among the highlights in Goderich is the **Historic Huron Gaol,** with walls 18 feet high and two feet thick, which also houses the **Huron County Museum,** 110 North St. (tel. 519/524-2686). Stop and stroll around the town, the most striking feature of which is the central octagonal space with the Huron County Courthouse at the center.

Bayfield is a pretty, well-preserved 19th-century town about 13 miles from Goderich and 40 miles from Stratford. Once a major grain shipping port, it became a quiet backwater when the railroad passed it by. Today the main square, high street, and Elgin Place are part of a Heritage Conservation District. Walk around and browse in the appealing stores—the information center has a walking-tour pamphlet that helps.

WHERE TO STAY

BENMILLER INN, RR 4, Goderich, ON, N7A 3Y1. Tel. 519/524-2191.
54 rms. A/C TV TEL
$ Rates (including continental breakfast): $105–$175 single or double; $225 deluxe suite. AE, MC, V.

The original wool mill, powered by a wheel, was built in 1877. Today it is the heart of this inn nestled in the Maitland River Valley and containing the Ivey Dining Room, Jonathan's Lounge, the reception area, and 13 accommodations. It was opened as an inn in 1974 and during the conversion many of the mill's parts were refashioned into decorations for the rooms. For example, lamps were created from gears and mirrors from pulley wheels. Jonathan's lounge is complete with a millwheel chandelier. The rooms feature barnboard siding, desks, floor lamps, heated ceramic tile in the bathrooms, and handmade quilts. Seventeen rooms are found in Gledhill House, the original millowner's home. Ground floor rooms here have pressed tin ceilings and all are extra-large by hotel standards. Four deluxe suites here have fireplaces and bidets and Jacuzzi bathtubs. Additional rooms are found in the River Mill, which is attached to a silo-style building containing the swimming pool, whirlpool, and running track. The dining room serves fine continental cuisine. The brick patio overlooking the gardens is a pleasant place to sit and regard the totem pole, which was brought here from British Columbia. Additional sports facilities include two tennis courts, billiards, bicycles, table tennis, and cross-country ski trails.

CLIFTON MANOR INN, 19 Clan Gregor Square, P. O. Box 454, Bayfield, ON, N0M 1G0. Tel. 519/565-2282. 5 rms (3 with bath).
$ Rates: $75–$110; $150 for the Mona Lisa room. No credit cards.

This elegant house was built in 1895 for the reve of Bayfield. The interior features ash wood, etched glass panels in the doors, and other attractive period details. Today it has many comforts that have been installed by owner Elizabeth Marquis—Oriental rugs, lamps, and comfortable sofas and love seats in the living room, elegant silver and sideboards in the dining room, and four comfortable accommodations, each named after an artist or composer. The Van Gogh room sports sunflower pillows and draperies along with a dresser and sidetable. The Renoir is charming, and its bathroom has a deep, six-foot-long tub. Elizabeth provides candles and bubble bath—a lovely romantic touch. All the rooms have cozy touches like mohair rugs, wingback chairs, fresh flowers, and so on. Currently a loft room is being converted into the Mona Lisa. Lilac bushes and fruit trees fill the yard. Afternoon tea is served. Breakfast consists of egg dishes like omelets or crêpes, plus fresh fruit often plucked from the very trees in the garden.

THE LITTLE INN AT BAYFIELD, Main St., P. O. Box 100, Bayfield, N0M 1G0. Tel. 519/565-2611. Fax 519/565-5474. 20 rms, 10 suites across the street. A/C MINIBAR
$ Rates (including breakfast): $85–$105 single; $100–$135 double; suites from $110 single, $175 double. Special packages available. AE, DC, ER, MC, V.

Although the inn was originally built in 1832, it has been thoroughly modernized. The older rooms in the main building are small and have only showers but they are comfortably furnished with oak or sleigh beds. Rooms in the newer section are larger and feature platform beds and modern furnishings. The suites across the street in the carriage house have platform beds, pine hutches, and similar furnishings but feature whirlpool bathrooms, propane gas fireplaces, and verandas. The restaurant is popular and is open for lunch and dinner seven days a week.

WHERE TO EAT

The **Benmiller Inn** (tel. 519/524-2191) has a good dining room. For casual dining, Bayfield offers several choices. The **Albion Hotel,** on Main Street (tel. 519/565-2641), features a fun, wall-length bar decorated with hundreds of baseball hats and other sports paraphernalia. It also has seven rooms available starting at $50 single or double. **Admiral Belfield's,** 5 Main St. (tel. 519/565-2326), is fun, too. A converted general store, it serves diner, deli, and pub fare. Jazz and other entertainment, too.

RED PUMP, Main St., Bayfield. Tel. 519/565-2576.
   Cuisine: INTERNATIONAL. **Reservations:** Recommended.
$ **Prices:** Main courses $18–$23. AE, MC, V.
   Open: May 1–May 24 weekend and Sept 1–Thanksgiving, lunch Tues–Sun noon–3pm, dinner Tues–Sun 5–10pm; May 24 weekend–Sept 1, lunch daily noon–3pm, dinner daily 5–10pm; Thanksgiving–December, lunch Thurs–Sun noon–3pm, dinner Thurs–Sun 5–9pm. **Closed:** Jan–Apr.

The food at this attractive restaurant is exciting and eclectic. Typical main dishes might include steamed chicken breast and scallops with pine nut, red pepper, tomato, and balsamic vinegar sauce; barbecued fish; and tiger shrimp stuffed with crab and served with risotto cakes.

4. ST. MARY'S

15 miles (24km) S of Stratford

GETTING THERE   By Train   The Amtrak/VIA Toronto-Chicago train stops in St. Mary's.

By Car   From London take Highway 4 North to Highway 7 East. Exit off 7 to St. Mary's.

ESSENTIALS   For tourist information, contact St. Mary's Tourism, P.O. Box 998, St. Mary's, ON, N4X 1B6 (tel. 519/284-3500 or 519/285-4763 for the recreation department).

This small town contains a lot of history and some remarkable stone architecture, much of it influenced by H. H. Richardson.

WHAT TO SEE & DO

Take a walk around town. Among the **architectural highlights** on Queen Street are the Town Hall (1891), the Andrews Building (1884) now housing Anstett's Jewellery, MacPherson's Craft Store (1855 and 1884), the Gothic Revival Opera House (1879), and the two Hutton blocks (1860s) that flank it on Water Street.
   The **Ross Pharmacy** is housed in the building where Timothy Eaton and his brothers operated a general store in the 1860s until Timothy decided that the kind of store he wanted to operate—based on cash and not barter and credit—would never succeed in St. Mary's, and he left in 1869 to open a store in Toronto and build the famous Eaton company.
   Some stores are worth browsing in town. At **MacPherson's,** at the corner of Queen and Water Streets (tel. 519/284-1741), you can stock up on every conceivable craft supply—beads, wicker, fabric flowers, doll-making materials, and stenciling supplies. Open Monday through Saturday from 9:30am to 5:30pm (on Friday until 9pm), and Sunday from noon to 5pm.
   Lovers of architecture and stone buildings in particular will enjoy the **Perth County Gallery,** 149 Queen St. East (tel. 519/284-3761), which has blueprints and drawings of many of St. Mary's landmarks.

At the **Wildwood Conservation Area,** three miles (five kilometers) east of St. Mary's, off Highways 7/19 (tel. 519/284-2292), there's camping (450 sites), picnicking, hiking trials, a beach and swimming, sailboarding and other boat rentals, fishing, and in winter, cross-country skiing. For information, contact the Upper Thames River Conservation Authority, R.R. 6, London, ON, N6A 4C1 (tel. 519/451-2800).

WHERE TO STAY & DINE

WESTOVER INN, 300 Thomas St. (P.O. Box 280), St. Mary's, ON, N0M 2V0. Tel. 519/284-2977. Fax 519/284-4043. 22 rms and suites. A/C TV TEL
$ Rates (including breakfast): $90–$145 single; $100–$160 double; $150–$275 suite. AE, ER, MC, V.

Graceful accommodations are provided in this Victorian manor house that was built in 1867 and features carved gingerbread decoration and leaded-glass windows. The house is set on 19 acres, making for a secluded retreat. Inside the limestone house, the rooms have been furnished in modern antique style with reproductions—cherry side tables, and cabinets housing the TVs. The decor is dusty rose and jade green; beds sport floral spreads. The bathrooms contain a full range of amenities. Some rooms, like Room 5, have balconies. Six rooms are located in the Manor itself, including a luxury suite with a whirlpool bathroom. Other accommodations are found in the Terrace (12), which was built in the '30s as a dormitory for the priests who attended what was then a seminary, and the Thames Cottage (4), a modern building containing two two-bedroom suites. Downstairs in the Manor, guests may use the comfortable lounge.

Dining/Entertainment: The elegant restaurant is gaining a reputation in the area for fine cuisine. Among the choices you might find fresh salmon, roast leg of Ontario lamb with garlic confit and thyme, or grilled escalopes of young turkey with sage-flavored potatoes and cranberry orange chutney. Prices range from $16 to $22. The appetizers might include assorted wild local mushrooms in phyllo pastry with aïoli and sage, and several soups. Desserts are enticing: profiteroles filled with chocolate and Kahlúa mousse, lemon tartlets in a shortbread crust, and more. Open daily from 8 to 11am for breakfast, 11:30am to 2pm for lunch (brunch on Sunday) and Monday to Saturday 5 to 8:30pm for dinner. There's a bar/lounge and delightful patio.

Facilities: Outdoor pool.

---

5. STRATFORD

93 miles W of Toronto; 28 miles W of Kitchener; 38 NE of London

GETTING THERE   By Train   Amtrak/VIA operate several daily trains along the Toronto-Kitchener-Stratford-London-Sarnia-Chicago route.

By Car   From Toronto take Highway 401 west to Interchange 278 at Kitchener. Follow Highway 8 west onto Highway 7/8 west to Stratford. From Detroit/Windsor follow Highway 401 East to Exit 218 at Ingersoll, to Highway 19 north and then to Highway 7 East. From Buffalo cross from Buffalo to Fort Erie and take QEW to Exit 100 West onto Highway 403. Take 403 west to Highway 6 north to Highway 401. Take 401 west and then pick up the directions above given from Toronto.

ESSENTIALS   For first-rate visitor information, go to the booth by the river on York Street at Erie (tel. 519/273-3352). It's open from May to early November from 10am to 5pm daily (until 8pm Thursday through Saturday). At other times, contact Tourism Stratford, P.O. Box 818, 88 Wellington St., Stratford, ON, N5A 6W1 (tel. 519/271-5140).

SPECIAL EVENTS   For details on the Stratford Festival, see below. In the last week of May, Festival City Days celebrates the opening of the festival with marching bands, floats, and clowns. In nearby New Hamburg in May, the annual Mennonite Relief Sale features some 300 quilts, an antiques auction, a large craft tent, and plenty of Mennonite food. Proceeds go to the Mennonite Central Committee to support its international relief work and service.

Home of the world-famous Stratford Festival, this city manages to capture the prime elements of the Bard's birthplace, from the swans on the Avon River to the grass banks that sweep down to it where you can picnic under a weeping willow before attending a Shakespeare play. It's a very pleasant town with some fine dining and, of course, the famous festival.

THE STRATFORD FESTIVAL

Since its modest beginnings on July 13, 1953, when *Richard III*, starring Sir Alec Guinness, was staged in a huge tent, Stratford's artistic directors have all built on the radical but faithfully classic base originally provided by Tyrone Guthrie to create a repertory theater with a glowing international reputation.

Stratford has three theaters: the **Festival Theatre,** 55 Queen St. in Queen's Park, with its dynamic thrust stage; the **Avon Theatre,** 99 Downie St., with a classic proscenium; and the **Tom Patterson Theatre,** an intimate 500-seat theater on Lakeside Drive.

World-famous for its Shakespearean productions, the festival also offers both classic and modern theatrical masterpieces. Recent productions have included Gilbert and Sullivan's *Mikado* (which went on to great success on Broadway), Thornton Wilder's *Our Town*, Chekhov's *Uncle Vanya, Timon of Athens* and *Measure for Measure* (both by Shakespeare), and *Les Belles Soeurs* by Michel Tremblay. Among the company's famous alumnae are such famous names as Maggie Smith, Sir Alec Guinness, Alan Bates, Christopher Plummer, Irene Worth, Julie Harris, and Gordon Thompson. Present stars include Nicholas Pennell, Brian Bedford, Pat Galloway, Goldie Semple, and Colm Feore.

Tom Patterson Theatre productions in particular are loved for their creative risk-taking and the excitement generated by the intimate space.

In addition to attending plays, visitors may enjoy "Meet the Festival," a series of informal discussions with members of the acting company, production, or administrative staff; "Post Performance Discussions" that follow Tuesday- and Thursday-evening performances; and Backstage Tours, offered every Sunday morning from mid-June to the end of October. The last cost $5 for adults, $2.50 for seniors and students (advance reservations recommended).

The season usually begins early in May and continues until mid-November. For tickets, call 519/273-1600; or write to the Stratford Festival, P.O. Box 520, Stratford, ON, N5A 6V2. Tickets are also available in the U.S. and Canada at Ticketron outlets. Telephone orders taken beginning in late February.

WHAT TO SEE & DO

Summer pleasures in Stratford beside theater? Within sight of the Festival Theatre, **Queen's Park** has picnic spots beneath tall shade trees or down by the water's edge where the swans and ducks will gather. To the east and west of the theater, footpaths follow both shores of the Avon River and Lake Victoria. Past the Orr Dam and the 90-year-old stone bridge, through a rustic gate once straw-thatched but now (for want of a thatcher) cedar-shingled, lies a very special park, the **Shakespearean Garden.**

Here in this formal English garden, where a sundial presented by the former mayor of England's Stratford-upon-Avon measures out the hours, you can relax and contemplate the herb and flower beds and the tranquil river lagoon, and muse on Shakespeare's bust by Toronto sculptor Cleeve Horne.

If you turn right onto Romeo Street North from Highways 7 and 8, as you come into Stratford, you'll find the **Gallery/Stratford,** 54 Romeo St. (tel. 519/271-5271), located in a lovely old building on the fringes of Confederation Park. Since it opened in 1967 it has naturally adopted a Canadian focus, mounting such shows as

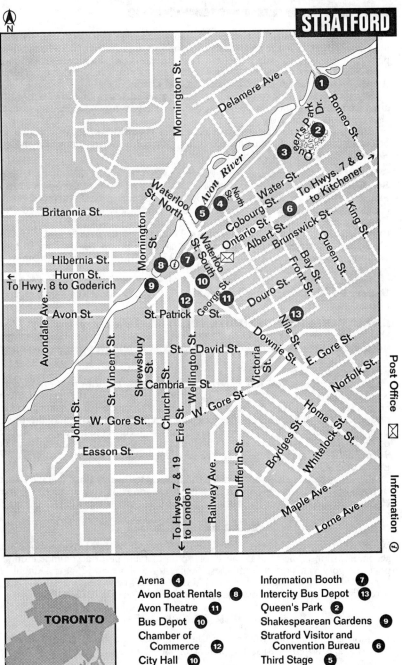

STRATFORD

N

Delamere Ave.

Mornington St.

Romeo St.

Queen's Park Dr.

To Hwys. 7 & 8 to Kitchener →

Avon River

Waterloo St. North

Mornington St.

Waterloo St. South

North St.

Water St.

Cobourg St.

Ontario St.

Albert St.

Brunswick St.

Bay St.

Front St.

Queen St.

King St.

Britannia St.

Hibernia St.

Huron St.

← To Hwy. 8 to Goderich

Avon St.

Avondale Ave.

St. Patrick

George St.

Douro St.

Nile St.

E. Gore St.

Norfolk St.

Downie St.

St. Vincent St.

Shrewsbury St.

Church St.

Wellington St.

David St.

Victoria St.

W. Gore St.

Cambria St.

John St.

W. Gore St.

Erie St.

Railway Ave.

Dufferin St.

Brydges St.

Home St.

Whitelock St.

Easson St.

To Hwys. 7 & 19 to London →

Maple Ave.

Lorne Ave.

Post Office ⊠

Information ⊙

TORONTO

← **Stratford**

Arena ④

Avon Boat Rentals ⑧

Avon Theatre ⑪

Bus Depot ⑩

Chamber of Commerce ⑫

City Hall ⑩

Festival Theatre ③

Gallery Stratford ①

Information Booth ⑦

Intercity Bus Depot ⑬

Queen's Park ②

Shakespearean Gardens ⑨

Stratford Visitor and Convention Bureau ⑥

Third Stage ⑤

Tourism Stratford ⑫

Train Station ⑬

"Québec-Ontario Crafts," "Twentieth-Century Canadian Drawing," and shows of individual artists. If you're an art lover, do stop in, for you're sure to find an unusual, personally satisfying show in one of the three galleries. Open Tuesday through Sunday from 9am to 6pm during the festival season, from 10am to 6pm at other times. Admission is $3 for adults, $2 for students and seniors.

Stratford is a historic town, and one-hour **guided tours** of early Stratford are given from July to Labor Day, Monday through Saturday leaving at 9:30am from the visitor's booth by the river.

Boat and canoe rentals are available at **The Boathouse,** located behind and below the information booth. Open daily from 10am in summer. Contact **Avon Boat Rentals,** 40 York St. (tel. 519/271-7739).

SHOPPING Browsing the many craft and gift shops is rewarding. **Village Studios,** 69 Ontario St. (tel. 519/271-7231), has a selection of Canadian crafts—Inuit and Iroquois art, leatherwork, sheepskin, wood carving, glass, and more. A stroll out along Ontario Street is particularly rewarding for antique lovers. At no. 286, **Paul Bennett** (tel. 519/273-3334) specializes in china, art glass, Oriental carpets, and early electric light fixtures. **Yesterday's Things,** 351 Ontario St. (tel. 519/271-5180), has a variety of antique jewelry and china as well as books. Back in town, **Gallery Indigena,** 151 Downie St. (tel. 519/271-7881), sells Native Canadian art, as well as paintings, prints, jewelry, and other craft items.

Props, 18 York St. (tel. 519/271-5666), has theatrical gifts, art, and interiors. **Gallery 96,** York Lane, behind Rundles (tel. 519/271-4660), is a cooperative gallery of regional artists.

A TRIP THROUGH MENNONITE COUNTRY Drive east on Highways 7/8 to Shakespeare, seven miles out of Stratford, and browse the shops and many antiques stores in this small and as-yet-unspoiled town. From here, drive north on Route 14 to Amulree. Turn right (east) onto County Road 15 toward Waterloo, which turns into Erb Street and takes you past the Seagram Museum.

From Waterloo, follow King Street north to Highway 86. Turn right onto County Road 17, follow it to County Road 22, and turn left. Take 22 north to County Road 86 and turn right to West Montrose and drive over Ontario's last remaining covered bridge. Built in 1881, it's 200 feet long and commonly referred to as the Kissing Bridge, a sobriquet it earned when it was lit only with coal-fired lamps. Double back on 86 to County Road 21 and take it into Elora. Drive northwest on County Road 7 to Salem and then south on Route 18, then 22 to Highway 86. Turn right and take it to Elmira and St. Jacobs.

Return by heading west on 17 through Linwood to County Road 7. Take 7 south through Millbank, with its famous cheese factory, and Poole to Highway 19. Follow Highway 19 through Gads Hill back to Stratford. The whole trip will take 2½ hours.

WHERE TO STAY

When you book your theater tickets, you can also, at no extra charge, book your accommodations. The festival can book you into the type of accommodation and price category you prefer, from guest homes for as little as $35 for a double to first-class hotels charging more than $125 double. Call or write the Festival Theatre Box Office, P.O. Box 520, Stratford, ON, N5A 6V2 (tel. 519/273-1600).

A PICK OF THE B&Bs

For more information on the Stratford bed-and-breakfast scene, write to **Tourism Stratford,** P.O. Box 818, 88 Wellington St., Stratford, ON, N5A 6W1 (tel. 519/271-5140).

ACRYLIC DREAMS, 66 Bay St., Stratford, ON, N5A 4K6. Tel. 519/271-7874. 4 rms (3 with bath). A/C

$ Rates (including full breakfast): $70 with shared bath; $80 and $85 double; $95 suite. No credit cards.

Acrylic Dreams has a funky, modern, artsy atmosphere thanks to its artist-owners. The house is furnished with cottage-style antiques except for the living room, which is furnished in New Wave with transparent acrylic furniture. Upstairs there's a suite with private bath and living room. On the ground floor, there are two doubles with bath plus a double with an antique iron-and-brass bed that shares a bathroom. The full breakfast will vary from day to day. It might bring, for example, orange juice and coffee, peaches with peach yogurt, scrambled eggs, and bagels (but no meat since the owners are vegetarians). There's a phone for guests' use and the suite has a TV.

AVONVIEW MANOR, 63 Avon St., Stratford, ON, N5A. 5N5. Tel. 519/273-4603. 4 rms (none with bath).
$ Rates (including full breakfast): $60 double. No credit cards.
Located on a quiet street in an Edwardian house, AvonView Manor has four rooms, with fans only, all attractively and individually furnished and sharing a bath. One room on the ground floor has a brass bed covered with a floral-pattern quilt and flouncy pillows, and is large enough for a couch and oak rocker. An oak staircase leads to the other rooms, one with a cherry acorn bed, cherry dresser, and love seat. A full breakfast is served in a bright dining room overlooking the garden in which the tables sport lace tablecloths. A kitchen equipped with an ironing board is available on the first floor. The living room is very comfortable, particularly in winter in front of the stone fireplace. Smoking is not allowed, except on the porch. Facilities include an outdoor pool.

BAKER HOUSE, 129 Brunswick St., Stratford, ON, N5A 3L9. Tel. 519/271-5644. 5 rms (1 with bath).
$ Rates (including continental breakfast): $63 double with shared bath; $75 double with private bath. No credit cards.
Baker House has four rooms sharing two baths, and one room with private bath. There's a comfy sitting room with plenty of slipcovered chairs and sofas, a small TV room, and a patio out back. An extended continental breakfast is served—fresh fruit, cereal, muffins, and croissants. No smoking.

BRUNSWICK HOUSE, 109 Brunswick St., Stratford, ON, N5A 3L9. Tel. 519/271-4546. six rms (none with bath).
$ Rates (including full breakfast): From $55 double. No credit cards.
Brunswick House is owned and operated by two writers, Geoff Hancock and Gay Allison. If you stay here you will enjoy very literary surroundings—portraits of Canadian authors and poetry on the walls, books everywhere, and the chance to run into a literary personality.
There are six rooms, sharing two baths, all nicely decorated and all with ceiling

---

AN IMPORTANT NOTE ON PRICES

Unless stated otherwise, **the prices cited in this guide are given in Canadian dollars,** which is good news for U.S. travelers because the Canadian dollar is worth 25% less than the American dollar, but buys nearly as much. As we go to press, $1 Canadian is worth 75¢ U.S., which means that your $100-a-night hotel room will cost only U.S. $75, and your $6 breakfast costs only U.S. $4.50.
Here's a quick table of equivalents:

Canadian $	U.S. $
$ 1	$ 0.75
5	3.75
10	7.50
20	15.00
50	37.50
80	60.00
100	75.00
200	150.00

fans. One is a family room with a double and two single beds. Each has a personal decorative touch—a Mennonite quilt, posters by an artist friend, a parasol atop a wardrobe. Smoking is restricted to the veranda.

DEACON HOUSE, 101 Brunswick St., Stratford, ON, N5A 3L9. Tel. 519/273-2052. 7 rms (3 with bath). A/C

$ Rates (including continental breakfast): $65 double without bath, $80 double with bath. V.

A shingle-style house, built in 1907 and home to a prominent surgeon, has been restored by Diane Hrysko and Mary Allen. The guest rooms are all decorated country style with iron and brass beds, quilts, pine hutches, oak rockers, and rope-style rugs. My favorites are the quirkily shaped units on the top floor. The living room with fireplace, TV, wingbacks, and sofa is comfortable. A bounteous continental breakfast is served.

FLINT'S INN, 220 Mornington St., Stratford, ON, N5A 5G5. Tel. 519/271-9579. 2 rms (none with bath), 1 suite (with bath). A/C

$ Rates: $60 double or twin; $80 suite. No credit cards.

The steep mansard-roofed Flint's Inn, built in 1862, has three rooms. One is a large suite with sun porch and balcony. Its iron-and-brass bed sports an old quilt and among the decorative features are an old butter churn and a bottle collection. It also has private bath and bar/refrigerator. The other two share a bathroom with a bidet. The double has an attractive window seat; the twin has chintz wallpaper, a brass-and-iron bed, dresser, and trunk at the foot of the bed. The living room, with its marble fireplace and pine furnishings, is inviting. At breakfast homemade muffins, juice, and coffee are accompanied by eggs Benedict or a similar offering. The garden is well kept and filled with the wonderful scent of lilac in season.

THE MAPLES, 220 Church St., Stratford, ON, N5A 2R6. Tel. 519/273-0810. 5 rms (1 with bath). A/C

$ Rates (including breakfast): $45 single; $60 double; $70 extra-large double with bath. Extra person $15. V.

Owner Jennifer Smith keeps five nice rooms—one extra-large quad, two triples, one double, and one single—and serves a breakfast consisting of juices, fruit or cheese, and homemade breads and muffins. One room has a private bath; the other rooms share two full baths. The house is a red-brick Victorian with a wraparound veranda.

WOODS VILLA, 62 John St. North, Stratford, ON, N5A 6K7. Tel. 519/271-4576. 5 rms (none with bath). A/C TV

$ Rates (including breakfast): $80 double. MC, V.

Woods Villa occupies a late-18th-century house. It's home to Ken Vinen, who enjoys collecting and restoring Wurlitzers, Victrolas, and player pianos, which are found throughout the house. In the large drawing room there are six—and they all work. Ken will happily demonstrate, drawing upon his vast library of early paper rolls and records.

There are five rooms sharing two bathrooms (four have fireplaces). Rooms are large and a good value, although they are not spectacularly furnished.

Ken has other hobbies and talents. At breakfast he may choose to make some homemade doughnuts or muffins, served along with fresh-fruit salad and five or so local cheeses. Barney and Fred, the macaws, add their comments. Guests are welcome to use the large outdoor heated pool, patio, and barbecue.

HOTELS/MOTELS

ALBERT PLACE, 23 Albert St., Stratford, ON, N5A 3K2. Tel. 519/273-5800. Fax 519/273-5008. 34 rms. A/C TV TEL

$ Rates: $75 double; $95 mini-suite, $115 luxury suite. MC, V.

The Albert Place is right across from the Avon Theatre. Rooms have high ceilings; some have separate sitting rooms, and most units are quite large. Furnishings are simple and modern.

BENTLEY'S INN, 99 Ontario St., Stratford, ON, N5A 3H1. Tel. 519/271-1121. 13 suites. A/C TV TEL
$ Rates: Apr–Nov $135 double; Nov–Apr $80 double. Summer weekends up to $290 double. Extra person $20. AE, DC, ER, MC, V. **Parking:** Free.
Bentley's has soundproofed luxurious duplex suites with bathrooms, two telephones, and fully equipped kitchenettes. Period English furnishings and attractive drawings, paintings, and costume designs on the walls make for a pleasant ambience. Five of the suites have skylights.

FESTIVAL MOTOR INN, 1144 Ontario St. (P.O. Box 811), Stratford, ON, N5A 6W1. Tel. 519/273-1150. Fax 519/273-2111. 151 rms. A/C TV TEL
$ Rates: Main building, $88 single, $89 double, $105 twin. Outside units (with no inside access and no refrigerator), $80 single, $85 double. New deluxe rooms $130–$160 double. Extra person $8; cot $6. Winter rates about 30% lower. AE, DC, MC, V.
With its black-and-white motel-style units, the Festival Motor Inn is set back off Highways 7 and 8 in 10 acres of nicely kept landscaped grounds. The place has an old English air with its stucco walls, Tudor-style beams, and high-back red settles in the lobby. The Tudor style is maintained throughout the large modern rooms, all with wall-to-wall carpeting, matching bedspreads and floor-to-ceiling drapes, reproductions of old masters on the walls, and full bathroom. Some of the bedrooms have charming bay windows with sheer curtains, and all rooms in the main building have refrigerators. Other facilities include two tennis courts, shuffleboard, dining room, coffee shop, and an indoor pool with outdoor patio.

QUEEN'S INN, 161 Ontario St., Stratford, ON, N5A 3H3. Tel. 519/271-1400. Fax 519/271-7373. 31 rms. A/C TV TEL
$ Rates: $90 small double; $120 room with queen-size bed; from $135–$180 suite May–Nov 15, $75–$90 Dec–Apr. AE, MC, V.
Conveniently located in the center of town, the Queen's Inn has recently been restored by the owner of the Elora Mill Inn. The rooms, all with private bath, have been pleasantly decorated in pastels and pine. Facilities include the Queen's Inn Pub and two restaurants—the Queen Victoria room and Queen's Table. The Queen's has always had a good reputation for traditional food.

SHAKESPEARE INN, P.O. Box 310, Shakespeare, ON, N0B 2P0. Tel. 519/625-8050. Fax 519/625-8358. 62 rms. A/C TV TEL
$ Rates: June–Oct $110 single or double; May and winter $80. ER, MC, V.
About 7½ miles (12km) outside Stratford, the Shakespeare Inn, on Route 1, offers nice modern rooms, all with queen-size beds. Coffee shop open from 8am to 10am.

WHERE TO DINE

EXPENSIVE

THE CHURCH, at the corner of Brunswick and Waterloo Sts. Tel. 519/273-3424.
Cuisine: CONTINENTAL. **Reservations:** Required. For dining during the festival, make your reservations in Mar–Apr when you buy your tickets— otherwise you'll be disappointed. Not needed for dining in Mar–Apr.
$ Prices: Summer prix-fixe dinner $38.50–$44.50. AE, ER, MC, V.
Open: Lunch Tues–Sun 11:30am–2pm; dinner Tues–Sun 5–9pm; after-theater 9pm–1am. May be open Mon if there's a musical performance or some other special event at the theaters.
    At The Church the decor is, well, awesome. The organ pipes and the altar are still intact, along with the vaulted roof, carved woodwork, and stained-glass windows, and you can sit in the nave or the side aisles and dine to the appropriate sounds of, usually, Bach. Fresh flowers, elegant table settings, and a huge table in the center graced with two silver samovars further enhance the experience.

In summer, there's a special four-course prix-fixe dinner, a luncheon on matinee days, and an after-theater menu. In winter, when things are a little calmer and crowds don't descend on The Church all at once, you can dine splendidly à la carte. Appetizers might include marinated "tea" smoked salmon with grilled sea scallops and shrimp in a pool of honey mustard sauce or chilled buckwheat noodles with goat cheese and avocado; or beluga caviar served on ice with frozen vodka. Among the selection of eight or so hot and cold entrées you might find a grain-fed chicken marinated Southeast Asian style, served with a snow pea–cashew spring roll in a roast sweet red pepper and ginger sauce; roast Washington State lamb, couscous, candied onion and parsnips in its natural jus with a hint of horseradish cream; or a selection of fish and shellfish in a scented stock made from vegetables, herbs, and spices. Desserts are equally exciting, like the rich white- and dark-chocolate mousse cake, or the iced Grand Marnier soufflé with orange-chocolate sauce.

The Belfry Bar, upstairs at The Church, is a popular pre- and posttheater gathering place. Besides cocktails and snacks, a full menu with main courses priced from $10 to $20, is available.

THE OLD PRUNE, 151 Albert St. Tel. 519/271-5052.
   Cuisine: CONTINENTAL. **Reservations:** Required.
$ Prices: Three-course prix fixe $43.50. ER, MC, V.
   Open: Lunch Wed–Sun 11:30am–1:30pm; dinner Tues–Sun 5–9pm. After-theater menu also available Fri–Sat from 9pm. Call ahead for winter hours.

Another of my Stratford favorites is run by two very charming, witty women—Marion Isherwood and Eleanor Kane. Set in a lovely Edwardian home, it has three dining rooms and a garden patio. Former Montrealers, the proprietors have brought with them some of that Québec flair, which is reflected in both decor and menu.

The chef selects the freshest local ingredients and creates such marvelous dinner dishes as a warm salad of duck leg confit with mashed potatoes and a creamy white peppercorn sauce on organic greens with a black currant and walnut oil vinaigrette, grilled Atlantic salmon with a horseradish crust, served with little beets, corn and champagne sauce, or grilled Ontario lamb with polenta fries and a roasted red pepper corn emulsion. Among the appetizers there might be house smoked salmon roulade with capers and spring onion vinaigrette or fresh goat's cheese in tomato aspic, with olives and marinated zucchini; both are outstanding. Desserts, too, are always inspired, like apricot strudel with sour cream ice cream or the fresh berry and blackberry clafoutis with vanilla ice cream. A more expensive, four-course menu gastronomique is also available along with a vegetarian menu. The Old Prune is also lovely for a late-night supper when such light specialties as vegetable lasagne, or tomato-saffron risotto with grilled sea scallops are offered. Similar dishes are available at lunch, priced from $8 to $12.

RUNDLES, 9 Cobourg St. Tel. 519/271-6442.
   Cuisine: INTERNATIONAL. **Reservations:** Required.
$ Prices: Three-course table d'hôte $42.50–$50. AE, ER, MC, V.
   Open: Lunch Wed and Sat–Sun noon–2:30pm; dinner Tues–Sun. On Fri–Sat an after-theater menu is available. **Closed:** During the winter the restaurant closes and functions occasionally as a cooking school until theater season comes again.

Rundles' large windows take advantage of its beautiful setting overlooking Lake Victoria. Its owner, Jim Morris, eats, sleeps, thinks, and dreams food, and chef Neil Baxter delivers exquisite cuisine to the table. The three-course table d'hôte, including appetizer, main course, dessert, and coffee, will always offer some palate-pleasing combination of flavors like the clear shrimp bouillon flavored with hot peppers and lemongrass and garnished with shiitake mushrooms and shrimp dumplings, or the barbecue skewered bay scallops and vegetables with sweet fries and salsa. Among the eight or so main dishes there might be grilled Atlantic salmon with lentils and caramelized onions, cumin, and fenugreek sauce; or crisp confit of duck, Japanese eggplant, and zucchini. As for dessert my choice would be the zesty lemon tarts, but the sherry trifle is also a dream. The dining area is very contemporary with its gray spotlighted tables, good cutlery and crystal, and contemporary art (including some bizarre sculpture by Victor Tinkl). The restaurant follows the theater schedule.

MODERATE

KEYSTONE ALLEY CAFE, 34 Brunswick St. Tel. 519/271-5645.
  Cuisine: CONTINENTAL. **Reservations:** Recommended.
  $ Prices: Appetizers $4–$7.50; main courses $12–$19. AE, DC, MC, V.
  Open: Lunch Mon 11am–3pm, Tues–Sat 11am–4pm; dinner Tues–Sat 5–9pm.
Actors from the theaters often stop in at the Keystone Alley Café for lunch—perhaps
soups, salads, burgers, sandwiches, New York cheesecake, or a choice from their daily
selection of muffins. Most items are under $7.
  At night there's a full dinner menu featuring eight or so items, such as breast of
chicken on a bed of leeks with a walnut cream sauce, a fish and a pasta of the day, and
grilled médaillons of pork with a port and blackberry scented jus.

OLDE ENGLISH PARLOUR, 101 Wellington St. Tel. 519/271-2772.
  Cuisine: CANADIAN/ENGLISH. **Reservations:** Recommended during theater
  season.
  $ Prices: Snacks under $8; main courses $10–$20. AE, MC, V.
  Open: Mon–Sat 11:30am–1am, Sun 10am–9pm.
For medium-priced fare, head for the Olde English Parlour. In this pubby atmosphere,
you can select sandwiches, steak-and-kidney pie, fish-and-chips, and other British
fare, along with burgers, seafood, and steaks.

WOLFY'S, 127 Downie St. Tel. 519/271-2991.
  Cuisine: ECLECTIC. **Reservations:** Recommended.
  $ Prices: Pretheater prix fixe $18.50–$26; à la carte main courses $12–$20. AE,
  MC, V.
  Open: Lunch Tues–Sun 11:30am–2pm; dinner Tues–Sat 5–8:30pm.
Wolfy's has won a loyal local and visitor following with its well-prepared, flavorful
cuisine. It's located in a former fish-and-chip shop and the original decor is still
evident—the booths, the counter and stools, and the old fish fryer serving as a display
cabinet in one corner. Yet it has a New Wave flavor. The walls are decorated with
vibrant art by Kato. On the limited menu might be found a rice and vegetable stir-fry
with peanut butter sauce, Caribbean pepper chicken, salmon with rhubarb relish,
shrimp with coconut-milk lemongrass broth, and rack of lamb with a salad of
different lettuces. Desserts are equally appealing. Caramelized walnut tart, peach-
nectarine fruit tart or the brownie with orange caramel sauce—a perennial favorite
that has survived for five years on the menu.

BUDGET

BENTLEY'S, 107 Ontario St. Tel. 519/271-1121.
  Cuisine: CANADIAN/ENGLISH. **Reservations:** Not accepted.
  $ Prices: Light fare $6–$8; main courses $12–$15. AE, DC, ER, MC, V.
  Open: Daily 11:30am–1am.
For budget dining and fun to boot, go to Bentley's, the local watering hole. In summer
you can sit on the garden terrace.
  In this atmosphere you can savor some light fare—deep-fried calamari, grilled
shrimp, vegetarian wontons, chicken fingers—along with sandwiches and salads,
which are served all day. Dinner items are more substantial, like roast chicken, baked
sole, sirloin, or prime rib.

CAFE MEDITERRANEAN, 10 Downie St. in the Festival Square building.
  Tel. 519/271-9590.
  Cuisine: LIGHT FARE. **Reservations:** Not accepted.
  $ Prices: Most items under $6. No credit cards.
  Open: Summer Mon 8am–5:30pm, Tues–Sat 8am–7:30pm, Sun 10am–2pm;
  winter Mon–Sat 8am–5:30pm.
The Café Mediterranean is great for made-to-order sandwiches, fruit flans, croissants
(cheese, almond, chocolate), quiches, salads, pastries, and crêpes. You can either take
them out or dine there while seated on director's chairs.

LET THEM EAT CAKE, 82 Wellington St. Tel. 519/273-4774.
  Cuisine: LIGHT FARE. **Reservations:** Not accepted.

$ Prices: Lunch items under $5; desserts $1–$4. MC, V.
   Open: Mon 7:30am–5pm, Tues–Fri 7:30am–9pm, Sat 8:30am–9pm, Sun 10am–5pm.

Let Them Eat Cake is great for breakfast (bagels, scones, and croissants), and lunch (soups, salads, sandwiches, quiche, and chicken potpie), but best of all for dessert only. There are about 30 to choose from—pecan pie, orange Bavarian cream, lemon bars, carrot cake, Black Forest cake, and chocolate cheesecake among them.

SPECIALTY DINING

For take-out, **Tastes,** 40 Wellington St. (tel. 519/273-6000), offers all kinds of salads—pasta, grain, vegetable—pâtés, fish, chicken, and meat entrées, soups, and breads and pastries. The shop also sells imported specialty foods. Open in summer Tuesday through Friday from 10am to 6pm, on Saturday from 9am to 5pm, and on Sunday from 11am to 2pm.

   Stratford is really a picnicking place. Take a hamper down to the banks of the river or into the parks. Plenty of places cater to this. **Rundles** will make you a supersophisticated hamper; **Café Mediterranean** has salads, quiches, crêpes, and flaky meat pies and pastries. Pop into this last and make up your own, or go to **Tastes.**

A NEARBY PLACE TO DINE IN NEW HAMBURG

WATERLOT, 17 Huron St., New Hamburg, ON, N0B 2G0. Tel. 519/662-2020.
   Cuisine: CONTINENTAL. **Reservations:** Recommended.
$ Prices: Appetizers $4–$7; main courses $13–$18.50. AE, ER, MC, V.
   Open: Lunch Tues–Sat 11:30am–2pm; dinner daily 5–10pm. Sun brunch seatings at 11:30am and 1:30pm.

Only 11 miles (18km) east of Stratford on Highway 8 in the village of New Hamburg, the Waterlot is located in an ornate 1846 brick home surrounded by gardens that sweep down to the willow-fringed millpond on the Nith River. The four wood-paneled dining rooms, each with a fireplace and bay window, contain cane bentwood chairs set at tables spread with linen cloths. There's also an attractive glass-enclosed café patio lounge.

   To start, the menu offers traditional soups and appetizers like pâté and escargots à la bourguignonne. Entrées include duck with garlic sauce, Dover sole, veal chop served with red-wine reduction and caramelized shallots, and rack of lamb seasoned with rosemary.

   Sunday is family day, when brunch is served at two sittings—11:30am and 1:30pm. For $16 you'll receive the usual brunch items plus pâtés, smoked fish, crêpes, chicken livers, and other dishes. Sunday evenings there's always prime rib and two hot specials from $18. At luncheon all items are under $9.

   Note: Two rooms tucked under the gables and furnished with antiques share a bathroom complete with marble shower and also a small sitting area under the cupola. They each rent for $70 double. There's also a suite that goes for $90 with a bedroom furnished with a white iron bed.

6. KITCHENER-WATERLOO

69 miles (115km) W of Toronto, 28 miles (45km) E of Stratford

GETTING THERE By Train Amtrak/VIA trains travel daily along the Toronto-Kitchener-Stratford-London-Sarnia-Chicago route.

By Bus From Toronto, Gray Coach (tel. 416/594-3310) operates daily buses to Kitchener via Guelph and Cambridge.

By Car From Toronto, take Highway 401 west to Highway 8 north.

ESSENTIALS For maps and detailed information on the area's attractions, stop in at the Kitchener-Waterloo Area Visitors and Convention Bureau, 2848 King St. East,

Kitchener, ON, N2A 1A5 (tel. 519/748-0800), between 9am and 5pm on weekdays only in winter, daily in summer.

SPECIAL EVENTS   Where you find Germans, there you find beer. From small beginnings in 1969, Oktoberfest now attracts over 600,000 people annually for nine days of celebration in early October. There are over 20 festival halls and tents serving frothy steins of beer, thick juicy sausages, and sauerkraut, accompanied by oompah music in the best Bavarian tradition. The fest also features over 50 cultural and sporting events, including the Miss Oktoberfest Pageant, with contestants from all over North America, an air show, an operetta, Musikfest, ethnic dance performances, and beer barrel races, to name just a few. Admission to the festival halls is $5, or up to $30 for an all-you-can-eat-all-night Bavarian smörgåsbord.

As the festival is so popular, rooms have to be reserved at least six months in advance (indeed, requests are received up to one year in advance). Accommodations in Kitchener-Waterloo itself are not always available, but Stratford, Guelph, Cambridge, or Hamilton is close enough. For information and reservations, call or write K-W Oktoberfest, Inc., P.O. Box 1053, Kitchener, ON, N2G 4G1 (tel. 519/576-0571).

The twin cities of Kitchener (pop. 135,000) and Waterloo (pop. 50,000) lie in the heartland of rural Ontario. Travel a few miles out of town and you can see fields being plowed by four-horse teams and families traveling to market by horse and buggy—the people of the twin cities are never far from their Mennonite heritage.

About 60% of the population is of German origin. The first German settlers were Pennsylvania Mennonites who came in Conestoga wagons around 1800. Abraham Erb, founder of Waterloo, left Pennsylvania with his family and possessions in 1806, while Benjamin Eby purchased the land on which Kitchener stands in 1807. Descendants of the Mennonites are still living and farming the area. Some still adhere to the old values—they do not drive cars, drink alcohol, vote, hold public office, serve in the armed forces, or use the courts to enforce personal rights. Listen for the gentle clip-clop of hooves upon the highway; look up and you will probably see a Mennonite couple, he in black suit and hat and she in bonnet and ankle-length skirt, riding proudly in an open buggy (with an umbrella if it's raining).

German immigration continued throughout the 19th and 20th centuries, and Kitchener-Waterloo's two drawing cards, the Farmer's Market and the Oktoberfest, still reflect the cities' ethnic heritage.

WHAT TO SEE & DO

IN KITCHENER

As you come into town along King Street (Highway 8), you'll pass the colorful **Rockway Gardens,** with their rockeries, flower beds, and illuminated fountains.

While you're visiting the market, you might pop over and see Canada's first **glockenspiel,** which is located at King and Benton Streets, right across from the Valhalla Inn lobby entrance. It depicts the fairy tale of Snow White and the Seven Dwarfs, and the 23 bells that form the carillon play a song each day at 12:15, 3, and 5pm.

FARMER'S MARKET, King and Weber St. N. (P.O. Box 443). Tel. 519/747-1830.

You'll find the Farmer's Market in the ultramodern Market Square Complex, which also houses 76 stores, among them Eaton's department store. The market started on May 25, 1839, and has been going strong ever since. The best way to see the market is to get up early on a Saturday morning (it starts at 6am), because by 8am the 350 stalls are booming with business and some of the best deals have already been made. Savor the sights, sounds, and scents. Sample some shoofly pie, apple butter, Kochcase (a cooked cheese ordered with or without caraway seeds), Baden Limburger, Wellesley cheddar, blueberry fritters, and in a class by itself, the region's sauerkraut. No cellophane packages here. Purchase homemade rugs, quilts, wood carvings, paintings, hand-carved toys, slippers, vests, mitts—the handsome creations of the local folk.

Admission: Free.

Open: Year-round Sat 7am–3pm; Thurs 7am–4pm; June–Aug Tues 8am–3pm as well.

WOODSIDE NATIONAL HISTORIC PARK, 528 Wellington St. North. Tel. 519/742-5273.

Drive down King Street, turn into Wellington Street, and continue until you reach Woodside National Historic Park, located on the left. From 1886 to 1893 this was the boyhood home of William Lyon Mackenzie King, prime minister of Canada from 1921 to 1930 and 1935 to 1948. The Victorian home with its 11½ acres of grounds has been restored to reflect the upper-middle-class lifestyle of the early 1890s. Each of the 14 rooms is elaborately decorated with bric-a-brac and personal belongings of the King family—plaster busts, beadwork, gilt-framed pictures suspended from picture rails. One can imagine the King family gathered around the piano in the parlor singing hymns and popular airs, or playing croquet on the front lawn. Interpreters demonstrate 19th-century activities and invite visitors to play Victorian games or listen to music played on the box grand piano. The park includes several acres of trees and lawn with picnic facilities.

Admission: Free.

Open: May 1–Jan 2 daily 10am–5pm; by appointment only Jan 3–Apr 30.

DOON HERITAGE CROSSROADS, Homer Watson Blvd. and Huron Rd. Tel. 519/748-1914.

Doon Heritage Crossroads represents a small Waterloo County village in the year 1914 before World War I. Costumed staff bring the era back to life, performing typical domestic, trade, and commercial activities in the more than 20 restored buildings including period homes, a dry goods and grocery store, post office, and tailor and blacksmith shops. Each weekend throughout the season numerous period events and programs are scheduled. In the museum, exhibits trace the history of the Waterloo region from prehistoric times to the present.

Admission: $5 adults, $3 seniors and students, $2 children 5–12; free for children under 5; $12.50 maximum for a family.

Open: May–Aug daily 10am–4:30pm; Sept–Dec Mon–Fri 10am–4:30pm. **Directions:** From Highway 401, exit at Homer Watson Boulevard (Interchange 275).

JOSEPH SCHNEIDER HAUS, 466 Queen St. South. Tel. 519/742-7752.

Here, Joseph bought land after his trek from Pennsylvania, and his second house (built ca. 1820) has been restored and features lively demonstrations of everyday activities and seasonal chores. It also houses a collection of German-Canadian folk art.

Admission: $1.75 adults, $1 seniors and students, 75¢ children, $4.50 families.

Open: May 18–Labor Day Mon–Sat 10am–5pm, Sun 1–5pm; Labor Day–May 16 Tues–Sat 10am–5pm, Sun 1–5pm.

IN WATERLOO

In Waterloo you might like to stop in at the **Waterloo County Farmer's Market,** held one mile north of Waterloo (just off Highway 86) on Weber Street at King Street every Saturday from 6am to 1pm and on Wednesday June through October 5 from 9am to 1pm. The **Stockyard Farmers' Market** (tel. 519/747-1830) is also held here on Saturday from 7am to 3pm and on Thursday from 7am to 4pm. On Tuesday and Thursday you can attend the livestock auctions of hogs, calves, dairy and beef cattle, and other animals. There's also a furniture and flea market on the premises.

The kids might also enjoy **Waterloo Park,** with its small animal menagerie of bears, deer, foxes, hawks, owls, peacocks, and wolves. Located off Albert Street, it's open all year and free, and the whole family can enjoy a picnic and a swim (in summer only).

The **University of Waterloo** (tel. 519/885-1211), Ontario's third-largest university, with 26,000 students, has much to offer the casual visitor—an art gallery, a biology–earth sciences museum, a museum of games, an optometry museum (all open weekdays from 9am to 4pm), and professional and amateur theater. Stop in at the information kiosk at the campus entrance on University Avenue south of King Street and ask for a campus map, a walking-tour guide, and parking information.

Also in Waterloo, the **Seagram Museum,** 57 Erb St. West (tel. 519/885-1857), traces the history of the distilling and wine-making industry and is located in the original Seagram distillery barrel warehouse. Open daily May 1 to October 31 from 10am to 6pm; Tuesday through Sunday from 10am to 6pm the rest of the year. Admission is free.

Two attractions have great family appeal. **Bingeman Park,** 1380 Victoria St. North, on the Grand River (tel. 519/744-1555), has a wave pool, water slides, go-karts, mini-golf, and more. Open May to September, weather permitting. Camping is available here, too, for $19 to $22 per day.

Sportsworld, 100 Sportsworld Dr., on Highway 8 north of Highway 401 (tel. 519/653-4442), is a 30-acre water theme park (with a wave pool, a giant water slide, and bumper boats) that also features go-karts, miniature golf, and an indoor driving range. Open daily from 10am to 10pm May to Labor Day (the water park opens in late May; the driving range is open all year). Admission to the water park is $11.80 for adults, $8.95 for children 5 to 11, and $1 children 1 to 4.

WHERE TO STAY

IN DOWNTOWN KITCHENER

VALHALLA INN, King and Benton Sts. (P.O. Box 4), Kitchener, ON, N2G 3W9. Tel. 519/744-4141, or toll free 800/268-2500. Fax 519/578-6889. 200 rms. A/C MINIBAR TV TEL

$ **Rates:** $95 single; $105 double; from $130 suite. Extra person $10. Children under 18 stay free in parents' room. Weekend packages available (except during Oktoberfest). AE, CB, DC, DISC, ER, MC, V. **Parking:** Free.

Across from the glockenspiel, the Valhalla Inn offers modern rooms with balconies. Furnished with dark colonial-style furniture, beige wall-to-wall carpeting, and pretty print spreads and curtains, they contain the usual amenities—color TVs with in-room movies, individually controlled air conditioning and heating, and full bathrooms. The hotel also has a sauna and an indoor pool surrounded by Astroturf and covered with a solarium dome (open from 10am to 10pm).

Dining facilities include a comfortable lobby bar, and Schatzi's. The fitness and recreation center also houses a fully equipped gymnasium, bowling lanes, billiards, table tennis, mini-golf, darts, tanning center, and three squash courts.

WALPER TERRACE HOTEL, 1 King St. West, Kitchener, ON, N2G 1A1. Tel. 519/745-4321. Fax 519/745-3625. 115 rms. A/C TV TEL

$ **Rates:** $85 single; $89 double; from $125 suite. Extra person $10. Children under 16 stay free in parents' room. AE, DC, DISC, ER, MC, V.

Situated in a historic landmark building, the Walper Terrace Hotel has been very nicely renovated. The rooms are tastefully decorated with candy-striped bedspreads and dark cherrywood furniture; each has a tile bathroom and a TV housed in a cabinet.

There are two restaurants: the Terrace Café, an airy dining spot with vaulted ceiling, stained-glass windows, and marble pillars; and La Galleria, an intimate cavelike dining room serving Italian cuisine.

ALONG KING STREET (HIGHWAY 8) IN KITCHENER

Along Highway 8 there are many motels and accommodations on both sides of the road.

BEST WESTERN CONESTOGA INN, 1333 Weber St. East, Kitchener, ON, N2A 1C2. Tel. 519/893-1234, or toll free 800/528-1234. Fax 519/893-2100. 102 rms. A/C TV TEL

$ **Rates:** $73–$83 single; $81–$91 double. Extra person $7. Children under 12 stay free in parents' room. AE, DC, DISC, ER, MC, V. **Parking:** Free.

If you're looking for a distinctly local flavor, try the Best Western Conestoga Inn, named after the finely crafted wagon introduced into the area by the Pennsylvania Dutch in the 1800s. It offers modern rooms, some in a tower; others are motel-style units with outside/inside access. There's an indoor pool, sauna, whirlpool, two lounges, and a restaurant.

In the Stein & Stave, you can view sports spectaculars on the big screen, and in the Hub there's dancing to a live band on most nights. The dining room is open all day serving everything from sandwiches to steaks.

HOLIDAY INN, 30 Fairway Rd. South, Kitchener, ON, N2A 2N2. Tel. 519/893-1211. Fax 519/894-8518. 182 rms. A/C TV TEL
$ Rates: $105–$115 single or double. AE, DC, DISC, ER, MC, V.
A good old standby, the Holiday Inn has well-appointed rooms decorated in modern style. This particular inn has a very pleasant outdoor pool, a slide and play area with climbing bars for the kids, barbecue facilities, an indoor pool, whirlpool, sauna, and exercise room. A dining room and lounge complete the facilities. Tower rooms have minibars.

JOURNEY'S END, 2899 King St. East, Kitchener, ON, N2A 1A6. Tel. 519/894-3500, or toll free 800/668-4200. Fax 519/894-1562. 101 rms. A/C TV TEL
$ Rates: $62.99 single; $70.99 double. AE, DC, ER, MC, V.
Journey's End has nice large rooms decorated tastefully in browns and beiges, all with fully tiled bathrooms. There are also Journey's End motels in Cambridge and Guelph.

RIVIERA MOTEL, 2808 King St. East, Kitchener, ON, N2A 1A5. Tel. 519/893-6641. 45 rms. A/C TV TEL
$ Rates: $36 single; $42 double; from $52 suite. Extra person $6. Children under 18 stay free in parents' room. AE, DC, ER, MC, V.
For a really nicely kept motel along this route, try the Riviera, with its chalet-style units, each sporting a brightly painted yellow door, and all set around a heated outdoor pool with its own grass picnic area. The rooms are tastefully decorated and contain modern furnishings; 28 of the 45 units have refrigerators.

TWO NEARBY PLACES TO STAY & DINE

LANGDON HALL, RR 3, Cambridge, ON, N3H 4R8. Tel. 519/740-2100, or toll-free 800/268-1898. Fax 519/740-8161. 36 rms, 7 suites. A/C TEL TV
$ Rates: $195–$230 single or double; from $320 suite. AE, DC, ER, MC, V.
The elegant house that stands at the head of the curving, tree-lined drive was completed in 1902 for Eugene Langdon Wilks, youngest son of Matthew and Eliza Astor Langdon, a granddaughter of John Jacob Astor. It remained in the family until 1987 when the transformation to a small country house hotel was begun. Today its 200 acres of lawns, gardens, and woodlands make for an ideal retreat. The main house, of red brick with classical pediment and Palladian-style windows, has a beautiful symmetry. Inside, a similar harmony is achieved. Throughout the emphasis is on comfort, rather than grandiosity, whether in the conservatory or the veranda, where tea is served, or in the lounge with its comfortable club chairs and Oriental rugs. The majority of the rooms are set around the cloister garden, which is filled with flowers. Each room is individually decorated; most have fireplaces. The furnishings are fine, consisting of handsome antique reproductions, mahogany wardrobes, ginger-jar porcelain lamps, wingchairs and armchairs upholstered with luxurious fabrics, fine Oriental rugs, gilt-framed pictures, and such nice touches as fresh flowers and terry bathrobes. The light and airy dining room overlooking the lily pond offers fine continental cuisine. Beyond the cloister down a trellis arcade and through a latch gate lies the herb and vegetable garden and beyond that the swimming pool (with an attractive poolhouse), the tennis court, and the croquet lawn. Other facilities include a whirlpool, a sauna, an exercise room, a billiard room, and cross-country ski trails.

OLDE HEIDELBERG BREWERY RESTAURANT AND MOTEL, 2 King St., Heidelberg, ON, N0B 1Y0. Tel. 519/699-4413. 16 rms. A/C TV
$ Rates: $47 single; $55 double. MC, V.
Some 7½ miles (12km) northwest of Kitchener, the Olde Heidelberg Brewery

Restaurant and Motel draws crowds to its tables for huge portions of ribs and pigs' tails, schnitzel and sauerkraut, sausage, and roast beef washed down with the home brew and accompanied by honky-tonk piano sing-alongs. Dinner dishes range from $7 to $9.

Open Monday through Thursday from 11am to midnight, on Friday and Saturday until 1am, and on Sunday from noon to 7pm.

The adjacent motel has rooms with color TV.

WHERE TO DINE
IN KITCHENER

BRITTANY, 24 Eby St. North, just off King St. Tel. 519/745-7001.
  Cuisine: FRENCH. **Reservations:** Recommended.
  $ **Prices:** Appetizers $3–$7.50; main courses $15–$20. AE, DC, MC, V.
  Open: Dinner Mon–Sat 5–10pm.

Downtown, Brittany was opened 14 years ago by owner-chef Jean-Pierre Gillet, who hails from Brittany. Located in an old two-story white-brick town house with rust-colored trim, the downstairs and upstairs dining areas are divided into three separate sections by the natural contours of the house. Coral tablecloths are exquisitely set and accented by flowers on every table, while the stucco walls are used to feature contemporary artists. It's simple, the essence of good taste, and an excellent setting for the superb food.

For dinner you might start with a cold marinated salmon with black peppercorn and ginger or perhaps a fish chowder flavored with saffron. Then you might progress to filet of beef tenderloin with three-peppercorn sauce, braised rabbit with Madeira sauce, or grilled chicken and scallops with a tarragon sauce. Finish off with an excellent crème caramel, cheesecake, or whatever Jean-Pierre is offering the day you visit. Only 40 minutes from Stratford, it's ideal for pretheater dinner.

CHARCOAL STEAK HOUSE, 2980 King St. East. Tel. 519/893-6570.
  Cuisine: STEAK. **Reservations:** Recommended.
  $ **Prices:** Steak $9–$20; seafood dishes $14–$26. AE, DC, ER, MC, V.
  Open: Mon–Fri 11am–11pm, Sat noon–11pm, Sun noon–10pm.

Out along King Street, opposite the Holiday Inn, stands the Charcoal Steak House, a large complex of six rooms, each decorated in a different style—among them the cellar room with wine-country murals, the hunt room with a stone fireplace, the hearth room with a butterfly collection on one wall, and the Parlour with a definite English flavor imparted by Windsor-style chairs and cozy fireplace. Each room provides a warm, attractive ambience for some really good steaks that range from a chopped sirloin to a New York sirloin, or seafood selections that might include salmon or lobster tails. If you're feeling adventurous, try a local delicacy—roasted pigs' tails (roasted in fruit juices, spices, and browned over charcoal, and basted with barbecue sauce). For dessert, try the Nesselrode pie, a light fluffy rum- and fruit-flavored dessert.

The **Lower Deck** (tel. 519/893-2911) serves scampi, swordfish, halibut, salmon, and lobster live from the tank for moderate prices. The daily catch is always a fine bet. Open Tuesday to Sunday evenings.

If you have to wait for a table or you just want a snack like a burger or a sub for under $10, then go into the **Library Lounge,** which also doubles as a piano bar. The lounge is open from 11:30am to midnight Monday through Wednesday, 11:30am to 1am Thursday and Friday, and 4pm to 1am Saturday.

SWISS CASTLE INN, 1508 King St. East. Tel. 519/744-2391.
  Cuisine: SWISS. **Reservations:** Not required.
  $ **Prices:** Main courses $11–$22. AE, DC, ER, MC, V.
  Open: Mon–Fri noon–11pm; Sat 4–11pm; Sun brunch 11:30am–2:30pm, dinner 4:30–9pm.

Out on King Street, the Swiss Castle Inn has a main dining room dominated by an octagonal open hearth and the colors red and white—red tablecloths and white napkins, red-and-white striped curtains over lattice windows—and cow bells. In this cozy atmosphere you can sample Swiss specialties, including Bunderfleisch appetizer (thin slices of air-cured beef), William Tell Platte (one smoked pork chop, one white sausage, and one piece of schnitzel served on a bed of sauerkraut), and fondues—beef bourguignon and seafood. The superspecial raclette (cheese, which you grill yourself in a special table oven, served with boiled potatoes, pickles, and onions) is available only if ordered a week in advance. Fish and steak dishes are also on the menu. For a perfect finale, try the Swiss chocolate-cherry cake. At lunchtime, try the daily special, the wienerschnitzel, or a quiche, all under $8.

IN WATERLOO

JANET LYNN'S BISTRO, 92 King St. South. Tel. 519/725-3440.
Cuisine: INTERNATIONAL/ECLECTIC. **Reservations:** Recommended.
$ Prices: Main courses $15–$20. AE, ER, MC, V.
Open: Lunch Mon–Fri 11:30am–2:30pm; dinner Mon–Sat 5–11pm.

⭐ A chic restaurant with dramatic decoration in tones of terra-cotta, purple, and saffron, including murals of English gardens, this bistro features a selective menu of usually about six or so entrées. The ingredients are fresh and are quite simply prepared—linguine with fresh seafood in a tomato basil sauce, grilled veal chop with ragoût of forest mushrooms, leek and potato Rösti, or sautéed slivers of pork tenderloin with peppercorn jus and spaetzle primavera. There's also always a pasta and fish of the day as well as one or two pizzas. Tempting appetizers include grilled spicy shrimp with avocado salsa and crisp shrimp chips. Desserts are also mouthwatering—fresh fruit flans, a specialty cheesecake, and chocolate sin cake that is really worthy of the name.

MARBLES, 8 William St. Tel. 519/885-4390.
Cuisine: BURGERS/LIGHT FARE. **Reservations:** Recommended on weekends.
$ Prices: Most items $4.50–$9. AE, MC, V.
Open: Mon–Thurs and Sat 11:30am–10pm, Fri 11:30am–11pm.

As you drive west along King Street, you probably won't even notice that you've crossed a boundary into Waterloo. One of the first budget eateries you'll come to is Marbles, just catercorner from the Labatts brewery. Brilliant colored marbles under glass form the serving counter.

The kids will enjoy the food—a foot-long hot dog smothered with fresh tomatoes and bacon slices, or any one of the eight or so burgers. There's a variety of salads also available, including spinach with bacon, egg, pink grapefruit, pine nuts, and orange-tarragon dressing, virtually a meal in itself. It's even fairly elegant with exposed brick, beams, carpeting, Formica tables, and hanging plants. Quiches, chicken fingers, and more are also available. The food is really fresh and imaginative, proving that you don't have to join the assembly line for budget fare.

---

7. ELMIRA & ST. JACOBS

These two small towns in the heart of the Mennonite farmlands can be visited from Kitchener-Waterloo or from Toronto. If you're driving from Toronto, take 401W to Highway 8 north to Highway 86.

For further information on the area, contact the **Elmira-Woolwich Chamber of Commerce,** 5 1st St. East, Elmira, ON, N3B 2E3 (tel. 519/669-2605).

ELMIRA

A charming town 14 miles north of Kitchener-Waterloo, Elmira (pop. 6,800) was one of the earliest settlements of Upper Canada. Set amid the rich farmlands of the Grand and Conestoga river valleys, it is a focal point for Mennonite farmers and craftspeople and home of a famous spring maple syrup festival, held the first Saturday in April, when the population swells to 40,000 and black-bonneted Mennonite women serve up flapjacks with syrup and offer handcrafted goods to all and sundry, while horse-drawn wagons take visitors off to the maple bush to see the sugaring off, from the tapping of the trees to the boiling of the syrup. Festivities usually start around 7am.

From June to August, Monday and Friday, harness racing is held at the **Elmira Raceway** in the Elmira fairgrounds.

A MENNONITE RESTAURANT & GIFT SHOP

STONE CROCK, 59 Church St. West. Tel. 519/669-1521.
  Cuisine: MENNONITE. **Reservations:** Not accepted.
  $ Prices: Lunch buffet $9.25; dinner buffet $12 weekdays, $13 weekends; à la carte main courses $4–$10. MC, V.
  Open: Mon–Sat 7am–8:30pm, Sun 11am–8:30pm (dinner buffet Mon–Fri 4:30–8:30pm and Sat–Sun from 3:30pm).

Be sure to stop at the Stone Crock for a savory taste of the past. Besides the popular buffet (soup, salads, cold cuts, cheeses, and several hot entrées) there's also an à la carte menu for breakfast, lunch, and dinner featuring eggs, sandwiches, roast beef, roast turkey and other dinners. The evening buffet includes coffee or beverage. The Elmira Stone Crock also has an in-house bakery and deli located next door and a gift shop.

ST. JACOBS

St. Jacobs, five miles (eight kilometers) north of Kitchener, has become a well-touristed small town. People are drawn by the shops—more than 80 in all—that are located in the **Country Mill** (once a flour and feed mill), the **Village Silos** (used to store grain for milling until 1974), the **Old Factory** (formerly a shoe company), the **Snyder Merchants** (built in the 1860s as a frontier general store), and **Riverworks,** located in another converted factory. There are blacksmiths, glassblowers, quilters, country crafts of all sorts, oak and pine furniture, stained glass, and more. Most are open from 10am to 6pm Monday through Saturday and 1 to 5pm on Sunday. Many close Monday in the winter.

In addition to shopping, the **Meetingplace,** 33 King St. (tel. 519/664-2103), shows audiovisuals about the Amish-Mennonite way of life. Open May to October, weekdays from 11am to 5pm, on Saturday from 10am to 5pm, and on Sunday from 1:30 to 5pm; November to April, weekends only from 11am to 4:30pm on Saturday and 2 to 4:30pm on Sunday.

The **Museum of Maple Syrup,** 8 Spring St., in the Old Factory, has an authentic sugar shack housing a storage tank, evaporator, and woodpile, plus tools and other artifacts related to maple syrup making. And, of course, while you're there, you'll want to purchase some!

WHERE TO STAY

BENJAMIN'S RESTAURANT AND INN, 17 King St., St. Jacobs, ON, N0B 2N0. Tel. 519/664-3731. Fax 519/664-2218. 9 rms. A/C TV TEL
  $ Rates (including continental breakfast): $85–$95 single; $95–$105 double. AE, ER, MC, V.

Benjamin's is located in a renovated 1852 building. Most of the rooms have been furnished with pine beds and modern handmade quilts, and have private bathrooms.

The dining rooms are stucco and tile with cherry furnishings and open-hearth fireplaces. At dinner about 10 items are offered, priced from $12 for pasta of the day to $16 for grilled strip steak marinated in ale and jalapeño smoked beans, speck and ancho chilies.

JAKOBSTETTEL GUEST HOUSE, 16 Isabella St., St. Jacobs, ON, N0B 2N0. Tel. 519/664-2208. Fax 519/664-1326. 12 rms. A/C TEL
  $ Rates (including breakfast): $85–$140 single; $100–$165 double. Extra person $15. AE, MC, V.

The Jakobstettel Guest House was originally built in 1898 by mill owner William Snider as a wedding gift for his wife and five daughters. The house stands on lovely grounds dotted with spruce and maple made even prettier by well-manicured lawns and a trellissed rose garden. There's also an outdoor pool, one tennis court, and 1¼ miles of trails. Bicycles are available. All rooms have been beautifully furnished with fine antique reproductions, individual chintz wallpapers, wing chairs, desks, wicker, and occasionally a brass or four-poster bed. Each room is different. It's a friendly place. A library, common room, and country kitchen are available for an even more comfortable stay. Muffins, fresh fruits, cheese, and coffee or tea are served for breakfast in the kitchen.

WHERE TO DINE

STONE CROCK, 41 King St. Tel. 519/664-2286.
   Cuisine: MENNONITE/CANADIAN. **Reservations:** Not accepted.
$ Prices: Main courses $8–$11. MC, V.
   Open: Mon–Sat 7am–8:30pm, Sun 11am–8:30pm; family-style dinner served 4:30–8:30pm.

Here at the original Stone Crock restaurant and gift shop, a traditional family-style dinner is served with a variety of salads and homemade bread with apple butter. Choose from a menu featuring sandwiches and fish-and-chips as well as the more traditional cabbage rolls, farmer's sausage, rolled ribs, roast beef, and turkey. There's an in-house gift shop also. The Stone Crock's Village Bakery and Meat & Cheese shop are right next door.

8. ELORA & FERGUS

If you're driving from Toronto, take Highway 401 west to Highway 6 north to 7 east, then back to 6 north into Fergus. From Fergus take Highway 18 west to Elora. Gray Line operates daily buses to Elora and Fergus from Toronto and Owen Sound.

ELORA

Elora has always been a special place. To the natives the gorge was a sacred site, home of spirits who dwelt within the great cliffs. Early explorers and Jesuit missionaries also wondered at the natural spectacle. As early as 1817 a few hardy settlers from Vermont and England had arrived and established farms along the riverbank, but it was Scotsman William Gilkinson who put the town on the map in 1832 when he purchased 14,000 acres on both sides of the Grand River and told his agent to build a mill and a general store. Gilkinson called it Elora, the name that his tea-planter brother, inspired by the Ellora Caves in India, had given to one of his ships. By the 1850s, encouraged by the water power afforded by the Grand, many settlers had arrived and the town developed into a commercial hub with a distillery, brewery, foundries, and furniture factories. Most of the houses that they built stand today. Many were built on nostalgia. In fact, St. John the Evangelist Church was built from a sketch of a church near Castle Conway in Wales sent by a settler's family. And inside this church are a set of communion vessels sent by Florence Nightingale to her cousin, who was the church's first pastor. For real insight into the town's history, pick up a walking tour brochure from the tourist booth on Mill Street.

WHAT TO SEE & DO

Besides picturesque **Mill Street,** where you can browse and chat in peace with only the sound of the river rushing by, Elora has the **Elora Gorge,** a 300-acre park on both sides of the 70-foot limestone gorge. Overhanging rock ledges, small caves, a waterfall, and the evergreen forest on its rim are just some of the scenic delights of the gorge. The park has facilities for camping and swimming, as well as nature trails, picnic areas, and playing fields. Located just west of Elora at the junction of the Grand and Irvine rivers, it is open from May 1 to October 15 from 10am to sunset. Admission is $2.75 per adult, $2.25 for seniors and students, $1.75 for children. To camp, for unserviced campsites, it's $7.75 per day day ($11 with water and electricity), plus the admission fee. For information, write or call the Grand River Conservation Authority, 400 Clyde Rd. (P.O. Box 729), Cambridge, ON, N1R 5W6 (tel. 519/621-2761).

An additional summer attraction is the **Elora Festival,** a three-week musical celebration beginning in late July. For more information, contact Three Centuries Festival, P.O. Box 990, Elora, ON, N0B 1S0 (tel. 519/846-0331).

WHERE TO STAY

ELORA MILL INN, 77 Mill St. West, Elora, ON, N0B 1S0. Tel. 519/846-5356. Fax 519/846-9180. 32 rms. A/C TV TEL

$ Rates: $100–$135 double; from $150 suite. Extra person $25. AE, ER, MC, V.

Many Torontonians seek escape at the Elora Mill Inn, located in a five-story gristmill built originally in 1870 and operated until 1974. Downstairs is a lounge overlooking the falls with the original exposed beams, a huge stone fireplace where a warm fire burns in winter, and pine Windsor-style chairs that go with the raw stone walls of the interior. Similar furniture and rusticity are retained in the upstairs dining areas.

Each guest room is furnished and shaped individually, with some four-posters, others with cannonball pine beds. Most beds are covered with quilts, and each room has a comfy rocker or hoopback chair. Some rooms in adjacent buildings are duplexes and have decks and river views. Many of the rooms in the inn have gorge views, and some units have fireplaces.

Dining/Entertainment: The dining room's eight or so appetizers might include pâté, cured Atlantic salmon, and Bermuda chowder, a spicy broth of fish, vegetables, spiced sausage, dark rum, and sherry-pepper. The main dishes, priced from $17 to $25, range from chateaubriand to chicken stuffed with spinach and Monterrey cheese and served with red currant sauce. Most popular is the prime rib cart. Among the desserts, the chocolate decadence, crème caramel, or shoofly pie are popular choices. At lunch, prices range from $6 for a vegetable pasty to $14 for a seven-ounce sirloin. The dining room serves lunch daily from 11:30am to 2:30pm, dinner Sunday to Thursday from 5 to 8pm, Friday from 5 to 9pm, Saturday from 5:30 to 9pm, and Sunday from 5:30 to 8pm.

GINGERBREAD HOUSE, 22 Metcalfe St. South, Elora, ON, N0B 1S5. Tel. 519/846-0521. 4 rms (sharing 3½ baths).

$ Rates (including breakfast): $55–$65 single; $75–$80 double. MC, V.

The Gingerbread House is operated by Petra Veveris, a very gracious, talented, and well-traveled woman who has an eye for decoration and design.

The house is filled with antiques and decorative objects acquired on her many traveling expeditions. There are four rooms sharing three baths, each comfortably furnished. The Marco Polo is filled with travel souvenirs from Ecuador, Peru, and Australia. Among the distinctive furnishings are a handsome pier mirror, a Biedermeier marquetry chair, and a sink stand. Other rooms are equally attractive and all have books and drinking glasses. Petra coddles her guests, providing such extras as dressing gowns and slippers. A lavish breakfast that might consist of fruit cocktail, waffles with fresh blueberries and sour cream, or a bacon, cheese, and mushroom omelet is served at a table set with German crystal and silver candlesticks. Wine is served on the back veranda every evening. There's also a suite available with fireplace, cathedral-ceilinged bedroom, bathroom, dining room, and small kitchen, which rents for $135.

WHERE TO DINE

METCALFE INN, 59 Metcalfe St., Elora, ON, N0B 1S0. Tel. 519/846-0081.

Cuisine: INTERNATIONAL. **Reservations:** Recommended on weekends.

$ Prices: Main courses $8–$17. AE, MC, V.

Open: Summer Mon–Sun 5–9pm, patio daily from 11am. Winter Tues–Sun 5–9pm.

The Metcalfe Inn has a casual dining room serving favorites like stir-fries, fajitas, seafood fettuccine, and pepper steak. At lunch, sandwiches and light entrées are all under $8. There's a large outdoor patio. In winter the room with the stone fireplace is cozy.

FERGUS

A pleasant town on the Upper Grand River Gorge, Fergus (pop. 7500) was originally known as Little Falls, but its name was changed for its Scottish immigrant founder, Adam Ferguson. There are over 250 fine old 1850s buildings to see—examples of Scottish limestone architecture—including the Foundry, which now houses the Fergus market, and the Breadalbane Inn, a favorite accommodation and dining establishment that appeals to those who are familiar with the warmth, style, and fare of British bed-and-breakfast inns.

The most noteworthy Fergus event is the **Fergus Scottish Festival,** which includes **Highland Games,** featuring pipe-band competitions, caber tossing, tug-of-war contests, and Highland dancing, and the North American Scottish Heavy Events, held usually on the second weekend in August. For more information on the games, contact Fergus Information Centre, P.O. Box 3, Fergus, ON, N1M 2W7 (tel. 519/843-5140).

While you're in Fergus, you may wish to visit **Templin Gardens,** an English-style garden on the banks of the Upper Gorge. The market is also a fun event to attend on Saturday or Sunday. Kids old and young love the **Great Teddy Bear Caper,** held on Victoria Day weekend each year. It's really a large garage sale to which people bring their favorite teddy bears, which are then judged and awarded prizes in particular categories.

WHERE TO STAY & DINE

BREADALBANE INN, 487 St. Andrew St. West, Fergus, ON, N1M 1P2. Tel. 519/843-4770.
  Cuisine: CANADIAN. **Reservations:** Recommended.
$ **Prices:** Main courses $13–$24. MC, V.
  Open: Lunch Tues–Fri noon–2pm; dinner Tues–Sun 5:30–9:30pm.

You can't miss the Breadalbane Inn, a delightful gray stone structure easily identified by the ornate grillwork around the front porch, the bay window jutting into the street, and the gleaming door knocker. Built by the Honorable Admiral Ferguson in 1860, it had variously served as a residence, nursing home, and rooming house for derelicts when Philip Cardinal, a mechanical engineer, and his wife, Jean, a home economics graduate, took it over 16 years ago. Inside you'll find two dining areas with French doors leading into the garden, which, if you're lucky, will be full of roses. Here you can dine at darkly polished tables set with cork placemats depicting hunting scenes or birds, to the strains of a Mozart or Mendelssohn violin concerto, and sip your coffee afterward from Royal Doulton china.

Philip and Jean quite obviously love what they are doing: They bake their own bread and take pains with everything. At dinner, try the French onion soup, and follow it with a fine-quality steak, or the charbroiled back ribs with honey-maple sauce. All entrées include relishes, home-baked bread, and baked potato Cardinal or french fries.

You can also enjoy an informal stay with Philip and Jean in one of their six rooms (five have private bath), all extremely comfortable and elegantly furnished with early Canadian-style furniture. For a large double with continental breakfast, expect to pay the grand sum of $90 double; for a smaller room, $80 double. In the back is an annex that contains a large bed-sitting room with bath and small kitchen. It rents for $100. If you enjoy this English bed-and-breakfast style of accommodation and a role as a responsible house guest, then this is the place for you.

CHAPTER 16

NORTH TO THE LAKELANDS & BEYOND

- **WHAT'S SPECIAL ABOUT THE NORTHERN LAKELANDS**
1. **BARRIE**
2. **FROM COLLINGWOOD (BLUE MOUNTAIN) TO TOBERMORY**
3. **MANITOULIN ISLAND**
4. **MIDLAND, ORILLIA, PENETANGUISHENE & PARRY SOUND**
5. **THE MUSKOKA LAKES**
6. **ALGONQUIN PARK**
7. **THE HALIBURTON REGION**
8. **SOME NORTHERN ONTARIO HIGHLIGHTS**

And where do Torontonians go whenever they feel the urge to flee their high-rises or dynamic, energy-packed downtown streets? Primarily, they head for the north—toward Georgian Bay, the wilderness of Algonquin Provincial Park, or the cottage-and-resort country of Huronia and the Muskoka Lakes, located about 130 miles north of the city, where they have ample opportunity to ride, hike, play golf, boat, fish, go antiquing, and swim in summer, and ski, snowmobile, and ice-fish in winter. To get there, take Highway 401 and turn north onto Highway 400 toward Barrie.

SEEING THE NORTHERN LAKELANDS

INFORMATION For information about Ontario, contact the **Ontario Ministry of Culture, Tourism, and Recreation**, 77 Bloor St. West, 9th floor, Toronto, ON, M7A 2R9 (tel. 416/314-0944, or toll free 800/ONTARIO from 9am to 8pm). The offices are open from 8:30am to 5pm Monday through Friday (daily from mid-May to mid-September).

A NOTE ON TAXES As you travel, keep in mind that Ontario has a provincial sales tax of 8%, plus a 5% accommodations tax—in addition to the national 7% GST.

ONTARIO PARKS There are 260 provincial parks in Ontario, offering ample opportunities for outdoor recreation. The daily in-season entry fee for a vehicle is $6; campsites cost anywhere from $13 to $18. For more information, contact the **Ontario Ministry of Natural Resources** (tel. 416/314-2000).

FARMSTAYS One way to really experience Ontario is to stay on a farm. Enjoy the home-cooked meals, the peace of the countryside, and the working rhythms of a dairy or mixed farm. There are all kinds of farms and locations to choose from. Rates average $35 to $60 double per night, $220 per week, all meals included. For information write to the **Ontario Vacation Farm Association**, R.R. 2, Alma,

WHAT'S SPECIAL ABOUT THE NORTHERN LAKELANDS

Natural Spectacles and Hideaways

☐ Manitoulin Island, a quiet, remote, and mystical spot where the native heritage lives on.

☐ The Muskoka Lakes and the handsome resorts that were built around them during the steamship era.

☐ Algonquin Provincial Park, 3000 square miles of pristine wilderness that's home to beaver, moose, bear, and deer.

Activities

☐ Canoeing along the routes in Algonquin and Quetico Provincial Parks and elsewhere in the region.

☐ Winter sports—skiing at Blue Mountain, snowmobiling the miles of trails around Parry Sound, and more.

☐ Hiking the Bruce Trail, and exploring the trails on Manitoulin and in the many wilderness parks.

☐ Fishing at remote fly-in camps or in the North Channel off Manitoulin Island.

Adventure Trips

☐ The Polar Bear Express, which travels to Moosonee on James Bay, gateway to the Arctic.

☐ The 114-mile Agawa Canyon train trip, at its very best in the fall.

ON, N0B 1A0. Or contact **Ontario Travel,** Ministry of Culture, Tourism, and Recreation, 77 Bloor St. West, 9th floor, Toronto, ON, M7A 2R9 (tel. 416/314-0944, or toll free 800/ONTARIO), where you can obtain a free "Farm Vacation Guide."

1. BARRIE

66 miles (107km) N of Toronto

GETTING THERE If you're driving from Toronto, take Highway 401 and then head north on Highway 400.

ESSENTIALS For information about Barrie, call 705/725-7280.

Barrie is the gateway to the north and primarily a convenient overnight stopping place for those leaving Toronto. If you do stop in Barrie, go into the **Simcoe County Museum and Archives** (tel. 705/728-3721), about five miles north of town on Highway 26, which traces the history of the area—Native Canadian, pioneer, and Victorian—in displays and reconstructions. It's open daily from 9am to 5pm Monday through Saturday and from 1 to 5pm on Sunday. Admission is $3 for adults, $2.75 for seniors, $2.25 for students, and $1.75 for elementary school children; preschoolers enter free.

WHERE TO STAY

BROOKDALE PARK INN, 150 Dunlop St. West, Barrie, ON, L4N 1B2. Tel. 705/721-5711. Fax 705/721-8947. 42 rms. TV TEL
$ Rates: $50 single; $60 double in the new section. MC, V.
Natural stone and chalet styling make the Brookdale Park Inn the most inviting local place to stay. Chalets are arranged around a tree-shaded court at the back of which is a secluded pool area sheltered by lilac and shrubbery. The rooms in the new building

are modern and fully equipped; the rooms in the older section are clean, well kept, and have been recently renovated.

JOURNEY'S END, 75 Hart Dr., Barrie, ON, L4N 5M3. Tel. 705/722-3600. Fax 705/722-4454. 60 rms. A/C TV TEL
$ Rates: $53.99 single; $61.99 double. AE, DC, ER, MC, V.
The Journey's End has typical rooms, each with a TV, a phone, a worktable, and a love seat.

RELAX INN, 55 Hart Dr., Barrie, ON, L4N 5M3. Tel. 705/734-9500. Fax 705/734-0622. 100 rms. A/C TV TEL
$ Rates: $60 single; $65 double; $80 suite. Extra person $6. Children under 17 stay free in parents' room. AE, DC, DISC, ER, MC, V.
The Relax Inn offers nicely appointed rooms, along with such facilities as an indoor pool and hot tub.

2. FROM COLLINGWOOD [BLUE MOUNTAIN] TO TOBERMORY

Collingwood: 106 miles (171km) NW of Toronto,
154 miles (248km) NE of London, 94 miles (151km) NE of Kitchener

GETTING THERE   By Car   From Toronto, take Highway 400 to Highway 26 west.

ESSENTIALS   For tourist information, call Georgian Triangle 705/445-7722.

Named after Admiral Collingwood, Nelson's second in command at Trafalgar, Collingwood first achieved prosperity as a Great Lakes port and shipbuilding town that turned out large lake carriers, and the many mansions and the Victorian main street are reminders of those days. Nestled at the base of Blue Mountain, today Collingwood is the center of Ontario's largest skiing area. And just east of Blue Mountain sweep nine miles of golden sands at Wasaga Beach.

WHAT TO SEE & DO

At **Blue Mountain Resorts,** R.R. 3, Collingwood (tel. 705/445-0231), there are 15 lifts, 96% snowmaking coverage on 31 trails, and three base lodges. In addition, there are three repair, rental, and ski shops, a ski school, and day care. Lift rates are $36 daily.

In summer the ☼ **Great Slide Ride,** installed in 1977, attracts enthusiasts. Anyone from 6 to 76 can zoom down 3,000 feet of asbestos-cement track aboard a mini-bobsled, weaving in and out of trees, and careening around high-banked hairpin curves. Naturally, you don't *have* to go at breakneck speed. The 10-minute ride to the top aboard the triple-chair lift treats you to a glorious panoramic view over Georgian Bay. The slide is open Victoria Day (late May) to Canadian Thanksgiving (U.S. Columbus Day) from 9:30am to dusk. Adults pay $3.75; children, $2.75; kids under 7, free; a book of four tickets costs $12 and $8, respectively.

On the **Tube Ride** you ride an inner tube down a series of waterfalls, ponds, and rapids that stretch over 400 feet. Kids must be at least 8 years old to ride.

Even more thrilling is the **Slipper Dipper water slide,** consisting of three flumes that loop and tunnel down 400 feet into a 3½-foot-deep splash-down pool. For this exhilarating pleasure adults pay $4.50 for five rides; children, $3.75. Open mid-June to Labor Day. Children must be at least 8 years old and 42 inches tall. An

---

AN IMPORTANT NOTE ON PRICES

Unless stated otherwise, **the prices cited in this guide are given in Canadian dollars,** which is good news for U.S. travelers because the Canadian dollar is worth 25% less than the American dollar, but buys nearly as much. As we go to press, $1 Canadian is worth 75¢ U.S., which means that your $100-a-night hotel room will cost only U.S. $75, and your $6 breakfast costs only U.S. $4.50.

Here's a quick table of equivalents:

Canadian $	U.S. $
$ 1	$ 0.75
5	3.75
10	7.50
20	15.00
50	37.50
80	60.00
100	75.00
200	150.00

---

all-day pass for unlimited rides on everything costs $16.95 for adults, $13.95 for kids 8 to 18, $7.95 for kids under 7.

Besides skiing, Blue Mountain is also famous for its **pottery,** and you can take a tour and watch it being made and perhaps buy a few seconds. Many of the creations have been inspired by the natural life of the area—the wing of a bird, the graceful neck of the heron, the silver-scaled fish of the rivers and lakes. A small group of artists began in 1949 using the native red clay dug along creek beds on the mountain. The pottery outlet is located at 2 Mountain Rd., on Highway 26 in Collingwood (tel. 705/445-3000).

Three miles east of Collingwood on Highway 26 at Theatre Road, the kids can enjoy testing their mettle and skills at **Blue Mountain Go-Karts** (tel. 705/445-2419). For the really small fry there are mini-karts, bumper boats, a batting cage, a pitching machine, plus mini-golf, a small touch-and-pet animal park, and a games arcade.

North beyond Collingwood stretches the **Bruce Peninsula.** The **Bruce Trail,** which starts at Queenston and crosses the Niagara escarpment, ends in Tobermory. The Bruce Trail Association (tel. 416/526-6821 in Hamilton) publishes a map that can be obtained from sporting goods stores specializing in outdoor activities.

From Tobermory you can also visit an underwater national park, **Fathom Five National Marine Park,** P.O. Box 189, Tobermory, ON, N0H 2R0 (tel. 519/596-2233), where numerous wrecks lie waiting for diving exploration. More accessible is **Flowerpot Island,** which can be visited by tour boat to view its weird and wonderful rock formations. Go for a couple of hours to hike and picnic. Boats leave from Tobermory harbor.

WHERE TO STAY

BEACONGLOW MOTEL, R.R. 3, Collingwood, ON, L9Y 3Z2. Tel. 705/445-1674. Fax 705/445-7176. 33 rms. A/C TV

$ Rates: Mini-condos from $120 per unit; motel and efficiency units from $50 double in summer and fall; $45 per person per night for a two-bedroom suite on winter weekends. Midweek and other packages available. Special weekly rates available. AE, MC, V.

You'll find a home away from home at the Beaconglow Motel, which has nicely furnished efficiency units that range in size from a compact one-bedroom with kitchenette to a three-bedroom/two-bathroom mini-condo with fully equipped kitchen (including coffee maker, microwave, and dishwasher) and living room with wood-burning fireplace. For fun there's an indoor pool, a whirlpool, a sauna, shuffleboard, a horseshoe pitch, a games room with two pool tables, and a library of 175 movies. Twenty-four of the units have telephones.

Note: For weekend or holiday stays, you should reserve at least three months ahead.

BEILD HOUSE, 64 Third St., Collingwood, ON, L9Y 1K5. Tel. 705/444-1522. Fax 705/444-2394. 17 rms (7 with bath).

$ Rates (including breakfast): $70–$130 weekends; $70–$95 mid-week. Special packages available. MC, V.

Bill Barclay and his wife Stephanie are the proud, enthusiastic owners of this handsome historic (1909) house. Bill is the one who prepares the breakfasts and gourmet dinners, while his wife creates the inviting decor. The downstairs common rooms are very comfortably furnished and personalized by their collections of folk art, quill boxes from Manitoulin, and sculptures by Stephanie's mother. The two fireplaces make the place cozy in winter. The rooms are each individually furnished with elegant pieces. Room 4 contains a bed that was owned by TRH the Duke and Duchess of Windsor, royal portraits, and a souvenir program of Prince Edward's trip to Canada in 1860. Room 7, the Marie Antoinette room, is a favorite, containing a canopied bed, gilded French mirrors and chairs, and, among other objets d'art, a striking pair of brilliantly colored Native American moccasins. The five rooms on the third floor share two bathrooms and are the least expensive. Beautiful quality fabrics are used throughout the house—not surprisingly, since Mrs. Barclay was formerly in the fashion business. Breakfast is sumptuous and the five-course dinner is even more so. It might feature scallops and shrimp au gratin to start followed by beef filet with bordelaise sauce or duck breast in cherry sauce with brandy.

BLUE MOUNTAIN INN, R.R. 3, Collingwood, ON, L9Y 3Z2. Tel. 705/445-0231. 102 rms. A/C TV TEL

$ Rates: Ski season $99 per person per night midweek, $139 per person per night weekends. Off-season $85 per room. Special packages available (see below). AE, MC, V.

Of course, you can stay right at Blue Mountain Inn, right at the base of the mountain, and beat the winter lift lines. Rooms are simply furnished, and have white cinderblock walls and little balconies facing the mountain and overlooking the tennis courts.

The inn offers a host of entertainment facilities including three lounges; a dining room; an indoor pool; squash, racquetball, and tennis courts; and an exercise room.

Five-day ski packages are available for as little as $325 per person, double occupancy, including five nights' accommodation, ski lessons, and skiing. Lift rates are $38 on weekends, $34 on weekdays. For more information, call 705/445-0231, or write Blue Mountain Resorts, R.R. 3, Collingwood, ON, L9Y 3Z2.

COLLINGWOOD ROADHOUSE INN, 461 Hume St., Collingwood, ON, L9Y 1W8. Tel. 705/445-4280. Fax 705/444-4750. 32 rms. A/C TV TEL

$ Rates: High season from $65 single or double; off-season $50 single or double. Extra person $5. Children under 12 stay free in parents' room. AE, MC, V.

Specializing in family accommodations, the Collingwood Roadhouse Inn offers rooms furnished in modern style. They face a grass courtyard where there's an outdoor pool.

HIGHWAYMAN INN, at the corner of 1st and High Sts., Collingwood, ON, L9Y 3J4. Tel. 705/444-2144. Fax 705/444-7772. 66 rms. A/C TV TEL

$ Rates: Weekdays $60 single, $65 double; weekends $65 single, $75 double. Children under 18 stay free in parents' room. Rates lower in spring and fall. AE, ER, MC, V.

The Highwayman Inn stands only minutes from the mountain, built in a mock Tudor style with lattice windows. In winter a fire blazes in the lobby's brick fireplace, which is studded with horse brasses, collars, and bridles; it provides a warm welcome to chilled skiers coming off the mountain. The restaurant, J. F. Kicks, offers the same glow, with DJ entertainment nightly. Rooms are ultramodern and fully appointed, and local telephone calls are free. For entertainment there's an indoor pool, a sauna, and also a floodlit tennis court.

MARINER MOTEL, 305 Hume St., Collingwood, ON, L9Y 1W2. Tel. 705/445-3330. 20 rms. A/C TV TEL
$ Rates: $55 single; $65 double. Off-season (spring) rates are lower. MC, V.
The Mariner's pleasantly decorated rooms are arranged in an L shape overlooking grass, trees, and (in season) lilacs. The rooms have color TVs and radios. The Mariner also has the added touch of a coffee room where you can have coffee or tea free, plus a breakfast room, which is as spick-and-span as any you'd ever wish to see.

WHERE TO DINE

CHEZ MICHEL, Highway 26 West, Craig Leaf (Box 1162, RR 1, Collingwood). Tel. 705/445-9441.
Cuisine: FRENCH. **Reservations:** Recommended.
$ Prices: Main courses $15–$18. MC, V.
Open: Lunch Wed–Mon 11:30am–2:30pm; dinner Mon and Wed–Sat 5:30–10pm, Sun 5:30–9pm.

Small and charming, Chez Michel has a very French air that's created by chef-proprietor Michel Masselin, who hails from Normandy. Floral tablecloths and sage green chairs set against cherry-colored walls make for a pretty background for some excellent, carefully prepared food. Among the specials you might find quail stuffed with goose liver pâté and served with a Madeira sauce or some other seasonal game dish along with more traditional favorites like coquilles St-Jacques, steak au poivre, and Cornish hen served with a blackcurrant sauce. There's a good wine list too, and desserts that are worth waiting for, like the marquise au chocolat or strawberries romanoff.

CHRISTOPHER'S, 167 Pine St. Tel. 705/445-7117.
Cuisine: FRENCH/CONTINENTAL. **Reservations:** Recommended.
$ Prices: Main courses $15–$19. AE, MC, V.
Open: Lunch daily 11am–2:30pm; dinner daily 5–10pm.
Dinner at Christopher's might find you sampling such dishes as grilled breast of chicken with mango and roasted pepper sauce, poached salmon with fennel beurre blanc or New York steak with a Dijon cream sauce in one of the handsome series of rooms in this Victorian town house. In summer afternoon tea is also served.

PEPPIS UPPER CRUST, 390 1st St. Tel. 705/445-0541.
Cuisine: PIZZA PLUS. **Reservations:** Recommended for large parties.
$ Prices: Pizzas $6–$25; pasta dishes under $7; steaks under $14. AE, DC, ER, MC, V.
Open: Sun–Thurs 11am–10pm, Fri–Sat 11am–11pm.
For budget dining, go to Peppis Upper Crust on Highway 26 in downtown Collingwood, for a pizza feast. Fifteen-inch pizzas are the highlight; various pastas and a range of steaks are also available. Booths, stained-glass lamps, and a pine interior create a comfortable atmosphere.

PINE STREET CAFE, 2 Schoolhouse Lane. Tel. 705/445-8242.
Cuisine: CANADIAN/CONTINENTAL. **Reservations:** Recommended.
$ Prices: Main courses $9–$17. AE, MC, V.
Open: Mon–Sat 11am–1am, Sun 5pm–1am.
A casual restaurant with a pleasant atmosphere for lunch or dinner, the Pine Street Café has a bar up front, three dining rooms decorated in gray/terracotta hues, and tables set with floral tablecloths. At lunch the choices include fajitas, pizzas, and pasta. For dinner choose from seafood gumbo and vegetable strudel to rack of lamb cutlets with a honey mint sauce. Jazz, blues, and other entertainment is featured too.

SPIKE AND SPOON, 637 Hurontario St. Tel. 705/445-2048.
Cuisine: CONTINENTAL. **Reservations:** Recommended. **Directions:** Enter Collingwood on Route 26; follow the signs to the business section past the

Collingwood Roadhouse Inn and Mariner Motel to Hurontario Street, where you turn left. The Spike and Spoon is on the left.

$ Prices: Main courses $13–$18. AE, MC, V.

Open: Lunch Tues–Fri noon–2pm; dinner Tues–Sat 5:30–9pm. **Closed:** Apr and Nov.

⭐ Set in an elegant mid-19th century red-brick house that once belonged to a Chicago millionaire named Hodgson, this restaurant offers food prepared with fresh ingredients and herbs that are grown in the yard out back. There are three dining rooms, each with a different atmosphere, plus a closed-in porch for pleasant summer dining. The bread and the desserts are all freshly made on the premises. At dinner the menu might list a chilled or hot soup, warm goat cheese and spinach in phyllo with a raspberry vinaigrette, or tortilla spring rolls filled with shrimp, chicken, and ginger, to start. Main courses might be baked orange roughy with vermouth, tomato, and leek; roast rack of lamb with mint, port wine, and grainy mustard; or quill noodles with pancetta, mushrooms, and onions in herbed tomato sauce.

SWISS ALPHORN, Highway 26 West, Craig Leaf. Tel. 705/445-8882.
   Cuisine: SWISS. **Reservations:** Not accepted.
   $ Prices: Main courses $14–$22. AE, MC, V.
   Open: Daily noon–10pm.

⭐ Bratwurst, wienerschnitzel, chicken Ticino, and cheese fondue are just some of the favorites served at this chalet-style restaurant, which is loaded with Swiss atmosphere. It's a very popular place and always crowded winter and summer. Save room for the Swiss crêpes with chocolate and almonds or the apple fritters.

3. MANITOULIN ISLAND

The island, named after the Great Indian Spirit Gitchi Manitou, is a place for those who seek a quiet, remote, and spiritual place, where life is slow and urban amusements are virtually nil.

For information about the island contact the **Manitoulin Tourism Association,** P.O. Box 119, Little Current, ON, P0P 1K0 (tel. 705/368-3021), or stop by the Information Centre at the Swing Bridge in Little Current. The island can be reached via ferry from Tobermory to South Baymouth, or by road across a swing bridge connecting Little Current to Great Cloche Island and via Highway 6 to Espanola. Ferries operate only from early May to mid-October with four a day in the summer months. The trip takes anywhere from 1¾ to 2 hours. Reservations are needed. One-way adult fare is $10.50; an average-size car costs $23 one way. For information call the **Owen Sound Transportation Company** at 519/376-6601 or contact the **Tobermory terminal** at 519/596-2510.

WHAT TO SEE & DO

The Indians have lived here for centuries and today you can visit the **Ojibwe Indian Reserve,** occupying the large peninsula on the eastern end of the island—although there really isn't that much to see unless you are genuinely interested in modern life on the reservation. It's home to about 2,500 people of Odawa, Ojibwe, and Potawotami descent and the area was never ceded to the government. Try to time your visit for the big ✪ **Wikwemikong Powwow,** which is held in August. For information contact the **Wikwemikong Heritage Organization** (tel. 705/859-2385). Other powows are also held during the year around the island. It is worth seeking out the few native art galleries like the ✪ **Kasheese Studios,** just outside West Bay at Highways 540 and 551 (tel. 705/377-4890), which is operated by artists in residence Blake Debassige and Shirley Cheechoo, and the **Ojibwe Cultural Foundation,** also just outside West Bay (tel. 705/377-4902), which opens erratically and then only until 4pm. You can also visit individual artists' studios.

The island is great for hiking, cycling, bird watching, boating, fishing, cross-country skiing, and just plain relaxing. In summer, fishing for chinook, coho, rainbow, lake trout, perch, and bass is excellent in Georgian Bay or any of the island lakes—Mindenmoya, Manitou, Kagawong, Tobacco, to name a few—and can be arranged through **Manitou Fishing Charters** in South Baymouth. A five-hour trip for four persons is $250. For information write Box 782, Azilda, ON, P0M 1B0 (tel. 705/983-2038 or 377-5270). Charters also operate from Meldrun Bay. Golf courses can be found in Mindemoya and Gore Bay.

Although there are several communities on the island, the highlights are scenic and mostly outside their perimeters, like the **Mississagi Lighthouse,** located at the western end of the island outside Meldrun Bay. Follow the signs that will take you about four miles down a dirt road past the limestone/dolomite quarry entrance (from which materials are still shipped across the Great Lakes) to the lighthouse, which is worth visiting to see how the lightkeeper lived before the advent of electricity when he and his family were warmed by a coal stove and lived in isolation before any roads were cut. A series of photographs show what may well be the wreck of La Salle's *Griffon.* There's a dining room open in summer. From the lighthouse several short trails lead along the shoreline. From the light you can see Cockburn island, which is inhabited supposedly by only two people who snowmobile to the mainland for supplies in winter.

There are several nature trails on the island. Among the more spectacular are **The Cup and Saucer Trail,** which starts 11 miles (18km) west of Little Current at the junction of Highway 540 and Bidwell Road. Also off Highway 540 lies the trail to **Bridal Veil Falls** as you enter the village of Kagawong. Halfway between Little Current and Manitowaning, stop at **Ten Mile Point** for the view over the North Channel, which is dotted with 20,000 islands. The best beach with showers/washrooms and other facilities is at **Providence Bay** on the south of the island.

Several galleries are well worth visiting. ✪ **Perivale Gallery,** RR 2, Spring Bay (tel. 705/377-4847), is the love of Sheila and Bob McMullan, who scour the country searching for the wonderful artists and craftspeople whose work they display in their log cabin/gallery overlooking Lake Kagawong. Glass, sculpture, paintings, engravings, fabrics, and ceramics fill the gallery. Everything is very fine, very carefully chosen, and aesthetically displayed by Sheila, who was an interior decorator for many years. From Spring Bay follow Perivale Road East for about two miles; turn right at the lake and keep following the dirt road until you see the gallery on the right. Open daily from 10am to 6pm from the May holiday to mid-September. **Dominion Bay Handcrafts,** Spring Bay (tel. 705/377-4625) is another store worth visiting for jewelry, knitwear, and other fashions. From Highway 542 follow the green Hettmann signs down to Dominion Bay.

WHERE TO STAY

Your best bet is to seek out one of several bed and breakfasts. The accommodations will most likely be plain and simple, like those at **Hill House,** P.O. Box 360, Gore Bay, ON, P0P 1K0 (tel. 705/282-2072). Otherwise, the very best accommodations on the island can be found at the following.

MANITOWANING LODGE & TENNIS RESORT, Box 160, Manitowaning, ON, P0P 1N0. Tel. 705/859-3136. Fax 705/859-3270.

$ Rates (including breakfast and dinner): $115–$160 per person. Lower rate is for standard room; the higher for a one-bedroom cabin with fireplace. Special tennis packages available. AE, MC, V. **Closed:** Canadian Thanksgiving to second Fri in May.

✪ An idyllic place that lacks the pretension of so many ooh-la-la resorts. It consists of a lodge and cottages set on 11 acres of spectacularly landscaped flower-filled gardens designed and tended by Gloria Barter, who manages the property with her husband, Peter. In 1989 their daughter and son-in law undertook to renovate the property and employed a number of artists who have created a whimsical, engaging decor with trompe l'oeil painting and furniture that sports handpainted scenes and designs. The buildings themselves have a delightful rustic air created by their beamed ceilings; in the lodge there's a large fieldstone fireplace with a huge carved mask of the Indian Spirit of Manitowaning looming above. The cottages are comfortably furnished with wicker or painted log furniture, beds with duvets and pillows, dhurries, log tables, and hand-painted furnishings. All have fireplaces. None has a TV or telephone—a real retreat.

The dining room is airy and light. Tables are set with French linens; white chairs painted with trailing ivy designs are original to the inn. The food features fine local meats like lamb, and, of course, fish. You might find Manitowaning poached trout, blackened snapper, or tournedos Henri IV, which you could precede with a warm salad of smoked goose with radicchio and snow peas. Lunch is served al fresco on the terrace overlooking the water. Breakfasts consist of eggs as well as fresh juice and breads. Facilities include four tennis courts with pro; a swimming pool surrounded by a deck and gardens set with chaise longues; a gym; mountain bikes; water sports; and great fishing in the area. There's a masseur on the premises. Open from the second Friday in May to Canadian Thanksgiving.

ROCK GARDEN TERRACE RESORT, RR 1, Spring Bay, ON, P0P 2B0. Tel. 705/377-4652. 18 motel units, 4 chalet suites. TV

$ Rates: Summer and winter $90–$105 single; $100–$120 double. Spring and fall rates slightly lower. Weekend and weekly packages available. MC, V.

This is a typical family resort with a Bavarian flair, located on the rocks above Lake Mindemoya. Most of the accommodations are in motel-style units furnished in contemporary style. There are also four log cabin–style suites.

The dining room has the atmosphere of an Austrian hunting lodge, with trophies displayed on the oak-paneled walls. The cuisine features some German-Austrian specialties like wienerschnitzel, sauerbraten, goulash, and beef rolladen. Facilities include a kidney-shaped pool, a whirlpool, a sauna, fitness facilities, a fishing dock, and games like outdoor shuffleboard and chess as well as bicycles, boats, and canoes for rent.

WHERE TO DINE

The island isn't exactly the place for fine dining. For more sophisticated food, go to the **Manitowaning Lodge and Tennis Resort** (tel. 705/859-3136) or the **Rock Garden Terrace Resort** (tel. 705/377-4642), both near Spring Bay. In Little Current, one of the nicest casual spots on the island for breakfast, lunch or dinner is **The Old English Pantry,** Water Street, Little Current (tel. 705/368-3341), which makes fresh-cut sandwiches, salads, pastries, muffins, and other baked goods that are served along with a fine selection of teas and coffees. At dinner you'll find a pasta and British dish of the day as well as savory pies and fresh fish. Afternoon cream teas are available and takeout picnic baskets, too. Open Monday to Thursday from 9am to 6pm and Friday and Saturday until 7pm (closed Sunday). Hours are extended in summer.

In West Bay, **Twin Bluffs Bar & Grill** (tel. 705/282-2000) offers sandwiches and other fare like fish and chips or veal parmigiana. There's also a pizza restaurant in the pavilion on the waterfront that offers inspiring water views complete with diving cormorants.

4. MIDLAND, ORILLIA, PENETANGUISHENE & PARRY SOUND

MIDLAND

The city's history goes back to 1639, when the Jesuits established a fortified mission to bring the word of God to the Huron tribe. The mission retreat of Sainte Marie Among the Hurons flourished for one decade only, for the Iroquois, jealous of the Huron-French trading relationship, increased their attacks at the end of the 1640s. In 1648, 2,000 Hurons and Father Daniel were killed, and in March of 1649 two villages were destroyed within six miles of Sainte Marie, and Father Brebeuf and Father Lalemant were tortured to death along with hundreds of Hurons. Eventually the Jesuits burned down their own mission and fled with the Hurons to Christian Island, about 20 miles away. But the winter of 1649 was harsh: Thousands of Hurons died, leaving only a few Jesuits and 300 Hurons to straggle back to Québec from whence they had come. Their mission had ended in tragedy and martyrdom. Had it been otherwise, the course of history might have changed, for it was 100 years before the Native Canadians saw whites again, and then they spoke a different language.

Midland lies 33 miles east of Barrie and 90 miles north of Toronto. If you're driving from Barrie, take Highway 400 to Highway 12W to Midland.

WHAT TO SEE & DO

Midland is the center for cruising through the beautifully scenic thousands of Georgian Islands, and **30,000 Island Cruises** (tel. 705/526-0161) offers 2½-hour cruises that follow the route of Brûlé, Champlain, and La Salle up through the inside passage to Georgian Bay. From July to Labor Day, boats usually leave the town dock three times a day. Admission: $13 for adults, $12 for seniors, and $7.50 for children.

SAINTE MARIE AMONG THE HURONS, five miles east of Midland. Tel. 705/526-7838.

Local history is recaptured at Sainte Marie Among the Hurons. The blacksmith stokes his forge, the carpenter squares a beam with a broadax, and the ringing church bell calls the missionaries to prayer, while a canoe enters the fortified water gate. A film also depicts the life of the missionaries. Special programs given in July and August include candlelight tours and also a 1½ hour canoeing trip (at extra cost).

Admission: $5.50 adults, $3.25 students, $3 seniors; free for children under 6.
Open: Mid-May to Oct daily 10am–5pm; last admission at 4pm. **Closed:** Nov to early May. **Directions:** Take Highway 12 five miles east of Midland and follow the Huronia Heritage signs.

MARTYRS' SHRINE, Hwy. 12. Tel. 705/526-3788.

Just east of Midland rise the twin spires of the Martyrs' Shrine, a memorial to the eight North American martyr saints. As six of these were missionaries at Sainte Marie, this imposing church was built on the hill overlooking the mission, and thousands make a pilgrimage here each year. The bronzed outdoor stations of the cross were imported from France.

Admission: $2 adults; free for children 15 and under.
Open: Mid-May to mid-Oct daily 8:30am–9pm. **Closed:** Rest of year.

WYE MARSH WILDLIFE CENTRE, Hwy. 12. (5km [3 miles] east of Midland). Tel. 705/526-7809.

Across from the Martyrs' Shrine, the Wye Marsh Wildlife Centre offers visitors the chance to explore (year-round) nature trails and a floating boardwalk that cut through marsh, field, and woods. Special guided canoe trips are available by reservation (tel. 705/526-7809) in July and August. In winter, cross-country skiing and snowshoeing are available. For information, write Highway 12 (P.O. Box 100), Midland, ON, L4R 4K6.

Admission: $4.50 adults, $3 students and seniors; free for children under 3.
Open: Victoria Day (late May)–Sept 4 daily 9am–6pm; other months daily 10am–4pm.

WHERE TO DINE

FREDA'S, 342 King St. Tel. 705/526-4851.

Cuisine: CONTINENTAL. **Reservations:** Recommended on weekends.
$ Prices: Appetizers $4–$8; main courses $14–$28. AE, MC, V.
Open: Lunch Tues–Fri 11:30am–2pm; dinner Tues–Sun 5:30–9pm.
At Freda's, located in an elegant home, you can choose from surf-and-turf, beef

Stroganoff, chicken Kiev, veal Cordon Bleu, and coquilles St-Jacques. Lunchtime offers a vast array of sandwiches, soups, and light entrées, priced from $6 to $9.

ORILLIA

En route to the Muskoka lakeland region, whether or not you come from Midland you will probably pass through Orillia, where you can visit Canadian author/humorist **Stephen Leacock's house** (tel. 705/326-9357), a green-and-white mansard-roofed and turreted structure with a central balcony overlooking the beautiful lawns and garden that sweep down to the lake. The interior is filled with heavy Victorian furniture reflecting the period when Leacock lived and worked here. It contains much original memorabilia. Admission is $4 for adults, $3.50 for seniors, $1 for students, and 50¢ for children 5 to 13. Open from the end of June to Labor Day from 10am to 7pm daily; by appointment only in other months.

If you're driving from Barrie, take Highway 11 to Orillia.

WHERE TO DINE

PAUL WEBER'S, Hwy. 11. Tel. 705/325-3696.
   Cuisine: BURGERS.
$ Prices: Burgers from $2.55. No credit cards.
   Open: Mid-Apr to Labor Day Sun–Thurs 10am–10pm, Fri 10am–midnight; other months Fri 11am–9pm, Sat 10am–4pm, Sun 11am–8pm.

From Orillia, head north on Highway 11, keeping a lookout for Paul Weber's hamburger place at the side of the road. Here, you can get a real burger with real french fries, not the frozen variety. I heartily recommend it. Take a breather and sit out under the trees at the picnic tables provided.

PENETANGUISHENE

This town on Georgian Bay is home to the **Historic Naval and Military Establishments,** a reconstructed 19th-century British outpost, complete with a fleet of schooners and costumed sailors and soldiers.

The outpost was founded in 1817 to provide a protective naval presence on the Upper Great Lakes. The military arrived in 1831 and stayed until 1856 when the British closed their base on Lake Huron. Today visitors enjoy horse-drawn wagon rides along the shoreline and visits to authentically furnished residences and workshops. Evening and afternoon excursions aboard the HMS Schooner *Bee* take sailors out into Georgian Bay for hands-on sail training. Visitors are also invited to row in a 19th-century-style gig out to the site of the sunken *Newash,* sister ship of the *Bee.* On Wednesday evening lantern walks are given.

The **King's Wharf Theatre** presents a full summer of professional theater, and there's also a dining room and gift shop. Open from May 22 to Labor Day from 10am to 5pm with last admission at 4:15pm. Admission is $5.75 for adults, $3.50 for students, and $3.25 for seniors. Follow Highway 400 to 93. Take 93 north to Penetanguishene. Turn right at the water and follow the ship logo.

The big event in the region for 1994 will be the **Georgian Bay Marine Heritage Festival,** when 150 marine events will be celebrated in 45 communities along the 350-mile shoreline of Georgian Bay from June 1 to September 30. The main focus is the Atlantic Challenge, an international sailing, rowing, seamanship, and navigation competition. The tall ships will visit and an array of marine heritage events will also be staged.

GEORGIAN BAY ISLAND NATIONAL PARK

The park consists of 50 islands in Georgian Bay and can be reached via boat from Honey Harbour. Swimming, fishing, and boating are the common pastimes. In summer, the boaters really do take over—if you're looking for a quiet retreat, look elsewhere. The park's center is located on the largest island, Beausoleil, which also has camping and other facilities. For more information call or write the Superintendent, Georgian Bay Islands National Park, Box 28, Honey Harbour, ON, P0E 1E0 (tel. 705/756-2415).

WHERE TO STAY

CHEZ VOUS CHEZ NOUS COUETTE ET CAFE, RR 3 (in Lafontaine), Penetang, ON, L0K 1P0. Tel. 705/533-2237. 7 rms.
$ Rates (including breakfast): $50 single; $65 double. No credit cards.

Georgette Robitaille takes care of the accommodations at this 50-acre working farm where she has personally decorated all of the seven rooms in different color schemes—gray, blue, lilac, aqua, and gold—many of them featuring her own paper tole art. Singles, doubles, and twins are available. There's a separate entrance to the guest rooms, which are incredibly clean and well-kept. Georgette is a fine baker and caters locally, so her breakfasts are excellent (muffins, eggs, fruit salad, homemade jam, and more) and pleasantly presented either in the dining room at the pine tables or in the kitchen if there are only a few guests.

THE PARRY SOUND AREA
WHAT TO SEE & DO

For information contact the **Parry Sound Area Chamber of Commerce** (tel. 705/746-4213 or the information centre at 705/378-5105). The greatest assets of the area (only 140 miles north of Toronto and 100 south of Sudbury) are its sports facilities and activities. There are, for example, loads of cross-country ski trails and more than 496 miles (800km) of well-groomed snowmobiling trails. Hikers can follow the 41-mile (66km) **Seguin Trail,** which meanders around several lakes south of Parry Sound. Nature lovers will head for ✪ **Killbear Provincial Park,** P.O. Box 71, Nobel, ON, P0G 1G0 (tel. 705/342-5492), farther north up Highway 69; it's over 4,000 glorious acres set in the middle of 30,000 islands. Swimming, fishing, hiking, boating, and flora and fauna watching are just some of the pursuits that can be enjoyed, along with camping at close to 900 sites in seven campgrounds. Canoeing and kayaking enthusiasts will want to join one of the programs/trips arranged by **White Squall,** R.R. 1, Nobel, ON, P0G 1G0 (tel. 705/342-5324). Day trips are $90; four-day trips start at $350 (prices include instruction, meals, and equipment). For the more sedate a three-hour cruise on the *Island Queen* through the 30,000 islands will satisfy. It leaves the town dock once or twice a day. For information contact **30,000 Island Cruise Lines,** 9 Bay St., Parry Sound, ON, P2A 1S4 (tel. 705/746-2311).

WHERE TO STAY

The following accommodation is exquisite and expensive, but there are other possibilities in the area. Contact the **Parry Sound & District Bed & Breakfast Association,** P.O. Box 71, Parry Sound, ON, P2A 2X2 for their accommodations listings, priced from $40 single and $50–$60 double. There's also a **Journey's End,** 118 Bowes St. (tel. 705/746-6221) and a modest, family-oriented **Resort Tapatoo,** Box 384, Parry Sound, ON, P2A 2X5 (tel. 705/378-2208), located at the edge of Otter Lake, which has cottages, rooms, and suites available.

INN AT MANITOU, McKellar, ON, P0G 1C0 Tel. 705/389-2171. Fax 705/389-3818. 32 rms, 1 three-bedroom country house.
$ Rates (including breakfast, lunch, and dinner): $209–$319 midweek, $219–$329 weekends per person per day based on double occupancy in July–Aug; $189–$269 and $209–$289 respectively in June and Sept; $169–$229 and $189–$249 respectively in May and Oct. A variety of special packages available. Special musical, cooking, and other events are scheduled also. **Closed:** Late Oct–early May.

Spectacular is the only way to describe the Inn at Manitou, although some folks may find this spa and tennis resort just too perfect. Everything about the foyer glows. Beyond the foyer and a sitting area, a veranda stretches around the rear of the building with wicker and bamboo chairs overlooking the tennis courts. Off the left of the foyer there's the very inviting Tea Room with a view of the lake in the distance. A steep staircase leads down to the swimming and boating dock. The space is luxuriously furnished in Franco-Oriental style with sofas and chairs upholstered in richly crimson-colored and patterned fabrics. The accommodations are located up the hill in several cedar lodges overlooking the lake—the setting is beautiful. Standard rooms are small and simple; deluxe units contain fireplaces, small sitting areas, and private sundecks, while the luxury rooms each feature a sizable living room with a fireplace, whirlpool bath, sauna, and private deck.

Dining/Entertainment: Downstairs in the main building you'll find the Club Lounge nightclub, a billiard room, and the open-to-view wine cellar, filled with fine vintages, where twice-weekly wine tastings are held. The resort's cuisine is renowned, too, and as much the reason for the distinguished Gold Shield that was awarded the property by the Relais and Châteaux organization. At dinner a casual three-course Bistro menu and a more elaborate five-course gourmet menu is offered along with a special spa menu. The first might feature such main dishes as ravioli of smoked trout with leeks and parmesan or roast grain-fed chicken with garlic and chevril butter. The second might offer hot Atlantic salmon mousse with caviar and chives among the appetizers, and follow with breast of duck and corn ravioli with green onion juice or rack of lamb stuffed with shiitake and crushed hazelnuts. Desserts range from caramelized banana terrine with vanilla ice cream and chocolate sauce to cold cream of Grand Marnier gratinated with brown sugar. Afterwards, guests can retire to the Tea Room for coffee, petit fours, and truffles.

Facilities: The spa facilities are in a separate building where a full range of body treatments—including herbal and mud wraps, massage therapy, and fitness activities—are offered. Other facilities include a swimming pool, 13 tennis courts (with 10 professional staff members), mountain bikes, sailboats, canoes, windsurfers, and exercise equipment, plus pitch-and-putt facilities and an instructional golfing range.

5. THE MUSKOKA LAKES

To settlers coming north in the 1850s, this region, with its 1,600-plus lakes north of the Severn River, presented peculiar problems. Part of the Canadian shield, the land was impossible for farming. Even at this early stage the wilderness aspect of the district attracted the sportsman and adventurer, like John Campbell and James Bain, who explored the three major lakes—Rosseau, Joseph, and Muskoka—and subsequently started the Muskoka Club, purchased an island in Lake Joseph, and began annual excursions to the district. Roads were difficult to cut and waterways became the main transportation. A. P. Cockburn put a fleet of steamers on the lakes and worked to get the railway to the lakehead in Gravenhurst in 1875. When the railway arrived in Huntsville in 1886, a Captain Marsh put a fleet of steamers on the North Muskoka Lakes—Vernon, Fairy, Peninsula, Mary, and Lake of Bays. Muskoka was effectively linked by water and rail to the urban centers in the south.

The area was wired for tourism and some folks gambled that people would pay to travel to the wilderness if they were wined and dined once they got there. The idea caught on and grand hotels like Clevelands House, Windermere House, and Deerhurst were opened, to name a few that have survived to this day. The lakes became the enclave of the well-to-do from Ontario and the United States. By 1903 there were eight big lake steamers, countless steam launches, and supply boats (floating grocery stores) serving a flourishing resort area.

And it continues today, even though the advent of the car ended the steamboat era and the grand hotel era. The rich are still here, but so are the many families in their summer cottages and the sophisticated young professionals from Toronto who also flock to the larger resorts. You'll note that many of the resorts don't look so impressive from the road—but just take a look at the other side and remember that they were built for steamship approach. The corridors are often very wide because, of course, they were originally built to accommodate huge steamer trunks.

GETTING THERE   VIA Rail (tel. toll free 800/361-3677) services Gravenhurst, Bracebridge, and Huntsville from Toronto's Union Station.

You can get there by car from the south via Highway 400 to Highway 11, from the east via Highways 12 and 169 to Highway 11, and from the north via Highway 11. It's about 100 miles (160km) from Toronto to Gravenhurst, nine miles (15km) from Gravenhurst to Bracebridge, 15½ miles (25km) from Bracebridge to Port Carling, and 21 miles (34km) from Bracebridge to Huntsville.

TOURIST INFORMATION   For information on the Muskoka region, call 705/645-3088, or toll free 800/267-9700; or contact **Muskoka Tourism,** 63 Kimberley Ave. (P.O. Box 1508), Bracebridge, ON, P1L 1R9.

MUSKOKA BED-AND-BREAKFAST   If you don't want to pay resort rates or restrict yourself to staying at an American Plan resort, then contact the **Muskoka Bed and Breakfast Association,** 175 Clairmont Rd., Gravenhurst, ON, P1P 1H9 (tel. 705/687-4511), which represents 25 or so bed-and-breakfasts throughout the area. Prices range from $30 to $50 single and $45 to $70 double.

SPORTS & RECREATION   The Muskoka District and Algonquin Provincial Park boast more than a thousand beautiful lakes, many of them with miles of connecting systems of waterways ideal for **canoeing.** For canoe route information in the park, contact Superintendent, Algonquin Provincial Park, Ministry of Natural Resources, P.O. Box 219, Whitney, ON, K0J 2M0 (tel. 705/633-5572).

Hiking trails abound in Arrowhead Provincial Park at Huntsville and the Resource Management Area on Highway 11, north of Bracebridge, and of course, in Algonquin Park.

FALL EVENTS   In the fall Muskoka has such dazzling scenery that Walt Disney had aerial photographs made of the region for the filming of his *Littlest Hobo,* the story of a vagabond cat. To celebrate its autumn beauty nearly all of Muskoka's towns stage fall fairs and other festivals. This is an especially good time to drive the Algonquin Route, that section of Highway 60 from the west gate to the east gate of Algonquin Park, known as the Frank MacDougall Parkway.

GRAVENHURST

Gravenhurst is the first town in Muskoka, both the first you reach if you're driving from Toronto and the first to achieve town status (in 1887 at the height of the logging boom). Most of the timber made its way to Muskoka Bay in Gravenhurst, to one of 15 mills that operated then. It was also the main terminus for the navigation company. Today it's home to the Muskoka Festival Theatre group, to the steamship *Segwun,* and the **Norman Bethune Memorial House,** the restored 1890 birthplace of Dr. Norman Bethune, 235 John St. (tel. 705/687-4261). In 1939 this surgeon, inventor, and humanitarian died tending the sick in China during the Chinese Revolution. Tours of the historic house include a modern exhibit on Bethune's life. A visitor center displays gifts from Chinese visitors and an orientation video is shown. Special events occur throughout the summer. A Victorian Christmas is celebrated from mid-December to December 31. The house is open from 10am to 5pm. Admission is free.

You can also cruise aboard the old steamship **RMS *Segwun*** (1887), which leaves from Gravenhurst, Port Carling, and also Clevelands House and Windermere. Aboard you'll find two lounges and a dining saloon for your enjoyment. The cruises on the lake vary from two hours (from $16.50) to a full day's outing ($47). For information, call or write: 820 Bay St., Gravenhurst, ON, P1P 1G7 (tel. 705/687-6667). Cruises operate from mid-June to mid-October.

Gravenhurst and Port Carling are home to the **Muskoka Festival.** A series of summer theater performances are given in the Gravenhurst Opera House (tel. 705/687-2762) and Port Carling Memorial Hall (tel. 705/765-3209). Tickets range from $14 to $20 for adults. For more information, contact: Muskoka Festival, P.O. Box 1055, Gravenhurst, ON, P1P 1X2 (tel. 705/687-7741).

WHERE TO STAY

MUSKOKA SANDS, Muskoka Beach Rd., Gravenhurst, ON, P1P 1R1. Tel. 705/687-2233. Fax 705/687-7474. 76 rms. A/C TV TEL **Directions:** From Highway 11 north take Gravenhurst Exit 169 (Bethune Drive) to Winewood Avenue and turn left. Then turn right onto Muskoka Beach Road for three miles (five kilometers).

$ Rates: Summer $170–$260 in lodge room or suite single or double. MAP rates also available. AE, DC, ER, MC, V.

In this large modern resort on Lake Muskoka, accommodations are either in the lodge or in a series of buildings scattered on the property. The rooms are handsomely furnished and the suites are luxurious, each with fully equipped kitchen, living room with fireplace, private deck, and bathroom with glass-brick accents and oval tub.

The dining room serves continental cuisine; Steamer Jakes is the downstairs dance bar. The Boathouse has an outdoor café deck. Facilities include a nicely landscaped outdoor pool, indoor pool, whirlpool, sauna, fitness room, games room, children's program (in July and August), squash and tennis courts, and waterfront sports.

Camping

Gravenhurst Reay Park and KOA Campground, R.R. 3, Gravenhurst, ON, P0C 1G0 (tel. 705/687-2333), has 750 acres of pine trees and meadows, plus a trout pond, two swimming pools, store, heated washrooms, hot showers, and laundry facilities. The 185 sites cost $17.50 for two people for an unserviced lot, plus $1.55 for electricity ($2 for 30-amp electricity) and 50¢ for water, or $5 more for a site with electricity, water, and sewer hookups. Extra people more than 5 years old pay $2. For recreation there's a nine-hole golf course, hiking trails, horseshoe pits, mini-golf, and boats for rent. Sites have fireplaces and picnic tables. The campground is located between Gravenhurst and Bracebridge on Highway 11. In winter, try the 10½ miles (17km) of groomed cross-country ski trails.

A Nearby Place to Stay & Dine

SEVERN RIVER INN, Cowbell Lane off Hwy. 11 (P.O. Box 44), Severn Bridge, ON, P0E 1N0. Tel. 705/689-6333. 10 rms (4 with bath), 2 suites. A/C

$ Rates (including breakfast): $65 single without bath, $70 single with bath; $70 double without bath, $75 double with bath. MC, V.

The Severn River Inn is 12 miles (19km) north of Orillia and nine miles (15km) south of Gravenhurst. It's located in a historic building that was built in 1906 and served as the local general store, post office, telephone exchange, and boardinghouse.

The rooms are all individually furnished. Pine and oak pieces, brass beds, flounce pillows, lace curtains, and quilts are found throughout. The suite contains a sitting room and the original old bathtub and pedestal sink.

Backgammon and cribbage are available in the lounge, which was originally the general store. Light meals, too.

Dining/Entertainment: The intimate restaurant is candlelit at night and the chintz and table settings affect a Victorian ambience. In summer the screened-in porch overlooking the river is a favored dining spot. The menu features contemporary continental cuisine—mango chicken with orange-port sauce, trout with lime-and-coriander butter, steak Maubeuge with mushroom-brandy-cream sauce—priced from $10 to $19. Appetizers might include coconut shrimp with mango or escargots with almond chablis. The dining room is open Wednesday through Sunday from noon to 3pm and 5:30 to 9pm; closed Thanksgiving to May 1.

WHERE TO DINE

ASCONA PLACE, Bethune Dr. Tel. 705/687-5906.
   Cuisine: FRENCH/CONTINENTAL. **Reservations:** Recommended.
$ Prices: Main courses $16–$21. AE, ER, MC, V.
   Open: Summer lunch daily 11:30am–2pm; dinner daily 5–9pm. **Closed:** Wed in other seasons.

Named after a small picturesque village in southern Switzerland, Ascona Place offers a pretty courtyard for outside dining in July and August. If you have to wait for a table or want to have a before-dinner cocktail, there's also an attractive lounge. The menu features classic cuisine plus one or two Swiss specialties, such as an éminé of veal Swiss-style in white wine and cream sauce with mushrooms. Other entrées include pan-fried pickerel and rack of lamb provençal. You may either dine in the wine cellar, a cozy nook hung with wine bottles, or in the larger Ascona Room, hung with Swiss banners, wicker lampshades, and a set of Swiss cow bells. Gateback chairs with blue seats and tablecloths complete the scene. Desserts are exquisite—Sachertorte, apple strudel, homemade meringues and sorbets, or an iced soufflé with French Marc de Bourgogne (all around $5). Lunchtime is a good time to try the cuisine, when most entrées are under $8.

BRACEBRIDGE

Headquarters for the district government, Bracebridge early became an important commercial center. Incorporated in 1875, it offered incentives for businesses to locate there and when the Anglo-Canadian and Beardmore companies were both operating, it was one of the largest centers of heavy leather-tanning in the British Empire. The town has a commanding position above Bracebridge Falls, which enabled hydro-electric power generation.

On the 45th parallel, Bracebridge is halfway between the equator and the North Pole and the community bills itself as Santa's summer home—and **Santa's Village** (tel. 705/645-2512), a must for kids from 2 to 70, is here to prove it. It's an imaginatively designed fantasyland full of delights, not the least of which are the frog litter bins that advertise "I love waste" and the Lost Adults Depot. You can wander through stands of pine trees to Elves' Island, a unique children's play area where the kids can crawl on a suspended net and over or through various modules—Punch Bag Forest, Cave Crawl, and Snake Tube Crawl, for instance. Rides, water attractions, roving entertainers are all part of the fun. Santa's Village is open mid-June to Labor Day only, daily from 10am to 6pm. Admission is $12 for adults, $8 for seniors and children 2 to 4, and free for children under 2.

WHERE TO STAY & DINE

INN AT THE FALLS, 17 Dominion St. (P.O. Box 1139), Bracebridge, ON, P1L 1R6. Tel. 705/645-2245. Fax 705/645-5093. 26 rms and suites. A/C TV TEL

$ Rates (including breakfast): $72–$110 single; $82–$158 double. AE, MC, V.

This is an attractive bed-and-breakfast inn hosted by an English couple, both of whom are hotel professionals. It's a lovely old Victorian house on a quiet street overlooking the Bracebridge Falls.

Each room is furnished differently with antique pieces and English chintz. For example, the William Mahaffy Suite has a comfortable sitting room with TV and telephone, and an upstairs bedroom with lace curtains and fringed lamps. The Mews rooms have a view of the falls, gas fireplaces, TV, telephone, and old Canadian prints on the walls. Beds have handsome white coverlets, and rooms contain louver closets and double sinks (one in the bathroom and one outside it). There are also four suites in a separate building complete with kitchenettes, and bedrooms furnished with queen four-posters. Two have fireplaces.

The gardens are inviting, filled with delphiniums, peonies, roses and spring flowers and there's also an outdoor heated pool.

Dining/Entertainment: The Pub is a popular local gathering place at lunch or dinner. In the winter the fire crackles and snaps, but in the summer the terrace is filled with flowers and umbrellaed tables. In the more elegant main dining room, with its floor-to-ceiling windows, the food is well recommended. At dinner prices range from $14 to $20 for such dishes as quenelles of smoked Muskoka trout, stuffed sole Véronique, veal marsala, and rack of lamb. The dining room is open daily from 6 to

9pm. The Pub is open from 11:30am to 10pm daily for food, staying open until midnight Monday through Saturday, until 11pm on Sunday.

PATTERSON KAYE LODGE, Golden Beach Rd., off Hwy. 118, R.R. 1, Bracebridge, ON, P0B 1C0. Tel. 705/645-4169. Fax 705/645-5720. 30 rms. A/C TV

$ Rates (including breakfast and dinner): High season $520–$640 per person per week, depending on the type of accommodation. Special weekend packages available, and also special reductions during certain weeks. European plan only winter and spring $100–$135. AE, MC, V.

For a secluded, casual lodge, ideal for families and not overdeveloped, Patterson Kaye Lodge fits the bill. Located on Lake Muskoka three miles west of town, the main lodge has a variety of rooms, while cottages of various sizes accommodating a total of 100 people are scattered around the property.

Facilities: Free waterskiing with instruction is run from the dock; there's a hot tub, two tennis courts, and a number of activities are arranged in which you may participate. Of course, there's plenty of fishing, golf, and riding nearby, and use of canoes, sailboats, and Windsurfers is free.

TAMWOOD RESORT, Hwy. 118, R.R. 1, Bracebridge, ON, P1L 1WB. Tel. 705/645-5172, or toll free 800/465-9166. 35 rms. A/C MINIBAR TV TEL

$ Rates: Three-night package $277–$340 per person; weekly rates $562–$675 per person. Special discount weeks available. AE, MC, V.

Tamwood Lodge is a moderate-size log lodge on Lake Muskoka, six miles west of town. The air-conditioned main lodge has 35 units, all simply but nicely decorated, and there are a few cottages. Then there are four deluxe loft accommodations, each stunningly appointed with pine interior, two bedrooms with a skylight, plus a loft area, an upstairs and downstairs bathroom, an efficiency kitchen, and a living room with Franklin stove leading out onto a balcony from which you can dive into Lake Muskoka. Three new waterfront units come complete with fireplaces. Knotty-pine furnishings and large granite fireplaces imbue the lounge and main dining room with character.

Facilities: There are facilities for swimming (both indoors and outdoors), fishing, tennis, volleyball, badminton, and shuffleboard, plus free waterskiing, sailing, and boating, and all the winter sports imaginable. There's also lots of family fun—such as baseball games, marshmallow roasts, and bingo—organized under the supervision of the sports and social director. Kids are also supervised. A fully equipped games room completes the picture.

PORT CARLING

As waterways became the main means of transportation in the region, Port Carling became, and still is, the hub of the lakes. It became a boatbuilding center when a lock was installed connecting Lakes Muskoka and Rosseau, and a canal between Lakes Rosseau and Joseph opened all three to navigation. The **Muskoka Lakes Museum** (tel. 705/765-5367) captures much of the flavor of this era. It's open Monday to Saturday 10am to 5pm, Sunday noon to 5pm from June to Canadian Thanksgiving (U.S. Columbus Day). Admission is $2.25 for adults, $1.25 for seniors and students.

WHERE TO STAY

CLEVELANDS HOUSE, Minett P.O., near Port Carling, ON, P0B 1G0. Tel. 705/765-3171. Fax 705/765-6296. Accommodates up to 450 people in 86 rooms, 21 suites, 30 bungalows, and several cottages. A/C TV TEL

$ Rates (including all meals): $135–$175 per person per night, $700–$1,000 per person per week. Cottages rent for a $3,500 minimum weekly rate. Rates depend on the number of people in the room and the type of accommodation. Special family-week off-season discounts and packages available. AE, MC, V.

The very name Clevelands House has a gracious ring to it, and indeed this resort has been providing the ultimate in luxury since 1869. It is much larger than the hostelries I recommended in nearby Bracebridge and is very much a full-facility resort. The lodge itself is a magnificent clapboard structure with a veranda that runs around the lakeside giving views over the well-kept flower gardens. There's a dance floor set out on the dock with a sun deck on top.

Accommodations vary in size and location and have solid old-fashioned furniture; the luxury suites, though, are supermodern, with private sun decks.

Facilities: Sixteen tennis, four shuffleboard, and three badminton courts; a nine-hole golf course; a huge children's playground and other activities; heated outdoor swimming pool; and good fishing, swimming, boating, and waterskiing on Lake Rosseau.

EDENVALE INN, Maple St., Port Carling, ON, P0B 1J0. Tel. 705/765-6435. Fax 705/765-6031. 18 rms. A/C TV TEL

$ Rates: $70 single; $90 double; from $150 suite. Extra person $15. AE, DC, ER, MC, V.

Right in Port Carling, overlooking the Indian River, the Edenvale Inn is a good value. Many of its rooms are large, containing beds and couches. They overlook the water and have access to a shared balcony. The fireside lounge is cozy and popular locally, and the summer outdoor deck sits out over the water.

SHERWOOD INN, P.O. Box 400, Lake Joseph, Port Carling, ON, P0B 1J0. Tel. 705/765-3131. Fax 705/765-6668. 30 rms. **Directions:** From Hwy. 400, take Hwy. 69 north to Foot's Bay. Turn right and take 169 south to Sherwood Rd. Turn left just before the junction of Hwy. 118. Or you can arrive via Gravenhurst and Bala or Bracebridge and Port Carling.

$ Rates (including breakfast and dinner): $168–$232 per person in cottages; $149–$186 in the inn. Rates based on double occupancy. Special packages available. AE, ER, MC, V.

Accommodations here are either in the lodge or in beachside cottages. The last are very appealing, with fieldstone fireplaces, comfortable armchairs, TVs, telephones, and screened porches overlooking the lake. Some are more luxurious than others and have additional features like VCRs or private docks. The older rooms in the lodge feature painted wood paneling while the newer wing has air conditioning and the rooms are furnished with wicker.

WINDERMERE HOUSE, off Muskoka Rte. 4, P.O. Box 68, Windermere, ON, P0B 1P0. Tel. 705/769-3611, or toll free 800/461-4283. Fax 705/769-2168. 78 rms. TEL

$ Rates (including breakfast and dinner): $75–$110 per person per night; unit with fireplace, fridge, TV, and private deck $125–$140 per person per night. Rates increase about 30% on weekends. Weekly rates and European Plan also available. AE, ER, MC, V.

This striking stone-and-clapboard turreted building overlooks lawns that sweep down to Lake Rosseau. Originally built in 1864, it was renovated in 1986. Out front stretches a long, broad veranda furnished with Adirondack chairs and geranium-filled window boxes. Rooms are variously furnished. Some are in the main house and some are located in cottages and buildings scattered around the property. Some have air conditioning, some only overhead fans. All have private bath and are furnished in modern style, some with a bamboo/rattan look. The dining room offers fine modern continental cuisine featuring such items at dinner as swordfish with a spiced black bean sauce or duck in rhubarb and port sauce, and is open to the public. There's nightly entertainment in the lounge.

Facilities: Outdoor swimming pool, tennis courts, golf, all kinds of water sports—fishing, windsurfing, sailing—and a full children's program. Room service is available from 7am to 10pm; laundry/dry cleaning. Children's program offered during July and August.

HUNTSVILLE

The town was named after first settler, Capt. George Hunt, who arrived in 1869, a temperance man who organized the first school, the first church, and the first retail store. He settled on the east side of the Muskoka River and later divided his land, selling off lots only to abstainers—which perhaps accounts for the flat roads that cut along the east side of the river while those on the west roll from hill to hill. In 1877 the construction of locks opened navigation on the Mary-Fairy-Vernon chain of lakes, and when the railway arrived in 1886 the town was incorporated. Lumber was the major industry and today it's Muskoka's biggest town with major manufacturing companies.

Some of the region's early history can be reviewed at the **Muskoka Pioneer Village and Museum** (tel. 705/789-7576), open June to Canadian Thanksgiving (U.S. Columbus Day), in summer from 10am to 4pm, in fall from 11am to 3pm, or by a visit to Brunel Locks in nearby Brunel. Some 20 miles (32km) east of Huntsville on Highway 60, **Ragged Falls** is worth a visit. Admission is $4 for adults, $2.75 for seniors, $2.25 for students and children; under 5 free.

Robinson's General Store (tel. 705/766-2415) in Dorset is so popular it was voted Canada's best country store. Wood stoves, dry goods, hardware, pine goods, and moccasins—you name it, it's here.

WHERE TO STAY

BLUE SPRUCE INN, on Hwy. 60 (R.R. 1), Dwight, ON, P0A 1H0. Tel. 705/635-2330. 10 motel rms, 15 cottages. A/C TV

$ Rates: High season (summer, all weekends, Christmas, and Easter) $75–$90 per night, $420–$510 per week motel; $90 per night, $510 per week one-bedroom cottage; $120 per night, $655 per week two-bedroom cottage; $135–$160 per night, $775–$875 per week three-bedroom cottage. Off-season rates reduced about 15%. MC, V.

On the fringes of Algonquin Provincial Park, the Blue Spruce Inn, 20 miles northeast of Huntsville, has nicely kept motel suites with separate kitchen areas, and cottages with wood-burning fireplaces. The lodge has a cozy lounge and games rooms. There's a beach with boating, a sun deck at the lake, and two tennis courts. In winter there's cross-country skiing, a large natural skating rink, toboggan hill, and snowmobiling for recreation.

CEDAR GROVE LODGE, P.O. Box 996, Huntsville, ON, P0A 1K0. Tel. 705/789-4036. Fax 705/789-6860. 8 rms (none with bath), 19 cabins. **Directions:** Take Grassmere Resort Road, off Highway 60.

$ Rates (including all meals): $80–$115 per person. Weekly rates and special packages available. AE, MC, V.

On Peninsula Lake, 7½ miles (12km) from Huntsville, Cedar Grove Lodge is a very attractive and well-maintained resort. The main lodge contains eight rooms sharing three bathrooms; the rest of the accommodations are one-, two-, or three-bedroom log cabins like the Hermit Thrush, which contains pine furnishings, a fieldstone fireplace, a porch overlooking the lake, bar/sink and refrigerator, and conveniently stored firewood; or the Chickadee, a smaller version of the same for two only.

The main lodge contains a comfortable large sitting room with stone fireplace, TV, and piano, along with the pretty lakeside dining room with lace-trimmed tablecloths on its tables. The facilities include two tennis courts, a hot tub, kid's beach, and games room. There's free waterskiing, plus sailboarding, canoeing, and windsurfing for an extra charge; cross-country skiing and skating on the lake are offered in winter.

DEERHURST RESORT, R.R. 4, Huntsville, ON, P0A 1K0. Tel. 705/789-6411, or toll free 800/441-1414. Fax 705/789-2431. 370 rms and suites. A/C TV TEL **Directions:** Take Canal Road off Highway 60 to Deerhurst Road.

$ Rates: $150–$210 double; $239–$269 suite. Extra person $25. AE, CB, DC, DISC, ER, MC, V.

Catering to well-heeled families, the Deerhurst Inn originally opened in 1896, but over the last decade it has expanded rapidly, scattering building units all over the property and catering to a slick, urban, mainly Toronto crowd. It's located on 800 acres of rolling landscape fronting on Peninsula Lake.

The guest rooms range from hotel rooms in the Terrace and Bayshore buildings to fully appointed one-, two-, or three-bedroom suites, many with fireplaces and/or whirlpool. These suites come fully equipped with all the comforts of home, including stereos, TVs, VCRs, and some have fully functioning kitchens complete with microwaves, dishwashers, and washer/dryers.

Dining/Entertainment: The turn-of-the-century main lodge features a living room lounge with a massive stone fireplace stretching the length of one wall, with comfy furnishings and leather sofas. The adjacent dining room offers romantic dining overlooking the lake (prices at dinner from $30 to $40, or $33 prix fixe), while the Piano Lounge and Cypress Bar provide a chic environment. Live entertainment highlights include a Las Vegas stage show and a comedy show, plus entertainment in the Piano Lounge, Four Winds nightclub, and also at Steamers Restaurant.

Facilities: The new indoor sports complex has four tennis courts, three squash courts, one racquetball court, an indoor pool, a whirlpool and sauna, and a full-service spa. Outdoor facilities include a pool, eight tennis courts, a beach, canoes, kayaks, sailboats, paddleboats, waterskiing, windsurfing, horseback riding, and two 18-hole golf courses. The full winter program includes on-site cross-country skiing, snowmobiling, dog-sledding, and downhill skiing at nearby Hidden Valley Highlands. A children's activity program operates during the summer and on weekends year-round.

GRANDVIEW INN, R.R. 4, Huntsville, ON, P0A 1K0. Tel. 705/789-4417. Fax 705/789-6882. 200 rms. A/C TV TEL
$ Rates: $140 single; $155 double; from $195 suite. Packages available. Children 18 and under stay free in parents' room. AE, ER, MC, V.

⭐ If Deerhurst is for the folks on the fast track, the Grandview Inn has a more measured pace. It's a smaller resort and care has been taken to retain the natural beauty and contours of the original farmstead even while providing the latest in resort facilities.

Eighty of the accommodations are traditional hotel-style rooms, but most units are suites located in a series of buildings, some right down beside the lake, others up on the hill with a view of the lake. All are spectacularly furnished. Each executive suite contains a kitchen, a dining area, a living room with a fireplace and access to an outside deck, a large bedroom, and a large bathroom with a whirlpool bath.

Dining/Entertainment: The Mews contains a reception area, a comfortable lounge/entertainment room furnished with sofas and wingbacks, and conference facilities. The main dining room, located in the original old farmhouse, is decorated in paisleys and English chintz, and has an inviting patio with an awning overlooking the gardens. At lunch, entrées range from $6 to $9. At dinner, steaks, seafood, and such items as Cajun red snapper or veal piccata are priced from $13 to $24. Snacks and light fare are also served in summer at the Dockside Restaurant right on the lake, and also at the golf clubhouse year-round.

Facilities: Sports facilities include an outdoor pool, a nine-hole golf course, two outdoor tennis courts, waterskiing, windsurfing, sailing, canoeing, and cross-country skiing. Mountain bikes are also available, and boat cruises are offered aboard a yacht. There's also a recreation center with an indoor pool, a tennis court, and an exercise room.

HIDDEN VALLEY RESORT HOTEL, Hidden Valley Rd. (R.R. 4), off Hwy. 60, Huntsville, ON, P0A 1K0. Tel. 705/789-2301. Fax 705/789-6586. 93 rms. A/C TV TEL
$ Rates: From $80 single; $90 double; from $120 suite. Extra person $15. Children under 18 stay free in parents' room. AE, CB, DC, DISC, ER, MC, V.

On a sheltered bay on Peninsula Lake, the Hidden Valley offers rooms boasting views over the lakes to crimson hills in fall. The name, though, is misleading because many of the rooms are motel-type accommodations. The resort has a series of lakeside condominiums that can be rented usually for several nights only; other accommodations are motel style. The one- to four-bedroom condos have fully equipped kitchens, wood-burning fireplaces, and large decks. There's a dining room and lounges.

Facilities: The hotel is located right at the base of a mountain that offers three chair lifts, a T-bar and rope tow, and 10 slopes. Snowmobiling and cross-country skiing are also available. Facilities include an indoor and an outdoor pool, a sauna, four tennis courts, one racquetball and two squash courts, a dock, sailing instruction, windsurfing, and boat rentals.

POW-WOW POINT LODGE, six miles east of Huntsville on Hwy. 60 (Box 387, R.R. 4), Huntsville, ON, P0A 1K0. Tel. 705/789-4951. Fax 705/789-7123. 27 rms.

$ Rates (including all meals): High season $105 per person double; off-season $85 per person. Weekly rates and other packages available. MC, V.

The accommodations at this small year-round family resort range from pine cottages and chalets (without TVs or phones, thank goodness) and motel-type rooms overlooking Peninsula Lake and Hidden Valley. The lodge itself has television in the main fireplace lounge, a recreation room, and a deck overlooking the lake. Facilities include an indoor pool, a tennis court, shuffleboard, a beach, fishing boats, boat cruises, and 7½ miles (12km) of cross-country ski trails. Golf, horseback riding, and alpine skiing are nearby.

6. ALGONQUIN PARK

Immediately east of Muskoka lie Algonquin Park's 3,000 square miles of wilderness—a haven for the naturalist, camper, and fishing and sports enthusiast, especially the canoeist (there are 1,000 miles of canoe routes). The park is a game sanctuary where moose, beaver, bear, and deer roam freely, but there is plenty of fishing for speckled, rainbow, and lake trout, and small-mouth black bass. It was the inspiration for the famous "Group of Seven" artists.

The **Algonquin Park Information Centre** (tel. 705/633-5572) on Highway 60 at the entrance to the park, sells canoe and hiking-trail maps and books about the park's flora and fauna. It's open Monday to Thursday from 7:30am to 5pm, Friday from 6am to 9pm, and Saturday and Sunday from 6am to 5pm. The **Museum of Logging** features a 15-minute audio visual presentation. Afterwards, walk the ¾-mile trail through the cambouse camp to the working dam and log shute.

It's worth stopping at the new **Algonquin Park Visitor Centre,** south of Highway 60, to become acquainted with the flora, fauna, and geology of the park. The center contains several galleries devoted to the natural history of the park, and occupies a ridge overlooking Sunday Creek Valley. There's a good bookstore also. Free admission.

There are several outfitters that will fully equip people to travel the network of rivers and lakes that make up much of the park. Among them are: **Algonquin Outfitters,** Oxtongue Lake (R.R. 1), Dwight, ON, P0A 1H0 (tel. 705/635-2243); and **Opeongo Outfitters,** Box 123, Whitney, ON, K0J 2M0 (tel. 613/637-5470). Complete canoe outfitting costs from $42 to $50 a day, depending on the length of trip and extent of equipment. Canoe rentals cost from $13 to $25 a day depending on the type.

WHERE TO STAY IN & NEAR THE PARK

AROWHON PINES, Algonquin Park, ON, P0A 1B0. Tel. 705/633-5661 in summer, 416/483-4393 in winter. Fax 705/633-5795 in summer, 416/483-4429 in winter. 50 rms.

$ Rates (including all meals): From $160 daily, $900 weekly, per person, double occupancy in standard accommodations. No credit cards. **Closed:** Mid-Oct to mid-May.

Arowhon Pines has to be one of the most entrancing places I have ever visited. Operated by a delightful couple, Eugene and Helen Kates, it's located eight miles off Highway 60 down a dirt road, so you're guaranteed total seclusion, quiet, and serenity. Cabins are dotted through the pine forests that surround the lake.

Each is furnished differently with assorted Canadian pine antiques, and each varies in layout, although they all have bedrooms with private baths, and sitting rooms with fireplaces. For example, Westview has vaulted cedar ceilings, a sitting room, and a bedroom complete with two bunk beds for the kids tucked away around the corner from the master bed. You can opt either for a private cottage or for one that contains anywhere from 2 to 12 bedrooms and shares a communal sitting room with a stone fireplace, oak table, and chest that serves as coffee table, among other furnishings. Sliding doors lead onto a deck. Other cabins might contain such interesting items as a butter churner or wicker love seat, as in Birchview, which has two bedrooms—one featuring a sleigh bed. There are no TVs and no telephones—just the sound of the loons, the gentle lap of the water, the croaking of the frogs, and the sound of oar paddles cutting the smooth surface of the lake.

Helen and Eugene are extremely gracious hosts and really do pay attention to the little details. Everything is artfully done, right down to the bark menus at mealtimes.

Dining/Entertainment: At the heart of the resort is a hexagonal dining room set down beside the lake with a veranda that runs along several sides. A huge fireplace is at the center of the room. The food is good, with fresh ingredients, and plenty of it. You select your own appetizers at dinner, which will consist of fresh salads and vegetables as well as a piping-hot soup. Main course will be a choice of meat or fish—perhaps prime English cut of beef served with horseradish (Helen hails from England) accompanied by crisply cooked beans flavored ever so delicately with mint and roast potatoes and Yorkshire pudding. No alcohol is allowed for sale in the park, so make sure to bring your own because the nearest liquor store is 25 miles away (the waiters will happily uncork it for you). Desserts are arranged on a harvest table—a wonderful spread of trifle, chocolate layer cake, almond tarts, fresh-fruit salad, and more. Breakfast brings a full selection—granola, fresh fruit, kippers, finnan haddie, pancakes—all cooked to order. Luncheon items are equally appealing, like the tourtière.

Facilities: Activities include early-morning swimming in the fresh clear water of the lake, canoeing, sailing, rowing, and windsurfing. There are also two tennis courts, a sauna, and a games room where a daily film is shown in the evening.

KILLARNEY LODGE, Algonquin Park, ON, P0A 1K0. Tel. 705/633-5551. Fax 705/633-5667 (summer only). 26 cabins. **Directions:** Enter the park on Highway 60 from either Dwight or Whitney.
$ **Rates** (including all meals): High season $130–$175 per person double. Off-season rates about 10% less. MC, V. **Closed:** Mid-Oct to mid-May.

The Killarney Lodge is not as secluded as Arowhon Pines (the highway is still visible and audible), but it, too, is a charming resort run by another lovely couple, Eric and Linda Miglin. The cabins all stand on a peninsula that juts out into the Lake of Two Rivers so that there's water all around. Each is made of pine logs and has a deck. Furnishings include old rockers, Ethan Allen–style beds, desks, chests, and rope rugs. A canoe comes with every cabin. Prices include all three home-style meals, served in an attractive rustic log dining room. The fare might include rainbow trout, pork loin, or prime rib.

SPECTACLE LAKE LODGE, P.O. Box 328, Barry's Bay, ON, K0J 1B0. Tel. 613/756-2324. Fax 613/756-7669.
Cuisine: CANADIAN. **Reservations:** Recommended in summer. **Directions:** Head 10.5 miles (17km) west of Barry's Bay, 22 miles (35km) east of Algonquin Park, south off Hwy. 60.
$ **Prices:** Main courses $11–$16. MC, V.
Open: Daily 8am–8pm. **Closed:** Last 2 weeks of Nov.

The lodge's rustic dining room looks out over the lake. Traditional fare includes salmon trout and orange roughy, as well as Italian favorites like spaghetti with meatballs and veal parmigiana. Breakfast and lunch are served, too.

There are also nine nicely kept cottages available for rent, some with full housekeeping facilities including fridge and stove. The rates are $37 to $47 per person ($67 to $77 per person with breakfast and dinner included). Canoe and pedal boats are available, too. Snowmobile rentals available.

Facilities include a comfortable sitting room with a hearth and games like cribbage available, as well as fine dining room and a decent wine cellar. Additional amenities include a health club, bikes, and a tennis court; all kinds of watersports are available, as is cross-country skiing in winter.

7. THE HALIBURTON REGION

East of Bracebridge along Highway 118 is the Haliburton Highlands, a region of lakes, mountains, and forests.

For information on the region, contact the **Haliburton Highlands Chamber of Commerce,** in Minden (tel. 705/286-1760). If you're relying on public transportation to get there, Can-Ar (tel. 416/393-7911) coaches operate daily from Toronto to Haliburton via Lindsay.

HALIBURTON VILLAGE

The **Haliburton Highlands Museum,** on Bayshore Acres Road, half a mile (one kilometer) north of the village off Highway 118 (tel. 705/457-2760), provides some insight into the lives of the pioneers who settled the region in the late 1800s—their homes and way of life. Open from 10am to 5pm: daily from Victoria Day (late May) to Canadian Thanksgiving (U.S. Columbus Day); in winter, Tuesday through Saturday only. Admission is $2 for adults, $1 for children.

Many artists and craftspeople have settled in the area and some of their works can be seen at the **Rail's End Gallery,** on York Street (tel. 705/457-2330), open Labor Day to July 1 Tuesday to Saturday 10am to 5pm; July 1 to Labor Day Monday to Saturday 10am to 5pm, Sunday noon to 4pm.

In Dorset, it's fun to visit **Robinson's General Store.** Also, stop by the **Leslie Frost Resources Centre,** seven miles (11km) south on Highway 35 (tel. 705/766-2451), for a guided tour of the site and buildings, with wildlife displays. Open weekdays all year.

AN EAGLE LAKE HIDEAWAY

SIR SAM'S INN, Eagle Lake P.O., ON, K0M 1M0. Tel. 705/754-2188.
Fax 705/754-4262 25 rms. **Directions:** Follow the signs to Sir Sam's ski area. From Highway 118, take Route 6 to Sir Sam's Road.

$ Rates (including breakfast and dinner): Summer $125–$145 per person weekdays, $249–$325 per person for a two-night weekend. Weekly rates available. In winter rates drop about 10%. AE, ER, MC, V.

 Sir Sam's takes some finding. That's the way politician and militarist Sir Sam Hughes probably wanted it when he built his 14-bedroom stone-and-timber mansion in 1917 in the woods above Eagle Lake.

Accommodations are either in the inn itself or in a series of new chalets or in two lakefront suites. The chalets have very fetching bed-sitting rooms with light-pine furnishings, wingback chairs, lush jade carpeting, wood-burning fireplace, cedar-lined bathrooms, small private decks, and such amenities as mini-refrigerators, alarm clocks, and kettles. Some have whirlpool baths. Rooms in the inn are a little more old-fashioned, except in the Hughes Wing where they are similar to the chalets with whirlpool bath and fireplace, but with bamboo furnishings. Room 6, which was Sir Sam's room, has French doors leading to a large porch furnished with wicker overlooking the gardens and lake. Room 9 has a whirlpool bath. The suites are fully equipped with full kitchens complete with microwave and dishwasher, and also contain whirlpools.

The atmosphere is friendly, yet sophisticated. There's a comfy sitting room in which the focal point is the large stone fireplace.

Dining/Entertainment: The pretty dining room with floral wallpaper and pink and blue table linens serves a prix-fixe dinner for $32.50 that might feature, for example, smoked salmon with capers or cognac pâté among its appetizers, salad, and roast venison tenderloin, or apricot-rosemary-glazed lamb chops, and filet mignon among the main courses. The Gunner's Bar sports Sir Sam's rifle on the wall and has a small dance floor.

Facilities: Facilities include an exercise room with a rowing machine and bicycle, two tennis courts, an outdoor pool overlooking the lake, a beach, and sailing, windsurfing, waterskiing, canoeing, paddleboats, and mountain bikes.

8. SOME NORTHERN ONTARIO HIGHLIGHTS

SUDBURY

A nickel-mining center with a population of 160,000, Sudbury is the largest metro area in northern Ontario. A rough-and-ready mining town, it has a landscape so barren that U.S. astronauts were trained here for lunar landings. Its most dubious claim to fame in Canada is that it was the first city to install parking meters in 1940; a pleasanter claim is that it was the first Ontario city to open an Olympic-size pool, at Laurentian University, where Alex Baumann trained before winning two gold medals at the Los Angeles Olympics in 1984.

The city lies about 102 miles (165km) northwest of Parry Sound up Highway 69. For information contact either the **Sudbury and District Chamber of Commerce** (tel. 705/673-7133) or the **Community Information Service and Convention and Visitors Service** (tel. 705/674-3141).

WHAT TO SEE & DO

The two major attractions are **Science North,** 100 Ramsey Lake Rd. (tel. 705/522-3701 or 522-3700 for recorded information) and **Big Nickel Mine.**

The first occupies two giant stainless steel snowflake-shaped buildings dramatically cut into a rock outcrop overlooking Lake Ramsey. Inside it provides opportunities to experiment: to simulate a hurricane, to monitor earthquakes on a seismograph, or to observe the sun through a solar telescope, to name only a few examples. In addition to the exhibits, a 3-D film and laser experience, *Shooting Star,* takes the audience on a journey back five billion years, charting the formation of the Sudbury Basin; a theatrical performance in another theater tells the story of the naturalist Grey Owl. There's also a water playground (where kids can play and adults can build a sailboat), space exploration and weather command centers, and a fossil identification workshop. Open year round daily in May and June from 9am to 5pm, July to Canadian Thanksgiving 9am to 6pm; call ahead for winter hours. Admission is $7.95 for adults, $5.25 for students and seniors, free for under 5s. A combined admission with the mine will save money.

At the **Big Nickel Mine,** visitors are taken underground for a 30-minute tour, where they learn about various mining methods, inspect a refuge station, and study a simulated blasting display. On the surface visitors can view a mineral processing station, measure their weight in gold, and enjoy some other video programs. Open May to Canadian Thanksgiving, same hours as Science North. Admission is $6.50 for adults, $4.25 for students and seniors, free for under 5s. A combined admission with Science North will save money.

The **Path of Discovery** is a two-hour bus tour that provides the only public access to INCO Ltd., the biggest nickel producer in the western world. On the tour visitors observe the surface processing facilities and one of the tallest smokestacks in the world. The tour is operated from July to Labor Day daily at 10am and 2pm.

Less than an hour's drive southwest of the city, ✪ **Killarney Provincial Park** offers camping and canoeing in a forested landscape on the shores of Georgian Bay. It's a wilderness park; hiking, canoeing, or skiing is the only way to get around. It's a popular place, so you'll need camping reservations. For information call 705/287-2900.

WHERE TO STAY

Your best bets for lodgings are the chains—**Journey's End,** at 2171 Regent St. South (tel. 705/522-1101) and at 440 2nd Ave. North (tel. 705/560-4502); **Holiday Inn,** 85 St. Anne's (tel. 705/675-1123); or **Venture Inn,** 1956 Regent St. South (tel. 705/522-7600). There's also the **Sheraton Caswell Inn,** at 1696 Regent St. South (tel. 705/522-3000).

COCHRANE & THE POLAR BEAR EXPRESS

⭐ The major, if not the only, reason for heading to Cochrane, 235 miles (380km) north of Sudbury, is to experience one of the great railroad/nature excursions—the Polar Bear Express to the Arctic. The train travels 186 miles (4½ hours) from Cochrane along the Abitibi and Moose Rivers (the latter, by the way, rises and falls six feet twice a day with the tides) to Moosonee on James Bay, gateway to the Arctic. Moosonee and Moose Factory, on an island in the river, will introduce you to frontier life—still a challenge, although it's easier today than when native Cree and fur traders traveled the rivers and wrenched a living from the land 300 years ago. You can take the cruiser *Polar Princess* or a freighter-canoe across to Moose Factory (site of the Hudson's Bay Company, founded in 1673) and see the 17th-century Anglican church and other sights. If you stay over, you can also visit **Fossil Island** and the **Shipsands Waterfowl Sanctuary.** Trains operate from the end of June to Labor Day. Tickets are limited because priority is given to the excursion passengers. Fares are $44 roundtrip for adults, $22 children ages 5 to 12. Various three-day/two-night and four-day/three-night packages are also offered from North Bay and Toronto. For information contact **Ontario Northland** at 555 Oak St. East, North Bay, ON P1B 8L3 (tel. 705/472-4500) or at Union Station, 65 Front St. West, Toronto, ON M5J 1E6 (tel. 416/314-3750).

SAULT STE. MARIE

From Sudbury it's 189 miles (305km) west along Highway 17 to Sault Ste. Marie, or the Soo, as it's affectionately called. The highlights of any visit are the Soo locks, the Agawa Canyon Train, and the **Bon Soo,** one of North America's biggest winter carnivals, celebrated in late January and early February.

For more travel information, contact the **Sault Ste. Marie Chamber of Commerce,** 360 Great Northern Rd., Sault Ste. Marie ON (tel. 705/949-7152) or the **Economic Development Corporation,** Civic Centre, 99 Foster Dr., P.O. Box 580, Sault Ste. Marie, ON P6A 5N1 (tel. 705/759-5432).

WHAT TO SEE & DO

The Soo, at the junction of Lakes Superior and Huron, actually straddles the border. The twin cities, one in Ontario and the other in Michigan, are separated by the St. Marys River rapids, and now joined by an international bridge. Originally the Northwest Fur Trading Company founded a post here in 1783, building a canal to bypass the rapids in 1797–99. That canal was replaced later by the famous **Soo locks**—four on the American side and one on the Canadian—which are part of the St. Lawrence Seaway system, which enables large international cargo ships to navigate from the Atlantic along the St. Lawrence to the Great Lakes. Lake Superior is about 23 feet higher than Lake Huron and the locks raise and lower the ships. There's a viewing station at both sets of locks or you can take a two- or three-hour cruise through the lock system daily from June to about October 10. For information, contact **Lock Tours Canada,** P.O. Box 424, Sault Ste. Marie, ON P6A 5M1 (tel. 705/253-9850).

At the turn of the century the Soo became industrialized with the establishment of a paper mill; the Great Lakes Power company, which harnessed power from the rapids; and the Algoma Steel Corporation. The Algoma Central Railway, which operates the ⭕ **Agawa Canyon Train Tours,** was established in 1901 to connect the iron ore mines at Michipicoten to Algoma Steel. Today this tour takes you on a 114-mile trip that ends at the Agawa Canyon, where you can spend a couple of hours taking in the spectacle of rock and waterfall. The most spectacular time to take the trip is in the fall from mid-September to mid-October. The train operates daily from early June through mid-October; January through March it operates weekends only. Fares are $44 for adults, $16.75 children and students (June–August) or $22 (September–October), and $7.80 for children under five. For information contact the Algoma Central Railway, 129 Bay St., Sault Ste. Marie, ON, P6A 1W7 (tel. 705/946-7300).

Another museum that provides insight into the local way of life is the **Ontario Bushplane Heritage Museum,** on Bay Street, next to the Government Dock (tel. 705/945-6242). Open daily in summer, weekends only in winter.

The surrounding area offers great fishing, snowmobiling, cross-country skiing, and other sports opportunities. For example, you can enjoy one-, four-, and seven-day kayaking trips with **Lake Superior Kayak Adventures,** 159 Shannon Rd., Sault Ste. Marie, ON P6A 4J9. For cross-country ski information, call the **Stokely Creek Ski Touring Centre,** at Stokely Creek Lodge, at Karalash Corners, Goulais River (tel. 705/649-3421). Call the tourist office for more sports information.

For scenery, drive the Lake Superior Drive, past Batchawana Bay and Alona Bay, to Agawa Bay in **Lake Superior Provincial Park,** which has camping facilities, and hiking and canoe routes. Several of the Group of Seven painted in the park. Farther along Route 17 lies **Pukaskwa National Park,** accessible on foot or by boat only. **Fort St. Joseph National Park,** on St. Joseph Island, lies between Michigan and Ontario, 31 miles (50km) east of the Soo.

WHERE TO STAY

Try the chains: the **Holiday Inn,** 208 St. Mary's River Dr. (tel. 705/949-0611), or **Journey's End,** 333 Great Northern Rd., ON P6B 4Z8 (tel. 705/759-8000). The **Ramada** (tel. 705/942-2500), has great facilities for families—waterslide, bowling, indoor golf, and more.

FROM THE SOO TO THUNDER BAY

From Sault Ste. Marie it's 428 miles (690km) west to Thunder Bay. Along the route atop Lake Superior, there are some stops worth making. **Wawa,** 142 miles (230km) north, is site of the famous salmon derby and serves as a supply center for canoeists, fishermen and other sports folks. Sixty-one miles farther on is **White River,** birthplace of Winnie the Pooh, with spectacular Magpie High Falls just outside. Another 167 miles (270km) will bring you to Nipigon and Nipigon Bay, offering fine rock, pine, and lake vistas. From here it's another 7.5 miles (12km) to **Ouimet Canyon,** a spectacular canyon 330 feet deep, 500 feet wide, and a mile long. About 15.5 miles (25km) on, next stop is **Sleeping Giant Provincial Park,** named after the rock formation that the Ojibwe Indians say is the Great Spirit Nana-bijou, who turned to stone after someone broke a promise to him. Take Route 587 south along the peninsula jutting into the lake. Facilities include camping. Just before you enter Thunder Bay, stop and honor Terry Fox at the **Monument and Scenic Lookout.** Not far from this spot he abandoned his heroic cross-Canada journey to raise money for cancer research.

THUNDER BAY

From this port city—an amalgam of Fort William and Port Arthur—wheat and other commodities are shipped out via the Great Lakes all over the world. The skyline is dominated by 15 grain elevators. You can't really grasp the city's role and its geography unless you take the **Harbor Cruise.** Other highlights include **Old Fort William,** about 10 miles outside the city where you can view 42 historic buildings. From 1803 to 1821 it was the headquarters of the North West Fur-Trading Company, which was later absorbed by the Hudson's Bay Company. **Kakabeka Falls,** a 130-foot-high waterfall, lies 18 miles out along the TransCanada Hwy.

From Thunder Bay it's 298 miles (480km) along the TransCanada Highway to **Kenora.** Several provincial parks dot the route: **Quetico, Sand Point Island,** and **Lake of the Woods.** Quetico boasts a maze of canoe routes and is a canoeists' paradise.

CHAPTER 17

WINNIPEG

Tough, sturdy, muscular, midwestern, Canada's Chicago—that's Winnipeg, capital of Manitoba. The solid cast-iron warehouses, stockyards, railroad depots, and grain elevators all testify to its historical role as a distribution and supply center, first for furs and then for agricultural products. It's a toiling city where about 600,000 inhabitants sizzle in summer and shovel in winter.

That's one side. The other is a city and populace that have produced a symphony orchestra that triumphed in New York, the first "Royal" ballet company in the British Commonwealth, and a theater and arts complex worthy of any national capital.

Many Winnipeggers have left their city, fanning east or west in search of fame—Len Cariou, Neil Young, John Hirsch, and Monty Hall—but they still talk about going back to Portage and Main, the windiest corner on the North American continent, to the city that nurtured them. There's something about Winnipeg that inspires gut loyalty and pride. Perhaps it has something to do with size, the human scale and communal spirit, or to quote stage director John Hirsch: "You can still be a mensch in Winnipeg—it's very difficult to be a mensch in a lot of places in the world today." And you know, he's right.

SOME HISTORY Native Canadians, herds of buffalo, a few trading posts, and forts were all that Lord Selkirk's first group of 70 colonists found in 1812 when they arrived on the banks of the Red River. The going was tough, and even after the first formal government of the Red River Settlement, centered on Fort Garry, was formed in 1835, it was another 24 years before the first steamboat navigated the upper Red River and reached the inhabitants.

During these early years, the 1869 Métis rebellion led by Louis Riel against the eastern government threw the colony into prominence and brought the Redcoats under Lord Garnet Wolseley to the region.

By 1873 the population had grown considerably and Winnipeg was incorporated as a city. With the coming of the Canadian Pacific Railway in 1886, Winnipeg became the gateway to the west and the destination for a tide of European immigrants—Ukrainians, Mennonites, Jews, Italians, Hungarians, and Poles. The rush for land was on and the city boomed. Speculation drove the cost of land to fantastic figures, and between 1904 and 1914 the population tripled, from 67,000 to 203,000. In those colorful days the streets were thronged with farmers, prospectors, trappers, speculators, promoters, immigrants, and all kinds of folk.

Of these halcyon years and those that followed in the 1920s, old-time residents nostalgically recall the hissing CPR steam engines shunting day and night, and cattle being driven through the streets on the way to the stockyards. Although the city has yielded its position as the world's most important grain center to Chicago, you can still

✓

WHAT'S SPECIAL ABOUT WINNIPEG

Attractions
- ☐ The Commodity Exchange, once the world's premier grain market, now trading oilseed, rapeseed, gold, and other commodities.
- ☐ The Manitoba Museum of Man & Nature, where pioneer and prairie life is recorded.
- ☐ The Royal Canadian Mint, where 18,000 coins an hour are stamped.

Architectural Highlights
- ☐ Wellington Crescent, once called the Park Avenue of the Prairies.
- ☐ The Church of the Precious Blood, designed in 1968 by Etienne Gaboury.
- ☐ The basilica of St. Boniface and the grave of Louis Riel.

Cultural Highlights
- ☐ The Inuit collection of art at the Winnipeg Art Gallery.
- ☐ The Royal Winnipeg Ballet, the second-oldest ballet company in North America.

Communities
- ☐ St. Boniface, the largest French community in western Canada.

Historical and Ethnic Heritage Landmarks
- ☐ Lower Fort Garry, a well-preserved stone fort dating to the 1830s.
- ☐ Steinbach Mennonite Heritage Village, portraying the way of life of the settlers who migrated from the Ukraine.
- ☐ Gimli, the hub of Icelandic culture in Manitoba, once the capital of New Iceland.

Natural Spectacles and Adventure Trips
- ☐ Riding Mountain National Park.
- ☐ The *Hudson Bay* train trip, which travels across the tundra to Churchill on the rim of the Bay, a mecca for nature lovers eager to see polar bears and beluga whales.

see the Exchange and the stockyards that laid the foundations for the thriving industrial city that Winnipeg is today.

1. ORIENTATION

ARRIVING Winnipeg International Airport (tel. 204/983-8410) is only about 20 minutes west-northwest from the city center (allow 30 to 40 minutes in rush hours). If you take a taxi downtown you'll pay around $10 to $15. Cheapest of all is the city bus ($1.20), which runs approximately every 15 minutes during the day, every• 22 minutes in the evenings, to Portage and Garry.

The following **airlines** have regular flights to and from Winnipeg: Air Canada, 355 Portage Ave. (tel. 204/943-9361); and Canadian Airlines International, 200 Portage Ave. (tel. 204/632-1250).

The **VIA Rail Canada** depot is at Main Street and Broadway. For information on train arrivals and departures, call 204/949-7400.

Greyhound Bus Lines and the bus depot are at 487 Portage Ave., at Colony (tel. 204/783-8840).

If you're driving, just to give you some idea of distance, it's 432 miles (697km) from Minneapolis, and 146 miles (235km) from Grand Forks, N.D.

TOURIST INFORMATION The following will supply you with information: **Travel Manitoba,** 7–155 Carlton St. (tel. 204/945-3777, or toll free 800/665-0040), open from 8am to 4:30pm Monday through Friday in winter, to 9pm daily from the third Monday in May to Labor Day; and **Tourism Winnipeg,** 232-375 York Ave., on the second floor of the Convention Centre (tel. 204/943-1970, or toll

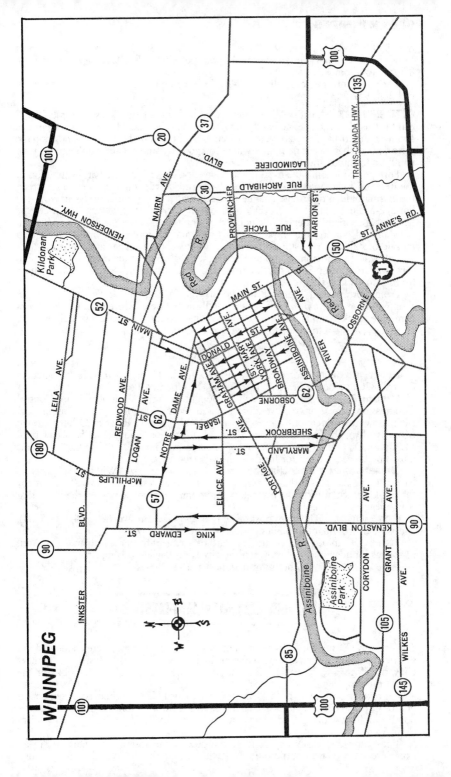

free 800/665-0204), open weekdays from 8:30am to 4:30pm, or at the Airport InfoCentre, Winnipeg International Airport (tel. 204/774-0031), open daily from 8:30am to 10pm.

For parks information, call 204/945-6784; for taped instant tourist information, call 204/942-2535.

CITY LAYOUT   A native Winnipegger who had come east once said to me, "I still can't get used to the confined and narrow streets in the east." When you see Portage and Main, each 132 feet wide (that's 10 yards off the width of a football field), and the eerie flatness that means no matter where you go you can see where you're going, then you'll understand why.

Portage and Main is the focal point of the city, which is situated at the junction of the Red and Assiniboine rivers. The Red River runs north-south, as does Main Street; the Assiniboine and Portage Avenue run east-west. Going north on Main from the Portage-Main junction will bring you to the City Hall, Exchange District, the Manitoba Centennial Centre (including the Manitoba Theatre Centre), the Museum of Man and Nature, the Ukrainian Museum, and on into the North End, once a mosaic of cultures, and still dotted with bulbous church domes and authentic delis visited by lost souls from Edmonton and west. (*Warning:* At night you are advised to stay away from Main Street north beyond the Arts Centre, unless you're reporting on fleabag hotels and skid row.)

From Portage and Main, if you go six blocks west along Portage, the main shopping drag, and two blocks south, you'll hit the new Convention Centre. From here, one block south and two blocks west brings you to the Legislative Building, the art gallery, and south, just across the river, to Osborne Village.

FAST FACTS

Emergencies   For medical assistance, dial 911 or call the Health Sciences Centre, 820 Sherbrook St. (tel. 204/774-6511). Open 24 hours.

Liquor Laws   Liquor can only be bought from the Manitoba Liquor Control Commission stores, or from vendors licensed by the Liquor Control Commission. Main downtown locations are: 923 Portage Ave. and 471 River at Osborne (open Monday through Thursday from 10am to 10pm, on Friday and Saturday until 11:30pm). On Sunday drinks may only be served with food, and the tab for drinks must not exceed the tab for food—otherwise forget it.

Newspapers and Magazines   For a city its size, Winnipeg is lucky to have two newspapers—the *Winnipeg Free Press* and the *Winnipeg Sun*—many foreign-language weeklies, plus eight community newspapers. Get the idea that Winnipeggers enjoy politics?

Post Office   The main post office is at 266 Graham Ave. (tel. 204/983-5481), and is open from 8am to 5:30pm Monday through Friday.

Time   Winnipeg is on central standard time except from the last Sunday in April to the last Sunday in October, when the city is on daylight saving time.

Weather   For weather information, dial 204/983-2050.

2. GETTING AROUND

The extensive Winnipeg Transit system makes it easy and cheap. There is a downtown shuttle (99 DASH), which visits many attractions for free. For information contact **City of Winnipeg Transit,** 421 Osborne St. (tel. 204/986-5700). Look for the DASH bus stop signs.

For regular buses, you need $1.20 in exact change (65¢ for children or seniors) to board. Call 204/986-5700 for route and schedule information, or visit the information booth in the Portage and Main concourse, open Monday to Friday from 9:45am to 5:45pm.

Taxis can most easily be found at the downtown hotels. As usual, they're an expensive form of transportation: $2.25 when the meter drops and $1.67 per mile thereafter. Try **Duffy's Taxi** (tel. 204/772-2451 or 204/775-0101), or **Unicity Taxi** (tel. 204/947-6611 or 204/942-3366).

Driving is no problem in Winnipeg, but watch out for the pedestrian walks marked with an X, and note that Manitoba has a stringent drunken driving law. A blood-alcohol level of 0.08 or higher means a conviction—don't take chances. You can also be fined for failure to fasten your seat belt.

For car rentals, **Tilden** is located downtown at 283 Ellice at Smith Street (tel. 204/942-3525) and also at the airport (tel. 204/783-2854). **Budget** has four offices: downtown at the corner of Ellice and Sherbrook (tel. 204/989-8505), at 1355 Regent Ave. (tel. 204/989-8520), at 1765 Sargent Ave. (tel. 204/989-8500), and at the airport (tel. 204/989-8510). **Avis** is located at 1350 King Edward (tel. 204/632-6615) and at 730 Portage Ave. in the Chrysler dealership (tel. 204/774-4581).

3. ACCOMMODATIONS

In the past, many hotels were established primarily to serve liquor, not to provide hospitality. As far as possible I have avoided such places, but it's still true that every hotel, first class or no, will have a large beverage room attached, which will be purely functional, somewhat loud, and often too boisterous for the average traveler.

Note: To all the rates that follow, add the 7% provincial sales tax and the GST. Both are refundable.

STAYING ON A FARM   To really get the feel of the prairies there's no better way than to stay for a while on a farm. The **Manitoba Country Vacations Association,** R.R. 1, Elm Creek, Winnipeg, MB, R0G 0N0 (tel. 204/436-2599), is the organization to contact for detailed information about farm accommodations. Rates average $50 a day for adults, $25 for children—a very reasonable price for such an exciting, authentic experience.

DOWNTOWN
EXPENSIVE

DELTA WINNIPEG, 288 Portage Ave. (at Smith St.), Winnipeg, MB, R3C 0B8. Tel. 204/956-0410, or toll free 800/877-1133 in the U.S. Fax 204/947-1129. 272 rms. A/C MINIBAR TV TEL
$ Rates: Weekdays $150 single or double. Weekend packages available. AE, DC, ER, MC, V. **Parking:** $6.50.
Two blocks west of the Westin stands the Delta Winnipeg. On floors 15 through 29 you'll find recently redecorated guest rooms, all with color TVs, hairdryers, coffee makers, and AM/FM radios.
Dining/Entertainment: Like the rooms, all the restaurants offer good views of the city. They include the candlelit, oak-paneled Signature's for fine dining and piano entertainment. On the main floor is Tillie's, where sports events are shown on a big TV screen.
Facilities: Other amenities include a lovely indoor pool with an outdoor deck, a whirlpool, a sauna, an exercise room, twin cinemas, and a free Children's Creative Centre (supervised on weekends) where kids can enjoy games, toys, and crafts activities. An indoor promenade connects the hotel to Eaton Place and Portage Place. A business lounge is on the 13th floor.

HOLIDAY INN CROWNE PLAZA, 350 St. Mary's Ave., Winnipeg, MB, R3C 3J2. Tel. 204/942-0551. Fax 204/943-8702. 389 rms. A/C MINIBAR TV TEL
$ Rates: $142 single; $157 double. Children under 18 stay free in parents' room. Weekend packages available. AE, DC, DISC, ER, MC, V. **Parking:** $7.50.
Right downtown and connected by skywalk to the Convention Centre, you'll find the Holiday Inn Crowne Plaza, with its rooms spread over 17 floors. The rooms are pleasantly decorated, and besides the usual accoutrements they offer remote-control

color TV with in-room movies. Poolside rooms are a couple of dollars more than standard rooms.

Dining/Entertainment: Dining facilities include J. J. Hargraves and Son, for all-day dining, and Between Friends, serving Mexican, Asian, and French food. There's also a piano bar, Tickers Lounge.

Services: 24-hour room service.

Facilities: There's a skylit indoor pool as well as an outdoor pool; both have been attractively designed with potted plants, terraces, and adjacent exercise facilities.

PLACE LOUIS RIEL ALL-SUITE HOTEL, 190 Smith St. (at St. Mary's), Winnipeg, MB, R3C 1J8. Tel. 204/947-6961. Fax 204/947-3029. 288 rms. A/C TV TEL

$ Rates: $115 single or double studio suite; $125 single or double one-bedroom suite. Extra person $10. Children under 16 stay free in parents' room. Weekend package available. AE, ER, MC, V. **Parking:** Free.

Right in the heart of downtown Winnipeg there's a bargain that shouldn't be passed up. At the Place Louis Riel All-Suite Hotel you can stay in a studio (with a sleeping/living area partitioned from the kitchen) or a beautifully furnished one- or two-bedroom suite. All come with a fully equipped kitchen (including a microwave and coffee maker) and dining area. For convenience, a laundry, grocery store, and restaurant and lounge are located on the ground floor of the 23-floor building.

SHERATON WINNIPEG, 161 Donald St., Winnipeg, MB, R3C 1M3. Tel. 204/942-5300, or toll free 800/325-3535. Fax 204/942-5300. 273 rms. A/C TV TEL

$ Rates: $155 double with one queen-size bed; $159 deluxe room. Extra person $15. Children 18 and under stay free in parents' room. Weekend and other discounts available. AE, DISC, ER, MC, V. **Parking:** $6.

One block from the Convention Centre and Eaton Place, the Sheraton offers large rooms furnished in pastels and appointed with remote-control TVs, two telephones, and hairdryers. There's an attractive restaurant, and off the lobby, a piano bar plus a whirlpool, sauna, swimming pool, and sun deck, as well as 24-hour room service. Guests can use the facilities at Broadview Fitness (squash, racquetball, running track).

WESTIN WINNIPEG, 2 Lombard Place, Winnipeg, MB, R3B 0Y3. Tel. 204/957-1350, or toll free 800/228-3000. Fax 204/949-1486. 350 rms. A/C MINIBAR TV TEL

AN IMPORTANT NOTE ON PRICES

Unless stated otherwise, **the prices cited in this guide are given in Canadian dollars,** which is good news for U.S. travelers because the Canadian dollar is worth 25% less than the American dollar, but buys nearly as much. As we go to press, $1 Canadian is worth 75¢ U.S., which means that your $100-a-night hotel room will cost only U.S. $75, and your $6 breakfast costs only U.S. $4.50.

Here's a quick table of equivalents:

Canadian $	U.S. $
$ 1	$ 0.75
5	3.75
10	7.50
20	15.00
50	37.50
80	60.00
100	75.00
200	150.00

$ Rates: $140 medium room; $160 deluxe room. Weekend packages available. AE, ER, MC, V. **Parking:** $7.50.

Right at the corner of Portage and Main rises the 21-story white concrete Westin Hotel Winnipeg, a few minutes' walk from the Manitoba Centennial Centre. Its rooms are furnished with white colonial-style pieces and the usual modern appointments.

Dining/Entertainment: The Velvet Glove, one of the top restaurants in Canada, features luxurious dining amid gilt-framed portraits, wood paneling, brass torchères, semicircular booths, and the soothing sounds of a harpist. Start your dinner with beluga malossol caviar or less extravagantly with the pâté maison, and continue with médaillons of reindeer, chicken and prawn Cajun, or any of the other gourmet dishes. Prices range from $19 to $30. Chocolate cherries, served with your coffee, are just part of the impeccable service, and if you desire that over-$100 bottle of wine, it's available.

For a more casual ambience, at breakfast or lunch, head for Chimes. Downstairs in the shopping concourse you'll find the Café Express coffee shop, open from 6:30am to 4pm daily.

Services: 24-hour room service.

Facilities: There's an indoor pool on the 21st floor, and a whirlpool, fitness center, and sauna, too.

MODERATE

BEST WESTERN CARLTON INN, 220 Carlton St., Winnipeg, MB, R3C 1P5. Tel. 204/942-0881. Fax 204/949-9312. 109 rms. A/C TV TEL
$ Rates: $56 single; $61 double. Extra person $3. Children under 12 stay free in parents' room. AE, DC, DISC, ER, MC, V. **Parking:** Free.

The Best Western has an excellent location just across from the Convention Centre, and offers an outdoor swimming pool and sun deck as well as a sauna.

Creating a Mediterranean mood is the inn's Greek restaurant, Mr. Greek (tel. 204/942-3000), serving Greek specialties as well as a regular menu.

CHARTERHOUSE, York and Hargrave Sts., Winnipeg, MB, R3C 0N9. Tel. 204/942-0101, or toll free 800/782-0175. Fax 204/956-0665. 90 rms. A/C TV TEL
$ Rates: $90 or double. Extra person $7. Seniors stay for $48 any night; children under 16 stay free in parents' room. Weekend package $49. AE, CB, DC, DISC, ER, MC, V. **Parking:** Free.

 Right downtown a block from the Convention Centre, the Charterhouse opened its doors in 1960 but has since been extensively remodeled and now offers attractively decorated rooms with all the modern accoutrements. Some 45 of them have balconies. There's an outdoor swimming pool and a deck/patio.

The Rib Room is well known locally for really good prime rib, ribs, steaks, and seafood. Dinner might begin with escargots bourguignons and continue with rack of lamb or Winnipeg goldeye or the locally famous ribs priced from $13 to $24. Reasonable table d'hôte meals are also available in this warm, wood-paneled room with its large copper-flued fireplace and otherwise simple table settings. The coffee shop is open from 7am to 11:30pm for hearty and inexpensive meals.

MARLBOROUGH WINNIPEG, 331 Smith St. (at Portage), Winnipeg, MB, R3B 2G9. Tel. 204/942-6411, or toll free 800/667-7666. Fax 204/942-2017. 148 rms. A/C TV TEL
$ Rates: $75 single or double. Extra person $7. Children under 18 stay free in parents' room. Special weekend (Fri–Sun) rates available. AE, DC, ER, MC, V. **Parking:** Free with room.

Originally built in 1914, the Marlborough retains its vaulted ceilings, stained-glass windows, and Victorian Gothic exterior, but offers all modern amenities. Most of the guest rooms have been recently renovated.

Dining/Entertainment: Victor's, a two-story-high room with Gothic arches, stained-glass windows, oak paneling, brass chandeliers, wingback chairs, and love seats, is for romantic dining. The menu lists gourmet items like steak/lobster combo and prawns Marco Polo (stuffed with coconut and chutney and fried in beer batter). Joanna's coffee shop, featuring a solid-oak hammerbeam ceiling, a row of iron lamps, and a distinctive clock, is comfortable for breakfast. And finally there's a cocktail lounge.

TRAVELODGE HOTEL WINNIPEG DOWNTOWN, 360 Colony St., Winnipeg, MB, R3B 2P3. Tel. 204/786-7011, or toll free 800/661-9563. Fax 204/772-1443. 160 rms. A/C TV TEL
$ Rates: $68 single; $75 double. Extra person $6. Children under 16 stay free in parents' room. AE, DC, DISC, ER, MC, V. **Parking:** $2.
Located on Portage at Colony, quite near the art gallery, the Travelodge offers rooms furnished in light oak, each with a bed, a desk, armchairs, and a table, decorated in gray and mauve. Bathrooms contain phones and full amenities. Other facilities include a restaurant, a whirlpool, and an indoor swimming pool.

BUDGET

GORDON DOWNTOWNER, 330 Kennedy St., Winnipeg, MB, R3B 2M6. Tel. 204/943-5581. Fax 204/338-4348. 40 rms. A/C TV TEL
$ Rates: $46–$48 single; $49–$52 double. Extra person $6. Children under 16 stay free in parents' room. AE, DC, ER, MC, V.
Probably the best budget hotel downtown is the Gordon Downtowner, part of Portage Place. The rooms have all been renovated recently. Added touches in each bathroom include an extra phone and sliding panels on the shower-bath. Amenities include a pub and a comfortable restaurant (open from 7am to 9pm) where you can get bacon, eggs, toast, and coffee for under $4.

NEAR THE RACETRACK

HOLIDAY INN AIRPORT WEST, 2520 Portage Ave., Winnipeg, MB, R3J 3T6. Tel. 204/885-4478, or toll free 800/665-0352. Fax 204/831-5734. 229 rms (19 suites). A/C TV TEL
$ Rates: $88 single; $98 double; $120 one-bedroom suite with kitchen. Extra person $10. Children under 18 stay free in parents' room. Weekend packages available. AE, DC, DISC, ER, MC, V. **Parking:** Free indoor parking.
Five minutes from the Assiniboia Downs racetrack, and a 10-minute drive from the airport, the Holiday Inn offers superb accommodations, with king-size, queen-size, or two double beds, and amenities including color TVs, clock radios, vanity mirrors with hairdryers, and remote-control pamper panels. One-bedroom suites have fully equipped kitchens, and deluxe apartments are furnished with king-size beds. Note the tropical fish that add a dash of color to the elevators and lobby.
Dining/Entertainment: Facilities include the brass-railed SOS Cocktail Lounge, where you can dance to live music or sit out on comfy couches; and Bell Bottoms Restaurant for all-day dining.
Services: Room service (available 6:30am to 11pm), free limousine service to and from the airport.
Facilities: The stunning tropical atrium contains an indoor pool, whirlpool, sauna, exercise room, and deck for that poolside refreshment. Supervised day room for children.

QUALITY INN WINNIPEG, 367 Ellice, at Carlton, Winnipeg, MB, R3B 1Y1. Tel. 204/956-0100. Fax 204/943-1375. 140 units. A/C TV TEL
$ Rates: $60 single; $68 double. Children under 10 stay free in parents' room. AE, ER, MC, V. **Parking:** Free.
This is a suite hotel, the front section containing 54 mini-suites with full kitchen facilities and daily maid service. The seven-story Tower houses 86 rooms with double, king-size, and queen-size beds, all well appointed and attractively decorated. Facilities include a restaurant, sports bar, whirlpool, and sauna. The hotel is conveniently located for Portage Place.

AWAY FROM THE CENTER
MODERATE

TRAVELODGE EAST, St. Anne's Rd. at Hwy. 1 East, Winnipeg, MB, R2M 0Y5. Tel. 204/255-6000. Fax 204/253-1563. 72 rms. A/C TV TEL
$ Rates: $59 single; $62 double for one person, $67 double for two people. Poolside accommodations $6 extra. Extra person $6. Children 17 and under stay free in parents' room. AE, ER, MC, V. **Parking:** Free.
TraveLodge East is located off on its own near the Canada Mint. Set well back from the highway, it offers attractive rooms with oak and cane furnishings and all modern amenities. Off the spacious tropically themed lobby (palms and wicker set the tone) is the Marquis, a moderately priced family dining room. There's an indoor pool, and oh yes, you can swing your arm at the automatic 12-lane bowling alley in the basement.

VISCOUNT GORT, 1670 Portage Ave., Winnipeg, MB, R3J 0C9. Tel. 204/775-0451. Fax 204/772-2161. 150 rms. A/C TV TEL
$ Rates: $60 single; $64 double. Extra person $6. Children under 18 stay free in parents' room. Weekend rates $56. AE, ER, MC, V. **Parking:** Free.
Viscount Gort offers attractively decorated rooms with all the modern amenities; some units have minibars, and most have balconies. Facilities include a swimming pool, a whirlpool, a sauna, and several eateries and nightspots.

Teddy's, the second-floor gourmet dining room, affects a mock-Tudor decor and ambience. And Weinberg and Wong, the hotel's coffee shop, serves (you guessed it) both bagels and bok choy—it's Chinese/Jewish. On weekends, the Viscount Gort presents a merrie medieval feast; mounds of food are eaten, 12th-century style, with your hands, while jesters and jugglers, magicians and musicians entertain. The cost is $30 per person. There's also a lobby bar.

The Gort's location is convenient—just minutes from the airport, across the street from Polo Park Shopping Centre, and a few blocks from the Winnipeg Arena/Stadium complex.

BUDGET

BOULEVARD MOTEL, 3120 Portage Ave., Winnipeg, MB, R3K 0Y3. Tel. 204/837-5891. 22 rms. A/C TV TEL
$ Rates: $35 single; $37 double; $41 kitchenette unit. Extra person $4. AE, DC, MC, V. **Parking:** Free.
On Portage Avenue, for a basic, clean motel accommodation with color TV, air conditioning, and phone (somewhat ancient in style), stop at the Boulevard Motel.

JOURNEY'S END, 3109 Pembina Hwy., Winnipeg, MB, R3T 4R6. Tel. 204/269-7390. Fax 204/261-7565. 80 rms. A/C TV TEL
$ Rates: $60.99 single; $69.99 double. AE, DC, ER, MC, V. **Parking:** Free.
For reliable, clean, and attractively decorated rooms, the Journey's End is hard to beat.

4. DINING

Not so long ago all the guidebooks advised that if you wanted to eat anything besides steak and potatoes you'd be out of luck in Winnipeg. Times have changed! For some time now it has been possible to eat very well and adventurously in Winnipeg.

For fine hotel dining, visit the **Velvet Glove** at the Westin Hotel Winnipeg, 2 Lombard Place (tel. 204/957-1350), or **Victor's** at the Marlborough Winnipeg, 331 Smith St. (tel. 204/942-6411).

Note: There's a 7% GST plus a 7% sales tax on any food bill above $6.

THE TOP RESTAURANTS

LA VIEILLE GARE, 630 Des Meurons, at bd. Provencher. Tel. 204/237-7072.

Cuisine: FRENCH. **Reservations:** Recommended.
$ Prices: Appetizers $5–$8; main courses $12–$27. AE, DC, ER, MC, V.
Open: Lunch Mon–Fri 11:30am–2pm; dinner daily 5–10pm.

La Vieille Gare is just that—a restaurant set in a 1914 railway station. Alongside is a 1912 dining car retaining its original fittings and glorious walnut interior, which serves as a cocktail lounge at night and a lunch spot during the day. I can heartily recommend the lunch specials, such as beef bourguignon, quenelles Nantua (a dumpling of crabmeat and northern pike mousseline braised in a white chablis sauce), or veal grandmère (sautéed with mushrooms, brandy, and cream). All are priced under $10.

In the main gold-on-brown dining room with its Louis XV–style chairs and a large central fireplace, you can enjoy the finer touches of candlelight and fresh flowers on your table. Appetizers include coquille thermidor with lobster, shrimp and scallops, escargots bourguignons, and frogs' legs in garlic butter or tomato-provençale sauce. Seafood is well represented on the menu—halibut forestière, trout amandine, scampis au Pernod, to name a few dishes. Chicken, veal, and steaks (including Diane and au poivre vert) complete the menu. For dessert, choose among the chocolate cheesecake, baba au rhum, strawberry Bavarian cream pie with Grand Marnier, or the very popular maple-sugar pie.

LE BEAUJOLAIS, 131 Provencher Blvd. at Taché in St. Boniface. Tel. 204/237-6276.
Cuisine: FRENCH. **Reservations:** Recommended.
$ Prices: Appetizers $7–$9; main courses $17–$25. AE, DC, ER, MC, V.
Open: Lunch Mon–Fri 11:30am–2:30pm; dinner daily 5–10pm.

Le Beaujolais is a comfortable French restaurant serving such traditional dishes as grilled chicken with sour-cherry sauce, veal tenderloin with lemon sauce, and rack of lamb.

RESTAURANT DUBROVNIK, 390 Assiniboine Ave. Tel. 204/944-0594.
Cuisine: CONTINENTAL. **Reservations:** Recommended.
$ Prices: Appetizers $7–$20; main courses $16–$24. AE, CB, DC, MC, V.
Open: Lunch Mon–Sat 11:30am–3pm; dinner daily 4:30–11pm.

At Restaurant Dubrovnik, one of my favorite Winnipeg restaurants, owner Milan Bodiroga has gone to great lengths to create a romantic setting for fine continental cuisine supplemented by Eastern European specialties. Having chosen a beautiful Victorian brick town house with working fireplaces and leaded-glass windows, he has enclosed the veranda to create a bi-level dining area; set tables in what used to be the living room, dining room, and center hall; and decorated tastefully with a few plants and colorful Yugoslav weavings, dolls, and gusle (ancient beautifully carved musical instruments, often inlaid with mother-of-pearl).

Start with the Russian borscht or the gibanica, a Yugoslavian pastry-cheese served with mixed greens and sour-cream dressing. Follow with darne of Atlantic salmon grilled or poached with fresh herb sauce or rack of lamb with rosemary. Finish with a coffee Dubrovnik (sljivovica, kruskovac bitters, with coffee, whipped cream, and chopped walnuts) and one of the many fine desserts like crêpes Suzette, cherries jubilee, and other French pastries, and you'll feel as though you've just returned from a vacation on the Mediterranean.

VICTOR'S, in the Marlborough Winnipeg Hotel, 331 Smith St. Tel. 204/947-2751.
Cuisine: CONTINENTAL. **Reservations:** Recommended.
$ Prices: Main courses $15–$22. AE, DC, ER, MC, V.
Open: Lunch Tues–Sat 11:30am–2pm; dinner Tues–Sat 5–9:30pm.

For many years Victor's, now in the Marlborough Winnipeg, was an Osborne Village landmark and dining hit with a reputation for fine cuisine, ambience, and service. Its location in this stately cathedral-ceilinged hotel room of polished mahogany with stained-glass windows continues the tradition. The menu is modern and imaginative, featuring such appetizers as carpaccio and crabmeat cakes with lime mayonnaise and mango relish. To follow, there are several pastas plus such entrées as herb-crusted Cornish hen with cheese polenta; veal médaillons with goose liver, balsamic vinegar sauce, and raspberries; broiled filet of beef with onion strudel; and bouillabaisse.

At lunch the good value is the daily special with soup or salad or you can choose from about 20 or so dishes including pizza with peppered shrimps and sun-dried tomatoes, pastas, sandwiches, and other light dishes.

DOWNTOWN

MODERATE

AMICI, 326 Broadway. Tel. 204/943-4997.
 Cuisine: CONTINENTAL/ITALIAN. **Reservations:** Recommended.
 $ Prices: Appetizers $5–$9; main courses $13–$32. AE, DC, ER, MC, V.
 Open: Lunch Mon–Fri 11:30am–2:30pm; dinner Mon–Thurs 5–10pm, Fri–Sat 5–11pm.

The atmosphere at Amici is plush and comfortable, the tablecloths are coral pink, and partitions are of frosted glass. There are 14 pastas to choose from—fettuccine al salmone or La Traviata (with scallops, red and green peppercorns, diced mango, and pimiento), linguine alla cinese (with black beans, ginger, jalapeño peppers, and chicken), or just plain spaghetti with tomato-basil sauce—as well as meat and fish dishes like médaillons of beef with a Barolo wine sauce, rack of lamb with fennel and tomato, or a fish of the day.

BOMBOLINIS, 326 Broadway. Tel. 204/943-5066.
 Cuisine: ITALIAN. **Reservations:** Recommended.
 $ Prices: Main courses $10–$15. AE, DC, ER, MC, V.
 Open: Mon–Thurs 11:30am–10pm, Fri 11:30am–11:30pm, Sat 4:30–11:30pm.
Bombolinis, downstairs from Amici, is billed as a wine bar, but it also offers a moderately priced menu. The dining room is divided by the bar: One side is light and airy facing the street; the other is more enclosed and cozy. Items include pane casareccio, a kind of pizza with a variety of toppings, about 14 pastas, and a limited selection of main courses like veal piccata, chicken parmigiana, and stracotto (beef tenderloin with raisins and pine nuts).

ICHIBAN, 189 Carlton St. Tel. 204/942-7493.
 Cuisine: JAPANESE. **Reservations:** Recommended.
 $ Prices: Appetizers $4–$5; main courses $13–$24. AE, DC, ER, MC, V.
 Open: Sun–Thurs 4:30–10pm, Fri–Sat 4:30–10:30pm.
Ichiban delights the eye as well as the taste buds with its garden atmosphere, the sounds of Japanese music, and water splashing over a waterwheel. You'll also love it if you're gregarious and have to share a teppan table where you watch the chef prepare your meal, producing steak Ichiban, ebi shrimp (prepared in butter, soya, lemon, and saké), chicken sesame, or the imperial dinner, which consists of gyunku (prime tenderloin), ise ebi (baby lobster), and niwatori (chicken). These dishes will also include an appetizer, soup, and sunomono (a salad of marinated cucumbers with shredded crabmeat).

OLD SWISS INN, 207 Edmonton St. Tel. 204/942-7725.
 Cuisine: SWISS. **Reservations:** Recommended.
 $ Prices: Appetizers $4–$8; main courses $12–$25. AE, DC, ER, MC, V.
 Open: Lunch Mon–Fri 11:30am–2:30pm; dinner Mon–Sat 5–9:30pm.
Expectations should match experience at the Old Swiss Inn, if a Swiss inn signifies unpretentious alpine warmth, wood paneling, pictures of mountain scenery, and Swiss specialties, for this is precisely what you'll find. At dinner, you might start with Swiss onion soup or cheese fondue and follow with quail périgourdine (stuffed with foie gras en croûte) or veal Zurich (with white wine and mushrooms), or the house specialty, fondue bourguignonne. At lunchtime you can have Bratwurst mit Rösti (Swiss fried potatoes).

BUDGET

KUM KOON GARDEN, 257 King St. Tel. 204/943-4655.
 Cuisine: CHINESE. **Reservations:** Recommended.

$ Prices: Main courses $7–$9. AE, MC, V.
　　Open: Lunch Mon–Fri 11am–3pm; dinner Mon–Thurs 5–11pm, Fri–Sat 5pm–1am, Sun 5–10pm.

You'll find many Chinese at Kum Koon Garden. The menu is long and varied, offering eight soups including egg drop with mushrooms ($4 for a large tureen) and special bean curd in a bowl ($5). For main dishes, there's a yummy shrimp with black-bean and garlic sauce, chicken in lemon sauce, beef with broccoli, and a most unusual fish lips with vegetable and assorted meat. At lunchtime there's a buffet and dim sum—sweet lotus bun, chicken in a bun, and so on.

SCHMECKER'S, 101 Mayfair, at Main St. Tel. 204/475-4751.
　　Cuisine: DELI. **Reservations:** Recommended.
$ Prices: Sandwiches and light fare under $6.25; main courses under $15. MC, V.
　　Open: Mon–Fri 11am–4am, Sat 8:30am–4am, Sun 8:30am–2am.

Schmecker's offers a wide range of fare from deli sandwiches, seafood, and steaks to Greek and Italian specialties. You might opt for light fare—a pastrami sandwich on rye or a bagel and cream cheese, both of which come with steak fries and coleslaw. More substantial specials might feature veal parmigiana, chicken Cordon Bleu, or souvlaki. For dessert there are delicious fresh-baked pastries and cakes. A wide variety of teas is also available. Schmecker's is a good place to know about since there aren't too many eating establishments in Winnipeg that stay open late.

SHANGRI-LA, on the second floor of the Convention Centre. Tel. 204/942-2281.
　　Cuisine: CHINESE. **Reservations:** Recommended, especially on weekends.
$ Prices: Main courses $7–$10. AE, MC, V.
　　Open: Mon–Thurs 11:30am–11pm, Fri–Sat 11:30am–midnight, Sun 11:30am–10pm.

Shangri-La is a popular spot, offering elegant Cantonese dining. Having started his first restaurant in 1972, Park Lee, who once worked as a bellhop at the Winnipeg Inn, now owns several establishments. The menu is extensive, with some unusual dishes like pork spareribs in black-bean and garlic sauce or bean cake and barbecued pork, along with chop suey, chow mein, and egg foo yung dishes.

OSBORNE VILLAGE

Old buildings in Osborne Village, located just behind the Legislative Building across the Assiniboine River, have been renovated to house some unique shopping and some of the prettiest and most reasonable restaurants in Winnipeg.

BASIL'S, 117 Osborne St. Tel. 204/453-8440.
　　Cuisine: LIGHT FARE. **Reservations:** Recommended.
$ Prices: Salads and main courses $8.50–$10. AE, DC, ER, MC, V.
　　Open: Mon–Thurs 11am–12:30am, Fri–Sat 11am–1:30am, Sun 3:30–11:30pm.

The boast on the menu "We do the unusual right" is very apropos of Basil's, and refers equally well to the food and the decor. As soon as you walk in you're faced with a cabinet full of delicious bakery items—éclairs, almond croissants, apple strudel, fruit tortes, almond chocolate, and Swiss zuger kirsch. Beyond the dessert showcase there are three dining areas, each with wonderfully textured wall hangings, macramé lampshades, and a lowered cedar ceiling. There's also a cocktail lounge and an open-air courtyard café. The food focuses on superfresh salads, and charbroiled chicken and beef. Side dishes include pasta salads, shrimp, potato skins, and ratatouille. And there are 12 different coffees available.

TEA COZY, 99 Osborne St. Tel. 204/475-1027.
　　Cuisine: LIGHT FARE. **Reservations:** Accepted.
$ Prices: Most items under $9. MC, V.
　　Open: Mon–Thurs 10am–6pm, Fri–Sat 10am–midnight, Sun 11am–6pm.

Upstairs at this address you'll find a charming tearoom, the Tea Cozy. During the day it serves such delights (especially to the English) as fresh-from-the-oven hot tea biscuits with Devonshire cream and strawberry preserves, and hot buttered crumpets, both of which I can heartily recommend. Sandwiches, quiche, and wienerschnitzel on toast are also available, as are daily specials—perhaps quiche and coq au vin—served with fresh-baked Irish soda bread and salad.

CHINATOWN

Winnipeg has a small Chinatown—one block bounded by King and Princess Streets and Rupert and James Avenues.

MARIGOLD, 245 King St. Tel. 204/944-9400.
   Cuisine: CHINESE. **Reservations:** Accepted.
   $ Prices: Most dishes $5–$12. AE, DC, ER, MC, V.
   Open: Mon–Thurs 11am–midnight, Fri–Sat 11am–1am, Sun 11am–9pm.
For Chinese food in elegant surroundings, go to Marigold in Chinatown Plaza, and sit yourself down in a modern brown upholstered chair that goes with the cream tablecloth and broadloom and sample some Cantonese fare. There are many soups to choose from, plus such specialties as beef with cashew nuts and sliced beef with ginger and green onions. Dim sum (about 30 selections) average $1.75 to $2.75 a plate; it's served from 11am to 3:30pm. There are also eight locations throughout the city.

BROADWAY & SHERBROOK STREET AREA
MODERATE

ACROPOLIS, 172 Sherbrook St. Tel. 204/775-8927.
   Cuisine: GREEK. **Reservations:** Recommended on weekends.
   $ Prices: Main courses $10–$18. AE, DC, ER, MC, V.
   Open: Mon–Thurs 11:30am–11pm, Fri–Sat 11:30am–midnight, Sun 4:30–9pm.
The name gives it away. The statues, fountains, and arcades merely confirm that Acropolis serves Greek food. Here you can watch lamb turn on the spit and the gyro slowly spinning, while you begin your meal with avgolemono soup, or more adventurously with octopus in oil and vinegar. Choose your main course from such specialties as arni (barbecued lamb), moussaka, and beef, pork, or chicken souvlaki, or grape leaves. There are also steak and seafood North American–style entrées. Or try the Greek God—a sampler of all major Greek dishes. Entrées come with soup or salad. For dessert there's galactomboureco (custard in phyllo with cinnamon) with Greek wild mountain tea. At lunchtime, and you can enjoy such things as a mini-souvlaki in a pita, or a Ulysses boat (gyro in a pita), as well as sandwiches, salads, and omelets.

BISTRO DANSK, 63 Sherbrook St. Tel. 204/775-5662.
   Cuisine: DANISH. **Reservations:** Recommended.
   $ Prices: Main courses $7.50–$13. V.
   Open: Lunch Mon–Sat 11am–3pm; dinner Mon–Sat 5–9:30pm.
In this warm chalet-style bistro, bright-red gate-back chairs complement the wooden tables and raffia placemats. The classical background music complements the unusually friendly and serene atmosphere. Main courses include seven superlative Danish specialties, such as frikadeller (Danish meat patties, made from ground veal and pork, served with red cabbage and potato salad), aeggekage (a Danish omelet with bacon, garnished with tomato and green onions, and served with home-baked Danish bread), and Cornish hen stuffed with walnuts and apricots. Dessert specials might include hazelnut pie. At lunchtime, besides salads and an omelet or two, there are nine or so open-face sandwiches available, served on homemade rye or white bread, most priced from $3 to $6.

INDIA CURRY HOUSE, 595 Broadway. Tel. 204/775-1150.
   Cuisine: INDIAN. **Reservations:** Required, especially on weekends.
   $ Prices: Main courses $6–$20. MC, V.
   Open: Lunch Mon–Fri 11am–2pm; dinner daily 5pm–midnight.
Not far around the corner on Broadway you'll find some excellent Indian cuisine at the popular India Curry House. Behind the unprepossessing exterior is a large, very low-lit room cut in half by a curtain of beads. The walls are decorated with batik pictures depicting mythology (lit creatively from behind). In the evening, start your meal with samosa or bhujia (meat patties or spiced vegetable fritters), and proceed to

the tandoori specialties or such entrées as chicken masala (cooked in eggs and curry sauce) or the chicken biryani with 21 spices. Lobster and crab curry can be ordered 48 hours in advance. All dinners include rice, onion, salad, and pappadum (crisp Indian bread). A choice of Indian sweets is available.

BUDGET

IMPRESSIONS CAFE, 102 Sherbrook. Tel. 204/772-8049.
   Cuisine: LIGHT FARE. **Reservations:** Not accepted.
   $ Prices: Most items under $9. V.
   Open: Mon–Fri 9am–midnight, Sat–Sun 10am–midnight.
Impressions Café is the kind of place where you can linger all day playing chess, reading, writing, or chatting. It's also the kind of place to clue into what's happening in the city culturally. Salads, sandwiches, and omelets are always available, along with specials like the falafel plate or the vegetarian lasagne. Wine and beer only.

MING COURT, 236 Edmonton St. Tel. 204/949-1087.
   Cuisine: CHINESE. **Reservations:** Recommended.
   $ Prices: Most dishes under $8. AE, DC, ER, MC, V.
   Open: Lunch Mon–Fri 11:30am–2:30pm; dinner Mon–Sat 5pm–1am, Sun 5–10pm.
A fine Chinese restaurant featuring northern cuisine, Ming Court, in a bi-level paneled room, has a pleasant atmosphere. It offers a variety of dishes, including beef with oyster sauce, moo shu pork, and lamb casserole.

THE NORTH END

The North End was once a thriving mosaic of cultures as evidenced by the delis that stretch along Main Street to which ex-Winnipeggers who have migrated to Montréal, Chicago, or Vancouver still return.

ALYCIA'S, 559 Cathedral. Tel. 204/582-8789.
   Cuisine: UKRAINIAN. **Reservations:** Recommended.
   $ Prices: Main courses $5–$9. AE, DC, ER, MC, V.
   Open: Mon–Sat 8am–8pm.
Alycia's, at the corner of McGregor, serves traditional home-style Ukrainian cuisine. Woven tablecloths cover the tables, and painted eggs and Ukrainian china decorate the small homey restaurant. Feast on pirogies, kolbassa, pickerel, hamburger, and roast turkey.

KELEKIS, 1100 Main St. Tel. 204/582-1786.
   Cuisine: BURGERS/HOT DOGS. **Reservations:** Not accepted.
   $ Prices: Burgers and hot dogs from $2.50; main courses under $10. No credit cards.
   Open: Mon–Sat 8am–midnight, Sun 9am–midnight.
Hamburgers and hot dogs are the attraction at this famous and always crowded spot, and they really are first class! More substantial dishes are available—for example, two grilled pork chops, deep-fried jumbo shrimp, or grilled ham steak (all served with coleslaw and either french fries or mashed potatoes).

OSCAR'S, 1204 Main St. Tel. 204/582-7128.
   Cuisine: DELI.
   $ Prices: Sandwiches $3.25. No credit cards.
   Open: Mon–Fri 8am–4pm, Sat 8am–3pm.
There's not a corned beef sandwich as good or as thick as those at Oscar's anywhere else on the North American continent. Thick slices of rye stuffed with either corned beef, turkey, roast beef, pastrami, or salami, go for incredibly low prices.

ALONG PORTAGE AVENUE

PARADISE RESTAURANT, 789 Portage Ave. Tel. 204/772-2539.
   Cuisine: ITALIAN. **Reservations:** Recommended.
   $ Prices: Pasta courses $7–$11; main courses $13–$16. AE, DC, ER, MC, V.

Open: Mon–Thurs 11am–12:30am, Fri 11am–1:30am, Sat 4pm–1:30am, Sun 4–11pm.

For Italian food, people swear by the Paradise Restaurant, where you can either order a pizza ($13 for a 12-inch pie with two toppings), or dine by candlelight in a warm room split down the middle by exposed brick walls with wrought-iron gates. The usual selection of pastas—cannelloni, spaghetti alla napoletana—and such specialties as veal scaloppine alla marsala, chicken cacciatore, or veal chops pizzaiola are available, along with special Paradise dishes such as melanzane piene (eggplant with meat filling). For dessert there's always spumoni.

RAE AND JERRY'S STEAKHOUSE, 1405 Portage Ave. Tel. 204/783-6155.

Cuisine: CANADIAN. **Reservations:** Recommended.

$ Prices: Appetizers $3–$7; main courses $16–$30. AE, DC, DISC, ER, MC, V.

Open: Mon–Sat 11am–midnight, Sun and holidays 11am–8:30pm.

Rae and Jerry's has been and remains a veritable Winnipeg institution. Set in a large low-lit room with slatted-wood walls and simple furniture, the restaurant serves complete dinners that include soup or juice, salad or vegetable, potato, and choice of beverage. Main dishes run the gamut from chicken Kiev to broiled lobster tail, with a lot of steaks, roast beef, and fish dishes in between. There's also a selection of sandwiches, hamburgers, and omelets (all under $7) for lunch.

AROUND TOWN

The restaurants that follow fit into no particular area but are well-known local eateries.

HAYNES CHICKEN SHACK, 257 Lulu St. Tel. 204/774-2764.

Cuisine: HOME COOKING. **Reservations:** Recommended.

$ Prices: Main courses $9–$13. MC, V.

Open: Lunch Mon–Fri noon–2:30pm; dinner Wed–Sun 5–11pm.

A small white house in the middle of a residential area somewhere between downtown and the airport, Haynes Chicken Shack offers good home-style cooking and a family welcome. The tasty home-style cooking includes southern fried chicken, barbecued spareribs, shrimp Créole, breaded shrimp, and T-bone steak. All these dishes come with french fries, coleslaw, and hot biscuits. For dessert there's ice cream.

MANDARIN, 613 Sargent Ave. Tel. 204/775-7819.

Cuisine: CHINESE. **Reservations:** Recommended.

$ Prices: Most items $6–$8. AE, MC, V.

Open: Dinner Tues–Sun 4–10pm.

Owner Hu Wang hails from northern China, and so Mandarin specializes in Szechuan-style cuisine such as shredded beef with Mandarin hot sauce and chicken with hot pickled pepper. Try one of the unusual soups—perhaps shredded meat and hot pickle soup. The two most famous dishes here, however, require one day's notice—the sizzling rice shrimp or Harvest in Snow, which can only be described as golden puffs of chicken and pork with other ingredients on a bed of angel-hair vermicelli, served with salad and eight pancakes (both are $26 for two). The Mandarin is attractive, its stucco walls hung with photos of old China.

Mr. Wang has another restaurant, **The River Mandarin,** at 252 River Ave. (tel. 204/284-8963); it's open Monday through Saturday from noon to midnight and is fancier and more expensive.

LITTLE INDIA BY THE UNIVERSITY

INDIA GARDENS, 764 McDermot Ave., at Emily St. Tel. 204/783-0306.

Cuisine: INDIAN. **Reservations:** Recommended.

$ Prices: Curries $7–$10; dinner buffets $6.95–$8.95. AE, ER, MC, V.

Open: Lunch Mon–Fri 11am–2pm; dinner Mon–Sat 5–9pm.

If you're looking for really good Indian food, served in a semielegant setting, then head for the University of Manitoba and India Gardens.

Don't be put off by the exterior. Inside, owner Kamal Mehra, who hails from New

Delhi, has installed comfortable upholstered chairs, a well-chosen beautiful Rajasthan tapestry, and several batik silk prints. It's a popular place (especially with the university medical students across the street), where people come for superlative curries. At lunch, besides the Indian specialties, you can have a deli sandwich for under $5. The regular vegetarian buffet every Tuesday night is a crowd pleaser and so, too, on Thursday is the mixed vegetable and meat buffet.

ST. BONIFACE

RED LANTERN, 302 Hamel Ave. Tel. 204/233-4841.
   Cuisine: CONTINENTAL. **Reservations:** Recommended.
$ Prices: Main courses $13–$17. AE, ER, MC, V.
   Open: Lunch daily 11am–2pm; dinner daily 5–10pm.
Over in St. Boniface there's a delightful little house called the Red Lantern that does indeed sport a red lantern without, and a long, narrow beamed two-tier dining room within that is cozy. The food is excellent, nicely presented, graciously served, and very reasonably priced. French background music adds to the atmosphere.

ON THE PEMBINA HIGHWAY

D' 8 SCHTOVE, 1842 Pembina Hwy. Tel. 204/275-2294.
   Cuisine: MENNONITE. **Reservations:** Accepted.
$ Prices: Main courses $6–$12. AE, DC, ER, MC, V.
   Open: Mon–Sat 8am–11pm, Sun 9am–11pm.
Occupying a large dining room decorated with brass and wood, this spot specializes in Mennonite fare. Start with one of the borschts—kommst borscht (cabbage with sausages) or summa borscht (with potato)—and follow with jebackte rebspaa (pork ribs baked in tomato sauce), holupche (cabbage rolls), beef Stroganoff, slices of smoked farmer sausage in sweet-and-sour sauce, or the wrenikje, more commonly known as pirogies. Top it all off with rhubarb or apple strudel.

5. ATTRACTIONS

THE TOP ATTRACTIONS

THE FORKS MARKET AREA

   At the junction of the Red and Assiniboine rivers, the Forks is a major city attraction. A community grew up here encouraged by the trade and river traffic during the fur-trading era; when the railroads came, the river traffic declined, and the Forks declined so that by the 1950s the area had become a railyard. In the late 1980s a $20 million redevelopment program was begun and the result can be seen today. At the core of the development is the Forks Market housed in buildings that once sheltered railroad cars and which are joined by an airy courtyard with a six-story glass tower overlooking the junction of the rivers. In the market fresh produce, meats, fish and specialty food are piled in colorful displays; there are also restaurants, specialty stores, and a variety of programs, exhibits, and events scheduled throughout the year. In summer visitors can stroll along the riverwalks; in winter there's free public skating on outdoor artificial ice or along groomed river trails. For program and other information call 204/943-7752, or 204/957-7618 for recorded information, updated weekly.

WINNIPEG ART GALLERY, 300 Memorial Blvd. Tel. 204/786-6641.

   Easily identifiable because of its triangular site and its bold prismatic mass (it looks like an iceberg or some other oceangoing object afloat) the gallery, opened in 1971, is most famous for its excellent collection of Inuit art and sculpture. Only a fraction is on display on the mezzanine. Note the wry vision of an artist such as Leah Qumaluk Povungnituk as contained in a stonecut of *Birds Stealing Kayak from Man.*
   The main thrust of the remaining collections are Canadiana—important recent shows have included *A Boundless Horizon: A Visual Record of Exploration and*

Settlement in the Manitoba Region, 1624–1874 and *Latitudes and Parallels— Focus on Contemporary Canadian Photography.*

Besides permanent and changing exhibits, the museum also organizes many artistic and cultural events: lectures, concerts (from folk to chamber and contemporary music), dance performances, films, and children's theater. A restaurant and cafeteria are located on the penthouse level as is the Sculpture Court—an outdoor area where large works are exhibited.

Admission: $3 adults, $2 students and seniors, $5 families; free for children age 12 and under.

Open: Sept–June Tues and Thurs–Sun 11am–5pm, Wed 11am–9pm. Late June to mid-Sept Thurs–Tues 11am–5pm, Wed 11am–9pm.

MANITOBA MUSEUM OF MAN AND NATURE, 190 Rupert Ave. Tel. 204/943-3139 for recorded information.

Part of the Manitoba Centennial Centre, the museum galleries depict aspects of local history, culture, and geology. The Earth History Gallery portrays the creation of the universe, the prehistoric era, the Ice Age, and the geologic formation of Manitoba. The Grasslands Gallery traces the history of the prairies from the days when Native Canadian tribes hunted the buffalo, through the fur-trading era, to the early settlement and the immigrant boom of the late 1800s. In the Urban Gallery, walk down a 1920s Winnipeg street past typical homes and businesses of the era. The Boreal Forest Gallery depicts Manitoba's most northerly forested region. Climb aboard the *Nonsuch,* a full-size replica of the 17th-century ketch that returned to England in 1669 with the first cargo of furs out of Hudson Bay. There's also an Arctic-Subarctic Gallery where the interdependence of Hudson Bay residents with their environment is explored. In each of these areas you'll find life-size exhibits such as a buffalo hunt, prehistoric creatures, pioneer life, pronghorn antelope, teepees, sod huts, log cabins—a fascinating place.

Admission: $3.50 adults, $2.50 students, $2.25 senior citizens and children ages 4–12.

Open: Victoria Day–Labor Day daily 10am–6pm. Labor Day–Victoria Day Tues–Sun 10am–4pm.

MANITOBA PLANETARIUM, 190 Rupert Ave. Tel. 204/943-3142 for recorded information, or 204/956-2830.

The planetarium, part of the Manitoba Museum of Man and Nature in the Manitoba Centennial Centre, offers a variety of multimedia feature shows in the 280-seat Star Theatre. You might explore cosmic catastrophes, speculate on the reality of UFOs, or travel to the edge of the universe, all in living-room comfort. Hundreds of projectors work in concert to fill the semicircular dome of the theater with stellar imagery, while the 154 separate projectors of the Zeiss planetarium instrument are geared so accurately that they can show the sky as our ancestors saw it thousands of years ago, or as people will see it far in the future. The Touch the Universe Gallery is a "hands-on" science gallery that encourages visitors to use their senses to experience the consequences of the laws of nature. Participants are encouraged to touch, pull, push, study, spin, walk into, talk to, and observe.

Admission: Planetarium $4 adults, $3 students, $2.25 seniors and children ages 4–12. Touch the Universe Gallery $3 adults, $2.25 students, $2 seniors and children 12 and under. Both are free for children 3 and under.

Open: Planetarium shows presented daily from mid-May to Labor Day, Tues–Sun the rest of the year. Touch the Universe open Victoria Day–Labor Day daily 10am–7pm; Sept 3–May 31 Tues–Fri 10am–4pm, Sat–Sun and holidays 10am–5pm.

IMPRESSIONS

With the thermometer at 30 below zero and the wind behind him, a man walking on Main Street in Winnipeg knows which side of him is which.
—STEPHEN LEACOCK, *MY DISCOVERY OF THE WEST*, 1937

THE UKRAINIAN CULTURAL AND EDUCATIONAL CENTRE, 184 Alexander Ave. East. Tel. 204/942-0218.

⭐ Just up the street from the Museum of Man and Nature is the Oseredok, or Ukrainian Centre, which devotes itself to conserving the artifacts and heritage of the Ukranian people. Housed in a restored old cast-iron building, it has a ground-floor boutique and reception area. The second-floor art gallery and fifth-floor museum are used for changing exhibits ranging from 18th-century icons to folk art (embroideries, weaving, Easter eggs, wood carving, ceramics, clothing, etc.). The center also offers lectures and film programs.

Admission: Free.
Open: Tues–Sat 10am–4pm, Sun 2–5pm.

ROYAL CANADIAN MINT, 520 Lagimodière Blvd. Tel. 204/257-3359.

The drive to the mint, which lies south of Winnipeg, will sketch and capture the feeling of the west—as you pass the Union stockyards, grain elevators, and boxcars etched against the horizon. At the end of your trip the mint rises up, a gleaming glass pyramid.

Here you will be taken on a truly mind-boggling tour of the engineering processes required to make money—the stages involved in producing dies, a roof crane lifting 4,000-pound strips of bronze and nickel, three 150-ton presses stamping out up to 8,800 coin blanks per minute, and the coining presses turning out up to 18,000 coins per hour to the telling machines that count the number for bagging. A bag of 5,000 dimes, by the way, weighs 23 pounds. The whole process from start to finish represents an extraordinary engineering feat, from the overhead cranes to the conveyor belt that carries the blanks up and down into the furnaces, dropping under the floors to deliver the metals from one room to the next, to the overhead monorail that delivers those same blanks to the coining presses. You will also see a film on contemporary minting operations.

Admission: $2 adults; free for children under 6.
Open: Tours given every 30 minutes Mon–Fri 9am–3pm. **Directions:** Take Main Street south over the Assiniboine/Red rivers, turn left onto Marion Street, and then right onto Lagimodière. You'll see the mint rise up just beyond the Trans Canada Highway (Route 135).

MORE ATTRACTIONS

THE GOLDEN BOY AND THE LEGISLATIVE BUILDING, 450 Broadway. Tel. 204/945-3700.

Author Jack Ludwig probably has captured the meaning of the Golden Boy to Winnipeggers when he said: "I was thinking about it as something corny and silly that has always been corny and silly. Yet, at the same time, it's spatially fixed. People change, people come, people go, people die. But the Golden Boy is like Keats' nightingale. Something so fixed it seems eternal, almost immortal. Golden Boy becomes as mythically important as a Keats nightingale or a Hopkins windhover" (*Speaking of Winnipeg*, edited by John Farr).

There he stands, 240 feet above ground atop the Legislative Building's dome, clutching a sheaf of wheat under his left arm and holding aloft in his right an eternally lit torch symbolizing the spirit of progress (remember, he was sculpted in 1914 or thereabouts, before progress became a dirty word). French sculptor Charles Gardet created his five-ton, 13½-foot bronze statue during World War I, which caused it a somewhat rough passage getting to Winnipeg. First the foundry was bombed, but the statue survived. Then the ship bound for New York was commandeered as a troop ship and the Golden Boy rolled around in the hold for two years, until he was safely delivered after the war to his current perch.

The building below is a magnificent classical Greek structure designed by British architect Frank Worthington Simon, who also designed the Liverpool Cotton Exchange, Liverpool University, and the buildings of the Edinburgh International Exhibition. Construction was completed in 1919. Enter the main lobby and you will be confronted by a grand marble staircase flanked by two enormous bronze buffalos, also the work of Gardet. Climb to the top of the staircase and look down from the legislative antehall into the Pool of the Black Star on the floor below. This chamber, with three steps leading down into it, is a perfect circle surrounded by 16 pillars, and is just one of many examples of the Egyptian influence evident in the building. Note also at the back of the antehall the Frank Brangwyn mural commemorating the First World War. The focal point of the whole building is, of course, the Legislative Chamber, where the 57 members of Manitoba's legislative assembly meet.

Before leaving the area, wander through the 31-acre grounds full of many species of trees, geraniums, and petunias, and note the statues that pay respect to Manitoba's many ethnic groups—Scotland's Robert Burns, French-Canadian Georges-Etienne Cartier, Iceland's Jon Sigurdson, and Ukrainian poet Taras Shevchenko.

Open: Building open spring and summer daily 8:30am–9pm, rest of the year 8:30am–8pm.

DALNAVERT, 61 Carlton St., between Broadway and Assiniboine Ave. Tel. 204/943-2835.

Just two blocks east of the Legislative Building stands one of the few surviving gracious Victorian homes that used to dominate the Winnipeg streetscape. The house has been restored to resemble its appearance in 1895, the year it was built for Hugh John Macdonald, the only son of Canada's first prime minister. It's a fine example of a late Victorian gingerbread house with wraparound veranda. At the time of construction the latest innovations—electric lighting, indoor plumbing, central hot water heating, and walk-in closets—were included. Throughout the house are beautiful stained-glass panels (whose softness of color cannot be duplicated today), elaborate wood paneling, high molded ceilings, wainscoting, and staircases, and masses of overstuffed furniture and ornate drapes. As you go through the house you'll probably wonder at the extraordinary amount of muscle power needed for housework in those days to operate such gadgets as the Dowswell Rocker washer, and how even functional appliances were things of beauty—note the waffle iron with its diamonds, hearts, clubs, and spades design. You can play a guessing game of "What Is It?" as you go around.

Admission: $3 adults, $2 senior citizens and students, $1.50 ages 13–18, $1 children 6–12, $7 families; free for children under 6.

Open: June–Aug Tues–Thurs and Sat–Sun 10am–6pm. Sept–Dec and Mar–May Tues–Thurs and Sat–Sun noon–5pm. Jan–Feb Sat–Sun noon–5pm.

THE COMMODITY EXCHANGE, on the fifth floor of the Commodity Exchange Tower, 360 Main St. Tel. 204/949-0495 to arrange a tour.

Originally organized in 1887 as a grain exchange, the Commodity Exchange changed its name in 1972 to reflect its expansion into oilseeds, rapeseed, and gold. The very crux of Winnipeg was right here: the world's premier grain market until World War II.

Come early, around 9:30am, or at 12:45pm, when you're more likely to see some feverish action on the floor. You have to view the proceedings from a glass-enclosed gallery overlooking the pit where buyers and sellers are jostling, yelling out figures, and gesticulating in apparent confusion, while above current Winnipeg and Chicago prices race by on ticker tape. The pits themselves are raised octagonal carpeted platforms, with descending steps on the inside—a shape that permits all buyers and sellers to see each other. Today the commodities traded include feed wheat, oats, barley, rye, and flaxseed. There are 300 members and 102 companies registered for trading privileges.

Admission: Free.

Open: Mon–Fri 9:30am–1:15pm.

WESTERN CANADA AVIATION MUSEUM, 958 Ferry Rd. Tel. 204/786-5503.

Among the historic flying treasures at the Western Canada Aviation Museum are Canada's first helicopter, designed and test-flown between 1935 and 1939, along with more than 30 other aircraft.

Admission: $2.50 adults, $1 students 6–17.

Open: Mon–Sat 10am–4pm, Sun and holidays 1–4pm.

GRANT'S OLD MILL, 2777 Portage Ave. Tel. 204/837-5761.

At the corner of Booth Drive stands the reconstruction of the original watermill built on Sturgeon Creek in 1829, which is believed to be the first watermill west of the Great Lakes and the first instance of the use of hydropower in Manitoba. Grist is ground daily during the summer and you can buy some in a souvenir bag if you like.

Admission: $1 adults, 75¢ students and seniors, 50¢ children under 12.

Open: June–Aug daily 10am–6pm; the rest of the year, by appointment only.

ASSINIBOIA DOWNS, 3975 Portage Ave. Tel. 204/885-3330.

The racetrack is open for Thoroughbred racing May to October and for simulcast racing November to April. You can dine in the Terrace Dining Room overlooking the track or drink in one of the four lounges. Post times are Wednesday, Friday, and Saturday at 7pm, and Sunday and holidays at 1:30pm.

The track is located nine miles (20 minutes) west of the city at the junction of Highway 1 West (Portage Avenue) and Highway 100 (Perimeter Highway).

Admission: $3 adults, $1.50 children 5–15 and seniors; free for children under 5. Clubhouse admission is $3 additional.

FORT WHYTE CENTRE, 1961 McCreary Rd., Fort Whyte. Tel. 204/989-8355.

About 15 minutes from downtown some old cement quarries have been converted into several lakes at Fort Whyte Centre, and now serve as an environmental educational facility. The freshwater aquarium has many local specimens from Manitoba lakes and streams, like the northern pike and walleye. There are self-guided nature trails, waterfowl gardens, and an interpretive center and gift shop.

Open: Mon–Fri 9am–5pm, Sat–Sun and holidays 10am–5pm.

STROLLS

THE EXCHANGE DISTRICT   The best way to explore this historic warehouse district is to join the walking tour that starts at the Museum of Man and Nature Tuesday through Sunday at 11am and 1:30pm. For more information, call 204/774-3514. View the buildings that were built during Winnipeg's boom years in the late 19th and early 20th centuries. Admission is $4 for adults, $2 for seniors and youths ages 12 to 17. Private group tours available.

WELLINGTON CRESCENT   For some insight into Winnipeg's history, drive down Wellington Crescent—the "Park Avenue of the Prairies" as it was once called—lined with mansions commissioned by the many entrepreneurs who built them during the city's great real estate booms of 1880–82. Land prices rocketed and thousands of dollars were made in literally minutes.

PORTAGE PLACE   Four blocks long, Portage Place contains 150 shops, a food court, three cinemas, and an IMAX theater. The whole complex is joined to downtown by several skywalks.

ST. BONIFACE   Across the river in St. Boniface, a street becomes a *rue* and a hello becomes *bonjour*. Here you'll find the largest French-language community in western Canada, dating from 1783 when Pierre Gaultier de Varennes established Fort Rouge at the junction of the Red and Assiniboine rivers. The junction became the center of a thriving fur trade for the North West Company, which rivaled and challenged the Hudson's Bay Company. In the early 19th century a religious presence was established and a church built in 1819 dedicated to Boniface. Later in 1846 four Grey Nuns arrived and began service in the west. The historic sites that can be viewed today relate to this period and later.

The original basilica was replaced in 1908, during Bishop Langevin's time, by a beautiful building that was destroyed by fire in 1968. The massive Gothic arches remain, and cradled within the shell of the old building is the new basilica built in 1972. In front of the cathedral, the cemetery is the resting place for many historical figures, most notably Louis Riel, whose grave is marked by a replica of a Red River cart. Riel, leader of the Métis uprising and president of the provincial government formed in 1869 to 1870, tried to prevent the transfer of the Red River settlement to Canada.

Another architectural highlight, at the corner of Kenny and Enfield, is the **Church**

of the Precious Blood (1968). Its design by Etienne Gaboury, with its conical wood-shingled roof spiraling into the sky, was inspired by the teepee shape.

COOL FOR KIDS

ASSINIBOINE PARK AND ZOO, Corydon Ave. Tel. 204/986-6921 or 204/986-3130.

Comprising 393 acres for playing, picnicking, or bicycling, the park also contains a miniature railway, a duck pond, an English garden (which opens in June), and a conservatory. During the winter you can enjoy skating on the pond and tobogganing.

The park's highlight, however, is a 100-acre zoo where the animals—bears, tigers, zebras, flamingos, buffalos, elk, moose—are kept in as natural an environment as possible. Some of the more exotic species on display here include Chinese red dogs, snow leopards, ruffed lemurs, and Irkutsk lynx. Many spectacular birds live and breed in the Tropical House. A special "Discovery Centre" for children is fun.

Admission: Mar–Sept $3 adults, $2.75 seniors, $1.50 children 13–17, $1 children 2–12. Oct–Feb $1 adults, seniors, and children; free for children under 2 year-round. Free to all Tues.

Open: Park daily dawn–dusk; zoo daily 10am–dusk. **Directions:** Take Portage Avenue west, turn left onto Kenaston Boulevard (Route 90) south, and then turn right onto Corydon.

FUN MOUNTAIN WATER SLIDE PARK, Hwy. 1 East. Tel. 204/255-3910.

Kids love the thrills at Fun Mountain Water Slide Park, four miles or so east of the mint. There are 10 slides as well as rides, including bumper boats, a giant hot tub, and kids' playground with a wading pool.

Admission: All day $11 adults, $8.50 children 12 and under, free for children 3 and under.

Open: June–Aug daily 10am–8pm, weather permitting.

CHILDREN'S MUSEUM, 109 Pacific Ave. Tel. 204/949-0109.

This museum is specially designed for 2- to 13-year-olds, with exhibit areas where kids can participate. At Under the Big Top they can run away to the circus and devise a show of their very own, they can discover how to operate and do business at the Grain Elevator, and they can gain greater awareness of their senses in Making Sense. In the TV studio they can create their own television shows, as performers or as technicians. Exploration of new technology is the focus of the spaceship, which has several computers aboard. There's also a graphics studio and a train station.

Admission: $2.95 adults; $2.50 children, students, and seniors.

Open: Mon–Fri 9:30am–5pm, Sat–Sun and holidays 11am–5pm.

SPECIAL EVENTS

Winnipeg's two largest events are the **Red River Exhibition,** usually held the last 10 days of June, and the **Folklorama,** a two-week cultural festival in August. The first celebrates and reflects the city's history, showcasing agricultural, horticultural, commercial, and industrial achievements. There is also a midway, a photography show, and a band competition that attracts concert and marching bands from around the world. For more information, contact Red River Exhibition, 876 St. James St., Winnipeg, MB, R3G 3J7 (tel. 204/772-9464).

Folklorama, a Festival of Nations, features over 40 ethnic pavilions celebrating ethnic culture, with traditional food, dancing, music, costumes, entertainment, and crafts. Two weeks long, it's held annually in August. For more information, contact Folklorama, Winnipeg Convention Centre, 375 York Ave., Winnipeg, MB, R3C 3J3 (tel. 204/982-6221, or toll free 800/665-0234).

The week-long **Festival du Voyageur** celebrates French Métis culture in St. Boniface (tel. 204/237-7692). It is usually held in February.

ORGANIZED TOURS

RIVER CRUISES During the summer, the cruise ships **MS *River Rouge*** and **MS *Paddlewheel Queen*** depart from their dock at Water and Gilroy at the foot of the Provencher Bridge on a variety of cruises including a sunset dinner-dance cruise beginning at 7pm and a moonlight version that leaves at 10pm (both $11). Two-hour sightseeing trips ($10) depart at 2pm, providing fine views of the city from the Red and Assiniboine rivers. A longer historic river cruise leaves at 9:30am, returning at 4pm. The cost is $17 for adults, $14.95 for seniors, and $9 for children. For more information call 204/947-6843.

A STEAM-TRAIN RIDE   A 1900 steam-era train, the **Prairie Dog Central,** will take you on a two-hour, 36-mile round-trip from Winnipeg to Grosse Isle, Manitoba. En route you really get a feel for the prairie and what it must have been like for late 19th-century immigrants to travel to and through the west. The train leaves on Sunday at 11am and 3pm June through September (adults pay $13; senior citizens and students 12 to 17, $11; children 2 to 11, $7).

Board the train at the CN St. James Station near 1661 Portage Ave. For more information, contact the Vintage Locomotive Society, P.O. Box 33021, L155–1485 Portage Ave., Winnipeg, MB, R3G 0W4 (tel. 204/832-5259).

SHOPPING

For those who like to spend a day shopping, Winnipeg offers several areas. Most interesting of the city's shopping centers is downtown's **Portage Place,** and the multilevel **Eaton Place** (between Graham and St. Mary's Avenues and Hargrave and Donald Streets). There are over 110 shops and services—apparel stores, eateries, fashion and footwear shops, gourmet markets, and book, record, jewelry, gift, toy, and craft stores. Open from 9:30am to 6pm on Tuesday, Wednesday, and Saturday, to 9:30pm on Monday, Thursday, and Friday.

Every Saturday and Sunday in the summer the **Old Market Square,** at Albert and Bannatyne, blossoms into a lively open-air market. Under canopied stalls, craftspeople, vendors, market gardeners, and local entertainers offer a variety of antiques, crafts, fresh foodstuffs, and music and magic in a heady celebration of summer.

Another area worth exploring is **Osborne Village,** behind the Legislative Building, where the boutiques and specialty shops are concentrated. Stop over to view the many artisan-owned shops displaying custom-made jewelry, handmade furniture, woven tapestries, Canadian art, wickerware, and more.

6. EVENING ENTERTAINMENT

THE PERFORMING ARTS
MAJOR PERFORMING ARTS COMPANIES

ROYAL WINNIPEG BALLET, 380 Graham Ave., at Edmonton St. Tel. 204/956-0183, or 204/956-2792 for the box office.

Of the three arts companies, the longest established has of course been the world-renowned Royal Winnipeg Ballet, which was founded in 1939 by two British immigrant ballet teachers, making it the second-oldest in North America (after San Francisco). By 1949 it was a professional troupe, and in 1953 was granted a royal charter. Today the company's repertoire contains both contemporary and classical works. A recent season included productions of Ashton's *The Dream, Giselle,* and *Anne of Green Gables.* The company performs at the Centennial Concert Hall, usually for a two-week period in October, November, December, March, and May.

Prices: Tickets $13–$37, with a 20% discount for students and senior citizens, and a 50% discount for children 12 and under.

WINNIPEG SYMPHONY ORCHESTRA, 555 Main St. Tel. 204/949-3950, or 204/949-3976 for the box office.

Established in 1947, the Winnipeg Symphony Orchestra made its debut in 1978 at Carnegie Hall in New York City. The prestige of the orchestra and the genuinely

superb acoustics of the Centennial Concert Hall have attracted such guest artists as Itzhak Perlman, Isaac Stern, Tracey Dahl, and Maureen Forrester. The season usually runs from September to mid-May.
Prices: Tickets $16–$30.

MANITOBA OPERA, Box 31027, Portage Place, 393 Portage Ave. Tel. 204/942-7479, or 204/957-7842 for the box office.
The Manitoba Opera gave its first performance in 1972 and has since settled down to a season of three operas each year at the Centennial Concert Hall with performances in November, February, and April. Recent seasons have included productions of *Don Giovanni* and *Tales of Hoffmann*. English surtitles are used.
Prices: Tickets from $19.

MAJOR CONCERT HALLS & AUDITORIUMS

In addition to the auditoriums in the Manitoba Centennial Centre, other places where you might find concerts being performed include: the **Winnipeg Art Gallery** (tel. 204/786-6641), which often features blues/jazz, chamber music, and contemporary music groups (ticket prices vary with the entertainment); touring artists and local groups perform at the **Pantages Playhouse Theatre,** 180 Market Ave. (tel. 204/986-3003); and the **Convention Centre,** 375 York Ave. (tel. 204/956-1720), for occasional popular and folk artists and light orchestral musical concerts.

MANITOBA CENTENNIAL CENTRE, 555 Main St. Tel. 204/956-1360.
The shining star on Winnipeg's cultural scene is the Manitoba Centennial Centre. The huge complex includes the Centennial Concert Hall (which features headliners like Dionne Warwick and Ray Charles), Manitoba Theatre Centre, the Museum of Man and Nature and the planetarium, the Warehouse Theatre, and the Playhouse Theatre. In the concert hall itself, works of art are highlighted. In the foyer Greta Dale's vast tile mural brilliantly represents the three major performing arts—dance, music, and drama—while the lobbies are enhanced by the murals of Tony Tascona that seem to represent the mathematical precision of music and huge wall hangings by Canadian artists Takao Tanabe and Kenneth Lochhead. The acoustics are considered fine and the no-center-aisle auditorium maximizes sight lines.
Prices: Tickets $15–$25 in the Centennial Concert Hall.

THEATER

Other city theaters include the **Gas Station Theatre,** 445 River Ave. (tel. 204/284-2757); and the **Celebrations Dinner Theatre Restaurant,** 1808 Wellington Ave. (tel. 204/786-4801).

MANITOBA THEATRE CENTRE, 174 Market Ave. Tel. 204/942-6537.
Acclaimed as the best regional theater in Canada, the Manitoba Theatre Centre began in 1958, operating in the rickety but spirited atmosphere of the old Dominion Theatre on Portage and Main. Today it has a modern theater seating 785 people on Market Avenue, adjacent to the Centennial Concert Hall. Ever since Tom Hendry and John Hirsch founded the group it has been dedicated to producing good serious theater, and over the years has performed all kinds of works. A recent season's offerings included *Heidi Chronicles* and *Macbeth*. Probably the most famous actor to have emerged from Winnipeg onto the Broadway stage and film is Len Cariou. The season usually contains six productions and runs from October to April.
Prices: Tickets $10–$32.

MTC WAREHOUSE, 140 Rupert St. Tel. 204/942-6537.
The MTC Warehouse performs the more experimental works in a 300-seat setting. It offers a four-play season from mid-October to mid-May. Recent productions have included *Burn This* and *My Children, My Africa*.

Prices: Tickets $13.75–$20.75.

RAINBOW STAGE, 2021 Main St. in Kildonan Park. Tel. 204/942-2091.
Write Rainbow Stage, 112 Market Ave., Suite 310, Winnipeg, MB, R3B 0P4 for tickets.

Canada's largest and oldest continuously operating outdoor theater, Rainbow Stage, marks its 40th anniversary in 1994. During July and August the stage presents two musical classics running about three weeks each.

Located on the banks of the Red River, Rainbow is easily accessible by bus or car. The park itself is quite delightful and contains landscaped gardens, picnic spots, cycling paths, outdoor swimming, and wading pools, as well as a restaurant and dining room overlooking a small artificial lake. Also in the park, look for the Witch's House from *Hansel and Gretel.*

Prices: Tickets $8–$18.

THE CLUB & MUSIC SCENE

Most of the nightlife action takes place either in the Exchange District or at the main downtown hotels: **Chimes,** in the Westin Hotel, for dancing to light, live music; **Manhattan's,** The Club, in the Holiday Inn Crowne Plaza for a younger scene with taped music and a live floor show; and **Windows,** in the Sheraton Winnipeg at 161 Donald St. (tel. 204/942-5300), for dancing to live music.

Rorie Street Marble Club, 65 Rorie St. (tel. 204/943-4222), combines live and taped music. Cover on weekends is $5. At **Norma Jean's,** 115 Bannatyne Ave. East (tel. 204/944-1600), a DJ plays dance tunes attracting a 20- to 35-year-old crowd. Cover charge of $4 Friday and Saturday.

Live rock bands play both upstairs and downstairs at the **Osborne Village Inn,** 160 Osborne St. (tel. 204/452-9824). Cover and minimum vary with the performer.

THE BAR SCENE

Again, most of the comfortable piano bars are found at the hotels—the **S.O.S.** at the Holiday Inn–Airport West, for example, or in the major downtown hotels.

Hy's, 216 Kennedy St. (tel. 204/942-1000), also has a plush and comfortable piano bar.

For drinking on a budget, you can't beat the **Keg,** 115 Garry St. (tel. 204/942-7619).

Sit back with shipboard friends and watch the city drift by as you glide along the Red and Assiniboine rivers on the **MS *River Rouge*** and dance to a live band. Dinners are available. For more information, call 204/947-6843.

CASINO GAMBLING

On the seventh floor of the Hotel Fort Garry visitors can play blackjack, baccarat, and roulette or pump coins into the 185 slot machines at the **Crystal Casino,** 222 Broadway Ave. (tel. 204/957-2600), an intimate, European-style casino accommodating about 380 players. Reservations are taken. Open Monday to Saturday from noon to 2am, Sunday from 2pm to 2am. Jacket and tie mandatory.

7. AROUND MANITOBA

LOWER FORT GARRY

This National Historic Park (tel. 204/983-3600), only 20 miles (32km) north of Winnipeg on Highway 9, is the only stone fort of the fur-trade era that's still intact. Built in the 1830s, it served primarily as an administrative center for the fur trade. At the center was the governor's residence, several warehouses including the fur loft, and the Men's House, where male employees of the company lived. Outside the compound are the service buildings—blacksmith's, engineer's, and so on. The place has been meticulously restored and staffed by volunteers who make candles and soap, forge horseshoes, locks, and bolts, and generally demonstrate the crafts and ways of life of an earlier time. An original York boat stands in a lean-to beside the fur-loft building. Hundreds of these once traveled the waterways from Hudson Bay to the Rockies and from the Red River to the Arctic carrying furs and trading goods.

The site is open daily from mid-May to Labor Day, and for weekends in September, from 10am to 6pm. Adults pay $3.25 for admission; children ages 5 to 16 and under, $1.50; under 5 and seniors over 65 enter free.

STEINBACH MENNONITE HERITAGE VILLAGE

About 30 miles (48km) outside Winnipeg, **Steinbach Mennonite Heritage Village,** located 1½ miles north of Steinbach on Highway 12 (tel. 204/326-9661), a 40-acre museum complex, is worth visiting. It's a whole complex of about 20 buildings, portraying the life of the Mennonite settlers who migrated from Ukraine to Manitoba in 1874. Seven thousand moved here between 1874 and 1880, establishing settlements like Kleefeld, Steinbach, Blumenort, and others. After World War I many moved on to Mexico and Uruguay when Manitoba closed all unregistered schools between 1922 and 1926, but they were replaced by another surge of emigrants fleeing the Russian Revolution. In the museum building, dioramas display daily life and the artifacts of the community—woodworking and sewing tools, sausage makers, clothes, medicines, and furnishings. Elsewhere in the complex visitors can view the windmill grinding grain (800 pounds an hour with a 25-m.p.h. wind), ride in an ox-drawn wagon, watch the blacksmith at work, or view any number of homes, agricultural machines, and so on.

The restaurant serves Mennonite food—a full meal of borscht, thick-sliced homemade brown bread, coleslaw, pirogies, and sausage, plus rhubarb crumble, at very reasonable prices.

The village is open in May from 10am to 5pm; in June, July, and August from 9am to 7pm; and in September from 10am to 5pm. On Sunday the gates do not open until noon. From October to April the village is open Monday to Friday from 10am to 4pm. Admission is $3.25 for adults, $2 for seniors, $1.50 for students, $1.25 for students in grades 1 to 6.

AROUND LAKE WINNIPEG

This 264-mile-long lake is the continent's seventh largest, and its shores harbor some interesting spots to visit. **Gimli,** 60 miles north of Winnipeg, is a farming and fishing community and the hub of Icelandic culture in Manitoba, which was established a century ago as the capital of New Iceland and for many years had its own government, school, and newspapers, and still celebrates an Icelandic festival on the first long weekend in August.

Gull Harbour, 110 miles (185km) northeast of Winnipeg on Hecla Island, was once a part of New Iceland and was, until recently, home for a small Icelandic-Canadian farming and fishing community. Today it's the site of Manitoba's newest provincial park, providing natural wilderness and excellent sporting opportunities—hiking, golf, fishing, camping, birdwatching, canoeing, swimming, hunting, cross-country skiing, snowshoeing, snowmobiling, tobogganing, and windsurfing.

Grand Rapids, 266 miles (425km) north of Winnipeg, is the home of a fish hatchery, major electric power-generating station, and a thriving Native Canadian community; and **Berens River,** on the eastern shore of the lake, is a remote (no all-weather roads connect it to the rest of Manitoba) community where one of Manitoba's largest and best-known reservations is located.

WHERE TO STAY IN GULL HARBOUR

GULL HARBOUR RESORT HOTEL, Box 1000, Riverton, MB, R0C 2R0. Tel. 204/475-2354. Fax 204/279-2000. 93 rms. A/C TV TEL

$ Rates: $100 single or double. Extra person $15. Children under 16 stay free in parents' room. Watch for specials year-round. AE, MC, V.

Though it boasts first-class resort facilities, Gull Harbour is unusual because it has really tried to retain the unspoiled nature of the island. Beaches and woods have been left intact, and outdoors and indoors almost seem to blend. Facilities include an indoor swimming pool, whirlpool, and sauna; badminton, volleyball, and basketball courts; a games room with pool tables, an 18-hole golf course, a putting green, mini-golf, tennis courts, skating rink, croquet, shuffleboard, and more. It's an ideal place to take the family.

WHITESHELL PROVINCIAL PARK

Less than two hours' drive from Winnipeg (90 miles, 144km, east) lies a network of a dozen rivers and over 200 lakes in a 1,000-square-mile park. Whiteshell offers unlimited opportunity for outdoor activity—swimming, scuba diving, sailing, windsurfing, waterskiing, fishing, hiking, golfing, horseback riding, tennis, and birdwatching, as well as winter sports. Within the park lies one of Canada's most modern recreational townsite developments, **Falcon Lake,** where tennis courts, an 18-hole golf course, and a ski resort are just some of the facilities. Most of the resorts and lodges in the park charge anywhere from $45 to $100 double ($200 to $625 per week) for a cabin. Camping facilities abound. For more information, contact Travel Manitoba, Dept. 4018, 155 Carlton St., Winnipeg, MB, R3C 3H8 (tel. 204/945-3777).

RIDING MOUNTAIN NATIONAL PARK

About 155 miles (248km) northwest of the city you can indulge in the same outdoor activities plus cross-country and downhill skiing at Mount Agassiz on the east side of the park, but in dramatically different surroundings. Riding Mountain is set in the highlands, atop a giant wooded escarpment that affords shelter to wildlife—elk, deer, beaver, and bear. Accommodations for all budgets and facilities are centered in Wasagaming. You'll find tennis courts, lawn bowling greens, a children's playground, and a log-cabin movie theater in the Wasagaming Visitor Centre beside Clear Lake. There's also a dance hall, picnic areas with stoves, and a bandshell down by the lake for Sunday-afternoon concerts. At the lake itself you can rent a boat, canoe, or paddleboat, and swim at the main beach.

For campers, the Wasagaming campground has electricity and three-way hookups, toilet buildings with showers, kitchen shelters, and a sewage-disposal station nearby. Rates are $9.50 unserviced, $12.50 with electricity, $14 full service. Other campgrounds are at Lake Katherine, Moon Lake, and Lake Audy.

The visitor center is open daily in the summer from 9am to 8pm. For information, call or write: Superintendent, Riding Mountain National Park, Wasagaming, MB, R0J 2H0 (tel. 204/848-2811). Outlying campgrounds are $6.50, site only. Entry to the park is $5 daily, $10 for a four-day pass, $30 for an annual permit good for all Canadian national parks. Golf at the park's 18-hole course costs about $17 a day.

WHERE TO STAY

ELKHORN RESORT, Clear Lake, MB, R0J 2H0. Tel. 204/848-2802. Fax 204/848-2109. 60 rms. A/C TV TEL

$ Rates: Lodge room $109 double, $120 double with fireplace. Extra person $15. Children under 17 stay free in parents' room. Lower off-season rates available. Three-bedroom chalet $225 per night; less off-season (Mar to mid-May and mid-Oct to mid-Dec). AE, DC, ER, MC, V.

This year-round lodge is just on the edge of Wasagaming with easy access to the park, overlooking quiet fields and forest. It's a wonderful place for families. At the ranch there's a common room where in the evenings you can join a game of bridge or cribbage. In addition there's a swimming pool, a nine-hole golf course, and a dining room with a lovely view over nearby stables.

Each of the rooms in the lodge itself is large and comfortable, pleasantly furnished in pine, country style. Also on the property are several fully equipped three-bedroom chalets (with fireplace, radio, fire extinguisher, toaster, dishwasher, microwave, and balcony with barbecue) designed after quonsets.

THE FAR NORTH

The best way to explore the north is aboard **VIA Rail's** *Hudson Bay* as it travels from Winnipeg, through the Pas, a mecca for fishing enthusiasts, and the mining community of Thompson to Churchill. No other land route has yet penetrated this remote region, which is covered with lakes, forests, and frozen tundra.

One of the largest grain-exporting terminals in the world, **Churchill** has a skyline dominated by grain elevators. You can watch the grain being unloaded from boxcars onto ships—perhaps 25 million bushels of wheat and barley clear the port in only 12 to 14 weeks of frantic nonstop operation. From Churchill you can travel independently to Eskimo Point, home of an Inuit community to view the polar bears and other wildlife in the region. Best time for the bears is mid-October to mid-November. In Churchill itself you can take a boat ride to Fort Prince of Wales and get the chance to observe beluga whales.

The trip takes a couple of days, with the train leaving Winnipeg at about 10pm and arriving 34 hours later in Churchill. A round-trip ticket costs $328 per person. In addition, the cheapest sleeping berth is $142. For more information, contact your travel agent or VIA (tel. toll free 800/361-3677).

Churchill is also serviced by **Canadian Airlines International** (tel. 204/632-2811).

CHAPTER 18

THE TWIN CITIES OF SASKATCHEWAN

- **WHAT'S SPECIAL ABOUT SASKATCHEWAN**
1. **REGINA**
2. **SASKATOON**

Five times the size of New York state, with a population of about one million, Saskatchewan is the center of Canada's prairie provinces and produces 60% of Canada's wheat.

For the tourist, it provides a hunting and fishing paradise in the northern lakes and forests, several summer playgrounds, including Prince Albert National Park and 31 provincial parks, and the cities of Regina and Saskatoon.

SOME PROVINCIAL HISTORY The first settlers of the province were Native Canadian hunting-and-gathering tribes—Chipewyans, Blackfoot, and Cree. At the end of the 17th century, Henry Kelsey entered the prairies and Saskatchewan—the first white man ever to do so. Soon others followed in search of furs, and among the first to settle were the Métis, of mixed European and Native Canadian blood. In 1872 the Canadian government offered free land to anyone who would settle what was then known as the Northwest Territories, but it was not until the arrival of the Central Pacific Railway in 1882 that the floodgates of immigration were opened and the British, Germans, Ukrainians, Scandinavians, French, and other Europeans poured in. Regina was established as the seat of the territorial government and headquarters of the Northwest Mounted Police. The Métis did not accept the takeover of the area by the eastern government, and in 1885 Louis Riel led them in a rebellion in northern Saskatchewan, which was suppressed by Major-General Middleton at the Battle of Batoche (Riel was later executed in Regina). Immigration continued apace, wheat production soared, and in 1905 Saskatchewan was created, with its capital at Regina.

Saskatchewan's steady growth was interrupted by the depression, when it was even more badly hit than other provinces because of nine years of drought and crop failure. After driving through southern Saskatchewan in the summer of 1934, a Regina newspaper reporter wrote (quoted in Prof. Edward McCourt's book *Saskatchewan*), "For miles there was scarcely a thing growing to be seen . . . Gaunt cattle and horses with little save their skins to cover their bones stalked about the denuded acres, weakly seeking to crop the malign Frenchweed which seemed to be maintaining some sickly growth. When the miserable animals moved it seemed as if their frames rattled. The few people in evidence in the little towns appeared haggard and hopeless."

The worst year of all was 1937, when the temperature reached 114°. In Regina, according to Professor McCourt, bathers in Wascana Creek could not get from the water to the bathhouses without being coated with dust, and an apocryphal story tells of a baseball player who set off from home plate, turning up three miles away on the prairies.

Such hardship breeds a stoic pride, independence, and pessimism, which may

WHAT'S SPECIAL ABOUT SASKATCHEWAN

Activities
- ☐ Freshwater fishing in more than 50,000 lakes, with more than 200 fishing camps, many of them accessible only by float plane or boat.
- ☐ Canoeing the Churchill River or the many routes through Prince Albert National Park and Lac La Ronge and Clearwater River provincial parks.

Natural Playgrounds
- ☐ Prince Albert National Park, home to bison, elk, moose, and caribou and the second-largest pelican colony in North America. Famous naturalist Grey Owl also resided here in the 1930s.

Museums/Ethnic Heritage Sites
- ☐ Saskatoon's Western Development Museum, in which pioneer days are revisited.

- ☐ Saskatoon's Ukrainian Museum, which tells an immigrant story and displays a fine textile collection.
- ☐ Regina's RCMP barracks, where the recruits to the Mounties, who "always get their man," are trained.
- ☐ Regina's Science Centre, featuring more than 80 hands-on exhibits and an IMAX theater.

Historic Monuments
- ☐ Batoche, site of the last stand of the Metis in 1885.
- ☐ Fort Battleford National Historic Site, the frontier outpost that sheltered 500 settlers during the Northwest Rebellion.
- ☐ The long-running Trial of Louis Riel in Regina, which tells the story of the Northwest Rebellion's leader and his trial.

account for both the suspicion of government and the willingness to indulge in political and social experiments that has characterized the province's recent history. Saskatchewan, remember, elected the first socialist government in Canada—in 1944.

SEEING SASKATCHEWAN

INFORMATION For information on the region, contact **Tourism Saskatchewan,** 1919 Saskatchewan Dr., Regina, SK, S4P 3V7 (tel. 306/787-2300). This department offers toll-free travel-counseling service year-round (tel. toll free 800/667-7191), from 8am to 7pm Monday through Friday, 10am to 4pm Saturday.

A NOTE ON TAXES Saskatchewan has a non-refundable 7% provincial sales tax in addition to the 7% federal GST.

A NOTE ON CLIMATE Summers can be simply magnificent, with warm sunny days and cool refreshing evenings and nights. The climate is on the dry side. Summer temperatures average 70° to 80°F. Average winter temperatures are 0° to 9°F. I think you can guess the best time to go.

SPECIAL SASKATCHEWAN ACTIVITIES The province of Saskatchewan covers a quarter of a million square miles. This huge space is inhabited by only a million people, most of whom are concentrated in the southern grain belt. Much of the rest of the province is taken up by forests; 100,000 lakes; and wilderness areas that afford spectacular canoeing, sportfishing, hiking, and camping opportunities. Three million acres are given over to parks—one million alone to Prince Albert National Park. La Rouge, Wollaston, and Reindeer are just a few of the lakes that are filled with northern pike and walleye so thickly that you can practically pluck them from the clear waters. Two hundred fishing lodges cater to the sportfisherman, many of them employing Native Canadian guides who have hunted, fished, and trapped these lakes all of their lives.

Canoeing To some it comes as a surprise that Saskatchewan has 31,000 square miles of water. The northern water routes offer a challenge to both novice and expert. So 55 canoe routes have been mapped, which will take you through terrain that has not changed since the era of explorers and fur traders. You can get to all but three of the routes by road. Various outfitters will supply tent, camping equipment, and canoe, look after your car, and transport you to the starting point for your canoe trip. Most of them are located in either Flin Flon or Lac La Ronge, 250 miles (400km) north of Saskatoon.

Churchill River Canoe Outfitters, P.O. Box 1110, La Ronge, SK, S0J 1L0 (tel. 306/635-4420), offers a selection of canoe camping tours. Available for rent are canoes and kayaks ($23 a day), paddles, life jackets, and all the gear for a wilderness expedition. Cabins are also available for rent from $50 to $170 per night.

For more general information about canoeing vacations and lists of canoe outfitters, write to **Tourism Saskatchewan,** 1919 Saskatchewan Dr. (main floor), Regina, SK, S4P 3V7 (tel. 306/787-2300, or toll free 800/667-7191).

Fishing   For the fishing enthusiast the same clear cold northern lakes hold out the chance of catching walleye, northern pike, four species of trout, and arctic grayling. There are over 300 northern outfitters—both fly-in and drive-in camps—offering equipment, accommodation, and experienced guides to take you to the best fishing spots. And while you're in the north you might catch the spectacular aurora borealis.

Rates for packages vary, but you can reckon it will cost anywhere between $800 and $5,000 a week per person, including transportation, meals, boat, guide, and accommodations. Contact the **Saskatchewan Outfitters Association,** P.O. Box 2016, Prince Albert, SK, S6V 6R1 (tel. 306/763-5434). Boat and motor will cost about $65 a day, and guide services run about $70 a day. For more information, write to **Tourism Saskatchewan,** 1919 Saskatchewan Dr., Regina, SK, S4P 3V7 (tel. toll free 800/667-7191).

Adults 16 and over must obtain an annual fishing license: $32.10 for nonresidents, $16.03 for Canadians. These can be purchased at special vendors, including most stores selling fishing equipment, and from Saskatchewan Environment and Resource Management offices, 3211 Albert St., Regina, SK S4S 5W6 (tel. 306/787-2700).

THE PROVINCIAL PARKS   Saskatchewan has 31 such parks where you can camp for $10 unelectrified, $14 electrified in addition to a $6 entry fee.

Duck Mountain, Cypress Hills, Greenwater Lake, and Moose Mountain offer cabin accommodations: Rates average $40 to $60 for a one-bedroom cabin, $48 to $90 for a two-bedroom, with some nonmoderns (that is, with an outdoor toilet) renting for about $25.

For information, contact the park superintendant at each: **Cypress Hills Provincial Park,** P.O. Box 850, Maple Creek, SK, S0N 1N0 (tel. 306/662-4411); **Duck Mountain Provincial Park,** P.O. Box 39, Kamsack, SK, S0A 1S0 (tel. 306/542-3482); **Greenwater Lake Provincial Park,** P.O. Box 430, Porcupine Plain, SK, S0E 1H0 (tel. 306/278-2972); **Moose Mountain Provincial Park,** P.O. Box 100, Carlyle, SK, S0C 0R0 (tel. 306/577-2131).

I recommend that you call ahead to Tourism Saskatchewan (tel. 306/787-2300, or toll free 800/667-3674 within Saskatchewan) to rate your chances of getting a campsite.

FARM STAYS   Staying on a farm is another way to acquaint yourself with the down-to-earth folks on the prairie. Costs average $30 to $40 a day with all three meals included or $20 to $25 without meals. For information, contact **Saskatchewan Country Vacations Association,** Box 654, Gull Lake, SK, S0N 1A0 (tel. 306/672-3970), or Tourism Saskatchewan, 1919 Saskatchewan Dr., Regina SK, S4P 3V7 (tel. toll free 800/667-7191).

---

1. REGINA

160 miles (259km) SE of Saskatoon; 355 miles (573km) W of Winnipeg

GETTING THERE   By Plane   Regina's airport is located only 15 minutes from

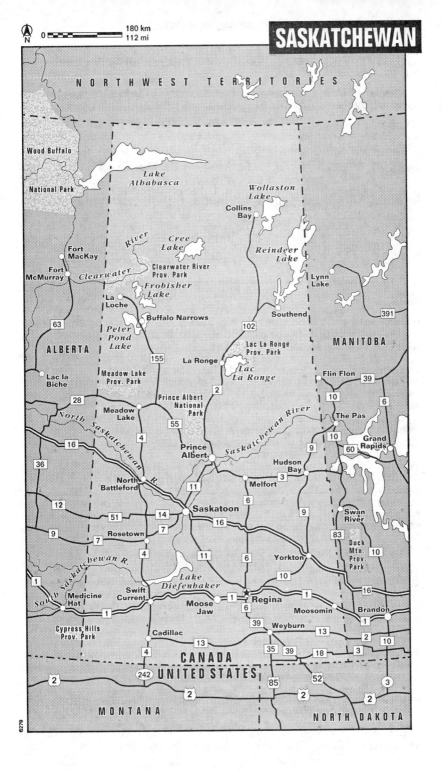

SASKATCHEWAN

0 ___ 180 km
___ 112 mi
N

NORTHWEST TERRITORIES

Wood Buffalo

National Park

Lake Athabasca

River

Cree Lake

Fort MacKay

Fort McMurray

Clearwater

Clearwater River Prov. Park

Frobisher Lake

La Loche

63

Peter Pond Lake

Buffalo Narrows

ALBERTA

155

Meadow Lake Prov. Park

Lac la Biche

28

Meadow Lake

4

55

Prince Albert National Park

North Saskatchewan

16

36

North Battleford

12

51

14

Rosetown

7

9

7

4

1

South Saskatchewan R.

Medicine Hat

Swift Current

1

Cypress Hills Prov. Park

Cadillac

4

242

2

MONTANA

Wollaston Lake

Collins Bay

Reindeer Lake

Lynn Lake

Southend

102

391

MANITOBA

Lac La Ronge Prov. Park

La Ronge

Lac La Ronge

2

Flin Flon

39

10

6

The Pas

Grand Rapids

60

Prince Albert

Saskatchewan River

11

Melfort

6

Hudson Bay

3

9

10

9

Swan River

83

Saskatoon

16

Duck Mtn. Prov. Park

10

11

6

Yorkton

10

Lake Diefenbaker

★ Regina

1

1

16

Moose Jaw

6

Moosomin

Brandon

1

39

Weyburn

13

2

10

13

35

39

18

3

CANADA

UNITED STATES

85

52

3

2

2

2

NORTH DAKOTA

downtown, west of the city. Air Canada has offices at 2015 12th Ave. (tel. 306/525-4711) and has flights going east-west. For Canadian Airlines International, call 306/569-2307.

By Train   VIA Rail operates out of the station at 1880 Saskatchewan Dr., at Rose Street (tel. toll free 800/561-8630 in Canada only).

By Bus   The bus depot is located at 2041 Hamilton St. For the Saskatchewan Transportation Company, offering bus service around the province, call 306/787-3340; ditto for Greyhound, call 306/787-3340.

SPECIAL EVENTS   During the first week of June, **Mosaic** celebrates the many ethnic groups that now live in the city. Special passports entitle visitors to enter pavilions and experience the food, crafts, and entertainment of each group. In June the **Big Valley Rodeo** is held. Regina's **Buffalo Days,** usually held the first week in August, recalls the time when this noble beast roamed the west. Throughout the city, businesses and individuals dress in Old West style, while the fair itself sparkles with a midway, grandstand shows, big-name entertainers, livestock competitions, beard-growing contests, and much, much more. For more information, contact Buffalo Days, P.O. Box 167, Exhibition Park, Regina, SK, S4P 2Z6 (tel. 306/781-9200).

———————————————————

Originally named Pile O'Bones after the heap of buffalo skeletons the first settlers found (Native Canadians had amassed the bones in the belief that they would lure the vanished buffalo back again), the city has Princess Louise, daughter of Queen Victoria, to thank for its more regal name. She named it in her mother's honor in 1882 when it became the capital of the Northwest Territories.

The original town site was not widely acclaimed. According to Professor McCourt, it was severely criticized by the Canadian press: "There is no water in the creek, a series of shallow stagnant pools . . . of a dark brown, brackish appearance," reported the Toronto *Globe and Mail,* while an exasperated editor of *Forest and Stream* wrote, "I have never in all my travels seen so wretched a site for a town."

Despite the questionable water supply, the barren prairie landscape, and the infamous Regina mud, the town grew. It only really hit the national headlines three times: first, when Louis Riel was hanged in November 1885; second, in June 1912 when a cyclone tore through the city, killing 28 and injuring 200; and third, when the Royal Canadian Mounted Police (RCMP) clashed with strikers from the labor camps of British Columbia who were en route to Ottawa. In the battle, hundreds were injured when stones, bricks, and clubs were met with gunfire and tear gas.

Today it is the provincial capital, with a population of 179,000, and although it still has a certain prairie feel, it's becoming more sophisticated. So take no notice of those who whisper of Regina as the last stop on any itinerary. It has some good hotels, a burgeoning selection of restaurants, and some rather interesting attractions.

ORIENTATION

INFORMATION   For on-the-spot Regina information, write **Tourism Regina,** P.O. Box 3355, Regina, SK, S4P 3H1 (tel. 306/789-5099), or visit the Visitor Information Centre on Highway 1 East located just west of CKCK-TV. It's open from 8:30am to 4:30pm year-round, with extended hours to 7pm from mid-May to Labor Day.

Or contact **Tourism Saskatchewan,** 1919 Saskatchewan Dr., Regina, SK, S4P 3V7 (tel. 306/787-2300 in Regina). This department offers toll-free travel-counseling service year-round (tel. toll free 800/667-7191), from 8am to 7pm Monday through Friday, 10am to 4pm Saturday.

CITY LAYOUT   The two main streets are Victoria Avenue, which runs east-west, and Albert Street, which runs north-south. South of the intersection lies the Wascana Centre, a 2,300-acre park that also contains the Legislative Building, the University of Regina, the Diefenbaker Homestead, the Natural History Museum, the Norman Mackenzie Art Gallery, Saskatchewan Centre of the Arts, and the waterfowl park.

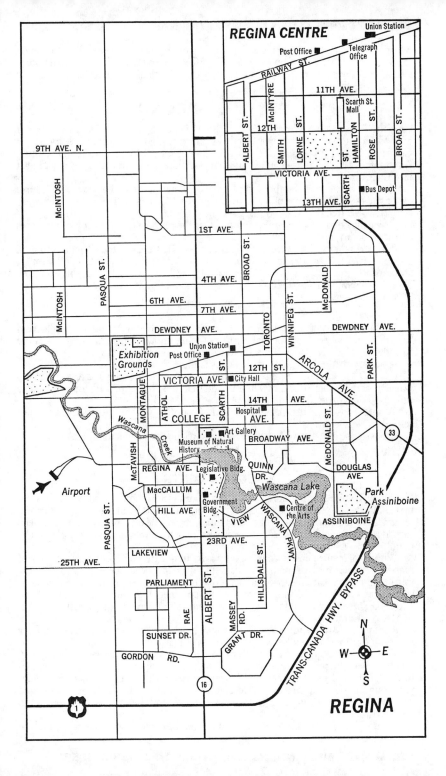

REGINA CENTRE

Union Station
Post Office
Telegraph Office
RAILWAY ST.
11TH AVE.
McINTYRE
Scarth St. Mall
12TH
ALBERT ST.
SMITH
LORNE ST.
ST. HAMILTON
ROSE ST.
BROAD ST.
VICTORIA AVE.
SCARTH
Bus Depot
13TH AVE.

9TH AVE. N.
McINTOSH
1ST AVE.
BROAD ST.
4TH AVE.
McDONALD
McINTOSH
PASQUA ST.
6TH AVE.
7TH AVE.
DEWDNEY AVE.
WINNIPEG ST.
DEWDNEY AVE.
PARK ST.
Exhibition Grounds
Union Station
Post Office
TORONTO
ARCOLA
12TH ST.
VICTORIA AVE.
City Hall
AVE.
33
MONTAGUE
ATHOL
SCARTH
14TH AVE.
Hospital
COLLEGE
McDONALD ST.
Art Gallery
BROADWAY AVE.
Museum of Natural History
McTAVISH
QUINN DR.
DOUGLAS AVE.
Wascana Creek
REGINA AVE.
Legislative Bldg.
Wascana Lake
Park Assiniboine
Airport
MacCALLUM
Government Bldg.
Centre of the Arts
ASSINIBOINE
HILL AVE.
VIEW
PASQUA ST.
23RD AVE.
LAKEVIEW
HILLSDALE ST.
WASCANA PKWY.
25TH AVE.
PARLIAMENT
ALBERT ST.
RAE
MASSEY RD.
SUNSET DR.
GRANT DR.
GORDON RD.
TRANS-CANADA HWY. BYPASS
16
N
W E
S
1
REGINA

Most of the downtown hotels stretch along Victoria Avenue between Albert Street on the west and Broad Street on the east. The RCMP barracks are located to the north and west of the downtown area. Lewvan Drive (also called the Ring Road) allows you to circle the city by car.

GETTING AROUND

Regina Transit, 333 Winnipeg St. (tel. 306/777-RIDE), operates 15 bus routes that make it easy to get around. For schedules and maps, go to the Transit Information Centre at 2124 11th Ave. in the old Merchant Bank building in Cornwall Centre. Adult fare is $1.10, 55¢ for elementary school children, 65¢ for high schoolers. Exact fare is required.

Taxis can most easily be found at downtown hotels. They are of course expensive—$2.10 when you get in and 10¢ per 120 meters (135 yards) thereafter. **Regina Cab** (tel. 306/543-3333) is the most used.

Driving is not a problem in Regina, but you should note that the province requires all motorists to wear seat belts.

For car rentals, here are a few addresses: **Dollar,** at the Regina Inn (tel. 306/525-1377); **Budget,** at the Airport Service Centre (tel. 306/522-9292); **Hertz,** at the airport (tel. 306/791-9131); **Tilden,** 3476 Saskatchewan Dr. at Elphinstone (tel. 306/757-4696); and **Avis,** 2010 Victoria Ave. (tel. 306/757-1653).

FAST FACTS

Business Hours   Regular store hours are 9am to 6pm Monday, Tuesday, and Saturday, and Wednesday through Friday evening until 9:30pm. Banking hours are Monday through Thursday from 10am to 3pm, to 6pm on Friday.

Newspapers   Regina's daily paper is the *Leader Post.*

Post Office   For postal service, there's a convenient outlet at 2200 Saskatchewan Dr. across from the Cornwall Parkade (tel. 306/761-6307). It's open Monday through Friday from 8am to 5pm.

Taxes   Provincial sales tax and GST are both 7%. The provincial tax is not refundable.

Useful Telephone Numbers   For telephone information, dial 113.

WHAT TO SEE & DO
WASCANA CENTRE

Certainly Regina did not start out with a bounty of natural assets, which is what makes Wascana Centre, a 2,300-acre park right in the middle of the city, practically a testament to the indomitable will of the human spirit. The muddy little creek has been turned into a glorious parkland, where every tree that grows was physically planted by man.

Within the center lies a **waterfowl park,** frequented by 60 or more species of marsh and water birds. A really interesting project was begun here in 1953 with the introduction of a pair of Canada geese. Now there are more than 150 breeding pairs, some of which remain during the winter, while others migrate as far south as New Mexico. There's a naturalist on duty from 8am to 4:30pm weekdays; call 306/522-3661 for information.

Another delightful spot is **Willow Island,** a picnic island reached by a small ferry from the overlook west of Broad Street on Wascana Drive.

Wascana Place, the headquarters building for Wascana Centre Authority (tel. 306/522-3661), open Monday from 8am to 4:30pm, Tuesday to Saturday from 8am to 6pm, Sunday 1 to 4pm. Hours are extended from May to Labor Day. It provides year-round public information services and a gift shop with Saskatchewan art and craft work. The intriguing architecture invites a visit and is enhanced by a tour up to the fourth-level observation deck.

Besides the natural features mentioned above, the center also contains the bulk of the city's attractions.

LEGISLATIVE BUILDING, Wascana Centre. Tel. 306/787-5358.

Start at the Legislative Building, a stately building that was built in 1908–12 for only $2 million in an English Renaissance and Louis XVI style (parts of the building also strongly remind one of the palace of Versailles). Designed in the shape of a cross, the building is crowned by a 226-foot-high dome. Once inside, note that on the main floor and main rotunda 34 kinds of marble were used—white-veined from Québec for the staircase, Italian on the walls, Vermont on the floor and baseboards, and Connemara for the pillar bases. The pillars were obtained from Cyprus and were cut and shaped in Québec.

The mural above the rotunda, entitled *Before the White Man Came,* depicts aboriginal people in the Qu'Appelle Valley preparing to attack a herd of buffalo on the opposite shore. Rooms of interest include the Legislative Assembly Chamber, the 300,000-volume library, and the art galleries in the basement and on the first floor.

Tours: Tours leave every half hour 8am–4:30pm in winter, 8am–7pm in summer.
Open: Summer daily 8am–9pm; winter daily 8am–5pm.

MUSEUM OF NATURAL HISTORY, Wascana Centre. Tel. 306/787-2815.

A recent fire at the Museum of Natural History destroyed much of its content, including the marvelous diorama showcases displaying realistic exhibits of bugling elk, caribou, wolf, and golden eagles in flight. Currently much of the museum is closed except for the Earth Sciences Gallery, which is devoted to geography, geology, and paleontology, including models of dinosaurs such as Tyrannosaurus rex. On weekends the Paleo Pit is open, with hands-on exhibits including fossils that can be examined through a microscope. The First Nation's Gallery, devoted to the local native heritage, reopened in 1993, and it is hoped that the whole museum will reopen in about 1997.

Admission: Free.
Open: May 1–Labor Day daily 9am–8:30pm; Labor Day–Apr 30 daily 9am–4:30pm. **Closed:** Christmas Day.

MACKENZIE ART GALLERY, 3475 Albert St., at Hillsdale. Tel. 306/522-4242.

The art gallery's collection has been built upon the legacy of Norman MacKenzie, a Regina lawyer who began collecting works of art in about 1900. It was not until 1957 that the gallery was completed. The approximately 1,600 works concentrate on Canadian artists, especially such Saskatchewan painters as James Henderson and Inglis Sheldon-Williams; contemporary American artists; and 15th- to 19th-century European paintings, drawings, and prints. The gallery also offers a round of cultural events—films, music, dance, lectures.

Admission: Free.
Open: Fri–Tues 11am–6pm, Wed–Thurs 11am–10pm.

DIEFENBAKER HOMESTEAD HOUSE, Wascana Centre. Tel. 306/522-3661.

Also in the park stands the Diefenbaker Homestead House, the original home of Prime Minister Diefenbaker, which has been moved from Borden, Saskatchewan. It is furnished in pioneer style and contains some original family articles.

Admission: Free.
Open: Daily 10am–7pm. **Closed:** Labor Day to Victoria Day.

SASKATCHEWAN SPORTS HALL OF FAME AND MUSEUM, 2205 Victoria Ave. Tel. 306/780-9232.

At the Saskatchewan Sports Hall of Fame, you'll see pictures, trophies, and memorabilia of those individuals and teams that have contributed either nationally or locally to the province's sports reputation.

Admission: Free.
Open: May–Oct Mon–Fri 9am–5pm, Sat–Sun 1–5pm; Nov–Apr Mon–Fri 9am–5pm.

MORE ATTRACTIONS

For downtown shopping, **Cromwell Centre** has more than 100 stores (all chains), with Eaton's as the anchor.

SASKATCHEWAN SCIENCE CENTRE, Winnipeg St. and Wascana Dr. Tel. 306/791-7900.
The Saskatchewan Science Centre is home to two great attractions: The Power-house of Discovery and the Kramer IMAX Theatre. The first is located in the renovated City of Regina Powerhouse on the north shore of Wascana Lake. It houses more than 70 thought-provoking, fun, hands-on exhibits that demonstrate basic scientific principles, ranging from a hot-air balloon that rises three stories in the central mezzanine to exhibits where visitors can test their strength, reaction time, and balance, or ponder a variety of optical illusions and visual tricks. Live science demonstrations are also given daily.

The adjacent IMAX theater shows films on a five-story screen accompanied by thrilling six-channel surround-sound. Call for show times (most are in the afternoon).

Admission: Powerhouse of Discovery $7 adults, $5.50 seniors and youths 18 and under, $2 children under 5. IMAX theater $6.50 adults, $4.25 youths and seniors, $3 children 5 and under. Combination tickets to both attractions $16.50 adults, $11.75 youths and seniors, $7.50 children 5 and under.

Open: Summer Mon–Thurs 9am–6pm, Fri–Sat 9am–9pm, Sun 10am–7:30pm; winter Tues–Fri 9am–5pm, Sat–Sun and holidays noon–6pm.

RCMP "DEPOT" DIVISION AND MUSEUM, off Lewvan Dr. at 11th Ave. (P.O. Box 6500, Regina, SK, S4S 2H3). Tel. 306/780-5838.
This fascinating museum traces the history of the Royal Canadian Mounted Police since 1874, when they began the Great March West to stop liquor traffic and enforce the law in the Northwest Territories. They did so at a time when organized law enforcement anywhere in the world was less than 50 years old. The museum uses replicas, newspaper articles, artifacts, uniforms, weaponry, and mementos to display the lives of the early Mounties and the pioneers, and goes on to trace their role in the 1885 Riel Rebellion, the Klondike Gold Rush (when the simple requirements laid down by the Northwest Mounted Police probably saved the lives of many foolhardy gold diggers who came pitifully ill equipped), the Prohibition era (when they sought out stills), the First and Second World Wars, the 1935 Regina labor riot (when they faced weapons made out of solid-steel pipe and the like), and in the capture of the mad trapper (who was chased in Arctic temperatures for 54 days in 1931–32), right up to the last dog patrol in 1969, the entry of women into the force in May 1974, and the use of the snowmobile. A computerized history display and other visitor-participation displays appeal to kids.

Kids, and adults too, will probably love to role-play in the cockpit of the de Havilland single-engine Otter from the Air Services Division, and also to see an audiovisual presentation of training.

Besides the museum there is a tour that takes in the chapel and, when possible, recruits in training. The highlight is the Sergeant Major's Parade, which normally takes place around 12:45pm Monday through Friday. The schedule is tentative, so call before you go.

Admission: Free.
Open: June 1–Sept 15 daily 8am–6:45pm; rest of the year, daily 10am–4:45pm.
Closed: Christmas Day.

THE TRIAL OF LOUIS RIEL

Louis Riel was tried and hanged in Regina in 1885. Bitter arguments have been fought between those who regard Riel as a patriot and martyr and those who regard him as a rebel. Whatever the opinion, Riel certainly raises some extremely deep and discomforting questions. As G. F. Stanley, professor of history at the Royal Military College, Kingston, has written, "The mere mention of his name bares those latent religious and racial animosities which seem to lie so close to the surface of Canadian politics."

Even though he took up the cause of the mixed-blood population of the west, French-speaking Canadians often regarded him as a martyr and English-speaking Canadians damned him as a madman. Written by John Coulter, *The Trial of Louis Riel* is a play based on the actual court records of the historical trial. It is presented

Wednesday to Friday at the Mackenzie Art Gallery during August. Certainly thought-provoking, the play raises such issues as language rights, prejudice, and justice. Tickets are $9. For reservations call 306/522-4242 or 306/525-1185.

WHERE TO STAY

Remember to add 7% PST and 7% GST tax to the rates below.

DOWNTOWN

Expensive

DELTA REGINA, 1818 Victoria Ave., Regina, SK, S4P 0R1. Tel. 306/ 569-1666. Fax 306/525-3550. 251 rms. A/C TV TEL
$ Rates: $130 single; $140 double. Children under 18 stay free in parents' room. Weekend packages available. AE, DC, ER, MC, V. **Parking:** $3.
The Delta Regina has a natural and graceful air that you'll notice the minute you walk into the lobby with its earth-color stone walls and pastel-colored coffee plaza with plants scattered around. Off this lobby lies the Cellar, where you can dine seated inside an oak vat under lamps created from wine casks—you even have your own personal dimmer. In the Fireside Lounge, sit around an open firepit on soft velour banquettes and enjoy nightly entertainment and dancing; the decor evokes a railroad parlor car. Another facility is the Village Pub, for darts, backgammon, and of course, drinks. To complete the picture, there's the luxurious Oasis on the second floor, housing saunas, sunlamps, whirlpool, miniature golf, and an indoor pool under a solarium dome. The hotel also has a children's play area.
The rooms are attractively decorated in jade and mauve with modern furnishings and all the usual facilities, including push-button phones and clock radios.

HOTEL SASKATCHEWAN, 2125 Victoria Ave., at Scarth, Regina, SK, S4P 0S3. Tel. 306/522-7691. Fax 306/757-5521. 200 rms. A/C MINIBAR TV TEL
$ Rates: $135 single; $155 double. Extra person $15. Children under 12 stay free in parents' room. AE, CB, DC, DISC, ER, MC, V. **Parking:** Free.
The ivy-covered limestone exterior of the Hotel Saskatchewan has a rather solid old-world air about it that provides a satisfying prelude to the modern comfort within. The large, almost heart-shaped clock that hangs in the lobby is original to the 1927 Georgian-style building.
The rooms have elegant high ceilings and decorative moldings; all bathrooms contain a hairdryer and an additional phone. A fully equipped fitness center with sauna is available.
The long narrow lobby leads to the L-shaped Ranch Room, with terraced seating highlighted by brick archways, wooden pillars, stately windows, and a coffered oak ceiling with brass chandeliers. The menu specializes in grills, seafood, veal, and chicken dishes (from $15 to $22) at dinner and a lighter selection at lunchtime. In the Monarch Lounge, Victorian furniture (plush sofas, tables with carved pedestal bases) creates a tasteful and restful setting for a quiet drink.

RAMADA RENAISSANCE, 1919 Saskatchewan Dr., Regina, SK, S4P 4H2. Tel. 306/525-5255. Fax 306/781-7188. 255 rms. A/C MINIBAR TV TEL
$ Rates: $130 single; $140 double. Extra person $10. Children under 16 stay free in parents' room. Weekend rates available. AE, DC, ER, MC, V. **Parking:** Free.
Conveniently located downtown in the Saskatchewan Trade and Convention Centre, the Ramada Renaissance is adjacent to two large retail malls, the Cornwall Centre and the Galleria. The rooms are modern and elegantly appointed with color TVs, marble vanities, sitting areas, and desks.
There are two restaurants—the casual Summerfields's and the more formal Capital's as well as Caper's Lounge for cocktails. Facilities include the Waterworks

Recreation Complex with three-story indoor water slide, swimming pool, and whirlpool.

REGINA INN, Victoria Ave. and Broad St., Regina, SK, S4P 1Y2. Tel. 306/525-6767, or toll free 800/667-8162 in Canada. Fax 306/525-3630. 240 rms. A/C MINIBAR TV TEL

$ Rates: $140 single or double. Extra person $10. Children under 18 stay free in parents' room. Weekend family rates from $65 per night. AE, DC, ER, MC. **Parking:** Free indoor parking.

The Regina Inn occupies an entire block and offers numerous facilities within. Its rooms, most with balconies, have contemporary decor with a warm pink or earth-tone color scheme. All of the rooms have louvered closets, color TVs, and clock radios. Guests enjoy the two outdoor hot tubs, sun deck, and a health club.

Just off the pretty lobby, with its plants and stone-walled fountain, the Courtyard is an enjoyable place for dining at any time of the day, surrounded by pink decor and bamboo and plant accents. On the other side of the lobby, the lounge is a pleasant end-of-the-day cocktail spot, and on Friday and Saturday evening the original California Club, Regina's number-one nightspot, swings to the sounds from the '50s and '60s.

Moderate

CHELTON INN, 1907 11th Ave., Regina, SK, S4P 0J2. Tel. 306/569-4600, or toll free 800/667-9922 in Canada. Fax 306/569-4531. 56 rms. A/C MINIBAR TV TEL

$ Rates: $74–$104 single; $79–$115 double. Top prices are for suites. Weekend rates available. AE, DC, ER, MC, V. **Parking:** Free.

The Chelton Inn is very conveniently located right downtown and is also small enough to provide friendly personal service. The rooms, all very large, sport modern furnishings. A bed-sitting room will contain table, chairs, drawers, and couch, as well as a sink, fridge, and private bathroom. Even the smallest rooms are bright and spacious compared to most other accommodations. Suites have a separate bedroom and living area.

The dining room is a local favorite for continental cuisine. Lithographs and large chandeliers impart a certain elegance to the room. There's a separate comfortable lounge up front.

VICTORIA INN, 1717 Victoria Ave., Regina, SK, S4P 0P9. Tel. 306/757-0663, or toll free 800/667-8190. Fax 306/757-0672. 126 rms. A/C TV TEL

$ Rates: $54 single; $64 double. Extra person $5. Children 12 and under stay free in parents' room. AE, ER, MC, V. **Parking:** Free.

Standing across from the Regina Inn is the seven-story-high Victoria Inn. All rooms feature contemporary furniture, color-coordinated spreads and curtains, and the usual accoutrements, including color TVs and radios. Rooms at the back of the hotel are quieter and might be preferred. There's a lounge and restaurant.

ALONG ALBERT STREET

If you are coming from the U.S. border you'll probably come into Regina along Albert Street South, which presents several accommodations choices.

LANDMARK INN, 4150 Albert St., Regina, SK, S4S 3R8. Tel. 306/586-5363. Fax 306/586-0901. 188 rms. A/C TV TEL

$ Rates: $70 single; $80 double. Children under 18 stay free in parents' room. Weekend specials available. AE, DC, ER, MC, V. **Parking:** Free.

The most luxurious accommodation on the strip is the Landmark Inn. From the road it looks long, low, and sleekly modern, and the interior consolidates that impression. It offers a selection of dining and entertaining establishments. You can play darts or dance to Top 40 tunes at Checkers, an olde English pub with horse brasses and hunting prints. The Wheatsheaf serves as all-day coffee shop. There's also an al fresco beer garden called Scotland Yard, and an attractive recreation center with indoor pool, water slide, sauna, whirlpool, and video games.

The rooms are pleasantly decorated with floral spreads and curtains, modern furniture, clock radios, and color TVs with sports and movie stations.

REGINA TRAVELODGE, 4177 Albert St., Regina, SK, S4S 3R6. Tel. 306/586-3443. Fax 306/586-9311. 200 rms. A/C TV TEL

$ Rates: $73 single; $79 double. Extra person $5. Children under 18 stay free in parents' room. AE, DC, DISC, ER, MC, V. **Parking:** Free.

The Regina TraveLodge has been completely renovated. On the premises is Oscar's restaurant, serving breakfast, lunch, and dinner and specializing in prime rib, steaks, and seafood. The rooms are contemporary in style. Facilities include pool, water slide, and whirlpool.

RELAX INN, 4025 Albert St., Regina, SK, S4S 3R6. Tel. 306/586-2663. Fax 306/584-1345. 84 rms. A/C TV TEL

$ Rates: $45 single; $50 double. Extra person $6. Children under 18 stay free in parents' room. AE, DC, ER, MC, V. **Parking:** Free.

When you enter the Relax Inn, you're quite likely to see people splashing around in the indoor pool, visible off the lobby. The area is tropically landscaped with lush greenery. Beyond the pool area you'll find the coffee shop, offering lighter fare from 7am to 11pm. The rooms are decorated in warm tones.

SEVEN OAKS MOTOR INN, 777 Albert St., Regina, SK, S4R 2P6. Tel. 306/757-0121. Fax 306/565-2577. 156 rms. A/C TV TEL

$ Rates: $60–$75 single; $65–$145 double. Extra person $5. Children under 16 stay free in parents' room. AE, ER, MC, V. **Parking:** Free.

The Seven Oaks features a water slide and a whirlpool in a central pool area surrounded by modern, well-furnished, and fully equipped rooms. Room decor features brightly colored drapes and spreads and burnt-orange shag carpeting; each unit's color TV has special sports, music, and movie channels. Third-floor executive rooms have queen-size beds and complimentary breakfast. Other facilities include Julie's Lounge for cocktails, Seven's Club for dancing to recorded music, and a family restaurant. There's also a fitness room with Universal and cycle machines.

AROUND TOWN

Moderate

JOURNEY'S END, 3221 E. Eastgate Dr., Regina, SK, S4N 0T0. Tel. and fax 306/789-5522. 100 rms. A/C TV TEL

$ Rates: $56.99 single; $64.99 double. AE, DC, ER, MC, V. **Parking:** Free.

For nicely furnished modern accommodations, it's hard to beat Journey's End, which charges surprisingly low rates for its well-equipped rooms.

TRAVELODGE REGINA EAST, 1110 E. Victoria Ave., Regina, SK, S4P 0N7. Tel. 306/565-0455. Fax 306/569-0012. 190 rms. A/C TV TEL

$ Rates: $49.95 single; $57.95 double. Extra person $6. Children under 18 stay free in parents' room. AE, DC, DISC, ER, MC, V. **Parking:** Free.

The Relax Inn offers rooms spread over three floors, all with color TVs, stucco walls, ultramodern furniture, and rose and blue color schemes. Bathrooms have colorful patterned floor tiles. Off the lobby is an indoor swimming pool and whirlpool, and a family restaurant adjoins.

Budget

TURGEON INTERNATIONAL HOSTEL, 2310 McIntyre St., Regina, SK, S4P 2S2. Tel. 306/791-8165. 50 beds. A/C

$ Rates: $10 members; $15 nonmembers. MC, V. **Parking:** Free.

Regina is fortunate to have one of the best, if not *the* best, youth hostel I've ever seen. It's the Turgeon International Hostel, located in a handsome 1907 town house adjacent to Wascana Centre. Inside, the place sparkles throughout. Accommodations are in dormitories with three or four bunks; the top floor has two larger dorms, and each dorm has access to a deck. Downstairs there's a comfortable sitting room worthy of any inn, with couches in front of the oak fireplace and plenty of magazines and books. In fact, the hostel acts as a resource center for travelers. The basement contains an impeccably clean dining and cooking area with electric stoves, as well as a laundry. Picnic tables are available in the backyard. A gem!

It's open year-round, daily from 7 to 10am and 5pm to midnight, with lights out at 11:30pm.

WHERE TO DINE

Not so long ago travelers in Regina had to content themselves with steak and Chinese food or else go hungry. Not quite so anymore.

DOWNTOWN

BARTLEBY'S, 1920 Broad St. Tel. 306/565-0040.
Cuisine: CANADIAN. **Reservations:** Recommended.
$ Prices: Main courses $7–$14. AE, DC, ER, MC, V.
Open: Mon–Sat noon–1am, Sun noon–midnight.

Barry Armstrong and his partners have amassed a wealth of Victoriana at Bartleby's, and created an interesting, lively eating spot and popular bar crammed with Canadiana, stained-glass panels, treadle tables, old advertisements, bicycles hanging from the ceiling, and such.

At dinner you might have prime rib, baby back ribs, lasagne, perch filet, or chicken teriyaki followed by cheesecake or mud pie for dessert. At lunchtime there's a selection of sandwiches, plus soups and burgers.

C C LLOYD'S, in the Chelton Inn, 1907 11th Ave. Tel. 306/569-4650.
Cuisine: CONTINENTAL. **Reservations:** Recommended.
$ Prices: Main courses $12–$23. AE, DC, ER, MC, V.
Open: Mon–Sat 7am–9pm, Sun 8am–2pm.

C C Lloyd's draws a strong local following. The cuisine served is classic—lobster provençale, orange roughy, filet of beef Madeira, chicken Cordon Bleu, and veal Oscar. There is also, of course, a selection of steaks. Among the appetizers, try the salmon and crab pâté en croûte, the mousse of chicken liver Madeira, or a warm quail salad. Desserts are equally classic—strawberry savarin, pear in red wine sauce, and crème caramel.

THE DIPLOMAT, 2032 Broad St. Tel. 306/359-3366.
Cuisine: CANADIAN. **Reservations:** Recommended.
$ Prices: Main courses $16–$25. AE, DC, ER, MC, V.
Open: Lunch Mon–Fri 11:30am–2pm; dinner Mon–Sat 4pm–midnight.

The Diplomat is one of Regina's elegant steakhouses. The room features semicircular banquettes and tables set with pink cloths, burgundy napkins, and tiny lanterns. Around the room hang portraits of eminent-looking prime ministers; there's a fireplace and lounge up front. The main attractions on the menu are the steaks—20-ounce porterhouse, 18-ounce T-bone—along with chicken Cordon Bleu, duck à l'orange, and other typical favorites.

GOLF'S STEAK HOUSE, 1945 Victoria Ave., at Hamilton St. Tel. 306/525-5808.
Cuisine: CANADIAN. **Reservations:** Required.
$ Prices: Main courses $10–$36. AE, DC, ER, MC, V.
Open: Lunch Mon–Fri 11:30am–2pm; dinner Mon–Sat 4:30pm–midnight, Sun and holidays 4:30–11pm.

In this venerable Regina institution, the atmosphere is decidedly plush (note the large fireplace, the piano and antique organ, the heavy gilt-framed paintings, and the high-backed carved-oak Charles II–style chairs). The menu offers traditional steakhouse fare. Start with smoked salmon or shrimp scampi before moving on to stuffed trout, baby back ribs, or any number of steaks. All dishes are served with soup, salad, hot garlic bread, and baked potato with sour cream, chives, and crisp Canadian bacon. For dessert there's a special treat, baked Alaska.

MIEKA'S, 1810 Smith St. Tel. 306/522-6700.
   Cuisine: INTERNATIONAL. **Reservations:** Recommended.
$ Prices: Main courses $10–$17. DC, ER, MC, V.
   Open: Tues–Thurs 11:30am–10pm, Fri–Sat 11:30am–11:30pm.

⭐ Mieka's belongs to 38-year-old Mieka Wiens who, upon her return from studying at the London Cordon Bleu cookery school, decided to open a rather different and experimental restaurant, at least for Regina. The decor, created by her architect father to her specifications, is light and airy, with lithographs and tasteful contemporary art on the white walls. The ceiling has been dropped, and the room is lit at night by lamps and candles. Fig trees and other plants add splashes of color to the evenness of tone created by the white Arborite tables and Naugahyde armchairs.

The comfortable bar serves standard drinks, imported red and white wine, plus champagne by the glass (or half-liter), and several good wines and champagne by the bottle at reasonable prices.

But it is the food that is really exciting—light and fresh, seasonal, and homemade. For instance, in August or September you're likely to find pumpkin soup featured on the menu. Otherwise, there's a selection of imaginative sandwiches—pepper steak with pimiento mayonnaise or a Dagwood (with herb-and-spice cream cheese, pâté, cucumber, tomato, and lettuce, garnished with green-pepper rings). Salads are also featured—Saskatchewan wild rice and chicken, for example, along with several daily specials. Dinner might begin with empanaditas (small Spanish cheese turnovers) and proceed to scallops in red pepper sherry sauce, roast pork loin with honey mustard bourbon sauce, or orange-ginger sautéed chicken.

At a recent lunch I enjoyed sweet-potato soup that was filled with diced sweet potato and vegetables, and flavored with a hint of curry. The salad that followed included a variety of greens, flecked with peanuts and chunks of sharp Cheddar cheese dressed with a herb vinaigrette. To finish, the mango-and-lime dessert was superb, and there are other yummy desserts (from $3.50) such as hazelnut raspberry devil's food cake.

EVENING ENTERTAINMENT

Hardly Canada's nightlife capital, the city does have one or two spots for dancing, most often located in the hotels, plus a marvelous cultural center in the middle of Wascana Park.

SASKATCHEWAN CENTRE OF THE ARTS On the southern shore of Wascana Lake stands the modern Saskatchewan Centre of the Arts (tel. 306/565-4500 or for the box office 306/525-9999), which opened in 1970. It contains two theaters and a large hall: the 2,029-seat Centennial Theatre; the smaller Jubilee Theatre, used for theater-in-the-round, proscenium performances, and recitals; and Hanbidgel Hall, 12,200 square feet of convention and banquet space. Offerings at the center are varied—from Men at Work, to Harry Belafonte, to dance performances, and the Regina Symphony Orchestra. Tickets vary in price depending on the show, and can range from $25 to $55 for first-run musicals and comedies. The center box office at 200 Lakeshore Dr. (tel. 306/525-9999) is open from 11am to 5:30pm Monday through Saturday.

THEATER The **Globe Theatre,** Old City Hall, 1801 Scarth St. (tel. 306/525-6400), is a theater-in-the-round. The Globe presents six mainstage plays each October-to-April season. Productions run the gamut from classics (Shakespeare, Molière, Shaw, etc.) to modern dramas, musicals, and comedies. Ticket prices range from $8 to $17.

THE CLUB & BAR SCENE A slightly older crowd (25 to 35, can you believe) frequents the **Manhattan Club,** upstairs at 2300 Dewdney St. (tel. 306/359-7771). Open Thursday and Saturday only.

The college crowd favors **Checker's,** at the Landmark Inn, 4150 Albert St. (tel. 306/586-5363), a comfortable, rustic, and relaxed dance spot. In summer, the outdoor area called Scotland Yard is also crowded.

For more relaxed entertainment, the piano at the **Regina Inn** lounge or the Delta Regina's **Fireside Lounge** provides welcome relief. Open Monday through Saturday from 11am to 1am.

---

2. SASKATOON

160 miles (259km) NW of Regina;
482 miles (777km) NW of Winnipeg

GETTING THERE   By Plane   Air Canada, 123 Second Ave. South (tel. 306/653-6392), and Canadian Airlines International (tel. 306/665-7688) fly in and out of the one-terminal airport.

By Train   VIA Rail trains leave from and arrive at the station in the west end of the city on Chappel Drive. For information, call 306/384-5665; for reservations, toll free 800/561-8630 in Canada.

By Bus   Greyhound bus services can be reached at 306/933-8000. Buses depart and arrive at the terminal at 50 23rd St. East.

SPECIAL EVENTS   Saskatoon's **Exhibition,** usually held the second week of July, provides some grand agricultural spectacles, such as the threshing competition in which steam power is pitted against gas—sometimes with unexpected results—and the tractor-pulling competition, when standard farm tractors are used to pull a steel sled weighted down with a water tank. The pay-one-price admission of $7 ($5 seniors and youths 11 to 15, children under 11 free) includes the Great American High Dive (Olympic medal winners in a high-dive show), racing armadillos (or similar), and super dog show, Thoroughbred racing, and much, much more. Country-and-western to rock-and-roll entertainment. Face painting, magicians, clowns, games, and a midway for the kids. A full schedule of agricultural events is held, and there's a casino, midway, and other attractions. For more information, contact Saskatoon PrairieLand Exhibition Corporation, P.O. Box 6010, Saskatoon, SK, S7K 4E4 (tel. 306/931-7149).

A **Folkfest** is held mid-August, celebrating the many ethnic groups in the city, and the **Prairieland Pro Rodeo** is held at the Exhibition Stadium in fall.

Saskatoon (pop. 184,000) is rapidly throwing off its frontier look and transforming itself into a progressive city on the plains. Although the city has much to recommend it both scenically and culturally, what always strikes me most on any visit are the amazing qualities of its people—friendly, and very genuine in their caring for others. That certainly makes it a great place for visitors!

In 1979, when the first edition of this book was researched, agriculture was still very much the dominant focus of the city, and there were still reminders of its hunting and trapping days. It was still very much a frontier town, but increasingly the city is attracting more industry, and in particular mining companies, standing as it does at the center of a vast mining region that yields potash, uranium, petroleum, gas, and gold. Key Lake, for example, is the largest uranium mine outside Russia.

I don't want to convey the wrong impression. There's still a distinctly western air to the town. Downtown streets are broad and dusty, dotted in summer with many a pickup truck. Those same downtown streets just seem to disappear on the edge of town into the prairie, where grain elevators and telegraph poles become the only reference points and the sky your only company. But the city is definitely changing.

Scenically Saskatoon possesses some distinct natural advantages. The Lower Saskatchewan River cuts a swath through the city, spanned by several graceful bridges. Both riverbanks have mercifully been kept free of development and so offer pleasant retreats within the city, especially along the Meewasin Valley, which runs for miles along the riverbank and makes for great strolling, cycling, and jogging.

SOME HISTORY   Saskatoon was originally founded in 1882 as a teetotaler's haven by John Lake and a group of Ontario Methodists who were granted 200,000 acres on and about the present site of the city. Since the grant stipulated that odd-numbered sections of the land had to be reserved for free homesteads, the colony did not remain teetotal for long.

Minnetonka was the settlement's original name, but Lake was so taken with the red berries that were abundant in the area that he renamed it Saskatoon in their honor.

In its early days the settlement lost out in the struggle for the railroad, which passed 150 miles south, thereby leaving Saskatoon in the backwaters until 1890 when the railroad finally penetrated from Moose Jaw. Even then it was not until the 1900s, when the agricultural potential of the surrounding area was realized, that the city was incorporated (1906) and it experienced a boom that saw, among other things, the founding of the University of Saskatchewan in 1907. The university has long been a pioneer in high-technology medicine, having been one of the major developers of cobalt-60 treatment for cancer and also of laser-beam eye surgery.

ORIENTATION

TOURIST INFORMATION For answers to all your travel problems, drop into **Tourism Saskatoon.** During the summer (from around May 18 to the end of August), tourist booths are open at Avenue C North at 47th Street, Highway 11 South at Grasswood Road, and Highway 7 at 11th Street West. Tourism Saskatoon is located at 102–310 Idylwyld Dr. North (P.O. Box 369), Saskatoon, SK, S7K 3L3 (tel. 306/242-1206), open Monday to Friday, 8:30am to 5pm (in summer Saturday 9am to 4:30pm).

CITY LAYOUT The main thing to remember when moving around town is that 22nd Street divides the city into northern and southern sections, and Idylwyld Drive divides east from west.

The South Saskatchewan River cuts a diagonal north-south swath through the city. The main downtown area lies on the west bank; the University of Saskatchewan and the long neon-sign-crazed 8th Street dominate the east bank.

Streets are laid out in a numbered grid system—22nd Street divides north and south designated streets; Idylwyld Drive divides, in a similar fashion, east from west. First Street through 18th Street lie on the east side of the river; 19th Street and up, on the west bank in the downtown area. Spadina Crescent runs along the west bank of the river, where you'll find such landmarks as the Bessborough Hotel, the Ukrainian Museum, and the art gallery.

GETTING AROUND

You probably won't need to use transportation too often except to visit the University of Saskatchewan and the Western Development Museum, but there's a perfectly adequate system of buses operated by the **Saskatoon Transit System,** 301 24th St. West at Avenue C (tel. 306/975-3100), which require $1.10 in exact change. For routes and schedules, contact the office.

Taxis are, as usual, expensive—$1.90 when you step inside and 10¢ every 120 meters (135 yards)—but here are the names of two companies: **Saskatoon Radio Cab** (tel. 306/242-1221) and **United Cabs** (tel. 306/652-2222), which also operates the limousine to the airport ($6 from downtown hotels).

Car-rental companies: **Avis,** 2130 Airport Dr. (tel. 306/652-3434); **Budget,** 234 First Ave. South, 2215 Ave. C North (tel. 306/244-7925); **Hertz,** 2323 8th St. East (tel. 306/373-1161); and **Tilden,** 321 21st St. East (tel. 306/652-3355).

IMPRESSIONS

The Lord said 'let there be wheat' and Saskatchewan was born.
—STEPHEN LEACOCK, *MY DISCOVERY OF AMERICA,* 1937

FAST FACTS

Business Hours Banking hours are Monday through Thursday from 10am to 4pm, on Friday to 5pm. Stores are open Monday through Saturday from 9am to 6pm, on Thursday until 9pm.

Emergencies Hospitals include St. Paul's, 1702 20th St. West (tel. 306/382-3220); Saskatoon City Hospital, 701 Queen St. (tel. 306/242-6681); and University Hospital, University Grounds (tel. 306/244-2323).

Liquor Stores Liquor stores are located at 401 20th St. West (tel. 306/933-5312; open from 11am to 6pm daily except Sunday), and 1701 Idylwyld Dr. North (tel. 306/933-5319; open from 11am to 6pm daily except Monday and Sunday, to 9pm on Thursday).

Newspapers and Magazines The daily newspaper, the *Star-Phoenix,* has a circulation of 60,000; there's also a weekly paper, the *Western Producer.*

Post Office The post office is located at 202 Fourth Ave. North (tel. 306/668-6723), and is open Monday through Friday from 8am to 5pm.

Taxes There's a 7% provincial tax in Saskatchewan.

WHAT TO SEE & DO

MENDEL ART GALLERY AND CIVIC CONSERVATORY, 950 Spadina Crescent East. Tel. 306/975-7610.

Housed in a visually striking modern building overlooking the South Saskatchewan River, a short walk from downtown, the Mendel Art Gallery and Civic Conservatory has a good permanent collection of Canadian paintings, sculpture, watercolors, and graphics, including works by Emily Carr, David Milne, and Lawren S. Harris, as well as more modern works by artists like David Craven, Greg Curnoe, Toni Onley, and Dorothy Knowles.

The gallery also arranges special shows, plus lecture, recital, and film programs. It also houses a conservatory with a fountain coolly playing amid a variety of exotic plants and tropical trees.

Admission: Free.

Open: Daily 10am–9pm. **Closed:** Christmas Day.

UKRAINIAN MUSEUM OF CANADA, 910 Spadina Crescent East. Tel. 306/244-3800.

Reminiscent of a Ukrainian home in western Canada at the turn of the century, this museum preserves the Ukrainian heritage as expressed and contained in such items as clothing, linens, tools, books, photographs, documents, wooden folk art, ceramics, pysanky (Easter eggs), and other treasures and art forms brought from the "old homeland" by Ukrainian immigrants to Canada.

Admission: $2 adults, $1 seniors, 50¢ children 6–12.

Open: Mon–Sat 10am–5pm, Sun 1–5pm.

WESTERN DEVELOPMENT MUSEUM, 2610 Lorne Ave. South. Tel. 306/931-1910.

✪ The energetic years of Saskatchewan settlement are vividly portrayed by "Boomtown 1910," an authentic replica of prairie community life as it was lived in the year 1910. Step onto the main street of Boomtown, and the memories of an earlier age flood the senses. Browse through the shops crammed with the unfamiliar goods of days gone by; savor the past through the intermingling of mysterious aromas that permeate the drugstore; step aside as you hear the clip-clop of a passing horse and buggy; or wander down to Boomtown Station drawn by the low wail of an approaching steam locomotive. The week-long Saskatoon Exhibition, held in mid-July, is a special time when the Saskatoon Museum truly comes to life, as Boomtown is manned by volunteers in authentic costume and many of the pieces of vintage equipment are pressed into service once again. The museum also houses a collection of vintage cars, from the 1905 Cadillac touring car to the Edsel and Ford Fairlane. While you're here, contemplate the old farm machinery and imagine the huge steam tractors slowly chugging across the horizon, their whistles tooting and funnels pumping steam.

Admission: $4 adults, $3 seniors, $1.50 children 5–12, $10 families.

Open: Daily 9am–5pm. **Directions:** Take Idylwyld Drive south to the Lorne Avenue exit and follow Lorne Avenue south until you see the museum on the right. **Bus:** No. 1 from the 23rd Street Bus Mall between Second and Third Avenues.

FORESTRY FARM PARK AND ZOO, 1903 Forest Dr. Tel. 306/975-3382.

This is an excellent site for a barbecue, after which you can wander around and view the 300 or so species of Canadian and Saskatchewan wildlife gathered here. Wolf, coyote, fox, bear, raccoon, eagle, owl, and hawk, different kinds of deer, caribou, elk, and bison all have their home here. There's a children's zoo, too.

During the winter you can cross-country ski the 2½-mile trail. During the summer there's a large sports field to play in. And if you don't feel like picnicking, there's a food concession in the park.

Admission: $2.50 adults, $1.75 students and senior citizens, $1.25 children under 12.

Open: May 1–Labor Day daily 9am–9pm; Labor Day–Apr 30 daily 10am–4pm. **Directions:** It's located in northeast Saskatoon; follow the signs on Attridge Drive from Circle Drive.

MORE ATTRACTIONS

The **University of Saskatchewan** (tel. 306/244-4343) occupies a dramatic 2,550-acre site overlooking the South Saskatchewan River and is attended by some 15,000 students. The actual campus buildings are set on 360 acres while the rest of the area is largely given over to the University Farm and experimental plots. Tours of the university campus can be taken from May through August (call 306/966-8385 for information). Some of the more interesting highlights include the **biology museum** (open weekdays from 8:30am to 4:30pm), which combines live and fossil exhibits (fish, amphibians, birds, and mammals, plus full-size replicas of dinosaurs and flying reptiles) to trace the evolution of prairie flora and fauna. The kids really appreciate this museum, for they can view close up bush babies, ferrets, rattlesnakes, crocodiles, various fish and bird species, and beautiful sea anemones and sponges. The **Rt. Hon. John G. Diefenbaker Centre** contains the papers and memorabilia of one of Canada's best-known prime ministers (open from 9:30am to 4:30pm weekdays and 12:30 to 5pm on Saturday, Sunday, and holidays). The **Observatory** (open Saturday evenings from 8 to 11pm) houses the Duncan telescope; the **Little Stone Schoolhouse** was built in 1887 and served as the city's first school and community center (open May to June, weekdays from 9:30am to 4pm; July 1 to Labor Day, weekends only, from 12:30 to 5pm). For more information, contact the High School Liaison Office, University of Saskatchewan, Saskatoon, SK, S7N 0W0 (tel. 306/966-8385). Special tours of the research farm, engineering building, and other sites can be arranged.

To get there, take bus no. 2 or 7 from downtown at 23rd Street and Second Avenue.

For a change of pace, head for the bandstand south of the Bessborough Hotel and hop aboard the luxurious 28-foot pontoon riverboat **WW Northcote River Cruiser** (tel. 306/665-1818) and cruise for an hour along the South Saskatchewan River. From May to September, cruises begin every hour on the hour from 1 to 8pm, except at 5pm.

SHOPPING

Several opportunities for shopping under one roof can be found downtown in the **Midtown Plaza** and at the **Scotia Centre.** Other outlying malls include the huge new **Circle Park Plaza,** which is filled with 71 independent (rather than chain) stores.

The **gift shops** at the art gallery and also at the Western Development Museum both have good-quality attractive gifts.

For Canadian gifts, stop in at **The Trading Post,** 226 Second Ave. South (tel.

306/653-1769), which carries Inuit soapstone carvings, Native Canadian art, Cowichan sweaters, beadwork, and more.

WHERE TO STAY

Remember to add 7% PST and 7% GST tax to the rates below.

DOWNTOWN

Very Expensive

RAMADA HOTEL DOWNTOWN SASKATOON, 405 20th St. East, Saskatoon, SK, S7K 6X6. Tel. 306/665-3322, or toll free 800/228-2828. Fax 306/665-5531. 291 rms. A/C TV TEL

$ Rates: From $130 single; from $140 double. Extra person $10. Children under 16 stay free in parents' room. Weekend packages available. AE, DC, ER, MC, V. **Parking:** Free.

Offering a riverside location in the heart of downtown, the Ramada is Saskatoon's newest luxury property. The skylit lobby is gracious and inviting with its handsome ash/oak walls, pink marble staircase and ornamentation, and bubbling fountain. Its rooms are well appointed, decorated attractively in pastel colors, and equipped with cable color TVs and all other modern amenities. About a third of the rooms offer river views. The corner rooms are particularly attractive.

Guests enjoy a three-story recreation complex containing a large indoor swimming pool, two indoor water slides, a sauna, and a whirlpool. Jogging and cross-country ski trails adjoin the property.

There are ample food and beverage facilities. Whiteside's, an intimate gourmet dining room, features pretty floral banquettes, pink-clothed tables, and French/continental haute cuisine. Bamboo and greenery set the tone in the pleasant coffee shop. Off the lobby, Caper's lounge is screened by plant settings.

Expensive

DELTA BESSBOROUGH, 601 Spadina Crescent East, Saskatoon, SK, S7K 3G8. Tel. 306/244-5521. Fax 306/653-2458. 227 rms and suites. A/C MINIBAR TV TEL

$ Rates: $100 single; $110 double. Higher rates for suite. Extra person $10. Weekend package $69 per night single or double. Children under 18 stay free in parents' room. AE, MC, V. **Parking:** Free.

An elegant and gracious hostelry built in 1930 and finished in 1935, the Bessborough was dashingly constructed to look like a French château, with a copper roof and turrets. Inside, each of the rooms is different, although all have venerable oak entrance doors and antique or traditional furniture. Front rooms are large and most have bay windows. Riverside rooms are smaller, but the views across the Saskatchewan River are lovely. All modern amenities are present and accounted for. Other facilities include an outdoor swimming pool set in landscaped grounds that sweep down to the river, an indoor pool with whirlpool, sauna, exercise room, and a riverview coffee shop called Gardens Bistro.

On the ground floor, the Samurai Japanese Steakhouse provides an extremely soothing lounge for that quiet drink and the opportunity to sample Japanese-style steaks and seafood. The most popular item on the menu is the Shogun special, a combination of steak, chicken, and lobster for $26.

HOLIDAY INN, 90 22nd St. East, Saskatoon, SK, S7K 3X6. Tel. 306/244-2311. Fax 306/664-2234. 187 rms. A/C TV TEL

$ Rates: $99 single; $109 double. Extra person $10. Children under 19 stay free in parents' room. Weekend packages available. AE, DC, ER, MC, V. **Parking:** Free.

Really conveniently located, the Holiday Inn stands opposite the Eaton's complex and Centennial Auditorium. The rooms feature the usual Holiday Inn appurtenances: large double or king-size beds, color TVs with in-room movies, radio consoles and alarm clocks, clotheslines in the bathrooms, Scandinavian-style furniture, and color-coordinated fabrics.

R. J. Willoughby offers varied all-day dining; a cocktail lounge adjoins. The restaurant has the finest reputation of any in the city (see my dining recommendations). Facilities also include an indoor pool, whirlpool, and sauna, and a sun deck.

SHERATON CAVALIER, 612 Spadina Crescent East, Saskatoon, SK, S7K 3G9. Tel. 306/652-6770, or toll free 800/325-3535. Fax 306/244-1739. 250 rms. A/C MINIBAR TV TEL

$ Rates: $98 single; $108 double. Children under 18 stay free in parents' room. Weekend packages available. AE, DC, ER, MC, V. **Parking:** Free, indoor.

Just across the street from the Bessborough is the Sheraton Cavalier, a white eight-story structure that contains rooms sporting louvered closets, radios, color TVs, and coffee makers. For businesspeople there's a special executive floor plus six executive rooms—each furnished with Murphy beds, fridge, sink/bar, as well as desk, table, and couch—that can double as meeting rooms.

The hotel also has a top range of facilities, including a complete resort complex with adult and kiddie swimming pools. Here, two extraordinary attractions are the two more than 250-foot-long water slides that attract many happy families, particularly on winter weekends. Also saunas, whirlpool, exercise room, sun deck, games room, and snack bar.

The elegant dining room is Benedict's, with etched-glass panels and a menu priced from $16 to $27 for steak and lobster. Windows Café serves breakfast, lunch, and dinner and overlooks the river. Entertainment and dancing are found in Lorenzo's Piano Lounge. The Barley Bin Pub has snacks, games, and is a good drinking spot.

Moderate

PARK TOWN HOTEL, 924 Spadina Crescent East, Saskatoon, SK, S7K 3H5. Tel. 306/244-5564. Fax 306/665-8698. 109 rms. A/C TV TEL

$ Rates: $70 single; $78 double. Extra person $8. Children under 15 stay free in parents' room. Weekend package $55 per night single or double. AE, CB, DC, DISC, ER, MC, V. **Parking:** Free.

Not quite so central to downtown but still conveniently located is the Park Town Hotel, a modern establishment, part of which was built in 1955, the rest in 1977. It stands just by the bridge over the river to the university, and offers rooms that are currently being renovated, decked out with brass and oak accents, pastel bedspreads and curtains, and shower/tubs in the bathrooms. Local phone calls are free.

Facilities include an attractive indoor pool, sauna, and whirlpool, surrounded by carpeting dotted with garden furniture, various shrubs, and potted plants; colorful banners hang from the ceiling girders. There's also a pleasant family dining room where you can enjoy a good brunch buffet (for $8) or a steak, seafood, or poultry dinner (from $12), plus a lounge.

Budget

KING GEORGE HOTEL, 157 Second Ave. North, Saskatoon, SK, S7K 2A9. Tel. 306/244-6133. Fax 306/652-4672. 104 rms. A/C TV TEL

$ Rates: $44 single; $50 double. Extra person $5. Children under 8 stay free in parents' room. Weekend package $40 single or double. AE, DC, ER, MC, V. **Parking:** Free covered parking.

The King George is an outstanding example of an old downtown hotel that has survived the vicissitudes of time and changing economies and continues to provide basic hospitality. Don't be put off by the somewhat austere exterior, dating to 1911. The whole place was renovated in the 1960s. And recently three of the four floors of rooms were redecorated with new curtains, rugs, and bedspreads. They also feature modern conveniences—color TVs, radios, large closets, and shuttered showers instead of the usual curtained variety.

In the basement, Downstairs at the KG serves steaks, veal Cordon Bleu, and similar items. Prices range from $8 to $15. For fun there's the karaoke sing-along bar and Szyd's, a western-style bar.

THE SENATOR, 243 21st St. East, Saskatoon, SK, S7K 0B7. Tel. 306/244-6141. Fax 306/244-1559. 44 rms. A/C TV TEL

$ Rates: $38 single; $40 double. Family and weekend rates available. AE, DC, ER, MC, V. **Parking:** Free.

The Senator has withstood the test of time and continues to cater to a primarily family trade. Built in 1908 at the corner of 21st Street East and Third Avenue South, it's recognized by its tiled exterior and portico with Corinthian columns. In the lobby there's a wonderful marble newel post at the bottom of the staircase that leads to the rooms on the two floors above. The rooms are furnished in early Scandinavian and contain modern color TVs, radios, and private baths, but each one is different in size and style.

The licensed dining room, Flanagans, with its large chandelier, gilt-framed pictures and wood paneling offers a hearty breakfast, lunch, or dinner. Good, wholesome, and large breakfasts—bacon, ham, or sausage, two eggs, toast, coffee, and jam—are available. At lunch salads—creamy tarragon seafood or strawberry romaine with poppyseed dressing—and sandwiches, are listed with pastas and light entrées like grilled salmon. Dinner features such dishes as New York steak or red snapper with a Caribbean Créole sauce. For dessert try the cappuccino caribou, an espresso-flavored custard on a chocolate base with Belgian chocolate sprinkled on top. *Note:* The dining room is open only from 7am to 9pm.

AROUND TOWN
Moderate

SASKATOON TRAVELODGE, 106 Circle Dr. West, Saskatoon, SK, S7L 4L6. Tel. 306/242-8881, or toll free 800/255-3050. Fax 306/665-7378. 220 rms. A/C TV TEL
$ Rates: $67 single; $72 double. Extra person $5. Children under 17 stay free in parents' room. Cribs free; rollaway beds $7. AE, DC, ER, MC, V. **Parking:** Free.
Still farther north on Idylwyld Drive from the other choices listed here, at the junction of Circle Drive, you'll find the white stucco Saskatoon TraveLodge, an outstanding member of the hotel chain. The lobby features a skylight, a marble front desk, lots of mirrors, and forest-green ottomans.

The rooms, each with either a vanity or small bar area, are variously decorated in brown carpeting with brown floral bedspreads or in burgundy or kingfisher blue. Some rooms have sitting areas and the bed is separated from the rest of the room with a half wall for comfortable effect. There are also 33 no-smoking rooms.

The hotel has an especially attractive pool area with skylit ceiling, tropical gardens, whirlpool, sauna, and poolside rooms with balconies. Another pool in the new section has a 250-foot-long water slide and an additional whirlpool. Dining facilities include the Heritage room for reasonably priced luncheons, dinners, and Sunday brunch buffets. Semicircular booths and low lighting create the atmosphere in Oscar's lounge.

Budget

CONFEDERATION INN, 3330 Fairlight Dr., Saskatoon, SK, S7M 3Y4. Tel. 306/384-2882. Fax 306/384-0773. 40 rms. A/C TV TEL
$ Rates: $44 single; $46 double. Extra person $2. Children under 16 stay free in parents' room. Cots $5. AE, ER, MC, V. **Parking:** Free.
One of the best buys in Saskatoon is found at the Confederation Inn. Standing well back from the road, the inn offers rooms decorated in red with Spanish-style modern furniture. The restaurant on the premises is open from 7am to 8pm daily (the $9 Sunday brunch here is popular). There's also a lounge-bar and indoor pool.

JOURNEY'S END, 2155 Northridge Dr., Saskatoon, SK, S7L 6X6. Tel. 306/934-1122. Fax 304/934-6539. 80 rms. A/C TV TEL
$ Rates: $52.99 single; $60.99 double. AE, DC, ER, MC, V. **Parking:** Free.
For a pleasant, fairly priced room, the Journey's End is a good choice.

WHERE TO DINE

Fourteen years ago when the first edition of this guide came out, Saskatoon was primarily steakhouse country. If you didn't like steak and seafood, you could forget eating. But as the city has grown more sophisticated, so, too, has the restaurant scene.

It's true that steakhouses still predominate, but some interesting restaurant arrivals are tipping the balance away from the red-meat-only prejudice.

EXPENSIVE

COUSIN NIKS, 1110 Grosvenor Ave., between 7th and 8th Sts. Tel. 306/374-2020.
    Cuisine: GREEK/CANADIAN. **Reservations:** Recommended.
$ Prices: Main courses $15–$33. AE, MC, V.
    Open: Dinner daily 5–11pm.

If you have only one dinner in Saskatoon, seek out the not-to-be-missed Cousin Niks. Here you'll find a delightful setting: an open courtyard garden lit from above and made even more charming by the sound of the splashing fountain. Greek rugs add color to the predominantly white color scheme.

A variety of steak and seafood dishes are offered, from filet of sole in oil and lemon-oregano sauce to lobster tails in drawn butter. Main-course prices include avgolemono soup, Greek salad, fresh seasonal fruit, and coffee. A guest book testifies to the happiness of departing gourmets.

This is also a very pleasant spot to stop for a cocktail in the piano lounge.

JOHN'S PRIME RIB, 401 21st St. East. Tel. 306/244-6384.
    Cuisine: STEAK/SEAFOOD. **Reservations:** Recommended.
$ Prices: Main courses $14–$25. AE, DC, ER, MC, V.
    Open: Mon–Fri 11:30am–10:30pm, Sat 4:30–11pm.

John's serves the best the Canadian prairies can offer. The room has been partitioned to provide intimate dining, and the pleasant surroundings are enhanced by a display of wines, original watercolors of prairie scenes, and art prints. The menu concentrates on prime rib, steaks, and seafood, from filet of sole to steak and lobster tail in drawn butter. Appetizers run from onion soup to jumbo shrimp cocktail. Desserts include an intriguing congo pie, a rich combination of chocolate cake with custard filling and chocolate icing, topped with whipped cream and chocolate sauce. At lunchtime there are dishes from $6 to $12, all served with soup, rolls and butter, and potatoes, and also a selection of sandwiches.

MODERATE

ARTFUL DODGER, 119 Fourth Ave. South. Tel. 306/653-2577.
    Cuisine: ENGLISH PUB. **Reservations:** Recommended at lunch.
$ Prices: Main courses $5–$15. AE, MC, V.
    Open: Mon–Sat 11am–1:30am.

The Artful Dodger is designed to re-create a Dickensian atmosphere. Start with French onion soup, and follow with shepherd's pie, Cornish pastry, steak-and-kidney pie, fish-and-chips, or heartier fare, like T-bone or New York steak. Finish with a fine sherry trifle. Some excellent British beers are on hand to enhance the dishes, and while you're here you might enjoy a game of darts, backgammon, or shuffleboard in the bar area.

There are live bands Monday to Saturday from 9pm.

THE CAVE, 2720 8th St. East. Tel. 306/374-5090.
    Cuisine: STEAK/SEAFOOD. **Reservations:** Recommended.
$ Prices: Appetizers $6–$11; main courses $7–$26. AE, MC, V.
    Open: Daily 11am–11:30pm.

Perhaps the most originally designed Saskatoon restaurant is the Cave, for spelunkular dining among stalagmites and stalactites. The restaurant has three dining areas, each with intimate semicircular booths and each part of a labyrinthine design. At the very back of the restaurant is an area filled with plants, where water spills down over the rocks and light comes in from above via tiny portholes. The kids will adore it and the food as well, for they can gorge themselves on 10- or 14-inch pizzas, or spaghetti with clam, tomato, mushroom, or meatball sauce, while the older folks can savor the charcoal-broiled steaks, prime rib, and seafood.

ST. TROPEZ BISTRO, 243 Third Ave. South. Tel. 306/652-1250.

Cuisine: CONTINENTAL. **Reservations:** Recommended.
$ **Prices:** Appetizers $5; main courses $11–$19. AE, MC, V.
Open: Lunch Mon–Sat 11am–2pm; dinner Mon–Sat 4:30–10pm.

One of my favorite downtown restaurants is St. Tropez Bistro. The background music is classical or French, and the tables are covered in Laura Ashley–style floral-design prints and adorned with ceramic vases of flowers.

At lunchtime various sandwiches, quiches, and crêpes (from $7 to $9) are available. The bread, by the way, is home-baked. At night, you can choose from a variety of crêpes and quiches and such specials as veal piccata, sole amandine, and spinach chicken. Also available are cheese soufflé or cheese fondue ($26 for two), and rich chocolate fondue with fresh fruit ($13 for two).

This is one place where you can find out what's happening culturally in Saskatoon, too.

SASKATOON STATION PLACE, 221 Idylwyld Dr. North. Tel. 306/244-7777.
Cuisine: STEAK/SEAFOOD. **Reservations:** Recommended on weekends.
$ **Prices:** Main courses $10–$30. AE, ER, MC, V.
Open: Mon–Sat 10:45am–midnight, Sun and holidays 10am–10pm. Sun brunch served 10am–2pm.

Saskatoon Station Place is a terrific place to sample traditional Canadian beef supplemented by some Greek specialties. Predinner cocktails are available from the ornately carved bar. Just make yourself comfortable in the plush railroad coach complete with stained-glass accents and brass luggage racks overhead. The newspaper-style menu lists primarily steaks and seafood. For example, there are Greek-style spareribs and several souvlakis. The steaks are good and fairly priced. Eight or so seafood dishes run from lobster tails to halibut steak. Start with stuffed mushrooms or scampi.

BUDGET

ADONIS, 103B Third Ave. South. Tel. 306/652-9598.
Cuisine: MIDDLE EASTERN. **Reservations:** Accepted only for parties of 10 or more.
$ **Prices:** Main courses $10–$13. AE, MC, V.
Open: Mon–Sat 9am–8pm.

The really fresh ingredients used at Adonis make for some excellent food at breakfast, lunch, or dinner. During the day you order at the counter, but at night the room is transformed by the simple addition of tablecloths and candlelight. In summer the sidewalk café is one of Saskatoon's few, or so it seems. At lunch, choose among falafel, hummus, donair, and a variety of fresh salads and sandwiches. Be sure to taste the baklava—crisp, sweet, and rolled rather than layered—absolutely addictive. At dinner the menu offers an array of North African and Middle Eastern specialties—dolmathes, couscous, steak Andalousia (with onions, garlic, tomatoes, green pepper, and red wine sauce), and a variety of kebabs. To start, try the escargots in a mushroom cap or the avocados stuffed with shrimp and topped with royal sauce.

BOOMTOWN CAFE, 2610 Lorne Ave. South. Tel. 306/931-1910.
Cuisine: CANADIAN. **Reservations:** Not accepted.
$ **Prices:** Most items $4–$6. MC, V.
Open: Mon–Fri 7:30am–5pm, Sat–Sun 9am–5pm.

At the Western Development Museum there's a pretty ginghamy café serving pioneer-style food—that is, such items as cabbage borscht, cabbage rolls, buffalo stew, or buffalo burgers, all at very reasonable prices. If they're in season, try the Saskatoon berry tarts—delicious and absolutely unique to this region. It's self-service.

GIBSON'S FISH AND CHIPS, in Cumberland Shopping Square, 1501 8th St. Tel. 306/374-1411.
$ **Prices:** Fish-and-chips $7. MC, V.
Open: Mon–Sat 10:30am–8pm, Sun 4–8pm.

When Mr. Gibson (an ex-Royal Canadian Air Force chap) retired from the service, he came back from England with a secret recipe and established a very authentic fish-and-chips outlet. Here you can either sit down at booths or else take out good helpings of fish-and-chips, or scallops, shrimps, or clams and chips, which will be placed in a box and wrapped in real newspaper as well as doused in real malt vinegar. Certainly worth stopping by if you appreciate the real thing.

TRAEGERS, in Cumberland Square, 1515 8th St. East. Tel. 306/374-7881.
    Cuisine: LIGHT FARE/DESSERTS. **Reservations:** Recommended at lunch.
$ Prices: Sandwiches and light fare $4–$8. MC, V.
    Open: Mon–Sat 8am–9pm, Sun 9am–8pm.
Traegers makes a very pleasant breakfast, lunch, afternoon tea, and supper spot. The offerings include croissant sandwiches, salads, quiche, pâté, a ploughman's lunch, a salami platter, and so on. It's the bakery items, though, that really excite—the croissants, bagels, and croque-monsieurs in the early morning, and the richly delicious desserts like amaretto-chocolate cheesecake, Black Forest torte, florentines, and hazelnut-chocolate square. And to top it all off, take some of the freshly made chocolates, sold by the quarter pound.

EVENING ENTERTAINMENT

There's not an awful lot of nightlife activity in Saskatoon, but the **Saskatoon Centennial Auditorium,** 35 22nd St. East (tel. 306/938-7800), provides a superb 2,003-seat theater where the Saskatoon Symphony (tel. 306/665-6414) regularly performs in a September-to-April season. Other offerings here might include the National Ballet, a production of *The Pirates of Penzance,* and headliners like Bill Cosby and Nana Mouskouri. Tickets range from $15 to $55, depending on the performer.

Among local theater companies, the **Persephone Theatre,** 2802 Rusholme Rd. (tel. 306/384-7727), offers six shows per fall-to-spring season (dramas, comedies, and musicals; tickets are $10 to $22.50); **Nightcap Productions,** 317 Hilliard St. East (tel. 306/653-2300), produces Shakespeare on the Saskatchewan annually during July and August in two tents overlooking the river. Plays vary. Tickets are $16 for adults, $14 for seniors and students, $10 for children 6 to 12.

Art galleries include the **Photographers Gallery** (tel. 306/244-8018) and **A.K.A.** (tel. 306/652-0044), which features modern and local artists and hosts the occasional literary event—also dance and music performances. Both are at 12 23rd St. East, and open Tuesday through Saturday from noon to 5pm.

For dancing to Top 40 video entertainment, go to the **Top of the Inn** in the Sheraton hotel. It makes a fun evening.

For quiet drinking and conversation, you can't beat the **Samurai** lounge in the Bessborough Hotel (tel. 306/244-5521). Other pleasant lounges include **Cousin Niks** (tel. 306/374-2020), whence a comfortable piano bar. For a more pubby atmosphere, try the **Artful Dodger** on Fourth Avenue South (tel. 306/653-2577).

Country, not surprisingly, is big in Saskatoon. The most popular of the crop are the **Texas "T,"** 3331 8th St. East (tel. 306/373-8080), which affects a corrallike decor and features live country bands (both Canadian and up-from-Nashville groups). Kick up your heels from 5pm to 1:30am. A cover (about $5) is charged sometimes.

Marquis Downs racetrack, at the corner of Ruth Street and St. Henry Avenue (tel. 306/242-6100), is open for 79 racing days from mid-May to mid-October. The clubhouse shelters a terraced brass restaurant granting a great view of the paddock and track. General admission is $3.50.

EASY EXCURSIONS FROM SASKATOON

FORT BATTLEFORD NATIONAL HISTORIC PARK This site lies about 86 miles (138km), a 1½-hour drive, northwest of Saskatoon on Highway 16. In 1876 when the district headquarters of the Northwest Mounted Police was established here, the area was still the exclusive domain of Native Canadians, bison, and a handful of white traders. The government, which had received the

Northwest Territories from the Hudson's Bay Company in 1870, wanted farmers to settle the land and open the west. Policing the area was necessary, hence the fort you see today was built in 1876 and remained in use until 1924.

Inside the palisade you'll find four buildings that can be visited, but first stop in at the interpretative gallery where you can walk through a display that relates the role of the mounted police in the history of the area from the fur-trading era, through early settlement and treaty negotiations with the Native Canadians, to the panorama of events that led to the North West Rebellion of 1885. You'll see a Red River cart, the type that was used to transport police supplies into the west; excerpts from the local Saskatchewan *Herald;* a typical settler's log-cabin home, which is amazingly tiny; articles of the fur trade; and an 1876 Gatling gun.

Besides the guardhouse (1887) containing a cell block and the sick horse stable (1898), visit the Officers' Quarters (1886), which now contains a display of vintage musical instruments and a room furnished in period style. Perhaps the most interesting house is the Commanding Officer's Residence (1877), which, even though it looks terribly comfortable today, was certainly not so in the 1880s, as Superintendant Walker lamented in 1879: "This morning with the thermometer 37 degrees below, water was frozen on top of the stove in my bedroom . . ." Much Victoriana here, and many interesting artifacts to see.

Open from 9am to 5pm Monday through Saturday and 10am to 6pm on Sunday and holidays during May, June, September, and October until Canadian Thanksgiving (U.S. Columbus Day); from 9am to 6pm daily in July and August. Call 306/937-2621 for further information. Admission is free.

PRINCE ALBERT NATIONAL PARK   This million-acre wilderness park lying 150 miles (240km) north of Saskatoon and 57 miles (91km) north of Prince Albert, offers outdoor experiences from canoeing and backpacking to nature hikes, picnicking, and swimming. The opportunities for seeing and photographing wildlife are good.

In the **Visitor Service Centre** of Waskesiu, the location of the park headquarters, you'll find an 18-hole golf course, tennis courts, riding stables, bowling greens, and a paddle wheeler that tours Waskesiu Lake. The park Nature Centre presents the award-winning audiovisual program *Up North* daily during July and August. Together with the participatory exhibits at the center and naturalist-led programs, it's an excellent way to discover a hint of what awaits you in the park.

Accommodations range from lodges, hotels, motels, and cabins (rates starting at $35 double, rising to $150 for a suite sleeping six to eight people) to serviced and unserviced campgrounds (rates of $8 to $14). Most of the cabins and lodges are old, quaint, and rustic in style—often containing stone fireplaces. Vehicle entry fees are $20 for an annual permit, $10 for a four-day permit, and $5 daily. Fisherfolk require a national park fishing license.

For more information, contact Prince Albert National Park, P.O. Box 100, Waskesiu Lake, SK, S0J 2Y0 (tel. 306/663-5322).

ALBERTA

Stretching from the Northwest Territories to the U.S. border of Montana in the south, flanked by the Rocky Mountains in the west and the province of Saskatchewan in the east, Alberta is a very young, very big, very beautiful chunk of North America—and also a very empty one. Measuring 255,285 square miles, the province is almost as large as Texas, but, with under two million inhabitants, it has fewer people than Philadelphia.

More than half the population lives in Edmonton and Calgary, leaving the rest of the province a tremendous amount of elbow room, breathing space, and unspoiled scenery.

The country was originally called Rupert's Land, a fur franchise of the Hudson's Bay Company first explored by a white scout named Anthony Henday, who penetrated far enough to see "shining mountains" in the distance—the first glimpse of the Canadian Rockies. Although fur traders and trappers formed the vanguard of white penetration, missionaries like Fr. Albert Lacombe opened the country to settlement.

They did it by making friends with the natives, particularly the powerful Blackfoot, a union of warrior tribes as formidable as the Sioux. Rupert's Land only became part of Canada in 1869, when the Hudson's Bay Company sold out to the government. Law and order, in the shape of the Northwest Mounted Police, didn't arrive until five years later. Meanwhile Alberta went through its wildest and bloodiest period, with fur and whisky traders moving up from Montana Territory and establishing such aptly named outposts as Fort Whoop-Up.

While the Mounties threw out the whisky peddlers, Father Lacombe established schools, churches, and good relations with the Blackfoot. So good, in fact, that an agreement with the tribes in 1880 made it possible to build the transcontinental railroad without firing a shot.

There isn't much left of earlier sources of Alberta's wealth, furs and gold. But the later ones are in evidence wherever you go: cattle, wheat, and oil. To which, in fairness, we must add tourism.

SEEING ALBERTA

INFORMATION For information about the entire province, contact **Alberta Economic Development and Tourism,** City Centre, 10155 102nd St., Edmonton, AB, T5J 4L6 (tel. toll free 800/661-8888).

A NOTE ON TAXES Alberta, you'll be pleased to know, has no provincial sales tax. There's only the national 7% GST, plus a 5% accommodations tax.

RANCH & FARM VACATIONS Alberta offers a variety of ranch and farm vacations, divided into guest ranches, working ranches, working farms, and hobby farms. Typical of the guest ranches is **Rafter Six,** about 50 miles west of Calgary. There is a log chalet, stables, swimming pool, and barbecue facilities, with accommodations for 60 people in the lodge and individual cabins. Bed and (hearty) breakfast costs from $39 to $59 per person. Contact Rafter Six Ranch Resort, Seebe, AB, T0L 1X0 (tel. 403/673-3622).

For a working farm, there's **Broadview,** 36 miles south of Edmonton, which has accommodations in the farm home as well as tent and trailer camping. Apart from farm activities, you can swim, boat, and golf nearby. Rates for room and board are

WHAT'S SPECIAL ABOUT ALBERTA

Nature
- ☐ The train trip through the Rocky Mountains, viewing the most grandiose scenery on earth.
- ☐ Close encounters with bears, elk, moose, and mountain sheep in Banff and Jasper National Parks.
- ☐ Roaming herds of huge shaggy wood buffalo on Elk Island.

Museums
- ☐ Fort Edmonton Park, Canada's largest historical park, which takes you back to the pioneer era.
- ☐ The Royal Tyrell Museum of Palaeontology near Drumheller, with 50 dinosaur skeletons in prehistoric settings.
- ☐ Calgary's wonderful zoo, one of the finest of its kind in North America.
- ☐ The Glenbow Museum in Calgary, housing an art gallery, ethnological exhibits, and a superb gun collection—something for every taste.

Sights
- ☐ Head-Smashed-In Buffalo Jump, an interpretive site showing hunting techniques used by Indians for 6,000 years. Declared a World Heritage Site by UNESCO.

- ☐ West Edmonton Mall, the world's largest shopping/entertainment complex. A mixture of department store and Disneyland, it contains a submarine fleet and indoor rollercoaster.
- ☐ Calgary Tower, a giant pillar that offers breathtaking views from the observation terrace and revolving restaurant.

Cuisine
- ☐ Alberta beef served in the form of the best steaks anywhere—bar none.

Entertainment
- ☐ Edmonton's Citadel, a complex housing five live theaters and a restaurant.
- ☐ The Calgary Stampede. The whole town turns into a combination of rodeo, carnival, and three-ring circus.
- ☐ Klondike Days, Edmonton's answer to the above. Annual gold-rush fever with parades, vaudeville, and street performers thrown in.

$35 a day (children up to 6, half price). Contact R. Young, R.R. 2, Millet, AB, T0C 1Z0 (tel. 403/387-4963).

RIVER TRIPS   The craft used by **North Saskatchewan River Canoe Trips** are standard 10-person boats on the scenic river. Everything from life jackets to food and guide is provided, including transportation to and from the nearest town. You can go for an evening, for a day, overnight, or for seven days. For details, contact Merle Pederson (tel. 403/845-7878).

On the **Tar Island River Cruise,** you cruise up the Peace River in a covered twin-jet craft for about 45 miles, stay overnight in comfortable tent cabins on a secluded island, and return the next day. Cruises operate throughout the summer months daily, departing in the early afternoon. Trips cost $117 per adult, $60 per child, meals included, with discounts given to groups. For details, contact David Crawford, P.O. Box 5070, Peace River, AB, T8S 1R7 (tel. 403/624-4295).

---

1. CALGARY

726 miles (1,200km) NE of Seattle, 634 miles (1,020km) NE of Vancouver

GETTING THERE   By Plane   Calgary International Airport lies five miles

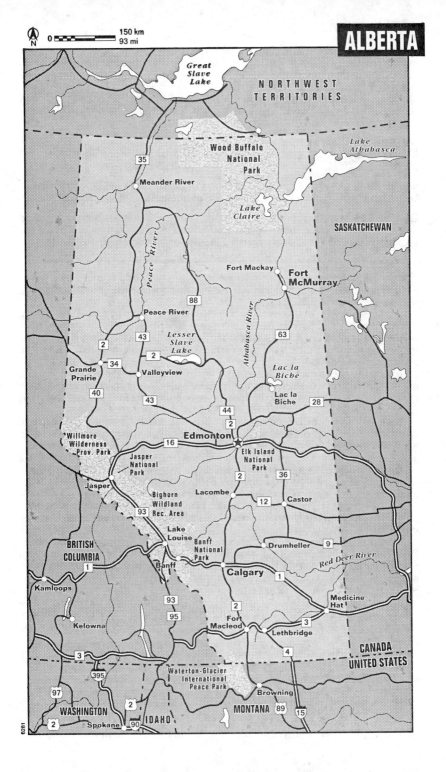

ALBERTA

0   150 km
     93 mi

N

Great
Slave
Lake

NORTHWEST
TERRITORIES

Wood Buffalo
National
Park

Lake
Athabasca

35

Meander River

Lake
Claire

SASKATCHEWAN

Peace River

Fort Mackay

Fort
McMurray

88

Peace River

Athabasca River

43

63

2

Lesser
Slave
Lake

34

2

Lac la
Biche

Grande
Prairie

Valleyview

Lac la
Biche

40

43

28

44

2

Willmore
Wilderness
Prov. Park

16

Edmonton

Elk Island
National
Park

Jasper
National
Park

2

36

Jasper

Bighorn
Wildland
Rec. Area

Lacombe

12

Castor

93

Lake
Louise

Banff
National
Park

Drumheller

9

BRITISH
COLUMBIA

1

Banff

Calgary

Red Deer River

1

Kamloops

93

Medicine
Hat

95

Kelowna

Fort
Macleod

2

3

Lethbridge

3

395

4

CANADA
UNITED STATES

97

Waterton-Glacier
International
Peace Park

Browning

WASHINGTON

2

IDAHO

MONTANA

89

15

2

Spokane

90

northeast of the city. You can go through U.S. Customs right here if you're flying home via Calgary. The airport is served by Air Canada, Canadian Airlines, Delta, American Airlines, United, KLM, Time Air, Air B.C., and Horizon, plus several commuter lines. A shuttle service to and from Edmonton is run by Air Canada and Canadian Airlines, which leaves on the half hour in the mornings, on the hour the rest of the day for the 36-minute hop. The one-way fare is $150. Cab fare to downtown hotels comes to around $19.

By Train   You can take a scenic train ride from Vancouver on the Rocky Mountaineer service, operated by the Great Canadian Rail Tour Company (tel. toll free 800/665-7245).

By Bus   Bus service to and from all points in Canada and the U.S. is provided by Greyhound Lines, located in Calgary at 877 Greyhound Way SW (tel. 403/260-0877).

By Car   From the U.S. border in the south, Highway 2 runs to Calgary. The same excellent road continues north to Edmonton (via Red Deer). From Vancouver you take the Trans Canada Highway through the Rocky Mountains via Banff.

Calgary is a phenomenon—the only metropolis in the world founded by a police force, and surely the only city of 700,000 people anywhere whose inhabitants refer to it affectionately as a "cowtown."

It takes a little while before you catch on to what they mean by that. At first glance this young urban giant, flexing steel-and-concrete muscles, seems as far removed from anything pastoral as Los Angeles is from the angels. What the locals are saying is that the heart and soul of their town has remained rural—wealth, high-rises, and traffic jams notwithstanding.

And in that they are right. Calgary is the friendliest place on the map, a city whose population consists of welcoming committees, where motorists smile after getting their fenders dented, where everybody seems to be competing for a National Niceness Award, and bus drivers tell you to "have a happy day" as if they cared.

It's a city that lives largely on oil but lives for that huge annual razzle-dazzle celebrated as the Calgary Stampede. A place where high-powered business executives who have never ridden a horse wear cowboy boots and invite you home for dinner after bumping into you at a street corner. Where a cop, seeing you lost, will walk you all the way to wherever you want to go and give a running commentary on the sights en route. Where a waitress may show you photos of her kids between courses and a total stranger may offer to share his umbrella to save you a drenching.

Niceness, however, doth not a city make. One famous Canadian author described Calgary as "looking like it was uncrated only an hour before you got there." And he isn't altogether wrong.

Historically Calgary dates back just over a century. It was born in the summer of 1875, when a detachment of the Northwest Mounted Police, advancing westward, reached the confluence of the Bow and Elbow rivers. They built a solid log fort there, and by the end of the year the fortified spot had attracted 600 settlers.

Gradually the lush prairie lands around the settlement drew tremendous beef herds, many of them from the overgrazed U.S. ranches in the south. Calgary grew into a cattle metropolis, a big meat-packing center, large by rancher standards—but not by any other. When World War II closed, it numbered barely 100,000 souls and life was placid.

The oil boom erupted in the late 1960s, and in one decade the pace and complexion of the city utterly changed. Alberta produces nearly all the oil in Canada, earning provincials the nickname of "blue-eyed Arabs." And about 80% of the country's oil and subsidiary companies have their headquarters in Calgary—or are trying to get them there. Modern Calgary is thus a little more than 25 years old, at the diaper stage of urban development.

The population shot up and is growing at a pace that makes statisticians dizzy. In 1978 alone, $1 billion worth of construction was added to the skyline, creating office

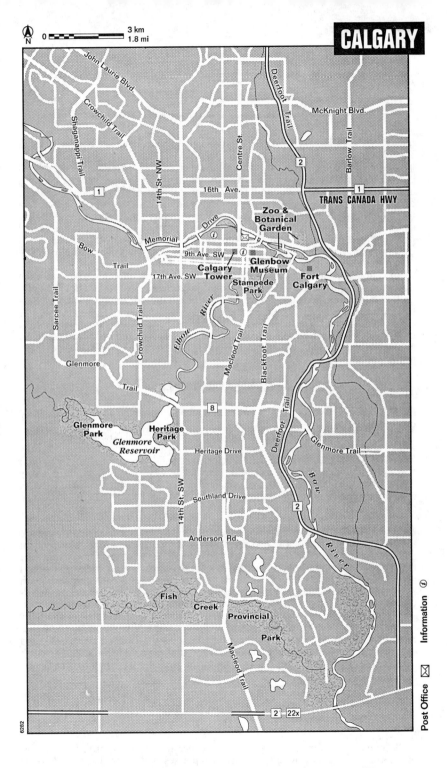

CALGARY

0 ___ 3 km
1.8 mi

N

John Laurie Blvd.

Crowchild Trail

Shaganappi Trail

14th St. NW

Centre St.

McKnight Blvd.

Barlow Trail

2

1

TRANS CANADA HWY

16th Ave.

Drive

Memorial

Bow

Trail

Zoo &
Botanical
Garden

9th Ave. SW

17th Ave. SW

Calgary
Tower

Glenbow
Museum

Stampede
Park

Fort
Calgary

Sarcee Trail

Crowchild Trail

Elbow River

Macleod Trail

Blackfoot Trail

Glenmore

Trail

Deerfoot Trail

8

Glenmore Trail

Glenmore
Park

Heritage
Park

Glenmore
Reservoir

Heritage Drive

Bow

14th St. SW

Southland Drive

2

Anderson Rd.

River

Fish

Creek

Provincial

Park

Macleod Trail

2 22x

6282

Post Office ⊠   Information ⓘ

IMPRESSIONS

They say of Calgary that it's going to look really great when it finally gets uncrated.
—ROBERT FOX, BBC RADIO, 1981

---

high-rises, hotel blocks, walkways, and shopping centers so fast that even locals weren't sure what was around the next corner.

The recession caused by the world's oil glut has cooled Calgary's overheated growth considerably. But—at least from the visitor's angle—this enhanced the city's attractiveness. The once-ubiquitous rooftop cranes that marred its skyline have largely disappeared. The ever-present clouds of cement dust that accompanied the construction boom have blown away. And instead of new luxury restaurants, Calgary is now sprouting a welcome crop of small family eateries together with outdoor cafés and neighborhood taverns. The bursting of the oil bubble may grieve local developers and cause an exodus of transient workers, but it has made Calgary a vastly more enjoyable spot to drop in on.

In February 1988 Calgary was the site of the Winter Olympics, which gave it the opportunity to roll out the welcome mat on a truly international scale. The city outdid itself in hospitality, erecting a whole network of facilities for the occasion, including the Canada Olympic Park, by the Trans Canada Highway, some 15 minutes west of downtown. The park was the site of the ski-jumping, bobsled, and skiing events, and it contains the Olympic Hall of Fame, now one of Calgary's proudest landmarks. So even if you didn't make it to the games, you can admire some of the marvels they left in their wake.

ORIENTATION

ARRIVING   The Airporter bus takes you downtown from the airport for $7.50. By cab it's around $19.

The Greyhound Bus depot is at 850 16th St. SW (tel. 403/260-0877).

TOURIST INFORMATION   The Visitor Information Centre provides you with free literature, maps, and information about the city. It's run by the Calgary Convention & Visitors Bureau, whose main office is at 237 Eighth Ave. SE. It operates a useful, no-charge Accommodation Bureau (tel. toll free 800/661-1678), something of a rarity in Canada.

CITY LAYOUT   Central Calgary lies between the Bow River in the north and the Elbow River to the south. The two rivers meet at the eastern end of the city, forming St. George's Island, which houses a park and the zoo. South of the island stands Fort Calgary, birthplace of the city. The Bow River makes a bend north of downtown, and in this bend nestles Prince's Island with another park. Between Ninth and Tenth Avenues run the Canadian Pacific Railway tracks, and south of the tracks stretch Central Park and Stampede Park, scene of Calgary's greatest annual festival.

For sheer muddle, central Calgary's street-numbering system is matched only by central London—which has the excuse of being some 900 years older. The city is divided into four segments: northeast (NE), southeast (SE), northwest (NW), and southwest (SW), with avenues running east-west and streets north-south. The north and south numbers begin at Centre Avenue, the east and west numbers at Centre Street—a recipe for confusion if ever there was one.

Even if you faithfully remember that downtown Calgary consists of one-way streets and make sure of driving the right way, you're in for a hair-raising shock. For Seventh Avenue, which goes west-east, has one lane on which buses and taxis hurtle toward you east to west! That's their privilege. So pull over, try to control your shaking hands, and smile.

Beyond the downtown area the going gets easier. In fact, beautiful. Calgary nudges the foothills between the Rocky Mountains to the west and the endless prairies to the east. A short drive northeast lie the Drumheller Badlands, an awesome configuration that yielded the dinosaur skeletons you'll see in the city museums. This is also the direction of the Calgary International Airport. Northwest, just across the Bow River, spreads the lovely campus of the University of Calgary. Southwest runs a vast pattern of parks, golf courses, and nature trails surrounding the sparkling Glenmore Reservoir. And farther south begins the rich rural landscape of farming communities and baronial cattle ranches.

Your best orientation point is the cloud-pushing Calgary Tower, at Ninth Avenue and Centre Street. Looking across the avenue, you're facing due north. You have the post office on your left, the Convention Centre opposite, and City Hall two blocks up on the right.

GETTING AROUND

Within the city, transportation is provided by the **Calgary Transit System** (tel. 403/276-7801), with the smilingest drivers extant. The system uses buses, plus one of the finest streetcar runs on the globe. There was a time when electric vehicles were being phased out all over the world but then the gasoline crunch arrived and many municipalities were given no choice but to resurrect them. The Calgary breed is a rolling example of how comfortable a mode of transport they can provide. The cars are sleekly beautiful, clean, silent, and nonpolluting. You can transfer from streetcars to buses on the same ticket. The ride costs $1.50 for adults, 90¢ for children, but it's free in the downtown stretch between 10th Street and City Hall.

Car-rental firms include: **Tilden,** located at 114 Fifth Ave. SE (tel. 403/263-6386) as well as at five other locations, including the airport; **Budget,** 140 6th Ave. SE (tel. 403/263-0505); and **Hertz,** 113 Seventh Ave. SE (tel. 403/221-1681).

Downtown Calgary was designed to be a motorist's nirvana but in places it requires a course in speed-reading. Traffic lights proliferate like tropical fungi, blossoming in clusters of six or more at some intersections. Some road junctions are festooned with so many signs, arrows, instructions, and admonitions that it takes minutes of reading before you dare proceed. Meanwhile the traffic piles up for blocks behind you. In other cities your fellow drivers would desire to lynch you. Here they smile by conditioned reflex.

To summon a taxi, call Checker Cabs (tel. 403/299-9999), Red Top Cabs (tel. 403/250-9222), or Yellow Cabs (tel. 403/250-8311).

FAST FACTS

American Express   There's an office at 421 7th Ave. SW (tel. 403/261-5085).

Climate   Because of its high altitude the city is dry and very sunny as well as windy, and even in summer it tends to be cool in the shade. Summer "heat" is a relative matter here. July and August, the warmest months, rarely climb above 75°F or so.

Hospitals   If you need medical care, try General Hospital, 841 Centre Ave. (tel. 403/268-9111).

Newspapers   Calgary's two dailies, the *Calgary Herald* and the *Calgary Sun,* are both morning papers.

Police   The 24-hour number is 403/266-1234.

Post Office   Try calling 403/292-5434 to find the branch nearest you.

THE CALGARY STAMPEDE

Every year, during the month of July, Calgary puts on the biggest, wildest, woolliest western fling on earth. To call the stampede a show would be a misnomer. The whole town, plus several more towns of visitors, participate by going mildly crazy for the occasion, donning western gear, whooping, hollering, dancing, and generally behaving uproariously.

Many of the organized events spill out into the streets, but most of them take place in **Stampede Park,** a show, sports, and exhibition ground that was built for just that purpose. Portions of the park become amusement areas, whirling, spinning, and rotating with the latest rides. Other parts are set aside especially for the kids, who romp through Kids' World and the Petting Zoo. Still other areas have concerts, livestock shows, food and handcraft exhibitions, free lectures, and dance performances.

The top attractions, though, are the stampede regulars, which always draw immense and fanatically enthusiastic audiences. Some of the attractions are held during the daytime, some in the evening. At the world-famous **Chuckwagon Race** you'll see old-time western cook wagons thundering around the track in a fury of dust and pounding hooves, competing eagerly for more than $300,000 in prize money.

The rodeo events of the Calgary Stampede are the biggest and roughest of their kind in all of North America. Cowboys from all over the continent take part in such competitions as riding bucking broncos and bulls, roping calves, and wrestling steers for prize money totaling more than $500,000. At night the arena becomes a blaze of lights when the **Stampede Stage Show**—the largest outdoor extravaganza in the world—takes over with precision-kicking dancers, clowns, bands, and gamour spectacles.

On top of that, the stampede offers a food fair, an art show, dancing exhibitions, an International Bazaar, a gambling casino, lotteries, and free entertainment on several stages.

Let me tell you right from the start that the whole city of Calgary is absolutely *packed* for the occasion, not just to the rafters but way out into the surrounding countryside. Reserving accommodation well ahead is essential—as many months ahead as you can possibly foresee your arrival. (For lodging, phone Calgary's Accommodation Bureau toll free at 800/661-1678.)

The same advice applies to reserving tickets for all of the park events. Tickets cost between $5 and $25, depending on the event and the seats and whether it is afternoon or evening. Tickets can be booked for any number of particular events or in one block covering all of them. For mail-order bookings, contact the **Calgary Exhibition & Stampede,** P.O. Box 1860, Station M, Calgary, AB, T2P 2M7 (tel. toll free 800/661-1260).

WHAT TO SEE & DO

THE TOP ATTRACTIONS

GLENBOW MUSEUM, 130 Ninth Ave. SE, at 1st St. Tel. 403/264-8300.

The Grenbow Museum, a most impressive complex, was created in order to exhibit, under one roof, the art and history of humankind. Beautifully displayed and spread over three floors, this ambitious museum devotes one floor to art, one to the history of western Canada, and others to West Africa and minerology. You can spend days here, constantly finding fascinating items you'd overlooked before: exotic carvings and ceramics from every part of the globe; hundreds of Native Canadian artifacts; paintings and sculpture by famous artists, both local and on tour; a stunning array of medieval armor, including mounted knights looking like apparitions from Star Wars; one of the largest gun collections in existence; trophies and weapons from two world wars; historic Canadian prints, letters, and documents; and so on.

Admission: $4.50 adults, $3 children; $1 to all on Sat.
Open: Tues–Sun 10am–6pm.

FORT CALGARY HISTORIC PARK, 750 Ninth Ave. SE. Tel. 403/290-1875.

On the occasion of the city's centennial in 1975, Fort Calgary became a public park of 40 acres, spread around the ruins of the original Mounted Police stronghold. The focal point is the Interpretive Centre (open daily 9am to 5pm), a fantastic life-size audiovisual kaleidoscope that takes you back from modern Calgary to the sights, sounds, and—you'd swear—smells of the prairies. The auditorium features multiscreen presentations of the life, adventures, and hardships of the Mounties a century ago—the rigors of their westward march and the almost unbelievable isolation and loneliness these pioneer troopers endured.

Admission: $2 adults, $1 youths; children under 6 free.
Open: Daily 9am–5pm. **LRT:** Bridgeland.

CALGARY ZOO AND PREHISTORIC PARK, 1300 Zoo Rd. NE. Tel. 403/232-9300.

On St. George's Island in the Bow River lies one of the largest and most thoughtfully designed zoos in North America. The Calgary Zoo comes as close to providing natural habitats for its denizens as is technically possible. You view environments rather than confines. You'll particularly want to see the troop of eight majestic lowland gorillas who produced babies in 1993—among the few born in captivity. The latest development is the "slice of Canadian Wilderness," featuring woodland, mountain, prairie, and Arctic backgrounds for its inhabitants. Adjoining the zoo is the Prehistoric Park, a three-dimensional textbook of ancient dinosaur habitats populated by 28 amazingly realistic "terrible lizards" (which is what the term means). The zoo's exotic butterfly garden harbors 40,000 blooming tulips in springtime.

Admission: $7.50 adults, $3.75 children.
Open: Daily 9am–6pm. **LRT:** Zoo station.

ALBERTA SCIENCE CENTRE, 701 11th St. SW. Tel. 403/221-3700.

A fascinating combination of exhibitions, planetarium, and live theater under one roof. The science-oriented exhibits change, but always invite visitors to push, pull, talk, listen, and play. This is a hands-on gallery with audience participation. The 360-degree Star Theatre opens windows to the universe, leaping back in time to the birth of our galaxies. The Pleiades Mystery Theatre features live stage productions from the Miss Marple and Sherlock Holmes genre . . . scientific sleuthing if you stretch the term a bit.

Admission: Exhibits and star shows adults $5.50, children $4.25. Pleiades Theatre $10.50–$12.90.
Open: Spring–fall daily 10am–8pm; winter daily 10am–5pm.

HERITAGE PARK, 1900 Heritage Dr., west of 14th St. SW. Tel. 403/259-1900.

On a peninsula jutting into Glenmore Reservoir, some 60 acres have been turned back in time. It's a Canadian pioneer township of the early 1900s, painstakingly re-created down to the almost-forgotten but then-popular sarsaparilla served over the counters. Walk down the main street and admire the "latest" fashions, drop in at the authentically curlicued soda fountain, stop at the elaborate hotel, watch the blacksmith at work, or sit on the cracker barrel of the general store. The layout includes a Hudson's Bay Company fort, a Native Canadian village, mining camp, old-time ranch, steam trains, streetcars, a horse-drawn bus, and a paddle wheeler that chugs you around Glenmore Reservoir. The town is not just for looking—you can join in the activities.

Admission: $6 adults, $3 children.
Open: May–Oct. 11 Mon–Fri 10am–4pm, Sat–Sun 10am–6pm. **LRT:** Heritage station, then bus 20 to Northmount.

CALGARY TOWER, Ninth Ave. and Centre St. SW. Tel. 403/266-7171.

Reaching 626 feet into the sky, this Calgary landmark is topped by an observation terrace offering unparalleled views of the city and the mountains and prairies beyond. A stairway from the terrace leads to the cocktail lounge for panoramic liquors. Photography from up here is fantastic—on a clear day you can practically snap tomorrow. The high-speed elevator whisks you to the top in just 63 seconds.

Admission: Elevator ride $3.75 adults, $1.75 children.
Open: Daily 8:30am–midnight.

MORE ATTRACTIONS

STAMPEDE PARK, 17th Ave. and 2nd St. SE. Tel. toll free 800/661-1260.

This is the center of action for the annual Calgary Stampede, held every July. But it also has a vast variety of events throughout the rest of the year. These include ice shows; circuses; rock concerts; dog, horse, and livestock shows; antique sales; NHL hockey matches; and wrestling, boxing, gymnastics, harness racing, and track shows. For information on what's going on, consult the newspapers or call the number above. **LRT:** Victoria Park.

OLYMPIC HALL OF FAME, Olympic Park at 16th Ave. North. Tel. 403/247-5455.

A lasting memento of Calgary's role as host of the 1988 Winter Olympic Games stands in the Olympic Park. Three floors of exhibits contain the world's largest collection of Olympic souvenirs, such as the torch used to bring the flame from Greece, costumes and sporting equipment used by the athletes, superb action photographs, and a gallery of all medal winners since the revival of the Olympic Games in 1924. Also shown is a video presentation of the games and their history. **Admission:** $3.50 adults, $2.50 children. **Open:** Daily 10am–5pm. **Directions:** Take Highway 1 west.

CALAWAY PARK, six miles west of downtown on the Trans Canada Hwy. Tel. 403/240-3822.

The 70-acre Calaway Park has all the thrills, loops, bumps, and squeals of the traditional fairground, with a bunch of new ones added. There's a huge double-corkscrew roller coaster, a 200-foot dry water slide, a haunted house, a hollow-log ride over waterfalls, a petting farm, and an absolutely bewildering 18,000-square-foot maze. Also live entertainers and a dozen eateries. **Admission** (including all rides): $14.95 adults, $8.95 children. **Open:** May–Oct daily 11am–6pm. (Call ahead to check first.)

GRAIN ACADEMY, in Plus 15, at Roundup Centre, Stampede Park. Tel. 403/263-4594.

This is an exhibition run by the Alberta Wheat Pool and devoted to one of Alberta's three most lucrative commodities—wheat. Features include a model train set showing grain transportation from the prairies over the Rockies to the coast, a working model grain elevator, and documentary films. **Admission:** Free. **Open:** Mon–Fri 10am–4pm, Sat noon–4pm. **LRT:** Victoria Park.

DEVONIAN GARDENS, Eighth Ave. Mall between 2nd and 3rd Sts. SW.

Another almost-unique attraction in downtown Calgary, the gardens are a patch of paradise, an enclosed 2½-acre park, like a gigantic glass house, 46 feet above street level. Laid out in natural contours with a mile of pathways and a central stage for musical performances, the gardens contain 20,000 plants (mostly imported from Florida), a reflecting pool, a sun garden, children's playground, sculpture court, and water garden. In this lushly green retreat Calgary has found the perfect antidote to the din and dust of its building boom. **Admission:** Free. **Open:** Daily 9am–9pm.

CALGARY AERO SPACE MUSEUM, 64 McTavish Place NE. Tel. 403/250-3752.

A small feast for aeronautics buffs, the Calgary Aero Space Museum places you amid World War II memorabilia with very little diversion into "space." You see aircraft engines, crew logbooks, air force uniforms, some fascinating action photos, plus the way this battleworn equipment was restored and made museum-worthy. **Admission:** $5 adults, $2 students, children free. **Open:** Mon–Fri 10am–5pm, Sat–Sun noon–5pm. **LRT:** Whitehorn, then bus 57.

MUSEUM OF MOVIE ART, 3600 21st St. NE, no. 9. Tel. 403/250-7588.

The nostalgia nook for fans cinematic houses some 10,000 vintage movie posters and photos, some dating back to the 1920s. The museum sells classic posters. **Admission:** $1, but the price is refunded with any purchase. **Open:** Tues–Sat 10am–5:30pm. **LRT:** Barlow, then bus 33.

FISH HATCHERY, 1440 17A St. SE.

The Fish Hatchery was designed to provide 5.5 million fish per year to stock

Alberta's lakes and streams. It's the focal point of the province's expanding sportfishing industry, calculated to satisfy fishing requirements for the next decade— hopefully.

Admission: Free.
Open: Daily till dusk.

FISH CREEK PARK, Canyon Meadows Dr. and Macleod Trail SE. Tel. 403/297-5293.

On the outskirts of town, but easily accessible, Fish Creek Park is one of the largest urban parks in the world (actually, a kind of metropolitan wildlife reserve). Spreading over 2,900 acres, it provides a sheltered habitat for a vast variety of animals and birds. You can learn about them by joining in the walks and slide presentations given by park interpreters. For information on their schedules and planned activities, visit the Administration Office or call the number above.

Bus: 52, 11, or 78.

ALBERTA COLLEGE OF ART, 1407 14th Ave. NW. Tel. 403/284-7600.

This remarkably versatile art gallery concentrates on contemporary art forms. Apart from a permanent collection, the gallery features various shows, two- or three-dimensional or multimedia. For information on current presentations, phone 403/284-1600.

Admission: Free.
Open: Tues–Sat 10am–6pm.

MUTTART GALLERY, 1221 2nd St. SW, in the Memorial Library. Tel. 403/266-2764.

The Muttart Gallery is another contemporary art gallery, but with special emphasis on the contribution of local talent. A good place to see Calgary's share in the modern art scene.

Admission: Free.
Open: Tues–Sat noon–5pm.

CHINESE CULTURAL CENTRE, 197 1st St. SW. Tel. 403/262-5071.

The new landmark and focal point of Calgary's Chinatown, this impressive structure is topped by a great central dome patterned after the Temple of Heaven in Beijing. The center houses exhibits, lecture halls, classrooms, a library, and special-ized retail shops as well as a restaurant, gym, and bookstore. It covers 70,000 square feet and offers an overview of historical and contemporary Chinese cultural (and commercial) life, displayed underneath a gleaming gold dragon hovering 60 feet above the floor.

Admission: Free.
Open: Daily 9:30am–9pm. **Bus:** 2, 3, or 17.

MUSEUM OF THE REGIMENTS, 4520 Crowchild Trail SW. Tel. 403/ 240-7674.

The largest military museum in western Canada tells the story of four famous Canadian regiments from the turn of the century to this day. This it does through a series of lifelike miniature and full-size displays showing incidents in which the regiments figured and individual deeds by their members in combat ranging from the Boer War in 1900 to World War II and contemporary peacekeeping actions. You also see videos, weapons, uniforms, medals, and photographs relating the history of the regiments and hear the actual voices of the combatants describing their experiences.

Admission: By donation.
Open: Thurs–Tues 10am–4pm (check first). **Bus:** 13 to 50th Avenue, then walk five blocks north.

ORGANIZED TOURS

Gray Line (Brewster) (tel. 403/762-6700) offers city sightseeing tours as well as three- to 15-hour excursions to the Canadian Rockies.

Tour C2 takes in the city sights, covering 30 miles in four hours; a running commentary provides the historical background. You start at the Palliser Hotel at 1:20pm, and go to Fort Calgary, Heritage Park, and Scotsman's Hill, which overlooks

Stampede Park and the core of downtown. Fares include admission prices: Adults are $32; children, $16.

There are four tours to the Rockies, Calgary's western neighbors, all of them touching Banff. Tour C10 is the longest, covering 350 miles in 15 hours and visiting the famous Columbia Icefield (optional snocoach ride on the glacier). The tour starts at the Skyline at 6:25am. Adults pay $69.50; children, $34.75.

SHOPPING

Calgary's retail scene is, like everything else, in a surge of expansion and flux. As more and more small stores give way to high-rises, retailing is becoming concentrated in huge shopping centers and arcades. This development makes shopping more comfortable and quicker in cold weather (Calgary has a long, hard winter), but it leads to a certain loss of individualism, the dwindling away of those intriguing one-of-a-kind establishments travel writers—and tourists—love.

A positive feature of the growth explosion is the "Plus-15" system, a series of enclosed walkways 15 feet above street level connecting buildings, which enables you to conduct a shopping expedition in living-room comfort, regardless of weather conditions.

A major portion of **Eighth Avenue** has been turned into a pedestrian zone called **Stephen Avenue Mall,** closed to most vehicles. While not terribly chic or impressive, it's a very comfortable stretch for shopping.

Calgary has one thoroughfare that qualifies as a chic and trendy strip—or is getting there, anyway. The stretch of **17th Avenue** between approximately 5th and 9th Streets SW has developed a mix of specialty shops, boutiques, cafés, bars, restaurants, and delis that makes sauntering, browsing, and stepping in one of the great urban pleasures. Here you'll find a store devoted entirely to cookbooks, another dealing in out-of-print rarities, a superb (and expensive) chocolate shop, antique dealers, a wine boutique, and restaurants for afternoon tea, gourmet meals, and vegetarian food. There are art shops, jewelry stores, porcelain specialists, dessert dispensaries, and some of the best cosmopolitan eateries in town.

Adjacent is **Mount Royal Village,** an outstandingly handsome shopping center, brick-paved, quarry-tiled, illuminated by diffused rays from a skylight, crammed with 40 specialists in the funky, the dressy, the elegant, the "in," and the beautiful.

Other specialty retailers are scattered around town.

COTTAGE CRAFT GIFTS, 6503 Elbow Dr. SW. Tel. 403/252-3797.

Cottage Craft Gifts has one of Canada's largest selections of Inuit sculptures, carvings, and prints, and other Native Canadian artifacts—all absolutely authentic and marked with official labels to prove it. Open daily noon to 5pm, with extended hours on Thursday to 8:30pm.

WESTERN OUTFITTERS, 128 Eighth Ave. SE. Tel. 403/266-3656.

This place could be called Calgary's cowboy headquarters since it stocks everything that a cowpoke (working or dude) might need, with the exception of cows. It offers a vast range of cowboy boots, including the famous handcrafted "Tony Lama."

WHERE TO STAY

Until a few years ago lucky Alberta had no such thing as a sales tax. Then, in response to dwindling oil revenues, the provincial government slapped a 5% charge on hotel bills and other transactions, sending up prices accordingly. While the oil boom lasted, Calgary had mushroomed with swank hotel giants, which displaced many of the older, smaller, and humbler hostelries. As a result, most of the budget establishments were pushed out of the downtown area and into the suburbs, a shift that is taking place in other parts of the globe as well.

BED-AND-BREAKFAST Lists of B&B accommodations are available from two sources. **Alberta Bed & Breakfast,** P.O. Box 15477, M.P.O., Vancouver, BC, V6B 5B2 (tel. 604/944-1793), has a large selection of B&B establishments throughout Alberta, with rates starting at $40 a day for singles, $45 for doubles.

Alternatively, listings are supplied by the **Calgary Convention & Visitors Bureau,** 237 Eighth Ave. SE (tel. toll free 800/661-1678). You can choose from 35 or more registered "hosts" in the Calgary area, each listing marked with details like "no-smoking home" and geographical location. A sample: "Host #106. Shared bathroom, Close to University. Two-minute walk to LRT. Spacious TV room with pool table. Single $30, double $50."

Other listings include places like **Inglewood,** 1006 8th Ave. SE, Calgary, AB, T2G 0M4 (tel. 403/262-6750). This is one of the few establishments that was built with B&B in mind and consists of four bedrooms with private baths. The Victorian-style home, located a few minutes from the Calgary Zoo, also has a shared TV lounge and serves "full breakfast prepared by a certified chef." The building is no-smoking and rooms cost $45 for singles, $60 for doubles. MasterCard and VISA are accepted.

EXPENSIVE

DELTA BOW VALLEY, 209 Fourth Ave. SE, Calgary, AB, T2G 0C6. Tel. 403/266-1980. Fax 403/266-0007. 400 rms and suites. A/C MINIBAR TV TEL
$ Rates: $145 single; $160 double; $190 suite. Special weekend rate $85 per night, including complimentary gifts for children. Children under 18 stay free in parents' room. AE, DC, ER, MC, V. **Parking:** $6.50 per weekday; free on weekends.

⭐ Chocolate brown and massive, this huge 24-story edifice of world-class luxury has an interior decor that ranges from svelte to spectacular. The lobby is vast and soothingly quiet despite all traffic. The Conservatory dining room boasts some of the finest table decorations in town, while the pleasantly casual coffee shop evokes a rather quaint country-store image. There is a cocktail lounge with a tropical garden setting and sophisticated keyboard sounds, an indoor pool, sauna, whirlpool, two outdoor patios, a gift shop, and a highly imaginative children's activity center.

The Delta has 400 guest rooms (and several no-smoking floors), all with individual climate controls. Rooms come in two sizes—large and huge—and are equipped with spacious beds and subtle lighting arrangements that include an unusual standing lamp. Folding-door closets offer ample hanging space, and the bathrooms feature thick terry robes, piles of oversize towels, and a platter of excellent soaps, bath gels, shampoos, and a lint cloth. This is one of the very few hotels that puts live plants in the bedrooms, providing a welcome touch of greenery. Room service is not only impeccable but—a rarity—punctual.

INTERNATIONAL, 220 Fourth Ave. SW, Calgary, AB, T2P 0H5. Tel. 403/265-9600, or toll free 800/223-0888. Fax 403/265-6949. 247 suites. A/C MINIBAR TV TEL
$ Rates: $116–$154 single; $130–$172 double. AE, CB, DC, ER, MC, V. **Parking:** $3 per day.

⭐ A soaring white tower with a breathtaking view from the upper balconies, the International is 35 stories of sheer splendor mellowed by good taste. The hotel has suites only, in various sizes, each with separate bed and living rooms, private balcony, and superb bathroom. The decor is in carefully matched colors, the modernistic prints on the walls chosen with an expert eye, plus the accoutrements—caressing carpeting, wide and wonderful beds, coffee makers, and huge walk-in closets.

The International features a most intriguing three-level bar that blends with the hotel, a grill decorated in the richest 1930s style, an indoor pool and saunas, and an all-pervasive aura of low-key luxury.

PALLISER, Ninth Ave. and 1st St. SW, Calgary, AB, T2P 2M3. Tel. 403/262-1234, or toll free 800/268-9411. Fax 403/260-1260. 406 rms and suites. A/C TV TEL
$ Rates: $180–$225 single; $200–$245 double; from $190 suite. AE, DC, ER, MC, V.
Opened in 1914 as one of a chain of deluxe railroad hostelries, the Palliser still adds a

sumptuous Edwardian touch to Canada's tourist scene. In a city where most luxury comes in high-rises, the square triple towers of the Palliser stand as a monument of the time when 12 stories were considered pretty tall masonry. You'll feel like a cattle baron come to town as soon as you enter the lobby, a vast chrome-and-white expanse glowing with crystal chandeliers, guarded by alabaster lions, and equipped with a burnished-brass Royal Mail box that seems designed for regal missives.

The Palliser's dining room has vaulted ceilings, a massive stone fireplace, and hand-tooled leather panels on real teakwood beams. The little café on the boulevard level downstairs bakes its own French bread and the lounge bar, with towering windows, looks like a gentlemen's West End club of the type Lord Peter Wimsey might have patronized. The modern touches are reserved for the basement boulevard and the bedrooms and suites. All rooms come equipped with every comfort and entertainment device known to travelers. And your room-service tray comes with a single perfect rose in the middle.

SKYLINE PLAZA, 110 Ninth Ave. SE, at Centre St., Calgary, AB, T2G 5A6. Tel. 403/266-7331, or toll free 800/661-7776. Fax 403/262-8442. 385 rms and suites. A/C MINIBAR TV TEL

$ Rates: From $139 single; from $149 double; from $170 suite. Ask about special weekend rates. AE, CB, DC, DISC, ER, MC, V. **Parking:** $9 a day.

The Skyline Plaza is a haven of discreet gorgeousness with the accent on personalized service (including 24-hour room service that really functions around the clock). It has a tropical garden terrace and an indoor pool with greenery that makes it resemble a jungle setting. Each of the two dining rooms has a distinct personality, one a family-style buffet, the other a temple for gourmets (and priced accordingly). A fireside cocktail bar, the Plaza Lounge, is the spot for cocktails and conversation; and the ultra-plush Silver Slipper offers country rock entertainment and a large-screen TV.

The bedrooms and suites come in restful greens and browns. Each has enough space for a theatrical wardrobe, lighting fixtures to suit your moods, and well-equipped bathrooms, including blow dryers. And the hotel connects with the promenade boutiques, stores, and theaters of Palliser Square, in case you want to go shopping without facing the weather.

WESTIN HOTEL, 320 Fourth Ave. SW, Calgary, AB, T2P 2S6. Tel. 403/266-1611, or toll free 800/228-3000. 525 rms and suites. A/C MINIBAR TV TEL

$ Rates: $125–$139 single; $145–$159 double; $155–$700 suite. AE, DC, ER, MC, V. **Parking:** $6 a day.

The Westin is a massive modern luxury block in the heart of the financial district. You could hold a diplomatic reception in the huge pink, green, and gold lobby, which is connected by heated skywalks with major shopping, oil, gas, and banking centers. There's a fabulous panoramic indoor swimming pool with sauna and whirlpool at the rooftop. Also, there are no fewer than seven eating and imbibing establishments, from a buffet to the exquisitely furbished Owl's Nest dining palace. The bedrooms and suites are decorated in lightly delicate pastel hues. You'll be spoiled with an array of special bathroom amenities, oversize towels, fluffy bathrobes, complimentary shoe-shines, and in-room movies. The ultra-deluxe Tower rooms come equipped with stocked minibars and decorative houseplants. Every room has supremely comfortable armchairs.

MODERATE

LORD NELSON INN, 1020 Eighth Ave. SW, Calgary, AB, T2P 1J3. Tel. 403/269-8262. Fax 403/269-4868. 55 rms and suites. TV TEL

$ Rates: $59 single; $65 double; $75 suite. AE, ER, MC, V.

The Lord Nelson is a modern nine-story structure with a widely visible sign and recently renovated guest rooms and suites. The inn has a small cozy lobby with red-brick pillars and comfortable armchairs. Adjoining are a fast-service coffee shop, and the Pub, a tavern with outdoor patio. Bedrooms come in tastefully matched color schemes and with excellent bathrooms, plus cable color TV sets, and if you wish, room service.

PRINCE ROYAL INN, 618 Fifth Ave. SW, Calgary, AB, T2P 0M7. Tel. 403/263-0520, or toll free 800/661-1592. Fax 403/298-4888. 301 suites. TV TEL

$ Rates (including breakfast): $80–$110 single or double. Ask about special weekly rates. AE, DC, ER, MC, V. **Parking:** Free.

Originally built as an apartment block, this "princely inn" offers self-contained suites (studio, or one- or two-bedroom) equipped with everything required to set up some pretty plush housekeeping. The suites come with vast beds, large mirrors, concentrated lighting over tables and bedsides, deep armchairs, and a multitude of drawers and hanging spaces. Kitchens come with all utensils, including coffee percolators and tea kettles. Bathrooms greet you with complimentary toiletries and mirrors illuminated by dressing-room lights. The TV sets have the latest in-house movies (including some "strictly adult" fare). The 28 floors house a health club with sauna, a smart main-floor restaurant, and a delightful garden patio with tables and sunshade umbrellas. The maid service is exceptionally smooth. For business travelers there is secretarial service, a photocopier, and several fax machines.

QUALITY HOTEL, 888 Seventh Ave. SW, Calgary, AB, T2P 3J3. Tel. 403/237-8626, or toll free 800/663-6900. Fax 403/290-1238. 300 rms. TV TEL
$ Rates: $96.75 single; $99.75 double. AE, DC, DISC, ER, MC, V.

A brown twin structure with a barely visible sign to reveal its hotel identity, the Quality is the most luxurious establishment in the moderate price bracket. The place offers everything you would expect in the deluxe class: smooth and speedy room service, a sumptuous restaurant, a smart coffee shop, a tavern, a cocktail lounge, a sauna, and a terrific indoor pool under a glass roof, complete with Jacuzzi and health club. It's also ideally situated, directly opposite Calgary's most charming miniature park and with the rapid transit trolleys stopping at the doorstep.

The lobby welcomes you with an intimate settee corner, ideal for impromptu conference huddles. The bedrooms (10 of which come with kitchenettes) come in nicely matched color schemes of light-wood furniture and russet carpeting, plus—on the upper floors—magnificent city views. You'll get a TV with bedside controls, an excellent writing desk, gift shampoo in the bathroom, and an electric bedside clock. Additionally, the corridors are almost soundless, and the elevator service is outstanding.

AN IMPORTANT NOTE ON PRICES

Unless stated otherwise, **the prices cited in this guide are given in Canadian dollars,** which is good news for U.S. travelers because the Canadian dollar is worth 25% less than the American dollar, but buys nearly as much. As we go to press, $1 Canadian is worth 75¢ U.S., which means that your $100-a-night hotel room will cost only U.S. $75, and your $6 breakfast costs only U.S. $4.50.

Here's a quick table of equivalents:

Canadian $	U.S. $
$ 1	$ 0.75
5	3.75
10	7.50
20	15.00
50	37.50
80	60.00
100	75.00
200	150.00

RAMADA HOTEL DOWNTOWN, 708 Eighth Ave. SW, Calgary, AB, T2P 1H2. Tel. 403/263-7600, or toll free 800/268-8998. Fax 403/237-6127. 200 rms. TV TEL
$ Rates: $79–$89 single; $89–$99 double. AE, DC, ER, MC, V.
In this colorful modernistic downtowner there's a delightful outdoor rooftop patio with swimming pool, trees, and wind shelters. A favorite with conventions, the Ramada is located in the heart of the business community, has two restaurants on the premises, and provides some thoughtful extras, such as complimentary hors d'oeuvres served in the lounge, and backgammon, checkers, and other games for guest entertainment. The bedrooms are big, airy, and cheerfully furnished. Room service functions 16 hours daily.

Macleod Trail

Once this was a cattle track but now it's a roaring expressway that runs from downtown Calgary south through wide-open suburbia until it becomes the highway leading to the U.S. border. The northern portions of this endless, pulsating roadway are lined with inns and motels—from upper middle range to economy. All of them have fast and frequent bus connections to downtown.

ELBOW RIVER INN, 1919 Macleod Trail South, Calgary, AB, T2G 4S1. Tel. 403/269-6771. Fax 403/237-5181. 78 rms. TV TEL
$ Rates: $69 single; $89 double. AE, CB, DC, ER, MC, V. **Parking:** Free.
The Elbow River Inn is the Macleod Trail establishment closest to downtown. The only local hotel on the banks of the little Elbow River, the inn has a pleasantly furnished lobby and a lovely dining room with a view of the water. There is also a restaurant offering hearty home-style cooking and a gambling casino operating six days a week until midnight. The bedrooms, all with bath, are simply furnished, but come equipped with color TVs. It's a good comfortable hostelry with near-budget rates.

FLAMINGO MOTEL, 7505 Macleod Trail, Calgary, AB, T2H 0L8. Tel. 403/252-4401. Fax 403/252-2780. 72 rms. A/C TV TEL
$ Rates: $42 single; $48–$52 double. Extra person $7. AE, DC, DISC, ER, MC, V. **Parking:** Free.
 The Flamingo is a white two-story building with an indoor pool opening out to a patio. There's no restaurant on the premises, but there are two next door. The Flamingo has a sauna and a coin laundry, and 32 of the units offer kitchenettes. The rooms are spacious and well carpeted, with compact bathrooms, lots of quality towels, plus excellent lighting from three low, strategically placed ceiling lamps. And there are small couches (apart from the beds), newish furnishings, a large open hanging space, and very colorful oil paintings as wall decorations.

HOLIDAY INN SOUTH, 4206 Macleod Trail SE, Calgary, AB, T2G 2R7. Tel. 403/287-2700, or toll free 800/661-1889. Fax 403/243-4721. 153 rms. A/C TV TEL
$ Rates: $79 single; $84 double. Special weekend rates available. AE, CB, DC, DISC, ER, MC, V. **Parking:** Free.
A recently renovated property with an LRT (light-rail station) right outside the door, the Holiday Inn is decorated in sophisticated pastel shades and is located only a short stroll away from an oasis of parkland. The softly lit lobby is a charmer, the restaurant and lounge are elegantly furnished, and the heated indoor pool ideal for unwinding. The hotel also offers valet and secretarial services and a coin laundry. The 150 guest rooms, temperature-controlled, are decorated in soul-soothing green and peach hues, and have good-quality carpeting and ample wardrobe space. Room service is available at your command.

PARKVIEW INN, 3630 Macleod Trail, Calgary, AB, T2G 2P9. Tel. 403/243-4651. Fax 403/948-3631. 45 rms. A/C TV TEL
$ Rates: $46 single; $46–$55 double or kitchenette. AE, DC, MC, V. **Parking:** Free.

The Parkview is a two-story pastel-colored place, as attractive inside as out. A large swimming pool is set amid green lawns sprinkled with bushes, tables, and sunshades. The units (10 with kitchenette) are fitted with decorative orange carpets in pleasing contrast to the white plaster walls. Each sports prints on the walls, a small writing desk with lamp, open hanging spaces, intimate bedside lamps, and compact bathroom. Razor plugs are outside the bathroom, but within cord range of the mirror. There's no charge for local calls. The management here is unusually attentive, even by Calgary standards of niceness.

STAMPEDER INN, 3828 Macleod Trail, Calgary, AB, T2G 2R2. Tel. 403/243-5531. Fax 403/243-6962. 102 rms. A/C TV TEL

$ Rates: $63 single; $68 double. Children under 12 stay free in parents' room. AE, DC, MC, V. **Parking:** Free.

The Stampeder is a mirror image of modern Calgary. From a modest little establishment it expanded into a vast, highly contemporary assemblage of restaurants, bars, hair salon, retail stores, dry-cleaning shop, convention facilities, and two wings of guest rooms. The dining room serves a buffet dinner that rates separate mention in the dining section below—it's famous.

The bedrooms are separated into the simpler old wing and the deluxe new wing. The 102 rooms combine spaciousness with conveniences such as automatic wake-up service, air conditioning, push-button telephone, extra-long beds, color TV, and clock radio. Furnishings are elegant, bathrooms have automatically timed ventilators, and the management supplies thoughtful trifles like miniature sewing kits and complimentary shampoo.

Motel Village

Northwest of downtown, Motel Village is a triangle of 10 motels, plus restaurants, stores, and gas stations, forming a self-contained hamlet near the University of Calgary. Enclosed by Crowchild Trail, the Trans Canada Highway, and Highway 1A, the village is arranged so that most of the costlier establishments flank the highway; the more economical lie off Crowchild Trail, offering a wide choice of accommodations in a small area with good transportation connections. Below are a couple of samplers.

THE HIGHLANDER, 1818 16th Ave. NW, Calgary, AB, T2M 0L8. Tel. 403/289-1961, or toll free 800/661-9564. Fax 403/289-3901. 130 rms. A/C TV TEL

$ Rates: $69 single; $75 double. Children under 16 stay free in parents' room. AE, DC, ER, MC, V. **Parking:** Free.

On the same avenue, but well outside the Motel Village, stands the Highlander. A large, sprawling, very attractive complex, the Highlander is as much a dining and dancing center as an accommodations spot (see "Evening Entertainment," below). The place has a spacious and sumptuous lobby, a modern coffee shop, an atmospheric tavern, a smart restaurant, a tartan-hued lounge, and an action-packed video-tech disco. The hotel provides room service, laundry and dry cleaning, plus a large, heated outdoor pool. The rooms are excellently furnished and have ceiling lights, desk lights, and bedside lamps. The Scottish motif, which permeates the entire establishment, doesn't reach the sleeping chambers, which are kept in soothing pastel tones.

PANAMA MOTOR INN, 2440 16th Ave. NW, Calgary, AB, T2M 0M5. Tel. 403/289-2561. Fax 403/282-9713. 55 rms. A/C TV TEL

$ Rates: $45–$68 single; $48–$68 double. AE, DC, DISC, ER, MC, V. **Parking:** Free.

The Mexican hacienda look of the Panama Motor Inn seems to belong somewhere farther south than Alberta. Flanked by Highway 1 and Crowchild Trail, this establishment offers some real luxury touches over and above its price bracket: a sauna, a restaurant open around the clock, a hairdresser on the premises. There's no charge for local calls, and 18 of the rooms come equipped with kitchenette at no extra cost. Furnishings are ultramodern and pastel-hued, carpeting is exceptionally plush, and the open clothes-hanging spaces exceptionally roomy.

ROYAL WAYNE MOTOR INN, 2416 16th Ave. NW, Calgary, AB, T2M
  0M5. Tel. 403/289-6651. Fax 403/289-6709. 52 rms. TV TEL
$ Rates: $44–$60 single or double. AE, DC, MC, V. **Parking:** Free.

A two-story white-and-brown structure flanking an enormous parking lot, the Wayne offers a heated outdoor pool, a family-style restaurant, and medium-sized units. All of them come equipped with color TV, telephone (local calls are free), and modern bathrooms. There are ample furnishings, including a writing desk with mirror, table and chairs, and large walk-in closets. There's an attractive lounge on the premises as well as conference rooms for business meetings.

BUDGET

The pickings are deplorably slim in this category downtown, since many of the older buildings, which usually supply economy lodgings, have been torn down. That's the reverse effect of any boom, oil or other.

ST. REGIS HOTEL, 124 Seventh Ave. SE, Calgary, AB, T2G 0H5. Tel.
  403/262-4641. 100 rms (50 with bath). TEL
$ Rates: $24–$48 single or double. Children under 13 stay free in parents' room.
  MC, V.

The St. Regis, a whitish six-story structure with a brick front, is right in the center of town. The building also houses a dance club and the hotel has a very lively bar trade. The lobby is simple, garnished with metal chairs and vending machines, but the corridors are spacious, well kept, and remarkably quiet, as is the elevator. The bedrooms (half with private bath, some with TV) have bedside lamps and vast closets. Furnishings are modern and fairly basic, and the bathrooms, rather old-fashioned but equipped with every necessity.

The Ys

Calgary's YMCA no longer takes residents.

YWCA, 320 Fifth Ave. SE, Calgary, AB, T2G 0E5. Tel. 403/232-1599.
  Fax 403/263-4681. 40 rms. TEL
$ Rates: $25–$30 single; $30–$40 double; $15 per person in bunk room. MC, V.
  Parking: $1 per hour, free after 8:30pm and on Sun.

The YWCA accepts women guests only. There's a visitors' lounge with tables, magazines, and TV, and a renovated lobby. The cafeteria is open seven days a week. The bedrooms are nicely carpeted and equipped with dressing tables, wardrobes, and bedside lights, all in cheerful color patterns. Accommodations range from rooms with private bath to a simple dormitory, giving a wide choice of rates. A full health and fitness facility is on the premises.

College Accommodations

UNIVERSITY OF CALGARY, 2500 University Dr. NW, Calgary, AB, T2N
  1N4. Tel. 403/220-3210. Fax 403/282-8443.
$ Rates: $27 single; $36 double; $22–$42 per person suite. MC, V. **Parking:** $2 a
  day. **Closed:** Sept–Apr.

The 314-acre campus of the University of Calgary is parklike and offers a vast variety of sports and cultural attractions. Visitors are accommodated May to August, and facilities are excellent, including restaurants, meeting rooms, and one- to four-bedroom suites. The campus is beside the Light Rail Transit Line (LRT).

Campgrounds and Trailer Parks

The **Calgary West KOA,** on the Trans Canada Highway West (Box 10, Site 12, SS#1), Calgary, AB, T2M 4N3 (tel. 403/288-0411), allows tents and pets, and has washrooms, toilets, laundry, a dumping station, hot showers, groceries, and a pool. Prices for two people are $21 per night; tent sites are $16 per night.

WHERE TO DINE

The only thing "cowtown"-like about Calgary's culinary scene is the profusion of steakhouses serving the superlative Alberta beef. This is certainly a red-meat metropolis, not a very happy hunting ground for vegetarians. But one of the brighter side effects of the oil boom has been the restaurant boom that accompanied it. In the course of five or six years Calgary changed from a determinedly parochial eating spot to an astonishingly cosmopolitan one, catering to the taste buds of the United Nations.

Most of the international establishments are very new, very plush, and rather expensive, tailored to an executive clientele. In the cheaper brackets the fare gets more conservative, and in the cheapest it's the old hamburger–hot dog routine, but with the redeeming feature that the quality of the meat, even there, is unusually high.

EXPENSIVE

I would have to stretch this bracket to three times its length to include all of Calgary's top-rankers. In addition to the listings below, there's **Caesar's,** 512 Fourth Ave. SW (tel. 403/264-1222), a sumptuous steakhouse with a Roman motif; **La Caille on the Bow,** 805 First Ave. SW (tel. 403/262-5554), for traditional French fare and what may be Alberta's choicest wine cellar; and **The Owl's Nest,** at the Westin Hotel, Fourth Avenue and 3rd Street (tel. 403/266-1611), for three-star chic and European flavor.

INN ON LAKE BONAVISTA, 747 Lake Bonavista Dr. SE. Tel. 403/271-6711.
   Cuisine: INTERNATIONAL. **Reservations:** Recommended.
$ **Prices:** Appetizers $3.50–$8.95; main courses $9.95–$26. AE, MC, V.
   Open: Lunch Mon–Fri 11:30am–2pm; dinner daily 5pm–1am.

It's hard to decide whether patrons come here for the panoramic view over the lake or the fare presented by head chef Joseph Fernandez. Both are memorable. The view extends to the Rockies, which overlook the lake. The fare includes far-famed house specialties like frogs' legs à la bordelaise, duck in orange sauce, a downright fabulous rack of lamb, and chateaubriand to which the quality of Alberta beef imparts a poetic flavor. The inn consists of several parts that blend into a "night out" rather than merely a meal. The Crystal and Newport dining rooms, possibly the most elegant in town, take care of the food and wine segment. For cocktails, dancing, romancing, and postprandial chatter you drift to the lower-level Show Boat Lounge. You definitely don't come here for a hurried pretheater snack.

THE KING AND I, 820 11th Ave. SW. Tel. 403/264-7241.
   Cuisine: THAI. **Reservations:** Accepted.
$ **Prices:** Main courses $6.95–$18.95. AE, DC, ER, MC, V.
   Open: Mon–Thurs 11:30am–10:30pm, Fri 11:30am–11:30pm, Sat 4:30–11:30pm, Sun 4:30–9:30pm.

This restaurant first introduced Thai cuisine to Calgary and still turns on the heat in carefully measured nuances. You get precisely the degree of spiciness you ask for. You also get considerable help in interpreting the menu. It's a calmly beautiful establishment, decorated in rose and blue-green, ornamented with abstract wall paintings and banners waving from the ceiling. Chicken and seafood predominate—one of the outstanding dishes is chicken filet sautéed with eggplant and peanuts in chili bean sauce. For the more seasoned palates there are eight regional curry courses, ranging from mild to downright devilish.

LA CHAUMIERE, 121 17th Ave. SE. Tel. 403/228-5690.
   Cuisine: FRENCH. **Reservations:** Recommended.
$ **Prices:** Appetizers $5.75–$39; main courses $17.50–$23. AE, ER, MC, V.
   Open: Lunch Mon–Fri noon–2pm; dinner Mon–Sat 6pm–midnight.

Winner of half a dozen awards for culinary excellence, La Chaumière is a subtly lit, discreetly luxurious temple of gourmetry, and a popular rendezvous for Alberta's upper-crust diners and their business friends. Dining here is an occasion to dress up for and La Chaumière is one of the few spots in town that enforces a dress code: Men must wear jackets and ties. And the after-dinner port comes in two vintages—either 20 or 40 years old. Hors d'oeuvres include beluga caviar on ice and a wonderfully aromatic duckling pâté with hazelnuts. Soup may be bisque d'homard, made from *fresh* lobster. You can choose from main courses such as trois médaillons de veau (médaillons of veal with sweetbreads and kidney), sole amandine, or the outstanding rack of lamb roasted with Provence herbs. If you have room for dessert, try a dreamy petit pyramid of tiny profiteroles filled with the finest chocolate, and served in vanilla sauce. A feast like this would cost between $40 and $60, excluding wine.

PANORAMA ROOM, 101 Ninth Ave. SW. Tel. 403/266-7171.
   Cuisine: INTERNATIONAL. **Reservations:** Accepted.
$ Prices: Appetizers $4.95–$8.25; main courses $18.50–$23.75. AE, DC, MC, V.
   Open: Breakfast daily 7:30–11am; lunch daily noon–3pm; dinner daily 5–10pm.
The Panorama sits atop Calgary's chief landmark, Calgary Tower. This vast and resplendent revolving restaurant with seating for 176 gives you a panoramic view from your table—from city to prairies to mountains and back again. The decor, subdued lighting, and background music enhance the romantic effect, but the view from the curved picture windows is the main attraction, not to be surpassed by an interior designer's skill.

You might start with the veal pâté and pheasant galantine, served with spiced apricot glaze. Then perhaps the roast breast of duck in orange sauce or the pork médaillons with blueberry chutney. And for dessert, try either the three-fruit sorbet or the double-chocolate terrine soaked in Grand Marnier. A three-course meal will come to around $28, not including wine.

QUINCY'S, 609 Seventh Ave. SW. Tel. 403/264-1000.
   Cuisine: INTERNATIONAL. **Reservations:** Recommended.
$ Prices: Appetizers $4–$8; main courses $17–$24. AE, DC, ER, MC, V.
   Open: Mon–Fri 11am–midnight, Sat 4pm–midnight.
This place used to be Oliver's—after the little Dickensian waif who wanted "some more." The current cuisine is something wee Oliver couldn't even have dreamt about. The specialties are New York strip steak flamed at your table, chateaubriand bouquetière or crispy roast duckling served with black cherries. Quincy's counts among the silkiest dineries in town, a haven of soundless carpets, oak paneling, and the most flattering lights in the province. Service is simultaneously attentive and unobtrusive, and after dinner you can dance to live piano or ensemble music.

MODERATE

BUZZARDS, 140 10th Ave. SW. Tel. 403/264-6969.
   Cuisine: INTERNATIONAL. **Reservations:** Accepted.
$ Prices: Most items $7–$10. AE, DC, ER, MC, V.
   Open: Mon–Wed 11:30am–midnight, Thurs–Sat 11:30am–2am, Sun 1–9pm.
Calgary's first wine bar when it opened in 1980, Buzzards has since expanded and now carries a selection of beers that fills an entire menu page, including a wondrous brew called Buzzard Breath Ale, blended exclusively for this establishment and dispensed at $3.50 per 16-ounce mug. The range of beers includes imports from New Zealand, Australia, Mexico, Jamaica, the Philippines, China, Japan, Scotland, Ireland, Austria, and more. Comestibles include stuffed trout, spicy killer prawns, various Oriental stir-fries, New York steak sandwiches, beef teriyaki, and 10 breeds of hamburgers. Buzzards has also become a local meeting and mingling institution, attracting a fanatically devoted and youngish clientele.

DIVINO, 817 1st St. SW. Tel. 403/263-5869.
   Cuisine: NOUVELLE. **Reservations:** Accepted.
$ Prices: Appetizers $4–$7; main courses $9–$12. AE, MC, V.
   Open: Mon–Sat 11:30am–11:30pm.
A delightful oddity, Divino is housed in a landmark building (the Grain Exchange) and run by a famous entrepreneur named Witold Twardowski. Among its peculiarities is the menu, in which all prices are given in even dollars. The wall decorations are also unique—contemporary abstract art, changed regularly, and all for sale. The fare is both unusual and tasty—steamed mussels in ginger and garlic broth, broccoli salad

with toasted almonds and ginger dressing, and items like lamb, spinach, and goat cheese baked in tortillas. For dessert, try the apple-and-ginger crumble.

FRANCISCO'S, in the Hospitality Inn South, 135 Southland Dr. SE. Tel. 403/278-5050.
   Cuisine: MEXICAN. **Reservations:** Accepted.
   $ Prices: Appetizers $4–$6; main courses $7–$12. AE, DC, MC, V.
   Open: Lunch daily 11:30am–2:30pm; dinner daily 5:30pm "till late."

Francisco's is a slice of real Mexico tucked away in the handsome atrium wing of the Hospitality Inn. The plants, pool, and sound of rushing water provide an unusually pleasant backdrop to some highly spiced dining. And there's an adjacent piano bar to drift to for a nightcap, mellow keyboard sounds, and a spot of socializing. The restaurant serves not only the standard chili rellenos, chimichangas, and enchiladas (which are excellent), but also some interesting regional specialties from various Mexican states. Sauces and seasoning have the genuine south-of-the-border tang—a rarity in Canada. Dinner will cost you around $21.

FRANZL'S GASTHAUS, 2417 4th St. SW. Tel. 403/228-6882.
   Cuisine: GERMAN. **Reservations:** Accepted.
   $ Prices: Appetizers $3.50–$5; main courses $10–$15.50. AE, DC, MC, V.
   Open: Lunch Mon–Sat 11am–2pm; dinner Mon–Sat 5pm–1am.

 As German as its shingle, Franz's Gasthaus is a vast and immensely elaborate "wursthaus" with one of the biggest bars this side of Bavaria. Waitresses wear dirndl costumes, garlanded pillars support the low ceiling, and one wall is entirely covered with highly colored Bavarian town and country scenes. A three-piece lederhosen band blows, beats, and squeezes Teutonic airs interspersed with tangos. The dance floor is always in use and the atmosphere is as *gemütlich* as huge helpings of beer can make it. The food is not only excellent but authentic. You'll find the rarely encountered—and quite delicious—Pilsner beer soup here. There's also a wonderful steak tartare, and if that's too raw for your palate, pick the Rindsrouladen (stuffed beef slices). The Gasthaus offers an encyclopedic list of German beers and wines, including the celebrated "boot of beer," a glass boot that holds six bottles.

GINSENG HOUSE, 1201 1st St. SW, at the corner of 12th Ave. Tel. 403/265-8088.
   Cuisine: KOREAN. **Reservations:** Accepted.
   $ Prices: Appetizers $1.25–$7.95; main courses $7.95–$12.95. AE, MC, V.
   Open: Lunch Mon–Fri 11am–2pm; dinner daily 4:30–11pm.

Fashioned like a Japanese teahouse, Ginseng House is decorated in deep blues and burgundy. This establishment offers Korean cuisine in all its spicy splendor, which means a maximum of marinading and a minimum of cooking oil used in preparation. The entrées are cooked at the tables and served up with rice and a very spicy side dish called kimchee, made from bean sprouts and cabbage. The menu features more than 100 Korean and Peking dishes, and includes ginger beef, goo-man-doo (deep-fried dumplings), marinated beef or pork, and a tingling concoction of nine kinds of vegetables called yae-chae-bok-kum. This palate adventure won't break your purse.

LIN YEN GARDEN, 5802 Macleod Trail South. Tel. 403/253-2721.
   Cuisine: CHINESE. **Reservations:** Accepted.
   $ Prices: Appetizers $3–$6; main courses $6–$12. AE, DC, MC, V.
   Open: Mon–Sat 5pm–1am, Sun 5–9pm.

Only some of Calgary's Chinese establishments are situated in Chinatown, which is too small to house them all. The Lin Yen Garden hides behind plum-colored drapes and has a split personality. Asian touches are supplied by bamboo partitions and Chinese prints on the walls. Western influences come in the form of taped pop music, metal chairs, and table mats showing (of all things) an illustrated "Century of Fire-fighting." The Garden serves chop suey, chow mein, and other standards, but also a variety of connoisseur pleasers. Try the chicken balls with crushed walnuts, the steamed pork spareribs in sweet plum sauce, or the chow steak kue (steak fried in oyster sauce with Chinese greens).

MONTY'S PENGUIN PUB, 606 1st St. SW. Tel. 403/264-5154.

Cuisine: DELI. **Reservations:** Accepted.
$ Prices: Sandwiches $4.95–$7.90; main courses $7.90–$10.20.
Open: Daily 6:30am–midnight.

Monty's is the wealthier offshoot or a little deli that outgrew its premises. Come and taste, and you'll see why. The new Monty's (named after owner Jim Monument) has Czech white-oak furniture, draped street windows, romantic lighting, and hanging greenery, enclosed by cozy paneling. The veal parmesan is splendid, and the hot roast beef sandwich contains one-quarter pound of meat.

SANTORINI, 1502 Centre St. North. Tel. 403/276-8363.
Cuisine: GREEK. **Reservations:** Accepted.
$ Prices: Appetizers $1.50–$7.95; main courses $8.25–$14.95. AE, DC, MC, V.
Open: Tues–Sun 11am–11pm.

The attractions of this open-armed, blue-and-white Greek taverna include patio dining, tremendous conviviality, bouzouki music, and on occasion, a belly dancer. The whole place sparkles and suggests a much warmer clime than that in which it is situated. The fare comes on huge platters and includes all the traditional Greek palate pleasers like kalamaria, spanakopita, souvlaki, and baklava. If you want to get a taste roundup, order the mezethes, a selection of hot and cold goodies that covers almost the entire range. Dinner, including a glass of wine, comes to around $20.

STAMPEDER INN BUFFET, 3828 Macleod Trail. Tel. 403/243-5531.
Cuisine: CANADIAN. **Reservations:** Accepted.
$ Prices: Buffet $10.95 per adult; children pay 90¢ less for every year under 10. AE, DC, MC, V.
Open: Daily 10am–2pm.

This famous spread is laid in the Stampeder's new dining room, which is partitioned into small sections to create intimacy, and paneled in light woods, scattered with greenery, the tables lit by glass-shielded candles. The buffet is one of the best arranged I've seen: an impressive choice of salads flanked by cold cuts of ham, beef, pork, and salami. Then the hot portions: piles of roast beef, fried chicken, fried fish, breaded veal, honey-garlic spareribs, and roast pork, accompanied by mashed potatoes and four kinds of vegetables. Finally there are the fruit tarts and French pastries.

SULTAN'S TENT, 909 17th Ave. SW. Tel. 403/244-2333.
Cuisine: MIDDLE EASTERN. **Reservations:** Accepted.
$ Prices: Appetizers $4–$6; main courses $8–$12. AE, ER, MC, V.
Open: Dinner Mon–Sat 5:30–11pm.

The Sultan's Tent is a North African oasis, where the menus come in Arabic script with English translations. The trappings are richly Middle Eastern and the cuisine as authentic as Western palates will accept. Harira with lentils, chickpeas, and exotic spices, and rich lamb couscous are followed by baklava of overwhelming sweetness and aromatic mint tea. A typical meal comes to around $19.

UNICORN, 304 Eighth Ave. SW. Tel. 403/233-2666.
Cuisine: ENGLISH. **Reservations:** Accepted.
$ Prices: Appetizers $5.95–$6.95; main courses $7.25–$11.95. AE, MC, V.
Open: Daily 11am–9pm.

The Unicorn is an Anglo-Irish pub-restaurant with a most un-English no-smoking section in the pub. You go downstairs through a gateway decorated with the signed photos of celebrities who have entered before you. The interior is dark and the pub fittings are delightfully authentic, the atmosphere relaxed, and the fare—both solid and liquid—hearty. You can eat shepherd's pie for $5.95. Most dishes are in this price range, but you can also get a lamb curry for $9.95. The establishment is divided into the tavern part, where "pub grub" is served, and a small, more chic dining section, kept separate from the bar carousers. It's immensely popular and usually crowded, particularly around lunchtime.

Chinatown

Calgary's Chinatown occupies a little over two blocks at the south end of the Centre Street Bridge. Although small, it is packed with stores and restaurants and—like everything in this town—is busily transforming itself. The eateries are of very good quality, but unfortunately don't put their menus in the window. Another thing: I didn't see anybody except the Chinese and yours truly eating with chopsticks. Perhaps the waiters should give some impromptu lessons to their Western clientele.

SILVER DRAGON, 106 Third Ave. SE. Tel. 403/264-5326.

Cuisine: CHINESE. **Reservations:** Recommended.
$ Prices: Appetizers $4–$6; main courses $7.95–$12.95. AE, DC, ER, MC, V.
Open: Mon–Sat 10:30am–midnight, Sun 9:30am–10:30pm.

The huge L-shaped, very elaborate dining room at the Silver Dragon is packed with Chinese families—a first-rate culinary recommendation. Excellent air conditioning helps as well. The low ceiling is crisscrossed with ornamented beams, Chinese paintings decorate the walls, soft carpeting mellows the sounds of many little feet, and the wooden chairs, nicely upholstered, make for extra comfort. The dining room is up a flight of stairs and there's a committee of potted plants to welcome you in the downstairs lobby. Try the Chinese sausages or garlic dry spareribs for starters. Then perhaps the chicken with ginger or vegetables in crabmeat sauce. For dessert, order the almond jelly with fruit cocktail. Your meal will come to between $18 and $20.

BUDGET

PIED PICKLE, 522 Sixth Ave. SW. Tel. 403/234-0054.

Cuisine: DELI. **Reservations:** Accepted.
$ Prices: Most items $4.95–$11.95. AE, DC, ER, MC, V.
Open: Mon–Sat 11am–midnight.

There's nothing remotely formal about this cross between a Jewish deli and a chuckwagon diner, which is surprisingly quiet. Comprising a bar and a large restaurant, gleaming clean and softly carpeted, decorated with hanging plants and wagon wheels, the establishment boasts a hilarious menu featuring edible personalities like "Napoleon Bonapickle" and "Wild Dill Hickock." There's home-made chicken soup, lox and bagels, and don't forget to order the wonderfully crisp and ungreasy potato pancakes with your meal.

THE PROSPECTOR, 205 Eighth Ave. SW. Tel. 403/263-4909.

Cuisine: INTERNATIONAL. **Reservations:** Accepted.
$ Prices: Appetizers $5.75–$6; main courses $7.95–$9.95. AE, DC, ER, MC, V.
Open: Daily 7am–midnight.

Located in the pedestrian mall, the Prospector used to be the western-style hangout of the blue-jean brigade—but no longer. The establishment has acquired an entirely new image, shed most of the western trappings, and now has an outdoor patio and a huge indoor TV screen. You are now met by a host and ushered to a linen-covered table. Only the prices have remained in the budget bracket. The Prospector serves breakfast all day, seven brands of burgers, plus a large selection of steak and pasta dishes.

SPECIALTY DINING

The ✪ **Alberta Food Fair,** 304 The Lancaster, Stephen Avenue Mall, Eighth Avenue SW at 2nd Street (tel. 403/294-3839), is a kind of culinary supermarket situated on the second floor of an otherwise very ordinary office building. The place is a total surprise: Little marble-top tables with very comfortable chairs alongside windows overlook the bustling mall below. Food is dispensed from 17 kiosks, catering to cosmopolitan palates, and manages to be both tasty and cheap: omelets—savory or sweet—from $2.90 to $4.95, oven fresh pizzas from $2 up to $9, Chinese specialties from wonton soup to funn noodles, curry dishes around $4 to $5, plus tacos and burritos. It's tremendously popular with the office lunch crowd and for good reason.

Open 6am to 6pm Saturday through Wednesday, to 9pm on Thursday and Friday.

The ✪ **River Café** is a unique establishment in Calgary and perhaps in all Canada. An eatery where *all* the seating is outside! Located in Prince's Island Park (tel. 403/261-7670), this modernistic antidote to air-conditioned claustrophobia has an extended roof that provides rain shelter and outdoor heaters to take the chill out of cool nights. But it's still a daring experiment that seems to have paid off—judging by the fact that you'd better reserve seats beforehand. The fare is a long way from the usual park café cuisine: smoked trout with apricot mousse, garlic and ginger mussels, lamb burgers with Cambazola cheese, and an outstanding combination salad of artichoke hearts, roasted peppers, and almonds with Gorgonzola dressing. Dishes range from $4 to $15, with salads going for around $6. The copious amounts of fresh air come gratis. Open daily from 11:30am to 11pm.

EVENING ENTERTAINMENT
THE PERFORMING ARTS

If there is anything that will effectively demolish Calgary's "cowtown" image, it's its performing arts scene. Calgary offers far more in the music and live stage line than most U.S. cities the same size or bigger. The trouble is that these low-key pleasures tend to be overshadowed by the more garish aspects of nightlife—meaning that they only get a fraction of the publicity and none of the neons. The listing below will give you an idea of the selection available. For current programs, check the newspapers or the little weekly *Action,* a publication devoted to the city's leisure and available in hotel lobbies.

CALGARY CENTRE FOR PERFORMING ARTS, 205 Eighth Ave. SE. Tel. 403/294-7455.

The Centre for Performing Arts gives the city the kind of cultural hub that many places twice as big still lack. The center houses the 1,800-seat Jack Singer Concert Hall, home of the Calgary Philharmonic Orchestra; the Max Bell Theatre; Theatre Calgary, Alberta Theatre Projects, and the Martha Cohen Theatre, which puts on some avant-garde and innovative performances. Call the center or consult the newspapers for what is currently being performed by whom.

Prices: Tickets $15–$36.

JUBILEE AUDITORIUM, 14th Ave. and 14th St. NW. Tel. 403/297-8000.

This magnificent performance hall seats 2,719 people. An acoustic marvel, the auditorium is located high on a hill with a panoramic view no other institution of its kind in the world enjoys. Open for visitors daily (no charge). The Southern Alberta Opera Association performs three operas each year at the auditorium. Periodic productions by the young Alberta Ballet Company are also part of the auditorium's varied programs.

Prices: Ticket prices vary with performance.

THE CLUB & BAR SCENE

Calgary's nightlife, more than that of most Canadian cities, is awash with dance clubs. Some clubs have distinct characteristics, but the majority are the standard mélange of rock/pop/western now found the world over. The samples below are merely a few raisins gleaned from a very large pie.

BLACKFOOT INN, 5940 Blackfoot Trail SE. Tel. 403/252-2253.

The Blackfoot Inn, like several other local establishments, is a conglomerate of hotel, restaurant, and entertainment spot under one roof. It houses Yuk Yuk's Komedy Kabaret, devoted to verbal humor—sometimes pretty broad—and attracts a devoted legion of fans. For good measure the establishment also contains the Other Side, a kind of adult sports lounge with darts, pool tables, lottery terminals, and an extra-large video screen.

CAFE CALABASH, 107 10A St. NW. Tel. 403/270-2266.

Café Calabash has a lot of laid-back California ambience. Upstairs is a restaurant; downstairs is Panama Joe's Piano Bar, where you can enjoy some fairly sophisticated ivory work nightly and jam sessions on Saturday afternoons. Reserve a table—the place gets packed.

HIGHLANDER MOTOR MOTEL, 1818 16th Ave. NW. Tel. 403/289-1961.

The Highlander houses The Yard, one of the town's leading dance clubs, which features the latest New York video presentations, plus an excellent snack bar. A mixed bag of entertainers, from rock to soul, take turns in the restaurants and taverns of this versatile hostelry.

LOOSE MOOSE THEATRE COMPANY, 2003 McKnight Blvd. NE. Tel. 403/291-5682.

The Loose Moose Theatre Company features improvisational comedy; sometimes hilarious, sometimes less so. Saturday and Sunday at 8pm.

Admission: $6.

STAGE WEST, 727 42nd Ave. SE. Tel. 403/243-6642.

This vastly successful dinner theater puts on polished performances as well as delectable buffet fare. I saw a revival of *Play It Again, Sam* there that made me believe the management had signed up Bogey's ghost. The buffet functions from 6 to 8pm, then the show starts. Performances Tuesday through Sunday.

Admission: Varies.

MORE ENTERTAINMENT

GAMBLING There are several legitimate gambling casinos in Calgary, whose proceeds go wholly or partially to charities. None of them imposes a cover charge.

Tower Casino, Lower Level Tower Centre, Ninth Avenue and Centre Street, offers roulette, blackjack, baccarat, and poker with $1 minimum wagers. Open Monday to Saturday from 11am to midnight.

Cash Casino Place, 4040B Blackfoot Trail SE, operates with a restaurant on the premises Monday through Saturday from noon to midnight.

Elbow River Inn Casino, 1919 Macleod Trail South, is part of a hotel by the same name (see "Where to Stay," above). It offers the usual games plus a variation called red dog. Minimum stake is a buck, the maximum $100. Open Monday through Saturday 11:30am to midnight.

ELECTRIC AVENUE This is the label bestowed on the stretch of 11th Avenue between 4th and 8th Streets SW. Crammed into these few blocks are some 25 bars and cabarets, plus about 20 hot-dog stands. Together they constitute Calgary's "Scarlet Strip," frowned on by the police and beloved by the ten thousand or so revelers who turn it into the city's longest-running party. Electric Avenue is entirely a matter of taste—and age. If you're under 30 and out for a wild night, immune to cacophonic din, and not overly concerned about crashing bottles, this is your territory. Otherwise it's easily avoided. Electric Avenue does not straddle any well-trodden tourist trails.

EASY EXCURSIONS FROM CALGARY

DRUMHELLER & THE BADLANDS Drumheller lies 88 miles northeast of Calgary (take Highway 9) amid a landscape that resembles a canvas by Salvador Dalí. The so-called Badlands is a patch of semiarid desert sprinkled with cacti and weird pillars called Hoodoos that give you the impression of walking on the surface of the moon. Adjoining this eroded scenery, however, are lush prairie farmlands with sparkling waters and roadside campgrounds. In a single day you can tour two entirely different worlds.

The Drumheller Valley was a tropical marshland some 150 million years ago, a stomping ground for the colossal reptiles that scientists have been digging for out there at an amazing rate. The town prides itself on the prevalence of these long-dead lizards, and you meet them all over the place. At the bridge crossing the Red Deer River on Highway 9 stands a life-size replica of the fearsome *Tyrannosaurus rex*—great for photographs.

Four miles northwest of Drumheller on the north Dinosaur Trail is the **Royal Tyrell Museum of Palaeontology** (tel. 403/823-7707). Opened in 1985, this museum displays the most extensive range of dinosaur specimens in the world. It offers far more than impressive skeletons. You walk through a prehistoric garden, watch a video, and see museum technicians preparing fossils. It's a compressed journey through time that traces life from its earliest forms to the evolution of man. The museum is also a renowned research facility where teams of scientists study all forms of ancient life. The museum is open daily in summer from 9am to 9pm, in winter Tuesday to Sunday from 10am to 5pm. Admission is $5 for adults, $2 for children; free on Tuesday.

The **Dinosaur Trail** is a scenic loop leading past most of Drumheller's attractions. This includes the "Largest Little Church in the World," an edifice that seats 10,000 people—but only six at a time.

Just outside Drumheller, on Highway 56, lies the **Dinosaur Provincial Park.** A World Heritage Site, this 15,000-acre expanse contains a huge dinosaur graveyard as well as the Field Station of the Royal Tyrell Museum. This is a laboratory for the preparation of fossil specimens before they are transferred to the museum. You can book a guided bus tour through the park at the **Drumheller Valley Tourism Bureau,** 703-2nd Ave. West (tel. 403/823-6300).

FORT MACLEOD   South of Calgary, a little over two hours by bus, stands what once was the western terminal of the Northwest Mounted Police in 1884. Named after Colonel Macleod, the redcoat commander who brought peace to Canada's west, the fort is still patrolled by Mounties in their traditional uniforms, one of the few places in Canada to see them. The fort is filled with fascinating material on the frontier period. Among its treasured documents is the rule sheet of the old Macleod Hotel, written in 1882: "All guests are requested to rise at 6am. This is imperative as the sheets are needed for tablecloths. Assaults on the cook are prohibited. Boarders who get killed will not be allowed to remain in the house."

LETHBRIDGE   East of Fort Macleod lies Lethbridge, a delightful garden city and popular convention site (it gets more annual hours of sunshine than most places in Canada). The pride of Lethbridge is the **Nikka Yuko Japanese Garden.** Its pavilion and dainty bell tower were constructed by Japanese artisans without nails or bolts. One of the largest Japanese gardens in North America, the place has Japanese in kimonos who pose for photos by the beautifully carved bridge.

2. BANFF & JASPER NATIONAL PARKS

Straddling the border between British Columbia and Alberta are two of the greatest nature reserves on the face of the globe. I say two because these wonderlands were founded at different times and have separate administrations. But for all practical purposes they are one very big unit and should be regarded as such.

The Banff and Jasper National Parks comprise 6,764 square miles carved out of the Canadian Rockies and boast a resident population of around 8,000. Their annual tourist flow, however, tops two million. The Rocky Mountains spill over into British Columbia to the west and the adjoining Willmore Wilderness Park to the north. But geographically both parks lie within Alberta, a province that has set aside 4% of its entire surface for national parkland.

Describing these parks is one of the most frustrating tasks that can face a writer. It's like trying to picture the vivid color of a tropical sunset in a black-and-white photograph or conveying the soul-stirring grandeur of a Beethoven symphony on typewriter keys. The feeble best I can say is that you will take those impressions of white peaks towering over green forests, of river torrents and silent blue lakes, of leaping mountain sheep and waddling bear cubs home with you to warm your heart on gray and dismal city days that may follow.

ORIENTATION   Banff is the senior of the two parks, founded as a modest 10-square-mile reserve by Canada's first prime minister, Sir John A. Macdonald, in 1885. Jasper, now Canada's biggest mountain park, was established in 1907, although it already boasted a "guesthouse" of sorts in the 1840s. A visiting painter described it as "composed of two rooms of about fourteen and fifteen feet square. One of them is used by all comers and goers, Indians, voyageurs and traders, men, women and children being huddled together indiscriminately, the other room being devoted to the exclusive occupation of Colin Fraser (postmaster) and his family, consisting of a Cree squaw and nine interesting half-breed children."

The parks form an irregular ribbon running from **Mount Sir Douglas** in the south to the **Resthaven Mountains** in the extreme north. They are traversed by one of the finest highway systems in Canada, plus innumerable nature trails leading to the more remote valleys and peaks. The two "capitals," Banff and Jasper, lie 178 miles apart, connected by Highway 93, one of the most scenic routes you'll ever roll on. Banff lies a mere 81 miles (135km) from Calgary via Highway 1A; Jasper, 225 miles (375km) from Edmonton on Route 16, the famous Yellowhead Highway.

Air Canada and **Canadian Airlines International** fly regularly to the parks. Or you can come by **VIA Rail** or **Greyhound Bus** from Calgary or Edmonton or from Vancouver and Prince Rupert in British Columbia. Rental cars are obtainable from **Tilden,** at the corner of Cariboo and Lynx Streets, Banff (tel. 403/762-2688), or from **Budget,** at the corner of Wolf and Bear Streets, Banff (tel. 403/762-3345).

Admission to both parks costs $5 per vehicle and is good for two days.

SEASONS The parks have two peak seasons, when hotels charge top rates and restaurants are jammed. The first is summer, from mid-June to the end of August, when it doesn't get terribly hot, rarely above 70°F, though the sun rays are powerful at this altitude. The other peak time is winter, from December to February, which is the skiing season; and this is probably the finest skiing terrain in all of Canada. March through May is decidedly off-season: Hotels offer bargain room rates and you can choose the best table in any eatery. There is plenty of rain throughout the year, so don't forget to bring some suitable rainwear.

LOOKING AT ANIMALS—AND VICE VERSA The parklands are swarming with wildlife, some of it meandering along and across highways and hiking trails, within easy camera range. Here I would like to pass on the fervent plea uttered all summer long by the game wardens: **Don't feed the animals, and don't touch them!** There is, for a start, a fine of up to $500 for feeding *any* wildlife. There is also a distinct possibility that you may end up paying more than cash for disregarding this warning.

It isn't easy to resist the blissfully fearless bighorn sheep, mountain goats, soft-eyed deer, and lumbering moose you meet. (Very little chance of meeting the coyotes, lynx, and occasional wolves, since they give humans a wide berth.) But the stuff you feed them can kill them. Bighorns get accustomed to summer handouts of bread, candy, potato chips, and marshmallows, when they should be grazing on the high-protein vegetation that will help them survive the winter. As a result, scores of sheep and goats, weakened by improper nutrition, lie dying in the Rocky Mountain snows.

Moose entail additional risks. They have been known to take over entire picnics after being given an initial snack, chase off the picnickers, and eat up everything in sight—including cutlery, dishes, and the tablecloth.

But it is the bears that pose the worst problems. The parks contain two breeds: the big grizzly, standing up to seven feet on its hind legs, and the smaller black bear, about five feet long. The little one, strangely enough, causes most of the trouble—or rather, human behavior toward it does.

The grizzly spends most of the summer in high alpine ranges, well away from tourist haunts. As one of North America's largest carnivores, its appearance and reputation are awesome enough to make visitors beat a retreat on sight. But the less formidable black bear is a born clown with tremendous audience appeal, and takes to human company like a squirrel.

At the Jasper Lodge golf course, a bear mother taught her cubs how to turn on water sprinklers so they could enjoy cooling showers. The cubs liked it so much that eventually the management had to hire someone to follow the bear family—at a safe distance—and shut off the sprinklers.

The black bear's cuddly looks and circus antics, plus its knack for begging and rummaging through garbage cans, tend to obscure the fact that these are wild animals: powerful, faster than a horse, and completely unpredictable. They are omnivorous, meaning that they eat everything—including human beings.

Hiking in bear country (and virtually all parkland is bear country) entails certain precautions that you ignore at your peril. Never hike alone, and never take a dog along. Dogs often yap at bears, then when the animal charges, run toward their owners for protection, bringing the pursuer with them. Use a telephoto lens when taking pictures. Bears in the wild have a set tolerance range which, when encroached upon, may bring on an attack. Above all, *never* go near a cub. The mother is usually close by, and a female defending her young is the most ferocious creature you'll ever face—and quite probably your last.

BANFF

The town lies 4,538 feet above sea level at the foot of **Cascade Mountain,** which looms so close that it seems to be peering into your bedroom window. Actually there are mountains all around, but the others aren't nearly as imposing.

Getting your bearings is easy. The main street—**Banff Avenue**—starts at the southern end of town at the Bow River and runs north for the entire length until it is swallowed by the Trans Canada Highway. The **Banff Tourism Bureau** is located at 224 Banff Ave. (tel. 403/762-8421). Just beyond the river stands the **Administration Building** and about halfway up the avenue is the **Park Information Centre.** Along that broad, bright, and bustling thoroughfare, which looks like an alpine village street without potholes, you'll find most of the hotels, restaurants, stores, office buildings, and nightspots the town possesses. At the northwestern edge of town is the **railroad station,** and a little farther northwest the road branches off to **Lake Louise** and Jasper. In the opposite direction, northeast, lies the **airstrip,** and past it, the highway going to Calgary.

The **Greyhound and Brewster Bus Depot** is located at the corner of Gopher and Lynx Streets (tel. 403/762-2286). **Banff Taxi & Tours** is at 230 Lynx St. (tel. 403/762-4444).

In passing, let me introduce you to **Rocky M. Ram,** Banff's town symbol and official greeter. Rocky is an enormous bighorn sheep, wearing hiking shorts, horns, and an expression of permanent incredulity. He's hard to get away from.

WHAT TO SEE & DO

Apart from helicopter excursions (which can be bumpy and are always expensive), the only way to get an overall view of a mountain landscape is by cable car. Banff Park is well provided with them, ranging from open chair lifts to glass-enclosed gondolas. The **Sulphur Mountain Gondola Lift** (tel. 403/762-2523) has its lower terminal two miles southeast of Banff on Mountain Avenue, by car, cab, or Grayline bus. The gondolas are roomy, safe, and fully enclosed; the panorama is stunning. At the upper terminal there's the famous Summit Restaurant for panoramic dining, and hiking trails along the mountain ridges. Rides cost $8.50 for adults, half for children (those under 5 ride free).

The **Lake Louise Gondola** (tel. 403/522-3555) offers a 10-minute ride and is located at Lake Louise, just off the Trans Canada Highway, 35 miles west of Banff. From the château the route is marked in red. The cars here are Swiss gondolas, probably the most comfortable anywhere. You arrive at the Whitehorn Lodge, 6,700 feet above the valley floor. The round-trip costs $8 for adults, half that for children, but the ride operates only from early June to late September.

The **Buffalo Paddocks** are located just outside Banff across the Trans Canada Highway, a large enclosure housing a small herd of the big shaggies that once roamed America's prairies in countless millions. (Strictly speaking, these animals are bison, not buffalo. The buffalo is indigenous only to Africa and Asia.) Now they're nearly all gone, except for the scattered groups in nature parks. The best time to visit them is early evening, since the bison stay hidden among the trees during the heat of the day.

The **Natural History Museum,** Clock Tower Village, Banff Avenue (tel. 403/762-4747), has interesting displays of early forms of life on earth, dating from the Canadian dinosaurs of 350 million years ago, plus the "authentic" model of a Sasquatch, local version of the Abominable Snowman. The museum makes regular film and slide presentations on the origins of the earth—the birth of our planet. Open daily from 10am to 8 or 10pm; admission is $2 for adults, half price for children.

The **Luxton Museum** (tel. 403/762-2388) is housed in a log fort south of the Bow River, just across the bridge. Devoted to Canada's native populations, it shows realistic dioramas, a sun-dance exhibit, artifacts, weaponry, and ornaments. Adults pay $3.50; children, $2. The museum is open daily from 9am to 9pm.

The **Whyte Museum,** 111 Bear St., (tel. 403/762-2291), stands as a memorial to the pioneers of the Canadian Rockies. It houses the historical archives, the Banff library, and an art gallery with changing exhibits—prints, paintings, and statuary pertaining to the mountains of western Canada. Afternoon tea is served in front of a fireplace Friday through Sunday. Admission is $3 for adults, $2 for students. Open daily 10am to 6pm.

The **Auto Tape Tour** is available from The Thunderbird in Sundance Mall, at 215 Banff Ave. This rental tape plus player gives you a running commentary to accompany several scenic routes while you're driving over them, and offers an enormous amount of incidental information: Native Canadian and animal facts and legends, what glaciers are, the various life zones of the parks, and facts about the mountains, trees, and plants you see. The driver sets the pace, so you start and stop as you wish. It costs $13 for either Banff or Jasper, $26 for both.

One-day **rafting trips** from Lake Louise on 17-foot rafts are strictly participation fun (everybody paddles). An experienced guide acts as steersman and instructor, so even beginners can't go far wrong. The price of the trip, from $49 up, includes lunch en route. For information, contact **Glacier Raft Co.,** P.O. Box 428, Golden, BC, V0A 1H0 (tel. 604/344-6521).

The **Upper Hot Springs Pool** (tel. 403/762-2056), at the top of Mountain Avenue 1½ miles west of Banff, is a rather grandiose thermal swimming pool and adjoining cave that constitute the actual birthplace of Banff National Park. It was the prospect of creating a bathing resort here that made government workers blast a tunnel into the cave in 1886 and dedicate the area as a national park—the world's third and Canada's first. When the natural hot springs became known they were rumored to be a cure-all for nearly everything from gunshot wounds to lead poisoning. Today people don't swim in the warm water to be "cured" of anything, but merely to enjoy the mineral-rich, almost tropical feeling of the pool and the lush vegetation all around. Open from April 8 to September 2, daily from noon to 9pm. Adults pay $3, children $2, and you can get a therapeutic massage for $17.

Heli-hiking, by **Mountain Wings** (tel. 403/378-6465), provides one of the most exciting and visually stunning jaunts the parks have to offer. A helicopter lifts hiking groups to the most scenic alplands, and a guide then leads them to glaciers, mountain peaks, and wildflower meadows. In this fashion you can visit four or five outstanding locations in one day. The choppers are based in Banff and Canmore. A tour of Mount Rundle and Banff costs $75.

The most popular daytime activities in the parks are hiking, fishing, boating, and horseback and bicycle riding, not necessarily in that order. All of them are lavishly catered to. Most of the lakes and streams in the parks are open to **fishing** (a license can be bought at all park information centers and park warden offices).

Hiking trails abound, 18 easy ones near Banff alone, all taking less than half a day to complete. My favorite is the **Golf Course Loop,** five miles round-trip to the Spray Bridge; at dawn and dusk you often see coyote, elk, and deer in the area. **Rental bikes** are available at 226 Bear St. at $6.50 per hour, $26 a day; horses for trail riding by the hour, half day, or full day, at the **stables** across from Banff Recreation Grounds.

WHERE TO STAY

If you prefer to stay in bed-and-breakfast inns, you can get a list of fairly economical establishments from the **Banff Tourism Bureau,** 224 Banff Ave. (tel. 403/762-8421). These places are screened for quality and should be booked well ahead of arrival. Some are open all year, some only from June to September or October. They accommodate from four to 30 guests, some have private baths, some kitchen units, and all serve hearty breakfasts that go with mountain appetites.

One example is **Ⓢ A Good Nite's Rest,** 437 Marten St., Banff, AB, T0L 0C0 (tel. 403/762-2984). Open year-round, this place offers a variety of rooms, including a large suite with a balcony. Will take a total of 20 guests in five rooms, at rates of $35 to $95 per room. Amenities include TV and coffee maker. Contact Denise Sykes.

In Town

BANFF PARK LODGE, 222 Lynx St., Banff, AB, T0L 0C0. Tel. 403/762-4433, or toll free 800/661-9266. Fax 403/762-3553. 211 rms. A/C MINIBAR TV TEL

$ **Rates:** High season (summer) $95–$175 single or double. Rates change three times annually. AE, CB, DC, ER, MC, V.

★ A large, handsome cedar-and-oak structure with a strongly cosmopolitan air, the Banff Park Lodge is popular with overseas travelers. Behind a simple frontage lies a beautifully wood-paneled and richly carpeted lobby, denoting a mixture of elegance, utility, and comfort. The lodge has one formal and one family-style restaurant, a cocktail lounge, an indoor swimming pool with whirlpool, and 10 convention rooms. The guest rooms are spacious, decorated in pleasing earth tones and exceptionally well furnished. All come with balconies (views vary with location), two basins (one inside, one outside the bathroom), artfully placed lighting arrangements, remote-control TV, and an all-in-one radio-clock-telephone. All rooms have king-size beds and delightfully springy couches. Some rooms have their own bathtub-sized Jacuzzi as well.

BANFF SPRINGS HOTEL, Spray Ave. (P.O. Box 960), Banff, AB, T0L 0C0. Tel. 403/762-2211. Fax 403/762-2211. 850 rms and suites. MINIBAR TV TEL

$ **Rates:** $130–$324 single or double; from $405 suite. AE, DC, DISC, ER, MC, V.

★ Standing south of the Bow River where it joins the Spray River, the Banff Springs Hotel could pass as a suburb under one roof. Resembling a cross between Camelot and a Scottish laird's stronghold, the place even has a mysterious "sealed room" somewhere on the premises (during rebuilding in 1928 the workmen neglected to put in the required door and later forgot the location of the chamber!).

Set in a fabulous landscape of twin rivers ringed by mountain ranges, the Springs greets you with a reception hall of such baronial splendor that you're not in the least surprised to learn that it maintains a staff of 925 and holds medieval banquets for convention groups. It houses 15 different food outlets, from palatial to functional, an espresso bar, three cocktail lounges, a post office, a beauty salon, a barbershop, 50 stores and boutiques, and an Olympic-size indoor pool and a panoramic one outside. The golf course is considered one of the most scenic in the world and has an added attraction in the shape of a bear named Victoria, who visits it regularly, accompanied by her latest litter of cubs.

The guest rooms are decorated in matching orange, white, and red, some with canopy beds and lanterns on the walls, all of them charming. "Regal" is the only word to describe the suites.

CARIBOU LODGE, 521 Banff Ave., Banff, AB, T0L 0C0. Tel. 403/762-5887, or toll free 800/563-8764. 207 rms and suites. TV TEL

$ **Rates:** High season $120–$160 single; $135–$190 double. Up to two children can share parents' room free. Rates change four times annually. AE, DC, ER, MC, V.

★ One of the newest establishments in town, the Caribou—green-roofed, with gables, wooden balconies, outdoor patio, and mansard windows—has a Swiss chalet look that blends well with the alpine landscape. The interior, though, is imposing, including a vast lobby with gleaming slate floor, woodwork of peeled logs, and a huge fireplace. Adjoining restaurant and cocktail bar. The lodge also houses a hot tub, sauna, and whirlpool. The bedrooms are not large but they're finely furnished with rustic pinewood chairs, beds with down comforters, and large wall mirrors. There are bedside, desk, and table lamps; private balconies; remote control TVs; and clock radios. The open closets could be bigger, but there are plenty of drawers. The bathrooms are spacious and ultramodern, with brilliant lighting, electric hairdryers, and a heap of complimentary toiletries.

CHARLTON'S CEDAR COURT, 513 Banff Ave., Banff, AB, T0C 0C0. Tel. 403/762-4485. Fax 403/762-2744. 63 rms. TV TEL

$ Rates: $115–$140 standard single or double; $150 loft unit. AE, DC, ER, MC, V. Four blocks from "downtown" is a romantic log cabin covering a deluxe core. The units are connected by a balcony running the entire length of the place and offering superb views of the mountain backdrop. There is a beautiful, heated indoor swimming pool with steambath and spa, satellite TV with a special movie channel, and two-story loft units with an upstairs bedroom connected by a spiral stairway. The rooms have neat little writing desks, cunningly angled bathroom mirrors, hairdryers, and large hanging recesses allowing for any amount of clothing. Sixteen apartments also have kitchenettes. The hotel has no restaurant, but serves complimentary morning coffee. For breakfast guests can go to the Evergreen Court, two lots down the road.

HOMESTEAD INN, 217 Lynx St., Banff, AB, T0L 0C0. Tel. 403/762-4471. Fax 403/762-8877. 27 rms. TV TEL
$ Rates: High season (summer) $89–$95 single or double. Extra person $10. Rates change three times yearly. AE, MC, V.
Though the Homestead Inn looks and feels like an alpine chalet, it actually stands two blocks from the center of town, with Melissa's Missteak, one of Banff's oldest and best restaurants, right next door. You have a choice between two styles of rooms, differing in price, decor, and sleeping facilities but each tastefully furnished and equipped with couches, armchairs, and stylish bathroom.

INNS OF BANFF PARK, 600 Banff Ave., Banff, AB, T0L 0C0. Tel. 403/762-4581. Fax 403/762-2434. 262 rms. TV TEL
$ Rates (depending on season and view): $62–$170 single or double. Extra person $15. Children under 16 free. AE, DC, ER, MC, V.
This complex of interconnected cedarwood chalets combines beautiful alpine architecture with the latest in hotel comfort—a charming blend of rusticity and streamlining. Those deceptively bucolic frontages hide all the expected luxury-resort facilities: a glassed-in cocktail lounge, a heated indoor swimming pool, a sumptuous restaurant, a sauna, a whirlpool, and a squash court. The rooms are large and in carefully harmonized color schemes; private balconies offer you panoramic views. The bathrooms are equipped with masses of soft towels, free shampoo, and possibly the best showers in the Rockies. The only trouble with this much spoiling is that you may not want to venture outside.

MOUNT ROYAL, 138 Banff Ave., Banff, AB, T0L 0C0. Tel. 403/762-3331. Fax 403/762-8938. 125 rms. TV TEL
$ Rates: High season $135 single or double. Children under 14 stay free in parents' room. AE, DC, MC, V.
The Mount Royal occupies the central corner of Banff Avenue and constitutes the hub of downtown. The hotel is much larger than the number of guest rooms indicates because everything in it is generously proportioned. A hive of holiday activity, the Royal has an appropriately alpine cocktail lounge, a smartly modern lobby, and an intimate, elegant dining room. Bedrooms are spacious and excellently furnished with writing desks, large closets, lots of bed pillows, and night desks with lamps. Beautiful scenic prints decorate the walls, and there is a brand-new health club on the premises.

RED CARPET INN, 425 Banff Ave., Banff, AB, T0L 0C0. Tel. 403/762-4184. Fax 403/762-4894. 52 rms. TV TEL
$ Rates: High season (summer) $75 single; $90 double. AE, MC, V.
A handsome brown three-story alpine-style building, the Red Carpet Inn has a balcony running along the upper floors and a small lobby. There's no restaurant on the premises, but an excellent one right next door. The front rooms get some street noise along with majestic views; in the rear it's only views. The wall-to-wall carpeting is springy, beds and furniture ample and new. Some rooms have enormous mirrors taking up an entire wall, and all come with streamlined bathrooms (including automatic heat lamps). The open closets are rather small, the towel supply lavish. There's good illumination from desk and bedside lamps.

YWCA, 102 Spray Ave., Banff, AB, T0L 0C0. Tel. 403/762-3560. Fax 403/762-2602.

$ Rates: $16 bunk in a dorm room (sleeping bag required); $41–$53 double. MC, V.

By way of contrast to the other listings here, you can get economy accommodations at the YWCA. A bright, modern building with good amenities, the Y welcomes both sexes—singly, in couples, or in family groups—with accommodations in private or dorm rooms, as required. Some units have private baths. There's also an assembly room with a TV, and a guest laundry on the premises.

Out of Town

CHATEAU LAKE LOUISE, Lake Louise, AB, T0L 1E0. Tel. 403/522-3511.
Fax 403/522-3894. 513 rms. TV TEL
$ Rates: $155–$320 single or double. Rates depend on whether you want a view of the lake or of the mountains. AE, DC, DISC, ER, MC, V. **Parking:** $5.35 a day.

The Château Lake Louise lies 35 miles west of Banff in a setting that can only be described as magical. It's a storybook castle perched a mile high in the Rockies, surrounded by forest-clad snowcapped mountains, mirrored in a lake as green as an emerald—a lake undisturbed by the screech of outboard motors, shimmering like a gem amid the towering mountains.

The Château is a massive, graceful structure, blue roofed and furnished with Edwardian sumptuousness. The two restaurants have enormous stone fireplaces as well as a spectacular view of Victoria Glacier. The lake is too chilly for swimming but ideal for canoes (rentable at $4 an hour). Château guests can enjoy a tea dance in the afternoon, cabaret entertainment at night, and memorable cuisine. Facilities include an indoor pool, a rooftop restaurant, a Jacuzzi, a tanning salon, boutiques, and outstanding room service.

The bedrooms are decorated in modern pastel hues and are superbly carpeted. All are temperature controlled and furnished with discreet elegance. The mountain view from the windows should rank as part of the decor—perhaps the best part.

LAKE LOUISE INN, 210 Village Rd., P.O. Box 209, Lake Louise, AB, T0L 1E0. Tel. 403/522-3791. Fax 403/522-2018. 220 rms and lodges. TV TEL
$ Rates: High season (summer) $120–$195 double. Six other seasonal rates as low as $70–$130 in fall. AE, MC, V.

The Lake Louise Inn stands in a wooded eight-acre estate, five driving minutes from the fabled lake and 35 miles from Banff. It consists of four distinct parts in different rate brackets: the inn, the Pinery, the lodge apartments and the Executive building—each comfortable, though the Pinery rooms are smaller and simpler. There's forest all around and snowcapped mountains peering over the trees outside your window. The complex also houses a restaurant, bars, a beautiful indoor swimming pool, a sauna, a boutique, and convention facilities.

The inn (three stories, no elevator) offers rather sumptuous rusticity, with polished wood furniture and bathrooms featuring separate outside handbasins and mirrors. Movies are shown nightly on the inn's TV channel.

WHERE TO DINE

For a place its size, Banff is remarkably well supplied with eateries in all price brackets, and the culinary standard is well above the usual tourist-resort level. As in most resorts, however, prices tend to be slightly higher than in their urban equivalents. You pay for the mountain air that gives you an appetite.

BALKAN RESTAURANT, 120 Banff Ave. Tel. 403/762-3454.
Cuisine: GREEK. **Reservations:** Accepted.
$ Prices: Appetizers $4.95–$7.95; main courses $9.95–$15.95. AE, MC, V.
Open: Daily 11am–11pm.

Up a flight of stairs you'll find this airy blue-and-white dining room with windows overlooking the street below. Blue rafters on the ceiling and Greek folk tunes in the background blend into a pleasantly atmospheric whole. The Greek, German, French, and Californian wines dispensed from the bar help nicely. The fare consists of reliable Hellenic favorites, well prepared and served with a flourish. The Greek platter (for two) consists of a small mountain of beef souvlaki, ribs, moussaka, lamb chops, tomatoes, and salad. If you're dining alone you can't do better than the logo stifado (rabbit stew) with onions and red wine.

CABOOSE, at the railroad depot, Elk and Lynx Sts. Tel. 403/762-3622.
 Cuisine: AMERICAN. **Reservations:** Accepted.
 $ Prices: Appetizers $5.95; main courses $9.95–$22.95. AE, DC, ER, MC.
 Open: Dinner daily 5–10pm.

What is now Banff was originally a railroad camp in the Bow River valley known as Siding 29. This restaurant was first a log cabin and then a railway station. The Caboose wraps you in the nostalgia of steam engines and the romance of the iron horse when steam ruled. The salad bar is served on a porter's cart, but otherwise the fittings are strictly "First Class Sleeper." Menu choices include Rocky Mountain trout, steak and lobster, New York strip steak, and crab legs, with soup and self-help salad included in the price.

ELITE VILLA STEAK HOUSE, 117 Banff Ave. Tel. 403/762-2414.
 Cuisine: STEAK/ALBERTAN. **Reservations:** Accepted.
 $ Prices: Appetizers $3.95–$6.95; main courses $9.95–$38.95. AE, MC, V.
 Open: Dinner daily 5:30–10pm.

This is one of the oldest and finest beef dispensaries in the Rockies. Beautifully decorated with a high-vaulted ceiling, vivid blue table linen, and comfortable armchairs, the place has a vaguely Spanish air, helped by the little candle lamps flickering at the tables and the bullfight posters displayed on the center pillar. But the cuisine is solidly Albertan and goes well beyond the steak range. You could try the stuffed Cornish game hen, which is just as tangy as the traditional prime rib of beef. Main courses come with soup and salad. To end your meal, try the Coffee Wellington (with "somewhat secret" ingredients).

GIORGIO'S, 219 Banff Ave. Tel. 403/762-5114.
 Cuisine: ITALIAN. **Reservations:** Accepted.
 $ Prices: Pasta courses $9–$9.50; pizza $8.50–$16.75. AE, MC, V.
 Open: Dinner daily 4:30–10pm.

Giorgio's is a cozy eatery dimly lit by low-hanging pink-gleaming lamps over the tables. Divided into a counter section and table portion (both comfortable), Giorgio's serves authentic old-country specialties at eminently reasonable prices. Wonderful crisp rolls—a delicacy themselves—come with your meal. Don't miss the gnocchi alla piemontese (potato dumplings in meat sauce) or the Sicilian cassata. And the espresso here is the real thing.

GRIZZLY HOUSE, 207 Banff Ave. Tel. 403/762-4055.
 Cuisine: FONDUE. **Reservations:** Recommended.
 $ Prices: Appetizers $7.50–$11.95; main courses $14.95–$55.95. MC, V.
 Open: Daily 11:30am–midnight.

The Grizzly House has nothing to do with bears except a rustic log-cabin atmosphere. The specialty here is Swiss fondue—from cheese to hot chocolate, with everything in between, including seafood and buffalo fondue (at $29.95). The setting is supremely cozy and the fare excellent, but be warned: A tradition exists according to which any man who drops a morsel into the fondue pot must buy drinks all around. If the mishap befalls a woman, she owes a kiss to all men at the table. So eat with caution. Other house specialties include buffalo, venison, alligator, and rattlesnake.

GUIDO'S, 116 Banff Ave. Tel. 403/762-4002.
 Cuisine: ITALIAN. **Reservations:** Recommended.
 $ Prices: Appetizers $4.25–$7.50; main courses $8.50–$16.50. AE, MC, V.
 Open: Dinner daily 5–10pm.

Guido's serves lots of things besides pasta. Every meal is accompanied by a wooden platter with crusty Italian bread and butter. The dining room is one floor up, so you get a lively view of the street below as you dine. It's a large, handsome place with a low wood ceiling, leather upholstered chairs and eating booths, and lights disguised as gas lanterns. A well-stocked bar in the background and a very Italian rear wall festooned with copperware gleaming in the "candle" light add to the mood. A glass of the decent house wine is a must at $4. Fettuccine Alfredo is outstanding and it arrives in enormous heaps; another good bet is the piccata milanese.

PARIS RESTAURANT, 114 Banff Ave. Tel. 403/762-3554.
Cuisine: INTERNATIONAL. **Reservations:** Accepted.
$ Prices: Appetizers $4.95; main courses $8.75–$15.95. AE, MC, V.
Open: Restaurant daily 11am–10:30pm. Café daily 11am–9pm.

⭐ The Paris Restaurant is also part Vienna—both portions delectable. A large alpine establishment with wooden beams, nicely upholstered chairs, and intimate dining niches, it boasts exceptionally smooth service along with outstanding cuisine. The menu is profusely international: wienerschnitzel, veal Cordon Bleu, pepper steak Madagascar, shrimp indienne, and pork à la forestière. Thursday and Friday are "Seafood Nights," devoted to feasts of lobster and other marine inhabitants. The tanks with live lobsters near the entrance are proof that you're getting them fresh.

The **Paris Café,** the adjoining part of the above dinery, is a bright, tiny, and charming snack corner with a narrow outside passage where you can sip coffee in the sunshine beneath colored umbrellas. It serves possibly the finest cappuccino in town, plus positively poetic apple strudel at $2.25 a plate.

ROSE AND CROWN, 202 Banff Ave. Tel. 403/762-2121.
Cuisine: ENGLISH. **Reservations:** Accepted.
$ Prices: Main courses $6.95–$10.95. AE, MC, V.
Open: Daily 11am–2am.
The Rose and Crown is a plush English pub transplanted into the Rockies. You climb a flight of stairs into a dual hostelry, both portions hung, cluttered, and festooned with wondrous memorabilia. As the menu explains, these artifacts were "accumulated in years of mindless and careless gathering." The pub interior occupies the right side, complete with stone fireplace, dart boards, and antiquated comic prints on the walls. The left part is a rather chic but not very expensive restaurant, where you can enjoy steak-and-kidney pie, chicken curry, and a truly aromatic English sherry trifle.

THEATRE BISTRO, in the Wolf and Bear Street Mall. Tel. 403/762-8900.
Cuisine: INTERNATIONAL. **Reservations:** Accepted.
$ Prices: Appetizers $3.75–$7.50; main courses $9–$16.50. AE, MC, V.
Open: Daily noon–midnight.
Located next to the Lux Theatre, this smart little eatery reflects the adjacent entertainment by means of artistic blowups of screen celebrities along the walls. The interior is oxblood and forest green, with half-curtained windows facing the street. An extensive wine list includes Canadian brands as well as Californian and French imports. You'll dine well and not too dearly under intimate cloth-shaded lamps. Choose the tangy house pâté, then perhaps the chicken curry Casimir (with fresh fruits and rice). Entrées are accompanied by crisp, fresh rolls. Dinner will cost around $19, not including potables.

TICINO, 205 Wolf St. Tel. 403/762-3848.
Cuisine: SWISS/ITALIAN. **Reservations:** Accepted.
$ Prices: Appetizers $4.60–$7.80; main courses $10.80–$19.80. AE, MC, V.
Open: Lunch daily noon–3pm; dinner daily 5–11pm.
The Ticino features a dual menu, Swiss-Italian, with a roughly equal number of selections from both. Elegantly paneled in dark woods, it has impeccable Swiss service, an impressive list of imported wines, and some of the best-laid tables in the Rockies. The fare, understandably, concentrates on veal dishes, fondues, and steaks. The veal médaillons in rich tomato sauce are a good bet, and you get a wonderfully aromatic beef fondue for two for $18.80 per person. Leave room for the zabaglione—light, frothy, and irresistible.

THE YARD, 137 Banff Ave. Tel. 403/762-5678.
Cuisine: TEX-MEX/CAJUN. **Reservations:** Accepted.
$ Prices: Appetizers $3.50–$7.95; main courses $8.95–$17.95. AE, MC, V.
Open: Lunch daily 11am–4:30pm; dinner daily 4:30–10:30pm.

✪ The Yard is a culinary surprise in this region: a freewheeling mix of Tex-Mex and Cajun cooking. It's hard to decide which is better, but in any case try to grab one of the window tables that offer great views along with the comestibles. The cooking takes place in an open kitchen, right under your eyes, and certainly sends appetites soaring. Choose from the Cajun-style blackened fish, the tacos stuffed with charbroiled beef, the tiger prawns, the enchiladas, the refreshing sorbets prepared with fresh fruit . . . it's a happy mélange and tremendously popular, as you can tell by the crowds.

EVENING ENTERTAINMENT

THE PERFORMING ARTS The **Banff Centre,** St. Julien Road (tel. 403/762-6300), is a remarkable year-round institution devoted to art and entertainment in the widest sense. From June through August annually the center hosts a Festival of the Arts, offering a stimulating mixture of drama, opera, jazz, ballet, classical and pop music, singing, and the visual arts. Tickets for some of the events cost $6 to $20; a great many are free. In winter the center shows the Festival of Mountain Films. Find out what's currently on by getting the program at the Banff Tourism Bureau or by calling the center.

THE CLUB & BAR SCENE Banff has a surprising amount of nightlife, all taking place at the larger hotels and restaurants. Quality ranges from excellent to below mediocre, as personified by young men with skeleton-key voices belaboring electric guitars as if they had a grudge against them.

The Works, at the Banff Springs Hotel, is a full-fledged disco, and the **Silver City,** 110 Banff Ave., has nightly dancing to DJ music and live bands to 2am. The **Rose and Crown** pub brings on live entertainers all week, their offerings aided by a huge video screen. At **Tommy's Pasta Emporium,** 209 Banff Ave., you can dance till 2:30am, and the **Voyager Inn,** 555 Banff Ave., presents a frequently changing lineup of talent Monday through Saturday to midnight. **Wild Bill's,** the "legendary saloon" at 203 Banff Ave., puts on live bands nightly from 8pm to midnight.

FROM BANFF TO JASPER

It's not really fair to say that the best thing about Jasper is the trip from Banff, except that the journey between the two park "capitals" is so grandiose that nothing—or very little—can match it as an experience.

Despite the excellent grading of the highway, it's a slow road—because you can't help stopping every few minutes to gaze at what surrounds it—animals: ambling bighorn sheep, mountain goats fighting head-banging duels, elks with huge shovel antlers, momma bears with cubs . . . all guaranteed to halt traffic and set cameras clicking.

From Lake Louise on, you travel the **Columbia Icefields Parkway,** which commands the most majestic scenery in the Rockies. The highway snakes through deep valleys between mountain ranges, skirted by the glaciers spawned by the icefield. You pass within a mile of the **Athabasca Glacier,** a white tongue of the Columbia Icefield that once covered most of Canada. It began retreating about 10,000 years ago but still forms the largest accumulation of ice in the Rocky Mountains. All around, the jagged rocks rise upward, striped with gushing waterfalls, dotted at intervals by calm green lakes. Occasionally you can watch the mountain goats picking their way with their delicate little hoofs over seemingly vertical stone walls as if they were treading level ground.

JASPER

Jasper Townsite is smaller and cozier than Banff. The main street, **Connaught Drive,** runs alongside the Canadian National Railway tracks. There's a tiny trim railroad station, looking as if designed for electric toy trains, where Jasper the Bear, symbol and mascot of the town, waves you a welcome.

The tracks run due north before they start the long easterly sweep that leads to Edmonton. Jasper, in fact, is the hub of the **Yellowhead Highway System** that links it with Vancouver, Prince George, and Edmonton, and is therefore an important communication point. Luckily you don't notice much of that—the little town has retained all the tranquillity you'd expect from an alpine resort. Right in the center, surrounded by delightful shady gardens, are the **Parks Information Offices.** East of town flows the **Athabasca River,** and beyond it lies **Lac Beauvert** with Jasper Park Lodge, adjoining one of the world's finest golf courses. That's the scene of the annual Totem Pole Golf Tournament, whose most celebrated competitor was Bing Crosby. The totem pole in question, named after Queen Charlotte, stands at the railroad station and is reputedly the largest in existence today.

The **post office** is at the corner of Patricia and Elm Streets, and **Tilden Rental Cars** is at 638 Connaught Dr. (tel. 403/852-3798). Taxis and buses can be caught at **Brewster Transport** on Connaught Drive (tel. 403/852-3332). Rental bicycles, canoes, fishing supplies, and licenses can be found at **Sandy's** and **Jasper Park Lodge.** For additional information, stop in at **Jasper Tourism,** 632 Connaught Dr. (tel. 403/852-3585).

WHAT TO SEE & DO

One of Jasper's delightful sidelights is the framed descriptions of local attractions from the laborious but highly evocative pens of fourth-grade students, tacked up all over the place. Read and chuckle.

The **Jasper Tramway** (tel. 403/852-3093) starts at the foot of **Whistler's Mountain,** four miles south of Jasper off Highway 93. The large red cars, each carrying a conductor, are the only reversible type found in the national parks. Each takes 30 passengers and hoists them 1¼ miles up to the summit in a breathtaking sky ride. The size of the cars permits them to take on baby carriages, wheelchairs, or the family dog. The unfolding panorama is grandiose. At the upper terminal you step out into alpine tundra, the region above the tree line where some flowers take 25 years to blossom, a wonderful picnic area carpeted with mountain grass and alive with squirrels. But please don't pick the flowers. The ride costs adults $9.65; children, half price.

At the Tramway's upper terminal you can encounter the beasties Whistler's Mountain is named for. The **"Whistlers"** (actually hoary marmots) are furry little critters that grow up to two feet long. They live in rock piles near the terminal and warn each other with sharp whistles when you approach their domain (hence their name). Whistlers are gentle but very shy. The terminal is one of the few places where they'll let you get within camera range before diving into their burrows. In winter the marmots hibernate en masse, sealing the entrance of their home, clustering into tightly packed clumps, and snoozing until spring.

Maligne Lake is an incredibly blue mountain lake 45 minutes east of Jasper. The Maligne Narrows is one of the most photographed beauty spots in the world. The Native Canadians, who called it Chaba Imne, had a superstitious awe of the region. The white man (in this case a white woman, Mary Schaffer) did not discover Maligne until 1908. Today regular buses go to the "hidden lake," and a summer lodge at the shore provides edibles, potables, and fishing equipment. Boat cruises—in either glass-enclosed or open craft—show you the entire lake area. Tickets cost $27 for adults, half price for children.

A phenomenal body of water, **Medicine Lake,** northwest of Maligne, exists only in summer! The lake appears regularly every spring, grows five miles long and 60 feet deep, then vanishes in the fall, leaving only a dry gravel bed through the winter. The reason for this annual wonder is the drainage from the Maligne system, which remains constant during warmer weather but is reduced to a trickle when the cold stops the melting process of the snowfields.

The **Columbia Icefield** sprawls over an area of 130 square miles and in places reaches depths of 2,000 to 3,000 feet! It thrusts out slowly moving rivers of ice into the valleys below—the glaciers, which rank among the most awe-inspiring spectacles nature provides. One of them, the enormous **Athabasca Glacier,** is six miles long and about 1,100 feet deep near the center. The **Columbia Icefield Chalet** stands adjacent to this mass on the Icefield Parkway, 63 miles south of Jasper. The chalet is the base for a fleet of peculiar vehicles specially designed to crawl around glaciers. They come in two sizes: big snocoaches, looking like tour buses mounted on sets of

Caterpillar tracks, and the small snowmobiles, which resemble enclosed army half-tracks with round bull's-eye windows. Operated by expert drivers familiar with the crevasses, moraines, and moulins of the terrain, they give you a 45-minute tour of the Athabasca with a fascinating commentary on its characteristics. Rides cost $18.50. At the turnaround point you get a chance to stomp around on the ice, toss a few snowballs (in midsummer), and take half a million pictures.

The **Miette Hot Springs** lie 36 miles northeast of Jasper by one of the best animal-spotting routes in the park. Watch for elk, deer, coyotes, and moose en route. The hot mineral springs can be enjoyed in a beautiful swimming pool, surrounded by forest and a grandiose mountain backdrop. Campgrounds and an attractive lodge with refreshments are nearby. During summer the pool remains open from 8:30am to 10:30pm. Admission is $2.50 for adults, $1.25 for children.

Horseback-riding facilities abound in the Jasper area, catering to every constitution from green tenderfeet to roughriders. To mention only one sample: **Jasper Park Riding Academy,** at Jasper Park Lodge (tel. 403/852-5794), features 1½-hour rides for $20, 4½-hour skyline jaunts for $45, all the way to pack trips lasting several days.

Tours and Excursions

The **Brewster Transport Co.** operates tours from Banff (tel. 403/762-6700) and Jasper (tel. 403/852-3332), covering most of the outstanding beauty spots in both parks. A few sample packages:

Banff to Jasper (or vice versa): Some 9½ hours through unmatched scenery, the trip takes in Lake Louise and a view of the icefield along the parkway. (The return trip requires an overnight stay, not included in the price.) One-way fare is $59.50; round-trip, $83.

Columbia Icefield: A 7½-hour tour from Banff. You stop at the Icefield Chalet and get time off for lunch and a snocoach ride up the glacier (not included in the tour price). Adults pay $59.50; children, half price.

ON HORSEBACK One of the most exhilarating experiences the parks can offer is trail riding. It has the added advantage of being available to the tenderest of tenderfeet—those who have never sat on a horse before. The guides take your riding prowess (or lack of it) into account and select foothill trails slow enough to keep you mounted. And the special mountain trail horses used are steady, reliable animals not given to sudden antics.

One of the largest riding outfits in Alberta is **Warner & MacKenzie,** Trail Rider Store, 132 Banff Ave. (tel. 403/762-4551). They offer local rides by the hour and half day, and overnight to six-day pack trips that vary with the seasons, as do the rates. A four-day trip in September is $396 per rider; July to August, $450, including guides, horses, tents, meals, etc. You supply your own sleeping bag and personal articles.

FISHING Currie's Guiding Ltd. (tel. 403/852-5650) conducts fishing excursions to the magically beautiful Maligne Lake. These are for a minimum of two people and cost $125 per person for an eight-hour day. Tackle, bait, and boat rentals are included in the price, as well as full lunches. Inquire about the special single and group rates.

CLIMBING The **Jasper Climbing School,** 806 Connaught Dr. (tel. 403/852-3964), offers beginner, intermediate, and advanced climbing courses under the expert guidance of Hans Schwarz. Basics are taught at a two-day course at the foot of Mount Morro, 12 miles from Jasper, for $80. Food, transport, and accommodations (in private homes) are extra.

WHERE TO STAY

Expensive

AMETHYST LODGE, 200 Connaught Dr. (P.O. Box 1200), Jasper, AB, T0E 1E0. Tel. 403/852-3394. Fax 403/852-5198. 97 rms. A/C TV TEL
$ Rates: $130 single; $135 double; $195 suite. AE, CB, MC, V.
In the central block of Jasper, the Amethyst Lodge is a brightly modernistic establishment with glassed-in stairways. Rooms are centrally air-conditioned and

elevators serve the three floors. There's nothing alpine about the pastel-colored dining room and ultramodern cocktail lounge with swivel chairs and leather settees. The guest rooms are quite spacious, excellently carpeted, and fitted with very ample sliding-door closets. The streamlined bathrooms have heat lamps, and lighting arrangements are unusually good for a resort hotel.

CHATEAU JASPER, 96 Geikie St., Jasper, AB, T0E 1E0. Tel. 403/852-5644, or toll free 800/661-9323. Fax 403/852-4860. 120 rms and suites. TV TEL
$ Rates: $199 single or double; $255–$315 suite. Kitchenette units $15 extra. AE, DC, ER, MC, V.

 There's a world-class hotel discreetly hidden behind the Château Jasper's rustic log-cabin frontage. The disguise drops as soon as you step inside. The château enfolds you in subtly understated elegance, characterized by the handcrafted furnishings in the bedrooms. The grounds are beautifully landscaped with colorful floral patches scattered through the courtyards. The dining room gleams in subdued russet hues; the swimming pool, sheltered behind glass, has a health spa; and there's an upper sun deck for a fast mountain tan.

The deluxe guest rooms have classic decor, French quilted bedspreads, and possibly the softest carpeting in the Rockies. The even more deluxe suites come with private double Jacuzzis, wet bars, and gilded faucets. TV sets are cabinet-sized (with in-house movie channels), and the bathrooms are huge, equipped with complimentary lotions and twin basins. There is a complimentary shuttle bus to the train and bus station.

JASPER INN, 98 Geikie St. (P.O. Box 879), Jasper, AB, T0E 1E0. Tel. 403/852-4461. Fax 403/852-5916. 14 rms. TV TEL
$ Rates: Summer $119 single in economy wing, $154 single in deluxe upper chalet. Extra person $10. AE, DC, ER, MC, V.
Standing on the northern fringe of town, this large, modern, luxurious complex offers chalet and inn accommodation in units housing from one to six guests. The low-slung stone-and-wood structure is set amid shrubs, trees, and flowering hedges, and has a plush indoor pool, sauna, whirlpool, steamroom, and two restaurants.

Most of the units come with lavishly equipped kitchenettes (including wine glasses). In the chalet they are actually condo-type apartments, with fireplace, living room, and sleeping loft up an interior stairway, which gives you the feeling of inhabiting a private cottage. The oaken roof beams spread a delightful woodsy aroma that's wonderful to sleep by. Private balconies overlooking the treetops add the right velvet touches.

LOBSTICK LODGE, Geikie and Juniper Sts. (P.O. Box 1200), Jasper, AB, T0E 1E0. Tel. 403/852-4431. Fax 403/852-4142. 138 rms. TV TEL
$ Rates: $126 single; $131 double. Kitchenette units $15 extra. Children under 15 stay free in parents' room. AE, DC, ER, MC, V.
The Lobstick Lodge has the mountain-chalet look that blends beautifully with the peaks framing it like a picture postcard. Big and modern, with swimming pool, whirlpool, outdoor hot tub, patio, guest laundry (but no room service), the Lobstick is an ideal family hostelry, featuring babysitting arrangements among its other attractions. There is a splendidly designed lounge with fireplace for adult relaxation. Of the guest rooms, 43 have all-electric kitchenettes. The rooms are generously proportioned, decorated in pleasing rust and beige tones, some equipped with day couches and such thoughtful extra touches as a special reading corner with a three-way hanging lamp. The bathrooms have virtually splash-proof folding shower screens.

SAWRIDGE HOTEL, 82 Connaught Dr., Jasper, AB, T0E 1E0. Tel. 403/852-5111. Fax 403/852-5942. 154 rms. TV TEL
$ Rates: $131 single or double; $150–$170 suite. AE, ER, MC, V.
 Behind the rustic stone and timber front of the Sawridge Hotel lie facilities expertly designed to spoil you. The lobby is vast and tranquil. In the rear stretches what may be the most beautiful dining room in town—a huge multitiered expanse of white-clothed tables and flowering greenery extending into a central atrium illuminated by softly filtered light from the glass ceiling. The Sawridge has guest rooms, decorated in brown and beige, with little balconies where you can

greet the morning sun. Closets are spacious, the wall and table light fixtures excellently placed, the bathrooms equipped with shampoos, body lotions, and handy sewing kits. The hotel also has an informal coffee shop, an indoor swimming pool, indoor and outdoor Jacuzzis, a cocktail lounge, and a swinging nightclub with dancing and live entertainers.

TONQUIN MOTOR INN, P.O. Box 658, Jasper, AB, T0E 1E0. Tel. 403/852-4987. Fax 403/852-4413. A/C TV TEL
$ Rates: $114–$134 single or double. AE, MC, V.

The Tonquin stands at the eastern end of Connaught Drive, well away from any "midtown" bustle. Built in deluxe log-cabin style, surrounded by shady trees, the place also houses the plush Prime Rib Village restaurant. Sun decks and lawns for sprawling, a coin laundry, combined with babysitting arrangements and hot tubs, as well as several executive suites, make this a pretty velvety holiday spot. Twenty of the units have their own kitchens. The bedrooms are on the small side, tastefully furnished and delightfully quiet. Six rooms are equipped for the special needs of the disabled. A recently opened new wing houses another 134 units.

Moderate

ATHABASCA, Patricia and Miette Sts., Jasper, AB, T0E 1E0. Tel. 403/852-3386. 61 rms (39 with bath). TV TEL
$ Rates: $46–$79 single; $77–$91 double; $75 triple. AE, DC, MC, V.

The Athabasca has a lobby like a hunting lodge, with a stone fireplace, rows of trophy heads of deer, elk, and bighorn, and a tavern alongside. A gray stone corner building with a homey old-timer's air, the hotel has a large beautiful dining room, a small and trim coffee shop, and a handsomely decorated lounge with nightly entertainment. Each of the bedrooms has a mountain view, although only half have private bath. The rooms are of fair size, the furnishing ample but not luxurious—armchairs, writing table, and walk-in closet, plus TV and radio.

MARMOT LODGE, 86 Connaught Dr., Jasper, AB, T0E 1E0. Tel. 403/852-4471, or toll free 800/661-6521. Fax 403/852-3280. 106 rms and suites. TV TEL
$ Rates: From $115–$145 single or double; $150–$325 one- to three-room suite. AE, DC, MC, V.

Located at the eastern end of Jasper's main street, this lavishly equipped holiday retreat combines the amenities of a big-city establishment with considerable rustic charm. The Marmot has a barbecue patio, a bright and upbeat dining room, a den lounge featuring nightly entertainment, and a heated, picture-windowed pool with sauna and whirlpool. The bedrooms come softly carpeted and colorful and are virtually soundproof. The two-part bathrooms have an extra sink, and the excellent lighting fixtures shed illumination wherever needed (other hotels, please copy). The open hanging space is rather small, but there is ample storage space in eight drawers. You get heaps of snowy towels, free shampoo, and color TV with Spectravision.

WHISTLERS INN, Connaught Dr., Jasper, AB, T0E 1E0. Tel. 403/852-3361. Fax 403/852-4993. 44 rms. TV TEL
$ Rates: High season, $109–$139 single or double. Extra person $10. AE, ER, MC, V.

The Whistlers Inn occupies the central corner of town and is correspondingly busy. With a pavilion-shaped drugstore in front and a restaurant, lounge, coffee shop, and pancake house on the premises, Whistlers is probably the most walked-through patch in the Rockies. The lobby has comfortable armchairs and is an ideal situation for a rendezvous. The same building also houses the wildlife museum.

The bedrooms are nice, modern, and airy, hung with landscapes, and equipped with color TVs, radios, and very good bathrooms. The open hanging space is large, and there is a sauna and Jacuzzi on the premises.

A Nearby Ranch

BLACK CAT GUEST RANCH, P.O. Box 6267, Hinton, AB, T7V 1X6. Tel. 403/865-3084. Fax 403/865-1924. 16 rms.

$ Rates (including all meals): Summer $90 single; $150 double; off-season $58 per person double. MC, V.

The Black Cat Guest Ranch is a wilderness retreat 35 miles northeast of Jasper. Set in superb mountain scenery, this rustic relaxer offers guest units, each with private bath, huge windows, and an unspoiled view of the Rocky ranges. There's a big central living room grouped around a large fireplace, and a separate dining room where the fare is family-style home cooking, the portions measured for fresh-air appetites. Activities include hikes, horseback riding, canoe rentals, murder-mystery weekends, and fishing. The ranch staff will meet your train or bus at Hinton.

Park Campgrounds

There are over 20 campgrounds in the region of Banff and Jasper National Parks, providing a total of some 5,000 campsites. You need a special permit to camp anywhere in the parks outside the regular campgrounds—a regulation necessary because of fire hazards (contact the Parks Information Office for permits). The campgrounds range from completely unserviced sites to those providing water, power, sewer connections, laundry facilities, gas, and groceries. The usual fees are $7 per night at unserviced sites, up to $15 for full-service hookups.

WHERE TO DINE

Expensive

VILLA CARUSO, Connaught Dr. Tel. 403/852-3920.
   Cuisine: ITALIAN. **Reservations:** Accepted.
$ Prices: Appetizers $5.95–$7.95; main courses $9.95–$31.95. AE, MC, V.
   Open: Daily 11am–midnight.

The Villa Caruso is a very handsome Italian hostelry overlooking the main street and the mountains beyond. Dark-wood ceilings and light-wood walls and pillars combine stylishness with an air of leisurely dignity accented by gleaming white table linen, upholstered armchairs, and mellow candle flames. An elegant little bar in the corner and appropriate Italian background music add to the flavor. The cuisine is—not surprisingly—outstanding. Your order comes accompanied by onion soup or salad and a memorable garlic toast. The specialty is spareribs served on a wood platter with baked potato; alternatively, try the fettuccine Alfredo.

Moderate

FIDDLE RIVER, 620 Connaught Dr. Tel. 403/852-3032.
   Cuisine: SEAFOOD. **Reservations:** Accepted.
$ Prices: Appetizers $4.95–$8.95; main courses $12.95–$23.95. AE, MC, V.
   Open: Dinner daily 5pm–midnight.

This rustic-looking upstairs retreat has panoramic windows viewing the Jasper railroad station and the mountain range beyond. The ceiling and furniture are done in country pinewood. The chalkboard with daily specials is brought to your table for closer perusal. The fare is fresh and subtly flavorful, the bread that comes with it excellent. (Blah bread is the weakest part of Rocky Mountain cuisine.) You can choose from river-fresh salmon or curried crab, fried squid, Bangkok tiger shrimps, or shrimp and scallop pesto. There's also a good selection of house wines—Australian, Californian, French, or Chilean. They cost $3.95 to $5.25 per glass, but you can also sample several "taste glasses" for a dollar each—an admirable practice that should be more widely followed.

L AND W, Hazel and Patricia Sts. Tel. 403/852-4114.
   Cuisine: GREEK/ITALIAN/CANADIAN. **Reservations:** Accepted.
$ Prices: Appetizers $3.75–$7.25; main courses $8.25–$18.50. AE, DC, MC, V.
   Open: Daily 11am "till everyone leaves."

L and W looks like a stone cottage with two glass houses attached, plus a beautiful patio for al fresco dining (or breakfasting or lunching). You walk through a stone archway into the glass houses. The carpets are deep green, the tables and chairs a light wicker. The patio has supercomfortable garden chairs, colored umbrellas, and a charming little fountain. The entire decor looks much pricier than the actual menu, a rare phenomenon. The cuisine includes rainbow trout, cabbage rolls, and a selection of 19 pizzas.

SOMETHING ELSE, 621 Patricia St. Tel. 403/852-3850.
   Cuisine: INTERNATIONAL/PIZZA. **Reservations:** Recommended.
$ **Prices:** Appetizers $6.25–$7.75; main courses $9.75–$15.95. AE, DC, ER, MC, V.
   Open: Daily 11am–midnight.

 Something Else is a mix of deluxe restaurant and pizza parlor, with a few jungle touches thrown in for good measure. The setting is stylish: intimate dining booths, half-curtained windows, and globular light bowls. But all around hanging plants and greenery cluster in profusion, and under the ceiling perch realistic looking parrots and toucans. The cuisine is equally paradoxical: prime Alberta steaks, fiery Louisiana jambalaya and mesquite chicken, Greek saganaki and moussaka, plus an array of 21 pizza varieties. A fun eatery, pleasantly relaxed and immensely popular—the stone bench outside for waiting patrons is rarely unoccupied.

TOKYO TOM'S, 410 Connaught Dr. Tel. 403/852-3780.
   Cuisine: JAPANESE. **Reservations:** Accepted.
$ **Prices:** Most items $3.95–$19.95. AE, MC, V.
   Open: Daily noon–11pm.
Tokyo Tom's is a slice of Japan, complete with sushi bar, a karaoke lounge, intimate nooks, and shoeless patrons, with soft Asian mood music in the background and service that is both fast and impeccable. The place has a studied simplicity that goes well with the traditional Japanese fare served: sukiyaki, sashimi, tempura, teriyaki. You can't do better than by ordering one of the five special dinners.

Budget

A & W, Connaught Dr. Tel. 403/852-4930.
   Cuisine: BURGERS. **Reservations:** Accepted.
$ **Prices:** Burgers $3.10–$4.05. No credit cards.
   Open: Mon–Sat 10am–10pm, Sun 10am–8pm.
This budget eatery doesn't look the part at all. New and wood paneled, with fringed lights above the tables and an inner ring of upholstered wooden seats grouped around a coal fire, the place is cozy and comfortable, perfect for lingering. The fare includes "Teen burgers," "Mozza burgers" (with mozzarella), and tacos.

MOUNTAIN FOODS CAFE, Connaught Dr. Tel. 403/852-4050.
   Cuisine: DELI. **Reservations:** Not accepted.
$ **Prices:** Appetizers $3.50; main courses $5.95–$9.95. MC, V.
   Open: Daily 8am–10pm.
This small deli and cafeteria is health-oriented, though it does sell beer and wine. Brightly trim and squeaky clean, the place serves counter meals as well as at the tables, and the fare is wholesome and tasty at the same time. This includes outstanding soups like navy bean and lentil, hearty beef stew with toast, and salads from the extensive salad bar. An entire meal will come to less than $12.

EVENING ENTERTAINMENT

Nearly all of Jasper's nightlife can be found in the bars and lounges of hotels, motels, and inns. Live entertainment ranges from solo performers to full-fledged combos.
   The **Night Club** of the Athabasca Hotel, 510 Patricia St. (tel. 403/852-3386), has a changing lineup of Top 40 bands, catering to a young and very relaxed clientele. There's a dance floor, and movies can be viewed on the large-screen TV in the Trophy room. In action Monday through Saturday to 2am.
   Champs is the dance club at the Sawridge Hotel, 82 Connaught Dr. (tel. 403/852-5111). Apart from the dance floor, dart games and pool are diversions. Monday to Saturday to 2am.

3. EDMONTON

320 miles (525km) N of the U.S. border, 176 miles (285km) N of Calgary

GETTING THERE   By Plane   Edmonton is served by major airlines, including Air Canada and Canadian Airlines International, which also operate the outstanding shuttle to Calgary, a no-reservation service of 17 flights a day, making the hop in 36 minutes for $150. The Edmonton International Airport lies 18 miles south of the city on Highway 2, about 45 driving minutes away. By cab the trip costs about $35; by Airporter bus, $11. North of downtown, but amazingly close to it, lies the Municipal Airport.

By Train   VIA Rail trains arrive at and depart from the CNR Station, 104th Avenue and 100th Street (tel. 403/429-5431).

By Bus   At 10324-103rd St. is the Greyhound Bus Depot.

By Car   Edmonton straddles the Yellowhead Highway, western Canada's great new interprovincial highway. This is an east-west route with excellent access from every compass point to other Canadian highways and U.S. Interstate highways. The Yellowhead route is also followed by the Canadian National Railways' transcontinental line through most of western Canada, using the famous domed lookout cars. Just west of Edmonton the Yellowhead is linked to the Alaska Highway.

A standing joke in Alberta has it that no rivalry exists between the province's two major cities, Edmonton and Calgary. Because both towns are utterly devoted to the cult of "niceness," they can't possibly admit to anything as abrasive as competitiveness. In point of fact, however, they're at it hammer and tongs, each scoring off the other at every given opportunity, running a neck-and-neck race for supremacy.

This works out splendidly for visitors, since the two places are constantly trying to outdo each other in hospitality. But it makes it hard—nay, impossible—to assess which of them is actually ahead.

Edmonton is the provincial capital but has a slightly smaller population, currently around 600,000. Calgary is growing faster and may lengthen its lead. Edmonton has slightly more political clout, but Calgary slightly more money. Calgary offers the world-famous annual stampede, while Edmonton is coming up fast with its yearly Klondike Days shindig. Edmonton is the technological and scientific center of the oil industry, Calgary the business and administrative one. Calgary smiles at you more, Edmonton feeds you better . . .

In one respect Edmonton has gained a very visible advantage. It began rebuilding its downtown area a decade sooner, which means that its core is now comfortably streamlined, whereas Calgary's is chaotic. But in a few years Calgary will have completed reconstruction and may emerge from the cement dust even more impressive.

Edmonton was founded as an armed and pallisaded trading post of the Hudson's Bay Company in 1795. Its customers were the formidable warriors of the Blackfoot tribal confederacy, and trading could be a somewhat nervous enterprise. When 2,000 mounted and feathered braves appeared on the skyline you never knew for certain whether they came to trade or to storm the stockade. So you primed the cannon and brought out the merchandise simultaneously—just in case.

Actually Edmonton House, as the post was called, had less trouble with its clients than with the supply line. Every scrap the outpost used had to come by freight canoe over 2,000 tortuous miles, and nothing got through in winter. From season to season the existence of the 165 men, women, and children in the "house" depended on whether they'd laid in enough supplies to last the winter months. Potatoes and vegetables were luxuries. The staple diet was buffalo meat—5 pounds a day for men, 2½ pounds for women, 1¼ pounds per child. The beef-eating habit has stayed with Edmontonians ever since.

Until 1870 Edmonton remained the most lucrative fur-trading post in the Hudson's Bay empire. Then the company sold the land to the Canadian government and the area was opened to pioneer settlement. The "house" expanded into a township, joined the outside world by means of telegraph wire, founded a newspaper, and got the law in the shape of the scarlet-coated Northwest Mounted Police, who put an end to the habit of settling disputed land claims by "Winchester arbitration."

In 1891 electricity and the railroad arrived from Calgary and utterly changed the little settlement. Floods of newcomers poured in, some to stay, others to populate the rich surrounding land. The Klondike gold rush made Edmonton the major supply center for goldseekers on the perilous Klondike Trail routes overland to Dawson City in the Yukon.

By 1905 when the Province of Alberta was created, Edmonton had around 8,000 souls and was one year old as a city. It got the nomination as capital of the new province largely because of its geographically central position. The older, bigger, and more southerly Calgary never quite got over the shock.

Edmonton grew in spurts, following a boom-and-bust pattern as exciting as it was unreliable. One moment people were lining up to buy blocks of land in the city and the next moment they were lining up outside soup kitchens. During World War II the boom came in the form of the Alaska Highway, with Edmonton as matériel base and temporary home of 50,000 American troops and construction workers.

The ultimate boom, however, gushed from the ground on a freezing afternoon in February 1947. That was when a drill at Leduc, 25 miles southwest of the city, sent a fountain of dirty-black crude oil soaring skyward. Some 10,000 other wells followed, all within a 100-mile radius of the city. In their wake came the petrochemical industry and the major refining and supply conglomerates. In two decades the population of the city quadrupled, its skyline mushroomed with glass-and-concrete office towers, a rapid-transit system was created, and a $150-million Civic Centre rose. Edmonton had become what it is today—the Oil Capital of Canada.

ORIENTATION

INFORMATION   For guidance on Edmonton and its attractions, contact **Edmonton Tourism,** 9797 Jasper Ave. (tel. 403/496-8400, or toll free 800/463-4667).

For information about the province as a whole, go to **Alberta Economic Development and Tourism,** 10155-102nd St., Edmonton, AB, T5J 4LG (tel. toll free 800/661-8888). This is one of the best-informed, most painstaking and helpful tourist offices in North America, ready to assist you with anything—from accommodations to zoos—as long as it's in Alberta.

CITY LAYOUT   Edmonton is located almost exactly in the center of Alberta. The Rocky Mountains stretch 200 miles to the west, to the south lie the foothills prairie, to the north the beautiful lake country and the Alaska Highway.

The winding **North Saskatchewan River** flows right through the heart of the city, dividing it into roughly equal portions. One of the young capital's greatest achievements is the way in which this river valley has been kept out of the grasp of commercial developers. Almost the entire valley has been turned into public parklands, forming 17 miles of greenery, sports, picnic, and recreation grounds within earshot of the busiest thoroughfares. You never lose sight of one or another of these multiple oases for office workers. Future generations will bless those powers-that-be for stubbornly hanging onto scenery that could so easily have withered into parking lots and factory sites. The river valley is ingeniously interwoven with a network of freeways connecting the two city portions, but so cleverly that the roadways above don't affect the green serenity of the parks below.

Edmonton's main street is the wide and seemingly endless **Jasper Avenue** (actually 101st Avenue), running north of the river. For some mysterious reason the high-numbered streets and avenues are the central ones while the low-numbered thoroughfares lie way out in the suburbs.

At 97th Street, on Jasper Avenue, rises the superb **Canada Place,** the only completely planned complex of its kind in Canada. At the northern approach to the **High Level Bridge,** surrounded by parkland, stand the buildings of the **Alberta Legislature,** seat of the provincial government. Across the bridge, to the west, stretches the vast campus of the **University of Alberta.** Running south in a straight line from **Queen Elizabeth Park** on the riverside is 104th Street, which becomes **Calgary Trail** and leads to the Edmonton International Airport.

Beneath the downtown core stretches a network of pedestrian walkways—called **pedways**—connecting hotels, restaurants, and shopping malls with the library, City Hall, and the Canadian National Railways station. These pedways not only avoid the surface traffic, they're also climate-controlled.

The "A" designations you'll notice for certain streets and avenues are a nuisance for anyone trying to get his bearings, since they interfere with block counts. But otherwise the layout of downtown Edmonton is a model of clarity.

GETTING AROUND

Edmonton's public transport is handled by **Edmonton Transit** (tel. 403/421-4636 for information), one of the finest outfits of its kind not only in Canada but on the North American continent. Transit operates the city buses as well as the new, silent, streamlined, and supremely comfortable **LRT** (Light Transit Line). This partly underground, partly aboveground electric rail service connects downtown Edmonton with northeastern Belvedere and has 10 stations. The downtown terminal, Central Station, lies underground at Jasper Avenue and 101st Street. It's spacious, spotless, handsomely decorated, and right in the heart of the busiest commercial section. The other end of the five-mile line is at 129th Avenue and Fort Road.

The LRT and the Transit buses have the same fares: $1.60 for adults, 70¢ for children during rush hours, and $1.35 in nonpeak hours for adults. You can transfer from one to the other at any given station on the same ticket. On weekdays from 9am to 3pm, downtown LRT travel is free between Churchill, Central, Bay, Corona, and Grandin stations.

CAR RENTALS You'll find **Tilden** at 10131-100A St. (tel. 403/422-6097) and at the airport (tel. 403/955-7232); **Budget,** at 10016-106th St. (tel. 403/428-6155); and **Hertz,** at 10815 Jasper Ave. (tel. 403/424-6408).

CYCLING With the possible exception of Amsterdam, no city in the world takes such tender care of its pedal pushers as Edmonton. The entire metropolitan area is sprinkled with cycling routes specially designed for clear visibility and for access to recreational facilities, schools, parks, commercial centers, and places of employment. They come in three clearly marked types: (1) bike paths, reserved exclusively for cyclists; (2) bike lanes, delineated portions of roadways meant for cyclists; and (3) bike routes, where cyclists have to share the roadways with other types of traffic. The **Capital Recreation Park,** the long ribbon of parks enfolding the North Saskatchewan River Valley, is a biker's paradise and the most ideal cycling area in Canada. The city has published a special Bikeways Map, showing cycling facilities, which you can get at the Visitor Information Centre.

FAST FACTS

American Express There's an office at 10305 Jasper Ave. (tel. 403/421-0608).

Climate The city tends to be sunny, windy, and cool. Midsummer temperatures average between 70° and 80°F, and at an altitude of 2,182 feet, even summer nights can be nippy.

Newspapers The *Edmonton Journal,* a morning paper, is the only daily.

Post Office The main post office is located at 103A Avenue at 99th Street.

KLONDIKE DAYS

The gold rush that sent an army of prospectors heading for the Yukon in 1898 put Edmonton "on the map," as they say. Although the actual goldfields lay 1,500 miles to the north, the little settlement became a giant supply store, resting place, and "recreation" ground for thousands of men stopping there en route before tackling the hazards of the Klondike Trail that led overland to Dawson City in the Yukon. Edmonton's population doubled in size, and its merchants, saloonkeepers, and ladies of easy virtue waxed rich in the process. But very few prospectors made their fortunes in the gold rush.

Since 1962 Edmonton has been celebrating the event with one of the greatest and most colorful extravaganzas staged in Canada. The Klondike Days are held annually in late July. Street festivities last five days, and the great Northlands Klondike Exposition goes on for another five.

Locals and visitors dress up in period costumes, street corners blossom with impromptu stages featuring anything from country bands to cancan girls, stage-coaches rattle through the streets, parades and floats wind from block to block. Buildings all over town disappear behind false storefronts displaying merchandise from yesteryear. Clerks and bank managers work disguised as camp gamblers; waitresses become red-gartered saloon waitresses. "Klondike Dollars" are the accepted coin of the realm for the duration (you can take those not spent home as souvenirs).

The 16,000-seat Coliseum holds nightly spectaculars of rock, pop, or western entertainment, using imported top stage stars and superstars. Northlands Park turns into Klondike Village, complete with old-time general store, barbershop, post office, and gambling saloon—legal for this occasion only. The Citadel Theatre drops serious stage endeavors for a moment and puts on hilarious melodramas with mustachioed villains to hiss and dashing heroes to cheer.

City Hall serves up immense "miners breakfasts" in the open air, massed marching bands compete in the streets, and down the North Saskatchewan River float more than 100 of the weirdest-looking home-built rafts ever seen, racing for the "World Championship of Sourdough River Rafting." Presiding over all the action is "Klondike Kate," chosen from all of America's nightclub talent for cyclonic energy, a leather larynx, Junoesque figure, and a wide repertoire of Klondike-style songs and dances.

WHAT TO SEE & DO
PARKS & ATTRACTIONS IN THE RIVER "GREEN BELT"

Edmonton's daylight action centers around that marvelous undulating ribbon of parkland that is the North Saskatchewan River Valley. The valley runs through the heart of the city, twisting, bending, and lush, providing totally unexpected vistas at every curve. The entire green belt on both sides of the river is a series of parks, sports grounds, recreation areas, and showplaces, and is in the process of developing more. By the time you get there, you may find a batch of new attractions that didn't exist when I researched this book.

It's impossible to lump the area into one segment. You have to take it piece by piece, park by park. The point to remember is that they all form one continuous strip along the river, connected by roads, bridges, bike paths, and hiking trails—and for boating folks, by the river itself.

The Major Parks

Dividing the actual parks from the other attractions, we have:

Borden Park: Swimming and wading pools, baseball diamond, fully equipped playground.

Victoria Park: 18-hole golf course, horseshoe pitch, picnic facilities, free outdoor skating in winter.

William Hawrelak Park: A unique children's fishing lake, stocked with rainbow trout. Only kids—or adults accompanied by such—can fish here. In winter the lake becomes a skating rink. The park also has paddleboats, an "Adventure" playground, and picnic and barbecue areas.

Emily Murphy Park: On the south bank of the river, with picnic facilities and two toboggan runs in winter.

Whitemud Park: On the south bank, with natural picnic areas around the creek, a riding academy with horses for trail rides, also a hang-gliding area—one of the biggest attractions for spectators and participants alike.

Kinsmen Park: The main feature here is the "Fitness Trail" for jogging, with interim exercise spots along the way (less energetic folks can picnic).

Rundle Park: A new development at the eastern edge of the city, with a family recreation center, eight tennis courts, roller skating, 18-hole golf course; also paddleboats, canoeing, and fishing.

The Major Attractions

The above list of parks is by no means comprehensive. But it does give you an idea of how wonderfully Edmontonians are utilizing the natural greenbelt they have so carefully preserved from becoming another strip of cement. Some of the attractions located within these park areas are listed below.

FORT EDMONTON PARK, on the Whitemud Frwy. at Fox Dr. Tel. 403/ 435-0755.

This is a detailed reconstruction of the old Fort Edmonton fur-trading post. Throughout the park you step into other re-created periods of the town's early history. On 1885 Street it's the Frontier Town, complete with blacksmith shop, saloon, general store, and Jasper House Hotel that serves hearty pioneer meals (but not at pioneer prices). 1905 Street has an antique photographic studio and fire hall equipped with appropriate engines. You can ride Edmonton streetcar no. 1, a stagecoach, or a steam locomotive. On 1920 Street, sip an old-fashioned ice-cream soda at Bill's "confectionary."

Admission: $6.25 adults, $3 children.
Open: Summer daily 10am–6pm. **Closed:** Oct–Apr. **Bus:** 32, 39, or 139.

JOHN JANZEN NATURE CENTRE, adjoining Fort Edmonton. Tel. 403/ 428-7900.

The John Janzen Nature Centre offers historic exhibits, hiking trails, and lessons in nature lore. You can go birdwatching, "shake hands" with a garter snake, observe a living beehive, and take courses from professionals in everything from building a log cabin to stalking and game tracking.

Admission: Free.
Open: Summer daily 9am–6pm. **Bus:** 32, 39, or 139.

VALLEY ZOO, in Laurier Park, 13315 Buena Vista Rd. Tel. 403/496- 6911.

In this charming combination of reality and fantasy, real-live beasties mingle with fairy-tale creations. Over 500 animals and birds are neighbors to the Three Little Pigs, Humpty Dumpty, and the inhabitants of Noah's Ark.

Admission: $4.75 adults, $2.50 children.
Open: Daily 10am–6pm. **Closed:** Weekdays in winter. **Bus:** 39, 54, or 139.

MUTTART CONSERVATORY, off James Macdonald Bridge at 98th Ave. and 96A St. Tel. 403/496-8755.

The conservatory is housed in a group of four pyramidical pavilions that look like science-fiction structures. Actually they house one of the finest floral displays in North America, but in a style quite different from other conservatories. Each pyramid contains a different climatic zone—the tropical one has an 18-foot waterfall as well. The Arid Pavilion has desert air and shows flowering cacti and their relatives. The temperate zone includes a cross section of plants from this global region. The fourth pyramid features changing ornamental displays of plants and blossoms. For good measure, there's also the Treehouse Café.

Admission: $4 adults, $2 children.
Open: Daily 11am–6pm. **Bus:** 51 or 55.

JOHN WALTER MUSEUM, 91 Ave. and Walterdale Rd., south of the 105th Street Bridge. Tel. 403/428-3033.

Housed on the site of Edmonton's first home on the south side of the river, built in 1874, this museum gives a glimpse of early Edmonton as well as knowledge of one of its first settlers. It is also the site of the town's first telegraph station.

Admission: Free.
Open: Sun only. Call ahead.

EDMONTON SPACE AND SCIENCE CENTRE, 11211–142nd St., Coronation Park. Tel. 403/452-9100 for information on IMAX movies.

This is probably the most advanced multipurpose facility of its kind in the world. It contains, among other wonders, the giant screen IMAX theater, the largest planetarium theater in Canada, plus many high-tech exhibit galleries and an observatory open on clear afternoons and evenings. The show programs include star shows, laser-light music concerts, and the special IMAX films that have to be seen to be believed.

Admission: $5 adults, $3 children. IMAX movies $7.50 adults, $4.50 children.
Open: Sun–Thurs 10am–10pm, Fri–Sat 10am–midnight. **Bus:** 17 or 22.

ALBERTA LEGISLATIVE BUILDING, 109th St. and 97th Ave. Tel. 403/ 427-7362.

The Alberta Legislative Building rises on the site of the early trading post from which the city grew. Surrounded by lovingly manicured lawns, formal gardens, and greenhouses, it overlooks the river valley. The seat of Alberta's government was completed in 1912, a stately Edwardian structure open to the public throughout the year. Conducted tours tell you about the functions of provincial lawmaking: Who does what, where, and for how long.

Tours: Free. Given daily every half hour 9am–5pm.
LRT: Grandin station.

ELSEWHERE IN THE CITY

Now we step outside the park belt for daytime action throughout the city. This being Edmonton, several of these attractions are also located in parkland, separate from the river valley.

PROVINCIAL MUSEUM, 12845-102nd Ave. Tel. 403/453-9100.

Modern and expertly laid out, this museum displays Alberta's natural and human history in four permanent galleries. The Habitat Groups show wildlife in natural settings, Indians and Fur Trade offers a glimpse of the region's original inhabitants, Natural History has fossils and dinosaurs, and History tells the pioneer story. The museum also presents artists and artisans and free film showings.

Admission: $3 adults, $1 children; free on Tues.
Open: Daily 9am–8pm. **Bus:** 1, 2, or 10.

VISTA 33, 10020-100th St. Tel. 403/493-3333.

Actually the head office of Alberta Government Telephones, this soaring square tower rises to 441 feet and has a helicopter landing pad on the roof. Vista 33, on the 33rd floor, commands an unsurpassed view: On clear days you can overlook some 2,500 square miles. Within this radius lives nearly a third of the population of Alberta! At night the lights of the city create a spectacular sight.

Part of Vista is the Telecommunication Museum, an intriguing mini-museum that displays telephonic instruments, starting with a tiny manual switchboard from 1906 to the fully automated marvels used today.

Admission: $1 adults, 50¢ children.
Open: Daily 10am–8pm.

EDMONTON ART GALLERY, 2 Sir Winston Churchill Sq. Tel. 403/422-6223.

The art gallery occupies a stately mansion right in the heart of downtown. The interior, however, is state-of-the-art modern, subtly lit and expertly arranged. Exhibits consist partly of contemporary Canadian art, partly of changing works on tour from every corner of the globe. The Gallery shop sells an eclectic array of items; from art books to handmade yo-yos.

Admission: $3 adults, $1.50 children; free on Thurs evening.
Open: Mon–Wed 10:30am–5pm, Thurs–Sun 11am–5pm.

NORTHLANDS, 118th Ave. and 74th St.

Northlands is a complex of parks, arenas, and buildings housing the Coliseum, Sportex, and Northland Parks racetrack, hosting a vast variety of sports events and other shows. The racetrack is the scene of the annual Canadian Derby as well as Thoroughbred and harness racing. In May there is the annual Horse Show, followed by a musical ride of the Royal Canadian Mounted Police—a superb equestrian spectacle apt to give amateur horseriders a massive inferiority complex.

LRT: Coliseum station.

RUTHERFORD HOUSE, 11153 Saskatchewan Dr., on the campus of the University of Alberta. Tel. 403/427-3995.

The home of Alberta's first premier, Alexander Rutherford, this lovingly preserved Edwardian building gleams with polished silver and gilt-framed oils. Around 1915 this mansion was the magnet for the social elite of the province: Today, guides dressed in period costumes convey some of the spirit of the times to visitors. There's also a tearoom on the premises.

Admission: Free, but donations encouraged.
Open: Summer daily 10am–6pm. **LRT:** University station.

WEST EDMONTON MALL, 8770-170th St. Tel. 403/444-5200.

⭐ You won't find many shopping malls mentioned in this book, but the West Edmonton Mall is something else. Although it contains more than 800 retail outlets, it looks and sounds more like a large slice of Disneyland that has somehow broken loose and drifted north. The locals modestly call it the "Eighth Wonder of the World."

More theme park than mall, the West Edmonton Mall houses the world's largest indoor amusement park, including a titanic indoor roller coaster, plus an enclosed wave-lake, complete with sandy beach and enough artificial waves to ride a surfboard on. It has walk-through bird aviaries, monkey and tiger habitats, a "petting zoo" with suitably cuddlesome inmates, a huge ice-skating palace, 19 (count 'em) movie theaters, a lagoon with performing dolphins, and several absolutely fabulous adventure rides (one of them by submarine to the ocean floor, another taking you through a series of underground caverns swarming with pirates, and still another simulating a white-water raft journey). In the middle of it all, an immense fountain with 19 computer-controlled jets weaves and dances in a musical-lights performance.

Some 500,000 visitors view the mall every week. There is a free bus service to the mall from 12 major hotels. Admission is gratis, but some of the rides are fairly expensive. Don't miss it.

Open: Daily. **Bus:** 10, 11, 12, or 16.

Old Strathcona

This historical district used to be a separate township, but was amalgamated with Edmonton in 1912. It lies around 82nd Avenue, between 103rd Street and 105th Street. Due to the efforts of the Old Strathcona Foundation, the area contains some of the best-preserved landmarks in the city. It's best seen on foot, guided by the brochures given out at the **Old Strathcona Foundation** office, 8331 104th St. (tel. 403/433-5866). Some of the most interesting landmarks are listed below. Other Old Strathcona landmarks include the **Princess Theatre,** 10337 Whyte Ave., opened in 1914 as a live stage, now a revival movie house; the **Dominion Hotel,** 10313 Whyte Ave., once one of the poshest hostelries in town, now a facsimile facade; and the **Fire Hall,** 10322 83rd Ave., dating back to the era when fire engines were horse-drawn and today the premises of the Walterdale Playhouse Theatre. Bus 8 or 46 will get you there.

THE MODEL AND TOY MUSEUM, 8603 104th St. Tel. 403/433-4512.

Displays over 400 scale models of famous buildings, ships, aircraft and trains, as well as dolls, birds, and metal toys.

Admission: By donation.
Open: Wed–Fri noon–8pm, Sat 10am–6pm, Sun 1–5pm.

C & E RAILWAY MUSEUM, 10447 86th Ave. Tel. 403/433-9739.

A replica of the old station built in 1891, it's exact to the last detail and a study ground for "iron horse" buffs.

Admission: By donation.
Open: Tues–Sat 11am–4pm. **Closed:** Sept–May.

TELEPHONE HISTORICAL INFORMATION CENTRE, 10437 83rd Ave. Tel. 403/441-2077.

A hands-on, interactive exhibition that tells the telephone story of Edmonton from 1885 to the present.

Admission: $1 adults, 50¢ children.
Open: Mon–Sat noon–4pm.

TOURS & EXCURSIONS

Royal Tours (tel. 403/488-9040) offers a variety of tours of the city and environs. All the tours feature pickups at certain downtown hotels.

The Historical Tour takes 3½ hours and includes the Alberta Legislature, the North Saskatchewan River Valley, and Fort Edmonton Park. Adults pay $23.50, children $12. The Ecological Tour is a 2½-hour jaunt through Edmonton's best residential areas, the Provincial Museum, University of Alberta, and the West Edmonton Mall. The price is $20 for adults, $11 for children. The Best of Edmonton features a combination of the two half-day tours, takes a full day, and costs $38 for adults, $20 for children.

The **North Saskatchewan Riverboat Company,** Edmonton Convention Centre, 9797 Jasper Ave. (tel. 403/424-2628), takes you up- and downstream from the Convention Centre six times a day. Their craft is a romantic 150-foot stern-wheeler riverboat with a bar and buffet on board. Tickets range from $8 to $28 per passenger, depending on the time of day or evening and the menu selection.

WHERE TO STAY

Having started its downtown facelift 10 years before its rival, Edmonton is that much better off than Calgary when it comes to providing tourist beds. This doesn't mean that the capital boasts many more hostelries. It does mean that the accommodations are better balanced at the lower-medium and budget end of the scale. Here even the older buildings now enjoy a measure of permanence and aren't threatened with bulldozing at any moment. So you're fairly safe in assuming that a hotel mentioned below will still be standing by the time you get there.

BED-AND-BREAKFAST ACCOMMODATIONS The old European B&B tradition is a latecomer in Alberta, but very efficiently organized—too efficiently for the taste of some visitors who prefer a more freewheeling approach. Here, instead of advertising individually, the host families register with agencies. From the tourist point of view, this has the advantage that all the listed accommodations are carefully screened, so you can get a row of choices without running your legs off. The drawback is that it virtually eliminates price competition. Nearly all B&Bs listed charge from $35 for singles, from $50 for doubles. Extra services such as laundry facilities, airport pickups, or babysitting entail extra charges.

The following agencies offer rooms with host families in Edmonton, Calgary, Banff, Jasper, and country areas: **Edmonton Bed & Breakfast,** 13814 110A Ave., Edmonton, AB, T5M 2M9 (tel. 403/455-2297); **Bed & Breakfast—Alberta's Gem,** 11216-48th Ave., Edmonton, AB, T6H 0C7 (tel. 403/434-6098); and **Holiday Home Accommodation,** 10808-54th Ave., Edmonton, AB, T6H 0T9 (tel. 403/436-4196).

FARM & RANCH ACCOMMODATIONS For the rustic at heart there are a number of farm operations that take in paying guests. These are not dude ranches but working farms, equipped with modern facilities and regularly inspected by the Alberta Hotel Association. Here are a few samples of farmstays available:

Rustic Ridge Ranch, Box 389, Evansburg, AB, T0E 0T0 (tel. 403/727-2042), is a mixed farm 70 miles west of Edmonton. It can accommodate up to eight people. There are barbecues on the veranda, campfire evenings with music, and fishing and swimming nearby. Room and breakfast is $30 for singles, $45 per couple.

Gwynalta Farm, Gwynne, AB, T0G 1L0 (tel. 403/352-3587), is a dairy farm accommodating four people. It has a lake that's perfect for boating and fishing (if you bring your own boat). The farm is close to Edmonton International Airport. Room and breakfast is $25 per person. Other meals are available for $5.

L. A. Triple B Guest Farm, Box 21, Hairy Hill, AB, T0B 1S0 (tel. 403/768-3877), is a 1,500-acre grain farm that has accommodation for eight people. Bread is baked fresh daily. There's croquet, lawn darts, billiards, and shuffleboard. Room and board is $50 per person, $90 per couple.

Some farms also have camping grounds and all offer bed-and-breakfast deals at correspondingly lower rates.

EXPENSIVE

CENTRE SUITE HOTEL, Eaton Centre, 10222 102nd St., Edmonton, AB T5J 4C5. Tel. 403/429-3900, or toll free 800/661-6655 in Canada. Fax 403/428-1566. 169 suites. A/C MINIBAR TV TEL
$ Rates: Standard or business suite $99–$160 single or double. Ask about special weekend rates. AE, DC, ER, MC, V. **Parking:** $7.50 per day.

This establishment forms part of the upscale Eaton Centre Mall in the heart of downtown. There are no rooms—only suites—and even the standard suites come with private Jacuzzis. Half the windows look into the mall, so you can stand behind the tinted one-way glass (in your pajamas, if you like) and watch the shopping action outside . . . a unique experience.

The suites enfold you in the lap of luxury with amenities like carefully matched color schemes, couches as well as armchairs, desks with personal computer hookup, elegant bathrooms with illuminated shaving or makeup mirrors, hairdryers, bath gels, body lotions, and fluffy bathrobes. Each sitting room and bedroom is equipped with separate telephones and Spectravision TV. The hotel provides a business center with photocopy and fax machines, an exercise room with steam bath and whirlpool, and a restaurant, Cocoa's where house guests receive 15% dinner discounts. And without having to stir out of doors there are the 120 retail shops of the mall, plus a movie theater, entertainment pub, and an indoor putting green. Hotel service, I should add, is exceptionally thoughtful and smooth.

HILTON INTERNATIONAL, 10235-101st St., Edmonton, AB, T5J 3E9. Tel. 403/428-7111, or toll free 800/263-9030. Fax 403/441-3098. 313 rms. A/C MINIBAR TV TEL
$ Rates: $89–$120 single or double. AE, DC, ER, MC, V. **Parking:** $9.90 a day.
The Hilton has the unique feature of having half the floors reserved for nonsmokers. The hotel is connected via overhead walkway with the Edmonton Centre shopping complex, so you can reach the stores without stepping outside. The showpiece here is the superlative Garden Lounge in the center of the lobby, lit by a skylight and set amid palms, ferns, and flower beds. An indoor pool with whirlpool and sauna, two celebrated restaurants, plus a disco and the 24-hour room service, complete the hotel facilities.

The guest rooms breathe discreet elegance. The decor is light gray and powder blue, and writing desks and bathroom sinks are topped with genuine marble. Despite the air conditioning, one window in each unit opens, a blessing for oxygen addicts like myself. You get bedside controls for the TV and radio, extra-large towels, and thoughtful touches like hideaway clotheslines, extra plugs for hairdryers, complimentary shower caps, and shampoo.

HOLIDAY INN CROWNE PLAZA, 10111 Bellamy Hill, Edmonton, AB, T5J 1N7. Tel. 403/428-6611, or toll free 800/661-8801. Fax 403/426-7625. 305 rms and suites. A/C TV TEL
$ Rates: $130 single; $145 double; $165–$450 suite. Weekend packages available. AE, CB, DC, ER, MC, V. **Parking:** $6.50 per day.

The Holiday Inn is the renamed and rejuvenated Château Lacombe—a round, ivory-colored tower soaring up 24 stories from the surrounding greenery, its dancing lights reflecting in the river below. The unusual design blends well with the city's dramatic skyline, yet it is instantly recognizable from afar—a perfect landmark.

The vast lobby is a study in serene beige and amber hues, suffused with the soft glow of chandeliers. The building is packed with facilities and amenities: two private executive floors, fitness center, boutique, cocktail lounges, no-smoking floors, plus a revolving restaurant, appropriately named La Ronde, at the top of the tower (see "Where to Dine," below). The bedrooms and suites come in delicate pastel tints. Bathrooms are stocked with hairdryers, shampoo, detergents, and sundry little extras and have lighting fixtures that can be adjusted from bright to dim.

HOTEL MACDONALD, 10065 100th St., Edmonton, AB, T5J 0N6. Tel. 403/424-5181, or toll free 800/828-7447. Fax 403/429-6481. 198 rms. A/C MINIBAR TV TEL

$ Rates: Regular room $170 single, $190 double; business class $185 single, $210 double. AE, DC, DISC, ER, MC, V. **Parking:** $12 a day.

⭐ The palatial Hotel Macdonald, named after Canada's first prime minister and opened in 1915, has reopened after a lengthy hibernation. And reopened in all its original splendor, which makes it the grandest of grandes dames in the province. It looks like a feudal château from the outside, and the interior houses a number of public rooms straight out of *The Great Gatsby*. High ceilings, majestic drapes, and crystal chandeliers grace the hotel, which boasts a ballroom fit for royalty, and a bar retreat that resembles an Edwardian gentlemen's club. The indoor swimming pool, with Roman pillars, adjoins a health club with a pro shop and juice bar, a sauna, a steamroom, and a separate wading pool for children.

There is an outdoor garden terrace for summer dining and an indoor dining room viewing the panoramic backdrop of the North Saskatchewan River valley. The guest rooms are furnished with subtle elegance and special attention to details, like eye-saving light fixtures, soothing color schemes, generous wardrobe space, and superbly sprung beds. Service throughout the hotel is smooth, prompt, and unobtrusive.

WESTIN HOTEL, 10135-100th St., Edmonton, AB, T5J 0N7. Tel. 403/426-3636, or toll free 800/228-3000. Fax 403/423-3785. 413 rms and suites. A/C TV TEL

$ Rates: $99–$139 single or double. Weekend special $90 per room, with $40 credit for food and beverages. AE, DC, ER, MC, V. **Parking:** $7.49 per day.

The Westin is an immense brown block of titanic beauty that manages to appear both huge and graceful. The softly lit lobby has a delightful cocktail bar in the center that's at least half garden, illuminated by star showers encased in waving nets. Impressive! The staff of this streamlined palace commands 29 languages. An underground shopping complex bustles, unheard, beneath your feet. The Carvery is the intimate and stylish main restaurant, but there's also the less formal Palm Court. And, of course, a luxurious swimming pool, whirlpool, and sauna.

The rooms and suites are large, decorated with some of the finest prints found on hotel walls; they contain burnt-orange carpeting, immense beds, alarm clocks, and a lot of other pampering gadgets. The bathrooms follow the pattern, with hideaway clotheslines, shower caps, and shampoo, plus heating lamps with attached timers (you can set them for just as long as it takes you to shower and dry yourself).

AN IMPORTANT NOTE ON PRICES

Unless stated otherwise, **the prices cited in this guide are given in Canadian dollars,** which is good news for U.S. travelers because the Canadian dollar is worth 25% less than the American dollar, but buys nearly as much. As we go to press, $1 Canadian is worth 75¢ U.S., which means that your $100-a-night hotel room will cost only U.S. $75, and your $6 breakfast costs only U.S. $4.50.

Here's a quick table of equivalents:

Canadian $	U.S. $
$ 1	$ 0.75
5	3.75
10	7.50
20	15.00
50	37.50
80	60.00
100	75.00
200	150.00

MODERATE

ALBERTA PLACE, 10049-103rd St., Edmonton, AB, T5J 2W7. Tel. 403/423-1565. Fax 403/426-6260. 85 units. TV TEL
$ Rates: $72 double bed-sitter; $82 double one-bedroom suite. Extra person $8. Children stay free in parents' room. AE, DC, ER, MC, V. **Parking:** Free.
This downtown apartment hotel is located in an ultramodern block and equipped with a small, smartly tasteful lobby. The building has a swimming pool (with hot tub and sauna), cable color TV, and suites of various sizes. The apartments are very well furnished in chrome and brown color schemes. They come with large open closets, writing desks, fine wall decorations, overhead and table lamps, comfortable beds, and armchairs. Kitchens are small and sparkling, refrigerators large, and there are serving counters as partitions. Everything to set up housekeeping is supplied.

AMBASSADOR MOTOR INN, 10041-106th St., Edmonton, AB, T5J 1G3. Tel. 403/423-1925. Fax 403/424-5302. 76 rms. A/C TV TEL
$ Rates: $45 single; $50–$54 double. Extra person $4. AE, ER, MC, V. **Parking:** Free.
There's a tavern attached to this very attractive small motor inn, but the tavern portion is kept completely separate from the hotel so none of the bar hurly-burly penetrates the living quarters. The smart, red-carpeted lobby has black leather armchairs and white cube tables, and an adjoining coffee shop doubles as a restaurant. The elevators are speedy and the guest rooms are models of contemporary comfort, all air-conditioned with individual controls, wall-to-wall carpets, and writing desks with lamp and mirror. The bathrooms, with tub and shower, have separate rooms for the sink and open hanging space.

CHERRYWOOD, 10010-104th St., Edmonton, AB, T5J 0Z1. Tel. 403/423-2450. Fax 403/426-6090. 138 rms. TV TEL
$ Rates: $55–$69 single or double. Children stay free in parents' room. AE, DC, ER, MC, V. **Parking:** $4 a day.
A sparkling white structure resting on blue pillars, the Cherrywood has a facade dominated by little balconies that give it a distinctly Mediterranean flavor. The lobby is spacious and modern, with an amiably old-fashioned touch supplied by a basket of apples free for the taking. The Cherrywood has a pleasantly informal restaurant, indoor pool, lavish exercise facilities, and bedroom VCRs with gratis movies ("adult" movies available for a fee). Each of the bedrooms has a private balcony, plus a remote-control TV.

CONTINENTAL INN, 16625 Stony Plain Rd., Edmonton, AB, T5P 4A8. Tel. 403/484-7751. Fax 403/484-9827. 60 rms. TV TEL
$ Rates: $40–$49 single; $44–$60 double. AE, DC, ER, MC, V. **Parking:** Free.
Located about 10 minutes from downtown on the Yellowhead route to Jasper Park, the Continental Inn is a huge, massively modern accommodation and entertainment complex. The inn contains a bar, restaurant, coffee shop, cocktail lounge, tavern, cabaret, a truly grand ballroom, and every conceivable convention facility, including an excellently laid-out lobby that combines vastness with comfort.
The inn has only 60 guest rooms, few for its size, but these are large and nicely furnished. Big front windows give maximum daylight, the decor is a pleasant beige and pink, hanging space is ample, and room service is excellent. The bathrooms are big and modern, with complimentary shower caps, shampoo, and boxes of tissues. (In Canada it's Scotties instead of Kleenex.)

EDMONTON INN, 11830 Kingsway Ave., Edmonton, AB, T5G 0X5. Tel. 403/454-9521. Fax 403/453-7360. 100 rms. A/C TV TEL
$ Rates: $95 single; $105 double. AE, MC, V. **Parking:** Free.
Although facing the Municipal Airport, the inn's bedrooms are so effectively soundproofed that they're actually quieter than most hotel rooms, which is fairly indicative of the entire establishment—one of the best-run hostelries in Canada. The inn has a wonderful shrubbery-shrouded courtyard bar with an indoor garden setting, a coffee bar that looks like a baronial country kitchen, a country-style saloon, a sports

bar, restaurant, and umpteen banquet chambers, meeting rooms, and ballrooms (which may be the reason why the lobby seems perpetually filled with blushing brides). While the downstairs portions are beehives of activities, the upstairs bedrooms are tranquil oases. Spacious and elegant, with exceptionally thick pile carpets, they contain bathrooms with enough surface space to lay out all your toilet utensils, something of a rarity. You get gratis shower caps, shampoo, and mountains of matches, plus excellent room service, and those wonderful granny armchairs the British call "comfy chairs." The inn is about a 10-minute drive from downtown.

EDMONTON RENAISSANCE, 10155-105th St., Edmonton, AB, T5J 1E2. Tel. 403/423-4811, or toll free 800/223-9898. Fax 403/423-3204. 300 rms. TV TEL

$ Rates: $110–$130 single or double. AE, DC, ER, MC, V. **Parking:** $6.50 a day.

The Renaissance is one of Edmonton's newest and liveliest hotels; the only sedate feature about it is the exterior. It's a white Riviera-style hostelry that welcomes you with a spacious green-carpeted lobby decorated with antique mirrors, desks, and a profusion of indoor plants. The Renaissance houses a heated indoor pool and sauna, two restaurants, a cocktail lounge, and a nightclub—all of which makes for a lot of action.

The bedrooms are spacious and light, most of them with small balconies. The carpeting is deep emerald, furnishings include luxurious chaise longues, and bathrooms come with separate outside sinks—very handy for double occupants. Also handy are the neat little writing tables with desk lamps, ideal for businesspeople doing a spot of homework.

LA BOHEME, 6427-112th Ave., Edmonton, AB, T5W 0N9. Tel. 403/474-5693. Fax 403/479-1871. 8 suites. MINIBAR TV TEL

$ Rates (including breakfast): $60 single; $75 double; $90 triple. AE, MC, V. **Parking:** Free.

La Bohème is a most unusual establishment. It started as a formidable restaurant and became a hotel as a hospitable afterthought. A modest brown three-story building that's a historical landmark, a five-minute drive from downtown, La Bohème was voted Premier French Restaurant in 1987, and a year later expanded into Edmonton's first European-style bed-and-breakfast inn. There are no rooms here—only suites of one and two bedrooms. All are newly renovated and furnished individually, and each suite has a character of its own. Downstairs, the hostelry has a celebrated wine cellar; upstairs, the rooms get fresh flowers and linen sheets along with outstanding service.

QUALITY INN, 10209-100th Ave., Edmonton, AB, T5J 0A1. Tel. 403/428-6442. Fax 403/428-6467. 72 rms. A/C TV TEL

$ Rates: From $54 single; from $64 double. Children under 18 stay free in parents' room. AE, DC, DISC, ER, MC, V. **Parking:** Free.

This remarkably versatile establishment lies behind an unassuming front. The Locker Room Pub on the premises exudes an air of sporting elegance; there's a separate restaurant. The guest rooms all have satellite TV, smart little writing desks, new carpeting, large open spaces to hang clothes, and couches. Some rooms have private Jacuzzis. The hotel also offers shuttle service to the airport.

RENFORD INN, 10425-100th Ave., Edmonton, AB, T5J 0A2. Tel. 403/423-5611. Fax 403/425-9791. 107 rms. A/C TV TEL

$ Rates: $69 single or double. Weekend rates $59 per day. AE, DC, ER, MC, V. **Parking:** Free.

Very contemporary and attractive, this representative of a Canadian hotel chain boasts a large array of facilities: restaurant, lounge, tavern, an English pub, as well as dry-cleaning service, laundry room, and a swimming pool with Jacuzzi. It welcomes you with a chic and spacious lobby, decorated with strange moving lights and positively embracing armchairs. The rooms all have color TVs and exceptionally good prints on the walls. The rooms are medium-sized, the furniture a stylish light wood, the open closets a trifle small. No overhead lights, but there are three table lamps. The smart streamlined bathrooms are equipped with automatic ventilators.

BUDGET

CECIL HOTEL, 10406 Jasper Ave., Edmonton, AB, T5J 1Z3. Tel. 403/ 428-7001. 52 rms (half with bath). TV TEL

$ Rates: $23 single without bath, $27 single with bath; $28 double without bath, $32 double with bath. Extra person $5.60. MC, V. **Parking:** Not available.

The Cecil is a small corner building with hewn-stone front and a tavern on the premises. The lobby is a rather Spartan affair, but the bedrooms are furnished nicely enough. Half of them have private bath or shower; the others, hot- and cold-water sinks. Carpeting is wall to wall, and there's fair hanging space in either closets or open arrangements, a small work desk, and a bedside lamp. A coffee shop is in the building.

MAYFAIR HOTEL, 10815 Jasper Ave., Edmonton, AB, T5J 2B2. Tel. 403/423-1650. Fax 403/425-6834. 97 rms. TV TEL

$ Rates: $49–$64 single or double. AE, ER, MC, V. **Parking:** $4.83 a day.

A white corner building with distinctive blue awnings over each window, this attractive hotel has been newly renovated and now houses a large family-style restaurant. The lobby is vast and plush, with red armchairs, brass chandeliers, and an electric fireplace. Bedrooms are a bit small, the furnishings strictly functional but ample. There are open closets and bedside lamps instead of ceiling lights. The bathrooms are compact and fluorescently lit.

SAXONY MOTOR INN, 15540 Stony Plain Rd., Edmonton, AB, T5P 3Z2. Tel. 403/484-3331. Fax 403/489-3774. 59 rms. A/C TV TEL

$ Rates: $54 single; $59 double. AE, DC, ER, MC, V. **Parking:** Free.

About 10 minutes from downtown, this dazzling white-and-blue structure with a display of international flags offers outstanding value. With sumptuous Spanish decor throughout, the Saxony houses a first-rate restaurant, a smart coffee shop, a cozy tavern, and a lounge, as well as a heated rooftop swimming pool, sauna, and sun terrace, and extensive convention and banquet facilities.

The rooms are large, with tiny balconies, all air-conditioned and very well appointed. You get king-size beds, leather armchairs, macrame on the walls, Indian prints, plus cable TV, radio, writing desk, and an open niche for hanging your clothes. Bathrooms are compact and streamlined.

The Ys

Both of Edmonton's Ys are housed in modern, pleasant buildings without any hint of the barracks flavor that permeates some of their counterparts elsewhere.

YMCA, 10030-102A Ave., Edmonton, AB, T5J 0G5. Tel. 403/421-9622. Fax 403/428-9469. 106 rms (some with bath).

$ Rates: $29 single; $40 double. MC, V.

The YMCA has a cafeteria, pool, weight room, gymnasium, and racquetball court, plus a TV lounge; it accommodates men, women, and couples. Only a few rooms have private bath (tub only). The rooms are small and trim, nicely carpeted, and cheerfully furnished with a small writing desk, a bedside table with lamp, and homey curtains. Telephones are in the lobby only.

YWCA, 10305-100th Ave., Edmonton, AB, T5J 0G5. Tel. 403/423-9922. Fax 403/425-7467. 4 beds in dorm, 85 rms (some with bath).

$ Rates: $27.50–$42.50 private room; $12.50 bunk in dorm; $5 sleeping bag. MC, V.

For women only, the YWCA has a cafeteria open seven days a week, as well as a pool. Accommodations range from a five-bed dormitory to singles with bath. Laundry facilities and TV lounge are available in the house. The public bathrooms are sparkling and the staff is exceptionally friendly. Reservations are advised.

WHERE TO DINE

Edmonton, as I said before, is very much a beef town, with a restaurant scene basking in the aroma of sizzling steaks. But over the past decade other, more cosmopolitan styles of cuisine have gained popularity, although not to the point of dominance. The city today has achieved a fine balance between the traditional American palate and its international alternatives—meaning that you can get both in every price bracket.

The following selections come from such a lengthy list of choices that they can only serve as samples. A handful among them are unique, one-of-a-kind establishments. The majority merely indicate a certain culinary genre that has a dozen or two other representatives, which I had to omit purely for space reasons.

EXPENSIVE

CLAUDE'S ON THE RIVER, 9797 Jasper Ave. Tel. 403/429-2900.
   Cuisine: FRENCH. **Reservations:** Recommended.
$ Prices: Appetizers $9.95–$12.75; main courses $18.25–$25.75. AE, CB, ER, MC, V.
   Open: Lunch Mon–Fri 11:30am–2pm; dinner Mon–Sat 5:30–11pm.
Claude's has a reputation for having the finest wine list in town. It's certainly the most informative: more than 100 choices, each adorned with a few expert comments that enable benighted patrons to shine as vintage sages. A velvety gourmetry, with background music whispering as softly as the ceiling fans and lighting intimate as a caress. Some of the outstanding house specialties are escargots in puff pastry and wine sauce, a magnificent seafood ragoût, rack of lamb in garlic sauce, and wickedly delicious fruit, ice, and chocolate desserts that make you forget the meaning of the word calorie. Service is as smooth and unobtrusive as the music.

LA BOHEME, 6427-112th Ave. Tel. 403/474-5693.
   Cuisine: FRENCH. **Reservations:** Required.
$ Prices: Appetizers $4.25–$8.25; main courses $14.50–$19.95. AE, MC, V.
   Open: Lunch Mon–Sat 11am–5pm; brunch Sun 11am–2:30pm; dinner Mon–Sat 5pm–midnight, Sun 5–9pm.
La Bohème is the restaurant that preceded the hotel by that name listed in "Where to Stay," above. It consists of two small, lace-curtained dining rooms. The cuisine is French, of course, and so is the wine selection, with particular accent on Rhône Valley vintages. The clam broth with a subtle saffron flavor makes a suitable opener. Then it's a very difficult choice between, say, the lamb cutlets grilled with herbs and Dijon mustard or the perfectly timed entrecôte steak in a Madeira and peppercorn sauce. To finish your meal, you can't do better than one of the pies—tangy and not oversweet. The restaurant also features some outstanding vegetarian entrées, such as a casserole of wild rice with provençale-style vegetables.

LA RONDE, in the Holiday Inn, 10111 Bellamy Hill. Tel. 403/428-6611.
   Cuisine: INTERNATIONAL. **Reservations:** Recommended.
$ Prices: Appetizers $7.50–$9.50; main courses $17.50–$29.95. AE, DC, ER, MC, V.
   Open: Dinner Tues–Sat 5:30–11pm; brunch Sun 10:30am–2pm.
Edmonton's only revolving restaurant is located atop the ivory tower of the Holiday Inn. Svelte and luxurious without being ornate, La Ronde achieves its glamour effect through the stunning panorama slowly unfolding below, plus quietly impeccable service. The establishment also has a dance floor, where all the revolving is done by the couples.

The cuisine is classic; nothing nouvelle about it. For appetizers, try escargots in garlic butter with mushrooms or a mélange of salmon, eel, and mackerel. For a soup, perhaps the chilled gazpacho or the teeming seafood bouillabaisse. Then the choices range from the mighty Alberta mixed grill, or veal and kidney vol-au-vent served with whisky-cream sauce, to the pan-fried breast of pheasant stuffed with chestnut and apricot purée. One unusual feature of La Ronde is that it serves a buffet Sunday brunch ($15.95 per bruncher). Of course, the panoramic views are on the house.

UNHEARDOF, 9602-82nd Ave. Tel. 403/432-0480.
   Cuisine: INTERNATIONAL. **Reservations:** Required.
$ Prices: Prix-fixe menus $34 and $42. AE, MC, V.
   Open: Dinner Tues–Sat 6:30–9pm.

Unheardof is a unique place, not only because of its name. It's the only deluxe restaurant I've come across in Canada that features a prix-fixe menu—or rather, two of them. The reason for this fixture also accounts for the culinary standard here: The limited choice enables the chef to use the highest-quality ingredients, prepare the meal from scratch, and yet have the first course ready almost as soon as the guests arrive. You get to choose between a $42 and a $34 meal—both superb, but one shorter than the other. When I ate there the opener was a hot crab soufflé of rare delicacy, followed by orange-flavored galantine of duck. Then came Vietnamese prawns, very large and stuffed with a wine-flavored purée of scallops. This was followed by chicken breasts filled with a sharp cheese, then beef tenderloin, fresh asparagus-and-leaf salad, and finally an absolutely magnificent chocolate torte with whipped cream. The entire meal was so perfectly and subtly blended that it resembled a symphony composed in a kitchen.

YEOMAN STEAK HOUSE, 10030-107th St. Tel. 403/423-1511.
   Cuisine: CANADIAN. **Reservations:** Accepted.
$ Prices: Appetizers $3.95–$5.95; main courses $10.95–$28.50. AE, DC, ER, MC, V.
   Open: Mon–Sat 11am–11pm, Sun 5–9pm.
The Yeoman Steak House is an unusually handsome establishment consisting of four dining rooms, each furnished in a subtly different style, all blending into a harmonious whole. You don't realize the size of the place—the glass partitions allow diners to see each other yet provide an air of intimacy for each section. The walls are hung with beautifully framed oils and prints, individually illuminated. The lower room has an open grill arranged rather like an altar to the gods of gastronomy. The service is silently attentive—and leisurely. Try, perhaps, the sweetbreads gourmet or the charcoal-broiled New York–cut steak. Finally—a must—the hot apple pie with rum sauce, which will give you an idea just how delicious dessert can be.

MODERATE

100A Street is a very special thoroughfare in culinary Edmonton. It has, in one block, no fewer than six first-rate restaurants in different price brackets. Unfortunately I don't have the space to describe them all as painstakingly as they deserve, but you can't go wrong—and won't wear out much shoe leather—by eating your way through them one by one. In addition to Bistro Praha and Geppetto's, described below, I like the **Mongolian Food Experience,** whose name aptly describes its cuisine.

BISTRO LA BODEGA, 10165-104th St. Tel. 403/429-0830.
   Cuisine: CONTINENTAL. **Reservations:** Accepted.
$ Prices: Appetizers $5.35–$6.50; main courses $14.95–$18.95. AE, MC, V.
   Open: Lunch Mon–Sat 11:30am–2:30pm; dinner Mon–Sat 5–11pm.
Here you'll find one of the very few wine bars in town, along with lashings of continental ambience and an illustrious chef-owner. Jurg Weber has the reputation of being one of Alberta's top kitchen wizards, and got his training in the Suvretta House of St. Moritz and the Palace Hotel of Gstaad, both Swiss havens for cultivated palates. You can order your wine by the glass or by the bottle, and the menu prices are kept well on the affordable side. Every weekend the Bodega features a chef's special, and alongside, the wine recommended for the dish. Thus the chicken Frangelico (veal and nut-filled chicken breast flamed with sweet Frangelico liqueur) should be accompanied by a soft, medium-dry Vouvray; the shrimp provençale, by a crisp German Oppenheimer.

BISTRO PRAHA, 10168-100A St. Tel. 403/424-4218.
   Cuisine: EASTERN EUROPEAN. **Reservations:** Accepted.
$ Prices: Appetizers $1.10–$4.95; main courses $12.90–$16.50. AE, DC, ER, MC, V.
   Open: Mon–Sat 11am–2am, Sun 5pm–1am.
This European-style café-restaurant is so relaxed, charming, and convenient that you can't help thinking how much the texture of life would be improved if the town had half a dozen more of the same. Spacious and quite simple, the

Praha has one wall covered by a landscape mural, some small framed pictures of Prague, and the kind of tables and chairs you'd find in a private home. The background music is Bach and Beethoven, the clientele cosmopolitan, appreciative, mainly young and mostly attractive. The cuisine is dreamy and the portions are colossal (the wienerschnitzel covers the entire plate—in two layers!). The Praha serves the finest tomato-and-onion salad in the West, and it comes as part of your meal. Choices include a rich cabbage soup, steak tartare, and a superb Naturschnitzel (meaning minus crumb crust). You get to choose among 12 brands of tea, and the Sachertorte is the way they dished it up in Old Vienna. Drop in for a meal or just a cuppa.

CAFE BUDAPEST, 10145-104th St. Tel. 403/426-4363.
   Cuisine: HUNGARIAN. **Reservations:** Accepted.
   $ Prices: Appetizers $5.95–$9.50; main courses $6.95–$15.95. AE, DC, ER, MC, V.
   Open: Mon–Sat 11:30am–10pm.

Easily spotted by its snowy white front and red awning, the Budapest has a simple yet stylish interior that manages to be both modernistic and cozy—not an easy feat—with large street windows that open wide on warm evenings, lazily spinning ceiling fans, white pillars, and some of the most comfortable seating facilities I've relaxed in. The Magyar touches are confined to the wall prints and the menu, plus melting violin strains in the background. The kettle goulash soup is a meal by itself—as it's supposed to be. Then your choice is between the equally ample chicken paprika, vads (sautéed sirloin), or the garlic-glazed médaillons called Gypsy steak. Try to leave room for the memorable punch torte.

THE CREPERIE, 10220-103rd St. Tel. 403/420-6656.
   Cuisine: CRÊPES. **Reservations:** Recommended.
   $ Prices: Crêpe dinners $7.75–$12.75. AE, DC, MC, V.
   Open: Mon–Sat 5–10:30pm, Sun 5–9pm.
Located in the Boardwalk Building downtown, the Crêperie has a large comfortable waiting room with park benches, and needs them—the curse of popularity. A charming, softly lit dining room wafting with delicious aromas is undoubtedly the magnet that keeps people rooted in those leather waiting chairs. There is a vast selection of crêpes, including beef and chicken bourguignon or crabmeat and smoked salmon.

EMERY'S, 10109-125th St. Tel. 403/482-7577.
   Cuisine: CONTINENTAL. **Reservations:** Accepted.
   $ Prices: Appetizers $5.95; main courses $8.95–$13.95. AE, DC, ER, MC, V.
   Open: Mon–Thurs 11:30am–10pm, Fri–Sat 11:30am–midnight, Sun 10:30am–3:30pm.

Housed in a stately two-story mansion overlooking a park, Emery's offers one of the most fashionable outdoor dining patios in Edmonton. But the interior is entertaining enough to make up for bad weather. The rooms are filled with artworks and knickknacks, there is a great fireplace, and a wall covered with tantalizing menus from long-past banquets, including one served to the king of Prussia in 1897. The fare is an even blend of continental specialties and nouvelle cuisine, beautifully presented. The salads are in a class by themselves. Eating here is like being invited to a wealthy home as a houseguest.

GEPPETTO'S, 10162-100A St. Tel. 403/426-1635.
   Cuisine: ITALIAN. **Reservations:** Accepted.
   $ Prices: Appetizers $4.95–$6.25; main courses $9.75–$14.95. AE, ER, MC, V.
   Open: Daily 11am–around midnight.
The menu at Geppetto's comes on a parchment scroll—a bit tricky to read but most romantic. High ceilings supported by tall pillars with floral designs give this place a Florentine air. Geppetto's has an outdoor patio with "Grand Marnier" umbrellas, but all the plants and potted palms are inside the premises. So, oddly enough, is the garden fountain. The overall effect of this reversal is both charming and endearing. The fare is top-notch throughout: zuppa alla cipolla (onion soup), osso buco, ravioli,

and a classic zabaglione for dessert. The excellent dry white Italian house wine comes for around $4 per glass. Hours are relaxed and flexible.

THE HARBIN, 10177-105th St. Tel. 403/424-3980.
   Cuisine: NORTHERN CHINESE. **Reservations:** Accepted.
$ Prices: Appetizers $1.75–$8; main courses $5.50–$10.95. AE, DC, MC, V.
   Open: Daily 11am–11pm.

★ Northern Chinese cuisine is still a novelty for Edmontonians, as is the Chinese beer that sets it off to perfection. But the growing popularity of both is proven by the fact that there are now two Harbins—the above downtowner and another in the Westend. Both take the wise precaution of marking their hotter dishes (which are *hot*) with a star, so as not to catch patrons unaware. Spacious, airy, with high ceilings, the white walls decorated with huge golden fans, the Harbin presents regional specialties like sha cha lamb (thinly sliced in a truly fiery sauce), string beef on the grill (with garlic black-bean sauce), pork dumplings in black vinegar, Szechuan beef sautéed with green peppers and carrots, or the special Harbin squid (deep-fried and sautéed with ginger). Helpings are huge and two courses constitute an ample meal.

HONG KONG DELIGHT, 10056-107th St. Tel. 403/423-3030.
   Cuisine: CHINESE. **Reservations:** Accepted.
$ Prices: Appetizers $1.75–$6.95; main courses $7.50–$18. AE, MC, V.
   Open: Mon–Fri 11am–midnight, Sat–Sun 5–10pm.

Hong Kong Delight is a tastefully furnished Chinese eatery featuring a minimum of Oriental trappings in its decor but pleasing authenticity in its cuisine. Lampshades in the shape of Chinese umbrellas share the ceiling with slowly revolving fans. The chairs are comfortably upholstered and there are charming wooden shutters sheltering you from the street view. Service is leisurely but attentive. I can highly recommend the deep-fried chicken wings, followed by Manchurian beef teppan (pan-fried filet of beef with green peppers, onions, and black bean sauce). As a finale, try the lychee fruit.

MARLOWE'S, 9828-101A Ave. Tel. 403/429-3338.
   Cuisine: CANADIAN. **Reservations:** Recommended.
$ Prices: Appetizers $4–$6; main courses $7.95–$13.95; Sun brunch buffet $6.95. AE, DC, MC, V.
   Open: Lunch daily 11am–2pm; dinner daily 5–9pm.

Marlowe's is located in the vast lobby of the Citadel Theatre, Alberta's number-one playhouse. Glassed-in, relaxed, and supremely comfortable, Marlowe's clientele ranges from theater patrons and actors to a dedicated lunchtime crowd. The big attraction is the weekday lunch and Sunday brunch buffet. The spread is impressive, including beef stew, chicken wings, salads, cheeses, fruit, and desserts, as well as an array of crêpes.

NINTH STREET BISTRO, 9910-109th St. Tel. 403/424-7219.
   Cuisine: CANADIAN/FRENCH. **Reservations:** Accepted.
$ Prices: Appetizers $3.95–$5.45; main courses $9.75–$12.95. AE, MC, V.
   Open: Daily 11am–11pm or midnight.

Apart from the misnomer, the Ninth Street Bistro is a remarkably tasteful dinery serving remarkably tasty meals: a long street-view window lined with potted plants, a solitary fan whirring on the brick ceiling, a glass vitrine filled with figurines to lend an antique touch, fresh flowers on every one of the lovingly polished dark-wood tables, and slender white pillars contrasting with the dark carpeting. The fare is an even mixture of Canadian and French: for instance, Montréal smoked meat or seafood St-Jacques, both equally excellent. The list of coffees is as impressive as the array of cocktails, including Spanish coffee (with brandy) or French (with Grand Marnier), as well as the undoubtedly finest cappuccino in Alberta.

RUSSIAN TEA ROOM, 10312 Jasper Ave. Tel. 403/426-0000.
   Cuisine: RUSSIAN. **Reservations:** Accepted.
$ Prices: Appetizers $4.95–$5.95; main courses $6.25–$14.95. AE, DC, MC, V.
   Open: Mon–Fri 9:30am–midnight, Sat 9:30am–1am, Sun 9:30am–11pm.

The Russian Tea Room is a somewhat misleading label for what is actually a splendidly versatile restaurant which also happens to serve Russian tea. The decor is beautiful: light pastel colors throughout, masses of greenery all around, excellent modern prints on the walls. There is a small smoking section, but the nonnicotiners get most of the space. The menu is thoroughly Russian, including 16 brands of vodka. The background music is classical. You can't start better than with the hot borscht, followed by either the pirozki or the very hearty Russian beef stew, and concluded by some of the most decadent tortes and pastries in North America.

STEAKBOARD, 10220-103rd St. Tel. 403/429-0886.

Cuisine: CANADIAN. **Reservations:** Accepted.

$ Prices: Appetizers $4.50–$6.50; main courses $8.95–$13.95. AE, DC, MC, V.

Open: Lunch Mon–Fri 11:30am–2pm; dinner daily 5–9pm.

In the Boardwalk Building, which is a complex of shops, offices, and eateries, you'll find the Steakboard. Divided into a large lounge and small dining room, both beautiful, it has a low black ceiling and brick walls decorated with movie-quality photos of Canadian scenes from the 1920s. An extensive salad bar occupies a central position, and glass-shielded candles glimmer on the tables. The svelte and cozy lounge features entertainers six nights a week. The dining room features items like jumbo prawns and prime rib of beef.

BUDGET

ASHOKA CURRY HOUSE, 0109-101st St. Tel. 403/424-7500.

Cuisine: EAST INDIAN. **Reservations:** Accepted.

$ Prices: Buffet style $6.95 at lunch, $11.95 at dinner. AE, DC, ER, MC, V.

Open: Mon–Fri 11am–10pm, Sat 5–11pm.

The Ashoka is unusual in several respects. First because it lies down a flight of stairs *inside* the LRT entrance on 101st Street. Secondly because it's the only curry dispensary with an English pub interior I have ever seen. The pub, called Maharaja, even has a pool table. Service is buffet style, with a smaller spread at lunchtime, a lavish one (20 items, including eight main courses) in the evening. The curry arrays are just hot enough to tickle—but not burn—your palate.

FRANK'S PLACE, 10048-101A Ave. Tel. 403/424-4795.

Cuisine: ITALIAN. **Reservations:** Accepted.

$ Prices: Main courses $5.50–$7.95. MC, V.

Open: Mon–Fri 11am–9pm, Sat 5–9pm.

Frank's Place shares the block with four other eateries, but keeps shorter hours and sticks to budget prices. With whitewashed walls, rural prints, and wooden shutters (but no windows), the place has a rustic look and a health-minded vegetarian air. The fare, however, is for the omniverous and includes beer and wine. You can get very good chicken cacciatore or spaghetti with seafood sauce.

GRANDMA LEE'S, 10109 Jasper Ave., at 106th St. Tel. 403/420-0906.

Cuisine: CANADIAN. **Reservations:** Not accepted.

$ Prices: Main courses $3.29–$4.15. No credit cards.

Open: Mon–Fri 6:30am–5pm.

 The bakery on the premises of this lovely old-fashioned country-style lunch place delivers baked goods fresh from the oven. Lit by "oil lamps" on the ceiling, it has wooden tables and chairs, and a wooden fence separating the food bar from the eating section. You get lasagne, casseroles, beef stew, and chicken pies, plus great sandwiches on thick slices of homemade bread and nondecadent pastries of the wholesome apple-pie kind.

HELLO DELI, 10725-124th St. Tel. 403/454-8527.

Cuisine: DELI.

$ Prices: Appetizers $3.95–$4.50; main courses $8.95–$9.95. AE, MC, V.

Open: Daily 11am–"late."

 Far and away the top deli in town, this place has the added virtue of having a dining room offering plenty of elbow space and popcorn served gratis. You have a choice between traditional deli fare, like hot smoked beef on rye and chicken matzoh-ball soup or nonethnic courses like honey-baked chicken or shrimp in a basket. Do try the authentic Russian borscht soup, followed by the brisket of beef served with latkes (potato pancakes). Then—if room permits—the poppyseed cake. Service is fast and amiable.

SHERLOCK HOLMES, 10012-101A Ave. Tel. 403/426-7784.
   Cuisine: ENGLISH. **Reservations:** Not accepted.
$ Prices: Appetizers $4–$6.50; main courses $6.35–$8.95. AE, DC, ER, MC, V.
   Open: Mon–Sat 11:30am–2am.

⑤ And now, as Monty Python says, for something completely different. The Sherlock Holmes is a tremendously popular English-style pub using the immortal gumshoe as a shingle. It's housed in a charming building with black crossbeams on whitewashed walls and a picket fence around the outdoor patio. The menus are decorated with illustrations from the original Holmes magazine series; the restaurant is adorned with a red English telephone booth, and signs indicating the Midland Bank, Norfolk Road, and sundry villages. Only the two constantly operating TV sets are out of character. You can get Mrs. Hudson's steak-and-kidney pie, calves' liver and onions, fish-and-chips, and—naturally—English ale and Guinness stout.

SPECIALTY DINING

The **Boardwalk market,** 102nd Avenue at 103rd Street, is actually the food section of a beautifully restored historic block that serves as an indoor market seven days a week. While the market sells anything from flower baskets to oil paintings, the edible section is a happy mélange of produce, meat, poultry, and seafood counters interspersed with top-grade, economy-priced snackeries. You can get steamed clams at $3.50 per dozen, Japanese sukiyaki for $4.50, Mongolian barbecued beef for $4.75, salad selections for 85¢, pizzas for $4, as well as German sausages, linguine, French pastries, Russian blintzes, etc. You also get a changing parade of musicians, singers, jugglers, and dancers, exactly as it used to be on the real old-time open-air marketplaces, only somewhat more hygienic.

   The market operates from 9:30am to 6pm Monday to Saturday.

   The **Sunday brunch** habit has spread across Canada like a benevolent epidemic. By and large this is because families are abandoning the traditional Sunday roast at home, along with the big leisurely breakfast, and combining both meals in one restaurant outing. As more hostelries opened up on Sunday and reaped full houses, the idea of such specials extended to later hours and slid into the afternoon and evening. Today these Sunday treats reach well into the dinner hour. The great advantage is the fact that brunch is invariably cheaper, giving even the moderately heeled a chance to taste some grandiose cuisine in places they wouldn't ordinarily frequent. Some of the top-bracket hotels and dineries make it a point of honor (and propaganda) to lay on superlative spreads for the Sabbath feast at very moderate tabs. Word, as they say, gets around. See the Sunday papers for what's being dished out where.

EVENING ENTERTAINMENT
THE PERFORMING ARTS

CITADEL THEATRE, 9828-101A Ave. Tel. 403/426-4811.
   A masterpiece of theatrical architecture, the Citadel is not a playhouse in the conventional sense but a community project encompassing virtually every form of showcraft. The complex takes up the entire city block adjacent to Sir Winston Churchill Square. It looks like a gigantic greenhouse: More than half is glass-walled, and even the awnings are glass. Apart from auditoriums, it also has a magnificent indoor garden with a waterfall, as well as a restaurant (see "Where to Dine," above). But the best feature of the complex is that it houses, under one roof, five different theaters adapted for different productions and distinct audiences, plus workshops and classrooms. The Citadel today is the largest, busiest, and most prolific theater in Canada.

   The stages comprise: the Shoctor Theatre, which is the main stage of the Citadel's subscription program; the Maclab Theatre, used chiefly as a young people's showcase; the Rice Theatre, designed for experimental and innovative productions; Zeidler Hall, primarily intended for films, lectures, and children's theater; and the Tucker

Amphitheatre, designed for concerts, recitals, and small lunchtime stage productions. The season, unfortunately, runs only from September through May.
Prices: Tickets $10–$45.

KAASA THEATRE, 11401-87th Ave. Tel. 403/451-8000.

This theater puts on a mixture of musicals and straight plays, mostly well-tried and popular material.
Prices: Tickets $14.

NORTHERN ALBERTA JUBILEE AUDITORIUM, 11455-87th Ave. Tel. 403/427-2760.

The Jubilee Auditorium is the setting for a great variety of concert and ballet performances. They range from the Edmonton Symphony Orchestra to the Conservatoire de Ballet and jazz specialties like A Nite in New Orleans.
Prices: Tickets $15–$30.

Dinner Theater

Edmonton has a pleasant abundance of theater restaurants. Different rules apply in the various establishments: In some your dinner tab includes the show; in others you pay extra. Three of the most popular are those listed below.

TEDDY'S MYSTERY DINNER CLUB, 11361 Jasper Ave. Tel. 403/488-0984.

Every Thursday Teddy's Restaurant becomes the scene of an interactive murder mystery. The actors mingle stealthily with the diners (you can't tell them apart) and the "murder" occurs around 8pm. The audience is drawn into the detective's Hercule Poirot–style investigation, and there's a prize for the person who correctly guesses the killer's identity.
Prices: Dinner plus homicide costs $35.

COMEDY WEST, 10545-82nd Ave. Tel. 403/439-1528.

Comedy West serves comedy along with the comestibles, either in the form of satirical sketches or hilarious improv soap operas. Shows Wednesday through Sunday, sometimes two different performances in one evening.
Prices: Vary.

STAGE WEST, in the Mayfield Inn, 16615-109th Ave. Tel. 403/483-4051.

This charming theater restaurant combines excellent food with lighthearted, often sumptuously equipped, stage productions. Shows go on at 8pm nightly and at brunchtime Sunday and Wednesday.
Prices: Tickets (including meals) $24–$47.25.

THE CLUB & BAR SCENE

Edmonton has a vast and colorful array of nocturnal action, but mostly so effervescent that it defies classification. Hardly any spots can be firmly labeled dance clubs, for instance. Most nighteries function as one thing one week and quite another the next. A café may be just that until evening, then turn into a restaurant and later still into a club with or minus a dance floor. Terms like "bar," "lounge," and "cabaret" are likewise interchangeable, the same place being one or the other in the course of one week.

The only way of dealing with such a fluid scenario is to dispense with labels and simply give you a list of samples, with the assurance that there are dozens more of the same ilk around town.

The country-and-western scene is the largest entertainment venue in town with new places opening up all the time. The music may be rustic but the hours are nightclub-urban.

COOK COUNTY SALOON, 8010-103rd St. Tel. 403/432-2665.

A changing lineup of western combos on Friday and Saturday.
Admission: $6.

DODGE CITY SALOON, 13103 Fort Rd. Tel. 403/437-4275.

The newest arrival on the country-music scene, featuring one of the largest dance floors in Edmonton. The bands play nightly from 9pm to 2am, and on Wednesdays there are free dance lessons.

GOOSE LOONIES, 6250-99th St. Tel. 403/438-5573.

Goose Loonies uses a cross-eyed goose as an emblem. It boasts North America's only computerized rainbow dance floor and has two levels of flashing lights and lasers.
Admission: Varies.

KINGSWAY INN, 10812 Kingsway Ave. Tel. 403/479-4266.

Here you get a taste of several styles. This entertainment center gives you a choice between hearing top Canadian and U.S. bands in their dining room, or cabaret dancing in the **Sumplacelse Cabaret,** or romantic vocalists in the **Tavern.** Shows six nights a week.

The **Rodeo Club** in the Kingsway Inn (tel. 403/479-4266), specializes in country-and-western music with a tinge of rock, featuring a changing cavalcade of performers, some local, many from the U.S. Wednesday night is Amateur Night.
Admission: $3 Fri–Sat only.

LONGRIDERS SALOON, 11733-78th St. Tel. 403/479-8700.

Country music six nights a week.
Admission: Free Tues–Thurs, $5 cover Fri–Sat.

SIDETRACK CAFE, 10333-112th St. Tel. 403/421-1326.

A local pioneer of outdoor eating, the Sidetrack Café has a double reputation as being a gourmet dinery (duck and mango pizza) and amazingly versatile nightspot. The lineup changes continually. You get an Australian rock group one week, a musical comedy troupe the next, a blues band the following, progressive jazz after that . . . and so on. The Sidetrack is a perfect example of why it's so difficult to divide Edmonton's nightlife into anything resembling neat brackets.
Admission: $10 cover.

SMOKEY JOE'S, 11607 Jasper Ave. Tel. 403/488-7538.

A pit barbecue downstairs and an entertainment lounge upstairs, featuring mainly rhythm and blues. In action Thursday through Saturday from 9:30pm to 2am.
Admission: Free.

21 CLUB, 9707-110th St. Tel. 403/488-8669.

Billed as an "adult" nightspot, the 21 specializes in "adult contemporary music"—meaning no acid rock or slam dancing—and has a mildly formal dress code that nixes tank tops or sandals. Open Thursday, Friday, and Saturday.
Admission: Free.

YARDBIRD SUITE, 10203-86th Ave. Tel. 403/432-0428.

The Yardbird features jazz groups Tuesday to Saturday from 9pm to 1am. The combos change, as do the cover charges.
Admission: Varies.

YUK YUK'S KOMEDY KABARET, at The Point, 7103-78th Ave. Tel. 403/466-2131.

The Edmonton branch of a national chain. Features professional stand-up comedians, sometimes very funny, sometimes mildly so. It offers (I quote) "Mindless escapism for the thinking Man . . . " Shows are Wednesday through Saturday: weeknights at 9pm, weekends at 8:30 and 11pm.
Admission: $6.50–$10.75.

GAMBLING

Gambling is a curious institution in Alberta. The money goes to charities (mostly) but the casinos are privately owned and—until recently—led a floating existence. Now they are located in permanent premises and have undergone considerable upscaling.

They offer pleasant surroundings, licensed lounges, no-smoking tables, and very amiable staff. The games are blackjack, roulette, baccarat, red dog, and sic bo; bets range from $1 to $100; and the play goes from Monday to Saturday, noon to midnight. Try your luck at **Casino ABS, City Centre,** 10549-102nd St. (tel. 403/424-WINS); or **Casino ABS, Southside,** 7055 Argyll Rd. (tel. 403/466-0199).

EASY EXCURSIONS FROM EDMONTON

Elk Island National Park (tel. 403/998-3686), located on the Yellowhead Highway, 20 miles east of Edmonton, is one of the most compact and prettiest of the national parks system. It protects one of Canada's most endangered ecosystems and is the home and roaming ground to North America's largest and smallest mammals: the wood buffalo and the pygmy shrew (a tiny creature half the size of a mouse, but with the disposition of a tiger). The park has hiking trails, campgrounds, golf courses, a lake, and a sandy beach. A one-day vehicle permit costs $5.

The **Ukrainian Cultural Heritage Village** (tel. 403/662-3640) is an open-air museum and a patch of living history 25 minutes east of Edmonton on Yellowhead Highway 16. The village has 30 restored historic buildings. Visitors learn what life was like for Ukrainian pioneers in the 1892–1930 era through costumed interpreters who re-create the daily activities of the period. Open from May 15 to September 6 every day from 10am to 6pm. Admission is $5 for adults, $2 for children (under 6 free).

Alberta Fairytale Grounds, a wooded 25-acre site, lie 19 miles west of Edmonton on Highway 16, then two miles north on Highway 779 (Stony Plain). The woods hide brightly colored fairy-tale displays showing Snow White, Cinderella, Sleeping Beauty, Little Red Riding Hood, and other favorites. Adults seem to enjoy them as much as their youngsters. Open daily May 15 to September 15, 10am to 6pm. For tour bookings call 403/963-3855. Admission is $4.50 for adults, $2.25 for children.

Father Lacombe Chapel, at St. Albert, 12 miles north of Edmonton on Highway 2, is the original log chapel built by Father Lacombe in 1861 in what was then a howling wilderness. One of the earliest pioneer structures in the province, it's open daily to 6pm; admission is free.

4. AROUND ALBERTA

The main magnets for visitors to Alberta (apart from the Calgary Stampede and Edmonton's Klondike Days) are the 53 provincial and five national parks. I have already detailed Banff and Jasper, and mentioned Elk Island.

Wood Buffalo National Park is the world's largest, measuring 17,300 square miles—bigger than Switzerland. Two-thirds lie inside Alberta, one-third in the Northwest Territories. The park was created for the specific purpose of preserving the last remaining herd of wood bison on earth. At the turn of the century these animals were near extinction. Today some 6,000 of the big shaggies roam their habitat, where you can see and snap them in droves.

The park is also the only known breeding ground for the majestic whooping crane. Some 50 of these birds live here from April until October before migrating to their winter range along the Gulf of Mexico.

Waterton Lakes National Park, in the southwestern corner of the province, is linked with Glacier National Park in neighboring Montana. Once the hunting ground of the Blackfoot, this 203-square-mile sanctuary has Upper Waterton Lake straddling the U.S. border. A lake steamer links the Montana with the Alberta shore. The park nestles against the eastern slopes of the Rockies and its animal life includes cougars, coyotes, bighorn sheep, and white-tailed deer.

Alberta has the greatest variety of geographical features among Canada's provinces: soaring mountain ranges, table-flat prairies, huge lakes, dense forests, and even a patch of subtropical oasis called **Cypress Hills.**

You can divide the province into four distinct areas, each with its special scenic attractions: first, the Canadian Rockies, in the west; then the land of rolling prairies and rich agriculture that starts at the U.S. border and reaches some 300 miles north; next the so-called parkland, with broad valleys, high ridges, lakes, streams, and small stands of timber; finally, the region comprising the whole northern half of the province—huge lakes and forests broken by tracts of open prairie and the sweeping terraces of the **Peace River Valley.**

Across the exact center of the province, east to west, runs the **Yellowhead Highway,** from Saskatchewan to British Columbia. This scenic route is named after an Iroquois trapper and scout with a trace of white blood that gave a blond tinge to his hair. His real name was Pierre Hatsinaton, but the French voyageurs called him Tête Jaune—Yellow Head. Tête Jaune worked as a guide for the Hudson's Bay Company and explored much of the route now followed by the highway that bears his name. Guiding ranked among the highest of high-risk occupations. In 1827, on the British Columbia side of the mountains, a swarm of the Beaver tribe fell upon Tête Jaune, his brother, their wives, and their children, and killed them all.

Rocky Mountain House, halfway between Edmonton and Calgary, is actually a town. Established in 1799 as a fort of the North West Company, the place exported great bales of otter, sable, fox, and other furs annually. Today this is one of the fastest-growing towns in the province, but has taken great care to preserve the landmarks of its colorful history.

At **Innisfail,** to the southeast, the Royal Canadian Mounted Police has its dog-training center (tel. 403/227-3346). The kennels are open to the public on weekdays between 9am and 4pm. But if you can manage to be in the area then, don't miss seeing these magnificent police shepherds. Call for times of training demonstrations.

Land of the Mighty Peace is the name given to the region around the confluence of the Peace and Smoky rivers. This is a land of gold-rush trails and explorers' passages, where summer twilight lingers until midnight and monuments to early explorers dot the landscape. The center of the region is the Peace River, some 300 miles northwest of Edmonton. A landmark of the town is the statue and grave marker of "Twelve-Foot Davis," on the river's east bank (Davis was a prospector who staked out a 12-foot claim between much larger ones during the Cariboo gold rush and dug out a bonanza). The **Peace River Museum** contains, among other memorabilia, a riverboat that used to ply the stream between Fort St. John and Vermillion.

Each July the annual jet-boat river races are run from Grande Cache to Peace River, with contestants coming from as far as Mexico and Australia. You can ride a jet boat by going on the **Tar Island River Cruise,** which runs from the town to Tar Island, about 40 miles downstream, and stops there overnight. (See "River Trips" earlier in this chapter.)

Alberta's lake country stretches from St. Paul, about 130 miles northeast of Edmonton, to the border of the Northwest Territories. Vast and beautiful, it gets emptier the farther north you go, and includes the **Wood Buffalo National Park.** This is big country in every sense of the word—the lakes are big, the fish are big, and the largest oil deposits in Canada are located here. There's wonderful lake and river fishing for trout, pike, perch, goldeye, and walleye.

The trading center of the area is **St. Paul,** which has constructed a world-famous centennial project—a "Flying Saucer Landing Pad," ready to receive whatever creatures may materialize from a *Close Encounter of the Third Kind.*

The curiously named **Head-Smashed-In Buffalo Jump** interpretive center is located in southern Alberta on Spring Point Road, 12 miles west of Highway 2, west of Fort Macleod (tel. 403/553-2731). It stands on top of a steep cliff over which the Native Canadians used to stampede herds of bison, the carcasses then providing them with meat, hides, and horns. The multimillion-dollar center, which opened in 1987, tells the story of these death drives by means of films and Native Canadian guide-lecturers. Designated a World Heritage Site, the center is open from 9am to 8pm during summer. Admission $5 per adult, $2 per child, but free on Tuesday.

At **Vegreville** stands the world's largest Ukrainian Easter egg, gaily painted and towering over 30 feet tall in Elk Park. This "pysanka" was constructed in 1974 to commemorate the 100th anniversary of the arrival of the Royal Canadian Mounted Police in Alberta. You can camp all around the egg and, if you get there early in July, watch the annual Ukrainian Festival with singing, music, and leg-throwing folk dances.

Lac La Biche is the communal heart of one of the greatest fishing areas in Canada. There are 50 shimmering lakes around the town, teeming with fish and game. In July and early August the Blue Feathers Fish Derby is held here, the biggest such event in the province.

If you want to get the feel of oil sand—more treasured than gold these days—go to **Fort McMurray,** the home of the Athabasca tar sands. The stuff is so rich in "black gold" that you can pick up a handful of sand and squeeze out oil. It's also a large and thriving community with motor hotels and golf courses.

At the entrance to the city stands the Fort McMurray Oil Sands Interpretive Centre (tel. 403/743-7167). The only attraction of its kind in the world, the center displays the entire range of activity in the oil sands industry, from mining to the separation of oil from the sands, by means of hands-on models and audiovisual presentations. Admission is free, and the center is open daily from 10am till 6pm in summer, till 4pm in winter.

Fort McMurray lies due north of Edmonton on Highway 63.

BRITISH COLUMBIA

Canada's most westerly province can be all things to all people—or pretty nearly so. Its outstanding characteristic is variety: scenically, climatically, and socially.

In the southwest, near the Washington State border, the country is densely populated, with large sophisticated cities, a sunny coastline dotted with resorts and belts of rich farmlands raising dairy cattle on lush pastures. But in the north, where the province borders Alaska and the Yukon, the settlements are tiny, and most of the land is a starkly beautiful wilderness ruled by bush pilots and pioneers. In between these extremes you get wide-open ranchlands with cowboys riding herd, ocean fjords as deep and blue as those of Norway, glacier icefields, huge birch and maple forests, thousands of lakes, valleys glowing with ripening fruit, vineyards on the hillsides, and a patch of genuine sand desert—the only one in Canada.

Holding the province together like two immense bolts are the Coast Mountains along the Pacific and the Canadian Rockies straddling the border with Alberta, culminating in their highest peak, Mount Robson.

British Columbia is a huge province of 366,255 square miles, more than twice the size of California, with a mere 2½ million people, most of them concentrated in the southern portion. This leaves the bulk of the province a thinly settled haven of natural wonders, a place to clear your eyes and lungs of the grit and grime of industrialized society and to reattune noise-deafened ears to birdcalls, rustling winds, and the burble of mountain streams.

Over a million acres of the province have been set aside in five national parks—four in the mountainous wilds of the east-central region, one on the west coast of Vancouver Island. Add to this the 11 million acres of provincial parks, which range from handkerchief proportions to huge, and you'll get an idea of how much British Columbians cherish and preserve their natural heritage.

They also cherish their historical heritage. Throughout the province you'll come across petroglyph sites. These are rock drawings made by unknown tribes in the primordial past, now carefully maintained as the earliest indicators of a human presence in the area.

The later explorers, fur traders, and pioneer settlers have their mementos in Fort Langley, a fully restored fur-trading post; in Fort Defiance on Vancouver Island; and in Fort James near Prince George. The Cariboo gold rush of the 1860s is preserved in Barkerville, a township that seems to have stepped out of a photograph of the gold dust boom years. Fort Steele is a living memorial to the Northwest Mounted Police, the entire fort re-created as a settlement of the 1890s, complete with steam train, general store, smithy, and saloons.

WHAT'S SPECIAL ABOUT BRITISH COLUMBIA

Attractions

- ☐ Vancouver's Canada Place, a giant edifice that looks like it's under full sail.
- ☐ The Royal British Columbia Museum in Victoria, where visitors can take a discovery trip into prehistory.
- ☐ The panoramic skyride on the Grouse Mountain cable train.
- ☐ The Capilano Suspension Bridge, billed as the Eighth Wonder of the World.
- ☐ Victoria's Butterfly World, where you walk among clouds of butterflies.
- ☐ The Omnimax Theatre in Vancouver's Science World, for film adventures beneath the world's largest dome screen.

Nature

- ☐ Whistler, the biggest ski mountain and the longest vertical drop in North America.
- ☐ Vancouver Island—where Vancouver *isn't*—but where the east coast is a garden and the west coast a wilderness.
- ☐ The Okanagan wine region, one of Canada's biggest surprises. It has the country's balmiest climate and produces remarkably fine vintages.
- ☐ Dawson Creek. In the far north of the province where grizzlies, moose, and caribou roam, you can see the fantastic spectacle of the northern lights fluttering across the sky.

Events/Festivals

- ☐ Vancouver Jazz Festival. An annual surge of syncopation, indoors and out.
- ☐ National Hockey League games from fall through spring.
- ☐ The International Grand Prix Bicycle Race. Cyclists from around the world whizzing over the cobblestones of Gastown each July.
- ☐ "Julyfest" in Kimberley, the highest city in Canada, which turns into a Bavarian alpine village.

Cool for Kids

- ☐ Victoria's Miniature World. An unsurpassed layout of historical themes showing 15,000 tiny participants.
- ☐ The For Kids Only supermarket on Granville Island, a complex of shops packed with toys, games, and the togs that go with them.
- ☐ The *St. Roch*, an erstwhile patrol vessel of the Royal Canadian Mounted Police, now an anchored museum you can clamber through.
- ☐ The Capilano Salmon Hatchery in North Vancouver where the life cycle of the chinook salmon unfolds before your eyes.

SEEING BRITISH COLUMBIA

INFORMATION Contact the helpful staff at **Discover British Columbia,** Parliament Building, Victoria, BC, V8V 1X4 (tel. toll free 800/663-6000), who'll be happy to answer your questions and send out brochures and maps. This office also offers a reservations service to help you book lodgings anywhere in the province; the available accommodations range from hotels and motels to a few inns.

A NOTE ON TAXES In addition to the 7% federal tax (GST), the province of British Columbia imposes a 7% sales tax on goods and services. You'll also be faced with an accommodations tax, which is 10% in Vancouver, Victoria, Whistler, Oak Bay, Smithers, Saanich, and Prince Rupert; elsewhere in the province the accommodations tax is 8%.

1. VANCOUVER

25 miles (40km) N of the U.S. border

GETTING THERE   By Plane   Vancouver's international airport is located on an island nine miles south of the city. The airport is served by Air Canada and Canadian Airlines as well as American Airlines, Continental, Delta, Horizon Air, and United. The trip downtown by Airport Express—the "Hustle Bus"—costs $8.25. By cab it's around $23. Air B.C. operates services from and to Victoria—either airport to airport or harbor to harbor (by seaplane). The flight takes 25 minutes. (See Section 2 of this chapter for details.)

By Train   The railroad station is at Main Street and Terminal Avenue (tel. toll free 800/561-8630). You can reach Vancouver by rail from Banff or Calgary, but there's no train service from the U.S.

By Bus   There's direct shuttle bus service from Seattle six times daily offered by Quick Shuttle (tel. 604/526-2836). Greyhound (tel. 604/662-3222) buses link Vancouver with most Canadian cities. The bus terminal is at the corner of Dunsmuir and Cambie Streets.

By Ferry   Sea connections with Vancouver Island are run by B.C. Ferries (tel. 604/669-1211). For details see Section 2 of this chapter.

By Car   Driving from Seattle, you take Highway 99 at the U.S.-Canadian border for the three-hour drive to Vancouver. This road takes you all the way into Granville Street and the downtown area. From the east, the Trans-Canada Highway (Highway 1) leads into Hastings Street.

SPECIAL EVENTS   July 1 brings Folkfest, British Columbia's major multicultural festival. Staged partly in Gastown, partly at the Orpheum Theatre, it's a whirl of native costumes, ethnic foods, and dance and choir performances. All events are free, but you have to pay for the cosmopolitan tidbits.

The Pacific National Exhibition, late August to Labor Day, a compendium of fun fair, exhibitions, displays, shows, and sports, and kicked off by a two-hour grand parade, is held at the Exhibition Grounds, with free indoor and outdoor entertainment. Highlights are the loggers' contests, with lumberjacks from all over the province competing in pole climbing and log burling.

Oktoberfest, weekends, late September to early October, is strictly Teutonic and very lively, with eating, drinking, and entertainment from early evening to 2am at the Exhibition Grounds. It features local and imported dance groups and oompah bands, genuine Tyrolean village music, and the famous Bavarian "pants-slappers" folk dancers.

In the extreme southwestern corner of British Columbia, there is a place where the mountains and ocean seem to have had a love affair and given birth to a city. The city is Vancouver, and few towns have been quite so wonderfully blessed with their setting as this one. Among the world's great harbor towns, only Rio de Janeiro can match its scenic combination of mountain peaks towering over silver-green waters, with the city nestling between.

Vancouver is a metropolis of unforgettable views, vistas of ocean and mountains that spring upon you when you least expect them. Because the city is hilly and the harbor splintered into scores of inlets, you can turn a busy downtown corner and find yourself faced with a panorama less fortunate urbanites have to drive for hours to glimpse.

Combine this setting with a relatively balmy climate, one of the world's finest natural deep-water ports, and a native passion for parks and greenery, and you'll understand why Vancouverites take a positively narcissistic delight in their habitat—an opinion, incidentally, that is continually reinforced by the legions of visitors flocking in summer and winter from every part of the continent.

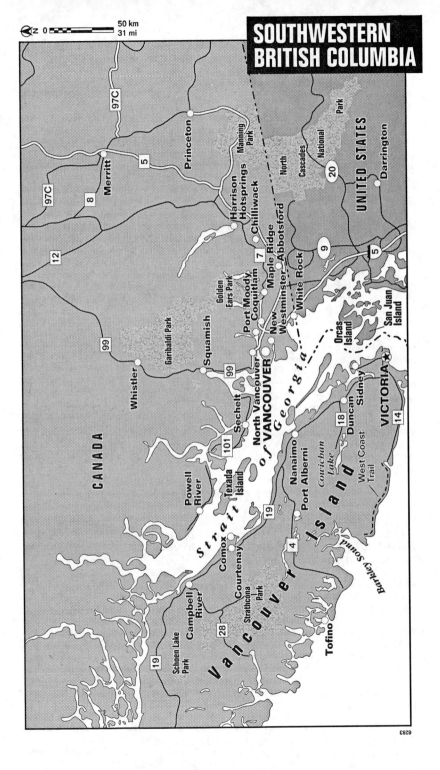

SOUTHWESTERN BRITISH COLUMBIA

0 — 50 km / 31 mi

UNITED STATES

CANADA

Darrington

San Juan Island

Orcas Island

VICTORIA

Sidney

Duncan

Cowichan Lake

West Coast Trail

Barkley Sound

Tofino

Port Alberni

Nanaimo

Courtenay

Comox

Campbell River

Strathcona Park

Schoen Lake Park

Powell River

Texada Island

Sechelt

Whistler

Squamish

Garibaldi Park

North Vancouver

VANCOUVER

New Westminster

Port Moody

Coquitlam

Golden Ears Park

Maple Ridge

Abbotsford

White Rock

Chilliwack

Harrison Hotsprings

Princeton

Merritt

Manning Park

North Cascades National Park

Vancouver Island

Strait of Georgia

97C

5

8

97C

12

99

101

19

28

4

18

14

9

5

20

7

6283

With around 1.2 million inhabitants Vancouver is—after Toronto and Montréal—the third-largest city in Canada. To complete Vancouver's delights are some of the best restaurants in the land. Add to that a fascinatingly cosmopolitan population: Vancouver's Chinatown is one of the biggest in North America, and portions of the main drag, Robson Street, are so thoroughly Europeanized that it bears the unofficial title "Robsonstrasse."

Vancouverites also possess that reverence for their past without which a city very quickly loses its character and becomes an anonymous assembly kit. Instead of leveling their oldest patch, which had deteriorated into a slum, they lovingly restored its crooked alleys, brushed, painted, and dry-cleaned them, and thus turned Gastown into a major tourist attraction, crammed with boutiques, galleries, and eateries, and boasting the only working steam clock on the continent.

Until about 15 years ago Vancouver had the reputation of being as dull as it was pretty. But as the downtown area changed from pokey provincial to streamlined splendiferous, the texture of the nightlife kept pace. Nowadays it's not only alive, but kicking up its heels in no uncertain fashion. Vancouverites have learned to eat late, drink late, and play late and hard. And in this they're merely treading in the footsteps of their colonial forebears who were—by all accounts—a rather rambunctious lot.

The city was named after Capt. George Vancouver, who took over the minute settlement of Nootka from the Spaniards in 1790. (Puget Sound, incidentally, got its name from Vancouver's lieutenant, Peter Puget, who helped him explore the area.) However, Vancouver was preceded by the township of New Westminster (today practically a suburb) and didn't come into being until the arrival of a very colorful Yorkshireman named John Deighton.

Mr. Deighton stepped ashore from a canoe, accompanied by his Native Canadian mistress, a dog, and a barrel of whisky. With the aid of the barrel's contents, plus a natural gift of gab, he persuaded some local sawmill workers to help him build a saloon—the first structure of future Vancouver! Other saloons, plus stores and a hotel, followed, the development attracted mainly by Deighton's unceasing eloquence, which earned him the nickname of "Gassy Jack."

By 1871 the community known as Gastown, after its honorary mayor, was as notorious for knifings and fistfights as for its indefatigable spokesman. But four years later respectability caught up with it. Gastown was incorporated as the city of Vancouver—counting 2,500 souls and a dozen saloons. Over the decades the center shifted south and Gastown became Vancouver's Skid Row, shunned by the saintlier majority, until its recent resurrection.

ORIENTATION

TOURIST INFORMATION For tourist information, try the **Vancouver Travel Info Centre,** Plaza Level, Waterfront Centre, 200 Burrard St., Vancouver, BC, V6C 2R7 (tel. 604/683-2000). The office is open Monday to Friday from 8:30am to 5pm, and on Saturdays from 9am to 5pm.

CITY LAYOUT Today's Vancouver, Canada's gateway to the Pacific, is centered on a tongue of land between the Burrard Inlet to the north and the Fraser River to the south, but sprawls out into vast suburbs in both directions. A galaxy of bridges—some magnificent, some mediocre—span the waterways, which cover the entire area like lacework. Overlooking the scene are the peaks of the Coast Mountains, which loom so close that they seem within climbing range from downtown. The nearest, Grouse Mountain, actually lies a 20-minute drive away.

Vancouver's focus and orientation point is **Robson Square.** A three-block complex of terraces, gardens, waterfalls, restaurants, exhibition halls, and government buildings, this is an absolutely ideal spot from which to get your bearings. It's almost the city's dead center.

Stand on the square's top terrace and look toward the old **Court House,** now an art gallery. You are now facing due west, toward the Pacific Ocean and **Stanley Park,** a wonderful green oasis the size of the entire downtown area.

To the north lies the **Burrard Inlet,** spanned by the First and Second Narrows bridges, which take you to suburban West and North Vancouver and, farther away, to Grouse Mountain. Your southern view is encircled by the crescent shape of **False Creek,** spanned by the Burrard and Granville bridges. On the far side lies **Vanier Park,** containing the Maritime Museum and the planetarium. To the west stretches the big and beautiful acreage of the **University of British Columbia.** Southwest, across an arm of the Fraser River and yet another bridge, is **Sea Island,** Richmond, where Vancouver International Airport is located. Due south there's a lot more of residential Vancouver and the road leading to **Tsawwassen,** departure point of the ferries sailing across the strait to Vancouver Island, seat of the provincial capital.

Due east runs the Trans Canada Highway, traversing the country from coast to coast, leading to the Fraser Valley and other beauty spots.

Downtown   Now back to your immediate surroundings. Running straight west, all the way to Stanley Park, is **Robson Street,** the main eating and shopping strip. Despite its Teutonic nickname, Robson isn't all that German, but Italian, French, Indian, Polish, and half a dozen other ethnic colorations. You can spend days strolling its length and constantly discover new variations.

Running vertically to the east is the **Granville Mall,** a reserve for the infantry carved out of Granville Street. As pedestrian malls go, it doesn't work too well: There are too few benches, too little greenery, not enough outdoor cafés (compared to, say, Rotterdam or Cologne), and portions of it have become rather tacky stomping grounds for teenagers, reeking of soggy chips and chicken batter. And although the mall is closed to all but privileged vehicles, there are so many of those—including cabs, squad cars, buses, ambulances, and delivery vans—that you still have to look right and left before crossing over.

Running west and east of you, through the mall, is **Georgia Street,** which contains the post office as well as some of the city's poshest hotels and stores. Northeast, close to the harborfront, lies **Gastown,** and adjoining it, **Chinatown.** A few blocks to the west of them is the VIA Railway Depot, the terminal for the Seabus, and the superbly designed **Harbour Centre,** which ranks as a major sight.

About half the downtown streets are one-way; if you're driving reconcile yourself to never getting from point to point by the shortest route.

GETTING AROUND

Vancouver is serviced by **B.C. Transit,** an excellent if rather expensive system of single-decker buses and trolleys, and by a variety of harbor ferries. These include the **Skytrain** and the famous **Seabus,** a science-fiction apparatus that skims you from the Granville waterfront station across Burrard Inlet to Lonsdale Quay in 12 breathless minutes. It runs every quarter hour during the day and costs $1.50.

The **Airport Express** runs from the airport and costs $8.25 (the same trip by cab would set you back about $21). **Bus** fare is by zone and costs $1.35 to $2.50, including transfers—and remember to have the exact change. For further B.C. Transit information, call 604/261-5100.

Cabs are plentiful (except when it's raining) and cheap compared to the rates you'll encounter way up north. Some of the major taxi companies are: Advance Cabs (tel. 604/876-5555), Black Top (tel. 604/683-4567), and Yellow Cabs (tel. 604/681-3311).

There's also a vast choice of **rental-car outfits.** But before giving you some sample addresses, let me give you a few words on driving in Vancouver. The city has a blitz mechanism for pedestrians—a little walking figure—which appears for about 15 seconds. Given the generally broad streets, not even the nimblest footslogger can scuttle across in the time permitted. So watch out for pedestrians dashing over after you've been given the go sign. Otherwise, traffic is very well regulated and urban speed limits are enforced. A right turn on a red light is legal. Motorists, on the whole, are well disciplined and bear no resemblance to the wheeled maniacs you'll meet in Québec. For rental cars, try: **Tilden,** 1140 Alberni St. (tel. 604/685-6111, or toll free 800/387-4747); **Budget,** 450 W. Georgia St. (tel. 604/668-7000); **Hertz,** 1128 Seymour St. (tel. 604/688-2411); or **Avis,** 757 Hornby St. (tel. 604/689-2847).

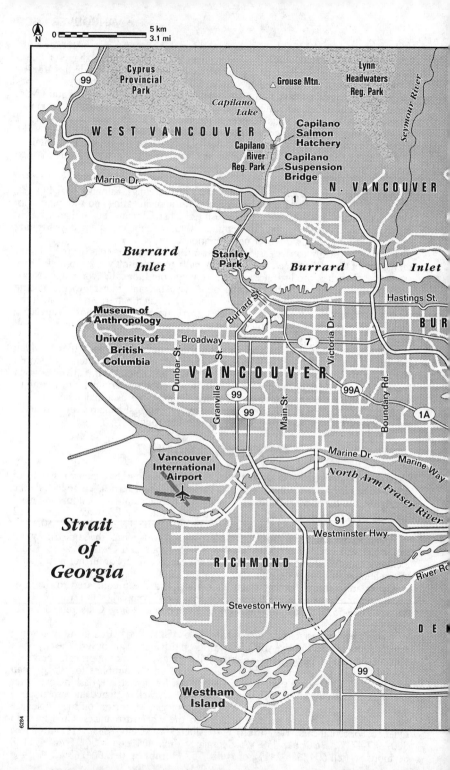

N

0 | 5 km
0 | 3.1 mi

Cyprus Provincial Park

Lynn Headwaters Reg. Park

△ Grouse Mtn.

Capilano Lake

Seymour River

99

WEST VANCOUVER

Capilano Salmon Hatchery

Capilano River Reg. Park

Capilano Suspension Bridge

Marine Dr.

1

N. VANCOUVER

Burrard Inlet

Stanley Park

Burrard *Inlet*

Hastings St.

Burrard St.

B U R

Museum of Anthropology

University of British Columbia

Broadway

Dunbar St.

Granville St.

V A N C O U V E R

7

Victoria Dr.

Boundary Rd.

99

99A

1A

99

Main St.

Marine Dr.

Marine Way

Vancouver International Airport

North Arm Fraser River

91

Westminster Hwy.

Strait of Georgia

RICHMOND

River Rd

D E N

Steveston Hwy.

99

Westham Island

6284

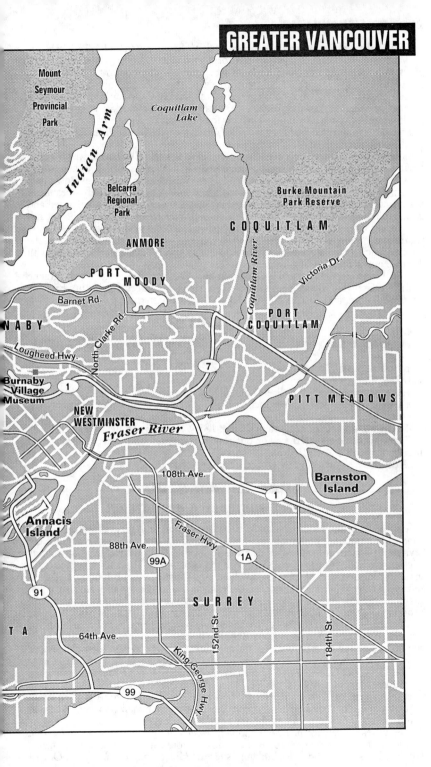

GREATER VANCOUVER

Mount Seymour Provincial Park

Indian Arm

Coquitlam Lake

Belcarra Regional Park

Burke Mountain Park Reserve

ANMORE

COQUITLAM

PORT MOODY

Barnet Rd.

Coquitlam River

Victoria Dr.

NABY

North Clarke Rd.

Lougheed Hwy.

PORT COQUITLAM

7

Burnaby Village Museum

1

PITT MEADOWS

NEW WESTMINSTER

Fraser River

108th Ave.

Barnston Island

1

Annacis Island

Fraser Hwy.

88th Ave.

99A

1A

91

SURREY

T A

64th Ave.

152nd St.

184th St.

King George Hwy.

99

The **Automobile Association** is at 999 W. Broadway (tel. 604/732-3911).

Vancouver is excellent **cycling** territory, particularly in the vast acreage of its parks. No American city that I know of pays as much attention to the needs of the pedal-pushers. Every park and a good many of the ordinary thoroughfares have special bike tracks. Bicycling today is one of the leading Canadian sports, and every second kid seems to be riding a bike, and more and more adults are getting into the saddle as well. Cycling is by far the best way to cover Vancouver's green portions, quite apart from the healthy exercise involved. You can rent bikes at **Robson Cycles,** 1463 Robson St. (tel. 687-2777), for $6 an hour.

The pride of Vancouver's transportation service is the **Skytrain,** which began operation just in time for the opening of the Expo '86 World's Fair. The train, which runs between Vancouver's waterfront and New Westminster, with four downtown stations, is a marvel of electronic engineering. It is completely automated—meaning it has no crew on board—glides silently along a special guideway, both elevated and underground, and has the cleanest, most comfortable cars I've ever sat in. But full automation has its drawbacks as well. The ticket machines at the stations frequently regurgitate perfectly good money. Unless you can substitute another bill for the rejected one, you're stuck—there are no human money changers. Fares vary with distance and start at $1.50.

The direct opposite are the **Aquabuses,** chugging from the Beach Avenue Marina to Granville Island. They look like something that's been floating in a bathtub, operate till 9pm, and cost $1.50 for adults, 75¢ for children.

FAST FACTS

American Express   There's an office at 1040 W. Georgia St. (tel. 604/669-2813).

Doctor and Dentist   For a doctor, call 604/683-2474; for a dentist, call 604/736-3621.

Emergencies   For police or ambulance emergencies, dial 911.

Post Office   The main branch of the post office is at 349 W. Georgia St. (tel. 604/662-5721).

Telegrams   The telegraph office is at 175 W. Cordova St. (tel. 604/681-4231).

Transit Information   For bus routes, schedules, and other transportation information, call 604/261-5100.

Weather   For recorded weather forecasts, dial 604/273-8331.

WHAT TO SEE & DO

EXPLORING GASTOWN & CHINATOWN

A few blocks from Harbour Centre lie Gastown and adjoining Chinatown, both bundles of attractions crammed into what is practically one compact area. (Take the Skytrain to Waterfront station, or take bus 1, 3, or 4.) Gastown radiates out from its brick-paved hub, **Maple Tree Square,** the spot where Vancouver began. It's a charming little tangle of eateries, galleries, and boutiques, clutching you like an amiable octopus, offering visual, edible, and audio treasures and junk in equal quantities. The air is filled with jazz, rock, a dozen ethnic aromas, and the chuffing and hooting from the Canadian Pacific tracks in the background. It's a fun place, with far too few seating facilities for footsore wanderers (a plot, mayhap, to make them pay for a chair somewhere?). The wondrous **Steam Clock,** however, works gratis. Operating on a one-cylinder steam engine, the apparatus plays the Westminster chimes and blows steam whistles every 15 minutes and, incidentally, also tells the time.

You can cover Gastown and Chinatown in one easy walking tour—stopping for appropriate refreshments, of course. The commercial center of Chinatown is a three-block area of West Pender Street, between Carrall and Gore. A kind of Asian "bazaar" quarter, dedicated to shopping and eating, it remains so completely in character that even the public telephone booths wear pagoda roofs.

The wares for sale include ivory and jade jewelry, gorgeous brocades, and exotic delicacies, cheek by jowl with some of the most fatuous rubbish north of the equator. The balcony style of the older buildings suggests Hong Kong or Singapore. One of them you'll find in Mr. Ripley's *Believe It or Not* bible. It's at the corner of Pender and Carrall—five feet ten inches wide, two stories high, and designated as the World's Thinnest Office Building. Do you know of a slimmer one?

THE PORT OF VANCOUVER

The Port of Vancouver, one of the biggest, busiest harbors on earth, can be seen from various angles and vantage points, revealing different aspects. From dry land there's the Vanterm, at the foot of Clark Drive, which has a public viewing area that shows the ultramodern container terminal in action. Other vantage points for marine buffs are at Centennial Pier and Granville Square. For a fast glimpse, take the Seabus from the terminal at the foot of Granville Street. For a more leisurely jaunt, **Harbour Ferries Ltd.** operates an old-time stern-wheeler that thumps around the port area in 75-minute tours from the north foot of Denman Street. (See "Tours and Excursions," later in this section.)

OTHER TOP ATTRACTIONS

HARBOUR CENTRE, 555 W. Hastings St. Tel. 604/689-0421.

Vancouver's landmark, the massive, soaring Harbour Centre, towers over the waterfront. The glass skylift whisks you 40 floors up to the Observation Deck, where the view is stunning, reinforced by angled observation windows and powerful telescopes. Admission includes a panoramic movie of the city's past and present, thrown on a 37-foot screen by 27 projectors and one computer.

The center also contains the Harbour Mall, with 50 specialty shops and a variety of eateries serving everything from snacks to gourmet dinners.

Admission: Skylift to observation deck $5.50 adults, $4.25 seniors, $4 students.

Open: Summer daily 8:30am–10:30pm; winter daily 10am–8pm. **Skytrain:** Waterfront Station.

STANLEY PARK, near W. Georgia St.

Rolling over 1,000 acres of woodlands, gardens, beaches, picnic sites, and nature trails, Stanley Park starts at the foot of West Georgia Street, and ranks as one of the best-designed, best-run, most thoroughly enjoyable green havens in the urbanized world. You could spend an entire vacation there. Encircled by a seven-mile seawall ideal for walking jaunts, the park houses tennis courts, miniature golf courses, a giant checkerboard, a midget railroad, lawn bowling greens, cricket pitches, a live theater, restaurants, coffee shops, and snack bars, and the Brockton Oval sports arena. Just offshore on a rock perches Vancouver's version of Copenhagen's *Little Mermaid—Girl in a Wetsuit.*

The park contains Vancouver's fairly unexciting zoo, a children's petting zoo, and the far more spectacular Aquarium, largest of its kind in Canada. It shows some 9,000 specimens of marine life and has a special pool for beluga whales—white, playful, and astonishingly noisy. The high spot of the exhibition is the Marine Mammal Complex, which stages regular performances by dolphins that look like animated torpedos and three personality-plus killer whales, Finna, Bjossa, and Hyak, who jostle each other for the limelight as much as for the fish.

Admission: Zoo free; Aquarium $8.88 adults, $5.84 children. **Bus:** 52.

CAPILANO SUSPENSION BRIDGE, 3735 Capilano Rd., North Vancouver. Tel. 604/985-7474.

The Capilano Suspension Bridge offers more thrills than a roller coaster. Hanging 230 feet up in the air, stretching 450 feet across the Capilano Canyon, and spectacularly illuminated at night, this is a dizzyingly wonderful experience and the source of some of the most fantastic photos ever taken.

Admission: Crossings $6.40 adults, $2 children.

Open: Daily 9am–5pm. **Bus:** 232.

CAPILANO FISH HATCHERY, Capilano River Park, just off Capilano Rd., North Vancouver. Tel. 604/666-1790.

This "fish farm," nestling in a forest setting, was designed to replenish the salmon

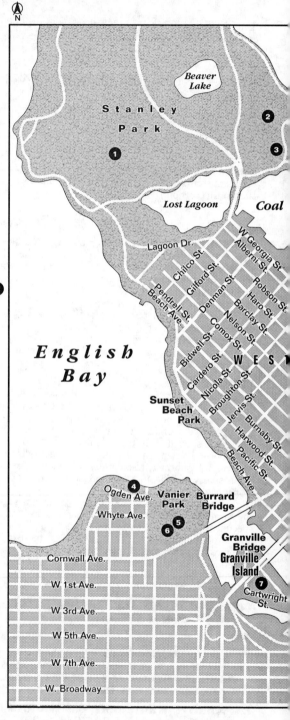

CENTRAL VANCOUVER ATTRACTIONS

Burrard

Inlet

Harbour

Canadian
National
S.S. Pier

Centennial Pier

9

10

W. Hastings St.

W. Pender St.

Melville St.

Bute St.

W. Cordova St.

Thurlow St.

11

Water St.

Railway St.

E N D

Dunsmuir St.

Powell St.

E. Cordova St.

Victory
Sq.

Post
Office

Abbott St.

Carrall St.

13

E. Hastings St.

Nelson
Park

8

W. Georgia St.

Robson
Sq.

15

Gore Ave.

Dunlevy Ave.

Burrard St.

Granville St.

Hornby St.

Seymour St.

Richards St.

Howe St.

Homer St.

Hamilton St.

Cambie St.

Bus
Depot

14

Main St.

Helmcken St.

Beatty St.

Stadium

Davie St.

Drake St.

Pacific Blvd.

12

Creek

Terminal Ave.

Cambie
St. Bridge

False

W 1st Ave.

Industrial Ave.

W 3rd Ave.

MOUNT

W 5th Ave.

PLEASANT

W 7th Ave.

FAIRVIEW

Information ⓘ

Post Office ⊠

6285

population of the Capilano River. You hear all about the salmon's remarkable life cycle and watch the fish, in various stages of development, swim in glass-fronted tanks, with each phase of the process explained in models, diagrams, and the live-water denizens.

Admission: Free.
Open: Daily 8am–dusk. **Bus:** 232.

GRANVILLE ISLAND, underneath the south end of Granville Street Bridge.

This tiny triangle of land situated underneath the south end of Granville Street Bridge represents the triumphant transformation of an industrial slum into a major culture, fun, and commerce attraction. At last count it housed three first-rate live theaters, the Arts Club, the Caroussel, and the Waterfront Theatre, several art galleries, restaurants, cocktail lounges, taverns, specialty stores, a playground with a wonderful water slide, and a miniature lake, plus remnants of industry.

Granville also has a famous Public Market, consisting of hundreds of covered stalls offering fresh vegetables, meat, baked goods, pasta, spices, prepared snacks, and handcraft items. After marketing you can slide straight into the dining and nightlife portion.

Open: Covered market Tues–Sun 9am–6pm. **Bus:** 4, 7, 10, or 14.

GROUSE MOUNTAIN.

The "Peak of Vancouver" is a combination resort and playground set amid some wondrous alpine scenery. You get up there by taking the Aerial Tramway from 6400 Nancy Greeneway at the end of Capilano Road in North Vancouver. This is a big, modern 100-passenger cable train that whisks you aloft on a panoramic six-minute ride. Then you can hike, picnic, take a helicopter, or visit the multimedia Theatre in the Sky. Admission includes the Skyride. If you dine at the Grouse Nest restaurant (tel. 604/984-0661) the Skyride comes gratis with your reservation.

Fare: $14.50 adults, $34.95 families.
Open: Skyride daily 9am–10pm. **Bus:** 232.

PLAYLAND, Exhibition Park, Hastings St., at Cassiar. Tel. 604/255-5161.

This joyously old-timey amusement park, dominated by the largest wooden roller coaster in Canada. Geared for family fun, Playland has 35 thrill rides—from mild to hair-raising—a petting zoo swarming with cuddly critters, two live musical revues, mini-golf, talent shows, clowns, plus popcorn, candy floss, skill games, and all the smells and shrieks that generate glee in kids and nostalgia in parents.

Admission: $5.50 adults, $3 juniors and seniors.
Open: 11am–10 or 11pm. Days vary seasonally; call ahead before visiting. **Bus:** 10, 14, or 16. **Closed:** Thanksgiving–Easter.

MORE ATTRACTIONS

B.C. SUGAR MUSEUM, 123 Rogers St. Tel. 604/253-2517.

This is a surprisingly interesting display, since the development of the sugar refinery closely parallels the historical growth of Vancouver. Here you can see old sugar-making equipment dating back to 1715, a plantation locomotive, intriguing ancient photographs, and a 20-minute documentary film.

Admission: Free.
Open: Mon–Fri 9am–4pm.

BLOEDEL CONSERVATORY, Cambie at 33rd Ave. in Queen Elizabeth Park.

Bloedel Conservatory has a magnificent triodectic dome—the first of its kind in the world—commanding a 360° view of the city and its environs. Beneath this transparent shelter thrive some 300 species of tropical plants as well as 50 kinds of birds. Sensitive climate controls and realistic settings simulate tropical jungle and desert environments to make the brightly hued inhabitants feel at home. The conservatory is beautifully illuminated at night.

Admission: $3 adults, $1.50 children.
Open: Daily 10am–8pm. **Bus:** 15.

CANADA PLACE, at the northern end of Burrard St.

Canada Place, which juts into the harbor, is a dazzling-white shopping, promenading, and entertainment complex built to resemble a multifunneled ocean liner at dock. The place houses the Board of Trade, the Convention Centre, a hotel, restaurants, cafés, specialty shops, and docking facilities for cruise ships.

At the very tip rises the CN IMAX Theatre, showing the largest motion-picture films ever made on a five-story-high screen. It's the closest thing to three-dimensional "feelies" yet produced. Double features are shown daily at 1 and 9:15pm. Adults pay $5.25; children, $4.25.

Skytrain: Waterfront station.

DR. SUN YAT-SEN CLASSICAL GARDEN, 578 Carrall St.

You can step into a realm of utter tranquillity by visiting the Dr. Sun Yat-sen Classical Garden. Tucked away behind sheltering walls in the heart of Chinatown, this oasis of beauty and contemplation was named after the founder of the Republic of China. It's a symphony of horticulture, architecture, and sculpturing, carefully blended for effect. A re-creation of a classical Ming dynasty garden, using materials and artisans brought over from China, this is the first of its genre ever built outside the Chinese mainland. Also on view is a video presentation showing the history of the Chinese in Vancouver.

Admission: $3.50 adults, $2.50 children.
Open: Daily 10am–4:30pm. **Bus:** 1, 3, 4, or 7.

MACMILLAN PLANETARIUM, 1100 Chestnut St. Tel. 604/736-4431.

Located near the ocean in Vanier Park, the planetarium presents programs on astronomy and fascinating laser-light shows.

Adjacent to the planetarium is the Gordon Southam Observatory, open on clear weekends and holidays, Tuesday through Sunday during the summer. Please note that the observatory hours are dependent on the weather. Call 604/736-4431 to find out if the building is open.

Admission: Planetarium programs $5.50 adults, $3.75 children; laser-light shows $7 for everyone; observatory free.
Open: Planetarium June–Sept daily. Call ahead for showtimes and exact winter hours. **Closed:** Mon in winter. **Bus:** 22.

MARITIME MUSEUM, 1905 Ogden Ave. Tel. 604/737-2211.

The Maritime Museum offers guided tours of the Arctic patrol vessel *St. Roch,* a nautical ugly duckling of amazing strength. Scores of other naval exhibits include a full-size replica of a ship's bridge, which you can visit.

Admission (including ticket to the Vancouver Museum): $5 adults, $2.50 students.
Open: Tues–Sun 10am–5pm. **Bus:** 22.

MUSEUM OF ANTHROPOLOGY, University of British Columbia, 6393 NW Marine Dr. Tel. 604/822-5087.

A masterpiece of specialized architecture, the Museum of Anthropology is a multimedia presentation rather than a standard museum. The exhibits include a famous Northwest Coast Native collection, a European ceramics collection, and fascinating material from Asia, Africa, the Pacific, and the Americas. It also contains some of the most impressive totem poles you'll ever see.

Admission: $5 adults, free for children under 6. Free on Tues 5–9pm.
Open: Tues–Sun 11am–5pm; July–Aug daily 11am–5pm. **Bus:** 4, 9, 10, or 14.

OMNIMAX THEATRE, 1455 Québec St. Tel. 604/875-OMNI.

Housed in the same complex as Science World, the Omnimax Theatre boasts the largest screen of its kind in the world, a huge domed auditorium showing special films that seem to engulf you in the action. Call for presentation times and current offerings. Separate tickets are required.

Tickets: $7 adults, $4.50 children.

POLICE MUSEUM, 240 E. Cordova St. Tel. 604/665-3346.

Appropriately housed in the old Coroner's Court, the darkly fascinating Police Museum tells the story of Vancouver's underworld. Most of the items were seized from local criminals, and they range from opium pipes and counterfeit currency to submachine guns, zip guns, pistols, and daggers, along with the photos of the men who wielded them.

Admission: $2 adults, children under 6 free.
Open: Mon–Sat 11:30am–4:30pm.

SCIENCE WORLD, 1455 Québec St. Tel. 604/268-6363.

This is a place of wonders that defies labeling. Housed in what used to be the World Expo Centre, this fascinating cross between a museum, a laboratory, and a laser show gives you a series of hands-on experiences it would take pages to detail. On your way through you can create a cyclone, lose your shadow, blow square bubbles, walk inside a camera, and step on sound. You can see a zucchini explode when zapped with a charge of 80,000 volts, stroll through the interior of a beaver lodge, compose music on an electric guitar, and run your hands through magnetic liquids. And these are only some of the encounters en route.

Admission: $7 adults, $4.50 children.
Open: Daily 10am–5pm. **Bus:** 3, 8, or 19.

STOCK EXCHANGE TOWER, 609 Granville St. Tel. 604/643-6590.

The Stock Exchange Tower has an unusual visitor center designed to give ordinary mortals a chance to see a computerized stock exchange in action. Individuals can take their own self-guided tours, although representatives are at hand to answer tricky questions. You watch the trading floor, view quotation terminals, and imbibe masses of financial information via literature, lectures, and huge graphic displays.

Admission: Free.
Open: Mon–Fri 6am–4pm.

VANCOUVER ART GALLERY, 750 Hornby St., at Robson. Tel. 604/682-5621.

Housed in one of the city's most splendid heritage buildings, the art gallery offers regularly changing exhibitions of important international and regional artworks. These include paintings, sculpture, graphics, photography, and video. A portion of the gallery's permanent collection covers four centuries of art. There is also an imaginative Children's Gallery, displaying past and current works of special interest to youngsters—a little touch other galleries might do well to copy. The permanent exhibits feature an unrivaled collection of the works of Emily Carr, one of Canada's greatest artists.

Admission: $4.75 adults, $2.50 students, free for children under 13. Thurs 5–9pm "pay what you can."
Open: Mon–Wed and Fri–Sat 10am–5pm, Thurs 10am–9pm, Sun noon–5pm.

VANCOUVER MUSEUM, 1100 Chestnut St., Vanier Park. Tel. 604/736-4431.

This is the largest civic museum in Canada. It shows the story of Vancouver's past as well as a thorough glimpse at warriors and weaponry from all over the world, plus changing exhibitions such as "The World of Children," with toys and mementos from around the globe. The gift shop here is a museum by itself.

Admission: $5 adults, $2.50 students. Free for seniors on Tues.
Open: Oct–Apr Tues–Sun 10am–5pm; May–Sept daily 10am–9pm. **Bus:** 22.

NEARBY ATTRACTIONS

HELL'S GATE AIRTRAM, at Fraser's Canyon. Tel. 604/867-9277.

Fraser Canyon, one of the province's natural wonders, lies 2½ driving hours from Vancouver, eastbound on Highway 1, 35 miles north of Hope. This is the site of the Hell's Gate Airtram, a ride you won't forget in a hurry. Swiss-built, the fully automated red tramcars descend on cables from highway level to directly above the roaring turbulence of the Fraser River where it leaps and roars through the 110-foot gorge—the spot through which some two million sockeye salmon pass each year on their way to the inland spawning grounds. There are fantastic camera angles from up there, plus a restaurant, gift shop, and observation platform.

Fare: $8 adults, $5 children.

Open: Daily 9am–5pm.

BURNABY VILLAGE MUSEUM, 6501 Deer Lake Ave., Burnaby. Tel. 604/293-6501.

This is an enchanting time capsule—an entire little township depicting British Columbia between 1890 and 1925. You can stroll along boardwalks, drop in on your grandparents' schoolhouse, watch an old-time blacksmith at work, shop in the general store, ride an antique carousel, and generally wallow in nostalgia. And it's only a 20-minute drive from Vancouver on Highway 7.

Admission: $5.25 adults, $3 children under 6.

Open: Daily 10am–4:30pm, but call first.

FORT LANGLEY NATIONAL HISTORIC PARK, 25 miles east of Vancouver, just off the Trans Canada Hwy, 232 St. exit. Tel. 604/888-4424.

This is the restored site of the trading post of the Hudson's Bay Company (1827–58), which served simultaneously as a stronghold. You see the furnishings, utensils, decorations, and log palisades of the place where the Crown Colony of British Columbia was proclaimed in 1858.

Also in Fort Langley is the Farm Machinery Museum, showing the implements of pioneering life in the colony. From crude plows and wooden kitchen utensils to early (hand-powered) stump pullers, pumping devices, vintage tractors, steam cultivators, and the first aircraft—a Tiger Moth—used in British Columbia for crop dusting.

Admission: $2.25 adults, $1 children.

Open: Summer daily 10am–4:30pm; winter Sun–Thurs 10am–4:30pm.

VANCOUVER GAME FARM, 5048-264th St., Aldergrove. Tel. 604/856-6825.

Eight miles from Fort Langley and 30 miles from Vancouver, close to Highway 1, these 120 acres of lush farmland boast 85 species of wild animals roaming in large paddocks or free. They include tigers, jaguars, lions, ostriches, buffalo, hippos, elephants, and camels, and those in "Babyland" are eminently touchable.

Admission: $9 adults, $7 children.

Open: Daily 8am–dusk.

CANADIAN MILITARY ENGINEERS MUSEUM, on the army base at Chilliwack, 55 miles east of Vancouver along the Trans Canada Hwy. Tel. 604/858-1462.

The museum houses a fascinating collection of military spectacles and gadgetry, including rows of archaic flintlocks and matchlocks—some of them looking more lethal for the user than for the target. There are weapons dating back to 1610, machine guns and mortars from both World Wars, authentic uniforms and medals, many dating back to the Zulu and Boer wars, and other displays from combat as recent as Kuwait.

Admission: By donation.

Open: June–Aug Mon–Fri 10am–4pm, Sun 1–4pm; Sept–May Sun 1–4pm. Call first.

GEORGE C. REIFEL MIGRATORY BIRD SANCTUARY, Westham Island, six miles west of Ladner, south of Vancouver. Tel. 604/946-6980.

A (rather windy) paradise for birdwatchers, the 850-acre sanctuary has an observation tower and two miles of pathways. Over 250 species pass through here, including great blue herons, trumpeter swans, hawks, eagles, peregrine falcons, owls, and coots. The species vary with the season, of course, but you get the greatest variety from September to November. July and August are the quietest months.

Admission: $3.25 adults; $1 children and seniors.

Open: Daily 9am–4pm.

TRANSPORTATION MUSEUM, 17790 [–]10 Highway, Cloverdale. Tel. 604/574-4191.

About 40 driving minutes east of Vancouver is a nostalgic cavalcade of historic vehicles. You can view an 1895 Burlington Victoria car, John Lennon's psychedelic Rolls-Royce, a plush Pullman coach, a 1913 streetcar, a sporting biplane, the immortal DC-3 transport workhorse, a fire truck, and a classic yellow hand-operated gasoline pump. Exhibits include old automobile movies, guaranteed to stir sentiments in all motoring fans.

Admission: $3 adults, $2 children.
Open: Daily 10am–5pm.

TOURS & EXCURSIONS

The **Constitution,** an authentic, white stern-wheeler, with tall smokestack and promenade deck, departs twice daily from the North Foot of Denman Street and circles the entire spectacular Vancouver harbor, accompanied by a running commentary on what you're seeing. Adults pay $15, children $12.50. For sailing times and bookings call 604/687-9558.

The **Royal Hudson** is a wonderfully cozy steam train that puffs and whistles from 1311 W. 1st St. in North Vancouver to the picturesque logging village of Squamish, leaving at 10am and returning at 3:30pm. The train, a delight for railroad buffs, is pulled by one of the mighty "2860" locomotives that huffed their way across all of Canada in the 1930s. The trip goes through some of the grandest scenery in the province. Round-trip tickets for adults are $32; for children, $9. For reservations, phone B.C. Rail at 604/984-5246.

A variety of sightseeing tours in and around Vancouver are run by **Gray Lines,** in the Hotel Vancouver, 900 W. Georgia St. (tel. 604/681-8687). The jaunts take in all the major sights, and prices include admission to most places.

Landsea Tours, 2596 Pandora St. (tel. 604/255-7272), is a minibus outfit that shows you the sights in small intimate groups instead of trainloads. Their main around-town tours run twice daily and take 3½ hours. Adults pay $30; children, $16.

Walking tours for confirmed footsloggers leave daily at 2pm from the Art Gallery Fountain on Georgia Street. Led by highly knowledgeable guides, these groups stroll through downtown, Gastown, and Chinatown, taking 1½ leisurely hours and costing $10 per participant. For details, call 604/324-6470.

Kids Tours, operated by experienced, reliable Vancouver college students, pick up and return children to major hotels. The excursions last three hours and go to the aquarium, zoo, planetarium, the Science and Technology Centre, etc. For bookings, call 604/327-1739.

Somewhat more turbulent are the river-raft trips organized by **Kumsheen Raft Adventures,** 281 Main St. (P.O. Box 30), Lytton, BC, V0K 1Z0 (tel. 604/455-2296). These are three-hour to three-day expeditions on motor-driven rubber rafts, combining the thrills of white-water rafting with the pleasures of swimming, hiking, picnicking, and sunbathing. The shortest one-day trips are through the Thompson River rapids and cost $96 for adults, $66 for kids. You will need a complete set of dry clothing for the return trip.

The Sunshine Coast starts a few miles west of North Vancouver—a scenic mingling of beaches, mountains, ocean inlets, and fishing harbors, where salmon and oysters are plentiful and the boating is superb. (The best time for oyster picking is spring or fall.) The best way to get to the Sunshine Coast is by ferry (phone 604/669-1211 for information). The beautiful white boats of the **B.C. Ferry Corporation** are equipped with picture windows, spacious lounges, promenade decks, and cafeterias. They depart from Horseshoe Bay, West Vancouver, 13 miles from downtown. And you may come back with enough trout, salmon, oysters, clams, and prawns to take care of your food bills for the next two days.

SHOPPING

The most impressive feature of Vancouver's retail trade is the magnificent underground shopping malls. They link vast portions of the downtown area in a network of subterranean stores and boutiques you can browse through on the wettest day without having to open your umbrella.

Biggest of the lot is the **Pacific Centre Mall,** which connects with the two main (aboveground) department stores and the Four Seasons Hotel. It also gives direct access to the **Vancouver Centre Mall.** Both these underground shopping towns lie below **Granville Mall,** where you have the majority of downtown movie houses.

The **Royal Centre Mall,** built under the Hyatt Regency Hotel, has two levels of high-class fashion stores, jewelry and gift shops, gourmet foods and restaurants. The **Harbour Centre Mall** lies beneath the aforementioned tower and another huge department store on the waterfront, and connects with Gastown.

Lonsdale Quay Market, at the foot of Lonsdale Avenue on the waterfront, is the newest, poshest, most versatile of Vancouver's shopping conglomerates. It sells virtually everything except automobiles. Lying adjacent to the Seabus terminal in North Vancouver, it features scores of stalls alongside the plushest of boutiques, Kid's Alley, specialty stores for youngsters, plus a hotel and four restaurants. The range extends from fresh produce to evening gowns, from salmon to silverware. Also strolling minstrels and one of the most spectacular views of the panoramic Vancouver skyline. Open seven days a week.

From the city's awesome array of specialty stores, a few samples:

Images, 164 Water St., Gastown (tel. 604/685-7046), is more art gallery than shop. Specializing in Native Canadian handwork—guaranteed authentic—the tastefully displayed treasures range from a superbly sculpted loon priced at $1,450 to argillite carvings. You can also buy Northwest Native Canadian masks, Inuit graphics, contemporary pottery, original water color paintings, limited-edition prints, and masses of ethnic jewelry. Open seven days a week.

For Inuit carvings—tiny white figures catching seals, fighting bears, harnessing sled dogs—local pottery, and art reproductions, try the **Arctic Loon,** 3095 Granville St.

In a town of generally dismal coffee, **Murchie's,** 970 Robson St., beckons like a lodestar—the aroma alone makes it worth entering. It sells a tremendous variety of coffee blends and tea mixtures in a traditional English setting that makes buying less a commercial and more a social transaction. Another branch, at 560 Cambie St., is a kind of museum of the "cup that cheers but not inebriates."

There are about half a dozen retailers who specialize in helping tourists take home some of the famous B.C. salmon—indubitably the world's finest. One of them is **Salmon Village,** 1057 Alberni St. (tel. 604/685-3378), open seven days. They gift-pack the fish for travel—soft and hot smoked, fresh frozen, whole, canned smoked, native-style smoked—and deliver it to either your hotel or the airport at no extra charge. Half-pound boxes cost $18.50.

WHERE TO STAY

Vancouver, being a tourist town par excellence, is crowded with visitors during peak season, July through the first half of September. But Vancouver has lots of hotels. And unlike the pattern in other Canadian cities, the cheaper ones are right downtown, not way out in the suburbs.

The **Canadian Hostelling Association** is at 1515 Discovery (tel. 604/224-7111).

Don't forget that there's a 10% accommodations tax in Vancouver.

VERY EXPENSIVE

DELTA PLACE, 645 Howe St., Vancouver, BC, V6C 2Y9. Tel. 604/687-1122, or toll free 800/268-1133. Fax 604/689-7044. 197 rms. A/C MINIBAR TV TEL

$ Rates: From $180 single; from $200 double; $1,100 duplex penthouse. AE, CB, DC, ER, MC, V. **Parking:** $12 per day.

The Delta Place is a link in the velvety chain of international hotels that have become a byword for discreet sumptuousness. Discreet is the right term: Service at the Delta Place is silent, unobtrusive, and ubiquitous. You'll notice that there are, for instance, hardly any signs in the hotel. But look like you don't know where you're going for just a moment and immediately a polite voice at your elbow inquires which particular facility you are seeking. This sets the tone of the place throughout.

The lobby is neither huge nor ornate, but it is furnished with the intimate, understated elegance of an ambassadorial drawing room. The bedrooms are furnished in genuine oak, and all are filled with deft little touches: umbrellas in the wardrobe, TV hidden in the cabinet, fluffy terrycloth robes in the bathroom, no fewer than three telephones (one in the bathroom), gargantuan tubs, and bedside consoles controlling everything. Small pets are welcome.

Dining/Entertainment: The restaurant, Le Café, is an award-winner. There's also an evening piano bar for intimate atmosphere.

Services: There's limousine service for whoever can afford it, and massage therapists are on call.

Facilities: Instead of having merely a swimming pool, the Delta Place has a glassed-in spa with steamroom, massage tables, racquetball courts, weight room, saunas, and sun deck. The hotel also operates a business center for executives.

FOUR SEASONS, 791 W. Georgia St., Vancouver, BC, V6C 2T4. Tel. 604/689-9333. Fax 604/684-4555. A/C MINIBAR TV TEL
$ Rates: $190–$215 single; $210–$235 double; from $265 suite. AE, CB, DC, ER, MC, V. **Parking:** $16 a day.

This midtown palace is so discreetly blended into the Pacific Centre complex that you could walk right past it without noticing. This is no accident—the entire international Four Seasons chain has an aversion to glaring neon signs and a penchant for subtly understated luxury that gives them a special mark of their own, like an artist's signature on a priceless painting.

The same leitmotif permeates their bedrooms. They're unostentatiously beautiful, graceful and sleek in pastel hues, with a lot of little touches that caress you like velvet: thick, fluffy bath towels, sink tops of genuine marble, a clock radio that wakes you with music, bedside TV controls, VCRs, and complimentary shampoos of top quality.

Dining/Entertainment: Apart from bedrooms you'll never want to leave, the Four Seasons has a world-class restaurant and possibly the most gorgeous cocktail bar in Canada. The Garden Lounge, beneath a huge skylight, is an indoor setting of trees, shrubs, and flowers, with a shimmering fountain at the center and a pianist in the background.

Services: There's 24-hour room service that is really service. The hotel will also clean your shoes overnight, and boasts a service desk that organizes anything—from bridge partners to bodyguards. There's also complimentary limo service in the downtown area.

HOTEL VANCOUVER, 900 W. Georgia St., Vancouver, BC, V6C 2W6. Tel. 604/684-3131, or toll free 800/268-9420. Fax 604/662-1929. 508 rms. A/C MINIBAR TV TEL
$ Rates: From $245 single or double; from $260 suite. AE, CB, DC, DISC, ER, MC, V. **Parking:** $13 a day.

A stately, massive landmark, dominating the skyline against a backdrop of mountains, this is the oldest and most traditional of the city's deluxe hostelries. Designed on a generous scale, the Vancouver has big everything: bedrooms, bathtubs, hallways, elevators—all giving you a feeling of wonderful spaciousness. The hotel breathes old-style comfort, starting with the mighty armchairs and svelte showcases in the brown-russet lobby, large enough to swallow up all bustle and retain an oasis-air of contemplative serenity.

The decor of the bedrooms is tastefully subdued—brown tones and light-gray carpets—and the thick, soundproof walls guarantee good slumber. You get magnificent views from the windows, magnifying shaving mirrors in the bathrooms, and impeccable service.

Dining/Entertainment: In the same building (which could house an entire village) there are two cocktail lounges, each with a distinctive atmosphere, a couple of fine dineries, and high above you the Panorama Roof, one of Vancouver's plushest food and dance spots.

HYATT REGENCY, 655 Burrard St., Vancouver, BC, V6C 2R7. Tel. 604/683-1234, or toll free 800/233-1234. Fax 604/689-3707. 644 rms and suites. A/C MINIBAR TV TEL

AN IMPORTANT NOTE ON PRICES

Unless stated otherwise, **the prices cited in this guide are given in Canadian dollars,** which is good news for U.S. travelers because the Canadian dollar is worth 25% less than the American dollar, but buys nearly as much. As we go to press, $1 Canadian is worth 75¢ U.S., which means that your $100-a-night hotel room will cost only U.S. $75, and your $6 breakfast costs only U.S. $4.50.

Here's a quick table of equivalents:

Canadian $	U.S. $
$ 1	$ 0.75
5	3.75
10	7.50
20	15.00
50	37.50
80	60.00
100	75.00
200	150.00

$ Rates: $175 single; $200 double; $425–$725 suite. AE, DC, ER, MC, V. **Parking:** $12.50 per day.

The Hyatt greets you with a stunning lobby. Vast and gleaming subtly in brown and beige, it sprawls into a sumptuous shopping arcade and features an outstanding staff, prepared to answer questions like "Where can I play racquetball?" in about 17 languages, including Czech and Indonesian.

The Hyatt is a gleaming white tower built over a huge shopping mall, which means that you need never stir from shelter. The rooms, all brightly elegant, come with electric blankets, carpeted bathrooms, digital clock radios, and refrigerators. The color TV sets screen house feature films on request, and the soundproofing is an engineering feat.

Dining/Entertainment: The hotel also offers two deluxe restaurants and a charmingly intimate bar.

Facilities: Outdoor heated pool, health club, 26 meeting rooms.

WESTIN BAYSHORE, 1601 W. Georgia St., Vancouver, BC, V6G 2V4. Tel. 604/682-3377. Fax 604/691-6959. 517 rms and suites. A/C MINIBAR TV TEL

$ Rates: $150–$200 single; $175–$225 double; from $255 suite. AE, CB, DC, ER, MC, V. **Parking:** $8.56 per day.

The Westin rises ivory-white against a resortlike background of ocean and mountains, with Stanley Park as a kind of garden extension. Yet it's almost right downtown, with the main shopping streets a few walking minutes away—a combination of every advantage Vancouver has to offer.

The bedrooms, beautifully light, have individual climate control, alarm clocks, and picture windows covering an entire wall. And the view below is of a dazzling array of luxury yachts (available for charter) bobbing at anchor along the marina.

Dining/Entertainment: There is a distinct Mediterranean touch to the place, particularly in the scenic Garden Lounge. Somehow the nautical trimmings of Trader Vic's blend nicely with the premises.

Facilities: The circular outdoor swimming pool is surrounded by a sun deck, lush greenery, and rock gardens. There's also an indoor pool and a health club.

MODERATE

Several of the establishments in this bracket have bottom rates nearly as high as those in the expensive category. But they're listed as "moderate" since they offer suites or apartments for the price of a room in the deluxe category.

BARCLAY HOTEL, 1348 Robson St., Vancouver, BC, V6E 1C5. Tel. 604/688-8850. Fax 604/688-2534. 85 rms. A/C TV TEL

$ Rates: $65 single; $85–$125 double. Rollaway beds $10 extra. Lower off-season rates. Special rates for AAA members and seniors. AE, DC, DISC, ER, MC, V. **Parking:** Limited; $5 a day.

The Barclay is housed in a small snowy-white three-story building with a distinct European air. The chairs in the white-tiled lobby are rococo style, and there's an adjacent bistro lounge with a glassed-in patio. The house restaurant serves French cuisine. The bedrooms are not large, but the space is expertly utilized and lighting arrangements are thoughtful. The rooms come with modern bathrooms; some have minibars as well. There is lots of hanging space everywhere and no-smoking rooms are available on request.

BOSMAN'S MOTOR HOTEL, 1060 Howe St., Vancouver, BC, V6Z 1P5. Tel. 604/682-3171, or toll free 800/663-7840. Fax 604/684-4010. 100 rms. A/C TV TEL

$ Rates: $54–$84 single; $59–$89 double. Extra person $10. Children under 12 stay free in parents' room. AE, CB, DC, ER, MC, V. **Parking:** Free.

A sleek modern four-story structure at the edge of downtown just a few minutes' stroll from Stanley Park, this is a motor hotel par excellence, with every convenience and no ambience to speak of. It has a beautiful heated outdoor pool, a smart lounge that doubles as a piano bar, and a highly efficient dining room. The bedrooms are quite spacious, equipped with good-quality motel furniture, and decorated in pleasing russet and walnut hues. The traffic noise of the busy thoroughfare outside doesn't penetrate the sleeping quarters.

DAYS INN, 921 W. Pender St., Vancouver, BC, V6C 1M2. Tel. 604/681-4335. Fax 604/681-7808. 85 rms and suites. TV TEL

$ Rates: $95 single; $95–$135 double; $135–$155 suite with microwave oven. AE, DC, DISC, ER, MC, V. **Parking:** Free.

The Days Inn is an older downtown establishment that has been beautifully renovated and updated. A light-brown, seven-story structure, the inn now houses a restaurant, a cocktail lounge with large TV screen, and a charming Edwardian-style English pub with "gaslight" illumination. The bedrooms (no-smoking on request) are medium-sized, with light color tones. All come equipped with remote-control TV and clock radios. Two bedside lamps and a cluster of ceiling lights grouped around the fan look after your eye comfort. Closets are walk-in, the bathrooms small but modern, and there is a guest laundry.

GREENBRIER, 1393 Robson St., Vancouver, BC, V6E 1C6. Tel. 604/683-4558. 32 apts. TV TEL

$ Rates: $58 single; $68 double. Each extra person $5. AE, MC, V. **Parking:** Free.

This apartment hotel features a very indifferent lobby and exterior, but surprisingly good living quarters. A smallish three-story building, the Greenbrier has self-contained units, each with a large kitchen, medium-size sitting room, and small bedroom. The furniture is neither new nor glamorous, but ample. Each unit has one huge walk-in closet plus a little one, bedroom with dressing table and good bedside lights, kitchen with dining table, electric range, and wonderfully spacious refrigerator, and spick-and-span bathroom with tub and shower. The units are nicely carpeted and they'll accommodate up to five persons, although this maximum may be a bit of a crunch.

HOTEL GEORGIA, 801 W. Georgia St., Vancouver, BC, V6C 1P7. Tel. 604/682-5566. Fax 604/682-8192. 313 rms. TV TEL

$ Rates: $120–$160 single; $130–$170 double; from $250 deluxe unit. Children under 16 stay free in parents' room. AE, DC, ER, MC, V. **Parking:** $12 a day.

Standing squarely in the heart of downtown Vancouver, the Hotel Georgia is as busy as a crossroads. A massive, red-brick corner building, the Georgia has an impressive wood-paneled lobby with a genuine fireplace, beautiful chandeliers, and heavy carpeting. Apart from a vast array of facilities, the hotel has an exceptionally friendly and helpful staff.

There is a candlelit restaurant for serious dining, an Olde English pub filled with good cheer and folksy entertainment, and a patio lounge devoted to business luncheons. Bedrooms are of medium size and not overly modern, the bathrooms tiny but well equipped.

PACIFIC PALISADES HOTEL, 1277 Robson St., Vancouver, BC, V6E 1C4. Tel. 604/688-0461, or toll free 800/663-1815. Fax 604/688-4374. 233 units. MINIBAR TV TEL

$ Rates: From $145 single; from $165 double. Children under 16 stay free in parents' room. AE, CB, DC, ER, V. **Parking:** $8 per day.

This handsome, centrally located establishment just fits into the "moderate" price range because all units are suites with their own kitchenettes. Preparing your own meals is a big cost-cutter. The Pacific has all the facilities of a luxury hotel: a glass-roofed 55-foot swimming pool, health spa, badminton court, weight room, whirlpool, and Finnish sauna; conference chambers with audiovisual equipment, a sidewalk patio, and an elegantly laid-back restaurant. The suites are divided into studios, executive and penthouse. All are spacious, with excellent couches and armchairs, ample closet space and—for the most part—panoramic views. Each unit comes with at least two telephones (on which you can leave voice messages) and bathrooms fitted with special makeup mirrors and hairdryers and stocked with free toiletries and bathrobes. The kitchenettes have microwave ovens, coffee makers, and minibars. The hotel also rents out bicycles, which you can ride safely in nearby Stanley Park.

RIVIERA MOTOR INN, 1431 Robson St., Vancouver, BC, V6G 1C1. Tel. 604/685-1301. 14 studios, 26 one-bedroom apts. TV TEL

$ Rates: From $68 single; from $78 double. Extra person $10. AE, DC, DISC, ER, MC, V. **Parking:** Free.

Directly opposite the Sheraton stands the Riviera Motor Inn. An up-to-the-minute former apartment block converted into an apartment hotel, this is an exceptionally good nest for lengthier stays, with its small lobby, impeccably maintained corridors, and apartment units. The units have everything that makes for complete independence: kitchens fully equipped with cooking and eating utensils, all-electric ranges with ovens, dining areas, and refrigerators. The bedrooms are spacious and airy, with little balconies, three hanging closets, wide beds, and lots of elbow room, all in bright, modern pastel shades. Chamber service is included in the rates, and the beautiful views from the upper floors come free.

SHERATON-LANDMARK, 1400 Robson St., Vancouver, BC, V6G 1B9. Tel. 604/687-0511. Fax 604/687-2801. 358 rms and suites. A/C TV TEL

$ Rates: $125–$175 single; $125–$195 double; $225–$450 suite. AE, CB, DC, DISC, ER, MC, V. **Parking:** $4.30 per day.

The Sheraton prides itself on being Vancouver's tallest hotel—a soaring tower of 42 floors with a revolving restaurant at the peak (see "Where to Dine," later in this section). The lobby is fairly small and unimpressive, but the hotel houses well-equipped rooms, saunas, a cocktail lounge, penthouse suites, no fewer than 20 meeting rooms, an underground garage, and a foreign exchange bank. It also has airport limousine service, superfast elevators, and excellent soundproofing.

The bedrooms are of medium size, and all have private balconies, cable TV and radio, piped-in music, and walk-in closets. The bathrooms come with heat lamps to give you an after-shower glow, and some boast refrigerators as well.

SUNSET INN, 1111 Burnaby St., Vancouver, BC, V6E 1P4. Tel. 604/684-8763. Fax 604/669-3340. 50 studios and one-bedroom suites. TV TEL

$ Rates: Studios $78–$108; one-bedroom suites $88–$118 per night, $528–$708 per week. AE, DC, ER, MC, V. **Parking:** Free.

This is a charmer of an apartment hotel, located in a quiet backwater of the busy West End. A tall gray modern structure, the inn offers completely self-contained apartments, nicely furnished in striking contemporary color schemes, and each with a little balcony, color TV, and thermostat heat control.

Kitchens and bathrooms are excellently equipped: all-electric, with every utensil you might need, including toaster, coffee maker, can opener, and knives that actually cut. The living rooms are spacious and designed to catch all the sunshine available.

The beds are comfortable, the closet space more than ample, the carpeting deep green and wall to wall. There are leather settees and armchairs as well as a dining table, with handy shelves hidden behind folding doors. The entire layout keeps the correct balance between clutter and bareness, and the lighting fixtures could serve as models for those establishments which assume that tourists never do anything but watch television in their abodes.

SYLVIA HOTEL, 1154 Gilford St., Vancouver, BC, V6G 2P6. Tel. 604/681-9321. 115 rms. TV TEL
$ Rates: From $55 single; from $60 double; $82–$95 triple; from $82 bed-sitter with fully equipped kitchen. AE, DC, MC, V. **Parking:** $3 per 24 hours.

 Gray-stoned and ivy-wreathed, the Sylvia Hotel resembles a town mansion nestling at English Bay on the fringe of Stanley Park. With one side overlooking the bay, the other the park, the place feels like a green retreat from urban dins. The reception lobby sets the tone: restful, subtly lit, with red carpets, ivory drapes, and wonderfully comfortable sofa chairs. There's an adjoining restaurant and cocktail lounge with the same atmosphere. The staff is charming, the service impeccable.

The bedrooms (some with captivating bay views) all have bath and shower, plus TV set. The furnishings and fittings are beautiful as well as ample: writing desks with twin lights, dressing tables with mirrors, open closet space, good springy beds, all in tastefully matched color schemes. The Sylvia, as you may have guessed, is popular; during summer you'd be wise to book eight weeks ahead.

BUDGET

Hotels

DOMINION HOTEL, 210 Abbott St., Vancouver, BC, V6B 2K8. Tel. 604/681-6666. Fax 604/681-5855. 40 rms (half with bath or shower). TV TEL
$ Rates: $39 single; $49 double. AE, DISC, MC, V. **Parking:** Not available.

Located in historic Gastown, this red- and white-brick restoration of an 1899 hostelry houses a treasure of nostalgic trivia. The Lamplighter pub downstairs was the first public bar in Vancouver to serve women. The lobby armchairs were once plush-covered recliners in which gentlemen had their shoes cleaned. An antique hotel sled and an ancient washing machine stand in the corridor. Stairways are suitably majestic but—despite modernization—the three-story hotel has no elevator.

The bedrooms are not period pieces, but simple and neatly furnished, equipped with color TVs, writing desks, bedside lamps, and open hanging spaces. About half of them come with private bathrooms; the rest use two communal facilities on each floor.

KINGSTON HOTEL, 757 Richards St., Vancouver, BC, V6B 3A6. Tel. 604/684-9024. Fax 604/684-9917. 60 rms (some with bath). TEL
$ Rates: $35–$50 single; $40–$75 double. Extra person $5–$10. 10% discount for students and seniors. AE, MC, V. **Parking:** Overnight, free.

The Kingston must rank among the best accommodation bargains in town. A small, modern, spick-and-span bed-and-breakfast hostelry, the Kingston is run by the tremendously house-proud Fred O'Hagan. Breakfast includes fruit juice and is served in a neat little lounge, and there is a special dessert menu for room service. The hotel has three floors and no elevator, but has a Swedish sauna, a guest laundry, and outdoor tables. The bedrooms have either private bath or hot-and-cold water handbasins; those with bath also have color TV. The rooms are small and trim, nicely carpeted, equipped with desk lights and basic furniture.

NELSON PLACE HOTEL, 1006 Granville St., Vancouver, BC, V6Z 1LS. Tel. 604/681-6341. 100 rms. TV TEL
$ Rates: $40–$50 single; $45–$55 double. Children under 12 stay free in parents' room. AE, DC, MC, V. **Parking:** Free.
There's a faintly nautical air about the Nelson Place Hotel, which invites you to "lay

anchor" there. The 100 bedrooms are rather narrow and have no ceiling lights, only table and bedside illumination. The bathrooms are spacious, modern, and fluorescently lit, there's lots of hanging space, the decor is a pleasing soft brown, and the walls are hung with intriguingly ancient maps of the world. The hotel stands on the fringe of a rather seedy part of town.

NIAGARA HOTEL, 435 W. Pender St., Vancouver, BC, V6B 1V2. Tel. 604/688-7574. Fax 604/687-5180. 99 rms (40 with bath). TEL
$ Rates: From $32 single; from $35 double; ($10 extra with bath). Children under 12 stay free in parents' room. AE, V. **Parking:** Not available.
The Niagara has an attractive hewn-stone facade, no restaurant on the premises, but a busy pub that serves cafeteria lunches daily except Sunday. Almost half the bedrooms come with private bath; for the others there's a bathroom on each floor. The rooms are small and rather sparsely furnished; all of them, however, have wall-to-wall carpet, bedside lights, dressing table, and color TV. They have large open closets with ample hanging space, although the rooms themselves are fairly small.

PATRICIA HOTEL, 403 E. Hastings St., Vancouver, BC, V6A 1P6. Tel. 604/255-4301. Fax 604/254-7154. 195 rms (all with bath). TV TEL
$ Rates: $32–$49 single; $44–$59 double. Winter rates up to 50% lower. MC, V. **Parking:** Free.

This large square six-story building has a very pleasant lobby equipped with gray settees. The corridors are plain, but spotless and quiet. There's no dining room, but a pub on the premises serves three home-cooked economy-priced meals a day. All bedrooms have either bath or shower, ventilating fan, and color TV. Furnishings are simple and well maintained, the carpeting good, the walk-in closets or open hanging spaces quite ample. About two-thirds of the rooms offer fine views of the city.

ST. REGIS HOTEL, 602 Dunsmuir St., Vancouver, BC, V6B 1Y6. Tel. 604/681-1135. Fax 604/683-1126. 84 rms (all with bath). TV TEL
$ Rates: $60 single; $65 double. Extra person $5. The management allows small pets (but "No reptiles, please"). AE, CB, DC, DISC, ER, MC, V. **Parking:** Within five blocks.
The St. Regis offers a lot for its rates. There's a restaurant, a pub, and a bar lounge on the premises (the latter featuring adult entertainment); rooms come with bath and shower, and all have color TV and dial phone. The lobby is large and fairly bare, but with ample seating facilities and vending machines. Corridors are impeccably kept, well carpeted, and quiet. The bedrooms come nicely furnished, with green carpets, nice wide beds, and much hanging space in open closets. You get a writing desk with

---

Ⓕ FROMMER'S COOL FOR KIDS: HOTELS

Westin Bayshore *(see p. 713)* An ideal oasis for (well-heeled) families. The Westin has a huge outdoor pool, vast lawns, a marina with sailing charters, bikes for rent, plus a busy seaplane base on the doorstep.

Pacific Palisades *(see p. 715)* Well equipped to keep youngsters entertained, with a badminton court, table tennis, an extra-large swimming pool, rowing, and rentable bicycles.

Sylvia Hotel *(see p. 716)* The hotel itself has no special facilities for kids, except perfect location. Overlooking English Bay on the fringe of Stanley Park, the Sylvia has the biggest playground in town as a front yard, so to speak.

desk lamp, bedside lamps, and a compact, modern fluorescently lit bathroom. Each corridor has a soft-drink machine in case of night thirst.

The Ys

YMCA, 955 Burrard St., Vancouver, BC, V6Z 1Y2. Tel. 604/681-0221.
111 rms (none with bath).
$ Rates: $29–$31 single; $51–$54 double. MC, V. **Parking:** Not available.
The YMCA has a vast and somewhat bleak guest lounge, with metal furniture, linoleum floors, a showcase full of athletic trophies, half a dozen pay phones, and as many vending machines. There is also a swimming pool, gym, steamroom, and racquetball court, plus a coffee shop. The bedrooms are spotless, bright, and equipped with the basics. No liquor is allowed on the premises. One-third of the rooms have TVs.

YWCA, 580 Burrard St., Vancouver, BC, V6C 2K9. Tel. 604/662-8188.
Fax 604/681-2550. 180 rms (some with bath). TEL
$ Rates: $44–$52 single; $64–$69 double. 10% discount for seniors. MC, V.
Parking: Nearby.
The YWCA is considerably frillier than the nearby YMCA. Housed in a brightly modern residence, 13 stories high, it has a welcoming lobby with comfortable settees, cozy TV lounges, kitchen facilities, swimming pool, and sauna (for women only). The cafeteria is a neon-lit, linoleum-floored affair offering meals for about $6 per helping, but the bedrooms come with armchairs, and some with private baths.

Bed-and-Breakfast

You can arrange to stay in this type of accommodation by contacting an agency that has a list of private homes in Vancouver or in rural British Columbia that take in B&B guests. All listings have been inspected and approved.

A Home Away from Home, 1441 Howard Ave., Burnaby, BC, V5B 3S2 (tel. 604/294-1760; fax 604/294-0799), handles all types of B&B accommodations—singles, couples, and families. It also arranges special lodgings for the disabled and those on diets or suffering from allergies. Rates offered are from $45 for singles, from $55 for doubles, from $65 for suites. Extra persons sharing rooms pay $15 to $25; children under 12, $10 to $20. A deposit equal to one night's stay is required on reservations.

A Hostel

GLOBETROTTER'S INN, 170 West Esplanade, North Vancouver, BC, V7N 1A3. Tel. 604/988-5141.
$ Rates: $13 per person in the dormitory; $27 single room; $38 double room with private bath. No credit cards. **Parking:** Not available.
Located on the scenic North Shore, a few minutes' walk from the Seabus terminal, this simple but versatile hostel has a fully equipped kitchen, dining room, and laundry.

College Accommodations

The **University of British Columbia** has a gorgeous near-shore setting overlooking English Bay, about 15 minutes from downtown by the no. 10 bus, which runs to the campus every 10 minutes. The layout embraces 100 acres of rose gardens, alpine trails, and wooded paths, the second-largest library in Canada, a superb Aquatic Centre, the Museum of Anthropology, botanical gardens, jogging tracks, tennis courts, and golf courses. The entire location is a tourist attraction in its own right.

UBC has 2,000 single rooms at the **Walter Gage Residence,** 5961 Student Union Mall, Vancouver, BC, V6T 2C9 (tel. 604/822-1010). Singles run from $29 for rooms to $80 for suites. Lodgings are available all year, and you can get very good and fairly cheap meals on campus. Parking costs $10 per day. MasterCard and VISA are accepted.

WHERE TO DINE

Vancouver boasts such a variety of eateries (over 1,500) that it's quite impossible to include more than a fraction of them in the space available. Assume, therefore, that for each establishment listed there are three, four, or a dozen more that had to be omitted. This applies especially to the French and Chinese restaurants, which flourish all over town.

It was also impossible to find a clear dividing line between dining and entertainment spots, since some of the best eating houses also put on great entertainment at night. Consequently you'll find some of them mentioned here, others in "Evening Entertainment," below.

Above all, you should sample the Sunday brunches, a local institution so highly competitive that it inspires every hostelry to lay on its best.

EXPENSIVE

The listings below are merely a smattering of what's being dished out on Vancouver's groaning board. Others in the same class include the **Three Greenhorns,** 1030 Denman St. (tel. 604/688-8655), for seafood; **Truffles,** 655 Burrard St. (tel. 604/687-6543), for gourmet fare in deluxe surroundings; and the **Ten-Sixty-Six,** 1066 W. Hastings St. (tel. 604/689-1066), for possibly the finest West Coast bouillabaisse you'll ever dream about.

CAFE DE PARIS, 751 Denman St. Tel. 604/687-1418.
   Cuisine: FRENCH. **Reservations:** Accepted.
$ Prices: Appetizers $3.95–$6.95; main courses $13.95–$18.95. AE, ER, MC, V.
   Open: Lunch Mon–Fri 11:30am–2pm; dinner daily 5:30–10pm.

The Café de Paris may be the most authentic French restaurant in Canada outside Québec. Not so much in terms of cuisine (which isn't "haute" by any means) but in general ambience, from the marble tabletops to the parquet flooring and the little gesture of turning the lights lower around 10pm. The fare is characteristic French bistro cooking of the provincial type—thoroughly delicious. You can recognize it by the quality of the pommes frites; every one a crackling gem. The onion soup is the powerful brew you used to get at four in the morning around the Paris markets. After that you have a difficult choice between the veal with mushrooms in Calvados cream sauce or the superlatively flavored rabbit in a cream and mustard sauce. The choice gets harder still when the dessert trolley comes a-wheeling. The menu here is quite short, but you have to fight the urge to eat your way from the top left to the bottom right corner.

CHATEAU MADRID, 1277 Howe St. Tel. 604/684-8814.
   Cuisine: SPANISH. **Reservations:** Accepted.
$ Prices: Appetizers $3–$6; main courses $12–$16. AE, DC, ER, MC, V.
   Open: Dinner Tues–Sat 6–11pm.
Château Madrid is located above the much more economical Bodega, forming a kind of Spanish downtown complex. The Madrid, however, is the original Spanish dinery in Vancouver, a sumptuous culinary retreat glowing with candlelight reflected from copper pots hanging from rough-hewn oak beams. The house specialty is paella, which seems to contain every subtle delicacy that can be found in and beside the Mediterranean. For an appetizer try the mussels marinated in white wine, and for a finale, the café Madrid, the house specialty coffee, which tastes downright poetic.

MULVANEY'S, 1535 Johnston St., on Granville Island. Tel. 604/685-6571.
   Cuisine: CAJUN/CREOLE. **Reservations:** Required.
$ Prices: Appetizers $5.95–$7.25; main courses $12.25–$19.95. AE, DC, ER, MC, V.
   Open: Lunch daily 11:30am–2:30pm; dinner daily from 5:30pm.
Mulvaney's was already flourishing when Granville Island (see "What to See and Do," above) was still an industrial wasteland. This restaurant was an act of courage that paid off—based on the idea that quality will prevail regardless of surroundings. Now that the "island" has blossomed into a popular attraction, Mulvaney's can claim pioneering status. The restaurant is beautifully situated, overlooking a tranquil waterway, the decor a smart mélange of swathed fabrics and rampant greenery. The

food is New Orleans at its finest. Cajun and Créole specialties include Cajun cioppino (mixed ocean edibles poached in white wine and herbs), seafood gumbo, blackened redfish (served in butter sauce), and a splendiferous rack of lamb basted in Créole mustard. Standing next to the Arts Club Theatre and the famed island market, Mulvaney's gets the patrons of both. After your meal you can dance off the calories.

THE PROW, Canada Place. Tel. 604/684-1339.
   Cuisine: SEAFOOD. **Reservations:** Accepted.
$ Prices: Appetizers $4.95–$6.95; main courses $10.95–$19.50. AE, MC, V.
   Open: Lunch daily 11:30am–2:30pm; dinner daily 5:30–10:30pm.
Canada Place, Vancouver's landmark, juts into the harbor like a ship in full sail with the Prow perched at the very tip. The view it offers is that of a lookout in the bows of a windjammer, high above the water, with Burrard Inlet and the city below you, the surrounding mountains in the distance. There are marine craft weaving all around and frequently a majestic cruise liner tied up at the promenade alongside.
   Seafood seems the logical fare here, although the restaurant also serves an array of terra firma victuals. Appetizers come hot or cold, according to taste, but you couldn't do better than the smoked salmon, served in horseradish cream and with house-baked black bread. Fish dishes—all fresh—include a subtly sweetish red snapper marinated in soy and ginger, and the regal "zarzuela," a special mix of fish, prawns, scallops, crab, clams, and mussels simmered in white wine. The dessert list is famous for originality. Try—if you have room—the brown-bread ice cream or the remarkable hazelnut mousse rendered aromatic and pleasantly alcoholic with Frangelico.

SEASONS, Queen Elizabeth Park, 33rd and Cambie Sts. Tel. 604/874-8008.
   Cuisine: CANADIAN. **Reservations:** Recommended.
$ Prices: Appetizers $5.75–$7.50; main courses $12.95–$19.95. AE, ER, MC, V.
   Open: Lunch daily 11:30am–2:30pm; dinner daily 5:30pm–"closing."
⭐ This, the second of Vancouver's great park restaurants, gained international attention when Presidents Clinton and Yeltsin had their diplomatic dinner there. It's a toss-up whether the place was chosen for its setting or its cuisine. The Seasons nestles in a garden, the picture windows of the dining room overlooking the city skyline and the North Shore mountains beyond. It's enchanting in daylight and almost magical at night, when the lights of the city are reflected by the tall white candles on the tables. The decor has an understated elegance of its own—ornamentation is left to the beautifully arranged indoor greenery and the all-round views.
   The menu is surprisingly short, the wine list very long, and both accentuate a classic culinary tradition. Appetizers feature an oyster stew of fresh Pacific oysters in cream and a plate of mushrooms stuffed with crab, shrimp, and green onions. Main courses include a magnificent rack of lamb scented with rosemary, médaillons of Montréal veal with wild mushrooms in sage-butter sauce, and lightly seared prawns served in Pernod and a light peppercorn dressing. This is Pacific Northwest cuisine at its finest and freshest—even the ravioli, filled with Dungeness crab and spinach, have a distinct West Coast individuality.

THE TEAHOUSE, Ferguson Point, in Stanley Park. Tel. 604/669-3281.
   Cuisine: FRENCH/AMERICAN. **Reservations:** Required.
$ Prices: Appetizers $5.75–$6.95; main courses $8.95–$19.95. AE, MC, V.
   Open: Lunch daily 11:30am–2:30pm; dinner daily 5pm–closing.
⭐ Once upon a time this really was a modest little afternoon teahouse. Since then it has blossomed into a decidedly svelte establishment. The decor resembles a rustic French château, the cuisine is haute, the setting idyllic. You can dine in the conservatory (under glass) or in the exquisitely furnished drawing room, enjoying a panoramic view of English Bay, West Vancouver, and the mountain ranges beyond.
   Appetizers include escargots in a light garlic butter or mushrooms stuffed with shrimp and cheese. There's a superb fish soup: Pernod-flavored broth teeming with

shrimp, mussels, and chunks of salmon. After that the choice gets really difficult. Perhaps the steak tartare, the traditional roast duck à l'orange, or the rack of lamb with fresh rosemary, served in Martini and Rossi sauce.

MODERATE
Along Robson Street

This is one of the world's most versatile eating strips, as you'll see by the string of samples below. Robson Street, and the area bordering on it, contains an inordinate proportion of Vancouver's dineries, with a heavy accent on European fare. The cuisine is generally excellent, the prices moderate, the choice pleasantly dazzling. The samples given here add up to only a fraction of what this street offers.

HEIDELBERG HOUSE, 1164 Robson St. Tel. 604/682-1661.
   Cuisine: GERMAN. **Reservations:** Accepted.
$ **Prices:** Appetizers $3.25; main courses $7.95–$10.50. AE, DC, DISC, ER, MC, V.
   Open: Daily 9am–midnight.
Heidelberg House used to be one of two restaurants by the same name on the same street. The second is now Maxl. This one is a cozy, dimly lit, wood-paneled hostelry, festooned with big and little stags' heads and antlers, alpine murals, and a large aquarium in the anteroom. There's an impressive bar in the rear, menu prices are moderate, and the helpings generous. With the main course you get soup (the broccoli soup is outstanding), a small salad, plus crispy German kaiser rolls. The Heidelberg is famous for its schnitzels and its apple strudel. Don't leave out the superb pan-fried potatoes.

LITTLE FRANK'S, 1487 Robson St. Tel. 604/687-7210.
   Cuisine: ITALIAN. **Reservations:** Accepted.
$ **Prices:** Appetizers $2.85–$6.50; main courses $9.50–$25.90. AE, MC, V.
   Open: Lunch Mon–Fri 11:30am–2pm; dinner daily 5–10pm.
This place, named after proprietor Frank Sorace, takes you to Italy. A handsome white-walled dining room, flowers on the tables, floral upholstery, and floral wall decorations supply an indoor garden air. The specialty of the house is a rather wonderful platter of scampi, lightly broiled in their split shells, bathed in an aromatic butter-and-garlic sauce. But Frank's is versatile. You can get a much cheaper meal by sticking to the pasta dishes or the fragrant calamari or steamed clams.

MONTEREY LOUNGE, in the Pacific Palisades Hotel, 1277 Robson St. Tel. 604/684-1277.
   Cuisine: INTERNATIONAL. **Reservations:** Accepted.
$ **Prices:** Appetizers $3.95–$6.95; main courses $6.95–$15.95. AE, CB, DC, DISC, ER, MC, V.
   Open: Dinner daily 6pm–1am.
The Monterey Lounge dispenses cuisine far above the usual hotel fare. A large bay window overlooks a courtyard with cherry trees, and the vegetables served come fresh from the roof garden of the hotel. The menu offers a choice between gourmet and moderate meals, both innovatively prepared and elegantly served. In the first bracket you get items like grilled claypot salmon and roasted breast of duck with sun-dried cherries. In the second category there's skillet-roasted breast of chicken and grilled Italian sausages with ratatouille.

PEPITAS, 1170 Robson St. Tel. 604/669-4736.
   Cuisine: MEXICAN. **Reservations:** Recommended.
$ **Prices:** Appetizers $3.95–$6.95; main courses $9.95–$18.50. AE, MC, V.
   Open: Dinner daily 6pm–11pm or 1am.
Dimly lit, permanently packed, and filled with joyous Latin brass music, Pepitas is one of the most popular feasting spots in town. The walls are decked with a profusion of posters, sombreros, beads, blankets, and ceramics, the menus are bilingual, and the

patrons almost as lively as the decor. You get the entire range of Mexican delicacies (chips and salsa on the house) plus the traditional combinaciones of tacos, tostada, burrito, and chile relleno. For something more fancy try the besugo a la plancha—red snapper grilled in garlic butter. There's dancing to live music six nights a week.

ROBSON GRILL, 1675 Robson St. Tel. 604/681-8030.
   Cuisine: CANADIAN. **Reservations:** Accepted.
$ Prices: Appetizers $5.50–$8.75; main courses $8.25–$24.95. AE, DC, DISC, MC, V.
   Open: Daily 11:30am–midnight or 1am.
The Robson Grill is a large, very attractive cross between a tavern and a restaurant. The fare is Anglo-Canadian, in sharp contrast to most of the Robson Street eateries. In the center there's a four-sided bar, and a dining and drinking patio outside; in the rear, a little band platform for nightly entertainment. You can drink at the bar or dine in stylish comfort at the tables. The house game pâté is as good as anything made in France. After that, try the original salmon Wellington—fresh salmon baked in pastry. The music, plus dancing, comes gratis.

SAIGON, 1500 Robson St. Tel. 604/682-8020.
   Cuisine: VIETNAMESE. **Reservations:** Accepted.
$ Prices: Appetizers $3.50–$3.75; main courses $7.95–$12.95. AE, DC, MC, V.
   Open: Daily 11am–midnight.
Saigon, is, of course, Vietnamese, but with an extensive vegetarian tone. Large and tastefully plain, the Saigon has no Asian imprint except in the general atmosphere. The only decorations are sprigs of foliage above the low, soft, rattan-shielded lamps. Prices here are modest, the helpings huge, the service both speedy and exceptionally courteous. A long and varied selection of potables includes 18 brands of beer and 18 after-dinner liqueurs. The Vietnamese wonton soup can be followed with an immense beef on rice noodles dish, or perhaps the Vegetarian Delight, a subtle blending of plants and spices.

In Gastown

The next batch of eateries are all in Gastown, where the numbers and variety are almost as profuse as on Robson Street, although considerably more touristy.

BROTHER'S, 1 Water St. Tel. 604/683-9124.
   Cuisine: INTERNATIONAL. **Reservations:** Accepted.
$ Prices: Appetizers $4.95–$8.95; main courses $8.95–$15.95. AE, MC, V.
   Open: Lunch daily 11:30am–4pm; dinner daily 4–11pm.
Brother's is a solid restaurant thinly disguised as a monastery. (Although the very idea may seem bizarre here, Europe has scores of genuine monasteries operating illustrious beer gardens and wine cellars.) Brother's has most of the trimmings in the form of stained glass, heavy-hewn tables, frescoes, and waiters garbed in somber monks' robes. Dishes include Brother Julian's clam chowder, Brother Antonio's pepperoni, Monastery burgers, and Brother Herman's Ribs (don't worry, they're beef). The "devilishly tasty" desserts include a satanically rich Black Forest cake.

KILIMANJARO, 332 Water St. Tel. 604/681-9913.
   Cuisine: AFRICAN. **Reservations:** Accepted.
$ Prices: Appetizers $3.95–$6.95; main courses $11.95–$21.95. AE, DC, ER, MC, V.
   Open: Lunch daily 11:30am–3pm; dinner daily 5–11pm.
The striking interior at Kilimanjaro is painted in red and jungle green and supported by soaring pillars, and the walls are hung with some outstanding pieces of tribal art. There's also a huge photo montage of one exceedingly irritated elephant. The cuisine is an Afro-Indian mixture, reflecting the owner's; background—he's an Indian from Uganda. Order mitabaki, a Swahili specialty of spiced crab in a pastry shell, or coconut fish soup, a surprisingly harmonious

combination. Or try the plantains steamed in banana leaves, served with beef stew. Don't forget the Snows of Kilimanjaro (shades of Hemingway) dessert—homemade vanilla ice cream topped with saffron and liqueur.

LE RAILCAR, 106 Carrall St. Tel. 604/669-5422.
Cuisine: FRENCH. **Reservations:** Recommended.
$ Prices: Appetizers $4.25–$6.95; main courses $10.95–$18.95. AE, DC, ER, MC, V.
Open: Dinner daily 5:30–10pm.

 Le Railcar is exactly what the name indicates: a converted Canadian Pacific dining coach (from 1929), restored to its steam-age splendor and turned into a stationary restaurant. Additional elbow space was created by coupling on an extra section, which looks like part of the original car. For realistic sound effects you have the working locomotives of the real railroad shunting on the nearby tracks. You eat off Orient Express china by candlelight and get panoramic views through flower-wreathed windows. The cuisine is *Orient Express* quality, the background music French chansons. I recommend the country pâté followed by the rack of lamb. I also recommend reservations—the traveling public comes in droves.

MAHARAJAH, 137A Water St. Tel. 604/685-6714.
Cuisine: INDIAN. **Reservations:** Accepted.
$ Prices: Appetizers $3.95–$5.95; main courses $12.95–$14.75. AE, DC, MC.
Open: Daily 11am–11pm.
Maharajah is a smallish Indian restaurant with outdoor tables under green umbrellas, the interior quiet and cool beneath soundless ceiling fans. Decorations are tastefully subdued: crossed swords, brass plates, and golden idols on the walls, pointed archways and long mirrors making the room appear much larger than it is. The restaurant offers daily specials such as beef, chicken, or vegetable curries served mild, hot, or extra-hot.

THE OLD SPAGHETTI FACTORY, 53 Water St. Tel. 604/684-1288.
Cuisine: ITALIAN. **Reservations:** Accepted.
$ Prices: Appetizers $2.35–$4.50; main courses $6.95–$11.85. AE, MC, V.
Open: Mon–Sat 11:30am–11:30pm, Sun 11:30am–10pm.
The eye-shattering mélange of antique trappings, gadgets, and contraptions here would take the rest of this chapter to list. The main item is a genuine 1910 streetcar, which once rattled around Vancouver but now serves as a dining car. Do make a point of having your leg pulled by the menu's glowing description of "vintage spaghetti harvests" in southern Italy. And please admire the mustachioed portrait of "Guilelmo Marrconi, Inventor of Wireless Spaghetti." There are nine makes of spaghetti dished out, all of them including salad, sourdough bread, coffee, and ice cream. The most expensive selection comes with meatballs, and there's an allegedly secret-recipe homemade lasagne.

In Chinatown

It's only a block or so from Gastown to Chinatown, which virtually consists of eateries. The cuisine is mostly Cantonese and generally excellent, although you do miss the Mandarin, Hunan, and Mongolian subtleties if you happen to hail from San Francisco. On the other hand, the Vancouver clan has come up with a few innovations of its own—such as Chinese smörgåsbord.

NOODLE MAKERS, 122 Powell St. Tel. 604/683-9196.
Cuisine: CHINESE. **Reservations:** Accepted.
$ Prices: Appetizers $5.95; main courses $9.95–$16.50. AE, CB, DC, ER, MC, V.
Open: Lunch Mon–Fri 11:30am–2pm; dinner daily from 5pm.

 Noodle Makers could pass for a museum and certainly constitutes a landmark. Run by four noodle-making brothers, the establishment is filled with artifacts used by the early Chinese immigrants in Canada. But the place of honor goes to a beautiful 30-foot fish pond, glittering with expensive goldfish that are trained to feed at the sound of a gong struck at 7:30 and 9:30pm daily. The background sounds are a soothing blend of running water and soft Asian music. The restaurant has a small select menu of gourmet dishes—lemon chicken and empress filet are outstanding.

PHNOM PENH, 244 E. Georgia St. Tel. 604/682-5777.
  Cuisine: CAMBODIAN. **Reservations:** Accepted.
$ Prices: Appetizers $5; main courses $8–$13. DC, MC.
  Open: Wed–Mon 10am–9:30pm.

Cambodian cooking strikes a delicate balance between Vietnamese and the spicier Thai cuisine. An excellent place in which to become acquainted with its palate pleasures is Phnom Penh, where a few items on the menu require a certain adventurousness, such as the jellyfish salad. Phnom Penh is light and spotless, decorated with silk flowers and furnished with dining booths as well as tables. If you haven't eaten Cambodian before, try the superb hot-and-sour soup first, then perhaps the prawns in garlic butter. As a highlight, try either the thin marinated "butter beef," cooked in a slightly sweet juice, or the chicken flavored with lemongrass and herbs together with a dish of crispy dry rice noodles. The meal might make you a convert to Cambodian cuisine.

Elsewhere Around Town

BRIDGES, Granville Island. Tel. 604/687-4400.
  Cuisine: INTERNATIONAL. **Reservations:** Recommended.
$ Prices: Appetizers $6.25–$9.95; main courses $8.75–$19.
  Open: Dinner daily 5:30pm–11pm or 1am.

 Located on Vancouver's downtown pleasure peninsula, across from the famous market, Bridges is an immense yellow structure housing three distinct restaurants. Choose between the formal elegance of the main dining room (with appropriate prices), the relaxed bistro ambience of the wine bar (serving wines by the glass or bottle), or the even more relaxed pub, where fishermen regale each other with the size of the one that got away. For good measure there's also a vast garden terrace overlooking False Creek and the Expo '86 site. You pay according to which dining room you choose to eat in, but the place is so popular that this choice is frequently governed by space availability.

CARLISLES, 793 Jervis St., off Robson. Tel. 604/687-4335.
  Cuisine: POULTRY/MEXICAN. **Reservations:** Accepted.
$ Prices: Appetizers $2.95–$7.95; main courses $4.95–$12.95. AE, MC, V.
  Open: Daily 11:30am–11pm or 1am.

Carlisles made its reputation with a "secret" broasted chicken dish in which the bird is pressure-cooked with the skin off, then served crisp and lightly spiced and virtually free of cholesterol. Since then the restaurant has added a range of other dishes, notably the Mexican fajitas. You put these together yourselves; they're sautéed in tequila, broiled with peppers and onions, and dished up in a hot iron skillet.

MOZART RESTAURANT, Robson Sq. Tel. 604/688-6869.
  Cuisine: CONTINENTAL. **Reservations:** Accepted.
$ Prices: Appetizers $4.95–$8.95; main courses $9.95–$15.95. AE, V.
  Open: Mon–Sat 10am–8pm.

Mozart Restaurant is a beautiful European-style dinery, not particularly Austrian—it could just as well stand in Stockholm or Amsterdam. It has a large umbrella-shaded patio outside, gleaming chandeliers and snowy table linen inside, plus picture windows overlooking the square. One wall covered by a colorful mural shows young Mozart playing before a bewigged and enchanted audience. Although this is one of the plushest eating places in town, it is not particularly expensive. The desserts, which are masterpieces, are correspondingly pricey. Choices are vast, but I heartily recommend the breast of veal Cordon Bleu or the pan-fried Bratwurst. Among those stunning desserts—try the cherries and buttercream mousse or the Romanoff parfait. Your check arrives in a discreetly classy red-leather wallet.

NANIWA-YA, 745 Thurlow St. Tel. 604/681-7307.
  Cuisine: JAPANESE. **Reservations:** Accepted.

$ Prices: Appetizers $3.50–$5.50; main courses $9–$14.50. AE, DC, ER, MC, V.
Open: Lunch Mon–Fri 11:30am–2:30pm; dinner daily 5:30–11pm.

 The name means Osaka-shop, but the interior is actually designed to resemble a Japanese country inn, though it's doubtful whether Japanese rural diners get to eat off the celebrated Arita-Yaki brand crockery, as you do here. The chief attractions are the tanks with bubbling seawater from which you can choose your own crabs, shrimp, lobsters, oysters, abalone, or fish, which are then cooked and served in the restaurant's special sauces. The fare is not exactly cheap, but the care taken with the preparation is immense and the hospitality doesn't so much please as enfold you. Assorted sashimi (bite-sized pieces of raw fish) dinners are available, and the sushi plates look like edible artworks.

QUILICUM, 1724 Davie St. Tel. 604/681-7044.
Cuisine: NATIVE CANADIAN. **Reservations:** Recommended.
$ Prices: Appetizers $5.95–$7.95; main courses $13.95–$28.95. AE, MC, V.
Open: Lunch Mon–Fri 11:30am–2:30pm; dinner daily 5–9:30pm.

This establishment serves West Coast Native Canadian fare, suitably modified, of course, because the native tribes ate their food without seasoning—healthy no doubt, but not very agreeable to our jaded palates. You descend a flight of stairs into a spotless basement, simply furnished with wooden benches and tables, decorated with a few Native Canadian artworks. The background tapes are rhythmic Native Canadian chants. Taste the bannock bread and a plate of the hearty caribou soup. Then feast on either the barbecued goat ribs in fruit sauce or the baked duck with cabbage and juniper sauce. In conclusion try the fresh berries in season.

SCANWICH, 750 W. Pender St. Tel. 604/683-6219.
Cuisine: SCANDINAVIAN. **Reservations:** Not accepted.
$ Prices: Sandwiches $4.25–$7.25. No credit cards.
Open: Mon–Fri 10am–4pm.

Scanwich is actually a Scandinavian food center and incidentally serves far and away the best coffee downtown. Charmingly decorated with hand-picked prints and posters (the table mats are 19th-century works of art), the air filled with the lilt of pure Viennese schmalz, and airmailed copies of Scandinavian dailies on the racks, it provides style and comfort in equal quantities. The famous "scanwiches" are justly so—shrimp, Danish salami, house pâté, ham, and Danish cheese on thinly shaved slices of excellent bread. Unfortunately they're so good and so minute that you need about three to pacify a middling appetite. Nordic beers are available.

TOPANGA, 2904 W. Fourth Ave. Tel. 604/733-3713.
Cuisine: MEXICAN. **Reservations:** Not accepted.
$ Prices: Appetizers $3–$7; main courses $8.50–$17. MC, V.
Open: Mon–Sat 11:30am–10pm.

There's a touch of Mexico—California style—at the Topanga. It looks like a cross between a café and a desert adobe hut, and suggests blazing sunshine even when it's freezing. The Topanga serves nearly all the standard favorites and prepares them in an open kitchen area: chiles rellenos, enchiladas, burritos, tostadas, and tacos, all including refried beans and rice, mostly topped with avocado sauce and sour cream. They're best consumed in combination plates, followed by Mexican hot chocolate or hibiscus-cinnamon tea with homemade cake.

ZUNI CAFE, 1221 Thurlow St. Tel. 604/681-3521.
Cuisine: CAJUN/THAI/MEX. **Reservations:** Accepted.
$ Prices: Appetizers $4.50–$5.95; main courses $9.95–$17.95. AE, MC, V.
Open: Dinner daily 5:30–10:30pm.

A small white structure with a yellow awning, the Zuni Café boasts an interior that's bright, cheerful, and imbued with a bohemian touch. One the walls there's a changing gallery of original paintings and sketches by local artists. The Zuni's decor is easier described than the fare: an astonishing mix of cuisines that make dining somewhat adventurous. You might start with baked onion pie or goat cheese in spicy black bean sauce. Go on to Oriental spiced lamb marinated in ginger, garlic, and rice wine; or the Cajun seafood stew of oysters, scallops, and salmon in light cream.

The dishes are preferably accompanied by wines from California, Australia, Chile, and Spain.

BUDGET

CAFE KAVKAZ, 1696 Robson St. Tel. 604/662-8777.
   Cuisine: UKRAINIAN. **Reservations:** Not accepted.
$ **Prices:** All dishes $3.27–$5.61. No credit cards.
   Open: Daily noon–10pm.

 A small white-on-white snack bar, almost bare of decoration, Café Kavkaz has a few tables along a counter inside, a few more on the pavement outside. What the place lacks in decor it makes up in flavor. The pelmeni (Russian ravioli) are outstanding. They come 12 to a plate and the menu describes them as "very interesting." Other standard favorites of the genre are cabbage rolls, plov, and hearty fried sausages, all served correctly with Russian tea with lemon and sugar. (If you want to do it exactly right, you must put a lump of sugar between your teeth and suck the tea through it. Takes a bit of practice.)

DUTCH PANNEKOEK HOUSE, 1260 Davie St. Tel. 604/669-8211.
   Cuisine: DUTCH. **Reservations:** Not accepted.
$ **Prices:** Pancakes $4.55–$7.75. No credit cards.
   Open: Breakfast and lunch Mon–Fri 8am–2:30pm, Sat–Sun 8am–4pm.

 This was the first of its breed in North America, introducing the Dutch version of the French crêpe, which is vastly more substantial—in fact, a solid meal on its own. The house offers 36 varieties from bacon, mushroom, and cheese, to apple, ginger, and strawberry with whipped cream—all of them platter size.

FRESGO INN, 1126 Davie St. Tel. 604/689-1332.
   Cuisine: CANADIAN. **Reservations:** Not accepted.
$ **Prices:** Hamburgers $4.30–$6.95. No credit cards.
   Open: Mon–Sat 8am–2am, Sun 9am–11pm.
The Fresgo Inn is a superior breed of cafeteria and a very bustling place. Handsomely decorated with ferns and creepers, a stained-glass lighting fixture, and a buffet that resembles a tiled cottage, its only jarring note an uninterrupted stream of canned music, it serves quite excellent chicken potpie, outstanding stew, and a classy array of hamburgers, plus enormous breakfasts with all the works.

THE JOLLY TAXPAYER, 828 W. Hastings St. Tel. 604/681-3574.
   Cuisine: ENGLISH. **Reservations:** Not accepted.
$ **Prices:** Most items $3.50–$6.50. MC, V.
   Open: Mon–Sat 10am–midnight, Sun 11am–midnight.
A very English pub with a shingle depicting a smiling gentleman dressed only in a barrel, the Jolly Taxpayer has a comforting atmosphere, eight kinds of draft beer, a jukebox, a pool table, and nightly dancing. Also the range of pub fare that even barrel-clad patrons can afford: steak-and-kidney pie, homemade soup plus sandwich, beef stew, meat loaf with mashed potatoes, and very tasty cabbage rolls at similar rates.

NONYA BABA, 1091 Davie St. Tel. 604/687-3398.
   Cuisine: MALAYSIAN. **Reservations:** Accepted.
$ **Prices:** All items $3.50–$9. MC, V.
   Open: Daily noon–9pm.

 Nonya Baba is a tiny establishment selling the kind of red-hot specialties dispensed at Singapore street stalls. This definitely no-smoking place (it tells you so every few feet), with spotless tables under fluorescent lights, is operated by two women named Lim—one cooks, the other serves. You get genuine blistering Malaysian fare at rock-bottom prices: like kway teow (a large platter laden with sausages, rice, fishcakes, noodles, and bean sprouts), oysters fried in flour with eggs and spices, fried rice with squid and shrimps, etc.

ROOSTER'S QUARTERS, 836 Denman St. Tel. 604/689-8023.
   Cuisine: FRENCH CANADIAN. **Reservations:** Not accepted.

FROMMER'S COOL FOR KIDS: RESTAURANTS

The Old Spaghetti Factory *(see p. 723)* Kids love the decor as much as the fare in this chain of "factories." The menu alone keeps them amused until the food arrives.

Noodle Makers *(see p. 723)* The big attraction here is the timed feeding of the goldfish—who rise when a gong is struck.

Dutch Pannekoek House *(see p. 726)* Pancakes have always been a favorite of the younger set. Here they come in 36 varieties, more than you're likely to encounter anywhere else.

Island Charters *(see p. 727)* The daytime lunch cruises on sleek white yachts are irresistible for children, particularly in sunny weather when the coastal waters are swarming with pleasure craft of all shapes and sizes.

Food Fairs *(see p. 728)* It doesn't matter which one you pick; juniors go for the variety of stalls, the idea of tasting a bit here and a bite there. And they haven't the slightest aversion to plastic cutlery.

$ Prices: Quarter chicken $7.25; half chicken $9.98. No credit cards.
Open: Daily 11:30am–11pm.

Rooster's Quarters is an awesomely popular French Canadian chicken dispensary that has folks lining up for tables every mealtime. There's nothing French about the decor—it's all devoted to golf caps, clubs, and cups (the owner is a passionate putter). But the grand attraction here is the superlative Montréal-style barbecued chicken: crunchy crisp on top, meltingly tender below, the way fowl should be roasted. It's possibly the best of its kind in Vancouver. The portion comes with french fries of like quality, coleslaw, and a soft bun (which you can safely ignore—portions are big). The fare is worth the wait.

A TASTE OF JAMAICA, 941 Davie St. Tel. 604/683-3464.
Cuisine: WEST INDIAN. **Reservations:** Not accepted.
$ Prices: Main courses $1.50–$7.75. No credit cards.
Open: Mon–Sat 11am–11pm, Sun 4–11pm.

Rather exotic, and cheap to boot, is A Taste of Jamaica. A tiny storefront specializing in West Indian fare, the place has only five tables, a rainbow-hued wall, and a display of art prints, some of them excellent. Otherwise simplicity reigns, down to the plastic knives and forks. The dishes are tangy and authentic—curried goat with rice and salad, or red snapper with boiled plantains. Juices include mango, papaya, and guava. Banana cake is only $1.

SPECIALTY DINING

MEALS AFLOAT If you fancy dining or lunching aboard a white motor yacht with panoramic picture windows, make your booking through **Island Charters, 104–1676 Duranleau** (tel. 604/688-6625). You have a choice between the two-hour lunch cruise or the 3½-hour dinner cruise, both of which let you view the best offshore angles of Vancouver along with your meal. The yachts cruise in calm water and have open deck space as well as cover. The fare is light and tasty, including salmon, marinated chicken, and excellent salads. Lunch costs $24.95, the sunset dinner $39.95, and cruises go out twice daily Sunday to Friday.

REVOLVING RESTAURANTS Vancouver has the unique distinction of possessing two revolving restaurants offering changing panoramas along with the comestibles. The **Harbour House Revolving Restaurant** crowns the top of the Harbour

Centre (tel. 604/669-2220; see "What to See and Do," above); **Cloud 9** (tel. 604/687-0511), sits 42 stories up in the Sheraton-Landmark Hotel at 1400 Robson St. It's hard to decide here what's more impressive, the fare or the view. The restaurant, 564 feet above sea level, takes one hour and 25 minutes to complete a turn, weighs 200 tons, and is propelled by two remarkably tiny electric motors.

At Cloud 9, between gazing in turn at the city, the bays, and the islands beyond, I imbibed a Bermuda-style fish chowder, sesame prawns and ginger, and mango ice-cream cake. Altogether, the cost was $32. Cloud 9 is open six days a week to 1am, on Sunday to 10pm.

FOOD FAIRS   There are at least half a dozen of these around Vancouver, and more spring up by the month. All of them consist of separate stalls selling international specialties at economy prices. Seating and eating facilities range from very comfortable to middling Spartan. It's hard to pick out a "best among them, but one of the most varied is in the landmark **Harbour Centre**, 555 W. Hastings St. Here you can browse from Hawaiian chicken to Ukrainian cabbage rolls, from burritos, tacos, and enchiladas to fish-and-chips, Vietnamese rice pilaf, and teriyaki beef. All items cost between $2.50 and $5, so the browsing won't break you. Open Monday to Saturday 10am to 7pm.

EVENING ENTERTAINMENT

The performing arts are thriving in Vancouver, although visitors from the U.S. often run into shows that closed on Broadway (or off Broadway) a couple of seasons ago. Check the daily papers or the gratis weekly publication *Vancouver Guideline* for what's on where, with whom, and for how long.

THE PERFORMING ARTS

ARTS CLUB THEATRE, Granville Island. Tel. 604/687-1644.
The Arts Club Theatre is actually a duo of establishments as well as one of the greatest theatrical success stories in Canada. The Granville Island Mainstage shows full-scale comedies, dramas, and musicals. Latest arrival is the Revue Theatre Stage, also on Granville Island, just beside the Public Market, an intimate cabaret-style showplace featuring musical revues to an audience sipping drinks at tables thoughtfully placed on tiered levels. The Granville Island Stage also offers the Backstage Lounge, with outdoor patio, a licensed bar, and live bands entertaining patrons after weekend performances.
Prices: Tickets for either stage $14–$26, with discounts for students and seniors.

BACK ALLEY THEATRE, 751 Thurlow St. Tel. 604/688-7013.
The Back Alley Theatre is an intimate little place specializing in evening and late-night comedy performances of the renowned improvisational troupe called Vancouver Theatre Sports League—often hilariously satiric and always amusing.
Prices: Tickets $6–$13.

PRESENTATION HOUSE THEATRE/GALLERY, 333 Chesterfield Ave., in North Vancouver. Tel. 604/986-1351.
This historic building houses a photo-related art gallery, a professional theater offering drama and comedy, and various musical programs.
Prices: Tickets $9–$12; two-for-one offers may be available.

QUEEN ELIZABETH THEATRE, THE ORPHEUM, AND THE VANCOUVER PLAYHOUSE, 600 Hamilton St. Tel. 604/280-4444.
Vancouver's three civic theaters, all located in the heart of downtown, provide the focal point of the city's live stage entertainment. A vast, beautiful, expertly designed stage complex, this center provides tremendous variety, including grand opera, ballet, Broadway musicals, symphony, drama, rock, recitals, and international plus Canadian theater productions.
Prices: Tickets $5.25–$35.

ROBSON SQUARE CONFERENCE CENTRE, 800 Robson St. Tel. 604/660-2830.

This ultramodern showcase-cum-exhibition area contains two theaters and an outdoor stage area, serving for almost everything from pop concerts and dance performances to avant-garde theatricals, ethnic cultural events, trade and product shows.

Prices: Mostly free.

STUDIO 58, 100 W. 49th Ave. Tel. 604/324-5227.

Studio 58 is the stomping ground of Vancouver Community College's Theatre Arts program. It's comfortable and intimate, presenting a year-round cycle of classics, modern stage hits, and occasional musicals.

Prices: Ticket prices vary.

VANCOUVER EAST CULTURAL CENTRE, 1895 Venables St. Tel. 604/ 254-9578.

This medium-size all-purpose performance space presents both adult and children's theater, jazz, folk, and classical music, ballet, and dance seven days a week.

Prices: Tickets $4–$22.

THE CLUB & BAR SCENE

Vancouver's nightlife is awash with bars and clubs. Some have live bands while others have DJs who spin platters. The list below offers only a few samples of Vancouver's nightlife. Clubs spring up and shut down, and change offerings and addresses with dazzling rapidity. A glance at a Saturday paper will give you a couple of dozen additional choices.

BIG BAMBOO, 1236 W. Broadway. Tel. 604/733-2220.

A nightspot with a sushi bar and "classy casual" dress code (whatever that means), Big Bamboo offers some unusual entertainments, such as rival band contests, hypnosis demonstrations, and organized dinner cruises. There's a special ladies' "night out" on Wednesday. There's action Monday to Saturday from 7pm to 2am.

Admission: $5–$7.

COMMODORE, 870 Granville Mall. Tel. 604/681-7838.

A huge entertainment complex geared to a high decibel range and a young clientele, Commodore presents celebrity bands and solo performers from all over America and overseas belting out anything from rock to reggae. The Commodore becomes a disco on Tuesday nights, and holds dance parties on Friday. Open seven nights a week.

Admission: $5 and up.

DRAC'S DUNGEON, 1238 Davie St. Tel. 604/689-1222.

One of the most original theatrical enterprises anywhere, founded and run by a dynamic Aussie "sheila" named Marilyn (Maz) Gering, this hilarious horror revue features Count Dracula and Associates in 2½ hours of glorious insanity, accompanied by (I quote) "five courses from the cauldrons of the dungeon kitchen and bloodcurdling cocktails." The hair-raising proceeds Tuesday to Saturday and the management guarantees audience participation and abuse. Reservations are essential.

Admission: Show and dinner $36 Tues–Thurs, $38 Fri–Sat.

LUNATIC FRINGE, 315 E. Broadway. Tel. 604/876-7003.

There's live rock and roll seven nights a week plus a changing lineup of local bands and guest outfits from Seattle. The doors open at 8pm. Very laid-back, but neither lunatic nor particularly fringey.

Admission: $5–$7.

MADISON'S, 398 Richards St. Tel. 604/687-5007.

This remarkably versatile place changes complexion five evenings a week. There's "classic" 1970-style dancing on Wednesday, guest artists on Thursday, ladies' night—with male exotic dancers—on Friday, and hot dance tracks and global alternatives on Saturday. The Madison, open from 9pm to 2am, also has three bars and a dual-level dance floor. It's casual dress weekdays, somewhat more formal weekends.

Admission: $4 weeknights, $7–$8 Fri–Sat.

NOTORIOUS, 364 Water St., Gastown. Tel. 604/684-1968.

Notorious covers the bases all the way from disco dancing to spaghetti-eating contests, from ladies' "nites" with erotic male dancers to bikini contests and dart games.

Admission: Varies with the offerings, $2–$7.

PUFFIN'S, in the Pacific Palisades Hotel, 1277 Robson St. Tel. 604/ 688-0461.

Puffin's is possibly the most popular piano lounge in Vancouver, thanks to an ivory tickler with a limitless repertoire of sing-alongs and hum-alongs. Most of his numbers echo the 1950s; most of his cheering, clapping patrons are in their 30s and 40s. The drinks are at bar prices, and there's action Monday through Saturday until 1am.

Admission: No cover.

PUNCHLINES THEATRE, 15 Water St., Gastown. Tel. 604/684-3015.

Punchlines is devoted to professional stand-up comedy five nights a week. Monday is Amateur Night for unknown talent (or lack of same). Punchlines presents a wondrously mixed bag of gags, though the quality varies considerably. Shows from 9:30pm Tuesday to Saturday.

Admission: $5–$10.70.

RICHARD'S, 1036 Richards St. Tel. 604/687-6794.

An upscale club with posh trimmings, Richard's enforces a mild dress code and offers valet parking. There's an astonishing range of entertainments: from Top 40 dance bands to prizefights, ladies' nights (with male models), rock groups, model contests, and dance exhibitions. Richard's is equipped with the latest video and laser system. It's open Monday to Saturday, and you'd better book ahead.

Admission: $2–$7, depending on offering.

THE ROXY, 932 Granville St. Tel. 604/684-7699.

The Roxy presents entertainment salads containing just about everything: weekly theme parties, old movies, stand-up comedy, local talent shows, variety bills, rock bands, dancing—you name it, they've got it. Call to find out what's on.

Admission: $4–$5 Thurs–Sat.

TOWN PUMP, 66 Water St., Gastown. Tel. 604/683-6695.

One of Vancouver's favorite mingling grounds. Aided by an immense selection of local and imported beers, it has live bands as well as a piano lounge, and an antique collection thrown in for good measure. In action daily from 9pm to 1 or 2am.

Admission: $5–$20, depending on the act.

TWILIGHT ZONE, 7 Alexander St., Gastown. Tel. 604/682-8550.

The Twilight Zone features live rock bands alternating with "battling" DJs and caged go-go dancers. "Friendly slamming allowed." Open nightly from 9pm to 2am.

Admission: $4.

YUK YUK'S, 750 Pacific Blvd. Tel. 604/687-LAFF.

This is part of a Canada-wide chain of comedy institutions. Stand-up comics and amateurs with various degrees of talent and laughability. In action Wednesday through Saturday at 9pm.

Admission: $3–$11.

Jazz and Folk

BLARNEY STONE, 216 Carrall St. Tel. 604/687-4322.

An Irish pub–like creation transplanted to Gastown, the Blarney Stone serves savory Irish lamb stew for $6. The pub atmosphere is diluted by romantic soft lights, the bands switch between full-throated Irish and somewhat less hearty show ensembles, and the atmosphere stays relaxed and rollicking regardless of who's on.

Admission: No cover for diners; others $3–$4, depending on the night.

GEORGE V LOUNGE, in the Hotel Georgia, 801 W. Georgia St. Tel. 604/682-5566.

Various groups belt out Scottish airs with tremendous gusto, occasionally sliding

into American and English ditties. It's by far the best sing-along entertainment in town, and the management kindly provides a brochure with the opening verses of "Loch Lomond," "I Belong to Glasgow," "Alouette," etc., so you won't have to just hum. A beer costs a pittance.
Admission: Free.

HOLLYWOOD NORTH, 856 Seymour St. Tel. 604/682-7722.
   In this smooth jazz club the combos range from intimate trios to 17-piece big band. Open Monday to Saturday from 8pm to 1:30am.
Admission: $3–$5.

HOGAN'S ALLEY, 730 Main St. Tel. 604/689-8645.
   Hogan's Alley concentrates mainly on blues bands, both local and imported from south of the border, with live performers seven nights a week. There's a very knowledgeable clientele.
Admission: $2 Fri–Sat.

HOT JAZZ SOCIETY, 2120 Main St. Tel. 604/873-4131.
   Here jazz is presented in the widest form, from Dixieland to swing and progressive, depending on the night. The patrons are dedicated fans and the dance floor is permanently packed.
Admission: Varies.

CASINOS

During the past few years changes in government regulations have permitted the introduction of public gambling in British Columbia—with certain restrictions, to be sure. For mysterious reasons the use of dice remains banned, ruling out those games of chance that require them. The law also stipulates that no gaming room contain more than 15 tables, that bets be limited to a maximum of $5, and that a percentage of the proceeds go to charity.
   As a result Vancouver now boasts a sprinkling of perfectly legal casinos. They are not concentrated in a strip but scattered all over town and the suburbs. None of them offers a floor show or other diversions, the decor is mostly modest and devoid of glamour, and they close at 2am. But besides the familiar roulette and blackjack they run some novelty games that may be new to you. One of them is a Wheel of Fortune that has dollar bills of various denominations instead of numbers. The other is sic-bo, an Asian import in which you roll three balls onto a spinning wheel with six sets of dice faces, representing the numbers one through six. Bets are placed on the sum total of the spaces in which the balls lands. There's no skill involved—it's pure chance.
   The **Royal Diamond Casino,** 1195 Richards St. (tel. 604/685-2340), is informal and very friendly. It features a novelty called Canadian craps—a combination of craps and roulette. Open seven nights a week from 6pm to 2am.
   The **Great Canadian Casino,** in the Holiday Inn, 2477 Heather St. (tel. 604/872-5543), has blackjack, roulette, and sic-bo, and branches all over British Columbia. Open nightly from 6pm to 2am.

2. VICTORIA

85 miles (137km) across the Strait of Georgia from Vancouver

GETTING THERE   By Plane   Air service between Vancouver and Victoria airports is operated by Air Canada (tel. toll free 800/663-3721) and Canadian Airlines (tel. toll free 800/465-3611), each with 16 daily flights. From Seattle, Horizon Air (tel. toll free 800/547-9308) has seven flights daily. Air B.C. (tel. 604/360-9074) has a harbor-to-harbor service (by seaplane) between Vancouver and Victoria. Kenmore Air (tel. toll free 800/543-9595) operates a seaplane service eight times daily between Seattle and Victoria harbors. Flights from Vancouver to Victoria take around 35 minutes.

By Bus   Pacific Coach Lines (tel. 604/385-4411) has a daily connecting service between Vancouver and Victoria, using B.C. Ferries for the crossing (see below). The fare is $21.25 one way.

By Ship and Ferry   The most pleasurable way to reach Victoria is by ship, regardless of whether you come from the U.S. or the Canadian mainland. The ocean route takes in forested islands, snowcapped mountain ranges in the distance, and occasional sights of fishing eagles and sounding killer whales to enliven the passage. Sometimes the ship's engines are drowned out by the clicking of camera shutters. From the United States you can choose to come by Black Ball Transport, Port Angeles, Wash. (tel. 206/457-4491); Washington State Ferries, Seattle, Wash. (tel. 206/464-6400), or Victoria Clipper, Seattle, Wash. (tel. toll free 800/888-2535). The Port Angeles ferries carry 800 passengers and 100 cars, take about 1½ hours and cost $44 (U.S.). The clipper is an exciting high-speed jet catamaran that carries 300 passengers but no vehicles, and takes 2½ hours from Seattle's Pier 69 to Victoria's Inner Harbour. Adult passengers pay $49 (U.S.), children $24.50 (U.S.).

The Royal Sealink Express is a 302-passenger catamaran sailing four times daily between downtown Vancouver and downtown Victoria. These craft take no vehicles and make the crossing in 2½ hours. For reservations call 604/687-6925 in Vancouver. One-way tickets for adults are $39.95; for children, $19.95.

The vast majority of travelers go by B.C. Ferries (tel. 604/685-1021). These are large vessels, carrying 360 cars and buses and 1,500 passengers. They depart daily, usually on the hour, from 7am to 9pm, from Tsawwassen, a 45-minute drive from Vancouver. One-way fare for adults is $5.50, for children $2.50, and $20 per car. The ferries arrive at Swartz Bay, where you can catch Bus no. 70 to downtown Victoria.

When you cross from Vancouver to Victoria you could momentarily believe that you've crossed the Atlantic and stepped ashore at an English seaside town. The capital of British Columbia looks so much like a mirror image of Bournemouth, Brighton, or Torquay that you glance at the flags to reassure yourself you're still in Canada.

Those glaring red double-decker buses, Tudor-style homes, manicured lawns, tea shoppes, pubs, antiques stores, and bookshops are so inimitably British that it takes a while to sink in that they are, in fact, imitations. The massive gray stone edifice of the Parliament Buildings seems specifically designed to house an English assembly. Even the street illuminations have the mellow gaslight sheen of Victorian England. It's hard to imagine that this was once a gold-rush town and fur-trading post with a very far-from-genteel clientele.

But imitation or not, Victoria is a charmer, a not-so-little jewel of a town that somehow manages to retain the atmosphere of a seaside resort while edging close to 230,000 inhabitants. Having the mildest climate and the finest gardens in Canada helps. So do the millions of tourists who swarm in annually to wander beneath the baskets of blossoms that hang from the downtown lampposts. So does the picture-postcard panorama that Rudyard Kipling once described as "Brighton Pavilion with the Himalayas for a backdrop."

Victoria was founded in the 1840s as the new western headquarters of the Hudson's Bay Company. It changed from a trading post to a rip-roaring boomtown when it became the hub of activity generated by the 1858 gold rush in the Cariboo region of British Columbia. When the Canadian Pacific Railway was being built, British Columbia joined the country as a province (with Victoria as capital) on the promise that the railroad would link its seat of government with the others.

That promise, however, went the way of a great many others. The C.P. tracks terminated at Vancouver, on the mainland, leaving the capital a backwater "deprived" of industrial expansion. Today millions of people thank history for this deprivation. The lack of factory chimneys allowed Victoria to remain a garden spot, free from slums, smog, congestion, pollution, and din, and with a bare minimum of high-rises to ruin its pretty profile. Instead it blossomed into the "bit of the old country" dream of prosperous merchants, farmers, and retired company servants from England and Scotland who fell in love with the scenery and climate.

And when you see the spotless tiled pavements, green trees, and colored awnings of Government Street, the velvet lawns along the oceanfront, the little squares and romantic alleys of Old Town, you'll probably agree that mislaid promises can turn out to be blessings.

ORIENTATION

TOURIST INFORMATION Logically and geographically, the best launching pad for sightseeing is the **Visitor Information Centre,** 812 Wharf St., Victoria, BC, V8W 1T3 (tel. 604/382-2127), right on the waterfront. With a highly knowledgeable staff, unfailing helpfulness, and an immense stock of maps, timetables, brochures, and pamphlets, the center can save you valuable holiday time and shoe leather, as well as tipping you off to local sights you might have missed otherwise. It's open daily from 9am to 6pm.

CITY LAYOUT Victoria sits on the extreme southern tip of Vancouver Island, the largest island on the Pacific coast of North America. (The city of Vancouver is *not* on Vancouver Island.) Its spectacular doorstep is the Juan de Fuca Strait, a narrow strip of water wedged in between the island and the northern portion of Washington State, dotted with smaller islands and dominated by the snowcapped peaks of the Olympic Mountains. The city actually lies closer to the U.S. than to mainland Canada.

The center and social focal point of the capital is the **Empress Hotel,** a grande dame of such regality that you get the impression the town was built around it as an afterthought. From the portals of this edifice you overlook the **Inner Harbour,** a wonderful bustle of yachts, ferries, fishing boats, launches, and seaplanes. You are now facing due west.

A few steps south rises the green-domed stone majesty of the **Parliament Buildings,** facing an enormous wooden totem pole and housing the legislative apparatus of British Columbia. Cutting through the vast lawns around this building is **Government Street,** which, running north, takes you to the post office and the city's main shopping and entertainment area. This is **Old Town** and **downtown,** a tightly entwined duality of arcades, small squares, picturesque alleys, and wide commercial streets.

Farther to the north and east stretches what is known as **Greater Victoria,** more like a patchwork of townships and villages held together by parks and gardens. Northeast lies the **University of Victoria,** and due north the enchanting Butchart Gardens, the airport, and the town of **Sidney,** and at the very tip of the peninsula, **Swartz Bay,** arrival point of the ferry from Vancouver. The ferry from Seattle lands right downtown.

GETTING AROUND

The towns of the island are linked by **Island Coach Lines,** 700 Douglas St. (tel. 604/385-4411). There's also the **VIA Rail Canada** (tel. 604/383-4324), which operates daily between Victoria and Courtenay.

Greater Victoria has the **B.C. Transit** (tel. 604/382-6161) bus service, charging $1.25 to $1.75 per ride. There are also cab companies: **Blue Bird** (tel. 604/382-4235) or **United** (tel. 604/388-9935).

Car-rental outfits include: **Tilden,** 767 Douglas St. (tel. 604/386-1213), and **Budget,** 757 Douglas St. (tel. 604/388-5525). Budget also rents out motor scooters at $8 an hour, and bicycles at $4 an hour, $16 per day.

WHAT TO SEE & DO

Some of the top local sights lie on and around **Government Street,** which runs straight through **Old Town.** On the left is **Bastion Square,** once the stomping ground of bearded miners, roistering sailors, and—appropriately—the site of the municipal gallows. Today it's an enchantingly restored pedestrian mall, with the raucousness ironed out and the facelifted old buildings crammed with boutiques and restaurants.

In the 1200 block on Government Street, a little byway runs through to Broad Street. This is **Trounce Alley,** where those selfsame miners and mariners once clustered to spend their gold. A lot of paint, soap, and affection has gone into making this wee thoroughfare a kind of welcome mat. Lit by gas lamps, hung with heraldic crests, ablaze with flower baskets and potted shrubs, Trounce Alley now offers jewelry, fashions, edibles, and greeting cards.

For the city's senior sight, however, you have to backtrack past the Empress Hotel to the **Parliament Buildings.** Opened in 1898, flanked by the awesome wooden totem pole carvings of **Thunderbird Park,** the legislature of British Columbia bears a certain resemblance to the British House of Commons, at least in the ceremonial trappings. The Speaker sits on a kind of canopied throne, escorted there by a sergeant-at-arms, and the symbol of authority is a golden mace—now purely ornamental, but originally a very handy implement to use on the heads of obstreperous members who disturbed the assembly. Daily guided tours take you through the house, and at night the building is gorgeously illuminated.

Next to Parliament lies **Heritage Court,** a superb combination of concrete buildings and native plant gardens which you enter by stepping over the petrified prints of a dinosaur. The **Netherlands Carillon,** a gift from the Dutch nation, rises like a slender white column 88 feet from the mall floor, carrying bells weighing 10,612 pounds.

ROYAL BRITISH COLUMBIA MUSEUM, Heritage Court. Tel. 604/387-3701.

One side of Heritage Court is occupied by the Royal British Columbia Museum, the most fascinating institution of its kind in Canada, perhaps in North America. The word "museum" here is a misnomer. It's a magnificently organized, artistically arranged, and magically lit tour of discovery into the past, the very distant past as much as the very recent. You walk among prehistoric native tribes and extinct animals. See the full-scale, minutely detailed replica of Captain Vancouver's HMS *Discovery.* Peer into the 19th-century "Grand Hotel," with two floors of period rooms containing 5,000 artifacts, including the liquor bottles of the time. Gaze at the model "T" Ford in the City Garage of 1913, which looks like a Norman Rockwell painting. Experience the sights and sounds of a steam railway station—I could fill the chapter with this masterpiece of a museum.

Admission: $5 adults, $2 children.
Open: Summer daily 9:30am–7pm, winter daily 10am–5:30pm.

HELMCKEN HOUSE, beside the Royal B.C. Museum. Tel. 604/387-4697.

Designed and built by a physician in the 1850s, the oldest intact dwelling in Victoria is now a showcase of colonial life in the upper middle strata. It is intriguing to note how much smaller people were only 140 years ago—we bang our heads on their doorways, and all those lovely china doorknobs are slightly below our grasp. Follow the stereo taped tour.

Admission: $3.25 adults, $1.25 children.
Open: Daily 11am–5pm.

THE ART GALLERY, 1040 Moss St. Tel. 604/384-4101.

This Victorian mansion, about a mile east of downtown, contains an excellent collection of Asian art, some superb Inuit pieces, Egyptian statuary dating back to the 6th century B.C., and contemporary Canadian works.

Admission: $4 adults; children free.
Open: Mon–Sat 10am–5pm, Sun 1–5pm.

CRYSTAL GARDENS, 713 Douglas St. Tel. 604/381-1213.

This titanic glass edifice located right behind the Empress Hotel once housed the largest saltwater swimming pool in the British Empire. Today it's a wondrous mélange of tropical plants, tropical birds, exotic reptiles, waterfalls, curious little stores, a tea garden, art gallery, and restaurant. It's difficult to label, but delightful to experience—a kind of indoor discovery jaunt.

Admission: $5 adults, $3 children.
Open: Daily 10am–5:30pm.

UNDERSEA GARDENS, 490 Belleville St. Tel. 604/382-5717.

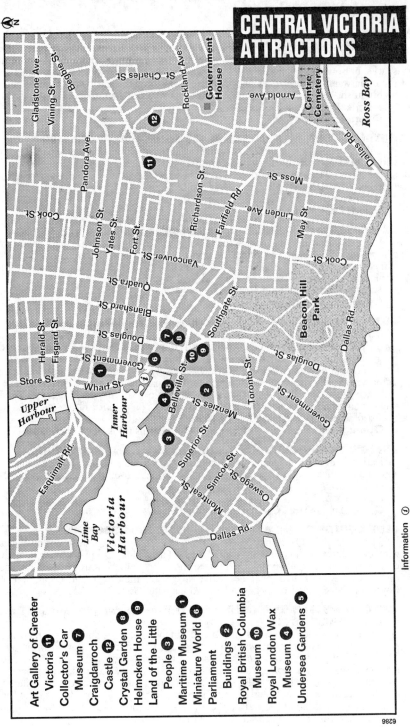

CENTRAL VICTORIA ATTRACTIONS

Ross Bay

Government House

Centre Cemetery

Beacon Hill Park

Upper Harbour

Inner Harbour

Lime Bay

Victoria Harbour

Gladstone Ave.
Bagde St.
Vining St.
St. Charles St.
Rockland Ave.
Arnold Ave.
Dallas Rd.
Pandora Ave.
Cook St.
Richardson St.
Fairfield Rd.
Moss St.
Linden Ave.
May St.
Cook St.
Johnson St.
Yates St.
Fort St.
Vancouver St.
Quadra St.
Southgate St.
Dallas Rd.
Herald St.
Fisgard St.
Blanshard St.
Douglas St.
Government St.
Store St.
Wharf St.
Belleville St.
Menzies St.
Toronto St.
Douglas St.
Government St.
Superior St.
Simcoe St.
Oswego St.
Montreal St.
Dallas Rd.
Esquimalt Rd.

Information ⓘ

Art Gallery of Greater Victoria **11**
Collector's Car Museum **7**
Craigdarroch Castle **12**
Crystal Garden **8**
Helmcken House **9**
Land of the Little People **3**
Maritime Museum **1**
Miniature World **6**
Parliament Buildings **2**
Royal British Columbia Museum **10**
Royal London Wax Museum **4**
Undersea Gardens **5**

6286

★ You walk down a gently sloping stairway to the bottom of the ocean at the Undersea Gardens. There, at eye level with the denizens, you see some 5,000 marine creatures feeding, playing, hunting, and mating. They include wolf eels, sharks, poisonous stonefish, flowerlike sea anemones, and salmon. The highlights are the underwater performances of scuba divers, featuring the star of the show: a huge, nightmarish, but remarkably photogenic octopus named Armstrong.

Admission: $6 adults, $2.75 children.
Open: Daily 9am–9pm.

ROYAL LONDON WAX MUSEUM, 470 Belleville St. Tel. 604/388-4461.

Directly opposite the Undersea Gardens stands the Royal London Wax Museum, with 300 figures from the works of Josephine Tussaud, magnificently gowned, amazingly lifelike, and set in dozens of scenes, including the obligatory Chamber of Horrors.

Admission: $6.50 adults, $3 children.
Open: Daily 9am–9pm.

COLLECTOR'S CAR MUSEUM, 813 Douglas St. Tel. 604/382-7180.

Just behind the Empress Hotel, the Classic Car Museum shows 60 years of vintage automobilia. The sheer functional beauty of some of those Rolls-Royces, Jaguars, Chryslers, and ancient Auburns makes you itch to get behind their wheels. Also on display are the Crown Jewels of England (replicas, of course).

Admission: $5 adults, $3 children.
Open: Daily noon–6pm.

BUTCHART GARDENS, 800 Benvenuto, off W. Saanich Rd. Tel. 604/652-5256.

★ The flowering gem of Vancouver Island is also a miracle of sorts. An abandoned limestone pit 14 miles north of Victoria has been transformed into a 50-acre Eden of blossoms, flowers, exotic shrubs, lawns, hedges, little bridges, and rare statuary. Actually there are six different gardens, each with an individual character, and each perfection. Illuminations, dancing fountains, Saturday-night fireworks, and evening entertainment make this a spot you simply don't want to leave.

Admission: $11 adults, $1.50 children.
Open: Summer daily 9am–10:30pm; other seasons till 4, 5, or 6pm. **Bus:** 75.

CRAIGFLOWER FARMHOUSE, 110 Island Hwy. Tel. 604/387-4697.

Dating from 1856, the manor was built for a farm bailiff and restored to its original appearance, including the household goods brought over from Scotland by its pioneering occupants.

Admission: Free.
Open: Thurs–Mon. Call for times. **Bus:** 14.

OLDE ENGLAND INN, 429 Lampson St. Tel. 604/388-4353.

Surrounding the Olde England Inn is a row of amazingly accurate Tudor dwellings with everything except the 16th-century dirt. The highlights are the painstakingly correct replicas of Shakespeare's birthplace and the equally famous thatched cottage of his wife, Anne Hathaway. The whole village was the dream and inspiration of Royal Air Force Squadron Leader Lane and his wife. **Bus:** 24 or 25.

VICTORIA BUTTERFLY WORLD, 1461 Benvenuto Ave., Brentwood Bay. Tel. 604/652-7811.

★ This paradisical patch lies en route to Butchart Gardens and is the largest live butterfly exhibit in the western hemisphere. Laid out in a gigantic atrium are tropical gardens with trees, pools, and waterfalls, swarming with butterflies from every part of the world. You walk among them and watch them sipping nectar, courting, basking, or laying their eggs. The setting is as exotic as the inhabitants, which include some astonishingly large species. Although the breeds originated in Asia, Africa, and South America, the insects were not taken from their home environment but bred on special rearing farms.

Admission: $6.50 adults, $3.50 children.
Open: Daily 10am–5pm. **Bus:** 75.

CRAIGDARROCH CASTLE, 1050 Joan Crescent. Tel. 604/592-5323.
This opulent mansion was built for coal baron Robert Dunsmuir in the 1880s. A prime example of ostentatious wealth, the 39-room structure is built like a medieval castle, turrets and all, and crammed with Persian carpets, antique furniture, stained glass, and expensive period paintings—a glimpse at how the very rich lived before income tax.
Admission: $5.50 adults, children by donation.
Open: Daily 9am-7:30pm. **Bus:** 10, 11, or 14.

MARITIME MUSEUM, Bastion Sq. Tel. 604/382-2869.
The downtown location of the Maritime Museum is marked by a huge anchor. The museum houses a wealth of artifacts and ship models connected with the province's nautical history, together with old naval uniforms, journals, and photographs—a must for shipping buffs.
Admission: $5 adults, $2 children.
Open: Daily 9:30am-4:30pm.

COOL FOR KIDS

MINIATURE WORLD, in the Empress Hotel, 649 Humboldt St. Tel. 604/385-9731.
There's a grave risk that you won't be able to get your kids—or yourself—out of the Miniature World. This is not only the most ingenious, but also the most accurate and artistic setup of its kind I've ever gaped at. The layout follows several themes—Fields of Glory, World of Dickens, Frontierland, the Canadian Pacific Railway, etc.—each so overwhelmingly detailed that you can spend hours discovering new minutiae. But the central masterpiece is The Wonderful World of the Circus. Four years in the making, this magical series of nostalgia-rousers includes 60 animations, 15,000 little people, and hundreds of buildings, the lighting and scenic effects so uncanny that you'd swear this was a live land of Lilliput. There's the circus in winter quarters, the Grand Parade through town, the performance under the Big Top, and an absolutely breathtaking Midway with 20 animated rides plus Buffalo Bill's Wild West Show shrunk to grasshopper dimensions. It's fabulous, so don't miss!
Admission: $6.50 adults, $4.50 children.
Open: Summer daily 8:30am-10pm; winter daily 9am-5pm.

LAND OF THE LITTLE PEOPLE, 321 Belleville St. Tel. 604/385-1735.
Another type of knee-high world is the Land of the Little People. Laid out in a charming garden setting is a series of toy delights: a collection of dollhouses, a model railroad (you can run it yourself), an English Village Green, a pond with playful Japanese koi fish, a 1900s-style Main Street, and a superb model of London's Tower Bridge. In between are waterfalls, Japanese dwarf bonsai trees and shrubs, a wishing pond, and a Belgian chocolate factory.
Admission: $2.75 adults, $2 children.
Open: Daily 10am-5pm.

ORGANIZED TOURS & EXCURSIONS

Vancouver Island measures about 12,400 square miles and has 350,000 inhabitants, more than half of them clustered in the extreme southern tip within or around Greater Victoria. This leaves quite a chunk of island to explore beyond the area of the capital. The most pleasant, leisurely, and luxurious way of doing it is by boat. The **British Columbia Ferry Corp.** runs cruises from Vancouver and from Victoria (tel. 604/386-3431 in Victoria).
Grayline, 700 Douglas St. (tel. 604/388-5248), runs a mixed fleet of sightseeing buses: authentic red double-deckers, imported from London, for the Victoria city jaunts, the customary parlor coaches for outside ventures. All tours depart from in front of the Empress Hotel.
The Grand City Tour departs every hour, takes in all the historic and scenic highlights of the capital (try to capture a seat on the top deck), and lasts 1½ hours. Tickets are $12.50 for adults, $6.25 for children. Tour 2A visits Butchart Gardens and

gives you a conducted tour through 30 acres of spectacular flowers, ponds, fountains, and waterfalls. The trip takes three hours and costs $27 for adults, $10.50 for children.

The **Tallyho,** 180 Goward Rd., does it in a more leisurely fashion. These are rubber-tired carriages with striped awnings above and two sturdy draft horses in front. You can't miss them—they leave every 15 minutes or so from opposite the Wax Museum, 490 Belleville St. You roll slowly and majestically through the town, the parks, and the harbor area while highly informative commentators tell you the story of quaint Victoria. The first tour leaves at 10am, the last at 7pm, and the jaunt costs $9.50 for adults, $4.75 for children (free if sitting on a lap).

Grayline Harbour Tours, 700 Douglas St. (tel. 604/388-5248), start at the boat launch in front of the Empress Hotel. The boats are deluxe sightseeing vessels with plenty of indoor/outdoor space. They show you the entire port area in a tour lasting an hour, fully narrated. Adults pay $9; children, $4.50.

For water excursions of quite a different kind you can go whale-watching with **Sea Coast Expeditions,** 1655 Ash Rd. (tel. 604/477-1818). The open boats have scheduled departures from Victoria's Inner Harbour May through September. They carry a biologist-guide and cruise the coastal waters looking for porpoises and killer whales. You also encounter harbor seals and swarms of marine birds. Protective suits (much needed) are provided and the round-trips go for 20 to 50 miles. You have a choice between a three-hour and a two-hour tour, one costing $70 for adults, $45 for children, the other $50 for adults, $25 for children. Reservations are advisable.

SPORTS & RECREATION

You can have a delightful day of **deep-sea fishing** in sheltered waters for $6 an hour (four-hour minimum). The 65-foot cruiser has an experienced skipper and a base at 1327 Beach Dr. (tel. 604/598-3369). Fishing license, tackle, and bait are available (for a small fee) at the dockside. The trips last 3½ hours and the coastal waters are scenic. Reservations are highly recommended.

SHOPPING

Downtown Victoria has several new shopping malls, all designed to blend beautifully with the old-world profile of the district. Latest on the scene is **Harbour Centre,** at Government and Courtney Streets. On two levels and air-conditioned, the square houses 25 shops selling women's and men's fashions, jewelry, and a huge variety of imports.

Market Square, at the harbor end of Johnson and Pandora Streets, is a converted and rejuvenated cluster of old theaters, hotels, and residential buildings turned into retail stores without loss of charm. Spread over three levels around a courtyard garden—with popcorn vendor, balloons, and occasional music—the place has 40 stores, restaurants, lounges, snackeries, hairdressers, and newsstands. This is summertime shopping at its nicest.

Victoria has department stores as well, but the accent here is on small, highly individualistic boutiques and specialty outlets, a large number of them dealing in imports—mostly from what used to be known as "Homeland & Empire."

At 64 Fort St. is **Victoria Handloom Ltd.** This store sells a magnificent range of Canadian handcraft products. You'll find collectors' pieces in handmade vases, bowls, and plates, beautiful jade wildlife figures, jewelry crafted by some of Canada's masters in the field, and salespeople who really know what they're selling.

Sasquatch, 1233 Government St., specializes in the famous Cowichan sweaters, bought directly from the homes of native women on Vancouver Island. Their buyer, who tours the reservation thrice weekly, is so expert that he can tell which garment was made by whom by looking at the finished piece. The sweaters come only in white, black, or gray, and are registered to guarantee authenticity.

WHERE TO STAY

Victoria, being a resort town, has the advantage of a vast selection of hostelries in central locations—most along the waterfront. It has the drawback that many of them get packed to the rafters during the peak summer season, July and August. If you intend visiting Victoria in that period, it would be a wise move to book ahead.

Don't forget that there's a 10% accommodations tax in Victoria.

EXPENSIVE

CHATEAU VICTORIA, 740 Burdett Ave., Victoria, BC, V8W 1B1. Tel. 604/382-4221, or toll free 800/663-5891. Fax 604/380-1950. 178 rms. TV TEL
$ Rates: $99 single; $126 double; $159–$189 one-bedroom suite. Special one- and two-night honeymoon packages available, including a bottle of imported champagne. AE, CB, DC, DISC, ER, MC, V. **Parking:** Free.

Dazzling white and ultramodern, this Mediterranean-style high-rise represents the last word in resort plushness. Despite caravansary bustle, the deeply carpeted lobby manages to appear elegant and tranquil. The hotel has a vast indoor swimming pool, and possibly the smoothest elevator system on the island. Thirty-two of the bedrooms have their own kitchens. All of them have small balconies, subtly soothing color schemes, and exceptionally spacious closets. Bathrooms come with large bars of soap (not the usual hotel wafers), illuminated mirrors, heat lamps, and fan.

Dining/Entertainment: The cocktail lounge has enough antique touches to give it a smoking-room atmosphere. The Parrot House rooftop restaurant combines prime cuisine with panoramic views.

Services: Free shuttle to and from downtown transport terminals.

Facilities: Vast indoor swimming pool, non-smoking floors.

EMPRESS HOTEL, 721 Government St., Victoria, BC, V8W 1W5. Tel. 604/384-8111, or toll free 800/441-1414. Fax 604/381-4334. 481 rms. A/C MINIBAR TV TEL
$ Rates: $190–$220 single; $215–$245 double; from $325 "Honeymoon Room." AE, DC, ER, MC, V. **Parking:** $9 a day.

The Empress Hotel doesn't need an address. It represents a cornerstone of Victoria, and you can no more easily miss it than you could accidentally brush past the harbor (although you might, possibly, mistake it for the legislature).

The Empress opened in 1908 and has kept enough period regality to make it an institution as much as a hotel. An ivy-banked gray stone structure, looking like a cross between a château and an art museum, the Empress has a huge lobby that even a couple of simultaneous tour busloads can't clutter completely. The hallways are lofty, the service smooth, with a touch of assured pride. The bedrooms have the stamp of serene and slightly subdued elegance that distinguishes hotels of this class—no screaming murals or canned Mantovani for this lady.

Dining/Entertainment: Tea in the lobby, served afternoons, is an occasion—like having a cuppa with a dowager queen: homemade scones and crumpets, Devonshire cream, silver teapots, and all, with the chance of a movie star or two hovering in the background (reservations are essential and the event costs $17.50). There's also one of the finest restaurants in town, an informal yet elegant garden café, and two bars.

Facilities: Indoor swimming pool, exercise room, ballroom.

GAMESDAY

During August 1994 the Commonwealth Games will be held in Victoria. Accommodation is expected to be rather tight for that period. Gamesday is an outfit specially set up for the occasion and will provide alternative lodgings in private homes. Apply to Gamesday, Victoria Tourism, 1175 Douglas St., Suite 110, Victoria, BC, V8W 2E1 (tel. toll free 800/663-2883).

EXECUTIVE HOUSE, 777 Douglas St., Victoria, BC, V8W 2B5. Tel. 604/388-5111, or toll free 800/663-7001. Fax 604/385-1323. 180 rms. TV TEL
$ Rates: $78–$159 single or double. Children under 18 free. AE, CB, DC, DISC, ER, MC, V. **Parking:** $2 daily.

This gleaming glass tower soars above the downtown area and features a small, smart lobby. Mostly ultramodern, but in top taste, the reception area is furnished with black leather settees that not only look good but rank among the most comfortable I've ever relaxed in.

The bedrooms, in matching blue, gray, and peach shades, are both elegant and streamlined. The open walk-in closet occupies an entire corner, and the little balconies provide wonderful views. There's a bedside clock radio, caressing carpeting, and in-room coffee and tea.

Dining/Entertainment: An arcade floor offers an oyster bar and banquet rooms, and an English pub-inspired grill, complete with Tiffany-style lamps and antiques.

Services: Complimentary shuttle to transport links.

Facilities: There's an excellent health spa with Jacuzzi and steamroom.

HARBOUR TOWERS, 345 Québec St., Victoria, BC, V8V 1W4. Tel. 604/385-2405, or toll free 800/663-5896. Fax 604/385-4453. 184 rms. TV TEL
$ Rates: $85–$106 single or double; $120–$500 suite. AE, CB, DC, ER, MC, V. **Parking:** $2 per day.

This hotel was designed for views. Most rooms have one, either across the harbor or the Juan de Fuca Strait—take your pick. Looking like a luxurious apartment block, the Towers' stylish reception lies off the lobby of the Impressions restaurant in the same building.

Victoria's fastest and most silent elevators waft you up to the bedrooms. The decor is pastel-colored and beautiful, the contemporary furnishings charming, the compact bathrooms equipped with heat lamps, but the views beat every other type of comfort—they make the rooms.

Dining/Entertainment: The restaurant serves West Coast cuisine.

Services: Complimentary shuttle service to downtown.

Facilities: Also on the premises are a swimming pool, hydrotherapy pool, and sauna.

HOTEL GRAND PACIFIC, 450 Québec St., Victoria, BC, V8V 1W5. Tel. 604/386-0450, or toll free 800/663-7550. Fax 604/386-8779. A/C MINIBAR TV TEL
$ Rates: $165 single or double; $260 suite. Extra person $15. AE, DC, DISC, ER, MC, V. **Parking:** Free.

A large green-roofed, European-style building, the Hotel Grand Pacific resembles a French turn-of-the-century structure, but is actually brand new. Behind the Edwardian front the interior is up-to-the-minute. Bedrooms have private balconies, spacious writing desks, coffee makers, and Spectravision movies. No-smoking rooms are available on request.

Dining/Entertainment: There's a vast and sophisticated dining room.

Facilities: The amenities include a lavishly equipped Business Centre, boardrooms with audiovisual systems, and a Fitness Spa that includes an Olympic-size swimming pool, massage room, racquetball courts, sauna, and whirlpool, plus a weight center with Universal Circuit training and an aerobics center with TV monitor.

MODERATE

BEACONSFIELD INN, 998 Humboldt St., Victoria, BC, V8V 2Z8. Tel. 604/384-4044. 12 rms.
$ Rates (including breakfast): $100–$198 single or double. MC, V. **Parking:** Free.

Billed as an "Edwardian hotel," this is a restored mansion built in the opulent style of 80 years ago. White with blue trimmings, in a quiet tree-lined residential location, the Beaconsfield retained its mansion exterior while upgrading the comforts inside. The rooms have private bathrooms (most un-Edwardian) and down comforters; the hotel has a library that serves as a social gathering spot, and the breakfast included in the rates is a full-fledged meal—none of your "continental" morning snacks. Each room has a different decor (and different price); some with fireplaces and private Jacuzzi.

CREST HARBOURVIEW INN, 455 Belleville St., Victoria, BC, V8V 1X3. Tel. 604/386-2421. Fax 604/386-8779. 84 rms. TV TEL

$ Rates: From $105 single; from $115 double. AE, DC, DISC, ER, MC, V. **Parking:** Free.

Standing directly across the street from the U.S. ferries, this hotel has Victoria's harbor on its doorstep. You can watch the day-long holiday promenade along the waterfront from the patio of the coffee shop, which serves excellent al fresco lunches. The same panoramic vista invades the dining lounge and cocktail bar. The bedrooms are pleasantly furnished: carpeted in scarlet hues and equipped with sliding-door wardrobes, comfy armchairs, and eight drawers to give you ample storage space. Three overhead and two desk lamps provide illumination. Guests get complimentary use of the luxuriously equipped Aquatic Centre at the Grand Pacific Hotel.

EMBASSY MOTOR INN, 520 Menzies St., Victoria, BC, V8V 2H4. Tel. 604/382-8161. Fax 604/382-4224. 103 rms. A/C TV TEL

$ Rates: $55–$125 single; $65–$125 double. Kitchen facilities $10 extra. Rates depend on the wing. AE, DC, MC, V. **Parking:** Free.

The Embassy Motor Inn is an intriguing duality consisting of an older, smaller unit overlooking the Inner Harbour and a soaring new tower addition overlooking everything. The rooms of the new wing have air conditioning and private balconies. The older units are somewhat simpler, but all come with fine carpeting, sliding-door closets, and excellent lighting. The inn has a heated outdoor pool, restaurant, and cocktail lounge.

INN ON THE HARBOUR, 427 Belleville St., Victoria, BC, V8V 1X3. Tel. and fax 604/386-3451. 69 rms. TV TEL

$ Rates: $57–$125. AE, DC, MC, V. **Parking:** Free.

The inn does indeed overlook the harbor and it offers an outdoor terrace café from which to watch the marine action with a drink in your hand and a sunshade over your head. A modern, comfortable four-story hostelry, the inn has a good seafood restaurant and a vaguely nautical cocktail lounge. The rooms are on the small side, nicely carpeted and comfortable, but not luxurious, with ornate hanging lamps and slip-proof bathtub. While there's only limited hanging space for two people, there are pleasing ocean views and very handy bedside TV switches.

INNER HARBOUR, 412 Québec St., Victoria, BC, V8V 1W5. Tel. and fax 604/384-5122, or toll free 800/528-1234. 65 rms, 7 suites. TV TEL

$ Rates (including continental breakfast): $99–$119 single or double; $139–$250 suite. AE, DC, DISC, ER, MC, V. **Parking:** Free.

 A red six-story former apartment block, the Inner Harbour—now a Best Western—has a kitchenette with every bedroom, plus amenities like a guest laundry, an extra-large Jacuzzi, an indoor sauna, and a heated outdoor swimming pool. The rooms have very attractive modern furnishings, vast beds, TV sets discreetly hidden in cupboards, and excellent illumination. The rooms come with little private balconies, writing desks, and clock radios with wakeup alarms. The sliding door wardrobes and deep drawers provide generous hanging and folding space; emerald green carpets and drapes, a cheerfully tranquil background. You get baskets filled with shampoos and body lotions in the bathrooms and electric coffee makers in the kitchens. You can prepare your own morning cuppa—the small breakfast room downstairs tends to get crowded.

OLDE ENGLAND INN, 429 Lampson St., Victoria, BC, V9A 5Y9. Tel. 604/388-4353. Fax 604/382-8311. 50 rms. TV TEL

$ Rates: $70–$98 single or double; $114–$180 special "Honeymoon Room." AE, DC, MC, V. **Parking:** Free.

The Olde England Inn lies five minutes by bus from downtown, but seems to have turned back the clock by four centuries. The hotel forms part of an entire Elizabethan village: a thatched, beamed, and shingled replica of Stratford in the reign of Queen Bess. The inn itself is a museum. You enter by a baronial hall, replete with suits of armor, ancient weaponry, banners, and a huge copper-canopied fireplace. The bedrooms are all individually furnished, some with antiques and authentic European canopy beds (used, we are told, by assorted continental monarchs). Standing on a bluff amid five acres of gorgeous grounds, the inn combines Tudor trappings with all-modern bathroom facilities. For good measure you also get magnificent vistas of sea and mountains.

ROYAL SCOT INN, 425 Québec St., Victoria, BC, V8V 1W7. Tel. 604/388-5463. Fax 604/388-5452. 178 rms. TV TEL
$ Rates: $99–$159 single or double. AE, DC, ER, MC, V. **Parking:** Free.
There's nothing very Scottish about this place except the shingle. A big, attractively modern motel with a great many facilities, the Scot serves traditional high tea as well as other meals, and has a heated indoor pool and a well-equipped health spa with exercise bikes, weight machines, Jacuzzi, and sauna. Most of the units come with their own fair-sized kitchens. Bedrooms are brightly contemporary and have Cablevision and exceptionally comfortable couches.

SHAMROCK MOTEL, 675 Superior St., Victoria, BC, V8V 1V1. Tel. 604/385-8768. Fax 604/385-1837. 15 rms. TV TEL
$ Rates: $79–$99 single or double. Extra person $10. AE, MC, V. **Parking:** Free.
This small corner building faces the vast green expanse of Beacon Hill Park. A large communal balcony runs along the entire front of the structure. Each of the units is self-contained, comprising a big sitting room, bedroom, bathroom, and all-electric kitchen with refrigerator and utensils—a real moneysaver for two or more people. The furnishings are comfortable if not stylish, with writing desks, sliding-door closets and cupboards, large and springy beds, standing, table, and bedside lamps, and somewhat lurid color prints on the walls.

BUDGET

ADMIRAL MOTEL, 257 Belleville St., Victoria, BC, V8V 1X1. Tel. and fax 604/388-6267. 29 rms. TV TEL
$ Rates: Summer $79–$125 double occupancy. Extra person $6. Children under 12 stay free in parents' room. AE, DISC, ER, MC, V. **Parking:** Free.
A small, quiet, modern establishment, the Admiral sits on the harborfront overlooking the water. Some of the units have their own kitchens and can house up to six

---

AN IMPORTANT NOTE ON PRICES

Unless stated otherwise, **the prices cited in this guide are given in Canadian dollars,** which is good news for U.S. travelers because the Canadian dollar is worth 25% less than the American dollar, but buys nearly as much. As we go to press, $1 Canadian is worth 75¢ U.S., which means that your $100-a-night hotel room will cost only U.S. $75, and your $6 breakfast costs only U.S. $4.50.

Here's a quick table of equivalents:

Canadian $	U.S. $
$ 1	$ 0.75
5	3.75
10	7.50
20	15.00
50	37.50
80	60.00
100	75.00
200	150.00

people. The rooms are quite attractive, the furnishings comfortable, lighting arrangements ample. All units have color cable TV.

HOTEL DOUGLAS, 1450 Douglas St., Victoria, BC, V8W 2G1. Tel. 604/383-4157. Fax 604/383-2279. 67 rms (half with bath). TV TEL
$ Rates: $55–$60 single; $65–$70 double. AE, DC, ER, MC, V. **Parking:** Free.
An elderly brick corner building, the Douglas, located downtown, has a small lobby offering seating facilities, a bar on one side, a coffee shop on the other. The elevator is good, the corridors quiet and well kept. The bedrooms are divided into regular and sleeping rooms—the latter are cheaper and share bath facilities in the hallways. Regular rooms come nicely furnished, and have modern bathrooms, large walk-in closets, and heavy window drapes. There's good illumination from ceiling, bedside, and desk lamps. All the rooms display framed religious texts of no particular denomination.

STRATHCONA HOTEL, 919 Douglas St., Victoria, BC, V8W 2C2. Tel. and fax 604/383-7137. 80 rms. TV TEL
$ Rates: $35–$75 single; $45–$85 double. AE, CB, DC, DISC, ER, MC, V. **Parking:** Free.
 This older structure also serves as a major entertainment center. It has a small lobby with touches of greenery and completely renovated bedrooms all nicely but functionally furnished, all with open closets, color TVs, and compact little bathrooms. Lighting facilities are good—overhead as well as bedside—and the carpeting is wall to wall. There's a lot of nocturnal action downstairs, but the sounds don't reach the living quarters.

VICTORIA PLAZA, 603 Pandora Ave., Victoria, BC, V8W 1N8. Tel. 604/386-3631. Fax 604/386-9452. 45 rms. TV TEL
$ Rates: Budget bunk bed $24 single; regular rooms $64.50 single, $69.50 double. AE, MC, V. **Parking:** Free.
A small, colorful, and modernistic establishment in the heart of downtown, the Victoria Plaza has a very lively entertainment portion, consisting of a pub featuring exotic dancers and a cabaret, plus a restaurant. The hotel also offers budget bunk beds (singles only).

On Gorge Road

Victoria's motel row is Gorge Road, about a mile north of the city center, with excellent bus connections to downtown. A rather industrialized and not overly handsome thoroughfare, Gorge Road is studded with hostelries in the medium and budget price ranges. Some of the selections there belong to the first, others to the second bracket, and you'll find them under the appropriate headings. But there are plenty more along the road.

CHESTNUT GROVE, 210 Gorge Rd. East, Victoria, BC, V9A 1L5. Tel. 604/385-3488. 18 rms. TV TEL
$ Rates: From $40 single; from $45 double. AE, MC, V. **Parking:** Free.
A small motel with a pretty blue and gray-stone frontage, the Chestnut also has a little pool in the rear. The units are modern and neat, 10 of them with private kitchen. You get wall-to-wall red carpets, extra-long beds, walnut-hued writing desks, and bathrooms with fiberglass tubs and heat lamps. Some rooms have an open hanging space instead of a closet.

MAPLE LEAF INN, 120 Gorge Rd. East, Victoria, BC, V9A 1L3. Tel. 604/388-9901. 64 rms. A/C TV TEL
$ Rates: $48 single; $56 double. Rooms with kitchenettes $10 extra. Extra person $8. AE, MC, V. **Parking:** Free.
The Maple Leaf Inn resembles a chalet with a swimming pool and sauna. About half of the units have their own kitchen, and all come equipped with queen-size beds or (on request) water beds. Very pleasantly furnished, they include bathrooms with heat lamps, large folding-door closets, message service, and complimentary morning coffee (rather rare in Canadian lodgings). Amenities include an outdoor pool and sauna.

PACIFIC ISLE MOTEL, 626 Gorge Rd. East, Victoria, BC, V8T 2W6. Tel. 604/385-3455. 24 rms. TV TEL

$ Rates: $35–$50 single; $38–$54 double. ER, MC, V. **Parking:** Free.

 The Pacific Isle looks very simple from the outside but contains good-size, well-maintained units, six with kitchen, and all with private bath, red carpeting, walk-in closets, and color TV. The kitchens are quite spacious and there's a little dinette to eat in. The motel has no restaurant, but a 24-hour diner lies just across the road.

BED-AND-BREAKFAST

Victoria abounds with this type of accommodation, and most considerably superior to the mainland breed. Many of the houses concerned are charmingly atmospheric period pieces, the hosts bestow more TLC on their guests, and you get greater variety in the rates charged.

ANDERSEN HOUSE, 301 Kingston St., Victoria, BC, V8V 1V5. Tel. 604/388-4565. 3 rms.

$ Rates (including breakfast): $65–$125 based on double occupancy. Extra person $15. MC, V.

Built in 1892 for a sea captain, Andersen House is a trim, modernized structure with high ceilings, stained-glass windows, and some original artwork. The three rooms are individually furnished (one is a self-contained apartment) and the place has a lovely English garden. Breakfast is hearty and the location is a few minutes from downtown. No smoking in the house and "children over 8 are welcome."

MARIDOU HOUSE, 116 Eberts St., Victoria, BC, V8S 3H7. Tel. 604/360-0747. Fax 604/598-1210. 3 rms, 1 suite.

$ Rates (including breakfast): $45–$95. Extra person $20. MC, V. **Parking:** Available.

An Edwardian home from the turn of the century, the Maridou has quiet sunny rooms furnished with antiques—and no TVs. There is a special Honeymoon Suite with a private Jacuzzi, but other rooms share bathroom. A large breakfast is served in the small dining room. The house stands half a block from the waterfront and has a bus stop at the door.

RENFREE COTTAGE, 149 Rendall St., Victoria, BC, V8V 2E3. Tel. 604/389-1598. 3 rms.

$ Rates: $75 single; $95 double. MC, V.

This cottage has been restored to combine period flavor with modern comfort. It has fireplaces and an antique chandelier, and private bath and kitchenette. The no-smoking rule of the house, however, is strictly 1990s.

WHYTE HOUSE, 155 Rendall St., Victoria, BC, V8V 2E3. Tel. 604/389-1598. 3 rms.

$ Rates: From $45 single; $100–$120 double. Children $15. Pets "considered" at $5. MC, V.

This Heritage Home, built in 1889, is adjoined by a beautiful flower garden. Guests get the entire upper floor, consisting of two bedrooms, living room, kitchen, bathroom, and private entrance. Breakfast choices range from "low calorie" to "full" (very).

THE Ys

YWCA, 880 Courtney St., Victoria, BC, V8W 1C4. Tel. 604/386-7511. 20 beds (no rms with private bath).

$ Rates: $31 single; $46 double. All charges payable in advance. MC, V. **Parking:** Not available.

 Victoria's YMCA and YWCA are both housed in the same building. Although providing facilities for both sexes, the residence part is for women only. A massive, modern brown-brick building with a bright, spacious lobby and inviting green leather settees, the Y has a cafeteria (closed on Sunday) and a total of 20 beds in single and double rooms. The rooms are bright and quite natty, but have neither private bath nor sink. There is a shared bathroom, and the telephone is likewise communal. A cozy TV lounge downstairs and coin laundry and a coed swimming pool are available.

A HOSTEL

INTERNATIONAL HOSTEL, 516 Yates St., Victoria, BC, V8W 1K8. Tel. 604/385-4511. Fax 604/385-3232. 104 beds.
$ Rates: $13.50 IYH members; $18.50 nonmembers.
Unlike most of the species, this International Hostel is situated right downtown. Simple but well equipped with two kitchens, TV lounge, games room, showers, and laundry facilities, the hostel has 104 beds, mostly in dormitories but also in four family rooms.

RV PARKS & CAMPGROUNDS

Maple Bank RV Park, 1 Maple Bank Rd., off Admirals Road (tel. 604/384-0441), located by the water, has a campground with electric hookups, showers, and a boat ramp. It's close to a shopping mall. Pets are welcome. Fees are $10 self-contained, $10 for tenting.
   West Bay RV Park, 453 Head St. (tel. 604/385-1831), just across the harbor, about 1¼ miles from downtown, has waterfront sites with full hookups, laundry, and hot showers. Oriented toward adults, West Bay has water taxi service to the Empress Hotel during the summer and arranges fishing charters and harbor cruises. No tents.

WHERE TO DINE

Victoria has a generally wonderful selection of eateries, ranging from deluxe gourmet chambers to economy quickies. As in most resort towns, the budget meals cost slightly more than the Canadian average, and during the high-pressure summer months the restaurants tend to get pretty crowded. There are some—but far too few—outdoor cafés, a deficiency the town shares with every Anglo-Saxon city on the face of the globe.

EXPENSIVE

ANTOINE'S, 2 Centennial Sq. Tel. 604/384-7055.
   Cuisine: FRENCH. **Reservations:** Accepted.
$ Prices: Appetizers $6.50–$7.50; main courses $16.50–$23.75. AE, MC, V.
   Open: Dinner daily 5:30–10pm.
Situated next to McPherson Playhouse is an after-theater restaurant in the classic tradition. You can, in fact, buy a special theater ticket and dinner package at the playhouse box office in one purchase—the only such arrangement I have come across. But dining at Antoine's is an event by itself. The floors are marble, the plates bone china, the glasses Waterford crystal, and the romantic illumination the product of sterling silver candelabra. The special feature here is a five-course dinner, which changes every week. (Coffee counts as a course.) I had barbecued pork slices wrapped in cabbage leaves and served with plum sauce, a crisply fresh garden salad, a bouillabaisse continental, containing a deliciously tangy array of ocean edibles, and a light and sweet orange mousse. The Theatre Menu, likewise changed weekly, is one course shorter.

CAPTAIN'S PALACE, 309 Belleville St. Tel. 604/388-9191.
   Cuisine: SEAFOOD. **Reservations:** Recommended.
$ Prices: Appetizers $6; main courses $12.95–$14.95. AE, DC, ER, MC, V.
   Open: Daily 7:30am–10pm.
The Captain's Palace has such a nautical trim that it would seem sacrilegious to order anything but seafood. The white-pillared, blue-roofed mansion dates from 1897, and you dine in the captain's living room, gazing at the sea through bay windows. The table spreads are works of art, the walls hung with the tall ships bearing the proud names of *Cutty Sark* and *Thermopylae*. The stained glass, frescoes, fireplaces, and built-in buffets evoke the era of the four-masters—at least the

plush side of it. The atmosphere is serene and leisurely, and so is the service: plenty of time to admire the superb oak-paneled foyer and vast antique collection of this city landmark. Try the steamed clams—served in their own juice—as gala premiere, followed by the fresh spring salmon steak poached in a court bouillon. For dessert, the Venetian cream is created from creams, brandy, and liqueurs.

The Palace is also a small Victorian hotel, and it's open for tea.

CHAUNEY'S, 614 Humboldt St. Tel. 604/385-4512.
   Cuisine: SEAFOOD. **Reservations:** Recommended.
$ **Prices:** Appetizers $3.95-$6.95; main courses $10.95-$21.95. AE, DC, ER, MC, V.
   Open: Lunch Mon–Fri 11:30am–2:30pm; dinner daily 5–10pm.
There are touches of Victoriana at Chauney's, although the host and chef are Dutch. Chauney's foyer is hung with outstanding feasting scenes and uniforms from the Crimean War, plus a changing array of contemporary art. The dining room breathes subdued luxury: a combination of swelling settees, soundless carpets, soft lighting, and a general air of total devotion to the pleasures of gastronomy and classical music. The menu carefully separates local seafood from the imported delicacies—a practice other establishments should follow. You can start with oysters Florentine and follow up with Nova Scotia lobster. For dessert, try possibly the richest Belgian chocolate ice cream on the island.

EMPRESS ROOM, in the Empress Hotel, 721 Government St. Tel. 604/384-8111.
   Cuisine: ENGLISH. **Reservations:** Recommended.
$ **Prices:** Appetizers $7.50-$10.25; main courses $23-$29.50. AE, DC, ER, MC, V.
   Open: Dinner daily 6–10pm.
⭐ In this palatial dining chamber, the chandeliers glow amber, the ornately carved wood ceiling might have been transplanted from a royal banquet hall, and George C. Scott could be dining at the next table. A pleasantly subdued pianist carries you through your courses. Service is in the grand tradition, and the fare matches the decor: cream of tomato and gin soup or smoked B.C. trout for starters; then, say, the breast of pheasant Aldergrove; then coffee and Grand Marnier.

MODERATE

CAFE MEXICO, 1425 Store St., Market Square. Tel. 604/386-5454.
   Cuisine: MEXICAN. **Reservations:** Recommended.
$ **Prices:** Appetizers $2.25-$6.50; main courses $3.25-$10.95. AE, MC, V.
   Open: Lunch daily 11:30am–2:30pm; dinner daily 5:30–11pm.
Red brick outside but cantina-style inside, the Café Mexico is spacious, relaxed, reasonably authentic, and highly popular. Cactus plants and bullfight posters supply south-of-the-border atmosphere. Some of the dishes have been modified for Anglo palates, others are pungent enough to satisfy purists. All the traditional Mexican favorites are on the menu and helpings are huge. Try the pollo chipolte (chicken with melted cheese), the chiles rellenos, and enchiladas.

CASA FINESTRA, 128 Johnson St. Tel. 604/386-8770.
   Cuisine: ITALIAN. **Reservations:** Accepted.
$ **Prices:** Appetizers $2.95-$4.95; main courses $7.50-$10.95. MC, V.
   Open: Daily 11:30am–11pm.
A corner building with an outdoor patio, the Casa generates a warm southern Italian ambience only slightly marred by noisy background music—mostly pops. White-washed walls, wooden floorboards, and low ceiling lamps make for a cozy intimate setting. Service is fast and smiling as well as efficient; an unusual combination. The herb bread comes in heaped baskets and in biblical style: with oil instead of butter. The house specialties are veal and chicken; pollo scaloppine cooked in olive oil and veal médaillons pan-fried in white wine with mushrooms and green onions. Excellent house wine by the glass.

CHERRY BANK HOTEL, 825 Burdett Ave. Tel. 604/385-5380.

Cuisine: RIBS. **Reservations:** Accepted.
$ Prices: Three-course rib specials $11.95. AE, DC, MC, V.
Open: Lunch daily 11:30am–2pm; dinner daily 5–9pm.
This atmospheric landmark hotel was built in 1897. Since the 1950s it has acquired local fame as Victoria's top-rated sparerib house. A welcome modern addition is the lounge patio where you eat periodically to the tunes of a pretty authentic honky-tonk piano. The spareribs come in king and queen sizes, and are accompanied by salad and garlic bread.

CHEZ PIERRE, 512 Yates St. Tel. 604/388-7711.
Cuisine: FRENCH. **Reservations:** Recommended.
$ Prices: Appetizers $6.95–$7.95; main courses $18.50–$24.50. AE, MC, V.
Open: Lunch Mon–Sat 11:30am–2:30pm; dinner Mon–Sat 5:30–9:30pm.
Chez Pierre stands in the very heart of Old Town, where it belongs. A small, delightfully authentic French dinery, it's a magnet for those locals who know about Gallic food and the tourists they tell about it. For all its reputation, the Pierre is not overly expensive—but it's frequently hard to get into. Don't miss the escargots; then try to make up your mind between the canard à l'orange (duck in orange sauce) or the rack of lamb, both terrific.

DA TANDOOR, 1010 Fort St. Tel. 604/384-6333.
Cuisine: INDIAN. **Reservations:** Accepted.
$ Prices: Appetizers $2.50–$7.95; main courses $7.95–$15.95. MC, V.
Open: Dinner daily 5–10:30pm.
Da Tandoor is an elaborately beautiful East Indian restaurant with a small dining patio in front. The interior gleams with ornamental copperware, wafted by an aromatic mixture of spices and incense, with soft, melancholy sitar strains in the background, and quietly impeccable service. The menu is vast and takes some studying. There are cold and hot appetizers like shrimp pakora (marinated in yogurt and ginger), a hearty mulligatawny soup, and plates of Indian tidbits called samosas. The lamb and beef dishes, like saag gosht, are offered, along with vegetarian selections. Special Indian desserts include rasmalai (sweetened cheese served with almonds).

JAPANESE VILLAGE, 734 Broughton St. Tel. 604/382-5165.
Cuisine: JAPANESE. **Reservations:** Accepted.
$ Prices: Appetizers $4–$5.75; main courses $15.25–$21.50. AE, CB, DC, ER, MC, V.
Open: Lunch Mon–Fri 11:30am–2pm; dinner daily 5–10:30pm.
Japanese Village features the traditional teppan tables with the cooking surfaces built into the top. The "tradition," however, is fairly new, since these tables were specifically designed for benighted Westerners whose legs rebelled against the standard Japanese floor-level facilities. The chefs prepare each meal at the table, combining cooking with juggling skills in a dazzling display of flashing knives and dissected vittles. You get all the famous teppan delicacies: shrimp, steak teriyaki, scallops, kamaboko, hibachi chicken, etc., fervently hoping that your chef's fingers won't be added to the menu (they haven't lost one yet). Your best bet here is one of the complete dinners that include samplings from most of the items.

KWONGTUNG, 548 Fisgard St. Tel. 604/381-1223.
Cuisine: CHINESE. **Reservations:** Accepted.
$ Prices: Appetizers $7.50–$9; main courses $8.50–$15.95. AE, MC, V.
Open: Lunch daily 11am–3pm; dinner daily 5–10pm.
Victoria's one-street Chinatown—Fisgard Street—virtually consists of restaurants wall to wall. This is a large, spacious upstairs dinery, with scarlet table linen and napkins that show and elucidate the Chinese zodiac. Tea arrives with your order. The large cocktail bar and extensive drink selection, plus huge portions, contribute to Wong's popularity. There is an excellent array of hot-pot dishes like ginger and onion beef or oysters with ginger and onions. Otherwise I'd recommend the honey-garlic spareribs or the breaded almond chicken. Chopsticks are available on request.

MILLOS, 716 Burdett St. Tel. 604/382-4422.
Cuisine: GREEK. **Reservations:** Accepted.

$ Prices: Appetizers $4.50–$6.95; main courses $11.95–$24.95. AE, DC, ER, MC, V.
Open: Lunch daily 11:30am–2pm; dinner daily 4:30–11pm.

When you see a shining white, red-shingled windmill with turning sails, you'll know it's Millos. The interior is a scenario of cool tiles, white walls, and green ferns, waiters in Greek costumes, and an aroma that hones your taste buds. You can't do better than the egg-and-lemon soup; then either the moussaka or the kota kapama (chicken slowly simmered in tomato sauce with wine). For dessert, try the classic baklava (which is Turkish) and Greek coffee (which is excellent).

THE NUTSHELL, 627 Fort St. Tel. 604/383-6142.
 Cuisine: ENGLISH/CANADIAN. **Reservations:** Accepted.
$ Prices: Main courses $6.25–$9.95. MC, V.
 Open: Mon–Sat 11am–8pm.

The Nutshell seems like a memento from an earlier, staider epoch of the island capital. A quiet, spick-and-span old-world dining room, fully air-conditioned, the Nutshell serves plain, economy-priced Anglo-Canadian fare at rather limited hours—definitely not for a night carouser. You can get three grilled lamb chops with two vegetables and steamed potato, or liver with bacon and fried onions. Homemade berry pie is offered in season.

OLDE ENGLAND INN, 429 Lampson St. Tel. 604/388-4353.
 Cuisine: ENGLISH. **Reservations:** Recommended.
$ Prices: Appetizers $6–$8; main courses $14–$30. AE, DC, MC, V.
 Open: Lunch daily 11:30am–3:30pm; dinner daily 5–9pm.

The dining room of the establishment listed in "Where to Stay," above, is so good that it rates a separate mention. It has the ambience of a baronial manor house (with appropriately costumed staff), snowy table linen, swords on the walls, with just enough informality to let you relax. The menu is in tune with the decor: Cumberland broth (consommé with mushrooms and laced with port), English mixed grill, rabbit pye (the traditional spelling) with juniper berries and currants, and a truly mighty roast loin of beef à la Henry VIII. In conclusion, try the classic English sherry trifle—which was invented by the very French M. Escoffier.

PABLO'S, 225 Québec St. Tel. 604/388-4255.
 Cuisine: SPANISH/FRENCH. **Reservations:** Recommended.
$ Prices: Appetizers $4.50–$8.95; main courses $13.95–$30. AE, MC, V.
 Open: Dinner daily 5:30–11pm.
Pablo's is housed in a beautifully refurbished old Edwardian home near the Inner Harbour. It's equally famous for its Spanish food and its Spanish coffee, presented with a kind of ritual fire dance by Pablo in person—quite scary if you're unprepared for the spectacle. The lobster here is live, and you can pick out your own feast. If you've had enough of seafood, go for the gazpacho soup, the marinated chicken tikka, and the crème caramel. Service tends to be leisurely.

THE RATHSKELLER, 1205 Quadra St. Tel. 604/386-9348.
 Cuisine: GERMAN. **Reservations:** Accepted.
$ Prices: Appetizers $4.25–$5.95; main courses $10.95–$15.95. AE, DC, MC, V.
 Open: Mon–Sat 11:30am–10pm, Sun 4:30–10pm.

The Rathskeller has the look of a real "keller" with a low ceiling resting on whitewashed pillars. You sit on wooden peasant chairs, surrounded by candle glow and heraldic emblems, listen to Bavarian brass and zither music, and admire the motto of the establishment: "The boss . . . is the cook!" The fare is authentic German, with a few western dishes for balance: soup with liver dumplings, beef roulade, seven varieties of schnitzel, rich cheesecake, and more. Instead of the customary beer (you can get a "boot" of it) you might try the delightfully tart B.C. cider.

RATTENBURY'S, at the corner of Douglas and Belleville Sts. Tel. 604/381-1333.
 Cuisine: INTERNATIONAL. **Reservations:** Accepted.
$ Prices: Appetizers $6.95–$9.95; main courses $8.50–$16.95. AE, MC, V.

Open: Daily 11:30am–10pm.

Rattenbury's is another of those famed Victorian charmers, but in a moderate price bracket. Housed in a historic mansion downtown, Rattenbury's boasts one of the largest selections of imported beers on the island, outstanding service, and an atmosphere simultaneously stylish and relaxed, plus a very pleasant outdoor eating area, where you can watch the city stroll by. The fare is mainly beef and seafood, the latter as fresh as it should be in a harbor town. The children's menu has puzzles kids can solve while waiting.

ROMEO'S, 760 Johnson St. Tel. 604/383-2121.
   Cuisine: PIZZA. **Reservations:** Accepted.
$ **Prices:** Pizzas $5.30–$20.95. AE, MC, V.
   Open: Daily 11am–3 or 4am.

Romeo's is probably the handsomest pizza place on the island—gleaming white, with glass walls, and well-groomed greenery growing all around. Romeo's serves a great many other dishes, but the pizzas, made with the house special tomato sauce, have been acclaimed as the best in town. They come in regular, medium, and large sizes, and 24 varieties, all with grated mozzarella.

SMITTY'S, 850 Douglas St. Tel. 604/383-5612.
   Cuisine: CANADIAN. **Reservations:** Accepted.
$ **Prices:** Most items $5.95–$8.95. MC, V.
   Open: Daily 6:30am–midnight.

A big, air-conditioned, and brightly lit establishment, Smitty's is a family eatery with the accent on the offspring. The place is nicely carpeted, has laminated tables and very fast service, and is generally a godsend for tourist groups. It serves 16 species of pancakes and waffles, as well as broiled steak sandwiches, fried shrimp, and other such.

SPECIALTY DINING

FISH & CHIPS   What pasta is to Italy, fish-and-chips is to England—and almost to Victoria. The number of fish-and-chip places in and around town is legion and the fare is cheap. But it's an acquired taste, and you will never acquire it if you're prejudiced against grease. And since the fish comes fried in batter there is a tendency for the batter to blot out the flavor of the fish. The quality dispensaries are those that make the batter light enough to enable you to actually taste the fish. This depends on the resident chefs—who change with great frequency. Try the **Cook Street Fish & Chips,** 252 Cook St. at Beacon Hill Park (tel. 604/384-1856). Portions, served with coleslaw, start at $4.95, and the place is open daily from 9am to 9pm.

A DELI   Deli dining is *not* a Victorian characteristic and you won't find many such establishments around town. But there is one right in the heart of tourist territory, and most of the time it's packed. **Sam's Deli,** 805 Government St. (tel. 604/382-8424), was one of the first to set up shop on the island and a pioneer of sidewalk café service. It is still one of the best people-watching vantages in Victoria. Don't expect New York–style noshables. This, after all, is the West Coast. People come for the huge shrimp sandwiches, the spinach and Caesar salads, the clam chowder, or the ploughman's platters. Above all, they come to sit on the outdoor patio and watch the sidewalk cavalcade. Open daily for breakfast, lunch, and dinner from 7:30am, on Sunday from 10am.

EVENING ENTERTAINMENT

You can find the current programs plus most of what's going on around town in a handy little weekly, *Visitor's Guide,* available in hotel lobbies. It not only keeps up with the food, drink, and entertainment scene, but features enlarged maps on which to locate the places mentioned.

THE PERFORMING ARTS

In addition to the listings below, several other auditoriums present considerably more mixed bags—anything from classical ballet to rock concerts, with the quality depending on who's performing what. The **McPherson Playhouse,** 3 Centennial Sq. (tel. 604/386-6121), has modern dance groups, musicals, drama festivals, and light opera. The **Memorial Arena,** 1925 Blanshard St. (tel. 604/361-0537), goes for rock concerts, circus performances, and wrestling bouts. The **Royal Theatre,** 805 Broughton St. (tel. 604/383-9711), is mainly devoted to plays and concerts.

THE BELFRY, 1291 Gladstone Ave. Tel. 604/385-6815.

My favorite live theater auditorium is this charming, small, and intimate professional playhouse, which maintains high standards of acting. Programs run the gamut of serious theater, from Eugene O'Neill and Harold Pinter to Sondheim musicals. It's dark on Monday.

Prices: Tickets $12–$15.

KALEIDOSCOPE PLAYHOUSE, 520 Herald St. Tel. 604/383-6183.

A modern theater with excellent acoustics, the Kaleidoscope is located in the heart of Victoria's Old Town. It hosts a wide variety of performances, from plays to dance shows and concerts. From September to May there's special fare for young audiences.

Prices: $12–$15.

PHOENIX THEATRES, University of Victoria. Tel. 604/721-8000.

The Phoenix Theatres are a remarkably versatile outfit, operating both as a playhouse and dinner theater (you don't have to eat to see the shows). Shows vary from comedy and fantasy to straight drama.

Prices: Tickets and dinner $18.

THEATRE INCONNU, 47 Market Sq. Tel. 604/380-1284.

Funky and versatile, this oddly named stage has a five-play summer season that covers almost the entire spectrum of performance art. One season included a one-man show, a thriller by a contemporary Canadian playwright, plus works by Chekhov, Molière, and Shakespeare.

Prices: Ticket prices vary.

THE CLUB & BAR SCENE

Until about a dozen years ago there was no such thing as a nightclub in the entire town. In fact, there was hardly any nightlife worth the title. Today Victoria is awash with clubs of all shapes and sizes. The trouble is that they keep changing their names at a dazzling rate, and I can't guarantee that any of those mentioned below will still bear the same label by the time you get to read this.

I found it quite impossible to distinguish among places calling themselves "cabarets," "nightclubs," or "discos." Lots of all three, but the labeling is so haphazard that I'll leave it to you to decide what tag belongs to which. (One reason for the confusion is that "cabaret," in Canada, refers to a certain type of liquor license and not to the brand of entertainment offered. Thus a so-called cabaret may consist of anything from a series of variety acts to one solitary combo without so much as a vocalist.)

HARPO'S, Bastion Sq. Tel. 604/385-5333.

This is currently the "in" place for Victoria's *jeunesse dorée* and it's correspondingly packed. Up a flight of stone steps, and permanently thronged, it has stand-up comics and top-name bands, many from the mainland: rock, blues, pop, and folk. There's dancing on an excellent floor. Open all week to 2am.

Admission: $3–$10.

HERMANN'S JAZZ CLUB, 753 View St. Tel. 604/388-9166.

The offerings at Hermann's run the gamut from Dixieland to swing, featuring a different combo Monday to Saturday nights. Most of the groups are Canadian, with an occasional import for variety. Also serves lunch and dinner.

Admission: Varies.

JULIE'S, 603 Pandora St. Tel. 604/386-3631.

Julie's has a different offering virtually every night, some with labels like Classic

Monday, Wicked Wednesday, Ladies' Nite, etc. There are fairly hectic dance parties Friday and Saturday, and usually a raunchy comedy turn on Sunday.
Admission: Free.

PAGLIACCI'S, 1011 Broad St. Tel. 604/386-1662.
Pagliacci's is a happy and convivial mixture of Italian restaurant, nightclub, and comedy showcase, with possibly the thickest and most enthusiastic clientele in town. Tables are close enough together to spoon your neighbor's soup and the vibes so good that you hardly need the laid-on entertainment, which can be almost anything from a rock group to a stand-up comic and points in between. The place never seems to be less than crowded seven days a week until 11pm or midnight.

STRATHCONA HOTEL, 919 Douglas St. Tel. 604/383-7137.
A good number of nightspots are housed in the remarkable entertainment complex centered by the Strathcona Hotel. **The Cuckoo's Nest** generates mighty volumes of sound, packs in a remarkably relaxed crowd, and stays open until 2am. Still under the same hospitable roof is a jumping lounge bar called **Big Bad John's,** and a British-style pub, **The Sticky Wicket,** a tavern dedicated to cricket.
Also located in this complex is **The Forge** (tel. 604/383-9913), Victoria's largest nightclub, which isn't so very large at that. The band attracts a wonderfully devoted clientele and there's a lot of dance floor and mike action from 9pm to 2am.
Admission: $4.

SWEETWATER, 27–570 Store St., Market Square. Tel. 604/383-7844.
Known as a "singles mingler," Sweetwater features classic tracks, Top 40s, the right kind of lighting, and whatever else gets people into a dancing mood. Stomps six nights a week from 8pm to 2am. Closed Sunday.
Admission: $2.

TALLYHO MOTOR INN, 3020 Douglas St. Tel. 604/386-6141.
The Tallyho Motor Inn puts on restaurant-theater performances Tuesday and Saturday at 8:30pm. The shows are mixed bags of stand-up comics, the dinners consistently good. (With the comedians you take your chance.)
Admission: Varies.

WILD ROVER, 569 Johnson St. Tel. 604/383-5000.
Billed as an "Irish Fun Spot," this upstairs restaurant/club serves an even mixture of Irish and Cajun specialties; both go equally well with Guinness and Harp beer. The entertainment is likewise a mixed bag: Dixieland jazz, sing-alongs, and changing bands. It all adds up to an atmosphere of pleasantly relaxed enjoyment, seven nights a week. Sunday jazz sessions from 4:30 to 7:30pm.
Admission: Free.

MORE ENTERTAINMENT

Great Canadian, 3366 Douglas St. (tel. 604/268-1000), is the island's gambling venture, very informal and laid-back, located in the Red Lion Inn. There are special tables for nonsmokers, but drinks are served to all players. You can try blackjack, roulette, or a variation called sic-bo. Open every night from 6pm to 2am.

EASY EXCURSIONS FROM VICTORIA

Duncan lies 38 miles north of Victoria up the Trans Canada Highway. The little town is the center of the rural Cowichan Valley (a Cowichan word meaning "warmed by the sun"), the area where the famed sweaters are knitted from naturally colored raw wool. The whole region is a forest, lake, and river playground, ideal for hiking, swimming, fishing, and camping. You can see the amazing **Glass Castle,** with a collection of 180,000 bottles, and **St. Francis Xavier Church,** an example of the community-built early pioneer churches.
Two miles north of Duncan is the **Forest Museum R.R. 4,** Trans Canada Highway (tel. 604/746-1251). Extending over 100 acres, this out- and indoor showpiece tells the story of wood better than a library of books. You can ride in a logging handcar and a narrow-gauge steam train, tour an old logging camp, watch

logging movies from the old days, and gaze at Douglas firs, five feet around and 180 feet tall, that were already a century old when Captain Cook landed on Vancouver Island in 1778. Open daily May to September from 9:30am to 6pm.

Nanaimo, the "sun porch of Canada," basks 69 miles north of Victoria on the same highway. Small and friendly, Nanaimo is a major deep-sea fishing port, but used to be a Hudson's Bay Company outpost. In 1853 the company men built the **Bastion,** a small fort-tower designed to protect the settlers against native attacks—which never came. But the tower has become a historical landmark and is open to visitors. Another stop is the **Centennial Museum,** which shares a building with the tourist bureau.

Parksville, 92 miles north of Victoria, is the major beach resort area of Vancouver Island, and reputedly has the warmest ocean swimming in Canada. There are miles and miles of white sandy beaches (never overcrowded), superb camping in Englishman River Park, and scenic forests with dark-green pools on the road to Port Alberni. For overnight stays there's the charming **Beach Acres Lodge,** originally the manor house of a country estate, now a guesthouse offering bedrooms with either private or semiprivate bath. Open from June 23 to Labor Day, one mile south of Parksville on Island Highway 1.

All the above places are served by **Island Coach Lines,** 700 Douglas St. (tel. 604/385-4411).

3. AROUND BRITISH COLUMBIA

THE BIG PEACE RIVER COUNTRY   The far north of the province—twice the size of Ohio—is inhabited by barely 50,000 people, but also by moose, caribou, black bear, grizzlies, lynx, beavers, wolverines, and eagles. It offers the fantastic spectacle of the northern lights, shimmering across the sky in a Niagara of changing colors. The center is **Fort St. John,** dating from 1798. At Dawson Creek stands the world's most photographed milestone: the **Mile Zero Post,** marking the start of the famous Alaska Highway.

KIMBERLEY   In the Rocky Mountains, 500 miles east of Vancouver, is the highest city in Canada—and one of the most amazing. The entire mining community of 8,000 people has been turned into a Bavarian alpine village! It's not terribly genuine, but there's enough likeness to make you believe you've stumbled into Central Europe by mistake. The core of the town is the Platzl (mall), with peasant-baroque storefronts, bubbling brook, flowers, and pedestrians wearing Lederhosen. In July the town celebrates its annual **"Julyfest,"** with parades, folk dances, international entertainment, and tidal waves of beer. While you're there you can inspect the world's largest lead and zinc mine.

OSOYOOS   In complete and startling contrast to the above, this is a Spanish desert town that makes you rub your eyes in disbelief. The pocket desert in question lies 252 miles east of Vancouver, two miles from the U.S. border. But sparkling **Lake Osoyoos** lies right alongside, and the region grows the earliest fruit crop in the country, including magnificent peaches. The Okanagan Valley, of which this is the southern tip, was once the road to the eastern goldfields, and you can still pan for gold there—occasionally even find some.

KSAN   This is an authentic village of the Gitskan tribe, reconstructed in every detail just outside the town of Hazelton and similar to the one that stood there when the first explorers came to the area, at the junction of the Skeena and Bulkley rivers. The village consists of four communal houses, and a **House of the Arts** and a **Carving House,** where you can see Native Canadian artists at work with leather, stone, wood, and cloth. The **House of Treasures** contains the tribal regalia of Gitskan chiefs. At the **Frog House** you can see the ingenious use the natives made of bones, skins, feathers, fur, stones, and bark to produce implements they needed before the introduction of European tools. A modern campground and trailer park adjoins the village, complete with power hookups, showers, and toilets. Ksan is operated as a joint enterprise of the Native Canadian association and the Canadian government. You reach Hazelton on Highway 16, running from Prince Rupert on the coast.

KAMLOOPS   Located 267 miles northeast of Vancouver, this is a small community spread out over 140 square miles—with several ranches right within the city limits. Nestling in a scenic valley, Kamloops lies surrounded by 2,000 lakes, offering some of the easiest and most rewarding fishing in all Canada. These are the homewaters of the famous Kamloops trout, and by a good rule of thumb the larger the lake, the bigger the trout. **Lake Shuswap** produces the biggest of all—up to 20 pounds. The nearby **Adams River** spawns the world's largest sockeye salmon. There is no general closed season here.

Kamloops has over 50 hotels and motels, while the entire region is peppered with dude ranches, chalets, motels, campsites, and trailer parks. It is served by **Air BC** (tel. 604/688-5515), **BC Rail** (tel. 604/631-3500), **VIA Rail** (tel. 604/640-3741), and **Greyhound** buses (tel. 604/662-3222) on a regularly scheduled basis.

THE CARIBOO GOLD RUSH COUNTRY   Actually called Cariboo Chilcotin, this is a huge chunk of land north of Vancouver stretching from the Pacific Ocean almost to the Rockies. Parts of it are ranch country, with working cowpokes and working guest ranches, including some of the biggest in North America. The Cariboo area abounds in gold-rush memorabilia—a historic museum in **Clinton,** and the overland telegraph and a gigantic waterwheel (used to pump out mine shafts) in **Quesnel.**

This is the gateway to **Barkerville,** restored almost exactly as it was in the gold-rush days. The main street consists of false-fronted shops, looking like props from a Hollywood horse opera. You can visit the uproarious Royal Theatre Review, take a bumpy ride in a stagecoach, or watch a reincarnation of Judge Begby (the notorious "hanging judge") presiding over his court. You can reach the area by train, bus, or plane from Vancouver, then take feeder buses to the various communities.

OKANAGAN   Some 240 miles northeast of Vancouver lies Canada's wine and fruit bowl, a region that surprises natives almost as much as foreign visitors. Blessed with the balmiest weather and highest percentage of sunshine in the country, Okanagan is a smiling ribbon of lakeshores, orchards, and wineries, producing some astonishingly fine vintages. The largest city of the region (not very large) is Kelowna, while north and south spreads some of the prettiest farming and vacation country on earth. You can go on wine-tasting tours or river and lake cruises, gorge on fresh fruit from the orchards, or visit bird sanctuaries and cheese factories. Also here, at Kelowna, is the **Father Pandosy Mission,** founded in 1859, the site of the valley's first vineyard and an operating gristmill dating back to 1877.

The Okanagan Valley is dotted with bed-and-breakfast establishments as friendly as the countryside. One of the most charming is **The Gables,** 2405 Bering Rd. (Box 1153), Kelowna, BC, V1Y 7P8 (tel. 604/768-4468), located six miles south of the town. This gingerbread-style house dating from 1910 was lovingly restored and is a recognized heritage site. Breakfast includes hot biscuits, homemade jams, and fresh fruit from the valley. Rates start at $40 for singles, $50 for doubles. You get to Kelowna by bus or car from Kamloops via Highway 97.

The town of Kelowna is the center of what few people know exists—Canada's wine industry. Canadian vintages are, unfortunately, a fairly well kept secret. Although the wine region can't compare in size to California's or Australia's, the quality of the products can stand any comparison. Decide for yourself. There are several winemakers in or just outside the town that offer tastings: Try **Calona Wineries,** 1125 Richter St. (tel. 604/762-9144); or **Cedar Creek Estate,** at the corner of Pandosy and Lakeshore Roads (tel. 604/764-8866), just off Highway 97, about five miles south of Kelowna.

THE NORTHWEST TERRITORIES

However you slice them, the Northwest Territories are a colossal chunk. Stretching from the 60th parallel to the North Pole, from Hudson Bay to the Arctic Ocean, they embrace 1.3 million square miles—more than twice the size of Alaska. The sheer stark loneliness of those landscapes of forests, lakes, mountains, arctic tundra, and northern taiga is overwhelming when you see them from the air.

For the Territories have over a million lakes and barely 55,000 people—three national parks, but only 63 communities, some of them numbering 50 to 80 souls. There is no other inhabited part of the earth where you stand a better chance of casting a line in unfished waters or treading a path no white person has stepped on before.

Yet the land is changing before our eyes. Mineral, oil, and gas exploration is preparing the industrialization to come; you can already discern the first signs of it here and there. The changes are creating a paradox, or rather a whole pattern of paradoxes. The Inuit live in prefabs instead of igloos and drive trucks and snowmobiles out to their traplines. But the money they spend in supermarkets is earned by ancestral hunting skills and their lifestyle remains based on the pursuit of migrating game animals and marine creatures.

You'll find modern tourist lodges, supplied by air, dotting half-explored regions of wilderness; dog teams sharing an airstrip with cargo planes; roaming herds of caribou streaming across brand-new all-weather highways; families dining on French cuisine in one spot and on walrus blubber in another; Inuit villages with rows of seaplanes moored alongside canoes.

SEEING THE NORTHWEST TERRITORIES

INFORMATION For information concerning almost anything in the Northwest Territories, contact the office of Economic Development and Tourism, Government of the N.W. Territories, P.O. Box 1320, Yellowknife, NT, X1A 2L9 (tel. 403/873-7200).

CLIMATE & SEASONS During the summer months the farther north you travel, the more daylight you get. Yellowknife, in the south, basks under 20 hours of sunshine a day, followed by four hours of milky twilight bright enough to read a newspaper by. But in northern Inuvik or Cambridge Bay the sun shines 24 hours around the clock. In winter, however, the northern sun doesn't rise above the horizon at all on certain days, while Yellowknifers have five hours of daylight.

The Northwest Territories are divided into two climatic zones: subarctic and arctic, and the division does not follow the Arctic Circle. And while there are permanent ice caps in the far northern islands, summer in the rest of the land gets considerably hotter than you might think. The average July and August temperatures run in the 60s and 70s, and the mercury has been known to climb into the 90s. You can go swimming in the lakes and rivers (although the water doesn't feel exactly

WHAT'S SPECIAL ABOUT
THE NORTHWEST TERRITORIES

People
- ☐ Here you can get a close-up of one of the world's least known and most interesting ethnic groups, the Inuit.

Nature
- ☐ The NWT has more polar bears—roughly 12,000—than any other region on earth.
- ☐ Two of the world's largest lakes, Great Bear and Great Slave, as well as Virginia Falls, which are twice the height of those at Niagara.
- ☐ Nahanni National Park, a legendary region of mystery deep in the heart of the Mackenzie Mountains. A real wilderness adventure for white-water canoeists, photographers, and trail hikers.

Northern Foods
- ☐ A cuisine that you'll rarely get to taste anywhere else, ranging from caribou stew and musk-ox steak to bannock and Eskimo doughnuts.

Native Arts and Crafts
- ☐ Inuit and Dene artisans turn out hauntingly beautiful art objects, ancient in design yet strangely modern in appearance. Their leather and needlework is unsurpassed in craftsmanship.

Natural Phenomena
- ☐ The NWT contains both the North Geographic and the North Magnetic Pole. The first—the Big Nail—is fixed. The second, which attracts compass needles, can move from year to year.
- ☐ More than 30 million acres in diamond claims have already been staked.

A Favorite Local Spot
- ☐ Lois Lane, a small thoroughfare in Yellowknife named after Superman's lady friend. Margot Kidder, the actress who played her in the movie, was born there.

Caribbean), but you can also get sudden cold snaps with freezing temperatures despite the almost constant daylight.

Even in summer you should bring a warm sweater or ski jacket—and don't forget a pair of really sturdy shoes or boots. In winter, with weather conditions truly arctic, you need the heavily insulated clothing and footwear you'll see in every Territorian closet. Avoid hobnailed boots—the metal can induce frostbite. And gentlemen tourists should bring a necktie. Some of the hotel dining rooms are surprisingly formal.

To give you an idea of the climatic contrasts: The highest recorded summer temperature was 97°F at Fort Simpson. The lowest winter temperature was −72°F in Shepard Bay.

ORGANIZED TOURS   One of Air Canada's connector airlines, **NWT Air,** P.O. Box 2435, Yellowknife, NT, X1A 2P8 (tel. 403/920-2165), offers **Touch the Arctic,** a selection of package tours. You won't be flying in bush planes; the aircraft used are Boeing 737 jets. All the tours start in either Edmonton or Winnipeg. From there you have 13 different choices. The Arctic Coast Adventure is a three-day jaunt to Coppermine, on the shores of the Arctic Ocean. You visit the Inuit community there, take a four-hour boat trip on the Coppermine River, take pictures by the light of the midnight sun, and shop for Inuit arts and crafts right at the source. The price, including transport and breakfasts, is $1,175. Another tour is a Naturalist trip to Banks Island, the "musk-ox capital" of the north. This one takes seven days and puts you down in Inuvik first, where you enjoy a boat trip on the Mackenzie River. From there you fly to Sachs Harbour and follow a professional guide to see the mighty musk-oxen, white foxes, and arctic hares in their wild habitat. Accommodation is in individual tents. The trip—all-inclusive—costs $2,950.

Cruise Canada's Arctic in the MS *Norweta,* a modern diesel-engine craft equipped with radar, and owned by **NWT Marine Group,** 5414 52nd St.,

Yellowknife, NT, X1A 3K1 (tel. 403/873-2489, or toll free 800/663-9157). This seven-day cruise begins in Yellowknife and explores the unspoiled, rarely visited east arm of the Great Slave Lake. It's leisurely exploration that includes a stop at the Chipewyan Dene community of Snowdrift for tea and bannock. Then you sail into remote channels and bays according to a pleasantly flexible schedule. The shoreline is virtually untouched wilderness, and you can view moose, bald eagles, peregrine falcons, wolves, and bears. For closer observation and shore excursions you use the *Zodiac* (open boat). Northern-style picnic lunches (lots of fresh lake fish) are provided and at night you sleep in the snug cabins of the *Norweta*. Cost of the cruise is $2,870 to $3,070 per person for double occupancy. The single supplement is $1,300 to $1,400.

HUNTING ADVENTURES   These are restricted by government regulations, but organized by dozens of local outfits. Nonresidents of the NWT have to employ one of three classes of outfitters (A, B, or C) to hunt for certain species of game. Thus only Class B outfitters can arrange hunts for wolf, wolverine, black bear, or grizzly. Only Class C can hunt musk-ox and polar bear. Hunting conditions can be pretty rugged and may require a fair degree of fitness.

Webb Outfitting, with a U.S. booking office at 2260 Sumneytown Pike, Harleysville, PA, 19348 (tel. 215/256-1118), can organize trips to hunt for caribou, wolverine, and wolf, 185 miles north of Yellowknife. Full meals, guides, and taxidermist service are available. Rates are all-inclusive from Yellowknife.

Tundra Camps, Box 1470EX, Yellowknife, NT, X1A 2P1 (tel. 403/920-4263), organizes spring and fall hunts for trophy musk-oxen, rifle or bow hunting, and special spring dogsled hunts for musk-oxen. Also hunt for barren-ground grizzly. The programs are all-inclusive, with experienced Inuit guides, boats, skidoos, aircraft based at camp.

1. AN OVERALL LOOK

THE PEOPLE   The earliest human inhabitants of the Northwest Territories were the ancestors of the Native Canadians (Indians) who entered Alaska from Siberia and moved into Canada about 10,000 years ago. Some 6,000 or so years later came the Inuit, also from Siberia via Alaska, and began wandering eastward across the Canadian Arctic.

Together they make up the majority of the Northwest Territories' population, particularly when you add the Métis—offspring of white and Native Canadian couples. All of them were originally nomadic, covering enormous distances in pursuit of migrating game animals. Today nearly all Dene and Inuit have permanent homes in their settlements, but many of them spend part of the year in remote tent camps, hunting, fishing, and trapping. And although nobody *lives* in igloos anymore, these snow houses are still being built as temporary shelters when the occasion arises. Countless hunting groups owe their lives to their ability to construct snow dwellings, for the Arctic storms blow huts and tents to smithereens but leave igloos intact.

"Survival" is the key word for Dene and Inuit. They learned to survive in conditions unimaginably harsh for southern societies, by means of skills that become more wondrous the better you know them. The early white explorers soon learned that in order to stay alive they had to copy those skills as best they could. Those who refused to "go native" rarely made it back.

The first known white man to penetrate the region was Martin Frobisher. His account of meeting the Inuit, written 400 years ago, is the earliest on record. About the same time, European whalers, hunting whales for their oil, were occasionally forced ashore by storms or shipwreck and depended on Inuit hospitality for survival. This almost legendary hospitality, extended to any stranger who came to them, remains an outstanding characteristic of the Inuit.

Whites only began to move into the Canadian Arctic in any number during the great "fur rush" in the late 18th century. In the wake of the fur hunters and traders came the missionaries, Roman Catholic and Anglican, who built churches and opened

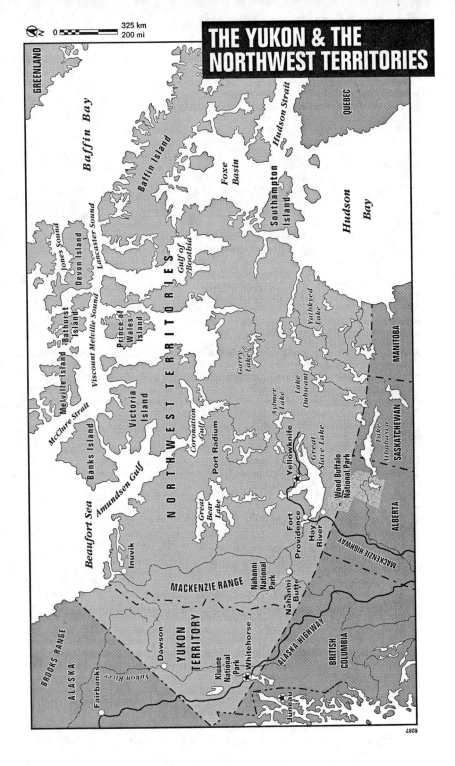

schools where lessons were given in the native languages. They also built hospitals, which became a desperate necessity because the Inuit—accustomed to a germ-free environment—were dying like flies from the measles, tuberculosis, scarlet fever, smallpox, and venereal diseases brought in by the whites. The same scourges were ravaging the Dene people.

For most of its recorded history, the far north was governed from afar, first by Great Britain, then by the Hudson's Bay Company, and from 1867 by the new Canadian government in Ottawa. At that time the Territories included all of the Yukon, Saskatchewan, Alberta, and huge parts of other provinces. The present boundaries were not drawn until 1920. Immense, isolated from the mainstream, administered by the Mounties on behalf of an absentee territorial council, the Northwest Territories were a textbook study of voiceless neglect.

Things began to change drastically when Territorians started electing their own council members. Today all 15 are chosen by local constituencies, and the commissioner resides in the territorial capital, shifted from Fort Smith to Yellowknife in 1967. You have only to glance at the expanding highways, the new shopping centers, schools, hospitals, government offices, and tourist facilities to realize that the era of the Yukon and Northwest Territories neglect is over. The Territories have joined Canada and the outside world in practice as well as in theory.

Tourism is one of the best barometers of this process, because the basis of a tourist industry is transportation and accommodation. About 15 years ago the Territories had about 600 visitors per year and only eight communities with hotels. Today the annual figure is 25,000. They find accommodation in 29 communities, including formerly isolated places with exotic names like Tuktoyaktuk and Pangnirtung. Tourist lodges over the same period increased from 12 to 70.

ANIMALS It's easy to confuse **caribou** with reindeer because the two species look very much alike. Actually, caribou are wild and still travel in huge migrating herds stretching to the horizon, sometimes numbering 100,000 or more. They form the major food and clothing supply for many of the native people whose lives are cycled around the movements of caribou herds. **Reindeer,** on the other hand, are strictly domestic animals, and imported ones at that. They were first brought into the Northwest Territories early in this century—contrary to the legend that had them helping Santa Claus on the North Pole since the invention of Christmas.

The mighty **musk-ox,** on the other hand, is indigenous to the Arctic. About 12,000 of them live on the northern islands—immense and prehistoric looking, the bulls weighing up to 1,300 pounds. They appear even larger than they are because they carry a mountain of the shaggiest fur in creation (they make the American buffalo look positively bald). This coat keeps them not only alive but comfortable in blizzard temperatures of 95° below zero. It is also the chief reason why the Inuit hunt them: There's no material quite like it. Underneath the shaggy outer coat musk-oxen have a silky-soft layer of underwool, called qiviut in Inuit. One pound of qiviut can be spun into a 40-strand thread 25 miles long! As light as it is soft, a sweater made from the stuff will keep its wearer warm in subzero weather. And it doesn't shrink when wet. Musk-ox bulls may not be pretty, but they're true gentlemen of the wild. In the worst storms they will face the wind, shielding the cows and calves with their huge bodies, standing on their feet as long as the gale lasts, sometimes for days, like hairy bulwarks.

The monarch of the Arctic, *Ursus maritimus,* the great white bear (Nanook, as the Inuit call him), has no such sentiments. Except for brief spring mating seasons he's a loner, constantly on the move and covering immense distances by ice and water in search of prey. **Polar bears** roam the Arctic coast and the shores of Hudson Bay, and you have to travel quite a ways over mighty tough country to see them in their

---

IMPRESSIONS

'Tain't nothin' but miles and miles of miles and miles.
—AMERICAN SERVICEMAN, QUOTED IN MALCOLM MACDONALD, *CANADIAN NORTH,* 1945

habitat. Weighing up to 1,450 pounds, they're the largest predators on the North American continent, and probably the most dangerous.

Polar bears are almost entirely carnivorous, but in an oddly selective fashion. Seals are their main diet, although the bears usually eat only the tough hide and the blubber underneath, leaving the meat and innards to foxes and other scavengers. They are surefooted on ice, fantastic swimmers, and aggressive enough to be given a very wide berth.

You can get a permit to hunt polar bears, but the total quota is 400 bears annually and only the local Inuit can decide how many of these are to be shot by tourists. You must use a native hunter as a guide, and you can't use mechanical vehicles. Thus a bear hunt may mean two weeks or more of bone-jarring travel over huge ice ridges on a dogsled, facing winds that rip tents apart like wet paper. With these restrictions, the great white bears are maintaining their numbers in Canada and appear in no danger of joining the list of endangered species.

The Northwest Territories are full of other animals much easier to observe than the bears. In the wooded regions you'll come across wolves and wolverines (harmless to humans, despite the legends about them), mink, lynx, otters, and beavers. The sleek and beautiful white or brown Arctic foxes live in ice regions as well as beneath the tree line and near settlements.

From mid-July to the end of August, seals, walruses, and whales are in their breeding grounds off the coast of Baffin Island and in Hudson Bay. And in the endless skies above there are eagles, hawks, huge owls, razor-billed auks, and ivory gulls. Also a gourmet-renowned little partridgelike bird called the ptarmigan, as delicious to eat as it is impossible to pronounce.

ART & CRAFTS These deserve a separate section here. The handwork of the Dene and Inuit people is absolutely unique, regardless whether the materials used are indigenous or imported. Many of them have utility value—you won't get finer, more painstakingly stitched cold-weather clothing anywhere in the world. A genuine muskrat parka, for instance, is not only wonderfully warm but has a stylish originality that puts it above fashion trends.

The art objects—sculpture, prints, and tapestries—are connoisseurs' delights and acknowledged investment values. Quite apart from the aesthetic pleasure you may derive from an exquisitely shaped walrus tusk carving, it's also a means of beating inflation. And the Northwest Territories is one of the few places where you can buy these items without paying a sales tax.

Most arts and crafts articles are handled through community cooperatives that take care of the making as well as the marketing, thus avoiding the excess cut of the middleman. This is an important business in the Territories, with sales averaging around $10 million a year. There are three official symbols stating clearly that a piece is a genuine Native Canadian object. Watch for them when buying. Some stores make a habit of mixing the genuine stuff with second-rate imitations.

Don't hesitate to ask retailers where a particular object comes from, what it's made of, and how it was made. They'll be glad to tell you, and frequently can even let you know who made it.

2. GETTING THERE & GETTING AROUND

BY PLANE The Northwest Territories are served by jets from Edmonton, Winnipeg, Calgary, and Montréal, with scheduled flights as far north as Resolute in the high Arctic. In summer this means virtually all daylight flying. Canadian Airlines International does the 1½-hour flight from Edmonton to Yellowknife 27 times weekly, to Inuvik eight times a week.

Within the Territories you have a large number of major and (very) minor airlines operating scheduled flights between communities. The bigger ones fly jets; the smaller outfits, four- to 50-passenger prop planes on wheels or on floats. Among them they serve virtually all populated centers in the Territories. You can also charter aircraft, ranging from three-passenger Cessnas to 50-passenger Dashes.

Here are some airline telephone numbers in Yellowknife: Canadian Airlines International (tel. toll free 800/661-1505), Air Canada (tel. 403/920-2500), Northward Airlines (tel. 403/873-5311), Northwest Territorial Airways (tel. toll free 800/661-8880), Ptarmigan Airways (tel. 403/873-4461), and Latham Island Airways (tel. 403/873-2891).

BY ROAD In 1960 the **Mackenzie Highway** reached Yellowknife from Edmonton, establishing a 941-mile link between the capitals of Alberta and the Northwest Territories. The drive north is fascinating, either by private car or thrice-weekly bus service. You cross two major rivers, neither of them bridged. In summer the crossing (five to 10 minutes) is by free car-ferry. In winter you drive over a completely safe ice bridge four to six feet thick. In spring and fall, however, there are periods of up to six weeks when thaw or freezing puts both facilities out of service. For information on ferry schedules or ice bridge conditions, call 403/873-7799 in Yellowknife.

The Territories have a fairly extensive net of all-weather gravel-surfaced highways connecting the major attractions. But there are a few important points to consider before you go motoring in what was quite recently the Arctic wild:

Driving distances are vast. From Yellowknife, it's 1,160 air miles to Cape Dorset, 1,405 miles to Frobisher Bay, 1,435 miles to Pangnirtung. Even the southerly old capital of Fort Smith is 190 miles off. There are long distances between service stops, gas prices are high, spare parts are severely limited, and human settlements en route are very sparse indeed.

You should always carry a tow rope, spare tire, matches, tools, first-aid kit, extra gas, oil, and water, and some extra food. In summer you won't need a flashlight since you get about 22 hours of daylight driving. Don't bother to bring a compass either: Near the magnetic pole they're not very reliable.

If you're unaccustomed to driving on gravel, remember to avoid sudden braking or abrupt steering movements—they can send you skidding. The great curse of gravel roads is dust, so don't accelerate too much when passing another motorist, and ease off the gas pedal when meeting another vehicle. A discourteous driver on a gravel road can enshroud you in a dust cloud as dense as a smoke screen and leave you virtually blinded for minutes.

---

3. YELLOWKNIFE

600 air miles (1,000km) and 981 road miles (1,620km) N of Edmonton,
272 miles (445km) S of the Arctic Circle

GETTING THERE **By Plane** Air Canada and Canadian Airlines International fly into Yellowknife from Edmonton (see Section 2 of this chapter). Yellowknife Airport is three miles northeast of the town, with service to downtown by airport limousine or City Cab taxi.

By Bus Greyhound (tel. 403/421-4211) runs a daily service (except Saturday) from Edmonton to Hay River, N.W.T. There you connect with Arctic Frontier Carriers (tel. 403/873-4892) bus service to Yellowknife.

By Car From Edmonton take Highway 16 to Grimshaw. From there the Mackenzie Highway leads to the NWT border, 295 miles north, and on to Yellowknife via Fort Providence. (See Section 2 of this chapter.)

In the Fort Providence area you may see a few huge wood bisons ambling across the road. They are highly photogenic, but keep your distance. They are not tame park animals and although generally harmless are thoroughly unpredictable, short-tempered, fast, and immensely powerful. What's more, as road users they have the right-of-way.

ESSENTIALS Information For information about the province in general, contact Economic Development and Tourism, Government of the N.W. Territories, P.O. Box 1320, Yellowknife, NT, X1A 2L9 (tel. 403/873-7200). For information on the town itself, contact the Chamber of Commerce, 4807 49th St., P.O. Box 90G, Yellowknife, NT, X1A 2N7 (tel. 403/920-4944).

Addresses The absence of full addresses, with streets and numbers, is something you'll notice immediately in Yellowknife. Every local knows where certain offices are located and they're only too willing to let visitors in on the secret. So why bother printing addresses?

Getting Around By City Cabs (tel. 403/873-4444), a ride to the airport costs about $10.

Tilden (tel. 403/873-2911) has a range of rental vehicles from full-size cars to half-ton four-speed vans. The number of cars available during the summer season is rather limited and the demand very high. You may have to settle for what's to be had rather than what you want. Try to book ahead as far as possible.

The capital of the Northwest Territories and the most northerly city in Canada lies on the north shore of Great Slave Lake. The site was originally occupied by the Dogrib tribe. The first white settlers didn't arrive until 1934, following the discovery of gold on the lake shores.

This first gold boom petered out in the 1940s, and Yellowknife dwindled nearly to a ghost town in its wake. But in 1945 came a second gold rush that put the place permanently on the map. Gold made this city, which lies 682 feet above sea level, and its landmarks are the two operating gold mines that flank it: Cominco and Giant Yellowknife, both open to visitors.

Most of the old gold-boom marks have gone—the bordellos, gambling dens, log-cabin banks, and never-closing bars are merely memories now. But the original Old Town is there, a crazy tangle of wooden shacks hugging the lakeshore rocks, surrounded by bush-pilot operations that fly sturdy little planes—on floats in summer, on skis in winter.

The city's expanding urban center, New Town, spreads above the old section, a busy hub of modern hotels, shopping centers, office blocks, and government buildings. Together the two towns count about 15,500 inhabitants, by far the largest community in the Territories.

Looking at the rows of parking meters along Franklin Avenue it's hard to believe that the city's first two cars were shipped in (by river barge) only in 1944. They had one mile of road to use between them, yet somehow managed to collide head-on!

Yellowknife has one main street which begins out of town as Old Airport Road, becomes Franklin Avenue in midtown, and continues as 50th Avenue for the remainder of its run (the avenues only go as low as 49th; I don't know what happened to the rest—maybe the gold prospectors carried them off). If you stand at the post office, at Franklin Avenue and 49th Street, you're at the geographical center, give or take a few blocks.

You are then facing northeast, the direction of **Old Town** and **Yellowknife Bay**. Behind you is Frame Lake, with the magnificent **Prince of Wales Northern Heritage Centre.** Beyond the lake, up on a hillside, is the airport, a cozy little affair with a licensed restaurant, washrooms, vending machines, and waiting passengers who all know each other.

Northwest is the direction of the **Giant Yellowknife Mine,** half a mile away, and from the west the great Mackenzie Highway runs in all the way from Edmonton. **Rat Lake** and the **Cominco Mine** lie southwest from where you're standing. Just off 49th Avenue (the streets get a bit embryonic hereabouts) stand the arena, city hall, and the Royal Canadian Mounted Police post.

Kam Lake Road branches off Old Airport Road at the southern end of town and from there leads to the **Eskimo Dog Research Foundation,** a colony of 100 canines whose job it is to preserve the indigenous kingmik breed, the world's original cold-weather pooch. And 48th Street leads into the **Ingraham Trail,** which is a bush road heading out toward dozens of spots where you can go fishing, hiking, and camping.

Yellowknife is still very much small town, and a frontier small town at that. This is changing rapidly as the population increases, but currently it gives the capital a distinctly rustic note. In Old Town, for instance, water is still delivered by truck—an advance from a few years ago when it was delivered by hand bucket, at 25¢ per pail.

But there is also a dramatic flavor about Yellowknife, one you don't usually encounter in little communities. It stems partly from the mushrooming high-rises, shopping malls, and public buildings, from the feeling of transformation and vitality that permeates the place. But mainly it comes from the sense of the endless boundless wilderness that starts at the town's doorstep and stretches all the way to the roof of the world.

WHAT TO SEE & DO

The ✪ **Prince of Wales Northern Heritage Centre,** on the shore of Frame Lake (tel. 403/873-7551), was inaugurated in 1979, a museum in a class all its own. "Museum" is really the wrong term—it's a showcase, archive, traveling exhibition, and information service rolled into one, a living interpretation and presentation of the heritage of the north, its land, people, and animals. The architecture alone is worth a visit. All levels are accessible by ramps—no stairways to climb. It incorporates a lookout platform with a panoramic view, and a wonderful rest lounge with brochures and armchairs to read them in. Few museums have anything like it.

The exhibits are three dimensional. You learn the history, background, and characteristics of the Dene and Inuit peoples, of the Métis and pioneer whites, through dioramas, artifacts, talking, reciting, and singing slide presentations. The story begins some 400 million years ago and ends with the present age. It depicts the human struggle with an environment so incredibly harsh that survival alone seems a historical accomplishment. And you get an idea of how the natives of the north did it—not by struggling against their environment but by harmonizing with it. Admission is free and it's open daily from June to August from 10:30am to 5:30pm; September through May it's open the same hours but only Tuesday to Friday.

The **Bush Pilot's Memorial** is a massive stone pillar rising above Old Town that pays tribute to the little band of airmen who opened up the far north. The surrounding cluster of shacks and cottages is the original Yellowknife, built on the shores of a narrow peninsula jutting into Great Slave Lake. It's not exactly a pretty place, but definitely intriguing. Sprinkled along the inlets are half a dozen bush-pilot operations, minuscule airlines flying charter planes as well as scheduled routes to outlying areas. The little float planes shunt around like taxis, and you can watch one landing or taking off every hour of the day.

Rising massively one block from the town's main intersection, the **Courthouse Building** is the seat of justice for the entire Northwest Territories—possibly the largest jurisdiction on the globe. It was not until the 1970s that a supreme court judge was named in the Territories, Judge Sissons, and some of his more famous cases are commemorated in intricate carvings on display in the building.

About 100 yards off the tip of the Old Town peninsula lies **Latham Island,** which you can reach by a causeway. The island has a Native Canadian community and a growing industrial area.

TOWN TOURS & LAKE CRUISES

Raven Tours, P.O. Box 2435, Yellowknife (tel. 403/873-4776), operates the "City of Gold" sightseeing tour over the town area. These three-hour tours are made in minivans driven by expert guides and run Monday through Saturday. Adults pay $25, children $12. The same company also offers a four-hour excursion to Cameron Falls that includes a stop at the Prelude Lake Lodge.

Sail North, P.O. Box 2497, Yellowknife (tel. 403/873-8019), operates a fleet of vessels on the Great Slave Lake. The *Naocha* is a handy little twin-engine motor cruiser that takes you on four-hour jaunts that include a fresh fish dinner ($47). You can cruise around Yellowknife Bay, see the floatplane base, the mines, and the Detah

Native Canadian village, or sail farther to scenic Naocha Bay. Tickets and departure times at the Yellowknife Trading Post on Latham Island.

HIKING, BOATING & RAFTING

The town is ringed by hiking trails, some gentle, some pretty rugged. The most popular branch out from the big Ingraham Trail, which starts at the Explorer Hotel and winds over 45 miles to Tibbet Lake, east of town. En route lie several territorial parks, two waterfalls, the Yellowknife Mine, and a bird habitat, plus lots of picnic sites, camping spots, boat rentals, and fishing spots.

You can rent canoes at **Sportsman,** on 50th Street and 52nd Avenue in Yellowknife (tel. 403/873-2911) for $30 a day. **Prelude Lake,** 20 miles east of town, is a wonderful setting for scenic boating and trout, pike, and arctic grayling fishing. At the lodge, motorboats rent for $9 to $11 an hour, and rafts for $9 to $10 an hour, depending on size.

But before you take to the water, a few words of advice: You must take warm, waterproof clothing, regardless of the temperature. Summer storms can blow up very quickly and drench you to the skin. You'll also need some insect repellent—blackflies and mosquitoes are the warm-weather curse of the north. Canoers are advised to bring mosquito headnets as well. If you camp on a water trip, pick an open island or sandbar where the lack of vegetation tends to discourage the winged pests.

SWIMMING

One of the biggest surprises for visitors and a source of pride for the locals is the **Ruth Inch Memorial Pool,** at the corner of Franklin Avenue and Forrest Drive (tel. 403/920-5683). Yes, it does get warm enough during July and August to make a dip very pleasant, and the pool offers more than mere swimming. You get a whirlpool, steamroom, and shower for $3.25. The pool is located beside the Yellowknife Community Arena.

SPECIAL EVENTS

The **Midnight Golf Tournament,** attended by visiting celebrities and local club swingers, is the only annual event of its kind that tees off at midnight, June 22. It's bright enough then to see individual sand grains on the "greens" (which are actually "browns"), but there are some unique handicaps. Thieving ravens, for instance, frequently hijack chip shots, and the entire course could be classified as one large sand trap.

The ✪ **Caribou Carnival,** held from March 17 to 25 annually, is a burst of spring fever after a very long, very frigid winter (part of the fever symptoms consist of the delusion that winter is over). For a solid week Yellowknife is thronged with parades, local talent shows, and skit revues with imported celebrities. Some fascinating and specifically Arctic contests include igloo building, Inuit wrestling, tea boiling, and the competition highlight: the **Canadian Championship Dog Derby.** A three-day, 150-mile dogsled race, with more than 200 huskies competing for the $30,000 prize, and their "mushers" running behind, yelling—well, maybe "porridge!" The carnival is kept "orderly" by swarms of helmeted Kariboo Kops, who swoop down on nonsmilers and other subversives, haul them off to kangaroo courts, and levy fines (which go to charity).

THE TOWN MASCOT

While he's not strictly speaking an attraction, I think I ought to mention **Raymond,** Yellowknife's unofficial heraldic bird. Raymond is a raven—or rather swarms of them. Large, gleaming black, and fitted with brass nerve and vocal cords, these popular pests put on daily shows for spectators—snatching bones from outraged dogs, bullying sea gulls, or knocking lids off garbage cans and arranging the contents in artistic patterns on the ground in a 50-foot radius. They'll also fly off with your golf ball while you're practicing on the (gravel and sand) course. Yet despite—or because of—his innumerable depredations, Raymond is the town mascot, his villainous features depicted on T-shirts, posters, and official brochures. Watch him sitting on a fence and squawking his own praises to heaven with all the leather-lunged smugness of a politician, and you'll understand why.

SHOPPING

Yellowknife is the main retail outlet for northern artwork and craft items, as well as the specialized clothing the climate demands. Some of it is so handsome and handy that sheer vanity will make you wear it in more southerly temperatures.

NORTHERN IMAGES, in the Yellowknife Mall, 50th Ave. Tel. 403/873-5944.

Northern Images is a link in the cooperative chain of stores by that name that stretches across the entire Canadian north. The premises are as attractive as they are interesting, exhibitions as much as markets. They feature authentic Native Canadian articles: apparel and carvings, graphic prints, silver jewelry, ornamental moose hair tuftings, and porcupine quill work. The items aren't cheap, but if you consider that they are handmade and have no provincial sales tax on them, they have definite bargain value. Boots run from $35; mukluks, the wonderfully soft and warm Inuit footwear, from $100 upward. Inuit parkas, the finest cold-weather coats made anywhere, cost between $350 and $500.

THE TRADING POST, 4 Lessard Dr., Latham Island. Tel. 403/873-3020.

Although fairly new, this log cabin-style emporium is the nearest thing to an old-time frontier store Yellowknife can offer. You drop in there not just to buy goods, but to have coffee and snacks, book cruises and excursions, listen to gossip, and collect information. The post has a wonderful viewing deck overlooking the water, and in summer gets quite enough sun to bask in. The goods on sale cover the entire range of northern specialties: Inuit and Dene arts and crafts, fur jackets, moccasins, scenic art prints, books with northern themes, jewelry, sculptings, and innumerable souvenirs. Hours are daily from 9am to 10pm.

WHERE TO STAY

Yellowknife now has over 450 hotel and motel rooms in a wide range of price brackets. Rates are generally somewhat higher than in the south, but this is eased by the fact that the Territories have no provincial sales tax. Hotel standards are good, in parts excellent, although you mustn't expect room service in most establishments.

EXPENSIVE

EXPLORER HOTEL, 48th St., Yellowknife, NT, X1A 2R3. Tel. 403/873-3531. Fax 403/873-2789. 128 rms. A/C TV TEL
$ Rates: $145 single; $160 double. AE, ER, MC, V.

The Explorer Hotel is a big, beautiful, snow-white structure overlooking the town in the manner of a guardian igloo. The Explorer is *the* hotel in the Northwest Territories, and it lets you know it the moment you step inside. The lobby has diffused and subtle lighting, indoor greenery, and wonderfully deep armchairs. The dining lounge is a local showpiece.

The guest rooms come furnished in dark wood and sea-green drapes; all equipped with color TVs and soft carpets. You get a writing desk, generous hanging space, chest of drawers, and a very handy closed cupboard for luggage. The small sparkling bathrooms have heat lamps with automatic timers. And the montages of Arctic scenery on the walls are worthy of a photographic award. No-smoking floor available. Shuttle van service to and from the airport.

YELLOWKNIFE INN, Franklin Ave., Yellowknife, NT, X1A 2N4. Tel. 403/873-2601. Fax 403/873-2602. 130 rms. TV TEL
$ Rates (including breakfast): $139 single; $159 double. AE, DC, ER, MC, V.

Founded by a two-fisted, wooden-legged, bighearted bootlegger, sailor, storekeeper, and character named Vic Ingraham, the Yellowknife is the second major hotel in town. The old hotel has been completely rebuilt and is now a plushly modern affair, but some of the old frontier spirit still lingers. This is partly due to the fact that it stands right next to the Legislative Assembly of the Territory and swarms with backslapping politicians, business executives, geologists, and prospectors. The lobby is a mine of information of what's going on in the region.

The rooms come with cable TV, some with minibars, and guest amenities that have won an International Hospitality award. The walls are decorated with Inuit art. Guests receive a pass to local fitness facilities and complimentary shuttle rides to and from the airport. The fourth floor is reserved for nonsmokers.

MODERATE

DISCOVERY INN, 4701 Franklin Ave., Yellowknife, NT, X1A 2N6. Tel. 403/873-4151. Fax 403/920-7948. 41 rms. A/C TV TEL

$ Rates: $90 single or double. AE, MC, V.

A small two-story modern brick building, with friendly awnings and huge neon sign, the Discovery Inn has a central downtown location and a number of permanent residents. There's a lively bar with pool table, video games, and nightly entertainment, plus a family restaurant. Six of the rooms come with kitchenettes; all come with cable TV.

THE EXECUTIVE, 4920 54th Ave., Yellowknife, NT, X1A 2P5. Tel. 403/920-3999. Fax 403/920-4716. 13 suites. TV TEL

$ Rates: $140 single or double occupancy of studio. AE, MC, V.

The Executive is a large frontier-style apartment building located two blocks from downtown. It rents complete spacious suites with washer, dryer, refrigerator, and dishwasher, plus cable TV. Also on the premises are a fully equipped gym and weight room, and a sauna and hot tub. If you're feeling energetic, you can join one of the fitness classes as well.

IGLOO INN, 4115 Franklin Ave. (P.O. Box 596), Yellowknife, NT, X1A 2N4. Tel. 403/873-8511. Fax 403/873-5547. 44 rms. TV TEL

$ Rates (including continental breakfast): $100 single; $105 double. AE, MC, V.

An attractive two-story wood structure, the Igloo is painted a vivid green and sits at the bottom of the hill road leading to Old Town. It has 44 units, 33 of them with kitchenettes, and also a breakfast room where the continental breakfast is gratis and complimentary coffee is served all day! All units come equipped with bath and shower, color TV, and dial telephone. Furnishings are in elegant light wood: smart little writing desks with mirrors, two armchairs, a table, and excellent lighting fixtures. The kitchen dinettes are pleasantly spacious, and the kitchens stocked with electric ranges and all necessary utensils. Bathrooms come with electric ventilators. Altogether, it's a great value for your money.

AN IMPORTANT NOTE ON PRICES

Unless stated otherwise, **the prices cited in this guide are given in Canadian dollars,** which is good news for U.S. travelers because the Canadian dollar is worth 25% less than the American dollar, but buys nearly as much. As we go to press, $1 Canadian is worth 75¢ U.S., which means that your $100-a-night hotel room will cost only U.S. $75, and your $6 breakfast costs only U.S. $4.50.

Here's a quick table of equivalents:

Canadian $	U.S. $
$ 1	$ 0.75
5	3.75
10	7.50
20	15.00
50	37.50
80	60.00
100	75.00
200	150.00

YWCA, 5004 54th St., Yellowknife, NT, X1A 2R6. Tel. 403/920-2777. Fax 403/873-9406. 30 rms. TV TEL

$ Rates: Hotel $75 single; $85 double. Extra person $10. Hostel $20. AE, MC, V.

A remarkably versatile and slightly confusing establishment, the YWCA and Bayview Apartment Hotel are located in a large, massive gravelstone building called Northern United Place. The Y's front desk is inside a side entrance. Both establishments come under the Y heading and take in both genders.

The Bayview offers modern, comfortably furnished suites, each with bathroom, fully equipped kitchenette, telephone and cable TV, as well as refrigerator and cutlery for up to four people. Hostel accommodation is in shared rooms. You'll find the Northern United Place two blocks from downtown opposite the Mildred Hall School on Franklin Avenue. The actual Y entrance is on 54th Street. The management is exceptionally amiable, even by Territorial standards.

BUDGET

In recent years Yellowknife has acquired a whole row of bed-and-breakfast establishments, where the breakfasts are as big as the hospitality. Some cater specifically to nonsmokers, and all expect you to share a bathroom.

BLUE RAVEN GUEST HOUSE, 37-B Otto Dr., Yellowknife, NT, X1A 2T9. Tel. 403/873-6328. Fax 403/920-4013. 2 rms (shared bath).

$ Rates: $60 single; $75 double. No credit cards.

The Blue Raven Guest House is a beautiful spacious home sitting atop Latham Island, with a large deck offering scenic views of the Great Slave Lake.

CAPTAIN RON'S, 8 Lessard Dr., Yellowknife, NT, X1A 2G5. Tel. 403/873-3746. 4 rms (shared bath).

$ Rates: $72 single; $88 double. MC, V.

Located on Latham Island on the shores of the Great Slave Lake, Captain Ron's is reached by causeway. It's a cozy and picturesque place with four guest rooms and a reading lounge with fireplace, and TV. You can arrange fishing trips with Captain Ron (he really exists and used to skipper a cruise vessel).

EVA AND ERIC HENDERSON, 114 Knutsen Ave., Yellowknife, NT, X1A 2Y4. Tel. 403/873-5779. Fax 403/873-6160. 3 rms (shared bath). TEL

$ Rates (including breakfast): $60 single; $70 double.

 Eva and Eric Henderson have three rooms available for nonsmokers. There's a shared lounge with color TV, a shared bathroom, a library, and northern foods for breakfast (if requested). Homemade jam and bread.

NEARBY LODGES & CAMPS

The Yellowknife region has half a dozen of these facilities ideal for fishing, boating, hiking, and wildlife watching. Accommodation standards are good, although not exactly luxurious. The rates quoted vary according to whether or not they include transportation, food, gear, or other essentials.

Blachford Lake Lodge, P.O. Box 1568, Yellowknife, NT, X1A 2P2 (tel. 403/873-3303), situated 60 air miles east of Yellowknife, accommodates 25 people in five housekeeping log cabins, offering lake fishing and hiking in summer, skiing and ice-fishing in winter, and a sauna all year. The rate of $145 per person includes accommodation and boats, but not transportation, food, or fishing equipment.

Meni Dene Lodge, General Delivery, Lac la Martre, NT, X0E 1P0 (tel. 403/573-3161), assures anglers of catching 20-pound lake fish. It is a full-service facility, accommodating 16 persons. Rates here cover all-inclusive packages from Yellowknife. The weekend package costs $1,065, the five-day package $1,585.

Prelude Lake Lodge, P.O. Box 596, Yellowknife, NT, X1A 2P8 (tel. 403/873-8511). Located off Highway 4 by the lakeshore 20 miles east of Yellowknife, it accommodates 15 people in housekeeping cabins and has a restaurant and store. The cabins cost from $55, but you pay extra for boats and transportation.

WHERE TO DINE

Yellowknife provides surprisingly good meals at prices that range 25% to 30% above prices in most of Canada. This is not surprising in view of the fact that the supply of fresh meat and produce must be airlifted part of the way for eight to 12 weeks of the year.

The capital is, let's face it, a hard-drinking town where most of the social life takes place in saloons—which, officially, don't exist at all. They're called lounge bars, cabarets, or what-have-you, but fulfill their purpose very gregariously until around 1am. However, 11 communities in the Territories have voted themselves bone dry: You can neither possess nor consume liquor in their areas, so check it out before visiting.

EXPENSIVE

FACTORS CLUB, in the Explorer Hotel, 48th St. Tel. 403/873-3531.
  Cuisine: INTERNATIONAL. **Reservations:** Recommended.
  $ Prices: Main courses $9.75–$33.95. AE, ER, MC, V.
  Open: Lunch Wed–Fri; dinner Mon–Sat 5–10pm.

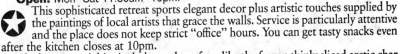 Factors proves quite a shock to those innocent visitors who expected log-cabin cuisine in the Territories. The logs are there all right, but on the ceiling and in the immense enclosed fireplace with copper chimney that forms the centerpiece. The vast and sumptuous room, heavily carpeted, functions on two levels, both overlooking the beautiful rock and tree landscape outside. The wooden chairs have leather upholstery and the walls are festooned with genuine pioneer kitchenware. The service is as smooth and silent as you'd find in top-ranking metropolitan dineries.

For an appetizer, try the jumbo shrimp in cocktail sauce, then move on to piccata of veal or the roasted quail with sautéed onions. For dessert, how about the Spanish coffee, a mixture of coffee, brandy, and Tía Maria? How's that for log-cabin fare?

THE OFFICE, 4915 50th St. Tel. 403/873-3750.
  Cuisine: CANADIAN/NORTHERN. **Reservations:** Recommended.
  $ Prices: Main courses $9–$26. AE, MC, V.
  Open: Mon–Sat 11:30am–10pm.

This sophisticated retreat sports elegant decor plus artistic touches supplied by the paintings of local artists that grace the walls. Service is particularly attentive and the place does not keep strict "office" hours. You can get tasty snacks even after the kitchen closes at 10pm.

The house specialties include northern fare, like the frozen thinly sliced arctic char and caribou steak. Otherwise the menu is top-grade Anglo: roast lamb, beef with Yorkshire pudding, roast duckling, and a large selection of seafood. The eggs Benedict served here is famous among the lunchtime crowd. And the Office puts on possibly the best salad bar in the north.

MODERATE

OUR PLACE, 50th Ave. and 50th St. Tel. 403/920-2265.
  Cuisine: NORTHERN. **Reservations:** Accepted.
  $ Prices: Main courses $6.95–$19.95. AE, MC, V.
  Open: Lunch Mon–Sat 11am–3pm; dinner Mon–Sat 6pm–midnight.

Our Place is actually a cocktail lounge, but it also dishes up some renowned northern specialties that lure patrons from very far afield. One of them is caribou vol au vent—thinly sliced meat slowly cooked in white wine sauce and served in a puff pastry shell. Or try the equally famous arctic char with lemon butter. Our Place also pours the only megadrinks in the north.

PARACHUTE RESTAURANT, Centre Square Mall, 5014 49th St. Tel. 403/873-6842.
  Cuisine: CHINESE/CONTINENTAL. **Reservations:** Recommended.
  $ Prices: Main courses $6–$12. MC, V.
  Open: Mon–Fri 7am–midnight, Sat–Sun 11am–midnight.

An astonishing culinary mix for breakfast, lunch, and dinner that ranges from

Cantonese wokery to French toast, from curry chicken on banana bread to homemade pasta; not forgetting hamburgers, seafood, and roast beef. The kitchen wizard behind this vittle variety was chosen Chef of the Year 1992, and you can taste the reason. A brightly polished eatery, the Parachute also has a lounge bar with imported beers on tap, serves homemade desserts, and puts on a locally famous Sunday brunch for around $10.

RED APPLE, in the Discovery Inn, Franklin Ave. Tel. 403/873-5859.
   Cuisine: CANADIAN/PIZZA/CHINESE. **Reservations:** Accepted.
$ Prices: Main courses $7–$12. AE, MC, V.
   Open: Mon–Thurs 6am–midnight, Fri–Sat 6am–1am, Sun 8am–11pm.
This is a rarity—a breakfast spot and family restaurant that also keeps late hours. Breakfast, in fact, is served all day in this pleasantly relaxed eatery with large viewing windows. The pizza selection is fairly small but the sizes hefty. You get a good array of predinner nibbles, English-style fish-and-chips, and hearty helpings of liver with onions, steaks, or breaded pork cutlets.

SAM'S MONKEY TREE, Range Lake Road Mall. Tel. 403/920-4914.
   Cuisine: INTERNATIONAL/CHINESE. **Reservations:** Accepted.
$ Prices: Most items $8–$14.95. MC, V.
   Open: Mon–Thurs 4–11pm, Fri 4–midnight, Sat–Sun 11am–10pm.
Sam's is actually two different establishments operating under one name, but serving quite distinct menus. The first is a pub restaurant with a country inn flavor, a dart board, and outdoor patio. The second is a standard Chinese eatery with take-out service and Cantonese fare. Between them the two manage to please most palates, including vegetarians'. They cover a remarkable range of goodies, from lasagne and vegetarian quiches to Greek chicken souvlaki, Ukrainian kolbassa and cabbage rolls, and beef stir-fry with garlic bread. On Sunday the pub portion spreads out a good-sized smörgåsbord.

WILDCAT CAFE, Willey Rd., in Old Town. Tel. 403/873-8850.
   Cuisine: NORTHERN. **Reservations:** Not accepted.
$ Prices: Main courses $7–$17. MC, V.
   Open: Mon–Sat 7am–9:30pm, Sun 10am–9pm. **Closed:** Winter.
⭐ The Wildcat Café is a visitors' "sight" as much as an eatery. A squat log cabin with a deliberately grizzled frontier look, the Wildcat was actually refurbished in the image of the original 1930s version. The atmospheric interior is reminiscent of Yellowknife in its pioneer days, and the café has been photographed, filmed, painted, and caricatured often enough to give it star rating. It serves up traditional northern fare like roast musk-ox and caribou stew, whitefish, and char.

BUDGET

THE LUNCHBOX, in the Yellowknife Centre Mall. Tel. 403/873-5004.
   Cuisine: CANADIAN. **Reservations:** Not accepted.
$ Prices: Main courses $5–$10. No credit cards.
   Open: Mon–Sat 7am–4pm.
 Fluorescently lit, streamlined, and plastic, this basement cafeteria provides fast, hygienic, cheap, and fairly good lunches for half the town's office workers. A solid breakfast of bacon, two eggs, and coffee costs $7.50; hamburgers around $7. Not exactly atmospheric, but bustling and efficient.

MIKE MARK'S, 51st St. and Franklin Ave. Tel. 403/873-3309.
   Cuisine: CHINESE. **Reservations:** Accepted.
$ Prices: Main courses $7–$11. MC, V.
   Open: Daily 11am–11pm.
Despite the Western label, Mike Mark's is a Chinese establishment, not exactly glamorous but tastefully decorated, with an extensive menu. The dining room has a bar on one side, steel chairs and yellow-draped tables on the other. The illumination comes from a multitude of tasseled lanterns. The low ceiling is artistically hung with fishnets and marine creatures. Deep-fried shrimp and mushroom gai kine are

excellent. Each diner gets one complimentary fortune cookie. There's a lengthy take-out menu in case you'd like to arrange a Chinese picnic.

EVENING ENTERTAINMENT

Yellowknife's nightlife revolves around a few bars and lounges in which most of the entertainment is self-generated. Several do employ professional vocalists or groups, but not on a regular basis. Sometimes the patrons put on turns of their own, usually uninvited. But the vibes are among the warmest you'll find anywhere, and the atmosphere pretty close to the fabled frontier spirit.

FLOAT BASE, at the corner of 50th Ave. and 51st St. Tel. 403/873-3034.

The Float Base is a jolly neighborhood pub beneath a bright-blue awning. It has a small intimate lounge with polished cedar tables and upholstered swivel chairs, and wall decorations in the form of pictures of old-time floatplanes. The Base shows sporting events on TV, has a corner for dart games, and features jam sessions and local entertainers with fair regularity. It also serves excellent cappuccino. Open Monday to Saturday from 3pm to 1am.

GOLD RANGE TAVERN, in the Gold Range Hotel, 5010 50th St. Tel. 403/873-4441.

Officially called Bad Sam's, this place is better known by its local nickname—"Strange Range." There is nothing really strange about it; the Gold Range is exactly what you'd expect to find in a northern frontier town. Except that Yellowknife has shed the "frontier" label quite a while back and become middling sedate.

Well, sedate the Gold Range is not. It's an occasionally rip-roaring tavern that attracts the whole gamut of native and visiting characters in search of some after-dinner whoopee. You get men in business suits and ladies in cocktail gowns bending elbows with haystack-bearded trappers, tattooed miners, hairy jocks in tank tops, lasses in skin-tight jeans, members of the Legislative Assembly, and T-shirted tourists. The nightly entertainment is supposedly country-and-western music, but that doesn't really describe it. Anybody is liable to join in with an offering—such as an elderly French Canadian fur trapper who comes to town on a snowmobile and accompanies himself on a plywood guitar. There is also dancing and a pool table, the second-highest per capita beer consumption in Canada, and—periodically—a brawl, very quickly subdued by the most efficient bouncers in the Territory. You don't come here for a quiet evening, but you can't say you've seen Yellowknife if you haven't seen the Strange Range.

AN EXCURSION TO A NATIVE CANADIAN SETTLEMENT

Detah, a Dogrib Dene village of about 160 people, lies just across the bay from Yellowknife. In summer the connection is either by freighter canoe across the lake or by an 11-mile road around the bay. In winter an ice road cuts across the lake that can accommodate cars, trucks, and snowmobiles as well as dog teams. There's nothing in the least "touristy" about Detah. It's a quiet traditional community whose people shun city life, even the Yellowknife version of same. They're friendly, cheerful, and hospitable, but there's no tourist accommodation or meal service in the village.

---

4. AROUND THE TERRITORIES

Of the 63 communities spread across the Territories, here are 10 that offer some accommodation and/or are of interest to the tourist.

COMMUNITIES Fort Smith Once the territorial capital, this town of 2,360 people is located one mile from the Alberta border and close to the **Wood Buffalo National Park.** The settlement was founded as a Hudson's Bay Company fur-trading post in 1874. The adventurous history of the place is portrayed in the **Northern Life Museum.** Famous for a spectacular series of four rapids on the Slave River and the nesting site of a colony of white pelicans, it has several hotels and restaurants. Pacific Western provides scheduled air service to the town.

Hay River   This port on the southern shore of Great Slave Lake, and on the Mackenzie Highway route, opposite Yellowknife, with 5,000 inhabitants, is a busy fishing harbor and summer dockside for the stream of barges carrying cargoes to the far-flung Arctic settlements in the north. Situated on a lake island facing the town is the only Dene reserve in the Territories. Some 33 miles to the south is the spectacular **Alexandra Falls,** where the Hay River plunges 106 feet and attracts camera bugs from all over Canada by the dramatic beauty of the spectacle. The town has tourist hotels and good restaurants.

Fort Simpson   Originally a trapping outpost for beaver and marten skins, this is now the ideal springboard for excursions into **Nahanni National Park.** It lies 230 miles west of Yellowknife on the Mackenzie Highway, and has a hotel and a lodge with restaurant facilities. Scheduled services are provided by four airlines.

Rae-Edzo   With about 1,400 people, this is the largest Dene settlement in the Territories. The Dene belong to the Dogrib tribe, and have banned the sale or consumption of liquor in the township. But since Rae lies only 68 miles northwest of Yellowknife, the prohibition doesn't entail much hardship. There is an interesting native craftshop as well as two motels and two cafés.

Inuvik   The name means "place of humans," and this is the second-largest community in the Northwest Territories, with a population of 3,200. Hewn out of the Arctic wilderness 680 miles northwest of Yellowknife, Inuvik was founded only in 1955 as the main supply base for the petrochemical exploration of the area. It's a modern community with hotels, restaurants, and jet air service from Edmonton and Yellowknife.

Every July 21 to July 25 the town becomes the site of the famous **Trans-Arctic Games,** biggest and most colorful of their kind. The games feature traditional Native Canadian sports, competitions, drumming, dancing, craft displays, and the unique "Good Woman" contest. Inuit women show their amazing skill at seal and muskrat skinning, bannock baking, sewing, and other abilities that traditionally made a "good woman," Arctic edition.

Frobisher Bay   Another "young" settlement, established as a U.S. Air Force airstrip in 1942, it now boasts a population of more than 2,500. Located on the east coast of the huge Baffin Island, 1,405 miles northeast of Yellowknife, it's a bustling and expanding place with the excellent **Nunuuta Museum** for Arctic arts and crafts, three hotels, and several restaurants. A celebrated **spring carnival** is held every April, featuring igloo building, ice sculpture, and reputedly the toughest snowmobile race in the world.

Cape Dorset   On the south coast of Baffin Island, 1,160 miles from Yellowknife, Cape Dorset has twice-weekly air service from Frobisher Bay. This is a world-renowned center of Inuit art and seat of the **West Baffin Eskimo Co-Operative,** which handles the stone carvings, prints, and lithographs that have given the place international standing. About 700 people live in the village, some still by hunting, trapping, and sealing. Tourist accommodation is available at the **Kingnait Inn** (tel. 819/897-8863).

Baker Lake   Another famous Inuit art center, located on the north shore of the huge lake at the approximate geographical center of Canada, this is the only island native community in the Northwest Territories and has about 1,000 people. The artisans here produce the highly regarded Baker Lake tapestries. Hotel accommodations are available, as well as scheduled air service. It's 585 miles northwest of Yellowknife.

Pangnirtung   Called "Pang" by Territorians and "the Switzerland of the Arctic" by tour promoters, Pangnirtung lies at the entrance of **Auyuittuq National Park** on Baffin Island, 1,435 miles from Yellowknife. In a beautiful scenic setting, surrounded by steeply rising mountains, "Pang" has about 900 people, living by fishing, sealing, walrus and caribou hunting, and the sale of their art and craft products. Room and board are available at the **Auyuittuq Lodge** (tel. 819/473-8611), and there's scheduled air service from Frobisher Bay.

Tuktoyaktuk   On the shores of the Beaufort Sea, 100 miles south of the permanent polar ice cap in the Arctic Ocean, and popularly known as "Tuk," this is a famous base for fur trappers and has a reindeer herd of 10,000 head, which means the finest reindeer steaks in the Territories. There are three hotels, and scheduled air service is from Inuvik.

NATIONAL PARKS   Wood Buffalo   The Northwest Territories share this park with Alberta, and the region is mentioned in Chapter 19. The main attraction is the roaming herd of 6,000 wood bison—the last in Canada—which are actually hybrids, the result of a mixture with the slightly smaller plains buffalo brought in from Alberta in 1923.

   The park has a campground and more than 30 miles of hiking trails. Park headquarters is in nearby Fort Smith, where you also have to buy whatever food you want on your excursion (none is available in the park—and you'd better not even think of buffalo stew).

Nahanni   A breathtaking, unspoiled wilderness of 1,840 square miles in the southwest corner of the Territories, accessible only by motorboat, canoe, or charter aircraft (see "Organized Tours" at the beginning of this chapter), this is a region of scenic grandeur and mystery. The **Nahanni River** claws its path through the mountain ranges and at **Virginia Falls** plunges down in a 316-foot cataract that is over twice the height of Niagara Falls! The whole scene is a dramatic composition of subarctic hot springs, white-water rapids, and cliffs soaring up vertically for 4,000 feet.

   The mystery stems from Native Canadian lore, which makes this the region of the legendary Bigfoot, and from the white man's tales about a hidden tropical valley containing gold nuggets the size of marbles. One man, Albert Fallie, spent his entire life searching for this gold bonanza. The three McLeod brothers set out to find it in 1905. Their headless skeletons were discovered three years later. The canyon in which they were found is called Headless Valley. The nearest accommodation is the log-cabin **Nahanni Mountain Lodge** (tel. 403/695-2505).

Auyuittuq   Pronounced "Ah-you-ee-tuk," which is Inuit for "the place that never melts," Auyuittuq is the world's first national park inside the Arctic Circle. But only about a quarter of the park's 8,300 square miles is covered by the fringes of the immense **Penny Ice Cap.** Most of the park consists of wonderful hiking scenery in deep, glacier-carved valleys and along spectacular fjords with sheer cliffs rising to 4,000 feet. From May through July this region has 24 hours of daylight—total darkness in midwinter.

   On land you can spot an occasional polar bear. In the coastal waters there are thousands of harp seals, walruses, belugas (white whales), and narwhals, an odd little whale with a long ivory spear on its face. There is a campground on the Weasel River delta equipped with tentsites, drinking water, and firewood, and six emergency shelters are in strategic locations. The park administration office is located in Pangnirtung. Hikers and climbers must register there.

CHAPTER 22

THE YUKON

- **WHAT'S SPECIAL ABOUT THE YUKON**
1. **THE GOLD RUSH**
2. **WHITEHORSE**
3. **DAWSON CITY**
4. **KLUANE NATIONAL PARK**

The verses of Robert W. Service, poet laureate of the north, paint the Yukon in the days of the Klondike gold rush that put it on the map. Well, the Yukon has grown considerably tamer since then, with hardships rather few and far between. But the land still beckons, casting a peculiar spell over visitors that no other part of Canada can quite match. There's a tang of adventure lingering in the Yukon air, despite motor roads, jetports, and deluxe hotels.

Once part of the Northwest Territories, the Yukon is now a separate territory bordering on British Columbia in the south and Alaska in the west (when locals refer to the U.S., they nearly always mean Alaska). Compared to the Northwest Territories it's a mere midget in size, but with 200,000 square miles the Yukon is more than twice as big as Wyoming.

The entire territory has a population of only 30,339—two-thirds of them living in the capital of Whitehorse. But every year it attracts over 300,000 visitors, or 13 times the total number of residents. Tourism is the area's second-largest business and, hopefully, after reading this chapter you'll understand why.

Far from being a barren, frigid landscape, the Yukon has some of the most colorful scenery in Canada: rolling green hillsides blazing with wildflowers, sparkling lakes studded with wooded islands, broad rushing streams swirling against a backdrop of snowcapped mountain ranges.

Some of the biggest herds of caribou in North America populate the northern plains. Mountain sheep clamber around the slopes and timber wolves roam the forests. Eagles draw slow circles in the sky and the rare peregrine falcon is still breeding in the more remote valleys. The lake and river fishing is unsurpassed anywhere.

SEEING THE YUKON

INFORMATION For general guidance about visiting the Yukon, including information on organized tours and sporting excursions, contact **Yukon Tourism,** P.O. Box 2703, Whitehorse, YT, Y1A 2C6 (tel. 403/667-5340).

CLIMATE & SEASONS The climate, at least in summer, is much milder than you'd expect in a territory whose northern toe dips into the Arctic Ocean. First of all it's very dry, so you don't have to worry about chilling dampness. In Whitehorse the summer average hovers around 58° Fahrenheit, sometimes climbing into the 70s and 80s in July. And you get hardly any darkness during the summer months, only a few hours of gray dusk from 11pm to 2am. In winter the mercury may dip as low as −60°, but never longer than a few days at a stretch.

As the myth about the Yukon's "perpetual ice and snow" is dispelled, more and more visitors are coming during the "shoulder seasons" of spring and fall, and during the actual winter for superb snowmobiling, snowshoeing, and cross-country skiing. Among the attractions of fall and winter visits is the absence then of mosquitoes and blackflies. Communities have a continued spraying program to keep them scarce, but out in the bush they keep you slapping unless you venture forth equipped with insect repellent.

GETTING THERE Perhaps the most striking contrast between the Yukon of the

WHAT'S SPECIAL ABOUT THE YUKON

Wildlife
- ☐ The Yukon swarms with wildlife— grizzly and black bears, moose, lynx, wolves, peregrine falcons, and herds of caribou.
- ☐ Trophy hunters can get bears, moose, and caribou—and strict regulations ensure that wildlife populations continue to flourish.

Natural Spectacles
- ☐ Kluane National Park, with the highest mountains in Canada and the largest nonpolar ice fields in the world.
- ☐ The Yukon River, winding through some of the most spectacular scenery on earth. Paddle your own canoe or cruise down by riverboat.
- ☐ The northern lights and the midnight sun. In winter there's a flickering sky show of red, green, and blue lights; in summer the sun shines through most of the night.

Ace Attractions
- ☐ Dawson City, a resurrected "ghost town" where the Klondike gold rush is replayed for tourists.

- ☐ The MacBride Museum in Whitehorse, with a fascinating collection of photos, utensils, maps, diagrams, and entire heritage buildings that present the Yukon's saga from prehistory to the present.

Routes through the Yukon
- ☐ The Chilkoot Trail, the legendary mountain road of the Klondike stampeders. You can rough it by hiking or take the White Pass railway in comfort.
- ☐ The Dempster Highway, the only public road in North America that runs across the Arctic Circle.

Unique Festivals
- ☐ Annual frolics like the Yukon Quest Dog Sled Race, the Klondike Outhouse Races, the Festival of Storytelling, and the Frostbite Music Festival.

People
- ☐ Yukon Indians of eight tribes, who act as guides and wilderness interpreters and produce superbly crafted artworks.

gold rush and ours is the ease of getting there. You can fly in, drive in, or sail in (by the Alaska Ferry to Port Chilkoot).

But the vast majority of visitors choose the air or road routes. **Canadian Airlines International** (tel. toll free 800/426-7000) has daily jet flights to Whitehorse from Calgary and Edmonton, costing $609.90. **Air Alaska** (tel. toll free 800/426-0333) links Whitehorse with Fairbanks, Juneau, and Anchorage.

Greyhound (tel. 403/667-2223) has bus service to Whitehorse from Vancouver and Edmonton. Over 90,000 private motorists every year choose to drive in on the Alaska Highway, which starts at Dawson Creek in British Columbia, taking you right into Whitehorse, some 918 miles north. It's a fairly good road through some very dramatic scenery, but in summer the dust is a nuisance and you have to watch the flying gravel that pits windshields and headlights.

If you're driving, it's a good idea to attach a bug or gravel screen and plastic headlight guards to your vehicle. And it's absolutely essential that your windshield wipers are operative and your washer reservoir full. The law requires that all automobiles drive with their headlights on while traveling on any Yukon highway.

For 24-hour highway information call 403/667-5893.

In summer dust can be a serious nuisance, particularly on gravel roads. When it becomes a problem, close all windows and turn on your heater fan. This builds up air pressure inside your vehicle and helps to keep the dust out. Keep cameras in plastic bags for protection.

April and May are the spring slush months when mud and water may render some road sections hazardous.

The winter months, from December to March, require a lot of special driving preparations. Your vehicle should be completely checked over and winterized. Snow tires, antifreeze, and winter-weight crankcase oil are a *must*. So are a circulating block heater and a battery blanket. Carry booster cables, a shovel, and a tow rope. Experienced northerners also carry tire chains, a can of gasoline antifreeze, an ax, kitchen matches, kindling wood, roadside flares, and sleeping bags.

Sailing to the Yukon is somewhat complicated by the fact that the Yukon has no seaports. The Alaska Marine Highway (tel. toll free 800/642-0066) carries passengers and vehicles from Prince Rupert in British Columbia to Skagway, Alaska. From Skagway you can take a motorcoach to Whitehorse, 110 miles north via the Klondike Highway.

ORGANIZED TOURS & EXCURSIONS   The Yukon Territory is one of the last great game reserves on the continent, literally teeming with wildlife. In order to keep it so, hunting permits are strictly controlled. All nonresidents must obtain a license and do their hunting accompanied by one of the Yukon's licensed guides. Most of these guides, however, also offer photo safaris, which require neither licenses nor permits.

The range of guided tours is immense—from comfortable coach travel to extremely strenuous sled-team and horseback adventures. Make sure you're in good physical shape before you venture on one of the latter. The listings below merely represent a few samples of the types of excursions available. For complete information, write to the province's tourism office (see "Information," above).

Rainbow Tours, Dept. AXY, 3089 Third Ave., Whitehorse, YT, Y1A 5B3 (tel. 403/668-5598), offers six different package journeys through the north for groups of no more than 12. It includes one trip right across the Arctic Circle, from Whitehorse to Inuvik.

The MV *Yukon Lou* sails down the Yukon River to Lake Laberge on 2½-hour luncheon trips or salmon barbecue excursions, both scenic and leisurely. The first costs $10.50; the second, $35. Contact Rainbow Tours.

Yukon Tours, Suite 200, 307 Jarvis St., Whitehorse, YT, Y1A 2H3 (tel. 403/667-7790), has guided canoe, boat, and fishing trips, horseback tours, and foot hikes throughout the Yukon. Ground and air transportation can be arranged, as well as special wildlife photo safaris.

Ecosummer Expeditions, Box 5095, Whitehorse, YT, Y1A 4Z2 (tel. 403/633-8453), takes guided backpacking and mountaineering parties to Kluane National Park. Wilderness canoe and raft trips throughout the Territory can also be arranged.

Atlas Tours, headquartered in the Westmark Hotel in Whitehorse (tel. 403/668-3161), operates a dozen excursions ranging from brief local jaunts to three-day fly-in fishing and kayaking expeditions as well as cruises to Glacier Bay. The shorter outings include Whitehorse City Sightseeing, which takes in all of the capital's historical landmarks and a trip to the Yukon Wildlife Preserve. The tour takes 3½ hours and costs $30 for adults, $15 for children. Their Skagway Excursion goes to Fraser by motorcoach, then changes to a vintage 1890s parlor car of the historic White Pass & Yukon Railway. The narrated journey chugs over trestles and through tunnels from the White Pass Summit to Skagway, Alaska. The trip takes five hours and the one-way fare is $115 for adults, $57.50 for children.

Coyote, P.O. Box 5210, Whitehorse (tel. 403/633-5006), run by Maureen Garrity and Cliff Dunaski, specializes in adventure travel. One of their trips, "Glaciers

---

IMPRESSIONS

There's a land where the mountains are nameless,
And the rivers all run God knows where;
There are lives that are erring and aimless,
And deaths that just hang by a hair;
There are hardships that nobody reckons;
There are valleys unpeopled and still;
There's a land—oh, it beckons and beckons,
And I want to go back—and I will.
—ROBERT W. SERVICE

and Grizzlies," goes by raft on the Alsek River through the section designated as a grizzly bear sanctuary and offers excellent bear viewing, ideal for camera shooting. The trip, labeled "suitable for all fitness levels," takes 2½ days and costs $550.

Canadian River Expeditions, 3524 W. 16th Ave., Vancouver, BC V6R 3C1, was founded in 1972 as Canada's first river-rafting outfitter. Their programs are carefully planned to highlight various ecosystems and environments and each trip is conducted by expert guides who pass on their knowledge of native culture and fauna to the participants.

One of their journeys is a six-day rafting and hiking expedition through the heart of the Kluane National Park. The emphasis is on natural history and the agenda includes the most spectacular part of the watershed of the Alsek River. The tour departs from Whitehorse and costs U.S. $1,420.

The same company also offers a helicopter portage over the glaciers on the upper Alsek and a sled expedition to the edge of Baffin Island's ice floe, using native Inuit guides. For further information call Dick Griffith (in Chicago) at 312/263-6481.

1. THE GOLD RUSH

There are two things you won't get away from as long as you linger in the Territory: the Klondike gold rush and the verses of Robert W. Service. One produced the other, and they combined to imprint the image of the Yukon on the outside world as well as the permanent inhabitants. Nobody is more gung ho on gold-rush lore and Service ballads than the locals, which is the highest compliment you can pay a bard.

Service may not have been a great poet in the literary sense, but he was a tremendously evocative one, depicting landscapes, characters, and emotions the way his contemporaries felt them, stirring echoes in their souls that an academically more brilliant wordsmith may never have aroused. I attended a local reading of "The Spell of the Yukon" and saw dozens of old-timers nodding their heads in fervent agreement with the lines—

> *I wanted the gold, and I got it—*
> *Came out with a fortune last fall,*
> *Yet somehow life's not what I thought it,*
> *And somehow the gold isn't all.*

These, I promise, will be the last Service stanzas I'll quote. But the point about "the gold isn't all" could be the motto of the Territory today. The gold is gone, give or take a few ounces, and the "spell of the Yukon" now lies in scenic grandeur, in the overwhelming friendliness of its people, and in the pervasive feeling that this is one of the last genuine frontier regions left on earth.

Still, gold made the Yukon, because few people ever knew of its existence before the mad scramble that was the greatest gold rush in recorded history. It began with a wild war whoop from the throats of three men—two Native Canadians and one white—that broke the silence of the Klondike Valley on the morning of August 17, 1896: "Gold!" they screamed, "gold—gold—gold . . ." and that cry rang through the Yukon, crossed to Alaska, and rippled down into the United States. Soon the whole world echoed with it, and people as far away as China and Australia began selling their household goods and homes to scrape together the fare to a place few of them had ever heard of before.

Some 100,000 men and women from every corner of the globe set out on the Klondike stampede, descending on a territory populated by a few hundred souls. Tens of thousands came by the Chilkpot Pass from Alaska—the shortest route, but also the toughest. Canadian law required each stampeder to carry 2,000 pounds of provisions up over the 3,000-foot summit. Sometimes it took 30 or more trips up a 45° slope to get all the baggage over, and the entire trail—with only one pack—takes about 3½ days to hike.

You can see amazing silent movies today showing the endless human chain scrambling up the steep incline in an unbroken line of black dots against the white snow. And you can still pick up some of the items they discarded en route—rotting boots, rusted horse's bits, tin mugs, and broken bottles. Many collapsed on the way, but the rest slogged on—on to the Klondike and the untold riches to be found there.

The riches were real enough. The Klondike fields proved to be the richest ever found anywhere. Before the big strike on Bonanza Creek, the handful of prospectors in the Territory had considered 10¢ worth of glitter per gold pan a reasonably good find—and gold was then valued at around $15 an ounce. But the Klondike stampeders were netting $300 to $400 in a single pan! What's more, unlike some gold that lies embedded in veins of hard rock, the Klondike stuff came in dust or nugget forms buried in creek beds. This placer gold, as it's called, didn't have to be milled—it was already in an almost pure state!

The trouble was that most of the clerks who dropped their pens and butchers who shed their aprons to join the rush came too late. By the time they had completed the backbreaking trip, all the profitable claims along the Klondike creeks were staked out and defended by grim men with guns in their fists. Claim jumping was the quickest way to harvest lead instead of nuggets.

But the stream of humanity kept surging in and within a few years the Territory had utterly changed. By 1898 a railroad was running from Skagway in Alaska across 110 miles of cliffed and gorged wilderness to the tiny hamlet of Whitehorse. It stopped there and hasn't progressed an inch since. From Whitehorse the "Trail of '98" led to Dawson City, springboard of the Klondike, 333 miles to the north.

Almost overnight Dawson boomed into a roaring, bustling, gambling, whoring metropolis of 30,000 people, thousands of them living in tents (today the place has a few hundred permanent residents, plus 100,000 annual tourists). And here gathered those who made fortunes from the rush without ever handling a pan: the supply merchants, the saloonkeepers, dance-hall girls, and cardsharps. Also some oddly peripheral characters such as barroom janitors, who "panned" the shavings they swept from the floors every night for the gold dust that had spilled to the ground. And a stocky 21-year-old former sailor from San Francisco who adopted a big mongrel dog in Dawson, then went home and wrote a book about him that sold half a million copies. The book was *The Call of the Wild* and the sailor, Jack London.

By 1903 over $500 million in gold had been shipped south from the Klondike and the rush petered out. A handful of millionaires bought mansions in Seattle, tens of thousands went home with empty pockets, thousands more lay dead in unmarked graves along the Yukon River. Dawson—"City" no longer—became a dreaming backwater haunted by 30,000 ghosts.

But the railroad still runs from Skagway to Fraser, and you can ride it. And on Bonanza Creek one free claim is left open for tourists—you can sluice a pan there and peer for tiny flakes of yellow in what was once the richest pay dirt on earth. You might be able to buy a drink with what you find.

2. WHITEHORSE

284 miles (457km) from the Alaska border (Beaver Creek);
1,287 miles (2,072km) NW of Edmonton

GETTING THERE By Plane The airport, placed on a rise above the city, is fair in size and now has a hotel and restaurant. It's served by Canadian Airlines International and Air Alaska. A limousine takes you to the downtown hotels for $5; cab fare is around $8.

ESSENTIALS Information Your first stop should logically be the Whitehorse Visitor Reception Centre, 302 Steele St. (tel. 403/667-7545), where you'll get a smiling reception plus armloads of information about hotels, restaurants, shopping, and excursions. The center is open daily from 8am to 8pm.

City Layout The city's layout generally can't be faulted: All streets run vertically, the avenues—First to Eighth—bisecting them horizontally, all roads running around the periphery. Public transit is handled by bright-green minibuses that touch the suburbs surrounding downtown. They operate from 7:45am to 3:45pm Monday to Friday. For information, call Whitehorse Transit (tel. 403/668-2831).

Getting Around If you need a taxi, try Yellow Cabs (tel. 403/668-4811). Automobiles are for rent from Tilden (tel. 403/668-2521), Avis (tel. 403/668-2136), and Whitehorse Motors (tel. 403/667-7866).

The capital of the Yukon is a late arrival on the scene. It was established only in the spring of 1900, fully two years after the stampeders had swarmed into Dawson City. But Whitehorse, located on the banks of the Yukon River, is the logical hub of the Territory and became the capital after Dawson fizzled out together with the gold.

The city has a curiously split personality. On the one hand it's a frontier outpost with a mere 20,000 residents living within a ridiculously large 162-square-mile area. On the other hand the tourist influx gives it an almost cosmopolitan tinge: a whiff of nightlife, some smart boutiques, gourmet restaurants, and international hotels.

The main street of Whitehorse is—you guessed it—Main Street, with four blocks of stores and a lot of traffic. Main Street runs into First Avenue at the site of the White Pass & Yukon Railroad station. Beyond the railroad tracks flows the Yukon River. A bridge crosses the river at the end of Second Avenue and to the right of the bridge lies the SS *Klondike,* one of the 250 stern-wheelers that once plied the river between Whitehorse and Dawson City.

On the left of Second Avenue, heading toward the bridge, stands the big and massive stone complex of the Territorial Government Building. One of the newest and best-equipped structures of its kind in Canada, it conveniently houses all territorial government departments, the legislature, public library, Territorial Archives, as well as the Tourism Branch information office. The Federal Building, housing the post office, stands at the corner of Third Avenue and Main Street.

WHAT TO SEE & DO

Log Skyscrapers are log cabins, three stories high, used as apartment buildings, possibly the only species of their kind anywhere. They're on Lambert Street at Third Avenue.

YUKON BOTANICAL GARDENS, at the junction of the Alaska Hwy. and S. Access Rd. Tel. 403/668-7972.

The botanical gardens are the pride of Whitehorse. This unique 22-acre showpiece presents a flora-fauna combination you will see nowhere else in the north. Floral displays include 17 varieties of wild orchids found in the Yukon. (Ignoramuses like myself always thought of them as strictly tropical flowers.)

The gardens include a lake teeming with rainbow trout and populated by swarms of northern waterfowl. Amid an array of shrubs, flowers, and trees indigenous to the region lies Old MacDonald's Farm, stocked with farm animals that blend with the otherwise manicured landscape.

Admission: $4.95 adults, $1 children.
Open: Daily 9am–9pm.

YUKON TRANSPORTATION MUSEUM, Whitehorse Airport, at mile 915 on the Alaska Hwy. Tel. 403/668-4792.

The transportation museum contains a gallery of the implements that helped to open up the Territory. Includes the historic aircraft, *Queen of the Yukon,* plus railroading exhibits that once served on the gold route.

Admission: $3 adults, $1 children.
Open: Daily 11am–8pm.

NORTHERN SPLENDOR REINDEER FARM, mile 10.5, Klondike Hwy. 2. Tel. 403/633-2996.

Situated off the Klondike Highway, about 30 driving minutes north of Whitehorse, is a farm that's the only one of its kind in the Yukon. You see a video on reindeer and watch the feedings between 8 and 10 in the morning.

Admission: $2.50 adults, $1 children.
Open: Daily 8am–9pm.

TAKHINI HOT SPRINGS, on the Klondike Hwy., six miles north of Whitehorse. Tel. 403/633-2706.

A swimming pool fed by natural hot springs and surrounded by rolling hills and hiking trails, the Takhini Hot Springs lie about 20 minutes from town. After swimming you can refresh yourself at the coffee shop.
Admission: $3 adults, $2 children.
Open: Daily 7am–10pm.

WHITEHORSE RAPIDS DAM, at the end of Nisutlin Dr., in suburban Riverdale.

This intriguing "fish ladder" allows the spawning salmon to bypass the dam on their tough journey upstream. Interpretive displays and an upper viewing deck show you the entire process by which the dam has ceased to be an obstruction to the salmon migration.
Admission: Free.
Open: Daily 8am–10pm.

YUKON NATIVE PRODUCTS, 4230 Fourth Ave. Tel. 403/668-5955.

This most unusual garment factory combines traditional native skills with the latest computer technology. You can watch the stylish double-shell Yukon parka being made. Also, view examples of mukluks, slippers, and beadwork found in the north.
Admission: Free.
Open: Daily 7:30am–8pm.

SS *KLONDIKE,* anchored at the Robert Campbell Bridge.

Largest of the 250 riverboats that chuffed up and down the Yukon River between 1866 and 1955, the *Klondike* is now a permanently dry-docked museum piece. The still majestic paddle wheeler is fully restored to almost its former glory.
Admission: Free.
Open: Daily 9am–5:30pm.

MACBRIDE MUSEUM, First Ave., at the corner of Wood St. Tel. 403/667-2709.

Within this museum compound you'll also find Sam McGee's Cabin (read Service's poem on the cremation of same) and the old Whitehorse Telegraph Office. The log-cabin museum is crammed with relics from the gold-rush era, and has a large display of Yukon wildlife. It's interesting material, lovingly arranged by a nonprofit society.
Admission: $3.25 adults, $1 children.
Open: Daily 10am–6pm.

OLD LOG CHURCH, Elliott St., at Third Ave.

When Whitehorse got its first resident priest in 1900, he lived and held services in a tent. By the next spring the Old Log Church and rectory were built, and both are currently the only buildings of that date in town still in use. The Old Log Church is now officially a cathedral—the only wooden cathedral in the world—and contains artifacts on the history of all churches in the Yukon. Mass is every Sunday evening; closed Sunday morning.
Admission: $2.50 adults, $1 children.
Open: Mon–Sat 9am–6pm, Sun noon–4pm.

CRUISES & EXCURSIONS

The ✪ MV *Schwatka* is a river craft that cruises the Yukon River through the famous Miles Canyon. This stretch—once the most hazardous section of water in the Territory—is now dammed and tamed, though it still offers fascinating wilderness scenery. The cruise takes two hours, accompanied by narration telling the story of the old wild river times. Adults pay $15, children $7.50. Book at **Rainbow Tours,** 3089 Third Ave. (tel. 403/668-5598).

The **Yukon Wildlife Preserve** covers hundreds of acres of forests and meadows. Roaming freely throughout are bison, moose, musk-ox, elk, snowy owls, and the rare peregrine falcon. Tours of the preserve depart daily and last 1½ hours. The cost is $18.50 for adults, $9.25 for children. Book through **Gray Line,** 208G Steele St. (tel. 403/668-3225).

A WHITEHORSE SPECIAL

In the downtown area you'll come across the **North-West Patrol**—students dressed up as 1898 Northwest Mounted Police troopers, but minus mustaches and with considerably friendlier grins. These are "Welcome Officers" in vintage garb: scarlet tunics and gold-striped trousers. Their main task is to provide visitor information. An additional duty is posing for tourist cameras.

WHERE TO STAY

Whitehorse has more than 20 hotels, motels, and chalets in and around the downtown area, including a couple just opposite the airport. This is far more than you'd expect in a place its size, and the accommodation standards come up to big-city levels in every respect. Rates, however, are higher than in the south—the city has few budget accommodations except in hostels, and bed-and-breakfast establishments.

EXPENSIVE

WESTMARK KLONDIKE INN, 2288 Second Ave., Whitehorse, YT, Y1A 1C8. Tel. 403/668-4747, or toll free 800/544-0970. Fax 403/667-7639. 98 rms. TV TEL
$ Rates: $118 single; $130 double. Children 12 and younger stay free in parents' room. AE, DC, MC, V. **Closed:** Oct–Apr.

An entertainment center as much as hotel, this large and attractively new building at the foot of Two Mile Hill stands framed against wooded mountain ranges that give it a picture-postcard backdrop. The beautifully carpeted foyer is a hive of action, the clocks on the wall indicating the different times around Canada (judging by the clientele, they should be showing the times around the globe). The inn has an outstanding coffee shop decorated with absorbing old gold-rush photos, upholstered wooden chairs, and wood chandeliers.

The guest rooms, of medium size, have a warm, soothing decor of burnt orange and deep reds. A low table is flanked by armchairs beneath a hanging lamp, and there's a smartly rustic writing desk, plus a smaller desk, twin bedside lamps, an abundance of drawers, and ultramodern bathrooms with electric ventilators.

WESTMARK WHITEHORSE, Second Ave. and Wood St. (P.O. Box 4250), Whitehorse, YT, Y1A 3T3. Tel. 403/668-4700, or toll free 800/478-1111. Fax 403/668-2789. 180 rms. TV TEL
$ Rates: $128 single; $140 double. Children under 12 stay free in parent's room. AE, MC, V.

Medium-sized and cozy, this representative of a national chain has one of the busiest lobbies in town, nicely fitted with deep leather armchairs and settees. There's a "mini-mall" alongside, housing a gift shop, deli, barber, and hairdresser, plus a travel agency. The lodge has a combination dining room and coffee shop, the most complete conference facilities in the Territory, and a very handsomely decorated cocktail lounge.

The guest rooms, including rooms for nonsmokers and the disabled, come with color TVs and radios. Each is handily divided into two parts, the front portion containing the bathroom and a dressing table with lights framing the mirror, theater fashion, plus hanging spaces; the rear has the beds, writing desk, table, and armchairs. One wall is wood-paneled and the decor kept in deep-brown and russet hues.

MODERATE

AIRLINE INN, 16 Burns Rd., Whitehorse, YT, Y1A 4Y9. Tel. 403/668-4400. Fax 403/668-2641. 30 rms. TV TEL
$ Rates: $75 single; $80 double. Children stay free in parents' room. AE, MC, V.
Just across the road from the airport, the Airline Inn is one of the most attractive

hostelries in town. The entire place is paneled in light woods, which give it the appearance of a mountain cabin. The upstairs cocktail lounge has a good view of the airport (you can see your plane taking off if you don't watch the clock). There's a small, very trim lobby with adjoining coffee shop-restaurant, deeply carpeted stairs, and a staff that acts like a welcoming committee.

The rooms have color TVs and dial phones, furniture that matches the paneling, and small settees. The mottled and beige decor blends in nicely, and the whole impression is ultramodern but devoid of stiffness: hanging bedlights, writing desks, bathrooms with heat lamps. The limousine to downtown stops at the door.

EDGEWATER HOTEL, 101 Main St., Whitehorse, YT, Y1A 2A7. Tel. 403/667-2572. Fax 403/668-3014. 30 rms. TV TEL
$ Rates: $99–$121 single or double. AE, ER, MC, V.

At the end of Main Street, overlooking the river, this miniature hotel has a distinct rustic charm of its own, plus an intriguingly contrasting dining room, the Cellar, with downright sumptuous appointments. The lobby and bedrooms are small and cozy, and there's a well-appointed lounge. The rooms are newly renovated, kept in soft pastel colors and equipped with extra-length beds and individual heat/air-conditioning units. The bathrooms are small but modern, and fitted with vanities.

GOLD RUSH INN, 411 Main St., Whitehorse, YT, Y1A 2A7. Tel. 403/668-4500. Fax 403/668-4432. 80 rms (24 with kitchenette). TV TEL
$ Rates: $106 single; $116 double. AE, DC, ER, MC, V.
Modern with a chaletlike frontage, the Gold Rush Inn has a very good dining room and a tavern. The lobby reflects the gold-rush era, but the rooms—furnished in different styles—are all attractive (no assembly-line decor here). Each has a fluorescently lit bathroom with electric ventilator. The rooms are surprisingly spacious, with excellent drapes and carpeting, large open hanging space, bedside lamps, and dressing tables with fluorescent lights. The kitchenettes come fully equipped.

REGINA HOTEL, 102 Wood St., Whitehorse, YT, Y1A 2E3. Tel. 403/667-7801. Fax 403/668-6075. 53 rms. TV TEL
$ Rates: $50–$66 single; $60–$90 double. Extra person $9. AE, ER, MC, V.
One of the oldest establishments in the Yukon, completely rebuilt in 1970, the Regina stands beside the Yukon River and breathes territorial tradition. The exterior is rather plain and has a frontier look, but the innards are charming as well as spacious and

---

AN IMPORTANT NOTE ON PRICES

Unless stated otherwise, **the prices cited in this guide are given in Canadian dollars,** which is good news for U.S. travelers because the Canadian dollar is worth 25% less than the American dollar, but buys nearly as much. As we go to press, $1 Canadian is worth 75¢ U.S., which means that your $100-a-night hotel room will cost only U.S. $75, and your $6 breakfast costs only U.S. $4.50.

Here's a quick table of equivalents:

Canadian $	U.S. $
$ 1	$ 0.75
5	3.75
10	7.50
20	15.00
50	37.50
80	60.00
100	75.00
200	150.00

lofty. The lobby is crowded with Old Yukon memorabilia, from hand-cranked telephones to moose antlers. There's a nicely intimate dining room open seven days a week.

The bedrooms give you plenty of elbow room. The decor is tastefully simple, hanging spaces large, and you can get a neat writing desk, dressing table, plus bedside and desk lamps. The bathrooms are fitted with heat lamps and electric ventilators.

TAKU HOTEL, 4109 Fourth Ave., Whitehorse, YT, Y1A 1H6. Tel. 403/ 668-4545. Fax 403/668-6538. 53 rms. TV TEL
$ Rates: $80 single or double. Children under 12 free. AE, DC, ER, MC, V.

 A small and neat hotel at the busiest downtown corner, the Taku has a very small lobby, but comfortable guest rooms, as well as a dining lounge and gift shop. Bedrooms are fitted with carpets and good standard furniture. There are handy wall mirrors (which many hotels lack) and fair-sized closets, bedside tables, and modern bathrooms.

YUKON INN, 4220 Fourth Ave., Whitehorse, YT, Y1A 1K1. Tel. 403/ 667-2527. Fax 403/668-7643. 98 rms. TV TEL
$ Rates: $85 single; $95–$110 double. AE, MC, V.
Another of the town's entertainment hives, this establishment features a dance club and cabaret lounge that draws swarms of "Yukon belles," most of whom come from somewhere else. The hotel also has a dining room, coffee shop, hair salon, and very pleasant bedrooms. Altogether it keeps a nice balance between catering to house guests and nightlife patrons.

The room decor is a delightful powder blue, and you get color TV, radio, and dial phone. Furnishings include a large dressing table with drawers and mirror, a standing lamp flanked by comfortable armchairs, a bedside lamp, and a very spacious closet with folding door. Bathrooms have heat lamps (with automatic timers) and electric ventilators.

BUDGET

BAKER'S BED & BREAKFAST, 84 11th Ave., Whitehorse, YT, Y1A 4J2. Tel. 403/633-2308. 2 rms (shared bath).
$ Rates: $50 single; $60 double. MC, V.
 Baker's Bed & Breakfast is a pleasantly quiet place located about three miles from downtown. The hearty breakfast here includes not only fresh fruit but home-baked goodies. There's a shared bathroom and fireplace.

PIONEER INN, 2141 Second Ave., Whitehorse, YT, Y1A 1C5. Tel. 403/668-2828. 30 rms (16 with kitchenettes). TV
$ Rates: $48.50 single; $58.85 double. MC, V.
The Pioneer Inn is a simple, clean, centrally located establishment that changes its name with disconcerting frequency. Furnishings, while not exactly stylish, are sufficient, the rates very moderate. Each room comes equipped with cable TV. No food served on the premises, but there is a pretty lively tavern with band entertainment.

CAMPGROUNDS & RV PARKS

There are five campgrounds in and around Whitehorse. The two samples below are the closest:

Downtown Sourdough Park, on Second Avenue north of Ogilvie (tel. 403/668-7938), has 146 campsites, most of them full-service, with showers, laundry, and a gift shop.

The **Robert Service Campground,** South Access Road (tel. 403/668-3721), offers 50 unserviced tentsites, plus firepits, washrooms, showers, and a picnic area. The rate is $13 per tent.

WHERE TO DINE

Whitehorse has a much greater variety of restaurants than hotels—you can get meals in every price range and quality. The top establishments measure up to any cuisine served in the south, and occasionally outshine them in hospitality and tender loving care. Food generally is more expensive here than in the provinces, and this goes for wine as well. Be happy you didn't come during the gold rush, when eggs sold for $25 each.

EXPENSIVE

ARIZONA CHARLIE'S, in the Klondike Inn, 2288 Second Ave. Tel. 403/668-4747.
Cuisine: INTERNATIONAL. **Reservations:** Recommended.
$ Prices: Main courses $12–$40. AE, DC, MC, V.
Open: Dinner daily 5:30–10pm.

Charlie's is named and decorated in honor of the fabulous entrepreneur who founded the Palace Grand Theatre in Dawson City during the gold rush (from his wall portrait he looks a little as if he might have sold somebody the Brooklyn Bridge). The place is decked out like a gaslight-age "entertainment palace," with red plush curtains, "gas" chandeliers, and curlicued alcoves. The foyer is festooned with wonderfully pompous Palace Grand production photos, including the "Tableau representing Great Britain and her Colonies at a Concert given in Aid of the widows and orphans created by the War with the Transvaal, February 15th, 1900."

Charlie Meadows must have been quite a gourmand, judging by the fare dished up in his honor: genuine turtle soup, superb tournedos Rossini, and concluding with a peach Melba that actually blends with the setting.

CELLAR DINING ROOM, in the Edgewater Hotel, 101 Main St. Tel. 403/667-2572.
Cuisine: CANADIAN. **Reservations:** Recommended.
$ Prices: Main courses $15.75–$30. AE, MC, V.
Open: Daily 6:30am–10pm.

This plush basement establishment has a big local reputation. The fare is strictly Anglo in the top-quality bracket, the choices between seafood and beef. You can't go wrong selecting either the king crab, lobster and prawns, or the excellent prime rib. Dress casually, but not *too* casually.

PANDA'S, 212 Main St. Tel. 403/667-2632.
Cuisine: FRENCH. **Reservations:** Recommended.
$ Prices: Main courses $15–$60. AE, MC, V.
Open: Dinner Mon–Sat 5:30–10pm.

Panda's is possibly the finest, and certainly the most romantic restaurant in the Territory. The decor is a mixture of restrained elegance enlivened by traditional Klondike touches, the service smoothly discreet. This is one of the few establishments in town to offer daily specials apart from the regular menu. Don't miss the escargots; they're just right and not too heavy on the garlic. The dress code is middling formal—gentlemen diners wear ties.

MODERATE

CASCA DINING ROOM, in the Gold Rush Inn, 411 Main St. Tel. 403/668-3864.
Cuisine: CANADIAN/CHINESE. **Reservations:** Accepted.
$ Prices: $4–$20. AE, DC, ER, MC, V.
Open: Daily 6am–10pm.

Divided into a Western and Eastern section (Tom's Kitchen), the Casca is named after the famous flagship of the Yukon River fleet, with one wall devoted to a mural of the old stern-wheeler. Green drapes at the street windows match the green table linen. Flower vases, attractively arranged, give the place a cheerful welcome look. The menu presents a difficult choice between the Chinese smörgåsbord and the salmon steak. Try the fine and rich Spanish coffee in conclusion.

CHINA GARDEN, 309 Jarvis St. Tel. 403/668-2899.
Cuisine: CHINESE. **Reservations:** Accepted.

$ Prices: Main courses $7.50–$16.75. MC, V.
Open: Daily 11:30am–11pm.

China Garden is a recently rehoused and redecorated dinery, agleam with lanterns, golden dragons, colored lights, and other Asian trimmings. It has one of the finest Chinese chefs in the Yukon and certainly the proudest proprietor, a combination that always spells great cuisine.

The fare is Cantonese and hot pot, the menu extensive. I particularly enjoyed the dry garlic spareribs, the curry beef, and the pan-fried squid with garlic and black bean sauce. The dessert selection is slim, but the ice cream with nuts and chocolate sauce hit the right spot. The China Garden has a bargain lunch smögåsbord—eight dishes for a total of $7.25.

EDDY'S, in the Town and Mountain Hotel, 401 Main St. Tel. 403/668-7644.

Cuisine: AMERICAN/CHINESE. **Reservations:** Accepted.
$ Prices: Main courses $6.95–$12.95. AE, MC, V.
Open: Dinner daily 5–10pm.

Eddy's is an American-Chinese establishment, the cuisine divided into roughly equal ethnic parts. The premises, in turn, are divided into a coffee shop and restaurant. The latter portion is small, simple, and attractive: chestnut-colored walls, wooden chairs, glass candleholders on the tables, and amber lights on the walls. The windows are discreetly curtained against the street. Hearty onion soup and delicious hot rolls come with the meal. On the Chinese side, the spareribs are excellent.

GOLDEN HORSE, 38 Lewes Blvd., Rendezvous Plaza. Tel. 403/668-7878.

Cuisine: CHINESE/WESTERN. **Reservations:** Accepted.
$ Prices: Main courses $9.95–$11. MC, V.
Open: Sun–Thurs 11am–10pm, Fri–Sat 11am–midnight.

The Golden Horse is devoted partly to Chinese, partly to Western cuisine, and both are excellent. The specialty here is the "live" seafood—swimming until you order it. You can then get the marine denizens prepared either Cantonese or American style. The Chinese smörgåsbord is a cheap option.

REGINA DINING ROOM, in the Regina Hotel, 102 Wood St. Tel. 403/667-7801, ext. 136.

Cuisine: CANADIAN. **Reservations:** Accepted.
$ Prices: $6.95–$13.95. AE, ER, MC, V.
Open: Breakfast, lunch, and dinner daily.

Simple, spacious, and colorful, with red-tiled walls and russet carpeting, this place serves solid and hearty northern fare for breakfast, lunch, and dinner. Dinner may begin with French onion soup or salad. Entrée choices include Yukon salmon served in parsley butter and the very hefty Monte Christo—a triple-decker of ham, cheese, and turkey dipped in egg and grilled to a golden brown. For dessert, try the homemade pie. Also serves special children's menus.

RUDY'S DINING ROOM, in the Airline Inn, 16 Burns Rd., opposite the airport. Tel. 403/668-4330.

Cuisine: CANADIAN/GERMAN. **Reservations:** Accepted.
$ Prices: Main courses $6–$40. AE, MC, V.
Open: Mon–Fri 7am–10pm.

Rudy's has a menu studded with aviation terminology, based (possibly) on the preferences of flying folk. There's a navigator's choice consisting of strips of beef, egg, baby shrimp, and cheese. Or the pilot's preference of broiled filet mignon rolled in cheese omelet and served with french fries. The oyster burger is served on homemade bread with a special sauce and potato chips. Rudy's also serves German specialties, such as schnitzel or sauerbraten.

SAM N ANDY'S, 506 Main St. Tel. 403/668-6994.

Cuisine: MEXICAN. **Reservations:** Accepted.
$ Prices: Main courses $4–$12. MC, V.
Open: Daily 11:30am–10:30pm.

A culinary surprise for this region is Sam n Andy's, which specializes in Mexican food, to eat in or take out. Another surprise feature is the outdoor dining patio.

BUDGET

MR. MIKE'S, 4114 Fourth Ave. Tel. 403/667-2242.
   Cuisine: STEAK. **Reservations:** Accepted.
$ Prices: Main courses $4.50–$14. MC, V.
   Open: Mon–Sat 11am–10pm.

 A steak cafeteria several rungs above the norm, with black-and-red decor, Mr. Mike's is a low wooden enclosure gently lit by hanging lamps. It has good carpeting, and charming photo blowups on the wall showing loving couples, kittens, and such like. The counter service is exceptionally pleasant, even in rush hours. Mike's also boasts a surprisingly extensive wine list, including the house "special blend."

THE POTBELLY, 106 Main St. Tel. 403/668-2323.
   Cuisine: DELI. **Reservations:** Not accepted.
$ Prices: Most items $4–$9. No credit cards.
   Open: Mon–Sat 9am–5pm.

The Potbelly offers deli-style cuisine, hot or cold, including a range of Swiss delicacies. It also serves soups, salads, wine, and beer. A meal here won't cost you more than $10.

EVENING ENTERTAINMENT

The top-of-the-bill attraction in Whitehorse is the **Frantic Follies,** a singing, dancing, clowning, and declaiming gold-rush revue that has become famous throughout the north. The show is a very entertaining mélange of skits, music-hall drollery, whooping, high-kicking, garter-flashing cancan dancers, sentimental ballads, and deadpan corn, interspersed with rolling recitations of Robert Service's poetry (I told you you couldn't get away from him). Shows take place nightly at the Westmark Whitehorse Hotel (see "Where to Stay," above). For reservations call 403/668-2042. Tickets cost $17.50 for adults, $8.75 for children.

The **Eldorado Revue** is solid family entertainment. A fast-moving cavalcade of gold-rush lore, songs, dances, skits, and dramatics, sprinkled with Robert Service's poetry. Performed nightly at 8pm at the Gold Rush Inn, 411 Main St. (tel. 403/668-6472). Tickets cost $15 for adults, $7.50 for children.

Sarsparilla Sisters, 144 Dalton Trail (tel. 403/668-5102), is another musical revue, this one telling a family history from the gold-rush era to the present. Performances Tuesday to Sunday at 7:30pm from May till late August. The locations shift around. Call to find out where it's playing. Tickets cost $8 for adults, $3.50 for children.

---

3. DAWSON CITY

333 miles (550km) NW of Whitehorse,
67 miles (110km) from the Alaska border

GETTING THERE   By Plane   From Whitehorse you can catch an Air North plane for the one-hour hop (tel. 403/668-2228).

By Bus   Atlas Tours and Rainbow Tours (see "Organized Tours and Excursions" at the beginning of this chapter) run motorcoaches from Whitehorse to Dawson.

By Car   From Alaska, take the Taylor Highway (Top of the World) from Chicken to Dawson. Well-maintained gravel surface, open from May 15 to September 19. The Klondike Highway runs from Skagway, Alaska, to Whitehorse and from there north to Dawson City via Carmacks and Stewart Crossing. From British Columbia: This is the long haul over the Alaska Highway from Dawson Creek (mile zero) to Whitehorse (888 miles), then to Dawson City (333 miles). Highway conditions range from excellent to fair.

ESSENTIALS   The Visitor Reception Centre, Front and King Streets (tel. 403/ 993-5566), provides you with information on all historic sights and attractions and puts on documentary slide shows and films about the gold rush. A walking tour of Dawson City, led by a highly knowledgeable guide, departs from the center four times a day. Free for all footsloggers.

Dawson is more of a paradox than a community today. Once the biggest Canadian city west of Winnipeg, with a population of 30,000, it withered to practically a ghost town after the stampeders stopped stampeding. In 1953 the seat of territorial government was shifted to Whitehorse, which might have spelled the end of Dawson—but didn't. For now, every summer, the influx of tourists more than matches the stream of gold rushers in its heyday. And while they don't scatter quite as much coin, their numbers grow larger instead of smaller each season.

The reason for this is the remarkable preservation and restoration work done by Parks Canada. Dawson today is the nearest thing to an authentic gold-rush town the world has to offer (with most of the seamy side dry-cleaned out). You can drop in for a drink at the Eldorado bar, ramble past ornately false-fronted buildings for a flutter at the tables in Diamond Tooth Gertie's Casino, head down to the banks of the Klondike River and take the highway southeast that leads to the claim sites at Bonanza Creek. It's a dream package, downtown nostalgia, for anyone who has ever fantasized about exchanging the feel of subway tokens for the weight of nuggets in his palm.

WHAT TO SEE & DO

PALACE GRAND THEATRE, King St. Tel. 403/993-6217.
Built at the height of the stampede by "Arizona Charlie" Meadows, this luxurious, flamboyant, tasteless opera house/dance hall had its slam-bang gala premiere in July 1899. Fitted with a Hollywood western-style false front incongruously at odds with the rafted roof and kitchen chairs, it now serves as showcase for the famous Gaslight Follies featuring assorted period "meller drammers" during which you are supposed to hiss the silk-cloaked villain and cheer the stalwart Mounted Police hero.
Admission: Tickets $11.50–$13.50.
Open: Performances May–Sept Wed–Mon nights at 8pm.

DIAMOND TOOTH GERTIE'S, Fourth and Queen Sts. Tel. 403/993- 5575.
Canada's only legal gambling casino north of the 60th parallel has an authentic gold-rush decor, from the shirt-sleeved honky-tonk pianist to the wooden floorboards. The games are blackjack, roulette, 21, red dog, and poker, as well as slot machines; the minimum stakes are low, the ambience friendly rather than tense. There's a maximum set limit of $100 per hand. The establishment also puts on two floor shows nightly: a riotous row of cancan dancers with swishing skirts and lots of black-hosed leg work.
Admission: $4.75.
Open: May–Sept daily 7pm–2am.

THE OLD POST OFFICE, at the corner of King St. and Third Ave.
The old post office has been completely restored to the way it was in 1900. Dawson originally had no post office, and in the early days of the rush, mail was handled by the Northwest Mounted Police in a tent. When the post office opened it was acclaimed a "miracle of the north" because mail usually arrived in one piece. (The regular post office is located between Princess and Queen Streets on Fifth Avenue.) You can still buy stamps and mail letters at the old edifice.

ROBERT SERVICE CABIN, Eighth Ave.
The bard lived in this two-room log cabin from 1909 to 1912. Set among trees on the lower slopes at the eastern end of town, the place today is the center of a permanent pilgrimage of Service admirers. They come to hear some of his most famous verses recited with suitable aplomb and in the right setting. In this cabin Service composed his third and final volume of *Songs of a Rolling Stone,* plus a

middling awful novel entitled *The Trail of Ninety-Eight*. Oddly enough, the bard of the gold rush neither took part in nor even saw the actual stampede. Born in England, he didn't arrive in Dawson until 1907—as a bank teller—when the rush was well and truly over. He got most of his plots by listening to old prospectors in the saloons, but the atmosphere he soaked in at the same time was genuine enough—and his imagination did the rest.

Admission: Free.

Open: Daily 9am–5pm; recitals daily at 10am and 3pm.

SS *KENO*, berthed beside the Bank of Commerce.

Built in Whitehorse, now permanently berthed at the Dawson waterfront, this high-structured riverboat dates from 1922. It was moved to its present site in 1960 and ran on a wood-burning boiler that supplied steam to the two engines that turned the stern wheel. This is one of the last riverboats to travel on the Yukon—there were once over 200 of them.

JACK LONDON'S CABIN, Eighth Ave.

Jack London lived in the Yukon less than a year—he left in June 1898 after a bout with scurvy—but his writings immortalized the north, particularly the animal stories like *White Fang*, and "The Son of Wolf." Recitations from his works and about him are given daily at 1pm.

Admission: Free.

Open: Daily 10am–5pm.

DISCOVERY CLAIM, Bonanza Creek Rd., mile 10.

This is the spot, now marked by a National Historic Sites cairn, where George Carmack, Skookum Jim, and Tagish Charlie found the gold that unleashed the Klondike Stampede in 1896. They staked out the first four claims (the fourth partner, Bob Henderson, wasn't present). Within a week Bonanza and Eldorado creeks had been staked out from end to end, but none of the later claims matched the wealth of the first. At Claim No. 17, just below Discovery, you can see one of the weird machines that ousted the hand-held pans. The huge ungainly elevator dredges were first used in New Zealand, and introduced in the Yukon in 1899. The one left in position is among the largest in North America and commenced operations in 1913. It could dig and sift 18,000 cubic yards in 24 hours, thus doing the work of an army of prospectors. You can do some panning yourself—at $5 per pan.

DAWSON CITY MUSEUM, Fifth Ave. Tel. 403/993-5219.

Located in the old Territorial Administration building, which became redundant when the capital was shifted to Whitehorse. Offers a well-presented look at the distant and recent past of the Dawson region, ranging from paleontological remains and the culture of the native Han people to the Klondike Mines railway. The museum has audiovisual presentations and a research library.

Admission: $3.25 adults, $2.25 students; small children free.

Open: June 1–Labor Day daily 10am–6pm.

TRAIL OF '98 MINI GOLF. Tel. 403/993-5664.

An unusual nine-hole mini-golf course with a historic Klondike theme. Located within a large picnic area southeast of town. With the admission you get free use of badminton courts and a horseshoe pit.

Open: May–Sept daily 7am–11pm.

Admission: $3.95 adults, $2.50 children.

RIVER CRUISES

The *Yukon Lou* docks off Front Street downtown and chugs past historic landmarks and the old Indian village of Moosehide on a 2½-hour cruise. Skipper and crew point out the highlights and spin yarns about the gold-rush days. Depart daily at 1pm from June to September. Tickets cost $10.50 for adults, $5.25 for children. Book at Gold City Tours (tel. 403/993-5175).

The *Yukon Queen* is a stately twin-deck craft carrying 49 passengers over the 108-mile stretch of river from Dawson City to Eagle, Alaska. Tickets include meals and cabins and the journey takes five hours downstream, six hours upstream. Runs daily from mid-May to mid-September. Passengers can choose either one-way or return trips. Adults pay $138 return, $85 one-way; children $69 return, $42.50 one-way. Book at Gray Line Yukon (tel. 403/668-3225).

WHERE TO STAY

There are about a dozen hotels, motels, and B&B establishments in Dawson City, most of them well appointed, none particularly cheap. Not all these facilities stay open all year, so check first.

DOWNTOWN HOTEL, corner of Second and Queen Sts., Dawson City, YT, Y0B 1G0. Tel. 403/993-5346. 60 rms. TV TEL
$ Rates: $109 single; $119 double. Extra person $10. AE, DC, MC, V.
A western-style building one block from Diamond Tooth Gertie's, the Downtown Hotel has rooms with cable TV and telephones, plus a restaurant, saloon, and a Jacuzzi.

EL DORADO HOTEL, Third Ave. and Princess St., Dawson City, YT, Y0B 1G0. Tel. 403/993-5451. 52 rms.
$ Rates: $102 single; $111 double; $120 triple. AE, DC, MC, V.
The El Dorado offers a dining room and a lounge bar. Its pluses include modern decor and a convenient downtown location.

WESTMARK INN, Fifth & Harper Sts., Dawson City, YT, Y0B 1G0. Tel. 403/993-5542. 136 rms.
$ Rates: $95 single; $110–$144 double. AE, MC, V.
The Westmark has 136 smartly furnished rooms, a Laundromat, a café with courtyard deck, a gift shop, and a traditional cocktail lounge.

4. KLUANE NATIONAL PARK

Tucked into the southwestern corner of the Yukon, two driving hours from Whitehorse, these 8,500 square miles of glaciers, marches, mountains, and sand dunes are Canada's largest national park, unsettled and virtually untouched wilderness. Bordering on Alaska in the west, Kluane contains Mount Logan and Mount St. Elias, respectively the second- and third-highest peaks in North America.

The park also contains an astonishing variety of wildlife. Large numbers of moose, wolves, red foxes, wolverines, lynx, otters, and beavers abound, plus black bears in the forested areas and lots of grizzlies in the major river valleys. The law makes it a serious offense to "feed and harass the bears," although personally I can't imagine someone trying to "harass" a grizzly.

Designated as a UNESCO World Heritage Site, Kluane Park lies 98 miles west of Whitehorse—take the Alaska Highway to Haines Junction. There, just outside the park's boundaries, you'll find the Visitor Reception Centre, which is open year-round (tel. 403/634-2345). The center has information on hiking trails and canoe routes and shows an award-winning audiovisual on the park. Admission to the park is free.

For overnight stays there is the **Kluane Park Inn,** Box 5400, Haines Junction, YT, Y0B 1L0 (tel. 403/634-2261). This is a modern motel with 20 rooms, all with private bath, charging $60 for singles, $65 for doubles.

Also at Haines Junction is the **Kluane R.V. Kampground** (tel. 403/634-2709). The spread has a tenting area, showers, Laundromat and convenience store, and sells fishing gear and licenses (which you'll need if you want to do any fishing).

Several companies operate one- to four-day tours of Kluane, including flightseeing and fishing trips with expert guides. To get the entire range of these organized trips contact **Yukon Tourism,** Box 2703, Whitehorse, YT, Y1A 2C6 (tel. 403/667-5340).

Key to province abbreviations: Alberta = AB; British Columbia = BC; Labrador = LB; Manitoba = MB; New Brunswick = NB; Newfoundland = NF; Northwest Territories = NT; Nova Scotia = NS; Ontario = ON; Prince Edward Island = P.E.I.; Québec = PQ; Saskatchewan = SK; The Yukon = YT.

Please Send Me the Books Checked Below:

FROMMER'S COMPREHENSIVE GUIDES
(Guides listing facilities from budget to deluxe,
with emphasis on the medium-priced)

	Retail Price	Code		Retail Price	Code
☐ Acapulco/Ixtapa/Taxco 1993–94	$15.00	C120	☐ Japan 1994–95 (Avail. 3/94)	$19.00	C144
☐ Alaska 1994–95	$17.00	C131	☐ Morocco 1992–93	$18.00	C021
☐ Arizona 1993–94	$18.00	C101	☐ Nepal 1994–95	$18.00	C126
☐ Australia 1992–93	$18.00	C002	☐ New England 1994 (Avail. 1/94)	$16.00	C137
☐ Austria 1993–94	$19.00	C119	☐ New Mexico 1993–94	$15.00	C117
☐ Bahamas 1994–95	$17.00	C121	☐ New York State 1994–95	$19.00	C133
☐ Belgium/Holland/ Luxembourg 1993–94	$18.00	C106	☐ Northwest 1994–95 (Avail. 2/94)	$17.00	C140
☐ Bermuda 1994–95	$15.00	C122	☐ Portugal 1994–95 (Avail. 2/94)	$17.00	C141
☐ Brazil 1993–94	$20.00	C111	☐ Puerto Rico 1993–94	$15.00	C103
☐ California 1994	$15.00	C134	☐ Puerto Vallarta/Manzanillo/ Guadalajara 1994–95 (Avail. 1/94)	$14.00	C028
☐ Canada 1994–95 (Avail. 4/94)	$19.00	C145	☐ Scandinavia 1993–94	$19.00	C135
☐ Caribbean 1994	$18.00	C123	☐ Scotland 1994–95 (Avail. 4/94)	$17.00	C146
☐ Carolinas/Georgia 1994–95	$17.00	C128	☐ South Pacific 1994–95 (Avail. 1/94)	$20.00	C138
☐ Colorado 1994–95 (Avail. 3/94)	$16.00	C143	☐ Spain 1993–94	$19.00	C115
☐ Cruises 1993–94	$19.00	C107	☐ Switzerland/Liechtenstein 1994–95 (Avail. 1/94)	$19.00	C139
☐ Delaware/Maryland 1994–95 (Avail. 1/94)	$15.00	C136	☐ Thailand 1992–93	$20.00	C033
☐ England 1994	$18.00	C129	☐ U.S.A. 1993–94	$19.00	C116
☐ Florida 1994	$18.00	C124	☐ Virgin Islands 1994–95	$13.00	C127
☐ France 1994–95	$20.00	C132	☐ Virginia 1994–95 (Avail. 2/94)	$14.00	C142
☐ Germany 1994	$19.00	C125	☐ Yucatán 1993–94	$18.00	C110
☐ Italy 1994	$19.00	C130			
☐ Jamaica/Barbados 1993–94	$15.00	C105			

FROMMER'S $-A-DAY GUIDES
(Guides to low-cost tourist accommodations and facilities)

	Retail Price	Code		Retail Price	Code
☐ Australia on $45 1993–94	$18.00	D102	☐ Israel on $45 1993–94	$18.00	D101
☐ Costa Rica/Guatemala/ Belize on $35 1993–94	$17.00	D108	☐ Mexico on $45 1994	$19.00	D116
☐ Eastern Europe on $30 1993–94	$18.00	D110	☐ New York on $70 1994–95 (Avail. 4/94)	$16.00	D120
☐ England on $60 1994	$18.00	D112	☐ New Zealand on $45 1993–94	$18.00	D103
☐ Europe on $50 1994	$19.00	D115	☐ Scotland/Wales on $50 1992–93	$18.00	D019
☐ Greece on $45 1993–94	$19.00	D100	☐ South America on $40 1993–94	$19.00	D109
☐ Hawaii on $75 1994	$19.00	D113	☐ Turkey on $40 1992–93	$22.00	D023
☐ India on $40 1992–93	$20.00	D010	☐ Washington, D.C. on $40 1994–95 (Avail. 2/94)	$17.00	D119
☐ Ireland on $45 1994–95 (Avail. 1/94)	$17.00	D117			

FROMMER'S CITY $-A-DAY GUIDES
(Pocket-size guides to low-cost tourist accommodations
and facilities)

	Retail Price	Code		Retail Price	Code
☐ Berlin on $40 1994–95	$12.00	D111	☐ Madrid on $50 1994–95 (Avail. 1/94)	$13.00	D118
☐ Copenhagen on $50 1992–93	$12.00	D003	☐ Paris on $50 1994–95	$12.00	D117
☐ London on $45 1994–95	$12.00	D114	☐ Stockholm on $50 1992–93	$13.00	D022

FROMMER'S WALKING TOURS
(With routes and detailed maps, these companion guides point out the places and pleasures that make a city unique)

	Retail Price	Code		Retail Price	Code
☐ Berlin	$12.00	W100	☐ Paris	$12.00	W103
☐ London	$12.00	W101	☐ San Francisco	$12.00	W104
☐ New York	$12.00	W102	☐ Washington, D.C.	$12.00	W105

FROMMER'S TOURING GUIDES
(Color-illustrated guides that include walking tours, cultural and historic sights, and practical information)

	Retail Price	Code		Retail Price	Code
☐ Amsterdam	$11.00	T001	☐ New York	$11.00	T008
☐ Barcelona	$14.00	T015	☐ Rome	$11.00	T010
☐ Brazil	$11.00	T003	☐ Scotland	$10.00	T011
☐ Florence	$ 9.00	T005	☐ Sicily	$15.00	T017
☐ Hong Kong/Singapore/			☐ Tokyo	$15.00	T016
Macau	$11.00	T006	☐ Turkey	$11.00	T013
☐ Kenya	$14.00	T018	☐ Venice	$ 9.00	T014
☐ London	$13.00	T007			

FROMMER'S FAMILY GUIDES

	Retail Price	Code		Retail Price	Code
☐ California with Kids	$18.00	F100	☐ San Francisco with Kids		
☐ Los Angeles with Kids			(Avail. 4/94)	$17.00	F104
(Avail. 4/94)	$17.00	F103	☐ Washington, D.C. with Kids		
☐ New York City with Kids			(Avail. 2/94)	$17.00	F102
(Avail. 2/94)	$18.00	F101			

FROMMER'S CITY GUIDES
(Pocket-size guides to sightseeing and tourist accommodations and facilities in all price ranges)

	Retail Price	Code		Retail Price	Code
☐ Amsterdam 1993–94	$13.00	S110	☐ Montréal/Québec		
☐ Athens 1993–94	$13.00	S114	City 1993–94	$13.00	S125
☐ Atlanta 1993–94	$13.00	S112	☐ Nashville/Memphis		
☐ Atlantic City/Cape			1994–95 (Avail. 4/94)	$13.00	S141
May 1993–94	$13.00	S130	☐ New Orleans 1993–94	$13.00	S103
☐ Bangkok 1992–93	$13.00	S005	☐ New York 1994 (Avail.		
☐ Barcelona/Majorca/Minorca/			1/94)	$13.00	S138
Ibiza 1993–94	$13.00	S115	☐ Orlando 1994	$13.00	S135
☐ Berlin 1993–94	$13.00	S116	☐ Paris 1993–94	$13.00	S109
☐ Boston 1993–94	$13.00	S117	☐ Philadelphia 1993–94	$13.00	S113
☐ Budapest 1994–95 (Avail.			☐ San Diego 1993–94	$13.00	S107
2/94)	$13.00	S139	☐ San Francisco 1994	$13.00	S133
☐ Chicago 1993–94	$13.00	S122	☐ Santa Fe/Taos/		
☐ Denver/Boulder/Colorado			Albuquerque 1993–94	$13.00	S108
Springs 1993–94	$13.00	S131	☐ Seattle/Portland 1994–95	$13.00	S137
☐ Dublin 1993–94	$13.00	S128	☐ St. Louis/Kansas		
☐ Hong Kong 1994–95			City 1993–94	$13.00	S127
(Avail. 4/94)	$13.00	S140	☐ Sydney 1993–94	$13.00	S129
☐ Honolulu/Oahu 1994	$13.00	S134	☐ Tampa/St.		
☐ Las Vegas 1993–94	$13.00	S121	Petersburg 1993–94	$13.00	S105
☐ London 1994	$13.00	S132	☐ Tokyo 1992–93	$13.00	S039
☐ Los Angeles 1993–94	$13.00	S123	☐ Toronto 1993–94	$13.00	S126
☐ Madrid/Costa del			☐ Vancouver/Victoria 1994–		
Sol 1993–94	$13.00	S124	95 (Avail. 1/94)	$13.00	S142
☐ Miami 1993–94	$13.00	S118	☐ Washington, D.C. 1994		
☐ Minneapolis/St.			(Avail. 1/94)	$13.00	S136
Paul 1993–94	$13.00	S119			

SPECIAL EDITIONS

	Retail Price	Code		Retail Price	Code
☐ Bed & Breakfast Southwest	$16.00	P100	☐ Caribbean Hideaways	$16.00	P103
☐ Bed & Breakfast Great American Cities (Avail. 1/94)	$16.00	P104	☐ National Park Guide 1994 (avail. 3/94)	$16.00	P105
			☐ Where to Stay U.S.A.	$15.00	P102

Please note: if the availability of a book is several months away, we may have back issues of guides to that particular destination. Call customer service at (815) 734-1104.